America's
TEST KITCHEN

THE COMPLETE
AMERICA'S TEST KITCHEN
TV SHOW COOKBOOK

2001-2013

THE COMPLETE AMERICA'S TEST KITCHEN TV SHOW COOKBOOK

2001 2013

BY THE EDITORS AT **AMERICA'S TEST KITCHEN**

PHOTOGRAPHY **CARL TREMBLAY, KELLER + KELLER, AND DANIEL J. VAN ACKERE**

AMERICA'S TEST KITCHEN
17 Station Street, Brookline, MA 02445

THE COMPLETE AMERICA'S TEST KITCHEN TV SHOW COOKBOOK:
Every recipe from the hit TV show with product ratings and a look behind the scenes

Revised Edition

ISBN-13: 978-1-936493-32-6   ISBN-10: 1-936493-32-2
ISSN 2162-6944
Hardcover: $39.95 US

Manufactured in the United States of America

10 9 8 7 6 5 4 3 2 1

Distributed by America's Test Kitchen
17 Station Street, Brookline, MA 02445

EDITORIAL DIRECTOR: Jack Bishop

EDITORIAL DIRECTOR, BOOKS: Elizabeth Carduff

EXECUTIVE EDITOR: Lori Galvin

SENIOR EDITORS: Louise Emerick and Rachel Toomey Kelsey

CONTRIBUTING EDITORS: Elizabeth Emery, Kate Hartke, and Barbara Wood

ASSISTANT EDITOR: Alyssa King

EDITORIAL ASSISTANT: Elizabeth Pohm

DESIGN DIRECTOR: Amy Klee

ART DIRECTOR: Greg Galvan

DESIGNERS: Tiffani Beckwith, Beverly Hsu, Erica Lee, and Katie Rezza

STAFF PHOTOGRAPHER: Daniel J. van Ackere

ADDITIONAL PHOTOGRAPHERS: Elisabeth O'Donnell and Peter Tannenbaum

FOOD STYLISTS: Marie Piraino and Mary Jane Sawyer

PRODUCTION DIRECTOR: Guy Rochford

SENIOR PRODUCTION MANAGER: Jessica Lindheimer Quirk

SENIOR PROJECT MANAGER: Alice Carpenter

TRAFFIC AND PRODUCTION COORDINATORS: Brittany Allen and Kate Hux

COLOR AND IMAGING SPECIALIST: Andrew Mannone

PRODUCTION AND IMAGING SPECIALISTS: Judy Blomquist, Heather Dube, and Lauren Pettapiece

COPYEDITOR: Cheryl Redmond

PROOFREADERS: Christine Corcoran Cox, Debra Hudak, and Jeffrey Schier

INDEXER: Elizabeth Parson

CONTENTS

PREFACE BY CHRISTOPHER KIMBALL   viii

WELCOME TO AMERICA'S TEST KITCHEN   x

CHAPTER 1   SOUP'S ON!   3

CHAPTER 2   SALAD DAYS   27

CHAPTER 3   EASY SKILLET SUPPERS   49

CHAPTER 4   ONE-DISH SUPPERS   61

CHAPTER 5   SIMPLY CHICKEN   83

CHAPTER 6   TALKING TURKEY AND ALL THE TRIMMINGS   111

CHAPTER 7   WE'LL HAVE THE STEAK   137

CHAPTER 8   PORK CHOPS EVERY DAY   149

CHAPTER 9   ROASTS AND MORE   163

CHAPTER 10   FAVORITE WAYS WITH FISH   189

CHAPTER 11   DINNER AT THE DINER   217

CHAPTER 12   WHO WANTS PASTA?   237

CHAPTER 13   BRINGING HOME ITALIAN FAVORITES   277

CHAPTER 14   THE FLAIR OF THE FRENCH   313

CHAPTER 15   TEX-MEX TONIGHT   345

CHAPTER 16   LET'S DO TAKEOUT   371

CHAPTER 17   IT'S GRILL TIME!   413

CHAPTER 18   SIDES OF PLENTY   475

CHAPTER 19   COME FOR BRUNCH   503

CHAPTER 20   PLEASE PASS THE BREAD   545

CHAPTER 21   COOKIE JAR FAVORITES   561

CHAPTER 22   A PIECE OF CAKE   593

CHAPTER 23   PUDDINGS AND SOUFFLÉS   639

CHAPTER 24   CLASSIC FRUIT DESSERTS   657

CHAPTER 25   KEEP YOUR FORK—THERE'S PIE!   679

THE AMERICA'S TEST KITCHEN SHOPPING GUIDE   707

THE 2013 SEASON   756

CONVERSIONS & EQUIVALENCIES   808

INDEX   810

PREFACE

My first experience riding a horse ended badly. The animal in question was my own horse, a Morgan, who realized instantly that I had no idea how to control 1,200 pounds of horseflesh. So he did the natural thing, which was to lope at an easy pace up to a small embankment and then stop dead, sending me flying into space. The good news was that my 10-year-old bones bent rather than snapped. I dusted myself off and got back on.

Flying off of horses was a constant theme during my childhood. My most spectacular fall was precipitated by an act of such extreme stupidity that I could have won a Darwin Award. One summer, as an aspiring hippie in Oregon, I managed to rope-halter a horse I chanced upon while crossing a large pasture and then hopped on its back without the benefit of saddle or bridle. A furious gallop ended in a spectacular arc that, of course, brought me rather harshly back to terra firma, only inches away from a large boulder. One might say that I have lived a charmed life, at least if survival is the key criterion.

As the host of *America's Test Kitchen*, I know that we have had our share of stumbles in the early years but we have always gotten back on our feet to do another segment and another season. If practice makes perfect, or almost perfect, then we stuck to it and so did you. Hopefully, we can make a better claim than "We survived!" since we are now the most-watched cooking show on public television.

After well over 300 episodes, hundreds of recipes, and 13 years we thought it would be a good time to publish *The Complete America's Test Kitchen TV Show Cookbook*. We have included EVERY recipe (more than 850) from all 13 years as well as a comprehensive guide to our product tastings and equipment testings, organized by category for easy reference, including photos of each of the winners.

I am not as young as I was when I stood in front of the TV cameras for the first time (watching early episodes is something I avoid), which means that I had forgotten some of the died-and-gone-to-heaven highlights from our 13 years. So preparing this book was a true trip down memory lane. The list includes Skillet Lasagna (just 40 minutes from start to finish and better than the oven-baked version), Chicken and Dumplings, Pan-Seared Thick Cut Steaks (unusual oven/stovetop method), Poached Salmon with Herb and

Caper Vinaigrette (so little liquid it's almost braised), Easier French Fries (started in cold, not hot, oil), Weeknight Bolognese, Italian-Style Grilled Chicken, French Chicken in a Pot (incredibly flavorful, moist meat), Well-Done Grilled Hamburgers (still juicy and tender), Barbecued Pulled Pork (finished in the oven), Creamy Mashed Potatoes, Blueberry Muffins (with a blueberry swirl), Molasses Spice Cookies with Dark Rum Glaze, Chocolate-Chunk Oatmeal Cookies with Pecans and Dried Cherries, Triple-Chocolate Mousse Cake, Applesauce Snack Cake, and our to-die-for Coconut Layer Cake.

Last weekend, I rode horseback with a neighbor through high mountain pastures that were just a few minutes from our farm. It was a neighbor's property and I had never ventured up the steep embankment just off the road and up into the hidden fields above. We loped through the high timothy, the Indian paintbrushes, and the daisies, rear ends firmly set in our saddles, boot heels down, comfortable with our horses and the ride. I had discovered another country, a magic valley that was just out my back door after a dozen years of similar rides just a stone's throw away.

Cooking is like that ride. It takes years to get comfortable, to figure out what you are doing, and to be certain that you can overcome almost any eventuality, whether it be a wood-chuck hole or a substitute ingredient. Years of accumulated experience—other rides and other recipes—are the bits and pieces that turn one from tentative to confident, from novice to professional.

The joy of cooking is that experience brings with it unexpected pleasure, moments when a recipe turns from everyday to transcendent. This book is a container of sorts; it holds all the steps, all the preparation that can take one from good cook to great cook, from putting food on the table to really enjoying the ride. One day, when you least expect it, you will be out and about and realize that you've found a whole new world, just around the corner.

Christopher Kimball
Founder and editor, *Cook's Illustrated* and *Cook's Country*
Host, *America's Test Kitchen* and
Cook's Country from America's Test Kitchen

WELCOME TO AMERICA'S TEST KITCHEN

This book has been tested, written, and edited by the folks at America's Test Kitchen, a very real 2,500-square-foot kitchen located just outside of Boston. It is the home of *Cook's Illustrated* and *Cook's Country* magazines and is the Monday-through-Friday destination for more than three dozen test cooks, editors, food scientists, tasters, and cookware specialists. Our mission is to test recipes over and over again until we understand how and why they work and until we arrive at the "best" version.

Our television show highlights the best recipes developed in the test kitchen during the past year—those recipes that our test kitchen staff makes at home time and time again. These recipes are accompanied by our most exhaustive equipment tests and our most interesting food tastings.

Christopher Kimball, the founder and editor of *Cook's Illustrated* magazine, is host of the show and asks the questions you might ask. It's the job of our chefs, Julia Collin Davison, Bridget Lancaster, Becky Hays, Bryan Roof, and Dan Souza to demonstrate our recipes. The chefs show Chris what works and what doesn't, and they explain why. In the process, they discuss (and show you) the best examples from our development process as well as the worst.

Adam Ried, our equipment expert, and Lisa McManus, our gadget guru, share the highlights from our detailed testing process in equipment corner segments. They bring with them our favorite (and least favorite) gadgets and tools. Jack Bishop is our ingredient expert. He has Chris taste our favorite (and least favorite) brands of common food products. Chris may not always enjoy these exercises (hot sauce isn't exactly as fun to taste as mozzarella or cocoa powder), but he usually learns something as Jack explains what makes one brand superior to another.

Although just 10 cooks and editors appear on the television show, another 50 people worked to make the show a reality. Executive Producer Melissa Baldino conceived and developed each episode with help from Associate Producer Stephanie Stender and Production Assistant Kaitlin Hammond. Rachael M. Stark and Debby Paddock assisted with all the historical recipe and photo research. Guy Crosby, our science expert on the show, researched the science behind the recipes. Along with the on-air crew, executive chefs Erin McMurrer and Keith Dresser helped plan and organize the 26 television episodes shot in May 2012 and ran the "back kitchen," where all the food that appeared on camera originated. Taizeth Sierra, Hannah Crowley, and Amy Graves organized the tasting and equipment segments.

During filming, chefs Andrea Geary, Nick Iverson, Andrew Janjigian, Lan Lam, Rebeccah Marsters, Suzannah McFerran, Rebecca Morris, Christie Morrison,

Chris O'Connor, Celeste Rogers, and Diane Unger and interns Amy DeMello and Alexxa Grattan cooked all the food needed on set. Cooks Sarah Gabriel, Carolynn Purpura MacKay, Sacha Madadian, Addy Parker, Cristin Walsh and interns Kelsey Branch, Joyce Liao, Blaire Newhard, and Lainey Seyler worked on-set developing recipes for our magazines and books. Assistant Test Kitchen Director Gina Nistico, Test Kitchen Manager Leah Rovner, and Senior Kitchen Assistant Meryl MacCormack were charged with making sure all the ingredients and kitchen equipment we needed were on hand. Kitchen assistants Maria Elena Delgado, Ena Gudiel, and Andrew Straaberg Finfrock also worked long hours. Chefs Dan Cellucci, Danielle DeSiato-Hallman, Sara Mayer, Ashley Moore, Kate Williams, and Dan Zuccarello helped coordinate the efforts of the kitchen with the television set by readying props, equipment, and food. Shannon Hatch, Kate May, and Christine Gordon led all tours of the test kitchen during filming.

Special thanks to director and editor Herb Sevush and director of photography Jan Maliszewski.

We also appreciate the hard work of the video production team, including Stephen Hussar, Michael McEachern, Peter Dingle, Roger Macie, Gilles Morin, Brenda Coffey, Ken Fraser, Joe Christofori, James Hirsch, Bob Hirsch, Griff Nash, Jeremy Bond, Eric Joslin, Heloise Borden, Amy Neben, and Ken Bauer. Thanks also to Nick Dakoulas, the second unit videographer.

We also would like to thank Nancy Bocchino, Bara Levin, and Victoria Yuen at WGBH Station Relations, and the team at American Public Television that presents the show: Cynthia Fenneman, Chris Funkhouser, Judy Barlow, and Tom Davison. Thanks also for production support from Elena Battista Malcom and DGA Productions, Boston, and Zebra Productions, New York.

DCS by Fisher & Paykel, Kohler, Diamond Crystal Salt, FOXY, Cooking.com, and Wente Vineyards helped underwrite the show, and we thank them for their support. We also thank Anne Traficante, Ann Naya, and Kate May for handling underwriter relations and Deborah Broide for managing publicity.

Meat was provided by Ronnie Savenor at Savenor's Market of Boston, Massachusetts. Fish was supplied by Ian Davison of Constitution Seafoods of Boston, Massachusetts. Live plants and garden items for the show were furnished by Mahoney's Garden Center of Brighton, Massachusetts. Aprons for Christopher Kimball were made by Nicole Romano and staff aprons were made by Crooked Brook. Props were designed and developed by Jay Layman, Christine Vo, and Erica Lee.

CHAPTER 1

SOUP'S ON!

Classic Chicken
Noodle Soup   4

Hearty Chicken
Noodle Soup   5

Old-Fashioned Slow-Cooker
Chicken Noodle Soup   6

Best Beef Stew   7

Our Favorite Chili   8

Quick Beef and
Vegetable Soup   10

Classic Cream of
Tomato Soup   11

Creamless Creamy
Tomato Soup   12

   Classic Croutons

Creamy Pea Soup   13

Creamy Mushroom
Soup   14

   Sautéed Wild
   Mushrooms

Butternut Squash Soup   15

Rustic Potato-Leek
Soup   16

Broccoli-Cheese Soup   16

Hearty Lentil Soup   17

Modern Ham and Split
Pea Soup   18

   Buttery Croutons

Hearty Ham and Split Pea
Soup with Potatoes   19

Mulligatawny Soup   20

Hearty Minestrone   21

Classic Gazpacho   22

   Garlic Croutons

Creamy Gazpacho
Andaluz   23

Lighter Corn Chowder   24

New England Clam
Chowder   25

CLASSIC CHICKEN NOODLE SOUP

WHY THIS RECIPE WORKS: Classic chicken noodle soup is one of *the* all-time comfort foods. We eat it to nurse a cold or pair it with a simple sandwich for a satisfying meal. But making chicken noodle soup from scratch can take all day. We wanted a simple recipe but we wanted to make it the old-fashioned way—starting with a whole chicken—rather than cheating with store-bought broth.

We began by cutting the chicken into small pieces that could be browned in batches. To develop additional flavor, we sweated the browned pieces in a covered pot with an onion, then simmered them for less than half an hour. Now we had a stock that just needed some salt and a bay leaf to round out its flavor. We reserved some of the skimmed fat from the stock to sauté aromatics and carrots for the soup, and we added in tender chicken breast pieces that had already been poached in our stock. For extra flavor, we cooked the egg noodles right in the soup pot so they could absorb rich, meaty flavor from the stock. With a final sprinkling of chopped parsley, our chicken noodle soup was complete—rich, homemade broth, moist pieces of chicken, tender vegetables, and perfectly cooked noodles.

Classic Chicken Noodle Soup

SERVES 6 TO 8

Make sure to reserve the chicken breast pieces until step 2; they should not be browned. If you use a cleaver, you will be able to cut up the chicken parts quickly. A chef's knife or kitchen shears will also work. Be sure to reserve 2 tablespoons of chicken fat for sautéing the aromatics in step 4; however, if you prefer not to use chicken fat, vegetable oil can be substituted.

STOCK
- 1 tablespoon vegetable oil
- 1 (4-pound) whole chicken, breast removed, split, and reserved; remaining chicken cut into 2-inch pieces (see note)
- 1 medium onion, chopped medium
- 2 quarts boiling water
- 2 teaspoons table salt
- 2 bay leaves

SOUP
- 2 tablespoons chicken fat, reserved from making stock, or vegetable oil (see note)
- 1 medium onion, chopped medium
- 1 large carrot, peeled and sliced ¼ inch thick
- 1 celery rib, sliced ¼ inch thick
- ½ teaspoon dried thyme
- 3 ounces egg noodles (about 2 cups)
- ¼ cup minced fresh parsley leaves
  Table salt and ground black pepper

1. FOR THE STOCK: Heat the oil in a large Dutch oven over medium-high heat until shimmering. Add half of the chicken pieces and cook until lightly browned, about 5 minutes per side. Transfer the cooked chicken to a bowl and repeat with the remaining chicken pieces; transfer to the bowl with the first batch. Add the onion and cook, stirring frequently, until the onion is translucent, 3 to 5 minutes. Return the chicken pieces to the pot. Reduce the heat to low, cover, and cook until the chicken releases its juices, about 20 minutes.

2. Increase the heat to high; add the boiling water, reserved chicken breast pieces, salt, and bay leaves. Reduce the heat to medium-low and simmer until the flavors have blended, about 20 minutes.

3. Remove the breast pieces from the pot. When cool, remove the skin and bones from the breast pieces and discard. Shred the meat with your fingers or two forks and set aside. Strain the stock through a fine-mesh strainer into a container, pressing on the solids to extract as much liquid as possible; discard the solids. Allow the liquid to settle about 5 minutes and skim off the fat; reserve 2 tablespoons, if desired (see note). (The shredded chicken, strained stock, and fat can be refrigerated in separate airtight containers for up to 2 days.)

4. FOR THE SOUP: Heat the reserved chicken fat in a large Dutch oven over medium-high heat. Add the onion, carrot, and celery and cook until softened, about 5 minutes. Add the thyme and reserved stock and simmer until the vegetables are tender, 10 to 15 minutes.

5. Add the noodles and reserved shredded chicken and cook until just tender, 5 to 8 minutes. Stir in the parsley, season with salt and pepper to taste, and serve.

HEARTY CHICKEN NOODLE SOUP

WHY THIS RECIPE WORKS: Sometimes we prefer a simple bowl of chicken soup—a brothy soup modestly enriched with chicken, noodles, and vegetables. Other times, a heartier version of chicken noodle soup is what we crave—one chock-full of chicken, noodles, and vegetables—a true meal in a bowl. We also wanted to find a way to produce such a soup without relying on a whole chicken for the stock.

We began by jump-starting the flavor of our soup with a mixture of store-bought chicken broth and water, but the broth-and-water base had a distinctly flat flavor. A few pounds of chicken parts created a wonderfully rich stock, but the method—browning the parts and then simmering them—was just too fussy for what we wanted here. Instead, we turned to a somewhat unlikely but more convenient substitute—store-bought ground chicken. Ground chicken offers more surface area and exponentially more flavor, providing a great-tasting stock when sautéed with aromatics and then simmered with the broth and water. All the stock needed was some body and thickening, which we got from a little cornstarch. With our broth down, we were ready to add the chicken (breasts that had been poached in the stock until just cooked through and then shredded), vegetables, and noodles. Along with onion, celery, and carrots, we further enriched the soup with potato and Swiss chard. Our streamlined hearty chicken noodle soup was now rich, and satisfying.

Hearty Chicken Noodle Soup

SERVES 4 TO 6

When skimming the fat off the stock, we prefer to leave a little bit on the surface to enhance the soup's flavor.

STOCK

- 1 tablespoon vegetable oil
- 1 pound ground chicken
- 1 small onion, chopped medium
- 1 medium carrot, peeled and chopped medium
- 1 celery rib, chopped medium
- 2 quarts low-sodium chicken broth
- 4 cups water
- 2 bay leaves
- 2 teaspoons table salt
- 2 (12-ounce) bone-in, skin-on chicken breast halves, cut in half crosswise

SOUP

- ¼ cup cold water
- 3 tablespoons cornstarch
- 1 small onion, halved and sliced thin
- 2 medium carrots, peeled, halved lengthwise, and cut crosswise into ¾-inch pieces
- 1 medium celery rib, halved lengthwise and cut crosswise into ½-inch pieces
- 1 medium russet potato (about 8 ounces), peeled and cut into ¾-inch cubes
- 1½ ounces egg noodles (about 1 cup)
- 4–6 Swiss chard leaves, ribs removed, torn into 1-inch pieces (about 2 cups; optional)
- 1 tablespoon minced fresh parsley leaves
  Table salt and ground black pepper

1. FOR THE STOCK: Heat the oil in a large Dutch oven over medium-high heat until shimmering. Add the ground chicken, onion, carrot, and celery. Cook, stirring frequently, until the chicken is no longer pink, 5 to 10 minutes (do not brown the chicken).

2. Reduce the heat to medium-low. Add the broth, water, bay leaves, salt, and chicken breasts; cover and cook for 30 minutes. Remove the lid, increase the heat to high, and bring to a boil. (If the liquid is already boiling when the lid is removed, remove the chicken breasts immediately and continue with the recipe.) Transfer the chicken breasts to a large plate and set aside. Continue to cook the stock for 20 minutes, adjusting the heat to maintain a gentle boil. Strain the stock through a fine-mesh strainer into a container, pressing on the solids to extract as much liquid as possible; discard the solids. Allow the liquid to settle about 5 minutes and skim off the fat (see note). (The strained stock can be refrigerated in an airtight container for up to 2 days or frozen for up to 3 months. The chicken breasts can be stored in a zipper-lock bag with the air squeezed out.)

3. FOR THE SOUP: Return the stock to a Dutch oven set over medium-high heat. In a small bowl, combine the water and cornstarch until a smooth slurry forms; stir into the stock and bring to a gentle boil. Add the onion, carrots, celery, and potato and cook until the potato pieces are almost tender, 10 to 15 minutes, adjusting the heat as necessary to maintain a gentle boil. Add the egg noodles and continue to cook until all the vegetables and noodles are tender, about 5 minutes longer.

4. Meanwhile, remove the skin and bones from the reserved cooked chicken and discard. Shred the meat with your fingers or two forks. Add the shredded chicken, Swiss chard (if using), and parsley to the soup and cook until heated through, about 2 minutes. Season with salt and pepper to taste and serve.

OLD-FASHIONED SLOW-COOKER CHICKEN NOODLE SOUP

WHY THIS RECIPE WORKS: Making chicken noodle soup with a deep, satisfying flavor requires a few tricks when using a slow cooker. First, we used a combination of bone-in chicken thighs and breasts; cooked and shredded breast meat was the perfect choice for the final soup, but bone-in thighs were key for giving the broth its deep flavor during the long cooking time. We found browning the chicken thighs before adding them to the slow cooker really maximized the flavor. To prevent the breast meat from overcooking we wrapped the chicken breast inside a foil packet. Since we were already dirtying a skillet to brown the chicken thighs, it was no effort to brown and soften the vegetables and aromatics as well, and this step was well worth the depth of flavor it lent. An unlikely ingredient, tomato paste, gave the soup body and brought out the savory notes of our soup. We cooked the noodles separately to ensure perfect texture and added them in at the end, along with frozen peas that we simply let sit in the soup for 5 minutes to heat through.

Old-Fashioned Slow-Cooker Chicken Noodle Soup

SERVES 6 TO 8

Do not try to cook the noodles in the slow cooker or they will turn out mushy and taste raw.

- 1½   pounds bone-in, skin-on chicken thighs, trimmed
        Table salt and ground black pepper
- 1   tablespoon vegetable oil
- 3   medium carrots, peeled and chopped medium
- 2   celery ribs, chopped medium
- 1   medium onion, minced
- 3   medium garlic cloves, minced or pressed through a garlic press (about 1 tablespoon)
- 1   tablespoon tomato paste
- 2   teaspoons minced fresh thyme leaves or ½ teaspoon dried
- ⅛   teaspoon red pepper flakes
- 8   cups low-sodium chicken broth
- 2   bay leaves
- 1   (12-ounce) bone-in, skin-on split chicken breast, trimmed
- 1½   ounces wide egg noodles (about 1 cup)
- ½   cup frozen peas
- 2   tablespoons minced fresh parsley leaves

1. Dry the chicken thighs with paper towels and season with salt and pepper. Heat the oil in a 12-inch skillet over medium-high heat until just smoking. Brown the chicken thighs well on both sides, 6 to 8 minutes. Transfer to a plate, let cool slightly, and discard the skin.

2. Pour off all but 1 tablespoon fat left in the skillet. Add the carrots, celery, and onion and cook over medium heat until the vegetables are softened, 7 to 10 minutes. Stir in the garlic, tomato paste, thyme, and red pepper flakes and cook until fragrant, about 30 seconds. Stir in 1 cup of the chicken broth, scraping up any browned bits; transfer to the slow cooker.

3. Stir the remaining 7 cups broth and the bay leaves into the slow cooker. Nestle the browned chicken thighs with any accumulated juice into the slow cooker. Season the chicken breast with salt and pepper and place on one side of a large piece of aluminum foil. Foil the foil over the chicken and crimp to seal the edges. Place the foil packet on top of the soup, pressing gently as needed to fit. Cover and cook until the chicken is tender, 4 to 6 hours on low.

4. Remove the foil packet, open it carefully (watch for steam), and transfer the chicken breast to a cutting board. Transfer the chicken thighs to a cutting board. Let all of the chicken cool slightly, then shred it into bite-size pieces with two forks, discarding the skin and bones. Let the soup settle for 5 minutes, then skim the fat from the surface using a large spoon. Discard the bay leaves.

5. Bring 4 quarts water to a boil in a large pot. Add 1 tablespoon salt and the noodles to the boiling water and cook until tender, then drain. Stir the cooked noodles, shredded chicken, and peas into the soup and let sit until heated through, about 5 minutes. Stir in the parsley, season with salt and pepper to taste, and serve.

BEST BEEF STEW

WHY THIS RECIPE WORKS: The taste of beef stew is rarely as complex as its rich aroma would lead you to believe. We wanted a rich-tasting but approachable beef stew with tender meat, flavorful vegetables, and a rich brown gravy that justified the time it took to prepare.

Step one for achieving rich meaty flavor is proper browning. If you crowd the pan, the meat ends up steaming in its own juices, so for a big pot of stew, it's important to sear the meat in two separate batches. After browning the beef (beefy-tasting chuck-eye is our preferred cut for stew), we caramelized the usual choices of onions and carrots, rather than just adding them raw to the broth.

Along with traditional stew components like garlic, red wine, and chicken broth, we added ingredients rich in glutamates like tomato paste, salt pork, and anchovies. Glutamates are compounds that give meat its savory taste and they contribute considerable flavor to the dish. To mimic the luxurious, mouth-coating texture of beef stews made with homemade stock (provided by the collagen in bones that is transformed into gelatin when simmered), we included powdered gelatin and flour. The rest of the recipe was simple. We added frozen pearl onions toward the end of cooking along with some frozen peas. As for potatoes, medium-starch Yukon Golds added halfway through cooking beat out starchy russets.

Best Beef Stew

SERVES 6 TO 8

Use a good-quality medium-bodied wine, such as a Côtes du Rhône or Pinot Noir, for this stew. Try to find beef that is well marbled with white veins of fat. Meat that is too lean will come out slightly dry. Four pounds of blade steaks, trimmed of gristle and silver skin, can be substituted for the chuck-eye roast. While the blade steak will yield slightly thinner pieces after trimming, it should still be cut into 1½-inch pieces. Look for salt pork that looks meaty and is roughly 75 percent lean.

- 2 medium garlic cloves, minced or pressed through a garlic press (about 2 teaspoons)
- 4 anchovy fillets, minced fine (about 2 teaspoons)
- 1 tablespoon tomato paste
- 1 (4-pound) boneless chuck-eye roast, trimmed of excess fat and cut into 1½-inch pieces
- 2 tablespoons vegetable oil
- 1 large onion, halved and sliced ⅛ inch thick
- 4 carrots, peeled and cut into 1-inch pieces
- ¼ cup unbleached all-purpose flour
- 2 cups red wine (see note)
- 2 cups low-sodium chicken broth
- 4 ounces salt pork (see note), rinsed of excess salt
- 2 bay leaves
- 4 sprigs fresh thyme
- 1 pound Yukon Gold potatoes, scrubbed and cut into 1-inch pieces
- 1½ cups frozen pearl onions, thawed
- 2 teaspoons (about 1 packet) unflavored powdered gelatin
- ½ cup water
- 1 cup frozen peas, thawed
- Table salt and ground black pepper

1. Adjust an oven rack to the lower-middle position and heat the oven to 300 degrees. Combine the garlic and anchovies in a small bowl and press the mixture with the back of a fork to form a paste. Stir in the tomato paste and set the mixture aside.

2. Pat the meat dry with paper towels (do not season the meat). Heat 1 tablespoon of the vegetable oil in a large Dutch oven over high heat until just starting to smoke. Add half of the beef and cook until well browned on all sides, about 8 minutes total, reducing the heat if the oil begins to smoke or the fond begins to burn. Transfer the beef to a large plate. Repeat with the remaining 1 tablespoon vegetable oil and remaining beef, leaving the second batch of meat in the pot after browning.

3. Reduce the heat to medium and return the first batch of beef to the pot. Add the onion and carrots to the pot and stir to combine with the beef. Cook, scraping the bottom of the pan to loosen any browned bits, until the onion is softened, 1 to 2 minutes. Add the garlic mixture and cook, stirring constantly, until fragrant, about 30 seconds. Add the flour and cook, stirring constantly, until no dry flour remains, about 30 seconds.

4. Slowly add the wine, scraping the bottom of the pan to loosen any browned bits. Increase the heat to high and allow the wine to simmer until thickened and slightly reduced, about 2 minutes. Stir in the broth, salt pork, bay leaves, and thyme. Bring to a simmer, cover, transfer to the oven, and cook for 1½ hours.

5. Remove the pot from the oven. Remove and discard the bay leaves and salt pork. Stir in the potatoes, cover, return the pot to the oven, and cook until the potatoes are almost tender, about 45 minutes.

6. Using a large spoon, skim any excess fat from the surface of the stew. Stir in the pearl onions. Cook over medium heat until the potatoes and onions are cooked through and the meat offers little resistance when poked with a fork (the meat should not be falling apart), about 15 minutes. Meanwhile, sprinkle the gelatin over the water in a small bowl and allow to soften for 5 minutes.

7. Increase the heat to high and stir in the softened gelatin mixture and the peas. Simmer until the gelatin is fully dissolved and the stew is thickened, about 3 minutes. Season with salt and pepper to taste. Serve. (The stew can be cooled, covered tightly, and refrigerated for up to 2 days. Reheat it gently before serving.)

OUR FAVORITE CHILI

WHY THIS RECIPE WORKS: Our goal in creating an "ultimate" beef chili was to determine which of the "secret ingredients" recommended by chili experts around the world were spot-on—and which were expendable. We started with the beef. Most recipes call for ground beef, but we preferred meaty blade steaks, which don't require much trimming and stayed in big chunks in our finished chili. For complex chile flavor, we traded in the commercial chili powder in favor of ground dried ancho and de árbol chiles; for a grassy heat, we added fresh jalapeños. Dried beans, brined before cooking, stayed creamy for the duration of cooking. Beer and chicken broth outperformed red wine, coffee, and beef broth as the liquid components. For balancing sweetness, light molasses beat out other offbeat ingredients (including prunes and Coca-Cola). And finally, for the right level of thickness, flour and peanut butter didn't perform as promised; instead, a small amount of ordinary cornmeal sealed the deal, providing just the right consistency in our ultimate beef chili.

Our Favorite Chili

SERVES 6 TO 8

A 4-pound chuck-eye roast, well trimmed of fat, can be substituted for the steak. Because much of the chili flavor is held in the fat of this dish, refrain from skimming fat from the surface. Dried New Mexican or guajillo chiles make a good substitute for the anchos; each dried de árbol may be replaced with ⅛ teaspoon cayenne pepper. If you prefer not to work with any whole dried chiles, the anchos and de árbols can be replaced with ½ cup commercial chili powder and ¼ to ½ teaspoon cayenne pepper, though the texture of the chili will be slightly compromised. Good choices for condiments include diced avocado, finely chopped red onion, chopped cilantro leaves, lime wedges, sour cream, and shredded Monterey Jack or cheddar cheese.

    Table salt
8 ounces dried pinto beans (1¼ cups), picked over and rinsed
6 dried ancho chiles, stemmed, seeded, and torn into 1-inch pieces
2-4 dried de árbol chiles, stemmed, seeded, and split into 2 pieces
3 tablespoons cornmeal
2 teaspoons dried oregano

2 teaspoons ground cumin

2 teaspoons cocoa powder

2½ cups low-sodium chicken broth

2 medium onions, cut into ¾-inch pieces

3 small jalapeño chiles, stemmed, seeded, and
cut into ½-inch pieces

3 tablespoons vegetable oil

4 medium garlic cloves, minced or pressed through a
garlic press (about 4 teaspoons)

1 (14.5-ounce) can diced tomatoes

2 teaspoons light molasses

3½ pounds blade steak, ¾ inch thick, trimmed and
cut into ¾-inch pieces

1 (12-ounce) bottle mild lager, such as Budweiser

1. Combine 3 tablespoons salt, 4 quarts water, and the beans in a Dutch oven and bring to a boil over high heat. Remove the pot from the heat, cover, and let sit for 1 hour. Drain and rinse well.

2. Adjust an oven rack to the lower-middle position and heat the oven to 300 degrees. Place the ancho chiles in a 12-inch skillet set over medium-high heat; toast, stirring frequently, until the flesh is fragrant, 4 to 6 minutes, reducing the heat if the chiles begin to smoke. Transfer to a food processor and cool. Do not wash out the skillet.

3. Add the de árbol chiles, cornmeal, oregano, cumin, cocoa, and ½ teaspoon salt to the food processor with the toasted ancho chiles; process until finely ground, about 2 minutes. With the processor running, slowly add ½ cup chicken broth until a smooth paste forms, about 45 seconds, scraping down the sides of the bowl as necessary. Transfer the paste to a small bowl. Place the onions in the now-empty processor and pulse until roughly chopped, about 4 pulses. Add the jalapeños and pulse until the consistency of chunky salsa, about 4 pulses, scraping down the bowl as necessary.

4. Heat 1 tablespoon oil in the Dutch oven over medium-high heat. Add the onion mixture and cook, stirring occasionally, until the moisture has evaporated and the vegetables are softened, 7 to 9 minutes. Add the garlic and cook until fragrant, about 1 minute. Add the chile paste, tomatoes, and molasses; stir until the chile paste is thoroughly combined. Add the remaining 2 cups chicken broth and the drained beans; bring to a boil, then reduce the heat to a simmer.

5. Meanwhile, heat 1 tablespoon more oil in the 12-inch skillet over medium-high heat until shimmering. Pat the beef dry with paper towels and sprinkle with 1 teaspoon salt. Add half of the beef and cook until browned on all sides, about 10 minutes. Transfer the meat to the Dutch oven. Add half of the beer to the skillet, scraping up any browned bits from the bottom of the skillet, and bring to a simmer. Transfer the beer to the Dutch oven. Repeat with the remaining 1 tablespoon oil, the remaining steak, and the remaining beer. Stir to combine and return the mixture to a simmer.

6. Cover the pot and transfer to the oven. Cook until the meat and beans are fully tender, 1½ to 2 hours. Let the chili stand, uncovered, for 10 minutes. Stir well, season with salt to taste, and serve. (The chili can be refrigerated for up to 3 days.)

QUICK BEEF AND VEGETABLE SOUP

WHY THIS RECIPE WORKS: Rich and hearty beef and vegetable soup with old-fashioned flavor is a snap to make—if you have a few hours free and several pounds of beef and bones hanging around. We wanted to find another way to develop the same flavors and textures in under an hour.

We knew the key to this recipe would be finding the right cut of meat, one that had great beefy flavor and that would cook up tender in a reasonable amount of time. Tender cuts, like strip steak and rib eye, became tough, livery, and chalky when simmered in soup. Sirloin tip steak was the best choice—when cut into small pieces, the meat was tender and offered the illusion of being cooked for hours, plus its meaty flavor imparted richness to the soup.

In place of labor-intensive homemade beef broth, we doctored store-bought beef broth with aromatics and lightened its flavor profile with chicken broth. To further boost the flavor of the beef, we added cremini mushrooms, tomato paste, soy sauce, and red wine, ingredients that are rich in glutamates, naturally occurring compounds that accentuate the meat's hearty flavor. To mimic the rich body of a homemade meat stock (made rich through the gelatin released by the meat bones' collagen during the long simmering process), we relied on powdered gelatin. Our beef and vegetable soup now had the same richness and flavor as cooked-all-day versions in a whole lot less time.

Quick Beef and Vegetable Soup

SERVES 4 TO 6

Choose whole sirloin tip steaks over ones that have been cut into small pieces for stir-fries. If sirloin tip steaks are unavailable, substitute blade or flank steak, removing any hard gristle or excess fat. Button mushrooms can be used in place of the cremini mushrooms, with some trade-off in flavor. If you like, add 1 cup frozen peas, frozen corn, or frozen cut green beans during the last 5 minutes of cooking. For a heartier soup, add 10 ounces red potatoes, cut into ½-inch pieces (2 cups), during the last 15 minutes of cooking.

1 pound sirloin tip steaks, trimmed of excess fat and cut into ½-inch pieces (see note)
2 tablespoons soy sauce
1 teaspoon vegetable oil
1 pound cremini mushrooms, stems trimmed, caps wiped clean, and quartered (see note)
1 large onion, chopped medium
2 tablespoons tomato paste
1 medium garlic clove, minced or pressed through a garlic press (about 1 teaspoon)
½ cup red wine
4 cups beef broth
1¾ cups low-sodium chicken broth
4 medium carrots, peeled and cut into ½-inch pieces
2 medium celery ribs, cut into ½-inch pieces
1 bay leaf
1 tablespoon unflavored powdered gelatin
½ cup cold water
2 tablespoons minced fresh parsley leaves
Table salt and ground black pepper

1. Combine the beef and soy sauce in a medium bowl; set aside for 15 minutes.

2. Heat the oil in a large Dutch oven over medium-high heat until just smoking. Add the mushrooms and onion; cook, stirring frequently, until the onion is browned and dark bits form on the pan bottom, 8 to 12 minutes. Transfer the vegetables to a bowl.

3. Add the beef and cook, stirring occasionally, until the liquid evaporates and the meat starts to brown, 6 to 10 minutes. Add the tomato paste and garlic; cook, stirring constantly, until fragrant, about 30 seconds. Add the red wine, scraping the bottom of the pot with a wooden spoon to loosen any browned bits, and cook until syrupy, 1 to 2 minutes.

4. Add the beef broth, chicken broth, carrots, celery, bay leaf, and browned mushrooms and onion; bring to a boil. Reduce the heat to low, cover, and simmer until the vegetables and meat are tender, 25 to 30 minutes. While the soup is simmering, sprinkle the gelatin over the cold water and let stand.

5. When the soup is finished, turn off the heat. Remove and discard the bay leaf. Add the gelatin mixture and stir until completely dissolved. Stir in the parsley, season with salt and pepper to taste, and serve.

CLASSIC CREAM OF TOMATO SOUP

WHY THIS RECIPE WORKS: Canned cream of tomato soup is a childhood favorite. But grown-up tastes deserve something better—and let's face it, the canned soup's overly sweet flavors are just not all that appealing today. We wanted a well-balanced cream of tomato soup, one with rich color, great tomato flavor, and a silky texture.

Right away, we turned to canned tomatoes; fresh tomatoes are at their best just a few months out of the year and we didn't want to restrict our soup-making to just one season. To coax the most flavor from our canned whole tomatoes, it was essential to roast them in the oven. The intense dry heat worked to evaporate surface liquids and concentrate the flavor, and a sprinkling of brown sugar encouraged caramelization. We cooked our roasted tomatoes with shallots, chicken broth, and reserved tomato juice to develop robust flavor, then pureed the tomatoes (with broth) to keep the deep red flavor of the tomato broth intact. Finished with heavy cream and a splash of brandy, this cream of tomato soup will satisfy everyone at the table.

Classic Cream of Tomato Soup
SERVES 6

Make sure to use canned whole tomatoes packed in juice. To obtain 3 cups of juice, use the packing juice as well as the liquid that falls from the tomatoes when they are seeded.

    2   (28-ounce) cans whole tomatoes packed in juice,
        drained, 3 cups juice reserved (see note)
    1½ tablespoons dark brown sugar
    4   tablespoons (½ stick) unsalted butter
    2   large shallots, minced (about ½ cup)
    1   tablespoon tomato paste
        Pinch ground allspice
    2   tablespoons unbleached all-purpose flour
    1¾ cups low-sodium chicken broth
    ½   cup heavy cream
    2   tablespoons brandy or dry sherry
        Table salt and cayenne pepper

1. Adjust an oven rack to the upper-middle position and heat the oven to 450 degrees. Line a large rimmed baking sheet with foil. With your fingers, carefully open the whole tomatoes over a fine-mesh strainer set in a bowl and push out the seeds, allowing the juices to fall through the strainer into the bowl; discard the seeds. Spread the seeded tomatoes in a single layer on the foil and sprinkle evenly with the brown sugar. Bake until all the liquid has evaporated and the tomatoes begin to color, about 30 minutes. Cool the tomatoes slightly, then peel them off the foil; transfer to a small bowl and set aside.

2. Melt the butter in a large saucepan over medium heat. Add the shallots, tomato paste, and allspice. Reduce the heat to low, cover, and cook, stirring occasionally, until the shallots are softened, 7 to 10 minutes. Add the flour and cook, stirring constantly, until thoroughly combined, about 30 seconds. Gradually add the chicken broth, whisking constantly to combine; stir in the reserved tomato juice and roasted tomatoes. Cover, increase the heat to medium, and bring to a boil. Reduce the heat to low and simmer, stirring occasionally, for 10 minutes.

3. Pour the mixture through a fine-mesh strainer into a medium bowl; rinse and dry the saucepan. Transfer the tomatoes and solids in the strainer to a blender; add 1 cup of the strained liquid and puree until smooth. Add the pureed mixture and the remaining strained liquid to the saucepan. Add the cream and warm over low heat until hot, about 3 minutes. Off the heat, stir in the brandy, season with salt and cayenne to taste, and serve. (The soup can be refrigerated in an airtight container for up to 2 days. Warm over low heat until hot; do not boil.)

CREAMLESS CREAMY TOMATO SOUP

WHY THIS RECIPE WORKS: Creamy tomato soup boasts a bright, sweet tomato flavor when done right, but not everyone is a fan of rich cream soups. We wanted to keep the sharp tomatoey flavor in this classic soup, but ditch the dairy and tame the tartness in other ways.

Our first step was to choose canned tomatoes over fresh tomatoes—canned are simply more consistent in flavor than your average supermarket tomato. We mashed whole tomatoes (preferred over diced or crushed for their concentrated flavor) with a potato masher, then combined them with aromatics sautéed in extra-virgin olive oil, not butter, which guaranteed bright, clean flavor. Stirring in some olive oil before pureeing our soup added back vital flavor that was lost when we cooked the oil. To combat the acid in the tomatoes, we added full-flavored brown sugar. And for an ultra-creamy texture without the cream, we pureed sandwich bread into the soup. For a final touch, we stirred chicken broth into the pot and simmered the soup briefly to give our creamless creamy tomato soup a rich and velvety feel.

Creamless Creamy Tomato Soup

SERVES 6

If half of the soup fills your blender more than halfway, process the soup in three batches, but do not add more olive oil for the third batch. You can also use a hand-held blender to process the soup directly in the pot. Serve this soup topped with Classic Croutons (recipe follows), if desired. For an even smoother soup, strain the pureed mixture through a fine-mesh strainer before stirring in the chicken broth in step 2.

- ¼ cup extra-virgin olive oil, plus extra for drizzling (see note)
- 1 medium onion, chopped medium
- 3 medium garlic cloves, minced or pressed through a garlic press (about 1 tablespoon)
  Pinch red pepper flakes (optional)
- 1 bay leaf
- 2 (28-ounce) cans whole tomatoes
- 3 slices high-quality white sandwich bread, crusts removed, torn into 1-inch pieces
- 1 tablespoon brown sugar
- 2 cups low-sodium chicken broth
- 2 tablespoons brandy (optional)
  Table salt and ground black pepper
- ¼ cup chopped fresh chives

1. Heat 2 tablespoons of the oil in a large Dutch oven over medium-high heat until shimmering. Add the onion, garlic, red pepper flakes (if using), and bay leaf. Cook, stirring frequently, until the onion is translucent, 3 to 5 minutes. Stir in the tomatoes with their juice. Using a potato masher, mash until no pieces bigger than 2 inches remain. Stir in the bread and sugar and bring the soup to a boil. Reduce the heat to medium and cook, stirring occasionally, until the bread is completely saturated and starts to break down, about 5 minutes. Remove and discard the bay leaf.

2. Transfer half of the soup to a blender. Add 1 tablespoon more oil and process until the soup is smooth and creamy, 2 to 3 minutes. Transfer to a large bowl and repeat with the remaining soup and the remaining 1 tablespoon oil. Rinse and dry the Dutch oven and return the soup to the pot. Stir in the chicken broth and brandy (if using). Return the soup to a boil and season with salt and pepper to taste. Ladle the soup into bowls, sprinkle with the chopped chives, drizzle with olive oil, and serve. (The soup, minus the garnish, can be refrigerated in an airtight container for up to 2 days. Warm over low heat until hot; do not boil.)

Classic Croutons

MAKES ABOUT 1½ CUPS

- 3 slices high-quality white sandwich bread, crusts removed, cut into ½-inch cubes (about 1½ cups)
- 1½ tablespoons olive oil
  Table salt and ground black pepper

1. Adjust an oven rack to the upper-middle position and heat the oven to 400 degrees. Combine the bread cubes and oil in a medium bowl and toss to coat. Season with salt and pepper to taste.

2. Spread the bread cubes in an even layer on a rimmed baking sheet and bake, stirring occasionally, until golden, 8 to 10 minutes. Cool on the baking sheet to room temperature. (The croutons can be stored in an airtight container or a plastic bag for up to 3 days.)

CREAMY PEA SOUP

WHY THIS RECIPE WORKS: Sweet pea soup is a labor of love—fresh peas are shelled, blanched, cooked with other vegetables, then passed through a sieve. We were after a fuss-free but still elegant version of this special soup. Our goal was a streamlined approach that would produce a soup with silky texture and real pea flavor.

Both garden and grocery store peas can be disappointing; fresh pods often reveal tough, starchy pellets that require a significant amount of time spent shelling. Instead, we decided to use frozen peas, which are processed at the height of ripeness, so their freshness and flavor is completely preserved. For maximum pea flavor, we ground the frozen peas in a food processor before adding them to our simple soup base of chicken broth and shallots. Adding some Boston lettuce leaves gave the soup a wonderfully frothy texture. And a small dose of heavy cream added richness. Now the focus is on the peas, not the work, with this easy recipe for creamy pea soup that highlights the natural sweetness of peas (even frozen ones).

Creamy Pea Soup

SERVES 4 TO 6

A few Classic Croutons (see page 12) are the perfect embellishment to this smooth soup.

- 4 tablespoons (½ stick) unsalted butter
- 4 large shallots, minced (about 1 cup), or 2 medium leeks, white and light green parts chopped fine and rinsed thoroughly (about 1⅓ cups)
- 2 tablespoons unbleached all-purpose flour
- 3½ cups low-sodium chicken broth
- 1½ pounds frozen peas (about 4½ cups), partially thawed at room temperature for 10 minutes
- 12 small leaves Boston lettuce (about 3 ounces), washed and dried
- ½ cup heavy cream
- Table salt and ground black pepper

1. Melt the butter in a large saucepan over low heat. Add the shallots and cook, covered, until softened, 8 to 10 minutes, stirring occasionally. Add the flour and cook, stirring constantly, until thoroughly combined, about 30 seconds. Whisking constantly, gradually add the chicken broth. Increase the heat to high and bring to a boil. Reduce the heat to medium-low and simmer for 3 to 5 minutes.

2. Meanwhile, process the peas in a food processor until coarsely chopped, about 20 seconds. Add the peas and lettuce to the saucepan. Increase the heat to medium-high, cover, and return to a simmer; cook for 3 minutes. Uncover, reduce the heat to medium-low, and continue to simmer 2 minutes longer.

3. Working in batches, puree the soup in a blender until smooth, filling the blender jar only halfway for each batch. Strain the soup through a fine-mesh strainer into a large bowl; discard the solids in the strainer. Rinse and dry the saucepan; return the pureed mixture to the saucepan and stir in the cream. Warm the soup over low heat until hot, about 3 minutes. Season with salt and pepper to taste and serve. (The soup can be refrigerated in an airtight container for up to 2 days. Warm over low heat until hot; do not boil.)

CREAMY MUSHROOM SOUP

WHY THIS RECIPE WORKS: Mushroom soups have great potential, but they often disappoint with their lackluster taste and less-than-stellar texture. We knew this pureed soup could be richly textured, neither too thick nor too thin, and showcase the deep, earthy flavor of mushrooms.

We chose to use readily available white mushrooms, which are often underestimated; fresh wild mushrooms were shelved because they can be expensive and difficult to find. To bring out the most flavor from the mushrooms, we had to slice them by hand (processing made for uneven and bruised pieces) and then sweat them in a covered pot with butter and shallots; roasted mushrooms were nixed because the juices released during roasting had browned on the pan and were lost, making for flavorless soup. Chicken broth proved a better addition than water for the liquid base, and dried porcini mushrooms amplified the mushroom flavor. After pureeing the soup, we added cream and a splash of Madeira for body. Our creamy mushroom soup was now texturally light and full of deep, rich flavor.

Creamy Mushroom Soup

SERVES 6 TO 8

The garnish of sautéed mushrooms (recipe follows) adds visual and textural appeal to this creamy soup.

- 6 tablespoons (¾ stick) unsalted butter
- 3 large shallots, minced (about ¾ cup)
- 1 medium garlic clove, minced or pressed through a garlic press (about 1 teaspoon)
- ½ teaspoon freshly grated nutmeg
- 2 pounds white mushrooms, wiped clean and sliced ¼ inch thick
- 4 cups hot water
- 3½ cups low-sodium chicken broth
- ½ ounce dried porcini mushrooms, rinsed well
- ⅓ cup Madeira or dry sherry
- 1 cup heavy cream
- 2 teaspoons juice from 1 lemon
  Table salt and ground black pepper
- 1 recipe Sautéed Wild Mushrooms, for garnish (recipe follows; see note)

1. Melt the butter in a large Dutch oven over medium-low heat. Add the shallots and sauté, stirring frequently, until softened, about 4 minutes. Stir in the garlic and nutmeg and cook until fragrant, about 30 seconds. Increase the heat to medium, add the white mushrooms, and stir to coat with the butter. Cook, stirring occasionally, until the mushrooms release some liquid, about 7 minutes. Reduce the heat to medium-low, cover the pot, and cook, stirring occasionally, until the mushrooms have released all their liquid, about 20 minutes.

2. Add the water, chicken broth, and porcini mushrooms. Cover, bring to a simmer, then reduce the heat to low and simmer until the mushrooms are fully tender, about 20 minutes.

3. Working in batches, puree the soup in a blender until smooth, filling the blender jar only halfway for each batch. Rinse and dry the pot; return the soup to the pot. Stir in the Madeira and cream and bring to a simmer over low heat. Add the lemon juice and season with salt and pepper to taste. Ladle the soup into bowls, garnish with sautéed wild mushrooms, and serve. (The soup, minus the garnish, can be refrigerated in an airtight container for up to 2 days. Warm over low heat until hot; do not boil.)

Sautéed Wild Mushrooms

MAKES ENOUGH TO GARNISH 6 TO 8 BOWLS OF SOUP

- 2 tablespoons unsalted butter
- 8 ounces shiitake, chanterelle, oyster, or cremini mushrooms, stems trimmed and discarded, mushrooms wiped clean and sliced thin
  Table salt and ground black pepper

1. Melt the butter in a medium skillet over low heat. Add the mushrooms and season with salt and pepper to taste. Cover and cook, stirring occasionally, until the mushrooms release their liquid, about 10 minutes for shiitakes and chanterelles, about 5 minutes for oysters, and about 9 minutes for cremini.

2. Uncover and continue to cook, stirring occasionally, until the liquid released by the mushrooms has evaporated and the mushrooms are browned, about 2 minutes for shiitakes, oysters, and cremini and about 3 minutes for chanterelles. Serve immediately as garnish for the soup.

BUTTERNUT SQUASH SOUP

WHY THIS RECIPE WORKS: Butternut squash soup strikes a perfect balance between nuttiness and sweetness. But getting that balance right depends on selecting just a few key ingredients so the sweet squash flavor can take center stage.

We found our answer to intense squash flavor in the squash's seeds and fibers. We sautéed shallots and butter with the seeds and fibers, simmered them in water, then used the liquid to steam the unpeeled quartered squash (thereby eliminating the pesky task of peeling raw squash). Once cooled, we scooped the flesh from the skin and pureed the squash with the steaming liquid (strained of seeds and fibers) for a soup with a perfectly smooth texture. A little dark brown sugar added to the soup also intensified the sweetness of the squash. Finally, we enriched the soup with a splash of heavy cream and a pinch of nutmeg to round out this velvety soup's rich flavors.

Butternut Squash Soup

SERVES 4 TO 6

Lightly toasted pumpkin seeds, drizzles of balsamic vinegar, or sprinklings of paprika make appealing accompaniments to this soup.

- 4 tablespoons (½ stick) unsalted butter
- 1 large shallot, minced (about ¼ cup)
- 3 pounds butternut squash (about 1 large squash), cut in half lengthwise, each half cut in half widthwise; seeds and fibers scraped out and reserved
- 6 cups water
  Table salt
- ½ cup heavy cream
- 1 teaspoon dark brown sugar
  Pinch grated nutmeg

1. Melt the butter in a large Dutch oven over medium-low heat. Add the shallot and cook, stirring frequently, until translucent, about 3 minutes. Add the seeds and fibers from the squash and cook, stirring occasionally, until the butter turns a saffron color, about 4 minutes.

2. Add the water and 1 teaspoon salt to the pot and bring to a boil over high heat. Reduce the heat to medium-low, place the squash, cut side down, in a steamer basket, and lower the basket into the pot. Cover and steam until the

squash is completely tender, about 30 minutes. Take the pot off the heat and use tongs to transfer the squash to a rimmed baking sheet. When cool enough to handle, use a large spoon to scrape the flesh from the skin. Reserve the squash flesh in a bowl and discard the skin.

3. Strain the steaming liquid through a fine-mesh strainer into a second bowl; discard the solids in the strainer. (You should have 2½ to 3 cups liquid.) Rinse and dry the pot.

4. Working in batches and filling the blender jar only halfway for each batch, puree the squash, adding enough reserved steaming liquid to obtain a smooth consistency. Transfer the puree to the clean pot and stir in the remaining steaming liquid, the cream, and brown sugar. Warm the soup over medium-low heat until hot, about 3 minutes. Stir in the nutmeg, season with salt to taste, and serve. (The soup can be refrigerated in an airtight container for up to 2 days. Warm over low heat until hot; do not boil.)

RUSTIC POTATO-LEEK SOUP

WHY THIS RECIPE WORKS: Rustic potato-leek soup often disappoints with soft, mealy potatoes and dingy, overcooked leeks. We wanted to perfect this soup so both ingredients would be at their best and the dish would retain its textural integrity and bright flavor.

We quickly eliminated potatoes with high or medium starch levels because they broke down too quickly in the chicken broth. Waxy, low-starch red potatoes were perfect—they kept their shape and didn't become waterlogged during cooking. To pump up the flavor of the soup, we used a substantial amount of leeks and sautéed both the white and light green parts in butter. Leeks and potatoes require different cooking times, so we staggered the cooking—leeks first, then potatoes, and then we removed the pot from the stove so the potatoes could gently cook through in the hot broth without becoming overcooked and mushy. We also added a bit of flour with the sautéed leeks to give our broth some body. At long last, we had a flavorful, oniony soup, full of perfectly cooked potatoes and sweet, tender leeks.

Rustic Potato-Leek Soup

SERVES 6

Leeks can vary in size; if your leeks have large white and light green parts, use the smaller amount of leeks given.

- **6 tablespoons (¾ stick) unsalted butter**
- **4–5 pounds leeks, white and light green parts only, halved lengthwise, sliced crosswise 1 inch thick, and rinsed thoroughly (about 11 cups; see note)**
- **1 tablespoon unbleached all-purpose flour**
- **5¼ cups low-sodium chicken broth**
- **1¾ pounds red potatoes (about 5 medium), peeled and cut into ¾-inch chunks**
- **1 bay leaf**
- **Table salt and ground black pepper**

1. Melt the butter in a large Dutch oven over medium-low heat. Add the leeks, increase the heat to medium, cover, and cook, stirring occasionally, until the leeks are tender but not mushy, 15 to 20 minutes; do not brown them. Add the flour and cook, stirring constantly, until thoroughly combined, about 2 minutes.

2. Increase the heat to high; whisking constantly, gradually add the broth. Add the potatoes and bay leaf, cover, and bring to a boil. Reduce the heat to medium-low and simmer, covered, until the potatoes are almost tender, 5 to 7 minutes. Remove the pot from the heat and let stand, covered, until the potatoes are tender, 10 to 15 minutes. Discard the bay leaf, season with salt and pepper to taste, and serve. (The soup can be refrigerated in an airtight container for up to 2 days. Warm over low heat until hot; do not boil.)

BROCCOLI-CHEESE SOUP

WHY THIS RECIPE WORKS: We were after a soup with pure broccoli flavor that wasn't hiding behind the cream or the cheese. Overcooked broccoli has a sulfurous flavor, but we discovered when we cooked our broccoli beyond the point of just overcooked—for a full hour—those sulfur-containing compounds broke down, leaving behind intense, nutty broccoli. Its texture was fairly soft, but that was perfect for use in a soup. Adding baking soda to the pot sped up the process, shortening the broccoli's cooking time to a mere 20 minutes. A little spinach lent bright green color to the soup without taking over the flavor. After adding cheddar and Parmesan, we had a soup so full of flavor and richness that it didn't even need the typical cream.

Broccoli-Cheese Soup

SERVES 6 TO 8

To make a vegetarian version of this soup, substitute vegetable broth for the chicken broth.

- **2 tablespoons unsalted butter**
- **2 pounds broccoli, florets chopped into 1-inch pieces, stems peeled and sliced ¼ inch thick**
- **1 medium onion, chopped coarse**
- **2 medium garlic cloves, minced or pressed through a garlic press (about 2 teaspoons)**
- **1½ teaspoons dry mustard**
- **Pinch cayenne pepper**
- **Table salt and ground black pepper**
- **3–4 cups water**
- **¼ teaspoon baking soda**
- **2 cups low-sodium chicken broth**

2 ounces baby spinach (about 2 cups)
3 ounces sharp cheddar cheese, shredded (about ¾ cup)
1½ ounces Parmesan cheese, grated fine (about ¾ cup), plus extra for serving
1 recipe Buttery Croutons (page 18)

1. Melt the butter in a Dutch oven over medium-high heat. Add the broccoli, onion, garlic, mustard, cayenne, and 1 teaspoon salt and cook, stirring frequently, until fragrant, about 6 minutes. Add 1 cup water and the baking soda. Bring to a simmer, cover, and cook until the broccoli is very soft, about 20 minutes, stirring once during cooking.

2. Add the broth and 2 cups more water and increase the heat to medium-high. When the mixture begins to simmer, stir in the spinach and cook until wilted, about 1 minute. Transfer half of the soup to a blender, add the cheddar and Parmesan, and process until smooth, about 1 minute. Transfer the soup to a medium bowl and repeat with the remaining soup. Return the soup to the Dutch oven, place over medium heat and bring to a simmer. Adjust the consistency of the soup with up to 1 cup water. Season with salt and pepper to taste. Serve, passing extra Parmesan.

HEARTY LENTIL SOUP

WHY THIS RECIPE WORKS: A hot bowl of lentil soup provides warm comfort on a cold day and, when properly prepared, tastes great—maybe even better—the next day. We wanted a hearty lentil soup worthy of a second bowl, not the tasteless variety we have so often encountered.

While *lentilles du Puy* are our top choice for lentil soup, almost any lentil (other than red lentils) can be used. To keep the lentils from losing their shape as they cooked, we sweated them with sautéed aromatic vegetables before adding chicken broth to the soup pot. These lentils stayed intact in our final soup, but their flavor was weak. Revisiting this step, we added canned tomatoes and crisp bacon, which gave our lentils a huge flavor boost. And because we cooked the bacon first, we could then use the rendered fat to sauté our vegetables and aromatics, which brought a nice smoky flavor to the soup. Looking for a not too smooth, or too thick, texture we pureed a few cups of the soup and added it back to the pot to warm through. Lentil soup needs plenty of acidity, so we used white wine as part of the broth and finished the soup with balsamic vinegar.

Hearty Lentil Soup
SERVES 4 TO 6

Lentilles du Puy, sometimes called French green lentils, are our first choice for this recipe, but brown, black, or regular green lentils are fine, too. Note that cooking times will vary depending on the type of lentils used. Be sure to rinse and then carefully sort through the lentils to remove any small stones.

3 ounces (3 slices) bacon, cut into ¼-inch pieces
1 large onion, minced
2 medium carrots, peeled and chopped medium
3 medium garlic cloves, minced or pressed through a garlic press (about 1 tablespoon)
1 (14.5-ounce) can diced tomatoes, drained
1 bay leaf
1 teaspoon minced fresh thyme leaves
1 cup (7 ounces) lentils, rinsed and picked over (see note)
1 teaspoon table salt
  Ground black pepper
½ cup dry white wine
4½ cups low-sodium chicken broth
1½ cups water
1½ teaspoons balsamic vinegar
3 tablespoons minced fresh parsley leaves

1. Fry the bacon in a large Dutch oven over medium-high heat, stirring occasionally, until the fat is rendered and the bacon is crisp, 3 to 4 minutes. Add the onion and carrots; cook, stirring occasionally, until the vegetables begin to soften, about 2 minutes. Add the garlic and cook until fragrant, about 30 seconds. Stir in the tomatoes, bay leaf, and thyme; cook until fragrant, about 30 seconds. Stir in the lentils, salt, and pepper to taste; cover, reduce the heat to medium-low, and cook until the vegetables are softened and the lentils have darkened, 8 to 10 minutes.

2. Uncover, increase the heat to high, add the wine, and bring to a simmer. Add the chicken broth and water; bring to a boil, cover partially, and reduce the heat to low. Simmer until the lentils are tender but still hold their shape, 30 to 35 minutes; discard the bay leaf.

3. Puree 3 cups of the soup in a blender until smooth, then return to the pot. Stir in the vinegar and heat the soup over medium-low heat until hot, about 5 minutes. Stir in 2 tablespoons of the parsley. Ladle the soup into bowls, garnish with the remaining parsley, and serve. (The soup, minus the garnish, can be refrigerated in an airtight container for up to 2 days. Warm over low heat until hot; do not boil.)

MODERN HAM AND SPLIT PEA SOUP

WHY THIS RECIPE WORKS: We wanted a spoon-coating, richly flavorful broth studded with tender shreds of sweet-smoky meat. To avoid having to bake a ham beforehand, we needed a substitute for the traditional ham bone. Ham hock made the soup greasy and was skimpy on the meat. Ham steak, however, was plenty meaty and infused the soup with a fuller pork flavor—and we could get away with using just 1 pound. Our soup still needed richness and smokiness, and adding a few strips of raw bacon to the pot did the job. Unsoaked peas broke down just as well as soaked and were better at absorbing the flavor of the soup, so we skipped the traditional soaking step. To dress up our recipe, we garnished it with a handful of fresh peas; their sweetness popped against the hearty, smoky broth. Fresh chopped mint leaves and a drizzle of good balsamic vinegar added visual appeal and punched up the flavors even more. Floating gently fried croutons on the surface rounded off our update of this classic soup.

Modern Ham and Split Pea Soup

SERVES 6 TO 8

Four ounces of regular sliced bacon can be used, but the thinner slices are a little harder to remove from the soup. Depending on the age and brand of split peas, the consistency of the soup may vary slightly. If the soup is too thin at the end of step 3, increase the heat and simmer, uncovered, until the desired consistency is reached. If it is too thick, thin it with a little water. In addition to sprinkling the soup with the Buttery Croutons, we also like to garnish it with fresh peas, chopped mint, and a drizzle of aged balsamic vinegar.

- 2 tablespoons unsalted butter
- 1 large onion, chopped fine
  Table salt and ground black pepper
- 2 medium garlic cloves, minced or pressed through a garlic press (about 2 teaspoons)
- 7 cups water
- 1 ham steak (about 1 pound), skin removed, cut into quarters
- 3 slices thick-cut bacon
- 1 pound (2 cups) green split peas, picked over and rinsed
- 2 sprigs fresh thyme
- 2 bay leaves
- 2 medium carrots, peeled and cut into ½-inch pieces
- 1 medium celery rib, cut into ½-inch pieces
- 1 recipe Buttery Croutons (recipe follows)

1. Heat the butter in a Dutch oven over medium-high heat. Add the onion and ½ teaspoon salt and cook, stirring frequently, until the onion is softened, about 3 to 4 minutes. Add the garlic and cook until fragrant, about 30 seconds. Add the water, ham steak, bacon, peas, thyme, and bay leaves. Increase the heat to high and bring to a simmer, stirring frequently to keep the peas from sticking to the bottom. Reduce the heat to low, cover, and simmer until the peas are tender but not falling apart, about 45 minutes.

2. Remove the ham steak, cover with aluminum foil or plastic wrap to prevent drying out, and set aside. Stir in the carrots and celery and continue to simmer, covered, until the vegetables are tender and the peas have almost completely broken down, about 30 minutes longer.

3. When cool enough to handle, shred the ham into small bite-size pieces. Remove and discard the thyme, bay leaves, and bacon slices. Stir the ham back into the soup and return to a simmer. Season with salt and pepper to taste and serve. (The soup can be refrigerated for up to 3 days. If necessary, thin it with water when reheating.)

Buttery Croutons

MAKES ABOUT 2 CUPS

- 3 tablespoons unsalted butter
- 1 tablespoon olive oil
- 3 large slices high-quality sandwich bread, cut into ½-inch cubes (about 2 cups)
  Table salt

Heat the butter and oil in a 12-inch skillet over medium heat. When the foaming subsides, add the bread cubes and cook, stirring frequently, until golden brown, about 10 minutes. Transfer the croutons to a paper towel–lined plate and season with salt to taste.

HEARTY HAM AND SPLIT PEA SOUP WITH POTATOES

WHY THIS RECIPE WORKS: Split pea soup tends to show up on the home cook's menu only when the previous meal (usually a holiday celebration) featured a big ham—and the leftovers are begging to be made into soup. We wanted a recipe for an old-fashioned ham and split pea soup that could be made anytime, with a readily available cut of ham that would also provide enough meat for really hearty soup. We found that we could get good, meaty ham stock with a picnic shoulder, a small, inexpensive cut that adds great flavor and provides plenty of meat for the soup (and some leftovers too). While it was easy enough to cook the peas in the ham stock, our vegetables benefited from a sauté in a separate pan. We had started out wanting a one-pot operation, but we found that caramelized vegetables gave this straightforward soup a richness and depth of flavor that had been missing—it was well worth the time spent washing an extra pan. Adding in a few red potatoes with the carrots, celery, and onions turned our soup into a truly satisfying meal.

Hearty Ham and Split Pea Soup with Potatoes
SERVES 6

Use an entire small 2½-pound smoked picnic portion ham if you can find one. Otherwise, buy a half-picnic ham and remove some meat, which you can roast and use in sandwiches, salads, or omelets. To remove the meat, loosen the large comma-shaped muscles on top of the ham with your fingers, then use a knife to cut the membrane separating the comma-shaped muscles from the rest of the ham.

- 1 (2½-pound) smoked bone-in picnic ham (see note)
- 4 bay leaves
- 3 quarts water
- 1 pound (2 cups) green split peas, picked over and rinsed
- 1 teaspoon dried thyme
- 2 tablespoons extra-virgin olive oil
- 2 medium onions, chopped medium
- 2 medium carrots, peeled and chopped medium
- 2 celery ribs, chopped medium
- 1 tablespoon unsalted butter
- 2 medium garlic cloves, minced or pressed through a garlic press (about 2 teaspoons)
    Pinch sugar
- 3 small red potatoes (about ½ pound), scrubbed and cut into ½-inch chunks
    Ground black pepper
    Minced red onion (optional)
    Balsamic vinegar

1. Place the ham in a large Dutch oven, add the bay leaves and water, cover, and bring to a boil over medium-high heat. Reduce the heat to low and simmer until the meat is tender and pulls away from the bone, 2 to 2½ hours. Remove the ham meat and bone from the pot and set aside.

2. Add the split peas and thyme to the stock. Bring to a boil, reduce the heat, and simmer, uncovered, until the peas are tender but not dissolved, about 45 minutes. While the vegetables are cooking, shred the meat with your fingers or two forks and set aside. Discard the rind and bone.

3. Meanwhile, heat the oil in a large skillet over medium-high heat until shimmering. Add the onions, carrots, and celery and sauté, stirring frequently, until most of the liquid evaporates and the vegetables begin to brown, 5 to 6 minutes. Reduce the heat to medium-low and add the butter, garlic, and sugar. Cook the vegetables, stirring frequently, until deeply browned, 30 to 35 minutes; set aside.

4. Add the sautéed vegetables, potatoes, and shredded ham to the pot with the split peas. Simmer until the potatoes are tender, the peas dissolve, and the soup thickens to the consistency of light cream, about 20 minutes. Season with pepper to taste. Discard the bay leaves and ladle the soup into bowls. Sprinkle with red onion (if using) and serve, passing balsamic vinegar separately. (The soup, minus the garnishes, can be refrigerated in an airtight container for up to 2 days. Warm over low heat until hot; do not boil.)

MULLIGATAWNY SOUP

WHY THIS RECIPE WORKS: As with many other dishes of Indian origin, mulligatawny soup is mildly spicy and richly flavored, with a number of spices in its lineup. We wanted an elegant, but potent, rendition of this classic soup, not the thin, raw-tasting version found in many restaurants.

Chicken broth proved to be the best base for this pureed vegetable-laden soup; beef broth was too strong and vegetable broth gave us an overly vegetal soup. For the spices, good-quality curry powder is a must, and a little cumin and cayenne pepper made for the perfect spice mix. Garlic, ginger, and coconut were a given—essentials in mulligatawny—but the best way to incorporate them wasn't immediately clear. We ended up adopting a technique common in Indian cooking—we pureed the raw garlic and ginger with water so they could be mixed into the soup for fresh bites of garlic and ginger. The best source for true coconut flavor turned out to be shredded unsweetened coconut.

Finally, to give the finished soup the right amount of body, we made a roux with our aromatics and pureed the soup with a banana, which imparted a rich, sweet flavor to the dish (a potato worked fine, too). A dollop of yogurt and sprinkling of cilantro were the crowning touches on our richly spiced, velvety mulligatawny.

Mulligatawny Soup

SERVES 6 TO 8

Leave the garlic and ginger puree from step 1 in the blender while making the soup; when the finished soup is pureed in the same blender, it will pick up a hit of spicy raw garlic and ginger. For a heartier soup, stir in cooked white rice.

- 4 medium garlic cloves, 2 peeled and 2 minced or pressed through a garlic press (see note)
- 1½ tablespoons minced or grated fresh ginger (see note)
- ¼ cup water
- 3 tablespoons unsalted butter
- 2 medium onions, chopped medium
- 1 teaspoon tomato paste
- ½ cup shredded unsweetened coconut
- ¼ cup unbleached all-purpose flour
- 1½ tablespoons curry powder
- 1 teaspoon ground cumin
- ¼ teaspoon cayenne pepper
- 7 cups low-sodium chicken broth
- 2 medium carrots, peeled and chopped medium
- 1 celery rib, chopped medium
- 1 medium very ripe banana (about 5 ounces), peeled, or 1 medium red potato (about 5 ounces), peeled and cut into 1-inch chunks
   Table salt and ground black pepper
   Plain yogurt
- 2 tablespoons minced fresh cilantro leaves

1. Puree the 2 peeled whole garlic cloves, 2 teaspoons of the ginger, and the water in a blender until smooth; leave the mixture in the blender and set aside.

2. Melt the butter in a large Dutch oven over medium heat. Add the onions and tomato paste and cook, stirring frequently, until the onions are softened and beginning to brown, about 3 minutes. Stir in the coconut and cook until fragrant, about 1 minute. Add the minced garlic, the remaining 2½ teaspoons ginger, the flour, curry powder, cumin, and cayenne; stir until evenly combined, about 1 minute. Whisking constantly, gradually add the chicken broth.

3. Add the carrots, celery, and banana to the pot. Increase the heat to medium-high and bring to a boil. Cover, reduce the heat to low, and simmer until the vegetables are tender, about 20 minutes.

4. Working in batches, puree the soup in the blender with the garlic and ginger until smooth, filling the blender jar only halfway for each batch. Wash and dry the pot. Return the pureed soup to the pot and season with salt and pepper to taste. Warm the soup over medium heat until hot, about 1 minute. Ladle the soup into bowls, spoon a dollop of yogurt over each bowl, sprinkle with the cilantro, and serve. (The soup, minus the garnishes, can be refrigerated in an airtight container for up to 3 days. Warm over low heat until hot; do not boil.)

HEARTY MINESTRONE

WHY THIS RECIPE WORKS: Excellent minestrone soup relies on fresh, perfectly ripe vegetables. But unless you've got access to a sun-drenched garden in the height of summer, you're stuck with lackluster supermarket offerings. We wanted a soup that squeezed every last ounce of flavor out of supermarket vegetables and was as satisfying as minestrone served in Italy.

To start, we limited our vegetables to a manageable six: the aromatic trio of onions, celery, and carrots; hearty cabbage; and fresh, summery zucchini and tomato, all simmered in water. We began our soup by sautéing some finely diced pancetta in a Dutch oven, then browned the vegetables in the rendered fat, which helped develop sweetness and also lent a rich flavor to the components. Before they were fully cooked, we removed the vegetables in order to prepare the starch. We decided to use cannellini beans (a favorite for their creamy texture and buttery flavor), which we soaked overnight in salted water to ensure they cooked evenly and turned out well seasoned. We added the soaked beans along with the cooking liquid (and a Parmesan rind) and simmered them together vigorously—this helped the beans release their starch to thicken the soup. Once the beans were tender, we returned the vegetables to the pot and simmered everything together until the vegetables were cooked through. And rather than using all water, we replaced a portion with chicken broth. But it wasn't until we landed on an unusual addition—V8 juice, rather than canned tomatoes—that our soup boasted consistent tomato and vegetable flavor in every spoonful.

Hearty Minestrone

SERVES 6 TO 8

If you are pressed for time you can "quick-brine" your beans. In step 1, combine the salt, water, and beans in a large Dutch oven and bring to a boil over high heat. Remove the pot from the heat, cover, and let stand 1 hour. Drain and rinse the beans and proceed with the recipe. We prefer cannellini beans, but navy or great Northern beans can be used. We prefer pancetta, but bacon can be used in its place. A Parmesan rind is added for flavor, but can be replaced with a 2-inch chunk of the cheese. In order for the starch from the beans to thicken the soup, it is important to maintain a vigorous simmer in step 3.

	Table salt
½	pound dried cannellini beans (about 1 cup), rinsed and picked over (see note)
1	tablespoon extra-virgin olive oil, plus extra for serving
3	ounces pancetta, cut into ¼-inch pieces (see note)
2	medium celery ribs, cut into ½-inch pieces (about ¾ cup)
1	medium carrot, peeled and cut into ½-inch pieces (about ¾ cup)
2	small onions, peeled and cut into ½-inch pieces (about 1½ cups)
1	medium zucchini, trimmed and cut into ½-inch pieces (about 1 cup)
½	small head green cabbage, halved, cored, and cut into ½-inch pieces (about 2 cups)
2	medium garlic cloves, minced or pressed through a garlic press (about 2 teaspoons)
⅛–¼	teaspoon red pepper flakes
8	cups water
2	cups low-sodium chicken broth
1	piece Parmesan cheese rind, about 5 by 2 inches (see note)
1	bay leaf
1½	cups V8 juice
½	cup chopped fresh basil leaves
	Ground black pepper
	Grated Parmesan cheese, for serving

1. Dissolve 1½ tablespoons salt in 2 quarts cold water in a large bowl or container. Add the beans and soak at room temperature for at least 8 hours and up to 24 hours. Drain the beans and rinse well.

2. Heat the oil and pancetta in a large Dutch oven over medium-high heat. Cook, stirring occasionally, until the pancetta is lightly browned and the fat has rendered, 3 to 5 minutes. Add the celery, carrot, onions, and zucchini; cook, stirring frequently, until the vegetables are softened and lightly browned, 5 to 9 minutes. Stir in the cabbage, garlic, ½ teaspoon salt, and red pepper flakes; continue to cook until the cabbage starts to wilt, 1 to 2 minutes longer. Transfer the vegetables to a rimmed baking sheet and set aside.

3. Add the soaked beans, water, broth, Parmesan rind, and bay leaf to the now-empty Dutch oven and bring to a boil over high heat. Reduce the heat and vigorously simmer, stirring occasionally, until the beans are fully tender and the liquid begins to thicken, 45 to 60 minutes.

4. Add the reserved vegetables and V8 juice to the pot; cook until the vegetables are soft, about 15 minutes. Discard the bay leaf and Parmesan rind, stir in the basil, and season with salt and pepper to taste. Serve with olive oil and grated Parmesan.

CLASSIC GAZPACHO

WHY THIS RECIPE WORKS: Spain's famous chilled soup, gazpacho, boasts bright flavors, distinct pieces of vegetables, and a bracing tomato broth. But all too often, gazpacho is either grainy with the addition of too much bread (a common thickener) or watery from an abundance of macerated vegetables. We were after a chunky gazpacho that was well seasoned with vibrant tomato flavor.

We had to figure out the best method for preparing the vegetables. Although it was a breeze to use, the blender broke down our vegetables beyond recognition. Next, we tried the food processor, but even this machine pulverized some of our tomatoes, and the resulting soup was closer to a slushie than a good gazpacho. For the best texture, we had to chop the vegetables by hand.

Tomatoes are the star player in this dish, and early on we decided that full, ripe beefsteaks were the best option. As for peppers, we preferred red over green for their sweeter flavor. Onion and garlic are usually too overpowering in gazpacho, so we kept to modest levels. A combination of tomato juice and ice cubes—to help chill the soup—provided the right amount of liquid for our broth. And instead of using bread as a thickener, we saved it to make croutons. Now our gazpacho was nice and chunky, and brightly flavored.

Classic Gazpacho

SERVES 8 TO 10

This recipe makes a large quantity, but it can be easily halved if you prefer. Traditionally, the same vegetables used in the soup are also used as garnish. If that appeals to you, cut additional vegetables while you prepare those called for in the recipe. Other garnish possibilities include Garlic Croutons (recipe follows), chopped pitted black olives, chopped Foolproof Hard-Cooked Eggs (see page 32), and finely diced avocado.

- 3 medium ripe beefsteak tomatoes (about 1½ pounds), cored and cut into ¼-inch cubes (about 4 cups)
- 2 medium red bell peppers (about 1 pound), stemmed, seeded, and cut into ¼-inch cubes (about 2 cups)

2   small cucumbers (about 1 pound), one peeled and the other with skin on, both seeded and cut into ¼-inch cubes (about 2 cups)

½   small sweet onion (such as Vidalia, Maui, or Walla Walla) or 2 large shallots, minced (about ½ cup)

2   medium garlic cloves, minced or pressed through a garlic press (about 2 teaspoons)

⅓   cup sherry vinegar
    Table salt and ground black pepper

5   cups tomato juice

8   ice cubes

1   teaspoon hot pepper sauce (optional)
    Extra-virgin olive oil, for serving

1. Combine the tomatoes, peppers, cucumbers, onion, garlic, vinegar, 2 teaspoons salt, and pepper to taste in a large (at least 4-quart) nonreactive bowl. Let stand until the vegetables just begin to release their juices, about 5 minutes. Stir in the tomato juice, ice cubes, and hot pepper sauce (if using). Cover tightly and refrigerate to blend flavors, at least 4 hours and up to 2 days.

2. Season with salt and pepper to taste and remove and discard any unmelted ice cubes. Serve cold, drizzling each portion with about 1 teaspoon olive oil and topping with the desired garnishes (see note).

Garlic Croutons
MAKES ABOUT 3 CUPS

3   tablespoons extra-virgin olive oil

3   medium garlic cloves, minced or pressed through a garlic press (about 1 tablespoon)

¼   teaspoon table salt

6   slices high-quality white sandwich bread, cut into ½-inch cubes (about 3 cups)

1. Adjust an oven rack to the middle position and heat the oven to 350 degrees. Combine the oil, garlic, and salt in a small bowl; let stand 20 minutes, then pour through a fine-mesh strainer into a medium bowl. Discard the garlic. Add the bread cubes to the bowl with the oil and toss to coat.

2. Spread the bread cubes in an even layer on a rimmed baking sheet and bake, stirring occasionally, until golden, about 15 minutes. Cool on the baking sheet to room temperature. (The croutons can be stored in an airtight container or a plastic bag for up to 1 day.)

GAZPACHO ANDALUZ

WHY THIS RECIPE WORKS: In the States, the classic "liquid salsa" style of gazpacho reigns supreme. But in Spain, the birthplace of gazpacho, a variety of styles abound. The most popular type by far comes from Andalusia, the southernmost region of the country. It starts with the same vegetables as its chunky cousin, but is blended with bread to give it some body. The result is a creamy, complex soup. But unless you have fresh, flavorful vegetables, in particular fresh, ripe tomatoes, this soup can be unremarkable and bland. So how could we ensure a flavorful gazpacho if we had to rely on supermarket tomatoes? In a word, salt. Salting gave our tomatoes—even mid-winter specimens—a deep, full flavor. Figuring the same process could only improve the cucumbers, onions, and bell peppers, we salted them as well. To maximize the flavor of our soup even more, we soaked the bread in a portion of the vegetables' exuded liquid, rather than water. With a garnish of chopped vegetables, fresh herbs, and drizzles of extra-virgin olive oil and sherry vinegar, this Spanish classic can be enjoyed any time of the year.

Creamy Gazpacho Andaluz
SERVES 4 TO 6

For ideal flavor, allow the gazpacho to sit in the refrigerator overnight. Serve the soup with additional extra-virgin olive oil, sherry vinegar, ground black pepper, and the reserved diced vegetables. Red wine vinegar can be substituted for the sherry vinegar. Although we prefer kosher salt in this soup, half the amount of table salt can be used.

3   pounds (about 6 medium) ripe tomatoes, cored

1   small cucumber, peeled, halved, and seeded

1   medium green bell pepper, halved, cored, and seeded

1   small red onion, peeled and halved

2   medium garlic cloves, peeled and quartered

1   small serrano chile, stemmed and halved lengthwise
    Kosher salt (see note)

1   slice high-quality white sandwich bread, crust removed, torn into 1-inch pieces

½   cup extra-virgin olive oil, plus extra for serving

2   tablespoons sherry vinegar, plus extra for serving (see note)

2   tablespoons finely minced parsley, chives, or basil leaves
    Ground black pepper

1. Roughly chop 2 pounds of the tomatoes, half of the cucumber, half of the bell pepper, and half of the onion and place in a large bowl. Add the garlic, chile, and 1½ teaspoons salt; toss until well combined. Set aside.

2. Cut the remaining tomatoes, cucumber, and pepper into ¼-inch dice; place the vegetables in a medium bowl. Mince the remaining onion and add to the diced vegetables. Toss with ½ teaspoon salt and transfer to a fine-mesh strainer set over a medium bowl. Set aside for 1 hour.

3. Transfer the drained diced vegetables to a medium bowl and set aside. Add the bread pieces to the exuded liquid (there should be about ¼ cup) and soak for 1 minute. Add the soaked bread and any remaining liquid to the roughly chopped vegetables and toss thoroughly to combine.

4. Transfer half of the vegetable-bread mixture to a blender and process for 30 seconds. With the blender running, slowly drizzle in ¼ cup of the oil and continue to blend until completely smooth, about 2 minutes. Strain the soup through a fine-mesh strainer into a large bowl, using the back of a ladle or rubber spatula to press the soup through the strainer. Repeat with the remaining vegetable-bread mixture and ¼ cup more olive oil.

5. Stir the vinegar, parsley, and half of the diced vegetables into the soup and season with salt and pepper to taste. Cover and refrigerate overnight or for at least 2 hours to chill completely and develop the flavors. Serve, passing the remaining diced vegetables, olive oil, vinegar, and pepper separately.

CORN CHOWDER

WHY THIS RECIPE WORKS: We were looking for a corn chowder recipe that would pack lots of corn flavor in every spoonful while still maintaining a satisfying, yet not too thick, chowder texture. Inspired by a recipe we found that juiced corn kernels, a trick that delivered pronounced corn flavor, we strained the scrapings and pulp from several cobs through a kitchen towel to get unadulterated corn juice (when we added the unstrained pulp to the pot, the soup curdled). This delivered the intense corn flavor we were after. We lightened things up by using water as our primary liquid, which allowed the pure corn flavor to shine through, then added just 1 cup of half-and-half to give our chowder the right richness. A sprinkling of basil before serving lent a fresh finish.

Lighter Corn Chowder

SERVES 6

When removing the kernels from the cob make sure to remove only the part of the kernel sticking out of the cob. Cutting deeper will result in too much fibrous material coming off the corn. Yukon Gold potatoes can be substituted for the red potatoes. Minced chives can be used in place of the basil.

- 8 ears corn, husks and silk removed
- 3 tablespoons unsalted butter
- 1 medium onion, chopped fine
- 4 ounces (about 4 slices) bacon, halved lengthwise, then cut crosswise into ¼-inch pieces
- 2 teaspoons minced fresh thyme leaves
  Table salt and ground black pepper
- ¼ cup unbleached all-purpose flour
- 5 cups water
- 12 ounces red potatoes, cut into ½-inch cubes
- 1 cup half-and-half
  Sugar
- 3 tablespoons chopped fresh basil leaves

1. Using a chef's knife, cut the kernels from the ears of corn; transfer to a bowl and set aside (you should have 5 to 6 cups). Holding the cobs over a second bowl, use the back of a butter knife to firmly scrape any pulp remaining on the cobs into the bowl (you should have 2 to 2½ cups of pulp). Transfer the pulp to the center of a clean kitchen towel set in a medium bowl. Wrap the towel tightly around the pulp and squeeze until dry. Discard the pulp in the towel and set the corn juice aside (you should have about ⅔ cup of juice).

2. Melt the butter in a Dutch oven over medium heat. Add the onion, bacon, thyme, 2 teaspoons salt, and 1 teaspoon pepper and cook, stirring frequently, until the onion is softened and beginning to brown, 8 to 10 minutes. Stir in the flour and cook, stirring constantly, for 2 minutes. Whisking constantly, gradually add the water and then bring to a boil. Add the corn kernels and the potatoes. Return to a simmer, reduce the heat to medium-low, and cook until the potatoes have softened, 15 to 18 minutes.

3. Transfer 2 cups of the chowder to a blender and process until smooth, 1 to 2 minutes. Return the puree to the pot, stir in the half-and-half, and return to a simmer. Remove the pot from the heat and stir in the reserved corn juice. Season with salt, pepper, and up to 1 tablespoon sugar to taste. Sprinkle with the basil and serve.

NEW ENGLAND CLAM CHOWDER

WHY THIS RECIPE WORKS: Good traditional chowder isn't that hard to make, but it can be daunting for the home cook. The biggest hurdle is a finicky ingredient that most people don't know how to work with—clams. We wanted to come up with a clam chowder that was economical, could be prepared quickly, and provided a simple method for working with the star ingredient.

We tested a variety of clams and ultimately found that medium-size hard-shell clams guaranteed the most clam flavor. Rather than shucking the raw clams (which can be tedious and time-consuming) and adding them to the pot, we steamed the clams to open them, then used the steaming liquid as our broth. The steamed clams had to be pulled from the pot when they had just opened; allowing them to open completely meant they would overcook quickly when returned to the soup to heat through. We found waxy red potatoes to be the best choice for our creamy chowder; high-starch potatoes, like russets, broke down too much. Bacon made a nice substitute for the traditional salt pork and gave our chowder great smoky flavor. As for the creaminess factor, using a modest amount of heavy cream instead of milk meant that we could use less dairy for a rich, creamy chowder that tasted distinctly of clams.

1. Bring 3 cups water to a boil in a large Dutch oven. Add the clams and cover with a tight-fitting lid. Cook for 5 minutes, uncover, and stir with a wooden spoon. Quickly cover the pot and steam until the clams just open, 2 to 4 minutes. (Don't let the clams open completely.) Transfer the clams to a large bowl and cool slightly; reserve the broth. Open the clams with a paring knife, holding the clams over a bowl to catch any juices. With the knife, sever the muscle that attaches the clam to the bottom shell and transfer the meat to a cutting board; discard the shells. Mince the clams and set aside. Pour the clam broth into a large bowl, holding back the last few tablespoons of broth in case of sediment; set the clam broth aside. (You should have about 5 cups. If not, add bottled clam juice or water to make this amount.) Rinse and dry the pot, then return the pot to the burner.

2. Fry the bacon in the pot over medium-low heat until the fat renders and the bacon crisps, 5 to 7 minutes. Add the onion and cook, stirring occasionally, until softened, about 5 minutes. Add the flour and stir until lightly colored, about 1 minute. Gradually whisk in the reserved clam broth. Add the potatoes, bay leaf, and thyme and simmer until the potatoes are tender, about 10 minutes. Add the clams, cream, parsley, and salt and pepper to taste; bring to a simmer. Remove from the heat, discard the bay leaf, and serve.

New England Clam Chowder

SERVES 6

Don't skip the step of scrubbing the clams; many clams have bits of sand embedded in their shells that can ruin a pot of chowder. To remove the sand, simply scrub them under cold, running water using a soft brush.

- 7 **pounds medium-size hard-shell clams, such as cherrystones, washed and scrubbed clean (see note)**
- 5 **ounces (about 3 slices) thick-cut bacon, cut into ¼-inch pieces**
- 1 **large onion, chopped medium**
- 2 **tablespoons unbleached all-purpose flour**
- 1½ **pounds red potatoes (about 4 medium), cut into ½-inch chunks**
- 1 **bay leaf**
- 1 **teaspoon fresh thyme leaves or ¼ teaspoon dried thyme**
- 1 **cup heavy cream**
- 2 **tablespoons minced fresh parsley leaves**
  Table salt and ground black pepper

CHAPTER 2

SALAD DAYS

Foolproof Vinaigrette 28

   Foolproof Lemon
   Vinaigrette

   Foolproof Balsamic-
   Mustard Vinaigrette

   Foolproof Walnut
   Vinaigrette

   Foolproof Herb
   Vinaigrette

Leafy Green Salad with Red
Wine Vinaigrette 29

Leafy Green Salad with Rich
and Creamy Blue Cheese
Dressing 30

Spicy Salad with Mustard
and Balsamic
Vinaigrette 30

Arugula Salad with Figs,
Prosciutto, Walnuts, and
Parmesan 31

Wilted Spinach Salad with
Warm Bacon Dressing 32

   Foolproof Hard-Cooked
   Eggs

Salad with Herbed Baked
Goat Cheese and
Vinaigrette 32

Almond-Crusted Chicken
with Wilted Spinach
Salad 33

Pan-Seared Scallops with
Wilted Spinach, Watercress,
and Orange Salad 35

Pear and Cranberry
Chopped Salad 36

Mediterranean Chopped
Salad 36

Fennel and Apple Chopped
Salad 36

Cherry Tomato Salad with
Feta and Olives 37

Italian Bread Salad
(Panzanella) 38

Classic Greek Salad 39

Sesame-Lemon Cucumber
Salad 40

Creamy Coleslaw 41

Creamy Buttermilk
Coleslaw 41

Confetti Cabbage Salad
with Spicy Peanut
Dressing 42

Cool and Creamy
Macaroni Salad 43

Pasta Salad with
Pesto 44

Antipasto Pasta Salad 44

Rice Salad with Oranges,
Olives, and Almonds 45

American Potato Salad with
Hard-Cooked Eggs and
Sweet Pickles 46

Austrian-Style Potato
Salad 47

FOOLPROOF VINAIGRETTES

WHY THIS RECIPE WORKS: Vinaigrettes often seem a little slipshod—harsh and bristling in one bite, dull and oily in the next. We were determined to nail down a formula for the perfect vinaigrette, one that would consistently yield a homogeneous, harmonious blend of bright vinegar and rich oil in every forkful.

For starters, top-notch ingredients are crucial. Balsamic vinegar works best with more assertive greens. Fruity extra-virgin olive oil is preferred as an all-purpose oil option, while walnut oil is best for nuttier vinaigrettes. As for mixing methods, whisking together the ingredients only gets you so far. A key ingredient—mayonnaise—is necessary to emulsify (bind together) the oil and vinegar for a stabilized, smooth dressing.

Foolproof Vinaigrette

MAKES ABOUT ¼ CUP, ENOUGH TO DRESS 8 TO 10 CUPS LIGHTLY PACKED GREENS

Red wine, white wine, or champagne vinegar will work in this recipe; however, it is important to use high-quality ingredients (see page 755 for our top-rated brands of white wine vinegar and red wine vinegar and page 747 for our top-rated brand of extra-virgin olive oil). This vinaigrette works with nearly any type of green (as do the walnut and herb variations). For a hint of garlic flavor, rub the inside of the salad bowl with a cut clove of garlic before adding the lettuce.

1 tablespoon wine vinegar (see note)
1½ teaspoons very finely minced shallot
½ teaspoon regular or light mayonnaise
½ teaspoon Dijon mustard
⅛ teaspoon table salt
  Ground black pepper
3 tablespoons extra-virgin olive oil (see note)

1. Combine the vinegar, shallot, mayonnaise, mustard, salt, and pepper to taste in a small nonreactive bowl. Whisk until the mixture is milky in appearance and no lumps of mayonnaise remain.

2. Place the oil in a small measuring cup so that it is easy to pour. Whisking constantly, very slowly drizzle the oil into the vinegar mixture. If pools of oil are gathering on the surface as you whisk, stop adding the oil and whisk the mixture well to combine, then resume whisking in the oil in a slow stream. The vinaigrette should be glossy and lightly thickened, with no pools of oil on its surface.

Foolproof Lemon Vinaigrette

This vinaigrette is best for dressing mild greens.

Follow the recipe for Foolproof Vinaigrette, substituting lemon juice for the vinegar, omitting the shallot, and adding ¼ teaspoon finely grated lemon zest and a pinch of sugar along with the salt and pepper.

Foolproof Balsamic-Mustard Vinaigrette

This vinaigrette is best for dressing assertive greens. See page 754 for our top-rated brand of balsamic vinegar.

Follow the recipe for Foolproof Vinaigrette, substituting balsamic vinegar for the wine vinegar, increasing the mustard to 2 teaspoons, and adding ½ teaspoon chopped fresh thyme along with the salt and pepper.

Foolproof Walnut Vinaigrette

Follow the recipe for Foolproof Vinaigrette, substituting 1½ tablespoons roasted walnut oil and 1½ tablespoons regular olive oil for the extra-virgin olive oil.

Foolproof Herb Vinaigrette

Follow the recipe for Foolproof Vinaigrette, adding 1 tablespoon minced fresh parsley leaves or chives and ½ teaspoon minced fresh thyme, tarragon, marjoram, or oregano leaves to the vinaigrette just before use.

LEAFY GREEN SALAD WITH RED WINE VINAIGRETTE

WHY THIS RECIPE WORKS: A leafy green salad with red wine vinaigrette is a vital recipe to have in your arsenal. We wanted to develop a recipe for this basic salad—a mix of well-chosen greens tossed with a light vinaigrette that was neither harsh nor oily.

Leafy green salads sound simple, but in reality, the dressing often soaks the greens, resulting in a muddy salad that's too acidic from the vinegar. We went back to the basics and revisited standard vinaigrette proportions. In most cases, 4 parts oil to 1 part vinegar produces the best balance of flavors in a vinaigrette, so that's where we started. Red wine vinegar was the foundation of our vinaigrette; with a sharp but clean flavor, this vinegar is a great choice for dressing salads. Before whisking the vinaigrette ingredients together, we added salt and pepper to the vinegar. This step mutes these seasonings a bit and prevents them from becoming too overpowering. With the right mix of salad greens—we like a combination of mild, delicate greens and peppery greens—this leafy salad makes the perfect complement to any main dish.

Leafy Green Salad with Red Wine Vinaigrette
SERVES 4 TO 6

For the best results, use at least two kinds of greens. A blend of mild, delicate greens, such as Boston and leaf lettuces, and peppery greens, such as arugula and watercress, is ideal. Romaine adds crunch and texture. If you like, add mild fresh herbs, such as chives, tarragon, or basil, in small amounts.

- 2¼   teaspoons red wine vinegar
- ⅛   teaspoon table salt
-     Pinch ground black pepper
- 3   tablespoons extra-virgin olive oil
- 8   cups mixed salad greens, washed, dried, and torn into bite-sized pieces (see note)

Combine the vinegar, salt, and pepper in a bowl; add the oil and whisk until combined. Place the greens in a large bowl, drizzle the vinaigrette over the greens, and toss to coat evenly. Serve.

LEAFY GREEN SALAD WITH RICH AND CREAMY BLUE CHEESE DRESSING

WHY THIS RECIPE WORKS: Cool and crunchy salad greens coated with creamy blue cheese dressing are simply irresistible. But getting the right proportion of dressing to greens can be tricky. Order this salad at a restaurant and it's likely you'll receive a plate of dressing-soaked greens. We wanted lettuce lightly napped with a creamy, tangy dressing.

Starting with the dressing, we found that the secret to proper flavor and texture was in using the right creamy components. We determined that three creamy ingredients were essential: mayonnaise to give the dressing body, sour cream to supply tang, and buttermilk to thin out and further reinforce the dressing's bold flavors. A bit of sugar brought some much-needed sweetness, and white wine vinegar gave our dressing some zing. As for the main ingredient, we ruled out really pungent blue cheeses as too overpowering; a mild blue cheese works best. For the right chunky consistency, we mixed the crumbled blue cheese with the buttermilk before adding any other ingredients.

Leafy Green Salad with Rich and Creamy Blue Cheese Dressing

SERVES 4 TO 6

Sturdy romaine and curly leaf lettuce hold up well to this thick dressing. In a pinch, whole milk can be used in place of the buttermilk; the dressing will be a bit lighter and milder in flavor, but will still taste good.

2½ ounces blue cheese, crumbled (about ½ cup)
  3 tablespoons buttermilk (see note)
  3 tablespoons sour cream
  2 tablespoons mayonnaise
  2 teaspoons white wine vinegar
  ¼ teaspoon sugar
  ⅛ teaspoon garlic powder
     Table salt and ground black pepper
 10 cups loosely packed sturdy salad greens, such as romaine or curly leaf lettuce, washed, dried, and torn into bite-size pieces (see note)

1. Mash the blue cheese and buttermilk in a small bowl with a fork until the mixture resembles cottage cheese with small curds. Stir in the sour cream, mayonnaise, vinegar, sugar, and garlic powder and season with salt and pepper to taste.

2. Place the greens in a large bowl. Pour the dressing over the greens and toss to coat evenly. Serve. (The dressing can be refrigerated in an airtight container for up to 2 weeks.)

SPICY SALAD WITH MUSTARD AND BALSAMIC VINAIGRETTE

WHY THIS RECIPE WORKS: Some salads act as humble introductions to the main course, while other salads demand attention and pack a flavor punch all their own. We had a craving for a bold salad, one using spicy and bitter greens dressed in a pungent, mustardy vinaigrette.

We started by focusing on the greens, and chose peppery greens like arugula and watercress. We envisioned this salad as standing up to rich main dishes, like fettuccine Alfredo or a hearty meat stew, so we used both balsamic vinegar and Dijon mustard as the acidic components. Minced shallot provided another strong flavor and added a bit of texture to our vinaigrette. We mixed the greens and vinaigrette together a little at a time to ensure that all the greens were well covered. Boldly flavored, this spicy salad with mustard and balsamic vinaigrette will wake up any dulled palate.

Spicy Salad with Mustard and Balsamic Vinaigrette

SERVES 8 TO 10

This salad makes a perfect partner to rich main dishes, like lasagna, because its bitter greens and zesty vinaigrette help to cut the richness.

  6 tablespoons extra-virgin olive oil
  4 teaspoons balsamic vinegar
  1 tablespoon Dijon mustard
  1 teaspoon finely minced shallot
  ¼ teaspoon table salt
  ⅛ teaspoon ground black pepper
 16 cups spicy greens, such as arugula, watercress, mizuna, and baby mustard greens, washed and dried

Whisk the oil, vinegar, mustard, shallot, salt, and pepper together in a bowl until combined. Place the greens in a large bowl, drizzle the dressing over the greens a little at a time, and toss to coat evenly, adding more vinaigrette if the greens seem dry. Serve.

ARUGULA SALAD

WHY THIS RECIPE WORKS: Unlike everyday iceberg lettuce, spicy arugula is more than just a leafy backdrop for salad garnishes. But arugula's complex, peppery flavor also makes it something of a challenge to pair with other ingredients. We wanted a truly outstanding arugula-based salad with co-starring ingredients that would stand up to these spicy greens.

Salad combinations with harsh, one-dimensional flavor profiles (adding radishes and lemon-buttermilk dressing to arugula, for example) struck out, with too much abrasive flavor. What we did like were the salads containing fruit and cheese, so we decided to pair our arugula with sweet and salty ingredients. Fried prosciutto strips and shaved Parmesan fit the bill when it came to upping the saltiness of our salad. A spoonful of jam added to the vinaigrette helped to emulsify the dressing and provided a sweet contrast to arugula's peppery bite. For additional sweetness, dried figs worked well and toasted walnuts delivered just the right amount of crunch.

Arugula Salad with Figs, Prosciutto, Walnuts, and Parmesan

SERVES 6

Although frying the prosciutto adds crisp texture to the salad, if you prefer, you can simply cut it into ribbons and use it as a garnish. Honey can be substituted for the jam in either of these salads.

- 4 tablespoons extra-virgin olive oil
- 2 ounces thinly sliced prosciutto, cut into ¼-inch strips
- 3 tablespoons balsamic vinegar
- 1 tablespoon raspberry jam
- ½ cup dried figs, stems removed, fruit chopped into ¼-inch pieces
- 1 small shallot, minced (about 1 tablespoon)
  Table salt and ground black pepper
- 5 ounces loosely packed baby arugula (about 5 cups), washed and dried
- ½ cup walnuts, toasted and chopped
- 2 ounces Parmesan cheese, shaved into thin strips with a vegetable peeler

1. Heat 1 tablespoon of the oil in a 10-inch nonstick skillet over medium heat; add the prosciutto and fry until crisp, stirring frequently, about 7 minutes. Using a slotted spoon, transfer to a paper towel–lined plate and set aside to cool.

2. Whisk the vinegar and jam together in a medium microwave-safe bowl until combined; stir in the figs. Cover with plastic wrap, cut several steam vents in the plastic, and microwave on high until the figs are plump, 30 seconds to 1 minute. Whisk in the remaining 3 tablespoons oil, the shallot, ¼ teaspoon salt, and ⅛ teaspoon pepper until combined. Cool to room temperature.

3. Toss the arugula with the vinaigrette in a large bowl; season with salt and pepper to taste. Divide the salad among individual plates; top each with a portion of the prosciutto, walnuts, and Parmesan. Serve.

WILTED SPINACH SALAD

WHY THIS RECIPE WORKS: Traditional wilted spinach salad, tossed with warm bacon dressing, makes for an appealing and elegant salad. But too often, this salad is a soggy mess of slimy spinach, bogged down from too much oil and too much heat. We wanted perfectly wilted spinach, a rich, balanced dressing, and crisp pieces of meaty bacon throughout.

Baby spinach was preferred over the mature variety for its tender, sweet qualities. Fried thick-cut bacon provided more textural interest than regular sliced bacon. And using the bacon fat left in the skillet to cook our onion and garlic gave the finished salad a smoky flavor. For the vinaigrette, a generous amount of cider vinegar, enhanced with sugar, cut the richness of the bacon fat. We found that pouring the hot vinaigrette right over the baby spinach provided enough heat to wilt the spinach without saturating it. With wedges of hard-cooked egg for some heartiness, this wilted spinach salad delivers on all fronts.

Wilted Spinach Salad with Warm Bacon Dressing
SERVES 4 TO 6

This salad comes together quickly, so have the ingredients ready before you begin cooking. When adding the vinegar mixture to the skillet, step back from the stovetop—the aroma is quite potent.

6	ounces baby spinach (about 6 cups), washed and dried
3	tablespoons cider vinegar
½	teaspoon sugar
¼	teaspoon ground black pepper
	Pinch table salt
10	ounces (about 8 slices) thick-cut bacon, cut into ½-inch pieces
½	medium red onion, chopped medium
1	small garlic clove, minced or pressed through a garlic press (about ½ teaspoon)
3	hard-cooked eggs (recipe follows), peeled and quartered

1. Place the spinach in a large bowl. Whisk the vinegar, sugar, pepper, and salt in a small bowl until the sugar dissolves; set aside.

2. Fry the bacon in a medium skillet over medium-high heat, stirring occasionally, until crisp, about 10 minutes. Using a slotted spoon, transfer the bacon to a paper towel–lined plate. Pour off all but 3 tablespoons of the bacon fat left in the pan. Add the onion to the skillet and cook over medium heat, stirring frequently, until softened, about 3 minutes. Stir in the garlic and cook until fragrant, about 15 seconds. Add the vinegar mixture, then remove the skillet from the heat. Working quickly, scrape the bottom of the skillet with a wooden spoon to loosen the browned bits. Pour the hot dressing over the spinach, add the bacon, and toss gently until the spinach is slightly wilted. Divide the salad among individual plates, arrange the egg quarters over each, and serve.

Foolproof Hard-Cooked Eggs
MAKES 3

You can double or triple this recipe as long as you use a pot large enough to hold the eggs in a single layer, covered by an inch of water.

3	large eggs

1. Place the eggs in a medium saucepan, cover with 1 inch of water, and bring to a boil over high heat. Remove the pan from the heat, cover, and let sit for 10 minutes. Meanwhile, fill a medium bowl with 1 quart water and one tray of ice cubes.

2. Transfer the eggs to the ice bath with a slotted spoon and let sit for 5 minutes. Peel the eggs.

BAKED GOAT CHEESE SALAD

WHY THIS RECIPE WORKS: Warm goat cheese salad has been a fixture on restaurant menus for years, featuring artisanal cheeses, organic greens, barrel-aged vinegars, and imported oils. But too often what arrives is an unremarkable salad at a price that defies reason. We wanted to bring this restaurant favorite home with creamy cheese rounds infused with the flavor of fresh herbs and surrounded by crisp, golden breading, all cradled in lightly dressed greens.

Ground Melba toasts (those ultra-dry and crispy crackers) made the crispiest crust for the goat cheese. After dipping the cheese rounds in beaten egg and herbs, we coated them with the crumbs, shaped them into attractive disks, and froze them to set the cheese and the crust. With the oven superhot and the cheese very cold, the cheese developed a crispy crust (with no oozing) and kept its shape, and a quick brush of olive oil on the outside of the disks lent flavor to the crumbs without turning them oily. A mix of greens paired well with the tangy flavor of the goat cheese, and a simple, light vinaigrette was all that was needed to finish this elegant salad.

Salad with Herbed Baked Goat Cheese and Vinaigrette
SERVES 6

The baked goat cheese should be served warm. Prepare the salad components while the cheese is in the freezer, then toss the greens and vinaigrette while the cheese cools a bit after baking.

GOAT CHEESE

- 3 ounces white Melba toasts (about 2 cups)
- 1 teaspoon ground black pepper
- 3 large eggs
- 2 tablespoons Dijon mustard
- 1 tablespoon chopped fresh thyme leaves
- 1 tablespoon chopped fresh chives
- 12 ounces goat cheese
- Extra-virgin olive oil

SALAD

- 6 tablespoons extra-virgin olive oil
- 2 tablespoons red wine vinegar
- 1 tablespoon Dijon mustard
- 1 teaspoon minced shallot
- ¼ teaspoon table salt
- Ground black pepper
- 14 cups mixed delicate and spicy salad greens, such as arugula, baby spinach, and frisée, washed and dried

1. FOR THE CHEESE: In a food processor, process the Melba toasts to fine, even crumbs, about 1½ minutes; transfer the crumbs to a medium bowl and stir in the pepper. Whisk the eggs and mustard in a second medium bowl until combined. Combine the thyme and chives in a small bowl.

2. Using dental floss or kitchen twine, divide the cheese into 12 equal pieces by slicing the log lengthwise through the middle and each half into six even pieces. Roll each piece of cheese into a ball; roll each ball in the combined fresh herbs to coat lightly. Transfer 6 pieces to the egg mixture and turn each piece to coat; transfer to the Melba crumbs and turn each piece to coat, pressing the crumbs into the cheese. Flatten each ball gently with your fingertips into a disk about 1½ inches wide and 1 inch thick and set on a baking sheet. Repeat with the remaining 6 pieces of cheese. Transfer the baking sheet to the freezer and freeze the disks until firm, about 30 minutes. Adjust an oven rack to the top position and heat the oven to 475 degrees.

3. FOR THE SALAD: Meanwhile, whisk the oil, vinegar, mustard, shallot, and salt in a small bowl until combined; season with pepper to taste. Set aside.

4. Remove the cheese from the freezer and brush the tops and sides evenly with olive oil. Bake until the crumbs are golden brown and the cheese is slightly soft, 7 to 9 minutes (or 9 to 12 minutes if the cheese is completely frozen). Using a thin metal spatula, transfer the cheese to a paper towel–lined plate and cool for 3 minutes.

5. Place the greens in a large bowl, drizzle the vinaigrette over them, and toss to coat. Divide the greens among individual plates; place two rounds of goat cheese on each salad and serve.

NUT-CRUSTED CHICKEN WITH SALAD GREENS

WHY THIS RECIPE WORKS: When leafy greens are paired with sautéed chicken, a simple salad becomes a satisfying, one-dish meal. We wanted to create an easy recipe for such a dish, and thought incorporating nuts in the coating of the chicken would make for a heartier, more elegant meal.

We started by pounding store-bought chicken breasts to the same thickness to ensure that they would cook evenly. Ground almonds paired with panko (Japanese-style bread crumbs) created a rich-tasting crust that was both light and crisp. After dipping the chicken breasts in eggs and the nut and panko mixture, we let them sit for a few minutes so the coating could set. Much like regular breaded chicken, the breasts had to be pan-fried in a fair amount of oil. Pan-frying can make a mess in a traditional skillet, so we used a nonstick pan. To make a quick salad with bright flavors, we heated orange slices to create a dressing in the skillet, then used the hot dressing to wilt the spinach.

Almond-Crusted Chicken with Wilted Spinach Salad

SERVES 4

Don't process the nuts longer than directed or they will turn pasty and oily.

CHICKEN

- 4 (5 to 6-ounce) boneless, skinless chicken breasts, trimmed
- Table salt and ground black pepper
- 1 cup sliced almonds
- ½ cup panko (Japanese-style bread crumbs)
- 2 large eggs
- 1 teaspoon Dijon mustard
- 1¼ teaspoons grated zest from 1 orange
- ¾ cup plus 2 tablespoons vegetable oil

SALAD

- 5 ounces baby spinach (about 5 cups)
- 2 medium oranges, peel and pith removed (see page 214), quartered and sliced ¼ inch thick
- 1 small shallot, minced (about 1 tablespoon)

1. FOR THE CHICKEN: Adjust an oven rack to the middle position and heat the oven to 200 degrees. Pound each breast between two sheets of plastic wrap to a uniform ½-inch thickness. Pat the chicken dry with paper towels and season with salt and pepper.

IS CHRIS REALLY A SUPER-TASTER?

The tasting segments offer Chris a chance to prove his mettle tasting supermarket ingredients. The setup is simple: Can Chris pick out the top-rated brand—the one chosen by the test kitchen's independent panel of tasters as the best? Jack brings the winner (along with some losers) to the tasting lab and asks Chris to taste samples and make a snap judgment. Chris doesn't know which brands are under those brown paper bags. And while our tasting panel takes as long as an hour sniffing, nibbling, and sipping as they form their opinions, Chris has about five minutes—and just one take—to get it right.

Despite Jack's best efforts to trip him up, Chris picks out the winner more often than not. It turns out Chris, like a small percentage of people around the world, is a super-taster. His palate is packed with more tastebuds per square inch than the average person. This makes him sensitive to nuances in flavor. It also makes Chris overly sensitive to heat. In fact, any tasting that relies on spice (think hot sauce or barbecue sauce) is likely to go Jack's way because Chris can't stand even the slightest hint of heat. While most cooks like their chili moderately spicy, Chris prefers it very tame. Well, no one is perfect.

2. Process the almonds in a food processor to fine crumbs, about 10 seconds (do not overprocess; see note). Toss the nuts with the panko in a shallow dish. Whisk the eggs, mustard, 1 teaspoon of the orange zest, ½ teaspoon salt, and ¼ teaspoon pepper together in another shallow dish. Working with 1 chicken breast at a time, dip the chicken into the egg mixture, turning to coat well and allowing the excess to drip off, then coat with the nut mixture, pressing gently so that the nuts adhere. Place the breaded chicken in a single layer on a wire rack set over a rimmed baking sheet and let sit for 5 minutes.

3. Heat 6 tablespoons of the oil in a 12-inch nonstick skillet over medium heat until shimmering. Add 2 of the chicken breasts and cook until browned on both

sides, 4 to 6 minutes total. Drain the chicken briefly on a paper towel–lined plate, then transfer to a clean wire rack set over a rimmed baking sheet and keep warm in the oven. Discard the oil and wipe out the skillet with paper towels. Repeat with 6 tablespoons more oil and the remaining chicken. Discard the oil and wipe out the skillet with paper towels.

4. FOR THE SALAD: Place the spinach in a large bowl. Heat 1 tablespoon more oil in the skillet over high heat until just smoking. Add the orange slices and cook until lightly browned around the edges, 1½ to 2 minutes. Remove the pan from the heat and add the remaining 1 tablespoon oil, the shallot, remaining ¼ teaspoon zest, ¼ teaspoon salt, and ⅛ teaspoon pepper and allow residual heat to soften the shallot, about 30 seconds. Pour the warm dressing with the oranges over the spinach and toss gently. Divide the greens among individual plates. Remove the chicken from the oven, set a cutlet over each portion, and serve.

WARM SPINACH SALAD WITH PAN-SEARED SCALLOPS

WHY THIS RECIPE WORKS: Attempts to make perfectly seared, caramelized sea scallops usually result in overcooking these tender mollusks, rendering them rubbery and tough. We wanted a concentrated, nutty, rich-colored crust encasing an interior of sweet, creamy, perfectly cooked scallop meat. And for a complete meal, we wanted to incorporate our scallops into a main course salad that would be both elegant and satisfying.

We tackled the scallops first: To get scallops with a crusty exterior, using the unprocessed variety is a must. We found it was essential to dry the scallops thoroughly before adding them to the pan, to further guard against the scallops steaming rather than searing. Equally important is to avoid crowding the pan. We cooked the scallops in batches, browning each batch on just one side, then returned them all to the skillet at once to cook through on the other side, so that each salad would have hot, not tepid, scallops.

For the salad, we liked baby spinach and watercress for easy prep and moist, tender greens. A bright dressing with sherry vinegar and fresh orange complemented the rich scallops. For a finishing touch, toasted sliced almonds lent our salad nutty flavor and welcome crunch.

Pan-Seared Scallops with Wilted Spinach, Watercress, and Orange Salad

SERVES 4

Sea scallops can vary dramatically in size from 1 to 1½ ounces each. A dinner portion, therefore, can range from four to six scallops per person. To ensure that the scallops cook at the same rate, be sure to buy scallops of similar size. Note that scallops have a small, rough-textured, crescent-shaped muscle that toughens once cooked. It's easy to remove—simply peel it from the side of each scallop before cooking.

SALAD

- 5 ounces baby spinach (about 5 cups)
- 4 ounces watercress or arugula (about 4 cups)
- ¾ cup sliced almonds, toasted

SCALLOPS

- 1½ pounds large sea scallops (16 to 24 scallops), tendons removed (see note)
- Table salt and ground black pepper
- ¼ cup vegetable oil

DRESSING

- 3 tablespoons extra-virgin olive oil
- ½ medium red onion, sliced thin
- 1 teaspoon minced fresh thyme leaves
- 2 large oranges, peel and pith removed (see page 214), quartered and sliced ¼ inch thick
- 2 tablespoons sherry vinegar

1. FOR THE SALAD: Toss the spinach, watercress, and almonds together in a large bowl; set aside.

2. FOR THE SCALLOPS: Place the scallops on a dish towel–lined plate or baking sheet and season with salt and pepper. Lay a single layer of paper towels over the scallops; set aside.

3. Add 2 tablespoons of the vegetable oil to a 12-inch skillet and heat over high heat until just smoking. Meanwhile, press the paper towel flush to the scallops to dry. Add half of the scallops to the skillet, dry side facing down, and cook until evenly golden, 1 to 2 minutes. Using tongs, transfer the scallops, browned side facing up, to a large plate; set aside. Wipe out the skillet using a wad of paper towels. Repeat with the remaining 2 tablespoons oil and the remaining scallops. Once the first side is golden, turn the heat to medium, turn the scallops over with tongs, and return the first batch of scallops to the pan, golden side facing up. Cook until the sides on all the scallops have firmed up and all but the middle third of each scallop is

opaque, 30 to 60 seconds longer. Transfer all the scallops to a clean, large plate; set aside.

4. FOR THE DRESSING: Wipe the skillet clean with a wad of paper towels. Add the olive oil, onion, thyme, and ½ teaspoon salt to the skillet and return to medium-high heat; cook until the onion is slightly softened, about 1 minute. Add the oranges and vinegar to the pan and swirl to incorporate. Remove from the heat.

5. TO FINISH THE SALAD: Pour the warm dressing over the salad mixture and gently toss to wilt. Divide the spinach salad among four plates and arrange the scallops on top. Serve immediately.

BETTER CHOPPED SALADS

WHY THIS RECIPE WORKS: Chopped salads are often little better than a random collection of cut-up produce from the crisper drawer exuding moisture that turns the salad watery and bland. We wanted lively, thoughtfully chosen compositions of lettuce, vegetables, and perhaps fruit—cut into bite-size pieces—with supporting players like nuts and cheese contributing hearty flavors and textures. Salting some of the vegetables—cucumbers and tomatoes—to remove excess moisture was an important first step. As for the dressing, most recipes we tried called for a ratio of 3 parts oil to 1 part vinegar, but we found that a more assertive blend of equal parts oil and vinegar was far better at delivering the bright, acidic kick needed in salads boasting hearty flavors and chunky textures. We also found that marinating ingredients such as bell peppers, onions, and fruit in the dressing for 5 minutes before adding cheese and other tender components brought a welcome flavor boost.

Pear and Cranberry Chopped Salad

SERVES 4 TO 6

Chopped dried cherries can be substituted for the cranberries.

- 1 cucumber, peeled, halved lengthwise, seeded, and cut into ½-inch dice (about 1¼ cups; see page 40)
  Table salt
- 3 tablespoons extra-virgin olive oil
- 3 tablespoons sherry vinegar
- 1 red bell pepper, stemmed, seeded, and cut into ¼-inch pieces (about 1 cup)
- 1 ripe but firm pear, cut into ¼-inch pieces (about 1 cup)
- ½ small red onion, minced (about ¼ cup)
- ½ cup dried cranberries
- 1 romaine heart, cut into ½-inch pieces (about 3 cups)
- 4 ounces blue cheese, crumbled (about 1 cup)
- ½ cup pistachios, toasted and chopped coarse
  Ground black pepper

1. Combine the cucumber and ½ teaspoon salt in a colander set over a bowl and drain for 15 minutes.

2. Whisk the oil and vinegar together in a large bowl. Add the drained cucumber, bell pepper, pear, onion, and cranberries. Toss and let stand at room temperature to blend the flavors, 5 minutes.

3. Add the romaine, blue cheese, and pistachios and toss to combine. Season with salt and pepper to taste and serve.

Mediterranean Chopped Salad

SERVES 4 TO 6

For information on our top-rated brand of feta cheese, see page 738.

- 1 cucumber, peeled, halved lengthwise, seeded, and cut into ½-inch dice (about 1¼ cups; see page 40)
- 1 pint grape tomatoes, quartered (about 1½ cups)
  Table salt
- 3 tablespoons extra-virgin olive oil
- 3 tablespoons red wine vinegar
- 1 medium garlic clove, minced or pressed through a garlic press (about 1 teaspoon)
- 1 (15-ounce) can chickpeas, drained and rinsed
- ½ cup pitted kalamata olives, chopped
- ½ small red onion, minced (about ¼ cup)
- ½ cup chopped fresh parsley leaves
- 1 romaine heart, cut into ½-inch pieces (about 3 cups)
- 4 ounces feta cheese, crumbled (about 1 cup)
  Ground black pepper

1. Combine the cucumber, tomatoes, and 1 teaspoon salt in a colander set over a bowl and drain for 15 minutes.

2. Whisk the oil, vinegar, and garlic together in a large bowl. Add the drained cucumber and tomatoes, chickpeas, olives, onion, and parsley. Toss and let stand at room temperature to blend the flavors, 5 minutes.

3. Add the romaine and feta and toss to combine. Season with salt and pepper to taste and serve.

Fennel and Apple Chopped Salad

SERVES 4 TO 6

Braeburn, Jonagold, or Red Delicious apples all work well here. The cheese is sprinkled on the salads after plating because goat cheese tends to clump when tossed.

- 1 cucumber, peeled, halved lengthwise, seeded, and cut into ½-inch dice (about 1¼ cups; see page 40)
  Table salt
- 3 tablespoons extra-virgin olive oil
- 3 tablespoons white wine vinegar
- 1 fennel bulb, halved lengthwise, cored, and cut into ¼-inch dice (about 1½ cups; see page 37)
- 2 apples, cored and cut into ¼-inch dice (about 2 cups; see note)
- ½ small red onion, minced (about ¼ cup)

¼ cup chopped fresh tarragon leaves

1 romaine heart, cut into ½-inch pieces (about 3 cups)

½ cup chopped walnuts, toasted
   Ground back pepper

4 ounces crumbled goat cheese (about 1 cup)

1. Combine the cucumber and ½ teaspoon salt in a colander set over a bowl and drain for 15 minutes.

2. Whisk the oil and vinegar together in a large bowl. Add the drained cucumber, fennel, apples, onion, and tarragon. Toss and let stand at room temperature to blend the flavors, 5 minutes.

3. Add the romaine and walnuts and toss to combine. Season with salt and pepper to taste. Divide the salad among individual plates; top each with some goat cheese and serve.

NOTES FROM THE TEST KITCHEN

TRIMMING AND CORING FENNEL

1. Cut off the stems and feathery fronds.

2. Trim a very thin slice from the base of the bulb and remove any tough or blemished outer layers.

3. After cutting the bulb in half through the base, use a small, sharp knife to remove the pyramid-shaped core. Slice or chop the fennel as directed.

CHERRY TOMATO SALAD

WHY THIS RECIPE WORKS: Cherry tomatoes are sweet, juicy, and available year-round—and especially tempting during those cold winter months when summer seems eons away. We wanted an easy recipe that would make the most of their sweetness so we could enjoy fresh tomatoes anytime we wanted.

Simply slicing cherry tomatoes in half and sprucing them up with vinaigrette resulted in a waterlogged salad with no flavor at all. To prevent this soggy, watery outcome, we quartered the tomatoes, salted them, and then took them for a spin in a salad spinner to remove as much of the jelly and seeds as possible. Reducing the jelly with red wine vinegar concentrated its flavor, and adding olive oil made for a dressing that brought the tomato flavor to the forefront. The tomatoes and vinaigrette were well flavored, but the salad lacked texture. Cucumber contributed welcome crunch, while chopped olives and crumbled feta added a briny touch that brought the whole dish together.

Cherry Tomato Salad with Feta and Olives
SERVES 4 TO 6

If in-season cherry tomatoes are unavailable, substitute vine-ripened cherry tomatoes or grape tomatoes from the supermarket. Cut grape tomatoes in half along the equator (rather than quartering them). If you don't have a salad spinner, after the salted tomatoes have stood for 30 minutes, wrap the bowl tightly with plastic wrap and gently shake to remove seeds and excess liquid. Strain the liquid and proceed with the recipe as directed. The amount of liquid given off by the tomatoes will depend on their ripeness. If you have less than ½ cup juice after spinning, proceed with the recipe using the entire amount of juice and reduce it to 3 tablespoons as directed (the cooking time will be shorter).

2 pints ripe cherry tomatoes, quartered (about 4 cups; see note)

½ teaspoon sugar
   Table salt

1 medium shallot, minced (about 3 tablespoons)

1 tablespoon red wine vinegar

2 medium garlic cloves, minced or pressed through a garlic press (about 2 teaspoons)

½ teaspoon dried oregano

2 tablespoons extra-virgin olive oil
   Ground black pepper

1 small cucumber, peeled, halved lengthwise, seeded, and cut into ½-inch pieces (see page 40)
½ cup chopped pitted kalamata olives
4 ounces feta cheese, crumbled (about 1 cup)
3 tablespoons chopped fresh parsley leaves

1. Toss the tomatoes, sugar, and ¼ teaspoon salt in a medium bowl; let stand for 30 minutes. Transfer the tomatoes to a salad spinner and spin until the seeds and excess liquid have been removed, 45 to 60 seconds, stirring to redistribute the tomatoes several times during spinning. Return the tomatoes to the bowl and set aside. Strain the tomato liquid through a fine-mesh strainer into a liquid measuring cup, pressing on the solids to extract as much liquid as possible.

2. Bring ½ cup of the tomato liquid (discard any extra), the shallot, vinegar, garlic, and oregano to a simmer in a small saucepan over medium heat. Simmer until reduced to 3 tablespoons, 6 to 8 minutes. Transfer the mixture to a small bowl and cool to room temperature, about 5 minutes. Whisk in the oil until combined and season with salt and pepper to taste.

3. Add the cucumber, olives, feta, parsley, and dressing to the bowl with the tomatoes; toss gently and serve.

ITALIAN BREAD SALAD

WHY THIS RECIPE WORKS: When the rustic Italian bread salad panzanella is done well, the sweet juice of the tomatoes mixes with a bright-tasting vinaigrette, moistening chunks of thick-crusted bread until they're soft and just a little chewy—but the line between lightly moistened and unpleasantly soggy is very thin. Toasting fresh bread in the oven, rather than using the traditional day-old bread, was a good start. With this method, the bread lost enough moisture in the oven to absorb the dressing without getting waterlogged. A 10-minute soak in the flavorful dressing yielded perfectly moistened, nutty-tasting bread ready to be tossed with the tomatoes, which we salted to intensify their flavor. A thinly sliced cucumber and shallot for crunch and bite plus a handful of chopped fresh basil perfected our salad.

Italian Bread Salad (Panzanella)
SERVES 4

The success of this recipe depends on high-quality ingredients, including ripe, in-season tomatoes and fruity olive oil. Fresh basil is also a must. Your bread may vary in density, so you may not need the entire loaf for this recipe.

1 (1-pound) loaf rustic Italian or French bread, cut or torn into 1-inch pieces (about 6 cups)
½ cup extra-virgin olive oil
  Table salt and ground black pepper
1½ pounds tomatoes, cored, seeded, and cut into 1-inch pieces
3 tablespoons red wine vinegar
1 medium cucumber, peeled, halved lengthwise, seeded, and sliced thin (see page 40)
1 medium shallot, sliced thin
¼ cup chopped fresh basil leaves

1. Adjust an oven rack to the middle position and heat the oven to 400 degrees. Toss the bread pieces with 2 tablespoons of the oil and ¼ teaspoon salt; arrange the bread in a single layer on a rimmed baking sheet. Toast the bread pieces until just starting to turn light golden, 15 to 20 minutes, stirring halfway through baking. Set aside and let cool to room temperature.

2. Gently toss the tomatoes and ½ teaspoon salt in a large bowl. Transfer to a colander set over a bowl; set aside to drain for 15 minutes, tossing occasionally.

3. Whisk the remaining 6 tablespoons oil, the vinegar, and ¼ teaspoon pepper into the tomato juices. Add the bread pieces, toss to coat, and let stand for 10 minutes, tossing occasionally.

4. Add the tomatoes, cucumber, shallot, and basil to the bowl with the bread pieces and toss to coat. Season with salt and pepper to taste and serve immediately.

GREEK SALAD

WHY THIS RECIPE WORKS: Most versions of Greek salad consist of iceberg lettuce, chunks of green pepper, and a few pale wedges of tomato, sparsely dotted with cubes of feta and garnished with one forlorn olive of questionable heritage. We wanted a salad with crisp ingredients and bold flavors—married with a lively, herb-infused dressing.

A combination of lemon juice, red wine vinegar, garlic, and olive oil made a rich, zesty vinaigrette, and oregano lent it fresh herb flavor. To give our salad a flavorful foundation, we marinated onion and cucumber slices in the vinaigrette. This step also served to mute the sting of raw onion in the salad. We swapped in crisp, flavorful romaine for the iceberg. And along with sliced tomatoes, we added jarred roasted red peppers for a bit of sweetness. A handful of kalamata olives and tangy feta cheese lent the traditional touches, and torn mint and parsley leaves gave our salad a fresh finish.

Classic Greek Salad

SERVES 6 TO 8

Marinating the onion and cucumber in the vinaigrette tones down the onion's harshness and flavors the cucumber. For efficiency, prepare the other salad ingredients while the onion and cucumber marinate.

VINAIGRETTE

    6   tablespoons extra-virgin olive oil
    3   tablespoons red wine vinegar
    2   teaspoons minced fresh oregano leaves
 1½   teaspoons juice from 1 lemon
    1   medium garlic clove, minced or pressed through a
        garlic press (about 1 teaspoon)
    ½   teaspoon table salt
    ⅛   teaspoon ground black pepper

SALAD

    ½   medium red onion, sliced thin (about ¾ cup)
    1   medium cucumber, peeled, halved lengthwise, seeded,
        and sliced ⅛ inch thick (see page 40)
    2   romaine hearts, washed, dried, and torn into 1½-inch
        pieces (about 8 cups)
    2   medium, firm, ripe tomatoes (6 ounces each), cored,
        seeded, and each tomato cut into 12 wedges
    6   ounces jarred roasted red bell peppers, cut into
        2 by ½-inch strips (about 1 cup)
    ¼   cup loosely packed fresh parsley leaves, torn
    ¼   cup loosely packed fresh mint leaves, torn
  20   large pitted kalamata olives, quartered
    5   ounces feta cheese, crumbled (about 1¼ cups)

1. FOR THE VINAIGRETTE: Whisk the oil, vinegar, oregano, lemon juice, garlic, salt, and pepper in a large bowl until combined.

2. Add the onion and cucumber to the vinaigrette and toss; let stand to blend the flavors, about 20 minutes.

3. FOR THE SALAD: Add the romaine, tomatoes, peppers, parsley, and mint to the bowl with the onions and cucumbers; toss to coat with the vinaigrette.

4. Transfer the salad to a serving bowl or platter; sprinkle the olives and feta over the salad and serve.

CUCUMBER SALAD

WHY THIS RECIPE WORKS: More often than not, by the time you eat a cucumber salad, the cucumbers have gone soft and watery, having lost their crunchy texture and released enough liquid to dilute the dressing and turn it flavorless. This phenomenon made the primary goal of our cucumber salad easy to identify: Maximize the crunch.

Because water makes cucumbers lose their texture, we had to salt and weight the seeded and sliced cucumbers to draw off excess moisture. For extra insurance, we also rinsed them and patted them dry. Then we tossed the cucumbers with a rice vinegar, lemon juice, and sesame oil vinaigrette, a flavorful combination that stood up to the superior crunch of our cucumbers. Toasted sesame seeds added even more textural interest.

Sesame-Lemon Cucumber Salad

SERVES 4

Mild rice vinegar works well in this Asian-inspired dressing.

- 3 medium cucumbers (about 2 pounds), peeled, halved lengthwise, seeded, and sliced ¼ inch thick (see photos)
- 1 tablespoon table salt
- ¼ cup rice vinegar (see note)
- 2 tablespoons toasted sesame oil
- 1 tablespoon juice from 1 lemon
- 1 tablespoon sesame seeds, toasted
- 2 teaspoons sugar
- ⅛ teaspoon red pepper flakes

1. Toss the cucumbers with the salt in a colander set over a large bowl. Weight the cucumbers with a gallon-sized zipper-lock bag filled with water; drain for 1 to 3 hours. Rinse and pat dry.

2. Whisk the remaining ingredients together in a medium bowl. Add the cucumbers; toss to coat. Serve chilled or at room temperature.

NOTES FROM THE TEST KITCHEN

SEEDING CUCUMBERS

Peel the cucumber, cut it in half lengthwise, and scoop out the seeds with a spoon.

CHOPPING CUCUMBERS

1. Cut each half crosswise into 2 to 3-inch pieces.

2. Place the pieces cut side up on a cutting board, then slice them lengthwise into even batons.

3. Cut the batons crosswise into an even dice.

CREAMY COLESLAW

WHY THIS RECIPE WORKS: No other food embodies an outdoor grillfest quite like coleslaw. This summery salad offers a crunch and creaminess that contrasts well with sweet and savory barbecued meats and vegetables. But, despite its simplicity, coleslaw can be tough to get just right. Usually, the coleslaw ends up limp and sitting in a pool of water. We wanted a recipe for a crisp salad and a creamy dressing that wouldn't be waterlogged. To prevent the salad from getting watery, we salted the cabbage until it wilted, then rinsed and dried it. Removing the excess water helped to keep our dressing thick and creamy, and ensured that the cabbage stayed crunchy in the slaw. For the dressing, we used a combination of mayonnaise and low-acidity rice vinegar; these made a creamy dressing that was flavorful but not too harsh. All our coleslaw needed now were a few grinds of black pepper and some shredded carrot for color, further crunch, and a little sweetness.

Creamy Coleslaw

SERVES 4

If you like caraway or celery seeds, add ¼ teaspoon of either with the mayonnaise and vinegar. If you like a tangier slaw, replace some or all of the mayonnaise with an equal amount of sour cream. To serve the coleslaw immediately, rinse the salted cabbage and carrot in a large bowl of ice water, drain them in a colander, pick out any ice cubes, then pat the vegetables dry before dressing.

- 1 pound red or green cabbage (about ½ medium head), shredded (about 6 cups; see page 42)
- 1 large carrot, peeled and shredded
- 1 teaspoon table salt
- ½ small onion, minced
- ½ cup mayonnaise (see note)
- 2 tablespoons rice vinegar
   Ground black pepper

1. Toss the cabbage and carrot with the salt in a colander set over a medium bowl. Let stand until the cabbage wilts, at least 1 hour or up to 4 hours. Rinse the cabbage and carrot under cold running water (or in a large bowl of ice water if serving immediately). Press, but do not squeeze, to drain; pat dry with paper towels.

2. Combine the cabbage, carrot, onion, mayonnaise, and vinegar in a medium bowl; toss to coat and season with pepper to taste. Serve chilled or at room temperature. (The coleslaw can be refrigerated in an airtight container for up to 2 days.)

BUTTERMILK COLESLAW

WHY THIS RECIPE WORKS: Order barbecue down South, and you won't just get coleslaw on the side, you'll get buttermilk coleslaw. Unlike all-mayonnaise coleslaw, buttermilk coleslaw is coated in a light, creamy, and refreshingly tart dressing. We wanted a recipe that showcased the best attributes of this side salad: a pickle-crisp texture and a tangy dressing.

To prevent watery coleslaw, we salted, rinsed, and dried our shredded cabbage. This also gave us the texture we wanted—as the salted cabbage sat, moisture was pulled out of it, wilting it to the right crispy texture. For a tangy dressing that clung to the cabbage and didn't pool at the bottom of the bowl, we supplemented the buttermilk with mayonnaise and sour cream. For finishing touches, we added shredded carrot, which contributed both color and sweetness. The mild flavor of shallot was a welcome addition, and sugar, mustard, and cider vinegar amped up the slaw's tanginess.

Creamy Buttermilk Coleslaw

SERVES 4

To serve the coleslaw immediately, rinse the salted cabbage in a large bowl of ice water, drain it in a colander, pick out any ice cubes, then pat the cabbage dry before dressing.

- 1 pound red or green cabbage (about ½ medium head), shredded (about 6 cups; see page 42)
   Table salt
- 1 large carrot, peeled and shredded
- ½ cup buttermilk
- 2 tablespoons mayonnaise
- 2 tablespoons sour cream
- 1 small shallot, minced (about 1 tablespoon)
- 2 tablespoons minced fresh parsley leaves
- ½ teaspoon cider vinegar
- ¼ teaspoon Dijon mustard
- ½ teaspoon sugar
- ⅛ teaspoon ground black pepper

1. Toss the cabbage with 1 teaspoon salt in a colander set over a medium bowl. Let stand until the cabbage wilts, at least 1 hour or up to 4 hours. Rinse the cabbage under cold running water (or in a large bowl of ice water if serving immediately). Press, but do not squeeze, to drain; pat dry with paper towels. Transfer the cabbage to a large bowl; add the carrot.

2. Combine the remaining ingredients with ¼ teaspoon salt in a small bowl. Pour the buttermilk dressing over the cabbage and carrot and toss to coat. Serve chilled or at room temperature. (The coleslaw can be refrigerated in an airtight container for up to 2 days.)

CABBAGE SALAD

WHY THIS RECIPE WORKS: Cabbage makes a great salad—not just as coleslaw but as a crunchy, flavorful, dress-up kind of salad. We aimed to develop an Asian-inspired cabbage salad that incorporated spicy, sweet flavors for a salad side dish that was a refreshing change from the same old slaw.

Salting the cabbage and setting it over a colander helped to extract excess liquid, which otherwise would dilute the potent flavors of the dressing. Shredded carrot gave the salad some sweetness, and radishes brought a peppery crunch. For the dressing, we started with smooth peanut butter for its rich flavor and velvety texture. Rice vinegar and soy sauce provided bright, tangy notes. White sugar would have contributed too much sweetness, but a small amount of honey was just right. Last touches to the dressing came in the form of a spicy jalapeño chile and fresh ginger. Processed to a smooth consistency, our spicy peanut dressing provided the perfect lush coating to the crisp vegetables.

Confetti Cabbage Salad with Spicy Peanut Dressing

SERVES 6

Serve this Asian-inspired cabbage salad with simple pork or chicken dishes. To serve the salad immediately, rinse the salted cabbage and carrot in a large bowl of ice water, drain them in a colander, pick out any ice cubes, then pat the vegetables dry before dressing.

- 1 pound red or green cabbage (about ½ medium head), shredded (about 6 cups; see photos)
- 1 large carrot, peeled and shredded
  Table salt
- 2 tablespoons smooth peanut butter
- 2 tablespoons peanut oil
- 2 tablespoons rice vinegar
- 1 tablespoon soy sauce
- 1 teaspoon honey

- 2 medium garlic cloves, minced or pressed through a garlic press (about 2 teaspoons)
- 1½ tablespoons minced or grated fresh ginger
- ½ jalapeño chile, seeds and ribs removed
- 4 medium radishes, halved lengthwise and sliced thin
- 4 scallions, sliced thin

1. Toss the cabbage and carrot with 1 teaspoon salt in a colander set over a medium bowl. Let stand until the cabbage wilts, at least 1 hour or up to 4 hours. Rinse the cabbage and carrot under cold running water (or in a large bowl of ice water if serving immediately). Press, but do not squeeze, to drain; pat dry with paper towels.

2. Process the peanut butter, oil, vinegar, soy sauce, honey, garlic, ginger, and jalapeño in a food processor until smooth. Combine the cabbage, carrot, radishes, scallions, and dressing in a medium bowl; toss to coat. Season with salt to taste. Cover and refrigerate; serve chilled. (The salad can be refrigerated in an airtight container for up to 2 days.)

NOTES FROM THE TEST KITCHEN

SHREDDING CABBAGE

1. Cut the cabbage into quarters, then trim and discard the hard core.

2. Separate the cabbage into small stacks of leaves that flatten when pressed.

3. Use a chef's knife to cut each stack of cabbage leaves into thin shreds.

MACARONI SALAD

WHY THIS RECIPE WORKS: Macaroni salad seems simple enough—toss elbow macaroni and a few seasonings with a mayo-based dressing. So why does this picnic salad often fall short, with mushy pasta and a bland, ho-hum dressing? We set out to make a picnic-worthy macaroni salad with tender pasta and a creamy, well-seasoned dressing.

First we had to get the pasta texture just right. To do this, we didn't drain the macaroni as thoroughly as we could have; the excess water is absorbed by the pasta as it sits and this prevents the finished salad from drying out. Also, cooking the macaroni to a point where it still has some bite left means the pasta won't get too soft when mixed with the mayonnaise. For the most flavor, we seasoned the pasta first—before adding the mayonnaise—so that the seasonings could penetrate and flavor the macaroni. Garlic powder added flavor to the salad (fresh garlic was too harsh), and lemon juice and Dijon mustard enlivened the creamy dressing.

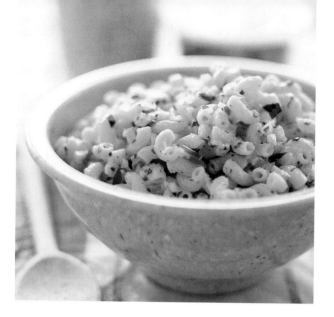

Cool and Creamy Macaroni Salad
SERVES 8 TO 10

Don't drain the macaroni too well before adding the other ingredients—a little extra moisture will keep the salad from drying out. If you've made the salad ahead of time, simply stir in a little warm water to loosen the texture before serving.

    Table salt
  1 pound elbow macaroni
  ½ small red onion, minced
  1 celery rib, chopped fine
  ¼ cup minced fresh parsley leaves
  2 tablespoons juice from 1 lemon
  1 tablespoon Dijon mustard
  ⅛ teaspoon garlic powder
    Pinch cayenne pepper
1½ cups mayonnaise
    Ground black pepper

1. Bring 4 quarts water to a boil in a large pot. Stir 1 tablespoon salt and the pasta into the boiling water and cook, stirring often, until nearly tender, about 5 minutes. Drain the pasta and rinse with cold water until cool, then drain briefly so that the macaroni remains moist. Transfer to a large bowl.

2. Stir in the onion, celery, parsley, lemon juice, mustard, garlic powder, and cayenne and let sit until the flavors are absorbed, about 2 minutes. Add the mayonnaise and let sit until the salad is no longer watery, 5 to 10 minutes. Season with salt and pepper to taste and serve. (The salad can be refrigerated in an airtight container for up to 2 days.)

PASTA SALAD WITH PESTO

WHY THIS RECIPE WORKS: Pasta salad with pesto should be light and refreshing, not dry and dull. We decided to perfect pesto pasta salad—and keep it fresh, green, garlicky, and full of herbal flavor.

Using a pasta shape with a textured surface, like farfalle, guaranteed that the pesto wouldn't slide off. To ensure that the pesto coated the pasta, we didn't rinse the pasta after cooking. Instead, we spread the pasta to cool in a single layer on a baking sheet; a splash of oil helped prevent the pasta from sticking. For the pesto, we blanched the garlic to tame its harsh bite. Lots of basil made for vibrant herb flavor, and to keep the green color from fading, we added mild-tasting baby spinach, which lent the salad a vivid green color but didn't overpower the basil. For a creamy, not greasy, pesto, we enriched it with mayonnaise. Lemon juice brightened the pesto's flavor, and extra pine nuts, folded into the salad, provided an additional hit of nutty flavor and a pleasant crunchy texture.

Pasta Salad with Pesto

SERVES 8 TO 10

This salad is best served the day it is made; if it's been refrigerated, bring it to room temperature before serving. The pesto can be made a day ahead—just cook the garlic in a small saucepan of boiling water for 1 minute.

- 2 medium garlic cloves, unpeeled
  Table salt
- 1 pound farfalle (bow-tie pasta)
- ¼ cup plus 1 tablespoon extra-virgin olive oil
- 3 cups packed fresh basil leaves (about 4 ounces)
- 1 cup packed baby spinach (about 1 ounce)
- ¾ cup pine nuts (3¾ ounces), toasted
- 2 tablespoons juice from 1 lemon
- ½ teaspoon ground black pepper
- 1½ ounces Parmesan cheese, finely grated (about ¾ cup), plus extra for serving
- 6 tablespoons mayonnaise
- 1 pint cherry tomatoes, quartered, or grape tomatoes, halved (optional)

1. Bring 4 quarts water to a boil in a large pot. Add the garlic to the boiling water and let cook for 1 minute. Remove the garlic with a slotted spoon and rinse under cold water; set aside to cool. Stir 1 tablespoon salt and the pasta into the boiling water and cook, stirring often, until the pasta is just past al dente. Reserve ¼ cup of the pasta cooking water, drain the pasta, toss with 1 tablespoon of the oil, spread in a single layer on a rimmed baking sheet, and cool to room temperature, about 30 minutes.

2. Peel and mince the garlic or press it through a garlic press. Process the garlic, basil, spinach, ¼ cup of the nuts, lemon juice, pepper, remaining ¼ cup oil, and 1 teaspoon salt in a food processor until smooth, scraping down the sides of the workbowl as necessary. Add the Parmesan and mayonnaise and process until thoroughly combined. Transfer the mixture to a large serving bowl. Cover and refrigerate until ready to assemble the salad.

3. Toss the pasta with the pesto, adding the reserved pasta water, 1 tablespoon at a time, until the pesto evenly coats the pasta. Fold in the remaining ½ cup nuts and the tomatoes (if using). Serve, passing extra Parmesan separately.

ANTIPASTO PASTA SALAD

WHY THIS RECIPE WORKS: We love the traditional antipasto platter served at Italian restaurants, chock-full of cured meats, cheese, and pickled vegetables. It's a full-flavored and satisfying dish—and something that we thought would translate well to a hearty pasta salad.

We quickly decided that short, curly pasta was the best shape to use, as its curves held on to the salad's other components, making for a more cohesive dish. Quickly rendering the meats in the microwave helped to keep this salad from becoming greasy. We used an increased ratio of vinegar to oil in the dressing—the sharp, acidic flavor cut the richness of the meats and cheese for a brighter-tasting salad. For well-seasoned pasta, we tossed the hot pasta with the dressing—hot pasta absorbs dressing better than cold pasta. Slicing the meat into thick strips meant that its hearty flavor wasn't lost among the other ingredients. And grating the cheese, rather than cubing it, made for evenly distributed sharp flavor throughout the salad.

Antipasto Pasta Salad

SERVES 6 TO 8

We also liked the addition of 1 cup chopped pitted kalamata olives or 1 cup jarred artichokes, drained and quartered, to this salad.

- 8 ounces sliced pepperoni, cut into ¼-inch strips
- 8 ounces thick-sliced sopresatta or salami, halved and cut into ¼-inch strips
- 10 tablespoons red wine vinegar
- 6 tablespoons extra-virgin olive oil
- 3 tablespoons mayonnaise
- 1 (12-ounce) jar pepperoncini, drained (2 tablespoons liquid reserved), stemmed, and chopped coarse
- 4 garlic cloves, minced or pressed through a garlic press (about 4 teaspoons)
- ¼ teaspoon red pepper flakes
  Table salt and ground black pepper
- 1 pound short, curly pasta, such as fusilli or campanelle
- 1 pound white mushrooms, wiped clean and quartered
- 4 ounces aged provolone cheese, grated (about 1 cup)
- 1 (12-ounce) jar roasted red peppers, drained, patted dry, and chopped coarse
- 1 cup minced fresh basil leaves

1. Bring 4 quarts water to a boil in a large pot. Place the pepperoni on a large paper towel–lined plate. Cover with another paper towel and place the sopresatta on top. Cover with another paper towel and microwave on high power for 1 minute. Discard the paper towels and set the pepperoni and sopresatta aside.

2. Whisk 5 tablespoons of the vinegar, the oil, mayonnaise, pepperoncini liquid, garlic, red pepper flakes, ½ teaspoon salt, and ½ teaspoon pepper together in a medium bowl.

3. Stir 1 tablespoon salt and the pasta into the boiling water and cook, stirring often, until the pasta is just past al dente. Drain the pasta and return it to the pot. Pour ½ cup of the dressing and the remaining 5 tablespoons vinegar over the pasta and toss to combine; season with salt and pepper to taste. Spread the pasta in a single layer on a rimmed baking sheet and cool to room temperature, about 30 minutes.

4. Meanwhile, bring the remaining dressing to a simmer in a large skillet over medium-high heat. Add the mushrooms and cook until lightly browned, about 8 minutes. Transfer to a large bowl and cool to room temperature.

5. Add the meat, provolone, peppers, basil, and pasta to the mushrooms and toss to combine. Season with salt and pepper to taste and serve.

RICE SALAD

WHY THIS RECIPE WORKS: Rice makes a light, refreshing salad when dressed properly and studded with vegetables—and it makes a nice change from pasta salad. But unlike pasta, rice can't stand up to assertive flavors or be bogged down by a heavy vinaigrette. To get rice salad just right, we would have to include a few bright, tangy ingredients and use a light hand when making the dressing.

To start out with as much flavor as possible, we toasted the rice to intensify its flavor and then boiled it in a large amount of water, as we would pasta. This method kept the rice tender when cool. To dry the rice, we spread it out on a large baking sheet—this guaranteed that the rice didn't clump or become waterlogged. As for the vinaigrette, restraint was key. We used small amounts of oil, vinegar, and seasonings to complement, but not overshadow, the grains of rice. Orange segments, slivered almonds, and chopped olives gave the salad character and textural interest. And a brief rest to blend the flavors yielded a rice salad that was bright and balanced.

Rice Salad with Oranges, Olives, and Almonds
SERVES 6 TO 8

Taste the rice as it nears the end of its cooking time; it should be cooked through and firm, but not crunchy. Be careful not to overcook the rice or the grains will be blown out.

1½ cups long-grain or basmati rice
    Table salt
2   tablespoons extra-virgin olive oil
¼   teaspoon grated zest plus 1 tablespoon juice from
    1 orange
2   teaspoons sherry vinegar
1   small garlic clove, minced or pressed through a
    garlic press (about ½ teaspoon)
½   teaspoon ground black pepper
2   medium oranges, peel and pith removed, and cut
    into segments (see page 214)
⅓   cup chopped pitted green olives
⅓   cup slivered almonds, toasted
2   tablespoons fresh oregano leaves, minced

1. Bring 4 quarts water to a boil in a large pot. Heat a medium skillet over medium heat until hot, about 3 minutes; add the rice and toast, stirring frequently, until faintly fragrant and some grains turn opaque, about 5 minutes.

2. Stir 1½ teaspoons salt and the rice into the boiling water. Cook, uncovered, until the rice is tender but not soft, 8 to 10 minutes for long-grain rice or about 15 minutes for basmati (see note). Line a rimmed baking sheet with foil or parchment paper. Drain the rice in a colander and spread on the prepared baking sheet. Cool while preparing the salad ingredients.

3. Whisk the oil, orange zest and juice, vinegar, garlic, 1 teaspoon salt, and pepper together in a small bowl. Combine the rice, oranges, olives, almonds, and oregano in a large bowl; drizzle the dressing over the salad and toss to combine. Let stand for 20 minutes to blend the flavors, and serve.

AMERICAN POTATO SALAD

WHY THIS RECIPE WORKS: Few salads make a splash at potlucks or picnics the way potato salad does—this classic, all-American side always seems to disappear first. We wanted a recipe for a traditional, creamy (read: mayonnaise-based) potato salad that looked good—no mushy, sloppy spuds—and tasted even better.

We began by choosing red potatoes. The skin adds color to a typically monochromatic salad. We boiled them whole for best flavor and then used a serrated knife to cut the potatoes into fork-friendly chunks—the serrated

edge helps prevent the skins from tearing for a nicer presentation. While the potatoes were still warm, we drizzled them with vinegar and added a sprinkle of salt and pepper; this preseasoning gave the finished salad more flavor. When the potatoes were cool, we folded in the final traditional touches—mayonnaise, pickles, and red onion—for a perfect potluck potato salad, with a creamy dressing and firm bites of potato.

American Potato Salad with Hard-Cooked Eggs and Sweet Pickles

SERVES 4 TO 6

Use sweet pickles, not relish, for the best results. For potatoes that cook through at the same rate, buy potatoes that are roughly the same size.

- 2 **pounds red potatoes (about 6 medium), scrubbed (see note)**
- ¼ **cup red wine vinegar**
  Table salt and ground black pepper
- ½ **cup mayonnaise**
- ¼ **cup sweet pickles, chopped fine (see note)**
- 3 **hard-cooked eggs (see page 32), peeled and cut into ½-inch pieces**
- 1 **celery rib, chopped fine**
- 2 **tablespoons minced red onion**
- 2 **tablespoons minced fresh parsley leaves**
- 2 **teaspoons Dijon mustard**

1. Place the potatoes in a large saucepan, cover with 1 inch of water, and bring to a boil over medium-high heat. Reduce the heat to medium and simmer, stirring occasionally, until the potatoes are tender (a paring knife can be slipped in and out of the potatoes with little resistance), 25 to 30 minutes.

2. Drain the potatoes and cool slightly; peel if desired. Cut the potatoes into ¾-inch pieces, using a serrated knife, while still warm, rinsing the knife occasionally in warm water to remove starch.

3. Combine the potatoes, vinegar, ½ teaspoon salt, and ¼ teaspoon pepper in a large bowl and toss gently. Cover and refrigerate until cool, about 20 minutes.

4. Meanwhile, combine the remaining ingredients and salt and pepper to taste. Add the potatoes, stir gently to combine, and serve. (The salad can be refrigerated in an airtight container for up to 1 day.)

AUSTRIAN POTATO SALAD

WHY THIS RECIPE WORKS: Austrian-style potato salad, seasoned with vinegar and mustard for a tart-and-tangy flavor, can be a welcome change of pace from traditional creamy potato salad. The ingredients might be different, but the goals are the same: keeping the salad saucy and the potatoes tender but not so tender they fall apart.

This style of potato salad calls on the starch from the potatoes along with an unexpected ingredient, chicken broth, to create the lush, flavor-packed dressing. After cooking the sliced potatoes in broth, which we cut with an equal amount of water, we reduced the cooking liquid and mixed it with vinegar, mustard, chives, and cornichons for best flavor. To give the dressing more body, and impart a rustic, country-style texture, we mashed in a small amount of our cooked potatoes. After mixing the rest of the sliced potatoes (which retained their shape but were soft and tender) with the thick vinaigrette, we had a luxurious, rich, and very different kind of potato salad.

Austrian-Style Potato Salad

SERVES 4 TO 6

If you can't find cornichons, chopped kosher dill pickles can be used in their place. To maintain its consistency, don't refrigerate the salad; it should be served within a few hours of preparation.

- 2 **pounds Yukon Gold potatoes (about 4 medium), peeled, quartered, and sliced ½ inch thick**
- 1 **cup low-sodium chicken broth**
- 2 **tablespoons white wine vinegar**
- 1 **tablespoon sugar**
  Table salt
- ¼ **cup vegetable oil**
- 1 **small red onion, minced**
- 6 **cornichons, minced (about 2 tablespoons; see note)**
- 2 **tablespoons minced fresh chives**
- 1 **tablespoon Dijon mustard**
  Ground black pepper

1. Bring 1 cup water, the potatoes, broth, 1 tablespoon of the vinegar, the sugar, and 1 teaspoon salt to a boil in a 12-inch skillet over high heat. Reduce the heat to medium-low, cover, and cook until the potatoes are tender (a paring knife can be slipped in and out of the potatoes with little resistance), 15 to 17 minutes. Remove the cover, increase the heat to high, and cook until the liquid has reduced, about 2 minutes.

2. Drain the potatoes in a colander set over a large bowl, reserving the cooking liquid. Set the potatoes aside. Pour off all but ½ cup cooking liquid (if ½ cup liquid does not remain, add water to make this amount). Whisk the cooking liquid, the remaining 1 tablespoon vinegar, the oil, onion, cornichons, chives, and mustard together in a large bowl.

3. Add ½ cup of the cooked potatoes to the bowl with the cooking liquid mixture and mash with a potato masher until a thick vinaigrette forms (the mixture will be slightly chunky). Add the remaining potatoes, stirring gently to combine. Season with salt and pepper to taste. Serve warm or at room temperature.

CHAPTER 3

EASY SKILLET SUPPERS

Skillet Baked Ziti 50

Skillet Chicken, Broccoli,
and Ziti 51

Skillet Lasagna 52

Skillet Chicken Pot Pie with
Biscuit Topping 53

Skillet Tamale Pie 54

Skillet Beef
Stroganoff 55

Skillet-Roasted Chicken
Breasts with Potatoes 56

Skillet Chicken and Rice
with Peas and Scallions 57

Skillet Chicken and Rice
with Broccoli and
Cheddar 58

Skillet Curried Chicken
and Rice 58

Skillet Jambalaya 59

SKILLET BAKED ZITI

WHY THIS RECIPE WORKS: Baked ziti, a hearty combination of pasta, tomato sauce, and gooey cheese, can be time-consuming and fussy, between making the sauce, boiling the pasta, and then assembling and baking the dish. We were looking for a method that would give us the same delicious results but in less time and without watching over, or dirtying, a multitude of pots.

Instead of preparing the components of the dish separately, we found we could get all our cooking done in a skillet—including the pasta. How did we do it? We thinned the sauce with water so that the pasta cooked through in the sauce without drying out. (And the thin sauce reduced to a nicely thick consistency.) To start building the sauce, we sautéed lots of garlic with red pepper flakes, then added crushed tomatoes, water, and the ziti. When the pasta was almost tender (it would finish cooking in the oven), we added some heavy cream, for richness and body, and shredded mozzarella cheese. A little grated Parmesan boosted the cheesy flavor, and minced fresh basil and pepper were all the seasonings we needed to finish our skillet version of this family favorite.

Skillet Baked Ziti

SERVES 4

To complete this recipe in 30 minutes, preheat your oven before assembling the ingredients. If your skillet is not ovensafe, transfer the pasta mixture to a shallow 2-quart casserole dish before sprinkling with the cheese and baking. Packaged preshredded mozzarella is a real time-saver here. Penne can be used in place of the ziti.

- 1 tablespoon olive oil
- 6 medium garlic cloves, minced or pressed through a garlic press (about 2 tablespoons)
- ¼ teaspoon red pepper flakes
  Table salt
- 1 (28-ounce) can crushed tomatoes
- 3 cups water
- 12 ounces ziti (3¾ cups; see note)
- ½ cup heavy cream
- 1 ounce Parmesan cheese, grated (about ½ cup)
- ¼ cup minced fresh basil leaves
  Ground black pepper
- 4 ounces whole milk mozzarella cheese, shredded (about 1 cup; see note)

1. Adjust an oven rack to the middle position and heat the oven to 475 degrees.

2. Heat the oil in a 12-inch ovensafe nonstick skillet over medium-high heat until hot. Add the garlic, red pepper flakes, and ½ teaspoon salt and sauté until fragrant, about 1 minute. Add the crushed tomatoes, water, ziti, and ½ teaspoon salt. Cover and cook, stirring often and adjusting the heat as needed to maintain a vigorous simmer, until the ziti is almost tender, 15 to 18 minutes.

3. Stir in the cream, Parmesan, and basil. Season with salt and pepper to taste. Sprinkle the mozzarella evenly over the ziti. Transfer the skillet to the oven and bake until the cheese has melted and browned, about 10 minutes. Using potholders (the skillet handle will be hot), remove the skillet from the oven. Serve.

SKILLET CHICKEN, BROCCOLI, AND ZITI

WHY THIS RECIPE WORKS: This classic restaurant dish rarely lives up to its promise. The flavors are mediocre, the texture suffers from overcooking (bone-dry chicken), or the sauce is oily and contains an overpowering amount of garlic. Our challenge would lie in getting the flavors and textures just right: well-seasoned, tender chunks of chicken, crisp broccoli, and pasta in a light, fresh-flavored sauce. At the same time, we wanted to streamline its preparation for an easy weeknight dinner.

To start, we turned to our skillet to make short work of this dish. First we browned pieces of skinless, boneless chicken breasts in the skillet, then we removed the chicken to build our sauce. (Briefly cooking the chicken, then reheating it later in the sauce would keep it from overcooking.) We started with a base of sautéed onion, a modest amount of garlic, oregano, and red pepper flakes. And to keep all our work limited to the skillet, we cooked the pasta right in the sauce. The broccoli went in next, along with chopped sun-dried tomatoes for depth of flavor. We then covered the skillet and simmered everything just until the broccoli turned bright green. At this point, we returned the chicken to the pan to finish cooking.

A few final touches: a little heavy cream made the sauce silky without obscuring the flavor of the broccoli and chicken. Grated Asiago cheese enriched the sauce and gave it a pleasantly tangy flavor. And a little lemon juice added a bright note. Our chicken, broccoli, and ziti not only boasted a great balance of flavors and textures, but it was quick and easy to prepare as well.

Skillet Chicken, Broccoli, and Ziti

SERVES 4

This recipe also works well with 8 ounces of penne. Parmesan cheese can be substituted for the Asiago.

- 1 **pound boneless, skinless chicken breasts, cut into 1-inch pieces**
  Table salt and ground black pepper
- 2 **tablespoons vegetable or olive oil**
- 1 **medium onion, minced**
- 3 **medium garlic cloves, minced or pressed through a garlic press (about 1 tablespoon)**
- ¼ **teaspoon dried oregano**
- ⅛ **teaspoon red pepper flakes**
- 8 **ounces ziti (2½ cups; see note)**
- 2¾ **cups water**
- 1⅔ **cups low-sodium chicken broth**
- 12 **ounces broccoli florets (4 cups)**
- ¼ **cup oil-packed sun-dried tomatoes, rinsed and chopped coarse**
- ½ **cup heavy cream**
- 1 **ounce Asiago cheese, grated (about ½ cup), plus extra for serving (see note)**
- 1 **tablespoon juice from 1 lemon**

1. Season the chicken with salt and pepper. Heat 1 tablespoon of the oil in a 12-inch nonstick skillet over medium-high heat until just smoking. Add the chicken in a single layer and cook for 1 minute without stirring. Stir the chicken and continue to cook until most, but not all, of the pink color has disappeared and the chicken is lightly browned around the edges, 1 to 2 minutes longer. Transfer the chicken to a clean bowl and set aside.

2. Add the remaining 1 tablespoon oil, the onion, and ½ teaspoon salt to the skillet. Return the skillet to medium-high heat and cook, stirring often, until the onion is softened, 2 to 5 minutes. Stir in the garlic, oregano, and red pepper flakes and cook until fragrant, about 30 seconds.

3. Add the ziti, 2 cups of the water, and the broth. Bring to a boil over high heat and cook until the liquid is very thick and syrupy and almost completely absorbed, 12 to 15 minutes.

4. Add the broccoli, sun-dried tomatoes, and the remaining ¾ cup water. Cover, reduce the heat to medium, and cook until the broccoli turns bright green and is almost tender, 3 to 5 minutes.

5. Uncover and return the heat to high. Stir in the cream, Asiago, and reserved chicken with any accumulated juices and continue to simmer, uncovered, until the sauce is thickened and the chicken is cooked and heated through, 1 to 2 minutes. Off the heat, stir in the lemon juice and season with salt and pepper to taste. Serve, passing more grated Asiago at the table, if desired.

SKILLET LASAGNA

WHY THIS RECIPE WORKS: Lasagna isn't usually a dish you can throw together at the last minute. Even with no-boil noodles, it takes a good amount of time to get the components just right. Our goal was to transform traditional baked lasagna into a stovetop skillet dish without losing any of its flavor or appeal.

We built a hearty, flavorful meat sauce with onions, garlic, red pepper flakes, and meatloaf mix (a more flavorful alternative to plain ground beef). A large can of diced tomatoes along with tomato sauce provided juicy tomato flavor and a nicely chunky texture. We scattered regular curly-edged lasagna noodles, broken into pieces, over the top of the sauce (smaller pieces are easier to eat and serve). We then diluted the sauce with a little water so that the noodles would cook through. After a 20-minute simmer with the lid on, the pasta was tender, the sauce was properly thickened, and it was time for the cheese. Stirring Parmesan into the dish worked well, but we discovered that the sweet creaminess of ricotta was lost unless we placed it in heaping tablespoonfuls on top of the lasagna. Replacing the lid and letting the cheese warm through for several minutes was the final step for this super-easy one-pan dish.

Skillet Lasagna

SERVES 4 TO 6

Meatloaf mix is a combination of ground beef, pork, and veal, sold prepackaged in many supermarkets. If it's unavailable, use ground beef. A skillet with a tight-fitting lid works best for this recipe.

- 1 (28-ounce) can diced tomatoes
  Water
- 1 tablespoon olive oil
- 1 medium onion, minced
  Table salt
- 3 medium garlic cloves, minced or pressed through a garlic press (about 1 tablespoon)
- ⅛ teaspoon red pepper flakes
- 1 pound meatloaf mix (see note)
- 10 curly-edged lasagna noodles, broken into 2-inch lengths
- 1 (8-ounce) can tomato sauce
- 1 ounce Parmesan cheese, grated (½ cup), plus extra for serving
  Ground black pepper
- 1 cup ricotta cheese
- 3 tablespoons chopped fresh basil leaves

1. Pour the tomatoes with their juice into a 4-cup liquid measuring cup. Add water until the mixture measures 4 cups.

2. Heat the oil in a 12-inch nonstick skillet over medium heat until shimmering. Add the onion and ½ teaspoon salt and cook until the onion begins to brown, 6 to 8 minutes. Stir in the garlic and red pepper flakes and cook until fragrant, about 30 seconds. Add the ground meat and cook, breaking apart the meat, until no longer pink, about 4 minutes.

3. Scatter the pasta over the meat but do not stir. Pour the diced tomatoes with their juice and the tomato sauce over the pasta. Cover and bring to a simmer. Reduce the heat to medium-low and simmer, stirring occasionally, until the pasta is tender, about 20 minutes.

4. Remove the skillet from the heat and stir in all but 2 tablespoons of the Parmesan. Season with salt and pepper to taste. Dot with heaping tablespoons of the ricotta, cover, and let stand off the heat for 5 minutes. Sprinkle with the basil and the remaining 2 tablespoons Parmesan. Serve.

SKILLET CHICKEN POT PIE

WHY THIS RECIPE WORKS: Quick versions of chicken pot pie are often plagued by dried-out leftover chicken, bland sauce made with canned soup, and biscuits popped out of a tube. We saw no reason why pot pie couldn't be a whole lot better. We wanted moist chicken, a richly flavored sauce, and a homemade biscuit crust.

Instead of the refrigerated biscuit dough used in most recipes, we turned to homemade biscuits, and it was easy enough to put together a simple dough for baking powder biscuits. We just whisked the dry ingredients together and stirred in heavy cream, kneaded the dough briefly, and cut it into rounds (wedges would also work fine). We then popped the biscuits into the oven to bake, while we turned to the filling.

Next, we decided to contain all our cooking to a skillet for ease of preparation. We first sautéed skinless, boneless breasts in butter, keeping the heat at medium so the exterior wouldn't toughen. We set the chicken aside after it was browned and started the sauce in the skillet with onion, celery, thyme, vermouth, and chicken broth—ingredients that contributed lots of flavor. Flour thickened the liquid, and heavy cream gave it richness and a lush texture. Gently simmering the browned chicken in this sauce not only enhanced the flavor of the sauce but also kept the chicken juicy. Using frozen peas and carrots made quick work of the vegetables. All that was left to do was to assemble our pie by placing the hot biscuits over the filling in the skillet. Our flavorful, meaty stew with tender biscuits on top was not only delicious but also fast and easy.

Skillet Chicken Pot Pie with Biscuit Topping

SERVES 4

If you don't have time to make your own biscuits for the topping, use packaged refrigerated biscuits and bake them according to the package instructions. We prefer the flavor of Pillsbury Golden Homestyle Biscuits but you can use your favorite brand (you will need anywhere from four to eight biscuits depending on their size). This pot pie can be served in a large pie plate with the biscuits arranged on top, or served directly from the skillet.

BISCUITS

- 2 cups (10 ounces) unbleached all-purpose flour, plus extra for the work surface
- 2 teaspoons sugar
- 2 teaspoons baking powder
- ½ teaspoon table salt
- 1½ cups heavy cream

FILLING

- 1½ pounds boneless, skinless chicken breasts
  Table salt and ground black pepper
- 4 tablespoons (½ stick) unsalted butter
- 1 medium onion, minced
- 1 celery rib, sliced thin
- ¼ cup unbleached all-purpose flour
- ¼ cup dry vermouth or dry white wine
- 2 cups low-sodium chicken broth
- ½ cup heavy cream
- 1½ teaspoons minced fresh thyme leaves
- 2 cups frozen pea-carrot medley, thawed

1. FOR THE BISCUITS: Adjust an oven rack to the upper-middle position and heat the oven to 450 degrees. Line a baking sheet with parchment paper and set aside.

2. Whisk the flour, sugar, baking powder, and salt together in a large bowl. Stir in the cream with a wooden spoon until a dough forms, about 30 seconds. Turn the dough out onto a lightly floured work surface and gather into a ball. Knead the dough briefly until smooth, about 30 seconds.

3. Pat the dough into a ¾-inch-thick circle. Cut the biscuits into rounds using a 2½-inch biscuit cutter or cut into eight wedges using a knife.

4. Place the biscuits on the prepared baking sheet. Bake until golden brown, about 15 minutes. Set aside on a wire rack.

5. FOR THE FILLING: While the biscuits bake, pat the chicken dry with paper towels and season with salt and pepper. Melt 2 tablespoons of the butter in a 12-inch skillet over medium heat until the foam subsides. Brown the

SKILLETS AREN'T JUST FOR THE STOVETOP

Take a walk through our test kitchen and you'll see stacks of skillets—small, medium, large, traditional and nonstick—all of them ovensafe. They're undoubtedly the most useful pans in the test kitchen. We use a skillet to cook everything from burgers, steaks, and chicken to eggs, stir-fries, and sauces. But that's not all. We use skillets to cook a host of other dishes that are started on the stovetop and finished in the oven, turning typically long-cooking dishes like roast chicken and baked ziti into weeknight meals. How do we do it? We brown chicken parts on the stovetop and then slide the chicken into the oven to finish cooking through. And for baked ziti? We cook the pasta right in sauce on the stovetop, add the cheese, then pop it into the oven to brown. Both dishes take only about 30 minutes from start to finish.

For most recipes the test kitchen prefers a 12-inch skillet. This large size is the most versatile because it can accommodate a big steak or all of the pieces of a cut-up 3-pound chicken. Look for a skillet that weighs about 3 or 4 pounds. Lighter weight pans performed poorly in the test kitchen and cooked food unevenly. Pans in the 3 to 4-pound range browned foods beautifully and have enough heft for heat retention and structural integrity, but not so much that they are difficult to lift or manipulate. A word of caution: When moving a skillet from the oven to the stovetop, remember that the skillet (and handle) will be hot for some time. To remind ourselves of this (after more than a few burns), we wrap a dry towel around the handle right after we pull it from the oven or slide an oven mitt over it. For more information on skillets and recommended brands of both traditional and nonstick skillets, see page 710.

chicken lightly on both sides, about 5 minutes total. Transfer the chicken to a clean plate.

6. Add the remaining 2 tablespoons butter to the skillet and return to medium heat until melted. Add the onion, celery, and ½ teaspoon salt and cook until the onion is softened, about 5 minutes. Stir in the flour and cook, stirring constantly, until incorporated, about 1 minute.

7. Stir in the vermouth and cook until evaporated, about 30 seconds. Slowly whisk in the broth, cream, and thyme, and bring to a simmer. Nestle the chicken into the sauce, cover, and cook over medium-low heat until the thickest part of the breasts registers 160 to 165 degrees on an instant-read thermometer, 8 to 10 minutes.

8. Transfer the chicken to a plate. Stir the peas and carrots into the sauce and simmer until heated through, about 2 minutes. When the chicken is cool enough to handle, cut or shred it into bite-size pieces and return it to the skillet. Season the filling with salt and pepper to taste.

9. FOR SERVING: Transfer the filling to a large pie plate and arrange the biscuits over the top, or serve directly from the skillet, topping individual portions with the biscuits.

SKILLET TAMALE PIE

WHY THIS RECIPE WORKS: Tamale pie—lightly seasoned, tomatoey ground beef with cornbread topping—is easy to prepare and makes a satisfying supper. But in many recipes, the filling either tastes bland and one-dimensional or turns heavy. As for the cornbread topping, it's usually from a mix and tastes like it. We wanted a skillet tamale pie with a rich, well-seasoned filling and a cornbread topping with real corn flavor.

For the beef, we found 90 percent lean ground sirloin gave us a good balance of richness and flavor. We started by sautéing minced onion and garlic. For seasoning, we used a generous amount of chili powder, which we added to the aromatics in the skillet to "bloom," or intensify, its flavor. The addition of canned black beans made our pie heartier, and canned diced tomatoes contributed additional flavor and texture. Cheddar cheese stirred into the mixture enriched the filling and also helped thicken it, and some minced fresh cilantro contributed a bright, fresh note. And to finish our pie, we skipped the cornbread mix and instead devised an easy homemade version. We spread the cornbread batter over the filling in the skillet, put the skillet in the oven to bake through, and the result was crunchy, corny topping that perfectly complemented the spicy tamale filling.

Skillet Tamale Pie

SERVES 4

Parsley can be substituted for the cilantro, if desired.

TAMALE FILLING

- 2 tablespoons vegetable oil
- 1 medium onion, minced
- 2 tablespoons chili powder
  Table salt
- 2 medium garlic cloves, minced or pressed through a garlic press (about 2 teaspoons)
- 1 pound 90 percent lean ground sirloin
- 1 (15-ounce) can black beans, drained and rinsed
- 1 (14.5-ounce) can diced tomatoes, drained
- 4 ounces cheddar cheese, shredded (about 1 cup)
- 2 tablespoons minced fresh cilantro leaves (see note)
  Ground black pepper

CORNBREAD TOPPING

- ¾ cup (3¾ ounces) unbleached all-purpose flour
- ¾ cup (3¾ ounces) yellow cornmeal
- 3 tablespoons sugar
- ¾ teaspoon table salt
- ¾ teaspoon baking powder
- ¼ teaspoon baking soda
- ¾ cup buttermilk
- 1 large egg
- 3 tablespoons unsalted butter, melted and cooled

1. Adjust an oven rack to the middle position and heat the oven to 450 degrees.

2. FOR THE TAMALE FILLING: Heat the oil in a 12-inch ovensafe skillet over medium heat until shimmering. Add the onion, chili powder, and ½ teaspoon salt and cook until the onion is softened, about 5 minutes. Stir in the garlic and cook until fragrant, about 30 seconds.

3. Stir in the ground sirloin, beans, and tomatoes and bring to a simmer, breaking up the meat with a wooden spoon, about 5 minutes. Stir the cheddar and cilantro into the filling and season with salt and pepper to taste.

4. FOR THE CORNBREAD TOPPING: Whisk the flour, cornmeal, sugar, salt, baking powder, and baking soda together in a large bowl. In a separate bowl, whisk the buttermilk and egg together. Stir the buttermilk mixture into the flour mixture until uniform. Stir in the butter until just combined.

5. Dollop the cornbread batter evenly over the filling and spread into an even layer. Bake until the cornbread is cooked through in the center, 10 to 15 minutes. Using potholders (the skillet handle will be hot), remove the skillet from the oven. Serve.

SKILLET BEEF STROGANOFF

WHY THIS RECIPE WORKS: Beef stroganoff is more often associated with bad banquet fare than with a hearty, satisfying dinner. But originally, this dish was quite elegant and was even made with filet mignon. Our goal was twofold: find a less expensive option for the beef to turn it into a within-reach weeknight supper, and bring the too-rich, often gloppy sauce back to its refined roots.

We started with the beef. Blade steaks shrank too much during cooking; sirloin tips became tender and held their shape well, but the pieces of meat crinkled up oddly. We solved that problem by pounding the meat before cutting it into strips. We first seared the meat and removed it from the pan, then sautéed mushrooms and onion in the same pan. To finish cooking the beef, we built a braising liquid with equal amounts of chicken and beef broth (beef broth alone tasted flat) and a little flour to thicken the sauce. We didn't want to overload the dish with seasonings—they would mask the flavor of the beef and mushrooms—but we found that some brandy was essential. We then returned the meat to the sauce to cook through.

To avoid cooking the noodles separately, we borrowed our method of cooking pasta directly in sauce and added the egg noodles to the braising liquid. When the noodles were tender and the beef was cooked through, we added the final touches, sour cream and lemon juice—but off the heat so that it wouldn't curdle.

Skillet Beef Stroganoff
SERVES 4

To prepare the beef, pound it with a meat pounder to an even ½-inch thickness. Slice the meat, with the grain, into 2-inch strips, then slice each piece against the grain into ½-inch strips. Brandy can ignite if added to a hot, empty skillet. Be sure to add the brandy to the skillet after stirring in the broth.

1½ **pounds sirloin tips, pounded and cut into ½-inch strips (see note)**
 Table salt and ground black pepper
4 **tablespoons vegetable oil**
10 **ounces white mushrooms, wiped clean and sliced thin**
1 **medium onion, minced**
2 **tablespoons unbleached all-purpose flour**
1½ **cups low-sodium chicken broth**
1½ **cups beef broth**
⅓ **cup brandy (see note)**
6 **ounces wide egg noodles (4 cups)**
⅔ **cup sour cream**
2 **teaspoons juice from 1 lemon**

1. Pat the beef dry with paper towels and season with salt and pepper. Heat 1 tablespoon of the oil in a 12-inch skillet over medium-high heat until just smoking. Cook half of the beef until well browned, 3 to 4 minutes per side. Transfer to a medium bowl and repeat with 1 tablespoon more oil and the remaining beef.

2. Heat the remaining 2 tablespoons oil in the now-empty skillet until shimmering. Cook the mushrooms, onion, and ½ teaspoon salt until the liquid from the mushrooms has evaporated, about 8 minutes. (If the pan becomes too brown, pour the accumulated beef juices into the skillet.) Stir in the flour and cook for 30 seconds. Gradually stir in the broths, then the brandy, and return the beef and accumulated juices to the skillet. Bring to a simmer, cover, and cook over low heat until the beef is tender, 30 to 35 minutes.

3. Stir the noodles into the beef mixture, cover, and cook, stirring occasionally, until the noodles are tender, 10 to 12 minutes. Off the heat, stir in the sour cream and lemon juice. Season with salt and pepper to taste and serve.

SKILLET-ROASTED CHICKEN DINNER

WHY THIS RECIPE WORKS: Roasted chicken and potatoes are a favorite combination for Sunday dinner. But on a busy weeknight, who has time to prepare a meal that requires at least an hour in the oven? We wanted to come up with a skillet preparation that would give us juicy, tender chicken and crispy potatoes in about half an hour.

To start, we borrowed the restaurant method of browning meat on the stovetop and finishing it in the oven. We swapped in bone-in split breasts for the whole chicken and seared the chicken in a skillet. This turned the skin nicely brown and crisp. Next, we transferred the chicken to a baking dish in the oven to finish cooking through.

Meanwhile, we turned to the potatoes. We chose red potatoes because their skins are tender and don't require peeling. This saved some prep time, but we couldn't get them to cook in the same amount of time as the chicken. The microwave turned out to be the solution; while the chicken was browning, we tossed the potatoes with a little olive oil, salt, and pepper and microwaved them for a few minutes to jump-start the cooking process. Placing the potatoes in a single layer in the skillet—the same one in which we'd browned

the chicken—helped them cook up creamy and moist inside while their exteriors became crispy and caramelized, just when it was time to take the chicken out of the oven. Before serving, we drizzled a mixture of olive oil, lemon juice, garlic, red pepper flakes, and thyme over our chicken and potatoes for an extra hit of moisture and flavor. In about half an hour, we had re-created the great flavors of a Sunday roast chicken dinner.

Skillet-Roasted Chicken Breasts with Potatoes
SERVES 4

To complete this recipe in 30 minutes, preheat your oven before assembling the ingredients. If the split breasts are different sizes, check the smaller ones a few minutes early and remove them from the oven if they are done.

- 4 (10 to 12-ounce) bone-in, split chicken breasts
  Table salt and ground black pepper
- 6 tablespoons olive oil
- 1½ pounds red potatoes (4 to 5 medium), cut into 1-inch wedges
- 2 tablespoons juice from 1 lemon
- 1 medium garlic clove, minced or pressed through a garlic press (about 1 teaspoon)
- 1 teaspoon minced fresh thyme leaves
  Pinch red pepper flakes

1. Adjust an oven rack to the lowest position and heat the oven to 450 degrees.

2. Pat the chicken dry with paper towels and season with salt and pepper. Heat 1 tablespoon of the oil in a 12-inch nonstick skillet over medium-high heat until just smoking. Add the chicken, skin side down, and cook until deep golden, about 5 minutes.

3. Meanwhile, toss the potatoes with 1 more tablespoon of the oil, ½ teaspoon salt, and ¼ teaspoon pepper in a microwave-safe bowl. Cover tightly with plastic wrap. Microwave on high power until the potatoes begin to soften, 5 to 10 minutes, shaking the bowl (without removing the plastic) to toss the potatoes halfway through.

4. Transfer the chicken, skin side up, to a baking dish and bake until the thickest part of the breasts registers 160 to 165 degrees on an instant-read thermometer, 15 to 20 minutes.

5. While the chicken bakes, pour off any fat in the skillet, add 1 tablespoon more oil, and return to medium heat until shimmering. Drain the microwaved potatoes, then add to the skillet and cook, stirring occasionally, until golden brown and tender, about 10 minutes.

6. Whisk the remaining 3 tablespoons oil, the lemon juice, garlic, thyme, and red pepper flakes together. Drizzle the oil mixture over the chicken and potatoes before serving.

SKILLET CHICKEN AND RICE

WHY THIS RECIPE WORKS: There are lots of bad recipes out there for quick chicken and rice. Most contain leftover chicken, instant rice, and canned cream-of-something soup. We aimed to improve this dish all around and still deliver it to the table on time.

Boneless, skinless chicken breasts are definitely convenient, but we needed to prevent them from drying out. Dredging them in flour not only gave the chicken a nice brown crust but also kept the meat juicy inside. After browning the breasts on one side in a nonstick skillet, we removed them to deal with the rice. We first sautéed minced onion, garlic, and red pepper flakes in butter, then added the rice and stirred to coat the grains. Coating and toasting the rice this way before adding liquid is a technique that imparts deeper flavor and keeps the rice grains distinct and firm. We added a little white wine to the skillet for brightness. We then added chicken broth and returned the chicken to the skillet to cook through. When the chicken was done, we removed it from the skillet and finished cooking the rice. Off the heat, we added frozen peas, which cooked in a just couple of minutes, and stirred in lemon juice and sliced scallions for a fresh, bright flavor. In about 30 minutes, this dish was perfectly cooked, flavorful, and ready to serve. In addition, we developed two variations: one with cheddar and broccoli and the other with the spicy flavors of curry.

Skillet Chicken and Rice with Peas and Scallions
SERVES 4

Be sure to use chicken breasts that are roughly the same size to ensure even cooking.

> 4 **(6 to 8-ounce) boneless, skinless chicken breasts, trimmed (see note)**
>   **Table salt and ground black pepper**

½ **cup unbleached all-purpose flour**
2 **tablespoons vegetable oil**
2 **tablespoons unsalted butter**
1 **medium onion, minced**
3 **medium garlic cloves, minced or pressed through a garlic press (about 1 tablespoon)**
   Pinch red pepper flakes
1½ **cups long-grain white rice**
½ **cup dry white wine**
4½ **cups low-sodium chicken broth**
1 **cup frozen peas**
5 **scallions, sliced thin**
2 **tablespoons juice from 1 lemon**
   Lemon wedges, for serving

1. Pat the chicken dry with paper towels and season with salt and pepper. Dredge the chicken in the flour to coat and shake off any excess. Heat the oil in a 12-inch nonstick skillet over medium-high heat just until smoking. Brown the chicken well on one side, about 5 minutes. Transfer the chicken to a plate and set aside.

2. Off the heat, add the butter to the skillet, and swirl to melt. Add the onion and ½ teaspoon salt and return to medium-high heat until softened, 2 to 5 minutes. Stir in the garlic and red pepper flakes and cook until fragrant, about 30 seconds. Stir in the rice thoroughly and let toast for about 30 seconds.

3. Stir in the wine and let the rice absorb it completely, about 1 minute. Stir in the broth, scraping up any browned bits. Nestle the chicken into the rice, browned side up, and add any accumulated juices. Cover and cook over medium heat until the thickest part of the chicken registers 160 to 165 degrees on an instant-read thermometer, about 10 minutes.

4. Transfer the chicken to a clean plate. Gently brush off and discard any rice clinging to the chicken, then tent the chicken with foil and set aside. Return the skillet of rice to medium-low heat, cover, and continue to cook, stirring occasionally, until the liquid is absorbed and the rice is tender, 8 to 12 minutes longer.

5. Off the heat, sprinkle the peas over the rice, cover, and let warm through, about 2 minutes. Add the scallions and lemon juice to the rice. Season with salt and pepper to taste and serve with the chicken and lemon wedges.

Skillet Chicken and Rice with Broccoli and Cheddar

SERVES 4

Be sure to use chicken breasts that are roughly the same size to ensure even cooking.

- 4 (6 to 8-ounce) boneless, skinless chicken breasts, trimmed (see note)
  Table salt and ground black pepper
- ½ cup unbleached all-purpose flour
- 3 tablespoons vegetable oil
- 1 onion, minced
- 1½ cups long-grain white rice
- 3 garlic cloves, minced or pressed through a garlic press (about 1 tablespoon)
- 4½ cups low-sodium chicken broth
- 1 (10-ounce) package frozen broccoli florets, thawed
- 4 ounces cheddar cheese, shredded (about 1 cup)
- 1 teaspoon hot sauce

1. Pat the chicken dry with paper towels and season with salt and pepper. Dredge the chicken in the flour to coat and shake off any excess. Heat 2 tablespoons of the oil in a 12-inch nonstick skillet over medium-high heat until just smoking. Brown the chicken well on one side, about 5 minutes. Transfer the chicken to a plate and set aside.

2. Add the remaining 1 tablespoon oil to the skillet and return to medium-high heat until shimmering. Add the onion and ½ teaspoon salt and cook until softened, about 5 minutes. Stir in the rice and garlic and cook until fragrant, about 30 seconds.

3. Stir in the broth, scraping up any browned bits. Nestle the chicken and any accumulated juices into the rice, browned side up. Cover and cook over medium heat until the liquid is absorbed and the thickest part of the chicken registers 160 to 165 degrees on an instant-read thermometer, about 10 minutes.

4. Transfer the chicken to a clean plate. Gently brush off and discard any rice clinging to the chicken, then tent the chicken with foil and set aside. Return the skillet of rice to medium-low heat, cover, and continue to cook, stirring occasionally, until the liquid is absorbed and the rice is tender, 8 to 12 minutes longer.

5. Off the heat, gently fold the broccoli, ½ cup of the cheddar, and the hot sauce into the rice and season with salt and pepper to taste. Sprinkle the remaining ½ cup cheddar over the top, cover, and let sit until the cheese melts, about 2 minutes. Serve with the chicken.

Skillet Curried Chicken and Rice

SERVES 4

Be sure to use chicken breasts that are roughly the same size to ensure even cooking. The heat level of curry varies from brand to brand. If your curry powder is very spicy, you may need to reduce the amount.

- 4 (6 to 8-ounce) boneless, skinless chicken breasts, trimmed (see note)
  Table salt and ground black pepper
- ½ cup unbleached all-purpose flour
- 3 tablespoons vegetable oil
- 1 onion, minced
- 1 tablespoon curry powder (see note)
- 1½ cups long-grain white rice
- 3 garlic cloves, minced or pressed through a garlic press (about 1 tablespoon)
- 4½ cups low-sodium chicken broth
- 1 cup frozen peas, thawed
- ¼ cup raisins
- ¼ cup minced fresh cilantro leaves

1. Pat the chicken dry with paper towels and season with salt and pepper. Dredge the chicken in the flour to coat and shake off any excess. Heat 2 tablespoons of the oil in a 12-inch nonstick skillet over medium-high heat until just smoking. Brown the chicken well on one side, about 5 minutes. Transfer the chicken to a plate and set aside.

2. Add the remaining 1 tablespoon oil to the skillet and return to medium-high heat until shimmering. Add the onion, curry powder, and ½ teaspoon salt and cook until softened, about 5 minutes. Stir in the rice and garlic and cook until fragrant, about 30 seconds.

3. Stir in the broth, scraping up any browned bits. Nestle the chicken and any accumulated juices into the rice, browned side up. Cover and cook over medium heat until the liquid is absorbed and the thickest part of the chicken registers 160 to 165 degrees on an instant-read thermometer, about 10 minutes.

4. Transfer the chicken to a clean plate. Gently brush off and discard any rice clinging to the chicken, then tent the chicken with foil and set aside. Return the skillet of rice to medium-low heat, cover, and continue to cook, stirring occasionally, until the liquid is absorbed and the rice is tender, 8 to 12 minutes longer.

5. Off the heat, sprinkle the peas and raisins over the rice, cover, and let warm through, about 2 minutes. Add the cilantro and gently fold into the rice. Season with salt and pepper to taste and serve with the chicken.

SKILLET JAMBALAYA

WHY THIS RECIPE WORKS: Jambalaya, a hearty mix of chicken, andouille sausage, shrimp, and rice, is typically made in a Dutch oven and can take at least an hour to prepare. We wanted a quicker, easier version without sacrificing any of the complex flavors of this Creole classic.

Bone-in, skin-on chicken thighs rather than the typical whole cut-up chicken called for in many recipes saved us time and fuss. To mimic long-simmered flavor, we browned the sausage in the skillet, added the chicken, then cooked the vegetables in some of the rendered fat. We then stirred the rice in to coat it with the fat for deep flavor. For our cooking liquid, we relied on chicken broth and clam juice (to complement the shrimp). To prevent the shrimp from overcooking, we cooked it for only a few minutes, then allowed it to finish cooking through off the heat (the residual heat is hot enough to cook it through). Entirely made in a skillet, this jambalaya makes a fast and satisfying supper.

Skillet Jambalaya

SERVES 4 TO 6

If you cannot find andouille sausage, either chorizo or linguiça can be substituted. For a spicier jambalaya, you can add ¼ teaspoon of cayenne pepper along with the vegetables, and/or serve it with hot sauce.

- 4 bone-in, skin-on chicken thighs (about 1½ pounds), trimmed
  Table salt and ground black pepper
- 5 teaspoons vegetable oil
- ½ pound andouille sausage, halved lengthwise and sliced into ¼-inch pieces (see note)
- 1 medium onion, chopped medium
- 1 medium red bell pepper, stemmed, seeded, and chopped medium
- 5 medium garlic cloves, minced or pressed through a garlic press (about 1½ tablespoons)
- 1½ cups long-grain white rice
- 1 (14.5-ounce) can diced tomatoes, drained
- 1 (8-ounce) bottle clam juice
- 2½ cups low-sodium chicken broth
- 1 pound large shrimp (31 to 40 per pound), peeled and deveined (see page 205)
- 2 tablespoons chopped fresh parsley leaves

1. Dry the chicken thoroughly with paper towels, then season generously with salt and pepper. Heat 2 teaspoons of the oil in a 12-inch nonstick skillet over medium-high heat until just smoking. Carefully lay the chicken thighs in the skillet, skin-side down, and cook until golden, 4 to 6 minutes. Flip the chicken over and continue to cook until the second side is golden, about 3 minutes. Remove the pan from the heat and transfer the chicken to a plate. Using paper towels, remove and discard the browned chicken skin.

2. Pour off all but 2 teaspoons of the fat left in the skillet and return to medium-high heat until shimmering. Add the andouille and cook until lightly browned, about 3 minutes; transfer the sausage to a small bowl and set aside.

3. Add the remaining 3 teaspoons oil to the skillet and return to medium heat until shimmering. Add the onion, bell pepper, garlic, and ½ teaspoon salt; cook, scraping the browned bits off the bottom of the skillet, until the onion is softened, about 5 minutes. Add the rice and cook until the edges turn translucent, about 3 minutes. Stir in the tomatoes, clam juice, and chicken broth; bring to a simmer. Gently nestle the chicken and any accumulated juices into the rice. Cover, reduce the heat to low, and cook until the chicken is tender and cooked through, 30 to 35 minutes.

4. Transfer the chicken to a plate and cover with foil to keep warm. Stir the shrimp and sausage into the rice and continue to cook, covered, over low heat for 2 more minutes. Remove the skillet from the heat and let stand, covered, until the shrimp are fully cooked and the rice is tender, about 5 minutes. Meanwhile, shred the chicken into bite-size pieces. Stir the parsley and shredded chicken into the rice, season with salt and pepper to taste, and serve.

CHAPTER 4

ONE-DISH SUPPERS

Simple Pot Roast 62

Old-Fashioned
Pot Roast 63

Old-Fashioned Pot Roast
with Root Vegetables

Carbonnade à la Flamande
(Belgian Beef, Beer, and
Onion Stew) 64

Hungarian Beef Stew 65

Braised Beef Short Ribs 67

Slow-Cooker Beer-Braised
Short Ribs 68

Chicken and
Dumplings 69

Lighter Chicken and
Dumplings 70

Chicken Pot Pie with Savory
Crumble Topping 72

Greek Spinach and Feta Pie
(Spanakopita) 73

Moroccan Chicken with
Olives and Lemon 74

Moroccan Chicken with
Chickpeas and Apricots

Latino-Style Chicken and
Rice (Arroz con Pollo) 76

Latino-Style Chicken
and Rice with Bacon and
Roasted Red Peppers 77

Latino-Style Chicken
and Rice with Ham,
Peas, and Orange 77

Cuban-Style Black Beans
and Rice 78

Paella 79

Creole-Style Shrimp
and Sausage Gumbo 81

POT ROAST

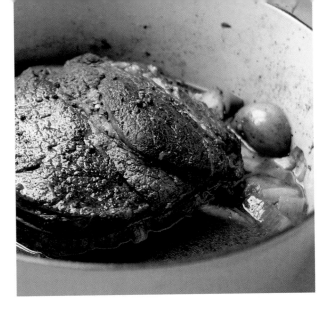

WHY THIS RECIPE WORKS: The long braise that a pot roast needs can result in either a succulent roast or a dry, bland disappointment. We wanted our pot roast to be fall-apart tender with a savory sauce—a meal that would be worth the wait.

We first determined that chuck-eye is the best choice for pot roast; its fat and connective tissue break down and keep the meat moist during the long oven stay. Browning the meat first was important for flavor as well as color. Caramelizing the vegetables with a little sugar added another layer of flavor. For the braising liquid, equal amounts of beef and chicken broth tasted best; and we added just enough water for the liquid to come about halfway up the sides of the roast and prevent it from drying out. Before we moved the roast into the oven, we covered the pot with foil and then covered with the lid for a tight seal, so no steam (or flavor) escaped. The secret to tenderness is in the cooking time. Cook the meat in the oven until it reaches 210 degrees internally, then cook it for an hour longer. The reward is moist, flavorful meat that is also remarkably tender.

Simple Pot Roast

SERVES 6 TO 8

Our favorite cut for pot roast is a chuck-eye roast. Most markets sell this roast with twine tied around the center; if necessary, do this yourself. Seven-bone and top-blade roasts are also good choices for this recipe. Remember to add only enough water to come halfway up the sides of these thinner roasts, and begin checking for doneness after 2 hours. If using a top-blade roast, tie it before cooking to keep it from falling apart. Mashed or boiled potatoes are a good accompaniment to pot roast.

- 1 (3½-pound) boneless chuck-eye roast (see note)
  Table salt and ground black pepper
- 2 tablespoons vegetable oil
- 1 medium onion, chopped medium
- 1 small carrot, chopped medium
- 1 small celery rib, chopped medium
- 2 medium garlic cloves, minced or pressed through a garlic press (about 2 teaspoons)
- 2 teaspoons sugar
- 1 cup low-sodium chicken broth
- 1 cup beef broth
- 1 sprig fresh thyme
- 1–1½ cups water
- ¼ cup dry red wine

1. Adjust an oven rack to the middle position and heat the oven to 300 degrees. Thoroughly pat the roast dry with paper towels; sprinkle generously with salt and pepper.

2. Heat the oil in a large Dutch oven over medium-high heat until shimmering but not smoking. Brown the roast thoroughly on all sides, reducing the heat if the fat begins to smoke, 8 to 10 minutes. Transfer the roast to a large plate; set aside. Reduce the heat to medium; add the onion, carrot, and celery to the pot and cook, stirring occasionally, until beginning to brown, 6 to 8 minutes. Add the garlic and sugar; cook until fragrant, about 30 seconds. Add the chicken and beef broths and thyme, scraping the bottom of the pan with a wooden spoon to loosen the browned bits. Return the roast and any accumulated juices to the pot; add enough water to come halfway up the sides of the roast. Place a large piece of foil over the pot and cover tightly with the lid; bring the liquid to a simmer over medium heat, then transfer the pot to the oven. Cook, turning the roast every 30 minutes, until fully tender and a meat fork or sharp knife easily slips in and out of the meat, 3½ to 4 hours.

3. Transfer the roast to a carving board; tent with foil to keep warm. Allow the liquid in the pot to settle for about 5 minutes, then use a wide spoon to skim the fat off the surface; discard the thyme sprig. Boil over high heat until reduced to about 1½ cups, about 8 minutes. Add the red wine and reduce again to 1½ cups, about 2 minutes. Season with salt and pepper to taste.

4. Using a chef's or carving knife, cut the meat into ½-inch-thick slices, or pull apart into large pieces; transfer the meat to a warmed serving platter and pour about ½ cup sauce over the meat. Serve, passing the remaining sauce separately.

OLD-FASHIONED BEEF POT ROAST

WHY THIS RECIPE WORKS: Pot roast can be boring and bland, full of dry, stringy meat, stubborn bits of fat, and wan gravy. We wanted a meltingly tender roast sauced in savory, full-bodied gravy.

To start, we separated the roast into two lobes, which allowed us to remove the knobs of fat that stubbornly refused to render and also shortened the cooking time. Salting the roast prior to cooking improved its flavor, as did sautéing the onion, celery, carrot, and garlic before we added them to the pot.

Some recipes use water as a pot roast cooking liquid but when we tried this, the gravy turned out as you'd expect—watery. We had better luck with beef broth. Other flavor-boosting ingredients went into the pot as well: garlic, tomato paste, red wine, thyme, and bay leaves. The resulting gravy boasted a rich, complex character but its flavor didn't stray from the dish's simple roots. Finally, sealing the pot with aluminum foil before securing the lid concentrated the steam for an even simmer and fork-tender meat.

Old-Fashioned Pot Roast

SERVES 6 TO 8

To separate the roast into two pieces, simply pull apart at the natural seam and then trim away any large knobs of fat. The roast can be made up to 2 days ahead: Follow the recipe through step 4, transferring the cooked roasts to a large bowl and straining the liquid as directed in step 5. Transfer the vegetables to the bowl with the roasts, cover with plastic wrap, cut vents in the plastic, and refrigerate overnight or up to 48 hours. One hour before serving, adjust the oven rack to the middle position and heat the oven to 325 degrees. Transfer the cold roasts to a carving board, slice them against the grain into ½-inch-thick slices, place them in a 13 by 9-inch baking dish, cover tightly with foil, and bake until heated through, about 45 minutes. While the roasts heat, puree the sauce and vegetables as directed in step 5. Bring the sauce to a simmer and finish as directed in step 6 before serving with the meat.

- 1 (3½ to 4-pound) boneless chuck-eye roast, pulled into 2 pieces at the natural seam and fat trimmed (see note)
  Table salt and ground black pepper
- 2 tablespoons unsalted butter
- 2 medium onions, halved and sliced thin (about 2 cups)
- 1 large carrot, peeled and chopped medium (about 1 cup)
- 1 celery rib, chopped medium (about ¾ cup)
- 2 medium garlic cloves, minced or pressed through a garlic press (about 2 teaspoons)
- 1 cup beef broth, plus 1 to 2 cups for the sauce
- ½ cup dry red wine, plus ¼ cup for the sauce
- 1 tablespoon tomato paste
- 1 bay leaf
- 1 sprig fresh thyme plus ¼ teaspoon chopped fresh thyme leaves
- 1 tablespoon balsamic vinegar

1. Sprinkle the pieces of meat with 1½ teaspoons salt, place on a wire rack set over a rimmed baking sheet and let stand at room temperature for 1 hour.

2. Adjust an oven rack to the lower-middle position and heat the oven to 300 degrees. Heat the butter in a heavy-bottomed Dutch oven over medium heat. When the foaming subsides, add the onions and cook, stirring occasionally, until softened and beginning to brown, 8 to 10 minutes. Add the carrot and celery and continue to cook, stirring occasionally, for 5 minutes longer. Add the garlic and cook until fragrant, about 30 seconds. Stir in 1 cup of the broth, ½ cup of the wine, the tomato paste, bay leaf, and thyme sprig; bring to a simmer.

3. Season the beef generously with pepper. Using three pieces of kitchen twine, tie each piece of meat into a loaf shape for even cooking.

4. Nestle the roasts on top of the vegetables. Place a large piece of foil over the pot and cover tightly with the lid; transfer the pot to the oven. Cook the roasts until fully tender and a sharp knife easily slips in and out of the meat, 3½ to 4 hours, turning the roasts halfway through cooking.

5. Transfer the roasts to a carving board and tent loosely with foil. Strain the liquid through a fine-mesh strainer into a 4-cup liquid measuring cup. Discard the thyme sprig and bay leaf. Transfer the vegetables to a blender. Allow the liquid to settle for 5 minutes, then skim any fat off the surface. Add the remaining beef broth as necessary to bring the total amount of liquid to 3 cups. Place the liquid in the blender with the vegetables and blend until smooth, about 2 minutes. Transfer the sauce to a medium saucepan and bring to a simmer over medium heat.

6. While the sauce heats, remove the twine from the roasts and slice them against the grain into ½-inch-thick slices. Transfer the meat to a large serving platter. Stir the chopped thyme, remaining ¼ cup wine, and the balsamic vinegar into the sauce and season with salt and pepper to taste. Serve immediately, passing the sauce separately.

Old-Fashioned Pot Roast with Root Vegetables

Follow the recipe for Old-Fashioned Pot Roast, adding 1 pound carrots, peeled and cut crosswise into 2-inch pieces, 1 pound parsnips, peeled and cut crosswise into 2-inch pieces, and 1½ pounds russet potatoes, peeled, halved lengthwise, and each half quartered, to the pot in step 4 after the roasts have cooked for 3 hours. Once the pot roast and vegetables are fully cooked, transfer any large pieces of carrot, parsnip, and potato to a serving platter using a slotted spoon, cover tightly with foil, and proceed with the recipe as directed.

BEEF CARBONNADE

WHY THIS RECIPE WORKS: Most recipes for this Belgian beef, onion, and beer stew go in one of two directions: In one version, the recipe masks its genuine flavors and, in others, the recipes rigidly adhere to the "three ingredients only" rule, so the stew is stripped down to a pale, tasteless version of itself. We wanted hearty chunks of beef and sliced sweet onion in a lightly thickened broth, laced with the malty flavor of beer.

Most recipes suggest using chuck-eye roast for the beef, but we tried several other cuts and found that top blade steak, which has a fair amount of marbling, provided the best texture and a "buttery" flavor that worked well alongside the onions and beer. White and red onions were too sweet in our stew; yellow onions worked better. The onions should be browned only lightly; overcaramelization caused them to disintegrate. An untraditional ingredient—tomato paste—gave the stew depth, as did garlic. Fresh thyme and bay leaves provided seasoning, and a splash of cider vinegar added the right level of

---

NOTES FROM THE TEST KITCHEN

TRIMMING BLADE STEAKS

To trim blade steaks, halve each steak lengthwise, leaving the gristle on one half. Then simply cut the gristle away.

---

acidity. Beer is a staple of Belgian cooking, and we found that it's less forgiving than wine when used in a stew. The light lagers we tried resulted in pale, watery stews; better were dark ales and stouts. But beer alone often made for bitter-tasting stew, so we included some broth; a combination of chicken and beef broth gave us more solid and complex flavor.

Carbonnade à la Flamande (Belgian Beef, Beer, and Onion Stew)
SERVES 6

Top blade steaks (also called blade or flatiron steaks) are our first choice, but any boneless roast from the chuck will work. If you end up using a chuck roast, look for the chuck-eye roast, an especially flavorful cut that can easily be trimmed and cut into 1-inch pieces. Buttered egg noodles or mashed potatoes make excellent accompaniments to carbonnade.

3½ pounds top blade steaks, 1 inch thick, trimmed of
    gristle and fat and cut into 1-inch pieces (see photo;
    see note)
    Table salt and ground black pepper
3 tablespoons vegetable oil
2 pounds yellow onions (about 4 medium), halved and
    sliced ¼ inch thick
1 tablespoon tomato paste
2 medium garlic cloves, minced or pressed through a
    garlic press (about 2 teaspoons)
3 tablespoons unbleached all-purpose flour
¾ cup low-sodium chicken broth
¾ cup beef broth
1½ cups (12-ounce bottle or can) dark beer or stout
4 sprigs fresh thyme, tied with kitchen twine
2 bay leaves
1 tablespoon cider vinegar

1. Adjust an oven rack to the lower-middle position and heat the oven to 300 degrees. Dry the beef thoroughly with paper towels, then season generously with salt and pepper. Heat 2 teaspoons of the oil in a large Dutch oven over medium-high heat until beginning to smoke; add about one third of the beef to the pot. Cook without moving the pieces until well browned, 2 to 3 minutes; using tongs, turn each piece and continue cooking until the second side is well browned, about 5 minutes longer. Transfer the browned beef to a medium bowl. Repeat with 2 teaspoons more oil and half of the remaining beef.

(If the drippings in the bottom of the pot are very dark, add ½ cup of the chicken or beef broth and scrape the pan bottom with a wooden spoon to loosen the browned bits; pour the liquid into the bowl with the browned beef, then proceed.) Repeat once more with 2 teaspoons more oil and the remaining beef.

2. Add the remaining 1 tablespoon oil to the now-empty Dutch oven; reduce the heat to medium-low. Add the onions, ½ teaspoon salt, and the tomato paste; cook, scraping the bottom of the pot with a wooden spoon to loosen the browned bits, until the onions have released some moisture, about 5 minutes. Increase the heat to medium and continue to cook, stirring occasionally, until the onions are lightly browned, 12 to 14 minutes. Stir in the garlic and cook until fragrant, about 30 seconds. Add the flour and stir until the onions are evenly coated and the flour is lightly browned, about 2 minutes. Stir in the broths, scraping the pan bottom to loosen any browned bits; stir in the beer, thyme, bay leaves, vinegar, browned beef with any accumulated juices, and salt and pepper to taste. Increase the heat to medium-high and bring to a full simmer, stirring occasionally; cover partially, then place the pot in the oven. Cook until a fork inserted into the beef meets little resistance, 2 to 2½ hours.

3. Discard the thyme and bay leaves. Season with salt and pepper to taste and serve. (The stew can be cooled and refrigerated in an airtight container for up to 4 days; reheat over medium-low heat.)

HUNGARIAN BEEF STEW

WHY THIS RECIPE WORKS: The Americanized versions of Hungarian goulash served in the United States bear little resemblance to the authentic dish. Sour cream has no place in the pot, nor do mushrooms, green peppers, or most herbs. We wanted the real deal—a simple dish of tender braised beef packed with paprika flavor.

To achieve the desired spicy intensity, some recipes call for as much as half a cup of paprika per three pounds of meat, but that much fine spice gave the dish a gritty, dusty texture. The chefs at a few Hungarian restaurants introduced us to paprika cream, a condiment as common in Hungarian cooking as the dried spice—but hard to find in the U.S. Instead, we created our own quick version by pureeing dried paprika with roasted red peppers and a little tomato paste and vinegar. This mixture imparted vibrant paprika flavor without any offensive grittiness.

As for the meat, after settling on chuck-eye roast, we bought a whole roast and cut it ourselves into uniform, large pieces to ensure even cooking. Since searing the meat first—normally standard stew protocol—competed with the paprika's brightness, we referred back to a trend we noticed in the goulash recipes gathered during research: skipping the sear. We tried this, softening the onions in the pot first, adding paprika paste, carrots, and then meat before placing the covered pot in the oven. Sure enough, the onions and meat provided enough liquid to stew the meat, and the bits of beef that cooked above the liquid line browned in the hot air. A bit of broth added near the end of cooking thinned out the stewing liquid to just the right consistency.

Hungarian Beef Stew

SERVES 6

Do not substitute hot, half-sharp, or smoked Spanish paprika for the sweet paprika in the stew, as they will compromise the flavor of the dish. Since paprika is vital to this recipe, it is best to use a fresh container. We prefer chuck-eye roast, but any boneless roast from the chuck will work. Cook the stew in a Dutch oven with a tight-fitting lid. (Alternatively, to ensure a tight seal, place a sheet of foil over the pot before adding the lid.) Serve the stew over boiled potatoes or egg noodles.

1   **boneless chuck-eye roast (about 3½ pounds), trimmed of excess fat and cut into 1½-inch cubes (see note)**
    Table salt

1 (12-ounce) jar roasted red peppers, drained and rinsed (about 1 cup)
⅓ cup sweet paprika (see note)
2 tablespoons tomato paste
1 tablespoon white vinegar
2 tablespoons vegetable oil
6 medium onions, minced (about 6 cups)
4 large carrots, peeled and cut into 1-inch-thick rounds (about 2 cups)
1 bay leaf
1 cup beef broth, warmed
¼ cup sour cream (optional)
    Ground black pepper

1. Adjust an oven rack to the lower-middle position and heat the oven to 325 degrees. Sprinkle the meat evenly with 1 teaspoon salt and let stand for 15 minutes. Process the roasted peppers, paprika, tomato paste, and 2 teaspoons of the vinegar in a food processor until smooth, 1 to 2 minutes, scraping down the sides as needed.

2. Combine the oil, onions, and 1 teaspoon salt in a large Dutch oven; cover and set over medium heat. Cook, stirring occasionally, until the onions have softened but have not yet begun to brown, 8 to 10 minutes. (If the onions begin to brown, reduce the heat to medium-low and stir in 1 tablespoon water.)

3. Stir in the paprika mixture; cook, stirring occasionally, until the onions stick to the bottom of the pan, about 2 minutes. Add the beef, carrots, and bay leaf; stir until the beef is well coated. Using a rubber spatula, scrape down the sides of the pot. Cover the pot and transfer to the oven. Cook until the meat is almost tender and the surface of the liquid is ½ inch below the top of the meat, 2 to 2½ hours, stirring every 30 minutes. Remove the pot from the oven and add enough beef broth that the surface of the liquid is ¼ inch from the top of the meat (the beef should not be fully submerged). Return the covered pot to the oven and continue to cook until a fork slips easily in and out of the beef, about 30 minutes longer.

4. Skim the fat off the surface using a wide spoon; stir in the remaining 1 teaspoon vinegar and the sour cream (if using). Remove the bay leaf, season with salt and pepper to taste, and serve. (The stew can be cooled, covered tightly, and refrigerated in an airtight container for up to 2 days; wait to add the optional sour cream until after reheating. Before reheating, skim the hardened fat from the surface and add enough water to the stew to thin it slightly.)

BRAISED SHORT RIBS

WHY THIS RECIPE WORKS: Short ribs have great flavor and luscious texture, but their excess fat can be a problem since so much fat is rendered during the ribs' stint in the oven. Most recipes call for resting them in the braising liquid overnight, so that the fat solidifies into an easy-to-remove layer. However, most people don't plan their dinners days in advance and skimming such a large amount of fat off with a spoon doesn't work well enough. The meat and sauce come out greasy, no matter how diligent one's spoon-wielding. We wanted a silky, grease-free sauce and fork-tender short rib meat, all in a few hours.

The first task was to choose the right rib. Instead of traditional bone-in short ribs, we used boneless short ribs, which rendered significantly less fat than bone-in. While we didn't miss much flavor from the bones, we did want the body that the bones' connective tissue added. To solve this, we sprinkled a bit of gelatin into the sauce to restore suppleness. We also wanted to ramp up the richness of the sauce. We jump-started flavor by reducing wine with browned aromatics (onions, garlic, and carrots) before using the liquid to cook the meat. This added the right intensity, but we needed another cup of liquid to keep the meat half-submerged—the right level for braises. More wine yielded too much wine flavor; we used beef broth instead. As for the excess fat, the level was low enough that we could strain and defat the liquid in a fat separator. Reducing the liquid concentrated the flavors and made for a rich, luxurious sauce for our fork-tender boneless short ribs.

Braised Beef Short Ribs

SERVES 6

Make sure that the ribs are at least 4 inches long and 1 inch thick. If boneless ribs are unavailable, substitute 7 pounds of bone-in beef short ribs at least 4 inches long with 1 inch of meat above the bone and bone them yourself (see photos).

3½ **pounds boneless beef short ribs, trimmed of excess fat (see note)**
    Table salt and ground black pepper
2   **tablespoons vegetable oil**
2   **large onions, sliced thin from pole to pole (about 4 cups)**
1   **tablespoon tomato paste**
6   **medium garlic cloves, peeled**
2   **cups red wine, such as Cabernet Sauvignon or Côtes du Rhône**
1   **cup beef broth**
4   **large carrots, peeled and cut crosswise into 2-inch pieces**
4   **sprigs fresh thyme**
1   **bay leaf**
¼   **cup cold water**
½   **teaspoon powdered gelatin**

1. Adjust an oven rack to the lower-middle position and heat the oven to 300 degrees. Pat the beef dry with paper towels and season with 2 teaspoons salt and 1 teaspoon pepper. Heat 1 tablespoon of the oil in a large Dutch oven over medium-high heat until smoking. Add half of the beef and cook, without stirring, until well browned, 4 to 6 minutes. Turn the beef and continue to cook on the second side until well browned, 4 to 6 minutes longer, reducing the heat if the fat begins to smoke. Transfer the beef to a medium bowl. Repeat with the remaining 1 tablespoon oil and the remaining meat.

2. Reduce the heat to medium, add the onions, and cook, stirring occasionally, until softened and beginning

to brown, 12 to 15 minutes. (If the onions begin to darken too quickly, add 1 to 2 tablespoons water to the pan.) Add the tomato paste and cook, stirring constantly, until it browns on the sides and bottom of the pan, about 2 minutes. Add the garlic and cook until aromatic, about 30 seconds. Increase the heat to medium-high, add the wine, and simmer, scraping the bottom of the pan with a wooden spoon to loosen the browned bits, until reduced by half, 8 to 10 minutes. Add the broth, carrots, thyme, and bay leaf. Add the beef and any accumulated juices to the pot; cover and bring to a simmer. Transfer the pot to the oven and cook, using tongs to turn the meat twice during cooking, until a fork slips easily in and out of the meat, 2 to 2½ hours.

3. Place the water in a small bowl and sprinkle the gelatin on top; let stand for at least 5 minutes. Using tongs, transfer the meat and carrots to a serving platter and tent with foil. Strain the cooking liquid through a fine-mesh strainer into a fat separator or bowl, pressing on the solids to extract as much liquid as possible; discard the solids. Allow the liquid to settle for about 5 minutes and strain off the fat. Return the cooking liquid to the Dutch oven and cook over medium heat until reduced to 1 cup, 5 to 10 minutes. Remove from the heat and stir in the gelatin mixture; season with salt and pepper to taste. Pour the sauce over the meat and carrots and serve.

NOTES FROM THE TEST KITCHEN

BONING SHORT RIBS

1. With a chef's knife as close as possible to the bone, carefully remove the meat.

2. Trim the excess hard fat and silver skin from both sides of the meat.

SLOW-COOKER BRAISED SHORT RIBS

WHY THIS RECIPE WORKS: Beef short ribs, which contain lots of fat and connective tissue, are ideal for long, slow cooking. We wanted to develop a recipe for the slow cooker that would produce meaty ribs in a rich, oniony sauce.

Thoroughly browning the ribs first gave us a good start. Next we browned lots of onions. Instead of stock or broth, we chose beer as the braising liquid, and dark beer worked best. Tomato paste and soy sauce intensified the taste and color of the sauce (flavors tend to become muted after hours in a slow cooker). But we thought the dish lacked balance. We found our solution in an unusual source: prunes. They melted into the sauce and were unidentifiable, but their sweetness balanced the other flavors nicely. Livened up just before serving with some Dijon mustard and fresh thyme, these slow-cooker short ribs had the rich, complex flavor we were looking for.

Slow-Cooker Beer-Braised Short Ribs

SERVES 4 TO 6

The only way to remove fat from the braising liquid is to prepare this recipe a day or two before you want to serve it. Luckily, the short ribs actually taste better if cooked in advance and then reheated in the defatted braising liquid.

- 5 pounds English-style beef short ribs (6 to 8 ribs), trimmed of excess fat
   Table salt and ground black pepper
- 2 tablespoons vegetable oil
- 2 tablespoons unsalted butter
- 3 pounds yellow onions (about 6 medium), halved and sliced thin
- 2 tablespoons tomato paste
- 2 (12-ounce) bottles dark beer
- 12 pitted prunes
- 2 tablespoons soy sauce
- 2 tablespoons Minute tapioca
- 2 bay leaves
- 2 teaspoons minced fresh thyme leaves
- 3 tablespoons Dijon mustard
- 2 tablespoons minced fresh parsley leaves

1. Season the ribs with salt and pepper. Heat the oil in a 12-inch skillet over medium-high heat until just smoking. Add half of the ribs, meaty side down, and cook until well browned, about 5 minutes. Turn each rib on one side and cook until well browned, about 1 minute. Repeat with the remaining sides. Transfer the ribs to a slow-cooker insert, arranging them meaty side down. Repeat with the remaining ribs.

2. Pour off all but 1 teaspoon fat from the skillet. Add the butter and reduce the heat to medium. When the butter has melted, add the onions and cook, stirring occasionally, until well browned, 25 to 30 minutes. Stir in the tomato paste and cook, coating the onions with the tomato paste, until the paste begins to brown, about 5 minutes. Stir in the beer, bring to a simmer, and cook, scraping the browned bits from the pan bottom with a wooden spoon, until the foaming subsides, about 5 minutes. Remove the skillet from the heat and stir in the prunes, soy sauce, tapioca, bay leaves, and 1 teaspoon of the thyme. Transfer to the slow-cooker insert.

3. Set the slow cooker on low, cover, and cook until the ribs are fork-tender, 10 to 11 hours. (Alternatively, cook on high for 4 to 5 hours.) Transfer the ribs to a baking dish and strain the liquid through a fine-mesh strainer into a bowl. Cover and refrigerate for at least 8 hours or up to 2 days.

4. When ready to serve, use a spoon to skim off the hardened fat from the liquid. Place the short ribs, meaty side down, and the liquid in a Dutch oven and reheat over medium heat until warmed through, about 20 minutes. Transfer the ribs to a serving platter. Whisk the mustard and remaining 1 teaspoon thyme into the sauce and season with salt and pepper to taste. Pour 1 cup of the sauce over the ribs. Sprinkle with the parsley and serve, passing the remaining sauce separately.

CHICKEN AND DUMPLINGS

WHY THIS RECIPE WORKS: Chicken and dumplings make chicken pot pie look easy. There's no disguising a leaden dumpling. One goal was to develop a dumpling that was light yet substantial, and tender yet durable. The other was to develop a well-rounded recipe that, like chicken pot pie, included vegetables, therein supplying the cook with a complete meal in one dish.

Dumplings can contain myriad ingredients, and there are just as many different ways to mix them. We tried them all—with disastrous results. But when we stumbled on a unique method of adding warm liquid rather than cold to the flour and fat, our dumplings were great—firm but light and fluffy. The reason? The heat expands and sets the flour so that the dumplings don't absorb liquid in the stew. The best-tasting dumplings were made with all-purpose flour, whole milk, and the chicken fat left from browning the chicken.

For the filling, we chose bone-in, skin-on chicken thighs for their deep flavor and added enough vegetables to make this dish into a meal. After browning the chicken and vegetables separately, we simmered them in the sauce until the chicken was done and the sauce thickened. We added some peas and parsley, then steamed the dumplings on top of everything until the dumplings turned light and tender.

Chicken and Dumplings

SERVES 6 TO 8

Don't use low-fat or fat-free milk in this recipe. Be sure to reserve 3 tablespoons of chicken fat for the dumplings in step 4; however, if you prefer not to use chicken fat, unsalted butter can be substituted. Start the dumpling dough only when you're ready to top the stew with the dumplings.

STEW

- 5 pounds bone-in, skin-on chicken thighs (about 12 thighs)
   Table salt and ground black pepper
- 4 teaspoons vegetable oil
- 4 tablespoons (½ stick) unsalted butter
- 4 carrots, peeled and sliced ¼ inch thick
- 2 celery ribs, sliced ¼ inch thick
- 1 medium onion, minced
- 6 tablespoons unbleached all-purpose flour
- ¼ cup dry sherry
- 4½ cups low-sodium chicken broth
- ¼ cup whole milk (see note)
- 1 teaspoon minced fresh thyme leaves
- 2 bay leaves
- 1 cup frozen green peas
- 3 tablespoons minced fresh parsley leaves

DUMPLINGS

- 2 cups unbleached all-purpose flour
- 1 tablespoon baking powder
- 1 teaspoon table salt
- 1 cup whole milk (see note)
- 3 tablespoons reserved chicken fat (see note)

1. FOR THE STEW: Pat the chicken dry with paper towels, then season with salt and pepper. Heat 2 teaspoons of the oil in a large Dutch oven over medium-high heat until just smoking. Add half of the chicken and cook until golden on both sides, about 10 minutes. Transfer the chicken to a plate and remove the browned skin. Pour off the chicken fat and reserve. Return the pot to medium-high heat and repeat with the remaining 2 teaspoons oil and the remaining chicken. Pour off and reserve any chicken fat.

2. Add the butter to the Dutch oven and melt over medium-high heat. Add the carrots, celery, onion, and ¼ teaspoon salt and cook until softened, about 7 minutes. Stir in the flour. Whisk in the sherry, scraping up any browned bits. Stir in the broth, milk, thyme, and bay leaves. Nestle the chicken, with any accumulated juices, into the pot. Cover and simmer until the chicken is fully cooked and tender, about 1 hour.

3. Transfer the chicken to a carving board. Discard the bay leaves. Allow the sauce to settle for a few minutes, then skim the fat from the surface using a wide spoon. Shred the chicken, discarding the bones, then return it to the stew.

4. FOR THE DUMPLINGS: Stir the flour, baking powder, and salt together. Microwave the milk and chicken fat in a microwave-safe bowl on high power until just warm (do not overheat), about 1 minute. Stir the warmed milk mixture into the flour mixture with a wooden spoon until incorporated and smooth.

5. Return the stew to a simmer, stir in the peas and parsley, and season with salt and pepper to taste. Following the photos, drop golf ball–sized dumplings over the top of the stew, about ¼ inch apart (you should have about 18 dumplings). Reduce the heat to low, cover, and cook until the dumplings have doubled in size, 15 to 18 minutes. Serve.

NOTES FROM THE TEST KITCHEN

ADDING THE DUMPLINGS

1. Gather a golf ball–sized portion of the dumpling batter onto a soup spoon, then push the dumpling onto the stew using a second spoon.

2. Cover the stew with the dumplings, leaving about ¼ inch between each.

3. When fully cooked, the dumplings will have doubled in size.

LIGHTER CHICKEN AND DUMPLINGS

WHY THIS RECIPE WORKS: A thick stew topped with sturdy dumplings was fine for our forebears, but we wanted dumplings as airy as drop biscuits in a light broth full of clean, concentrated chicken flavor.

For a streamlined rich and chickeny broth and tender meat, we poached browned chicken thighs in store-bought broth. To give our broth body, we added chicken wings to the pot. Boiling the wings converts the connective tissue in chicken wings to gelatin and thickens the broth. Dry sherry gave the broth complexity.

For dumplings as light as our drop biscuits yet sturdy enough to hold together in broth, we made some changes to our drop biscuit recipe—cutting back the buttermilk and eliminating the baking powder (which had led to overrising) were two steps in the right direction. And adding an egg white kept our dumplings from turning mushy. To help keep the dumplings intact, we waited until the broth was simmering to add them, which reduced their time in the broth and helped keep them whole. Finally, wrapping a kitchen towel around the lid of the Dutch oven trapped the moisture before it had a chance to drip down and saturate our light-as-air dumplings.

Lighter Chicken and Dumplings

SERVES 6

We strongly recommend buttermilk for the dumplings, but you can substitute ½ cup plain yogurt thinned with ¼ cup milk. If you want to include white meat (and don't mind losing a bit of flavor in the process), replace 2 chicken thighs with 2 boneless, skinless chicken breast halves (about 8 ounces each). Brown the chicken breasts along with the thighs and remove them from the stew once they reach an internal temperature of 160 to 165 degrees, 20 to 30 minutes. The collagen in the wings helps thicken the stew; do not omit or substitute. Since the wings yield only about 1 cup of meat, using their meat is optional.

STEW

- 2½ pounds bone-in, skin-on chicken thighs, trimmed
       Table salt and ground black pepper
- 2 teaspoons vegetable oil
- 2 small onions, minced
- 2 carrots, peeled and cut into ¾-inch pieces
- 1 celery rib, chopped fine

- ¼ cup dry sherry
- 6 cups low-sodium chicken broth
- 1 teaspoon minced fresh thyme leaves
- 1 pound chicken wings
- ¼ cup chopped fresh parsley leaves

DUMPLINGS
- 2 cups (10 ounces) unbleached all-purpose flour
- 1 teaspoon sugar
- 1 teaspoon table salt
- ½ teaspoon baking soda
- ¾ cup cold buttermilk (see note)
- 4 tablespoons (½ stick) unsalted butter, melted and cooled
- 1 large egg white

1. FOR THE STEW: Pat the chicken thighs dry with paper towels and season with 1 teaspoon salt and ¼ teaspoon pepper. Heat the oil in a large Dutch oven over medium-high heat until shimmering. Add the chicken thighs, skin side down, and cook until the skin is crisp and well browned, 5 to 7 minutes. Using tongs, turn the chicken pieces and brown the second side, 5 to 7 minutes longer; transfer to a large plate. Discard all but 1 teaspoon fat from the pot.

2. Add the onions, carrots, and celery to the pot. Cook, stirring occasionally, until caramelized, 7 to 9 minutes. Stir in the sherry, scraping up any browned bits. Stir in the broth and thyme. Return the chicken thighs, along with any accumulated juices, to the pot and add the chicken wings. Bring to a simmer, cover, and cook until the thigh meat offers no resistance when poked with the tip of a paring knife but still clings to the bones, 45 to 55 minutes.

3. Remove the pot from the heat and transfer the chicken to a cutting board. Allow the broth to settle for 5 minutes, then skim the fat from the surface using a wide spoon or ladle. When cool enough to handle, remove and discard the skin from the chicken. Using your fingers or a fork, pull the meat from the chicken thighs (and wings, if desired) and cut into 1-inch pieces. Return the meat to the pot.

4. FOR THE DUMPLINGS: Whisk the flour, sugar, salt, and baking soda in a large bowl. Combine the buttermilk and melted butter in a medium bowl, stirring until the butter forms small clumps. Whisk in the egg white. Add the buttermilk mixture to the dry ingredients and stir with a rubber spatula until just incorporated and the batter pulls away from the sides of the bowl.

5. Return the stew to a simmer, stir in the parsley, and season with salt and pepper to taste. Using a greased tablespoon measure (or #60 portion scoop), scoop level amounts of batter and drop them into the stew, spacing the dumplings about ¼ inch apart (you should have about 24 dumplings). Wrap the lid of the Dutch oven with a clean kitchen towel (keeping the towel away from the heat source) and cover the pot. Simmer gently until the dumplings have doubled in size and a toothpick inserted into the center comes out clean, 13 to 16 minutes. Serve immediately. (The stew can be prepared through step 3 up to 2 days in advance; bring the stew back to a simmer before proceeding with the recipe.)

CHICKEN POT PIE

WHY THIS RECIPE WORKS: As homey as chicken pot pie sounds, this dish is a production. You've got to cook and cut up a chicken, make a sauce, parcook vegetables, and all the while prepare, chill, and roll out pie crust. We wanted to streamline the dish and get it on the table in 90 minutes, tops. And, we wanted a completely homemade pie (no prefab crust) full of tender, juicy chicken and bright vegetables.

To start, we swapped out a whole chicken for easy-to-poach chicken breasts—and we used the poaching liquid as the base of our sauce. But to boost the sauce's flavor, we turned to a few ingredients rich in glutamates, naturally occurring flavor compounds that accentuate savory qualities. Sautéed mushrooms, soy sauce, and tomato paste did the trick, turning into caramelized fond that gave our sauce deep flavor. Sautéing the vegetables, a medley of onions, carrots, and celery, while the chicken rested, also boosted the filling's flavor. (Later we'd add quick-cooking frozen peas straight to the filling to warm through).

For the pot pie topping, we replaced traditional pastry with a savory crumble topping, enriched with grated cheese and pepper. To increase the crunch factor, we baked the crumble separately from the filling, then scattered it over the pot pie and slid it into the oven to warm through. Minutes later, our homemade pot pie emerged bubbling, fragrant, and topped with a crunchy, flavorful crust.

Chicken Pot Pie with Savory Crumble Topping

SERVES 6

This recipe relies on two unusual ingredients: soy sauce and tomato paste. Do not omit them. They don't convey their distinct tastes but greatly deepen the savory flavor of the filling. When making the topping, do not substitute milk or half-and-half for the heavy cream.

FILLING

- 1½ pounds boneless, skinless chicken breasts and/or thighs
- 3 cups low-sodium chicken broth
- 2 tablespoons vegetable oil
- 1 medium onion, minced
- 3 medium carrots, peeled and cut crosswise into ¼-inch-thick slices (about 1 cup)
- 2 small celery ribs, chopped fine
  Table salt and ground black pepper
- 10 ounces cremini mushrooms, stems trimmed, caps wiped clean and sliced thin
- 1 teaspoon soy sauce (see note)
- 1 teaspoon tomato paste (see note)
- 4 tablespoons (½ stick) unsalted butter
- ½ cup unbleached all-purpose flour
- 1 cup whole milk
- 2 teaspoons juice from 1 lemon
- 3 tablespoons minced fresh parsley leaves
- ¾ cup frozen baby peas

CRUMBLE TOPPING

- 2 cups (10 ounces) unbleached all-purpose flour
- 2 teaspoons baking powder
- ¾ teaspoon table salt
- ½ teaspoon ground black pepper
- ⅛ teaspoon cayenne pepper
- 6 tablespoons (¾ stick) unsalted butter, cut into ½-inch cubes and chilled
- 1 ounce Parmesan cheese, finely grated (about ½ cup)
- ¾ cup plus 2 tablespoons heavy cream (see note)

1. FOR THE CHICKEN: Bring the chicken and broth to a simmer in a covered Dutch oven over medium heat. Cook until the chicken is just done, 8 to 12 minutes. Transfer the cooked chicken to a large bowl. Pour the broth through a fine-mesh strainer into a liquid measuring cup and reserve. Do not wash the Dutch oven. Meanwhile, adjust an oven rack to the upper-middle position and heat the oven to 450 degrees.

2. FOR THE TOPPING: Combine the flour, baking powder, salt, black pepper, and cayenne in a large bowl. Sprinkle the butter pieces over the top of the flour. Using your fingers, rub the butter into the flour mixture until it resembles coarse cornmeal. Stir in the Parmesan. Add the cream and stir until just combined. Crumble the mixture into irregularly shaped pieces ranging from ½ to ¾ inch onto a parchment-lined rimmed baking sheet. Bake until fragrant and starting to brown, 10 to 13 minutes. Set aside.

3. FOR THE FILLING: Heat 1 tablespoon of the oil in the now-empty Dutch oven over medium heat until shimmering. Add the onion, carrots, celery, ¼ teaspoon salt, and ¼ teaspoon pepper; cover and cook, stirring occasionally, until just tender, 5 to 7 minutes. While the vegetables are cooking, shred the chicken into small bite-size pieces. Transfer the cooked vegetables to the bowl with the chicken; set aside.

4. Heat the remaining 1 tablespoon oil in the again-empty Dutch oven over medium heat until shimmering. Add the mushrooms; cover and cook, stirring occasionally, until the mushrooms have released their juices, about 5 minutes. Remove the cover, stir in the soy sauce and tomato paste. Increase the heat to medium-high and cook, stirring frequently, until the liquid has evaporated, the mushrooms are well browned, and a dark fond begins to form on the surface of the pan, about 5 minutes. Transfer the mushrooms to the bowl with the chicken and vegetables. Set aside.

5. Heat the butter in the again-empty Dutch oven over medium heat. When the foaming subsides, stir in the flour and cook for 1 minute. Slowly whisk in the reserved chicken broth and the milk. Bring to a simmer, scraping the pan bottom with a wooden spoon to loosen the browned bits, then continue to simmer until the sauce fully thickens, about 1 minute. Season with salt and pepper to taste. Remove from the heat and stir in the lemon juice and 2 tablespoons of the parsley.

6. Stir the chicken-vegetable mixture and peas into the sauce. Pour the mixture into a 13 by 9-inch baking dish or casserole dish of similar size. Scatter the crumble topping evenly over the filling. Bake on a rimmed baking sheet until the filling is bubbling and the topping is well browned, 12 to 15 minutes. Sprinkle with the remaining 1 tablespoon parsley and serve.

GREEK SPINACH AND FETA PIE

WHY THIS RECIPE WORKS: The roots of this savory dish run deep in Greek culture, yet most stateside versions are nothing more than soggy layers of phyllo with a sparse, bland filling. We wanted a casserole-style pie with a perfect balance of zesty spinach filling and shatteringly crisp, flaky phyllo crust—and we didn't want it to take all day. Using store-bought phyllo was an easy timesaver. Among the various spinach options (baby, frozen, mature curly-leaf), tasters favored the bold flavor of fresh curly-leaf spinach that had been microwaved, coarsely chopped, and squeezed of excess moisture. Crumbling the feta into fine pieces ensured a salty tang in every bite, while the addition of Greek yogurt buffered the assertiveness of the feta. We found that Pecorino Romano (a good stand-in for the traditional Greek hard sheep's milk cheese) added complexity to the filling and, when sprinkled between the sheets of phyllo, helped the flaky layers hold together. Using a baking sheet rather than a baking dish allowed excess moisture to easily evaporate, ensuring a crisp crust.

Greek Spinach and Feta Pie (Spanakopita)

SERVES 6 TO 8 AS A MAIN COURSE OR 10 TO 12 AS AN APPETIZER

It is important to rinse the feta; this step removes some of its salty brine, which would overwhelm the spinach. Full-fat sour cream can be substituted for whole-milk Greek yogurt. Phyllo dough is also available in larger 14 by 18-inch sheets; if using, cut them in half to make 14 by 9-inch sheets. Don't thaw the phyllo in the microwave; let it sit in the refrigerator overnight or on the countertop for 4 to 5 hours. The filling can be made up to 24 hours in advance and refrigerated. The assembled, unbaked spanakopita can be frozen on a baking sheet, wrapped well in plastic wrap, or cut in half crosswise and frozen in smaller sections on a plate. To bake, unwrap and increase the baking time by 5 to 10 minutes.

FILLING

- 1¼ pounds curly-leaf spinach, stemmed
- ¼ cup water
- 12 ounces feta cheese, rinsed, patted dry, and crumbled into fine pieces (about 3 cups)
- ¾ cup whole-milk Greek yogurt
- 4 scallions, sliced thin
- 2 large eggs, beaten
- ¼ cup minced fresh mint leaves
- 2 tablespoons minced fresh dill leaves
- 3 medium garlic cloves, minced or pressed through a garlic press (about 1 tablespoon)
- 1 teaspoon grated zest plus 1 tablespoon juice from 1 lemon
- 1 teaspoon ground nutmeg
- ½ teaspoon ground black pepper
- ¼ teaspoon table salt
- ⅛ teaspoon cayenne pepper

PHYLLO LAYERS

- 7 tablespoons unsalted butter, melted
- 8 ounces (14 by 9-inch) phyllo, thawed
- 1½ ounces Pecorino Romano cheese, grated (¾ cup)
- 2 teaspoons sesame seeds (optional)

1. FOR THE FILLING: Place the spinach and water in a large bowl and cover with a large dinner plate. Microwave until the spinach is wilted and decreased in volume by half, about 5 minutes. Using potholders, remove the bowl from the microwave and keep covered for 1 minute. Carefully remove the plate and transfer the spinach to a colander. Using the back of a rubber spatula, gently press the spinach against the colander to release the excess liquid. Transfer the spinach to a cutting board and chop coarse. Transfer the spinach to a clean kitchen towel and squeeze to remove excess water. Place the drained spinach in a large bowl. Add the remaining filling ingredients and mix until thoroughly combined.

2. FOR THE PHYLLO LAYERS: Adjust an oven rack to the lower-middle position and heat the oven to 425 degrees. Line a rimmed baking sheet with parchment paper. Using a pastry brush, lightly brush a 14 by 9-inch rectangle in the center of the parchment with melted butter to cover an area the same size as the phyllo. Lay 1 phyllo sheet on the buttered parchment and brush thoroughly with melted butter. Repeat with 9 more phyllo sheets, brushing each with butter (you should have a total of 10 layers of phyllo).

3. Spread the spinach mixture evenly over the phyllo, leaving a ¼-inch border on all sides. Cover the spinach with 6 more phyllo sheets, brushing each with butter and sprinkling each with about 2 tablespoons Pecorino cheese. Lay 2 more phyllo sheets on top, brushing each with butter (do not sprinkle these layers with Pecorino).

4. Working from the center outward, use the palms of your hands to compress the layers and press out any air pockets. Using a sharp knife, score the spanakopita through the top 3 layers of phyllo into 24 equal pieces. Sprinkle with the sesame seeds (if using). Bake until the phyllo is golden and crisp, 20 to 25 minutes. Cool on a baking sheet for 10 minutes or up to 2 hours. Slide the spanakopita, still on the parchment, onto a cutting board. Cut into squares and serve.

MOROCCAN CHICKEN

WHY THIS RECIPE WORKS: Time-consuming techniques and esoteric ingredients make cooking authentic Moroccan chicken a daunting proposition. We wanted a recipe that was ready in an hour and relied on supermarket staples. For depth and flavor, we used a mix of white and dark meat and browned the meat first. After removing the chicken from the pot, we sautéed onion, strips of lemon zest, garlic, and a spice blend in some oil and the browned bits left in the pot; this ensured that no flavor went to waste. A number of everyday spices were necessary to re-create the authentic notes in Moroccan chicken, including paprika, cumin, cayenne, ginger, coriander, and cinnamon; honey filled the bill for the missing sweetness. Greek green olives provided the meatiness and piquant flavor of hard-to-find Moroccan olives. Chopped cilantro, stirred in right before serving, was the perfect finishing touch to our exotic dinner.

Moroccan Chicken with Olives and Lemon

SERVES 4

Bone-in chicken parts can be substituted for the whole chicken. For best results, use four chicken thighs and two chicken breasts, each breast split in half; the dark meat contributes valuable flavor to the broth and should not be omitted. Use a vegetable peeler to remove wide strips of zest from the lemon before juicing it. Make sure to trim any white pith from the zest, as it can impart bitter flavor. If the olives are particularly salty, rinse them first. Serve with Simple Couscous (page 500).

- 1¼ teaspoons paprika
- ½ teaspoon ground cumin
- ½ teaspoon ground ginger
- ¼ teaspoon cayenne pepper
- ¼ teaspoon ground coriander
- ¼ teaspoon ground cinnamon
- 3 (2-inch) strips zest plus 3 tablespoons juice from 1 lemon
- 5 medium garlic cloves, minced or pressed through a garlic press (about 5 teaspoons)
- 1 (3½ to 4-pound) whole chicken, cut into 8 pieces (4 breast pieces, 2 thighs, 2 drumsticks), wings discarded, and trimmed
  Table salt and ground black pepper
- 1 tablespoon olive oil
- 1 large onion, halved and sliced ¼ inch thick
- 1¾ cups low-sodium chicken broth
- 1 tablespoon honey
- 2 medium carrots, peeled and cut crosswise into ½-inch-thick rounds, very large pieces cut into half-moons
- 1 cup cracked green olives, pitted and halved
- 2 tablespoons chopped fresh cilantro leaves

1. Combine the paprika, cumin, ginger, cayenne, coriander, and cinnamon in a small bowl and set aside. Mince 1 of the lemon zest strips, combine with 1 teaspoon of the minced garlic, and mince together until reduced to a fine paste; set aside.

2. Season both sides of the chicken pieces with salt and pepper. Heat the oil in a Dutch oven over medium-high heat until beginning to smoke. Brown the chicken pieces, skin side down, until deep golden, about 5 minutes; using tongs, flip the chicken pieces and brown on the second side, about 4 minutes longer. Transfer the chicken to a large plate; when cool enough to handle, remove and discard the skin. Pour off and discard all but 1 tablespoon fat from the pot.

3. Add the onion and the 2 remaining lemon zest strips to the pot and cook, stirring occasionally, until the onion slices have browned at the edges but still retain their shape, 5 to 7 minutes (add 1 tablespoon water if the pan gets too dark). Add the remaining 4 teaspoons garlic and cook, stirring, until fragrant, about 30 seconds. Add the spices and cook, stirring constantly, until darkened and very fragrant, 45 seconds to 1 minute. Stir in the broth and honey, scraping up the browned bits from the bottom of the pot. Add the thighs and drumsticks, reduce the heat to medium, and simmer for 5 minutes.

4. Add the carrots and breast pieces with any accumulated juices to the pot, arranging the breast pieces in a single layer on top of the carrots. Cover, reduce the heat to medium-low, and simmer until the breast pieces register 160 to 165 degrees, 10 to 15 minutes.

5. Transfer the chicken to a plate and tent with aluminum foil. Add the olives to the pot; increase the heat to medium-high and simmer until the liquid has thickened slightly and the carrots are tender, 4 to 6 minutes. Return the chicken to the pot and stir in the garlic mixture, lemon juice, and cilantro; season with salt and pepper to taste. Serve immediately.

Moroccan Chicken with Chickpeas and Apricots

Follow the recipe for Moroccan Chicken with Olives and Lemon, replacing 1 carrot with 1 cup dried apricots, halved, and replacing the olives with one 15-ounce can chickpeas, rinsed.

BEHIND THE SCENES

A PEEK INSIDE THE TEST KITCHEN FREEZER

Curious as to what we keep in our freezer? A whole lot more than you might think. In fact, we've found that some pantry staples are better preserved in the freezer. Here's a list of the more unusual items the test kitchen keeps on ice.

RIPE OR OVERRIPE BANANAS: Great to have for making banana bread or muffins, or drop them into a blender while still frozen for fruit smoothies. Peel bananas before freezing.

NUTS: Sealed in a zipper-lock freezer bag, nuts stay fresh tasting for months. And there's no need to defrost; frozen nuts chop just as easily as fresh.

HERBS: Dried bay leaves retain their potency much longer when stored in the freezer. Chopped fresh herbs such as parsley, sage, rosemary, and thyme can be covered with water in an ice cube tray and then frozen indefinitely. Keep the frozen cubes in a zipper-lock freezer bag until needed for sauces, soups, or stews. Homemade pesto can also be frozen in ice cube trays, and there's no need to add water.

BUTTER: When stored in the refrigerator, butter picks up off-odors and eventually turns rancid. You can prolong its life by storing it in the freezer. Transfer it to the refrigerator one stick at a time, as you need it.

DRY GOODS: Stored in the freezer, flour, bread crumbs, cornmeal, oats, and other grains are protected from humidity, bugs, and rancidity.

LATINO-STYLE CHICKEN AND RICE

WHY THIS RECIPE WORKS: The traditional way of cooking this bold-flavored cousin of American chicken and rice is time-consuming, requiring an overnight marinade of the chicken and then a long, slow stewing with rice and vegetables. Could we find a way to achieve the same results in a lot less time?

We began by choosing chicken thighs, not only for shopping convenience but also to ensure that all of the pieces would cook at the same rate—a problem when using a combination of white and dark meat. We poached the thighs in a broth preseasoned with a *sofrito*, a classic Latin American mixture of chopped onions and bell peppers. About half an hour before the chicken finished cooking, we added medium-grain rice (which we preferred over long-grain for its creamy texture), stirring it a few times to ensure even cooking. And for maximum flavor, we devised two marinades. Before cooking, we marinated the chicken quickly in garlic, oregano, and distilled white vinegar; after cooking we tossed the cooked chicken with olive oil, vinegar, and cilantro.

We had one final dilemma: how to give the dish its traditional orange hue that comes from infusing oil with achiote, a tropical seed not readily available in local grocery stores. Adding canned tomato sauce solved the problem.

Latino-Style Chicken and Rice (Arroz con Pollo)
SERVES 4 TO 6

To keep the dish from becoming greasy, remove any visible pockets of waxy yellow fat from the chicken and most of the skin, leaving just enough to protect the meat. To use long-grain rice instead of medium-grain, increase the amount of water added in step 2 from ¼ to ¾ cup and add the additional ¼ cup water in step 3 as needed. When removing the chicken from the bone in step 4, we found it better to use two spoons rather than two forks; forks tend to shred the meat, while spoons pull it apart in chunks.

6   medium garlic cloves, minced or pressed through a garlic press (about 2 tablespoons)
    Table salt and ground black pepper
1   tablespoon plus 2 teaspoons distilled white vinegar
½   teaspoon dried oregano
4   pounds bone-in, skin-on chicken thighs (about 10 thighs), trimmed (see note)
2   tablespoons olive oil
1   medium onion, minced
1   small green pepper, stemmed, seeded, and chopped fine
¼   teaspoon red pepper flakes
¼   cup minced fresh cilantro leaves
1¾ cups low-sodium chicken broth
1   (8-ounce) can tomato sauce
¼   cup water, plus more if needed (see note)
3   cups medium-grain rice (see note)
½   cup green manzanilla olives, pitted and halved
1   tablespoon capers
½   cup jarred pimentos, cut into 2 by ¼-inch strips
    Lemon wedges, for serving

1. Adjust an oven rack to the middle position and heat the oven to 350 degrees. Place the garlic and 1 teaspoon salt in a large bowl; using a rubber spatula, mix to make a smooth paste. Add 1 tablespoon of the vinegar, the oregano, and ½ teaspoon black pepper to the garlic-salt mixture; stir to combine. Place the chicken in the bowl with the marinade. Coat the chicken pieces evenly with the marinade; set aside for 15 minutes.

2. Heat 1 tablespoon of the oil in a Dutch oven over medium heat until shimmering. Add the onion, green pepper, and red pepper flakes; cook, stirring occasionally, until the vegetables begin to soften, 4 to 8 minutes. Add 2 tablespoons of the cilantro; stir to combine. Push the vegetables to the sides of the pot and increase the heat to medium-high. Add the chicken to the clearing in the center of the pot, skin side down, in an even layer. Cook, without moving the chicken, until the outer layer of the meat becomes opaque, 2 to 4 minutes. (If the chicken begins to brown, reduce the heat to medium.) Using tongs, flip the chicken and cook on the second side until opaque, 2 to 4 minutes more. Add the broth, tomato sauce, and water; stir to combine. Bring to a simmer; cover, reduce the heat to medium-low, and simmer for 20 minutes.

3. Add the rice, olives, capers, and ¾ teaspoon salt; stir well. Bring to a simmer, cover, and place the pot in the oven. After 10 minutes, remove the pot from the oven and stir the chicken and rice once from the bottom up. Cover and return the pot to the oven. After another 10 minutes, stir once more, adding another ¼ cup water if the rice appears dry and the bottom of the pot is beginning to burn. Cover and return the pot to the oven; cook until the rice has absorbed all the liquid and is tender but still holds its shape and the thickest part of the thighs registers 175 degrees on an instant-read thermometer, about 10 minutes longer.

4. Using tongs, remove the chicken from the pot; replace the lid and set the pot aside. Remove and discard the chicken skin; using two spoons, pull the meat off the bones in large chunks. Using your fingers, remove the remaining fat and any dark veins from the chicken pieces. Place the chicken in a large bowl and toss with the remaining 1 tablespoon oil, remaining 2 teaspoons vinegar, remaining 2 tablespoons cilantro, and the pimentos; season with salt and pepper to taste. Place the chicken on top of the rice, cover, and let stand until warmed through, about 5 minutes. Serve, passing the lemon wedges separately.

Latino-Style Chicken and Rice with Bacon and Roasted Red Peppers

Bacon adds a welcome layer of richness, and red peppers bring subtle sweet flavor and color to this variation. To use long-grain rice, increase the amount of water to ¾ cup in step 2 and the salt added in step 3 to 1 teaspoon.

1. Follow the recipe for Latino-Style Chicken and Rice through step 1, substituting 2 teaspoons sweet paprika for the oregano and sherry vinegar for the white vinegar.

2. Fry 4 ounces (about 4 strips) bacon, cut into ½-inch pieces, in a Dutch oven over medium heat until crisp, 6 to 8 minutes. Using a slotted spoon, transfer the bacon to a paper towel–lined plate; pour off all but 1 tablespoon bacon fat. Continue with step 2, substituting 1 small red pepper, chopped fine, and 1 medium carrot, chopped fine, for the green pepper and sautéing the vegetables in the bacon fat.

3. Continue with the recipe, substituting ¼ cup minced fresh parsley leaves for the cilantro, omitting the olives and capers, and substituting ½ cup roasted red peppers, cut into 2 by ¼-inch strips, for the pimentos. Garnish the chicken and rice with the reserved bacon before serving.

Latino-Style Chicken and Rice with Ham, Peas, and Orange

Ham gives this variation further richness, and orange zest and juice provide a bright accent. To use long-grain rice, increase the amount of water to ¾ cup in step 2 and the salt added in step 3 to 1 teaspoon.

1. Follow the recipe for Latino-Style Chicken and Rice through step 1, substituting 1 tablespoon ground cumin for the oregano.

2. Continue with step 2, adding 8 ounces ham steak or Canadian bacon, cut into ½-inch pieces (about 1½ cups), with the onion, green pepper, and red pepper flakes.

3. With a vegetable peeler, remove three 3-inch strips of zest from 1 orange. Continue with step 3, adding the orange zest with the rice, olives, capers, and salt. Add 1 cup frozen peas to the pot with ¼ cup water, if necessary, after stirring the contents of the pot the second time.

4. In step 4, add 3 tablespoons juice from 1 orange to the bowl with the olive oil, vinegar, cilantro, and pimentos and proceed with the recipe.

CUBAN-STYLE BLACK BEANS AND RICE

WHY THIS RECIPE WORKS: Beans and rice is a familiar combination the world over, but Cuban black beans and rice is unique in that the rice is cooked in the inky concentrated liquid left over from cooking the beans, which renders the grains just as flavorful. For our own version, we expanded on this method, simmering a portion of the *sofrito* (the traditional combination of garlic, bell pepper, and onion) with our beans to infuse them with flavor and then using the liquid to cook our rice and beans together. Lightly browning the remaining sofrito vegetables and spices with rendered salt pork added complex, meaty flavor, and finishing the dish in the oven eliminated the crusty bottom that can form when the dish is cooked on the stove.

Cuban-Style Black Beans and Rice

SERVES 6 TO 8

It is important to use lean—not fatty—salt pork. If you can't find it, substitute 6 slices of bacon. If using bacon, decrease the cooking time in step 4 to 8 minutes. You will need a Dutch oven with a tight-fitting lid for this recipe. For a vegetarian version of this recipe, use water instead of chicken broth, omit the salt pork, add 1 tablespoon tomato paste with the vegetables in step 4, and increase the amount of salt in step 5 to 1½ teaspoons.

> Table salt
> 6½ ounces dried black beans (1 cup), picked over and rinsed
> 2 cups low-sodium chicken broth
> 2 cups water
> 2 large green bell peppers, stemmed, seeded, and halved
> 1 large onion, halved at equator and peeled, root end left intact
> 1 head garlic, 5 medium cloves minced or pressed through a garlic press (about 5 teaspoons), remaining head halved at equator with skin left intact
> 2 bay leaves
> 1½ cups long-grain white rice
> 2 tablespoons olive oil
> 6 ounces lean salt pork, cut into ¼-inch dice (see note)
> 4 teaspoons ground cumin
> 1 tablespoon minced fresh oregano leaves

> 2 tablespoons red wine vinegar
> 2 scallions, sliced thin, for serving
> Lime wedges, for serving

1. Dissolve 1½ tablespoons salt in 2 quarts cold water in a large bowl or container. Add the beans and soak at room temperature for at least 8 hours or up to 24 hours. Drain and rinse well.

2. In a Dutch oven, stir together the drained beans, broth, water, 1 bell pepper half, 1 onion half (with root end), the halved garlic head, bay leaves, and 1 teaspoon salt. Bring to a simmer over medium-high heat, cover, and reduce the heat to low. Cook until the beans are just soft, 30 to 35 minutes. Using tongs, remove and discard the pepper, onion, garlic, and bay leaves. Drain the beans in a colander set over a large bowl, reserving 2½ cups bean cooking liquid. (If you don't have enough bean cooking liquid, add water to equal 2½ cups.) Do not wash out the Dutch oven.

3. Adjust an oven rack to the middle position and heat the oven to 350 degrees. Place the rice in a large fine-mesh strainer and rinse under cold running water until the water runs clear, about 1½ minutes. Shake the strainer vigorously to remove all excess water; set the rice aside. Cut the remaining peppers and onion into 2-inch pieces and process in a food processor until broken into rough ¼-inch pieces, about 8 pulses, scraping down the bowl as necessary; set the vegetables aside.

4. In the now-empty Dutch oven, heat 1 tablespoon oil and the salt pork over medium-low heat and cook, stirring frequently, until lightly browned and rendered, 15 to 20 minutes. Add the remaining 1 tablespoon oil, the chopped bell peppers and onion, cumin, and oregano. Increase the heat to medium and continue to cook, stirring frequently, until the vegetables are softened and beginning to brown, 10 to 15 minutes longer. Add the minced garlic and cook, stirring constantly, until fragrant, about 1 minute. Add the rice and stir to coat, about 30 seconds.

5. Stir in the beans, reserved bean cooking liquid, vinegar, and ½ teaspoon salt. Increase the heat to medium-high and bring to a simmer. Cover and transfer to the oven. Cook until the liquid is absorbed and the rice is tender, about 30 minutes. Fluff with a fork and let rest, uncovered, for 5 minutes. Serve, passing the scallions and lime wedges separately.

PAELLA

WHY THIS RECIPE WORKS: Paella can be a big hit at restaurants but an unwieldy production at home. Could we re-create this Spanish classic in two hours without using any fancy equipment?

The key to our paella was finding equipment and ingredients that stayed true to the dish's heritage. First, we substituted a Dutch oven for a single-purpose paella pan. Then we pared down our ingredients, dismissing lobster (too much work), diced pork (sausage would be enough), fish (flakes too easily), rabbit and snails (too unconventional). We were left with chorizo, chicken (boneless, skinless thighs), shrimp (marinated in a garlic–olive oil mixture), and mussels (favored over scallops, clams, and calamari). We next simplified our *sofrito*—in this Spanish version, a combination of onions, garlic, and tomatoes—by mincing a can of drained diced tomatoes rather than seeding and grating a fresh tomato.

For the rice, we found we preferred short-grain varieties. Valencia was our favorite, with Italian Arborio a close second. Sautéing the rice in the same pot used to brown the meat and make the sofrito boosted its flavor. For the cooking liquid and seasonings, we chose chicken broth, white wine, saffron, and a bay leaf. Once the rice had absorbed almost all the liquid, we added the mussels, shrimp, and peas to the mix. The result? A colorful, streamlined, yet flavorful rendition of the Spanish classic.

Paella
SERVES 6

Use a Dutch oven that is 11 to 12 inches in diameter with at least a 6-quart capacity. Dry-cured Spanish chorizo is the sausage of choice for paella, but fresh chorizo or linguiça is an acceptable substitute.

Soccarat, a layer of crusty browned rice that forms on the bottom of the pan, is a traditional part of paella. In our version, soccarat does not develop because most of the cooking is done in the oven. We have provided instructions to develop soccarat in step 5; if you prefer, skip this step and go directly from step 4 to step 6.

- 1 pound extra-large shrimp (21 to 25 per pound), peeled and deveined (see page 205)
  Table salt and ground black pepper
- 2 tablespoons olive oil, plus extra as needed
- 8-9 medium garlic cloves, minced or pressed through a garlic press (2 generous tablespoons)
- 1 pound boneless, skinless chicken thighs (about 4 thighs), trimmed and halved crosswise
- 1 red bell pepper, stemmed, seeded, and cut pole to pole into ½-inch-wide strips
- 8 ounces Spanish chorizo, sliced ½ inch thick on the bias (see note)
- 1 medium onion, minced
- 1 (14.5-ounce) can diced tomatoes, drained, minced, and drained again
- 2 cups Valencia or Arborio rice
- 3 cups low-sodium chicken broth
- ⅓ cup dry white wine
- ½ teaspoon saffron threads, crumbled
- 1 bay leaf
- 1 dozen mussels, scrubbed and debearded
- ½ cup frozen peas, thawed
- 2 tablespoons chopped fresh parsley leaves
- 1 lemon, cut into wedges, for serving

1. Adjust an oven rack to the lower-middle position and heat the oven to 350 degrees. Toss the shrimp, ¼ teaspoon salt, ¼ teaspoon pepper, 1 tablespoon of the oil, and 1 teaspoon of the garlic in a medium bowl; cover with plastic wrap and refrigerate until needed. Season the chicken thighs with salt and pepper; set aside.

2. Heat 2 teaspoons more oil in a large Dutch oven over medium-high heat until shimmering but not smoking. Add the pepper strips and cook, stirring occasionally, until the skin begins to blister and turn spotty black, 3 to 4 minutes. Transfer the pepper to a small plate and set aside.

3. Add the remaining 1 teaspoon oil to the now-empty Dutch oven; heat the oil until shimmering but not smoking. Add the chicken pieces in a single layer; cook, without moving the pieces, until browned, about 3 minutes. Turn the pieces and brown on the second side, about 3 minutes longer; transfer the chicken to a medium bowl. Reduce the heat to medium and add the chorizo to the pot; cook, stirring frequently, until deeply browned and the fat begins to render, 4 to 5 minutes. Transfer the chorizo to the bowl with the chicken and set aside.

4. Add enough oil to the fat in the Dutch oven to equal 2 tablespoons; heat over medium heat until shimmering but not smoking. Add the onion and cook, stirring frequently, until softened, about 3 minutes; stir in the remaining garlic and cook until fragrant, about 1 minute. Stir in the tomatoes; cook until the mixture begins to darken and thicken slightly, about 3 minutes. Stir in the rice and cook until the grains are well coated with the tomato mixture, 1 to 2 minutes. Stir in the chicken broth, wine, saffron, bay leaf, and ½ teaspoon salt. Return the chicken and chorizo to the pot, increase the heat to medium-high, and bring to a boil, uncovered, stirring occasionally. Cover the pot and transfer it to the oven; cook until the rice absorbs almost all of the liquid, about 15 minutes. Remove the pot from the oven (close the oven door to retain heat). Uncover the pot; scatter the shrimp over the rice, insert the mussels, hinged side down, into the rice (so they stand upright), arrange the bell pepper strips in a pinwheel pattern, and scatter the peas over the top. Cover and return to the oven; cook until the shrimp are opaque and the mussels have opened, 10 to 12 minutes.

5. OPTIONAL: If soccarat is desired (see note), set the Dutch oven, uncovered, over medium-high heat for about 5 minutes, rotating the pot 180 degrees after about 2 minutes for even browning.

6. Let the paella stand, covered, for about 5 minutes. Discard any mussels that have not opened and the bay leaf, if it can be easily removed. Sprinkle with the parsley and serve, passing the lemon wedges separately.

CREOLE-STYLE GUMBO

WHY THIS RECIPE WORKS: With shrimp, sausage, and vegetables in a deeply flavored, rich brown sauce with a touch of heat, gumbo is a unique one-pot meal. We wanted a foolproof, streamlined technique for gumbo that featured a thick, smooth sauce with lots of well-seasoned vegetables, meat, and fish.

The basis of gumbo is the roux, which is flour cooked in fat. For a deep, dark roux in half the time, we heated the oil before adding the flour. We also added the roux to room-temperature shrimp stock (supplemented with clam juice) to prevent separating. Although tomatoes are traditional in gumbo, our tasters didn't think they were necessary—but garlic was, and lots of it. Some cayenne pepper added the requisite heat. We added spicy andouille sausage and simmered everything for half an hour, tossing in the shrimp only during the last few minutes of cooking. You can add filé powder if you like, but our gumbo is delicious even without it.

Creole-Style Shrimp and Sausage Gumbo

SERVES 6 TO 8

Making a dark roux can be dangerous, as the mixture reaches temperatures in excess of 400 degrees. Therefore, use a deep pot for cooking the roux and long-handled utensils for stirring it, and be careful not to splash it on yourself. One secret to smooth gumbo is adding shrimp stock that is neither too hot nor too cold to the roux. For a stock that is at the right temperature when the roux is done, start preparing it before you tend to the vegetables and other ingredients, strain it, and then give it a head start on cooling by immediately adding the ice water and clam juice. So that your constant stirring of the roux will not be interrupted, start the roux only after you've made the stock. Alternatively, you can make the stock well ahead of time and bring it back to room temperature before using it. Spicy andouille sausage is a Louisiana specialty that may not be available everywhere; kielbasa or any fully cooked smoked sausage makes a fine substitute. Gumbo is traditionally served over white rice.

- 1½ **pounds small shrimp (51 to 60 per pound), shells removed and reserved**
- 3½ **cups ice water**
- 1 **(8-ounce) bottle clam juice**
- ½ **cup vegetable oil**
- ½ **cup all-purpose flour, preferably bleached**
- 2 **medium onions, minced**
- 1 **medium red bell pepper, stemmed, seeded, and chopped fine**
- 1 **medium celery rib, chopped fine**
- 6 **medium garlic cloves, minced or pressed through a garlic press (about 2 tablespoons)**
- 1 **teaspoon dried thyme**
  Table salt
  Cayenne pepper
- 2 **bay leaves**
- 1 **pound smoked sausage, such as andouille or kielbasa (see note), sliced ¼ inch thick**
- ½ **cup minced fresh parsley leaves**
- 4 **medium scallions, white and green parts, sliced thin**
  Ground black pepper

1. Bring the reserved shrimp shells and 4½ cups water to a boil in a stockpot or large saucepan over medium-high heat. Reduce the heat to medium-low and simmer for 20 minutes. Strain the stock and add the ice water and clam juice (you should have about 2 quarts of tepid stock, 100 to 110 degrees); discard the shells. Set the stock aside.

2. Heat the oil in a Dutch oven or large, heavy-bottomed saucepan over medium-high heat until it registers 200 degrees on an instant-read thermometer, 1½ to 2 minutes. Reduce the heat to medium and gradually stir in the flour with a wooden spatula or spoon, making sure to work out any lumps that may form. Continue stirring constantly, reaching into the corners of the pan, until the mixture has a toasty aroma and is deep reddish brown, about 20 minutes. (The roux will thin as it cooks; if it begins to smoke, remove the pan from the heat and stir the roux constantly to cool slightly.)

3. Add the onions, bell pepper, celery, garlic, thyme, 1 teaspoon salt, and ¼ teaspoon cayenne to the roux and cook, stirring frequently, until the vegetables soften, 8 to 10 minutes. Add 4 cups of the reserved stock in a slow, steady stream while stirring vigorously. Stir in the remaining 4 cups of stock. Increase the heat to high and bring to a boil. Reduce the heat to medium-low, skim the foam from the surface with a wide spoon, add the bay leaves, and simmer, uncovered, skimming the foam as it rises to the surface, about 30 minutes. (The mixture can be covered and set aside for several hours. Reheat when ready to proceed.)

4. Stir in the sausage and continue simmering to blend the flavors, about 30 minutes. Stir in the shrimp and simmer until cooked through, about 5 minutes. Off the heat, stir in the parsley and scallions and season with salt, black pepper, and cayenne to taste. Discard the bay leaves and serve immediately.

CHAPTER 5

SIMPLY CHICKEN

Sautéed Chicken Cutlets with Mustard-Cider Sauce 84

Breaded Chicken Cutlets 84

Chicken Milanese

Nut-Crusted Chicken Breasts with Lemon and Thyme 85

Nut-Crusted Chicken Breasts with Orange and Oregano

Stuffed Chicken Cutlets with Ham and Cheddar 86

Pan-Seared Chicken Breasts 88

Lemon and Chive Pan Sauce

Chicken Kiev 89

Sweet and Tangy Oven-Barbecued Chicken 91

Spice-Rubbed Picnic Chicken 92

Pan-Roasted Chicken Breasts with Sage-Vermouth Sauce 93

Perfect Roast Chicken 94

Weeknight Roast Chicken 94

Tarragon-Lemon Pan Sauce

Thyme–Sherry Vinegar Pan Sauce

Crisp-Skinned Roast Chicken 96

Classic Roast Lemon Chicken 97

Glazed Roast Chicken 99

Stovetop Roast Chicken with Lemon-Herb Sauce 100

High-Roast Butterflied Chicken with Potatoes 101

Mustard-Garlic Butter with Thyme

"Stuffed" Roast Butterflied Chicken 103

Mushroom-Leek Bread Stuffing with Herbs

Peruvian Roast Chicken with Garlic and Lime 104

Spicy Mayonnaise

Crispy Fried Chicken 105

Easier Fried Chicken 107

Oven-Fried Chicken 108

Buffalo Wings 109

SAUTÉED CHICKEN CUTLETS

WHY THIS RECIPE WORKS: Sautéed super-thin cutlets are satisfying midweek fare, except when they are tough and dry. We wanted juicy, ultrathin sautéed chicken cutlets, paired with a sauce that complements, rather than overpowers, the meat.

For evenly sized cutlets, we took a two-step approach. We halved the chicken breasts horizontally before pounding them to an even thickness under plastic wrap. Halving and pounding the breasts ensures that they cook at the same rate, and turn out moist, tender, and juicy. To further ensure the cutlets turned out juicy, we browned them on only one side. And for the sauce, we kept the flavors simple, relying on the sweet, tangy combination of apple cider and cider vinegar complemented with the kick of whole grain mustard.

Sautéed Chicken Cutlets with Mustard-Cider Sauce

SERVES 4

To make slicing the chicken easier, freeze it for 15 minutes.

CHICKEN

- 4 (6 to 8-ounce) boneless, skinless chicken breasts, tenderloins removed and breasts trimmed
  Table salt and ground black pepper
- 2 tablespoons vegetable oil

MUSTARD-CIDER SAUCE

- 2 teaspoons vegetable oil
- 1 medium shallot, minced (about 3 tablespoons)
- 1¼ cups apple cider
- 2 tablespoons cider vinegar
- 2 teaspoons whole grain mustard
- 2 teaspoons minced fresh parsley leaves
- 2 tablespoons unsalted butter
  Table salt and ground black pepper

1. FOR THE CHICKEN: Adjust an oven rack to the middle position and heat the oven to 200 degrees. Halve the chicken horizontally, then cover the chicken halves with plastic wrap and use a meat pounder to pound the cutlets to an even ¼-inch thickness. Season both sides of each cutlet with salt and pepper. Heat 1 tablespoon of the oil in a 12-inch skillet over medium-high heat until just smoking. Place four cutlets in the skillet and cook without moving them until browned, about 2 minutes. Using a spatula, flip the cutlets and continue to cook until the

second sides are opaque, 15 to 20 seconds. Transfer to a large heatproof plate. Add the remaining 1 tablespoon oil to the now-empty skillet and repeat to cook the remaining cutlets. Cover the plate loosely with foil and transfer it to the oven to keep warm while making the sauce.

2. FOR THE SAUCE: Off the heat, add the oil and shallot to the hot skillet. Using residual heat, cook, stirring constantly, until softened, about 30 seconds. Set the skillet over medium-high heat and add the cider and vinegar. Bring to a simmer, scraping the pan bottom with a wooden spoon to loosen any browned bits. Simmer until reduced to ½ cup, 6 to 7 minutes. Off the heat, stir in the mustard and parsley; whisk in the butter 1 tablespoon at a time. Season with salt and pepper to taste and serve immediately with the cutlets.

BREADED CHICKEN CUTLETS

WHY THIS RECIPE WORKS: Breaded chicken cutlets, for all their apparent simplicity, can be problematic. Too often, they end up with either an underdone or burnt coating, which falls off the tasteless, rubbery chicken underneath. We wanted chicken cutlets with flavorful meat and a crunchy crust that would adhere nicely to the meat.

To ensure even cooking, we flattened the chicken breasts to ½ inch; thin enough to cook evenly, but thick enough to make a hearty, crisp cutlet. To prevent crust separation, we coated the chicken with flour, an egg and oil mixture, and flavorful, fresh bread crumbs. We then let them sit for five minutes to help set the crust. For the crispiest coating, we fried the cutlets in batches in vegetable oil. And for a tasty variation, we added Parmesan for a version of the classic Italian dish Chicken Milanese.

Breaded Chicken Cutlets

SERVES 4

If you'd rather not prepare fresh bread crumbs, use panko, the extra-crisp Japanese bread crumbs. The chicken is cooked in batches of two because the crust is noticeably more crisp if the pan is not overcrowded. Note that these cutlets are a bit thicker than others in the chapter and should not be halved horizontally.

- 4 (5 to 6-ounce) boneless, skinless chicken breasts, tenderloins removed and breasts trimmed
  Table salt and ground black pepper
- 3 slices high-quality white sandwich bread, torn into quarters

¾ cup unbleached all-purpose flour

2 large eggs

1 tablespoon plus ¾ cup vegetable oil

   Lemon wedges, for serving

1. Use a meat pounder to pound the chicken breasts to an even ½-inch thickness. Sprinkle the cutlets with salt and pepper and set aside. Set a large wire rack over a large baking sheet and set aside.

2. Adjust an oven rack to the lower-middle position, set a heatproof plate on the rack, and heat the oven to 200 degrees. Process the bread in a food processor until evenly fine-textured, 20 to 30 seconds. Transfer the crumbs to a pie plate or shallow dish. Spread the flour in a second plate. Beat the eggs with 1 tablespoon of the oil in a third plate.

3. Working with one cutlet at a time, dredge each cutlet in the flour, shaking off the excess. Using tongs, dip both sides of the cutlets in the egg mixture, allowing the excess to drip off. Dip both sides of the cutlets in the bread crumbs, pressing the crumbs with your fingers to form an even, cohesive coat. Place the breaded cutlets on the wire rack and allow the coating to dry for about 5 minutes.

4. Meanwhile, heat 6 tablespoons more oil in a 12-inch nonstick skillet over medium-high heat until shimmering but not smoking, about 2 minutes. Lay 2 cutlets gently in the skillet; cook until deep golden brown and crisp on the first side, gently pressing down on the cutlets with a metal spatula, about 2½ minutes. Using tongs, flip the cutlets, reduce the heat to medium, and continue to cook until the meat feels firm when pressed gently and the second side is deep golden brown and crisp, 2½ to 3 minutes longer. Line the warmed plate with a double layer of paper towels and set the cutlets on top; return the plate to the oven.

5. Discard the oil in the skillet and wipe the skillet clean with paper towels. Repeat step 4 using the remaining 6 tablespoons oil and remaining cutlets; serve with lemon wedges.

Chicken Milanese

Though Parmesan is classic in this dish, use Pecorino Romano if you prefer a more tangy flavor. Keep a close eye on the cutlets as they brown to make sure the cheese does not burn.

Follow the recipe for Breaded Chicken Cutlets, substituting ¼ cup finely grated Parmesan cheese for an equal amount of bread crumbs.

NUT-CRUSTED CHICKEN BREASTS

WHY THIS RECIPE WORKS: Adding chopped nuts to a coating is a great way to add robust flavor to otherwise lean and mild boneless, skinless chicken breasts. But nut coatings are often dense and leaden, and the rich flavor of the nuts rarely comes through. Using a combination of chopped almonds and panko bread crumbs—rather than all nuts—kept the coating light and crunchy, and the bread crumbs helped the coating adhere. Instead of frying the breaded breasts, we found that baking them in the oven was not only easier but also helped the meat stay juicy and ensured an even golden crust. But it wasn't until we cooked the coating in browned butter prior to breading the chicken that we finally achieved the deep nutty flavor we sought.

Nut-Crusted Chicken Breasts with Lemon and Thyme

SERVES 4

This recipe is best with almonds but works well with any type of nut. We prefer kosher salt in this recipe. If using table salt, reduce salt amounts by half.

4 (6 to 8-ounce) boneless, skinless chicken breasts, tenderloins removed and breasts trimmed
   Kosher salt

1 cup almonds, chopped coarse

4 tablespoons (½ stick) unsalted butter

1 medium shallot, minced (about 3 tablespoons)

1 cup panko bread crumbs

2 teaspoons finely grated zest from 1 lemon, zested lemon cut into wedges

1 teaspoon minced fresh thyme leaves

⅛ teaspoon cayenne pepper
1 cup unbleached all-purpose flour
3 large eggs
2 teaspoons Dijon mustard
¼ teaspoon ground black pepper

1. Adjust the oven rack to the lower-middle position and heat the oven to 350 degrees. Set a wire rack in a rimmed baking sheet. Pat the chicken dry with paper towels. Using a fork, poke the thickest half of the breasts 5 to 6 times and sprinkle with ½ teaspoon salt. Transfer the breasts to the prepared wire rack and refrigerate, uncovered, while preparing the coating.

2. Pulse the almonds in a food processor until they resemble coarse meal, about 20 pulses. Melt the butter in a 12-inch skillet over medium heat, swirling occasionally, until the butter is browned and releases a nutty aroma, 4 to 5 minutes. Add the shallot and ½ teaspoon salt and cook, stirring constantly, until just beginning to brown, about 3 minutes. Reduce the heat to medium-low, add the bread crumbs and ground almonds and cook, stirring often, until golden brown, 10 to 12 minutes. Transfer the panko mixture to a shallow dish or pie plate and stir in the lemon zest, thyme, and cayenne. Place the flour in a second dish. Lightly beat the eggs, mustard, and black pepper together in a third dish.

3. Pat the chicken dry with paper towels. Working with one breast at a time, dredge the chicken in the flour, shaking off the excess, then coat with the egg mixture, allowing the excess to drip off. Coat all sides of the breast with the panko mixture, pressing gently so that the crumbs adhere. Return the breaded breasts to the wire rack.

4. Bake until the chicken registers 160 degrees on an instant-read thermometer, 20 to 25 minutes. Let the chicken rest for 5 minutes before serving with the lemon wedges.

Nut-Crusted Chicken Breasts with Orange and Oregano

This version works particularly well with pistachios or hazelnuts.

Follow the recipe for Nut-Crusted Chicken Breasts with Lemon and Thyme, substituting 1 teaspoon orange zest for the lemon zest (reserving the orange wedges for the garnish) and 1 teaspoon oregano for the thyme.

STUFFED CHICKEN CUTLETS

WHY THIS RECIPE WORKS: Cutlets that are stuffed and breaded are special-occasion food. The filling moistens the chicken from the inside with a creamy, tasty sauce, while the crust makes a crunchy counterpoint. The problem is that these bundles can leak and getting the right proportion of filling to cutlet can be tricky. We wanted stuffed chicken cutlets with a creamy filling that wouldn't turn runny and flavors that would complement, not overpower, the chicken. And we wanted the crust to be crisp all over and completely seal in the filling so that none leaked out.

We pounded the chicken breasts thin so they rolled easily and cooked evenly. A combination of cream cheese and cheddar mixed with onion, garlic, and fresh thyme gave us a creamy, well-flavored filling. Thin-sliced ham added another layer of flavor to our cutlets. Before we breaded the cutlets, we chilled them in the refrigerator to help the filling set—this step prevented leaks during cooking. For perfectly cooked stuffed cutlets, we sautéed them just until brown, then moved them into the oven to finish cooking through.

Stuffed Chicken Cutlets with Ham and Cheddar
SERVES 4

To make slicing the chicken easier, freeze it for 15 minutes. The cutlets can be filled and rolled in advance, then refrigerated for up to 24 hours. To dry fresh bread crumbs, spread them out on a baking sheet and bake in a 200-degree oven, stirring occasionally, for 30 minutes. Removing some moisture from the crumbs cuts down on splattering when the breaded cutlets are pan-fried.

FILLING
1 tablespoon unsalted butter
1 small onion, minced
1 small garlic clove, minced or pressed through a garlic press (about ½ teaspoon)
4 ounces cream cheese, softened
1 teaspoon minced fresh thyme leaves
2 ounces cheddar cheese, shredded (about ½ cup)
  Table salt and ground black pepper
4 slices (about 4 ounces) thin-sliced cooked deli ham

CHICKEN
4 (5 to 6-ounce) boneless, skinless chicken breasts, tenderloins removed and breasts trimmed
  Table salt and ground black pepper
¾ cup unbleached all-purpose flour

2 large eggs

1 tablespoon plus ¾ cup vegetable oil

4 slices high-quality white sandwich bread, pulsed in a food processor to coarse crumbs and dried (see note)

1. FOR THE FILLING: Melt the butter in a medium skillet over low heat; add the onion and cook, stirring occasionally, until deep golden brown, 15 to 20 minutes. Stir in the garlic and cook until fragrant, about 30 seconds longer; set aside.

2. In a medium bowl and using an electric mixer, beat the cream cheese on medium speed until light and fluffy, about 1 minute. Stir in the onion mixture, thyme, and cheddar; season with salt and pepper to taste and set aside.

3. Following the photos, butterfly each chicken breast and pound between two sheets of plastic wrap to a uniform ¼-inch thickness. Pound the outer perimeter to ⅛ inch. Place the chicken cutlets, smooth side down, on a work surface and season with salt and pepper. Spread each cutlet with one-quarter of the cheese mixture, then place 1 slice of ham on top of the cheese, folding the ham as necessary to fit onto the surface of the cutlet. Roll up each cutlet from the tapered end, folding in the edges to form a neat cylinder. Refrigerate until the filling is firm, at least 1 hour.

4. FOR THE CHICKEN: Adjust an oven rack to the lower-middle position and heat the oven to 450 degrees. Set a large wire rack over a large baking sheet and set aside. Place the flour in a pie plate or shallow dish. Beat the eggs with 1 tablespoon of the oil in a second plate. Spread the bread crumbs in a third plate. Dredge 1 chicken roll in the flour, shaking off the excess, then coat with the egg mixture, allowing the excess to drip off. Coat all sides of the chicken roll with the bread crumbs, pressing gently so that the crumbs adhere. Place on the wire rack and repeat the flouring and breading with the remaining chicken. Allow the coating to dry for about 5 minutes. Transfer the chicken to a plate. Wipe the wire rack and baking sheet clean and set aside.

5. Heat the remaining ¾ cup oil in a 10-inch nonstick skillet over medium-high heat until shimmering, but not smoking. Using tongs, carefully add the chicken, seam side down, to the pan, and cook until medium golden brown, about 2 minutes. Turn each roll and cook until medium golden brown on all sides, 2 to 3 minutes longer. Transfer the chicken rolls, seam side down, to the now-clean wire rack on the baking sheet; bake until deep golden brown and an instant-read thermometer inserted into the center of a roll registers 160 to 165 degrees, about 15 minutes. Let stand for 5 minutes before slicing each roll crosswise on the diagonal with a serrated knife into five pieces; arrange on individual dinner plates and serve.

NOTES FROM THE TEST KITCHEN

BUTTERFLYING CHICKEN BREASTS

1. Starting on the thinnest side, butterfly the breast by slicing it lengthwise almost in half. Open the breast up to create a single flat breast. (To make cutlets, continue to cut through the meat until you have two cutlets.)

2. With the breast or cutlet in a zipper-lock bag or between sheets of plastic wrap, pound (starting at the center) to ¼-inch thickness. Pound the outer perimeter to ⅛ inch.

PAN-SEARED CHICKEN BREASTS

WHY THIS RECIPE WORKS: A boneless, skinless chicken breast doesn't have the bone and skin to protect it from the intensity of a hot pan. Inevitably, it emerges moist in the middle and dry at the edges, with an exterior that's leathery and tough. We wanted a boneless, skinless chicken breast that was every bit as flavorful, moist, and tender as its skin-on counterpart.

We decided to utilize a technique that we've used successfully in the test kitchen with thick-cut steaks (see page 140), where we gently parcook the meat in the oven and then sear it on the stovetop. First, we salted the chicken to help it retain more moisture as it cooked. To expedite the process we poked holes in the breasts, creating channels for the salt to reach the interior of the chicken as it parcooked. We then placed the breasts in a baking dish and covered it tightly with foil. In this enclosed environment, any moisture released by the chicken stayed trapped under the foil, keeping the exterior from drying out without becoming so overly wet that it couldn't brown quickly.

The next step was figuring out how to achieve a crisp, even crust on our parcooked breasts. We turned to a Chinese cooking technique called velveting, in which meat is dipped in a mixture of oil and cornstarch to create a thin protective layer that keeps the protein moist and tender, even when exposed to ultra-high heat. We replaced the oil with butter (for flavor) and mixed flour in with the cornstarch to avoid any pasty flavor. The coating helped the chicken make better contact with the hot skillet, creating a thin, browned, crisp veneer that kept the breast's exterior as moist as the interior.

Pan-Seared Chicken Breasts
SERVES 4

For the best results, buy similarly sized chicken breasts. If your breasts have the tenderloin attached, leave it in place and follow the upper range of baking time in step 1. For optimal texture, sear the chicken immediately after removing it from the oven.

    4 (6 to 8-ounce) boneless, skinless chicken breasts,
       trimmed (see note)
    1 teaspoon table salt
    1 tablespoon vegetable oil
    2 tablespoons unsalted butter, melted
    1 tablespoon unbleached all-purpose flour
    1 teaspoon cornstarch
    ½ teaspoon ground black pepper
    1 recipe Lemon and Chive Pan Sauce (optional;
       recipe follows)

1. Adjust an oven rack to the lower-middle position and heat the oven to 275 degrees. Use a fork to poke the thickest half of each breast five to six times, then sprinkle each breast with ¼ teaspoon salt. Place the chicken, skinned side down, in a 13 by 9-inch baking dish and cover tightly with foil. Bake until the chicken registers 145 to 150 degrees on an instant-read thermometer, 30 to 40 minutes.

2. Remove the chicken from the oven and transfer, skinned side up, to a paper towel–lined plate and pat dry with paper towels. Heat the oil in a 12-inch skillet over medium-high heat until smoking. While the pan is heating, whisk the butter, flour, cornstarch, and pepper together in a small bowl. Lightly brush the tops of the chicken with half of the butter mixture. Place the chicken in the skillet, coated side down, and cook until browned, 3 to 4 minutes. While the chicken browns, brush the second side with the remaining butter mixture. Using tongs, flip the chicken, reduce the heat to medium, and cook until the second side is browned and the chicken registers 160 to 165 degrees, 3 to 4 minutes. Transfer the chicken to a platter and let rest while preparing the pan sauce (if not making the pan sauce, let the chicken rest for 5 minutes before serving).

Lemon and Chive Pan Sauce
MAKES ABOUT ¾ CUP

    1 medium shallot, minced (about 3 tablespoons)
    1 teaspoon unbleached all-purpose flour
    1 cup low-sodium chicken broth
    1 tablespoon juice from 1 lemon
    1 tablespoon minced fresh chives
    1 tablespoon unsalted butter, chilled
       Table salt and ground black pepper

Add the shallot to the empty skillet and cook over medium heat until softened, about 2 minutes. Add the flour and cook, stirring constantly, for 30 seconds. Add the broth, increase the heat to medium-high, and bring to a simmer, scraping the pan bottom to loosen the browned bits. Simmer rapidly until reduced to ¾ cup, 3 to 5 minutes. Stir in any accumulated chicken juices, return to a simmer, and cook for 30 seconds. Off the heat, whisk in the lemon juice, chives, and butter; season with salt and pepper to taste. Spoon the sauce over the chicken and serve immediately.

CHICKEN KIEV

WHY THIS RECIPE WORKS: Chicken Kiev is a recipe that elevates the humdrum boneless, skinless chicken breast to star status. Traditionally, the dish is a crisp fried chicken breast encasing a buttery herb sauce that dramatically oozes out when knife meets fork. But today, the dish has sunk to the level of bad banquet food—a greasy, bread crumb–coated chicken breast whose meat is dry and chalky despite the butter filling. This was a dish that truly needed its greatness restored.

We found that butterflying the chicken breasts, then pounding them thin—and even thinner at the edges—helped created chicken bundles that wouldn't leak the butter filling. Instead of deep-frying the chicken as is traditionally done, we chose to oven-fry the chicken. This made for a crisp, rather than greasy, Kiev. Toasting the bread crumbs prior to breading the chicken helped mimic the flavorful, golden brown crust of the original. All we had left to do was to perk up the plain filling. Traditional recipes stuff the Kievs with butter spiked with nothing more than parsley and chives, but we found that minced shallots were more flavorful than chives and a small amount of minced tarragon added a pleasant hint of sweetness. A squeeze of lemon juice tamed the rich butter with a bit of acidity and Dijon mustard, whisked into the egg wash (for coating the chicken), provided another layer of flavor for a chicken Kiev that was anything but bland.

Chicken Kiev

SERVES 4

To make slicing the chicken easier, freeze it for 15 minutes. Unbaked, breaded chicken Kievs can be refrigerated overnight and baked the next day or frozen for up to one month. To cook frozen chicken Kievs, increase the baking time to 50 to 55 minutes (do not thaw the chicken).

HERB BUTTER

- 8 tablespoons (1 stick) unsalted butter, softened
- 1 tablespoon juice from 1 lemon
- 1 small shallot, minced (about 1 tablespoon)
- 1 tablespoon minced fresh parsley leaves
- ½ teaspoon minced fresh tarragon leaves
- ⅜ teaspoon table salt
- ⅛ teaspoon ground black pepper

CHICKEN

- 4 slices high-quality white sandwich bread, torn into quarters
  Table salt and ground black pepper
- 2 tablespoons vegetable oil
- 4 (7 to 8-ounce) boneless, skinless chicken breasts, tenderloins removed and breasts trimmed
- 1 cup unbleached all-purpose flour
- 3 large eggs, beaten
- 1 teaspoon Dijon mustard

1. FOR THE HERB BUTTER: Mix the ingredients in a medium bowl with a rubber spatula until thoroughly combined. Following the photo on page 90, form into a 2 by 3-inch rectangle on a sheet of plastic wrap; wrap tightly and refrigerate until firm, about 1 hour.

2. FOR THE CHICKEN: Adjust an oven rack to the lower-middle position and heat the oven to 300 degrees. Add half of the bread to a food processor and pulse until the bread is coarsely ground, about 16 pulses. Transfer the crumbs to a large bowl and repeat with the remaining bread. Add ⅛ teaspoon salt and ⅛ teaspoon pepper to the bread crumbs. Add the oil and toss until the crumbs are evenly coated. Spread the crumbs on a rimmed baking sheet and bake until golden brown and dry, about 25 minutes, stirring twice during the baking time. Cool to room temperature.

3. Following the photos on page 87, butterfly each chicken breast and pound between two sheets of plastic wrap to a uniform ¼-inch thickness. Pound the outer perimeter to ⅛ inch. Unwrap the herb butter and cut it into four rectangular pieces. Following the photos on page 90, place a chicken breast, cut side up, on a

SHAPING THE BUTTER FOR CHICKEN KIEV

Shape the butter mixture into a 2 by 3-inch rectangle on plastic wrap, then wrap tightly and refrigerate until firm, about 1 hour.

ASSEMBLING CHICKEN KIEV

1. Cut the butter into four rectangular pieces. Place one butter piece near the tapered end of the cutlet.

2. Roll up the tapered end of the chicken over the butter, then fold in the sides and continue rolling, pressing on the seam to seal. Repeat with the remaining butter pieces and cutlets. The chicken is now ready to be breaded.

work surface; season both sides with salt and pepper. Place one piece of butter in the center of the bottom half of the breast. Roll the bottom edge of the chicken over the butter, then fold in the sides and continue rolling to form a neat, tight package, pressing on the seam to seal. Repeat with the remaining butter and chicken. Refrigerate the chicken, uncovered, to allow the edges to seal, about 1 hour.

4. Adjust an oven rack to the middle position and heat the oven to 350 degrees. Set a large wire rack over a large baking sheet and set aside. Place the flour, eggs, and bread crumbs in separate pie plates or shallow dishes.

Season the flour with ¼ teaspoon salt and ⅛ teaspoon pepper; season the bread crumbs with ½ teaspoon salt and ¼ teaspoon pepper. Add the mustard to the eggs and whisk to combine. Dredge 1 chicken roll in the flour, shaking off the excess, then coat with the egg mixture, allowing the excess to drip off. Coat all sides of the chicken roll with the bread crumbs, pressing gently so that the crumbs adhere. Place on the wire rack set over a rimmed baking sheet. Repeat the flouring and breading with the remaining chicken rolls.

5. Bake until the center of the chicken registers 160 to 165 degrees on an instant-read thermometer, 40 to 45 minutes. Let rest for 5 minutes on the wire rack before serving.

OVEN-BARBECUED CHICKEN

WHY THIS RECIPE WORKS: Smoky, tender, and tangy, barbecued chicken is a real crowd pleaser. What do you do when a craving for this summertime favorite strikes in midwinter? Oven-barbecued chicken is the obvious solution. But while recipes for this dish abound, so do the disappointments: tough, rubbery, or unevenly cooked chicken in sauces ranging from pasty and candy-sweet to greasy, stale, thin, or commercial-tasting.

We started with boneless, skinless chicken breasts; the mild white meat is a perfect backdrop for the sauce. (Skinless breasts also meant that we wouldn't have to deal with the problem of flabby skin.) We lightly seared the chicken breasts in a skillet, then removed them from the pan to make a simple but flavorful barbecue sauce with pantry ingredients like grated onion, ketchup, Worcestershire sauce, mustard, molasses, and maple syrup. When we returned the chicken to the pan, the sauce clung nicely to the meat, thanks to the light searing we had given the chicken. We slid the chicken and sauce, still in the skillet, into the oven to cook through. Finally, for a nicely caramelized coating on the sauce, we finished the chicken under the high heat of the broiler. The result? Juicy chicken, thickly coated with a pleasantly tangy barbecue sauce.

Sweet and Tangy Oven-Barbecued Chicken

SERVES 4

Real maple syrup is preferable to imitation syrup, and "mild" or "original" molasses is preferable to darker, more bitter types. Use a rasp-style grater or the fine holes of a box grater to grate the onion. Make this recipe only in an in-oven broiler; do not use a drawer-type broiler. Broiling times may differ from one oven to another, so we urge you to check the chicken for doneness after only 3 minutes of broiling. You may also have to lower the oven rack if your broiler runs very hot. It is important to remove the chicken from the oven before switching to the broiler setting to allow the broiler element to come up to temperature.

- 1 cup ketchup
- 3 tablespoons molasses (see note)
- 3 tablespoons cider vinegar
- 2 tablespoons finely grated onion (see note)
- 2 tablespoons Worcestershire sauce
- 2 tablespoons Dijon mustard
- 2 tablespoons maple syrup (see note)
- 1 teaspoon chili powder
- ¼ teaspoon cayenne pepper
- 4 (5 to 6-ounce) boneless, skinless chicken breasts, tenderloins removed and breasts trimmed
  Table salt and ground black pepper
- 1 tablespoon vegetable oil

1. Adjust an oven rack to the upper-middle position, about 5 inches from the heating element, and heat the oven to 325 degrees. Whisk the ketchup, molasses, vinegar, onion, Worcestershire sauce, mustard, maple syrup, chili powder, and cayenne together in a small bowl; set aside. Pat the chicken dry with paper towels and season with salt and pepper.

2. Heat the oil in a 12-inch ovensafe skillet over high heat until just smoking. Add the chicken, smooth side down, and cook until very light golden, 1 to 2 minutes; using tongs, turn the chicken and cook until very light golden on the second side, 1 to 2 minutes longer. Transfer the chicken to a plate and set aside.

3. Discard the fat in the skillet; off the heat, add the sauce mixture and, using a wooden spoon, scrape up the browned bits on the bottom of the skillet. Simmer the sauce over medium heat, stirring frequently with a heatproof spatula, until the sauce is thick and glossy and a spatula leaves a clear trail in the sauce, about 4 minutes. Off the heat, return the chicken to the skillet and turn to coat thickly with the sauce; set the chicken pieces smooth side up and spoon extra sauce over each piece to create a thick coating.

4. Place the skillet in the oven and cook until the thickest part of the breasts registers 130 degrees on an instant-read thermometer, 8 to 12 minutes. Remove the skillet from the oven, turn the oven to broil, and heat for 5 minutes. Once the broiler is heated, place the skillet back in the oven and broil the chicken until the thickest part of the breasts registers 160 to 165 degrees, 3 to 8 minutes longer. Transfer the chicken to a platter and let rest for 5 minutes. Meanwhile, whisk the sauce in the skillet to recombine and transfer to a small bowl. Serve the chicken, passing the extra sauce separately.

PICNIC CHICKEN

WHY THIS RECIPE WORKS: Cold barbecued picnic chicken presents numerous challenges: the meat may be dry, the skin flabby, and the chicken covered with a sticky, messy sauce. We wanted a recipe for chicken that would be easy to pack (and eat) for a picnic, chicken with moist, tender meat flavored with robust spicy and slightly sweet barbecue flavors.

We first threw out the idea of a sticky sauce, substituting a robust dry rub (brown sugar, chili powder, paprika, and pepper) that reproduced the flavors of a good barbecue sauce. We partly solved the flabby skin problem by diligently trimming the chicken pieces as well as by slitting the skin before cooking (which allowed the excess fat to render). But the skin was still flabby from the moisture contributed by our traditional brine (we brine most poultry for better flavor and moister meat). We tried eliminating the brine, adding salt to the rub, and applying it the night before. Sure enough, when we oven-roasted the chicken the next day, we found the meat well seasoned throughout and very moist. Best of all, the skin was flavorful, delicate, and definitely not flabby.

Spice-Rubbed Picnic Chicken

SERVES 8

If you plan to serve the chicken later on the same day that you cook it, refrigerate it immediately after it has cooled, then let it come back to room temperature before serving. On the breast pieces, we use toothpicks to secure the skin, which otherwise shrinks considerably in the oven, leaving the meat exposed and prone to drying out. We think the extra effort is justified, but you can omit this step. This recipe halves easily.

    5   pounds bone-in, skin-on chicken parts (split breasts, thighs, drumsticks, or a mix, with breasts cut into 3 pieces or halved if small), trimmed of excess fat and skin
    3   tablespoons brown sugar
    2   tablespoons chili powder
    2   tablespoons sweet paprika
    2   tablespoons kosher salt
    2   teaspoons ground black pepper
¼–½   teaspoon cayenne pepper

1. Use a sharp knife to make two or three short slashes in the skin of each piece of chicken, taking care not to cut into the meat. Combine the sugar, chili powder, paprika, salt, and pepper in a small bowl and mix thoroughly. Coat the chicken pieces with the spices, gently lifting the skin to distribute the spice rub underneath but leaving it attached to the chicken. Transfer the chicken, skin side up, to a wire rack set over a large, rimmed baking sheet, lightly tent it with foil, and refrigerate for at least 6 hours or up to 24 hours.

2. If desired, secure the skin of each breast piece with two or three toothpicks placed near the edges of the skin (see note).

3. Adjust an oven rack to the middle position and heat the oven to 425 degrees. Roast the chicken until the thickest part of the smallest piece registers 140 degrees on an instant-read thermometer, 15 to 20 minutes. Increase the oven temperature to 500 degrees and continue roasting until the chicken is browned and crisp and the thickest part of the breasts registers 160 to 165 degrees, 5 to 8 minutes longer, removing the pieces from the oven and transferring them to a clean wire rack as they finish cooking. Continue to roast the thighs and/or drumsticks, if using, until the thickest part of the meat registers 175 degrees, about 5 minutes longer. Remove from the oven, transfer the chicken to a rack, and cool completely before refrigerating or serving.

PAN-ROASTED CHICKEN BREASTS

WHY THIS RECIPE WORKS: Cooking bone-in, skin-on chicken breasts can be a challenge. They are difficult to sauté or cook through on the stovetop because of their uneven shape. We wanted to find a method that would produce crisp skin, moist meat, and a quick, flavorful pan sauce.

We chose whole breasts, then split them ourselves to control their size. We brined the breasts for maximum moistness and then seared them on the stovetop before letting them cook through in a 450-degree oven. For the pan sauce, we sautéed minced shallot in the same skillet used to cook the chicken, so we could take advantage of the flavorful browned bits left in the pan. We deglazed the pan with chicken broth and vermouth, then added fresh sage for a sauce with deep herbal flavor. Butter whisked into the sauce after it had reduced lent the sauce body and richness—a perfect partner to our moist, juicy chicken.

NOTES FROM THE TEST KITCHEN

TRIMMING SPLIT CHICKEN BREASTS

Using kitchen shears, trim off the rib sections from each breast, following the vertical line of fat from the tapered end of the breast up to the socket where the wing was attached.

Pan-Roasted Chicken Breasts with Sage-Vermouth Sauce

SERVES 4

We prefer to split whole chicken breasts ourselves because store-bought split chicken breasts are often sloppily butchered. However, if you prefer to purchase split chicken breasts, try to choose 10 to 12-ounce pieces with skin intact. If split breasts are of different sizes, check the smaller ones a few minutes early to see if they are cooking more quickly, and remove them from the skillet when they are done.

CHICKEN

- ½ cup table salt
- 2 (1½-pound) whole bone-in, skin-on chicken breasts, split in half along breast bone and trimmed of rib sections
  Ground black pepper
- 1 teaspoon vegetable oil

SAGE-VERMOUTH SAUCE

- 1 large shallot, minced (about 4 tablespoons)
- ¾ cup low-sodium chicken broth
- ½ cup dry vermouth
- 4 medium fresh sage leaves, each leaf torn in half
- 3 tablespoons unsalted butter, cut into 3 pieces
  Table salt and ground black pepper

1. FOR THE CHICKEN: Dissolve the salt in 2 quarts cold water in a large container; submerge the chicken in the brine, cover, and refrigerate for about 30 minutes. Rinse the chicken well and pat dry with paper towels. Season the chicken with pepper.

2. Adjust an oven rack to the lowest position and heat the oven to 450 degrees.

3. Heat the oil in a 12-inch ovensafe skillet over medium-high heat until beginning to smoke. Brown the chicken, skin side down, until deep golden, about 5 minutes; turn the chicken and brown until golden on the second side, about 3 minutes longer. Turn the chicken skin side down and place the skillet in the oven. Roast until the thickest part of the breasts registers 160 to 165 degrees on an instant-read thermometer, 15 to 18 minutes. Transfer the chicken to a platter, and let it rest while making the sauce. (If you're not making the sauce, let the chicken rest for 5 minutes before serving.)

4. FOR THE SAUCE: Using a potholder to protect your hands from the hot skillet handle, pour off all but 1 teaspoon of the fat from the skillet; add the shallot, then set the skillet over medium-high heat and cook, stirring frequently, until the shallot is softened, about 1½ minutes. Add the chicken broth, vermouth, and sage; increase the heat to high and simmer rapidly, scraping the skillet bottom with a wooden spoon to loosen the browned bits, until slightly thickened and reduced to about ¾ cup, about 5 minutes. Pour the accumulated chicken juices into the skillet, reduce the heat to medium, and whisk in the butter 1 piece at a time; season with salt and pepper to taste and discard the sage. Spoon the sauce around the chicken breasts and serve immediately.

PERFECT ROAST CHICKEN

WHY THIS RECIPE WORKS: Most home-cooked chickens are either grossly overcooked or so underdone that they resemble an avian version of steak tartare. We wanted a method for producing perfectly roasted chicken, where the white meat cooks up juicy and tender, but with a hint of chew, and the dark meat is fully cooked, all the way to the bone.

For maximum juiciness and well-seasoned meat, we brined the chicken. And for further flavor and a moisture boost to the delicate breast, we rubbed butter under the skin and over the breast. Trussing and continuous basting both proved unnecessary for this ideal chicken. In fact, basting turned its skin greasy and chewy. We had hoped that the bird wouldn't have to be turned while cooking, but we found it was a must for even cooking. In the end, we found that roasting the bird for 15 minutes on each side and then putting it on its back rendered perfectly cooked white and dark meat as well as golden, crunchy skin.

Perfect Roast Chicken

SERVES 2 TO 3

If using a kosher chicken, skip the brining process and begin with step 2. We recommend using a V-rack to roast the chicken. If you don't have a V-rack, set the bird on a regular roasting rack and use balls of aluminum foil to keep the roasting chicken propped up on its side.

- ½ cup table salt
- ½ cup sugar
- 1 (3½ to 4-pound) whole chicken, giblets discarded (see note)
- 2 tablespoons unsalted butter, softened
- 1 tablespoon olive oil
  Ground black pepper

1. Dissolve the salt and sugar in 2 quarts cold water in a large container. Submerge the chicken in the brine, cover, and refrigerate for 1 hour.

2. Adjust an oven rack to the lower-middle position, place a roasting pan on the rack, and heat the oven to 400 degrees. Coat a V-rack with vegetable oil spray and set aside (see note). Remove the chicken from the brine, rinse well, and pat dry with paper towels.

3. Following the photo, use your fingers to gently loosen the center portion of the skin covering each breast; place the butter under the skin, directly on the meat in the center of each breast. Gently press on the skin to distribute the butter over the meat. Tuck the wings behind the back. Rub the skin with the oil, season with pepper, and place the chicken, wing side up, on the prepared V-rack. Place the V-rack in the preheated roasting pan and roast for 15 minutes.

4. Remove the roasting pan from the oven and, using two large wads of paper towels, rotate the chicken so that the opposite wing side is facing up. Return the roasting pan to the oven and roast for another 15 minutes.

NOTES FROM THE TEST KITCHEN

APPLYING BUTTER UNDER THE SKIN

Loosen the skin on the breasts and thighs of the chicken by sliding your fingers between the skin and meat.

---

5. Using two large wads of paper towels, rotate the chicken again so that the breast side is facing up and continue to roast until the thickest part of the breasts registers 160 to 165 degrees and the thickest part of the thighs registers 175 degrees on an instant-read thermometer, 20 to 25 minutes longer. Transfer the chicken to a carving board and let rest for 10 minutes. Carve the chicken and serve.

WEEKNIGHT ROAST CHICKEN

WHY THIS RECIPE WORKS: Roast chicken is often described as a simple dish, and it is, at least in terms of flavor—when done properly, the rich flavor and juicy meat of the chicken need little adornment. But the actual process of preparing and roasting chicken is anything but simple; recipes often call for complicated trussing techniques and rotating the bird multiple times during the course of cooking. And the most time-consuming part is salting or brining the bird, a step that ensures juiciness and well-seasoned meat. We wanted to find a way to get roast chicken on the table in just an hour without sacrificing flavor. After systematically testing the various components and steps of a typical recipe, we found we could just tie the legs together and tuck the wings underneath. We also discovered we could skip both the V-rack and flipping the chicken by using a preheated skillet and placing the chicken breast side up; this gave the thighs a jump-start on cooking. Starting the chicken in a 450-degree oven and then turning the oven off while the chicken finished cooking slowed the evaporation of juices, ensuring moist, tender meat.

Weeknight Roast Chicken

SERVES 4

We prefer to use a 3½ to 4-pound chicken for this recipe; however this method can be used to cook a larger chicken. If roasting a larger bird, increase the cooking time in step 2 to 35 to 40 minutes. If you choose to serve the chicken with one of the pan sauces that follow, don't wash the skillet after removing the chicken. Prepare the pan sauce while resting the chicken.

- 1 tablespoon kosher salt
- ½ teaspoon ground black pepper
- 1 (3½ to 4-pound) whole chicken, giblets removed and discarded
- 1 tablespoon olive oil
- 1 recipe pan sauce (optional; recipes follow)

1. Adjust an oven rack to the middle position, place a 12-inch ovensafe skillet on the rack, and heat the oven to 450 degrees. Combine the salt and pepper in a bowl. Pat the chicken dry with paper towels and rub the entire surface with the oil. Sprinkle evenly all over with the salt mixture and rub in the mixture with your hands to coat evenly. Tie the legs together with twine and tuck the wing tips behind the back.

2. Transfer the chicken, breast side up, to the preheated skillet in the oven. Roast the chicken until the thickest part of the breasts registers 120 degrees and the thickest part of the thighs registers 135 degrees on an instant-read thermometer, 25 to 35 minutes. Turn off the oven and leave the chicken in the oven until the breasts register 160 degrees and the thighs register 175 degrees, 25 to 35 minutes.

3. Transfer the chicken to a carving board and rest, uncovered, for 20 minutes. Carve and serve with pan sauce.

Tarragon-Lemon Pan Sauce
MAKES ABOUT ¾ CUP

- 1 medium shallot, minced (about 3 tablespoons)
- 1 cup low-sodium chicken broth
- 2 teaspoons Dijon mustard
- 2 tablespoons unsalted butter
- 2 teaspoons chopped fresh tarragon leaves
- 2 teaspoons juice from 1 lemon
  Ground black pepper

While the chicken rests, remove all but 1 tablespoon of fat from the now-empty skillet using a large kitchen spoon, leaving any browned bits and juices in the skillet. Place the skillet over medium-high heat, add the shallot, and cook until softened, about 2 minutes. Stir in the chicken broth and mustard, scraping the skillet bottom with a wooden spoon to loosen the browned bits. Cook until reduced to ¾ cup, about 3 minutes. Off the heat, whisk in the butter, tarragon and lemon juice. Season with pepper to taste; cover and keep warm.

Thyme-Sherry Vinegar Pan Sauce
MAKES ABOUT ¾ CUP

- 1 medium shallot, minced (about 3 tablespoons)
- 2 medium garlic cloves, minced or pressed through a garlic press (about 2 teaspoons)
- 2 teaspoons chopped fresh thyme leaves

NOTES FROM THE TEST KITCHEN

CARVING A WHOLE CHICKEN

1. Cut the chicken where the leg meets the breast, then pull the leg quarter away. Push up on the joint, then carefully cut through it to remove the leg quarter.

2. Cut through the joint that connects the drumstick to the thigh. Repeat on the second side to remove the other leg.

3. Cut down along one side of the breastbone, pulling the breast meat away from the bone.

4. Remove the wing from the breast by cutting through the wing joint. Slice the breast into attractive slices.

- 1 cup low-sodium chicken broth
- 2 teaspoons Dijon mustard
- 2 tablespoons unsalted butter
- 2 teaspoons sherry vinegar
  Ground black pepper

While the chicken rests, remove all but 1 tablespoon of fat from the now-empty skillet, leaving any browned bits and juices in the skillet. Place the skillet over medium-high heat, add the shallot, garlic, and thyme, and cook until softened, about 2 minutes. Stir in the chicken broth and mustard, scraping the skillet bottom with a wooden spoon to loosen the browned bits. Cook until reduced to ¾ cup, about 3 minutes. Off the heat, whisk in the butter and vinegar. Season with pepper to taste; cover and keep warm.

CRISP-SKINNED ROAST CHICKEN

WHY THIS RECIPE WORKS: During roasting, juices and rendered fat can accumulate beneath the chicken skin and turn it wet and flabby. We wanted a juicy roasted chicken with skin that would crackle against your teeth with every bite.

A five-step process was the solution. We first cut an incision down the chicken's back to allow fat to escape and then loosened the skin from the thighs and breasts, poking holes in the fat deposits to allow multiple channels for excess fat and juices to escape. And since skin can't brown until all the surface moisture evaporates, we added baking powder to our salt rub. This helped dehydrate the skin and enhanced the effects of our fourth step: overnight air-drying. Finally, we roasted the bird at high heat to speed the browning. To prevent our kitchen from filling with smoke from the pan drippings, we placed a sheet of foil with holes punched into it under the chicken to shield the rendered fat from direct oven heat. The final result? Roast chicken with tender, juicy meat and the crispest skin ever.

Crisp-Skinned Roast Chicken

SERVES 2 TO 3

Do not brine the bird; it will prevent the skin from becoming crisp. The sheet of foil between the roasting pan and V-rack will keep the drippings from burning and smoking.

- 1 (3½ to 4-pound) whole chicken, giblets discarded (see note)
- 1 tablespoon kosher salt or 1½ teaspoons table salt
- 1 teaspoon baking powder
- ½ teaspoon ground black pepper

1. Place the chicken, breast side down, on a work surface. Following the photos, use the tip of a sharp knife to make four 1-inch incisions along the back of the chicken. Using your fingers or the handle of a wooden spoon, separate

PREPARING CRISP ROAST CHICKEN

1. Cut incisions in the skin along the chicken's back for the fat to escape.

2. Loosen the skin from the thighs and breast to allow rendering fat to trickle out the openings.

3. Poke holes in the skin of the breast and thighs to create additional channels for fat and juices to escape.

4. Rub a mixture of baking powder and salt into the skin and air-dry the chicken in the refrigerator to help the skin crisp and brown.

the skin from the thighs and breast, being careful not to break the skin. Using a metal skewer, poke 15 to 20 holes in the fat deposits on top of the breast halves and thighs. Tuck the wings behind the back.

2. Combine the salt, baking powder, and pepper in a small bowl. Pat the chicken dry with paper towels and sprinkle all over with the salt mixture. Rub in the mixture with your hands, coating the entire surface evenly. Set the chicken, breast side up, in a V-rack set on a rimmed baking sheet and refrigerate, uncovered, for at least 12 hours or up to 24 hours.

3. Adjust an oven rack to the lowest position and heat the oven to 450 degrees. Using a paring knife, poke 20 holes about 1½ inches apart in a 16 by 12-inch piece of foil. Place the foil loosely in a large roasting pan. Flip the chicken so the breast side faces down, and set the V-rack in the roasting pan on top of the foil. Roast the chicken for 25 minutes.

4. Remove the roasting pan from the oven. Using two large wads of paper towels, rotate the chicken breast side up. Continue to roast until the thickest part of the breasts registers 135 degrees on an instant-read thermometer, 15 to 25 minutes.

5. Increase the oven temperature to 500 degrees. Continue to roast until the skin is golden brown and crisp and the thickest part of the breasts registers 160 to 165 degrees and the thickest part of the thighs registers 175 degrees, 10 to 20 minutes.

6. Transfer the chicken to a carving board and let rest, uncovered, for 20 minutes. Carve the chicken following the illustrations on page 95 and serve immediately.

CLASSIC ROAST LEMON CHICKEN

WHY THIS RECIPE WORKS: Simple as it sounds, roast lemon chicken can disappoint if the chicken is dry and uninteresting, tastes nothing like lemon, or, even worse, is bursting with citric acidity. The accompanying pan sauce usually suffers a similar fate: bland and lacking lemon or overly harsh. We wanted a way to bring out the full potential of this dish. The chicken should be evenly roasted and moist, with crispy skin, and the lemon flavor should be bright and pure, with no trace of bitterness.

We brined the chicken for extra juiciness. Then we filled the chicken cavity with a cut-up lemon and garlic cloves. To further ensure a juicy bird, we found that the roasting technique was key. We started the chicken breast side down in a moderately hot oven, then flipped it breast side up, added some broth to prevent the drippings from burning, and raised the oven temperature for the remainder of the cooking time. Once the chicken was cooked, we cut it into four pieces and broiled the pieces to get an evenly crisped skin. For the truest lemon flavor, we added a squirt of fresh lemon juice to a simple pan sauce of chicken broth, butter, and fresh herbs.

Classic Roast Lemon Chicken

SERVES 3 TO 4

If using a kosher chicken, skip the brining process and begin with step 2. Broiling the fully roasted and quartered chicken skin side up as it sits in a shallow pool of sauce crisps and browns the skin while keeping the meat succulent. If you decide to skip the broiling step, go directly from quartering the chicken to finishing the sauce with lemon juice, butter, and herbs.

½   cup table salt
1   (3½ to 4-pound) whole chicken, giblets discarded
2   lemons
6   medium garlic cloves, crushed and peeled
4   tablespoons (½ stick) unsalted butter, 2 tablespoons melted and 2 tablespoons chilled and cut into 2 pieces
     Ground black pepper
1¾ cups low-sodium chicken broth
1   tablespoon minced fresh parsley leaves
1   teaspoon minced fresh thyme leaves

1. Dissolve the salt in 2 quarts cold water in a large container. Submerge the chicken in the brine, cover, and refrigerate for 1 hour. Remove the chicken from the brine, rinse well, and pat dry with paper towels.

2. Adjust an oven rack to the lower-middle position; heat the oven to 375 degrees. Spray a V-rack with vegetable oil spray and set in a roasting pan.

3. Cut 1 of the lemons lengthwise into quarters. Place the lemon quarters and garlic in the cavity of the chicken. Brush the breast side of the chicken with 1 tablespoon of the melted butter and season generously with pepper. Place the chicken, breast side down, in the V-rack, then

SHOPPING FOR CHICKEN—WHAT YOU NEED TO KNOW

Every good chicken dish starts with high-quality, fresh chicken. But there are an overwhelming number of choices at the super-market—so how do you recognize superior poultry? Here are a few tips the test kitchen has learned over time. If you're buying bone-less, skinless chicken breasts, you should be aware that breasts of different sizes are often packaged together, and it's usually impossible to tell what you've bought until you've opened the package. If possible, buy chicken breasts individually. If that isn't an option, pound the thicker ends of the larger pieces of chicken to match those of the smaller pieces. Some breasts will still be larger than others, but pounding will help make their thickness the same and ensure even cooking. As for chicken parts—say for making a dish such as fried chicken or stew—we prefer to butcher our own birds rather than buy pack-aged parts. Not only is this a less expensive option, but the parts will be consistently sized. (We also use this approach with stew meat—there's no guarantee that packaged stew meat is going to be cut into even-sized pieces or be from the same cut or even the same cow!) And what about ground chicken? Prepackaged ground chicken is made from either dark or white meat or a mix of the two. Higher-end markets often grind their chicken to order, so the choice is yours. In most of our testing, we found ground white meat chicken to be exceedingly dry and almost void of flavor. The dark meat was more flavorful and juicy due to its higher fat content. For our recommended brands of chicken, see page 740.

brush the back with the remaining 1 tablespoon melted butter and season generously with pepper.

4. Roast the chicken for 40 minutes. Remove the roast-ing pan from the oven; increase the oven temperature to 450 degrees. Using two large wads of paper towels, rotate the chicken breast side up; add 1 cup of the chicken broth to the roasting pan. Return the roasting pan to the oven and continue roasting until the thickest part of the breasts registers 160 to 165 degrees and the thickest part of the thighs registers 175 degrees on an instant-read thermome-ter, 35 to 40 minutes longer. Remove the roasting pan from the oven; tip the V-rack to let the juices from the chicken cavity run into the roasting pan. Transfer the chicken to a

carving board and let rest, uncovered, while making the sauce. Remove the V-rack from the roasting pan.

5. Adjust the oven rack to the upper-middle position and heat the broiler. Skim the fat from the drippings in the roasting pan, add the remaining ¾ cup chicken broth, and set the roasting pan on a burner over high heat. Simmer the liquid, scraping the pan bottom with a wooden spoon to loosen the browned bits, until reduced to ½ cup, about 4 minutes; set aside off the heat.

6. Discard the lemons and garlic from the chicken cavity. Following photos 1 and 3 on page 95, cut the chicken into quarters. Pour the accumulated chicken juices into the roasting pan, then place the chicken quarters, skin side up, into the sauce in the roasting pan; broil the chicken until the skin is crisp and deep golden brown, 3 to 5 minutes. Transfer the chicken to a serving platter.

7. Halve the remaining lemon lengthwise; squeeze the juice of one half into the roasting pan; cut the remaining half into four wedges and set aside. Whisk the remaining 2 tablespoons butter into the sauce until combined; stir in the parsley and thyme. Season with salt and pepper to taste. Serve the chicken with the pan sauce and lemon wedges.

GLAZED ROAST CHICKEN

WHY THIS RECIPE WORKS: Glazed chicken might sound simple but actually turns up a host of troubles, as the problems inherent in roasting chicken (dry breast meat, flabby skin, big deposits of fat under the skin) are com-pounded by the glaze (won't stick to the meat, burns in patches, introduces moisture to already flabby skin). We wanted evenly glazed roast chicken with crisp skin and moist, tender meat.

We started with a large roaster chicken. We separated the skin from the meat and pricked holes in the fat deposits to allow rendered fat to escape, then rubbed it with salt and baking powder—to dehydrate the skin and help it to crisp—and we roasted the chicken straddled on top of a beer can set in a roasting pan (a popular grill-ing technique). The technique seemed like a winner— no awkward flipping, glazing every nook and cranny was easy, and fat dripped freely out of the bird. But cutting into the chicken revealed that the breast, now exposed to the high oven heat for the entire cooking time, was dry and tough. Two techniques solved these problems. First, we rested the chicken before putting it in the oven for a final blast of heat—the skin came out crisper than before and the breast meat was perfectly cooked. Second, we thickened our glaze with a little cornstarch and reduced it to a syrupy consistency, then applied it before the final five minutes of roasting. The result? Moist, tender chicken with deeply flavorful, crisp, glazed skin.

Glazed Roast Chicken

SERVES 4 TO 6

For best results, use a 16-ounce can of beer. A larger can will work, but avoid using a 12-ounce can, as it will not support the weight of the chicken. A vertical roaster can be used in place of the beer can, but we recommend only using a model that can be placed in a roasting pan. Taste your marmalade before using it; if it is overly sweet, reduce the amount of maple syrup in the glaze by 2 tablespoons. Trappist Seville Orange Marmalade is the test kitchen's preferred brand.

CHICKEN

- 1 (6 to 7-pound) whole chicken, giblets discarded
- 2½ teaspoons table salt
- 1 teaspoon baking powder
- 1 teaspoon ground black pepper
- 1 (16-ounce) can beer (see note)

GLAZE

- 1 tablespoon water
- 1 teaspoon cornstarch
- ½ cup maple syrup
- ½ cup orange marmalade (see note)
- ¼ cup cider vinegar
- 2 tablespoons unsalted butter
- 2 tablespoons Dijon mustard
- 1 teaspoon ground black pepper

1. FOR THE CHICKEN: Place the chicken, breast side down, on a work surface. Following the photos on page 96, use the tip of a sharp knife to make four 1-inch incisions along the back of the chicken. Using your fingers or the handle of a wooden spoon, separate the skin from the thighs and breast, being careful not to break the skin. Using a metal skewer, poke 15 to 20 holes in the fat deposits on top of the breast halves and thighs. Tuck the wings behind the back.

2. Combine the salt, baking powder, and pepper in a small bowl. Pat the chicken dry with paper towels and sprinkle evenly all over with the salt mixture. Rub in the mixture with your hands, coating the entire surface evenly. Set the chicken, breast side up, on a rimmed baking sheet and refrigerate, uncovered, for 30 to 60 minutes. Mean-

while, adjust an oven rack to the lowest position and heat the oven to 325 degrees.

3. Open the beer can and pour out (or drink) about half of the liquid. Spray the can lightly with vegetable oil spray and place in the middle of a roasting pan. Slide the chicken over the can so the drumsticks reach down to the bottom of the can, the chicken stands upright, and the breast is perpendicular to the bottom of the pan. Roast until the skin starts to turn golden and the thickest part of the breasts registers 140 degrees on an instant-read thermometer, 75 to 90 minutes. Carefully remove the chicken and pan from the oven and increase the oven temperature to 500 degrees.

4. FOR THE GLAZE: While the chicken cooks, stir the water and cornstarch together in a small bowl until no lumps remain; set aside. Bring the remaining glaze ingredients to a simmer in a medium saucepan over medium-high heat. Cook, stirring occasionally, until reduced to ¾ cup, 6 to 8 minutes. Slowly whisk the cornstarch mixture into the glaze. Return to a simmer and cook for 1 minute. Remove the pan from the heat.

5. When the oven is heated to 500 degrees, place 1½ cups water in the bottom of the roasting pan and return to the oven. Roast until the entire chicken skin is browned and crisp, the thickest part of the breasts registers 160 to 165 degrees, and the thickest part of the thighs registers 175 degrees on an instant-read thermometer, 24 to 30 minutes. Check the chicken halfway through roasting; if the top is becoming too dark, place a 7-inch square piece of foil over the neck and wingtips of the chicken and continue to roast (if the pan begins to smoke and sizzle, add ½ cup water to the roasting pan).

6. Brush the chicken with ¼ cup of the glaze and continue to roast until browned and sticky, about 5 minutes. (If the glaze has become stiff, return to low heat to soften.) Carefully remove the chicken from the oven, transfer the chicken, still on the can, to a carving board, and brush with ¼ cup more glaze. Let rest for 20 minutes.

7. While the chicken rests, strain the juices from the pan through a fine-mesh strainer into a fat separator; allow the liquid to settle for 5 minutes. Whisk ½ cup juices into the remaining ¼ cup glaze in a saucepan and set over low heat. Using a kitchen towel, carefully lift the chicken off the can and onto a platter or carving board. Following the photos on page 95, carve the chicken, adding any accumulated juices to the sauce. Serve, passing the sauce separately.

STOVETOP ROAST CHICKEN

WHY THIS RECIPE WORKS: Roasting chicken in the oven is the usual route to crisp skin and moist meat, but sometimes you want your oven for something else. Cooking chicken pieces in a skillet easily yields a flavorful pan sauce, but the skin on the chicken is often flabby and the meat unevenly cooked. We wanted to combine the best aspects of both roasted and skillet-cooked chicken. Our goals were ambitious: crisp, golden skin; evenly cooked, juicy meat; and a flavorful sauce—all produced in a single large skillet that would never go into the oven.

We started with a standard set of mixed chicken parts: four breast halves, two drumsticks, and two thighs. We tested a variety of approaches to achieve moist meat and crisp skin, but ran into numerous problems. One method—steaming the raw chicken in broth and then searing it in a hot pan, skin side down—crisped the skin but caused it to shrink dramatically. To avoid this, we found that searing the chicken first and then steaming was the answer. After steaming, we poured off all the liquid from the pan (reserving it to use for the pan sauce) and returned the chicken to sear again skin side down. This second searing produced the deep, russet-hued crisp skin we had hoped for. After removing the finished chicken, we set out to make our pan sauce with shallot, lemon, and fresh herbs. This quick pan sauce was the perfect complement to our tender roast chicken with crisp skin.

Stovetop Roast Chicken with Lemon-Herb Sauce

SERVES 4

Use a splatter screen when browning the chicken.

CHICKEN
- 3½ pounds bone-in, skin-on chicken pieces (split breasts cut in half, drumsticks, and/or thighs), trimmed
  Table salt and ground black pepper
- 1 tablespoon vegetable oil
- ¾–1¼ cups low-sodium chicken broth

LEMON-HERB SAUCE
- 1 teaspoon vegetable oil
- 1 medium shallot, minced (about 3 tablespoons)
- 1 teaspoon unbleached all-purpose flour
- 1½ tablespoons minced fresh parsley leaves
- 1½ tablespoons minced fresh chives
- 1 tablespoon juice from 1 lemon
- 1 tablespoon unsalted butter, chilled
  Table salt and ground black pepper

1. FOR THE CHICKEN: Pat the chicken dry with paper towels and season with salt and pepper. Heat 2 teaspoons of the oil in a 12-inch nonstick skillet over medium-high heat until just smoking. Add the chicken pieces skin side down and cook without moving until golden brown, 5 to 8 minutes.

2. Using tongs, flip the chicken pieces skin side up. Reduce the heat to medium-low, add ¾ cup of the broth to the skillet, cover, and cook until the thickest part of the breasts registers 155 degrees and the thickest part of the thighs/drumsticks registers 170 degrees on an instant-read thermometer, 10 to 16 minutes. Transfer the chicken to a plate, skin side up.

3. Pour off the liquid from the skillet into a 2-cup measuring cup and reserve. Wipe out the skillet with paper towels. Add the remaining 1 teaspoon oil to the skillet and heat over medium-high heat until shimmering. Return the chicken pieces skin side down and cook undisturbed until the skin is deep golden brown and crisp, the thickest part of the breasts registers 160 to 165 degrees, and the thickest part of the thighs/drumsticks registers 175 degrees, 4 to 7 minutes. Transfer to a serving platter and tent loosely with foil. Using a spoon, skim any fat from the reserved cooking liquid and add enough broth to measure ¾ cup.

4. FOR THE SAUCE: Heat the oil in the now-empty skillet over low heat. Add the shallot and cook, stirring frequently, until softened, about 2 minutes. Add the flour and cook, stirring constantly, for 30 seconds. Increase the heat to medium-high, add the reserved cooking liquid, and bring to a simmer, scraping the skillet bottom with a wooden spoon to loosen any browned bits. Simmer rapidly until reduced to ½ cup, 2 to 3 minutes. Stir in any accumulated juices from the resting chicken; return to a simmer and cook for 30 seconds. Off the heat, whisk in the parsley, chives, lemon juice, and butter; season with salt and pepper to taste. Pour the sauce around the chicken and serve immediately.

HIGH-ROAST CHICKEN

WHY THIS RECIPE WORKS: "High roasting"—cooking a bird at temperatures in excess of 450 degrees—is supposed to produce tastier chicken with crisper skin in record time. But recipes we've tried overcook the bird while producing enough smoke to be mistaken for a five-alarm fire. We wanted to improve upon this method for a quick roasted chicken with skin that is crisp and tanned to a deep golden hue and meat that is irresistibly tender and moist. And while we were at it, we wanted roasted potatoes too.

We began by brining the chicken for moist, well-seasoned meat. Then we butterflied the chicken, which allowed for more even and faster roasting. We found that we were able to add moisture and flavor to the chicken by rubbing flavored herb butter under the skin. (Some recipes instruct rubbing the butter over the skin, but the herbs burn and the butter doesn't season the meat.) We cooked the chicken on top of a broiler pan with a bottom attached. In the bottom of the pan under the chicken, we placed a layer of potatoes. To ensure that the potatoes cooked through, we sliced them thin—⅛ to ¼ inch

thick. As the chicken cooked, the potatoes absorbed the juices from the chicken and became well seasoned. In just one hour we had roast chicken with spectacularly crisp skin and moist meat—and potatoes too.

High-Roast Butterflied Chicken with Potatoes
SERVES 2 TO 3

If using a kosher bird, skip the brining process and begin with step 2. Because you'll be cooking the chicken under high heat, it's important that you rinse it thoroughly before proceeding—otherwise, the sugar remaining on the skin from the brine will caramelize and ultimately burn. For this cooking technique, russet potatoes offer the best potato flavor, but Yukon Golds develop a beautiful color and retain their shape better after cooking. Either works well in this recipe. A food processor makes quick and easy work of slicing the potatoes.

CHICKEN AND BRINE
½ cup table salt
½ cup sugar
1 (3½ to 4-pound) whole chicken, giblets discarded (see note)
1 recipe Mustard-Garlic Butter with Thyme (recipe follows)
1 tablespoon olive oil
   Ground black pepper

POTATOES
2½ pounds russet or Yukon Gold potatoes (4 to 5 medium), peeled and sliced ⅛ to ¼ inch thick (see note)
1 tablespoon olive oil
½ teaspoon table salt
⅛ teaspoon ground black pepper

1. FOR THE CHICKEN AND BRINE: Dissolve the salt and sugar in 2 quarts cold water in a large container. Submerge the chicken in the brine, cover, and refrigerate for 1 hour.

2. Adjust an oven rack to the lower-middle position and heat the oven to 500 degrees. Line a broiler-pan bottom with foil. Remove the chicken from the brine, rinse well, and pat dry with paper towels. Following the photos on page 102, remove the backbone from the chicken, pound the chicken to a fairly even thickness, and tuck the wings behind the back.

3. Use your fingers to gently loosen the center portion of skin covering each side of the breast. Place the butter mixture under the skin, directly on the meat in the center of each side. Gently press on the skin to distribute the butter over the meat. Rub the skin with the oil and season with pepper. Place the chicken on the broiler-pan top and push each leg up to rest between the thigh and breast.

4. FOR THE POTATOES: Toss the potatoes with the oil, salt, and pepper. Spread the potatoes in an even layer in the prepared broiler-pan bottom. Place the broiler-pan top with the chicken on top.

5. Roast the chicken until just beginning to brown, about 20 minutes. Rotate the pan and continue to roast until the skin is crisped and deep brown and the thickest part of the breasts registers 160 to 165 degrees and the thickest part of the thighs registers 175 degrees on an instant-read thermometer, 20 to 25 minutes longer. Transfer the chicken to a carving board and let rest for 10 minutes.

NOTES FROM THE TEST KITCHEN

BUTTERFLYING A CHICKEN

1. With the breast side down, cut along each side of the backbone and remove it.

2. Turn the chicken breast side up. Open the chicken on the work surface. Use the heel of your hand to flatten the breastbone.

3. Cover the chicken with plastic wrap, then pound it with a meat pounder to a fairly even thickness.

6. While the chicken rests, remove the broiler-pan top and, using paper towels, soak up any excess grease from the potatoes. Transfer the potatoes to a serving platter. Carve the chicken, transfer to the platter with the potatoes, and serve.

Mustard-Garlic Butter with Thyme
MAKES ABOUT 3 TABLESPOONS

- **2 tablespoons unsalted butter, softened**
- **1 tablespoon Dijon mustard**
- **1 medium garlic clove, minced or pressed through a garlic press (about 1 teaspoon)**
- **1 teaspoon minced fresh thyme leaves**
  Pinch ground black pepper

Mash all the ingredients together in a small bowl.

"STUFFED" ROAST CHICKEN

WHY THIS RECIPE WORKS: Stuffed roast chicken can be a conundrum—it's either a perfectly cooked bird filled with lukewarm stuffing (risking salmonella) or safe-to-eat stuffing packed in parched poultry. And given the small cavity of a roasting chicken, there's often no more than a few tablespoons of stuffing per person. We wanted our stuffed roast chicken to produce both flavorful white and dark chicken meat along with an ample amount of intensely flavored stuffing. And we wanted to solve the problem of cooking the stuffing to a safe temperature without drying out the delicate breast meat of the chicken.

We ensured moist, savory meat by brining the bird before we stuffed and roasted it. While the chicken was brining, we jazzed up the stuffing mix by replacing the customary onion with a thinly sliced leek, adding it along with celery, mushrooms, minced garlic, fresh sage, thyme, and parsley, and chicken broth. Our most creative solution, however, was to make an aluminum foil bowl, mound the stuffing into it, and place the chicken—after butterflying it—on top. This improvised cooking vessel allowed the stuffing to become moist and flavorful throughout from the chicken juices, while also becoming brown and chewy on the bottom. And cleanup was a snap.

registers 160 to 165 degrees, and the thickest part of the thighs registers 175 degrees on an instant-read thermometer, 25 to 35 minutes longer. Transfer the chicken to a carving board and let rest for 10 minutes.

4. While the chicken rests, transfer the stuffing to a serving bowl and fluff. Cover the stuffing with foil to keep warm. Carve the chicken and serve with the stuffing.

Mushroom-Leek Bread Stuffing with Herbs

MAKES ABOUT 6 CUPS

The dried bread cubes for this stuffing can be stored in an airtight container for up to 1 week.

- 6 **slices high-quality white sandwich bread, cut into ¼-inch cubes**
- 2 **tablespoons unsalted butter**
- 1 **leek, white and light green parts only, halved lengthwise, sliced ⅛ inch thick, and rinsed thoroughly**
- 1 **celery rib, chopped fine**
- 8 **ounces white mushrooms, wiped clean and chopped medium**
- ¼ **cup minced fresh parsley leaves**
- 2 **medium garlic cloves, minced or pressed through a garlic press (about 2 teaspoons)**
- ½ **teaspoon minced fresh sage leaves or ¼ teaspoon dried sage**
- ½ **teaspoon minced fresh thyme leaves or ¼ teaspoon dried thyme**
- ½ **cup plus 2 tablespoons low-sodium chicken broth**
- 1 **large egg**
- ½ **teaspoon table salt**
- ½ **teaspoon ground black pepper**

1. Adjust an oven rack to the middle position and heat the oven to 250 degrees. Spread the bread cubes in a single layer on a rimmed baking sheet. Bake until thoroughly dried but not browned, about 30 minutes, stirring halfway through the baking time.

2. Meanwhile, melt the butter in a 12-inch skillet over medium-high heat. Add the leek, celery, and mushrooms and cook, stirring occasionally, until the vegetables begin to brown, 6 to 8 minutes. Stir in the parsley, garlic, sage, and thyme and cook until fragrant, about 30 seconds.

3. Whisk the broth, egg, salt, and pepper together in a large bowl. Add the bread cubes and leek–mushroom mixture and toss gently until evenly moistened and combined. Use as directed.

"Stuffed" Roast Butterflied Chicken

SERVES 4 TO 6

If using a kosher bird, skip the brining process and begin with step 2. Use a traditional (not nonstick) roasting pan to prepare this recipe. When arranging the chicken over the stuffing, it should extend past the edges of the bowl so that most of the fat renders into the roasting pan.

- ½ **cup table salt**
- ½ **cup sugar**
- 1 **(5 to 6-pound) whole chicken, giblets discarded (see note)**
- 1 **tablespoon olive oil**
  Ground black pepper
- 1 **recipe Mushroom-Leek Bread Stuffing with Herbs (recipe follows)**

1. Dissolve the salt and sugar in 2 quarts cold water in a large container. Submerge the chicken in the brine, cover, and refrigerate for 1½ hours.

2. Adjust an oven rack to the lower-middle position and heat the oven to 450 degrees. Remove the chicken from the brine, rinse well, and pat dry with paper towels. Following the photos on page 102, remove the backbone from the chicken, pound the chicken to a fairly even thickness, and tuck the wings behind the back. Rub the skin with the oil and season with pepper.

3. To make the foil bowl, place two 12-inch squares of foil on top of each other. Fold the edges to construct an 8 by 6-inch bowl. Coat the inside of the bowl with vegetable oil spray, and place the bowl in a roasting pan. Gently mound and pack the stuffing into the foil bowl and position the chicken over the stuffing. Roast the chicken until just beginning to brown, about 30 minutes. Rotate the pan and continue to roast until the skin is crisped and deep golden brown, the thickest part of the breasts

PERUVIAN ROAST CHICKEN

WHY THIS RECIPE WORKS: Authentic versions of Peruvian garlic-lime chicken require a wood-fired oven and hard-to-find ingredients. We wanted to replicate this robustly flavored dish using an oven and supermarket staples. A paste of salt, garlic, oil, lime zest, and cumin rubbed underneath and on top of the skin produced well-seasoned meat and a heady flavor. To this basic paste we added fresh mint (replacing the black mint paste called for in authentic recipes), oregano, pepper, and minced habanero chile for tangy spice, while a little smoked paprika subtly mimicked the smokiness we were missing from the rotisserie. Roasting the chicken vertically allowed it to cook evenly, while using two different oven temperatures helped us achieve both moist meat and well-browned skin.

NOTES FROM THE TEST KITCHEN

FLAVORING PERUVIAN ROAST CHICKEN

1. Wearing gloves while working with the chiles, loosen the chicken skin from over the thighs and breast and rub half of the paste directly over the meat.

2. Spread the remaining paste over the skin of the entire chicken.

3. Place the chicken in a gallon-size zipper-lock bag; refrigerate for at least 6 or up to 24 hours.

Peruvian Roast Chicken with Garlic and Lime
SERVES 3 TO 4

If habanero chiles are unavailable, 1 tablespoon of minced serrano chile can be substituted. Wear gloves when working with hot chiles. This recipe calls for a vertical poultry roaster. If you don't have one, substitute a 12-ounce can of beer. Open the beer and pour out (or drink) about half of the liquid. Spray the can lightly with vegetable oil spray and proceed with the recipe. Serve with Spicy Mayonnaise (recipe follows).

- ¼ cup fresh mint leaves
- 6 medium garlic cloves, chopped coarse
- 3 tablespoons extra-virgin olive oil
- 1 tablespoon table salt
- 1 tablespoon ground black pepper
- 1 tablespoon ground cumin
- 1 tablespoon sugar
- 2 teaspoons smoked paprika
- 2 teaspoons dried oregano
- 2 teaspoons finely grated zest plus ¼ cup juice from 2 limes
- 1 teaspoon minced habanero chile
- 1 (3½ to 4-pound) whole chicken, giblets discarded
- 1 cup Spicy Mayonnaise (recipe follows)

1. Process all the ingredients except the chicken and mayonnaise in a blender until a smooth paste forms, 10 to 20 seconds. Following the photos, use your fingers to gently loosen the skin covering the breast and thighs; place half of the paste under the skin, directly on the meat of the breast and thighs. Gently press on the skin to distribute the paste over the meat. Spread the entire exterior surface of the chicken with the remaining paste. Tuck the wings behind the back. Place the chicken in a 1-gallon zipper-lock bag and refrigerate for at least 6 hours or up to 24 hours.

2. Adjust an oven rack to the lowest position and heat the oven to 325 degrees. Place a vertical roaster on a rimmed baking sheet. Slide the chicken onto the vertical roaster so the drumsticks reach down to the bottom of the roaster, the chicken stands upright, and the breast is perpendicular to the bottom of the pan. Roast the chicken until the skin just begins to turn golden and the thickest part of the breast registers 140 degrees, 45 to 55 minutes. Carefully remove the chicken and the pan from the oven and increase the oven temperature to 500 degrees.

3. Once the oven has reached 500 degrees, place 1 cup water in the bottom of the baking sheet and continue to roast until the entire chicken skin is browned and crisp, the breast registers 160 degrees, and the thighs register

175 degrees, about 20 minutes, rotating the pan halfway through roasting. Check the chicken halfway through roasting; if the top is becoming too dark, place a 7-inch square piece of aluminum foil over the neck and wingtips of the chicken and continue to roast (if the pan begins to smoke and sizzle, add additional water to the pan).

4. Carefully remove the chicken from the oven and let rest, still on the vertical roaster, for 20 minutes. Using 2 large wads of paper towels, carefully lift the chicken off the vertical roaster and onto a carving board. Carve the chicken and serve, passing the Spicy Mayonnaise separately.

Spicy Mayonnaise

MAKES ABOUT 1 CUP

If you have concerns about consuming raw eggs, ¼ cup of an egg substitute can be used in place of the egg.

- 1 large egg
- 2 tablespoons water
- 1 tablespoon minced onion
- 1 tablespoon juice from 1 lime
- 1 tablespoon minced fresh cilantro leaves
- 1 tablespoon minced jarred jalapeños
- 1 medium garlic clove, minced or pressed through a garlic press (about 1 teaspoon)
- 1 teaspoon yellow mustard
- ¼ teaspoon table salt
- 1 cup vegetable oil

Process all the ingredients except the oil in a food processor until combined, about 5 seconds. With the machine running, slowly drizzle in the oil in a steady stream until a mayonnaise-like consistency is reached, scraping down the bowl as necessary.

FRIED CHICKEN

WHY THIS RECIPE WORKS: Frying chicken at home is a daunting task, with its messy preparation and spattering hot fat. In the end, the chicken often ends up disappointingly greasy, with a peeling crust and dry, tasteless meat. We wanted fried chicken worthy of the mess and splatter: moist, seasoned meat coated with a delicious, crispy mahogany crust.

We soaked chicken parts in a seasoned buttermilk brine for ultimate flavor and juiciness. Then we air-dried the brined chicken parts to help ensure a crisp skin. Flour made the crispest coating. We found that peanut oil can withstand the demands of frying and has the most neutral flavor of all the oils tested. Vegetable oil was a close runner-up. As for frying the chicken, we found that a Dutch oven worked best. With its high sides and lid, a Dutch oven minimizes splatters and retains heat that helps the chicken cook through.

Crispy Fried Chicken

SERVES 4 TO 6

Avoid using kosher chicken in this recipe or it will be too salty. Maintaining an even oil temperature is key. After the chicken is added to the pot, the temperature will drop dramatically, and most of the frying will be done at about 325 degrees. Use an instant-read thermometer with a high upper range; a clip-on candy/deep-fry thermometer is fine, too, though it can be clipped to the pot only for the uncovered portion of frying.

CHICKEN
- ½ cup table salt
- ¼ cup sugar
- 2 tablespoons paprika
- 7 cups buttermilk
- 3 medium garlic heads, cloves separated and smashed
- 3 bay leaves, crumbled
- 4 pounds bone-in, skin-on chicken pieces (split breasts cut in half, drumsticks, and/or thighs), trimmed (see note)
- 3–4 quarts peanut oil or vegetable oil, for frying

COATING
- 4 cups (20 ounces) unbleached all-purpose flour
- 1 large egg
- 1 teaspoon baking powder
- ½ teaspoon baking soda
- 1 cup buttermilk

1. FOR THE CHICKEN: Dissolve the salt, sugar, and paprika in the buttermilk in a large container. Add the garlic and bay leaves, submerge the chicken in the brine, cover, and refrigerate for 2 to 3 hours.

2. Rinse the chicken well and place in a single layer on a wire rack set over a rimmed baking sheet. Refrigerate uncovered for 2 hours. (At this point, the chicken can be covered with plastic wrap and refrigerated for up to 6 more hours.)

3. Adjust an oven rack to the middle position and heat the oven to 200 degrees. In a large Dutch oven, heat 2 inches of oil over medium-high heat to 375 degrees (see note).

4. FOR THE COATING: Place the flour in a shallow dish. Whisk the egg, baking powder, and baking soda together in a medium bowl, then whisk in the buttermilk (the mixture will bubble and foam). Working with 3 chicken pieces at a time, dredge in the flour, shaking off the excess, then coat with the egg mixture, allowing the excess to drip off. Finally, coat with flour again, shake off the excess, and return to the wire rack.

5. When the oil is hot, add half of the chicken pieces to the pot, skin side down, cover, and fry until deep golden brown, 7 to 11 minutes, adjusting the heat as necessary to maintain an oil temperature of about 325 degrees. (After

4 minutes, check the chicken pieces for even browning and rearrange if some pieces are browning faster than others.) Turn the chicken pieces over and continue to cook until the thickest part of the breasts registers 160 to 165 degrees and the thickest part of the thighs or drumsticks registers 175 degrees on an instant-read thermometer, 6 to 8 minutes. Drain the chicken briefly on a paper towel–lined plate, then transfer to a clean wire rack set over a rimmed baking sheet and keep warm in the oven.

6. Return the oil to 375 degrees (if necessary) over medium-high heat and repeat with the remaining chicken pieces. Serve.

EASIER FRIED CHICKEN

WHY THIS RECIPE WORKS: Crackling-crisp, golden-brown, and juicy—what's not to love about fried chicken? In a word, frying. Heating—and then cleaning up—more than a quart of fat on the stovetop is more trouble than most home cooks care to bother with. We wanted to find a way to prepare fried chicken—golden brown and crisp with a buttermilk- and flour-based coating—without having to heat up a pot full of fat.

To season the meat and ensure it turned out juicy, we soaked chicken parts in a buttermilk brine (buttermilk heavily seasoned with salt). We also incorporated baking powder, an unconventional ingredient in fried chicken, into our dredging mixture (flour seasoned with garlic powder, paprika, and cayenne pepper). As the chicken fries, the baking powder releases carbon dioxide gas, leavening the crust and increasing its surface area, keeping it light and crisp. And while most dredging mixtures contain purely dry ingredients, we added a little buttermilk to our mixture because the small clumps of batter it forms turn ultra-crisp once fried.

To streamline frying the chicken, we turned to a hybrid method where we fried the chicken until just lightly browned on both sides in less than half the amount of oil we'd typically use. Then we transferred the chicken to a wire rack set over a baking sheet and slid it into the oven to finish cooking through. Setting the chicken on a rack promoted air circulation all around the meat for an evenly crisp crust. And with a lot less oil to deal with post-frying, cleanup was a breeze.

Easier Fried Chicken

SERVES 4

A whole 4-pound chicken, cut into eight pieces, can be used instead of the chicken parts. Skinless chicken pieces are also an acceptable substitute, but the meat will come out slightly drier. A Dutch oven with an 11-inch diameter can be used in place of the straight-sided sauté pan.

1¼ **cups buttermilk**
     Table salt
     Dash of hot sauce
3   **teaspoons ground black pepper**
1   **teaspoon garlic powder**
1   **teaspoon paprika**
¼   **teaspoon cayenne pepper**
3½   **pounds bone-in, skin-on chicken parts (breasts, thighs, and drumsticks, or a mix, with breasts cut in half), trimmed of excess fat (see note)**
2   **cups unbleached all-purpose flour**
2   **teaspoons baking powder**
1¾   **cups vegetable oil**

1. Whisk 1 cup of the buttermilk, 1 tablespoon salt, the hot sauce, 1 teaspoon of the black pepper, ¼ teaspoon of the garlic powder, ¼ teaspoon of the paprika, and a pinch of cayenne together in a large bowl. Add the chicken pieces and turn to coat. Refrigerate, covered, for at least 1 hour or up to overnight.

2. Adjust an oven rack to the middle position and heat the oven to 400 degrees. Whisk the flour, baking powder, 1 teaspoon salt, and the remaining 2 teaspoons black pepper, the remaining ¾ teaspoon garlic powder, the remaining

¾ teaspoon paprika, and the remaining cayenne together in a large bowl. Add the remaining ¼ cup buttermilk to the flour mixture and mix with your fingers until combined and small clumps form. Working with one piece at a time, dredge the chicken pieces in the flour mixture, pressing the mixture onto the pieces to form a thick, even coating. Place the dredged chicken on a large plate, skin side up.

3. Heat the oil in an 11-inch straight-sided sauté pan over medium-high heat to 375 degrees, about 5 minutes. Carefully place the chicken pieces in the pan, skin side down, and cook until golden brown, 3 to 5 minutes. Carefully flip the chicken pieces and continue to cook until golden brown on the second side, 2 to 4 minutes longer. Transfer the chicken to a wire rack set over a rimmed baking sheet. Bake the chicken until an instant-read thermometer inserted into the thickest part of the chicken registers 160 degrees for the breasts and 175 for the legs and thighs, 15 to 20 minutes. (Smaller pieces may cook faster than larger pieces. Remove the chicken pieces from the oven as they reach the correct temperature.) Let the chicken rest for 5 minutes before serving.

OVEN-FRIED CHICKEN

WHY THIS RECIPE WORKS: Oven-fried chicken never seems to taste as good as the real thing. The coating, often plain bread crumbs or cornflakes, just never gets as crunchy or as flavorful as a deep-fried coating does. We wanted a good alternative to regular fried chicken—one that would have real crunch and good flavor, and wouldn't taste like diet food.

We soaked bone-in chicken legs and thighs in a buttermilk brine to achieve maximum juiciness and flavor in the meat. And we removed the skin from the chicken before brining because it simply didn't render in the oven and turned flabby. A mixture of eggs and mustard helped the crumbs stick to the chicken and encouraged the formation of a crunchy crust. Melba toast crumbs made the crispest coating. We baked the chicken on a wire rack set over a baking sheet that we had lined with foil. This method allowed heat to circulate around the chicken during baking, resulting in crisp chicken all over without turning. As a bonus, the foil protected the pan, which made cleanup quick and easy.

Oven-Fried Chicken

SERVES 4

Avoid using kosher chicken in this recipe or it will be too salty. If you don't want to buy whole chicken legs and cut them into drumsticks and thighs, simply buy four drumsticks and four thighs. To make Melba toast crumbs, place the toasts in a heavy-duty zipper-lock freezer bag, seal, and pound with a meat pounder or other heavy blunt object. Leave some crumbs in the mixture the size of pebbles, but most should resemble coarse sand.

CHICKEN

- ½ cup plus 2 tablespoons table salt
- ¼ cup sugar
- 2 tablespoons paprika
- 3 medium heads garlic, cloves separated
- 3 bay leaves, crumbled
- 7 cups buttermilk
- 4 whole chicken legs, separated into drumsticks and thighs and skin removed (see note)

COATING

- ¼ cup vegetable oil
- 1 box (about 5 ounces) plain Melba toast, crushed (see note)
- 2 large eggs
- 1 tablespoon Dijon mustard
- 1 teaspoon dried thyme
- ¾ teaspoon table salt
- ½ teaspoon ground black pepper
- ½ teaspoon dried oregano
- ¼ teaspoon garlic powder
- ¼ teaspoon cayenne pepper (optional)

1. FOR THE CHICKEN: In a large zipper-lock bag, combine the salt, sugar, paprika, garlic cloves, and bay leaves. With a flat meat pounder, smash the garlic into the salt and spice mixture thoroughly. Pour the mixture into a large container. Add the buttermilk and stir until the salt and sugar are completely dissolved. Submerge the chicken in the brine and refrigerate for 2 to 3 hours. Rinse the chicken well and place on a large wire rack set over a rimmed baking sheet. Refrigerate uncovered for 2 hours. (After 2 hours, the chicken can be covered with plastic wrap and refrigerated up to 6 hours longer.)

2. Adjust an oven rack to the upper-middle position and heat the oven to 400 degrees. Line a large, rimmed baking sheet with foil and set a large wire rack over the pan.

3. FOR THE COATING: Drizzle the oil over the Melba toast crumbs in a pie plate or shallow dish; toss well to coat. Mix the eggs, mustard, thyme, salt, pepper, oregano, garlic powder, and cayenne (if using) with a fork in a second plate.

4. Working with one piece at a time, coat the chicken on both sides with the egg mixture. Set the chicken in the Melba crumbs, sprinkle the crumbs over the chicken, and press to coat. Turn the chicken over and repeat on the other side. Gently shake off the excess and place on the rack. Bake until the chicken is deep nutty brown and the thickest part of a piece registers 175 degrees on an instant-read thermometer, about 40 minutes. Serve.

BUFFALO WINGS

WHY THIS RECIPE WORKS: Buffalo wings are the ultimate bar snack. Great wings boast juicy meat, a crisp coating, and a spicy, slightly sweet, and vinegary sauce. But dry, flabby wings are often the norm and the sauce can be scorchingly hot. We wanted perfectly cooked wings, coated in a well-seasoned sauce—good enough to serve with our homemade creamy blue cheese dressing.

We coated the wings with cornstarch for a supercrisp exterior and deep-fried (rather than roasting, sautéing, or pan-frying) the wings for the best texture. Then we deepened the flavor of the traditional hot sauce by adding brown sugar and cider vinegar. And for heat, we chose Frank's RedHot Original Sauce, which is traditional, but not very spicy, so we added a little Tabasco for even more kick.

Buffalo Wings

SERVES 6 TO 8

Frank's RedHot Original Sauce is not terribly spicy. We like to combine it with a more potent hot sauce, such as Tabasco, to bring up the heat.

SAUCE

- 4 tablespoons (½ stick) unsalted butter
- ½ cup Frank's RedHot Original Sauce (see note)
- 2 tablespoons Tabasco or other hot sauce, plus more to taste (see note)
- 1 tablespoon packed dark brown sugar
- 2 teaspoons cider vinegar

WINGS

- 1–2 quarts peanut oil, for frying
- 3 tablespoons cornstarch
- 1 teaspoon table salt
- 1 teaspoon ground black pepper
- 1 teaspoon cayenne pepper
- 18 chicken wings (about 3 pounds), wings separated into 2 parts at joint and wingtips removed (see photos)

VEGETABLES AND DRESSING

- 2 medium carrots, peeled and cut into thin sticks
- 4 medium celery ribs, cut into thin sticks
- 1 recipe Rich and Creamy Blue Cheese Dressing (see page 30)

1. FOR THE SAUCE: Melt the butter in a small saucepan over low heat. Whisk in the hot sauces, brown sugar, and vinegar until combined. Remove from the heat and set aside.

2. FOR THE WINGS: Heat the oven to 200 degrees. Line a baking sheet with paper towels. In a large Dutch oven fitted with a clip-on candy thermometer, heat 2½ inches of oil over medium-high heat to 360 degrees. While the oil heats, combine the cornstarch, salt, black pepper, and cayenne in a small bowl. Dry the chicken with paper towels and place the pieces in a large mixing bowl. Sprinkle the spice mixture over the wings and toss with a rubber spatula until evenly coated. Fry half of the chicken wings until golden and crisp, 10 to 12 minutes. With a slotted spoon, transfer the fried chicken wings to the prepared baking sheet. Keep the first batch of chicken warm in the oven while frying the remaining wings.

3. TO SERVE: Pour the sauce mixture into a large bowl, add the chicken wings, and toss until the wings are uniformly coated. Serve immediately with the carrot and celery sticks and blue cheese dressing on the side.

NOTES FROM THE TEST KITCHEN

CUTTING UP CHICKEN WINGS

1. Cut into the skin between the larger sections of the wing until you hit the joint.

2. Bend back the two sections to pop and break the joint.

3. Cut through the skin and flesh to completely separate the two meaty portions.

4. Hack off the wingtip and discard.

CHAPTER 6

TALKING TURKEY AND ALL THE TRIMMINGS

Classic Roast Turkey 112

   Giblet Pan Gravy

Roast Turkey for a Crowd 114

   Giblet Pan Gravy for a Crowd

Old-Fashioned Stuffed Turkey 115

   Make-Ahead Turkey Gravy

Classic Roast Stuffed Turkey 118

   Bread Stuffing with Bacon, Apples, Sage, and Caramelized Onions

Slow-Roasted Turkey with Gravy 119

Crisp-Skin High-Roast Butterflied Turkey with Sausage Dressing 120

   Golden Corn Bread

   Turkey Gravy

Roast Salted Turkey 123

Herbed Roast Turkey 125

   All-Purpose Turkey Gravy

Braised Turkey 127

Grill-Roasted Turkey 128

Grill–Roasted Boneless Turkey Breast 130

Classic Cranberry Sauce 131

Baked Bread Stuffing with Sausage, Dried Cherries, and Pecans 132

   Baked Bread Stuffing with Leeks, Bacon, and Apple

   Baked Bread Stuffing with Fresh Herbs

Classic Green Bean Casserole 133

Quick Green Bean "Casserole" 134

Candied Sweet Potato Casserole 135

MORE RECIPES FOR ROUNDING OUT YOUR HOLIDAY MEAL

Cream Biscuits 546

Rustic Dinner Rolls 547

Classic Mashed Potatoes 487

Creamy Mashed Potatoes 489

Fluffy Mashed Potatoes 490

Classic Apple Pie 685

Deep Dish Apple Pie 686

Pumpkin Pie 693

Spiced Pumpkin Cheesecake 636

CLASSIC ROAST TURKEY

WHY THIS RECIPE WORKS: Few of us want to take chances when cooking the holiday bird. We wanted to find a way that guaranteed moist, flavorful meat and bronzed skin—a true holiday table centerpiece.

First we brined our turkey, which helped prevent the meat from drying out and also seasoned it right to the bone. After brining, we rinsed the bird of excess salt and let it rest on a wire rack in the refrigerator so that the skin dried out. This step helped ensure the skin would cook up crisp, not flabby. Placing the turkey on a V-rack allowed for air circulation all around so that the bird cooked evenly. And turning the turkey three times also helped to ensure even cooking. Finally, once the turkey was cooked, we waited 30 minutes before carving it. That might seem like a long time, but it allowed the juices in the turkey to redistribute so that, once carved, each slice was moist and full of flavor.

Classic Roast Turkey

SERVES 10 TO 12

Resist the temptation to tent the roasted turkey with foil while it rests on the carving board. Covering the bird will make the skin soggy.

- 2   **cups table salt**
- 1   **(12 to 14-pound) turkey; giblets, neck, and tailpiece removed and reserved for gravy**
- 2   **medium onions, chopped coarse**
- 2   **medium carrots, chopped coarse**
- 2   **celery ribs, chopped coarse**
- 6   **sprigs fresh thyme**
- 3   **tablespoons unsalted butter, melted**
- 1   **cup water, plus more as needed**
- 1   **recipe Giblet Pan Gravy (recipe follows)**

1. Dissolve the salt in 2 gallons cold water in a large container. Submerge the turkey in the brine, cover, and refrigerate or store in a very cool spot (40 degrees or less) for 4 to 6 hours.

2. Set a wire rack over a large rimmed baking sheet. Remove the turkey from the brine and rinse it well. Pat the turkey dry, inside and out, with paper towels. Place the turkey on the prepared baking sheet. Refrigerate, uncovered, for at least 8 hours or overnight.

3. Adjust an oven rack to the lowest position and heat the oven to 400 degrees. Line a V-rack with heavy duty foil and poke several holes in the foil. Set the V-rack in

a roasting pan and spray the foil with vegetable oil spray.

4. Toss half of the onions, carrots, celery, and thyme with 1 tablespoon of the melted butter in a medium bowl and place inside the turkey. Tie the legs together with kitchen twine and tuck the wings under the bird. Scatter the remaining vegetables into the roasting pan.

5. Pour 1 cup water over the vegetable mixture. Brush the turkey breast with 1 tablespoon more melted butter, then place the turkey, breast side down, on the V-rack. Brush with the remaining 1 tablespoon melted butter.

6. Roast the turkey for 45 minutes. Remove the pan from the oven; baste with juices from the pan. With a dish towel in each hand, turn the turkey leg/thigh side up. If the liquid in the pan has totally evaporated, add another ½ cup water. Return the turkey to the oven and roast for 15 minutes. Remove the turkey from the oven again, baste, and turn the other leg/thigh side up; roast for another 15 minutes. Remove the turkey from the oven for a final time, baste, and turn it breast side up; roast until the thickest part of the breast registers 160 to 165 degrees and the thickest part of the thigh registers 175 degrees on an instant-read thermometer, 30 to 45 minutes.

7. Remove the turkey from the oven. Gently tip the turkey so that any accumulated juices in the cavity run into the roasting pan. Transfer the turkey to a carving board and let rest, uncovered, for 30 minutes. Carve the turkey and serve with the gravy.

Giblet Pan Gravy

MAKES ABOUT 6 CUPS

Complete step 1 up to a day ahead, if desired. Begin step 3 once the bird has been removed from the oven and is resting on a carving board.

- 1 tablespoon vegetable oil
  Reserved turkey giblets, neck, and tailpiece
- 1 medium onion, chopped
- 4 cups low-sodium chicken broth
- 2 cups water
- 2 sprigs fresh thyme
- 8 sprigs fresh parsley
- 3 tablespoons unsalted butter
- ¼ cup unbleached all-purpose flour
- 1 cup dry white wine
  Table salt and ground black pepper

1. Heat the oil in a large Dutch oven over medium heat until shimmering; add the giblets, neck, and tailpiece, and cook until golden and fragrant, about 5 minutes. Add the onion and continue to cook until softened, 3 to 4 minutes longer. Reduce the heat to low, cover, and cook until the turkey parts and onion release their juices, about 15 minutes. Add the broth, water, and herbs, bring to a boil, and adjust the heat to low. Simmer, uncovered, skimming any impurities that may rise to the surface, until the broth is rich and flavorful, about 30 minutes longer. Strain the broth into a large container and reserve the giblets. When cool enough to handle, chop the giblets. Refrigerate the giblets and broth until ready to use. (The broth can be stored in the refrigerator in an airtight container for up to 1 day.)

2. While the turkey is roasting, return the reserved turkey broth to a simmer. Heat the butter in a large saucepan over medium-low heat. Vigorously whisk in the flour (the mixture will froth and then thin out again). Cook slowly, stirring constantly, until nutty brown and fragrant, 10 to 15 minutes. Vigorously whisk all but 1 cup of the hot broth into the flour mixture. Bring to a boil, then continue to simmer, stirring occasionally, until the gravy is lightly thickened and very flavorful, about 30 minutes longer. Set aside until the turkey is done.

3. When the turkey has been transferred to a carving board to rest, spoon out and discard as much fat as possible from the roasting pan, leaving the caramelized herbs and vegetables. Place the roasting pan over two burners set

on medium-high heat. Return the gravy to a simmer. Add the wine to the roasting pan of caramelized vegetables, scraping up any browned bits with a wooden spoon, and boil until reduced by half, about 5 minutes. Add the remaining 1 cup turkey broth and continue to simmer for 15 minutes; strain the pan juices into the gravy, pressing as much juice as possible out of the vegetables. Stir the reserved giblets into the gravy and return to a boil. Season with salt and pepper to taste and serve.

ROAST TURKEY FOR A CROWD

WHY THIS RECIPE WORKS: Unless you have access to multiple ovens, only a very large turkey will do when you've got a crowd coming to dinner. But finding a container large enough to brine a gargantuan bird can be tricky. And turning the bird in the oven, our usual method for evenly cooked meat, can be hot, heavy, and dangerous. We wanted the Norman Rockwell picture of perfection: a crisp, mahogany skin wrapped around tender, moist meat. And it had to be easy to prepare in a real home kitchen.

We chose a Butterball turkey, which has already been brined for juicy flavor (a kosher bird, which has been salted, works well too). A combination of high and low heat resulted in a tender, juicy bird with deeply browned skin. We made the meat and pan drippings more flavorful with the addition of onion, carrot, and celery. A quartered lemon added bright, clean flavor. After roasting, we allowed the turkey to rest so the juices would redistribute, but didn't tent it with foil so the skin wouldn't become soggy. Serve with Giblet Pan Gravy for a Crowd (recipe follows).

Roast Turkey for a Crowd

SERVES ABOUT 20

Rotating the bird helps produce moist, evenly cooked meat, but for the sake of ease, you may opt not to rotate it. In that case, skip the step of lining the V-rack with foil and roast the bird breast side up for the entire cooking time. Because we do not brine the bird, we had the best results with a frozen Butterball (injected with salt and water) or a kosher bird (soaked in salt water during processing).

- 3 medium onions, chopped coarse
- 3 medium carrots, chopped coarse
- 3 celery ribs, chopped coarse
- 1 lemon, quartered
- 2 sprigs fresh thyme
- 5 tablespoons unsalted butter, melted
- 1 (18 to 22-pound) frozen Butterball or kosher turkey (see note); giblets, neck, and tailpiece removed and reserved for gravy (recipe follows)
- 1 cup water, plus more as needed
- 1 teaspoon table salt
- 1 teaspoon ground black pepper
- 1 recipe Giblet Pan Gravy for a Crowd (recipe follows)

1. Adjust an oven rack to the lowest position. Heat the oven to 425 degrees. Line a large V-rack with heavy-duty foil and poke several holes in the foil. Set the V-rack in a large roasting pan and spray the foil with vegetable oil spray.

2. Toss half of the onions, carrots, celery, lemon, and thyme with 1 tablespoon of the melted butter in a medium bowl and place inside the turkey. Tie the legs together with kitchen twine and tuck the wings under the bird. Scatter the remaining vegetables into the roasting pan.

3. Pour 1 cup water over the vegetable mixture. Brush the turkey breast with 2 tablespoons more of the melted butter, then sprinkle with half of the salt and half of the pepper. Place the turkey, breast side down, on the V-rack. Brush with the remaining 2 tablespoons melted butter and sprinkle with the remaining salt and pepper.

4. Roast the turkey for 1 hour. Remove the pan from the oven; baste with juices from the pan. With a dish towel in each hand, turn the turkey breast side up. If the liquid in the pan has totally evaporated, add another ½ cup water. Lower the oven temperature to 325 degrees. Return the turkey to the oven and continue to roast until the thickest part of the breast registers 160 to 165 degrees and the thickest part of the thigh registers 175 degrees on an instant-read thermometer, about 2 hours longer.

5. Remove the turkey from the oven. Gently tip the turkey up so that any accumulated juices in the cavity run into the roasting pan. Transfer the turkey to a carving board. Let rest, uncovered, for 35 to 40 minutes. Carve the turkey and serve with the gravy.

Giblet Pan Gravy for a Crowd

MAKES ABOUT 8 CUPS

Complete step 1 up to a day ahead, if desired. Begin step 3 once the bird has been removed from the oven and is resting on a carving board.

- 1 tablespoon vegetable oil
- Reserved turkey giblets, neck, and tailpiece
- 1 medium onion, unpeeled and chopped
- 6 cups low-sodium chicken broth
- 3 cups water
- 2 sprigs fresh thyme
- 8 sprigs fresh parsley
- 5 tablespoons unsalted butter
- ¼ cup plus 2 tablespoons unbleached all-purpose flour
- 1½ cups dry white wine
- Table salt and ground black pepper

1. Heat the oil in a large Dutch oven over medium heat until shimmering; add the giblets, neck, and tailpiece, and cook until golden and fragrant, about 5 minutes. Add the onion and continue to cook until softened, 3 to 4 minutes longer. Reduce the heat to low, cover, and cook until the turkey parts and onion release their juices, about 15 minutes. Add the broth, water, and herbs, bring to a boil, and adjust the heat to low. Simmer, uncovered, skimming any impurities that may rise to the surface, until the broth is rich and flavorful, about 30 minutes longer. Strain the broth into a large container and reserve the giblets. When cool enough to handle, chop the giblets. Refrigerate the giblets and broth until ready to use. (The broth can be stored in the refrigerator in an airtight container for up to 1 day.)

2. While the turkey is roasting, return the reserved turkey broth to a simmer. Heat the butter in a large saucepan over medium-low heat. Vigorously whisk in the flour (the mixture will froth and then thin out again). Cook slowly, stirring constantly, until nutty brown and fragrant, 10 to 15 minutes. Vigorously whisk all but 2 cups of the hot broth into the flour mixture. Bring to a boil, then continue to simmer, stirring occasionally, until the gravy is lightly thickened and very flavorful, about 35 minutes longer. Set aside until the turkey is done.

3. When the turkey has been transferred to a carving board to rest, spoon out and discard as much fat as possible from the roasting pan, leaving the caramelized herbs and vegetables. Place the roasting pan over two burners set on medium-high heat. Return the gravy to a simmer. Add the wine to the roasting pan of caramelized vegetables, scraping up any browned bits with a wooden spoon, and boil until reduced by half, about 7 minutes. Add the remaining 2 cups turkey broth and continue to simmer for 15 minutes; strain the pan juices into the gravy, pressing as much juice as possible out of the vegetables. Stir the reserved giblets into the gravy and return to a boil. Season with salt and pepper to taste and serve.

OLD-FASHIONED STUFFED TURKEY

WHY THIS RECIPE WORKS: Perfecting one aspect of a roast turkey usually comes at the cost of another. Crisp skin means dry white meat. Brining adds moisture, but can turn the skin soggy. And stuffing the cavity compounds the headache, slowing the roasting time and upping the chance for uneven cooking. We wanted a turkey with everything: juicy meat, crisply burnished skin, and rich-flavored stuffing that cooked inside the bird.

Unwilling to sacrifice crisp skin, we opted for salting over brining. Salting initially draws moisture out of the meat, but after a long rest in the refrigerator, all the moisture gets slowly drawn back in, seasoning the meat and helping it retain moisture. Next we turned to slow roasting and started the bird in a relatively low oven, then cranked the temperature to give it a final blast of skin-crisping heat and to bring the center up to temperature. It worked beautifully, yielding breast meat that was moist and tender. For even crispier skin, we massaged it with a baking powder and salt rub. The baking powder dehydrates the skin and raises its pH, making it more conducive to browning. We also poked holes in the skin to help rendering fat escape.

And for extra flavor, we draped the bird with meaty salt pork, which we removed and drained before cranking up the heat so the bird didn't taste too smoky. To make sure the stuffing was cooked through, we started half of it in the bird to give it meaty flavor, then combined it with the uncooked batch to finish baking it while the turkey rested.

Old-Fashioned Stuffed Turkey

SERVES 10 TO 12

Table salt is not recommended for this recipe because it is too fine. To roast a kosher or self-basting turkey (such as a frozen Butterball), do not salt it in step 1. Look for salt pork that is roughly equal parts fat and lean meat. The bread can be toasted up to 1 day in advance. Serve with Make-Ahead Turkey Gravy (recipe follows).

TURKEY

- **1** (12 to 14-pound) turkey, giblets and neck reserved for gravy, if making (see note)
- **3** tablespoons plus 2 teaspoons kosher salt (see note)
- **2** teaspoons baking powder
- **12** ounces salt pork, cut into ¼-inch-thick slices and rinsed (see note)

STUFFING

1½ **pounds (about 15 slices) high-quality white sandwich bread, cut into ½-inch cubes (about 12 cups)**

4 **tablespoons (½ stick) unsalted butter, plus extra for the baking dish**

1 **medium onion, minced**

2 **celery ribs, chopped fine**

Kosher salt and ground black pepper

2 **tablespoons minced fresh thyme leaves**

1 **tablespoon minced fresh marjoram leaves**

1 **tablespoon minced fresh sage leaves**

1½ **cups low-sodium chicken broth**

1 **36-inch square cheesecloth, folded in quarters**

2 **large eggs**

1. FOR THE TURKEY: Following the photos on page 124, use your fingers or the handle of a wooden spoon to separate the turkey skin from the meat on the breast, legs, thighs, and back; avoid breaking the skin. Rub 1 tablespoon of the salt evenly inside the cavity of the turkey, 1½ teaspoons salt under the skin of each breast half, and 1½ teaspoons salt under the skin of each leg. Wrap the turkey tightly with plastic wrap; refrigerate for 24 to 48 hours.

2. FOR THE STUFFING: Adjust an oven rack to the lowest position and heat the oven to 250 degrees. Spread the bread cubes in a single layer on a rimmed baking sheet; bake until the edges have dried but the centers are slightly moist (the cubes should yield to pressure), about 45 minutes, stirring several times during baking. Transfer to a large bowl and increase the oven temperature to 325 degrees.

3. While the bread dries, heat the butter in a 12-inch skillet over medium-high heat; when the foaming subsides, add the onion, celery, 2 teaspoons salt, and 1 teaspoon pepper; cook, stirring occasionally, until the vegetables begin to soften and brown slightly, 7 to 10 minutes. Stir in the herbs; cook until fragrant, about 1 minute. Add the vegetables to the bowl with the dried bread; add 1 cup of the broth and toss until evenly moistened.

4. TO ROAST THE TURKEY: Combine the remaining 2 teaspoons salt and the baking powder in a small bowl. Remove the turkey from the refrigerator and unwrap. Thoroughly dry the turkey inside and out with paper towels. Using a skewer, poke 15 to 20 holes in the fat deposits on top of the breast halves and thighs, 4 to 5 holes in each deposit. Sprinkle the surface of the turkey with the salt–baking powder mixture and rub in the mixture with your hands, coating the skin evenly. Tuck the wings underneath the turkey. Line the turkey cavity with the cheesecloth, pack with 4 to 5 cups stuffing, and tie the ends of the cheesecloth together. Cover the remaining stuffing with plastic wrap and refrigerate. Using kitchen twine, loosely tie the turkey legs together. Place the turkey breast side down in a V-rack set in a roasting pan and drape the salt pork slices over the back.

5. Roast the turkey breast side down until the thickest part of the breast registers 130 degrees on an instant-read thermometer, 2 to 2½ hours. Remove the roasting pan from the oven and increase the oven temperature to 450 degrees. Transfer the turkey in the V-rack to a rimmed baking sheet. Remove and discard the salt pork. Using clean potholders or kitchen towels, rotate the turkey breast side up. Cut the twine binding the legs and remove the stuffing bag; empty into the reserved stuffing in the bowl. Pour the drippings from the roasting pan into a fat separator and reserve for gravy, if making.

6. Once the oven has come to temperature, return the turkey in the V-rack to the roasting pan and roast until the skin is golden brown and crisp, the thickest part of the breast registers 160 degrees, and the thickest part of the thigh registers 175 degrees, about 45 minutes, rotating the pan halfway through. Transfer the turkey to a carving board and let rest, uncovered, for 30 minutes.

7. While the turkey rests, reduce the oven temperature to 400 degrees. Whisk the eggs and remaining ½ cup broth together in a small bowl. Pour the egg mixture over the stuffing and toss to combine, breaking up any large chunks; spread in a buttered 13 by 9-inch baking dish. Bake until the stuffing registers 165 degrees and the top is golden brown, about 15 minutes. Carve the turkey and serve with the stuffing.

Make-Ahead Turkey Gravy

MAKES ABOUT 2 QUARTS

Note that the optional roast turkey drippings may be quite salty—add them carefully to the gravy in step 4 so the gravy does not become too salty.

- 6 turkey thighs, trimmed, or 9 wings, separated at the joints
- 2 medium carrots, chopped coarse
- 2 medium celery ribs, chopped coarse
- 2 medium onions, chopped coarse
- 1 head garlic, halved
  Vegetable oil spray
- 10 cups low-sodium chicken broth, plus extra as needed
- 2 cups dry white wine
- 12 sprigs fresh thyme
  Unsalted butter, as needed
- 1 cup unbleached all-purpose flour
  Table salt and ground black pepper
  Defatted drippings from Old-Fashioned Stuffed Turkey (page 115; optional)

NOTES FROM THE TEST KITCHEN

STUFFING A TURKEY

1. After placing 4 to 5 cups of the preheated stuffing into the turkey, use metal skewers (or cut bamboo skewers) and thread them through the skin on both sides of the cavity to seal the cavity shut.

2. Center a 2-foot piece of kitchen twine on the top skewer and then cross the twine as you wrap each end of it around and under the skewers. Loosely tie the legs together with another short piece of twine.

3. Flip the turkey over onto its breast. Stuff the neck cavity loosely with approximately 1 cup of stuffing. Pull the skin flap over and use a skewer to pin the flap to the turkey.

1. Adjust an oven rack to the middle position and heat the oven to 450 degrees. Toss the thighs, carrots, celery, onions, and garlic together in a roasting pan and spray with vegetable oil spray. Roast, stirring occasionally, until well browned, 1½ to 1¾ hours.

2. Transfer the contents of the roasting pan to a large Dutch oven. Add the broth, wine, and thyme and bring to a boil, skimming as needed. Reduce to a gentle simmer and cook until the broth is brown and flavorful and measures about 8 cups when strained, about 1½ hours. Strain the broth through a fine-mesh strainer into a large container, pressing on the solids to extract as much liquid as possible; discard the solids. (The turkey broth can be cooled and refrigerated in an airtight container for up to 2 days or frozen for up to 1 month.)

3. Let the strained turkey broth settle (if necessary) then spoon off and reserve ½ cup of the fat that has risen to the top (add butter as needed if short on turkey fat). Heat the fat in a Dutch oven over medium-high heat until bubbling. Whisk in the flour and cook, whisking constantly, until well browned, 3 to 7 minutes.

4. Slowly whisk in the turkey broth and bring to a boil. Reduce to a simmer and cook until the gravy is very thick, 10 to 15 minutes. Add the defatted drippings (if using) to taste, then season with salt and pepper to taste and serve. (The gravy can be refrigerated in an airtight container for up to 2 days; reheat gently, adding additional chicken broth as needed to adjust the consistency).

CLASSIC ROAST STUFFED TURKEY

WHY THIS RECIPE WORKS: There is something undeniably festive about a stuffed roasted turkey. Every year, though, we are warned that for health and safety reasons, turkeys are best roasted unstuffed. Despite these warnings, many cooks continue to stuff their holiday bird. For the sake of flavorful, moist, turkey-infused stuffing, these cooks sacrifice perfectly cooked breast meat and risk food-borne illness from underdone stuffing. We wanted to find a way to safely and successfully roast a stuffed turkey, making sure that the breast meat would be succulent and the stuffing fully cooked.

At the outset, we decided to limit our turkey to a maximum of 14 pounds, because it is just too difficult to safely stuff and roast a larger bird. In most recipes, the breast meat is a bone-dry 180 degrees by the time the stuffing reaches a safe 165 degrees. We got around this by heating the stuffing in the microwave before placing half of it in the bird to give it a head start on cooking. We baked the remaining stuffing separately in a casserole dish; this ensured that there would be enough stuffing to go around. We also brined the bird to add flavor and moisture (brining did not, as we feared, make the stuffing soggy or overly salty).

Classic Roast Stuffed Turkey
SERVES 10 TO 12

A 12 to 14-pound turkey will accommodate approximately half of the stuffing. Bake the remainder in a casserole dish while the bird rests before carving. If serving with Giblet Pan Gravy (page 113), note that you can complete step 1 up to a day ahead, if desired. Begin step 3 once the bird has been removed from the oven and is resting on a carving board.

- 2 **cups table salt**
- 1 **(12 to 14-pound) turkey; giblets, neck, and tailpiece removed and reserved for gravy (see page 113)**
- 2 **medium onions, chopped coarse**
- 1 **medium carrot, chopped coarse**
- 1 **celery rib, chopped coarse**
- 4 **sprigs fresh thyme**
- 1 **cup water, plus more as needed**
- 12 **cups prepared stuffing (recipe follows)**
- 3 **tablespoons unsalted butter, plus extra for the casserole dish and foil**
- ¼ **cup low-sodium chicken broth**
- 1 **recipe Giblet Pan Gravy (page 113)**

1. Dissolve the salt in 2 gallons cold water in a large container. Submerge the turkey in the brine, cover, and refrigerate or store in a very cool spot (40 degrees or less) for 4 to 6 hours.

2. Set a wire rack over a large rimmed baking sheet. Remove the turkey from the brine and rinse it well. Pat the turkey dry inside and out with paper towels. Place the turkey on the prepared baking sheet. Refrigerate, uncovered, and air-dry for at least 8 hours or overnight.

3. Adjust an oven rack to the lowest position and heat the oven to 400 degrees. Line a V-rack with heavy-duty foil and poke several holes in the foil. Set the V-rack inside a roasting pan and spray the foil with vegetable oil spray. Scatter the onions, carrot, celery, and thyme in the roasting pan. Pour 1 cup water over the vegetable mixture.

4. Place half of the stuffing in a buttered medium casserole dish, dot the surface with 1 tablespoon of the butter, cover with foil, and refrigerate until ready to use. Microwave the remaining stuffing on high power, stirring two

or three times, until very hot (120 to 130 degrees on an instant-read thermometer), 6 to 8 minutes. Spoon 4 to 5 cups of stuffing into the turkey cavity until very loosely packed. Following the photos on page 117, secure the skin flap over the cavity opening with skewers. Melt the remaining 2 tablespoons butter. Tuck the wings under the bird, brush the turkey breast with half of the melted butter, then turn the turkey breast side down. Fill the neck cavity with the remaining heated stuffing and secure the skin flap over the opening. Place the turkey, breast side down, on the V-rack. Brush with the remaining butter.

5. Roast the turkey for 1 hour, then reduce the temperature to 250 degrees and roast for 2 hours longer, adding water if the pan becomes dry. Remove the pan from the oven (close the oven door) and, with a dish towel in each hand, turn the bird breast side up, and baste (the temperature of the thickest part of the breast should be 145 to 150 degrees). Increase the oven temperature to 400 degrees; continue to roast until the thickest part of the breast registers 160 to 165 degrees, the thickest part of the thigh registers 175 degrees, and the center of the stuffing registers 165 degrees on an instant-read thermometer, 1 to 1½ hours longer. Remove the turkey from the oven, transfer to a carving board, and let rest for 30 minutes.

6. Add the broth to the dish of reserved stuffing, replace the foil, and bake until hot throughout, about 20 minutes. Remove the foil; continue to bake until the stuffing forms a golden brown crust, about 15 minutes longer.

7. Carve the turkey and serve with the stuffing and the gravy.

Bread Stuffing with Bacon, Apples, Sage, and Caramelized Onions
MAKES ABOUT 12 CUPS

To dry the bread, spread the cubes out onto 2 large baking sheets and dry in a 300-degree oven for 30 to 60 minutes. Let the bread cool before using in the stuffing.

- 1 **pound bacon, cut crosswise into ¼-inch strips**
- 6 **medium onions, sliced thin (about 7 cups)**
- 1 **teaspoon table salt**
- 2 **Granny Smith apples, peeled, cored, and cut into ½-inch cubes (about 2 cups)**
- ½ **cup fresh parsley leaves, chopped fine**
- 3 **tablespoons minced fresh sage leaves**
- ½ **teaspoon ground black pepper**
- 3 **pounds high-quality white sandwich bread, cut into ¾-inch cubes (about 12 cups)**
- 1 **cup low-sodium chicken broth**
- 3 **large eggs, lightly beaten**

1. Cook the bacon in a large skillet or Dutch oven over medium heat until crisp and browned, about 12 minutes. Remove the bacon from the pan with a slotted spoon and drain on paper towels. Discard all but 3 tablespoons of the rendered bacon fat.

2. Increase the heat to medium-high and add the onions and ¼ teaspoon of the salt. Cook the onions until golden in color, making sure to stir occasionally and scrape the sides and bottom of the pan, about 20 minutes. Reduce the heat to medium and continue to cook, stirring more often to prevent burning, until the onions are deep golden brown, another 5 minutes. Add the apples and continue to cook for another 5 minutes. Transfer the contents of the pan to a large bowl.

3. Add the parsley, sage, remaining ¾ teaspoon salt, and the pepper to the bowl and mix to combine. Add the bread cubes.

4. Whisk the broth and eggs together in a small bowl. Pour the mixture over the bread cubes. Gently toss to evenly distribute the ingredients.

SLOW-ROASTED TURKEY WITH GRAVY

WHY THIS RECIPE WORKS: Roasting a whole turkey is a race to keep the white meat from drying out while the dark meat cooks through. We wanted no less than the perfect turkey recipe—an approach that would get our fowl from supermarket to table in just a few hours. We required meat as moist as prime rib and with crisp, crackling skin, and it all needed to be accompanied by rich gravy. For a greater challenge, we wanted to do it without salting the turkey or brining it, both of which take the better part of a day.

First, we roasted two nonbrined turkeys, one using our standard high-heat method and the other at 275 degrees the entire time. The outer layers of the high-heat breast dried out, but the slow-roasted breast cooked through moist, even without a brine. Coordinating the cooking between the breast and legs and thighs, however, was a problem. Instead we discovered that swapping in turkey parts for a whole turkey would help ensure the breast and thighs cooked through at about the same time. We roasted a breast and two leg quarters (thighs and drumsticks) on a rack over a baking sheet to promote air circulation. The results? Tender, juicy meat.

We next had to tackle crisping the skin. Most recipes achieve crisp skin by starting the bird in a hot oven to brown it, then lowering the heat. But that meant a higher oven temperature, which meant dried-out meat. Instead, we let the turkey cool before popping it back in the oven to crisp the skin. This turned out a perfect turkey from center to edge surrounded by flawless, crisp skin.

Slow-Roasted Turkey with Gravy

SERVES 10 TO 12

Instead of drumsticks and thighs, you may use 2 whole leg quarters, 1½ to 2 pounds each. The recipe will also work with turkey breast alone; in step 2, reduce the butter to 1½ tablespoons, the salt to 1½ teaspoons, and the pepper to 1 teaspoon. If you are roasting kosher or self-basting turkey parts, season the turkey with only 1½ teaspoons salt.

TURKEY

- 3 medium onions, chopped medium
- 3 medium celery ribs, chopped medium
- 2 medium carrots, peeled and chopped medium
- 5 sprigs fresh thyme
- 5 medium garlic cloves, peeled and halved
- 1 cup low-sodium chicken broth
- 1 (5 to 7-pound) whole bone-in, skin-on turkey breast, trimmed (see note)
- 4 pounds turkey drumsticks and thighs, trimmed (see note)
- 3 tablespoons unsalted butter, melted
- 1 tablespoon table salt
- 2 teaspoons ground black pepper

GRAVY

- 2 cups low-sodium chicken broth
- 3 tablespoons unsalted butter
- 3 tablespoons unbleached all-purpose flour
- 2 bay leaves
  Table salt and ground black pepper

1. FOR THE TURKEY: Adjust an oven rack to the lower-middle position and heat the oven to 275 degrees. Arrange the onions, celery, carrots, thyme, and garlic in an even layer on a large rimmed baking sheet. Pour the broth into the baking sheet. Place a wire rack on top of the vegetables.

2. Pat the turkey pieces dry with paper towels. Brush the turkey pieces on all sides with the melted butter. Sprinkle the salt and pepper evenly over the turkey. Place the breast, skin side down, and the drumsticks and thighs, skin side up, on the rack on the vegetable-filled baking sheet, leaving at least ¼ inch between the pieces.

3. Roast the turkey pieces for 1 hour. With a dish towel in each hand, turn the turkey breast skin side up. Continue roasting until the thickest part of the breast registers 160 to 165 degrees the thickest part of the thigh registers 175 degrees on an instant-read thermometer, 1 to 2 hours longer. Remove the baking sheet from the oven and transfer the rack with the turkey to a second baking sheet. Allow the pieces to rest for at least 30 minutes or up to 1½ hours.

4. FOR THE GRAVY: Strain the vegetables and liquid from the baking sheet through a colander set in a large bowl. Press the solids with the back of a spatula to extract as much liquid as possible. Discard the vegetables. Transfer the liquid in the bowl to a 4-cup liquid measuring cup. Add the chicken broth to the measuring cup (you should have about 3 cups liquid).

5. In a medium saucepan, heat the butter over medium-high heat; add the flour and cook, stirring constantly, until the flour is dark golden brown and fragrant, about 5 minutes. Whisk in the broth mixture and bay leaves and gradually bring to a boil. Reduce the heat to medium-low and simmer, stirring occasionally, until the gravy is thick and reduced to 2 cups, 15 to 20 minutes. Discard the bay leaves. Remove the gravy from the heat and season with salt and pepper to taste. Keep the gravy warm.

6. TO SERVE: Heat the oven to 500 degrees. Place the baking sheet with the turkey in the oven. Roast until the skin is golden brown and crisp, about 15 minutes. Transfer the turkey to a carving board and let rest, uncovered, for 20 minutes. Carve and serve with the gravy.

CRISP-SKIN HIGH-ROAST TURKEY

WHY THIS RECIPE WORKS: High-roasting (oven-roasting at very high temperatures for the sake of speed and flavor) a turkey presents the home cook with two potential problems: billowing smoke from incinerated pan drippings and torched breast meat. We wanted to find a way to prepare a high-roast turkey with crisp, picture-perfect skin and moist, evenly cooked meat in less than two hours—without setting off the smoke alarm.

We butterflied the turkey for crisp skin and evenly cooked meat, and then roasted it on a broiler pan set over the stuffing—which absorbed the drippings. This step helped season the stuffing and kept the kitchen from filling with smoke. These techniques let us crank up the heat to get the bird done in record time. To complement our moist, crisp-skinned turkey, we made a corn bread and sausage stuffing that was both rich and easy to prepare.

Crisp-Skin High-Roast Butterflied Turkey with Sausage Dressing
SERVES 10 TO 12

The dressing can be made with corn bread or white bread, but note that they are not used in equal amounts. The turkey is roasted in a broiler pan top, or a sturdy wire rack, set in a 16 by 12-inch disposable aluminum roasting pan. If using a wire rack, choose one that measures about 17 by 11 inches so that it will span the roasting pan and sit above the dressing in the pan.

TURKEY
- 1 cup table salt
- 1 cup sugar
- 1 (12 to 14-pound) turkey; giblets, neck, and tailpiece removed and reserved for gravy; turkey butterflied (see page 121) and backbone and rib bones reserved for gravy
- 1 tablespoon unsalted butter, melted

SAUSAGE DRESSING
- 12 cups corn bread (recipe follows) broken into 1-inch pieces (include crumbs), or 18 cups 1-inch challah or Italian bread cubes (from about 1½ loaves)
- 1¾ cups low-sodium chicken broth
- 1 cup half-and-half
- 2 large eggs, beaten lightly
- 12 ounces bulk pork sausage, broken into 1-inch pieces

- 3 **medium onions, minced (about 3 cups)**
- 3 **celery ribs, chopped fine (about 1½ cups)**
- 2 **tablespoons unsalted butter**
- 2 **tablespoons minced fresh thyme leaves**
- 2 **tablespoons minced fresh sage leaves**
- 3 **medium garlic cloves, minced or pressed through a garlic press (about 1 tablespoon)**
- 1½ **teaspoons table salt**
- 2 **teaspoons ground black pepper**
- 1 **recipe Turkey Gravy (see page 122)**

1. TO BRINE THE TURKEY: Dissolve the salt and sugar in 2 gallons cold water in a large container. Submerge the turkey in the brine and refrigerate or store in a very cool spot (40 degrees or less) for 4 to 6 hours.

2. TO PREPARE THE DRESSING: While the turkey brines, adjust the oven racks to the upper-middle and lower-middle positions and heat the oven to 250 degrees. Spread the bread in an even layer on two rimmed baking sheets and dry in the oven for 50 to 60 minutes for corn bread or 40 to 50 minutes for challah or Italian bread.

3. Place the bread in a large bowl. Whisk the broth, half-and-half, and eggs together in a medium bowl; pour over the bread and toss very gently to coat so that the bread does not break into smaller pieces. Set aside.

4. Heat a 12-inch skillet over medium-high heat until hot, about 1½ minutes. Add the sausage and cook, stirring occasionally, until the sausage loses its raw color, 5 to 7 minutes. With a slotted spoon, transfer the sausage to a medium bowl. Add half the onions and celery to the fat in the skillet; sauté, stirring occasionally, over medium-high heat until softened, about 5 minutes. Transfer the onion mixture to the bowl with the sausage. Return the skillet to the heat and add the butter; when melted add the remaining onions and celery and sauté, stirring occasionally, until softened, about 5 minutes. Stir in the thyme, sage, and garlic; cook until fragrant, about 30 seconds; add the salt and pepper. Add this mixture along with the sausage and onion mixture to the bread and stir gently to combine (try not to break the bread into smaller pieces).

5. Spray a 16 by 12-inch disposable aluminum roasting pan with vegetable oil spray. Transfer the dressing to the roasting pan and spread in an even layer. Cover the pan with foil and refrigerate while preparing the turkey.

6. TO PREPARE THE TURKEY FOR ROASTING: Remove the turkey from the brine and rinse it well. Position the turkey on a broiler pan top or wire rack (see note); thoroughly pat the surface of the turkey dry with paper towels. Place the broiler pan top with the turkey on top of the roasting pan with the dressing; refrigerate, uncovered, for 8 to 24 hours.

NOTES FROM THE TEST KITCHEN

PREPARING THE BUTTERFLIED TURKEY

1. Holding the turkey upright with the backbone facing front, use a hacking motion to cut through the turkey directly to one side of the backbone with a chef's knife.

2. Holding the backbone with one hand, hack through the turkey directly to the other side of the backbone; the backbone will fall away.

3. Using kitchen scissors, cut out the rib plate and remove any small pieces of bone.

4. Place the turkey, breast side up, on a cutting board and cover with plastic wrap. With a large rolling pin, whack the breastbone until it cracks and the turkey flattens.

5. After brining and rinsing, place the turkey, breast side up, on a wire rack set over a rimmed baking sheet. Tuck the wings under the turkey. Push the legs up to rest between the thigh and breast. Tie the legs together.

7. TO ROAST THE TURKEY WITH THE DRESSING: Adjust an oven rack to the lower-middle position and heat the oven to 450 degrees. Remove the broiler pan top with the turkey and remove the foil from the dressing; place the broiler pan top with the turkey on the dressing in the roasting pan. Brush the turkey with the melted butter. Roast the turkey until the turkey skin is crisp and deep brown and the thickest part of the breast registers 160 to 165 degrees and the thickest part of the thigh registers 175 degrees on an instant-read thermometer, 1 hour 20 minutes to 1 hour 40 minutes, rotating the pan from front to back after 40 minutes.

8. Transfer the broiler pan top with the turkey to a carving board, tent loosely with foil, and let rest for 20 minutes. Meanwhile, adjust an oven rack to the upper-middle position, place the roasting pan with the dressing back in the oven, and bake until golden brown, about 10 minutes. Carve the turkey and serve with the dressing and gravy.

Golden Corn Bread

MAKES ABOUT 16 CUPS CRUMBLED CORN BREAD

You need about three-quarters of this recipe for the dressing; the rest is for nibbling.

>   4   tablespoons (½ stick) unsalted butter, melted,
>   plus extra for the baking dish
>   4   large eggs
>   1⅓ cups buttermilk
>   1⅓ cups milk
>   2   cups yellow cornmeal
>   2   cups (10 ounces) unbleached all-purpose flour
>   2   tablespoons sugar
>   4   teaspoons baking powder
>   1   teaspoon baking soda
>   1   teaspoon table salt

1. Adjust an oven rack to the middle position and heat the oven to 375 degrees. Grease a 13 by 9-inch baking dish with butter.

2. Beat the eggs in medium bowl; whisk in the buttermilk and milk.

3. Whisk the cornmeal, flour, sugar, baking powder, baking soda, and salt together in a large bowl. Push the dry ingredients up the sides of the bowl to make a well, then pour the egg and milk mixture into the well and stir with a whisk until just combined; stir in the melted butter.

4. Pour the batter into the prepared baking dish. Bake until the top is golden brown and the edges have pulled away from the sides of the pan, 30 to 40 minutes.

5. Transfer the baking dish to a wire rack and cool to room temperature before using, about 1 hour.

Turkey Gravy

MAKES ABOUT 4 CUPS

Because this gravy doesn't use drippings from the roasted turkey but instead uses the trimmings from butterflying the bird, the gravy can conveniently be made a day in advance (while the turkey brines and air-dries in the refrigerator) and then reheated before serving.

>   Reserved giblets, neck, tailpiece, and backbone and
>   rib bones from the turkey (see note)
>   2   small onions, chopped coarse
>   1   medium carrot, cut into 1-inch pieces
>   1   celery rib, cut into 1-inch pieces
>   6   garlic cloves, unpeeled
>   3½ cups low-sodium chicken broth
>   3   cups water
>   2   cups dry white wine
>   6   sprigs fresh thyme
>   ¼   cup unbleached all-purpose flour
>   Table salt and ground black pepper

1. Heat the oven to 450 degrees. Adjust an oven rack to the middle position. Place the turkey trimmings, onions, carrot, celery, and garlic in a large roasting pan or broiler pan bottom. Spray lightly with vegetable oil spray and toss to combine. Roast, stirring every 10 minutes, until well browned, 40 to 50 minutes.

2. Remove the pan from the oven and place over two burners set at high heat; add the chicken broth and bring to a boil, scraping up the browned bits on the bottom of the pan with a wooden spoon.

3. Transfer the contents of the pan to a large saucepan. Add the water, wine, and thyme; bring to a boil over high heat. Reduce the heat to low and simmer until reduced by half, about 1½ hours. Strain the stock into a large measuring cup or container. Cool to room temperature; cover with plastic wrap, and refrigerate until the fat congeals on the surface, about 2 hours.

4. Skim the fat from the stock using a soup spoon; reserve the fat. Pour the stock through a fine-mesh strainer to remove remaining bits of fat. Bring the stock to a simmer in a medium saucepan over medium-high heat.

5. In a second medium saucepan, heat ¼ cup reserved turkey fat over medium-high heat until bubbling; whisk in the flour and cook, whisking constantly, until combined and honey-colored, about 2 minutes. Continuing to whisk constantly, gradually add the hot stock; bring to a boil, then reduce the heat to medium-low and simmer, stirring occasionally, until slightly thickened, about 5 minutes. Season with salt and pepper to taste. (The gravy can be stored in an airtight container in the refrigerator for up to 1 day. While the turkey is resting, heat the gravy in a medium saucepan over medium heat until hot, about 8 minutes.)

salt is too fine and is not recommended for this recipe. If you are roasting a kosher or self-basting turkey (such as a frozen Butterball), do not salt it; it already contains a good amount of sodium. If serving with Giblet Pan Gravy (page 113), note that you can complete step 1 of the gravy recipe up to a day ahead, if desired. Begin step 3 once the bird has been removed from the oven and is resting on a carving board.

ROAST SALTED TURKEY

WHY THIS RECIPE WORKS: Brining is the best way to guarantee a moist turkey, but it isn't always the most practical way, especially if you have limited refrigerator space. We wanted to develop an alternative method to brining that would both season the meat and keep it moist.

Instead of brining, we turned to salting—it seasons the meat, but no bucket is required. We wanted to make sure the salt penetrated the meat, but we didn't want to tear the skin. We found that either chopsticks or the handle of a wooden spoon worked well to help us gently separate the skin from the meat. To ensure moist breast meat, we chilled the breast by placing a small bag of ice inside the cavity against the breast and setting the turkey, breast side down, on ice. This trick brought down the temperature of the breast, thus allowing it to cook through over a longer period in the oven (more in line with the cooking time of the dark meat) without drying out.

Roast Salted Turkey

SERVES 10 TO 12

This recipe was developed and tested using Diamond Crystal Kosher Salt. If you have Morton's Kosher Salt, which is denser than Diamond Crystal, use only 4½ teaspoons of salt in the cavity, 2¼ teaspoons of salt per each half of the breast, and 1 teaspoon of salt per leg. Table

1 **(12 to 14-pound) turkey; giblets, neck, and tailpiece removed and reserved for gravy (see page 113)**
5 **tablespoons kosher salt (see note)**
1 **(5-pound) bag ice cubes**
4 **tablespoons (½ stick) unsalted butter, melted**
3 **medium onions, chopped coarse**
2 **medium carrots, chopped coarse**
2 **celery ribs, chopped coarse**
6 **sprigs fresh thyme**
1 **cup water, plus more as needed**

1. Following the photos on page 124, carefully separate the turkey skin from the meat on the breast, legs, thighs, and back; avoid breaking the skin. Then rub 2 tablespoons of the salt evenly inside the cavity of the turkey, 1 tablespoon more salt under the skin of each breast half, and 1½ teaspoons more salt under the skin of each leg. Wrap the turkey tightly with plastic wrap; refrigerate for 24 to 48 hours.

2. Remove the turkey from the refrigerator. Rinse off any excess salt between the meat and skin and in the cavity, then pat dry inside and out with paper towels. Add ice to two 1-gallon zipper-lock bags until each is half full. Place the bags in a large roasting pan and lay the turkey, breast side down, on top of the ice. Add ice to two 1-quart zipper-lock bags until each is one-third full; place one bag of ice in the large cavity of the turkey and the other bag in the neck cavity. (Make sure that the ice touches the

ICING THE TURKEY BREAST

Cooling the breast down with ice ensures that it will cook more slowly than the legs and thighs, preventing the breast meat from drying out. Place bags of ice underneath the breast and inside both the large cavity and the neck area.

HOW TO SALT A TURKEY

1. Use a chopstick or a thin wooden spoon handle to separate the skin from the meat over the breast, legs, thighs, and back.

2. Rub 2 tablespoons kosher salt inside the main cavity.

3. Lift the skin and apply 1 tablespoon kosher salt over each breast half, placing half of the salt on each end of each breast, then massaging the salt evenly over the meat.

4. Apply 1½ teaspoons kosher salt over the top and bottom of each leg.

breast only, not the thighs or legs; see the photo.) Keep the turkey on ice for 1 hour (the roasting pan should remain on the counter).

3. Meanwhile, adjust an oven rack to the lowest position and heat the oven to 425 degrees. Line a large V-rack with heavy-duty foil and poke several holes in the foil. Set the V-rack in a roasting pan and spray the foil with vegetable oil spray.

4. Remove the turkey from the ice and pat dry with paper towels (discard the ice). Tuck the tips of the drumsticks into the skin at the tail to secure and tuck the wings under the bird. Brush the turkey breast with 2 tablespoons of the melted butter. Scatter the vegetables and thyme in the roasting pan and pour 1 cup water over the vegetable mixture. Place the turkey, breast side down, on the V-rack. Brush the turkey with the remaining 2 tablespoons melted butter.

5. Roast the turkey for 45 minutes. Remove the pan from the oven (close the oven door to retain the oven heat) and reduce the oven temperature to 325 degrees. With a dish towel in each hand, rotate the turkey breast side up; continue to roast until the thickest part of the breast registers 160 to 165 degrees and the thickest part of the thigh registers 175 degrees on an instant-read thermometer, 1 to 1½ hours longer. Transfer the turkey to a carving board and let rest, uncovered, for 30 minutes. Carve the turkey and serve with the gravy (see note).

HERBED ROAST TURKEY

WHY THIS RECIPE WORKS: Throwing a bunch of herbs into the cavity of a turkey or rubbing the outside of the bird with a savory paste only flirts with great herb flavor—it doesn't infuse that flavor into each and every bite. We wanted an intensely herby turkey, one with a powerful, aromatic flavor that permeated well beyond the meat's surface.

First we tried an intense brine, but it made the bird taste more pickled than infused with herbs. Next, we pumped the paste into the bird with a syringe, which created nothing but ugly blobs of overwhelmingly strong, raw-tasting herbs. Then we tried a technique we had developed for stuffing a thick-cut pork chop. We made a vertical slit in the breast meat and, using a paring knife, created an expansive pocket by sweeping the blade back and forth. This created a void into which we could rub a small amount of herb paste. This along with three other herbal applications—underneath the skin, inside the cavity, and over the skin—made for a successful four-pronged approach that gave every bite of turkey herb flavor. The herb paste itself, balanced with small amounts of pungent herbs (sage and rosemary) and greater amounts of softer flavors (thyme and parsley), also included lemon zest for a fresh, bright note and olive oil and Dijon mustard to make it spreadable. This was a moist roast turkey packed with bright herb flavor—a fresh alternative to the usual holiday bird.

Herbed Roast Turkey

SERVES 10 TO 12

If you have the time and the refrigerator space, air-drying produces extremely crisp skin and is worth the effort. After brining, rinsing, and patting the turkey dry, place the turkey, breast side up, on a wire rack set over a rimmed baking sheet and refrigerate, uncovered, for 8 to 24 hours. Proceed with the recipe. Serve with All-Purpose Turkey Gravy (recipe follows).

TURKEY AND BRINE

- 2 **cups table salt**
- 1 **(12 to 14-pound) turkey; giblets, neck, and tailpiece removed and discarded**

HERB PASTE

- 1¼ **cups roughly chopped fresh parsley leaves**
- 4 **teaspoons minced fresh thyme leaves**
- 2 **teaspoons roughly chopped fresh sage leaves**
- 1½ **teaspoons minced fresh rosemary leaves**
- 1 **medium shallot, minced (about 3 tablespoons)**
- 2 **medium garlic cloves, minced or pressed through a garlic press (about 2 teaspoons)**
- ¾ **teaspoon grated zest from 1 lemon**
- ¾ **teaspoon table salt**
- 1 **teaspoon ground black pepper**
- ¼ **cup olive oil**
- 1 **teaspoon Dijon mustard**
- 1 **recipe All-Purpose Turkey Gravy**

1. FOR THE TURKEY AND BRINE: Dissolve the salt in 2 gallons cold water in a large container. Submerge the turkey in the brine, cover, and refrigerate or store in a very cool spot (40 degrees or less) for 4 to 6 hours.

NOTES FROM THE TEST KITCHEN

APPLYING HERB PASTE TO THE TURKEY

1. Carefully separate the skin from the meat on the breast, thigh, and drumstick areas.

2. Rub the herb paste under the skin and directly onto the flesh, distributing it evenly.

3. Make a 1½-inch slit in each breast. Swing a knife tip through the breast to create a large pocket.

4. Place a thin layer of paste inside each pocket.

5. Rub the remaining paste inside the turkey cavity and on the skin.

NOTES FROM THE TEST KITCHEN

CARVING THE BREAST

The wings and legs on our Herbed Roast Turkey can be carved just as they would be on any other turkey, but the breast, which is stuffed with herb paste, needs some special attention. Here's how to ensure that every slice has a nice swirl of herbs.

1. With the wings facing toward you, cut along both sides of the breastbone, slicing from the tip of the breastbone to the cutting board.

2. Gently pull each breast half away to expose the wishbone. Then pull and remove the wishbone.

3. Using the knife tip, cut along the rib cage to remove the breast completely.

4. Place the entire breast half on a carving board and cut on the bias into thin slices. Repeat steps 3 and 4 on the other side.

2. Remove the turkey from the brine and rinse it well. Pat dry inside and out with paper towels. Place the turkey, breast side up, on a wire rack set over a rimmed baking sheet or roasting pan and refrigerate, uncovered, for 30 minutes. (Alternatively, air-dry the turkey; see note.)

3. FOR THE HERB PASTE: Pulse the parsley, thyme, sage, rosemary, shallot, garlic, lemon zest, salt, and pepper together in a food processor until a coarse paste is formed, 10 pulses. Add the olive oil and mustard; continue to pulse until the mixture forms a smooth paste, 10 to twelve 2-second pulses; scrape the sides of the processor bowl with a rubber spatula after 5 pulses. Transfer the mixture to a small bowl.

4. TO PREPARE THE TURKEY: Adjust an oven rack to the lowest position and heat the oven to 400 degrees. Line a large V-rack with heavy-duty foil and poke several holes in the foil. Set the V-rack in a large roasting pan and spray the foil with vegetable oil spray. Remove the turkey from the refrigerator and wipe away any water collected in the baking sheet; set the turkey, breast side up, on the baking sheet.

5. Following the photos on page 125, use your hands to carefully loosen the skin from the meat of the breast, thighs, and drumsticks. Using your fingers or a spoon, slip 1½ tablespoons of the paste under the breast skin on each side of the turkey. Using your fingers, distribute the paste under the skin over the breast, thigh, and drumstick meat.

6. Using a sharp paring knife, cut a 1½-inch vertical slit into the thickest part of each side of the breast. Starting from the top of the incision, swing the knife tip down to create a 4 to 5-inch pocket within the flesh. Place 1 tablespoon more paste in the pocket of each side of the breast; using your fingers, rub the paste in a thin, even layer.

7. Rub 1 tablespoon more paste inside the turkey cavity. Rotate the turkey breast side down; apply half the remaining herb paste to the turkey skin; flip the turkey breast side up and apply the remaining herb paste to the skin, pressing and patting to make the paste adhere; reapply the herb paste that falls onto the baking sheet. Tuck the tips of the drumsticks into the skin at the tail to secure, and tuck the wings under the bird.

8. TO ROAST THE TURKEY: Place the turkey, breast side down, on the V-rack. Roast the turkey for 45 minutes.

9. Remove the pan from the oven (close the oven door to retain the oven heat). With a dish towel in each hand, rotate the turkey breast side up. Continue to roast until the thickest part of the breast registers 160 to 165 degrees and the thickest part of the thigh registers 175 degrees on an instant-read thermometer, 50 to 60 minutes longer. Transfer the turkey to a carving board and let rest, uncovered, for 30 minutes. Following the photos, carve the turkey and serve with the gravy.

All-Purpose Turkey Gravy

MAKES ABOUT 2 CUPS

Adding drippings from the roasted turkey will enhance the flavor of the gravy.

- 1 small carrot, peeled and chopped coarse
- 1 small celery rib, chopped coarse
- 1 small onion, chopped coarse
- 3 tablespoons unsalted butter
- ¼ cup unbleached all-purpose flour
- 2 cups low-sodium chicken broth
- 2 cups beef broth
- 1 bay leaf
- 2 sprigs fresh thyme
- 5 whole black peppercorns
  Defatted pan drippings from Herbed Roast Turkey (optional; see note)
  Table salt and ground black pepper

1. Pulse the carrot into ¼-inch pieces in a food processor, about 5 pulses. Add the celery and onion and continue to pulse until all of the vegetables are chopped fine, 5 pulses.

2. Melt the butter in a large saucepan over medium-high heat. Add the vegetables and cook, stirring often, until softened and well browned, about 7 minutes. Reduce the heat to medium, stir in the flour, and cook, stirring constantly, until well browned, about 5 minutes.

3. Gradually whisk in the broths until smooth. Bring to a boil, skimming any foam that rises to the surface. Add the bay leaf, thyme, and peppercorns. Reduce the heat to medium-low and simmer, stirring occasionally, until the gravy is thickened and measures about 3 cups, 20 to 25 minutes. Stir in any juices from the roasted meat (if using) and continue to simmer the gravy as needed to re-thicken.

4. Strain the gravy through a fine-mesh strainer into a serving pitcher, pressing on the solids to extract as much liquid as possible; discard the solids. Season the gravy with salt and pepper to taste and cover to keep warm until needed.

BRAISED TURKEY

WHY THIS RECIPE WORKS: Separating turkey into parts and braising it for the holiday meal? It may sound heretical if you've never presented anything but a whole roasted bird at the table, but this break from tradition has a lot going for it. Roasting a large turkey is always a race to get the denser, fattier thighs and legs to come up to the ideal temperature of around 175 degrees before the leaner, more delicate breast dries out, once its temperature climbs past 160 degrees. An intact, upright bird compounds this problem because the slower-cooking thighs are shielded from the heat. So we wondered if there was an easier way to get perfectly cooked turkey on the table without sacrificing flavor. Turkey parts provided a neat solution to the problem by giving both types of meat more even exposure to the heat—and without any cumbersome turning. Better yet, braising the pieces in a flavorful liquid created rich, ready-made gravy and infused the meat with all of its complex flavors. When we tasted this deeply flavored, moist and tender turkey, we found we didn't miss the traditional whole bird at all.

Braised Turkey

SERVES 10 TO 12

Instead of drumsticks and thighs, you may use 2 whole leg quarters, 1½ to 2 pounds each. The recipe will also work with turkey breast alone; in step 1, reduce the amount of salt and sugar to ½ cup each, and the amount of water to 4 quarts. If you are braising kosher or self-basting turkey parts, skip the brining step, and instead season the turkey parts with 1½ teaspoons salt.

BRAISED TURKEY

- Table salt and ground black pepper
- 1 cup sugar
- 1 (5 to 7-pound) whole bone-in, skin-on turkey breast, trimmed
- 4 pounds turkey drumsticks and thighs, trimmed
- 3 medium onions, chopped medium
- 3 medium celery ribs, chopped medium
- 2 medium carrots, peeled and chopped medium
- 6 medium garlic cloves, peeled and crushed
- 2 bay leaves
- 6 sprigs fresh thyme
- 6 sprigs fresh parsley
- ½ ounce dried porcini mushrooms, rinsed
- 4 tablespoons (½ stick) unsalted butter, melted
- 4 cups low-sodium chicken broth
- 1 cup dry white wine

GRAVY

3 tablespoons unbleached all-purpose flour
Table salt and ground black pepper

1. FOR THE TURKEY: Dissolve 1 cup salt and the sugar in 2 gallons cold water in a large container. Submerge the turkey pieces in the brine, cover, and refrigerate for 3 to 6 hours.

2. Adjust an oven rack to the lower-middle position and heat the oven to 500 degrees. Remove the turkey from the brine and pat dry with paper towels. Toss the onions, celery, carrots, garlic, bay leaves, thyme, parsley, porcini, and 2 tablespoons of the melted butter in a large roasting pan; arrange in an even layer. Brush the turkey pieces with the remaining 2 tablespoons melted butter and season with pepper. Place the turkey pieces, skin side up, over the vegetables, leaving at least ¼ inch between the pieces. Roast until the skin is lightly browned, about 20 minutes.

3. While the turkey is roasting, bring the broth and wine to a simmer in a medium saucepan over medium heat. Cover and keep warm.

4. Remove the turkey from the oven and reduce the oven temperature to 325 degrees. Pour the broth mixture around the turkey pieces (it should come about three-quarters of the way up the legs and thighs.) Place a 12 by 16-inch piece of parchment paper over the turkey pieces. Cover the roasting pan tightly with aluminum foil. Return the covered roasting pan to the oven and cook until the breast registers 160 degrees and the thighs register 175 degrees on an instant-read thermometer, 1½ to 2 hours. Transfer the turkey to a carving board, tent loosely with foil, and let rest for 20 minutes.

5. FOR THE GRAVY: Strain the vegetables and liquid from the roasting pan through a fine-mesh strainer set in a large bowl. Press the solids with the back of a spatula to extract as much liquid as possible. Discard the vegetables. Transfer the liquid to a fat separator and allow to settle for 5 minutes. Reserve 3 tablespoons fat and measure off 3 cups broth (use any remaining broth for another use.)

6. Heat 3 tablespoons reserved turkey fat in a medium saucepan over medium-high heat; add the flour and cook, stirring constantly, until the flour is dark golden brown and fragrant, about 5 minutes. Whisk in 3 cups braising liquid and bring to a boil. Reduce the heat to medium-low and simmer, stirring occasionally, until the gravy is thick and reduced to 2 cups, 15 to 20 minutes. Remove the gravy from the heat and season with salt and pepper to taste.

7. Carve the turkey and serve, passing the gravy separately.

GRILL-ROASTED TURKEY

WHY THIS RECIPE WORKS: Grill-roasting a turkey can be hard to manage. Cooking times can vary depending on the weather, and it's much easier to burn the bird's skin on a grill. There also remain the usual problems inherent to roasting a turkey: dry, overcooked breast meat and undercooked thighs.

But grill-roasting can produce the best-tasting, best-looking turkey ever, with crispy skin and moist meat wonderfully perfumed with smoke. We wanted to take the guesswork out of preparing the holiday bird on the grill.

Because the skin on larger birds will burn before the meat is done, we chose a small turkey (less than 14 pounds). We ditched stuffing the turkey or trussing it—both can lead to burnt skin and undercooked meat. To season the meat and help prevent it from drying out on the grill, we brined the turkey. To protect the skin and promote slow cooking, we placed the turkey on the opposite side of the glowing coals or lit gas burner. Using a V-rack also helped, as it improved air circulation. And we turned the turkey three times instead of twice; this way, all four sides received equal exposure to the hot side of the grill for evenly bronzed skin.

Grill-Roasted Turkey for a Charcoal Grill
SERVES 10 TO 12

The total cooking time is 2 to 2½ hours, depending on the size of the bird, the ambient conditions (the bird will require more time on a cool, windy day), and the intensity of the fire. Check the internal temperature in the thigh when rotating the bird at the 1-hour-and-45-minute mark. If the thigh is nearly up to temperature (the final temperature should be 175 degrees), check the temperature again after about 15 minutes. If the thigh is still well below temperature (145 degrees or cooler), don't bother checking the bird again for at least another 30 minutes.

1 cup table salt
1 (12 to 14-pound) turkey; giblets, neck, and tailpiece
removed and wings tucked under the bird
6 (3-inch) wood chunks
2 tablespoons unsalted butter, melted

1. Dissolve the salt in 2 gallons cold water in a large container. Submerge the turkey in the brine, cover, and refrigerate or store in a very cool spot (40 degrees or less) for 12 hours or overnight.

2. Toward the end of brining, soak the wood chunks in cold water to cover for 1 hour; drain.

3. Light a large chimney starter filled three-quarters with charcoal (about 4½ quarts) and allow to burn until the coals are partially covered with a layer of ash, about 20 minutes. Open the bottom grill vents completely.

4. Meanwhile, spray a V-rack with vegetable oil spray. Remove the turkey from the brine and rinse inside and out under cool running water to remove all traces of salt. Pat the turkey dry with paper towels; brush both sides with melted butter. Set the turkey, breast side down, in the V-rack.

5. Build a single-banked fire by banking the coals over half of the grill, piling them up two or three coals high, leaving the other half empty. Place three of the wood chunks on top of the charcoal. Set the cooking grate in place, open the lid vents halfway, and cover the grill. Heat the grate until hot, about 5 minutes, turning the lid so that the vents are opposite the wood chunks to draw smoke through the grill.

6. Position the V-rack with the turkey on the side of the grill opposite the fire. Cover and cook for 1 hour.

7. Remove the lid from the grill. Using thick potholders, transfer the V-rack with the turkey to a large rimmed baking sheet or roasting pan. Remove the cooking grate and place 12 new pieces of charcoal and the three remaining wood chunks on top of the coals; replace the grate. With a dish towel in each hand, flip the turkey breast side up in the rack. Return the V-rack with the turkey to the cool part of the grill so that the leg and wing that were facing the coals are now facing away. Cover and cook for 45 minutes.

8. Using thick potholders, carefully turn the V-rack with the turkey (the breast remains up) so that the leg and wing that were facing the coals are now facing away from the coals. Insert an instant-read thermometer into each thigh to check the temperature and gauge how much longer the turkey must cook (see note).

9. Cover and continue to cook until the thickest part of the thigh registers 175 degrees on an instant-read thermometer, 15 to 45 minutes longer.

10. Remove the turkey from the grill, cover loosely with foil, and let rest for 30 minutes. Carve and serve.

Grill-Roasted Turkey for a Gas Grill

The total cooking time is 2 to 2½ hours, depending on the size of the bird, the ambient conditions (the bird will require more time on a cool, windy day), and the intensity of the fire. Check the internal temperature in the thigh when rotating the bird at the 1-hour-and-45-minute

THE MECHANICS OF BRINING

Anyone who watches our show knows that we love to brine. Brining not only helps prevent delicate meat like chicken, turkey, and pork from drying out, it also seasons the meat for better flavor. What equipment do you need for brining? A clean container that's large enough to accommodate the meat and brine. For large containers (such as a washtub or cooler) that won't fit in a refrigerator, you need ice packs to keep the temperature at 40 degrees F. For a whole chicken, the test kitchen likes to use a Cambro storage container, which is a large, clear bucket marked with level graduations—Cambros make handy containers for rising bread dough, too. (Look for these containers at restaurant supply stores or online.)

As for brining tips, we've got a few after 15 years. After pulling your turkey out of the brine, rinse it thoroughly to get rid of the excess salt on the surface. And pat it dry to prevent soggy skin. You can also place the turkey on a wire rack set on a baking sheet and allow it to dry overnight in the refrigerator—this will further encourage crispy skin during roasting. And as for the salt, the test kitchen prefers table salt. Kosher salt works fine, but the size of the grains varies between the two major brands, which can make recipe testing (and writing) difficult. The ratio of salt to water varies a bit from recipe to recipe, but generally the test kitchen uses 1 cup table salt to 2 gallons of water (this is enough brine for a 12 to 14-pound turkey).

mark. If the thigh is nearly up to temperature (the final temperature should be 175 degrees), check the temperature again after about 15 minutes. If the thigh is still well below temperature (145 degrees or cooler), don't bother checking the bird again for at least another 30 minutes.

Follow the recipe for Grill-Roasted Turkey on a Charcoal Grill through step 4, making the following changes: Cover 3 cups wood chips with water and soak for 30 minutes, then drain. Place the soaked wood chips in a small disposable aluminum pan; set the pan on the burner that will remain on. Turn all the burners to high, close the lid, and heat the grill until the chips smoke heavily, about 20 minutes. Turn off the burner(s) without the wood chips. Place the turkey over the cool part of the grill and proceed as directed in step 6.

GRILL-ROASTED TURKEY BREAST

WHY THIS RECIPE WORKS: Grill-roasting a turkey breast makes a nice change from the same old oven-roasted holiday bird. And unleashing the smoky fire of the grill on mild-mannered turkey breast is bound to add great flavor. The problem is that unlike fatty pork butt or brisket, which turns moist and tender after a stint on the grill, ultra-lean turkey breast easily dries out. Plus its irregular shape can lead to uneven cooking. We wanted to develop a recipe that would deliver a grill-roasted breast with all the richness and juiciness we associate with the thighs and legs, along with crisp, well-rendered skin, and meat that was moist all the way through.

We began by salting our turkey breast. Salting, much like brining, imparts flavor and moisture to the meat. When meat is salted, its juices are initially drawn out of the flesh and beads of liquid pool on its surface. Eventually, the salty liquid slowly migrates back into the meat, keeping it moist as it cooks. We grill-roasted the turkey breast over a modified two-level fire, starting the meat over the cool side of the grill and later moving it to the hot side to finish cooking. Although most of the meat turned out moist and flavorful, there were still desiccated spots on the tapered ends of the breast and in places where the skin didn't completely cover the meat. Inspired by a restaurant technique, we reshaped our turkey breast like a roulade so that it would cook through evenly. After carefully removing the skin, we rolled the boneless turkey breast into a tight cylinder. Then we rewrapped the skin around the roulade of meat to completely cover and protect it. Our roast held its shape beautifully on the grill and, once carved, the roulade revealed moist, evenly cooked meat and crisp skin.

Charcoal Grill-Roasted Boneless Turkey Breast
SERVES 6 TO 8

We prefer either a natural (unbrined) or kosher turkey breast for this recipe. Using a kosher turkey breast (rubbed with salt and rinsed during processing) or self-basting turkey breast (injected with salt and water) eliminates the need for salting in step 2. If the breast has a pop-up timer, remove it before cooking.

1 (5 to 7-pound) whole bone-in, skin-on turkey breast (see note)
2 teaspoons table salt (see note)
½ cup wood chips (optional)
1 teaspoon vegetable oil, plus extra for the cooking grate
   Ground black pepper

1. Set a wire rack over a large rimmed baking sheet and set aside. Following photos 1 and 2 on page 131, remove the skin from the breast meat and then remove the breasts from the bone structure (discard the bones or save for stock).

2. Sprinkle the entire surface of each breast half with 1 teaspoon of the salt. Following photos 3 and 4 on page 131, assemble and tie the turkey roast. Place the roast on the prepared baking sheet and refrigerate, uncovered, for 1 hour.

3. Meanwhile, if using, soak the wood chips in cold water to cover for 30 minutes; drain. Light a large chimney starter filled with charcoal (about 6 quarts) and allow to burn until the coals are partially covered with a layer of ash, about 20 minutes. Build a modified two-level fire by arranging all the coals over one half of the grill, leaving the other half empty. Sprinkle the wood chips (if using) over the coals. Set the cooking grate in place, cover, and heat the grate until hot, about 5 minutes. Use a grill brush to scrape the grate clean. Dip a wad of paper towels in the oil; holding the wad with tongs, oil the cooking grate.

4. Rub the surface of the roast with 1 teaspoon oil and season with pepper. Place the roast on the cooler side of the grill. Cover the grill and cook until an instant-read thermometer inserted into the thickest part of the roast registers 150 degrees, 40 to 60 minutes, turning the roast 180 degrees halfway through the cooking time.

5. Slide the roast to the hot side of the grill and cook, uncovered, until the roast is browned and the skin is crisp on all sides, 2 to 2½ minutes per side (8 to 10 minutes total). Transfer the roast to a carving board and let rest, uncovered, for 20 minutes. Cut into ½-inch-thick slices, removing the twine as you cut. Serve.

TURNING A BONE-IN TURKEY BREAST INTO A BONELESS TURKEY ROAST

1. Starting at one side of the breast and using your fingers to separate the skin from the meat, peel the skin off the breast meat and reserve.

2. Using the tip of a knife, cut along the rib cage to remove each breast half completely.

3. Arrange one breast, cut side up; top with the second breast, cut side down, the thick end over the tapered end. Drape the skin over the breasts and tuck the ends under.

4. Tie a 3-foot piece of kitchen twine lengthwise around the roast. Then, tie five to seven pieces of twine at 1-inch intervals crosswise along the roast, starting at its center, then at either end, and then filling in the rest.

Gas Grill–Roasted Boneless Turkey Breast

Follow the recipe for Charcoal Grill–Roasted Boneless Turkey Breast through step 2. If using wood chips, place them in a disposable aluminum pie plate and place the pie plate on the primary burner and reposition the cooking grate(s). Turn all the burners to high, close the lid, and heat the grill until hot, about 15 minutes. Scrape the cooking grate clean with a grill brush. Dip a wad of paper towels in the oil; holding the wad with tongs, wipe the cooking grate. Leave the primary burner on high and turn off the other burner(s). Continue with the recipe from step 4, placing the roast seam side up on the side opposite the primary burner and cooking with the lid down in step 5.

CRANBERRY SAUCE

WHY THIS RECIPE WORKS: The best cranberry sauce has a clean, pure cranberry flavor, with enough sweetness to temper the assertively tart fruit but not so much that the sauce is cloying or candylike. The texture should be that of a soft gel, neither too liquidy nor too stiff, cushioning some softened but still intact berries.

For the most part, it turned out that simpler was better. We used white table sugar, which, unlike brown sugar, honey, or syrup, balanced the tartness of the cranberries without adding a flavor profile of its own. Simpler was also better when it came to liquid: water proved the best choice. We also discovered that adding just a pinch of salt brought out an unexpected sweetness in the berries, heightening the flavor of the sauce overall.

Classic Cranberry Sauce

MAKES 2¼ CUPS

If you've got frozen cranberries, do not defrost them before use; just pick through them and add about 2 minutes to the simmering time.

- 1 cup (7 ounces) sugar
- ¾ cup water
- ¼ teaspoon table salt
- 1 (12-ounce) bag cranberries, picked through (see note)

Bring the sugar, water, and salt to a boil in a medium saucepan over high heat, stirring occasionally to dissolve the sugar. Stir in the cranberries; return to a boil. Reduce the heat to medium; simmer until saucy and slightly thickened, and about two-thirds of the berries have popped open, about 5 minutes. Transfer to a medium bowl, cool to room temperature, and serve. (The cranberry sauce can be covered and refrigerated for up to 7 days; let stand at room temperature for 30 minutes before serving.)

BAKED BREAD STUFFING

WHY THIS RECIPE WORKS: Stuffing baked in a dish definitely has appeal—you can make as much as you want and you don't have to time its doneness to coincide with the doneness of the meat—but it lacks the rich flavor from the bird's juices. As the base for our stuffing we chose ordinary sandwich bread, which we "staled" in a low oven; this would allow it to soak up plenty of liquid. To infuse the stuffing with meaty turkey flavor, we browned turkey wings on the stovetop, then we used the same pan to sauté the aromatics. When we placed the stuffing in a baking dish, we arranged the seared wings on top—as they cooked, their rendered fat infused the stuffing with rich flavor. Covering the baking dish with foil prevented the top of the stuffing from drying out, while placing a baking sheet underneath the dish protected the bottom layer from the oven's heat.

Baked Bread Stuffing with Sausage, Dried Cherries, and Pecans

SERVES 10 TO 12

Two pounds of chicken wings can be substituted for the turkey wings. If using chicken wings, separate them into 2 sections (it's not necessary to separate the tips) and poke each segment 4 to 5 times. Also, increase the amount of broth to 3 cups, reduce the amount of butter to 2 tablespoons, and cook the stuffing for only 60 minutes (the wings should register over 175 degrees at the end of cooking). Use the meat from the cooked wings to make salad or soup. The bread can be toasted up to 1 day in advance.

2 pounds hearty white sandwich bread, cut into ½-inch cubes (16 cups)
3 pounds turkey wings, divided at joints
2 teaspoons vegetable oil
1 pound bulk pork sausage
4 tablespoons (½ stick) unsalted butter
1 large onion, chopped fine
3 medium celery ribs, minced
   Table salt
2 tablespoons minced fresh thyme
2 tablespoons minced fresh sage
1 teaspoon ground black pepper
2½ cups low-sodium chicken broth
3 large eggs
1 cup dried cherries
1 cup pecan halves, toasted and chopped fine

1. Adjust the oven racks to the upper-middle and lower-middle positions and heat the oven to 250 degrees. Spread the bread cubes in an even layer on 2 rimmed baking sheets. Bake until the edges have dried but the centers are slightly moist (the cubes should yield to pressure), 45 to 60 minutes, stirring several times during baking. Transfer the dried bread to a large bowl and increase the oven temperature to 375 degrees.

2. While the bread dries, use a paring knife to poke 10 to 15 holes in each wing segment. Heat the oil in a 12-inch skillet over medium-high heat until shimmering. Add the wings in a single layer and cook until golden brown on both sides, 8 to 12 minutes. Transfer the wings to a separate bowl and set aside.

3. Return the now-empty skillet to medium-high heat, add the sausage, and cook, breaking it up into ½-inch pieces with a wooden spoon, until browned, 5 to 7 minutes. Remove the sausage with a slotted spoon and transfer to a paper towel–lined plate.

4. Melt the butter in the fat left in the skillet over medium heat. Add the onion, celery, and ½ teaspoon salt and cook, stirring occasionally, until the vegetables are softened, 7 to 9 minutes. Stir in the thyme, sage, and pepper and cook until fragrant, about 30 seconds. Stir in 1 cup of the broth, scraping up any browned bits, and bring to a simmer. Add the vegetable mixture to the bowl with the dried bread and toss to combine.

5. Grease a 13 by 9-inch baking dish. Whisk the eggs, remaining 1½ cups broth, 1½ teaspoons salt, and any accumulated juices from the wings together in a bowl. Add the egg mixture, cherries, pecans, and sausage to the bread mixture and toss to combine; transfer to the prepared baking dish. Arrange the wings on top of the stuffing, cover tightly with aluminum foil, and place the baking dish on a rimmed baking sheet.

6. Bake on the lower rack until the wings register 175 degrees, 60 to 75 minutes. (The stuffing can be held at room temperature for up to 4 hours. To finish, remove the wings from the stuffing and re-cover the stuffing tightly with foil. Heat on a rimmed baking sheet in a 375-degree oven until hot, 20 to 25 minutes. Remove the foil, fluff with a fork, and serve immediately.)

7. Remove the foil and transfer the wings to a dinner plate to reserve for another use. Gently fluff the stuffing with a fork. Let rest for 5 minutes before serving.

Baked Bread Stuffing with Leeks, Bacon, and Apple

Follow the recipe for Baked Bread Stuffing with Sausage, Dried Cherries, and Pecans, substituting 12 ounces bacon, cut into ½-inch pieces, for the sausage. In step 3, cook the bacon in a skillet until crisp, about 5 minutes. Remove the bacon with a slotted spoon and transfer to a paper towel–lined plate; pour off all but 2 tablespoons fat from the skillet. Proceed with the recipe from step 4, substituting 2 leeks, white and light green parts, sliced thin, for the onion, and 3 Granny Smith apples, cut into ¼-inch pieces, for the dried cherries. Omit the pecans.

Baked Bread Stuffing with Fresh Herbs

Follow the recipe for Baked Bread Stuffing with Sausage, Dried Cherries, and Pecans, omitting the sausage. After the browned turkey wings have been removed in step 2, increase the butter to 6 tablespoons and melt it in the skillet over medium heat. Proceed with the recipe from step 4, substituting 3 tablespoons chopped fresh parsley for the dried cherries and pecans.

GREEN BEAN CASSEROLE

WHY THIS RECIPE WORKS: The classic combination of green beans, condensed soup, and canned onions isn't bad. But for a holiday centered on homemade food, shouldn't every dish be great? We wanted to upgrade green bean casserole to give it fresh, homemade flavor.

Our first tasting determined that we definitely needed to use fresh green beans rather than frozen or canned beans. A preliminary blanching and shocking prepared the beans to finish cooking perfectly in the casserole, enabling them to keep a consistent texture and retain their beautiful green color. For our sauce, we made a mushroom variation of the classic French velouté sauce (chicken broth thickened with a roux made from butter and flour, then finished with heavy cream). Our biggest challenge was the onion topping. Ultimately we found that the canned onions couldn't be entirely replaced without sacrificing the level of convenience we thought appropriate to the dish, but we masked their "commercial" flavor with freshly made buttered bread crumbs.

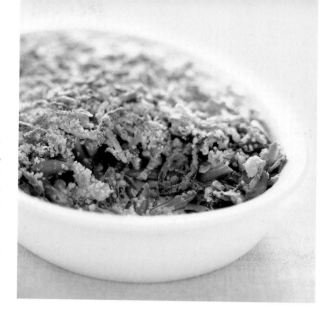

Classic Green Bean Casserole

SERVES 8 TO 10

All the components of this dish can be cooked ahead of time. The assembled casserole needs only 15 minutes in a 375-degree oven to warm through and brown.

TOPPING

- 4 slices high-quality white sandwich bread, torn into quarters
- 2 tablespoons unsalted butter, softened
- ¼ teaspoon table salt
- ⅛ teaspoon ground black pepper
- 3 cups canned fried onions (about 6 ounces)

BEANS

- Table salt
- 2 pounds green beans, ends trimmed, cut on the diagonal into 2-inch pieces
- ½ ounce dried porcini mushrooms
- 6 tablespoons (¾ stick) unsalted butter
- 1 medium onion, minced
- 3 medium garlic cloves, minced or pressed through a garlic press (about 1 tablespoon)
- 12 ounces white button mushrooms, wiped clean and sliced ¼ inch thick
- 12 ounces cremini mushrooms, wiped clean and sliced ¼ inch thick
- 2 tablespoons minced fresh thyme leaves
- ¼ teaspoon ground black pepper
- 2 tablespoons unbleached all-purpose flour
- 1 cup low-sodium chicken broth
- 2 cups heavy cream

1. FOR THE TOPPING: Pulse the bread, butter, salt, and pepper in a food processor until the mixture resembles coarse crumbs, 10 to 15 pulses. Transfer to a large bowl and toss with the onions; set aside.

2. FOR THE BEANS: Heat the oven to 375 degrees. Bring 4 quarts water to a boil in a large pot. Add 2 tablespoons salt and the beans. Cook until bright green and slightly crunchy, 4 to 5 minutes. Drain the beans and plunge immediately into a large bowl filled with ice water to stop cooking. Spread the beans out onto a paper towel–lined baking sheet to drain.

3. Meanwhile, cover the dried porcini with ½ cup hot tap water in a small microwave-safe bowl; cover with plastic wrap, cut several steam vents with a paring knife, and microwave on high power for 30 seconds. Let stand until the mushrooms soften, about 5 minutes. Lift the mushrooms from the liquid with a fork and mince using a chef's knife (you should have about 2 tablespoons). Pour the liquid through a paper towel–lined sieve and reserve.

4. Melt the butter in a large nonstick skillet over medium-high heat. Add the onion, garlic, button mushrooms, and cremini mushrooms and cook until the mushrooms release their moisture, about 2 minutes. Add the porcini mushrooms along with their strained soaking liquid, the thyme, 1 teaspoon salt, and the pepper and cook until all the mushrooms are tender and the liquid has reduced to 2 tablespoons, about 5 minutes. Add the flour and cook for 1 minute. Stir in the chicken broth and reduce the heat to medium. Stir in the cream and simmer gently until the sauce has the consistency of dense soup, about 15 minutes.

5. Arrange the beans in a 3-quart gratin dish. Pour the mushroom mixture over the beans and mix to coat the beans evenly. Sprinkle with the bread-crumb mixture and bake until the top is golden brown and the sauce is bubbling around the edges, about 15 minutes. Serve immediately.

QUICK GREEN BEAN CASSEROLE

WHY THIS RECIPE WORKS: We love traditional green bean casserole, but we wanted a streamlined technique for preparing the dish—one with tender beans in a tasty sauce worthy of a holiday spread and yet speedy enough for a last-minute supper.

Rather than using two pots—one for the beans and one for the sauce—we cooked both in just one pot, a skillet. First, we built a sauce in the skillet with onion, garlic, chicken broth, cream, and a little flour; then we added the beans along with thyme and bay leaves, covered

them, and allowed them to steam until the beans were almost done. We then stirred in meaty browned cremini mushrooms and thickened the sauce by uncovering the skillet during the final phase of cooking. And instead of canned fried onions, we sprinkled crunchy fried sliced shallots over our easy, tasty skillet casserole.

Quick Green Bean "Casserole"

SERVES 8

3	large shallots, sliced thin (about 1 cup)
	Table salt and ground black pepper
3	tablespoons unbleached all-purpose flour
5	tablespoons vegetable oil
10	ounces cremini mushrooms, wiped clean and sliced ¼ inch thick
2	tablespoons unsalted butter
1	medium onion, minced
2	medium garlic cloves, minced or pressed through a garlic press (about 2 teaspoons)
1½	pounds green beans, trimmed
3	sprigs fresh thyme
2	bay leaves
¾	cup heavy cream
¾	cup low-sodium chicken broth

1. Toss the shallots with ¼ teaspoon salt, ⅛ teaspoon pepper, and 2 tablespoons of the flour in a bowl. Heat 3 tablespoons of the oil in a 12-inch nonstick skillet over medium-high heat until smoking; add the shallots and cook, stirring frequently, until golden and crisp, about 5 minutes. Transfer the shallots with the oil to a baking sheet lined with paper towels.

2. Wipe out the skillet and return to medium-high heat. Add the remaining 2 tablespoons oil, the mushrooms, and ¼ teaspoon salt; cook, stirring occasionally, until the mushrooms are well browned, about 8 minutes. Transfer to a plate and set aside.

3. Wipe out the skillet. Melt the butter in the skillet over medium heat, then add the onion and cook, stirring occasionally, until the edges begin to brown, about 2 minutes. Stir in the garlic and remaining 1 tablespoon flour; toss in the green beans, thyme, and bay leaves. Add the cream and chicken broth, increase the heat to medium-high, cover, and cook until the beans are partly tender but still crisp at the center, about 4 minutes. Add the mushrooms and continue to cook, uncovered, until the green beans are tender, about 4 minutes. Off the heat, discard the bay leaves and thyme; season with salt and pepper to taste. Transfer to a serving dish, sprinkle evenly with the shallots, and serve.

CANDIED SWEET POTATO CASSEROLE

WHY THIS RECIPE WORKS: Sweet potato casserole is often claimed as a must-have at the Thanksgiving table. Kids love this sweet, sticky dish, but adults long for a side dish with more restrained sweetness, rather than one that could double as dessert. We set out to develop a sweet potato casserole with a bit of a savory accent to please everyone.

For the best texture and flavor, we steamed the sweet potatoes on the stovetop with a little water, butter, and brown sugar. We kept the other flavorings simple—just salt and pepper. In the topping, we used whole pecans instead of chopped; this gave the casserole a better texture and appearance. And a little cayenne and cumin lent a hit of spice to the topping that offset the sweetness of the potato.

Candied Sweet Potato Casserole

SERVES 10 TO 12

For a more intense molasses flavor, use dark brown sugar in place of light brown sugar.

SWEET POTATOES

- 8 tablespoons (1 stick) unsalted butter, cut into 1-inch chunks
- 5 pounds sweet potatoes (about 8 medium), peeled and cut into 1-inch cubes
- 1 cup (7 ounces) packed light brown sugar (see note)
- ½ cup water
- 1½ teaspoons table salt
- ½ teaspoon ground black pepper

PECAN TOPPING

- 2 cups pecan halves
- ½ cup packed (3½ ounces) light brown sugar (see note)
- 1 egg white, lightly beaten
- ⅛ teaspoon table salt
- Pinch cayenne pepper
- Pinch ground cumin

1. FOR THE SWEET POTATOES: Melt the butter in a large Dutch oven over medium-high heat. Add the sweet potatoes, brown sugar, water, salt, and black pepper; bring to a simmer. Reduce the heat to medium-low, cover, and cook, stirring often, until the sweet potatoes are tender (a paring knife can be slipped into and out of the center of the potatoes with very little resistance), 45 to 60 minutes.

2. When the sweet potatoes are tender, remove the lid and bring the sauce to a rapid simmer over medium-high heat. Continue to simmer until the sauce has reduced to a glaze, 7 to 10 minutes.

3. FOR THE TOPPING: Meanwhile, mix all the ingredients for the topping together in a medium bowl; set aside.

4. Adjust an oven rack to the middle position and heat the oven to 450 degrees. Pour the potato mixture into a 13 by 9-inch baking dish (or a shallow casserole dish of similar size). Spread the topping over the potatoes. Bake until the pecans are toasted and crisp, 10 to 15 minutes. Serve immediately.

CHAPTER 7

WE'LL HAVE THE STEAK

Pan-Seared Steaks 138

    Red Wine Pan Sauce

    Shallot Butter Sauce

Restaurant-Style Herb Sauce for Pan-Seared Steaks 139

Restaurant-Style Brandy and Green-Peppercorn Sauce for Pan-Seared Steaks 139

Restaurant-Style Port Wine Sauce for Pan-Seared Steaks 140

Sauce Base 140

Pan-Seared Thick-Cut Steaks 141

    Red Wine–Mushroom Pan Sauce

    Thai Chili Butter

Pan-Seared Inexpensive Steaks 142

    Tomato-Caper Pan Sauce

    Mustard-Cream Pan Sauce

Pan-Seared Filet Mignon 144

    Madeira Pan Sauce with Mustard and Anchovies

    Argentinian-Style Fresh Parsley and Garlic Sauce (Chimichurri)

Pepper-Crusted Filet Mignon 145

    Port-Cherry Reduction

    Blue Cheese–Chive Butter

Flank Steak and Arugula Sandwiches with Red Onion 147

    Garlic-Soy Mayonnaise

PAN-SEARED STEAKS

WHY THIS RECIPE WORKS: The flavor of a juicy, grilled steak is hard to beat. We wanted to produce outstanding steaks—indoors—that were every bit as good as those cooked on the grill, with a flavorful crust and perfectly cooked, rosy meat.

We found that heating a heavy-bottomed skillet until very hot is essential for a good sear and, thus, a good crust. Thoroughly drying the steaks is also key—soggy steaks will steam, not sear. For best flavor, we seasoned the steaks with salt and pepper prior to cooking. And we reduced the heat before adding the steaks—the skillet was still hot, but not so hot that it burned the fond (the browned bits left in the pan), which we used to make a pan sauce. After removing the steaks from the pan, we let them rest for five minutes, enough time to prepare the pan sauce and allow the juices in the meat to redistribute.

Pan-Seared Steaks

SERVES 4

Serve these steaks with either Red Wine Pan Sauce or Shallot Butter Sauce (recipes follow). Prepare all the sauce ingredients before starting the steaks and don't wash the skillet after cooking the steaks; the fat left in the pan will be used for the sauce. Note that the wine reduction used in the red wine sauce should be started before the steaks are cooked.

- 1 tablespoon vegetable oil
- 4 (8-ounce) boneless strip or rib-eye steaks, each 1 to 1¼ inches thick, thoroughly dried with paper towels
  Table salt and ground black pepper

1. Heat the oil in a 12-inch skillet over high heat until just smoking. Meanwhile, season both sides of the steaks with salt and pepper.

2. Lay the steaks in the pan, leaving ¼ inch of space between them; reduce the heat to medium-high and cook, not moving the steaks until well browned, about 4 minutes. Using tongs, flip the steaks; cook until the center of the steaks registers 120 degrees on an instant-read thermometer for rare (4 minutes), 125 degrees for medium-rare (5 minutes), or 130 degrees for medium (6 minutes). Transfer the steaks to a large plate, tent with foil, and let rest for 5 minutes while preparing one of the pan sauces.

Red Wine Pan Sauce

MAKES ABOUT ½ CUP

Start cooking the steaks when the wine has almost finished reducing. Use a smooth, medium-bodied, fruity wine, such as a Côtes du Rhône.

WINE REDUCTION

- 1 cup red wine (see note)
- 1 medium shallot, minced (about 3 tablespoons)
- 2 white mushrooms, wiped clean and chopped fine (about 3 tablespoons)
- 1 small carrot, chopped fine (about 2 tablespoons)
- 1 bay leaf
- 3 sprigs fresh parsley

SAUCE

- 1 medium shallot, minced (about 3 tablespoons)
- ½ cup low-sodium chicken broth
- ½ cup low-sodium beef broth
- 3 tablespoons cold unsalted butter, cut into 6 pieces
- ½ teaspoon fresh thyme leaves
  Table salt and ground black pepper

1. FOR THE WINE REDUCTION: Heat the wine, shallot, mushrooms, carrot, bay leaf, and parsley in a 12-inch skillet over low heat; cook, without simmering (the liquid should be steaming but not bubbling), until the entire mixture reduces to 1 cup, 15 to 20 minutes. Strain through a fine-mesh strainer and return the liquid (about ½ cup) to the clean skillet. Continue to cook over low heat, without simmering, until the liquid is reduced to 2 tablespoons, 15 to 20 minutes. Transfer the reduction to a bowl.

2. FOR THE SAUCE: Follow the recipe for Pan-Seared Steaks. After removing the steaks from the skillet, add the shallot and cook over low heat until softened, about 1 minute. Turn the heat to high; add the chicken and beef broths. Bring to a boil, scraping up the browned bits on the pan bottom with a wooden spoon, until the liquid is reduced to 2 tablespoons, about 6 minutes. Turn the heat to medium-low, gently whisk in the reserved wine reduction and any accumulated juices from the plate with the steaks. Whisk in the butter, one piece at a time, until melted and the sauce is thickened and glossy; add the thyme and season with salt and pepper to taste. Spoon the sauce over the steaks and serve immediately.

Shallot Butter Sauce
MAKES ABOUT ½ CUP

- 2 medium shallots, minced (about ⅓ cup)
- 4 tablespoons (½ stick) cold unsalted butter, cut into 4 pieces
- 1 teaspoon juice from 1 lemon
- 1 teaspoon minced fresh parsley leaves
  Table salt and ground black pepper

Follow the recipe for Pan-Seared Steaks. After removing the steaks from the skillet, add the shallots and cook over low heat until softened, about 1 minute. Turn the heat to medium-low; stir in the butter, scraping up the browned bits on the pan bottom with a wooden spoon. When the butter is just melted, stir in the lemon juice and parsley; season with salt and pepper to taste. Spoon the sauce over the steaks and serve immediately.

RESTAURANT-STYLE STEAK SAUCE

WHY THIS RECIPE WORKS: We love the ultra-rich flavor and glossy consistency that a classic French demi-glace (a savory, full-bodied reduction traditionally made from veal bones and stock) adds to a sauce, but making it is a time-consuming process usually left to the expertise of professional cooks. We wanted to find a shortcut for making demi-glace at home, so that we could use it as the base of a variety of great sauces for crusty, pan-seared steaks. Chopping up vegetables (to increase their surface area, thus providing more opportunity for flavorful browning) as well as adding mushrooms, tomato paste, and seasonings to red wine and beef broth was a good start, but it wasn't enough. To replicate the meaty flavor and unctuous gelatin given up by roasted bones, we sautéed ground beef with the tomato paste and stirred powdered gelatin into the final reduction. Since it was easy to freeze and use again, making a big batch of our Sauce Base was worth our while; we made enough for two recipes of steak sauce and came up with variations that would make us want to eat steak every night.

Restaurant-Style Herb Sauce for Pan-Seared Steaks
SERVES 4

We like this sauce with strip or rib-eye steaks, but it will work with any type of pan-seared steak.

- 1 recipe Pan-Seared Steaks (page 138)
- 1 small shallot, minced (about 1 tablespoon)
- ½ cup white wine
- ¼ cup Sauce Base (½ recipe; recipe follows)
- ¼ teaspoon white wine vinegar
- 1½ teaspoons minced fresh chives
- 1½ teaspoons minced fresh parsley leaves
- 1 teaspoon minced fresh tarragon leaves
- 1 tablespoon unsalted butter
  Table salt and ground black pepper

After transferring the steaks to a plate to rest, return the now-empty skillet to medium-low heat; add the shallot and cook, stirring constantly, until lightly browned, about 2 minutes. Add the wine and bring to a simmer, scraping the bottom of the skillet with a wooden spoon to loosen any browned bits. Add the Sauce Base, vinegar, and any accumulated juices from the steaks; return to a simmer and cook until slightly reduced, about 1 minute. Off the heat, whisk in the chives, parsley, tarragon, and butter; season with salt and pepper to taste. Spoon the sauce over the steaks and serve.

Restaurant-Style Brandy and Green-Peppercorn Sauce for Pan-Seared Steaks
SERVES 4

- 1 recipe Pan-Seared Steaks (page 138)
- 1 small shallot, minced (about 1 tablespoon)
- ½ cup brandy
- ¼ cup Sauce Base (½ recipe; recipe follows)
- ¼ teaspoon red wine vinegar
- ¼ cup heavy cream
- 2 tablespoons green peppercorns, rinsed
- ¼ teaspoon chopped fresh thyme leaves
  Table salt and ground black pepper

After transferring the steaks to a plate to rest, return the now-empty skillet to medium-low heat; add the shallot and cook, stirring constantly, until lightly browned, about 2 minutes. Add the brandy and bring to a simmer, scraping the bottom of the skillet with a wooden spoon to loosen any browned bits. Add the Sauce Base, vinegar, heavy cream, peppercorns, thyme, and any accumulated juices from the steaks; return to a simmer and cook until slightly reduced, about 1 minute. Off the heat, season with salt and pepper to taste. Spoon the sauce over the steaks and serve.

Restaurant-Style Port Wine Sauce for Pan-Seared Steaks

SERVES 4

- 1 recipe Pan-Seared Steaks (page 138)
- 1 small shallot, minced (about 1 tablespoon)
- ½ cup ruby port
- ¼ cup Sauce Base (½ recipe; recipe follows)
- ¼ teaspoon balsamic vinegar
- ¼ teaspoon chopped fresh thyme leaves
- 1 tablespoon unsalted butter
  Table salt and ground black pepper

After transferring the steaks to a plate to rest, return the now-empty skillet to medium-low heat; add the shallot and cook, stirring constantly, until lightly browned, about 2 minutes. Add the port and bring to a simmer, scraping the bottom of the skillet with a wooden spoon to loosen any browned bits. Add the Sauce Base, vinegar, and any accumulated juices from the steaks; return to a simmer and cook until slightly reduced, about 1 minute. Off the heat, whisk in the thyme and butter; season with salt and pepper to taste. Spoon the sauce over the steaks and serve.

Sauce Base

MAKES ½ CUP

The sauce base recipe yields more than called for in the sauce recipes; leftovers can be refrigerated in an airtight container for up to 3 days or frozen for up to 1 month.

- 1 small onion, peeled and cut into rough ½-inch pieces
- 1 small carrot, peeled and cut into rough ½-inch pieces
- 8 ounces cremini mushrooms, trimmed and halved
- 2 medium garlic cloves, peeled
- 1 tablespoon vegetable oil
- 8 ounces 85 percent lean ground beef

- 1 tablespoon tomato paste
- 2 cups dry red wine
- 4 cups beef broth
- 4 sprigs fresh thyme
- 2 bay leaves
- 2 teaspoons whole black peppercorns
- 5 teaspoons unflavored gelatin

1. Pulse the onion, carrot, mushrooms, and garlic in a food processor into ⅛-inch pieces, 10 to 12 pulses, scraping down the sides as needed.

2. Heat the oil in a Dutch oven over medium-high heat until shimmering; add the beef and tomato paste and cook, stirring frequently, until the beef is well browned, 8 to 10 minutes. Add the vegetable mixture and cook, stirring occasionally, until any exuded moisture has evaporated, about 8 minutes. Add the wine and bring to a simmer, scraping the bottom of the pot with a wooden spoon to loosen any browned bits. Add the broth, thyme, bay leaves, and peppercorns; bring to a boil. Reduce the heat and gently boil, occasionally scraping the bottom and sides of the pot and skimming fat from the surface, until reduced to 2 cups, 20 to 25 minutes.

3. Strain the mixture through a fine-mesh strainer set over a small saucepan, pressing on the solids with a rubber spatula to extract as much liquid as possible (you should have about 1 cup stock). Sprinkle the gelatin over the stock and stir to dissolve. Place the saucepan over medium-high heat and bring the stock to a boil. Gently boil, stirring occasionally, until reduced to ½ cup, 5 to 7 minutes. Remove from the heat and cover to keep warm.

PAN-SEARED THICK-CUT STEAKS

WHY THIS RECIPE WORKS: A nicely charred thick-cut steak certainly looks appealing. But cutting into the steak to find that the rosy meat is confined to a measly spot in the center—with the rest a thick band of overcooked gray—is a great disappointment. We wanted to find a surefire method for pan-searing thick-cut steaks that could deliver both a flavorful crust and juicy, perfectly pink meat throughout.

We found it was essential to sear the steaks quickly to keep the meat directly under the crust from turning gray. But we'd need to take an untraditional approach for these thick-cut steaks and sear them at the end of cooking, rather than at the beginning. We began by moving the steaks straight from the fridge into a 275-degree oven, which not only warmed them to 95 degrees but also dried the meat thoroughly—dry meat is essential for a well-browned crust. At this temperature, when the steak met the hot skillet, it developed a beautiful brown crust in less than four minutes, while the rest of the meat stayed pink, juicy, and tender.

Pan-Seared Thick-Cut Steaks

SERVES 4

Rib-eye or filet mignon of similar thickness can be substituted for strip steaks. If using filet mignon, buying a 2-pound center-cut tenderloin roast and portioning it into four 8-ounce steaks yourself will produce more consistent results. If using filet mignon, increase the oven time by about 5 minutes. When cooking lean strip steaks (without an external fat cap) or filet mignon, add an extra tablespoon of oil to the pan. To serve the steaks with the Red Wine–Mushroom Pan Sauce (recipe follows), prepare all the sauce ingredients while the steaks are in the oven, and don't wash the skillet after cooking the steaks.

- 2 (1-pound) boneless strip steaks, each 1½ to 1¾ inches thick (see note)
  Table salt and ground black pepper
- 1 tablespoon vegetable oil

1. Adjust an oven rack to the middle position and heat the oven to 275 degrees. Pat the steaks dry with paper towels. Cut each steak in half vertically to create four 8-ounce steaks. Season the steaks liberally with salt and pepper; using your hands, gently shape into a uniform thickness. Place the steaks on a wire rack set over a rimmed baking

sheet; transfer the baking sheet to the oven. Cook until an instant-read thermometer inserted horizontally into the center of the steaks registers 90 to 95 degrees for rare to medium-rare (20 to 25 minutes), or 100 to 105 degrees for medium (25 to 30 minutes).

2. Heat the oil in a 12-inch skillet over high heat until smoking. Place the steaks in the skillet and sear until well browned and crusty, 1½ to 2 minutes, lifting once halfway through to redistribute the fat underneath each steak. (Reduce the heat if the fond begins to burn.) Using tongs, turn the steaks and cook until well browned on the second side, 2 to 2½ minutes. Transfer the steaks to a clean rack and reduce the heat under the pan to medium. Use tongs to stand 2 steaks on their sides. Holding the steaks together, return to the skillet and sear on all edges until browned, about 1½ minutes (see photo on page 142). Repeat with the remaining 2 steaks.

3. Return the steaks to the wire rack and let rest, loosely tented with foil, for about 10 minutes. If desired, cook the sauce in the now-empty skillet. Serve immediately.

Red Wine–Mushroom Pan Sauce

MAKES ABOUT 1 CUP

Prepare all the ingredients for the pan sauce while the steaks are in the oven.

- 1 tablespoon vegetable oil
- 8 ounces white mushrooms, wiped clean and sliced thin (about 3 cups)
- 1 small shallot, minced (about 1 tablespoon)
- 1 cup dry red wine
- ½ cup low-sodium chicken broth
- 1 tablespoon balsamic vinegar
- 1 teaspoon Dijon mustard
- 2 tablespoons cold unsalted butter, cut into 4 pieces
- 1 teaspoon minced fresh thyme leaves
  Table salt and ground black pepper

Follow the recipe for Pan-Seared Thick-Cut Steaks. After removing the steaks from the skillet, pour off the fat from the skillet. Heat the oil over medium-high heat until just smoking. Add the mushrooms and cook, stirring occasionally, until beginning to brown and the liquid has evaporated, about 5 minutes. Add the shallot and cook, stirring frequently, until beginning to soften, about 1 minute. Increase the heat to high; add the red wine and broth, scraping the bottom of the skillet with a wooden spoon to loosen any browned bits. Simmer rapidly until

SEARING TWO STEAKS AT ONCE

Use tongs to sear the sides of two steaks at the same time.

the liquid and mushrooms are reduced to 1 cup, about 6 minutes. Add the vinegar, mustard, and any juices from the resting steaks; cook until thickened, about 1 minute. Off the heat, whisk in the butter and thyme; season with salt and pepper to taste. Spoon the sauce over the steaks and serve immediately.

Thai Chili Butter

MAKES ABOUT ⅓ CUP

Prepare all the ingredients for the butter while the steaks are in the oven. If red curry paste isn't available, increase the chili-garlic sauce to 2½ teaspoons.

- 4 tablespoons (½ stick) unsalted butter, softened
- 1 tablespoon chopped fresh cilantro leaves
- 2 teaspoons Asian chili-garlic sauce (preferably Thai)
- 1½ teaspoons thinly sliced scallion, green part only (from 1 scallion)
- 1 small garlic clove, minced or pressed through a garlic press (about ½ teaspoon)
- ½ teaspoon red curry paste (preferably Thai; see note)
- 2 teaspoons juice from 1 lime
  Table salt

Beat the butter vigorously with a spoon until soft and fluffy. Add the cilantro, chili-garlic sauce, scallion, garlic, and red curry paste; beat to incorporate. Add the lime juice a little at a time, beating vigorously between each addition until fully incorporated. Add salt to taste. Spoon a dollop over each steak, giving it time to melt before serving.

PAN-SEARED INEXPENSIVE STEAKS

WHY THIS RECIPE WORKS: Buying cheap steak can be a gamble and a lesson in confusion. Names differ from region to region, some cuts are wonderfully tender while others are hopelessly tough, and some recipes recommend cuts that are almost impossible to find, leaving the consumer to make a blind substitution. We wanted inexpensive steak with the flavor and texture to rival its pricey counterparts.

We first visited meat purveyors to learn what makes some steaks more expensive than others as well as to decipher all the different names. After sorting through the confusion, we were left with a list of 12 candidates. We cooked them as we would any steak, creating a nice sear on both sides without overcooking or allowing the browned bits in the pan to burn. Tasters judged most to be too tough and/or lacking beefy flavor, while others were livery or gamy. We tried a variety of preparation methods—salting, aging, tenderizing, marinating—but none really improved flavor and texture. In the end, only two cuts earned favored status: boneless shell sirloin steak (aka top butt) and flap meat steak (aka sirloin tips). To prepare the steak, season the steaks simply with salt and pepper and start with a very hot skillet. Allow the meat to rest before slicing. Slice the steak thin, against the grain and on the bias, to ensure the tenderest meat.

Pan-Seared Inexpensive Steaks

SERVES 4

Serve these steaks with Tomato-Caper Pan Sauce or Mustard-Cream Pan Sauce (recipes follow). Prepare all of the sauce ingredients before cooking the steaks, and don't wash the skillet after removing the steaks; the sauce will use some of the fat left in the pan. To serve two instead of four, use a 10-inch skillet to cook a 1-pound steak and halve the sauce ingredients. Bear in mind that even those tasters who usually prefer rare beef preferred these steaks cooked medium-rare or medium because the texture is firmer and not quite so chewy. The times in the recipe are for 1¼-inch-thick steaks.

- 2 tablespoons vegetable oil
- 2 1-pound whole boneless shell sirloin steaks (top butt) or whole flap meat steaks, each about 1¼ inches thick
  Table salt and ground black pepper

1. Heat the oil in a heavy-bottomed 12-inch skillet over medium-high heat until smoking. Meanwhile, season both sides of the steaks with salt and pepper. Place the steaks in the skillet; cook, without moving the steaks, until well browned, about 2 minutes. Using tongs, flip the steaks; reduce the heat to medium. Cook until well browned on the second side and the center of the steaks registers 125 degrees on an instant-read thermometer for medium-rare (about 5 minutes) or 130 degrees for medium (about 6 minutes).

2. Transfer the steaks to a large plate and tent loosely with foil; let rest for about 10 minutes. Meanwhile, prepare the pan sauce, if making.

3. Using a sharp chef's knife or carving knife, slice the steak about ¼ inch thick against the grain on the bias, arrange on a platter or on individual plates, and spoon some sauce (if using) over each steak; serve immediately.

Tomato-Caper Pan Sauce

MAKES ABOUT ¾ CUP

If ripe fresh tomatoes are not available, substitute 2 to 3 canned whole tomatoes, seeded and cut into ¼-inch pieces.

- 1 **medium shallot, minced (about 3 tablespoons)**
- 1 **teaspoon unbleached all-purpose flour**
- 2 **tablespoons dry white wine**
- 1 **cup low-sodium chicken broth**
- 2 **tablespoons capers, drained**
- 1 **medium ripe tomato, seeded and cut into ¼-inch dice (about ¼ cup; see note)**
- ¼ **cup minced fresh parsley leaves**
  Table salt and ground black pepper

Follow the recipe for Pan-Seared Inexpensive Steaks. After removing the steaks from the skillet, pour off all but 1 tablespoon of the fat. Return the skillet to low heat and add the shallot; cook, stirring frequently, until beginning to brown, 2 to 3 minutes. Sprinkle the flour over the shallot; cook, stirring constantly, until combined, about 1 minute. Add the wine and increase the heat to medium-high; simmer rapidly, scraping up the browned bits on the pan bottom with a wooden spoon. Simmer until the liquid is reduced to a glaze, about 30 seconds; add the broth and simmer until reduced to ⅔ cup, about 4 minutes. Reduce the heat to medium; add the capers, tomato, and any meat juices that have accumulated on the plate and cook until the flavors are blended, about

1 minute. Stir in the parsley and season with salt and pepper to taste; spoon the sauce over the sliced steak and serve immediately.

Mustard-Cream Pan Sauce

MAKES ABOUT ¾ CUP

- 1 **medium shallot, minced (about 3 tablespoons)**
- 2 **tablespoons dry white wine**
- ½ **cup low-sodium chicken broth**
- 6 **tablespoons heavy cream**
- 3 **tablespoons grainy Dijon mustard**
  Table salt and ground black pepper

Follow the recipe for Pan-Seared Inexpensive Steaks. After removing the steaks from the skillet, pour off all but 1 tablespoon of the fat. Return the skillet to low heat and add the shallot; cook, stirring frequently, until beginning to brown, 2 to 3 minutes. Add the wine and increase the heat to medium-high; simmer rapidly, scraping up the browned bits on the pan bottom with a wooden spoon. Simmer until the liquid is reduced to a glaze, about 30 seconds; add the broth and simmer until reduced to ¼ cup, about 3 minutes. Add the cream and any meat juices that have accumulated on the plate; cook until heated through, about 1 minute. Stir in the mustard; season with salt and pepper to taste. Spoon over the sliced steak and serve immediately.

PAN-SEARED FILET MIGNON

WHY THIS RECIPE WORKS: Many cooks feel that filet mignon should be reserved for a celebratory restaurant meal rather than a less-expensive home-cooked meal. We wanted to replicate the best restaurant filet at home, with a rich, brown crust and a tender interior, topped with a quick but luscious pan sauce.

For a great crust, we patted the steaks dry before searing them in a very hot skillet. Then we transferred the meat to a hot oven to cook through. Finishing the steak in the oven prevents the richly flavored browned bits in the bottom of the pan from burning and gives the cook time to start the sauce, which can be made in minutes while the steaks rest.

Pan-Seared Filet Mignon
SERVES 4

If you are making one of the sauces, have all the sauce ingredients ready before searing the steaks, and don't wash the skillet after removing the steaks. Begin the sauce while the steaks are in the oven. To cook six steaks instead of four, use a 12-inch pan and use 6 teaspoons of olive oil.

    4   (7 to 8-ounce) center-cut filets mignons, 1½ inches thick,
        each dried thoroughly with paper towels
    4   teaspoons olive oil
        Table salt and ground black pepper

1. Adjust an oven rack to the lower-middle position, place a large rimmed baking sheet on the oven rack, and heat the oven to 450 degrees. When the oven reaches 450 degrees, heat a large skillet over high heat on the stovetop until very hot.

2. Meanwhile, rub each side of the steaks with ½ teaspoon oil and sprinkle generously with salt and pepper. Place the steaks in the hot skillet and cook, without moving the steaks, until well browned and a nice crust has formed, about 3 minutes. Turn the steaks with tongs and cook until well browned and a nice crust has formed on the second side, about 3 minutes longer. Remove the pan from the heat and use tongs to transfer the steaks to the hot baking sheet in the oven.

3. Roast until the center of the steaks registers 120 degrees on an instant-read thermometer for rare (4 to 5 minutes), 125 degrees for medium-rare (6 to 8 minutes), or 130 degrees for medium (8 to 10 minutes). Transfer the steaks to a large plate; loosely tent with foil and let rest for about 10 minutes before serving.

Madeira Pan Sauce with Mustard and Anchovies
MAKES ABOUT ⅔ CUP

If you do not have Madeira on hand, sherry makes a fine substitute. The accumulated pan juices from the steaks in the oven are incorporated into the reduction. If the steaks haven't finished cooking once the sauce has reduced, simply set the sauce aside until the steaks (and accumulated juices) are ready.

    1   medium shallot, minced (about 3 tablespoons)
    1   cup Madeira (see note)
    2   anchovy fillets, minced to a paste
        (about 1 teaspoon)
    1   tablespoon minced fresh parsley leaves
    1   tablespoon minced fresh thyme leaves
    1   tablespoon Dijon mustard
    1   tablespoon juice from 1 lemon
    3   tablespoons unsalted butter, softened
        Table salt and ground black pepper

Follow the recipe for Pan-Seared Filet Mignon. While the steaks are in the oven, set the skillet over medium-low heat; add the shallot and cook, stirring constantly, until softened, about 1 minute. Add the Madeira, increase the heat to high, and scrape the pan bottom with a wooden spoon to loosen the browned bits. Simmer until the liquid is reduced to about ⅓ cup, 6 to 8 minutes. Add the accumulated juices from the baking sheet and reduce the liquid 1 minute longer. Off the heat, whisk in the anchovies, parsley, thyme, mustard, lemon juice, and butter until the butter has melted and the sauce is slightly thickened. Season with salt and pepper to taste, spoon the sauce over the steaks, and serve immediately.

Argentinian-Style Fresh Parsley and Garlic Sauce (Chimichurri)

MAKES ABOUT 1 CUP

For best results use flat-leaf parsley.

- 1 cup packed fresh parsley leaves from one large bunch, washed and dried (see note)
- 5 medium garlic cloves, peeled
- ½ cup extra-virgin olive oil
- ¼ cup red wine vinegar
- 2 tablespoons water
- 1 small red onion, finely minced
- 1 teaspoon table salt
- ¼ teaspoon red pepper flakes

Pulse the parsley and garlic in a food processor, stopping as necessary to scrape down the sides of the bowl with a rubber spatula, until the garlic and parsley are chopped fine, about 20 pulses; transfer to a medium bowl. Whisk in the oil, vinegar, water, onion, salt, and red pepper flakes until thoroughly blended. Spoon about 2 tablespoons over each steak and serve. (This sauce tastes best when used fresh but can be refrigerated, with plastic wrap pressed directly on the surface, for up to 3 days.)

PEPPER-CRUSTED FILET MIGNON

WHY THIS RECIPE WORKS: Filet mignon is ultra-tender, but it has only mild beefy flavor. Chefs often compensate by wrapping the delicate meat in bacon or puff pastry, serving it with rich wine sauces or flavored butter, or giving it a crust of cracked black peppercorns. We decided to pursue the peppercorn approach and found several problems to solve: The peppercorns tend to fall off in the pan, interfere with the meat's browning, and—when used in sufficient quantity to create a real crust—deliver punishing pungency.

Our first step was to mellow the peppercorns' heat by gently simmering them in olive oil. We then created a well-browned and attractive pepper crust using a two-step process: First, we rubbed the raw steaks with a paste of the cooked cracked peppercorns, salt, and oil, then we pressed the paste into each steak through a sheet of plastic wrap. We let the steaks sit, covered, for an hour before cooking. The paste not only added flavor to the meat but drew out the meat's own beefy flavor. While the steaks sat wrapped and covered in paste, we had plenty of time to simmer a rich reduction sauce—though a flavored butter also made an excellent accompaniment.

Pepper-Crusted Filet Mignon

SERVES 4

If you prefer a very mild pepper flavor, drain the cooled peppercorns in a fine-mesh strainer in step 1, toss them with 5 tablespoons of fresh oil, add the salt, and proceed. Serve with Port-Cherry Reduction or Blue Cheese–Chive Butter (recipes follow).

- 5 tablespoons black peppercorns, cracked
- 5 tablespoons plus 2 teaspoons olive oil
- 1½ teaspoons table salt
- 4 (7 to 8-ounce) center-cut filets mignons, 1½ to 2 inches thick, each dried thoroughly with paper towels

1. Heat the peppercorns and 5 tablespoons of the oil in a small saucepan over low heat until faint bubbles appear. Continue to cook at a bare simmer, swirling the pan occasionally, until the pepper is fragrant, 7 to 10 minutes. Remove from the heat and set aside to cool. When the mixture is at room temperature, add the salt and stir to combine. Rub the steaks with the pepper mixture, thoroughly coating the top and bottom of each steak with

We've all seen recipe instructions such as "Reduce sauce to ½ cup" or "Simmer until broth is reduced to 2 cups." Those directions are clear, but when you look into a pan of sauce, can you really discern volume? Unless you have wizard-like abilities, the answer is probably "No."

Here in the test kitchen, we know that getting the right amount of sauce can make or break a dish, and to be sure of success we keep a heatproof liquid measuring cup next to the stove. As the sauce appears to be getting near the targeted amount, we pour it into the cup to get an exact measure. If it needs more time on the stove, back into the pan it goes until just the right amount is obtained. No guessing, no problem.

the peppercorns. Cover the steaks with plastic wrap and press gently to make sure the peppercorns adhere; let stand at room temperature for 1 hour.

2. Meanwhile, adjust an oven rack to the middle position, place a rimmed baking sheet on the oven rack, and heat the oven to 450 degrees. Heat the remaining 2 teaspoons oil in a 12-inch heavy-bottomed skillet over medium-high heat until faint smoke appears. Place the steaks in the skillet and cook, without moving the steaks, until a dark brown crust has formed, 3 to 4 minutes. Using tongs, turn the steaks and cook until well browned on the second side, about 3 minutes. Remove the pan from the heat and transfer the steaks to the hot baking sheet. Roast until the center of the steaks registers 120 degrees on an instant-read thermometer for rare (3 to 5 minutes), 125 degrees for medium-rare (5 to 7 minutes), and 130 degrees for medium (7 to 9 minutes). Transfer the steaks to a wire rack and let rest, loosely tented with foil, for about 10 minutes before serving.

Port-Cherry Reduction

MAKES ABOUT 1 CUP

1½ cups port
½ cup balsamic vinegar
½ cup dried tart cherries
1 large shallot, minced (about 4 tablespoons)
2 sprigs fresh thyme
1 tablespoon unsalted butter
   Table salt

1. Combine the port, balsamic vinegar, cherries, shallot, and thyme in a medium saucepan; simmer over medium-low heat until the liquid is reduced to ⅓ cup, about 30 minutes. Set aside, covered.

2. While the steaks are resting, reheat the sauce. Off the heat, remove the thyme, then whisk in the butter until melted. Season with salt to taste. Serve, passing the sauce at the table with the steak.

Blue Cheese–Chive Butter

MAKES ABOUT ½ CUP

3 tablespoons unsalted butter, softened
⅓ cup crumbled mild blue cheese, at room temperature
⅛ teaspoon table salt
2 tablespoons minced fresh chives

Combine the butter, cheese, and salt in a medium bowl and mix with a stiff rubber spatula until smooth. Fold in the chives. While the steaks are resting, spoon 1 to 2 tablespoons of the butter on each one.

STEAK SANDWICHES

WHY THIS RECIPE WORKS: Steak sandwiches run the gamut from oversized "bombs" with greasy, gristly meat (break out the napkins) to precious restaurant concoctions (hold the truffle butter, please) with a price tag to match. We wanted to find a satisfying steak sandwich with some middle ground—easy to eat and gussied up with flavorful, but not costly, ingredients.

We started with the choice of steak, and flank steak won out over all other cuts. It's relatively inexpensive, lean, and tender, as long as the meat is cooked correctly. For a flavorful browned crust, we generously seasoned the steak with salt and pepper and then pan-seared it in a very hot skillet on both sides until browned. To keep the steak tender and juicy, we allowed the meat to rest and then sliced it thin across the grain. Soft, squishy bread needn't apply here—only a crusty French baguette or similar artisan-style bread would do. We slathered the bread with mayonnaise doctored with soy sauce, honey, garlic, and ginger. And to finish, thinly sliced onion and arugula scattered on top of the steak provided a little spicy bite.

Flank Steak and Arugula Sandwiches with Red Onion

SERVES 4

For juicy, tender meat, be sure to let the steak rest for 10 minutes after cooking and slice the steak thin across the grain.

- 1½ pounds flank steak, trimmed of excess fat and patted dry with paper towels
  Table salt and ground black pepper
- 1 tablespoon vegetable oil
- 1 baguette, cut into four 5-inch lengths, each piece split into top and bottom pieces
- 1 recipe Garlic-Soy Mayonnaise (recipe follows)
- ½ small red onion, sliced thin
- 3 ounces arugula, stemmed, washed, and dried (about 3 cups)

1. Heat a 12-inch skillet over high heat until very hot, about 4 minutes. While the skillet is heating, season the steak generously with salt and pepper. Add the oil to the pan and swirl to coat the bottom. Lay the steak in the pan and cook without moving it until well browned, about 5 minutes. Using tongs, flip the steak; cook until well browned on the second side, about 5 minutes longer. Transfer the steak to a carving board, tent with foil, and let rest for 10 minutes. Cut the steak into ¼-inch slices on the bias against the grain.

2. Spread each baguette piece with 1 tablespoon mayonnaise; portion the steak over the bottom pieces of the bread and sprinkle with salt and pepper to taste. Evenly divide the onion and arugula over the steak; top each with a baguette piece and serve.

Garlic-Soy Mayonnaise

MAKES ABOUT ½ CUP

Blue Plate is the test kitchen's favorite brand of mayonnaise—read why on page 745.

- ½ cup mayonnaise
- 1 tablespoon soy sauce
- 1 teaspoon minced or grated fresh ginger
- ½ teaspoon honey
- 1 small garlic clove, minced or pressed through a garlic press (about ½ teaspoon)
- ½ teaspoon toasted sesame oil

Mix all the ingredients together in a small bowl. (The mayonnaise can be covered and refrigerated for up to 1 day.)

NOTES FROM THE TEST KITCHEN

SLICING FLANK STEAK

Once the steak has rested, slice the meat across the grain into thin pieces.

CHAPTER 8

PORK CHOPS EVERY DAY

Sautéed Pork Cutlets with
Mustard-Cider Sauce   150

Crispy Pan-Fried
Pork Chops   151

Pan-Seared Thick-Cut
Pork Chops   152

Garlic and Thyme Sauce

Oven-Roasted
Pork Chops   153

Lemon-Caper Sauce

Skillet-Barbecued
Pork Chops   154

Cider-Glazed
Pork Chops   156

Smothered
Pork Chops   157

Crunchy Baked
Pork Chops   158

Stuffed Pork Chops   160

Quick All-Purpose Gravy

Ginger-Apple Chutney

SAUTÉED PORK CUTLETS

WHY THIS RECIPE WORKS: Lean pork cutlets are flavorless without proper browning, but by the time the cutlets take on any color, they're dry and lacking any tenderness. We wanted tender, browned cutlets with meaty flavor and a rich pan sauce to accompany them.

Instead of supermarket pork cutlets, we opted for a meatier-tasting cut: boneless country-style spare ribs. These ribs combine a large portion of the flavorful shoulder meat with minimal connective tissue and only a bit of bland tenderloin. Even better, because the ribs are sold portioned into relatively small pieces, they require little work to be fashioned into cutlets. To guard against dry meat, we brined our cutlets to help them retain moisture. A quick brine worked well, but the retained moisture kept the meat so wet that it steamed, cooking the cutlets all the way through before they had a chance to brown. To trigger faster browning, we added sugar to the brine. The sugar in the brine helped the cutlets develop a golden-brown exterior without sweetening them too much. And for an even darker crust, we cooked the cutlets in a combination of olive oil and butter. The sugars and milk proteins in the butter promote browning and boost flavor.

Sautéed Pork Cutlets with Mustard-Cider Sauce
SERVES 4

We prefer natural to enhanced pork (pork that has been injected with a salt solution to increase moistness and flavor). If the pork is enhanced, do not brine. Look for ribs that are 3 to 5 inches long. Cut ribs over 5 inches in half crosswise before slicing them lengthwise to make pounding more manageable.

Table salt and ground black pepper
1½ teaspoons sugar
1½ pounds boneless country-style pork spareribs, trimmed (see note)
1½ tablespoons unsalted butter, cut into 6 equal pieces
1 small shallot, minced (about 1 tablespoon)
1 teaspoon unbleached all-purpose flour
1 teaspoon dry mustard
½ cup low-sodium beef or chicken broth
¼ cup apple cider
½ teaspoon minced fresh sage
1 tablespoon olive oil
2 teaspoons whole-grain mustard

1. Dissolve 1 tablespoon salt and the sugar in 2 cups water in a medium bowl. Cut each pork rib lengthwise into 2 or 3 cutlets about ⅜ inch wide. Gently pound the cutlets to ¼-inch thickness between two layers of plastic wrap. Submerge the cutlets in the brine, cover with plastic wrap, and refrigerate for 30 minutes. (Do not overbrine.)

2. Meanwhile, melt 2 pieces of the butter in a small saucepan over medium heat. Add the shallot and cook until softened, about 1½ minutes. Stir in the flour and dry mustard and cook for 30 seconds. Gradually whisk in the broth, smoothing out any lumps. Stir in the cider and sage, bring to a boil, then reduce to a gentle simmer and cook for 5 minutes. Remove the pan from the heat, cover, and set aside.

3. Adjust an oven rack to the middle position and heat the oven to 200 degrees. Remove the cutlets from the brine, dry thoroughly with paper towels, and season with pepper. Heat the oil in a 12-inch skillet over medium-high heat until just smoking. Add 1 piece more butter, let it melt, then quickly lay half of the cutlets in the skillet. Cook until browned on the first side, 1 to 2 minutes.

4. Using tongs, flip the cutlets and continue to cook until browned on the second side, 1 to 2 minutes. Transfer the cutlets to a large plate and keep warm in the oven. Repeat with the remaining cutlets and 1 piece more butter.

5. Return the empty skillet to medium heat, add the reserved broth mixture, and bring to a simmer. Cook, scraping up the browned bits, until the sauce is slightly thickened and has reduced to about ½ cup, about 2 minutes. Stir in any accumulated pork juices and simmer for 30 seconds longer.

6. Off the heat, whisk in the whole-grain mustard and remaining 2 pieces butter. Season the sauce with salt and pepper to taste, spoon it over the cutlets, and serve immediately.

CRISPY PAN-FRIED PORK CHOPS

WHY THIS RECIPE WORKS: A breaded coating can be just the thing to give lean, bland pork chops a flavor boost—but not when it turns gummy and flakes off the meat. Using boneless chops was fast and easy. Dipping the chops in cornstarch was our first step toward creating an ultra-crisp sheath. Buttermilk brought a lighter texture and tangy flavor to the breading, and minced garlic and mustard perked up the breading's flavor. Crushed cornflakes added a craggy texture to the pork chops, especially once we combined them with more cornstarch. Finally, to ensure that our breading adhered to the chops, we gave the meat a short rest and we lightly scored the pork chops before adding them to the pan.

Crispy Pan-Fried Pork Chops

SERVES 4

We prefer natural to enhanced pork (pork that has been injected with a salt solution to increase moistness and flavor) for this recipe. Don't let the chops drain on the paper towels for longer than 30 seconds, or the heat will steam the crust and make it soggy. You can substitute ¾ cup store-bought cornflake crumbs for the whole cornflakes. If using crumbs, omit the processing step and mix the crumbs with the cornstarch, salt, and pepper.

- ⅔ cup cornstarch
- 1 cup buttermilk
- 2 tablespoons Dijon mustard
- 1 medium garlic clove, minced or pressed through a garlic press (about 1 teaspoon)
- 3 cups cornflakes
  Table salt and ground black pepper
- 8 (3 to 4-ounce) boneless pork chops, ½ to ¾ inch thick, trimmed
- ⅔ cup vegetable oil
  Lemon wedges, for serving

1. Place ⅓ cup of the cornstarch in a shallow dish or pie plate. In a second shallow dish, whisk the buttermilk, mustard, and garlic until combined. Process the cornflakes, ½ teaspoon salt, ½ teaspoon pepper, and the remaining ⅓ cup cornstarch in a food processor until the cornflakes are finely ground, about 10 seconds. Transfer the cornflake mixture to a third shallow dish.

2. Adjust the oven rack to the middle position and heat the oven to 200 degrees. With a sharp knife, cut 1/16-inch-deep slits on both sides of the chops, spaced ½ inch apart, in a crosshatch pattern. Season the chops with salt and pepper. Dredge 1 chop in cornstarch; shake off the excess. Using tongs, coat with the buttermilk mixture; let excess drip off. Coat with the cornflake mixture; gently pat off excess. Transfer the coated chop to a wire rack set in a rimmed baking sheet and repeat with the remaining 7 chops. Let the coated chops stand for 10 minutes.

3. Heat ⅓ cup of the oil in a 12-inch nonstick skillet over medium-high heat until shimmering. Place 4 chops in the skillet and cook until golden brown and crisp, 2 to 5 minutes. Carefully flip the chops and continue to cook until the second side is golden brown, crispy, and the chops register 145 degrees on an instant-read thermometer, 2 to 5 minutes longer. Transfer the chops to a paper towel–lined plate and let drain for 30 seconds on each side. Transfer to a clean wire rack set in a rimmed baking sheet, then transfer to the oven to keep warm. Discard the oil in the skillet and wipe clean with paper towels. Repeat the process with the remaining ⅓ cup oil and 4 pork chops. Serve with the lemon wedges.

PAN-SEARED THICK-CUT PORK CHOPS

WHY THIS RECIPE WORKS: Pan-seared thick-cut pork chops boast a juicy interior and crisp, browned exterior. Usually, though, they aren't prepared well and fall flat on both fronts. We wanted a simple skillet-roasting recipe that would give us plump, juicy meat and a well-formed crust every time.

Instead of brining our chops, we salted the meat and let it rest for almost an hour. This helped to draw out additional moisture, which would be pulled back in later to produce juicy, well-seasoned meat. Instead of cooking our chops on the stovetop, we turned to the oven. Slow-roasting the chops at a gentle temperature broke down connective tissue and tenderized the meat. This step also dried the exterior of the chops, creating a thin outer layer that, when seared, caramelized and turned into the crisp crust that we were after. For a completely browned crust, we seared the sides of the chops as well, using tongs to hold them up on their edges. While the cooked chops rested, we created a simple wine and garlic sauce using the browned bits left behind in the pan; now, we had the perfect rich, tangy accompaniment to our chops' tender meat and crisp surface.

Pan-Seared Thick-Cut Pork Chops
SERVES 4

We prefer natural to enhanced pork (pork that has been injected with a salt solution to increase moistness and flavor) for this recipe. If using enhanced pork, skip the salting in step 1. To serve the pork chops with the Garlic and Thyme Sauce (recipe follows), have all the sauce ingredients ready to go and don't wash the skillet after browning the chops; begin the sauce, using the fat left behind from browning the chops, when you set them aside to rest.

4 (12-ounce) bone-in rib loin pork chops, about 1½ inches thick, trimmed of excess fat (see note)
   Table salt and ground black pepper (see note)
1–2 tablespoons vegetable oil

1. Adjust an oven rack to the middle position and heat the oven to 275 degrees. Pat the chops dry with paper towels. Following the photo on page 156, use a sharp knife to cut two slits, about 2 inches apart, through the outer layer of fat and silver skin of each chop (do not cut into the meat of the chops). Sprinkle each chop with ½ teaspoon salt. Place the chops on a wire rack set over a rimmed baking sheet and let stand at room temperature for 45 minutes.

2. Season the chops with pepper; transfer the baking sheet to the oven. Cook until the center of the chops registers 120 to 125 degrees on an instant-read thermometer, 30 to 45 minutes.

3. Heat 1 tablespoon oil in a 12-inch skillet over high heat until smoking. Place 2 chops in the skillet and sear until well browned, 2 to 3 minutes, lifting once halfway through to redistribute the fat underneath each chop. (Reduce the heat if the browned bits on the pan bottom start to burn.) Flip the chops and cook until the second side is well browned, 2 to 3 minutes longer. Transfer the chops to a plate and repeat with the remaining 2 chops, adding 1 tablespoon more oil if the pan is dry.

4. Reduce the heat to medium. Using tongs, stand 2 pork chops on their sides. Hold them together with the tongs, return them to the skillet, and sear the sides (do not sear the bone side) until browned and the center of the chops registers 140 to 145 degrees on an instant-read thermometer, about 1½ minutes. Repeat with the remaining 2 chops. Transfer the chops to a platter, cover loosely with foil, and let rest until the internal temperature reaches 150 degrees, about 5 minutes, or while preparing the pan sauce.

Garlic and Thyme Sauce
MAKES ABOUT ½ CUP

- 1 large shallot, minced (about 4 tablespoons)
- 2 medium garlic cloves, minced or pressed through a garlic press (about 2 teaspoons)
- ¾ cup low-sodium chicken broth
- ½ cup dry white wine
- 1 teaspoon minced fresh thyme leaves
- ¼ teaspoon white wine vinegar
- 3 tablespoons unsalted butter, chilled and cut into 3 pieces
- Table salt and ground black pepper

Follow the recipe for Pan-Seared Thick-Cut Pork Chops. Pour off all but 1 teaspoon oil from the pan used to cook the chops and return the pan to medium heat. Add the shallot and garlic and cook, stirring constantly, until softened, about 1 minute. Add the broth and wine, scraping up any browned bits. Bring to a simmer and cook until the sauce measures ½ cup, 6 to 7 minutes. Off the heat, stir in the thyme and vinegar; whisk in the butter, 1 tablespoon at a time. Season with salt and pepper to taste and serve with the pork chops.

OVEN-ROASTED PORK CHOPS

WHY THIS RECIPE WORKS: Tender, juicy pork chops make for a satisfying dinner, but most home cooks pass up thick chops at the market because they assume the cooking time will be long. However, roasting these chops in a blazing hot oven (their thickness prevents them from drying out) cuts down on cooking time and frees up the stovetop so you can make an easy pan sauce at the same time.

We chose extra-thick rib loin pork chops and flavored them with a brown sugar and salt brine. We found that our thick chops couldn't go straight into the oven—they had to be cooked in three stages. First, we seared them in a hot pan to give them a nicely browned crust, then we transferred them to a preheated pan in the oven to cook most of the way through, and finally we moved them to a platter and covered them with foil to gently come up to serving temperature (while the meat stayed moist and tender). This last step also gave us time to make a speedy lemon-caper sauce right in the pan using the fond (browned bits) left behind from searing the chops.

Oven-Roasted Pork Chops
SERVES 4

We prefer natural to enhanced pork (pork that has been injected with a salt solution to increase moistness and flavor) for this recipe. If using enhanced pork, skip the brining in step 1. To serve the pork chops with the Lemon-Caper Sauce (recipe follows), have all the sauce ingredients ready to go and don't wash the skillet after browning the chops; begin the sauce, using the fat left behind from browning the chops, after the pork chops come out of the oven and are resting.

- ¾ cup (5¼ ounces) dark brown sugar
- ¼ cup table salt
- 10 medium garlic cloves, crushed
- 4 bay leaves, crumbled
- 8 whole cloves
- 3 tablespoons whole black peppercorns, crushed
- 4 (12-ounce) bone-in rib loin pork chops, about 1½ inches thick, trimmed of excess fat (see note)
- 2 tablespoons vegetable oil

1. Dissolve the sugar and salt in 6 cups cold water in a large bowl or container. Add the garlic, bay leaves, cloves, and peppercorns. Submerge the chops in the brine, cover with plastic wrap, and refrigerate for 1 hour. Remove the chops from the brine, rinse, and pat dry with paper towels. Following the photo on page 156, use a sharp knife to cut two slits, about 2 inches apart, through the outer layer of fat and silver skin of each chop (do not cut into the meat of the chops).

2. Adjust an oven rack to the lower-middle position, place a rimmed baking sheet on the rack, and heat the oven to 450 degrees. When the oven reaches 450 degrees, heat the oil in a 12-inch skillet over high heat until shimmering. Place the chops in the skillet and cook until well browned, about 2 minutes. Flip the chops and continue to cook until the second side is well browned, about 2 minutes longer.

3. Transfer the chops to the baking sheet in the oven. Roast until the center of the chops registers 140 to 145 degrees on an instant-read thermometer, about 15 minutes, turning the chops over once halfway through the cooking time. Transfer the chops to a platter, cover loosely with foil, and let rest until the internal temperature registers 150 degrees on an instant-read thermometer, 5 to 10 minutes or while preparing the pan sauce.

Lemon-Caper Sauce

MAKES ABOUT ½ CUP

- 1 medium shallot, minced (about 3 tablespoons)
- 1 cup low-sodium chicken broth
- ¼ cup juice from 2 lemons
- 2 tablespoons capers, drained
- 3 tablespoons unsalted butter, softened

Follow the recipe for Oven-Roasted Pork Chops. After removing the chops from the pan, add the shallot and cook over medium heat until softened, about 30 seconds. Increase the heat to high and stir in the broth, scraping up any browned bits. Add the lemon juice and capers, bring to a simmer, and cook until the sauce measures ⅓ cup, 3 to 4 minutes. Off the heat, whisk in the butter; serve with the pork chops.

SKILLET-BARBECUED PORK CHOPS

WHY THIS RECIPE WORKS: One of our favorite summer flavors is that of charred, salty-sweet grilled pork chops coated with spicy barbecue sauce. But because winter sometimes seems endless, we wanted to come up with an indoor method for replicating the tangy, sweet burnished crust and juicy meat of grilled chops.

Brining the chops first ensured that our meat would be juicy and well seasoned. We quickly learned that searing the chops in a blazing hot skillet and then turning the heat down once they had developed a nice crust only made the test kitchen smoky. Instead, we coated the chops with a dry spice rub—the rub charred rather than the pork chops and gave the meat the flavor and appearance of real barbecue. To prevent the rub from blackening, we cooked the chops over medium heat and used a nonstick skillet. Homemade barbecue sauce, made with ketchup, molasses, onion, and just a few other ingredients, provided a tangy flavor that contrasted nicely with the tender meat, and some reserved spice rub gave the sauce a spicy kick. A touch of liquid smoke gave our barbecue sauce more grill flavor. Finally, we brushed our chops with a small amount of sauce for a second sear so the sauce would caramelize and intensify in flavor—just as it would on the grill.

Skillet-Barbecued Pork Chops

SERVES 4

We prefer natural to enhanced pork (pork that has been injected with a salt solution to increase moistness and flavor) for this recipe. If using enhanced pork, skip the brining in step 1 and add ½ teaspoon salt to the spice rub. Grate the onion on the large holes of a box grater. In step 5, check your chops after 3 minutes. If you don't hear a definite sizzle and the chops have not started to brown on the underside, increase the heat to medium-high and continue cooking as directed (follow the indicated temperatures for the remainder of the recipe).

PORK CHOPS

- ½ cup table salt (see note)
- 4 (8 to 10-ounce) bone-in rib loin pork chops, ¾ to 1 inch thick, trimmed of excess fat (see note)
- 4 teaspoons vegetable oil

SPICE RUB

- 1 tablespoon paprika
- 1 tablespoon brown sugar
- 2 teaspoons ground coriander
- 1 teaspoon ground cumin
- 1 teaspoon ground black pepper

SAUCE

- ½ cup ketchup
- 3 tablespoons light or mild molasses
- 2 tablespoons grated onion (see note)
- 2 tablespoons Worcestershire sauce
- 2 tablespoons Dijon mustard
- 1 tablespoon cider vinegar
- 1 tablespoon brown sugar
- 1 teaspoon liquid smoke

1. FOR THE PORK CHOPS: Dissolve the salt in 2 quarts cold water in a large bowl or container. Submerge the chops in the brine, cover with plastic wrap, and refrigerate for 30 minutes.

2. FOR THE SPICE RUB: Combine the rub ingredients in a small bowl. Measure 2 teaspoons of the mixture into a medium bowl and set aside for the sauce. Transfer the remaining spice rub to a large plate.

3. FOR THE SAUCE: Whisk the sauce ingredients in the bowl with the reserved spice mixture until thoroughly combined; set aside.

4. Remove the chops from the brine, rinse, and pat dry with paper towels. Following the photo on page 156, use a sharp knife to cut two slits, about 2 inches apart, through the outer layer of fat and silver skin of each chop (do not cut into the meat of the chops). Coat both sides of the chops with the spice rub, pressing gently so the rub adheres. Shake off the excess rub.

5. Heat 1 tablespoon of the oil in a 12-inch nonstick skillet over medium heat until just smoking. Place the chops in the skillet in a pinwheel pattern, with the ribs pointing toward the center, and cook until browned and charred in spots, 5 to 8 minutes. Flip the chops and continue to cook until the second side is browned and the center of the chops registers 130 degrees on an instant-read thermometer, 4 to 8 minutes. Remove the skillet from the heat and transfer the chops to a plate. Lightly brush the top of each chop with 2 teaspoons of the sauce.

6. Wipe out the pan with paper towels and return to medium heat. Add the remaining 1 teaspoon oil and heat until just smoking. Add the chops to the pan, sauce side down, and cook without moving them until the sauce has caramelized and charred in spots, about 1 minute. While cooking, lightly brush the top of each chop with 2 more teaspoons sauce. Flip the chops and cook until the second side is charred and caramelized and the center of the chops registers 140 to 145 degrees on an instant-read thermometer, 1 to 2 minutes.

BEHIND THE SCENES

KOSHER? YES. ENHANCED? NO.

In the test kitchen we often brine chicken and pork to ensure moist, well-seasoned meat. But there are options at the store that allow you to skip this step. For chicken, that means buying a kosher bird. Koshering is a process similar to brining; it involves coating the chicken with salt to draw out any impurities. Kosher birds are also all-natural and contain no hormones or antibiotics. In a side-by-side taste test of all kinds of chicken, Empire brand kosher birds rated highest.

Some people are surprised that pork is lean and prone to drying out. In fact, today's pork is 50 percent leaner than its 1950s counterpart, and less fat means less flavor and moisture. The industry has addressed this issue by introducing enhanced pork, which is meat injected with a solution of water, salt, and sodium phosphate. The idea is to both season the pork and prevent it from drying out. We've conducted countless tests comparing "enhanced" pork to natural pork and unequivocally prefer the latter. Natural pork has a better flavor and, if it's cooked correctly, moisture isn't an issue. We also strongly recommend brining most cuts of pork, which lends both moisture and seasoning to the meat. Manufacturers don't use the terms "enhanced" or "natural" on package labels, but if the pork has been enhanced it will have an ingredient list. Natural pork contains just pork and won't have an ingredient list. While natural pork benefits from brining, enhanced pork should not be brined because it's already pretty salty.

7. Transfer the chops back to the plate, cover loosely with foil, and let rest until the center of the chops registers 150 degrees on an instant-read thermometer, about 5 minutes.

8. Meanwhile, add the remaining sauce to the pan and cook over medium heat, scraping up any browned bits, until thickened and it measures ⅔ cup, about 3 minutes. Brush each chop with 1 tablespoon of the sauce and serve, passing the remaining sauce separately.

GLAZED PORK CHOPS

WHY THIS RECIPE WORKS: Thin boneless pork chops are readily available straight from the meat case—no butcher required. Plus they cook fast and are a bargain compared to other meats. But because they do cook quickly, they're prone to overcooking. We wanted to combine the convenience and speed of thin boneless pork chops with the flavor and moist, juicy interior of their thicker, bone-in counterparts.

To cook pork chops on the stove, it's best to stick with thin chops. Before searing the chops, it's important to cut through the fat and silver skin, which create a bowing effect (especially pronounced with thin chops) as it contracts. We found the chops needed an initial quick sear—we didn't want them to cook all the way through just yet but we still wanted a nicely browned side. A sweet and sticky glaze of cider, brown sugar, soy sauce, vinegar, and mustard went into the pan to finish cooking the chops. Not only did the sauce give the chops rich flavor, but it also reduced down to a nice, thick glaze, which perfectly coated the juicy, tender chops.

Cider-Glazed Pork Chops

SERVES 4

We prefer natural to enhanced pork (pork that has been injected with a salt solution to increase moistness and flavor) for this recipe, though either will work here. If your chops are on the thinner side, check their internal temperature after the initial sear. If they are already at the 140-degree mark, remove them from the skillet and allow them to rest, covered loosely with foil, for 5 minutes, then add the accumulated juices and glaze ingredients to the skillet and proceed with step 4. If your chops are a little thicker than we specify, you may need to increase the simmering time in step 3.

NOTES FROM THE TEST KITCHEN

HOW TO PREVENT CURLED PORK CHOPS

Whether your pork chops are boneless or bone-in, you can use the same technique to prevent them from buckling in a hot pan or oven. Simply cut two slits, about 2 inches apart, through one side of each chop.

GLAZE
- ½ cup distilled white vinegar or cider vinegar
- ⅓ cup (2⅓ ounces) light brown sugar
- ⅓ cup apple cider or apple juice
- 2 tablespoons Dijon mustard
- 1 tablespoon soy sauce
  Pinch cayenne pepper

PORK CHOPS
- 4 (5 to 7-ounce) boneless center-cut or loin pork chops, ½ to ¾ inch thick, trimmed of excess fat (see note)
  Table salt and ground black pepper
- 1 tablespoon vegetable oil

1. FOR THE GLAZE: Combine the glaze ingredients in a medium bowl and set aside.

2. FOR THE PORK CHOPS: Following the photo, use a sharp knife to cut two slits, about 2 inches apart, through the outer layer of fat and silver skin of each chop (do not cut into the meat of the chops). Pat the chops dry with paper towels and season with salt and pepper. Heat the oil in a 12-inch skillet over medium-high heat until smoking. Add the chops to the skillet and cook until well browned, 4 to 6 minutes. Flip the chops and cook 1 minute longer; transfer the chops to a platter and pour off any oil in the skillet. (Check the internal temperature of the thinner chops; see note.)

3. Return the chops to the skillet, browned side up, and add the glaze mixture; cook over medium heat until the center of the chops registers 140 to 145 degrees on an instant-read thermometer, 5 to 8 minutes. Remove the skillet from the heat; transfer the chops to a clean platter, cover loosely with foil, and let rest until the center of the chops registers 150 degrees on an instant-read thermometer, about 5 minutes.

4. Stir any accumulated meat juices from the plate into the glaze in the skillet and simmer, whisking constantly, until the glaze has thickened, 2 to 6 minutes. Return the chops to the skillet and turn to coat both sides with the glaze. Transfer the chops back to the plate, browned side up, spread the remaining glaze over the top, and serve.

SMOTHERED PORK CHOPS

WHY THIS RECIPE WORKS: Tender, flavorful chops stand up very well to rich, hearty gravy. But most of the time, the gravy misses the mark—it's either so thick you can't find the pork chop, or so thin and watery that the meat seems to be floating on the plate. We wanted a foolproof recipe for juicy chops smothered in rich gravy with a satiny, thick texture.

For a nice balance with the gravy and to allow for the best absorption of the gravy's flavors, we used thin, not thick, rib chops. Browning them well left meaty browned bits in the pan, essential for making a flavorful gravy. To build further flavor, we made a nut-brown, bacony roux. Thinly sliced yellow onions contributed a significant amount of moisture to the gravy. Garlic, thyme, and bay leaves rounded out the flavorful gravy; we skipped the salt because we had already salted the onions to encourage their browning and so they would give up liquid. For the tenderest chops, we combined the sauce and browned chops in the pan and braised them for half an hour. Not only did the lengthy braise result in moist, tender chops, it also allowed the gravy to thicken and its flavors to meld, so the chops had a rich, velvety coating when served.

Smothered Pork Chops

SERVES 4

We prefer natural to enhanced pork (pork that has been injected with a salt solution to increase moistness and flavor) for this recipe, though either will work here. Serve smothered chops with egg noodles or mashed potatoes to soak up the rich gravy.

- 3 ounces bacon (about 3 slices), cut into ¼-inch pieces
- 2 tablespoons unbleached all-purpose flour
- 1¾ cups low-sodium chicken broth
- 2 tablespoons vegetable oil, plus more as needed
- 4 (7-ounce) bone-in rib loin pork chops, ½ to ¾ inch thick, trimmed of excess fat (see note)
  Ground black pepper
- 2 medium yellow onions, halved and sliced thin (about 3½ cups)
  Table salt

- 2 tablespoons water
- 2 medium garlic cloves, minced or pressed through a garlic press (about 2 teaspoons)
- 1 teaspoon minced fresh thyme leaves
- 2 bay leaves
- 1 tablespoon minced fresh parsley leaves

1. Fry the bacon in a small saucepan over medium heat, stirring occasionally, until crisp, 8 to 10 minutes. Using a slotted spoon, transfer the bacon to a paper towel–lined plate, leaving the fat in the saucepan (you should have 2 tablespoons bacon fat; if not, add oil to make this amount). Whisk in the flour and cook over medium-low heat until golden, about 5 minutes. Whisk in the broth and bring to a boil, stirring occasionally, over medium-high heat; cover and set aside off the heat.

2. Heat 1 tablespoon of the oil in a 12-inch skillet over high heat until smoking. Pat the chops dry with paper towels. Following the photo on page 156, use a sharp knife to cut two slits, about 2 inches apart, through the outer layer of fat and silver skin of each chop (do not cut into the meat of the chops). Sprinkle each chop with ½ teaspoon pepper. Brown the chops in a single layer until browned on the first side, about 3 minutes. Flip the chops and cook until the second side is browned, about 3 minutes longer. Transfer the chops to a plate and set aside.

3. Add the remaining 1 tablespoon oil to the skillet and return to medium heat until shimmering. Add the onions, ¼ teaspoon salt, and the water, scraping up any browned bits, and cook until lightly browned, about 5 minutes. Stir in the garlic and thyme and cook until fragrant, about 30 seconds longer. Return the chops to the skillet and cover with the onions. Add the reserved sauce, the bay leaves, and any accumulated meat juices from the plate to the skillet. Cover and simmer over low heat until the chops are tender and a paring knife inserted into the chops meets little resistance, about 30 minutes.

4. Transfer the chops to a platter and cover loosely with foil. Simmer the sauce over medium-high heat, stirring frequently, until thickened, about 5 minutes. Discard the bay leaves, stir in the parsley, and season with salt and pepper to taste. Cover the chops with the sauce, sprinkle with the reserved bacon, and serve.

CRUNCHY BAKED PORK CHOPS

WHY THIS RECIPE WORKS: When done right, baked, breaded pork chops are the ultimate comfort food—juicy, tender chops covered with a well-seasoned, crunchy crust. We were on a mission to perfect these chops and avoid the common missteps of a soggy, flavorless crust, flabby meat, and a coating that just won't stay on.

We used center-cut boneless loin chops—which are easy to find and affordable—and brined them so the meat would stay moist and juicy. For the coating, only fresh bread crumbs would do; we toasted them first for crispness, then doctored them with garlic, shallots, Parmesan cheese, and minced herbs for flavor. To form a strong adhering agent for the crumbs, and prevent the chops from ending up bald in patches, we made a quick batterlike mixture by whisking flour and mustard into egg whites; whole eggs were a no-go because their higher amount of fat made for a soft, puffy layer under the bread crumbs. Baking the breaded chops on a wire rack set over a baking sheet allowed air to circulate completely around the chops, keeping the bottom crumbs crisp. Out of the oven, these chops were tender and moist, with a crisp coating that stayed put, even through some heavy knife-and-fork action.

Crunchy Baked Pork Chops

SERVES 4

We prefer natural to enhanced pork (pork that has been injected with a salt solution to increase moistness and flavor) for this recipe. If using enhanced pork, skip the brining in step 1. The breaded chops can be frozen for up to 1 week. They don't need to be thawed before baking; simply increase the cooking time in step 5 to 35 to 40 minutes.

> Table salt
> 4 (6 to 8-ounce) boneless center-cut or loin pork chops, ¾ to 1 inch thick, trimmed of excess fat (see note)
> 4 slices high-quality white sandwich bread, torn into 1-inch pieces
> 2 tablespoons vegetable oil
> 1 small shallot, minced (about 1 tablespoon)
> 3 medium garlic cloves, minced or pressed through a garlic press (about 1 tablespoon)
> Ground black pepper
> 2 tablespoons grated Parmesan cheese
> 2 tablespoons minced fresh parsley leaves
> ½ teaspoon minced fresh thyme leaves
> ¼ cup plus 6 tablespoons unbleached all-purpose flour
> 3 large egg whites
> 3 tablespoons Dijon mustard
> Lemon wedges, for serving

1. Adjust an oven rack to the middle position and heat the oven to 350 degrees. Dissolve ¼ cup salt in 4 cups cold water in a medium bowl or gallon-sized zipper-lock bag. Submerge the chops in the brine, cover the container with plastic wrap or seal the bag, and refrigerate for 30 minutes. Remove the chops from the brine, rinse, and pat dry with paper towels.

2. Meanwhile, pulse the bread in a food processor to coarse crumbs, about 8 pulses (you should have about 3½ cups crumbs). Transfer the crumbs to a rimmed baking sheet, add the oil, shallot, garlic, ¼ teaspoon salt, and ¼ teaspoon pepper, and toss until the crumbs are evenly coated with the oil. Bake until golden brown and dry, about 15 minutes, stirring twice during the baking time. (Do not turn off the oven.) Cool to room temperature. Toss the crumbs with the Parmesan, parsley, and thyme. (The bread-crumb mixture can be stored in an airtight container for up to 3 days.)

3. Place ¼ cup of the flour in a pie plate. In a second pie plate, whisk the egg whites and mustard together; add the remaining 6 tablespoons flour and whisk until almost smooth, with pea-sized lumps remaining.

4. Increase the oven temperature to 425 degrees. Spray a wire rack with vegetable oil spray and place over a rimmed baking sheet. Season the chops with pepper. Dredge 1 pork chop in the flour; shake off the excess. Using tongs, coat with the egg mixture; let the excess drip off. Coat all sides of the chop with the bread-crumb mixture, pressing gently so that a thick layer of crumbs adheres to the chop. Transfer the breaded chop to the wire rack. Repeat with the remaining 3 chops.

5. Bake until the center of the chops registers 140 to 145 degrees on an instant-read thermometer, about 20 minutes. Let rest on the rack for 5 minutes; serve with the lemon wedges.

STUFFED PORK CHOPS

WHY THIS RECIPE WORKS: Thick-cut pork chops make the perfect home for a simple stuffing. Unfortunately, most stuffed pork chops are extremely dry and bland, with a filling that looks like it's trying to escape. We wanted the stuffing to be especially flavorful and rich to offset the mildness of the pork, and we wanted the chops to be moist and juicy.

Our stuffing was easy enough to make—we used a simple combination of aromatic vegetables, herbs, and fresh bread. But the stuffing was so loose, it crumbled and spilled out over the plate when the chops were served. Clearly, we needed a binder. Instead of eggs, we chose cream, which added richness and enough moisture to bring the stuffing together. Because the stuffing didn't contain eggs, the chops could be cooked to a lower (and more palatable) internal temperature, making for tender

WHY IS THAT PORK STILL PINK?

In the test kitchen, we steer clear of dishes like Parchingly Dry Pork Chops and No-Pink Pork Loin. But there's a reason that older recipes recommend cooking pork to startlingly high internal temperatures. Years ago, when pork quality was inconsistent and trichinosis concerns ran high, pink pork was considered a safety risk, thus most recipes recommended cooking pork to 190 degrees. Today, however, the risk of trichinosis is nearly nonexistent in the United States. What's more, even when the trichinosis parasite is present, it is killed when the temperature of the meat rises to 137 degrees.

Both the U.S. Department of Agriculture and the National Pork Board recommend cooking pork to a final internal temperature of 160 degrees. If you are concerned about contamination with salmonella (which is possible in any type of meat), you must cook the pork to 160 degrees to be certain that all potential pathogens are eliminated. Unfortunately, given the leanness of today's pork, these recommendations result in dry, tough meat. (In fact, today's pork has 50 percent less fat than it did 50 years ago, which explains why older recipes that called for cooking pork to 190 degrees weren't a total disaster—all that fat kept even overcooked pork moist.)

In the test kitchen, we have found cooking modern pork beyond 150 degrees to be a waste of time and money. We cook pork to an internal temperature of 140 to 145 degrees—the meat will still be slightly rosy in the center and juicy. As the meat rests and juices are redistributed throughout the meat, the internal temperature will continue to climb to the final serving temperature of 150. Of course, if safety is your top concern, cook all meat (including pork) until it is well-done; that is, when the internal temperature reaches 160 degrees.

and juicy meat. After brining the chops and creating a small "pocket" to hold the stuffing, we started them in a skillet to develop a nice brown crust but finished cooking them through on a baking sheet in a hot oven. A sweet chutney of ginger, apples, and apple cider provided a nice contrast to the savory filling.

For an alternative to chutney, flavorful gravy (sans big roast) is ideal for draping over the stuffed chops. Thoroughly browning both the aromatic vegetables and the flour added significant flavor, as did the inclusion of two kinds of broth: beef and chicken.

NOTES FROM THE TEST KITCHEN

STUFFING PORK CHOPS

1. Using a paring knife, trim away the excess fat and connective tissue around the edge of the meat.

2. With the knife positioned as shown, insert the blade through the center of the side of the chop until the tip touches the bone.

3. Swing the tip of the blade through the middle of the chop to create a pocket (the opening should be about 1 inch wide).

4. With your fingers, gently press the stuffing mixture into the pocket, without enlarging the opening.

Stuffed Pork Chops

SERVES 4

We prefer natural to enhanced pork (pork that has been injected with a salt solution to increase moistness and flavor) for this recipe, though either will work here. Serve these pork chops with Quick All-Purpose Gravy or Ginger-Apple Chutney (recipes follow). The gravy is best made before you start the chops and reheated as needed. If you choose to serve the chops with the chutney, prepare it in the skillet used to cook the chops while the chops are in the oven.

PORK CHOPS

- 4 (12-ounce) bone-in rib loin pork chops, about 1½ inches thick, trimmed of excess fat (see note)
- ¾ cup packed light brown sugar
- ¼ cup table salt
  Ground black pepper
- 1 tablespoon vegetable oil

STUFFING

- 3 tablespoons unsalted butter
- 1 small onion, minced
- 1 celery rib, chopped fine
- ½ teaspoon table salt
- 1 tablespoon minced fresh parsley leaves
- 2 medium garlic cloves, minced or pressed through a garlic press (about 2 teaspoons)
- 2 teaspoons minced fresh thyme leaves
- 2 slices high-quality white sandwich bread, cut into ¼-inch cubes (about 2 cups)
- 2 tablespoons heavy cream
  Ground black pepper

1. FOR THE PORK CHOPS: Following the photos, cut a small pocket through the side of each chop. Dissolve the sugar and salt in 6 cups cold water in a large bowl or container. Submerge the chops in the brine, cover with plastic wrap, and refrigerate for 1 hour.

2. FOR THE STUFFING: Melt the butter in a 12-inch skillet over medium heat. Add the onion, celery, and salt and cook until the vegetables are softened, 6 to 8 minutes. Add the parsley, garlic, and thyme and cook until fragrant, about 30 seconds. Transfer to a medium bowl and toss with the bread cubes, cream, and ⅛ teaspoon pepper. Mix, lightly pressing the mixture against the sides of the bowl, until it comes together.

3. Adjust an oven rack to the lower-middle position, place a rimmed baking sheet on the rack, and heat the oven to 450 degrees. Remove the chops from the brine, rinse, and pat dry with paper towels. Place one-quarter of the stuffing (about ⅓ cup) in the pocket of each pork chop. Season the chops with pepper.

4. Heat the oil in a 12-inch skillet over high heat until shimmering. Place the chops in the skillet and cook until well browned, about 3 minutes. Flip the chops and cook until the second side is well browned, about 2 minutes longer.

5. Transfer the chops to the baking sheet in the oven. Roast until the center of the chops registers 140 degrees on an instant-read thermometer, about 15 minutes, turning the chops over halfway through the cooking time. Transfer the chops to a plate, cover loosely with foil, and let rest for 5 to 10 minutes. Serve.

Quick All-Purpose Gravy

MAKES 2 CUPS

This gravy can be served with almost any type of meat and with mashed potatoes as well. The recipe can be doubled. If doubling it, use a Dutch oven so that the vegetables brown properly and increase the cooking times by roughly half. The finished gravy can be frozen. To thaw it, place the gravy and 1 tablespoon of water in a saucepan over low heat and slowly bring it to a simmer. It may appear broken or curdled as it thaws, but a vigorous whisking will recombine it.

- 3 **tablespoons unsalted butter**
- 1 **onion, minced**
- 1 **small carrot, peeled and chopped fine**
- 1 **celery rib, chopped fine**
- ¼ **cup unbleached all-purpose flour**
- 2 **cups low-sodium chicken broth**
- 2 **cups beef broth**
- 1 **bay leaf**
- ¼ **teaspoon dried thyme**
- 5 **whole black peppercorns**
  Table salt and ground black pepper

1. Melt the butter in a large saucepan over medium-high heat. Add the onion, carrot, and celery and cook, stirring frequently, until softened, about 7 minutes. Reduce the heat to medium, add the flour, and cook, stirring constantly, until thoroughly browned, about 5 minutes. Gradually whisk in the broths and bring to a boil, skimming off any foam that forms on the surface. Add the bay leaf, thyme, and peppercorns and simmer, stirring occasionally, until thickened and reduced to 3 cups, 20 to 25 minutes.

2. Strain the gravy through a fine-mesh strainer into a clean saucepan, pressing on the solids to extract as much liquid as possible; discard the solids. Season with salt and pepper to taste and serve with the pork chops.

Ginger-Apple Chutney

MAKES ABOUT 3½ CUPS

If you want more heat, add a little more cayenne pepper.

- 1 **tablespoon vegetable oil**
- 1 **small onion, chopped medium**
- 2 **Granny Smith apples, peeled, cored, and cut into ½-inch pieces**
- 1 **tablespoon minced ginger**
- ¼ **teaspoon ground allspice**
- ⅛ **teaspoon cayenne pepper (see note)**
- 1 **cup apple cider**
- ¼ **cup (1¾ ounces) packed light brown sugar**
  Table salt and ground black pepper

Follow the recipe for Stuffed Pork Chops. After removing the chops from the pan, pour off any fat left in the skillet. Heat the oil over medium-high heat until shimmering. Add the onion and apples and cook, stirring occasionally, until softened, about 10 minutes. Add the ginger, allspice, and cayenne and cook until fragrant, about 30 seconds. Add the cider and sugar and bring to a boil, scraping up any browned bits, until the cider is slightly thickened, about 4 minutes. Season with salt and pepper to taste and serve with the pork chops.

CHAPTER 9

ROASTS AND MORE

Slow-Roasted Beef 164

    Horseradish Cream Sauce

Roast Beef Tenderloin 165

    Shallot and Parsley Butter

    Chipotle and Garlic Butter
    with Lime and Cilantro

Horseradish-Crusted Beef
Tenderloin 166

Roast Beef Tenderloin
with Caramelized Onion
and Mushroom
Stuffing 168

Prime Rib 170

Onion-Braised Beef
Brisket 171

Thick-Cut Pork Tenderloin
Medallions 172

    Maple-Mustard Sauce

    Apple Cider Sauce

Breaded Pork Cutlets
(Pork Schnitzel) 174

Pan-Seared Oven-Roasted
Pork Tenderloins 175

    Dried Cherry–Port
    Sauce with Onions
    and Marmalade

    Garlicky Lime Sauce
    with Cilantro

Maple-Glazed Pork
Tenderloin 177

French-Style Pot-Roasted
Pork Loin 178

Maple-Glazed
Pork Roast 179

    Maple-Glazed Pork Roast
    with Rosemary

    Maple-Glazed Pork Roast
    with Orange Essence

    Maple-Glazed Pork Roast
    with Star Anise

    Maple-Glazed Pork Roast
    with Smoked Paprika

Garlic-Studded Roast
Pork Loin 180

    Mustard–Shallot Sauce
    with Thyme

Slow-Cooker Pork Loin
with Cranberries and
Orange 181

Slow-Roasted Pork
Shoulder with Peach
Sauce 182

Indoor Pulled Pork with
Sweet and Tangy
Barbecue Sauce 183

    Lexington Vinegar
    Barbecue Sauce

    South Carolina Mustard
    Barbecue Sauce

Roast Fresh Ham 185

    Cider and Brown
    Sugar Glaze

    Spicy Pineapple-Ginger
    Glaze

    Coca-Cola Glaze with
    Lime and Jalapeño

    Orange, Cinnamon, and
    Star Anise Glaze

Glazed Spiral-Sliced
Ham 187

    Maple-Orange Glaze

    Cherry-Port Glaze

SLOW-ROASTED BEEF

WHY THIS RECIPE WORKS: Roasting inexpensive beef usually yields tough meat best suited for sandwiches. We wanted to take an inexpensive cut and turn it into a tender, rosy, beefy-tasting roast worthy of Sunday dinner.

First, we selected the best cut for our roast. Our favorite, the eye round, has good flavor and tenderness and a uniform shape that guarantees even cooking. Next, we chose between the two classic methods for roasting meat—high and fast or low and slow. Low temperature was the way to go. Keeping the meat's internal temperature below 122 degrees as long as possible allowed the meat's enzymes to act as natural tenderizers, breaking down its tough connective tissue (this action stops at 122 degrees). Since most ovens don't heat below 200 degrees, we needed to devise a special method to lengthen this tenderizing period. We roasted the meat at 225 degrees (after searing it to give the meat a crusty exterior) and shut off the oven when the roast reached 115 degrees. The meat stayed below 122 degrees an extra 30 minutes, allowing the enzymes to continue their work before the temperature reached 130 degrees for medium-rare. As for seasoning, we found that salting the meat a full 24 hours before roasting made it even more tender and seasoned the roast throughout.

Slow-Roasted Beef

SERVES 6 TO 8

We don't recommend cooking this roast past medium. Open the oven door as little as possible and remove the roast from the oven while taking its temperature. If the roast has not reached the desired temperature in the time specified in step 3, heat the oven to 225 degrees for 5 minutes, shut it off, and continue to cook the roast to the desired temperature. For a smaller (2½ to 3½-pound) roast, reduce the amount of pepper to 1½ teaspoons. For a 4½ to 6-pound roast, cut in half crosswise before cooking to create two smaller roasts. Slice the roast as thin as possible and serve with Horseradish Cream Sauce, if desired (recipe follows).

- 1 (3½ to 4½-pound) boneless eye-round roast (see note)
- 2 teaspoons table salt
- 1 tablespoon plus 2 teaspoons vegetable oil
- 2 teaspoons ground black pepper (see note)

BEHIND THE SCENES

SALTING—THE SECRET TO JUICY ROASTS

We're big advocates of brining in the test kitchen (see "How Brining Saved Thanksgiving" on page 113). But brining works best for lean types of meat like poultry and pork. Is there an alternative to brining for fattier meats like beef? There is— salting. Salting is a kind of "dry brine" in which meat is rubbed with salt and then refrigerated for several hours. How does salting do its work? Initially, the salt draws out moisture from the meat, and this moisture mixes with the salt to form a shallow brine. Over time, the salt migrates from the shallow brine into the meat, just as it does in our usual brining technique. Once inside the meat, the salt changes the structure of the muscle fibers, allowing the meat to hold on to more water, so that it turns out juicy and well-seasoned.

We tried salting in developing our Slow-Roasted Beef and found that salting for 24 hours worked best—the results were remarkable. In addition to the slow-cooking technique we use in this recipe, salting helped transform our bargain eye round into a tender, juicy roast that rivals beef tenderloin. (Note that smaller cuts of meat, like steak, do not need to be salted nearly as long—about 40 minutes is sufficient.)

1. Sprinkle all sides of the roast evenly with the salt. Wrap with plastic wrap and refrigerate for 18 to 24 hours.

2. Adjust an oven rack to the middle position and heat the oven to 225 degrees. Pat the roast dry with paper towels; rub with 2 teaspoons of the oil and sprinkle all sides evenly with the pepper. Heat the remaining 1 tablespoon oil in a 12-inch skillet over medium-high heat until starting to smoke. Sear the roast until browned on all sides, 3 to 4 minutes per side. Transfer the roast to a wire rack set over a rimmed baking sheet. Roast until the center of the roast registers 115 degrees on an instant-read thermometer for medium-rare (1¼ to 1¾ hours), or 125 degrees for medium (1¾ to 2¼ hours).

3. Turn the oven off; leave the roast in the oven, without opening the door, until the center of the roast registers

130 degrees for medium-rare or 140 degrees for medium, 30 to 50 minutes longer. Transfer the roast to a carving board and let rest for 15 minutes. Slice the meat crosswise as thin as possible and serve with the sauce, if using.

Horseradish Cream Sauce

MAKES ABOUT 1 CUP

See page 743 for information on our recommended brand of prepared horseradish.

- ½ **cup heavy cream, chilled**
- ½ **cup prepared horseradish**
- 1 **teaspoon table salt**
- ⅛ **teaspoon ground black pepper**

Whisk the cream in a medium bowl until thickened but not yet holding soft peaks, 1 to 2 minutes. Gently fold in the horseradish, salt, and pepper. Transfer to a serving bowl and refrigerate for at least 30 minutes or up to 1 hour before serving.

ROAST BEEF TENDERLOIN

WHY THIS RECIPE WORKS: There's nothing like the buttery texture of a roasted beef tenderloin. Ideally, it has rosy meat all the way through and a deep brown crust; too often, though, this roast has only one or the other. We wanted a technique that produced perfectly cooked and deeply flavored meat—without too much fuss.

Tenderloins come whole or center-cut, and the obvious choice was the latter; it's already trimmed, and it lacks the narrow "tail" of the whole cut. We first tried searing the meat in the oven as many recipes recommend, but it never browned evenly and came out with a gray band of overcooked meat around the edge. Stovetop browning was better for producing a crust, but the roast still came out of the oven with that same gray band. The trick was to reverse the process, first roasting the meat in the oven, then searing at the end. The warmer surface of the meat browned in less time and so didn't overcook. Lowering the oven temperature eliminated the ring of overcooked meat altogether. To add flavor to this mild cut of beef, a simple technique of salting it before roasting worked wonders; rubbing the roast with a little softened butter added richness. A flavored butter served alongside was the final touch. With its uniformly rosy meat, deep brown crust, and beefy flavor, this beef tenderloin was worthy of its price tag.

Roast Beef Tenderloin

SERVES 4 TO 6

Ask your butcher to prepare a trimmed, center-cut Châteaubriand from the whole tenderloin, as this cut is not usually available without special ordering. If you are cooking for a crowd, this recipe can be doubled to make two roasts. Sear the roasts one after the other, wiping out the pan and adding new oil after searing the first roast. Both pieces of meat can be roasted on the same rack.

- 1 **(2-pound) beef tenderloin center-cut Châteaubriand, trimmed (see note)**
- 1 **teaspoon table salt**
- 1 **teaspoon coarsely ground black pepper**
- 2 **tablespoons unsalted butter, softened**
- 1 **tablespoon vegetable oil**
- 1 **recipe flavored butter (recipes follow)**

1. Using 12-inch lengths of kitchen twine, tie the roast crosswise at 1½-inch intervals. Sprinkle the roast evenly with the salt, cover loosely with plastic wrap, and let stand at room temperature for 1 hour. Meanwhile, adjust an oven rack to the middle position and heat the oven to 300 degrees.

2. Pat the roast dry with paper towels. Sprinkle the roast evenly with the pepper and spread the butter evenly over the surface. Transfer the roast to a wire rack set over a rimmed baking sheet. Roast until the center of the roast registers 125 degrees on an instant-read thermometer for medium-rare (40 to 55 minutes), or 135 degrees for medium (55 to 70 minutes), flipping the roast halfway through cooking.

3. Heat the oil in a 12-inch heavy-bottomed skillet over medium-high heat until just smoking. Place the roast in the skillet and sear until well browned on four sides, 1 to 2 minutes per side (a total of 4 to 8 minutes). Transfer the roast to a carving board and spread 2 tablespoons of the flavored butter evenly over the top of the roast; let rest for 15 minutes. Remove the twine and cut the meat crosswise into ½-inch-thick slices. Serve, passing the remaining flavored butter separately.

Shallot and Parsley Butter

MAKES ABOUT ½ CUP

- 4 tablespoons (½ stick) unsalted butter, softened
- 1 small shallot, minced (about 1 tablespoon)
- 1 medium garlic clove, minced or pressed through a garlic press (about 1 teaspoon)
- 1 tablespoon finely chopped fresh parsley leaves
- ¼ teaspoon table salt
- ¼ teaspoon ground black pepper

Combine all the ingredients in a medium bowl.

Chipotle and Garlic Butter with Lime and Cilantro

MAKES ABOUT ½ CUP

- 5 tablespoons unsalted butter, softened
- 1 medium chipotle chile in adobo sauce, seeded and minced, with 1 teaspoon adobo sauce
- 1 medium garlic clove, minced or pressed through a garlic press (about 1 teaspoon)
- 1 teaspoon honey
- 1 teaspoon grated zest from 1 lime
- 1 tablespoon minced fresh cilantro leaves
- ½ teaspoon table salt

Combine all the ingredients in a medium bowl.

HORSERADISH-CRUSTED BEEF TENDERLOIN

WHY THIS RECIPE WORKS: A crisp horseradish crust contrasts nicely with the mild flavor of beef tenderloin, but most horseradish-crusted recipes are uninspired, and when carving time comes around, the crust falls off the meat in patches. We wanted to combine the bracing flavor of horseradish with a crisp, golden crust that would add textural contrast to rosy, medium-rare meat—and we wanted it to stick.

We chose to use a center-cut roast—also called a Châteaubriand—because its uniform shape cooks evenly. After lightly flouring the meat and applying a thin wash of egg white, we rolled the roast in crushed potato chips and panko bread crumbs mixed with horseradish, mayonnaise, shallot, garlic, and herbs. Potato chips may seem unusual, but they kept their crunch and contributed lots of flavor, particularly when we made our own by frying shredded potato in oil until browned and crisp. To make the crust adhere to the meat after being sliced, we replaced the egg white with gelatin. Because both meat and gelatin are made up of linear proteins that form tight bonds with each other, the gelatin mixture bound the bread crumbs firmly to the meat, yet yielded slightly as we cut it.

And to prevent the crust from turning soggy from meat juices released during cooking, we seared the meat in a hot skillet and let it rest so that its juices could drain off before applying the paste and the crumbs. Then we coated only the top and sides of the tenderloin, leaving an "opening" on the bottom for meat juices to escape as it roasted.

Horseradish-Crusted Beef Tenderloin

SERVES 6

If using table salt, reduce the amount in step 1 to 1½ teaspoons. Add the gelatin to the horseradish paste at the last moment or the mixture will become unspreadable. If desired, serve the roast with Horseradish Cream Sauce (page 165; you will need 2 jars of prepared horseradish for both the roast and sauce). If you choose to salt the tenderloin in advance, remove it from the refrigerator 1 hour before cooking. To make this recipe 1 day in advance, prepare it through step 3, but in step 2 do not toss the bread crumbs with the other ingredients until you are ready to sear the meat.

1   (2-pound) beef tenderloin center-cut Châteaubriand, trimmed of fat and silver skin
     Kosher salt (see note)
3   tablespoons panko (Japanese-style bread crumbs)
1   cup plus 2 teaspoons vegetable oil
1¼   teaspoons ground black pepper
1   small shallot, minced (about 1 tablespoon)
2   medium garlic cloves, minced or pressed through a garlic press (about 2 teaspoons)
¼   cup well-drained prepared horseradish (see note)
2   tablespoons minced fresh parsley leaves
½   teaspoon minced fresh thyme leaves
1   small russet potato (about 6 ounces), peeled and grated on the large holes of a box grater
1½   teaspoons mayonnaise
1½   teaspoons Dijon mustard
½   teaspoon powdered gelatin (see note)

1. Sprinkle the roast with 1 tablespoon salt, cover with plastic wrap, and let stand at room temperature for 1 hour or refrigerate for up to 24 hours. Adjust an oven rack to the middle position and heat the oven to 400 degrees.

2. Toss the bread crumbs with 2 teaspoons of the oil, ¼ teaspoon salt, and ¼ teaspoon of the pepper in a 10-inch nonstick skillet. Cook over medium heat, stirring frequently, until deep golden brown, 3 to 5 minutes. Transfer to a rimmed baking sheet and cool to room temperature (wipe out the skillet). Once cool, toss the bread crumbs with the shallot, garlic, 2 tablespoons of the horseradish, the parsley, and thyme.

3. Rinse the grated potato under cold water, then squeeze dry in a kitchen towel. Transfer the potatoes and remaining 1 cup oil to the skillet. Cook over high heat, stirring frequently, until the potatoes are golden brown and crisp, 6 to 8 minutes. Using a slotted spoon, transfer the potatoes to a paper towel–lined plate and season lightly with salt; let cool for 5 minutes. Reserve 1 tablespoon oil from the skillet and discard the remainder. Once the potatoes are cool, transfer to a quart-size zipper-lock bag and crush until coarsely ground. Transfer the potatoes to the baking sheet with the bread-crumb mixture and toss to combine.

4. Pat the exterior of the tenderloin dry with paper towels and sprinkle evenly with the remaining 1 teaspoon pepper. Heat the reserved 1 tablespoon oil in a 12-inch nonstick skillet over medium-high heat until just smoking. Sear the tenderloin until well browned on all sides, 5 to 7 minutes. Transfer to a wire rack set over a rimmed baking sheet and let rest for 10 minutes.

5. Combine the remaining 2 tablespoons horseradish, mayonnaise, and mustard in a small bowl. Just before coat-

ing the tenderloin, add the gelatin and stir to combine. Spread the horseradish paste on the top and sides of the meat, leaving the bottom and ends bare. Roll the coated sides of the tenderloin in the bread-crumb mixture, pressing gently so the crumbs adhere in an even layer that just covers the horseradish paste; pat off any excess.

6. Return the tenderloin to the wire rack. Roast until an instant-read thermometer inserted into the center of the roast registers 120 to 125 degrees for medium-rare, 25 to 30 minutes.

7. Transfer the roast to a carving board and let rest for 20 minutes. Carefully cut the meat crosswise into ½-inch-thick slices and serve.

ULTIMATE BEEF TENDERLOIN

WHY THIS RECIPE WORKS: Beef tenderloin is perfect holiday fare. Add a rich stuffing and you've got the ultimate main course—at least in theory. We found three problems with stuffed tenderloin. The tenderloin's thin, tapered shape made for uneven cooking; in the time it took to develop a nice crust, the meat overcooked; and "deluxe" fillings such as lobster and chanterelles were so chunky they fell out of the meat when sliced. We wanted a stuffed beef tenderloin with a deeply charred crust, a tender, rosy-pink interior, and an intensely flavored stuffing that stayed neatly rolled in the meat.

STUFFING AND TYING A TENDERLOIN

1. Insert a chef's knife about 1 inch from the bottom of the roast and cut horizontally, stopping just before the edge. Open the meat like a book.

2. Make another cut diagonally into the thicker portion of the roast. Open up this flap, smoothing out the butterflied rectangle of meat.

3. Spread the filling evenly over the entire surface, leaving a ½-inch border on all sides. Press the spinach leaves evenly on top of the filling.

4. Using both hands, gently but firmly roll up the stuffed tenderloin, making it as compact as possible without squeezing out the filling.

5. Evenly space eight pieces of kitchen twine (each about 14 inches) beneath the roast. Tie each strand tightly around the roast, starting with the ends.

We had determined for our Roast Beef Tenderloin recipe (page 165) that a center-cut tenderloin cooks more evenly than a whole one, and its cylindrical shape had an added advantage here as it made the roast easier to stuff. But making a slit in the roast didn't give us much room for stuffing; double-butterflying the meat, to open it up like a book, gave us more space. After we stuffed, rolled, and tied it, we rubbed the roast with salt, pepper, and olive oil, which added flavor and helped develop a good crust when we seared the meat. We could fit just a cupful of stuffing in the meat, so we knew the flavors had to be intense. Chunky stuffings fell out when the roast was sliced, and anything with bread in it became a sponge that soaked up the meat juice. We finally decided on woodsy cremini mushrooms and caramelized onions, seasoned with Madeira and garlic; this combination made a savory-sweet jamlike filling that spread easily on the meat and held together well. Baby spinach added color and freshness. This roast was juicy and flavorful, and the filling was the ultimate touch of luxury.

Roast Beef Tenderloin with Caramelized Onion and Mushroom Stuffing

SERVES 4 TO 6

The roast can be stuffed, rolled, and tied a day ahead, but don't season the exterior until you are ready to cook it. This recipe can be doubled to make two roasts. Sear the roasts one after the other, cleaning the pan and adding new oil after searing the first roast. Both pieces of meat can be roasted on the same rack.

STUFFING

- 8 ounces cremini mushrooms, cleaned, stems trimmed, and broken into rough pieces
- 1½ teaspoons unsalted butter
- 1½ teaspoons olive oil
- 1 medium onion, halved and sliced ¼ inch thick
- ¼ teaspoon table salt
- ⅛ teaspoon ground black pepper
- 1 medium garlic clove, minced or pressed through a garlic press (about 1 teaspoon)
- ½ cup Madeira or sweet Marsala wine

BEEF ROAST

- 1 (2 to 3-pound) beef tenderloin center-cut Châteaubriand, trimmed and butterflied (see photos) Table salt and ground black pepper

½ cup lightly packed baby spinach

3 tablespoons olive oil

HERB BUTTER

4 tablespoons (½ stick) unsalted butter, softened

1 tablespoon chopped fresh parsley leaves

¾ teaspoon chopped fresh thyme leaves

1 medium garlic clove, minced or pressed through a garlic press (about 1 teaspoon)

1 tablespoon whole grain mustard

⅛ teaspoon table salt

⅛ teaspoon ground black pepper

1. FOR THE STUFFING: Pulse the mushrooms in a food processor until coarsely chopped, about 6 pulses. Heat the butter and oil in a 12-inch nonstick skillet over medium-high heat. Add the onion, salt, and pepper; cook, stirring occasionally, until the onion begins to soften, about 5 minutes. Add the mushrooms and cook, stirring occasionally, until all the moisture has evaporated, 5 to 7 minutes. Reduce the heat to medium and continue to cook, stirring frequently, until the vegetables are deeply browned and sticky, about 10 minutes. Stir in the garlic and cook until fragrant, about 30 seconds. Slowly stir in the Madeira and cook, scraping the bottom of the skillet to loosen any browned bits, until the liquid has evaporated, 2 to 3 minutes. Transfer the onion-mushroom mixture to a plate and cool to room temperature.

2. FOR THE ROAST: Pat the tenderloin dry and season the cut side of the tenderloin liberally with salt and pepper. Following the photos on page 168, spread the cooled stuffing mixture over the interior of the beef, leaving a ½-inch border on all sides; press the spinach leaves on top of the stuffing. Roll the roast lengthwise, making it as compact as possible without squeezing out any filling. Evenly space eight pieces of kitchen twine (each about 14 inches) beneath the roast. Tie each strand tightly around the roast, starting with the ends.

3. In a small bowl, stir together 1 tablespoon of the olive oil, 1½ teaspoons salt, and 1½ teaspoons pepper. Rub the roast with the oil mixture and let stand at room temperature for 1 hour.

4. Adjust an oven rack to the middle position and heat the oven to 450 degrees. Heat the remaining 2 tablespoons olive oil in a 12-inch skillet over medium-high heat until smoking. Add the beef to the pan and cook until well browned on all sides, 8 to 10 minutes total. Transfer the beef to a wire rack set over a rimmed baking sheet and

GIVE THAT MEAT A REST

You'll never see anyone in the test kitchen cut into a roast, or any meat, straight from the oven. They always let it rest before slicing. Exposed to heat during cooking, proteins, which resemble coiled springs, undergo a radical transformation in which they uncoil and then reconnect to each other in haphazard structures. This process, called coagulation, is the reason that proteins become firm and lose moisture during the cooking process. The longer that proteins are exposed to heat, the tighter they coagulate and the more liquid they drive toward both the surface and the center of the meat, much like wringing a wet kitchen towel.

If you were to cut the meat immediately after removing it from the heat source, the liquid suspended between the interior proteins is driven toward the surface and would simply pool (or what many chefs call bleed) on the cutting board or plate because the proteins have not had time to relax. The best way to prevent this pooling of juices and a dry hunk of meat is to rest the roast. Although the process of coagulation is not reversible, allowing the protein molecules to relax after cooking slows the rate which they continue to squeeze the liquid between their tight coils and increases their capacity to retain moisture. A short rest on the cutting board will decrease the amount of liquid lost during carving by about 40 percent. There's another good reason to have some patience and let your meat rest—it allows you some time to finish the other components of dinner, which is especially useful around the holidays when there are typically loads of sides to get to the table too.

place in the oven. Roast until the thickest part of the roast registers 120 degrees on an instant-read thermometer for rare (16 to 18 minutes), or 125 degrees for medium-rare (20 to 22 minutes).

5. FOR THE BUTTER: While the meat roasts, combine all the ingredients in a small bowl. Transfer the tenderloin to a carving board; spread half of the butter evenly over the top of the roast. Loosely tent the roast with foil; let rest for 15 minutes. Cut the roast between the pieces of twine into thick slices. Remove the twine and serve, passing the remaining butter separately.

PRIME RIB

WHY THIS RECIPE WORKS: Most of us cook prime rib only once a year, if that, and don't want to risk experimenting with the cooking method—especially when the results are no better than mediocre. We thought that a special-occasion roast deserved better and wanted to find the best way to get the juicy, tender, rosy meat that prime rib should have.

The principal question for roasting prime rib was oven temperature, and our research turned up a wide range of recommendations. Most delivered meat that was well-done on the outside but increasingly rare toward the center—not too bad, but not exactly great. Surprisingly, the roast we cooked at a temperature of only 250 degrees was rosy from the center all the way out. Additionally, it retained more juice than a roast cooked at a higher temperature, and the internal temperature rose less during resting, so we had more control over the final degree of doneness. Searing before roasting gave us a crusty brown exterior. For seasoning, prime rib needs nothing more than salt and pepper. Now that we'd found a dependable cooking method, we could serve this once-a-year roast with confidence.

Prime Rib

SERVES 6 TO 8

With two pieces of kitchen twine running parallel to the bone, tie the roast at both ends to prevent the outer layer of meat from pulling away from the rib-eye muscle and overcooking.

> 1 (7-pound; 3-rib) standing rib roast, trimmed and tied (see note)
> Table salt and ground black pepper

1. Pat the roast dry with paper towels and season with salt and pepper. Cover the roast loosely with plastic wrap and let sit at room temperature for 1 to 2 hours.

2. Adjust an oven rack to the lowest position and heat the oven to 250 degrees. Heat a large roasting pan over two burners set at medium-high heat until hot, about 4 minutes. Place the roast in the hot pan and cook on all sides until nicely browned and about ½ cup fat has rendered, 6 to 8 minutes.

3. Remove the roast from the pan. Set a wire rack in the pan, then set the roast on the rack.

4. Place the roast in the oven and roast until the meat registers 125 degrees on an instant-read thermometer for rare, 130 degrees for medium-rare, and 140 degrees for

medium, 3 to 3½ hours. Remove the roast from the oven and tent with foil. Let stand for 20 to 30 minutes to allow the juices to redistribute evenly throughout the roast.

5. Remove the twine and set the roast on a carving board, with the rib bones at a 90-degree angle to the board. Following the photos, carve and serve immediately.

BRAISED BRISKET

WHY THIS RECIPE WORKS: Brisket is naturally flavorful, but because it is so lean, it requires long, slow braising to become tender—and the result is almost always stringy, dry meat. We wanted a better way to cook brisket so that it would remain moist, and we wanted to serve it with a flavorful sauce that would complement the beef, not disguise it.

The fat in a piece of brisket is all on the surface; there's no marbling to keep the interior moist. We needed to find a way to get the moisture inside. We tried many different types and amounts of liquids and a variety of cooking vessels and techniques, but no matter what we did, the meat was still dry. Could the answer lie in adding moisture after the long braise? We left the meat in the sauce after cooking it, and after about an hour there was a noticeable difference. Taking this discovery further, we refrigerated the cooked meat and sauce overnight. The meat reabsorbed some of the liquid, becoming more moist and easier to carve without shredding. The sauce—based on red wine, chicken broth, and lots of onions—had improved as well; the fat had risen to the surface and congealed, making it easier to remove. All we had to do was reheat the sliced meat in the sauce, and this hearty dish was ready.

Onion-Braised Beef Brisket

SERVES 6

This recipe requires a few hours of unattended cooking. It also requires advance preparation. After cooking, the brisket must stand overnight in the braising liquid that later becomes the sauce; this helps to keep the brisket moist and flavorful. Defatting the sauce is essential. If the fat has congealed into a layer on top of the sauce, it can be easily removed while cold. Sometimes, however, fragments of solid fat are dispersed throughout the sauce; in this case, the sauce should be skimmed of fat after reheating. If you prefer a spicy sauce, increase the amount of cayenne to ¼ teaspoon. You will need 18-inch-wide heavy-duty foil for this recipe. If you own an electric knife, it will make easy work of slicing the cold brisket.

If you would like to make and serve the brisket on the same day, after removing the brisket from the oven in step 4, reseal the foil and let the brisket stand at room temperature for an hour. Then transfer the brisket to a carving board and continue with the recipe to strain, defat, and reheat the sauce and slice the meat; because the brisket will still be hot, there will be no need to put it back into the oven once the reheated sauce is poured over it.

1   (4 to 5-pound) beef brisket, preferably flat cut
     Table salt and ground black pepper
1   teaspoon vegetable oil, plus more as needed
3   large onions (about 2½ pounds), halved and
     sliced ½ inch thick
1   tablespoon brown sugar
3   medium garlic cloves, minced or pressed through a
     garlic press (about 1 tablespoon)
1   tablespoon tomato paste
1   tablespoon paprika
⅛   teaspoon cayenne pepper (see note)
2   tablespoons unbleached all-purpose flour
1   cup low-sodium chicken broth
1   cup dry red wine
3   bay leaves
3   sprigs fresh thyme
2   teaspoons cider vinegar (to season the sauce
     before serving)

1. Adjust an oven rack to the lower-middle position and heat the oven to 300 degrees. Line a 13 by 9-inch baking dish with two 24-inch-long sheets of 18-inch-wide heavy-duty foil, positioning the sheets perpendicular to each other and allowing the excess foil to extend beyond the edges of the pan. Pat the brisket dry with paper towels. Place the brisket, fat side up, on a cutting board; using a dinner fork, poke holes in the meat through the fat layer about 1 inch apart. Season both sides of the brisket liberally with salt and pepper.

2. Heat 1 teaspoon oil in a 12-inch skillet over medium-high heat until the oil just begins to smoke. Place the brisket, fat side up, in the skillet (the brisket may climb up the sides of the skillet); weight the brisket with a heavy Dutch oven or cast-iron skillet and cook until well browned, about 7 minutes. Remove the Dutch oven; using tongs, flip the brisket and cook on the second side without the weight until well browned, about 7 minutes longer. Transfer the brisket to a platter.

3. Pour off all but 1 tablespoon fat from the pan (or, if the brisket is lean, add enough oil to the fat in the skillet to equal 1 tablespoon); stir in the onions, brown sugar, and ¼ teaspoon salt and cook over medium-high heat, stirring occasionally, until the onions are softened and golden, 10 to 12 minutes. Add the garlic and cook, stirring frequently, until fragrant, about 1 minute; add the tomato paste and cook, stirring to combine, until the paste darkens, about 2 minutes. Add the paprika and cayenne and cook, stirring constantly, until fragrant, about 1 minute. Sprinkle the flour over the onions and cook, stirring constantly, until well combined, about 2 minutes. Add the broth, wine, bay leaves, and thyme, stirring to scrape up the browned bits from the pan; bring to a simmer and simmer for about 5 minutes to fully thicken.

4. Pour the sauce and onions into the foil-lined baking dish. Nestle the brisket, fat side up, in the sauce and onions. Fold the foil extensions over and seal (do not tightly crimp the foil because it must later be opened to test for doneness). Place in the oven and cook until a fork can be inserted into and removed from the center of the brisket with no resistance, 3½ to 4 hours (when testing for doneness, open the foil with caution as the contents will be steaming). Carefully open the foil and let the brisket cool at room temperature for 20 to 30 minutes.

5. Transfer the brisket to a large bowl; set a mesh strainer over the bowl and strain the sauce over the brisket. Discard the bay leaves and thyme from the onions and transfer the onions to a small bowl. Cover both bowls with plastic wrap, cut vents in the plastic with a paring knife, and refrigerate overnight.

6. About 45 minutes before serving, adjust an oven rack to the lower-middle position and heat the oven to 350 degrees. While the oven heats, transfer the cold brisket to a carving board. Scrape off and discard any congealed fat from the sauce, then transfer the sauce to a medium saucepan and heat over medium heat until warm, skimming any fat on the surface with a wide shallow spoon (you should have about 2 cups of sauce without onions; if necessary, simmer the sauce over medium-high heat until reduced to 2 cups). While the sauce heats, use an electric knife, chef's knife, or carving knife to slice the brisket against the grain into ¼-inch-thick slices, trimming and discarding any excess fat, if desired; place the slices in a 13 by 9-inch baking dish. Stir the reserved onions and the vinegar into the warmed sauce and season with salt and pepper to taste. Pour the sauce over the brisket slices, cover the baking dish with foil, and bake until heated through, 25 to 30 minutes. Serve immediately.

SAUTÉED PORK TENDERLOIN

WHY THIS RECIPE WORKS: When cooked properly, ultra-lean pork tenderloin has a tenderness rivaling that of beef tenderloin; unfortunately it also has ultra-mild flavor. Long marinades and hybrid searing and roasting techniques help remedy the flavor deficiency, but they take the home cook a long way from the realm of the no-fuss meal. We wanted a recipe for a fast weeknight dinner that still offered maximum flavor.

Packaging and shape presented the first challenge: we needed to deal with the tenderloin's oblong, tapered shape as well as the fact that the tenderloins (which are usually sold in a pair in a vacuum pack) were almost guaranteed to be substantially different in weight and length. The solution was to cut them into 1½-inch-thick medal-

lions (the end pieces were scored, creating a small flap of meat that folded underneath the larger half to yield the right-sized medallion). To preserve their tidy cylindrical shape, we developed two approaches: tying the medallions or wrapping blanched bacon around them, fastened with toothpicks. We found we could create a beautiful sear on all sides of these neat packages in the time it took to reach an internal temperature of 140 to 145 degrees, and the searing process had the extra benefit of producing enough fond (flavorful browned bits) to create a few easy, flavorful pan sauces.

Thick-Cut Pork Tenderloin Medallions
SERVES 4 TO 6

We prefer natural to enhanced pork (pork that has been injected with a salt solution to increase moistness and flavor), though both will work in this recipe. Begin checking the doneness of smaller medallions 1 or 2 minutes early; they may need to be taken out of the pan a little sooner. Be sure not to rinse out the skillet if serving with a pan sauce (recipes follow).

> 2 (1 to 1¼-pound) pork tenderloins, trimmed, cut crosswise into 1½-inch pieces, and tied; thinner end pieces removed and tied together (see photos)
> Table salt and ground black pepper
> 2 tablespoons vegetable oil

1. Pat the pork medallions dry and season with salt and pepper.

2. Heat the oil in a 12-inch skillet over medium-high heat until shimmering. Add the pork and cook, without moving the pieces, until well browned, 3 to 5 minutes. Turn the pork and brown on the second side, 3 to 5 minutes more. Reduce the heat to medium. Using tongs, stand each piece on its side and cook, turning the pieces as necessary, until the sides are well browned and the internal temperature registers 140 to 145 degrees on an instant-read thermometer, 8 to 12 minutes. Transfer the pork to a platter, tent loosely with foil, and let rest until the temperature registers 150 degrees on an instant-read thermometer, while making a pan sauce (recipes follow). Serve with the sauce.

NOTES FROM THE TEST KITCHEN

TURNING THE TAILPIECE INTO A MEDALLION

1. Score the tenderloin's tapered tail end.

2. Fold in half at the incision.

3. Tie the medallion with kitchen twine, making sure the outer surfaces are flat.

TYING THICK MEDALLIONS

Thick medallions allow for more browning, but they can flop over in the pan. To prevent this, tie each piece with kitchen twine.

Maple-Mustard Sauce

MAKES ABOUT 1 CUP

- 2 teaspoons vegetable oil
- 1 medium onion, halved and sliced thin
- 1 cup low-sodium chicken broth
- ⅓ cup maple syrup
- 3 tablespoons balsamic vinegar
- 3 tablespoons whole grain mustard
  Table salt and ground black pepper

Pour off any fat from the skillet in which the pork was cooked. Add the oil and heat the skillet over medium heat until shimmering. Add the onion and cook, stirring occasionally, until softened and beginning to brown, 3 to 4 minutes. Increase the heat to medium-high and add the broth; bring to a simmer, scraping the bottom of the skillet with a wooden spoon to loosen any browned bits. Simmer until the liquid is reduced to ½ cup, 3 to 4 minutes. Add the maple syrup, vinegar, mustard, and any juices from the resting meat and cook until thickened and reduced to 1 cup, 3 to 4 minutes longer. Season with salt and pepper to taste, pour the sauce over the pork, and serve immediately.

Apple Cider Sauce

MAKES ABOUT 1¼ CUPS

Complete step 1 of this recipe either before or during the cooking of the pork, then finish the sauce while the pork rests.

- 1½ cups apple cider
- 1 cup low-sodium chicken broth
- 2 teaspoons cider vinegar
- 1 cinnamon stick
- 4 tablespoons (½ stick) unsalted butter, cut into 4 pieces
- 2 large shallots, minced (about ½ cup)
- 1 tart apple, such as Granny Smith, peeled, cored, and diced small
- ¼ cup Calvados or apple-flavored brandy
- 1 teaspoon minced fresh thyme leaves
  Table salt and ground black pepper

1. Combine the cider, broth, vinegar, and cinnamon stick in a medium saucepan; simmer over medium-high heat until the liquid is reduced to 1 cup, 10 to 12 minutes. Remove the cinnamon stick and discard. Set the sauce aside until the pork is cooked.

2. Pour off any fat from the skillet in which the pork was cooked. Add 1 tablespoon of the butter and heat over medium heat until melted. Add the shallots and apple and cook, stirring occasionally, until softened and beginning to brown, 1 to 2 minutes. Remove the skillet from the heat and add the Calvados. Return the skillet to the heat and cook for about 1 minute, scraping the bottom of the skillet with a wooden spoon to loosen any browned bits. Add the reduced cider mixture, any juices from the resting meat, and the thyme; increase the heat to medium-high and simmer until thickened and reduced to 1¼ cups, 3 to 4 minutes. Off the heat, whisk in the remaining 3 tablespoons butter and season with salt and pepper to taste. Pour the sauce over the pork and serve immediately.

BREADED PORK CUTLETS

WHY THIS RECIPE WORKS: While classic Wiener schnitzel features a thin, tender veal cutlet coated in ultrafine bread crumbs and then fried until puffy and golden brown, many recipes—to avoid the toughness and high price of veal—substitute pork. But too often these recipes yield dry, tough pork cutlets with greasy coatings. We wanted tender pork cutlets with the crisp, wrinkled, puffy coating that is Wiener schnitzel's signature.

Dismissing pork chops and prepackaged cutlets, we chose tenderloin, which has a mild flavor similar to veal and isn't tough. We cut the tenderloin crosswise on an angle into four pieces, which when pounded thin gave us long, narrow cutlets that would fit two at a time in the pan. Schnitzel is breaded with the usual flour, egg, and bread-crumb sequence of coatings, but we had to figure out how to get the characteristic puffiness and "rumpled" appearance of the finished cutlets; with good schnitzel you should be able to slide a knife between the meat and the coating. Drying bread in the microwave produced extra-dry crumbs that helped with the crispness, and a little vegetable oil whisked into the egg helped separate the coating from the meat.

But the real breakthrough was in the frying method: Instead of sautéing the cutlets, we cooked them in a Dutch oven in an inch of oil, shaking the pot to get some of the oil over the top of the meat. The extra heat quickly solidified the egg in the coating, so that the steam from the meat couldn't escape and puffed the coating instead. With the traditional schnitzel garnishes of lemon, parsley, capers, and a sieved hard-cooked egg, these cutlets, with their tender meat and crisp coating, delivered on all fronts.

Breaded Pork Cutlets (Pork Schnitzel)
SERVES 4

To make cutlets, cut the tenderloin in half on a 20-degree angle, then cut each piece in half again at the same angle. Cut the tapered tail pieces slightly thicker than the middle ones. Using 2 cups of oil for cooking may seem like a lot, but it is necessary to get an authentic, wrinkled texture on the finished cutlets. When properly cooked, the cutlets absorb very little oil. To ensure ample room for the cutlets as they fry, it is essential to use a Dutch oven with a large surface area. Although spaetzle is the traditional side dish, boiled potatoes or egg noodles also make terrific accompaniments.

- **7 slices high-quality white sandwich bread, crusts removed, cut into ¾-inch cubes (about 4 cups)**
- **½ cup unbleached all-purpose flour**
- **2 large eggs**
- **2 cups plus 1 tablespoon vegetable oil (see note)**
- **1 (1¼-pound) pork tenderloin, trimmed of fat and silver skin and tenderloin cut on an angle into 4 equal pieces (see note)**
- **Table salt and ground black pepper**

GARNISHES
- **1 lemon, cut into wedges**
- **2 tablespoons chopped fresh parsley leaves**
- **2 tablespoons capers, rinsed**
- **1 large hard-cooked egg (page 32), yolk and white separated and passed separately through a fine-mesh strainer (optional)**

1. Place the bread cubes on a large microwave-safe plate. Microwave on high power for 4 minutes, stirring well halfway through the cooking time. Microwave on medium power until the bread is dry and a few pieces start to lightly brown, 3 to 5 minutes longer, stirring every minute. Process the dry bread in a food processor to very fine crumbs, about 45 seconds. Transfer the bread crumbs to a shallow dish (you should have about 1¼ cups crumbs). Spread the flour in a second shallow dish. Beat the eggs with 1 tablespoon of the oil in a third shallow dish.

2. Place the pork, with one cut side down, between two sheets of plastic wrap and pound to an even thickness of between ⅛ and ¼ inch. Season the cutlets with salt and pepper. Working with one cutlet at a time, dredge the cutlets thoroughly in flour, shaking off the excess, then coat with the egg, allowing the excess to drip back into the dish to ensure a very thin coating, and coat evenly with the bread crumbs, pressing on the crumbs to adhere. Place the breaded cutlets in a single layer on a wire rack set over a baking sheet; let the coating dry for 5 minutes.

3. Heat the remaining 2 cups oil in a large Dutch oven over medium-high heat until it registers 375 degrees on an instant-read thermometer. Lay two cutlets, without overlapping, in the pan and cook, shaking the pan continuously and gently, until wrinkled and light golden brown on both sides, 1 to 2 minutes per side. Transfer the cutlets to a paper towel–lined plate and flip the cutlets several times to blot the excess oil. Repeat with the remaining cutlets. Serve immediately with the garnishes.

PAN-SEARED PORK TENDERLOIN

WHY THIS RECIPE WORKS: Because pork tenderloins are so lean, they cook relatively quickly and are therefore a good choice for an easy-to-prepare meal. But that same leanness means there's also less flavor. Grilling is often used to add more flavor, but we wanted an indoor preparation for pork tenderloins that would deliver a flavor boost to this quick-cooking roast.

Simply roasted in the oven, the pork tended to dry out and never achieved the dark brown crust we wanted. We got that crust when we seared the tenderloins on the stovetop—but then the pork wasn't cooked through. A combination of searing the meat in a skillet, then transferring the pork to the oven to finish cooking, produced a flavorful crust and well-cooked meat. The browned crust added some flavor, but we wanted more. A dry rub of just salt and pepper, left on for half an hour before searing, provided enough seasoning and further encouraged a browned crust, and a pan sauce made with the browned

bits left from sautéing was an additional flavor boost. Not only were these pork tenderloins delicious; they were also on the dinner table in about half an hour.

Pan-Seared Oven-Roasted Pork Tenderloins
SERVES 4

We prefer natural to enhanced pork (pork that has been injected with a salt solution to increase moisture and flavor) for this recipe. Enhanced pork can be used, but the meat won't brown as well. Because two are cooked at once, tenderloins larger than 1 pound apiece will not fit comfortably in a 12-inch skillet. If time permits, season the tenderloins up to 30 minutes before cooking; the seasonings will better penetrate the meat. The recipe will work in a nonstick or a traditional skillet. A pan sauce can be made while the tenderloins are in the oven (recipes follow); if you intend to make a sauce, make sure to prepare all of the sauce ingredients before cooking the pork.

> 2 (12 to 16-ounce) pork tenderloins, trimmed of fat and silver skin (see note)
> 1¼ teaspoons table salt
> ¾ teaspoon ground black pepper
> 2 teaspoons vegetable oil
> 1 recipe pan sauce (optional; recipes follow)

1. Adjust an oven rack to the middle position and heat the oven to 400 degrees. Sprinkle the tenderloins evenly with the salt and pepper; rub the seasoning into the meat. Heat the oil in a 12-inch skillet over medium-high heat until smoking. Place both tenderloins in the skillet; cook until well browned, about 3 minutes. Using tongs, rotate the tenderloins a quarter-turn; cook until well browned, 45 to 60 seconds. Repeat until all sides are browned, about 1 minute longer. Transfer the tenderloins to a rimmed baking sheet and place in the oven (reserve the skillet if making a pan sauce); roast until the internal temperature registers 140 to 145 degrees on an instant-read thermometer, 10 to 16 minutes. (Begin the pan sauce, if making, while the meat roasts.)

2. Transfer the tenderloins to a carving board and tent loosely with foil (continue with the pan sauce, if making); let rest until the internal temperature registers 150 degrees, 8 to 10 minutes. Cut the tenderloins crosswise into ½-inch-thick slices, arrange on a platter or individual plates, and spoon the sauce (if using) over; serve immediately.

Dried Cherry–Port Sauce with Onions and Marmalade

MAKES ABOUT ½ CUP

The flavors in this sauce are especially suited to the winter holiday season.

- 1 teaspoon vegetable oil
- 1 large onion, halved and sliced ½ inch thick (about 1½ cups)
- ¾ cup port
- ¾ cup dried cherries
- 2 tablespoons orange marmalade
- 3 tablespoons unsalted butter, cut into 3 pieces
  Table salt and ground black pepper

1. Immediately after placing the pork in the oven, add the oil to the still-hot skillet, swirl to coat, and set the skillet over medium-high heat; add the onion and cook, stirring frequently, until softened and browned around the edges, 5 to 7 minutes. (If the drippings are browning too quickly, add 2 tablespoons water and scrape up the browned bits with a wooden spoon.) Set the skillet aside off the heat.

2. While the pork is resting, set the skillet over medium-high heat and add the port and cherries; simmer, scraping up the browned bits with a wooden spoon, until the mixture is slightly thickened, 4 to 6 minutes. Add any accumulated pork juices and continue to simmer until thickened and reduced to about ⅓ cup, 2 to 4 minutes longer. Off the heat, whisk in the orange marmalade and butter, one piece at a time. Season with salt and pepper to taste.

Garlicky Lime Sauce with Cilantro

MAKES ABOUT ½ CUP

This assertive sauce is based on a Mexican sauce called *mojo de ajo*. A rasp grater is the best way to break down the garlic to a fine paste. Another option is to put the garlic through a press and then finish mincing it to a paste with a knife. If your garlic cloves contain green sprouts or shoots, remove the sprouts before grating—their flavor is bitter and hot. The initial cooking of the garlic off the heat will prevent scorching.

- 10 garlic cloves, peeled and grated to a fine paste on a rasp grater (about 2 tablespoons; see note)
- 2 tablespoons water
- 1 tablespoon vegetable oil
- ¼ teaspoon red pepper flakes
- 2 teaspoons light brown sugar
- ¼ cup chopped fresh cilantro leaves
- 3 tablespoons juice from 2 limes
- 1 tablespoon chopped fresh chives
- 4 tablespoons (½ stick) unsalted butter, cut into 4 pieces
  Table salt and ground black pepper

1. Immediately after placing the pork in the oven, mix the garlic paste with the water in a small bowl. Add the oil to the still-hot skillet and swirl to coat; off the heat, add the garlic paste and cook with the skillet's residual heat, scraping up the browned bits with a wooden spoon, until the sizzling subsides, about 2 minutes. Set the skillet over low heat and continue cooking, stirring frequently, until the garlic is sticky, 8 to 10 minutes; set the skillet aside off the heat.

2. While the pork is resting, set the skillet over medium heat; add the red pepper flakes and brown sugar to the skillet and cook until sticky and the sugar is dissolved, about 1 minute. Add the cilantro, lime juice, and chives; simmer to blend the flavors, 1 to 2 minutes. Add any accumulated pork juices and simmer for 1 minute longer. Off the heat, whisk in the butter, one piece at a time. Season with salt and pepper to taste.

MAPLE-GLAZED PORK TENDERLOIN

WHY THIS RECIPE WORKS: When done right, nothing can quite match pork tenderloin's fine-grained, buttery-smooth texture, but even when perfectly cooked, too often it's still sorely lacking in flavor. We thought a thick, sweet, fragrant glaze would be just the solution and decided it should feature New England's signature ingredient, maple syrup.

Getting the glaze right was comparatively easy: To temper the sweetness of the maple syrup, we added molasses, mustard, and a shot of bourbon; with a little cinnamon, cloves, and cayenne, the glaze was ready. To give the glaze something to hold on to, we rolled the tenderloins in a mixture of cornstarch and sugar before searing them. When we'd built a good crust in the skillet, we painted on some glaze and transferred the pork to the oven. It occurred to us that the painting analogy was a good one—why not put multiple coats on the tenderloins to get the best coverage? When the meat was nearly done, we put on more glaze, and we added yet another coat when the tenderloins were completely done. Finally, after letting the tenderloins rest, we glazed them one last time. Slicing into this roast revealed success: A thick maple glaze coated the meat.

Maple-Glazed Pork Tenderloin

SERVES 6

We prefer natural to enhanced pork (pork that has been injected with a salt solution to increase moistness and flavor) for this recipe. If your tenderloins are smaller than 1¼ pounds, reduce the cooking time in step 3 (and use an instant-read thermometer for best results). If the tenderloins don't fit in the skillet initially, let their ends curve toward each other; the meat will eventually shrink as it cooks. Make sure to cook the tenderloins until they turn deep golden brown in step 2 or they will appear pale after glazing. Be sure to pat off the cornstarch mixture thoroughly in step 1, as any excess will leave gummy spots on the tenderloins.

- ¾ cup maple syrup, preferably grade B
- ¼ cup light or mild molasses
- 2 tablespoons bourbon or brandy
- ⅛ teaspoon ground cinnamon
-   Pinch ground cloves
-   Pinch cayenne pepper
- ¼ cup cornstarch
- 2 tablespoons sugar
- 1 tablespoon table salt
- 2 teaspoons ground black pepper
- 2 (1¼ to 1½-pound) pork tenderloins (see note), trimmed of fat and silver skin
- 2 tablespoons vegetable oil
- 1 tablespoon whole grain mustard

1. Adjust an oven rack to the middle position and heat the oven to 375 degrees. Stir ½ cup of the maple syrup, the molasses, bourbon, cinnamon, cloves, and cayenne together in a 2-cup liquid measure; set aside. Whisk the cornstarch, sugar, salt, and black pepper in a small bowl until combined. Transfer the cornstarch mixture to a rimmed baking sheet. Pat the tenderloins dry with paper towels, then roll them in the cornstarch mixture until evenly coated on all sides. Thoroughly pat off the excess cornstarch mixture.

2. Heat the oil in a 12-inch heavy-bottomed nonstick skillet over medium-high heat until just beginning to smoke. Reduce the heat to medium and place both tenderloins in the skillet, leaving at least 1 inch between them. Cook until well browned on all sides, 8 to 12 minutes. Transfer the tenderloins to a wire rack set over a rimmed baking sheet.

3. Pour off the fat from the skillet and return to medium heat. Add the syrup mixture to the skillet, scraping up the browned bits with a wooden spoon, and cook until reduced to ½ cup, about 2 minutes. Transfer 2 tablespoons of the glaze to a small bowl and set aside. Using the remaining glaze, brush each tenderloin with approximately 1 tablespoon glaze. Roast the pork until the thickest part of the tenderloins registers 130 degrees on an instant-read thermometer, 12 to 20 minutes. Brush each tenderloin with another tablespoon of the glaze and continue to roast until the thickest part of the tenderloins registers 140 degrees, 2 to 4 minutes longer. Remove the tenderloins from the oven and brush each with the remaining glaze; let rest, uncovered, until the temperature reaches 150 degrees, about 10 minutes.

4. While the tenderloins rest, stir the remaining ¼ cup maple syrup and the mustard into the reserved 2 tablespoons glaze. Brush each tenderloin with 1 tablespoon mustard glaze. Transfer the meat to a carving board and slice into ¼-inch-thick pieces. Serve, passing the extra mustard glaze at the table.

FRENCH-STYLE POT-ROASTED PORK LOIN

WHY THIS RECIPE WORKS: *Enchaud Perigordine* is a fancy name for what's actually a relatively simple French dish: slow-cooked pork loin. Cooked in the oven in a covered casserole dish, the roast turns out incredibly moist and flavorful, with a rich jus to accompany it. At least it does when it's prepared in France. But while pigs in France are bred to have plenty of fat, their American counterparts are lean, which translates to a bland and stringy roast. To improve the flavor and texture of our center-cut loin, we lowered the oven temperature (to 225 degrees) and removed the roast from the oven when it was medium-rare. Searing just three sides of the roast, rather than all four, prevented the bottom of the roast from overcooking from direct contact with the pot. Butterflying the pork allowed us to salt a maximum amount of surface area for a roast that was thoroughly seasoned throughout. And while we eliminated the hard-to-find trotter (or pig's foot), we added butter for richness while a sprinkling of gelatin lent body to the sauce.

French-Style Pot-Roasted Pork Loin

SERVES 4 TO 6

We strongly prefer the flavor of natural pork in this recipe, but enhanced pork (injected with a salt solution) can be used. If using enhanced pork, reduce the salt to 2 teaspoons (1 teaspoon per side) in step 2. The pork can be prepared through step 2, wrapped in plastic wrap, and refrigerated for up to 2 days.

> 2 tablespoons unsalted butter, cut into 2 pieces
> 6 medium garlic cloves, sliced thin
> 1 (2½-pound) boneless center-cut pork loin roast, trimmed
> Kosher salt and ground black pepper
> 1 teaspoon sugar
> 2 teaspoons herbes de Provence
> 2 tablespoons vegetable oil
> 1 Granny Smith apple, peeled, cored, and cut into ¼-inch pieces
> 1 medium onion, chopped fine
> ⅓ cup dry white wine
> 2 sprigs fresh thyme
> 1 bay leaf
> 1 tablespoon unflavored gelatin
> ¼–¾ cup low-sodium chicken broth
> 1 tablespoon chopped fresh parsley leaves

1. Adjust an oven rack to the lower-middle position and heat the oven to 225 degrees. Melt 1 tablespoon of the butter in an 8-inch skillet over medium-low heat. Add half of the garlic and cook, stirring frequently, until golden, 5 to 7 minutes. Transfer the mixture to a bowl and refrigerate while preparing the pork.

2. Following the photos, butterfly the pork loin. Sprinkle 1 tablespoon salt evenly over both sides of the loin (½ tablespoon per side) and thoroughly rub into the pork until the surface is slightly tacky. Sprinkle the sugar evenly over the inside of the loin and then spread with the cooled toasted garlic mixture. Fold the roast back together and tie tightly with kitchen twine at 1-inch intervals. Sprinkle the tied roast evenly with the herbes de Provence and season with pepper.

3. Heat 1 tablespoon of the oil in a large Dutch oven over medium heat until just smoking. Add the roast, fat side down, and brown on the top and sides (do not the brown bottom of the roast), 5 to 8 minutes. Transfer to a large plate. Add the remaining 1 tablespoon oil, the apple, and onion; cook, stirring frequently, until the onion is softened and browned, 5 to 7 minutes. Stir in the remaining sliced garlic and cook until fragrant, about 30 seconds. Stir in the wine, thyme, and bay leaf, and cook for 30 seconds. Return the roast, fat side up, to the pot; place a large sheet of foil over the pot and cover tightly with the lid. Transfer the pot to the oven and cook until the pork registers 140 degrees on an instant-read thermometer, 50 to 90 minutes

4. Transfer the roast to a carving board, tent loosely with foil, and let rest for 20 minutes. While the pork rests, sprinkle the gelatin over ¼ cup chicken broth and let sit until the gelatin softens, about 5 minutes. Remove and discard the thyme sprigs and bay leaf from the jus. Pour the jus into a 2-cup measuring cup and, if necessary, add chicken broth to measure 1¼ cups. Return the jus to the pot and bring to a simmer over medium heat. Whisk the softened gelatin mixture, the remaining 1 tablespoon butter, and the parsley into the jus and season with salt and pepper to taste; remove from the heat and cover to keep warm. Slice the pork into ½-inch-thick slices, adding any accumulated juices to the sauce. Serve the pork, passing the sauce separately.

NOTES FROM THE TEST KITCHEN

DOUBLE-BUTTERFLYING A ROAST

1. Holding a chef's knife parallel to the cutting board, insert the knife one-third of the way up from the bottom of the roast and cut horizontally, stopping ½ inch before the edge. Open up the flap.

2. Make another horizontal cut into the thicker portion of the roast. Open up this flap, smoothing out the butterflied rectangle of meat.

MAPLE-GLAZED PORK ROAST

WHY THIS RECIPE WORKS: Maple-glazed pork roast often falls short of its savory-sweet promise. Many roasts turn out dry (a constant concern when cooking today's lean pork), but the glazes often present even bigger problems. Most are too thin to coat the pork properly, some are so sweet that they require a hotline to the dentist's office, and few have a pronounced maple flavor. We wanted a glistening roast, which, when sliced, would combine the juices from tender, well-seasoned pork with a rich maple glaze to create complex flavor in every bite.

For this dish we chose a blade-end loin roast, which has a deposit of fat that helps keep the meat moist. We tied it at intervals to make a neat bundle. Searing the roast first on the stovetop was a must for a brown, flavorful exterior. We then removed the pork so that we could use the browned bits in the skillet to build the glaze. Maple syrup, with complementary spices and a touch of cayenne pepper for heat, made a thick, clingy glaze. Instead of brushing the glaze onto the pork, however, we decided to keep things simple: Rather than hauling out our roasting pan, we returned the pork to the skillet, rolled it in the glaze to coat it, and put the whole thing into the oven. The smaller area of the skillet kept the glaze from spreading out and burning, and the glaze reduced nicely while the roast cooked. Rolling the roast in the glaze periodically ensured even coverage and resulted in a tender, juicy roast packed with maple flavor.

Maple-Glazed Pork Roast

SERVES 4 TO 6

We prefer natural to enhanced pork (pork that has been injected with a salt solution to increase moisture and flavor) for this recipe. We prefer a nonstick oven-safe skillet because it is much easier to clean than a traditional one. Whichever you use, remember that the handle will be blistering hot when you take it out of the oven, so be sure to use a potholder or oven mitt. Note that you should not trim the pork of its thin layer of fat. This dish is unapologetically sweet, so we recommend side dishes that take well to the sweetness. Garlicky sautéed greens, braised cabbage, and soft polenta are good choices.

⅓ cup maple syrup, preferably grade B
⅛ teaspoon ground cinnamon
  Pinch ground cloves
  Pinch cayenne pepper
1 (2½-pound) boneless blade-end pork loin roast, tied at 1½-inch intervals (see note)
¾ teaspoon table salt
½ teaspoon ground black pepper
2 teaspoons vegetable oil

1. Adjust an oven rack to the middle position and heat the oven to 325 degrees. Stir the maple syrup, cinnamon, cloves, and cayenne together in a measuring cup or small bowl and set aside. Pat the roast dry with paper towels, then sprinkle evenly with the salt and pepper.

2. Heat the oil in a heavy-bottomed ovensafe 10-inch nonstick skillet over medium-high heat until just beginning to smoke, about 3 minutes. Place the roast, fat side down, in the skillet and cook until well browned, about 3 minutes. Using tongs, rotate the roast a quarter-turn and cook until well browned, about 2½ minutes; repeat until the roast is well browned on all sides. Transfer the roast to a large plate. Reduce the heat to medium and pour off the fat from the skillet; add the maple syrup mixture and cook until fragrant, about 30 seconds (the syrup will bubble immediately). Turn off the heat and return the roast to the skillet; using tongs, roll the roast to coat with the glaze on all sides.

3. Place the skillet in the oven and roast until the center of the pork registers 140 to 145 degrees on an instant-read thermometer, 35 to 45 minutes, using tongs to roll and spin the roast to coat with the glaze twice during the roasting time.

Transfer the roast to a carving board; set the skillet aside to cool slightly to thicken the glaze, about 5 minutes. Pour the glaze over the roast and let rest for 15 minutes longer (the center of the loin should register 150 degrees on an instant-read thermometer). Remove the twine, cut the meat into ¼-inch slices, and serve immediately.

Maple-Glazed Pork Roast with Rosemary

Follow the recipe for Maple-Glazed Pork Roast, substituting 2 teaspoons minced fresh rosemary for the cinnamon, cloves, and cayenne.

Maple-Glazed Pork Roast with Orange Essence

Follow the recipe for Maple-Glazed Pork Roast, adding 1 tablespoon fresh grated orange zest to the maple syrup along with the spices.

Maple-Glazed Pork Roast with Star Anise

Follow the recipe for Maple-Glazed Pork Roast, adding 4 star anise pods to the maple syrup along with the spices.

Maple-Glazed Pork Roast with Smoked Paprika

Follow the recipe for Maple-Glazed Pork Roast, adding 2 teaspoons smoked hot paprika to the maple syrup along with the spices.

GARLIC-STUDDED ROAST PORK LOIN

WHY THIS RECIPE WORKS: Although it has a little more fat than pork tenderloin, a center loin pork roast is still quite lean and requires special handling to roast without drying out. We sought the best way to roast this cut so that the juices would remain inside the meat, not wind up on the carving board.

It turns out that a two-step roasting process is the key to juicy pork loin. After poking slivers of garlic into the meat and rubbing the surface with a mixture of thyme, cloves, salt, and pepper for extra flavor, we refrigerated the roast overnight. The next day we cranked up the oven to 475 degrees and added the pork directly from the fridge, leaving it for just half an hour before removing it. After we rested the roast, we returned it to the oven, this time at a lower temperature, to finish cooking. The texture of the meat was remarkably tender, and it had lost very little juice.

It turns out the reason this method works is that during the rest, the middle of the roast heats by conduction from the heat absorbed by the outside of the roast. When the meat goes back into the oven, the center cooks through but the outside doesn't overcook. A mustard-shallot sauce provides additional moisture and flavor, although the roast is so juicy and flavorful on its own, the sauce can be omitted.

Garlic-Studded Roast Pork Loin

SERVES 4 TO 6

We prefer natural to enhanced pork (pork that has been injected with a salt solution to increase moisture and flavor) for this recipe. For extra flavor and moisture, serve the sliced roast with the mustard-shallot sauce.

- 2 teaspoons dried thyme
- 2 teaspoons table salt
- 1 teaspoon ground black pepper
- ¼ teaspoon ground cloves or allspice
- 2 large garlic cloves, peeled and cut into slivers
- 1 (2¼-pound) boneless center loin pork roast, fat trimmed to about ⅛ inch thick and roast tied at 1½-inch intervals (see note)
- 1 recipe Mustard–Shallot Sauce with Thyme (optional; recipe follows)

1. Mix together the thyme, salt, pepper, and cloves. Coat the garlic slivers in the spice mixture. Poke slits in the roast with the point of a paring knife; insert the garlic slivers. Rub the remaining spice mixture onto the meat. Tie the roast with kitchen twine into a tight cylinder. Wrap the roast in plastic wrap and refrigerate for at least 2 hours or up to 24 hours.

2. Adjust an oven rack to the middle position and heat the oven to 475 degrees. Take the meat directly from the refrigerator, remove the plastic wrap, and place it on a wire rack set in a shallow roasting pan. Roast for exactly 30 minutes.

3. Remove the meat from the oven; immediately reduce the oven temperature to 325 degrees. Insert an instant-read thermometer at one end of the roast, going into the thickest part at the center (the temperature will range from 80 to 110 degrees); let the roast rest at room temperature, uncovered, for exactly 30 minutes. (At this point the roast's internal temperature will range from 115 to 140 degrees.) After this 30-minute rest, remove the thermometer, return the meat to the oven, and roast until the thickest part of the roast reaches an internal temperature of 140 to 145 degrees, 15 to 30 minutes longer, depending on the roast's internal temperature at the end of the resting period. Since the roast may cook unevenly, take temperature readings from a couple of locations, each time plunging the thermometer into the center of the meat and waiting 15 seconds.

4. Let the roast stand at room temperature, uncovered, for 15 to 20 minutes to finish cooking. (The temperature should register 150 degrees.) Remove the twine, slice the meat thin, and serve with the sauce (if using).

Mustard–Shallot Sauce with Thyme

MAKES ABOUT 1 CUP

Start making the sauce as soon as the roast comes out of the oven for the second time. Use a grainy, or country-style, mustard in this recipe. For extra body and richness, swirl another tablespoon or two of softened butter into the finished sauce.

- 2 **tablespoons unsalted butter (see note)**
- 4 **medium shallots, minced (about ¾ cup)**
- ¾ **cup dry white wine or dry vermouth**
- 1 **cup low-sodium chicken broth**
- ¾ **teaspoon minced fresh thyme leaves or ¼ teaspoon dried thyme, crumbled**
- ¼ **cup whole grain mustard (see note)**

Melt the butter in a medium skillet over medium-high heat. Add the shallots and sauté until softened, 3 to 4 minutes. Add the wine and boil until nearly evaporated, 8 to 10 minutes. Add the broth and thyme; boil until reduced by one third, about 5 minutes. Remove the pan from the heat and stir in the mustard. Serve immediately.

SLOW-COOKER PORK LOIN

WHY THIS RECIPE WORKS: Cooking a lean roast like a pork loin in a slow cooker is tricky because it can quickly turn overcooked and dry. The key to this recipe was to monitor the temperature of the roast after a few hours and take it out of the slow cooker as soon as it reached 145 degrees. Whether you're cooking a pork loin in the oven or the slow cooker, pairing the lean meat with a sauce gives it a lot more appeal. We paired our loin with both dried cranberries and whole canned cranberries. Cinnamon, orange juice, and orange zest livened up our easy-to-make sauce, which goes directly into the slow cooker. After cooking the loin, we reduced the braising liquid until it became a sweet sauce that paired perfectly with our juicy pork loin.

Slow-Cooker Pork Loin with Cranberries and Orange

SERVES 6

When choosing a pork loin, we prefer the blade-end—be sure to choose a fatter, shorter loin over the longer, skinnier ones. Use a vegetable peeler to remove wide strips of zest from the orange. Make sure to trim any white pith from the zest, as it can impart a bitter flavor.

- 1 **(4½ to 5-pound) boneless pork loin roast, trimmed and tied at 1-inch intervals**
   Table salt and ground black pepper
- 1 **tablespoon vegetable oil**
- 1 **(14-ounce) can whole berry cranberry sauce**
- ½ **cup dried cranberries**
- ½ **cup juice and 3 (3-inch-long) strips zest from 1 orange**
- ⅛ **teaspoon ground cinnamon**

1. Dry the pork with paper towels and season with salt and pepper. Heat the oil in a 12-inch skillet over medium-high heat until just smoking. Brown the pork well on all sides, 7 to 10 minutes.

2. Stir the cranberry sauce, cranberries, orange juice, orange zest, and cinnamon into the slow cooker. Nestle the browned pork into the slow cooker. Cover and cook until the pork is tender and registers 140 to 145 degrees on an instant-read thermometer, about 4 hours on low.

3. Transfer the pork to a cutting board, tent loosely with aluminum foil, and let rest for 10 minutes. Let the braising liquid settle for 5 minutes, then remove the fat from the surface using a large spoon. Discard the orange zest. Transfer the braising liquid to a saucepan and simmer until reduced to 2 cups, about 12 minutes. Season with salt and pepper to taste.

4. Remove the twine from the pork, slice into ½-inch-thick slices, and arrange on a serving platter. Spoon 1 cup sauce over the meat and serve with the remaining sauce.

SLOW-ROASTED PORK SHOULDER

WHY THIS RECIPE WORKS: To most modern-day cooks, "roast pork" equals the lean (and often bland) loin, which is typically gussied up with a glaze or chutney to compensate for its lack of fat (and flavor). We wanted to celebrate the glories of rich old-fashioned pork with the shoulder roast (also called Boston butt or pork butt). This tough cut is loaded with intramuscular fat that builds flavor and bastes the meat during roasting; outside, its thick fat cap renders to a bronze, bacon-like crust. Plus, at around $2 per pound, the shoulder offers value.

First, we salted the meat overnight—a technique we frequently use with large, tough roasts for improved texture and flavor. This helped, but to improve the roast's flavor even more, we turned to an idea taken from Chinese barbecue pork, where the meat is rubbed with a salt and sugar rub (we preferred brown sugar over white for its subtle molasses flavor and hints of caramel). As we hoped,

the sugar caramelized and helped crisp the fat cap, giving it a bronze hue. For an accompanying sauce, peaches, white wine, sugar, vinegar, and a couple of sprigs of fresh thyme added to the drippings and then reduced delivered on all fronts. To round out the sweetness, we finished it with a spoonful of whole grain mustard.

Slow-Roasted Pork Shoulder with Peach Sauce
SERVES 8 TO 12

We prefer natural pork to enhanced pork (pork that has been injected with a salt solution to increase moistness and flavor), though both will work in this recipe. Add more water to the roasting pan as necessary during the last hours of cooking to prevent the fond from burning.

PORK ROAST
- 1 **(6 to 8-pound) bone-in pork butt (see note)**
- ⅓ **cup kosher salt**
- ⅓ **cup packed light brown sugar**
- **Ground black pepper**

PEACH SAUCE
- 10 **ounces frozen peaches, cut into 1-inch chunks (about 2 cups) or 2 fresh peaches cut into ½-inch wedges**
- 2 **cups dry white wine**
- ½ **cup granulated sugar**
- ¼ **cup plus 1 tablespoon unseasoned rice vinegar**
- 2 **sprigs fresh thyme**
- 1 **tablespoon whole grain mustard**

1. FOR THE ROAST: Using a sharp knife, cut slits 1 inch apart in the fat cap of the roast in a crosshatch pattern, being careful not to cut into the meat. Combine the salt and brown sugar in a medium bowl. Rub the salt mixture over the entire pork shoulder and into the slits. Wrap the roast tightly in a double layer of plastic wrap, place on a rimmed baking sheet, and refrigerate for at least 12 hours or up to 24 hours.

2. Adjust an oven rack to the lowest position and heat the oven to 325 degrees. Unwrap the roast and brush off any excess salt mixture from the surface. Season the roast with pepper. Transfer the roast to a V-rack coated with vegetable oil spray set in a large roasting pan. Add 1 quart water to the roasting pan.

3. Cook the roast, basting twice during cooking, until the meat is extremely tender and an instant-read thermometer inserted into the roast near, but not touching, the bone registers 190 degrees, 5 to 6 hours. Transfer the roast to a carving board and let rest, loosely tented with foil, for 1 hour. Transfer the liquid in the roasting pan to a fat separator and let stand for 5 minutes. Pour off ¼ cup jus and reserve, then discard any remaining jus and fat.

4. FOR THE SAUCE: Bring the peaches, wine, granulated sugar, ¼ cup of the vinegar, the reserved defatted jus, and the thyme to a simmer in a small saucepan; cook, stirring occasionally, until reduced to 2 cups, about 30 minutes. Stir in the remaining 1 tablespoon vinegar and the mustard. Remove the thyme sprigs, cover the pan, and keep warm.

5. Using a sharp paring knife, cut around the inverted T-shaped bone, until it can be pulled free from the roast (use a clean kitchen towel to grasp the bone). Using a serrated knife, slice the roast. Serve, passing the sauce separately.

INDOOR PULLED PORK

WHY THIS RECIPE WORKS: In recipes, the phrase "indoor barbecue" is usually code for "braised in a Dutch oven with bottled barbecue sauce." Unfortunately, this results in mushy, waterlogged meat and candy-sweet sauce. We wanted moist, tender, shreddable meat with deep smoke flavor all the way through, plus a dark, richly seasoned crust, often referred to as bark.

Be it indoor or outdoor, with barbecue a good amount of fat is necessary for moisture and flavor, so we chose to use boneless Boston butt because of its high level of marbling. To mimic the moist heat of a covered grill, we came up with a dual cooking method: covering the pork for part of the oven time to speed up cooking and keep it moist, then uncovering it for the remainder of the time to help the meat develop a crust.

To achieve smoky flavor without an actual barbecue pit, we turned to liquid smoke, a natural product derived from condensing the moist smoke of smoldering wood chips. We found that adding it to our brine infused it with smoky flavor without tasting unnatural. For even more smokiness, we employed a dry rub and a wet rub, which we also fortified with smoky flavorings. To serve alongside our pork, we developed three sauces inspired by the variety of barbecue regions and styles: a classic sweet and tangy sauce, a vinegar sauce, and a mustard sauce, all of which we flavored with some of the pork's defatted cooking liquid.

Indoor Pulled Pork with Sweet and Tangy Barbecue Sauce

SERVES 6 TO 8

Sweet paprika may be substituted for smoked paprika. Covering the pork with parchment and then foil prevents the acidic mustard from eating holes in the foil. Serve the pork on hamburger rolls with pickle chips and thinly sliced onion. In place of the Sweet and Tangy Barbecue Sauce or the variations that follow, you can use 2 cups of your favorite barbecue sauce thinned with ½ cup of the defatted pork cooking liquid in step 5. The shredded and sauced pork can be cooled, tightly covered, and refrigerated for up to 2 days. Reheat it gently before serving.

PORK

- 1 cup plus 2 teaspoons table salt
- ½ cup plus 2 tablespoons sugar
- 3 tablespoons plus 2 teaspoons liquid smoke
- 1 5-pound boneless pork butt roast, cut in half horizontally (see page 184)
- ¼ cup yellow mustard
- 2 tablespoons ground black pepper
- 2 tablespoons smoked paprika (see note)
- 1 teaspoon cayenne pepper

SWEET AND TANGY BARBECUE SAUCE

- 1½ cups ketchup
- ¼ cup light or mild molasses
- 2 tablespoons Worcestershire sauce
- 1 tablespoon hot sauce
- ½ teaspoon table salt
- ½ teaspoon ground black pepper

1. FOR THE PORK: Dissolve 1 cup of the salt, ½ cup of the sugar, and 3 tablespoons of the liquid smoke in 1 gallon cold water in a large container. Submerge the pork in the brine, cover with plastic wrap, and refrigerate for 2 hours.

2. While the pork brines, combine the mustard and remaining 2 teaspoons liquid smoke in a small bowl; set aside. Combine the black pepper, paprika, remaining 2 tablespoons sugar, remaining 2 teaspoons salt, and cayenne in a second small bowl; set aside. Adjust an oven rack to the lower-middle position and heat the oven to 325 degrees.

3. Remove the pork from the brine and dry thoroughly with paper towels. Rub the mustard mixture over the entire surface of each piece of pork. Sprinkle the entire surface of each piece with the spice mixture. Place the pork on a wire rack set over a foil-lined rimmed baking sheet. Place a piece of parchment paper over the pork, then cover with a sheet of aluminum foil, sealing the edges to prevent moisture from escaping. Roast the pork for 3 hours.

4. Remove the pork from the oven; remove and discard the foil and parchment. Carefully pour off the liquid in the bottom of the baking sheet into a fat separator and reserve for the sauce. Return the pork to the oven and cook, uncovered, until well browned, tender, and the center of the roast registers 200 degrees on an instant-read thermometer, about 1½ hours. Transfer the pork to a serving dish, tent loosely with foil, and let rest for 20 minutes.

5. FOR THE SAUCE: While the pork rests, pour ½ cup of the defatted cooking liquid from the fat separator into a medium bowl; whisk in the sauce ingredients.

6. TO SERVE: Using two forks, shred the pork into bite-size pieces. Toss with 1 cup sauce and season with salt and pepper to taste. Serve, passing the remaining sauce separately.

NOTES FROM THE TEST KITCHEN

CUTTING A PORK BUTT IN HALF

Halving the pork increases its surface area, which creates more flavorful bark. Holding your knife parallel to the cutting board, press one hand flat against the top of the pork while cutting horizontally.

Lexington Vinegar Barbecue Sauce
MAKES ABOUT 2½ CUPS

- 1 **cup cider vinegar**
- ½ **cup ketchup**
- ½ **cup water**
- 1 **tablespoon sugar**
- ¾ **teaspoon table salt**
- ¾ **teaspoon red pepper flakes**
- ½ **teaspoon ground black pepper**

Combine all the ingredients in a medium bowl with ½ cup of the defatted cooking liquid in step 5 and whisk to combine.

South Carolina Mustard Barbecue Sauce
MAKES ABOUT 2½ CUPS

- 1 **cup yellow mustard**
- ½ **cup white vinegar**
- ¼ **cup packed light brown sugar**
- ¼ **cup Worcestershire sauce**
- 2 **tablespoons hot sauce**
- 1 **teaspoon table salt**
- 1 **teaspoon ground black pepper**

Combine all the ingredients in a medium bowl with ½ cup of the defatted cooking liquid in step 5 and whisk to combine.

ROAST HAM

WHY THIS RECIPE WORKS: Fresh ham is not cured like a Smithfield ham or salted and air-dried like prosciutto. It's not pressed or molded like a canned ham, and it's not smoked like a country ham. In fact, some people think there's no such thing as "fresh" ham. There is—and we wanted to find the best way to cook it for a roasted ham that boasted rich, moist meat and crackling crisp skin.

Fresh hams are large, so they're usually cut in half and sold as either the sirloin or the shank end; we chose the latter for its ease of carving. But even cut into these smaller roasts, fresh ham needs a long time in the oven, so the danger is drying out the meat. To prevent this, we brined our ham overnight. A garlic and herb rub added further flavor. We positioned the ham face down on a rack

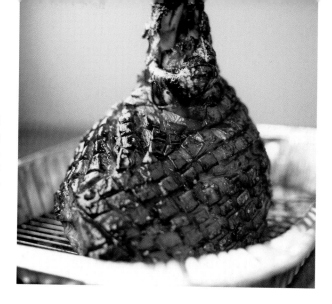

in a roasting pan; the rack allowed the heat to circulate all around the ham for more even cooking. A brief roasting at a high temperature followed by longer cooking at a lower temperature produced crunchy skin and succulent meat. The crowning touch was a sweet glaze, which we brushed on periodically while the meat roasted.

Roast Fresh Ham

SERVES 8 TO 10

Fresh ham comes from the pig's hind leg. Because a whole leg is quite large, it is usually cut into two sections. The sirloin, or butt, end is harder to carve than our favorite, the shank end. If you don't have room in your refrigerator, brine the ham in an insulated cooler or a small plastic garbage can; add five or six freezer packs to the brine to keep it well cooled.

ROAST

1 (6 to 8-pound) bone-in fresh half ham with skin, preferably shank end, rinsed (see note)

BRINE

3 cups packed brown sugar

2 cups table salt

2 heads garlic, cloves separated, lightly crushed and peeled

10 bay leaves

½ cup black peppercorns, crushed

GARLIC AND HERB RUB

1 cup lightly packed fresh sage leaves

½ cup parsley leaves

¼ cup olive oil

8 medium garlic cloves, peeled

½ tablespoon ground black pepper

1½ teaspoons table salt

GLAZE

1 recipe glaze (recipes follow)

1. FOR THE ROAST: Carefully slice through the skin and fat with a serrated knife, making a 1-inch diamond pattern. Be careful not to cut into the meat.

2. FOR THE BRINE: In a large container, dissolve the brown sugar and salt in 2 gallons cold water. Add the garlic, bay leaves, and crushed peppercorns. Submerge the ham in the brine and refrigerate for 8 to 24 hours.

3. Set a large disposable aluminum roasting pan on a baking sheet for extra support; place a flat wire rack in the roasting pan. Remove the ham from the brine; rinse under cold water and dry thoroughly with paper towels. Place the ham, wide cut side down, on the rack. (If using the sirloin end, place the ham skin side up.) Let the ham stand, uncovered, at room temperature for 1 hour.

4. FOR THE RUB: Meanwhile, adjust an oven rack to the lowest position and heat the oven to 500 degrees. Process the sage, parsley, oil, garlic, pepper, and salt in a food processor until the mixture forms a smooth paste, about 30 seconds. Rub all sides of the ham with the paste.

5. Roast the ham at 500 degrees for 20 minutes. Reduce the oven temperature to 350 degrees and continue to roast, brushing the ham with the glaze every 45 minutes, until the center of the ham registers 145 to 150 degrees on an instant-read thermometer, about 2½ hours longer. Remove from the oven and tent the ham loosely with foil and let stand until the center of the ham registers 155 to 160 degrees, 30 to 40 minutes. Carve and serve.

Cider and Brown Sugar Glaze

MAKES ABOUT 1⅓ CUPS

1 cup apple cider

2 cups packed brown sugar

5 whole cloves

Bring the cider, brown sugar, and cloves to a boil in a small saucepan over high heat; reduce the heat to medium-low and simmer until syrupy and reduced to about 1⅓ cups, 5 to 7 minutes. (The glaze will thicken as it cools between bastings; cook over medium heat for about 1 minute, stirring once or twice, before using.)

Spicy Pineapple-Ginger Glaze

MAKES ABOUT 1⅓ CUPS

- 1 cup pineapple juice
- 2 cups packed brown sugar
- 1 (1-inch) piece fresh ginger, grated (about 1 tablespoon)
- 1 tablespoon red pepper flakes

Bring the pineapple juice, brown sugar, ginger, and red pepper flakes to a boil in a small saucepan over high heat; reduce the heat to medium-low and simmer until syrupy and reduced to about 1⅓ cups, 5 to 7 minutes. (The glaze will thicken as it cools between bastings; cook over medium heat about for 1 minute, stirring once or twice, before using.)

Coca-Cola Glaze with Lime and Jalapeño

MAKES ABOUT 1⅓ CUPS

- 1 cup Coca-Cola
- ¼ cup juice from 2 limes
- 2 cups packed brown sugar
- 2 medium jalapeño chiles, cut crosswise into ¼-inch-thick slices

Bring the Coca-Cola, lime juice, brown sugar, and jalapeños to a boil in a small nonreactive saucepan over high heat; reduce the heat to medium-low and simmer until syrupy and reduced to about 1⅓ cups, 5 to 7 minutes. (The glaze will thicken as it cools between bastings; heat over medium heat for about 1 minute, stirring once or twice, before using.)

Orange, Cinnamon, and Star Anise Glaze

MAKES ABOUT 1⅓ CUPS

- 1 cup juice plus 1 tablespoon grated zest from 2 large oranges
- 2 cups packed brown sugar
- 4 pods star anise
- 1 (3-inch) cinnamon stick

Bring the orange juice, zest, brown sugar, star anise, and cinnamon stick to a boil in a small nonreactive saucepan over high heat; reduce the heat to medium-low and simmer until syrupy and reduced to about 1⅓ cups, 5 to 7 minutes. (The glaze will thicken as it cools between bastings; cook over medium heat for about 1 minute, stirring once or twice, before using.)

GLAZED HOLIDAY HAM

WHY THIS RECIPE WORKS: Nothing could be easier than heating up a cured ham, right? Well, we've made enough of them to know that as easy as it may be, the results are often leathery meat with an overly sweet glaze. We wanted to revisit the way to cook this roast to get moist meat accompanied by a glaze that didn't overwhelm it.

We have found that bone-in hams, labeled "with natural juices," have the best flavor, and spiral-sliced ones make carving a cinch. We knew that the longer the ham spent in the oven, the greater the chances we'd end up with dried-out meat, so we focused on reducing the cooking time. First we soaked the ham in hot water so that it wouldn't be ice-cold when it went into the oven; this step saved a full hour. Roasting the ham in an oven bag further reduced the cooking time, and using the bag had the added advantage of holding in moisture. For the glaze, we threw out the packet that came with our ham and made a fruit-based glaze with just a touch of sweetness to complement the moist, tender meat. This foolproof method will make the perfect holiday ham every time.

Glazed Spiral-Sliced Ham

SERVES 12 TO 14

You can bypass the 90-minute soaking time, but the heating time will increase to 18 to 20 minutes per pound for a cold ham. If there is a tear or hole in the ham's inner covering, wrap the ham in several layers of plastic wrap before soaking it in hot water. Instead of using the plastic oven bag, the ham may be placed cut side down in the roasting pan and covered tightly with foil, but you will need to add 3 to 4 minutes per pound to the heating time. If using an oven bag, be sure to cut slits in the bag so it does not burst.

1 **(7 to 10-pound) spiral-sliced bone-in half ham**
1 **large plastic oven bag (see note)**
1 **recipe glaze (recipes follow)**

1. Leaving the ham's inner plastic or foil covering intact, place the ham in a large container and cover with hot tap water; set aside for 45 minutes. Drain and cover again with hot tap water; set aside for another 45 minutes.

2. Adjust an oven rack to the lowest position and heat the oven to 250 degrees. Unwrap the ham; remove and discard the plastic disk covering the bone. Place the ham in the oven bag. Gather the top of the bag tightly so the bag fits snugly around the ham, tie the bag, and trim the excess plastic. Set the ham, cut side down, in a large roasting pan and cut four slits in the top of the bag with a paring knife.

3. Bake the ham until the center registers 100 degrees on an instant-read thermometer, 1 to 1½ hours (about 10 minutes per pound).

4. Remove the ham from the oven and increase the oven temperature to 350 degrees. Cut open the oven bag and roll back the sides to expose the ham. Brush the ham with one-third of the glaze and return to the oven until the glaze becomes sticky, about 10 minutes (if the glaze is too thick to brush, return it to the heat to loosen).

5. Remove the ham from the oven, transfer it to a carving board, and brush the entire ham with another third of the glaze. Let the ham rest, loosely tented with foil, for 15 minutes. While the ham rests, heat the remaining third of the glaze with 4 to 6 tablespoons of the ham juices until it forms a thick but fluid sauce. Carve and serve the ham, passing the sauce at the table.

Maple-Orange Glaze

MAKES 1 CUP

¾ **cup maple syrup**
½ **cup orange marmalade**
2 **tablespoons unsalted butter**
1 **tablespoon Dijon mustard**
1 **teaspoon ground black pepper**
¼ **teaspoon ground cinnamon**

Combine all the ingredients in a small saucepan. Cook over medium heat, stirring occasionally, until the mixture is thick, syrupy, and reduced to 1 cup, 5 to 10 minutes; set aside.

Cherry-Port Glaze

MAKES 1 CUP

½ **cup ruby port**
½ **cup cherry preserves**
1 **cup packed dark brown sugar**
1 **teaspoon ground black pepper**

Simmer the port in a small saucepan over medium heat until reduced to 2 tablespoons, about 5 minutes. Add the remaining ingredients and cook, stirring occasionally, until the sugar dissolves and the mixture is thick, syrupy, and reduced to 1 cup, 5 to 10 minutes; set aside.

CHAPTER 10

FAVORITE WAYS WITH FISH

Crunchy Oven-Fried
Fish   190

   Sweet and Tangy
   Tartar Sauce

Fish and Chips   191

Pan-Seared Salmon   192

   Sweet-and-Sour Chutney

Broiled Salmon with
Mustard and Crisp
Dilled Crust   193

Poached Salmon with Herb
and Caper Vinaigrette   194

Glazed Salmon   195

   Pomegranate-Balsamic
   Glaze

   Asian Barbecue Glaze

   Orange-Miso Glaze

   Soy-Mustard Glaze

Oven-Roasted
Salmon   197

   Tangerine and
   Ginger Relish

   Fresh Tomato Relish

   Spicy Cucumber Relish

Pan-Seared Sesame-Crusted
Tuna Steaks   198

   Ginger-Soy Sauce
   with Scallions

   Avocado-Orange Salsa

Pan-Roasted Halibut
Steaks   200

   Chipotle-Garlic Butter
   with Lime and Cilantro

   Chunky Cherry Tomato–
   Basil Vinaigrette

Pan-Roasted Thick-Cut
Fish Fillets   201

Baked Sole Fillets
with Herbs and
Bread Crumbs   202

Pan-Seared Scallops   203

   Lemon Brown
   Butter Sauce

Pan-Seared Shrimp   204

Pan-Seared Shrimp with
Garlic-Lemon Butter   205

Pan-Seared Shrimp with
Ginger-Hoisin Glaze   205

Pan-Seared Shrimp with
Chipotle-Lime Glaze   205

Garlicky Shrimp with
Buttered Bread
Crumbs   205

Spanish-Style Garlic
Shrimp   206

Greek-Style Shrimp with
Tomatoes and Feta   208

Shrimp Cocktail   209

Shrimp Salad   209

Shrimp Salad with Roasted
Red Pepper and Basil   210

Shrimp Salad with Avocado
and Orange   210

Flambéed Pan-Roasted
Lobster   210

Maryland Crab Cakes   212

   Creamy Chipotle
   Chile Sauce

Crab Towers with Avocado
and Gazpacho Salsas   213

Indoor Clambake   215

SUPER-CRISPY OVEN-FRIED FISH

WHY THIS RECIPE WORKS: The golden brown coating and moist, flaky flesh of batter-fried fish come at a price: the oil. Cooks have turned to the oven to avoid the bother of deep-fat frying, but oven-frying often falls short. The coating never gets very crisp and the fish usually ends up overcooked. We aimed to put the crunch back into oven-frying.

We used thick fillets so that the fish and coating would finish cooking at the same time. Flaky cod and haddock provided the best contrast to the crunchy exterior we envisioned. A conventional bound breading—flour, egg, and fresh bread crumbs—wasn't as crisp as we wanted, so we toasted the bread crumbs with a little butter. (Precooking the crumbs also ensured we wouldn't have to overcook the fish to get really crunchy crumbs.) Placing the coated fish on a wire rack while baking allowed air to circulate all around the fish, crisping all sides. We boosted flavor in two ways, adding shallots and parsley to the breading and horseradish, cayenne, and paprika to the egg wash. As a final touch, we whipped up a creamy tartar sauce with mayonnaise, capers, and sweet relish.

Crunchy Oven-Fried Fish

SERVES 4

To prevent overcooking, buy fish fillets that are at least 1 inch thick. The bread crumbs can be made up to 3 days in advance and stored at room temperature in a tightly sealed container (allow to cool fully before storing). Serve the dish with Sweet and Tangy Tartar Sauce (recipe follows).

- 4 slices high-quality white sandwich bread, torn into quarters
- 2 tablespoons unsalted butter, melted
  Table salt and ground black pepper
- 2 tablespoons minced fresh parsley leaves
- 1 small shallot, minced (about 1 tablespoon)
- ¼ cup plus 5 tablespoons unbleached all-purpose flour
- 2 large eggs
- 3 tablespoons mayonnaise
- 2 teaspoons prepared horseradish (optional)
- ½ teaspoon paprika
- ¼ teaspoon cayenne pepper (optional)
- 1¼ pounds cod, haddock, or other thick whitefish fillets (1 to 1½ inches thick), cut into 4 pieces (see note)
  Lemon wedges, for serving

1. Adjust an oven rack to the middle position and heat the oven to 350 degrees. Pulse the bread, butter, ¼ teaspoon salt, and ¼ teaspoon black pepper in a food processor until the bread is coarsely ground, about 8 pulses. Transfer to a rimmed baking sheet and bake until deep golden brown and dry, about 15 minutes, stirring twice during the baking time. Cool the crumbs to room temperature, about 10 minutes. Transfer the crumbs to a pie plate and toss with the parsley and shallot. Increase the oven temperature to 425 degrees.

2. Place ¼ cup of the flour in a second pie plate. In a third pie plate, whisk together the eggs, mayonnaise, horseradish (if using), paprika, cayenne (if using), and ¼ teaspoon black pepper until combined; whisk in the remaining 5 tablespoons flour until smooth.

3. Spray a wire rack with vegetable oil spray and place over a rimmed baking sheet. Dry the fish thoroughly with paper towels and season with salt and black pepper. Dredge 1 fillet in the flour; shake off the excess. Using tongs, coat the fillet with the egg mixture. Coat all sides of the fillet with the bread-crumb mixture, pressing gently so that a thick layer of crumbs adheres to the fish. Transfer the breaded fish to the wire rack. Repeat with the remaining 3 fillets.

4. Bake the fish until the center of the fillets registers 140 degrees on an instant-read thermometer, 18 to 25 minutes. Using a thin spatula, transfer the fillets to individual plates and serve immediately with the lemon wedges.

Sweet and Tangy Tartar Sauce

MAKES ABOUT 1 CUP

This sauce can be refrigerated, tightly covered, for up to 1 week.

- ¾ cup mayonnaise
- 2 tablespoons drained capers, minced
- 2 tablespoons sweet pickle relish
- 1 small shallot, minced (about 1 tablespoon)
- 1½ teaspoons distilled white vinegar
- ½ teaspoon Worcestershire sauce
- ½ teaspoon ground black pepper

Mix all the ingredients together in a small bowl. Cover the bowl with plastic wrap and let sit until the flavors meld, about 15 minutes. Stir again before serving.

FISH AND CHIPS

WHY THIS RECIPE WORKS: The fish and chips served at most American pubs are mediocre at best. But the alternative—deep-frying fish at home—can be a hassle and a mess. Plus, by the time the fries finish frying, the fish is cold. We wanted fish with a light, crisp crust and moist interior, and we wanted to serve both the fish and the fries at their prime.

Our first challenge was to come up with a batter that not only would protect the fish as it cooked (allowing it to steam gently) but would also provide the fish with a nicely crisp contrast. We discovered that a wet batter was the most effective way to coat and protect the fish. We liked beer—the traditional choice—as the liquid component. What was the best way to keep the coating crisp? The answer was a 3-1 ratio of flour to cornstarch, along with a teaspoon of baking powder. Still, the coating was so tender it puffed away from the fish as it cooked. A final coating of flour on top of the battered fish solved the problem.

To solve the second challenge—delivering the fish and fries while both are still hot—we cooked them alternately. First, we precooked the fries in the microwave, which not only lessened cooking time but removed excess moisture that could dilute the oil and diminish crisping. Then we gave the fries their first, quick fry in hot oil. While the potatoes were draining, we battered and fried the fish. Then, as the fish drained, we gave the fries a quick final fry.

Fish and Chips

SERVES 4

For safety, use a Dutch oven with at least a 7-quart capacity. Serve with traditional malt vinegar or with Sweet and Tangy Tartar Sauce (at left).

- 3 pounds russet potatoes (about 4 large potatoes), peeled, ends and sides squared off, and cut lengthwise into ½-inch by ½-inch fries (see page 340)
- 3 quarts plus ¼ cup peanut oil or canola oil
- 1½ cups unbleached all-purpose flour
- ½ cup cornstarch
- ½ teaspoon cayenne pepper
- ½ teaspoon paprika
- ⅛ teaspoon ground black pepper
  Table salt
- 1 teaspoon baking powder
- 1½ pounds cod or other thick whitefish fillets, such as hake or haddock, cut into eight 3-ounce pieces about 1 inch thick
- 1½ cups (12 ounces) cold beer

1. Place the cut fries in a large microwave-safe bowl, toss with ¼ cup of the oil, and cover with plastic wrap. Microwave on high power until the potatoes are partially translucent and pliable but still offer some resistance when pierced with the tip of a paring knife, 6 to 8 minutes, tossing them with a rubber spatula halfway through the cooking time. Carefully pull back the plastic wrap from the side farthest from you and drain the potatoes into a large mesh strainer set over a sink. Rinse well under cold running water. Spread the potatoes on a few clean kitchen towels and pat dry. Let rest until the fries have reached room temperature, at least 10 minutes or up to 1 hour.

2. While the fries cool, whisk the flour, cornstarch, cayenne, paprika, black pepper, and 2 teaspoons salt in a large mixing bowl; transfer ¾ cup of the mixture to a rimmed baking sheet. Add the baking powder to the bowl and whisk to combine.

3. In a large Dutch oven fitted with a clip-on candy thermometer, heat 2 quarts more oil over medium heat to 350 degrees. Add the fries to the hot oil and increase the heat to high. Fry, stirring with a mesh spider or slotted metal spoon, until the potatoes turn light golden and just begin to brown at the corners, 6 to 8 minutes. Transfer the fries to a thick paper bag or paper towels to drain.

4. Reduce the heat to medium-high, add the remaining 1 quart oil, and heat the oil to 375 degrees.

Meanwhile, thoroughly dry the fish with paper towels and dredge each piece in the flour mixture on the baking sheet; transfer the pieces to a wire rack, shaking off any excess flour. Add 1¼ cups of the beer to the flour mixture in the mixing bowl and stir until the mixture is just combined (the batter will be lumpy). Add the remaining ¼ cup beer as needed, 1 tablespoon at a time, whisking after each addition, until the batter falls from the whisk in a thin, steady stream and leaves a faint trail across the surface of the batter. Using tongs, dip 1 piece of fish in the batter and let the excess run off, shaking gently. Place the battered fish back on the baking sheet with the flour mixture and turn to coat both sides. Repeat with the remaining fish, keeping the pieces in a single layer on the baking sheet.

5. When the oil reaches 375 degrees, increase the heat to high and add the battered fish to the oil with the tongs, gently shaking off any excess flour. Fry, stirring occasionally, until golden brown, 7 to 8 minutes. Transfer the fish to a thick paper bag or paper towels to drain. Allow the oil to return to 375 degrees.

6. Add all of the fries back to the oil and fry until golden brown and crisp, 3 to 5 minutes. Transfer to a fresh paper bag or paper towels to drain. Season the fries with salt to taste and serve immediately with the fish.

PAN-SEARED SALMON

WHY THIS RECIPE WORKS: We love salmon cooked on the grill, but when the weather makes grilling unpleasant or impossible, we don't want to forgo serving this flavorful fish. We wanted a great recipe for pan-seared salmon with a crisp, even, golden brown crust.

Preheating the skillet over high heat and using just a teaspoon of neutral canola or vegetable oil (butter tended to burn and was too rich) produced the brown crust we wanted—no flour or other coating was necessary. To prevent burning, we turned the heat down just after adding the fillets. Allowing plenty of space around the fillets kept them from merely steaming. We flipped the fillets when they turned opaque from the bottom to about halfway up; there was no need to shake the pan or move the fish until then. We found that removing the salmon just before it was done prevented overcooking; residual heat brought it up to serving temperature. Simply seasoned and perfectly cooked, these salmon fillets were easy to make and just as good as any cooked on the grill.

Pan-Seared Salmon

SERVES 4

To ensure uniform pieces of fish that cook at the same rate, buy a whole center-cut fillet and cut it into four pieces. With the addition of the fish fillets, the pan temperature drops; compensate for the heat loss by keeping the heat on high for 30 seconds after adding them. If cooking two or three fillets instead of the full recipe of four, use a 10-inch skillet and medium-high heat for both preheating the pan and cooking the salmon. A splatter screen helps reduce the mess of pan-searing.

1 (1¾ to 2-pound) skinless salmon fillet, about 1½ inches
   at the thickest part (see note)
1 teaspoon canola or vegetable oil
   Table salt and ground black pepper
   Sweet-and-Sour Chutney (recipe follows) or lemon
   wedges, for serving

1. Use a sharp knife to trim any whitish fat from the belly of the fillet and cut it into four equal pieces. Heat the oil in a 12-inch skillet over high heat until shimmering but not smoking. Sprinkle the salmon with salt and pepper.

2. Add the fillets, skin-side down, and cook, without moving the fillets, until the pan regains lost heat, about 30 seconds. Reduce the heat to medium-high; continue to cook until the skin side is well browned and the bottom half of the fillets turns opaque, 4½ minutes. Turn the fillets and cook, without moving them, until they are no longer translucent on the exterior and are firm, but not hard, when gently squeezed, 3 minutes for medium-rare and 3½ minutes for medium. Remove the fillets from the pan; let stand for 1 minute. Pat the fillets with a paper towel to absorb excess fat on the surface, if desired. Serve immediately with the chutney or the lemon wedges.

Sweet-and-Sour Chutney

MAKES ABOUT ⅓ CUP

A little of this intensely flavored condiment goes a long way.

- 1 teaspoon fennel seeds
- ½ teaspoon ground cumin
- ½ teaspoon ground coriander
- ¼ teaspoon ground cardamom
- ¼ teaspoon paprika
- ¼ teaspoon table salt
- 2 teaspoons olive oil
- ½ medium onion, minced (about ½ cup)
- ¼ cup red wine vinegar
- 1 tablespoon sugar
- 1 tablespoon minced fresh parsley leaves

Mix the fennel, cumin, coriander, cardamom, paprika, and salt in a small bowl; set aside. Heat the oil in a medium skillet over medium heat; sauté the onion until soft, 3 to 4 minutes. Add the reserved spice mixture; sauté until fragrant, about 1 minute more. Increase the heat to medium-high and add the vinegar, sugar, and 2 tablespoons water; cook until the mixture reduces by about one third and reaches a syrupy consistency, about 1½ minutes. Stir in the parsley. Serve with the salmon.

BROILED SALMON

WHY THIS RECIPE WORKS: Cooking an entire side of salmon in the oven often results in fish that is either soggy or chalky. We wanted to pull off a crowd-pleasing side of salmon that is moist and firm, with a golden crumb crust that contrasts with the flavorful fish.

Most of the time, we achieve a crisp crust on salmon through pan-searing in a skillet on the stovetop. With a crumb crust, it made sense to use the broiler. A plain bread crumb-topping seemed bland, but when we toasted the crumbs and mixed in crushed potato chips and

chopped dill, the result was a crisp and flavorful coating. To get the crumb mixture to adhere to the fish, we relied on a thin layer of mustard. One problem: The crust burned by the time the fish was cooking through. We switched gears and broiled the fish almost unadorned (save for salt, pepper, and a bit of olive oil) until it was nearly done, then spread on the mustard and crumbs for a second run under the broiler to crisp the crust. To get the fish onto a platter in one piece, we lined a baking sheet with heavy-duty foil before adding the fish, creating a sling with which we could move it. Our two-step broiling method resulted in firm, moist fish and a flavorful crunchy topping.

Broiled Salmon with Mustard and Crisp Dilled Crust

SERVES 8 TO 10

If you prefer to cook a smaller 2-pound fillet, ask to have it cut from the thick center of the fillet, not the thin tail end, and begin checking doneness a minute earlier.

- 3 slices high-quality white sandwich bread, torn into quarters
- 4 ounces plain high-quality potato chips, crushed into rough ⅛-inch pieces (about 1 cup)
- 6 tablespoons chopped fresh dill
- 1 whole side salmon fillet, about 3½ pounds, white belly fat trimmed
- 1 teaspoon olive oil
  Table salt and ground black pepper
- 3 tablespoons Dijon mustard

1. Adjust one oven rack to the top position (about 3 inches from the heat source) and the second rack to the upper-middle position; heat the oven to 400 degrees.

2. Pulse the bread in a food processor to fairly even ¼-inch pieces about the size of Grape-Nuts cereal (you should have about 1 cup), about 10 pulses. Spread the crumbs evenly on a rimmed baking sheet; toast on the lower oven rack, shaking the pan once or twice, until golden brown and crisp, 4 to 5 minutes. Toss the bread crumbs, crushed potato chips, and dill together in a small bowl; set aside.

3. Change the oven setting to broil. Cut a piece of heavy-duty foil 6 inches longer than the fillet. Fold the foil lengthwise in thirds and place lengthwise on a rimmed baking sheet; position the salmon lengthwise on the foil, allowing the excess foil to overhang the baking sheet. Rub the fillet evenly with the oil; sprinkle with salt and pepper. Broil the salmon on the upper rack until the surface is spotty brown and the outer ½ inch of the thick end is opaque when gently flaked with a paring knife, 9 to 11 minutes. Remove the baking sheet from the oven, spread the fish evenly with the mustard, and press the bread-crumb mixture onto the fish. Return the baking sheet to the lower oven rack and continue broiling until the crust is deep golden brown, about 1 minute longer.

4. Grasping the ends of the foil sling, lift the salmon, sling and all, onto a platter. Slide an offset spatula under the thick end. Grasp the foil, press the spatula against the foil, and slide it under the fish down to the thin end, loosening the entire side of fish. Grasp the foil again, hold the spatula perpendicular to the fish to stabilize it, and pull the foil out from under the fish. Wipe the platter clean with a damp paper towel. Serve the salmon immediately.

FLAVORFUL POACHED SALMON

WHY THIS RECIPE WORKS: When salmon is poached incorrectly, not only is it dry, but the flavor is so washed out that not even the richest sauce can redeem it. We wanted irresistibly supple salmon accented by the delicate flavor of the poaching liquid, accompanied by a simple pan sauce—all in under half an hour.

We started our tests with a classic court-bouillon, which is made by boiling water, wine, herbs, vegetables, and aromatics and then straining out the solids. But discarding all those vegetables seemed wasteful for a simple weeknight supper. Using less liquid—poaching the salmon in just enough liquid to come half an inch up the side of the fillets—allowed us to cut back on the quantity of vegetables and aromatics; in fact, a couple of shallots, a few herbs, and some wine were all we needed to solve the flavor issue. However, the part of the salmon that wasn't submerged in liquid needed to be steamed for thorough cooking, and the low cooking tempera-ture required to poach the salmon evenly didn't create enough steam. The solution was to increase the ratio of wine to water. The additional alcohol lowered the liquid's boiling point, producing more vapor even at the lower temperature. Meanwhile, the bottom of the fillets had the opposite problem, overcooking due to direct contact with the pan. Resting the salmon fillets on top of lemon slices provided sufficient insulation. For a finishing touch, after removing the salmon, we reduced the liquid and added a few tablespoons of olive oil to create an easy vinaigrette-style sauce.

Poached Salmon with Herb and Caper Vinaigrette

SERVES 4

To ensure uniform pieces of fish that cook at the same rate, buy a whole center-cut fillet and cut it into four pieces. If a skinless whole fillet is unavailable, remove the skin yourself (see page 195) or follow the recipe as directed with a skin-on fillet, adding 3 to 4 minutes to the cooking time in step 2.

- 2 **lemons**
- 1 **large shallot, minced (about 4 tablespoons)**
- 2 **tablespoons minced fresh parsley leaves, stems reserved**
- 2 **tablespoons minced fresh tarragon leaves, stems reserved**
- ½ **cup dry white wine**
- ½ **cup water**
- 1 **(1¾ to 2-pound) skinless salmon fillet, about 1½ inches at the thickest part (see note)**
- 2 **tablespoons capers, rinsed and roughly chopped**
- 2 **tablespoons extra-virgin olive oil**
- 1 **tablespoon honey**
  Table salt and ground black pepper

1. Cut the top and bottom off 1 lemon; cut the lemon into eight to ten ¼-inch-thick slices. Cut the remain-ing lemon into eight wedges and set aside. Arrange the lemon slices in a single layer across the bottom of a 12-inch skillet. Scatter 2 tablespoons of the shallot and the herb stems evenly over the lemon slices. Add the wine and water.

2. Use a sharp knife to trim any whitish fat from the belly of the fillet and cut it into four equal pieces. Place the salmon fillets in the skillet, skinned side down, on top of the lemon slices. Set the pan over high heat and bring the liquid to a simmer. Reduce the heat to low, cover, and cook until the sides of the fillets are opaque but the center of the thickest part of the fillets is still translucent (or until the thickest part of the fillets registers 125 degrees on an instant-read thermometer), 11 to 16 minutes. Remove the pan from the heat and, using a spatula, carefully transfer the salmon and lemon slices to a paper towel–lined plate. Tent loosely with foil.

3. Return the pan to high heat and simmer the cooking liquid until slightly thickened and reduced to 2 tablespoons, 4 to 5 minutes. Meanwhile, combine the remaining 2 tablespoons shallot, the minced herbs, capers, olive oil, and honey in a medium bowl. Strain the reduced cooking liquid through a fine-mesh strainer into the bowl with the herb-caper mixture, pressing on the solids to extract as much liquid as possible. Whisk to combine and season with salt and pepper to taste.

4. Season the salmon lightly with salt and pepper. Using a spatula, carefully lift and tilt the salmon fillets to remove the lemon slices. Place the salmon on a serving platter or individual plates and spoon the vinaigrette over the top. Serve, passing the reserved lemon wedges separately.

NOTES FROM THE TEST KITCHEN

HOW TO SKIN A SALMON FILLET

1. Insert the blade of a sharp boning knife just above the skin about 1 inch from the end of the fillet. Cut through the nearest end, away from yourself, keeping the blade just above the skin.

2. Rotate the fish and grab the loose piece of skin. Run the knife between the flesh and skin, making sure the knife is just above the skin, until the skin is completely removed.

GLAZED SALMON

WHY THIS RECIPE WORKS: The traditional method for glazed salmon calls for broiling, but reaching into a broiling-hot oven every minute to baste the fish is a hassle and, even worse, the fillets often burn if your timing isn't spot-on. We wanted a foolproof method for glazed salmon that was succulent and pink throughout while keeping the slightly crusty, flavorful browned exterior typically achieved with broiling. First we found that reducing the temperature and gently baking the fish, instead of broiling, cooked the salmon perfectly. To rapidly caramelize the exterior of the fillets before they had a chance to toughen, we sprinkled the fillets with sugar and quickly pan-seared each side before transferring them to the oven. To ensure the glaze stayed put, we rubbed the fish with a mixture of cornstarch, brown sugar, and salt before searing.

Glazed Salmon

SERVES 4

To ensure uniform pieces of fish that cook at the same rate, buy a whole center-cut fillet and cut it into 4 pieces. Prepare the glaze before you cook the salmon. If your nonstick skillet isn't ovensafe, sear the salmon as directed in step 2, then transfer it to a rimmed baking sheet, glaze it, and bake as directed in step 3. You will need a 12-inch ovensafe nonstick skillet for this recipe.

1 teaspoon light brown sugar
½ teaspoon kosher salt
¼ teaspoon cornstarch
1 (1½ to 2-pound) skin-on salmon fillet, about 1½ inches thick
Ground black pepper
1 teaspoon vegetable oil
1 recipe glaze (recipes follow)

1. Adjust an oven rack to the middle position and heat the oven to 300 degrees. Combine the brown sugar, salt, and cornstarch in a small bowl. Use a sharp knife to remove any whitish fat from the belly of the salmon and cut the fillet into 4 equal pieces. Pat the fillets dry with paper towels and season with pepper. Sprinkle the brown sugar mixture evenly over the top of the flesh side of the salmon, rubbing to distribute.

2. Heat the oil in a 12-inch ovensafe nonstick skillet over medium-high heat until just smoking. Place the salmon, flesh side down, in the skillet and cook until well browned, about 1 minute. Using tongs, carefully flip the salmon and cook on the skin side for 1 minute.

3. Remove the skillet from the heat and spoon the glaze evenly over the salmon fillets. Transfer the skillet to the oven and cook until the fillets register 125 degrees on an instant-read thermometer (for medium-rare) and are still translucent when cut into with a paring knife, 7 to 10 minutes. Transfer the fillets to a platter or individual plates and serve.

Pomegranate-Balsamic Glaze

MAKES ABOUT ½ CUP

This fruity, tangy glaze is a perfect match for rich salmon.

- 3 tablespoons light brown sugar
- 3 tablespoons pomegranate juice
- 2 tablespoons balsamic vinegar
- 1 tablespoon whole grain mustard
- 1 teaspoon cornstarch
  Pinch cayenne pepper

Whisk the ingredients together in a small saucepan. Bring to a boil over medium-high heat; simmer until thickened, about 1 minute. Remove from the heat and cover to keep warm.

Asian Barbecue Glaze

MAKES ABOUT ½ CUP

Toasted sesame oil gives this teriyaki-like glaze rich flavor.

- 2 tablespoons ketchup
- 2 tablespoons hoisin sauce
- 2 tablespoons rice vinegar

- 2 tablespoons packed light brown sugar
- 1 tablespoon soy sauce
- 1 tablespoon toasted sesame oil
- 2 teaspoons Asian chili-garlic sauce
- 1 teaspoon minced or grated fresh ginger

Whisk the ingredients together in a small saucepan. Bring to a boil over medium-high heat; simmer until thickened, about 3 minutes. Remove from the heat and cover to keep warm.

Orange-Miso Glaze

MAKES ABOUT ½ CUP

Miso is a fermented soybean paste that adds deep flavor to foods. We prefer milder, white miso here, rather than the strong-flavored red miso.

- 1 teaspoon grated zest plus ¼ cup juice from 1 orange
- 2 tablespoons white miso
- 1 tablespoon light brown sugar
- 1 tablespoon rice vinegar
- 1 tablespoon whole grain mustard
- ¾ teaspoon cornstarch
  Pinch cayenne pepper

Whisk the ingredients together in a small saucepan. Bring to a boil over medium-high heat; simmer until thickened, about 1 minute. Remove from the heat and cover to keep warm.

Soy-Mustard Glaze

MAKES ABOUT ½ CUP

Mirin, a sweet Japanese rice wine, can be found in Asian markets and the international section of most supermarkets.

- 3 tablespoons light brown sugar
- 2 tablespoons soy sauce
- 2 tablespoons mirin (see note)
- 1 tablespoon sherry vinegar
- 1 tablespoon whole grain mustard
- 1 tablespoon water
- 1 teaspoon cornstarch
- ⅛ teaspoon red pepper flakes

Whisk the ingredients together in a small saucepan. Bring to a boil over medium-high heat; simmer until thickened, about 1 minute. Remove from the heat and cover to keep warm.

OVEN-ROASTED SALMON

WHY THIS RECIPE WORKS: Roasting a salmon fillet can create a brown exterior, but often at the risk of a dry, overcooked interior. The best roasted salmon should have moist, flavorful flesh inside, with a contrasting crisp texture on the outside.

To ensure that the salmon fillets would cook evenly, we cut a whole center-cut fillet into four pieces. We roasted the fish at a low temperature and achieved the buttery flesh we were after, but no browning—and the fillets were a little mushy from the rendered fat. Taking the opposite approach, we put the fish on a preheated baking sheet and started the oven at a high temperature to firm up and brown the exterior. This gave us a crust, but we still needed to get rid of the fat; cutting slits in the skin released the fat rendered by the high heat. Lowering the temperature as soon as we put the fish in the oven enabled it to cook through gradually after the initial blast of heat, so it didn't dry out. Now we had the contrast between moist interior and crisp brown exterior that we wanted. Salmon is rich and flavorful all on its own, but we devised a couple of easy no-cook relishes that can be served alongside for even more flavor.

Oven-Roasted Salmon

SERVES 4

To ensure uniform pieces of fish that cook at the same rate, buy a whole center-cut fillet and cut it into four pieces. If your knife is not sharp enough to easily cut through the skin, try a serrated knife. It is important to keep the skin on during cooking; remove it afterward if you choose not to serve it.

- 1 (1¾ to 2-pound) skin-on salmon fillet, about 1½ inches at the thickest part (see note)
- 2 teaspoons olive oil
  Table salt and ground black pepper
- 1 recipe relish (recipes follow)

1. Adjust an oven rack to the lowest position, place a rimmed baking sheet on the rack, and heat the oven to 500 degrees. Remove any whitish fat from the belly of the fillet and cut it into four equal pieces. Make four or five shallow slashes about an inch apart along the skin side of each piece, being careful not to cut into the flesh.

2. Pat the salmon dry with paper towels. Rub the fillets evenly with the oil and season liberally with salt and pepper. Reduce the oven temperature to 275 degrees and remove the baking sheet. Carefully place the salmon, skin-side down, on the baking sheet. Roast until the thickest part of the fillets is still translucent when cut into with a paring knife (or the thickest part of the fillets registers 125 degrees on an instant-read thermometer), 9 to 13 minutes. Transfer the fillets to individual plates or a platter. Top with relish and serve.

Tangerine and Ginger Relish

MAKES ABOUT 1¼ CUPS

- 4 tangerines, rind and pith removed and segments cut into ½-inch pieces (about 1 cup)
- 1 scallion, sliced thin (about ¼ cup)
- 1½ teaspoons minced or grated fresh ginger
- 2 teaspoons juice from 1 lemon
- 2 teaspoons extra-virgin olive oil
  Table salt and ground black pepper

1. Place the tangerines in a fine-mesh strainer set over a medium bowl and drain for 15 minutes.

2. Pour off all but 1 tablespoon tangerine juice from the bowl; whisk in the scallion, ginger, lemon juice, and oil. Stir in the tangerines and season with salt and pepper to taste.

Fresh Tomato Relish
MAKES ABOUT 1½ CUPS

- ¾ pound ripe tomatoes, cored, seeded, and cut into ¼-inch dice (about 1½ cups)
- 2 tablespoons chopped fresh basil leaves
- 1 small shallot, minced (about 1 tablespoon)
- 1 tablespoon extra-virgin olive oil
- 1 teaspoon red wine vinegar
- 1 small garlic clove, minced or pressed through a garlic press (about ½ teaspoon)
  Table salt and ground black pepper

Combine the tomatoes, basil, shallot, oil, vinegar, and garlic in a medium bowl. Season with salt and pepper to taste.

Spicy Cucumber Relish
MAKES ABOUT 2 CUPS

- 1 medium cucumber, peeled, seeded, and cut into ¼-inch dice (about 2 cups)
- 2 tablespoons minced fresh mint leaves
- 1 small shallot, minced (about 1 tablespoon)
- 1 serrano chile, seeds and ribs removed, chile minced (about 1 tablespoon)
- 1–2 tablespoons juice from 1 lime
  Table salt

Combine the cucumber, mint, shallot, chile, 1 tablespoon of the lime juice, and ¼ teaspoon salt in a medium bowl. Let sit at room temperature until the flavors meld, about 15 minutes. Season with additional lime juice and salt to taste.

PAN-SEARED TUNA STEAKS

WHY THIS RECIPE WORKS: Moist and rare in the middle with a seared crust, pan-seared tuna is a popular entrée in restaurants. This dish is so simple that we thought it would be easy to make at home, and set out to determine the best method.

Starting with high-quality tuna—sushi grade if possible—is paramount; we prefer the flavor of yellowfin. A thickness of at least an inch is necessary for the center of the tuna to be rare while the exterior browns. Before searing the tuna in a nonstick skillet, we rubbed the steaks with oil, then coated them with sesame seeds; the oil helped the seeds stick to the fish. The sesame seeds browned in the skillet and formed a beautiful, nutty-tasting crust. We learned that tuna, like beef, will continue to cook from residual heat when removed from the stove, so when the interior of the tuna was near the desired degree of doneness (about 110 degrees on an instant-read thermometer), we transferred it to a platter.

Pan-Seared Sesame-Crusted Tuna Steaks
SERVES 4

If you plan to serve the fish with the sauce or salsa (recipes follow), prepare it before cooking the fish. Most members of the test kitchen staff prefer their tuna steaks rare to medium-rare; the cooking times given in this recipe are for tuna steaks cooked to these two degrees of doneness. For tuna steaks cooked medium, observe the timing for medium-rare, then tent the steaks loosely with foil for 5 minutes before slicing. If you prefer tuna steaks cooked so rare that they are still cold in the center, try to purchase steaks that are 1½ inches thick and cook them according to the timing below for rare steaks. Bear in mind, though, that the cooking times below are estimates; check for doneness by nicking the fish with a paring knife. To cook only two steaks, use half as many sesame seeds, reduce the amount of oil to 2 teaspoons both on the fish and in the pan, use a 10-inch nonstick skillet, and follow the same cooking times.

¾ cup sesame seeds

4 (8-ounce) tuna steaks, preferably yellowfin, about 1 inch thick (see note)

2 tablespoons vegetable oil
Table salt and ground black pepper

1 recipe sauce or salsa (recipes follow)

1. Spread the sesame seeds in a shallow baking dish or pie plate. Pat the tuna steaks dry with a paper towel; use 1 tablespoon of the oil to rub both sides of the steaks, then sprinkle them with salt and pepper. Press both sides of each steak in the sesame seeds to coat.

2. Heat the remaining 1 tablespoon oil in a 12-inch non-stick skillet over high heat until just beginning to smoke and swirl to coat the pan. Add the tuna steaks and cook 30 seconds without moving the steaks. Reduce the heat to medium-high and continue to cook until the seeds are golden brown, about 1½ minutes. Using tongs, flip the tuna steaks carefully and cook, without moving them, until golden brown on the second side and the centers register 110 degrees on an instant-read thermometer for rare (about 1½ minutes), or 120 degrees for medium-rare (about 3 minutes). Serve with the sauce or salsa.

Ginger-Soy Sauce with Scallions

MAKES ABOUT 1 CUP

If available, serve pickled ginger and wasabi, passed separately, with the tuna and this sauce.

¼ cup soy sauce

¼ cup rice vinegar

¼ cup water

1 medium scallion, sliced thin

2½ teaspoons sugar

2 teaspoons minced or grated fresh ginger

1½ teaspoons toasted sesame oil

½ teaspoon red pepper flakes

Combine all the ingredients in a small bowl, stirring to dissolve the sugar.

Avocado-Orange Salsa

MAKES ABOUT 1 CUP

To keep the avocado from discoloring, prepare this salsa just before you cook the tuna steaks.

1 large orange, cut into segments (see page 214)

1 ripe avocado, pitted, peeled, and diced medium (see page 348)

2 tablespoons minced red onion

2 tablespoons minced fresh cilantro leaves

4 teaspoons juice from 1 to 2 limes

1 small jalapeño chile, stemmed, seeded, and minced
Table salt

Combine all the ingredients, including salt to taste, in a small nonreactive bowl.

PAN-ROASTED HALIBUT

WHY THIS RECIPE WORKS: Chefs often choose to braise halibut instead of pan-roasting or sautéing because this moist-heat cooking technique keeps the fish from drying out. The problem is that braising doesn't allow for browning, therefore producing a fish that the test kitchen considers bland-tasting. We didn't want to make any compromises on either texture or flavor, so we set out to develop a technique for pan-roasting halibut that would produce perfectly cooked, moist, and tender fish.

Halibut is most frequently sold as steaks, but there is quite a bit of range in size; to ensure that they cooked at the same rate, we chose steaks that were as close in size to each other as possible. We knew we could get a crust on the fish by pan-searing or oven-roasting, but neither technique proved satisfactory. A combination of the two proved best: browning on the stovetop and roasting in the oven. To be sure the steaks wouldn't overcook, we seared them on one side in a piping-hot skillet, then turned them over before placing them into the oven to finish cooking through. When they were done, the steaks were browned but still moist inside. To complement the lean fish, we paired the halibut with a rich flavored butter.

Pan-Roasted Halibut Steaks

SERVES 4 TO 6

If you plan to serve the fish with the flavored butter or vinaigrette (recipes follow), prepare it before cooking the fish. Even well-dried fish can cause the hot oil in the pan to splatter. You can minimize splattering by laying the halibut steaks in the pan gently and putting the edge closest to you in the pan first so that the far edge falls away from you.

2 tablespoons olive oil
2 (full) halibut steaks, about 1¼ inches thick and 10 to 12 inches long (about 2½ pounds total), gently rinsed, dried well with paper towels, and trimmed of cartilage at both ends (see photo)
  Table salt and ground black pepper
1 recipe flavored butter or vinaigrette (recipes follow)

1. Adjust an oven rack to the middle position and heat the oven to 425 degrees. When the oven reaches 425 degrees, heat the oil in a 12-inch ovensafe skillet over high heat until the oil just begins to smoke.

2. Meanwhile, sprinkle both sides of the halibut steaks generously with salt and pepper. Reduce the heat to medium-high and swirl the oil in the pan to distribute; carefully lay the steaks in the pan and sear, without moving them, until spotty brown, about 4 minutes. (If the steaks are thinner than 1¼ inches, check browning at 3½ minutes; thicker steaks of 1½ inches may require extra time, so check at 4½ minutes.) Off the heat, flip the steaks over in the pan using two thin-bladed metal spatulas.

3. Transfer the skillet to the oven and roast until an instant-read thermometer inserted into the steaks reads 140 degrees and the fish flakes loosen and the flesh is opaque when checked with the tip of a paring knife, about 9 minutes (thicker steaks may take up to 10 minutes). Remove the skillet from the oven. Remove the skin from

NOTES FROM THE TEST KITCHEN

TRIMMING AND SERVING FULL HALIBUT STEAKS

BEFORE COOKING: Cut off the cartilage at each end of the steaks to ensure that they will fit neatly in the pan and diminish the likelihood that the small bones located there will wind up on your dinner plate.

BEFORE SERVING: Remove the skin from the cooked steaks and separate the quadrants of meat from the bone by slipping a spatula gently between them.

the cooked steaks and separate each quadrant of meat from the bones by slipping a spatula or knife gently between them (see photo). Transfer the fish to a warm platter and serve with the flavored butter or vinaigrette.

Chipotle-Garlic Butter with Lime and Cilantro
MAKES ABOUT ¼ CUP

- 4 tablespoons (½ stick) unsalted butter, softened
- 1 medium chipotle chile in adobo sauce, seeded and minced, plus 1 teaspoon adobo sauce
- 2 teaspoons minced fresh cilantro leaves
- 1 medium garlic clove, minced or pressed through a garlic press (about 1 teaspoon)
- 1 teaspoon honey
- 1 teaspoon grated zest from 1 lime
- ½ teaspoon table salt

Beat the butter with a fork until light and fluffy. Stir in the remaining ingredients until thoroughly combined. Dollop a portion of the butter over the pieces of hot cooked fish and allow the butter to melt. Serve immediately.

Chunky Cherry Tomato–Basil Vinaigrette
MAKES ABOUT 1½ CUPS

- ½ pint cherry or grape tomatoes, each tomato quartered (about 1 cup)
- ¼ teaspoon table salt
- ¼ teaspoon ground black pepper
- 2 medium shallots, minced (about 6 tablespoons)
- 6 tablespoons extra-virgin olive oil
- 3 tablespoons juice from 1 lemon
- 2 tablespoons minced fresh basil leaves

Mix the tomatoes with the salt and pepper in a medium bowl; let stand until juicy and seasoned, about 10 minutes. Whisk the shallots, oil, lemon juice, and basil together in a small mixing bowl, pour the vinaigrette over the tomatoes, and toss to combine. Pour over the pieces of hot cooked fish and serve immediately.

PAN-ROASTED FISH FILLETS

WHY THIS RECIPE WORKS: Pan-roasted fish seems like a simple dish, but in reality it is usually only well executed by practiced chefs. At home, the dish often results in dry, overbaked fillets. We set out to develop a foolproof recipe for producing succulent, well-browned fillets.

From an initial round of testing, we knew we needed thick fillets; skinnier pieces end up overcooked by the time they've achieved a serious sear. We then turned to a common restaurant method to cook the fish: Sear the fillet in a hot pan, flip, then transfer it to a hot oven to finish cooking. The technique was sound, but to brown the fish quickly before the hot pan had a chance to dry out the fish's exterior we turned to a sprinkling of sugar. The idea is that sugar commingles with exuded juices from the fish, accelerating browning and giving the fish a rich color and deep flavor that's anything but sweet. We dusted a few fillets with a touch of granulated sugar and placed them in a hot skillet. A well-browned crust formed almost immediately, leaving no time for the interior to dry out. And after a short stay in the oven to finish cooking through, the fish emerged well-browned, tender and moist, and best of all, not one taster detected any out-of-place sweetness.

Pan-Roasted Thick-Cut Fish Fillets
SERVES 4

Thick white fish fillets with a meaty texture, like halibut, cod, sea bass, or red snapper, work best in this recipe. Because most fish fillets differ in thickness, some pieces may finish cooking before others—be sure to immediately remove any fillet that reaches 135 degrees. You will need an ovensafe nonstick skillet for this recipe. If you can't find skinless fillets, see page 195 for information on skinning fillets. Serve with lemon wedges or one of the relishes on pages 197–198.

- 4 (6 to 8-ounce) skinless white fish fillets, 1 to 1½ inches thick (see note)
  Table salt and ground black pepper
- ½ teaspoon sugar
- 1 tablespoon vegetable oil
  Lemon wedges or relish (see note), for serving

Adjust an oven rack to the middle position and heat the oven to 425 degrees. Dry the fish thoroughly with paper towels and season with salt and pepper. Sprinkle ⅛ teaspoon sugar evenly over one side of each fillet. Heat the oil in a

12-inch ovensafe nonstick skillet over high heat until smoking. Place the fillets in the skillet, sugared side down, and press down lightly to ensure even contact with the pan. Cook until browned, 1 to 1½ minutes. Using two spatulas, flip the fillets and transfer the skillet to the oven. Roast the fillets until the centers are just opaque and the fish registers 135 degrees on an instant-read thermometer, 7 to 10 minutes. Immediately transfer the fish to individual plates and serve with lemon wedges or relish.

BAKED SOLE FILLETS

WHY THIS RECIPE WORKS: We wanted a fuss-free, foolproof sole preparation that was suitable for a weeknight dinner yet impressive and elegant enough to serve to company. We found that rolling the fillets into compact bundles eased the transport from baking dish to plate and covering the baking dish with foil protected the delicate fish from the drying heat of the oven. To ramp up the fillets' mild flavor, we brushed them with Dijon mustard; seasoned them with salt, pepper, fresh herbs, and lemon zest; and drizzled them with melted butter and garlic. Then we rolled them up, drizzled them with more butter, and baked them. For texture, we added a mixture of herbs, butter, and panko bread crumbs to the sole at two intervals. We removed the foil before the fish was done cooking, basted the fillets with pan juices, topped them with most of the bread-crumb mixture, and then returned them to the oven uncovered. Just before serving, we sprinkled the remaining crumbs over the fillets.

Baked Sole Fillets with Herbs and Bread Crumbs

SERVES 6

Try to purchase fillets of similar size. If using smaller fillets (about 3 ounces each), serve 2 fillets per person and reduce the baking time in step 3 to 20 minutes. We strongly advise against using frozen fish in this recipe. Freezing can undermine the texture of the fish, making it hard to roll. Fresh basil or dill can be used in place of the tarragon.

- 3 tablespoons minced fresh parsley leaves
- 3 tablespoons minced fresh chives
- 1 tablespoon minced fresh tarragon leaves
- 1 teaspoon grated zest from 1 lemon
- 5 tablespoons unsalted butter, cut into 5 pieces
- 2 medium garlic cloves, minced or pressed through a garlic press (about 2 teaspoons)
- 6 (6-ounce) boneless, skinless sole or flounder fillets
  Table salt and ground black pepper
- 1 tablespoon Dijon mustard
- ⅔ cup panko bread crumbs
  Lemon wedges, for serving

1. Adjust an oven rack to the middle position and heat the oven to 325 degrees. Combine the parsley, chives, and tarragon in a small bowl. Reserve 1 tablespoon herb mixture; stir the lemon zest into the remaining herb mixture.

2. Heat 4 tablespoons of the butter in an 8-inch skillet over medium heat until just melted. Add half of the garlic and cook, stirring frequently, until fragrant, 1 to 2 minutes. Remove from the heat and set aside.

3. Pat the fillets dry with paper towels and season both sides with salt and pepper. Arrange the fillets, skinned side up, with the tail end pointing away from you. Spread ½ teaspoon mustard on each fillet, sprinkle each evenly with about 1 tablespoon of the herb–lemon zest mixture, and drizzle each with about 1½ teaspoons of the garlic butter. Tightly roll the fillets from the thick end to form cylinders. Set the fillets, seam side down, in a 13 by 9-inch baking dish. Drizzle the remaining garlic butter over the fillets, cover the baking dish with aluminum foil, and bake for 25 minutes. Wipe out the skillet but do not wash.

4. While the fillets are baking, melt the remaining 1 tablespoon butter in the now-empty skillet over medium heat. Add the panko and cook, stirring frequently, until the crumbs are deep golden brown, 5 to 8 minutes. Reduce the heat to low, add the remaining garlic, and cook, stirring constantly, until the garlic is fragrant and evenly distributed in the crumbs, about 1 minute. Transfer to a small bowl, stir in ¼ teaspoon salt, and season with pepper to taste. Let cool, then stir in the reserved 1 tablespoon herb mixture.

5. After the fillets have baked for 25 minutes, remove the baking dish from oven. Baste the fillets with melted garlic butter from the baking dish, sprinkle with all but 3 tablespoons of the bread crumbs, and continue to bake, uncovered, until the fillets register 135 degrees on an instant-read thermometer, 6 to 10 minutes longer. Using a thin metal spatula, transfer the fillets to plates, sprinkle with the remaining bread crumbs, and serve with the lemon wedges.

PAN-SEARED SCALLOPS

WHY THIS RECIPE WORKS: Producing, crisp-crusted restaurant-style scallops means overcoming two obstacles: chemically treated scallops and weak stovetops. We wanted to achieve superior pan-seared scallops that had a perfectly brown crust and no hint of off-flavors.

We decided to work with wet scallops (those that are chemically treated with STP, a solution of water and sodium tripolyphosphate, to increase shelf life and retain moisture) first. If we could develop a good recipe for finicky wet scallops, it would surely work with premium dry (untreated) scallops. We found that waiting to add the scallops to the skillet until the oil was beginning to smoke, cooking the scallops in two batches instead of one, and switching to a nonstick skillet (so that the browned bits formed a crust on the meat instead of sticking to the skillet) were all steps in the right direction. But it wasn't until we tried a common restaurant technique—butter basting—that our scallops really improved. We seared the scallops in oil on one side and added butter to the skillet after flipping them. (Butter contains milk proteins and sugars that brown rapidly when heated.) We then used a large spoon to ladle the foaming butter over the scallops. Waiting to add the butter ensured that it had just enough time to work its browning magic on the scallops, but not enough time to burn.

Next we addressed the lingering flavor of STP. Unable to rinse it away, we decided to mask it by soaking the scallops in a saltwater brine containing lemon juice. For dry scallops, we simply skipped the soaking step and proceeded with the recipe. It produced scallops that rivaled those made on a powerful restaurant range, with golden brown exteriors and juicy and tender interiors.

Pan-Seared Scallops

SERVES 4

We strongly recommend purchasing dry scallops (those without chemical additives). If you can only find wet scallops, soak them in a solution of 1 quart cold water, ¼ cup lemon juice, and 2 tablespoons table salt for 30 minutes before proceeding with step 1, and season the scallops with pepper only in step 2. Prepare the sauce (if serving) while the scallops dry (between steps 1 and 2) and keep it warm while cooking them.

- 1½ pounds dry sea scallops (about 16 scallops), tendons removed (see note)
  Table salt and ground black pepper
- 2 tablespoons vegetable oil
- 2 tablespoons unsalted butter
  Lemon wedges or Lemon Brown Butter Sauce (recipe follows)

NOTES FROM THE TEST KITCHEN

ARE YOUR SCALLOPS WET OR DRY?

If you are unsure whether your scallops are wet (treated with chemicals) or dry (untreated), conduct this quick test: Place 1 scallop on a paper towel–lined, microwave-safe plate and microwave on high power for 15 seconds. If the scallop is dry, it will exude very little water. If it is wet, there will be a sizable ring of moisture on the paper towel. (The microwaved scallop can be cooked as is.)

PREPPING SCALLOPS

The small, crescent-shaped muscle that is sometimes attached to the scallop will be incredibly tough when cooked. Use your fingers to peel this muscle away from the sides of each scallop before cooking.

1. Place the scallops on a rimmed baking sheet lined with a clean kitchen towel. Place a second clean kitchen towel on top of the scallops and press gently on the towel to blot the liquid. Let the scallops sit at room temperature for 10 minutes while the towels absorb the moisture.

2. Remove the second towel and sprinkle the scallops on both sides with salt and pepper. Heat 1 tablespoon of the oil in a 12-inch nonstick skillet over high heat until just smoking. Add half of the scallops in a single layer, flat side down, and cook, without moving, until well browned, 1½ to 2 minutes.

3. Add 1 tablespoon of the butter to the skillet. Using tongs, flip the scallops and continue to cook, using a large spoon to baste the scallops with the melted butter, tilting the skillet so the butter runs to one side, until the sides of the scallops are firm and the centers are opaque, 30 to 90 seconds longer (remove the smaller scallops from the pan as they finish cooking). Transfer the scallops to a large plate and tent loosely with foil. Wipe out the skillet with a wad of paper towels and repeat with the remaining 1 tablespoon oil, remaining scallops, and remaining 1 tablespoon butter. Serve immediately with lemon wedges or sauce.

Lemon Brown Butter Sauce

MAKES ABOUT ¼ CUP

- 4 tablespoons (½ stick) unsalted butter, cut into 4 pieces
- 1 small shallot, minced (about 1½ tablespoons)
- 1 tablespoon minced fresh parsley leaves
- ½ teaspoon minced fresh thyme leaves
- 2 teaspoons juice from 1 lemon
  Table salt and ground black pepper

Heat the butter in a small heavy-bottomed saucepan over medium heat and cook, swirling the pan constantly, until the butter turns dark golden brown and has a nutty aroma, 4 to 5 minutes. Add the shallot and cook until fragrant, about 30 seconds. Remove the pan from the heat and stir in the parsley, thyme, and lemon juice. Season with salt and pepper to taste. Cover to keep warm.

PAN-SEARED SHRIMP

WHY THIS RECIPE WORKS: A good recipe for pan-seared shrimp is hard to find. Of the handful of recipes we uncovered, the majority resulted in shrimp that were either dry and flavorless or pale, tough, and gummy. We wanted shrimp that were well caramelized but still moist, briny, and tender.

We peeled the shrimp first and tried using a brine to add moisture, but found that it inhibited browning. Instead, we seasoned the shrimp with salt, pepper, and sugar, which brought out their natural sweetness and aided in browning. We cooked the shrimp in batches in a large, piping-hot skillet and then paired them with thick, glazelike sauces with assertive ingredients and plenty of acidity as a foil for the shrimp's richness.

Pan-Seared Shrimp

SERVES 4

This recipe can also be prepared with large shrimp (31 to 40 per pound); the cooking time will be slightly shorter. Either a nonstick or a traditional skillet will work for this recipe, but a nonstick simplifies cleanup.

- 2 tablespoons vegetable oil
- 1½ pounds extra-large shrimp (21 to 25 per pound), peeled and deveined (see photos; see note)
- ¼ teaspoon table salt
- ¼ teaspoon ground black pepper
- ⅛ teaspoon sugar

Heat 1 tablespoon of the oil in a 12-inch skillet over high heat until smoking. Meanwhile, toss the shrimp, salt, pepper, and sugar in a medium bowl. Add half of the shrimp to the pan in a single layer and cook until spotty brown and the edges turn pink, about 1 minute. Remove the pan from the heat. Using tongs, flip each shrimp and let stand until all but the very center is opaque, about 30 seconds. Transfer the shrimp to a large plate. Repeat with the remaining 1 tablespoon oil and the remaining shrimp. After the second batch has stood off the heat, return the first batch to the skillet and toss to combine. Cover the skillet and let stand until the shrimp are cooked through, 1 to 2 minutes. Serve immediately.

Pan-Seared Shrimp with Garlic-Lemon Butter

Beat 3 tablespoons softened unsalted butter with a fork in a small bowl until light and fluffy. Stir in 1 medium garlic clove, minced or pressed through a garlic press, 1 tablespoon juice from 1 lemon, 2 tablespoons chopped fresh parsley leaves, and ⅛ teaspoon salt until combined. Follow the recipe for Pan-Seared Shrimp, adding the flavored butter when returning the first batch of shrimp to the skillet. Serve with lemon wedges, if desired.

Pan-Seared Shrimp with Ginger-Hoisin Glaze

Stir 2 tablespoons hoisin sauce, 1 tablespoon rice vinegar, 1½ teaspoons soy sauce, 2 teaspoons minced or grated fresh ginger, 2 teaspoons water, and 2 scallions, sliced thin, together in a small bowl. Follow the recipe for Pan-Seared Shrimp, substituting an equal amount of red pepper flakes for the black pepper and adding the hoisin mixture when returning the first batch of shrimp to the skillet.

Pan-Seared Shrimp with Chipotle-Lime Glaze

Stir 1 chipotle chile in adobo, minced, 2 teaspoons adobo sauce, 4 teaspoons brown sugar, 2 tablespoons juice from 1 lime, and 2 tablespoons chopped fresh cilantro leaves together in a small bowl. Follow the recipe for Pan-Seared Shrimp, adding the chipotle mixture when returning the first batch of shrimp to the skillet.

NOTES FROM THE TEST KITCHEN

DEVEINING SHRIMP

1. After removing the shell, use a paring knife to make a shallow cut along the back of the shrimp so that the vein is exposed.

2. Use the tip of the knife to lift the vein out of the shrimp. Discard the vein by wiping the blade against a paper towel.

GARLICKY SHRIMP WITH BREAD CRUMBS

WHY THIS RECIPE WORKS: Just about every all-purpose cookbook includes a recipe for a casserole of shrimp in a sherry-garlic sauce topped with bread crumbs, but the ones we tried produced rubbery shrimp and gluey toppings. We wanted all the potent flavors and contrasting textures that the name of this dish promises—tender, moist shrimp infused with garlic and blanketed with crisp, buttery bread crumbs.

Most recipes call for cooking the shrimp twice, first poaching them on the stovetop and then baking them in the casserole dish. No wonder they're usually overdone! Our experiments with skipping the poaching weren't very successful—the shrimp were just plain bland—so we abandoned the oven altogether and decided to make the entire dish in a skillet on top of the stove. After searing the shrimp on one side, sprinkled with a pinch of sugar to promote browning, we removed them to build the sauce; we would add the shrimp back at the end to heat through and finish cooking. For the sauce, we started with garlic. Sherry alone tasted too boozy, so we cut it with clam juice, which underscored the briny flavor of the shrimp. A pinch of flour and some butter thickened the sauce, and lemon juice brightened everything up. A chewy supermarket baguette made the perfect buttery bread crumbs; sprinkled on at the last minute, they were sturdy enough to stay crisp on the saucy shrimp. Our modernized skillet "casserole" was definitely an improvement on the tired old version.

Garlicky Shrimp with Buttered Bread Crumbs
SERVES 4

Vermouth can be substituted for the sherry. If using vermouth, increase the amount to ½ cup and reduce the amount of clam juice to ½ cup. To prepare this recipe in a 10-inch skillet, brown the shrimp in three batches for about 2 minutes each, using 2 teaspoons oil per batch. Serve the shrimp with rice and either broccoli or asparagus.

- 1 (3-inch) piece baguette, cut into small pieces
- 5 tablespoons unsalted butter, cut into 5 pieces
- 1 small shallot, minced (about 1 tablespoon)
  Table salt and ground black pepper
- 2 tablespoons minced fresh parsley leaves
- 2 pounds extra-large shrimp (21 to 25 per pound), peeled and deveined (see photo)
- ¼ teaspoon sugar
- 4 teaspoons vegetable oil

4 medium garlic cloves, minced or pressed through a garlic press (about 4 teaspoons)
⅛ teaspoon red pepper flakes
2 teaspoons unbleached all-purpose flour
⅔ cup bottled clam juice
⅓ cup dry sherry (see note)
2 teaspoons juice from 1 lemon, plus lemon wedges for serving

1. Pulse the bread in a food processor until coarsely ground, about 8 pulses; you should have about 1 cup crumbs. Melt 1 tablespoon of the butter in a 12-inch non-stick skillet over medium heat. Add the crumbs, shallot, ⅛ teaspoon salt, and ⅛ teaspoon pepper. Cook, stirring occasionally, until the bread crumbs are golden brown, 7 to 10 minutes. Stir in 1 tablespoon of the parsley and transfer to a plate to cool. Wipe out the skillet with paper towels.

2. Pat the shrimp dry with paper towels and toss with the sugar, ¼ teaspoon salt, and ¼ teaspoon pepper in a bowl. Return the skillet to high heat, add 2 teaspoons of the oil, and heat until shimmering. Add half of the shrimp in a single layer and cook until spotty brown and the edges turn pink, about 3 minutes (do not flip the shrimp). Remove the pan from heat and transfer the shrimp to a large plate. Wipe out the skillet with paper towels. Repeat with the remaining 2 teaspoons oil and remaining shrimp; transfer the shrimp to the plate.

3. Return the skillet to medium heat and add 1 tablespoon more butter. When melted, add the garlic and red pepper flakes; cook, stirring frequently, until the garlic just begins to color, about 1 minute. Add the flour and cook, stirring frequently, for 1 minute. Increase the heat to medium-high and slowly whisk in the clam juice and sherry. Bring to a simmer and cook until the mixture

reduces to ¾ cup, 3 to 4 minutes. Whisk in the remaining 3 tablespoons butter, 1 tablespoon at a time. Stir in the lemon juice and remaining 1 tablespoon parsley.

4. Reduce the heat to medium-low, return the shrimp to the pan, and toss to combine. Cook, covered, until the shrimp are pink and cooked through, 2 to 3 minutes. Uncover and sprinkle with the toasted bread crumbs. Serve with the lemon wedges.

SIZZLING GARLIC SHRIMP

WHY THIS RECIPE WORKS: Sizzling *gambas al ajillo* is a tempting dish served in tapas bars. We knew we would have to make some adjustments to re-create this dish as an appetizer to serve at home, but our work would pay off when we could savor the juicy shrimp in spicy, garlic-infused oil.

The shrimp in the Spanish original are completely submerged in oil and cooked slowly. We didn't want to use that much oil, so we added just enough to a skillet to come halfway up the sides of the shrimp. We cooked them over very low heat and turned them halfway through; these shrimp cooked as evenly as they would have if completely covered with oil. We built heady garlic flavor in three ways: We added raw minced garlic to a marinade, we browned smashed cloves in the oil in which the shrimp would be cooked, and we cooked slices of garlic along with the shrimp. We included the traditional bay leaf and red chile, and added sherry vinegar (rather than sherry) and parsley, all of which brightened the richness of the oil. Served with plenty of bread to soak up the extra juices and flavorful oil, these garlicky shrimp rival the best restaurant versions.

Spanish-Style Garlic Shrimp
SERVES 6

Serve the shrimp with crusty bread for dipping in the richly flavored olive oil. This dish can be served directly from the skillet (make sure to use a trivet) or, for a sizzling effect, transferred to an 8-inch cast-iron skillet that's been heated for 2 minutes over medium-high heat. We prefer the slightly sweet flavor of dried chiles in this recipe, but ¼ teaspoon sweet paprika can be substituted. If sherry vinegar is unavailable, use 2 teaspoons dry sherry and 1 teaspoon white vinegar.

14 medium garlic cloves, peeled
1 pound large shrimp (31 to 40 per pound), peeled,
   deveined (see page 205), and tails removed
8 tablespoons olive oil
½ teaspoon table salt
1 bay leaf
1 (2-inch) piece mild dried chile, such as New Mexico,
   roughly broken, seeds included (see note)
1½ teaspoons sherry vinegar (see note)
1 tablespoon minced fresh parsley leaves

1. Mince 2 of the garlic cloves with a chef's knife or garlic press. Toss the minced garlic with the shrimp, 2 tablespoons of the olive oil, and salt in a medium bowl. Let the shrimp marinate at room temperature for 30 minutes.

2. Meanwhile, using the flat side of a chef's knife, smash 4 more garlic cloves. Heat the smashed garlic with the remaining 6 tablespoons olive oil in a 12-inch skillet over medium-low heat, stirring occasionally, until the garlic is light golden brown, 4 to 7 minutes. Remove the pan from the heat and allow the oil to cool to room temperature. Using a slotted spoon, remove the smashed garlic from the skillet and discard.

3. Slice the remaining 8 garlic cloves thin. Return the skillet to low heat and add the sliced garlic, bay leaf, and chile. Cook, stirring occasionally, until the garlic is tender but not browned, 4 to 7 minutes. (If the garlic has not begun to sizzle after 3 minutes, increase the heat to medium-low.) Increase the heat to medium-low and add the shrimp with the marinade to the pan in a single layer. Cook the shrimp, undisturbed, until the oil starts to gently bubble, about 2 minutes. Using tongs, flip the shrimp and continue to cook until almost cooked through, about 2 minutes longer. Increase the heat to high and add the sherry vinegar and parsley. Cook, stirring constantly, until the shrimp are cooked through and the oil is bubbling vigorously, 15 to 20 seconds. Serve immediately, discarding the bay leaf.

GREEK SHRIMP

WHY THIS RECIPE WORKS: We can think of few examples where the unlikely combination of seafood and cheese marry as well as in Greece's shrimp *saganaki*. In this dish, sweet, briny shrimp are covered with a garlic-and-herb accented tomato sauce and topped with crumbles of creamy, salty feta cheese. Ordering this dish at a restaurant, however, can be a gamble. The shrimp can be tough and rubbery, the tomato sauce can turn out dull or overwhelming, and the feta can be lackluster. We set out to develop a foolproof version of this dish—one that is perfectly cooked and captures the bold and exuberant essence of Greek cuisine.

We started with the tomato sauce. Canned diced tomatoes along with sautéed onion and garlic provided our base. Dry white wine added acidity. Ouzo, the slightly sweet anise-flavored Greek liqueur, added welcome complexity when we simmered it in the sauce.

While the shrimp are typically layered with the tomato sauce and feta and baked, we found this method lacking. Since this should be a quick and easy dish, we opted to cook the shrimp right in the sauce; adding the shrimp raw to the sauce helped infuse them with the sauce's bright flavor. And for even more flavor, we marinated the shrimp with olive oil, ouzo, garlic, and lemon zest first while we made the sauce. Final touches included a generous sprinkling of feta over the sauced shrimp as well as a scattering of chopped fresh dill.

Greek-Style Shrimp with Tomatoes and Feta

SERVES 4 TO 6

This recipe works equally well with either jumbo shrimp (16 to 20 per pound) or extra-large shrimp (21 to 25 per pound); the cooking times in step 3 will vary slightly. Serve with crusty bread for soaking up the sauce.

1½ pounds shrimp, peeled and deveined (see page 205), tails left on, if desired (see note)
4 tablespoons extra-virgin olive oil
3 tablespoons ouzo
5 medium garlic cloves, minced or pressed through a garlic press (about 5 teaspoons)
1 teaspoon grated zest from 1 lemon
   Table salt and ground black pepper
1 small onion, diced medium
½ medium red bell pepper, stemmed, seeded, and diced medium
½ medium green bell pepper, stemmed, seeded, and diced medium
½ teaspoon red pepper flakes
1 (28-ounce) can diced tomatoes, drained, ⅓ cup juice reserved
¼ cup dry white wine
2 tablespoons coarsely chopped fresh parsley leaves
6 ounces feta cheese, preferably sheep's and/or goat's milk, crumbled (about 1½ cups)
2 tablespoons chopped fresh dill

1. Toss the shrimp, 1 tablespoon of the oil, 1 tablespoon of the ouzo, 1 teaspoon of the garlic, the lemon zest, ¼ teaspoon salt, and ⅛ teaspoon black pepper in a small bowl until well combined. Set aside while preparing the sauce.

2. Heat 2 tablespoons more oil in a 12-inch skillet over medium heat until shimmering. Add the onion, red and green bell peppers, and ¼ teaspoon salt and stir to combine. Cover the skillet and cook, stirring occasionally, until the vegetables release their moisture, 3 to 5 minutes. Uncover and continue to cook, stirring occasionally, until the moisture cooks off and the vegetables have softened, about 5 minutes longer. Add the remaining 4 teaspoons garlic and the red pepper flakes and cook until fragrant, about 1 minute. Add the tomatoes and reserved juice, the wine, and the remaining 2 tablespoons ouzo; increase the heat to medium-high and bring to a simmer. Reduce the heat to medium and simmer, stirring occasionally, until the flavors have melded and the sauce is slightly thickened (the sauce should not be completely dry), 5 to 8 minutes. Stir in the parsley and season with salt and pepper to taste.

3. Reduce the heat to medium-low and add the shrimp along with any accumulated liquid to the pan; stir to coat and distribute evenly. Cover and cook, stirring occasionally, until the shrimp are opaque throughout, 6 to 9 minutes for extra-large shrimp or 7 to 11 minutes for jumbo shrimp, adjusting the heat as needed to maintain a bare simmer. Remove the pan from the heat and sprinkle evenly with the feta. Drizzle the remaining 1 tablespoon oil evenly over the top and sprinkle with the dill. Serve immediately.

SHRIMP COCKTAIL

WHY THIS RECIPE WORKS: Nothing is more basic than shrimp cocktail and, given its simplicity, few dishes are more difficult to improve. Yet we set out to do just that, seeing three ways in which we might challenge tradition: work on the flavor of the shrimp, work on the cooking method for the shrimp, and produce a great cocktail sauce.

Shrimp cook very quickly, so there's little time to add flavor to them in the pan. We based our cooking liquid on shrimp stock, easily made by boiling the shells, and added wine, lemon juice, and herbs and spices. To keep the shrimp in contact with this flavorful liquid as long as possible without overcooking them, we brought the mixture to a boil, turned off the heat, and only then added the shrimp; the hot liquid cooked the shrimp slowly while they absorbed flavor from the stock. Turning to the sauce, we determined that the classic base, ketchup, is the best. We added horseradish, which is the usual ingredient for spicing up the sauce, but we also included chili powder, cayenne, and lemon juice for extra spiciness.

Shrimp Cocktail

SERVES 4

When using larger or smaller shrimp, increase or decrease, respectively, the cooking times for the shrimp by one to two minutes. When using such large shrimp, we find it wise to remove the large black vein. Use horseradish from a freshly opened bottle and mild chili powder for the best flavor in the sauce.

SHRIMP

  1   pound jumbo shrimp (16 to 20 per pound; see note), peeled, deveined (see page 205), and shells reserved
  1   teaspoon table salt
  1   cup dry white wine
  4   peppercorns
  5   coriander seeds
  ½   bay leaf
  5   sprigs fresh parsley
  1   sprig fresh tarragon
  1   teaspoon juice from 1 lemon

COCKTAIL SAUCE

  1   cup ketchup
  1   tablespoon juice from 1 small lemon
  2½ teaspoons prepared horseradish (see note)
  1   teaspoon ancho or other mild chili powder (see note)
      Pinch cayenne pepper
      Table salt and ground black pepper

1. FOR THE SHRIMP: Bring the reserved shells, 3 cups water, and salt to a boil in a medium saucepan over medium-high heat; reduce the heat to low, cover, and simmer until fragrant, about 20 minutes. Strain the stock through a fine-mesh strainer, pressing on the shells to extract all the liquid.

2. Bring the stock and remaining ingredients except the shrimp to a boil in a 3- or 4-quart saucepan over high heat; boil for 2 minutes. Turn off the heat and stir in the shrimp; cover and let stand until the shrimp are firm and pink, 8 to 10 minutes. Meanwhile, fill a large bowl with ice water. Drain the shrimp, reserving the stock for another use. Immediately transfer the shrimp to the ice water to stop cooking and chill thoroughly, about 3 minutes. Remove the shrimp from the ice water and pat dry with paper towels.

3. FOR THE SAUCE: Stir all the ingredients together in a small bowl; season with salt and pepper to taste. Serve the chilled shrimp with the cocktail sauce.

BETTER SHRIMP SALAD

WHY THIS RECIPE WORKS: Most shrimp salads drown in a sea of mayonnaise, in part to hide the rubbery, flavorless boiled shrimp. We wanted perfectly cooked shrimp without the extra work of grilling, roasting, or sautéing. And we needed to coat them with the perfect deli-style dressing—something creamy but not overwhelming.

Overcooking is the culprit when shrimp turn out rubbery. We found that starting the shrimp in cold water (with lemon, parsley, tarragon, pepper, sugar, and salt), then cooking them over very gentle heat, resulted in tender shrimp. The longer cooking time infused the shrimp with the flavors of the poached liquid. We didn't want to mask these tender, flavorful shrimp with too much dressing, so we scaled back the mayonnaise to a modest amount. Celery added a nice crunch, and shallot, herbs, and lemon juice perked up and rounded out the flavors.

Shrimp Salad

SERVES 4

This recipe can also be prepared with large shrimp (31 to 40 per pound); the cooking time will be 1 to 2 minutes shorter. The shrimp can be cooked up to 24 hours in advance, but hold off on dressing the salad until ready to serve. The recipe can be easily doubled; cook the shrimp in a 7-quart Dutch oven and increase the cooking time to 12 to 14 minutes. Serve the salad spooned over salad greens or on buttered and grilled buns.

  1   pound extra-large shrimp (21 to 25 per pound; see note), peeled and deveined (see page 205)
  ¼   cup plus 1 tablespoon juice from 2 to 3 lemons, spent halves reserved

5 sprigs fresh parsley plus 1 teaspoon minced fresh
  parsley leaves
3 sprigs fresh tarragon plus 1 teaspoon minced fresh
  tarragon leaves
1 teaspoon whole black peppercorns plus ground
  black pepper
1 tablespoon sugar
  Table salt
¼ cup mayonnaise
1 small celery rib, minced (about ⅓ cup)
1 small shallot, minced (about 1 tablespoon)

1. Combine the shrimp, ¼ cup of the lemon juice, the reserved lemon halves, parsley sprigs, tarragon sprigs, whole peppercorns, sugar, and 1 teaspoon salt with 2 cups cold water in a medium saucepan. Place the saucepan over medium heat and cook the shrimp, stirring several times, until pink, firm to the touch, and the centers are no longer translucent, 8 to 10 minutes (the water should be just bubbling around the edge of the pan and register 165 degrees on an instant-read thermometer). Remove the pan from the heat, cover, and let the shrimp sit in the broth for 2 minutes.

2. Meanwhile, fill a medium bowl with ice water. Drain the shrimp into a colander and discard the lemon halves, herbs, and spices. Immediately transfer the shrimp to the ice water to stop the cooking and chill thoroughly, about 3 minutes. Remove the shrimp from the ice water and pat dry with paper towels.

3. Whisk together the mayonnaise, celery, shallot, remaining 1 tablespoon lemon juice, the minced parsley, and minced tarragon in a medium bowl. Cut the shrimp in half lengthwise and then each half into thirds; add the shrimp to the mayonnaise mixture and toss to combine. Season with salt and pepper to taste and serve.

Shrimp Salad with Roasted Red Pepper and Basil

This Italian-style variation is especially good served over bitter greens.

Follow the recipe for Shrimp Salad, omitting the tarragon sprigs from the cooking liquid. Replace the celery, minced parsley, and minced tarragon with ⅓ cup thinly sliced jarred roasted red peppers, 2 teaspoons rinsed capers, and 3 tablespoons chopped fresh basil leaves.

Shrimp Salad with Avocado and Orange

Avocado and orange are a refreshing addition to this salad.

Follow the recipe for Shrimp Salad, omitting the tarragon sprigs from the cooking liquid. Replace the celery, minced parsley, and minced tarragon with 4 halved and thinly sliced radishes; 1 large orange, peeled and cut into ½-inch pieces; ½ ripe avocado, cut into ½-inch pieces; and 2 teaspoons minced fresh mint leaves.

FLAMBÉED PAN-ROASTED LOBSTER

WHY THIS RECIPE WORKS: Boiling and steaming are the usual ways of preparing lobster, and they're just fine. But we wanted an alternative cooking method that would be even tastier, and we didn't want to spend a whole lot more time in the kitchen. Our solution was a restaurant dish adapted for home cooking.

The New England restaurant chef Jasper White created a pan-roasted lobster dish that we took as our starting point. We quartered the lobsters and tossed them into a very hot skillet—shells down, so the meat wouldn't overcook—to pan-roast. The heat roasted the shells and permeated the lobster meat with intense flavor. To cook the exposed meat, we put the skillet under the broiler, returning it to the stovetop when the meat was cooked through. Now came the fun part: We flambéed the lobster with bourbon (carefully, of course!). A quick pan sauce, made in the skillet after we removed the lobsters, was the final touch; we used shallots, white wine, herbs, and, for unusual and intense flavor, the lobster tomalley. This way of cooking lobsters is a little more trouble than dunking them in a pot of boiling water, but we think the results are well worth it.

Flambéed Pan-Roasted Lobster
SERVES 2

If you want to prepare more than two lobsters, we suggest that you engage some help. This dish requires close attention, and managing multiple extremely hot pans can be tricky. Before flambéing, make sure to roll up long shirtsleeves, tie back long hair, turn off the exhaust fan (otherwise the fan may pull up the flames), and turn off any lit burners (this is critical if you have a gas stove). For equipment, you will need a large ovensafe skillet, oven mitts, a pair of tongs, and long fireplace or grill matches.

2 (1½ to 2-pound) live lobsters
2 tablespoons peanut or canola oil
¼ cup bourbon or cognac
6 tablespoons (¾ stick) unsalted butter, cut into 6 pieces
2 medium shallots, minced (about 6 tablespoons)
3 tablespoons dry white wine
1 teaspoon minced fresh tarragon leaves
1 tablespoon minced fresh chives
  Table salt and ground black pepper
  Lemon wedges, for serving (optional)

1. Following the photos, use a large heavy-duty chef's knife to quarter the lobsters. (Don't be put off if the lobsters continue to twitch a little after quartering; it's a reflexive movement.)

2. Adjust an oven rack so it is 6 inches from the broiler element and heat the broiler. Heat the peanut oil in a large ovensafe skillet over high heat until smoking. Add the lobster pieces, shell-side down, in a single layer and cook, without disturbing, until the shells are bright red and lightly browned, 2 to 3 minutes. Transfer the skillet to the broiler and cook until the tail meat is just opaque, about 2 minutes.

3. Carefully remove the pan from the oven and return it to the stovetop. Off the heat, pour the bourbon over the lobsters. Wait for 10 seconds, then light a long match and wave it over the skillet until the bourbon ignites. Return the pan to medium-high heat and shake it until the flames subside. Transfer the lobster pieces to a warmed serving bowl and tent with foil to keep warm.

4. Using tongs, remove any congealed albumen (white substance) from the skillet and add 2 tablespoons of the butter and the shallots. Cook, stirring constantly, until the shallots are softened and lightly browned, 1 to 2 minutes. Add the tomalley (if using) and white wine and stir until completely combined. Remove the skillet from the heat and add the tarragon and chives. Stirring constantly, add the remaining 4 tablespoons butter, 1 piece at a time, until fully emulsified. Season with salt and pepper to taste. Pour the sauce over the lobster pieces. Serve immediately, accompanied by the lemon wedges, if desired.

NOTES FROM THE TEST KITCHEN

PREPARING LOBSTER FOR PAN-ROASTING

1. Plunge a chef's knife into the body at the point where the shell forms a "T" to kill the lobster. Move the blade straight down through the head. (Freezing the lobster for 5 to 10 minutes first will sedate it.)

2. Turn the lobster around and, while holding the upper body with one hand, cut through the body toward the tail.

3. Remove and discard the stomach and intestinal tract. Reserve the green tomalley for the sauce, if desired.

4. Cut the tail from the body.

5. Twist off the claws from the body. Remove the rubber bands from the claws. (Don't be put off if the lobster continues to twitch a little; it's a reflexive movement.)

1 pound fresh jumbo lump crabmeat, carefully picked over to remove cartilage and shell fragments (see note)
4 scallions, green parts only, minced (about ½ cup)
1 tablespoon chopped fresh herb, such as cilantro, dill, basil, or parsley
1½ teaspoons Old Bay seasoning
2–4 tablespoons plain dry bread crumbs (see note)
¼ cup mayonnaise
 Table salt and ground white pepper
1 large egg
¼ cup unbleached all-purpose flour
¼ cup vegetable oil
 Sweet and Tangy Tartar Sauce (page 191), Creamy Chipotle Chile Sauce (recipe follows), or lemon wedges

MARYLAND CRAB CAKES

WHY THIS RECIPE WORKS: Making crab cakes at home is the only way to avoid the pricey crab-flecked dough balls that pass for crab cakes in many restaurants. We wanted cakes with a crisp brown exterior and creamy, well-seasoned filling that tasted of sweet crab, not filler.

Fresh crabmeat provided superior taste and texture, and we think jumbo lump crabmeat is worth the high price tag. Pasteurized crabmeat is not quite as good, but it is less expensive. At all costs, avoid the canned crabmeat sold near canned tuna. After experimenting with different binders, we settled on fine dry bread crumbs; their flavor is mild, they held the cakes together well, and they mixed easily with the crab. We used just a few tablespoons of crumbs so that the crab's flavor and texture would shine. An egg and some mayonnaise bound the cakes together. Old Bay is the traditional seasoning for crab; some herbs and white pepper were the only additions we found necessary. Carefully folding the ingredients together rather than stirring them kept the texture chunky rather than pasty, and a short chilling in the refrigerator ensured that the cakes wouldn't fall apart. Pan-frying in vegetable oil gave our crab cakes the crisp exterior we wanted, and the interior tasted intensely of crab.

Maryland Crab Cakes

SERVES 4

The amount of bread crumbs you add will depend on the crabmeat's juiciness. Start with the smallest amount, adjust the seasonings, then add the egg. If the cakes won't bind at this point, add more bread crumbs, 1 tablespoon at a time. If you can't find fresh jumbo lump crabmeat, pasteurized crabmeat, though not as good, is a decent substitute. Either a nonstick or a traditional skillet will work for this recipe, but a nonstick simplifies cleanup.

1. Gently mix the crabmeat, scallions, herb, Old Bay, 2 tablespoons of the bread crumbs, and the mayonnaise in a medium bowl, being careful not to break up the lumps of crab. Season with salt and white pepper to taste. Carefully fold in the egg with a rubber spatula until the mixture just clings together. Add more bread crumbs if necessary.

2. Divide the crab mixture into four portions and shape each into a fat, round cake, about 3 inches across and 1½ inches high. Arrange the cakes on a baking sheet lined with waxed or parchment paper; cover with plastic wrap and chill for at least 30 minutes. (The crab cakes can be refrigerated for up to 24 hours.)

3. Place the flour in a pie plate. Lightly dredge the crab cakes in the flour. Heat the oil in a large skillet over medium-high heat until hot but not smoking. Gently place the chilled crab cakes in the skillet; pan-fry until the outsides are crisp and browned, 4 to 5 minutes per side. Serve immediately with a sauce or lemon wedges.

Creamy Chipotle Chile Sauce

MAKES ABOUT ½ CUP

The addition of sour cream makes this sauce richer than traditional tartar sauce. The chipotles add smoky and spicy flavors.

¼ cup mayonnaise
¼ cup sour cream
2 teaspoons canned minced chipotle chiles in adobo sauce
1 small garlic clove, minced or pressed through a garlic press (about ½ teaspoon)
2 teaspoons minced fresh cilantro leaves
1 teaspoon juice from 1 lime

Mix all of the ingredients in a small bowl. Cover and refrigerate until the flavors blend, about 30 minutes. (The sauce can be refrigerated for up to 2 days.)

CRAB TOWERS WITH AVOCADO AND GAZPACHO SALSA

WHY THIS RECIPE WORKS: Sometimes a dish served in a restaurant is so delicious and impressive-looking that we just have to try to make it ourselves. A crab salad molded into towers, from the Mayflower Park Hotel in Seattle, is one such dish, but a hotel restaurant can easily handle the recipe's 35 ingredients. Was there a way to re-create the flavors and presentation at home, with fewer ingredients and a lot less effort?

By breaking down the recipe for this appetizer into its components—crab salad, avocado–hearts of palm salsa, and gazpacho salsa—we were able to address each one separately. For the crab salad, we used lump crabmeat mixed with a little mayonnaise and champagne vinaigrette. We eliminated the hearts of palm from the salsa; it was impossible to find any that tasted decent, and tasters felt the avocado alone worked quite well. For the gazpacho salsa, we used only one kind of bell pepper rather than two and omitted the diced lime and orange segments that were in the original recipe; we also cut back on some of the seasonings, limiting ourselves to sherry vinegar and olive oil. Garnishes were simplified to frisée and orange segments. Now that we'd streamlined the components, we had to assemble the dish. The restaurant uses timbale rings, but we found our workaday biscuit cutter did the job just fine.

Crab Towers with Avocado and Gazpacho Salsas

SERVES 6

You can prepare the crabmeat salad and gazpacho salsa several hours ahead of serving, but the avocado salsa should be prepared just before assembly.

CRABMEAT SALAD

- 3 tablespoons extra-virgin olive oil
- 1 tablespoon champagne vinegar
- 1 teaspoon minced or grated lemon zest
- ½ teaspoon Dijon mustard
- ½ teaspoon table salt
- ⅛ teaspoon ground black pepper
- 2 tablespoons mayonnaise
- 12 ounces lump or backfin Atlantic blue crabmeat, carefully picked over to remove cartilage and shell fragments

GAZPACHO SALSA

- 1 small yellow bell pepper, cored, seeded, and cut into ⅛-inch pieces (about ½ cup)
- ½ small cucumber, peeled if desired, seeded, and cut into ⅛-inch pieces (about ½ cup)
- 1 medium plum tomato, cored, seeded, and cut into ⅛-inch pieces (about ½ cup)
- 1 small celery rib, cut into ⅛-inch pieces (about ½ cup)
- ½ small red onion, minced (about ¼ cup)
- ½ small jalapeño chile, stemmed, seeded, and minced
- 1 tablespoon minced fresh cilantro leaves
- 2 tablespoons extra-virgin olive oil
- 1 tablespoon sherry vinegar
- ¾ teaspoon table salt
- ¼ teaspoon ground black pepper

AVOCADO SALSA

- 3 ripe avocados, pitted, peed, and cut into ¼-inch dice (see page 348)
- 2 tablespoons juice from 1 lime
- ¼ teaspoon ground coriander
- ½ teaspoon table salt
- ⅛ teaspoon ground black pepper

GARNISH

- 1 cup frisée
- 2 oranges, peeled using a paring knife and segmented (see page 214; optional)

1. FOR THE CRABMEAT SALAD: Whisk the olive oil, champagne vinegar, lemon zest, mustard, salt, and pepper together in a small bowl. Measure 3 tablespoons of the vinaigrette into a medium bowl and mix with the mayonnaise.

SEGMENTING ORANGES

1. Start by slicing a ½-inch piece from the top and bottom of the orange. With the fruit resting flat against a work surface, use a very sharp paring knife to slice off the rind, including the white pith.

2. Slip the knife blade between a membrane and one section of the fruit and slice to the center. Turn the blade so that it is facing out and slide the blade from the center out along the membrane to completely free the section.

ASSEMBLING CRAB TOWERS

1. Place the biscuit cutter in the center of the plate and, using the back of a soup spoon, press ⅓ cup of the Avocado Salsa evenly into the cutter. Lift the cutter off the plate slightly to reveal some but not all of the avocado.

2. Holding the cutter aloft, press ⅓ cup of the Crabmeat Salad evenly into the cutter, on top of the avocado. Lift the cutter farther off the plate and press ⅓ cup of the Gazpacho Salsa evenly into the cutter, on top of the crab.

3. Gently lift the cutter up and away from the plate to reveal the crab tower. Repeat with the remaining salsas and crabmeat salad.

Add the crabmeat to the mayonnaise mixture and toss to coat. Cover with plastic wrap and refrigerate until needed. Set the remaining vinaigrette aside.

2. FOR THE GAZPACHO SALSA: Toss the bell pepper, cucumber, tomato, celery, red onion, jalapeño, cilantro, olive oil, sherry vinegar, salt, and pepper in a medium bowl and set aside.

3. FOR THE AVOCADO SALSA: Toss the avocados, lime juice, coriander, salt, and pepper in a medium bowl and set aside.

4. TO ASSEMBLE: Place a 3-inch-wide round biscuit cutter in the center of an individual plate. Following the photos, press ⅓ cup of the Avocado Salsa into the bottom of the cutter using the back of a soup spoon. Lift the cutter off the plate slightly to reveal some but not all of the avocado. Holding the cutter aloft, press ⅓ cup of the Crabmeat Salad evenly into the cutter on top of the avocado. Lift the cutter further to reveal some but not all of the crab salad. Holding the cutter aloft, use a soup spoon to press ⅓ cup of the Gazpacho Salsa evenly into the cutter on top of the crab. Gently lift the cutter up and away from the plate to reveal the crab tower. Repeat the procedure five more times with the remaining ingredients.

5. Dress the frisée with the remaining champagne vinaigrette. Place a few sprigs of the dressed frisée on top of each crab tower and arrange the orange segments (if using) around the towers. Serve immediately.

INDOOR CLAMBAKE

WHY THIS RECIPE WORKS: A clambake is perhaps the ultimate seafood meal: clams, mussels, and lobster, nestled with sausage, corn, and potatoes, all steamed together with hot stones in a sand pit by the sea. A genuine clambake is an all-day affair and, of course, requires a beach. But we wanted to re-create the great flavors of the clambake indoors, so we could enjoy this flavorful feast without hours of preparation.

A large stockpot was the cooking vessel of choice. Many recipes suggest cooking the ingredients separately before adding them to the pot, but we found that with careful layering, we could cook everything in the same pot and have it all finish at the same time. And we didn't need to add water, because the shellfish released enough liquid to steam everything else. Sliced sausage went into the pot first (we liked kielbasa), so that it could sear before the steam was generated. Clams and mussels were next, wrapped in cheesecloth for easy removal. Then in went the potatoes, which would take the longest to cook; they were best placed near the heat source, and we cut them into 1-inch pieces to cook more quickly. Corn, with the husks left on to protect it from seafood flavors and lobster foam, was next, followed by the lobsters. It took less than half an hour for everything to cook—and we had all the elements of a clambake (minus the sand and surf) without having spent all day preparing them.

Indoor Clambake

SERVES 4 TO 6

Choose a large, narrow stockpot in which you can easily layer the ingredients. The recipe can be cut in half and layered in an 8-quart Dutch oven, but it should cook for the same amount of time. We prefer small littlenecks for this recipe. If your market carries larger clams, use 4 pounds. Mussels often contain a weedy beard protruding from the crack between the two shells. It's fairly small and can be difficult to tug out of place. To remove it easily, trap the beard between the side of a small paring knife and your thumb and pull to remove it. The flat surface of the knife gives you some leverage to remove the beard.

- 2 **pounds small littleneck or cherrystone clams, scrubbed (see note)**
- 2 **pounds mussels, shells scrubbed and beards removed (see note)**
- 1 **pound kielbasa, sliced into ⅓-inch-thick rounds**
- 1 **pound small new or red potatoes, scrubbed and cut into 1-inch pieces**
- 6 **medium ears corn, silk and all but the last layer of husk removed**
- 2 **(1½-pound) live lobsters**
- 8 **tablespoons (1 stick) salted butter, melted**

1. Place the clams and mussels on a large piece of cheesecloth and tie the ends together to secure; set aside. In a heavy-bottomed 12-quart stockpot, layer the sliced kielbasa, the sack of clams and mussels, the potatoes, the corn, and the lobsters on top of one another. Cover with the lid and place over high heat. Cook until the potatoes are tender (a paring knife can be slipped into and out of the center of a potato with little resistance), and the lobsters are bright red, 17 to 20 minutes.

2. Remove the pot from the heat and remove the lid (watch out for scalding steam). Remove the lobsters and set aside until cool enough to handle. Remove the corn from the pot and peel off the husks; arrange the ears on a large platter. Using a slotted spoon, remove the potatoes and arrange them on the platter with the corn. Transfer the clams and mussels to a large bowl and cut open the cheesecloth with scissors. Using a slotted spoon, remove the kielbasa from the pot and arrange it on the platter with the potatoes and corn. Pour the remaining steaming liquid in the pot over the clams and mussels. Using a kitchen towel to protect your hand, twist and remove the lobster tails, claws, and legs (if desired). Arrange the lobster parts on the platter. Serve immediately with the melted butter and napkins.

CHAPTER 11

DINNER AT THE DINER

Classic Tuna Salad 218

Tuna Salad with Balsamic Vinegar and Grapes 218

Curried Tuna Salad with Apples and Currants 218

Tuna Salad with Lime and Horseradish 218

Classic Grilled Cheese Sandwiches 219

Classic Macaroni and Cheese 220

Stovetop Macaroni and Cheese 221

Light Macaroni and Cheese 222

Turkey Tetrazzini 222

Cincinnati Chili 224

Chicken-Fried Steaks 225

Glazed All-Beef Meat Loaf 226

Meat Loaf with Brown Sugar–Ketchup Glaze 227

Classic Stuffed Bell Peppers 228

Best Old-Fashioned Burgers 229

Classic Burger Sauce

Juicy Pub-Style Burgers 231

Pub-Style Burger Sauce

Juicy Pub-Style Burgers with Crispy Shallots and Blue Cheese

Juicy Pub-Style Burgers with Peppered Bacon and Aged Cheddar

Juicy Pub-Style Burgers with Sautéed Onions and Smoked Cheddar

Juicy Pub-Style Burgers with Pan-Roasted Mushrooms and Gruyère

Oven-Fried Onion Rings 232

Steak Fries 233

Classic French Fries 234

Easier French Fries 235

Chive and Black Pepper Dipping Sauce

Belgian-Style Dipping Sauce

TUNA SALAD SANDWICHES

WHY THIS RECIPE WORKS: Tuna salads have been given a bad name by their typically mushy, watery, and bland condition. We wanted a tuna salad that was evenly textured, moist, and well seasoned.

We learned that there are three keys to a great tuna salad. The first is to drain the tuna thoroughly in a colander; don't just tip the water out of the can. Next, instead of using a fork, break up the tuna with your fingers for a finer, more even texture. Finally, season the tuna before adding the mayonnaise for maximum flavor. Some additions to tuna salad are a matter of taste, but we thought that small amounts of garlic and mustard added another dimension, and minced pickle was a piquant touch. In addition to classic tuna salad, we developed a few variations that include tuna with balsamic vinegar and grapes, another with curry and apples, and a third with lime and horseradish.

Classic Tuna Salad

MAKES ABOUT 2 CUPS, ENOUGH FOR 4 SANDWICHES

Our favorite canned tuna is Wild Planet Wild Albacore. For more information on why we like this brand, see page 754.

- 2 (6-ounce) cans solid white tuna in water (see note)
- 1 small celery rib, minced (about ¼ cup)
- 2 tablespoons juice from 1 lemon
- 2 tablespoons minced red onion
- 2 tablespoons minced dill or sweet pickles
- 2 tablespoons minced fresh parsley leaves
- ½ small garlic clove, minced or pressed through a garlic press (about ½ teaspoon)
- ½ teaspoon table salt
- ¼ teaspoon ground black pepper
- ½ cup mayonnaise
- ¼ teaspoon Dijon mustard

Drain the tuna in a colander and shred with your fingers until no clumps remain and the texture is fine and even. Transfer the tuna to a medium bowl and mix in the celery, lemon juice, onion, pickles, parsley, garlic, salt, and pepper until evenly blended. Fold in the mayonnaise and mustard until the tuna is evenly moistened. (The tuna salad can be refrigerated in an airtight container for up to 3 days.)

Tuna Salad with Balsamic Vinegar and Grapes

Follow the recipe for Classic Tuna Salad, omitting the lemon juice, pickles, garlic, and parsley and adding 2 tablespoons balsamic vinegar, 6 ounces halved red seedless grapes (about 1 cup), ¼ cup lightly toasted slivered almonds, and 2 teaspoons minced thyme leaves to the tuna along with the salt and pepper.

Curried Tuna Salad with Apples and Currants

Follow the recipe for Classic Tuna Salad, omitting the pickles, garlic, and parsley and adding 1 medium firm, juicy apple, cut into ¼-inch dice (about 1 cup), ¼ cup currants, and 2 tablespoons minced fresh basil leaves to the tuna along with the lemon juice, salt, and pepper; mix 1 tablespoon curry powder into the mayonnaise before folding into the tuna.

Tuna Salad with Lime and Horseradish

Follow the recipe for Classic Tuna Salad, omitting the lemon juice, pickles, and garlic and adding 2 tablespoons juice and ½ teaspoon grated zest from 1 lime and 3 tablespoons prepared horseradish to the tuna along with the salt and pepper.

GRILLED CHEESE SANDWICHES

WHY THIS RECIPE WORKS: The perfect grilled cheese sandwich consists of evenly melted cheese between slices of lacy-crisp, buttery bread, but most don't turn out that way. We set out to find the keys to getting that ideal sandwich every time.

Cutting slices from a block of cheese often produces uneven, scraggly pieces. We found that grating the cheese on a box grater enabled us to get an even layer of cheese onto the bread. Butter melted in the pan sometimes burned and didn't always coat the bread evenly, so we opted to butter the bread rather than the pan. And to coat the bread evenly and prevent it from tearing, we melted the butter first. Finally, we learned that the secret of a crisp exterior is low heat; the longer it takes for the bread to become golden, the crispier the bread will become—these are grilled cheese sandwiches worth the wait.

Classic Grilled Cheese Sandwiches
SERVES 2

The traditional grilled cheese sandwich usually uses a mild cheddar cheese, but our technique for this sandwich works with most any cheese. Grilled cheese sandwiches are best served hot out of the pan, though in a pinch they can be held, unsliced, for up to 20 minutes in a warm oven. If you want to make more than two sandwiches at once, get two skillets going or use an electric griddle set at medium-low (about 250 degrees), grilling 10 minutes per side. The possible variations on the basic grilled cheese sandwich are endless, but the extras are best sandwiched between the cheese. Try a few very thin slices of baked ham, prosciutto, turkey breast, or ripe, in-season tomato. Condiments such as Dijon mustard, pickle relish, or chutney can be spread on the bread instead of sandwiched in the cheese.

- **3** ounces cheese (preferably mild cheddar) or a combination of cheeses, shredded on the large holes of a box grater (about ¾ cup; see note)
- **4** slices high-quality white sandwich bread
- **2** tablespoons unsalted butter, melted

BEHIND THE SCENES

COOKS WHO CAN MAKE THE CUT

Our recipes are created by a team of test cooks—more than three dozen cooks in total—who spend their day mincing, roasting, tasting, and talking about food. So what does it take to join our army of test cooks? It goes without saying that you must love to cook. Everyone in the test kitchen has professional cooking experience (this usually includes work in a restaurant kitchen as well as a degree from one of the top cooking schools in the country). But in-depth food knowledge and cooking skills are just a start.

To get hired, you must have a passion for understanding how things work in the kitchen. A curious mind is essential, as are attention to detail and a scientific approach to problem solving. Our test cooks are continually developing hypotheses to explain how a recipe works and then devising a testing protocol to prove (or disprove) their theory. Finally, we look for cooks who understand the realities of cooking at home—with imperfect equipment, the usual distractions (kids, pets, and phone calls), and no one to wash the dishes.

So how do we find test cooks? Our test kitchen director, Erin McMurrer, has developed a bench test for potential hires—it's like an audition, with knives. Erin gives potential hires two of our published recipes and watches them as they set to work preparing them. Chop those onions when the recipe says to mince them, and you're in trouble. Use a dry measuring cup to measure milk, and you're in serious trouble. Shape cookie dough into ½-inch balls when the recipe says 1-inch balls, and you're in very serious trouble. But job candidates can save the day when the cooking is done and Erin asks them to analyze their success and failures during the bench test. A candidate who can thoughtfully examine his or her work (and figure out how to remedy problems) might just make the cut.

1. Heat a heavy 12-inch skillet over low to medium-low heat. Meanwhile, sprinkle the cheese evenly over two bread slices. Top each with a remaining bread slice, pressing down gently to set.

2. Brush the sandwich tops completely with half of the melted butter; place each sandwich, buttered side down, in the skillet. Brush the remaining side of each sandwich completely with the remaining butter. Cook until crisp and deep golden brown, 5 to 10 minutes per side, flipping the sandwiches back to the first side to reheat and crisp, about 15 seconds. Serve immediately.

CLASSIC MACARONI AND CHEESE

WHY THIS RECIPE WORKS: Old-fashioned macaroni and cheese takes no shortcuts. This family favorite should boast tender pasta in a smooth, creamy sauce with great cheese flavor. Too often, the dish, which is baked in the oven, dries out or curdles. We aimed to create a foolproof version.

We cooked the pasta until just past al dente and then combined it with a béchamel-based cheese sauce. For best flavor and a creamy texture, we used a combination of sharp cheddar and Monterey Jack. We combined the cooked pasta with the sauce and heated it through on the stovetop, rather than in the oven. This step helped ensure the dish didn't dry out, but remained smooth and creamy. And to give the dish a browned topping, we sprinkled it with bread crumbs and ran it briefly under the broiler.

Classic Macaroni and Cheese

SERVES 6 TO 8

It's crucial to cook the pasta until tender—that is, just past the al dente stage. Whole, low-fat, and skim milk all work well in this recipe. The recipe may be halved and baked in an 8-inch square, broiler-safe baking dish. If desired, offer celery salt or hot sauce for sprinkling at the table.

BREAD-CRUMB TOPPING
- **6** slices high-quality white sandwich bread, torn into quarters
- **3** tablespoons cold unsalted butter, cut into 6 pieces

MACARONI AND CHEESE
- **1** tablespoon plus 1 teaspoon table salt
- **1** pound elbow macaroni
- **5** tablespoons unsalted butter
- **6** tablespoons unbleached all-purpose flour
- **1½** teaspoons dry mustard
- **¼** teaspoon cayenne pepper (optional)
- **5** cups milk (see note)
- **8** ounces Monterey Jack cheese, shredded (about 2 cups)
- **8** ounces sharp cheddar cheese, shredded (about 2 cups)

1. FOR THE BREAD CRUMBS: Pulse the bread and butter in a food processor until coarsely ground, 10 to 15 pulses. Set aside.

2. FOR THE MACARONI AND CHEESE: Adjust an oven rack to the lower-middle position and heat the broiler. Bring 4 quarts water to a rolling boil in a large pot. Add 1 tablespoon of the salt and the macaroni and stir to separate the noodles. Cook until tender, drain, and set aside.

3. In the now-empty pot, melt the butter over medium-high heat. Add the flour, mustard, cayenne (if using), and remaining 1 teaspoon salt and whisk well to combine. Continue whisking until the mixture becomes fragrant and deepens in color, about 1 minute. Whisking constantly, gradually add the milk; bring the mixture to a boil, whisking constantly (the mixture must reach a full boil to fully thicken), then reduce the heat to medium and simmer, whisking occasionally, until thickened to the consistency of heavy cream, about 5 minutes. Off the heat, whisk in the cheeses until fully melted. Add the pasta and cook over medium-low heat, stirring constantly, until the mixture is steaming and heated through, about 6 minutes.

4. Transfer the mixture to a broiler-safe 13 by 9-inch baking dish and sprinkle with the bread crumbs. Broil until deep golden brown, 3 to 5 minutes. Cool for 5 minutes, then serve.

STOVETOP MACARONI AND CHEESE

WHY THIS RECIPE WORKS: Just about the only thing boxed macaroni and cheese has going for it is its fast prep—and the fact that kids will almost always gobble it up. We wanted a quick stovetop macaroni and cheese with an ultra-creamy texture and authentic cheese flavor—so good that it would satisfy everyone at the table.

We cooked the macaroni to just shy of al dente, then drained and combined it with butter and an egg custard mixture that included evaporated milk, eggs, hot sauce, and dry mustard. For the cheese we chose cheddar, American, or Monterey Jack—and plenty of it. We stirred the cheese into the macaroni mixture until thick and creamy and then topped the mixture with toasted homemade bread crumbs—the final touch to this easy-to-prepare family favorite.

Stovetop Macaroni and Cheese

SERVES 4

If you're in a hurry or prefer to sprinkle the dish with crumbled crackers (saltines aren't bad), you can skip the bread-crumb step.

BREAD-CRUMB TOPPING
- 3 slices high-quality white sandwich bread, torn into quarters
- 2 tablespoons unsalted butter
- Table salt

MACARONI AND CHEESE
- 2 large eggs
- 1 (12-ounce) can evaporated milk
- 2 teaspoons table salt
- ¼ teaspoon ground black pepper
- 1 teaspoon dry mustard, dissolved in 1 teaspoon water
- ¼ teaspoon hot sauce
- 8 ounces elbow macaroni (about 2 cups)
- 4 tablespoons (½ stick) unsalted butter
- 12 ounces sharp cheddar, American, or Monterey Jack cheese, shredded (about 3 cups)

1. FOR THE BREAD CRUMBS: Pulse the bread in a food processor until coarsely ground, 10 to 15 pulses. Melt the butter in a large skillet over medium heat. Add the bread crumbs and cook, tossing to coat with the butter, until the crumbs just begin to color, about 10 minutes. Season with salt to taste; set aside.

2. FOR THE MACARONI AND CHEESE: Mix the eggs, 1 cup of the evaporated milk, ½ teaspoon of the salt, the pepper, mustard mixture, and hot sauce in a small bowl; set aside.

3. Meanwhile, bring 2 quarts water to a boil in a large heavy-bottomed saucepan or Dutch oven. Add the remaining 1½ teaspoons salt and the macaroni; cook until almost tender but still a little firm to the bite. Drain and return to the pan over low heat. Add the butter; toss to melt.

4. Pour the egg mixture over the buttered noodles along with three-quarters of the cheese; stir until thoroughly combined and the cheese starts to melt. Gradually add the remaining ½ cup milk and the remaining cheese, stirring constantly, until the mixture is hot and creamy, about 5 minutes. Serve immediately, topped with the toasted bread crumbs.

LIGHT MACARONI AND CHEESE

WHY THIS RECIPE WORKS: Weighing in at about 650 calories and 40 grams of fat per serving, a bowl of homemade mac and cheese should really be a treat every once in a while, like a slice of cheesecake. But the truth is, most of us like to enjoy this family favorite a little more often. We aimed to develop a lighter version of mac and cheese—macaroni in a creamy (not rubbery or grainy), cheesy sauce—with a fraction of the calories.

We slashed both fat and calories by replacing full-fat cheddar with low-fat—its flavor and texture are vastly superior to nonfat cheddar. We also swapped in 2 percent milk for the whole milk and added 2 percent evaporated milk to ensure a creamy consistency. And we found that we could eliminate butter entirely by thickening the sauce with cornstarch instead of a classic roux. In the end, we cut the calories by almost half and the fat grams by 75 percent, turning full-fat macaroni and cheese into a dish you could eat every day.

Light Macaroni and Cheese

SERVES 4 TO 6

Don't be tempted to use either preshredded or nonfat cheddar cheese in this dish—the texture and flavor of the macaroni and cheese will suffer substantially. For best results, choose a low-fat cheddar cheese that is sold in block form and has roughly 50 percent of the fat and calories of regular cheese (we like Cracker Barrel brand).

> Table salt
> 8 ounces elbow macaroni (about 2 cups)
> 1 (12-ounce) can 2 percent reduced-fat evaporated milk
> ¾ cup 2 percent milk
> ¼ teaspoon dry mustard
> ⅛ teaspoon garlic powder or celery salt (optional)
> Pinch cayenne pepper
> 2 teaspoons cornstarch
> 8 ounces 50 percent light cheddar cheese, shredded (about 2 cups; see note)

1. Bring 2½ quarts water to a boil in a large saucepan. Stir in 2 teaspoons salt and the macaroni; cook until the pasta is completely cooked and tender, about 5 minutes. Drain the pasta and leave it in the colander; set aside.

2. Add the evaporated milk, ½ cup of the 2 percent milk, the mustard, garlic powder (if using), cayenne, and ½ teaspoon salt to the now-empty saucepan. Bring the mixture

to a boil, then reduce to a simmer. Whisk the cornstarch and remaining ¼ cup milk together, then whisk it into the simmering mixture. Continue to simmer, whisking constantly, until the sauce has thickened and is smooth, about 2 minutes.

3. Off the heat, gradually whisk in the cheddar until melted and smooth. Stir in the macaroni and let the macaroni and cheese sit off the heat until the sauce has thickened slightly, 2 to 5 minutes, before serving.

TURKEY TETRAZZINI

WHY THIS RECIPE WORKS: Overcooking is the inevitable fate of many casseroles, as the contents are usually cooked twice: once on their own and once again when joined with the other casserole ingredients. We wanted a casserole with a silky sauce, a generous portion of turkey meat, and noodles cooked just till done.

We found we could cut the second cooking down to just 15 minutes by baking the recipe in a shallow dish that would allow it to heat through quickly. Most recipes for turkey Tetrazzini call for a béchamel sauce, in which milk is added to a roux (a paste made from fat and flour that is then cooked on the stovetop). In switching to a velouté, which is based on chicken stock rather than milk, we brightened up the texture and the flavor. We also used less sauce than most recipes call for, giving the other ingredients a chance to express themselves. Still looking for brighter flavor, we spruced things up with a shot of sherry and a little lemon juice and nutmeg. Parmesan cheese provided tang and bite, and a full 2 teaspoons of fresh thyme helped to freshen the overall impression of the dish.

Turkey Tetrazzini

SERVES 8

Don't skimp on the salt and pepper; this dish needs aggressive seasoning.

BREAD-CRUMB TOPPING
> 6 slices high-quality white sandwich bread, torn into quarters
> 4 tablespoons (½ stick) unsalted butter, melted
> Pinch table salt
> ½ ounce Parmesan cheese, grated (about ¼ cup)

FILLING
> 8 tablespoons (1 stick) unsalted butter, plus extra for the baking dish

8 ounces white mushrooms, wiped cleaned and sliced thin (about 3 cups)

2 medium onions, minced
Table salt and ground black pepper (see note)

12 ounces spaghetti or other long-strand pasta, strands snapped in half

6 tablespoons unbleached all-purpose flour

3 cups low-sodium chicken broth

1½ ounces Parmesan cheese, grated (about ¾ cup)

¼ cup dry sherry

1 tablespoon juice from 1 lemon

2 teaspoons minced fresh thyme leaves

¼ teaspoon grated nutmeg

2 cups frozen peas

4 cups leftover cooked boneless turkey or chicken meat, cut into ¼-inch pieces

1. FOR THE TOPPING: Adjust an oven rack to the middle position and heat the oven to 350 degrees. Pulse the bread in a food processor until coarsely ground, 10 to 15 pulses. Mix the bread crumbs, butter, and salt in a small baking dish; bake until golden brown and crisp, 15 to 20 minutes. Cool to room temperature and mix with the Parmesan in a small bowl. Set aside.

2. FOR THE FILLING: Increase the oven temperature to 450 degrees. Melt 2 tablespoons of the butter in a large skillet over medium heat; add the mushrooms and onions and sauté, stirring frequently, until the liquid from the mushrooms evaporates, 12 to 15 minutes. Season with salt and pepper to taste; transfer the vegetables to a medium bowl and set aside. Clean the skillet.

3. Meanwhile, bring 4 quarts water to a boil in a large pot. Add 1 tablespoon salt and the pasta and cook until al dente. Reserve ¼ cup cooking water, drain the pasta, and return to the pot with the reserved liquid.

4. Melt the remaining 6 tablespoons butter in the clean skillet over medium heat. Whisk in the flour and cook, whisking constantly, until the flour turns golden, 1 to 2 minutes. Whisking constantly, gradually add the chicken broth. Increase the heat to medium-high and simmer until the mixture thickens, 3 to 4 minutes. Off the heat, whisk in the Parmesan, sherry, lemon juice, thyme, nutmeg, and ½ teaspoon salt. Add the sauce, sautéed vegetables, peas, and turkey to the pasta and mix well; season with salt and pepper to taste.

5. Turn the mixture into a buttered 13 by 9-inch gratin dish (or other shallow ovensafe baking dish of similar size), sprinkle evenly with the reserved bread crumbs, and bake until the bread crumbs brown and the mixture is bubbly, 13 to 15 minutes. Serve immediately.

CINCINNATI CHILI

WHY THIS RECIPE WORKS: This Midwestern diner specialty is an unusual marriage of American chili and Middle Eastern spices. For an easy weeknight meal, we wanted to pare the list of ingredients down to the essentials without compromising the distinctive character of the dish.

The beef in Cincinnati Chili isn't sautéed like the beef in other chilis, so there is no way to remove the fat. To avoid greasiness, we blanched ground chuck for half a minute, which got rid of most of the fat but still left plenty of flavor. The spices used in this chili vary from recipe to recipe. We settled on a limited palette starring chili powder, oregano, cinnamon, and cocoa powder, which we bloomed in hot oil for more depth of flavor. Water and tomato sauce are the traditional base for the sauce; we added chicken broth for balance. Vinegar and brown sugar livened things up. After a long simmer, the chili was ready to be served, and we couldn't think of a better way to do it than "five-way"—over spaghetti, topped with cheddar cheese, chopped onions, and kidney beans.

Cincinnati Chili

SERVES 6 TO 8

CHILI

2 teaspoons table salt, plus more to taste

1½ pounds 80 percent lean ground chuck

2 tablespoons vegetable oil

2 medium onions, minced

2 medium garlic cloves, minced or pressed through a garlic press (about 2 teaspoons)

2 tablespoons chili powder

2 teaspoons dried oregano

2 teaspoons cocoa powder

1½ teaspoons ground cinnamon

½ teaspoon cayenne pepper

½ teaspoon ground allspice

¼ teaspoon ground black pepper

2 cups tomato sauce

2 cups low-sodium chicken broth

2 cups water

2 tablespoons cider vinegar

2 teaspoons dark brown sugar

Hot sauce

ACCOMPANIMENTS

1 pound spaghetti, cooked, drained, and tossed with 2 tablespoons unsalted butter

12 ounces sharp cheddar cheese, shredded (about 3 cups)

1 (15-ounce) can red kidney beans, drained, rinsed, and warmed

1 medium onion, chopped

1. FOR THE CHILI: Bring 2 quarts water and 1 teaspoon of the salt to a boil in a large saucepan. Add the ground chuck, stirring vigorously to separate the meat into individual strands. As soon as the foam from the meat rises to the top (this takes about 30 seconds) and before the water returns to a boil, drain the meat into a strainer and set it aside.

2. Rinse and dry the empty saucepan. Set the pan over medium heat and add the oil. When the oil is warm, add the onions and cook, stirring frequently, until the onions are soft and browned around the edges, about 8 minutes. Add the garlic and cook until fragrant, about 1 minute. Stir in the chili powder, oregano, cocoa, cinnamon, cayenne, allspice, black pepper, and the remaining 1 teaspoon salt. Cook, stirring constantly, until the spices are fragrant, about 30 seconds. Stir in the tomato sauce, broth, water, vinegar, and sugar, scraping the pan bottom to remove any browned bits.

PRESS, DON'T MINCE, YOUR GARLIC

Newly hired test cooks (many of whom are fresh out of cooking school) often do a double take when they discover a test kitchen secret. When it comes to mincing garlic, we'd rather use a garlic press to do the job. Purists may insist on mincing their garlic the old-fashioned way (a chef's knife and cutting board), but let's face it—mincing garlic is quite a chore. First, its texture is defiantly sticky, so that little bits cling tenaciously to your cutting board, knife blade, and fingers. Second, despite the diminutive size of garlic cloves, mincing a couple of them finely and evenly is a time- and labor-intensive proposition. Enter the garlic press.

Most garlic presses share a common design, comprising two handles connected by a hinge. At the end of one handle is a small perforated hopper; at the end of the other is a plunger that fits snugly inside the hopper. The garlic cloves in the hopper get crushed by the descending plunger when you squeeze the handles together and the puree is extruded through the perforations in the bottom of the hopper. In thousands of hours of use in our test kitchen, we have found that this little tool delivers speed, ease, and a comfortable separation of garlic from fingers. (See page 714 for our recommended brand of garlic press.) And there are other advantages: A good garlic press breaks down the cloves more than an average cook would with a knife, resulting in a fuller, more pungent garlic flavor. A good garlic press also ensures a consistently fine texture, which in turns means better distribution throughout the dish. Lesson learned? They don't teach you everything in cooking school.

3. Add the blanched ground beef and increase the heat to high. As soon as the liquid boils, reduce the heat to medium-low and simmer, stirring occasionally, until the chili is deep red and has thickened slightly, about 1 hour. Season with salt and hot sauce to taste. (The chili can be refrigerated in an airtight container for up to 3 days. Bring to a simmer over medium-low heat before serving.)

4. TO SERVE: Divide the buttered spaghetti among individual bowls. Spoon the chili over the spaghetti and top with the cheese, beans, and onion. Serve immediately.

CHICKEN-FRIED STEAK

WHY THIS RECIPE WORKS: Although this truck-stop favorite often gets a bad rap, chicken-fried steak can be delicious when cooked just right. Poorly prepared versions feature dry, rubbery steaks that snap back with each bite, coated in damp, pale breading and topped with a bland, pasty white sauce. When cooked well, thin cutlets of beef are breaded and fried until a crisp, golden brown. The creamy gravy that accompanies the steak is well seasoned and not too thick. This was our goal.

A thin steak works best here, so we turned to cube steak and pounded the meat to an even thickness. What makes this steak special is the crisp coating. After trying a variety of coatings—Melba toast, corn flakes, panko, and the like—we determined simple was best. We dredged the steaks in heavily seasoned flour, dipped them in a thick buttermilk and egg mixture aerated with baking power and baking soda, and then returned them to the seasoned flour for a second coat. This coating fried up to an impressive dark mahogany color with a resilient texture to stand up to the gravy. For the gravy, we built in flavor by using the fried bits left in the pan after cooking the steaks and by making a roux. Onions and cayenne are traditional for the gravy, but we found that small additions of thyme and garlic also improved its flavor.

Chicken-Fried Steaks

SERVES 6

Getting the initial oil temperature to 375 degrees is key to the success of this recipe. Use an instant-read thermometer with a high upper range to check the temperature; a clip-on candy/deep-fry thermometer is also fine. If your Dutch oven measures 11 inches across (as ours does), you will need to fry the steaks in two batches.

STEAKS

- 3 cups unbleached all-purpose flour
  Table salt and ground black pepper
- ⅛ teaspoon cayenne pepper
- 1 large egg
- 1 teaspoon baking powder
- ½ teaspoon baking soda
- 1 cup buttermilk
- 6 (5-ounce) cube steaks, pounded ⅓ inch thick
- 4–5 cups peanut oil

CREAM GRAVY

- 1 medium onion, minced
- ⅛ teaspoon dried thyme
- 2 medium garlic cloves, minced or pressed through a garlic press (about 2 teaspoons)
- 3 tablespoons unbleached all-purpose flour
- ½ cup low-sodium chicken broth
- 2 cups whole milk
- ¾ teaspoon table salt
- ¼ teaspoon ground black pepper
  Pinch cayenne pepper

1. FOR THE STEAKS: Mix the flour, 5 teaspoons salt, 1 teaspoon black pepper, and the cayenne together in a large shallow dish. In a second large shallow dish, beat the egg, baking powder, and baking soda; stir in the buttermilk.

2. Set a wire rack over a large rimmed baking sheet. Pat the steaks dry with paper towels and sprinkle each side with salt and pepper. One at a time, drop the steaks into the flour and shake the dish to coat. Shake excess flour from each steak, then, using tongs, dip each steak into the egg mixture, turning to coat well and allowing the excess to drip off. Coat the steaks with flour again, shake off the excess, and place them on the wire rack.

3. Adjust an oven rack to the middle position, set a second wire rack over a second rimmed baking sheet, and place the sheet on the oven rack; heat the oven to 200 degrees. Line a large plate with a double layer of paper towels. Meanwhile, heat 1 inch of oil in a large (11-inch diameter) Dutch oven over medium-high heat to 375 degrees. Place 3 steaks in the oil and fry, turning once, until deep golden brown on each side, about 5 minutes (the oil temperature will drop to around 335 degrees). Transfer the steaks to the paper towel–lined plate to drain, then transfer them to the wire rack in the oven. Bring the oil back to 375 degrees and repeat the cooking and draining process (use fresh paper towels) with the 3 remaining steaks.

4. FOR THE GRAVY: Carefully pour the hot oil through a fine-mesh strainer into a clean pot. Return the browned bits from the strainer along with 2 tablespoons of the frying oil to the Dutch oven. Turn the heat to medium, add the onion and thyme, and cook until the onion has softened and is beginning to brown, 4 to 5 minutes. Add the garlic and cook until aromatic, about 30 seconds. Add the flour to the pan and stir until well combined and starting to dissolve, about 1 minute. Whisk in the broth, scraping any browned bits off the bottom of the pan. Whisk in the milk, salt, black pepper, and cayenne; bring to a simmer over medium-high heat. Cook until thickened (the gravy should have a loose consistency—it will thicken as it cools), about 5 minutes.

5. Transfer the chicken-fried steaks to individual plates. Spoon a generous amount of gravy over each steak. Serve immediately, passing any remaining gravy separately.

ALL-BEEF MEAT LOAF

WHY THIS RECIPE WORKS: Every all-beef meat loaf we've tasted has had the same problems—chewy texture and uninteresting flavor, making it more of a hamburger in the shape of a log than bonafide meat loaf. In the past, when we wanted a great meat loaf, we turned to a traditional meat-loaf mix consisting of beef, pork, and veal. Could we create an all-beef meat loaf to compete with this classic?

Supermarkets offer a wide selection of "ground beef," and after testing them alone and in combination we determined that equal parts of chuck (for moisture) and sirloin (for beefy flavor) were best. Beef has a livery taste that we wanted to subdue, and the usual dairy additions to meat loaf didn't work. Chicken broth, oddly enough, neutralized this off-flavor and provided moisture. For additional moisture and richness, we included mild-tasting Monterey Jack cheese, which also helped bind the mixture. To avoid pockets of oozing hot cheese in the meat loaf, we shredded the cheese and froze it briefly. Crushed saltines, our choice for the starchy filler, provided texture, but we felt our meat loaf needed more "sliceability." Surprisingly, gelatin gave us just the smooth, luxurious texture we sought. We seasoned the mixture with onions, celery, garlic (all sautéed), thyme, paprika, soy sauce, and mustard. A traditional ketchup glaze crowned our flavorful all-beef meat loaf.

Glazed All-Beef Meat Loaf

SERVES 6 TO 8

If you can't find chuck and/or sirloin, substitute 85 percent lean ground beef.

MEAT LOAF

- 3 ounces Monterey Jack cheese, shredded on the small holes of a box grater (about 1 cup)
- 1 tablespoon unsalted butter
- 1 medium onion, minced
- 1 medium celery rib, minced
- 2 teaspoons minced fresh thyme leaves
- 1 teaspoon paprika
- 1 medium garlic clove, minced or pressed through a garlic press (about 1 teaspoon)
- ¼ cup tomato juice
- ½ cup low-sodium chicken broth
- 2 large eggs
- ½ teaspoon unflavored powdered gelatin
- ⅔ cup crushed saltines
- 2 tablespoons minced fresh parsley leaves
- 1 tablespoon soy sauce
- 1 teaspoon Dijon mustard
- ¾ teaspoon table salt
- ½ teaspoon ground black pepper
- 1 pound 90 percent lean ground sirloin (see note)
- 1 pound 80 percent lean ground chuck (see note)

GLAZE

- ½ cup ketchup
- ¼ cup cider vinegar
- 3 tablespoons light brown sugar
- 1 teaspoon hot sauce
- ½ teaspoon ground coriander

1. FOR THE MEAT LOAF: Adjust an oven rack to the middle position and heat the oven to 375 degrees. Spread the cheese on a plate and place in the freezer until ready to use. To prepare the baking sheet, set a wire rack over a rimmed baking sheet. Fold a sheet of heavy-duty aluminum foil to form a 10 by 6-inch rectangle. Center the foil on the rack and poke holes in the foil with a skewer (about half an inch apart). Spray the foil with vegetable oil spray or use nonstick foil.

2. Melt the butter in a 10-inch skillet over medium-high heat; add the onion and celery and cook, stirring occasionally, until beginning to brown, 6 to 8 minutes. Add the thyme, paprika, and garlic and cook, stirring, until fragrant, about 1 minute. Reduce the heat to low and add the tomato juice. Cook, stirring to scrape up the browned bits from the pan, until thickened, about

1 minute. Transfer the mixture to a small bowl and set aside to cool.

3. Whisk the broth and eggs together in a large bowl until combined. Sprinkle the gelatin over the liquid and let stand for 5 minutes. Stir in the saltines, parsley, soy sauce, mustard, salt, pepper, and onion mixture. Crumble the frozen cheese into a coarse powder and sprinkle over the mixture. Add the sirloin and chuck; mix gently with your hands until thoroughly combined, about 1 minute. Transfer the meat to the foil rectangle and shape into a 10 by 6-inch oval about 2 inches high. Smooth the top and edges of the meat loaf with a moistened spatula. Bake until the center of the loaf registers 135 to 140 degrees on an instant-read thermometer, 55 to 65 minutes. Remove the meat loaf from the oven and turn on the broiler.

4. FOR THE GLAZE: While the meat loaf cooks, combine the glaze ingredients in a small saucepan; bring to a simmer over medium heat and cook, stirring, until thick and syrupy, about 5 minutes. Spread half of the glaze evenly over the cooked meat loaf with a rubber spatula; place under the broiler and cook until the glaze bubbles and begins to brown at the edges, about 5 minutes. Remove the meat loaf from the oven and spread evenly with the remaining glaze; place back under the broiler and cook until the glaze is again bubbling and beginning to brown, about 5 minutes more. Let the meat loaf cool for about 20 minutes before slicing.

CLASSIC MEAT LOAF

WHY THIS RECIPE WORKS: Not all meat loaves resemble Mom's. Some recipes go the canned soup route and, frankly, taste like it. Others become gussied up with ingredients that have no place in this humble family dish—canned pineapple, sun-dried tomatoes, and the like. Our goal was not to develop the ultimate meat loaf but to bring it back to its classic roots—a tender, well-seasoned loaf smothered with tangy sweet glaze.

We started, of course, with the meat. We determined that supermarkets haven't been selling "meat loaf mix" for no reason—a mixture of ground beef chuck, ground pork, and ground veal produced the best balance of flavors and textures. A starch turned out to be a necessity for binding the meat and giving it that classic meat loaf texture; cracker crumbs, quick-cooking oatmeal, and fresh bread crumbs all worked well. To prevent the filler from drying out the meat loaf, we knew we needed to add some moisture. After trying a host of options, we determined that whole milk and plain yogurt are equally acceptable. Finally, we realized that the pan in which the meat loaf baked made a big difference. A standard loaf pan traps the fat and stews the meat, and the juice bubbles up and destroys the glaze. Baking the meat loaf free-form in a shallow baking pan gave the loaf a good crust, preserved our sweet-tart glaze, and helped the bacon topping crisp nicely.

Meat Loaf with Brown Sugar–Ketchup Glaze
SERVES 6 TO 8

If you like, you can omit the bacon topping from the loaf. In this case, brush on half of the glaze before baking and the other half during the last 15 minutes of baking. If you choose not to special-order the mix of meat below, we recommend the standard meat loaf mix of equal parts beef, pork, and veal, available at most grocery stores. Lining the baking pan with foil makes for easier cleanup.

BROWN SUGAR–KETCHUP GLAZE
- ½ **cup ketchup or chili sauce**
- ¼ **cup brown sugar**
- 4 **teaspoons cider vinegar or white vinegar**

MEAT LOAF
- 2 **teaspoons vegetable oil**
- 1 **medium onion, chopped**
- 2 **medium garlic cloves, minced or pressed through a garlic press (about 2 teaspoons)**

2 large eggs

½ cup whole milk or plain yogurt, plus more as needed

2 teaspoons Dijon mustard

2 teaspoons Worcestershire sauce

1 teaspoon table salt

½ teaspoon ground black pepper

½ teaspoon dried thyme

¼ teaspoon hot sauce

2 pounds meat loaf mix (50 percent ground chuck, 25 percent ground pork, 25 percent ground veal; see note)

⅔ cup crushed saltine crackers (about 16) or quick oatmeal or 1⅓ cups fresh bread crumbs

⅓ cup minced fresh parsley leaves

6–8 ounces bacon (8 to 12 slices, depending on loaf shape) (see note)

1. FOR THE GLAZE: Mix all the ingredients together in a small saucepan; set aside.

2. FOR THE MEAT LOAF: Line a 13 by 9-inch baking pan with foil; set aside. Heat the oven to 350 degrees. Heat the oil in a medium skillet over medium heat until shimmering. Add the onion and garlic; sauté until softened, about 5 minutes. Set aside to cool while preparing the remaining ingredients.

3. Mix the eggs with the milk, mustard, Worcestershire sauce, salt, pepper, thyme, and hot sauce. Combine the egg mixture with the meat in a large bowl and add the crackers, parsley, and cooked onion and garlic; mix with a fork until evenly blended and the meat mixture does not stick to the bowl. (If necessary, add more milk, a couple of tablespoons at a time, until the mixture no longer sticks.)

4. Turn the meat mixture onto a work surface. With wet hands, pat the mixture into an approximately 9 by 5-inch loaf shape. Place on the prepared baking pan. Brush with half the glaze, then arrange the bacon slices, crosswise, over the loaf, overlapping them slightly and tucking only the bacon tip ends under the loaf.

5. Bake the loaf until the bacon is crisp and the center of the loaf registers 160 degrees on an instant-read thermometer, about 1 hour. Cool for at least 20 minutes. Simmer the remaining glaze over medium heat until thickened slightly. Slice the meat loaf and serve with the extra glaze passed separately.

STUFFED PEPPERS

WHY THIS RECIPE WORKS: A vegetable can be more than just a side dish, and stuffed peppers are a perfect case in point. But slimy or too-crunchy peppers and tasteless fillings can ruin the show. We wanted to revamp this dish to be a flavorful option for a weeknight dinner.

Cooking the peppers correctly is critical; they need to be sturdy enough to hold the filling but not crunchy and bitter. We found that blanching them before adding the filling gave us peppers that held their shape, had good color, and tasted sweeter. Rice is the classic stuffing for peppers, but alone it didn't have much flavor. Tastings of various fillings showed us that simpler is better for this dish; a mixture of rice and ground beef was the favorite. We cooked the rice in the water we'd used to blanch the peppers and for additional flavor, we included sautéed onion and garlic, tomatoes, cheddar cheese, and ketchup. We'd taken this recipe back to its 1950s version, but made it into a simple recipe suitable for today's busy cooks.

Classic Stuffed Bell Peppers

SERVES 4

When shopping for bell peppers to stuff, it's best to choose those with broad bases that will allow the peppers to stand up on their own. It's easier to fill the peppers after they have been placed in the baking dish because the sides of the dish will hold the peppers steady.

Table salt

4 medium red, yellow, or orange bell peppers (about 6 ounces each), ½ inch trimmed off tops, cores and seeds discarded (see note)

½ cup long-grain white rice

1½ tablespoons olive oil

1 medium onion, minced

12 ounces ground beef, preferably 80 percent lean ground chuck

3 medium garlic cloves, minced or pressed through a garlic press (about 1 tablespoon)

1 (14.5-ounce) can diced tomatoes, drained, ¼ cup juice reserved

5 ounces Monterey Jack cheese, shredded (about 1¼ cups)

2 tablespoons chopped fresh parsley leaves

Ground black pepper

¼ cup ketchup

1. Bring 4 quarts water to a boil in a large stockpot or Dutch oven over high heat. Add 1 tablespoon salt and the bell peppers. Cook until the peppers just begin to soften, about 3 minutes. Using a slotted spoon, remove the peppers from the pot, drain off the excess water, and place the peppers, cut side up, on paper towels. Return the water to a boil; add the rice and boil until tender, about 13 minutes. Drain the rice and transfer it to a large bowl; set aside.

2. Adjust an oven rack to the middle position and heat the oven to 350 degrees.

3. Meanwhile, heat the oil in a heavy-bottomed 12-inch skillet over medium-high heat until shimmering. Add the onion and cook, stirring occasionally, until softened and beginning to brown, about 5 minutes. Add the ground beef and cook, breaking the beef into small pieces with a spoon, until no longer pink, about 4 minutes. Stir in the garlic and cook until fragrant, about 30 seconds. Transfer the mixture to the bowl with the rice; stir in the tomatoes, 1 cup of the cheese, the parsley, and salt and pepper to taste.

4. Stir together the ketchup and the reserved tomato juice in a small bowl.

5. Place the peppers, cut side up, in a 9-inch square baking dish. Using a soup spoon, divide the filling evenly among the peppers. Spoon 2 tablespoons of the ketchup mixture over each filled pepper and sprinkle each with 1 tablespoon of the remaining ¼ cup cheese. Bake until the cheese is browned and the filling is heated through, 25 to 30 minutes. Serve immediately.

OLD-FASHIONED BURGERS

WHY THIS RECIPE WORKS: The burger you find at most drive-ins is a rubbery, thin, gray patty with little beef flavor. We wanted to create, at home, the classic drive-in burger. Made from freshly ground beef, cooked on a flat griddle, this style of burger is ultracrisp, ultrabrowned, and ultrabeefy. Topped with melted cheese and tangy sauce, it's the burger fast food restaurants wish they could produce.

We learned right off the bat that the thin patty typical of this burger style requires freshly ground meat. Prepackaged hamburger is ground very fine and packaged tightly, which produces dense, rubbery, and dry patties. For the meat, we settled on short ribs ground up with sirloin steak tips. Numerous grinding tests revealed that while beefiness depends on cut, juiciness corresponds to fat. Well-marbled short ribs added the perfect amount of fat to complement the beefy flavor from the sirloin tips. And if you don't have a meat grinder? The food processor works just fine as long as the meat is first chilled in the freezer until firm but still pliable. We still had to deal with a rubbery texture caused by meat collagen proteins shrinking and tightening when exposed to heat. To fight this, the meat needed to be as loosely packed as possible—not pressed but rather gently shaped into loose patties. To top our burgers, we went back to the tried-and-true flavors of a tangy and sweet Thousand Island–style dressing, American cheese, and thinly sliced onion.

Best Old-Fashioned Burgers

MAKES 4 BURGERS

Sirloin steak tips are also labeled "flap meat" by some butchers. Flank steak can be used in its place. This recipe yields juicy medium to medium-well burgers. If doubling the recipe, process the meat in three batches in step 2. Because the cooked burgers do not hold well, fry four burgers and serve them immediately before frying more. Or cook them in two pans. Extra patties can be frozen for up to 2 weeks. Stack the patties, separated by parchment paper, and wrap them in three layers of plastic wrap. Thaw burgers in a single layer on a baking sheet at room temperature for 30 minutes before cooking.

10 ounces sirloin steak tips, cut into 1-inch chunks (see note)
6 ounces boneless beef short ribs, cut into 1-inch chunks
Table salt and ground black pepper
1 tablespoon unsalted butter
4 soft hamburger buns

½ teaspoon vegetable oil

4 slices American cheese

Thinly sliced onion

1 recipe Classic Burger Sauce (recipe follows)

1. Place the beef chunks on a baking sheet in a single layer, leaving ½ inch of space around each chunk. Freeze the meat until very firm and starting to harden around the edges but still pliable, 15 to 25 minutes.

2. Place half of the meat in a food processor and pulse until the meat is coarsely ground, 10 to 15 pulses, stopping and redistributing the meat around the bowl as necessary to ensure the beef is evenly ground. Transfer the meat to a baking sheet by overturning the bowl, without touching the meat. Repeat the grinding with the remaining meat. Spread the meat over the sheet and inspect carefully, discarding any long strands of gristle or large chunks of hard meat or fat.

3. Gently separate the ground meat into four equal mounds. Without picking the meat up, with your fingers gently shape each mound into a loose patty ½ inch thick and 4 inches in diameter, leaving the edges and surface ragged. Season the top of each patty with salt and pepper. Using a spatula, flip the patties and season the other side. Refrigerate while toasting the buns.

4. Melt ½ tablespoon of the butter in a heavy-bottomed 12-inch skillet over medium heat. Add the bun tops, cut side down, and toast until light golden brown, about

2 minutes. Repeat with the remaining ½ tablespoon butter and the bun bottoms. Set the buns aside and wipe out the skillet with paper towels.

5. Return the skillet to high heat; add the oil and heat until just smoking. Using a spatula, transfer the burgers to the skillet and cook without moving them for 3 minutes. Using the spatula, flip the burgers over and cook for 1 minute. Top each patty with a slice of the cheese and continue to cook until the cheese is melted, about 1 minute longer.

6. Transfer the patties to the bun bottoms and top with the onion. Spread 2 teaspoons of the burger sauce on each bun top. Cover the burgers with the bun tops and serve immediately.

Classic Burger Sauce
MAKES ABOUT ¼ CUP

2 tablespoons mayonnaise

1 tablespoon ketchup

½ teaspoon sweet pickle relish

½ teaspoon sugar

½ teaspoon white vinegar

¼ teaspoon ground black pepper

Whisk all the ingredients together in a small bowl.

JUICY PUB-STYLE BURGERS

WHY THIS RECIPE WORKS: Few things are as satisfying as a thick, juicy pub-style burger. But avoiding the usual gray band of overcooked meat is a challenge. We wanted a patty that was well-seared, juicy, and evenly rosy from center to edge, with big beefy flavor. Grinding our own meat in the food processor was a must (freezing the meat until just firm helps the processor chop it cleanly), and we found that sirloin steak tips were the best cut for the job. To give the burgers just enough structure to hold their shape in the skillet, we cut the meat into small ½-inch chunks before grinding, and we lightly packed the meat into patties. A little melted butter improved their flavor and juiciness, but our biggest discovery came when we transferred the burgers from the stovetop to the oven to finish cooking—the stovetop provided intense heat for searing, while the oven's gentle ambient heat allowed for even cooking, thus eliminating the overcooked gray zone.

Juicy Pub-Style Burgers

SERVES 4

Sirloin steak tips are also labeled as "flap meat." When stirring the butter and pepper into the ground meat and shaping the patties, take care not to overwork the meat or the burgers will become dense. For the best flavor, season the burgers aggressively just before cooking. The burgers can be topped as desired, or try one of our variations that follow. The uncooked patties can be refrigerated for up to 1 day.

- 2 **pounds sirloin steak tips or boneless beef short ribs, trimmed and cut into ½-inch chunks**
- 4 **tablespoons unsalted butter (½ stick), melted and cooled slightly**
  Table salt and ground black pepper
- 1 **teaspoon vegetable oil**
- 4 **large hamburger buns, toasted and buttered**
- 1 **recipe Pub-Style Burger Sauce (optional; recipe follows)**

1. Place the beef chunks on a baking sheet in a single layer. Freeze the meat until very firm and starting to harden around the edges but still pliable, 15 to 25 minutes.

2. Place one-quarter of the meat in a food processor and pulse until finely ground into ¹⁄₁₆-inch pieces, about 35 pulses, stopping and redistributing the meat around the bowl as necessary to ensure the beef is evenly ground. Transfer the meat to the baking sheet by overturning the processor bowl and without directly touching the meat. Repeat grinding with the remaining 3 batches of meat. Spread the meat over the sheet and inspect carefully, discarding any long strands of gristle or large chunks of hard meat or fat.

3. Adjust an oven rack to the middle position and heat the oven to 300 degrees. Drizzle the melted butter over

the ground meat and add 1 teaspoon pepper. Gently toss with a fork to combine. Divide the meat into 4 lightly packed balls. Gently flatten into patties ¾ inch thick and about 4½ inches in diameter. Refrigerate the patties until ready to cook.

4. Season 1 side of the patties with salt and pepper. Using a spatula, flip the patties and season the other side. Heat the oil in a 12-inch skillet over high heat until just smoking. Using the spatula, transfer the burgers to the skillet and cook without moving for 2 minutes. Using the spatula, flip the burgers over and cook for 2 minutes longer. Transfer the patties to a rimmed baking sheet and bake until the burgers register 125 degrees (for medium-rare) on an instant-read thermometer, 3 to 5 minutes.

5. Transfer the burgers to a plate and let rest for 5 minutes. Transfer to the buns, top with Pub-Style Burger Sauce (if using), and serve.

Pub-Style Burger Sauce

MAKES ABOUT 1 CUP, ENOUGH TO TOP 4 BURGERS

- ¾ **cup mayonnaise**
- 2 **tablespoons soy sauce**
- 1 **tablespoon dark brown sugar**
- 1 **tablespoon Worcestershire sauce**
- 1 **tablespoon minced chives**
- 1 **medium garlic clove, minced or pressed through a garlic press (about 1 teaspoon)**
- ¾ **teaspoon ground black pepper**

Whisk all ingredients together in bowl.

Juicy Pub-Style Burgers with Crispy Shallots and Blue Cheese

Heat ½ cup vegetable oil and 3 thinly sliced shallots in a medium saucepan over high heat; cook, stirring frequently, until the shallots are golden, about 8 minutes. Using a slotted spoon, transfer the shallots to a paper towel–lined plate, season with table salt, and let drain until crisp, about 5 minutes. (The cooled shallots can be stored at room temperature in an airtight container for up to 3 days.) Follow the recipe for Juicy Pub-Style Burgers, topping each burger with 1 ounce crumbled blue cheese before transferring to the oven. Top with Pub-Style Burger Sauce and the crispy shallots just before serving.

Juicy Pub-Style Burgers with Peppered Bacon and Aged Cheddar

Adjust an oven rack to the middle position and heat the oven to 375 degrees. Arrange 6 bacon slices on a rimmed baking sheet and sprinkle with 2 teaspoons coarsely ground pepper. Place a second rimmed baking sheet on top of the bacon and bake until the bacon is crisp, 15 to 20 minutes. Transfer the bacon to a paper towel–lined plate and cool. Cut the bacon in half crosswise. Follow the recipe for Juicy Pub-Style Burgers, topping each burger with 1 ounce grated aged cheddar cheese before transferring to the oven. Top with Pub-Style Burger Sauce and the bacon just before serving.

Juicy Pub-Style Burgers with Sautéed Onions and Smoked Cheddar

Heat 2 tablespoons vegetable oil in a 12-inch skillet over medium-high heat until just smoking. Add 1 thinly sliced onion and ¼ teaspoon table salt; cook, stirring frequently, until softened and lightly browned, 5 to 7 minutes. Follow the recipe for Juicy Pub-Style Burgers, topping each burger with 1 ounce grated smoked cheddar cheese before transferring to the oven. Top with Pub-Style Burger Sauce and the onion just before serving.

Juicy Pub-Style Burgers with Pan-Roasted Mushrooms and Gruyère

Heat 2 tablespoons vegetable oil in a 12-inch skillet over medium-high heat until just smoking. Add 10 ounces thinly sliced cremini mushrooms, ¼ teaspoon table salt, and ¼ teaspoon pepper; cook, stirring frequently, until browned, 5 to 7 minutes. Add 1 minced shallot and 2 teaspoons minced thyme and cook until fragrant. Remove the skillet from the heat and stir in 2 tablespoons dry sherry. Follow the recipe for Juicy Pub-Style Burgers, topping each burger with 1 ounce grated Gruyère cheese before transferring to the oven. Top with Pub-Style Burger Sauce and the mushrooms just before serving.

OVEN-FRIED ONION RINGS

WHY THIS RECIPE WORKS: Fried onion rings are the perfect accompaniment to burgers, barbecue, and other casual fare. But who wants the mess and smell of deep-frying? We wanted an oven method that produced tender, sweet onions with a super-crunchy coating.

We made a batter with buttermilk, egg, and flour, but when we put the baking sheet in the oven the batter slid right off the onions. Coating the onion rings with flour first gave the batter something to cling to. But we wanted even more crunch. For an extra layer of coating, we turned to crushed saltines and crushed potato chips. We preheated the oil in the baking sheet before adding the coated onions so they'd start crisping right away. The result: crispy, crunchy oven-fried onion rings with deep-fried flavor.

Oven-Fried Onion Rings
SERVES 4 TO 6

Slice the onions into ½-inch-thick rounds, separate the rings, and discard any rings smaller than 2 inches in diameter.

- ½   cup unbleached all-purpose flour
- 1   large egg, at room temperature
- ½   cup buttermilk, at room temperature
- ½   teaspoon table salt
- ¼   teaspoon ground black pepper
- ¼   teaspoon cayenne pepper
- 30   saltine crackers
- 4   cups kettle-cooked potato chips
- 2   large yellow onions, cut into 24 large rings (see note)
- 6   tablespoons vegetable oil

1. Adjust the oven racks to the lower-middle and upper-middle positions and heat the oven to 450 degrees. Place ¼ cup of the flour in a shallow baking dish. Beat the egg and buttermilk in a medium bowl. Whisk the remaining ¼ cup flour, the salt, black pepper, and cayenne into the buttermilk mixture. Pulse the saltines and chips together in a food processor until finely ground; place in a separate shallow baking dish.

2. Working one at a time, dredge each onion ring in the flour, shaking off the excess. Dip in the buttermilk mixture, allowing the excess to drip back into the bowl, then drop into the crumb coating, turning the ring over to coat evenly. Transfer to a large plate. (At this point, the onion rings can be refrigerated for up to 1 hour. Let them sit at room temperature for 30 minutes before baking.)

3. Pour 3 tablespoons of the oil onto each of two rimmed baking sheets. Place in the oven and heat until just smoking, about 8 minutes. Carefully tilt the heated sheets to coat evenly with the oil, then arrange the onion rings on the sheets. Bake, flipping the onion rings over and switching and rotating the baking sheets halfway through baking, until golden brown on both sides, about 15 minutes. Briefly drain the onion rings on paper towels. Serve immediately.

STEAK FRIES

WHY THIS RECIPE WORKS: Thick spears of skin-on potato, steak fries are the heartier, more rustic cousins of the crisp, skinny french fry. But getting steak fries crisp on the outside and tender inside can be tricky—soggy steak fries are too often the norm. We wanted to find a way to achieve a steak fry with hearty potato flavor and great crunch.

We found that the dense starchiness of russet potatoes makes them the best variety for frying. We got the proper ratio of crisp exterior to tender interior when we cut them into ¾-inch wedges. As for the frying oil, peanut oil was our top choice. Chilling the potatoes in cold water before frying proved to be an essential step. Prepared this way, they cooked more slowly and evenly, without burning. Even after chilling, though, our fries were overcooked when we simply fried them in oil. A two-step process worked wonders. After chilling and drying the potatoes, we par-fried them at a lower temperature to cook the interiors without browning them.

Following a brief rest, we fried them again at a higher temperature to brown and crisp the exteriors. Neither greasy nor soggy, these fries boasted great flavor and crunch.

Steak Fries
SERVES 4

The potatoes must be soaked in cold water, fried once, cooled, and then fried a second time—so start this recipe at least one hour before dinner.

2½   pounds russet potatoes (about 4 large), scrubbed and cut lengthwise into ¾-inch-thick wedges (about 12 wedges per potato)
2   quarts peanut oil
Table salt and ground black pepper

1. Place the cut potatoes in a large bowl, cover with cold water by at least 1 inch, and then cover with ice cubes. Refrigerate for at least 30 minutes or up to 3 days.

2. In a large Dutch oven fitted with a clip-on candy thermometer, heat the oil over medium-low heat to 325 degrees. (The oil will bubble up when you add the potatoes, so be sure you have at least 3 inches of room at the top of the pot.)

3. Pour off the ice and water, quickly wrap the potatoes in a clean kitchen towel, and thoroughly pat them dry. Increase the heat to medium-high and add the potatoes, one handful at a time, to the hot oil. Fry, stirring with a Chinese skimmer or large-holed slotted spoon, until the potatoes are limp and soft and have turned from white to gold, about 10 minutes. (The oil temperature will drop 50 to 60 degrees during this frying.) Use the skimmer or slotted spoon to transfer the fries to a triple thickness of paper towels to drain; let rest for at least 10 minutes. (The fries can stand at room temperature for up to 2 hours.)

4. When ready to serve the fries, reheat the oil to 350 degrees. Using the paper towels as a funnel, pour the potatoes into the hot oil. Discard the paper towels and line a wire rack with another triple thickness of paper towels. Fry the potatoes, stirring fairly constantly, until medium brown and puffed, 8 to 10 minutes. Transfer to the paper towel–lined rack to drain. Season with salt and pepper to taste. Serve immediately.

CLASSIC FRENCH FRIES

WHY THIS RECIPE WORKS: Efforts to re-create restaurant-style fries at home have always disappointed, with fries that were greasy, droopy, or burnt on the outside and raw on the inside. We wanted to find a recipe and method for the home cook that would rival those cooked by professionals—crunchy fries with deep potato flavor.

As we found in developing our recipe for Steak Fries (page 233), russet potatoes were preferred for their dense texture and hearty flavor. Because these are starchy potatoes, it was important to rinse the starch off the surface after cutting the potatoes into fries. To achieve evenly cooked fries, we first refrigerated the cut potatoes in a bowl of ice water for at least 30 minutes and then took a double-fry approach. During the first fry, because the potatoes are nearly frozen, the potatoes can cook long and slow, which ensures a soft, rich-tasting interior. A quick second fry at a higher temperature crisped and colored the exterior. We used peanut oil for frying but felt our fries lacked the flavor imparted by lard. A little strained bacon grease gave our fries a touch of meaty flavor just like those found in our favorite restaurant fries.

Classic French Fries

SERVES 4

We prefer to peel the potatoes. Leaving the skin on keeps the potato from forming those little airy blisters that we like. Peeling the potato also allows the removal of any imperfections and greenish coloring. Once the potatoes are peeled and cut, plan on at least an hour before the fries are ready to eat.

2½ pounds russet potatoes (about 4 large), peeled and cut into ¼-inch by ¼-inch lengths (see page 340)
2 quarts peanut oil
¼ cup bacon fat, strained (optional)
Table salt and ground black pepper

1. Place the cut potatoes in a large bowl, cover with at least 1 inch of water, then cover with ice cubes. Refrigerate for at least 30 minutes or up to 3 days.

2. In a large Dutch oven fitted with a clip-on candy thermometer, heat the oil over medium-low heat to 325 degrees. (The oil will bubble up when you add the potatoes, so be sure you have at least 3 inches of room at the top of the pot.) Add the bacon grease (if using).

3. Pour off the ice and water, quickly wrap the potatoes in a clean kitchen towel, and thoroughly pat them dry. Increase the heat to medium-high and add the potatoes, one handful at a time, to the hot oil. Fry, stirring with a Chinese skimmer or large-holed slotted spoon, until the potatoes are limp and soft and have turned from white to gold, about 10 minutes. (The oil temperature will drop 50 to 60 degrees during this frying.) Use the skimmer or slotted spoon to transfer the fries to a triple thickness of paper towels to drain; let rest for at least 10 minutes. (The fries can stand at room temperature for up to 2 hours.)

4. When ready to serve the fries, reheat the oil to 350 degrees. Using the paper towels as a funnel, pour the potatoes into the hot oil. Discard the paper towels and line a wire rack with another triple thickness of paper towels. Fry the potatoes, stirring fairly constantly, until medium brown and puffed, about 1 minute. Transfer to the paper towel–lined rack to drain. Season with salt and pepper to taste. Serve immediately.

EASIER FRENCH FRIES

WHY THIS RECIPE WORKS: Our recipe for Classic French Fries works beautifully, but we'll admit that it sometimes seems like a lot of trouble. We challenged ourselves to devise a shortcut that would give us crisp, golden fries with less work.

Oven-frying is the usual "quick" method, but we wanted real french fries. We started with an unorthodox procedure of starting the cut potatoes in a few cups of cold oil. To our surprise, the fries were pretty good, if a little dry. Because russets are fairly dry potatoes, we wondered if a different type of potato would work better. Sure enough, Yukon Golds, which have more water and less starch, came out creamy and smooth inside and crisp outside. A bonus was their thin skin—we could save time by not having to peel the potatoes. We were almost there, but the fries tended to stick to the bottom of the pot and they also tended to clump. Stirring seemed like the obvious solution, but this tended to break the potatoes. After some experimentation, we found that leaving the fries undisturbed for 15 minutes, then stirring them, kept them from sticking and from breaking apart. Thinner batons were also less likely to stick. These fries had all the qualities of classic french fries, without all the bother.

Easier French Fries

SERVES 4

For those who like it, flavoring the oil with bacon fat gives the fries a mild meaty flavor. We prefer peanut oil for frying, but vegetable oil can be substituted. This recipe will not work with sweet potatoes or russets. Serve with dipping sauces (recipes follow), if desired.

- 2½ pounds Yukon Gold potatoes (about 6 medium), scrubbed, dried, sides squared off, and cut lengthwise into ¼-inch by ¼-inch batons (see page 340; see note)
- 6 cups peanut oil (see note)
- ¼ cup bacon fat, strained (optional; see note)
  Table salt

1. Combine the potatoes, oil, and bacon fat (if using) in a large Dutch oven. Cook over high heat until the oil has reached a rolling boil, about 5 minutes. Continue to cook, without stirring, until the potatoes are pale golden and the exteriors are beginning to crisp, about 15 minutes.

2. Using tongs, stir the potatoes, gently scraping up any that stick, and continue to cook, stirring occasionally, until golden and crisp, 5 to 10 minutes longer. Using a skimmer or slotted spoon, transfer the fries to a thick paper bag or paper towels. Season with salt to taste and serve immediately.

Chive and Black Pepper Dipping Sauce

MAKES ABOUT ½ CUP

- 5 tablespoons mayonnaise
- 3 tablespoons sour cream
- 2 tablespoons chopped fresh chives
- 1½ teaspoons juice from 1 lemon
- ¼ teaspoon table salt
- ¼ teaspoon ground black pepper

Whisk all the ingredients together in a small bowl.

Belgian-Style Dipping Sauce

MAKES ABOUT ½ CUP

- 5 tablespoons mayonnaise
- 3 tablespoons ketchup
- 1 medium garlic clove, minced or pressed through a garlic press (about 1 teaspoon)
- ½ teaspoon hot sauce or more to taste
- ¼ teaspoon table salt

Whisk all the ingredients together in a small bowl.

CHAPTER 12

WHO WANTS PASTA?

Pasta with Garlic and Oil 238

Spaghetti with Lemon and Olive Oil (al Limone) 238

Spaghetti with Pecorino Romano and Black Pepper 239

Pasta with Fresh Tomatoes and Herbs 240

Pasta and Fresh Tomato Sauce with Garlic and Basil 240

Pasta with Creamy Tomato Sauce 241

Pasta Caprese 242

Farfalle with Tomatoes, Olives, and Feta 243

Quick Tomato Sauce 244

Marinara Sauce 244

Spaghetti Puttanesca 245

Pasta with Tomato, Bacon, and Onion (Pasta all'Amatriciana) 246

Farfalle with Pesto 247

Pasta with Tomato and Almond Pesto (Pesto alla Trapanese) 247

Campanelle with Arugula, Goat Cheese, and Sun-Dried Tomato Pesto 248

Penne with Toasted Nut and Parsley Pesto

Spaghetti with Olive Pesto

Spring Vegetable Pasta 250

Campanelle with Asparagus, Basil, and Balsamic Glaze 251

Cavatappi with Asparagus, Arugula, Walnuts, and Blue Cheese

Pasta with Sautéed Mushrooms and Thyme 252

Orecchiette with Broccoli Rabe and Sausage 253

Garlicky Shrimp Pasta 254

Shrimp fra Diavolo 255

Pasta with Hearty Italian Meat Sauce (Sunday Gravy) 256

Simple Italian-Style Meat Sauce 257

Fettuccine with Slow-Simmered Bolognese Sauce 258

Pasta with Weeknight Bolognese Sauce 259

Pasta and Slow-Simmered Tomato Sauce with Meat 261

Spaghetti and Meatballs 262

Classic Spaghetti and Meatballs for a Crowd 263

Penne with Vodka Sauce (Penne alla Vodka) 264

Spaghetti alla Carbonara 265

Fettuccine Alfredo 266

Potato Gnocchi with Browned Butter and Sage Sauce 266

Gorgonzola-Cream Sauce

Parmesan Sauce with Pancetta and Walnuts

Creamy Baked Four-Cheese Pasta 269

Baked Ziti 270

Baked Manicotti 270

Four-Cheese Lasagna 272

Vegetable Lasagna 273

Lasagna with Hearty Tomato-Meat Sauce 274

PASTA WITH GARLIC AND OIL

WHY THIS RECIPE WORKS: Nothing sounds easier than pasta with olive oil and garlic, but too often this dish turns out oily or rife with burnt garlic. We were after a flawless version of this quick classic, with bright, deep garlic flavor and no trace of bitterness or harshness.

For a mellow flavor, we cooked most of the garlic over low heat until sticky and straw-colored; a modest amount of raw garlic added at the end brought in some potent fresh garlic flavor. Extra-virgin olive oil and reserved pasta cooking water helped to keep our garlic and pasta saucy. A splash of lemon juice and sprinkling of red pepper flakes added some spice and brightness to this simple, yet complex-flavored recipe.

Pasta with Garlic and Oil

SERVES 4 TO 6

For a twist on pasta with garlic and oil, try sprinkling toasted fresh bread crumbs over individual bowls, but prepare them in advance. Simply pulse two slices of high-quality white sandwich bread, torn into quarters, in a food processor to coarse crumbs. Combine with 2 tablespoons extra-virgin olive oil, season with salt and pepper, and bake on a rimmed baking sheet at 375 degrees until golden brown, 8 to 10 minutes.

  Table salt
1 pound spaghetti
6 tablespoons extra-virgin olive oil
12 medium garlic cloves, minced or pressed through a garlic press (about 4 tablespoons)
¾ teaspoon red pepper flakes
3 tablespoons chopped fresh parsley leaves
2 teaspoons juice from 1 lemon
½ cup grated Parmesan cheese (optional)

1. Bring 4 quarts water to a boil in a large pot. Add 1 tablespoon salt and the pasta to the boiling water and cook, stirring often, until al dente; reserve ⅓ cup of the cooking water then drain the pasta and return it to the pot.

2. Meanwhile, heat 3 tablespoons of the oil, 3 tablespoons of the garlic, and ½ teaspoon salt over low heat in a 10-inch nonstick skillet. Cook, stirring constantly, until the garlic is sticky and straw-colored, 10 to 12 minutes. Off the heat, stir in the remaining 1 tablespoon garlic, the red pepper flakes, parsley, lemon juice, and 2 tablespoons of the reserved pasta cooking water.

3. Transfer the drained pasta to a warm serving bowl; add the remaining 3 tablespoons oil and remaining reserved pasta cooking water and toss to combine. Add the garlic mixture and ¾ teaspoon salt; toss to combine. Serve, sprinkling individual bowls with Parmesan cheese, if desired.

SPAGHETTI AL LIMONE

WHY THIS RECIPE WORKS: Unaccustomed to the spotlight, lemon can turn temperamental in this quick Italian classic—unless you provide it with the perfect costars. We wanted a dish bursting with bright, bracing lemon flavor and moistened with just enough fruity olive oil to coat each delicate strand. Starting with lemon flavor, we found the window for the right amount of juice per pound of pasta was extremely small, and if we leaned more to either side, the lemon flavor became either too tart or barely noticeable. To boost the lemon's power without extra acidity, we added some grated zest to the sauce. As for the base of the sauce, we relied on an olive oil–cream sauce. The cream neutralized some of the acids in the juice while augmenting the oils responsible for the fruity, floral notes.

Spaghetti with Lemon and Olive Oil (al Limone)

SERVES 4

Letting this dish rest briefly before serving allows the flavors to develop and the sauce to thicken.

  Table salt and ground black pepper
1 pound spaghetti
¼ cup extra-virgin olive oil, plus extra for drizzling
1 medium shallot, minced (about 3 tablespoons)
¼ cup heavy cream
1 ounce Parmesan cheese, grated (about ½ cup), plus extra for serving
2 teaspoons grated zest plus ¼ cup juice from 2 lemons
2 tablespoons chopped fresh basil leaves

1. Bring 4 quarts water to a boil in a large pot. Add 1 tablespoon salt and the pasta to the boiling water and cook until al dente. Reserve 1¾ cups of the cooking water, then drain the pasta.

2. Heat 1 tablespoon of the oil in the now-empty pot over medium heat until shimmering. Add the shallot and ½ teaspoon salt and cook until softened, about 2 minutes.

Stir in 1½ cups of the reserved cooking water and the cream, bring to a simmer, and cook for 2 minutes. Off the heat, add the drained pasta, remaining 3 tablespoons oil, Parmesan, lemon zest, lemon juice, and ½ teaspoon pepper, and toss to combine.

3. Cover and let the pasta rest for 2 minutes, tossing frequently and adding the remaining cooking water as needed to adjust the consistency. Stir in the basil and season with salt and pepper to taste. Drizzle individual portions with oil and serve, passing the additional Parmesan separately.

SPAGHETTI WITH PECORINO ROMANO AND BLACK PEPPER

WHY THIS RECIPE WORKS: With just three main ingredients (cheese, pepper, and pasta), this Roman dish makes a delicious and quick pantry supper. But in versions we tried, the creamy sauce quickly turns into clumps of solidified cheese. We wanted a sauce that was intensely cheesy but also creamy and smooth.

Our science editor explained why the cheese clumps in this dish. Cheese consists mainly of three basic substances: fat, protein, and water. When a hard cheese like Pecorino, our cheese of choice, is heated, its fat begins to melt and its proteins soften. The fat acts as a sort of glue, fusing the proteins together. In order to coat the cheese and prevent the proteins from sticking together, we needed to introduce a starch into the mix.

It occurred to us that as pasta cooks, it releases starch into the water. We reduced the amount of water to concentrate the starch and whisked some of the cooking liquid into the cheese. This helped to a point, but we found we also needed an emulsifier—something to bind together the sauce. We turned to cream. By switching the butter for cream, we created a light, perfectly smooth sauce that had all the cheese flavor we wanted. Even after sitting on a table for a full five minutes, there wasn't a clump in sight.

Spaghetti with Pecorino Romano and Black Pepper
SERVES 4 TO 6

High-quality ingredients are essential in this dish, most importantly, imported Pecorino Romano. For a slightly less rich dish, substitute half-and-half for the heavy cream. Do not adjust the amount of water for cooking the pasta; the amount used is critical to the success of the recipe. Make sure to stir the pasta frequently while cooking so that it doesn't stick to the pot. Draining the pasta water into the serving bowl warms the bowl and helps keeps the dish hot until it is served. Letting the dish rest briefly before serving allows the flavors to develop and the sauce to thicken.

- 4 ounces Pecorino Romano, grated fine (about 2 cups), plus 2 ounces grated coarse (about 1 cup), for serving
- 1 pound spaghetti
  Table salt
- 2 tablespoons heavy cream
- 2 teaspoons extra-virgin olive oil
- 1½ teaspoons ground black pepper

1. Place the finely grated Pecorino in a medium bowl. Set a colander in a large bowl.

2. Bring 2 quarts water to a boil in a large Dutch oven. Add the pasta and 1½ teaspoons salt and cook, stirring frequently, until the pasta is al dente. Drain the pasta into the colander set in the bowl, reserving the cooking water. Pour 1½ cups of the cooking water into a liquid measuring cup and discard the remainder and then place the pasta in the empty bowl.

3. Slowly whisk 1 cup of the reserved pasta water into the finely grated Pecorino until smooth. Whisk in the cream, oil, and pepper. Gradually pour the cheese mixture over the pasta, tossing to coat. Let the pasta rest for 1 to 2 minutes, tossing frequently, adjusting the consistency with the remaining ½ cup reserved pasta cooking water as needed. Serve, passing the coarsely grated Pecorino separately.

TOMATOES—SKIP THE FRIDGE, PLEASE

We never store tomatoes in the refrigerator. Cold damages tomatoes in two ways: It destroys an enzyme that produces flavorful compounds, and it makes water in the tomato expand, rupturing cells and turning the flesh mealy. But what about storing a partially used tomato? We cut a dozen ripe tomatoes in two, stored half of each in the fridge, and kept the other half at room temperature (both were wrapped tightly in plastic wrap). After a few days, the halves at room temperature had begun to soften, while the refrigerated halves were still as firm as the day they were cut. Upon tasting, however, we found the refrigerated halves were bland and mealy compared with the never-refrigerated halves. Our advice? Keep cut tomatoes tightly wrapped at room temperature and consume them within a few days. The shelf life gained by refrigeration doesn't make up for the loss in flavor and texture.

PASTA WITH FRESH TOMATOES

WHY THIS RECIPE WORKS: Fully ripe tomatoes need little else besides high-quality olive oil and a smattering of fresh herbs to become a bright, summery dressing for pasta. We set out to create the perfect raw tomato sauce—ideal for a quick yet flavorful dinner.

Selecting the ripest tomatoes guarantees fresh flavor in the sauce, but to prevent their sweetness and acidity from taking over, we mixed in a generous amount of extra-virgin olive oil and a hefty amount of fresh herbs—you can use basil, parsley, cilantro, mint, oregano, or tarragon. We let the flavors of the tomatoes, olive oil, herbs, and some minced garlic blend while we cooked the pasta. Short pasta shapes that hold on to the chunky sauce work best.

Pasta with Fresh Tomatoes and Herbs

SERVES 4 TO 6

This chunky sauce works best with tubular pasta shapes, such as penne or fusilli. The success of this dish depends on using ripe, flavorful tomatoes.

1½ pounds ripe tomatoes (about 3 large), cored and cut into ½-inch pieces (see note)
¼ cup minced fresh herbs, such as basil, parsley, cilantro, mint, oregano, or tarragon
1 medium garlic clove, minced or pressed through a garlic press (about 1 teaspoon)
¼ cup extra-virgin olive oil
Table salt and ground black pepper
1 pound penne, fusilli, or other short tubular pasta (see note)

1. Combine the tomatoes, herbs, garlic, oil, and salt and pepper to taste in a medium bowl. Set aside.

2. Bring 4 quarts water to a boil in a large pot. Add 1 tablespoon salt and the pasta to the boiling water and cook, stirring often, until al dente. Reserve ½ cup of the cooking water then drain the pasta and return it to the pot. Add the tomatoes and toss to combine; adjust the consistency of the sauce with the reserved pasta cooking water as needed. Serve.

PASTA AND FRESH TOMATO SAUCE

WHY THIS RECIPE WORKS: The best fresh tomato sauces capture the contrasting sweet and tart flavors of ripe tomatoes. But often, these sauces get waterlogged from the tomato juice. We wanted a cooked sauce that allowed the flavors of the traditional players—tomatoes, basil, garlic, and oil—to meld, but not become watered down.

Quick cooking was the key to preserving fresh tomato flavor and creating a sauce that is both hearty and brightly flavored. To prevent unattractive pieces of curled-up tomato skin floating in our finished sauce, we simply peeled the tomatoes by boiling them and pulling off their skins. Seeded tomatoes made for a less watery start to the sauce, and cooking them down for a brief period facilitated the evaporation of any remaining liquid. Chopped fresh basil rounded out the flavors of the sauce, and a last-minute drizzle of olive oil brought a richness that complemented the sweetness of the tomatoes.

Pasta and Fresh Tomato Sauce with Garlic and Basil

SERVES 4 TO 6

To peel the tomatoes, dunk the cored tomatoes in a pot of boiling water until the skins split and begin to curl around the cored area, 15 to 30 seconds; transfer the tomatoes

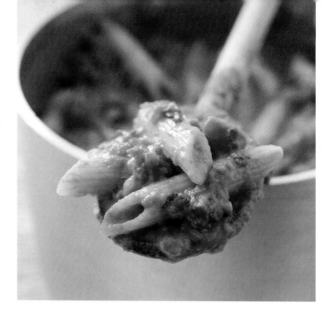

to a bowl of ice water, then peel off the skins with your fingers. This chunky sauce works best with tubular pasta shapes, such as penne or fusilli. If you'd like to serve it with spaghetti or linguine, puree the sauce in a blender or food processor before adding the basil. This recipe can be doubled and prepared in a 12-inch skillet.

- 3 tablespoons extra-virgin olive oil
- 2 medium garlic cloves, minced or pressed through a garlic press (about 2 teaspoons)
- 2 pounds ripe tomatoes (about 4 large), cored, peeled, seeded, and cut into ½-inch pieces (see note)
- 2 tablespoons chopped fresh basil leaves
  Table salt
- 1 pound penne, fusilli, or other short tubular pasta (see note)

1. Cook 2 tablespoons of the oil and the garlic in a 10-inch skillet over medium heat until fragrant, about 30 seconds. Stir in the tomatoes and cook over medium-high heat until the liquid released by the tomatoes evaporates and the tomato pieces form a chunky sauce, about 10 minutes. Stir in the basil and salt to taste; cover.

2. Meanwhile, bring 4 quarts water to a boil in a large pot. Add 1 tablespoon salt and the pasta to the boiling water and cook, stirring often, until al dente. Reserve ½ cup of the cooking water then drain the pasta and return it to the pot. Add ¼ cup of the reserved cooking water, the sauce, and the remaining 1 tablespoon oil and toss to combine. Adjust the consistency of the sauce with the remaining reserved pasta cooking water as needed. Serve.

PASTA WITH CREAMY TOMATO SAUCE

WHY THIS RECIPE WORKS: In the best examples of creamy tomato sauce, the acidity of fruity tomatoes is balanced with the richness of dairy; the worst deliver instant heartburn and make you wish the two elements had never met. We wanted a smooth, full-flavored tomato sauce enriched with, but not overwhelmed by, cream.

Readily available, canned crushed tomatoes trumped canned whole and diced tomatoes—they're bright in flavor, easy to puree in the food processor, and contain just the right amount of juice. Before adding the tomatoes to the pot, we cooked a few tablespoons of tomato paste with some onion and garlic, and added sun-dried tomatoes, to deepen the flavor of the sauce. A pinch of red pepper flakes, a splash of wine, and a little minced

prosciutto added depth and tamed some of the sauce's sweetness; a bit of reserved uncooked crushed tomatoes and another splash of wine stirred in before serving brought the sauce's ingredients together. As for the cream, traditional heavy cream can't be beat; we added it to the just-finished sauce to enrich it without subduing the bright tomato flavor.

Pasta with Creamy Tomato Sauce

SERVES 4 TO 6

Use high-quality crushed tomatoes; our favorite brands are Tuttorosso and Muir Glen.

- 3 tablespoons unsalted butter
- 1 small onion, minced
- 1 ounce prosciutto, minced (about 2 tablespoons)
- 1 bay leaf
  Pinch red pepper flakes
  Table salt
- 3 medium garlic cloves, minced or pressed through a garlic press (about 1 tablespoon)
- 2 ounces oil-packed sun-dried tomatoes, drained, rinsed, patted dry, and chopped coarse (about 3 tablespoons)
- 2 tablespoons tomato paste
- ¼ cup plus 2 tablespoons dry white wine
- 2 cups plus 2 tablespoons crushed tomatoes (from one 28-ounce can; see note)
- 1 pound ziti, penne, or other short tubular pasta
- ½ cup heavy cream
  Ground black pepper
- ¼ cup chopped fresh basil leaves
  Grated Parmesan cheese, for serving

1. Melt the butter in a medium saucepan over medium heat. Add the onion, prosciutto, bay leaf, red pepper flakes, and ¼ teaspoon salt; cook, stirring occasionally, until the onion is very soft and beginning to turn light gold, 8 to 12 minutes. Increase the heat to medium-high, add the garlic, and cook until fragrant, about 30 seconds. Stir in the sun-dried tomatoes and tomato paste and cook, stirring constantly, until slightly darkened, 1 to 2 minutes. Add ¼ cup of the wine and cook, stirring frequently, until the liquid has evaporated, 1 to 2 minutes.

2. Add 2 cups of the crushed tomatoes and bring to a simmer. Reduce the heat to low, partially cover, and cook, stirring occasionally, until the sauce is thickened, 25 to 30 minutes.

3. Meanwhile, bring 4 quarts water to a boil in a large pot. Add 1 tablespoon salt and the pasta to the boiling water and cook, stirring often, until al dente. Reserve ½ cup of the cooking water then drain the pasta and return it to the pot.

4. Remove the bay leaf from the sauce and discard. Stir the cream, remaining 2 tablespoons crushed tomatoes, and remaining 2 tablespoons wine into the sauce; season with salt and pepper to taste. Add the sauce to the pasta and adjust the consistency of the sauce with the reserved pasta cooking water as needed. Stir in the basil and serve, passing the Parmesan separately.

PASTA CAPRESE

WHY THIS RECIPE WORKS: The summer salad composed of creamy mozzarella, fresh basil, and sweet tomatoes has become so popular that we wanted to translate it to a simple-yet-elegant pasta dish, one in which the primary ingredients work in harmony with the pasta. Specifically, we wanted creamy pockets of milky mozzarella throughout the dish, rather than the chewy wads that can occur when cheese hits hot pasta. And we wanted to find a way to guarantee sweet tomato flavor, even when we were working with substandard tomatoes.

Supermarket mozzarella works well in this dish; the trick is to dice and freeze it for just 10 minutes before tossing it with the hot pasta to keep the cheese soft and creamy (instead of dry and clumpy). Otherwise, handmade mozzarella (minus the freezing step) works well. To boost the flavor of less-than-stellar tomatoes, we added a little sugar for sweetness and fresh lemon juice for brightness. Marinating the tomatoes and mozzarella with olive oil, minced shallot, salt, and a pinch of black pepper while the pasta was cooking added even more flavor. We decided not to cut corners with a substandard olive oil; because there are few flavors in this dish, the fruity nuances of a good extra-virgin olive oil really make a difference.

Pasta Caprese
SERVES 4 TO 6

This dish will be very warm, not hot. The success of this recipe depends on high-quality ingredients, including ripe, in-season tomatoes and a fruity olive oil (the test kitchen prefers Columela extra-virgin). Don't skip the step of freezing the mozzarella, as freezing prevents it from turning chewy when it comes in contact with the hot pasta. If handmade buffalo- or cow's-milk mozzarella is available (it's commonly found, packed in water, in gourmet and cheese shops), we highly recommend using it, but do not freeze it. Additional lemon juice or up to 1 teaspoon sugar can be added at the end to taste, depending on the ripeness of the tomatoes.

¼ cup extra-virgin olive oil (see note)
2–4 teaspoons juice from 1 lemon (see note)
1 small garlic clove, minced or pressed through a garlic press (about ½ teaspoon)
1 small shallot, minced (about 1 tablespoon)
Table salt and ground black pepper
1½ pounds ripe tomatoes (about 3 large), cored, seeded, and cut into ½-inch dice (see note)
12 ounces fresh mozzarella cheese, cut into ½-inch cubes (see note)
1 pound penne, fusilli, or campanelle
¼ cup chopped fresh basil leaves
1 teaspoon sugar (optional; see note)

1. Whisk the oil, 2 teaspoons of the lemon juice, the garlic, shallot, ½ teaspoon salt, and ¼ teaspoon pepper together in a large bowl. Add the tomatoes and gently toss to combine; set aside. Do not marinate the tomatoes for longer than 45 minutes.

2. While the tomatoes are marinating, place the mozzarella on a plate and freeze until slightly firm, about 10 minutes. Bring 4 quarts water to a boil in a large pot. Add

1 tablespoon salt and the pasta to the boiling water and cook, stirring often, until al dente. Drain well.

3. Add the pasta and mozzarella to the tomato mixture and gently toss to combine. Let stand for 5 minutes. Stir in the basil, season with salt and pepper to taste, and add additional lemon juice or sugar, if desired. Serve immediately.

PASTA WITH TOMATOES AND OLIVES

WHY THIS RECIPE WORKS: When tomatoes are in season, there's no better time to make a simple, fresh tomato sauce. We like the classic pairing of tomatoes and olives, so we set out to make an easy, not too watery, sauce with Mediterranean flavors.

Seeding the tomatoes rid them of excess moisture and prevented a watery sauce. Instead of peeling the tomato skins, we decided to leave them on so the chopped tomatoes would have some structural integrity and not disintegrate. By making a no-cook sauce—the other components were fresh mint, chopped kalamata olives, and feta—we were able to prepare it quickly while the drained pasta waited on the sidelines. The potent olives and feta added a bright zestiness to our pasta, and the mint amplified the sauce's freshness.

Farfalle with Tomatoes, Olives, and Feta
SERVES 4 TO 6

To prevent the feta from melting into the pasta, add it only after the tomatoes have been tossed with the pasta, which gives the mixture the opportunity to cool slightly.

> Table salt
> 1 **pound farfalle**
> 1½ **pounds ripe tomatoes (about 3 large), cored, seeded, and cut into ½-inch pieces**
> ½ **cup pitted kalamata olives, chopped coarse**
> ¼ **cup extra-virgin olive oil**
> 1 **tablespoon chopped fresh mint leaves**
> **Ground black pepper**
> 6 **ounces feta cheese, crumbled (about 1½ cups; see note)**

1. Bring 4 quarts water to a boil in a large pot. Add 1 tablespoon salt and the pasta to the boiling water and cook, stirring often, until al dente. Reserve ½ cup of the cooking water then drain the pasta and return it to the pot.

2. Meanwhile, combine the tomatoes, olives, oil, mint, ½ teaspoon salt, and ¼ teaspoon pepper in a medium bowl.

Add the sauce to the pasta and adjust the consistency of the sauce with the reserved pasta cooking water as needed. Add the feta and toss to combine. Season with salt and pepper to taste and serve.

QUICK TOMATO SAUCE

WHY THIS RECIPE WORKS: In a perfect world, garden-ripe tomatoes make the best quick tomato sauce. But that isn't a realistic option for most of the year. We wanted to create a complex, brightly flavored sauce with the next best alternative—canned tomatoes—that tasted of full, fruity tomatoes, in the time it took to boil pasta.

Choosing the right can of tomatoes was a critical first step. Crushed tomatoes were the best choice because they would save us the step of pureeing. We also shredded a small amount of onion on a box grater before sautéing; the shredded pieces cooked faster and became sweeter more quickly. We sautéed the onion in butter, which caramelizes when heated, and added garlic, sugar, and the crushed tomatoes, then simmered the sauce briefly. To make up for the lost fragrance of fresh tomatoes, we added chopped fresh basil and extra-virgin olive oil. Swirled in just before serving, these ingredients infused the sauce with fresh herbal flavor and a hit of richness.

Quick Tomato Sauce

MAKES ABOUT 3 CUPS

This recipe makes enough to sauce a pound of pasta. High-quality canned tomatoes will make a big difference in this sauce; our preferred brands of crushed tomatoes are Tuttorosso and Muir Glen. Grate the onion on the large holes of a box grater.

- 2 tablespoons unsalted butter
- ¼ cup grated onion (see note)
- ¼ teaspoon dried oregano
  - Table salt
- 2 medium garlic cloves, minced or pressed through a garlic press (about 2 teaspoons)
- 1 (28-ounce) can crushed tomatoes (see note)
- ¼ teaspoon sugar
- 2 tablespoons chopped fresh basil leaves
- 1 tablespoon extra-virgin olive oil
  - Ground black pepper

Melt the butter in a medium saucepan over medium heat. Add the onion, oregano, and ½ teaspoon salt; cook, stirring occasionally, until the liquid has evaporated and the onion is golden brown, about 5 minutes. Add the garlic and cook until fragrant, about 30 seconds. Stir in the tomatoes and sugar; bring to a simmer over high heat. Lower the heat to medium-low and simmer until slightly thickened, about 10 minutes. Off the heat, stir in the basil and oil; season with salt and pepper to taste.

MARINARA SAUCE

WHY THIS RECIPE WORKS: Making a tomato sauce with deep, complex flavor usually requires hours of simmering. We wanted to produce a multidimensional marinara sauce in under an hour, perfect for any night of the week.

Our first challenge was picking the right tomatoes. We found canned whole tomatoes, which we hand-crushed to remove the hard core, to be the best choice in terms of both flavor and texture. We boosted tomato flavor by sautéing the tomato pieces until they glazed the bottom of the pan, after which we added their liquid. We shortened the simmering time by using a skillet instead of a saucepan (the greater surface area of a skillet encourages faster evaporation and flavor concentration). Finally, we added just the right amount of sugar, red wine (we especially liked Chianti and Merlot), and, just before serving, a few uncooked canned tomatoes for texture, fresh basil for fresh herbal flavor, and olive oil for richness.

Marinara Sauce

MAKES 4 CUPS

You can figure on about 3 cups of sauce per pound of pasta. Chianti or Merlot work well for the dry red wine. Because canned tomatoes vary in acidity and saltiness, it's best to add salt, pepper, and sugar to taste just before serving. If you prefer a chunkier sauce, give it just three or four pulses in the food processor in step 4.

- 2 (28-ounce) cans whole tomatoes packed in juice
- 3 tablespoons extra-virgin olive oil
- 1 medium onion, minced
- 2 medium garlic cloves, minced or pressed through a garlic press (about 2 teaspoons)
- ½ teaspoon dried oregano
- ⅓ cup dry red wine (see note)
- 3 tablespoons chopped fresh basil leaves
  - Table salt and ground black pepper
- 1–2 teaspoons sugar, as needed (see note)

1. Pour the tomatoes into a strainer set over a large bowl. Open the tomatoes with your hands and remove and discard the fibrous cores; let the tomatoes drain excess liquid, about 5 minutes. Remove ¾ cup tomatoes from the strainer and set aside. Reserve 2½ cups tomato juice and discard the remainder.

2. Heat 2 tablespoons of the olive oil in a 12-inch skillet over medium heat until shimmering. Add the onion and cook, stirring occasionally, until softened and golden around the edges, 6 to 8 minutes. Add the garlic and oregano and cook, stirring constantly, until the garlic is fragrant, about 30 seconds.

3. Add the tomatoes from the strainer and increase the heat to medium-high. Cook, stirring every minute, until the liquid has evaporated and the tomatoes begin to stick to the bottom of the pan and browned bits form around the pan edges, 10 to 12 minutes. Add the wine and cook until thick and syrupy, about 1 minute. Add the reserved tomato juice and bring to a simmer; reduce the heat to medium and cook, stirring occasionally and loosening any browned bits, until the sauce is thickened, 8 to 10 minutes.

4. Transfer the sauce to a food processor and add the reserved tomatoes; process until slightly chunky, about 8 pulses. Return the sauce to the skillet, add the basil and remaining 1 tablespoon olive oil, and season with salt, pepper, and sugar to taste. (The sauce can be refrigerated in an airtight container for up to 3 days or frozen for up to 1 month.)

PASTA PUTTANESCA

WHY THIS RECIPE WORKS: Puttanesca is a gutsy tomato sauce punctuated by the brash, zesty flavors of garlic, anchovies, olives, and capers. But too often, the sauce comes off as too fishy, too garlicky, too briny, or just plain too salty. We wanted to harmonize the bold flavors in this Neapolitan dish and not let any one preside over the others.

For a sauce with the best tomato flavor and a slightly clingy consistency, we used canned diced tomatoes and kept the cooking time to a minimum to retain their fresh flavor and their meaty texture. To tame the garlic and prevent it from burning, we soaked minced garlic in a bit of water before sautéing it. Cooking the garlic and anchovies with red pepper flakes (before adding the tomatoes) helped their flavors bloom and added a subtle heat. We chose to add the olives and capers when the sauce was finished—this prevented them from disintegrating in the sauce. Reserved tomato juice from the canned tomatoes moistened the pasta, and a last-minute addition of minced parsley preserved the fresh flavors of the sauce.

Spaghetti Puttanesca

SERVES 4 TO 6

The pasta and sauce cook in about the same amount of time, so begin the sauce just after you add the pasta to the boiling water in step 1.

  3 **medium garlic cloves, minced or pressed through a garlic press (about 1 tablespoon)**
      Table salt
  1 **pound spaghetti**
  1 **(28-ounce) can diced tomatoes, drained and ½ cup juice reserved**
  2 **tablespoons extra-virgin olive oil, plus extra for drizzling**

USE YOUR NOODLE—PERFECT PASTA TIPS

We love pasta in the test kitchen. As a result, we're pretty opinionated about how we cook it. Here's what you need to know.

COOKING PASTA: Make sure you have all the necessary ingredients and utensils assembled before you begin. You'll need 4 quarts of water to cook 1 pound of dried pasta. Any less and the noodles may stick. Use a pot large enough to accommodate the water and pasta without boil-overs—we like an 8-quart pot. It's crucial to properly season the cooking water—we recommend 1 tablespoon table salt per 4 quarts water. Bring the water to a rolling boil before adding the salt and pasta and give it an immediate stir to prevent sticking. And don't add oil to the pot—oil will prevent sauce from sticking to the pasta.

DRAINING AND SERVING PASTA: If a sauce is too thick, we thin it with a little reserved pasta water. The trouble is, it's easy to forget to save some water. As a reminder, we place a measuring cup in the colander. As for draining pasta, just give it a shake or two. You don't want the pasta bone dry. The little bit of hot cooking water clinging to the pasta will help the sauce coat it. And if you're using a large serving bowl for the pasta, place it underneath the colander while draining the pasta. The hot water heats up the bowl, which keeps the pasta warmer longer.

  4 **teaspoons minced anchovy fillets (about 8 fillets)**
  1 **teaspoon red pepper flakes**
  ½ **cup pitted kalamata olives, chopped coarse**
  ¼ **cup minced fresh parsley leaves**
  3 **tablespoons capers, rinsed**

1. Combine the garlic with 1 tablespoon water in a small bowl; set aside. Bring 4 quarts water to a boil in a large pot. Add 1 tablespoon salt and the pasta to the boiling water and cook, stirring often, until al dente. Reserve ½ cup of the cooking water then drain the pasta and return it to the pot. Add ¼ cup of the reserved tomato juice and toss to combine.

2. Meanwhile, heat the oil, anchovies, garlic mixture, and red pepper flakes in a 12-inch skillet over medium heat. Cook, stirring frequently, until the garlic is fragrant, 2 to 3 minutes. Add the tomatoes and simmer until slightly thickened, about 8 minutes.

3. Stir the olives, parsley, and capers into the sauce. Pour the sauce over the pasta and toss to combine; adjust the consistency of the sauce with the remaining reserved tomato juice or reserved pasta cooking water as needed. Season with salt to taste, drizzle with 1 tablespoon oil, if desired, and serve immediately.

PASTA ALL'AMATRICIANA

WHY THIS RECIPE WORKS: Pasta all'Amatriciana is a classic Roman pasta dish that boasts a rich sauce containing tomato, bacon, onion, and Pecorino Romano cheese. Unfortunately, for a truly authentic dish, you need a specific type of bacon, *guanciale* (made from pork jowls), which is easy to find in central Italy but not so easy to locate in the States. We wanted to create a recipe that would do this classic sauce justice using ingredients found locally.

Thickly sliced pancetta (unsmoked Italian bacon) is the best substitute for guanciale but if you can't find pancetta, bacon works too. We cut the pancetta into strips and cooked them in a skillet until crisp, then built the sauce in the remaining fat. Canned diced tomatoes, onion, and red pepper flakes made up the sauce; we kept the pancetta separate until the end so it stayed crisp in the finished

dish. For the last steps, we tossed the crisp pancetta in with the tomato sauce and pasta (long-strand pasta, like bucatini or linguine, works best) and sprinkled grated Pecorino Romano cheese on top.

Pasta with Tomato, Bacon, and Onion (Pasta all'Amatriciana)
SERVES 4 TO 6

This dish is traditionally made with bucatini, also called perciatelli, which appear to be thick, round strands but are actually thin, extralong tubes. Linguine works fine, too. When buying pancetta, ask the butcher to slice it ¼ inch thick; if using bacon, buy slab bacon and cut it into ¼-inch-thick slices yourself. If the pancetta that you're using is very lean, it's unlikely that you will need to drain off any fat before adding the onion.

- **2** tablespoons extra-virgin olive oil
- **6** ounces pancetta or bacon, sliced ¼ inch thick and cut into strips 1 inch long and ¼ inch wide (see note)
- **1** medium onion, minced
- **½** teaspoon red pepper flakes, or to taste
- **1** (28-ounce) can diced tomatoes, drained and juice reserved
- **Table salt**
- **1** pound bucatini, perciatelli, or linguine (see note)
- **⅓** cup grated Pecorino Romano cheese

1. Bring 4 quarts water to a boil in a large pot.

2. Meanwhile, heat the oil in a 12-inch skillet over medium heat until shimmering. Add the pancetta and cook, stirring occasionally, until lightly browned and crisp, about 8 minutes. Using a slotted spoon, transfer the pancetta to a paper towel–lined plate; set aside. Pour off all but 2 tablespoons of fat from the skillet. Add the onion and cook over medium heat until softened, about 5 minutes. Add the red pepper flakes and cook, about 30 seconds. Stir in the tomatoes and reserved juice and simmer until slightly thickened, about 10 minutes.

3. While the sauce is simmering, add 1 tablespoon salt and the pasta to the boiling water and cook, stirring often, until al dente. Reserve ½ cup of the cooking water then drain the pasta and return it to the pot.

4. Add the pancetta to the sauce and season with salt to taste. Add the sauce to the pasta and toss over low heat to combine, about 30 seconds. Add the Pecorino and toss again. Adjust the consistency of the sauce with the reserved pasta cooking water as needed and serve immediately.

PASTA WITH PESTO

WHY THIS RECIPE WORKS: Pasta with pesto makes for a satisfying, summery meal. But getting pesto right isn't always so easy; the sauce can be anywhere from too thin and watery to too thick and overpoweringly garlicky. Our goal was to heighten the basil and subdue the garlic flavors in pesto so that each major element balanced the next.

We started by briefly blanching whole unpeeled garlic cloves to tame their flavor and prevent them from taking over the sauce. Then we bruised the basil in a plastic bag with a meat pounder (you could also use a rolling pin) to unlock its flavor; we found that this method released the most herbal flavors from the basil. With the basil flavor boosted and the garlic toned down, it was time to process the ingredients with toasted nuts and stir in the Parmesan. Finally, we reserved some of the pasta cooking water, which was essential to thin out the pesto once it had been added to the pasta. The water also softened and blended the flavors a bit, and highlighted the creaminess of the cheese and nuts.

Farfalle with Pesto

SERVES 4 TO 6

Basil usually darkens in homemade pesto, but you can preserve the green color by adding the optional parsley. For sharper flavor, substitute 1 tablespoon finely grated Pecorino Romano cheese for 1 tablespoon of the Parmesan. For a change from farfalle, try curly shapes, such as fusilli, which can trap bits of the pesto.

- 3 **medium garlic cloves, threaded on a skewer**
- 2 **cups packed fresh basil leaves**
- 2 **tablespoons fresh flat-leaf parsley leaves (optional; see note)**
- ¼ **cup pine nuts, walnuts, or almonds, toasted**
- 7 **tablespoons extra-virgin olive oil**
  Table salt
- ¼ **cup grated Parmesan (see note)**
- 1 **pound farfalle (see note)**

1. Bring 4 quarts water to a boil in a large pot. Lower the skewered garlic into the water and boil for 45 seconds. Immediately run the garlic under cold water. Remove the garlic from the skewer, peel, and mince.

2. Place the basil and parsley (if using) in a zipper-lock bag and pound with the flat side of a meat pounder or a rolling pin until all the leaves are bruised.

3. Process the nuts, garlic, basil, oil, and ½ teaspoon salt in a food processor until smooth, scraping down the sides of the workbowl as necessary. Transfer the mixture to a small bowl, stir in the cheese, and season with salt to taste. (The pesto can be covered with a sheet of plastic wrap pressed against the surface and refrigerated for up to 5 days.)

4. Add 1 tablespoon salt and the pasta to the boiling water and cook, stirring often, until al dente. Reserve ½ cup of the cooking water then drain the pasta and return it to the pot. Stir in ¼ cup reserved cooking water and the pesto; adjust the consistency of the sauce with the remaining reserved pasta cooking water as needed. Serve immediately.

PASTA WITH TOMATO AND ALMOND PESTO

WHY THIS RECIPE WORKS: In the Sicilian village of Trapani, there's a very different kind of pesto—it's basically pesto crossed with tomato sauce. Almonds replace pine nuts, but the big difference is the appearance of fresh tomatoes—not as the main ingredient, but as a fruity, sweet accent. We wanted a recipe for a clean, bright version of this sauce, not a chunky tomato salsa or thin, watery slush.

For an uncooked sauce, fresh tomatoes were best. Cherry and grape tomatoes proved equal contenders, sharing a similar brightness and juiciness that was far more reliable than that of their larger cousins. We processed the tomatoes with a handful of basil, garlic, and toasted almonds. The almonds contributed body and thickened the sauce while retaining just enough crunch to offset the tomatoes' pulpiness; using blanched, slivered almonds avoided the muddy flavor often contributed by papery skins. We added a scant amount of hot vinegar peppers for zing, then drizzled in olive oil in a slow, steady stream to emulsify the pesto. Parmesan was stirred in for the finishing touch to this light, bright, and texturally satisfying pesto.

Pasta with Tomato and Almond Pesto (Pesto alla Trapanese)

SERVES 4 TO 6

While we prefer linguine or spaghetti, any pasta shape will work here. You may substitute ½ teaspoon of red wine vinegar and ¼ teaspoon of red pepper flakes for the pepperoncini.

NONTRADITIONAL PESTOS

WHY THIS RECIPE WORKS: Pesto doesn't always mean basil, pine nuts, and Parmesan. We wanted to make quick pestos with a variety of other potent ingredients, like sun-dried tomatoes, goat cheese, and kalamata olives.

For pestos that were flavorful but not harsh, we tamed the garlic by toasting unpeeled cloves in a hot skillet or replaced most of it with sun-dried tomatoes. Then we processed the garlic or sun-dried tomatoes with olive oil, nuts, cheese, and olives, among other ingredients, to create smooth sauces that cling well to pasta. And to keep the pasta moist, we made sure to reserve some of the pasta cooking water to thin the pesto.

Table salt
1 pound linguine or spaghetti (see note)
¼ cup slivered almonds, toasted
12 ounces cherry or grape tomatoes (about 2½ cups)
½ cup packed fresh basil leaves
1 medium garlic clove, minced or pressed through a garlic press (about 1 teaspoon)
1 small pepperoncini (hot peppers in vinegar), stemmed, seeded, and minced (about ½ teaspoon; see note)
Pinch red pepper flakes (optional)
⅓ cup extra-virgin olive oil
1 ounce Parmesan cheese, grated (about ½ cup), plus extra for serving

1. Bring 4 quarts water to a boil in a large pot. Add 1 tablespoon salt and the pasta to the boiling water and cook, stirring often, until al dente. Reserve ½ cup of the cooking water then drain the pasta and return it to the pot.

2. Meanwhile, process the almonds, tomatoes, basil, garlic, pepperoncini, 1 teaspoon salt, and red pepper flakes (if using) in a food processor until smooth, about 1 minute. Scrape down the sides of the workbowl with a rubber spatula. With the machine running, slowly drizzle in the oil, about 30 seconds.

3. Add the pesto and ½ cup of the Parmesan to the cooked pasta and adjust the consistency of the sauce with the reserved pasta cooking water as needed. Serve immediately, passing extra Parmesan separately.

Campanelle with Arugula, Goat Cheese, and Sun-Dried Tomato Pesto

SERVES 4 TO 6

Make sure to rinse the herbs and seasonings from the sun-dried tomatoes. Farfalle can be substituted for the campanelle.

1 cup oil-packed sun-dried tomatoes (one 8½-ounce jar), drained, rinsed, patted dry, and chopped coarse (see note)
1 ounce Parmesan cheese, grated (about ½ cup)
6 tablespoons extra-virgin olive oil
¼ cup walnuts, toasted
1 small garlic clove, minced or pressed through a garlic press (about ½ teaspoon)
Table salt and ground black pepper
1 pound campanelle (see note)
1 medium bunch arugula, washed, dried, stemmed, and torn into bite-size pieces (about 6 cups)
3 ounces goat cheese, crumbled (about ¾ cup)

1. Process the sun-dried tomatoes, Parmesan, oil, walnuts, garlic, ½ teaspoon salt, and ⅛ teaspoon pepper in a food processor until smooth, scraping down the sides of the workbowl as necessary. Transfer the mixture to a small bowl and set aside.

2. Bring 4 quarts water to a boil in a large pot. Add 1 tablespoon salt and the pasta to the boiling water and cook, stirring often, until al dente. Reserve ¾ cup of the cooking water then drain the pasta and return it to the pot. Immediately stir in the arugula until wilted. Stir ½ cup of the reserved pasta cooking water into the pesto and add the pesto to the pasta. Toss to combine, adjusting the

consistency of the sauce with the remaining reserved pasta cooking water as needed. Serve immediately, sprinkling the cheese over individual bowls.

Penne with Toasted Nut and Parsley Pesto

SERVES 4 TO 6

Toasting the unpeeled garlic in a skillet reduces its harshness and gives it a mellow flavor that works well in pesto.

- 3 medium garlic cloves, unpeeled
- 1 cup pecans, walnuts, whole blanched almonds, skinned hazelnuts, unsalted pistachios, or pine nuts, or any combination thereof, toasted
- ½ cup packed fresh parsley leaves
- 7 tablespoons extra-virgin olive oil
- 1 ounce Parmesan cheese, grated (about ½ cup)
  Table salt and ground black pepper
- 1 pound penne

1. Toast the garlic in a small skillet over medium heat, shaking the pan occasionally, until softened and spotty brown, about 8 minutes; when cool, remove and discard the skins.

2. Process the garlic, nuts, parsley, and oil in a food processor until smooth, scraping down the sides of the workbowl as necessary. Transfer the mixture to a small bowl and stir in the Parmesan; season with salt and pepper to taste.

3. Bring 4 quarts water to a boil in a large pot. Add 1 tablespoon salt and the pasta to the boiling water and cook, stirring often, until al dente. Reserve ½ cup of the cooking water then drain the pasta and return it to the pot. Stir ¼ cup of the reserved pasta cooking water into the pesto and add the pesto to the pasta. Toss to combine, adjusting the consistency of the sauce with the remaining reserved pasta cooking water as needed. Serve immediately.

Spaghetti with Olive Pesto

SERVES 4 TO 6

This black pesto is called olivada in Italy. Make sure to use high-quality olives in this recipe. The anchovy adds flavor but not fishiness to the pesto and we recommend its inclusion.

- 3 medium garlic cloves, unpeeled
- 1½ cups pitted kalamata olives (see note)
- 1 ounce Parmesan cheese, grated (about ½ cup), plus extra for serving

- 6 tablespoons extra-virgin olive oil
- ¼ cup packed fresh parsley leaves
- 1 medium shallot, chopped coarse (about 3 tablespoons)
- 8 large basil leaves
- 1 tablespoon juice from 1 lemon
- 1 anchovy fillet, rinsed (optional; see note)
  Table salt and ground black pepper
- 1 pound spaghetti
  Lemon wedges, for serving

1. Toast the garlic in a small skillet over medium heat, shaking the pan occasionally, until the garlic is softened and spotty brown, about 8 minutes; when cool, remove and discard the skins.

2. Process the garlic, olives, ½ cup of the Parmesan, oil, parsley, shallot, basil, lemon juice, and anchovy (if using) in a food processor, scraping down the sides of the workbowl as necessary. Transfer the mixture to a small bowl and season with salt and pepper to taste.

3. Bring 4 quarts water to a boil in a large pot. Add 1 tablespoon salt and the pasta to the boiling water and cook, stirring often, until al dente. Reserve ½ cup of the cooking water then drain the pasta and return it to the pot. Stir ¼ cup of the reserved pasta cooking water into the pesto and add the pesto to the pasta. Toss to combine, adjusting the consistency of the sauce with the remaining reserved pasta cooking water as needed. Serve immediately, passing the lemon wedges and extra Parmesan separately.

SPRING VEGETABLE PASTA

WHY THIS RECIPE WORKS: In pasta primavera, the vegetables and pasta are tossed together in a sauce made with broth and heavy cream. We love this classic, but sometimes we want a lighter, brighter version—one with a creamy sauce, but without the cream. As for the vegetables, we wanted true spring vegetables. To start, we chose asparagus and green peas, adding chives for bite and garlic and leeks for depth and sweetness. For a deeply flavored sauce that would unify the pasta and vegetables, we borrowed a technique from risotto, lightly toasting the pasta in olive oil before cooking it in broth and white wine. The sauce flavored the pasta as it cooked while the pasta added starch to the sauce, thickening it without the need for heavy cream. This nontraditional approach gave us a light but creamy sauce with sweet, grassy flavors that paired perfectly with the vegetables. This was a dish that truly tasted like spring.

Spring Vegetable Pasta

SERVES 4 TO 6

Campanelle is our pasta of choice in this dish, but farfalle and penne are good substitutes.

1½ pounds leeks, white and light green parts halved lengthwise, sliced ½ inch thick, and washed; 3 cups coarsely chopped dark green parts, washed

1 pound asparagus, tough ends trimmed (see page 251), chopped coarse, and reserved, spears cut on bias into ½-inch lengths

2 cups frozen peas, thawed

4 medium garlic cloves, minced or pressed through a garlic press (about 4 teaspoons)

4 cups vegetable broth

1 cup water

2 tablespoons minced fresh mint leaves

2 tablespoons minced fresh chives

½ teaspoon grated zest plus 2 tablespoons juice from 1 lemon

6 tablespoons extra-virgin olive oil
Table salt and ground black pepper

¼ teaspoon red pepper flakes

1 pound campanelle (see note)

1 cup dry white wine

1 ounce grated Parmesan cheese (about ½ cup), plus extra for serving

1. Bring the leek greens, asparagus trimmings, 1 cup of the peas, half of the garlic, the broth, and water to simmer in a large saucepan. Reduce the heat to medium-low and simmer gently for 10 minutes. While the broth simmers, combine the mint, chives, and lemon zest in a bowl; set aside.

2. Strain the broth through a fine-mesh strainer into a large liquid measuring cup, pressing on the solids to extract as much liquid as possible (you should have 5 cups broth; add water as needed to measure 5 cups). Discard the solids and return the broth to the saucepan. Cover and keep warm.

3. Heat 2 tablespoons of the oil in a Dutch oven over medium heat until shimmering. Add the leeks and a pinch salt and cook, covered, stirring occasionally, until the leeks begin to brown, about 5 minutes. Add the asparagus spears and cook until the asparagus is crisp-tender, 4 to 6 minutes. Add the remaining garlic and the red pepper flakes and cook until fragrant, about 30 seconds. Add the remaining 1 cup peas and continue to cook for 1 minute longer. Transfer the vegetables to a plate and set aside. Wipe out the pot.

4. Heat the remaining ¼ cup oil in the now-empty pot over medium heat until shimmering. Add the pasta and cook, stirring often, until just beginning to brown, about 5 minutes. Add the wine and cook, stirring constantly, until absorbed, about 2 minutes.

5. When the wine is fully absorbed, add the warm broth and bring to a boil. Cook, stirring frequently, until most of the liquid is absorbed and the pasta is al dente, 8 to 10 minutes. Off the heat, stir in half of the herb mixture, the vegetables, lemon juice, and ½ cup of the Parmesan. Season with salt and pepper to taste and serve immediately, passing the additional Parmesan and the remaining herb mixture separately.

PASTA WITH ASPARAGUS

WHY THIS RECIPE WORKS: Asparagus is a natural starting point when trying to make a tomato-free vegetarian pasta sauce. Its sweet, vegetable flavor and quick-cooking nature is a terrific match to pasta. But more often than not, asparagus sauces are bland and boring. We wanted to keep it simple but make this dish livelier.

First, we focused on how to cook the asparagus. Boiling and steaming dilute the vegetable's grassy flavor, so they were out. Instead, we browned the asparagus in a hot skillet, after cutting it into bite-size pieces, for a sauce that's both quick and flavorful. The asparagus caramelized just a bit, and the heat brought out the flavors of the other ingredients, such as onions, walnuts, and garlic. To finish off the dish, we paired the asparagus with a balance of salty, sweet, and sour ingredients. In one dish, we teamed asparagus with balsamic vinegar, basil, and pecorino and in another, arugula, blue cheese, and apple worked well.

Campanelle with Asparagus, Basil, and Balsamic Glaze

SERVES 4 TO 6

Campanelle is a frilly trumpet-shaped pasta that pairs nicely with this sauce. If you cannot find it, fusilli works well, too. Use a vegetable peeler to shave the cheese.

    Table salt
1   pound campanelle (see note)
¾   cup balsamic vinegar
5   tablespoons extra-virgin olive oil
1   pound asparagus, tough ends trimmed (see photos),
    thick spears halved lengthwise and cut into
    1-inch lengths
1   medium red onion, halved and sliced thin (about
    1½ cups)
½   teaspoon ground black pepper
¼   teaspoon red pepper flakes
1   cup chopped fresh basil leaves
2   ounces Pecorino Romano cheese, shaved (about 1 cup;
    see note)
1   tablespoon juice from 1 lemon

1. Bring 4 quarts water to a boil in a large pot. Add 1 tablespoon salt and the pasta to the boiling water and cook, stirring often, until al dente. Reserve ½ cup of the cooking water then drain the pasta and return it to the pot.

2. While the pasta is cooking, bring the balsamic vinegar to a boil in an 8-inch skillet over medium-high heat; reduce the heat to medium and simmer gently until reduced to ¼ cup, 15 to 20 minutes.

3. Meanwhile, heat 2 tablespoons of the oil in a 12-inch nonstick skillet over high heat until smoking. Add the asparagus, onion, black pepper, red pepper flakes, and ½ teaspoon salt and stir to combine. Cook, without stirring, until the asparagus begins to brown, about 1 minute, then stir and continue to cook, stirring occasionally, until the asparagus is crisp-tender, about 4 minutes longer.

4. Add the asparagus mixture, basil, ½ cup of the Pecorino, the lemon juice, and the remaining 3 tablespoons oil to the pasta and toss to combine. Adjust the consistency of the sauce with the reserved pasta cooking water as needed. Serve immediately, drizzling 1 to 2 teaspoons balsamic glaze over individual servings and passing the remaining ½ cup Pecorino separately.

Cavatappi with Asparagus, Arugula, Walnuts, and Blue Cheese

SERVES 4 TO 6

Cavatappi is a short, tubular corkscrew-shaped pasta; penne is a fine substitute. The grated apple balances the other flavors in this dish.

    Table salt
1   pound cavatappi (see note)
5   tablespoons extra-virgin olive oil
1   pound asparagus, tough ends trimmed (see photos),
    thick spears halved lengthwise and cut into
    1-inch lengths
½   teaspoon ground black pepper
1   cup walnuts, chopped
4   cups lightly packed arugula leaves from 1 large bunch,
    washed and dried
6   ounces strong blue cheese, such as Roquefort, crumbled
    (about 1½ cups)
2   tablespoons cider vinegar
1   Granny Smith apple, peeled, for garnish

1. Bring 4 quarts water to a boil in a large pot. Add 1 tablespoon salt and the pasta to the boiling water and cook, stirring often, until al dente. Reserve ½ cup of the cooking water then drain the pasta and return it to the pot.

2. While the pasta is cooking, heat 2 tablespoons of the oil in a 12-inch nonstick skillet over high heat until smoking. Add the asparagus, pepper, and ½ teaspoon salt

---

NOTES FROM THE TEST KITCHEN

TRIMMING ASPARAGUS SPEARS

1. Before cooking asparagus, it's important to remove the tough ends. Remove one asparagus spear from the bunch and snap off the end.

2. Using the broken asparagus as a guide, trim off the ends of the remaining spears using a chef's knife.

and cook, without stirring, until the asparagus begins to brown, about 1 minute. Add the walnuts and continue to cook, stirring frequently, until the asparagus is crisp-tender and the nuts are toasted, about 4 minutes longer. Add the arugula and toss to wilt.

3. Add the asparagus mixture, blue cheese, vinegar, and the remaining 3 tablespoons oil to the pasta and toss to combine. Adjust the consistency of the sauce with the reserved pasta cooking water as needed. Serve immediately, grating the apple over individual servings.

PASTA WITH MUSHROOMS

WHY THIS RECIPE WORKS: Pasta with mushrooms can be watery and tasteless. But when done right, this dish transforms an ordinary box of pasta and a package of mushrooms into something special. We wanted to combine the intense flavor of sautéed mushrooms with a light cream sauce to create a woodsy, full-flavored pasta dish.

For optimum flavor and texture, we used a combination of shiitake and cremini mushrooms; cremini mushrooms provided richness and meatiness, and the shiitakes contributed hearty flavor and a pleasant, chewy texture. Cooking the mushrooms in a skillet (not in the sauce) improved their flavor; adding salt to the pan

helped the mushrooms release their juices and enhanced browning. We then added chicken broth and cream to the browned bits left in the skillet after the mushrooms were removed. Garlic, shallots, and thyme rounded out the flavors of our simple sauce, and lemon juice added brightness. We added the browned mushrooms back in for a chunky sauce that paired nicely with short pasta with lots of crevices—we liked either campanelle or farfalle.

Pasta with Sautéed Mushrooms and Thyme
SERVES 4 TO 6

Vegetable broth can be substituted for the chicken broth to make this dish vegetarian. If you add the pasta to the boiling water at the same time the cremini go into the skillet, the pasta and sauce will finish at the same time.

    Table salt
  1 **pound campanelle or farfalle**
  2 **tablespoons unsalted butter**
  2 **tablespoons extra-virgin olive oil**
  4 **large shallots, minced (about 1 cup)**
  3 **medium garlic cloves, minced or pressed through a garlic press (about 1 tablespoon)**
 10 **ounces shiitake mushrooms, stems discarded, caps wiped clean and sliced ¼ inch thick**
 10 **ounces cremini mushrooms, wiped clean and sliced ¼ inch thick**
  1 **tablespoon plus 1 teaspoon minced fresh thyme leaves**
 1¼ **cups low-sodium chicken broth (see note)**
  ½ **cup heavy cream**
  1 **tablespoon juice from 1 lemon**
    Ground black pepper
  2 **ounces Parmesan cheese, grated (about 1 cup)**
  2 **tablespoons minced fresh parsley leaves**

1. Bring 4 quarts water to a boil in a large pot. Add 1 tablespoon salt and the pasta to the boiling water and cook, stirring often, until al dente. Reserve ½ cup of the cooking water then drain the pasta and return it to the pot.

2. Meanwhile, melt the butter with the oil over medium heat in a 12-inch skillet. Add the shallots and cook, stirring occasionally, until softened and translucent, about 4 minutes. Add the garlic and cook until fragrant, about 30 seconds. Increase the heat to medium-high; add the shiitakes and cook, stirring occasionally, for 2 minutes. Add the cremini and ½ teaspoon salt; cook, stirring occasionally, until the moisture released by the mushrooms has evaporated and the mushrooms are golden brown, about 8 minutes. Add the thyme and cook until fragrant, about 30 seconds. Transfer the mushrooms to a bowl and set aside.

3. Add the chicken broth to the skillet and bring to a boil, scraping up the browned bits. Off the heat, stir in the cream and lemon juice and season with salt and pepper to taste.

4. Add the mushrooms, chicken broth mixture, cheese, and parsley to the pasta. Toss over medium–low heat until the cheese melts and the pasta absorbs most of the liquid, about 2 minutes. Adjust the consistency of the sauce with the reserved pasta cooking water as needed and serve immediately.

PASTA WITH BROCCOLI RABE AND SAUSAGE

WHY THIS RECIPE WORKS: In southern Italy, broccoli rabe and orecchiette, which translates loosely as "little ears," is a popular combination. The trick to this pasta dish is cooking the broccoli rabe just right and limiting the number of ingredients so that at the end, you have a moist and flavorful (but not oily) pasta dish.

For a hearty, filling dish, we decided to include some Italian sausage. Tasters preferred spicy Italian sausage to the sweet variety, but if you like less heat, the sweet sausage still makes for a satisfying dish. We started by browning the sausage in a skillet, then adding the broccoli rabe and chicken broth to absorb the rich, meaty flavors in the pan; covering the pan allowed us to steam the rabe with the other sauce ingredients. Besides eliminating the need for a separate pot to blanch the rabe, this cooking method doesn't wash away the pleasantly bitter flavor of this Italian vegetable. Some red pepper flakes amplified the heat from the sausage, and a drizzle of olive oil and freshly grated Parmesan cheese brought the whole dish together.

Orecchiette with Broccoli Rabe and Sausage

SERVES 4 TO 6

If you prefer to use broccoli instead of broccoli rabe in this recipe, use 2 pounds broccoli cut into 1-inch florets and increase the cooking time by several minutes. If you prefer a less spicy dish, use sweet Italian sausage.

Table salt
1 **pound orecchiette**
8 **ounces hot Italian sausage, casings removed (see note)**

6 **medium garlic cloves, minced or pressed through a garlic press (about 2 tablespoons)**
½ **teaspoon red pepper flakes**
1 **bunch broccoli rabe (about 1 pound), washed, trimmed, and cut into 1½-inch pieces (see note)**
½ **cup low-sodium chicken broth**
1 **tablespoon extra-virgin olive oil**
1 **ounce Parmesan cheese, grated (about ½ cup)**

1. Bring 4 quarts water to a boil in a large pot. Add 1 tablespoon salt and the pasta to the boiling water and cook, stirring often, until al dente. Reserve ½ cup of the cooking water then drain the pasta and return it to the pot.

2. While the pasta is cooking, cook the sausage until browned in a 12-inch nonstick skillet over medium–high heat, breaking it into ½-inch pieces with a wooden spoon, about 3 minutes. Stir in the garlic, red pepper flakes, and ½ teaspoon salt. Cook, stirring constantly, until the garlic is fragrant, about 1½ minutes. Add the broccoli rabe and chicken broth, cover, and cook until the broccoli rabe turns bright green, about 2 minutes. Uncover and cook, stirring frequently, until most of the broth has evaporated and the broccoli rabe is tender, 2 to 3 minutes.

3. Add the sausage mixture, oil, and cheese to the pasta and toss to combine. Adjust the consistency of the sauce with the reserved pasta cooking water as needed and serve immediately.

SHRIMP AND GARLIC WITH PASTA

WHY THIS RECIPE WORKS: In theory, garlic shrimp pasta has all the makings of an ideal weeknight meal—just toss a few quick-cooking ingredients with boiled pasta. In reality, delicate shrimp cooks fast, which translates to overcooked in a matter of seconds. Meanwhile, garlic can become overbearing or bitter, depending on how it's treated. Add to that the challenge of getting a brothy sauce to coat the pasta, and this simple recipe turns into a precarious balancing act. We wanted it all: al dente pasta and moist shrimp bound by a supple sauce infused with a deep garlic flavor.

For the best flavor and texture, we prefer to buy individually quick-frozen shrimp and thaw them ourselves. We settled on extra-large shrimp and marinated them with minced garlic before a quick sauté in garlic oil (olive oil we simmered with smashed garlic cloves). We also cut each shrimp into thirds before cooking to ensure that every bite of pasta had a tasty morsel of shrimp. With sweet low notes from the infused oil and brasher high notes from the minced garlic, we finally had a balanced, deeply layered garlic flavor. As for the sauce, to deglaze the pan, tasters preferred the clean taste of vermouth or white wine; bottled clam broth added complexity to the sauce. Using a chunky tubular pasta instead of traditional linguine made it easy to find the shrimp. To get the sauce to cling to the pasta, we simply stirred flour into the oil as a thickener just before adding the vermouth and clam juice and tossed in some cold butter to finish.

Garlicky Shrimp Pasta

SERVES 4 TO 6

Marinate the shrimp while you prepare the remaining ingredients. Any short tubular or curly pasta works well here. If you prefer more heat, use the greater amount of red pepper flakes given.

- 1 pound extra-large shrimp (21 to 25 per pound), peeled, deveined (see page 205), and each shrimp cut into 3 pieces
- 3 tablespoons olive oil
- 5 medium garlic cloves, minced or pressed through a garlic press (about 5 teaspoons), plus 4 medium garlic cloves, smashed
  Table salt
- 1 pound mezze rigatoni, fusilli, or campanelle (see note)
- ¼–½ teaspoon red pepper flakes (see note)
- 2 teaspoons unbleached all-purpose flour
- ½ cup dry vermouth or white wine
- ¾ cup clam juice
- ½ cup chopped fresh parsley leaves
- 3 tablespoons unsalted butter, cut into 3 pieces
- 1 teaspoon lemon juice, plus lemon wedges for serving
  Ground black pepper

1. Toss the shrimp, 1 tablespoon of the oil, 2 teaspoons of the minced garlic, and ¼ teaspoon salt in a medium bowl. Let the shrimp marinate at room temperature 20 minutes.

2. Heat the 4 smashed garlic cloves and the remaining 2 tablespoons oil in a 12-inch skillet over medium-low heat, stirring occasionally, until the garlic is light golden brown, 4 to 7 minutes. Remove the skillet from the heat and use a slotted spoon to remove the garlic from the skillet; discard the garlic. Set the skillet aside.

3. Bring 4 quarts water to a boil in a large pot. Add 1 tablespoon salt and the pasta to the boiling water and cook, stirring often, until al dente. Reserve ½ cup of the cooking water then drain the pasta and return it to the pot.

4. While the pasta cooks, return the skillet with the oil to medium heat; add the shrimp with the marinade to the skillet in a single layer. Cook the shrimp, undisturbed, until the oil starts to bubble gently, 1 to 2 minutes. Stir the shrimp and continue to cook until almost cooked through, about 1 minute longer. Using a slotted spoon, transfer the shrimp to a medium bowl. Add the remaining 3 teaspoons minced garlic and the red pepper flakes to the skillet and cook until fragrant, about 1 minute. Add the flour and cook, stirring constantly, for 1 minute; stir in the vermouth and cook for 1 minute. Add the clam juice and parsley; cook until the mixture starts to thicken, 1 to

2 minutes. Off the heat, whisk in the butter and lemon juice. Add the shrimp and sauce to the pasta and adjust the consistency of the sauce with the reserved pasta cooking water as needed. Season with black pepper to taste. Serve immediately, passing the lemon wedges separately.

SHRIMP FRA DIAVOLO

WHY THIS RECIPE WORKS: Most recipes for shrimp *fra diavolo* ("brother devil" in Italian) lack depth of flavor, with the star ingredients, shrimp and garlic, contributing little to an acidic, unbalanced tomato sauce. We wanted a shrimp fra diavolo with a seriously garlicky, spicy tomato sauce studded with sweet, firm shrimp.

Most fra diavolo recipes add raw shrimp to the finished sauce, but this doesn't infuse the shrimp with any flavor whatsoever. We seared the shrimp first to help them caramelize and enrich their sweetness. Following a brief sear with olive oil, salt, and red pepper flakes—the pepper flakes also benefited from the sear, as they took on a toasty, earthy note—we flambéed the shrimp with cognac. The combined forces of cognac and flame brought out the shrimp's sweet, tender notes and imbued our fra diavolo with the cognac's richness and complexity. We then sautéed the garlic slowly for a mellow nutty flavor, and reserved some raw garlic for a last-minute punch of heat and spice. Simmered diced tomatoes and a splash of white wine (balanced by a bit of sugar) completed our perfect fra diavolo in less than 30 minutes.

Shrimp fra Diavolo

SERVES 4 TO 6

One teaspoon of red pepper flakes will give the sauce a little kick, but you may want to add more depending on your taste. For safety notes on flambéing, see page 342.

Table salt
1 pound linguine or spaghetti
1 pound large shrimp (31 to 40 per pound), peeled and deveined (see page 205)
6 tablespoons extra-virgin olive oil
1 teaspoon red pepper flakes, plus more to taste (see note)
¼ cup cognac or brandy
12 medium garlic cloves, minced or pressed through a garlic press (about ¼ cup)
1 (28-ounce) can diced tomatoes, drained

1 cup dry white wine
½ teaspoon sugar
¼ cup minced fresh parsley leaves

1. Bring 4 quarts water to a boil in a large pot. Add 1 tablespoon salt and the pasta to the boiling water and cook, stirring often, until al dente. Reserve ½ cup of the cooking water then drain the pasta and return it to the pot.

2. Meanwhile, toss the shrimp with 2 tablespoons of the oil, ½ teaspoon of the red pepper flakes, and ¾ teaspoon salt. Heat a 12-inch skillet over high heat. Add the shrimp to the skillet in a single layer and cook, without stirring, until the bottoms of the shrimp turn spotty brown, about 30 seconds. Remove the skillet from the heat, flip the shrimp, and add the cognac; wait until the cognac has warmed slightly, about 5 seconds, and return the skillet to high heat. Wave a lit match over the skillet until the cognac ignites, shaking the pan to distribute the flame over the entire pan. When the flames subside (this will take 15 to 30 seconds), transfer the shrimp to a medium bowl and set aside. Let the skillet cool, off the heat, about 2 minutes.

3. Add 3 tablespoons more oil and 3 tablespoons of the garlic to the cooled skillet and cook over low heat, stirring constantly, until the garlic becomes sticky and straw colored, 7 to 10 minutes. Add the remaining red pepper flakes, ¾ teaspoon salt, the tomatoes, wine, and sugar, increase the heat to medium-high, and simmer until thickened, about 8 minutes.

4. Stir the shrimp with accumulated juices, the remaining 1 tablespoon garlic, and the parsley into the tomato sauce. Simmer until the shrimp have heated through, about 1 minute. Off the heat, stir in the remaining 1 tablespoon oil. Add ½ cup of the tomato sauce (no shrimp) to the pasta; toss to coat and adjust the consistency of the sauce with the reserved pasta cooking water as needed. Serve immediately, topping individual bowls with the sauce and shrimp.

PASTA WITH HEARTY ITALIAN MEAT SAUCE

WHY THIS RECIPE WORKS: Traditional "Sunday gravy" is more than just meat sauce—it's a labor of love, an all-day kitchen affair, involving several types of meat, a bunch of tomatoes, and at least one Italian grandmother. We wanted to honor this meaty extravaganza but shortcut the cooking so we could get this traditional dish on the table in a reasonable amount of time.

When you're using six or seven types of meat, the browning alone can take up to 40 minutes. Our first step was to limit the dish to just one kind of sausage and one pork cut—plus meatballs. Hot Italian links gave the sauce a mild kick; baby back ribs were our favorite cut of pork because they weren't too fatty and turned moist and tender in just a few hours. Meat loaf mix, a combination of ground beef, pork, and veal, produced juicy, tender meatballs, especially when mixed with a panade of bread and buttermilk. To further bump up flavor, we mixed in minced garlic, parsley, and red pepper flakes, plus an egg yolk for richness. To help the meatballs retain their shape we browned them first in a skillet before adding them to the sauce.

For the tomato sauce, canned crushed tomatoes were a winner, leading to a sauce with nice thickness and bright tomato flavor. Instead of merely browning the tomato paste for 30 seconds, we cooked it until it nearly blackened, which concentrated its sweetness. The sauce was still lacking some beefy undercurrents; the best booster turned out to be the simple, straightforward addition of an ingredient rarely found in tomato sauce: beef broth.

Pasta with Hearty Italian Meat Sauce (Sunday Gravy)

SERVES 8 TO 10

We prefer meat loaf mix (a combination of ground beef, pork, and veal) for the meatballs in this recipe. Ground beef may be substituted, but the meatballs won't be as flavorful. Six tablespoons of plain yogurt thinned with 2 tablespoons of milk can be substituted for the buttermilk. Our preferred brands of crushed tomatoes are Tuttorosso and Muir Glen. This recipe can be prepared through step 4 and then cooled and refrigerated in the Dutch oven for up to 2 days. To reheat, drizzle ½ cup water over the sauce (do not stir in) and warm on the lower-middle rack of a preheated 325-degree oven for 1 hour before proceeding with the recipe.

SAUCE

- 2 tablespoons olive oil
- 1 (2¼-pound) rack baby back ribs, cut into 2-rib sections
  Table salt and ground black pepper
- 1 pound hot Italian sausage links
- 2 medium onions, minced
- 1¼ teaspoons dried oregano
- 3 tablespoons tomato paste
- 4 medium garlic cloves, minced or pressed through a garlic press (about 4 teaspoons)
- 2 (28-ounce) cans crushed tomatoes (see note)
- ⅔ cup low-sodium beef broth

MEATBALLS AND PASTA

- 2 slices high-quality white sandwich bread, crusts removed and bread cut into ½-inch cubes
- ½ cup buttermilk (see note)
- ¼ cup chopped fresh parsley leaves
- 2 medium garlic cloves, minced or pressed through a garlic press (about 2 teaspoons)
- 1 large egg yolk
  Table salt
- ¼ teaspoon red pepper flakes
- 1 pound meat loaf mix (see note)
- 2 ounces thinly sliced prosciutto, minced
- 1 ounce Pecorino Romano cheese, grated (about ½ cup)
- ½ cup olive oil
- 1½ pounds spaghetti or linguine
- ¼ cup chopped fresh basil leaves
  Grated Parmesan cheese, for serving

1. FOR THE SAUCE: Adjust an oven rack to the lower-middle position and heat the oven to 325 degrees. Heat the oil in a large Dutch oven over medium-high heat until just smoking. Pat the ribs dry with paper towels and season with salt and pepper. Add half of the ribs to the pot and brown on both sides, 5 to 7 minutes total. Transfer the ribs to a large plate and repeat with the remaining ribs. After transferring the second batch of ribs to the plate, brown the sausages on all four sides, 5 to 7 minutes total. Transfer the sausages to the plate with the ribs.

2. Reduce the heat to medium, add the onions and oregano; cook, stirring occasionally, until beginning to brown, about 5 minutes. Add the tomato paste and cook, stirring constantly, until very dark, about 3 minutes. Stir in the garlic and cook until fragrant, about 30 seconds. Add the crushed tomatoes and broth, scraping up any browned bits. Return the ribs and sausage to the pot; bring to a simmer, cover, and transfer to the oven. Cook until the ribs are tender, about 2½ hours.

3. FOR THE MEATBALLS: Meanwhile, combine the bread cubes, buttermilk, parsley, garlic, egg yolk, ½ teaspoon salt, and the red pepper flakes in a medium bowl and mash with a fork until no bread chunks remain. Add the meat loaf mix, prosciutto, and Pecorino Romano to the bread mixture; mix with your hands until thoroughly combined. Divide the mixture into 12 pieces; roll into balls, transfer to a plate, cover with plastic wrap, and refrigerate until ready to use.

4. When the sauce is 30 minutes from being done, heat the oil in a large nonstick skillet over medium-high heat until shimmering. Add the meatballs and cook until well browned all over, 5 to 7 minutes. Transfer the meatballs to a paper towel–lined plate to drain briefly. Remove the sauce from the oven and skim the fat from the top with a large spoon. Transfer the browned meatballs to the sauce and gently submerge. Return the pot to the oven and continue cooking until the meatballs are just cooked through, about 15 minutes.

5. Meanwhile, bring 6 quarts water to a boil in a large pot. Add 2 tablespoons salt and the pasta to the boiling water and cook, stirring often, until al dente. Reserve ½ cup of the cooking water then drain the pasta and return it to the pot.

6. Using tongs, transfer the meatballs, ribs, and sausage to a serving platter and cut the sausages in half. Stir the basil into the sauce and season with salt and pepper to taste. Add 1 cup of the sauce and the reserved pasta cooking water to the pasta; toss to coat. Serve, passing the remaining sauce, meat platter, and Parmesan separately.

SIMPLE ITALIAN–STYLE MEAT SAUCE

WHY THIS RECIPE WORKS: Old-fashioned Italian-style meat sauces are on an old-fashioned time line—they require hours of simmering. But just giving browned ground beef, onions, garlic, and canned tomatoes a quick simmer produces lackluster flavor and meat with the texture of a rubber band. We wanted a quick, weeknight meat sauce with long-simmered flavor.

Our goal required concentrated flavor and tender meat. Browned chopped onions and mushrooms gave the sauce a rich base of flavor, and browning the mushrooms made them so soft and supple they practically disappeared into the finished sauce. Deglazing the pan with tomato paste and tomato juice further boosted flavor. To tenderize the meat, we incorporated a panade—a paste of bread and milk—into the meat before cooking; we combined the panade and the meat in a food processor to avoid chili-like chunks. We cooked the meat mixture just until it lost its raw color; any longer, and the meat would have turned dry and mealy. Finishing the meat in a combination of canned diced and crushed tomatoes gave us the best mix of textures. A handful of grated Parmesan, added just before serving, lent the sauce a tangy, complex character.

Simple Italian-Style Meat Sauce
MAKES ABOUT 6 CUPS

You can figure on about 3 cups of sauce per pound of pasta. Except for ground round (which tasters found spongy and bland), this recipe will work with most types of ground beef, as long as it is 85 percent lean. Use high-quality crushed tomatoes; our favorite brands are Tuttorosso and Muir Glen. If using dried oregano, add the entire amount with the canned tomato liquid in step 2.

- 4 ounces white mushrooms, wiped clean and broken into rough pieces
- 1 large slice high-quality white sandwich bread, torn into quarters
- 2 tablespoons whole milk
  Table salt and ground black pepper
- 1 pound 85 percent lean ground beef (see note)
- 1 tablespoon olive oil
- 1 medium onion, minced
- 6 medium garlic cloves, minced or pressed through a garlic press (about 2 tablespoons)
- 1 tablespoon tomato paste
- ¼ teaspoon red pepper flakes
- 1 (14.5-ounce) can diced tomatoes, drained, ¼ cup juice reserved

1   tablespoon minced fresh oregano leaves or 1 teaspoon dried oregano (see note)
1   (28-ounce) can crushed tomatoes (see note)
¼   cup grated Parmesan cheese

1. Pulse the mushrooms in a food processor until finely chopped, about 8 pulses, scraping down the sides of the workbowl as needed; transfer to a medium bowl. Add the bread, milk, ½ teaspoon salt, and ½ teaspoon black pepper to the food processor and pulse until a paste forms, about 8 pulses. Add the beef and pulse until the mixture is well combined, about 6 pulses.

2. Heat the oil in a large saucepan over medium-high heat until just smoking. Add the onion and mushrooms; cook, stirring frequently, until the vegetables are browned and dark bits form on the pan bottom, 6 to 12 minutes. Stir in the garlic, tomato paste, and red pepper flakes; cook until fragrant and the tomato paste starts to brown, about 1 minute. Add the ¼ cup reserved tomato juice and 2 teaspoons of the fresh oregano (if using dried, add the full amount), scraping the bottom of the pan with a wooden spoon to loosen the browned bits. Add the meat mixture and cook, breaking the meat into small pieces with a wooden spoon, until no longer pink, 2 to 4 minutes, making sure that the meat does not brown.

3. Stir in the diced and crushed tomatoes and bring to a simmer; reduce the heat to low and gently simmer until the sauce has thickened and the flavors have blended, about 30 minutes. Stir in the cheese and the remaining 1 teaspoon fresh oregano; season with salt and pepper to taste. (The sauce can be refrigerated in an airtight container for up to 3 days or frozen for up to 1 month.)

PASTA WITH CLASSIC BOLOGNESE SAUCE

WHY THIS RECIPE WORKS: Unlike meat sauces in which tomatoes dominate, Bolognese sauce is about the meat, with the tomatoes in a supporting role. We wanted a traditional recipe for this complexly flavored sauce, with rich meatiness up front and a good balance of sweet, salty, and acidic flavors.

We started simple—with just onions, carrots, and celery, sautéed in butter. A combination of meats, in the form of meat loaf mix, provided the right amount of meatiness. For the most tender texture, we cooked the meat just until it lost its pink color and didn't let it brown. For dairy, which is used to tenderize the meat

and give the sauce a sweet, appealing flavor, we used milk. Once the milk had reduced, we added white wine, which gave the sauce a delicate brightness. For the tomato element, diced canned tomatoes imparted sweet, acidic notes. Finally, we simmered the sauce at the lowest possible heat for about three hours and served it with rich, eggy fettuccine.

Fettuccine with Slow-Simmered Bolognese Sauce
SERVES 4

Don't drain the pasta of its cooking water too meticulously when using this sauce; a little water left clinging to the noodles will help distribute the very thick sauce evenly over the noodles, as will the addition of 2 tablespoons of butter along with the sauce. If doubling this recipe, increase the simmering times for the milk and the wine to 30 minutes each, and increase the simmering time once the tomatoes are added to 4 hours. You can substitute equal amounts of 80 percent lean ground beef, ground veal, and ground pork for the meat loaf mix (the total amount of meat should be ¾ pound).

5   tablespoons unsalted butter
2   tablespoons minced onion
2   tablespoons minced carrot
2   tablespoons minced celery
¾   pound meat loaf mix (see note)
      Table salt
1   cup whole milk
1   cup dry white wine
1   (28-ounce) can diced tomatoes
1   pound fresh or dried fettuccine
      Grated Parmesan cheese, for serving

1. Melt 3 tablespoons of the butter in a large Dutch oven over medium heat. Add the onion, carrot, and celery and cook until softened but not browned, about 6 minutes. Add the meat and ½ teaspoon salt; crumble the meat into tiny pieces with a wooden spoon. Cook, continuing to crumble the meat, just until it loses its raw color but has not yet browned, about 3 minutes.

2. Add the milk and simmer until the milk evaporates and only rendered fat remains, 10 to 15 minutes. Add the wine and simmer until the wine evaporates, 10 to 15 minutes longer. Add the tomatoes with their juice and bring to a simmer. Reduce the heat to low so that the sauce continues to simmer just barely, with an occasional bubble or two at the surface, until the liquid has evaporated, about

3 hours. Season with salt to taste. (The sauce can be refrigerated in an airtight container for up to 3 days or frozen for up to 1 month.)

3. Bring 4 quarts water to a boil in a large pot. Add 1 tablespoon salt and the pasta to the boiling water and cook, stirring often, until al dente. Reserve ½ cup of the cooking water then drain the pasta and return it to the pot. Add the sauce and remaining 2 tablespoons butter; toss to combine. Adjust the consistency of the sauce with the reserved pasta cooking water as needed. Serve, passing the Parmesan separately.

PASTA WITH STREAMLINED BOLOGNESE SAUCE

WHY THIS RECIPE WORKS: Bolognese, including our own recipe, gets its big flavor from braising ground meat and softened vegetables in slowly reducing milk, wine, and tomatoes. The process typically takes about three hours. But on a busy weeknight, we rarely have that much time to spend making dinner. We wanted to streamline Bolognese into a weeknight-friendly dinner—but keep all the lush, decadent flavor.

Using a food processor to chop the vegetables, including a big can of whole tomatoes with their juice, cut

down on preparation time. To develop sweetness in the sauce without the day-long simmering, we reduced white wine in a separate pan and added it to the sauce at the end; a little bit of sugar, stirred in with the garlic to help it caramelize, amplified the sweetness. Instead of browning the ground meat, we cooked it with milk, which helped to break down and soften the meat in a short amount of time. To beef up the meaty flavor of the sauce, we added chopped pancetta, dried porcini mushrooms, and the flavorful liquid left behind from rehydrating the mushrooms. In about an hour, our sauce was ready, with all the rich meatiness of a long-simmered Bolognese.

Pasta with Weeknight Bolognese Sauce
SERVES 4 TO 6

Sweet white wines such as Gewürztraminer, Riesling, and even white Zinfandel work especially well in this sauce. To obtain the best texture, be careful not to break up the meat too much when cooking it with the milk in step 4; with additional cooking and stirring, it will continue to break up. Just about any pasta shape complements this meaty sauce, but spaghetti and linguine are the test kitchen favorites. If using pancetta that has been sliced thin rather than cut into 1-inch chunks, reduce the processing time in step 3 from 30 seconds to about 5 seconds. You can substitute equal amounts of 80 percent lean ground beef, ground veal, and ground pork for the meat loaf mix (the total amount of meat should be 1¼ pounds).

- ½ ounce dried porcini mushrooms
- 1¼ cups sweet white wine (see note)
- ½ small carrot, peeled and chopped coarse (about ½ cup)
- ½ small onion, chopped coarse (about ¼ cup)
- 3 ounces pancetta, cut into 1-inch chunks (see note)
- 1 (28-ounce) can whole tomatoes
- 1½ tablespoons unsalted butter
- 1 teaspoon sugar
- 1 small garlic clove, minced or pressed through a garlic press (about ½ teaspoon)
- 1¼ pounds meat loaf mix (see note)
- 1½ cups whole milk
- 2 tablespoons tomato paste
  Table salt
- ⅛ teaspoon ground black pepper
- 1 pound pasta (see note)
  Grated Parmesan cheese, for serving

1. Combine the porcini and ½ cup water in a small microwave-safe bowl; cover the bowl with plastic wrap, cut three vents for steam with a knife, and microwave on high power for 30 seconds. Let stand until the mushrooms have softened, about 5 minutes. Transfer the mushrooms to a second small bowl and reserve the liquid; pour the liquid through a paper towel–lined mesh strainer. Set the mushrooms and the strained liquid aside.

2. Bring the wine to a simmer in a 10-inch nonstick skillet over medium heat; reduce the heat to low and continue to simmer until the wine is reduced to 2 tablespoons, about 20 minutes. Set aside.

3. Meanwhile, pulse the carrot in a food processor until broken down into ¼-inch pieces, about 10 pulses. Add the onion and pulse until the vegetables are broken down into ⅛-inch pieces, about 10 pulses. Transfer the vegetables to a small bowl. Process the reserved mushrooms until well ground, about 15 seconds, scraping down the sides of the workbowl as needed. Transfer the mushrooms to the bowl with the vegetables. Process the pancetta until the pieces are no larger than ¼ inch, 30 to 35 seconds, scraping down the sides of the workbowl as needed; transfer to a small bowl. Pulse the tomatoes with their juice until chopped fine, about 8 pulses.

4. Melt the butter in a 12-inch skillet over medium-high heat. Cook the pancetta, stirring frequently, until well browned, about 2 minutes. Add the carrot, onion, and mushrooms and cook, stirring frequently, until the vegetables are softened but not browned, about 4 minutes. Add the sugar and garlic and cook until fragrant, about 30 seconds. Add the meat, breaking it into 1-inch pieces with a wooden spoon, and cook for about 1 minute. Add

the milk and stir to break the meat into ½-inch pieces; bring to a simmer, reduce the heat to medium, and cook, stirring to break the meat into smaller pieces, until most of the liquid has evaporated and the meat begins to sizzle, 18 to 20 minutes. Stir in the tomato paste and cook until combined, about 1 minute. Add the tomatoes, reserved mushroom soaking liquid, ¼ teaspoon salt, and the pepper; bring to a simmer over medium-high heat, then reduce the heat to medium and simmer until the liquid is reduced and the sauce is thickened, 12 to 15 minutes. Stir in the reduced wine and simmer to blend the flavors, about 5 minutes.

5. Meanwhile, bring 4 quarts water to a boil in a large pot. Add 1 tablespoon salt and the pasta to the boiling water and cook, stirring often, until al dente. Reserve ½ cup of the cooking water then drain the pasta and return it to the pot. Add 2 cups of the sauce and 2 tablespoons of the reserved pasta cooking water to the pasta; toss to combine and adjust the consistency of the sauce with the remaining reserved pasta cooking water as needed. Serve immediately, topping individual bowls with ¼ cup sauce and passing the Parmesan separately.

PASTA AND SLOW-SIMMERED TOMATO SAUCE WITH MEAT

WHY THIS RECIPE WORKS: Slow-simmered Italian meat sauce—the kind without meatballs—relies on pork for rich flavor. But the pork found in supermarkets is so lean, we weren't convinced that any of the options could provide enough fat and flavor. So we set out to make a rich, flavorful meat sauce with fall-off-the-bone tender meat that was made from readily available supermarket products.

Today's pork chops turn dry and leathery when cooked for long periods, so instead we used a fattier cut. Country-style pork ribs turn meltingly tender when cooked for a long time and gave our tomato sauce a truly meaty flavor. Beef short ribs can also be used, but since they tend to be thicker than pork ribs, it's important to remember to let them cook a little longer. Red wine accentuated the meatiness of the sauce, which was built on a simple combination of sautéed onion and canned diced tomatoes.

NOTES FROM THE TEST KITCHEN

IMPROVISING A FLAME TAMER

A flame tamer fits over the burner to reduce the heat to a bare simmer. To make one, take a long sheet of heavy-duty aluminum foil and shape it into a 1-inch-thick ring. Make sure the ring is of an even thickness so that the pot will rest flat on it.

Pasta and Slow-Simmered Tomato Sauce with Meat (Sunday Gravy)

SERVES 4 TO 6

This sauce can be made with either beef or pork ribs. Depending on their size, you will need 4 or 5 ribs.

- 1 tablespoon olive oil
- 1½ pounds pork spareribs or country-style ribs or beef short ribs, trimmed of fat (see note)
- Table salt and ground black pepper
- 1 medium onion, minced
- ½ cup red wine
- 1 (28-ounce) can diced tomatoes
- 1 pound ziti, rigatoni, or other short tubular pasta
- Grated Parmesan cheese, for serving

1. Heat the oil in a 12-inch skillet over medium-high heat until shimmering. Season the ribs with salt and pepper and brown on all sides, turning occasionally, 8 to 10 minutes. Transfer the ribs to a plate; pour off all but 1 teaspoon fat from the skillet. Add the onion and cook until softened, 2 to 3 minutes. Add the wine and simmer, scraping up any browned bits, until the wine reduces to a glaze, about 2 minutes.

2. Return the ribs and accumulated juices to the skillet; add the tomatoes with their juice. Bring to a boil, then reduce the heat to low, cover, and simmer gently, turning the ribs several times, until the meat is very tender and falling off the bones, 1½ hours (for pork spareribs or country-style ribs) to 2 hours (for beef short ribs).

3. Transfer the ribs to a clean plate. When cool enough to handle, remove the meat from the bones and shred, discarding the fat and bones. Return the shredded meat to the sauce. Bring the sauce to a simmer over medium heat and cook, uncovered, until heated through and slightly thickened, about 5 minutes. Season with salt and pepper to taste. (The sauce can be refrigerated in an airtight container for up to 4 days or frozen for up to 2 months.)

4. Meanwhile, bring 4 quarts water to a boil in a large pot. Add 1 tablespoon salt and the pasta to the boiling water and cook, stirring often, until al dente. Reserve ½ cup of the cooking water then drain the pasta and return it to the pot. Add the sauce to the pasta and toss to combine. Adjust the consistency of the sauce with the reserved pasta cooking water as needed. Serve immediately, passing the Parmesan separately.

SPAGHETTI AND MEATBALLS

WHY THIS RECIPE WORKS: One of the problems with meatballs is that they're thought of as smaller, rounder versions of hamburgers. This would be fine if meatballs were cooked to rare or medium-rare, as most hamburgers are, but meatballs are usually cooked to well-done. This can leave them flavorless, dry, and dense, so they need some help to lighten their texture. What we were after was nothing short of great meatballs: crusty and dark brown on the outside and soft and moist on the inside.

White bread soaked in buttermilk added as a binder gave the meatballs a creamy texture and an appealing tang. Eggs were also important for texture and flavor; their fats and emulsifiers added moistness and richness. Egg yolks alone worked best and kept the meatballs moist and light; the whites just made the mixture sticky and hard to handle, with no other added benefits. Adding some ground pork to the usual ground beef enhanced the flavor. Broiling dried out the meatballs; pan-frying was the best way to brown the meatballs and kept the interior moist. Finally, building the tomato sauce on top of the browned bits left in the pan after frying the meatballs made for a hearty, robust-tasting sauce.

Spaghetti and Meatballs

SERVES 4 TO 6

The shaped meatballs can be covered with plastic wrap and refrigerated for several hours ahead of serving time; fry the meatballs and make the sauce at the last minute. If you don't have buttermilk, you can substitute 6 tablespoons of plain yogurt thinned with 2 tablespoons of milk.

MEATBALLS

- 2 slices high-quality white sandwich bread, crusts removed and bread torn into small pieces
- ½ cup buttermilk (see note)
- ¾ pound 85 percent lean ground beef
- ¼ pound ground pork
- ¼ cup grated Parmesan cheese
- 2 tablespoons minced fresh parsley leaves
- 1 large egg yolk
- 1 medium garlic clove, minced or pressed through a garlic press (about 1 teaspoon)
- ¾ teaspoon table salt
- ⅛ teaspoon ground black pepper
  Vegetable oil, for pan-frying

TOMATO SAUCE AND PASTA

- 2 tablespoons extra-virgin olive oil
- 1 medium garlic clove, minced or pressed through a garlic press (about 1 teaspoon)
- 1 (28-ounce) can crushed tomatoes
- 1 tablespoon minced fresh basil leaves
  Table salt and ground black pepper
- 1 pound spaghetti
  Grated Parmesan cheese, for serving

1. FOR THE MEATBALLS: Mash the bread and buttermilk to a smooth paste in a large bowl. Let stand for 10 minutes.

2. Add the beef, pork, cheese, parsley, egg yolk, garlic, salt, and pepper to the mashed bread; stir gently until uniform. Gently form into 1½-inch round meatballs (about 14 meatballs). (When forming the meatballs use a light touch; if you compact the meatballs too much, they can become dense and hard.)

3. Pour the vegetable oil into a 12-inch skillet until it measures a depth of ¼ inch. Heat over medium-high heat until shimmering. Add the meatballs in a single layer and cook until nicely browned on all sides, about 10 minutes. Transfer the meatballs to a paper towel–lined plate and discard the oil left in the skillet.

4. FOR THE SAUCE: Add the olive oil and garlic to the skillet and cook over medium heat, scraping up any browned bits, until fragrant, about 30 seconds. Add the tomatoes with their juice, bring to a simmer, and cook until the sauce thickens, about 10 minutes. Stir in the basil and season with salt and pepper to taste. Add the meatballs and simmer, turning them occasionally, until heated through, about 5 minutes.

5. Meanwhile, bring 4 quarts water to a boil in a large pot. Add 1 tablespoon salt and the pasta to the boiling water and cook, stirring often, until al dente. Reserve ½ cup of the cooking water then drain the pasta and return it to the pot. Stir in several large spoonfuls of the tomato sauce (without meatballs) over the pasta and toss to coat. Adjust the consistency of the sauce with the reserved pasta cooking water as needed. Serve immediately, topping individual bowls with more tomato sauce and several meatballs and passing the Parmesan separately.

NOTES FROM THE TEST KITCHEN

MAKING MEATBALLS

1. Use a fork to mash the bread and buttermilk into a smooth paste.

2. Working with 3 tablespoons of the meatball mixture at a time, form the mixture into a 1½-inch ball by gently rolling it between your palms.

3. Fry the meatballs, turning every so often, until they are a crusty golden brown all over.

SPAGHETTI AND MEATBALLS FOR A CROWD

WHY THIS RECIPE WORKS: Making spaghetti and meatballs to serve a crowd can try the patience of even the toughest Italian grandmother. We sought an easier way. We found that roasting our meatballs on a wire rack, rather than frying them in batches, made our recipe faster and cleaner. Adding some powdered gelatin to a mix of ground chuck and ground pork served to plump the meatballs and lent them a soft richness with minimal work. Prosciutto gave the meatballs extra meatiness, and a panade, which we made with panko, kept the meat moist and prevented it from getting tough. To create a rich, flavorful sauce, we braised the meatballs in marinara sauce for about an hour. And to make sure the sauce didn't overreduce, we swapped half of the crushed tomatoes in our marinara recipe for an equal portion of tomato juice.

Classic Spaghetti and Meatballs for a Crowd

SERVES 12

If you don't have buttermilk, you can substitute 1 cup whole-milk plain yogurt thinned with ½ cup whole milk. Grate the onion on the large holes of a box grater. You can cook the pasta in two separate pots if you do not have a large enough pot to cook all of the pasta together. Once cooked, the sauce and the meatballs can be cooled and refrigerated for up to 2 days. To reheat, drizzle ½ cup of water over the sauce, without stirring, and reheat on the lower-middle rack of a 325-degree oven for 1 hour.

MEATBALLS

- 2¼ cups panko bread crumbs
- 1½ cups buttermilk (see note)
- 1½ teaspoons unflavored gelatin
- 3 tablespoons water
- 2 pounds 85 percent lean ground beef
- 1 pound ground pork
- 6 ounces thinly sliced prosciutto, chopped fine
- 3 large eggs
- 3 ounces Parmesan cheese, grated (about 1½ cups)
- 6 tablespoons minced fresh parsley leaves
- 3 medium garlic cloves, minced or pressed through a garlic press (about 1 tablespoon)
- 1½ teaspoons table salt
- ½ teaspoon ground black pepper

SAUCE

- 3 tablespoons extra-virgin olive oil
- 1 large onion, grated
- 6 medium garlic cloves, minced or pressed through a garlic press (about 2 tablespoons)
- 1 teaspoon dried oregano
- ½ teaspoon red pepper flakes
- 3 (28-ounce) cans crushed tomatoes
- 6 cups tomato juice
- 6 tablespoons dry white wine
- Table salt and ground black pepper
- ½ cup minced fresh basil leaves
- 3 tablespoons minced fresh parsley leaves
- Sugar

- 3 pounds spaghetti
- 2 tablespoons table salt
- Grated Parmesan cheese, for serving

1. FOR THE MEATBALLS: Adjust the oven racks to the lower-middle and upper-middle positions and heat the oven to 450 degrees. Set 2 wire racks in 2 aluminum foil–lined rimmed baking sheets and spray the racks with vegetable oil spray.

2. Combine the bread crumbs and buttermilk in a large bowl and let sit, mashing occasionally with a fork, until a smooth paste forms, about 10 minutes. Meanwhile, sprinkle the gelatin over the water in a small bowl and allow to soften for 5 minutes.

3. Mix the ground beef, ground pork, prosciutto, eggs, Parmesan, parsley, garlic, salt, pepper, and gelatin mixture into the bread-crumb mixture using your hands. Pinch off and roll the mixture into 2-inch meatballs (about 40 meatballs total) and arrange on the prepared sheets. Bake until well browned, about 30 minutes, switching and rotating the sheets halfway through baking.

4. FOR THE SAUCE: While the meatballs bake, heat the oil in a Dutch oven over medium heat until shimmering. Add the onion and cook until softened and lightly browned, 5 to 7 minutes. Stir in the garlic, oregano, and red pepper flakes and cook until fragrant, about 30 seconds. Stir in the crushed tomatoes, tomato juice, wine, 1½ teaspoons salt, and ¼ teaspoon pepper, bring to a simmer, and cook until thickened slightly, about 15 minutes.

5. Remove the meatballs from the oven and reduce the oven temperature to 300 degrees. Gently nestle the meatballs into the sauce. Cover, transfer to the oven, and cook until the meatballs are firm and the sauce has thickened, about 1 hour.

6. Meanwhile, bring 10 quarts water to boil in a 12-quart pot. Add the pasta and salt and cook, stirring often, until al dente. Reserve ½ cup of the cooking water, then drain the pasta and return it to the pot.

7. Gently stir the basil and parsley into the sauce and season with sugar, salt, and pepper to taste. Add 2 cups of the sauce (without meatballs) to the pasta and toss to combine, adding the reserved cooking water to adjust the consistency as needed. Serve, topping individual portions with more tomato sauce and several meatballs and passing the Parmesan separately.

PENNE WITH VODKA SAUCE

WHY THIS RECIPE WORKS: Splashes of vodka and cream can turn run-of-the-mill tomato sauce into luxurious restaurant fare—or a heavy, boozy mistake. Despite the simple ingredients, we found recipes for *penne alla vodka* gave us results that varied widely. Many were absurdly rich (with more cream than tomatoes) and others were too harsh from a heavy hand with the vodka. We wanted to fine-tune this modern classic to strike the right balance of sweet, tangy, spicy, and creamy.

To achieve a sauce with the right consistency, we pureed half the tomatoes (which helped the sauce cling

nicely to the pasta) and cut the rest into chunks. For sweetness, we added sautéed minced onions; for depth of flavor, we used a bit of tomato paste. We found we needed a liberal amount of vodka to cut through the richness and add "zinginess" to the sauce, but we needed to add it to the tomatoes early on to allow the alcohol to mostly (but not completely) cook off and prevent a boozy flavor. Adding a little heavy cream to the sauce gave it a nice consistency, and we finished cooking the penne in the sauce to encourage cohesiveness.

Penne with Vodka Sauce (Penne alla Vodka)
SERVES 4 TO 6

So that the sauce and pasta finish cooking at the same time, drop the pasta into the boiling water just after adding the vodka to the sauce.

  1 **(28-ounce) can whole tomatoes, drained, juice reserved**
  2 **tablespoons olive oil**
  ½ **small onion, minced**
  1 **tablespoon tomato paste**
  2 **medium garlic cloves, minced or pressed through a garlic press (about 2 teaspoons)**
  ¼ **teaspoon red pepper flakes**
  Table salt
  ⅓ **cup vodka**
  ½ **cup heavy cream**
  1 **pound penne**
  2 **tablespoons minced fresh basil leaves**
  Grated Parmesan cheese, for serving

1. Puree half of the tomatoes in a food processor until smooth. Dice the remaining tomatoes into ½-inch pieces, discarding the cores. Combine the pureed and diced tomatoes in a liquid measuring cup (you should have about 1⅔ cups). Add the reserved juice to equal 2 cups.

2. Heat the oil in a large saucepan over medium heat until shimmering. Add the onion and tomato paste and cook, stirring occasionally, until the onion is light golden around the edges, about 3 minutes. Add the garlic and red pepper flakes; cook, stirring constantly, until fragrant, about 30 seconds.

3. Stir in the tomatoes and ½ teaspoon salt. Remove the pan from the heat and add the vodka. Return the pan to medium-high heat and simmer briskly until the alcohol flavor is cooked off, 8 to 10 minutes; stir frequently and lower the heat to medium if the simmering becomes too vigorous. Stir in the cream and cook until hot, about 1 minute.

4. Meanwhile, bring 4 quarts water to a boil in a large pot. Add 1 tablespoon salt and the pasta to the boiling water. Cook, stirring often, until just shy of al dente. Reserve ½ cup of the cooking water then drain the pasta and return it to the pot. Add the sauce to the pasta and toss over medium heat until the pasta absorbs some of the sauce, 1 to 2 minutes. Adjust the consistency of the sauce with the reserved pasta cooking water as needed. Stir in the basil and season with salt to taste. Serve immediately, passing the Parmesan separately.

SPAGHETTI ALLA CARBONARA

WHY THIS RECIPE WORKS: Standard carbonara is often a lackluster spaghetti dish; it's either covered in a leaden sauce or riddled with dry bits of cheese. To add to the problems, if the dish gets to the table a few minutes too late, the sauce congeals and the pasta turns rubbery. We set out to make the sauce silky and smooth.

Eggs form the base of the lush, silky sauce, so we used three whole eggs to guarantee superior texture and richness. A combination of Pecorino Romano, with its distinctly sharp flavor, and Parmesan, with its sweet, nutty flavor, provided the most bite and creaminess. Raw garlic balanced the richness of the eggs and cheese. In place of the traditional *guanciale* (salt-cured pork jowl), we used American bacon, which gave our dish the perfect crunch and a hint of sweetness and smoke. Skipping the heavy cream—which deadened the flavor of the cheeses—we added white wine to achieve a rich, translucent sauce. Pouring the cheese and egg mixture right over the hot pasta in a warmed serving bowl helped ensure that everyone at the table could enjoy a perfectly coated portion of pasta and sauce.

Spaghetti alla Carbonara
SERVES 4 TO 6

Although we call for spaghetti in this recipe, you can substitute linguine or fettuccine.

 ¼ **cup extra-virgin olive oil**
 8 **ounces (about 8 slices) bacon, halved lengthwise and cut into ¼-inch pieces**
 ½ **cup dry white wine**
 3 **large eggs**
1½ **ounces Parmesan cheese, grated (about ¾ cup)**
 ¼ **cup grated Pecorino Romano cheese**
 1 **large garlic clove, minced or pressed through a garlic press (about 1½ teaspoons)**
 1 **pound spaghetti (see note)**
    Table salt and ground black pepper

1. Adjust an oven rack to the lower-middle position, set an ovensafe serving bowl on the rack, and heat the oven to 200 degrees. Bring 4 quarts water to a boil in a large pot.

2. While the water is heating, heat the oil in a large skillet over medium heat until shimmering. Add the bacon and cook, stirring occasionally, until crisp, about 8 minutes. Add the wine and simmer until it is slightly reduced, 6 to 8 minutes. Remove from the heat and cover. Whisk the eggs, cheeses, and garlic together in a small bowl; set aside.

3. When the water comes to a boil, add 1 tablespoon salt and the pasta. Cook, stirring often, until al dente. Reserve ½ cup of the cooking water; drain the pasta. Remove the warm bowl from the oven and add the pasta. Immediately pour the egg and bacon mixtures over the pasta, season with salt and pepper to taste, and toss to coat; adjust the consistency of the sauce with the reserved pasta cooking water as needed. Serve immediately.

FETTUCCINE ALFREDO

WHY THIS RECIPE WORKS: Fettuccine Alfredo—tender pasta bathed in a silky, creamy cheese sauce—always sounds so tempting. But too often, restaurant-style fettuccine Alfredo means gargantuan portions, overcooked pasta, and a sauce that quickly congeals in the bowl (or your stomach). We were after a better Alfredo, with a luxurious sauce that remained supple and velvety from the first bite of pasta to the last.

We first discovered that fresh pasta was essential as a base—dried noodles didn't hold on to the sauce, and the delicate nature of fresh pasta brought a more sophisticated tone to the dish. Turning our attention to the sauce, we found that a light hand was necessary when adding two of the richer ingredients: the cheese and the butter. Smaller amounts were sufficient to add distinctive flavor without being overwhelming. To manage the heavy cream, we reduced a portion of it, then added the remaining amount uncooked. This technique produced not only a luxurious texture but also a fresher flavor. A pinch of freshly grated nutmeg added a spicy, sweet undertone to this elegant dish.

Fettuccine Alfredo

SERVES 4 TO 6

Fresh pasta is the best choice for this dish; supermarkets sell 9-ounce containers of fresh pasta in the refrigerated section. When boiling the pasta, undercook it slightly (just shy of al dente) because the pasta cooks an additional minute or two in the sauce just before serving. Note that fettuccine Alfredo must be served immediately; it does not hold or reheat well.

- 1½ cups heavy cream
- 2 tablespoons unsalted butter
  Table salt
- ¼ teaspoon ground black pepper
- 9 ounces fresh fettuccine (see note)
- 1½ ounces Parmesan cheese, grated (about ¾ cup)
- ⅛ teaspoon grated nutmeg

1. Bring 1 cup of the heavy cream and the butter to a simmer in a medium saucepan over medium heat; reduce the heat to low and simmer gently until the mixture reduces to ⅔ cup, 12 to 15 minutes. Off the heat, stir in the remaining ½ cup cream, ½ teaspoon salt, and the pepper.

2. While the cream reduces, bring 4 quarts water to a boil in a large pot. Add 1 tablespoon salt and the pasta to the boiling water and cook, stirring often, until just shy of al dente. Reserve ¼ cup of the cooking water then drain the pasta and return it to the pot.

3. Meanwhile, return the cream mixture to a simmer over medium-high heat; reduce the heat to low and add the pasta, cheese, and nutmeg to the cream mixture. Cook over low heat, tossing the pasta to combine, until the cheese is melted, the sauce coats the pasta, and the pasta is just al dente, 1 to 2 minutes. Stir in the reserved pasta cooking water and toss to coat; the sauce may look thin but will gradually thicken as the pasta is served. Serve immediately.

POTATO GNOCCHI

WHY THIS RECIPE WORKS: Good potato gnocchi are something of a culinary paradox, light, airy pillows created from dense, starchy ingredients. The method is simple: knead mashed potatoes into a dough with a minimum of flour; shape; and boil for a minute. And yet the potential pitfalls are numerous (lumpy mashed potatoes, too much or too little flour, a heavy hand when kneading, and bland flavor). We wanted a foolproof recipe for impossibly light gnocchi with unmistakable potato flavor. Baking russets (parcooked in the microwave for speed and ease) produced intensely flavored potatoes—an excellent start to our gnocchi base. To avoid lumps, which can cause gnocchi to break apart during cooking, we turned to a ricer for a smooth, supple mash. While many recipes offer a range of flour to use, which ups the chances of overworking the dough (and producing leaden gnocchi), we used an exact amount based on the ratio of potato to flour so that our gnocchi dough was mixed as little as possible. And we found that an egg, while not traditional, tenderized our gnocchi further, delivering delicate pillow-like dumplings.

Potato Gnocchi with Browned Butter and Sage Sauce

SERVES 4

Gnocchi, like many baking recipes, require accurate measurement to achieve the proper texture; it's best to weigh the potatoes and flour. After processing, you may have slightly more than the 3 cups (16 ounces) of potatoes required for this recipe; do not be tempted to use more than 3 cups. If you prefer, replace the browned butter sauce with Gorgonzola-Cream Sauce or Parmesan Sauce with Pancetta and Walnuts (recipes follow).

POTATO GNOCCHI

- **2** pounds russet potatoes
- **1** large egg, lightly beaten
- **¾** cup plus 1 tablespoon (4 ounces) unbleached all-purpose flour, plus extra for the work surface
  Table salt

BROWN BUTTER AND SAGE SAUCE

- **4** tablespoons (½ stick) unsalted butter, cut into 4 pieces
- **1** small shallot, minced (about 2 tablespoons)
- **1** teaspoon minced fresh sage leaves
- **1½** teaspoons juice from 1 lemon
- **¼** teaspoon table salt

1. FOR THE GNOCCHI: Adjust an oven rack to the middle position and heat the oven to 450 degrees. Poke each potato 8 times with a paring knife over the entire surface. Place the potatoes on a plate and microwave until slightly softened at the ends, about 10 minutes, flipping the potatoes halfway through cooking. Transfer the potatoes directly to the oven rack and bake until a skewer glides easily through the flesh and the potatoes yield to gentle pressure, 18 to 20 minutes.

2. Hold a potato with a pot holder or kitchen towel and peel with a paring knife. Process the potato through a ricer or food mill onto a rimmed baking sheet. Repeat with the remaining potatoes. Gently spread the riced potatoes into an even layer and cool for 5 minutes.

3. Transfer 3 cups (16 ounces) warm potatoes to a large bowl. Using a fork, gently stir in the egg until just combined. Sprinkle the flour and 1 teaspoon salt over the potato mixture. Using a fork, gently combine until no pockets of dry flour remain. Press the mixture into a rough dough, transfer to a lightly floured work surface and gently knead until smooth but slightly sticky, about 1 minute, lightly dusting the work surface with flour as needed to prevent sticking.

4. Line 2 rimmed baking sheets with parchment paper and dust liberally with flour. Cut the dough into 8 pieces. Lightly dust the work surface with flour. Gently roll one piece of dough into a ½-inch-thick rope, dusting with flour to prevent sticking. Cut the rope into ¾-inch lengths. Following the photo, hold a fork, with the tines facing down, in one hand and press the side of each piece of dough against the ridged surface with your thumb to make an indentation in the center; roll the dough down and off the tines to form ridges. Transfer the formed gnocchi to the prepared sheets and repeat with the remaining dough.

5. FOR THE SAUCE: Melt the butter in a 12-inch skillet over medium-high heat, swirling occasionally, until the butter is browned and releases a nutty aroma, about 1½ minutes. Off the heat, add the shallot and sage, stirring until the shallot is fragrant, about 1 minute. Stir in the lemon juice and the salt and cover to keep warm.

6. Bring 4 quarts water to a boil in a large pot. Add 1 tablespoon salt. Using the parchment paper as a sling, add half of the gnocchi and cook until firm and just cooked through, about 90 seconds (the gnocchi should float to the surface after about 1 minute). Remove the gnocchi with a slotted spoon, transfer to the skillet with the sauce, and cover to keep warm. Repeat with the remaining gnocchi and transfer to the skillet. Gently toss the gnocchi with the sauce to combine, and serve.

NOTES FROM THE TEST KITCHEN

MAKING RIDGES ON GNOCCHI

To make ridges on gnocchi, hold a fork with the tines facing down. Press each dough piece (cut side down) against the tines with your thumb to make an indentation. Roll the dumpling down the tines to create ridges on the sides.

Gorgonzola-Cream Sauce

MAKES ABOUT 1 CUP

Adjust the consistency of the sauce with up to 2 tablespoons cooking water before adding the gnocchi to it.

- ¾ cup heavy cream
- ¼ cup dry white wine
- 4 ounces Gorgonzola cheese, crumbled (about 1 cup)
- 2 tablespoons minced fresh chives
  Table salt and ground black pepper

Bring the cream and wine to a simmer in a 12-inch skillet over medium-high heat. Gradually add the Gorgonzola while whisking constantly and cook until melted and the sauce is thickened, 2 to 3 minutes. Stir in the chives and season with salt and pepper to taste. Remove from the heat and cover to keep warm.

Parmesan Sauce with Pancetta and Walnuts

MAKES ABOUT 1 CUP

Serve gnocchi prepared with this sauce with extra grated Parmesan cheese on the side.

- ½ cup low-sodium chicken broth
- 1 ounce Parmesan cheese, grated (about ½ cup)
- ¼ cup heavy cream
- 2 large egg yolks
- ⅛ teaspoon ground black pepper
- 2 teaspoons olive oil
- 3 ounces pancetta, chopped fine
- ½ cup walnuts, chopped coarse
  Table salt

Whisk the broth, Parmesan, cream, yolks, and pepper together in a bowl until smooth. Heat the oil in a 12-inch skillet over medium heat until shimmering. Add the pancetta and cook until crisp, 5 to 7 minutes. Stir in the walnuts and cook until golden and fragrant, about 1 minute. Off the heat, gradually add the broth mixture, whisking constantly. Return the skillet to medium heat and cook, stirring often, until the sauce is thickened slightly, 2 to 4 minutes. Season with salt to taste. Remove from the heat and cover to keep warm.

BAKED CHEESY PASTA CASSEROLE

WHY THIS RECIPE WORKS: We love macaroni and cheese (who doesn't?), but sometimes we want a more adult version than the typical neon orange mac and cheese. Enter the classic Italian iteration of macaroni and cheese, *pasta ai quattro formaggi*, made with four cheeses and heavy cream. We set out to make a four-cheese creamy pasta casserole with great flavor, properly cooked pasta, and a crisp bread-crumb topping.

The cheese was first up for consideration; for the best flavor and texture, we used Italian fontina, Gorgonzola, Pecorino Romano, and Parmesan cheeses. Heating the cheese and cream together made a greasy, curdled mess, so instead we built a basic white sauce (a béchamel) by cooking butter with flour and then adding cream. Combining the hot sauce and pasta with the cheese—and not cooking the cheese in the sauce—preserved the fresh flavor of the different cheeses. Knowing the pasta would spend some time in the oven, we drained it before it was al dente so it wouldn't turn to mush when baked. Topped with bread crumbs and more Parmesan, and baked briefly in a very hot oven, our pasta dinner was silky smooth and rich but not heavy—a grown-up, sophisticated version of macaroni and cheese with Italian flavors.

Creamy Baked Four-Cheese Pasta

SERVES 4 TO 6

To streamline the process, prepare the bread-crumb topping and shred, crumble, and grate the cheeses while you wait for the pasta water to boil.

- 2 slices high-quality white sandwich bread, torn into quarters
- 1 ounce Parmesan cheese, grated (about ½ cup) Table salt and ground black pepper
- 4 ounces Italian fontina cheese, rind removed, shredded (about 1 cup)
- 3 ounces Gorgonzola cheese, crumbled (about ¾ cup)
- 1 ounce Pecorino Romano cheese, grated (about ½ cup)
- 1 pound penne
- 2 teaspoons unsalted butter
- 2 teaspoons unbleached all-purpose flour
- 1½ cups heavy cream

1. Pulse the bread in a food processor to coarse crumbs, about 10 to 15 pulses. Transfer to a small bowl. Stir in ¼ cup of the Parmesan, ¼ teaspoon salt, and ⅛ teaspoon pepper; set aside.

2. Adjust an oven rack to the middle position and heat the oven to 500 degrees.

3. Bring 4 quarts water to a boil in a large pot. Combine the remaining ¼ cup Parmesan and the fontina, Gorgonzola, and Pecorino Romano cheeses in a large bowl; set aside. Add 1 tablespoon salt and the pasta to the boiling water and cook, stirring often.

4. While the pasta is cooking, melt the butter in a small saucepan over medium-low heat. Whisk in the flour until no lumps remain, about 30 seconds. Gradually whisk in the cream, increase the heat to medium, and bring to a boil, stirring occasionally; reduce the heat to medium-low and simmer for 1 minute longer. Stir in ¼ teaspoon salt and ¼ teaspoon pepper; cover and set aside.

5. When the pasta is just shy of al dente, drain it, leaving it slightly wet. Add the pasta to the bowl with the cheeses; immediately pour the cream mixture over, then cover the bowl and let stand for 3 minutes. Uncover the bowl and stir with a rubber spatula, scraping the bottom of the bowl, until the cheeses are melted and the mixture is thoroughly combined.

6. Transfer the pasta to a 13 by 9-inch baking dish, then sprinkle evenly with the reserved bread crumbs, pressing down lightly. Bake until the topping is golden brown, about 7 minutes. Serve immediately.

BAKED ZITI

WHY THIS RECIPE WORKS: Most versions of baked ziti seem like they went directly from the pantry into the oven, calling for little more than cooked pasta, jarred tomato sauce, a container of ricotta, and some preshredded cheese. The results: overcooked ziti in a dull, grainy sauce topped with a rubbery mass of mozzarella. We wanted to rescue baked ziti so we could have perfectly al dente pasta, a rich and flavorful sauce, and melted cheese in every bite.

For a sauce that's big on flavor and light on prep, we cooked sautéed garlic with two canned products—diced tomatoes and tomato sauce. Fresh basil and dried oregano added aromatic flavor. Just when the tomato sauce seemed perfect, we added ricotta, and a familiar problem reared its head: Rather than baking up creamy and rich, the ricotta was grainy and dulled the sauce. Cottage cheese was the best choice for a replacement—its curds have a texture similar to ricotta, but are creamier and tangier. For more flavor, we combined the cottage cheese with eggs, Parmesan, and heavy cream thickened with cornstarch. Adding this milky, tangy mixture to the tomato sauce produced a sauce that was bright, rich, and creamy.

When it came to the pasta, we undercooked it and then baked it with a generous amount of sauce for perfectly al dente pasta and plenty of sauce left to keep our baked ziti moist. As for the mozzarella, we cut it into small cubes instead of shredding it, which dotted the finished casserole with gooey bits of cheese.

Baked Ziti

SERVES 8 TO 10

We prefer baked ziti made with heavy cream, but whole milk can be substituted by increasing the amount of cornstarch to 2 teaspoons and increasing the cooking time in step 3 by 1 to 2 minutes. Our preferred brand of mozzarella is Sorrento Whole Milk Mozzarella. Part-skim mozzarella can also be used.

- 1 **pound whole-milk or 1 percent cottage cheese**
- 2 **large eggs, lightly beaten**
- 3 **ounces Parmesan cheese, grated (about 1½ cups)**
  Table salt
- 1 **pound ziti or other short tubular pasta**
- 2 **tablespoons extra-virgin olive oil**
- 5 **medium garlic cloves, minced or pressed through a garlic press (about 5 teaspoons)**
- 1 **(28-ounce) can tomato sauce**
- 1 **(14.5-ounce) can diced tomatoes**
- 1 **teaspoon dried oregano**
- ½ **cup plus 2 tablespoons chopped fresh basil leaves**
- 1 **teaspoon sugar**
  Ground black pepper
- ¾ **teaspoon cornstarch**
- 1 **cup heavy cream (see note)**
- 8 **ounces whole-milk mozzarella cheese, cut into ¼-inch pieces (about 1½ cups; see note)**

1. Adjust an oven rack to the middle position and heat the oven to 350 degrees. Whisk the cottage cheese, eggs, and 1 cup of the Parmesan together in a medium bowl; set aside. Bring 4 quarts water to a boil in a large pot. Add 1 tablespoon salt and the pasta; cook, stirring occasionally, until the pasta begins to soften but is not yet cooked through, 5 to 7 minutes. Drain the pasta and leave in the colander (do not wash the pot).

2. Meanwhile, heat the oil and garlic in a 12-inch skillet over medium heat until the garlic is fragrant but not brown, about 2 minutes. Stir in the tomato sauce, diced tomatoes, and oregano; simmer until thickened, about 10 minutes. Off the heat, stir in ½ cup of the basil and the sugar; season with salt and pepper to taste.

3. Stir the cornstarch and heavy cream together in a small bowl; transfer the mixture to the now-empty pasta pot set over medium heat. Bring to a simmer and cook until thickened, 3 to 4 minutes. Remove the pot from the heat and add the cottage cheese mixture, 1 cup of the

tomato sauce, and ¾ cup of the mozzarella; stir to combine. Add the pasta and stir to coat thoroughly with the sauce.

4. Transfer the pasta to a 13 by 9-inch baking dish and spread the remaining tomato sauce evenly over the pasta. Sprinkle the remaining ¾ cup mozzarella and remaining ½ cup Parmesan over the top. Cover the baking dish tightly with foil and bake for 30 minutes.

5. Remove the foil and continue to cook until the cheese is bubbling and beginning to brown, about 30 minutes longer. Cool for 20 minutes. Sprinkle with the remaining 2 tablespoons basil and serve.

MANICOTTI

WHY THIS RECIPE WORKS: Despite being composed of a straightforward collection of ingredients (pasta, cheese, and tomato sauce), manicotti is surprisingly fussy to prepare. Blanching, shocking, draining, and stuffing slippery pasta requires a lot of patience and time. We wanted an easy-to-prepare recipe that still produced great-tasting manicotti.

Our biggest challenge was filling the slippery manicotti tubes. We solved the problem by discarding the tubes completely and spreading the filling onto a lasagna noodle, which we then rolled up. For the lasagna noodles, we found that the no-boil variety were ideal. We soaked the noodles in boiling water for 5 minutes until pliable, then used the tip of a knife to separate them and prevent sticking. For the cheese filling, we taste-tested several ricottas and found that part-skim had an ideal level of richness. Eggs, Parmesan, and an ample amount of mozzarella added richness, flavor, and structure to the ricotta filling. For a quick but brightly flavored tomato sauce, we pureed canned diced tomatoes and simmered them until slightly thickened with sautéed garlic and red pepper flakes, then finished the sauce with fresh basil.

Baked Manicotti

SERVES 6 TO 8

We prefer Barilla no-boil lasagna noodles for their delicate texture resembling fresh pasta. Note that Pasta Defino and Ronzoni brands contain only 12 no-boil noodles per package; the recipe requires 16 noodles.

The manicotti can be prepared through step 5, covered with a sheet of parchment paper, wrapped in aluminum foil, and refrigerated for up to 3 days or frozen for up to 1 month. (If frozen, thaw the manicotti in the refrigerator for 1 to 2 days.) To bake, remove the parchment, replace the aluminum foil, and increase the baking time to 1 to 1¼ hours.

TOMATO SAUCE

- 2 (28-ounce) cans diced tomatoes
- 2 tablespoons extra-virgin olive oil
- 3 medium garlic cloves, minced or pressed through a garlic press (about 1 tablespoon)
- ½ teaspoon red pepper flakes (optional)
  Table salt
- 2 tablespoons chopped fresh basil leaves

CHEESE FILLING AND PASTA

- 3 cups part-skim ricotta cheese
- 4 ounces Parmesan cheese, grated (about 2 cups)
- 8 ounces whole-milk mozzarella cheese, shredded (about 2 cups)
- 2 large eggs, lightly beaten
- 2 tablespoons chopped fresh parsley leaves
- 2 tablespoons chopped fresh basil leaves
- ¾ teaspoon table salt
- ½ teaspoon ground black pepper
- 16 no-boil lasagna noodles (see note)

1. FOR THE SAUCE: Adjust an oven rack to the middle position and heat the oven to 375 degrees. Pulse 1 can of the tomatoes with their juice in a food processor until coarsely chopped, 3 to 4 pulses. Transfer to a bowl. Repeat with the remaining can of tomatoes.

2. Heat the oil, garlic, and red pepper flakes (if using) in a large saucepan over medium heat until fragrant but not brown, 1 to 2 minutes. Stir in the tomatoes and ½ teaspoon salt and simmer until thickened slightly, about 15 minutes. Stir in the basil; season with salt to taste.

3. FOR THE CHEESE FILLING: Combine the ricotta, 1 cup of the Parmesan, the mozzarella, eggs, parsley, basil, salt, and pepper in a medium bowl; set aside.

4. Pour 2 inches boiling water into a 13 by 9-inch broiler-safe baking dish. Slip the noodles into the water, one at a time, and let them soak until pliable, about 5 minutes, separating them with the tip of a knife to prevent sticking. Remove the noodles from the water and place in a single layer on clean kitchen towels. Discard the water and dry the baking dish.

5. Spread the bottom of the baking dish evenly with 1½ cups of the sauce. Using a spoon, spread ¼ cup of the cheese mixture evenly onto the bottom three-quarters of each noodle (with the short side facing you), leaving the top quarter of the noodle exposed. Roll into a tube shape and arrange in the baking dish, seam side down. Top evenly with the remaining sauce, making certain that the pasta is completely covered.

6. Cover the baking dish tightly with foil and bake until bubbling, about 40 minutes. Remove the baking dish from the oven and remove the foil. Adjust the oven rack to the uppermost position (about 6 inches from the heating element) and heat the broiler. Sprinkle the manicotti evenly with the remaining 1 cup Parmesan. Broil until the cheese is spotty brown, 4 to 6 minutes. Cool for 15 minutes; cut into pieces and serve.

FOUR-CHEESE LASAGNA

WHY THIS RECIPE WORKS: Cheese lasagna offers an elegant alternative to meat-laden, red sauce lasagna. But some cheese lasagna is just heavy and bland, due to the use of plain-tasting cheeses. And even those with good cheese flavor can have soupy, dry, or greasy textures. We wanted a robust cheese lasagna with great structure, creamy texture, and maximum flavor.

For the best cheese flavor, we settled on a combination of fontina, Parmesan, Gorgonzola, and Gruyère cheeses. We found that making the white sauce (a béchamel) with a high ratio of flour to butter created a thick binder that provided enough heft to keep the lasagna layers together.

And replacing some of the milk with chicken broth was the key to balancing the richness of the sauce and bringing the cheese flavor forward. But the real secret of a great four-cheese lasagna proved to be a fifth cheese. While ricotta didn't add much flavor, it gave the lasagna body without making the dish heavy and starchy. Our final challenge was to keep the baking time short enough to avoid harming this delicate pasta dish. Both presoaking the no-boil noodles and using a low-heat/high-heat baking method—baking at a moderate temperature and then briefly broiling to brown the top—kept the lasagna from overbaking.

Four-Cheese Lasagna

SERVES 10

It's important not to overbake the lasagna. Once the sauce starts bubbling around the edges, uncover the lasagna and turn the oven to broil. If your lasagna pan is not broiler-safe, brown the lasagna at 500 degrees for about 10 minutes. Whole milk is best in the sauce, but skim and low-fat milk also work. Supermarket-brand cheeses work fine in this recipe. The Gorgonzola may be omitted, but the flavor of the lasagna won't be as complex. We prefer Barilla no-boil lasagna noodles for their delicate texture resembling fresh pasta. Note that Pasta Defino and Ronzoni brands contain only 12 no-boil noodles per package; this recipe requires 15 noodles. This lasagna is very rich; serve small portions with a green salad.

    6   ounces Gruyère cheese, shredded (about 1½ cups)
    2   ounces Parmesan cheese, grated (about 1 cup)
 1½   cups part-skim ricotta cheese
    1   large egg, lightly beaten
    2   tablespoons plus 2 teaspoons minced fresh parsley leaves
  ¼   teaspoon ground black pepper
    3   tablespoons unsalted butter
    1   medium shallot, minced (about 2 tablespoons)
    1   medium garlic clove, minced or pressed through a garlic press (about 1 teaspoon)
  ⅓   cup unbleached all-purpose flour
 2½   cups whole milk (see note)
 1½   cups low-sodium chicken broth
  ½   teaspoon table salt
    1   bay leaf
        Pinch cayenne pepper

   15   no-boil lasagna noodles (see note)
    8   ounces fontina cheese, rind removed, shredded (about 2 cups)
    3   ounces Gorgonzola cheese, crumbled fine (about ¾ cup; see note)

1. Place the Gruyère and ½ cup of the Parmesan in a large ovensafe bowl. Combine the ricotta, egg, 2 tablespoons of the parsley, and the black pepper in a medium bowl. Set both bowls aside.

2. Melt the butter in a medium saucepan over medium heat; add the shallot and garlic and cook, stirring frequently, until beginning to soften, about 2 minutes. Add the flour and cook, stirring constantly, until thoroughly combined, about 1½ minutes; the mixture should not brown. Gradually whisk in the milk and broth; increase the heat to medium-high and bring to a full boil, whisking frequently. Add the salt, bay leaf, and cayenne; reduce the heat to medium-low and simmer until the sauce thickens and coats the back of a spoon, about 10 minutes, stirring occasionally with a heatproof rubber spatula or wooden spoon and making sure to scrape the bottom and corners of the saucepan.

3. Remove the saucepan from the heat and discard the bay leaf. Gradually whisk ¼ cup of the sauce into the ricotta mixture. Pour the remaining sauce over the Gruyère mixture and stir until smooth; set aside.

4. Adjust an oven rack to the upper-middle position and heat the oven to 350 degrees. Pour 2 inches boiling water into a 13 by 9-inch broiler-safe baking dish. Slip the noodles into the water, one at a time, and let them soak until pliable, about 5 minutes, separating them with the tip of a knife to prevent sticking. Remove the noodles from the water and place in a single layer on clean kitchen towels. Discard the water, dry the baking dish, and spray lightly with vegetable oil spray.

5. Spread the bottom of the baking dish evenly with ½ cup of the sauce. Place 3 noodles in a single layer on top of the sauce. Spread ½ cup of the ricotta mixture evenly over the noodles and sprinkle evenly with ½ cup of the fontina and 3 tablespoons of the Gorgonzola. Drizzle ½ cup of the sauce evenly over the cheese. Repeat the layering of noodles, ricotta, fontina, Gorgonzola, and sauce three more times. Place the final 3 noodles on top and cover completely with the remaining sauce, spreading with a rubber spatula and allowing it to spill over the noodles. Sprinkle evenly with the remaining ½ cup Parmesan.

6. Spray a large sheet of foil with vegetable oil spray and cover the lasagna; bake until the edges are just bubbling, 25 to 30 minutes, rotating the pan halfway through the baking time. Remove the foil and turn the oven to broil. Broil until the surface is spotty brown, 3 to 5 minutes. Cool for 15 minutes. Sprinkle with the remaining 2 teaspoons parsley; cut into pieces and serve.

GREAT VEGETABLE LASAGNA

WHY THIS RECIPE WORKS: For a complex vegetable lasagna with bold flavor, we started with a summery mix of zucchini, yellow squash, and eggplant, salting and microwaving the eggplant and sautéing all of the vegetables to cut down on excess moisture and deepen their flavor. Garlic, spinach, and olives added textural contrast and flavor without much work. We dialed up the typical cheese filling by switching mild-mannered ricotta for tangy cottage cheese mixed with heavy cream for richness and Parmesan and garlic for added flavor. Our creamy, quick no-cook tomato sauce brought enough moisture to our lasagna that we found that we could skip the usual step of soaking the no-boil noodles before assembling the dish.

Vegetable Lasagna

SERVES 8 TO 10

Part-skim mozzarella can also be used in this recipe, but avoid preshredded cheese, as it does not melt well. We prefer kosher salt because it clings best to the eggplant. If using table salt, reduce salt amounts by half. To make assembly easier, the roasted vegetable filling can be made ahead and stored in the refrigerator for up to one day.

TOMATO SAUCE

- 1 (28-ounce) can crushed tomatoes
- ¼ cup minced fresh basil leaves
- 2 tablespoons extra-virgin olive oil
- 2 medium garlic cloves, minced or pressed through a garlic press (about 2 teaspoons)
- 1 teaspoon kosher salt
- ¼ teaspoon red pepper flakes

CREAM SAUCE

- 8 ounces whole-milk cottage cheese (about 1 cup)
- 1 cup heavy cream
- 4 ounces Parmesan cheese, grated (about 2 cups)
- 2 medium garlic cloves, minced or pressed through a garlic press (about 2 teaspoons)
- 1 teaspoon cornstarch
- ½ teaspoon kosher salt
- ½ teaspoon ground black pepper

VEGETABLE FILLING

- 1½ pounds eggplant, peeled and cut into ½-inch pieces
  Kosher salt and ground black pepper
- 1 pound zucchini, cut into ½-inch pieces
- 1 pound yellow squash, cut into ½-inch pieces
- 5 tablespoons plus 1 teaspoon extra-virgin olive oil
- 4 medium garlic cloves, minced or pressed through a garlic press (about 4 teaspoons)
- 1 tablespoon minced fresh thyme leaves
- 12 ounces baby spinach (12 cups)
- ½ cup pitted kalamata olives, minced
- 12 ounces whole-milk mozzarella cheese, shredded (about 3 cups)

- 12 no-boil lasagna noodles
- 2 tablespoons chopped fresh basil leaves

1. FOR THE TOMATO SAUCE: Whisk all the ingredients together in a bowl; set aside.

2. FOR THE CREAM SAUCE: Whisk all the ingredients together in a separate bowl; set aside.

3. FOR THE FILLING: Adjust an oven rack to the middle position and heat the oven to 375 degrees. Toss the eggplant with 1 teaspoon kosher salt in a large bowl. Line the surface of a large plate with a double layer of coffee filters and lightly spray with vegetable oil spray. Spread the eggplant in an even layer over the coffee filters; wipe out and reserve the bowl. Microwave the eggplant, uncovered, until dry to the touch and slightly shriveled, about 10 minutes, tossing halfway through cooking. Cool slightly. Return the eggplant to the bowl and toss with the zucchini and summer squash.

4. Combine 1 tablespoon of the oil, the garlic, and thyme in a small bowl. Heat 2 tablespoons more oil in a 12-inch nonstick skillet over medium-high heat until shimmering. Add half of the eggplant mixture, ¼ teaspoon kosher salt, and ¼ teaspoon pepper and cook, stirring occasionally, until the vegetables are lightly browned, about 7 minutes. Clear the center of the skillet, add half of the garlic mixture, and cook, mashing with a spatula, until fragrant, about 30 seconds. Stir the garlic mixture into the vegetables and transfer to a medium bowl. Repeat with the remaining eggplant mixture, 2 tablespoons more oil, and the remaining garlic mixture; transfer to the bowl.

5. Heat the remaining 1 teaspoon oil in the now-empty skillet over medium-high heat until shimmering. Add the spinach and cook, stirring frequently, until wilted, about 3 minutes. Transfer the spinach to a paper towel–lined plate and drain for 2 minutes. Stir into the eggplant mixture.

6. Grease a 13 by 9-inch baking dish. Spread 1 cup of the tomato sauce evenly over the bottom of the dish. Arrange 4 noodles on top of the sauce (the noodles will overlap). Spread half of the vegetable mixture over the noodles, followed by half of the olives. Spoon half of the cream sauce over the top and sprinkle with 1 cup of the mozzarella. Repeat the layering with 4 more noodles, 1 cup more tomato sauce, the remaining vegetables, remaining olives, remaining cream sauce and 1 cup more mozzarella. For the final layer, arrange the remaining 4 noodles on top and cover completely with the remaining tomato sauce. Sprinkle with the remaining 1 cup mozzarella.

7. Cover the dish tightly with aluminum foil that has been sprayed with vegetable oil spray and bake until the edges are just bubbling, about 35 minutes, rotating the dish halfway through baking. Cool the lasagna for 25 minutes, then sprinkle with the basil and serve.

LASAGNA WITH MEAT SAUCE

WHY THIS RECIPE WORKS: Traditional meaty lasagna is one of the best comfort foods out there. Unfortunately, this hearty dish takes the better part of a day to make (not very comforting, if you ask us). The noodles must be boiled and the sauce slow-cooked. Then, once the cheese filling is mixed, the ingredients must be carefully layered before the whole thing is baked. We wanted a really good meat lasagna, with all of the rich, hearty meatiness of an all-day lasagna, but ready in a lot less time.

We made a speedy meaty tomato sauce by simmering onion, garlic, and meat loaf mix (a combination of ground beef, pork, and veal) together for about 15 minutes. Adding some heavy cream created a richer, creamier, more cohesive sauce; we stirred in pureed and diced tomatoes for a luxurious, soft sauce with chunks of tomatoes. Using no-boil lasagna noodles eliminated the tedious process of boiling and draining the pasta. For a classic cheese layer, we combined ricotta cheese, Parmesan cheese, fresh basil, and an egg, which helped thicken and bind the mixture; a layer of shredded mozzarella upped the creaminess and cheesiness of the filling. Covering the lasagna with foil before baking helped to soften the noodles; removing it during the last half-hour of baking ensured that the cheeses were properly browned.

Lasagna with Hearty Tomato-Meat Sauce

SERVES 6 TO 8

You can substitute equal amounts of 80 percent lean ground beef, ground veal, and ground pork for the meat loaf mix (the total amount of meat should be 1 pound). The assembled, unbaked lasagna will keep in the freezer for up to 2 months; wrap it tightly with plastic wrap, then foil, before freezing. To bake, defrost it in the refrigerator for up to 2 days and bake as directed, extending the covered baking time by 5 to 10 minutes.

TOMATO-MEAT SAUCE

 1 tablespoon olive oil
 1 medium onion, minced
 6 medium garlic cloves, minced or pressed through a
   garlic press (about 2 tablespoons)
 1 pound meat loaf mix (see note)
 ½ teaspoon table salt
 ½ teaspoon ground black pepper

¼ cup heavy cream
1 (28-ounce) can tomato puree
1 (28-ounce) can diced tomatoes, drained

CHEESE FILLING AND PASTA
1¾ cups whole-milk or part-skim ricotta cheese
2½ ounces Parmesan cheese, grated (about 1¼ cups)
½ cup chopped fresh basil leaves
1 large egg, lightly beaten
½ teaspoon table salt
½ teaspoon ground black pepper
12 no-boil lasagna noodles
1 pound whole-milk mozzarella cheese, shredded
(about 4 cups)

1. Adjust an oven rack to the middle position and heat the oven to 375 degrees.

2. FOR THE SAUCE: Heat the oil in a large Dutch oven over medium heat until shimmering. Add the onion and cook, stirring occasionally, until softened but not browned, about 2 minutes. Add the garlic and cook until fragrant, about 2 minutes. Increase the heat to medium-high and add the meat loaf mix, salt, and pepper; cook, breaking the meat into small pieces with a wooden spoon, until the meat loses its raw color but has not browned, about 4 minutes. Add the cream and simmer, stirring occasionally, until the liquid evaporates and only rendered fat remains, about 4 minutes. Add the tomato puree and diced tomatoes and bring to a simmer; reduce the heat to low and simmer until the flavors have blended, about 3 minutes. Set aside. (The cooled sauce can be refrigerated in an airtight container for up to 2 days; reheat before assembling the lasagna.)

3. FOR THE CHEESE FILLING: Combine the ricotta, 1 cup of the Parmesan, the basil, egg, salt, and pepper in a medium bowl; set aside.

4. Spread the bottom of a 13 by 9-inch baking dish evenly with ¼ cup of the meat sauce (avoiding large chunks of meat). Place 3 noodles in a single layer on top of the sauce. Spread each noodle evenly with 3 tablespoons of the ricotta mixture and sprinkle the entire layer

BEHIND THE SCENES

A FRESH CRUSH IS BEST

We're always looking for ways to make our kitchen work more efficient and will often prep recipes in advance if we know we've got a lot of recipes to get through on a given day. But noticing that garlic can develop a particularly strong odor if minced too far in advance, we decided to run a quick test. We used garlic in three different applications: lightly cooked in Pasta with Garlic and Oil (page 238); raw, when stirred into mayonnaise; and as a subtle flavoring in a vinaigrette. For each recipe, we used freshly minced garlic, garlic that had been minced six hours in advance, and garlic that had been minced the day before. Both the six-hour-old and one-day-old minced garlic were so powerful they overwhelmed the other flavors in the dish.

Turns out, garlic flavor comes from a compound called allicin, which is not formed until after the garlic's cells are ruptured. As soon as you cut into garlic, the allicin will start to build and build until its flavor becomes overwhelmingly strong. So if you're going to prep a recipe in advance, make sure to leave the garlic cloves whole until the last minute.

evenly with 1 cup of the mozzarella cheese. Spread the cheese evenly with 1½ cups of the meat sauce. Repeat the layering of noodles, ricotta, mozzarella, and sauce two more times. Place the remaining 3 noodles on top of the sauce, spread evenly with the remaining sauce, sprinkle with the remaining 1 cup mozzarella, then sprinkle with the remaining ¼ cup Parmesan. Spray a large sheet of foil with vegetable oil spray and cover the lasagna.

5. Bake for 15 minutes, then remove the foil. Continue to bake until the cheese is spotty brown and the sauce is bubbling, about 25 minutes longer. Cool the lasagna for 10 minutes; cut into pieces and serve.

CHAPTER 13

BRINGING HOME ITALIAN FAVORITES

Rosemary Focaccia   278

Crisp Thin-Crust Pizza   280

   Quick Tomato Sauce
for Pizza

New York–Style Thin-Crust
Pizza   281

Deep-Dish Pizza with
Tomatoes, Mozzarella,
and Basil   283

Chicago-Style Deep-Dish
Pizza   284

Pepperoni Pan Pizza   286

Pizza Bianca   287

Grilled Tomato and
Cheese Pizzas   288

   Spicy Garlic Oil

Tomato and Mozzarella
Tart   291

Classic Garlic Bread   292

Cheesy Garlic Bread   292

Frico   293

Italian Pasta and Bean Soup
(Pasta e Fagioli)   294

Hearty Tuscan Bean
Stew   295

Eggplant Parmesan   296

Basic Polenta   297

Mushroom Risotto   298

Butternut Squash
Risotto   299

Chicken Marsala   300

Lighter Chicken
Parmesan   301

   Simple Tomato Sauce

Chicken Piccata   302

Parmesan-Crusted Chicken
Cutlets   303

Chicken Francese   304

Chicken Saltimbocca   305

Chicken Canzanese   306

Italian-Style Grilled
Chicken   307

Pork Chops with Vinegar
and Sweet Peppers   308

Osso Buco   309

Beef Braised in Barolo   310

Shrimp Scampi   311

FOCACCIA

WHY THIS RECIPE WORKS: Most of the focaccia we see in the States is heavy, thick, and strewn with pizza-like toppings. We wanted a lighter loaf, crisp-crusted and airy on the inside and topped with just a smattering of herbs.

To start, we focused on flavor. To get the benefits of a long fermentation with minimal effort, many bakers use a "preferment" (also known as a "sponge," "starter," or *biga* in Italian): a mixture of flour, water, and a small amount of yeast that rests (often overnight) before being incorporated into the dough. We followed suit, but the interiors of the loaves weren't as tender and airy as we wanted. We wondered if our stand mixer was developing too much gluten (the strong, elastic network of cross-linked proteins that give bread its crumb structure). Instead we turned to a more gentle approach, one we learned while developing our Almost No-Knead Bread (page 553). In this method, a high hydration level (the weight of the water in relation to the weight of the flour) and a long autolysis (the dough resting process) take advantage of the enzymes naturally present in the wheat to produce the same effect as kneading.

This method worked to a point—our loaves were light and airy, but squat. To improve the structure, we turned

the dough (folding in the edges of the dough toward the middle) at regular intervals while it proofed. But to cut back on the long proofing time (three hours) and hasten gluten development, we followed the advice of research, which suggested holding back the salt when mixing our dough, adding it in later. (Salt inhibits flour from absorbing water and slows down the activity of the enzymes responsible for developing gluten.) The results were dramatic—we were able to shave an hour off our proofing time.

To give our loaves a flavorful, crisp crust, we oiled the baking pans and added coarse salt for flavor and an extra crunchy texture. This focaccia was a revelation: crackly crisp on the bottom, deeply browned on top, with an interior that was open and airy.

Rosemary Focaccia

MAKES TWO 9-INCH ROUND LOAVES

If you don't have a baking stone, bake the bread on an overturned, preheated rimmed baking sheet set on the upper-middle oven rack. The bread can be kept for up to 2 days well-wrapped at room temperature or frozen for several months wrapped in foil and placed in a zipper-lock bag.

BIGA

- ½ cup (2½ ounces) unbleached all-purpose flour
- ⅓ cup (2⅔ ounces) warm water (100–110 degrees)
- ¼ teaspoon instant or rapid-rise yeast

DOUGH

- 2½ cups (12½ ounces) unbleached all-purpose flour, plus extra for shaping
- 1¼ cups (10 ounces) warm water (100–110 degrees)
- 1 teaspoon instant or rapid-rise yeast
  Kosher salt
- 4 tablespoons extra-virgin olive oil
- 2 tablespoons chopped fresh rosemary leaves

1. FOR THE BIGA: Combine the flour, water, and yeast in a large bowl and stir with a wooden spoon until a uniform mass forms and no dry flour remains, about 1 minute. Cover the bowl tightly with plastic wrap and let stand at room temperature (about 70 degrees) overnight (at least 8 hours or up to 24 hours). Use immediately or store in the refrigerator for up to 3 days (allow to stand at room temperature for 30 minutes before proceeding with the recipe).

2. **FOR THE DOUGH:** Stir the flour, water, and yeast into the biga with a wooden spoon until a uniform mass forms and no dry flour remains, about 1 minute. Cover with plastic wrap and let rise at room temperature for 15 minutes.

3. Sprinkle 2 teaspoons salt over the dough; stir into the dough until thoroughly incorporated, about 1 minute. Cover with plastic wrap and let rise at room temperature for 30 minutes. Spray a rubber spatula or bowl scraper with vegetable oil spray; fold the partially risen dough over itself by gently lifting and folding the edge of the dough toward the middle. Turn the bowl 90 degrees; fold again. Turn the bowl and fold the dough six more times (for a total of eight turns). Cover with plastic wrap and let rise for 30 minutes. Repeat the folding, turning, and rising two more times, for a total of three 30-minute rises. Meanwhile, adjust an oven rack to the upper-middle position, place a baking stone on the rack, and heat the oven to 500 degrees, at least 30 minutes before baking.

4. Gently transfer the dough to a lightly floured work surface. Lightly dust the top of the dough with flour and divide it in half. Shape each piece of dough into a 5-inch round by gently tucking under the edges. Coat two 9-inch round cake pans with 2 tablespoons olive oil each. Sprinkle each pan with ½ teaspoon kosher salt. Place a round of dough in one pan, top side down; slide the dough around the pan to coat the bottom and sides, then flip the dough over. Repeat with the second piece of dough in the second pan. Cover the pans with plastic wrap and let rest for 5 minutes.

5. Using your fingertips, press the dough out toward the edges of the pan, taking care not to tear it. (If the dough resists stretching, let it relax for 5 to 10 minutes before trying to stretch it again.) Using a dinner fork, poke the entire surface of the dough 25 to 30 times, popping any large bubbles. Sprinkle the rosemary evenly over the top of the dough. Let the dough rest in the pan until slightly bubbly, 5 to 10 minutes.

6. Place the pans on the baking stone and lower the oven temperature to 450 degrees. Bake until the tops are golden brown, 25 to 28 minutes, switching the placement of the pans halfway through the baking time. Transfer the pans to a wire rack and let cool for 5 minutes. Remove the loaves from the pans and place on the wire rack. Brush the tops with any oil remaining in the pans. Cool for 30 minutes before serving.

NOTES FROM THE TEST KITCHEN

KEY STEPS TO MAKING FOCACCIA

1. Fold the partially risen dough over itself by gently lifting and folding the edge of the dough toward the middle. Turn the bowl 90 degrees; fold again. Turn the bowl and fold dough six more times (for a total of eight turns).

2. Cover with plastic wrap and let rise for 30 minutes. Repeat stretching, folding, and rising two more times, for a total of three 30-minute rises.

3. Dust the dough with flour and divide in half. Shape the halves into 5-inch rounds. Place the rounds in the oiled pans and slide around to coat the dough. Flip and repeat. Cover the pans with plastic wrap and let rest for 5 minutes.

4. Using your fingertips, press the dough out toward the edges of the pan, taking care not to tear it. (If the dough resists stretching, let it relax for 5 to 10 minutes before trying to stretch it again.)

5. Using a dinner fork, poke the surface of the dough 25 to 30 times. Deflate any remaining bubbles of dough with a fork. Sprinkle the rosemary over the dough. Let rest until slightly bubbly, 5 to 10 minutes, before baking.

THIN-CRUST PIZZA

WHY THIS RECIPE WORKS: Few dishes say "Italian" better than a slice of pizza. At one end of the pizza spectrum is crisp-crust Neapolitan-style pizza. We aimed to develop the ultimate version, one with a shatteringly crisp, wafer-thin crust with a deeply caramelized flavor that bears no trace of raw yeast or flour.

For a pizza dough that comes together quickly and easily, we turned to the food processor. Letting the dough rise slowly in the refrigerator overnight made it easier to handle the next day, and it developed good flavor from the slow fermentation. For the thinnest crust possible, we used a rolling pin. A sheet of plastic wrap on top of the dough made rolling easier; we didn't need to add more flour to prevent sticking. This slim crust can't handle heavy toppings, nor should it. A thin layer of tomato sauce and a sprinkling of mozzarella pack lots of flavor.

Crisp Thin-Crust Pizza
SERVES 6 TO 8

Note that the pizza dough needs to be started at least 1 day before serving. Keep in mind that it is more important for the rolled dough to be of even thinness than to be a perfect circle. For topping the pizzas, we recommend buying shrink-wrapped mozzarella from the supermarket; do not use fresh because it is too moist and will make the crust soggy. If you don't have a pizza stone, bake the pizza on a rimless or overturned baking sheet that has been preheated just like the pizza stone.

DOUGH
- 1¾–2 cups (8¾ to 10 ounces) unbleached all-purpose flour, plus extra for the work surface
- ½ teaspoon instant or rapid-rise yeast
- ½ teaspoon honey
- ½ teaspoon table salt
- ¼ cup olive oil
- ¾ cup warm water (110 degrees)

TOPPINGS
- 1 cup Quick Tomato Sauce for Pizza (recipe follows)
- 8 ounces whole-milk mozzarella cheese, shredded (about 2 cups; see note)

1. FOR THE DOUGH: Pulse 1¾ cups of the flour, the yeast, honey, and salt in a food processor (fitted with the dough blade, if possible) until combined, about 5 pulses. With the machine running, pour the oil and then the water through the feed tube and process until the dough forms a ball, about 30 seconds. If after 30 seconds the dough is sticky and clings to the blade, add the remaining ¼ cup flour 1 tablespoon at a time. Turn the dough out onto a work surface.

2. Divide the dough in half and place each piece in a gallon-size, heavy-duty zipper-lock bag and seal. Refrigerate overnight or up to 48 hours.

3. TO MAKE THE PIZZA: One hour before baking the pizza, adjust an oven rack to the lowest position, set a pizza stone on the rack, and heat the oven to 500 degrees.

4. Remove the dough from the plastic bags. Set each piece in the center of a lightly floured large sheet of parchment paper. Cover each with two 18-inch lengths of plastic wrap, overlapping them in the center; let the dough rest for 10 minutes.

5. Setting one piece of dough aside, roll the other into a 14-inch round with an even thickness, using the tackiness of the dough against the parchment to help roll it. If the parchment wrinkles, flip the dough sandwich over and smooth the wrinkles with a metal bench scraper.

6. Peel the plastic wrap off the top of the rolled dough. Spread ½ cup of the tomato sauce to the edges of the dough. Sprinkle with 1 cup of the cheese.

7. Slip the dough with the parchment onto a pizza peel or rimless baking sheet. Slide the pizza, parchment and all, onto the hot pizza stone. Bake until a deep golden brown, about 10 minutes. Remove the pizza from the oven with a pizza peel or pull the parchment with the pizza onto a baking sheet. Transfer the pizza to a cutting board, slide the parchment out from under the pizza, and slide it onto a wire rack. Cool for 2 minutes until crisp; slide to a cutting board, cut into wedges, and serve.

8. While the first pizza is baking, repeat steps 5 and 6 to roll and top the second pizza; allow the baking stone to reheat for 15 minutes after baking the first pizza, then repeat step 7 to bake the second pizza.

Quick Tomato Sauce for Pizza
MAKES ABOUT 1½ CUPS

For pizza, you want the smoothest possible sauce. Start with crushed tomatoes and puree them in a food processor before cooking them with the garlic and oil. This recipe makes a bit more sauce than needed to sauce two thin-crust pizzas.

1 (14.5-ounce) can crushed tomatoes
1 tablespoon olive oil
1 medium garlic clove, minced or pressed through a
   garlic press (about 1 teaspoon)
   Table salt and ground black pepper

1. Process the tomatoes in a food processor until smooth, about 5 pulses.

2. Heat the oil and garlic in a medium saucepan over medium heat until the garlic is fragrant, about 30 seconds. Stir in the tomatoes; bring to a simmer and cook, uncovered, until the sauce thickens, about 15 minutes. Season with salt and pepper to taste.

NEW YORK–STYLE THIN-CRUST PIZZA

WHY THIS RECIPE WORKS: With home ovens that reach only 500 degrees and dough that's impossible to stretch thin, even the savviest cooks can struggle to produce parlor-quality pizza. We were in pursuit of a simple-to-make pizza with a New York–style crust: thin, crisp, and spottily charred on the exterior; tender yet chewy within. High-protein bread flour gave us a chewy, nicely tanned pizza crust and the right ratio of flour to water to yeast gave us dough that was easy to stretch and retained moisture as it baked. We kneaded the dough quickly in a food processor then let it proof in the refrigerator for a few hours to develop its flavors. After we shaped and topped the pizza, it went onto a blazing hot baking stone to cook. Placing the stone near the top of the oven was a surprising improvement, allowing the top of the pizza to brown as well as the bottom. In minutes we had a pizza with everything in sync: a thoroughly crisp, browned crust with a slightly chewy texture, just like a good parlor slice.

New York–Style Thin-Crust Pizza
SERVES 4 TO 6

If you don't own a baking stone, bake the pizzas on a rimless or overturned baking sheet that has been preheated just like the pizza stone. If you don't own a pizza peel, stretch the dough on a large sheet of lightly floured parchment paper, transfer to a rimless or overturned baking sheet, and slide the pizza with the parchment onto the hot pizza stone. You can shape the second dough round while the first pizza bakes, but don't add the toppings until just before baking. It's important to use ice water in the dough to prevent it from overheating in the food processor. Semolina flour is ideal for dusting the peel; use it in place of bread flour if you have it. The sauce will yield more than needed in the recipe; extra sauce can be refrigerated for up to 1 week or frozen for up to 1 month.

DOUGH
3 cups (16½ ounces) bread flour, plus extra for the
   work surface
2 teaspoons sugar
½ teaspoon instant or rapid-rise yeast
1⅓ cups ice water
1 tablespoon vegetable oil
1½ teaspoons table salt

SAUCE
1 (28-ounce) can whole tomatoes, drained
1 tablespoon extra-virgin olive oil
2 medium garlic cloves, minced or pressed through a
   garlic press (about 2 teaspoons)
1 teaspoon red wine vinegar
1 teaspoon table salt
1 teaspoon dried oregano
¼ teaspoon ground black pepper

CHEESE
1 ounce Parmesan cheese, grated fine (about ½ cup)
8 ounces whole-milk mozzarella, shredded (about 2 cups)

1. FOR THE DOUGH: Pulse the flour, sugar, and yeast in a food processor (fitted with the dough blade, if possible) until combined, about 5 pulses. With the food processor running, slowly add the water; process until the dough is just combined and no dry flour remains, about 10 seconds. Let the dough sit for 10 minutes.

2. Add the oil and salt to the dough and process until the dough forms a satiny, sticky ball that clears the sides of the bowl, 30 to 60 seconds. Transfer the dough to a lightly oiled work surface and knead briefly by hand until smooth, about 1 minute. Shape the dough into a tight ball and place in a large, lightly oiled bowl; cover the bowl tightly with plastic wrap and refrigerate for at least 24 hours or up to 3 days.

3. FOR THE SAUCE: Process all the ingredients in the clean bowl of the food processor until smooth, about 30 seconds. Transfer to a bowl and refrigerate until ready to use.

4. TO BAKE THE PIZZA: One hour before baking, adjust an oven rack to the upper-middle position (the rack should be 4 to 5 inches from the broiler), set a baking stone on the rack, and heat the oven to 500 degrees. Transfer the dough to a clean work surface and divide in half.

NOTES FROM THE TEST KITCHEN

TOPPING TIPS

Our New York–Style Thin-Crust Pizza is great with just tomato sauce, shredded mozzarella, and Parmesan, but additional toppings are always an option—provided they're prepared correctly and added judiciously. (An overloaded pie will bake up soggy.) Here are a few guidelines for how to handle different types of toppings:

HEARTY VEGETABLES

Aim for a maximum of 6 ounces per pie, spread out in a single layer. Vegetables such as onions, peppers, and mushrooms should be thinly sliced and lightly sautéed (or microwaved for a minute or two along with a little olive oil) before using.

DELICATE VEGETABLES AND HERBS

Leafy greens and herbs like spinach and basil are best placed beneath the cheese to protect them or added raw to the fully cooked pizza.

MEATS

Proteins (no more than 4 ounces per pie) should be precooked and drained to remove excess fat. We like to poach meats like sausage (broken up into ½-inch chunks), pepperoni, or ground beef for 4 to 5 minutes in a wide skillet along with ¼ cup of water, which helps to render the fat while keeping the meat moist.

With cupped palms, form each half into a smooth, tight ball. Place the balls of dough on a lightly greased baking sheet, spacing them at least 3 inches apart; cover loosely with greased plastic wrap and let sit for 1 hour.

5. Coat 1 ball of dough generously with flour and place on a well-floured work surface (keep the other ball covered). Use your fingertips to gently flatten the dough into an 8-inch disk, leaving 1 inch of the outer edge slightly thicker than the center. Using your hands, gently stretch the disk into a 12-inch round, working along the edges and giving the disk quarter turns. Transfer the dough to a well-floured pizza peel and stretch into a 13-inch round. Using the back of a spoon or ladle, spread ½ cup of the tomato sauce in a thin layer over the surface of the dough, leaving a ¼-inch border around the edge. Sprinkle ¼ cup of the Parmesan evenly over the sauce, followed by 1 cup of the mozzarella. Slide the pizza carefully onto the baking stone and bake until the crust is well browned and the cheese is bubbly and beginning to brown, 10 to 12 minutes, rotating the pizza halfway through baking. Transfer the pizza to a wire rack and let cool for 5 minutes before slicing and serving. Repeat step 5 to shape, top, and bake the second pizza.

DEEP-DISH PIZZA

WHY THIS RECIPE WORKS: Unlike its thin-crust cousin, deep-dish pizza has a soft, chewy, thick crust and can stand up to substantial toppings. We wanted to try our hand at making this restaurant-style pizza at home. We were after a recipe that didn't require a lot of fuss, and our pizza had to taste better than takeout.

Most of the allure of deep-dish pizza is in the crust, so it was important to get it right. After trying numerous ingredients and techniques, we discovered that a boiled potato gave the crust exactly the right qualities: It was soft and moist, yet with a bit of chew and good structure. The potato even made the unbaked dough easier to handle. To keep the outside of the crust from toughening during baking, we added a generous amount of olive oil to the pan before putting in the dough. Topping the pizza before it went into the oven weighed down the crust so that it didn't rise much and became dense, so we baked the crust untopped for a few minutes first. Our deep-dish crust wasn't just a platform for the topping; it had great flavor and texture of its own.

Deep-Dish Pizza with Tomatoes, Mozzarella, and Basil

SERVES 4

Prepare the topping while the dough is rising so the two will be ready at the same time. Baking the pizza in a deep-dish pan on a hot pizza stone will help produce a crisp, well-browned bottom crust. If you don't have a pizza stone, use an overturned or heavy rimless baking sheet. The amount of oil used to grease the pan may seem excessive, but it helps brown the crust while also preventing sticking. If you don't have a 14-inch deep-dish pizza pan, use two 10-inch cake pans. Grease them with 2 tablespoons oil each; divide the pizza dough in half and pat each half into a 9-inch round. Use shrink-wrapped supermarket cheese rather than fresh mozzarella.

DOUGH

- 1 medium russet potato (about 9 ounces), peeled and quartered
- 3¼–3½ cups (16¼ to 17½ ounces) unbleached all-purpose flour
- 1¾ teaspoons table salt
- 1½ teaspoons instant or rapid-rise yeast
- 6 tablespoons olive oil, plus extra for oiling the bowl (see note)
- 1 cup warm water (110 degrees)

TOPPING

- 1½ pounds plum tomatoes (5 to 6 medium), cored, seeded, and cut into 1-inch pieces
- 2 medium garlic cloves, minced or pressed through a garlic press (about 2 teaspoons)
  Table salt and ground black pepper
- 6 ounces whole-milk mozzarella cheese, shredded (about 1½ cups; see note)
- 1¼ ounces Parmesan cheese, grated (about ⅔ cup)
- 3 tablespoons shredded fresh basil leaves

1. FOR THE DOUGH: Bring 4 cups water and the potato to a boil in a small saucepan over medium-high heat; cook until tender, 10 to 15 minutes. Drain and cool until the potato can be handled; press the potato through the fine disk of a potato ricer or grate it on the large holes of a box grater. Measure 1⅓ cups lightly packed potato; discard the remaining potato.

2. Process 3¼ cups of the flour, the potato, salt and yeast in a food processor (fitted with the dough blade, if possible) until combined, about 5 seconds. With the motor running, pour 2 tablespoons of the oil and then the water through the feed tube and process until the dough comes together in a ball, about 30 seconds. If after 30 seconds the dough is sticky and clings to the blade, add the remaining ¼ cup flour 1 tablespoon at a time. Lightly coat a medium bowl with oil. Transfer the dough to the bowl; cover tightly with plastic wrap and set in a warm spot until doubled in volume, 1½ to 2 hours.

3. Meanwhile, mix the tomatoes and garlic together in a medium bowl; season with salt and pepper to taste and set aside.

4. Oil the bottom of a 14-inch deep-dish pizza pan with the remaining 4 tablespoons olive oil. Remove the dough from the oven and gently punch it down; turn the dough onto a clean, dry work surface and pat it into a 12-inch round. Transfer the round to the oiled pan, cover with plastic wrap, and let rest until the dough no longer resists shaping, about 10 minutes.

5. Adjust the oven racks to the lowest and top positions, set a pizza stone on the lower rack, and heat the oven to 500 degrees. Uncover the dough and pull it into the edges and up the sides of the pan to form a 1-inch-high lip. Cover with plastic wrap; let rise in a warm, draft-free spot until doubled in size, about 30 minutes. Uncover the dough and prick it generously with a fork. Reduce the oven temperature to 425 degrees, place the pan with the pizza on the hot pizza stone, and bake until dry and lightly browned, about 15 minutes. Add the tomato mixture, followed by the mozzarella, then the Parmesan. Bake the pizza on the stone or baking sheet until the cheese melts, 10 to 15 minutes (5 to 10 minutes for 10-inch pizzas). Move the pizza to the top rack and bake until the cheese is spotty golden brown, about 5 minutes longer. Cool for 5 minutes, then, holding the pizza pan at an angle with a potholder, use a wide spatula to slide the pizza from the pan to a cutting board, cut into wedges, and serve.

CHICAGO DEEP-DISH PIZZA

WHY THIS RECIPE WORKS: Recipes for the sort of deep-dish pizzas with crusts like buttery pastries you can only get in Chicago pizzerias are staunchly protected by the people who make them. We would have to invent our own recipe for the best deep-dish pizza Chicago has to offer: one that boasts a thick, crisp crust with an airy, flaky interior, and a rich taste that can hold its own under any kind of topping.

The recipes we came across in our research sounded a lot like classic pizza dough, with cornmeal added for crunch and butter for tenderness and flavor. These crusts weren't bad, but they weren't as flaky as a Chicago-made crust. To increase the flakiness factor, we turned to laminating. This baking term refers to the layering of butter and dough to create ultra-flaky pastries through a sequence of rolling and folding. A combination of adding melted butter to the dough and spreading the rolled out dough with softened butter before folding it did the trick. This crust was a huge improvement. Our only additional tweak was adding oil to each pan to crisp the edges.

With our crust all set, we turned to the toppings. Following Chicago tradition, we covered the dough with freshly shredded mozzarella and then topped the cheese with our thick, quick-to-make tomato sauce. The cheese formed a consistent barrier between the crust and our sauce, which prevented our thick, flavorful crust from turning soggy.

Chicago-Style Deep-Dish Pizza
MAKES TWO 9-INCH PIZZAS

You will need a stand mixer with a dough hook for this recipe. Place a damp kitchen towel under the mixer and watch it at all times during kneading to prevent it from wobbling off the counter. Handle the dough with slightly oiled hands to prevent sticking. The test kitchen prefers Sorrento Whole Milk Mozzarella; part-skim mozzarella can also be used, but avoid preshredded cheese here. Our preferred brands of crushed tomatoes are Tuttorosso and Muir Glen. Grate the onion on the large holes of a box grater.

DOUGH
- 3¼ cups (16¼ ounces) unbleached all-purpose flour
- ½ cup (2¾ ounces) yellow cornmeal
- 2¼ teaspoons (about 1 envelope) instant or rapid-rise yeast
- 2 teaspoons sugar
- 1½ teaspoons table salt
- 1¼ cups water, room temperature
- 3 tablespoons unsalted butter, melted, plus 4 tablespoons, softened
- 1 teaspoon plus 4 tablespoons olive oil

SAUCE
- 2 tablespoons unsalted butter
- ¼ cup grated onion (see note)
- ¼ teaspoon dried oregano
  Table salt and ground black pepper
- 2 medium garlic cloves, minced or pressed through a garlic press (about 2 teaspoons)
- 1 (28-ounce) can crushed tomatoes (see note)
- ¼ teaspoon sugar
- 2 tablespoons chopped fresh basil
- 1 tablespoon extra-virgin olive oil

TOPPINGS
- 1 pound mozzarella, shredded (about 4 cups; see note)
- ¼ cup grated Parmesan cheese

1. FOR THE DOUGH: Mix the flour, cornmeal, yeast, sugar, and salt in the bowl of a stand mixer fitted with the dough hook on low speed until incorporated, about 1 minute. Add the water and melted butter and mix on low speed until fully combined, 1 to 2 minutes, scraping the sides and bottom of the bowl as needed. Increase the speed to medium and knead until the dough is glossy and smooth and pulls away from sides of the bowl, 4 to 5 minutes. (The dough will only pull away from the sides while the mixer is on. When the mixer is off, the dough will fall back to the sides.)

2. Using your fingers, coat a large bowl with 1 teaspoon of the olive oil, rubbing excess oil from your fingers onto the blade of a rubber spatula. Using the oiled spatula, transfer the dough to the oiled bowl, turning once to oil the top. Cover the bowl tightly with plastic wrap. Let the dough rise at room temperature until nearly doubled in volume, 45 to 60 minutes.

3. FOR THE SAUCE: While the dough rises, heat the butter in a medium saucepan over medium heat until melted. Add the onion, oregano, and ½ teaspoon salt and cook, stirring occasionally, until the liquid has evaporated and the onion is golden brown, about 5 minutes. Add the garlic and cook until fragrant, about 30 seconds. Stir in the tomatoes and sugar, increase the heat to high, and bring to a simmer. Lower the heat to medium-low and simmer until the sauce has reduced to 2½ cups, 25 to 30 minutes. Off the heat, stir in the basil and oil, then season with salt and pepper to taste.

4. TO LAMINATE THE DOUGH: Adjust an oven rack to the lowest position and heat the oven to 425 degrees. Using a rubber spatula, turn the dough out onto a dry work surface and roll into a 15 by 12-inch rectangle. Following the photos, use an offset spatula to spread the softened butter over the surface of the dough, leaving a ½-inch border along the edges. Starting at the short end, roll the dough into a tight cylinder. With the seam side down, flatten the cylinder into an 18 by 4-inch rectangle. Cut the rectangle in half crosswise. Working with one half, fold the dough into thirds like a business letter, then pinch the seams together to form a ball. Repeat with the remaining half of the dough. Return the dough balls to the oiled bowl, cover tightly with plastic wrap, and let rise in the refrigerator until nearly doubled in volume, 40 to 50 minutes.

5. Coat two 9-inch round cake pans with 2 tablespoons olive oil each. Transfer one dough ball to a dry work surface and roll out into a 13-inch disk about ¼ inch thick. Transfer the dough round to a cake pan by rolling the dough loosely around the rolling pin, then unrolling the dough into the pan. Lightly press the dough into the pan, working it into the corners and 1 inch up the sides. If the dough resists stretching, let it relax for 5 minutes before trying again. Repeat with the remaining dough ball.

6. For each pizza, sprinkle 2 cups of the mozzarella evenly over the surface of the dough. Spread 1¼ cups of the tomato sauce over the cheese and sprinkle 2 tablespoons of the Parmesan over the sauce for each pizza. Bake until the crust is golden brown, 20 to 30 minutes. Remove the pizza from the oven and let rest for 10 minutes before slicing and serving.

NOTES FROM THE TEST KITCHEN

MAKING DEEP-DISH PIZZA CRUST

1. After rolling out the dough into a 15 by 12-inch rectangle, spread the softened butter over the dough, leaving a ½-inch border along the edges.

2. Roll the dough into a tight cylinder, starting at the short end closest to you.

3. Flatten the dough cylinder into an 18 by 4-inch rectangle, then halve the cylinder crosswise.

4. Fold each dough half into thirds to form a ball, pinch the seams shut, and let the dough balls rise in the refrigerator for 40 to 50 minutes.

5. After rolling each ball of dough into a 13-inch disk about ¼ inch thick, transfer the dough disks to the oiled pans and lightly press the dough into the pans, working it into the corners and up the sides.

THE TEST KITCHEN'S TOP FIVE ESSENTIAL KITCHEN TOOLS

Face it: Americans are crazy about gadgets. Since the time of Benjamin Franklin, we have valued the ingenuity of the inventor who designs a simple tool that makes the execution of an everyday task easier. But as anyone who watches late-night television knows, America's love of the gadget can—and does—go too far at times. No one needs a syringe to inject marinades into meat.

So how do you know which gadgets work and which ones don't? That's where we can help. Here's our list of five gadgets you might not own, but really should. (See pages 709–719 for recommended brands.)

1. DIGITAL INSTANT-READ THERMOMETER: How else do you know when food is done? And, because it's digital, it works in seconds so your hands don't tarry in hot spots like the oven or grill.

2. LOCKING TONGS: Don't use a fork. Sturdy, long-handled tongs (with scalloped edges that won't pierce food) can turn, flip, rotate, stir, and more.

3. GARLIC PRESS: Stop kidding yourself. You're never going to mince garlic finely and evenly enough. A garlic press ensures consistent (and perfect) results every time.

4. OVEN THERMOMETER: News flash—your oven probably isn't properly calibrated. How do we know? We tested 20 home ovens and only a handful came close. You could pay big bucks to get your oven serviced by a professional or spend a few dollars on an oven thermometer so cookies don't burn and roasts are perfectly cooked.

5. KNIFE SHARPENER: Using dull knives is slow and unsafe. You wouldn't drive a car with nearly flat tires, would you? A fancy electric sharpener is nice, but even a good (and cheap) manual sharpener is far better than nothing.

PEPPERONI PAN PIZZA

WHY THIS RECIPE WORKS: Great pan pizza—named for the pan in which the dough rises and is cooked—has an irresistible crust that's crisp on the bottom and soft and chewy in the middle. A generous amount of oil poured into the pan creates the crisp bottom; getting the soft interior is harder to figure out. We found the secret in a novel ingredient: skim milk. Milk is often used in tender yeast breads, and when we tried it in our pan pizza dough, we got a tender crust with just the right chew. Whole milk worked fine as well, but dough made with skim milk rose better and baked up especially soft and light. Just a few teaspoons of sugar gave the yeast a jump start and improved the flavor of the dough. Rising the dough in a warmed oven sped up the process to just 30 minutes. We were determined to top our pizza with the quintessential pepperoni, but when just plopped on the pizza and baked, the pepperoni floated in pools of orange grease. We tried frying it, but this made it too crisp and turned it an ugly shade of brown. The solution was to use the microwave to render the excess fat before baking. Topped with chewy, spicy pepperoni, mozzarella, and a quick, fresh tomato sauce (and ready in just 90 minutes), this pizza beat delivery hands down.

Pepperoni Pan Pizza
MAKES TWO 9-INCH PIZZAS

DOUGH
- ½ cup olive oil
- ¾ cup skim milk plus 2 additional tablespoons, warmed to 110 degrees
- 2 teaspoons sugar
- 2⅓ cups (11⅝ ounces) unbleached all-purpose flour, plus extra for the work surface
- 1 envelope instant yeast
- ½ teaspoon table salt

TOPPING
- 1 (3.5-ounce) package sliced pepperoni
- 1½ cups Quick Tomato Sauce for Pizza (page 280)
- 12 ounces shredded part-skim mozzarella cheese (about 3 cups)

1. TO MAKE THE DOUGH: Adjust an oven rack to the lowest position and heat the oven to 200 degrees. When the oven reaches 200 degrees, turn it off. Lightly coat a large bowl with vegetable oil spray. Coat each of two 9-inch cake pans with 3 tablespoons of the oil.

2. Mix the milk, sugar, and remaining 2 tablespoons oil in a measuring cup. Mix the flour, yeast, and salt in a stand mixer fitted with the dough hook. Turn the machine to low and slowly add the milk mixture. After the dough comes together, increase the speed to medium-low and mix until the dough is shiny and smooth, about 5 minutes. Turn the dough onto a lightly floured work surface, gently shape into a ball, and place in the greased bowl. Cover with plastic wrap and place in the warm oven until doubled in size, about 30 minutes.

3. TO SHAPE AND TOP THE DOUGH: Transfer the dough to a lightly floured work surface, divide it in half, and lightly roll each half into a ball. Working with 1 dough ball at a time, roll and shape the dough into a 9½-inch round and press into the oiled pans. Cover with plastic wrap and set in a warm spot (not in the oven) until puffy and slightly risen, about 20 minutes. Meanwhile, heat the oven to 400 degrees.

4. While the dough rises, put half of the pepperoni in a single layer on a microwave-safe plate lined with 2 paper towels. Cover with 2 more paper towels and microwave on high for 30 seconds. Discard the towels and set the pepperoni aside; repeat with new paper towels and the remaining pepperoni.

5. Remove the plastic wrap from the dough. Ladle ¾ cup of the sauce on each round, leaving a ½-inch border around the edges. Sprinkle each with 1½ cups of the cheese and top with the pepperoni. Bake until the cheese is melted and the pepperoni is browning around the edges, about 20 minutes. Remove from the oven; let the pizzas rest in the pans for 1 minute. Using a spatula, transfer the pizzas to a cutting board and cut each into 8 wedges. Serve.

NOTES FROM THE TEST KITCHEN

PIZZA DOUGH WITHOUT A MIXER

In step 2, mix the flour, yeast, and salt together in a large bowl. Make a well in the flour, then pour the milk mixture into the well. Using a wooden spoon, stir until the dough becomes shaggy and difficult to stir. Turn out onto a heavily floured work surface and knead, incorporating any shaggy scraps. Knead until the dough is smooth, about 10 minutes. Shape into a ball and proceed as directed.

PIZZA BIANCA

WHY THIS RECIPE WORKS: The Roman version of pizza has a crust like no other we've ever tasted: crisp but extraordinarily chewy. It's so good on its own that it is usually topped with just olive oil, rosemary, and kosher salt. We wanted to figure out how we could enjoy this marvel without taking a trip to Italy.

This pizza dough contains significantly more water than other styles, which is the secret to its chewy texture. But extra-wet doughs require more kneading, and we wanted to make this dish at home in a reasonable amount of time. Instead of a long knead, we let the dough rest for 20 minutes, which let us get away with just 10 minutes of kneading. After an initial rise, the dough was still sticky; we couldn't roll it out, but it was easy to pour out then press onto a baking sheet. After letting the dough rest briefly, we baked the crust, adding just kosher salt, oil, and rosemary to remain true to the authentic version.

Pizza Bianca
SERVES 6 TO 8

Serve the pizza by itself as a snack, or with soup or salad as a light entrée. Once the dough has been placed in the oiled bowl, it can be transferred to the refrigerator and kept for up to 24 hours. Bring the dough to room temperature, 2 to 2½ hours, before proceeding with step 4 of the recipe. While kneading the dough on high speed, the mixer tends to wobble and walk on the countertop. Place a towel or shelf liner under the mixer and watch it at all times while mixing. Handle the dough with lightly oiled hands. Resist flouring your fingers or the dough might stick further. This recipe was developed using an

18 by 13-inch baking sheet. Smaller baking sheets can be used, but because the pizza will be thicker, baking times will be longer. If you don't have a pizza stone, bake the pizza on a rimless or overturned baking sheet that has been preheated just like the pizza stone.

3 cups (15 ounces) unbleached all-purpose flour
1⅔ cups water, at room temperature
1¼ teaspoons table salt
1½ teaspoons instant or rapid-rise yeast
1¼ teaspoons sugar
5 tablespoons extra-virgin olive oil
1 teaspoon kosher salt
2 tablespoons whole fresh rosemary leaves

1. Mix the flour, water, and table salt in the bowl of a stand mixer fitted with the dough hook on low speed until no areas of dry flour remain, 3 to 4 minutes, occasionally scraping down the sides of the bowl. Turn off the mixer and let the dough rest for 20 minutes.

2. Sprinkle the yeast and sugar over the dough. Knead on low speed until fully combined, 1 to 2 minutes, occasionally scraping down the sides of the bowl. Increase the mixer speed to high and knead until the dough is glossy and smooth and pulls away from the sides of the bowl, 6 to 10 minutes. (The dough will pull away from the sides only while the mixer is on. When the mixer is off, the dough will fall back to the sides.)

3. Using your fingers, coat a large bowl with 1 tablespoon of the oil, rubbing the excess oil from your fingers onto the blade of a rubber spatula. Using the oiled spatula, transfer the dough to the bowl and pour 1 tablespoon more oil over the top. Flip the dough over once so that it is well coated with the oil; cover tightly with plastic wrap. Let the dough rise at room temperature until nearly tripled in volume and large bubbles have formed, 2 to 2½ hours.

4. One hour before baking the pizza, adjust an oven rack to the middle position, place a pizza stone on the rack, and heat the oven to 450 degrees.

5. Coat a rimmed baking sheet with 2 tablespoons more oil. Using a rubber spatula, turn the dough out onto the baking sheet along with any oil in the bowl. Using your fingertips, press the dough out toward the edges of the baking sheet, taking care not to tear it. (The dough will not fit snugly into corners. If the dough resists stretching, let it relax for 5 to 10 minutes before trying to stretch it again.) Let the dough rest until slightly

bubbly, 5 to 10 minutes. Using a dinner fork, poke the surface of the dough 30 to 40 times and sprinkle with the kosher salt.

6. Bake until golden brown, 20 to 30 minutes, sprinkling the rosemary over the top and rotating the baking sheet halfway through baking. Using a metal spatula, transfer the pizza to a cutting board. Brush the dough lightly with the remaining 1 tablespoon oil. Slice and serve immediately.

GRILLED PIZZA

WHY THIS RECIPE WORKS: Most homemade versions of this restaurant classic disappoint with charred crusts and sauce and cheese that drip onto the coals. We set out to find the secret to great grilled pizza at home.

Regular pizza dough stuck to the cooking grate and burned easily. We found that the dough has to be both thinner and sturdier to work on the grill. We used high-protein bread flour to strengthen the dough, and adding water made it easier to stretch. The crust also needed more flavor to stand up to the heat of the fire, so we added extra salt, a little whole wheat flour, and some olive oil. The oil in the dough also kept the crust from sticking to the cooking grate. Salted chopped tomatoes rather than sauce and a mixture of soft fontina (which has more flavor than mozzarella) and nutty Parmesan made a flavorful but light topping that didn't weigh down the crust or make it soggy. Spicy garlic oil and a scattering of fresh basil added complexity without heaviness. Full of flavor and with a cracker-crisp crust, these grilled pizzas are as good as any we've had in a restaurant.

Grilled Tomato and Cheese Pizzas for a Charcoal Grill

SERVES 4

The pizzas cook very quickly on the grill, so before you begin, be sure to have all the equipment and ingredients you need at hand. Equipment includes a pizza peel (or a rimless baking sheet), a pair of tongs, a paring knife, a large cutting board, and a pastry brush; ingredients include all the toppings and a small bowl of flour for dusting. The pizzas are best served hot off the grill but can be kept warm for 20 to 30 minutes on a wire rack in a 200-degree oven.

DOUGH

- 1 cup water, at room temperature
- 2 tablespoons olive oil, plus extra for oiling the bowl
- 2 cups (11 ounces) bread flour, plus extra for the work surface
- 1 tablespoon whole wheat flour (optional)
- 2 teaspoons sugar
- 1¼ teaspoons table salt
- 1 teaspoon instant or rapid-rise yeast

TOPPING

- 1½ pounds plum tomatoes (5 to 6 medium), cored, seeded, and cut into ½-inch pieces
- ¾ teaspoon table salt
- 6 ounces fontina cheese, shredded (about 1½ cups)
- 1½ ounces Parmesan cheese, grated fine (about ¾ cup)
  Vegetable oil for the cooking grate
- 1 recipe Spicy Garlic Oil (recipe follows)
- ½ cup chopped fresh basil leaves
  Kosher salt

1. FOR THE DOUGH: Combine the water and 2 tablespoons olive oil in a liquid measuring cup. Process 1¾ cups of the bread flour, the whole wheat flour (if using), sugar, salt, and yeast in a food processor (fitted with the dough blade, if possible) until combined, about 5 seconds. With the machine running, pour the oil and water mixture through the feed tube and process until the dough forms a ball, about 1½ minutes. If after 1½ minutes the dough is sticky and clings to the blade, add the remaining ¼ cup flour 1 tablespoon at a time. Lightly coat a medium bowl with olive oil. Transfer the dough to the bowl; cover tightly with plastic wrap and set in a warm spot until doubled in volume, 1½ to 2 hours.

2. When the dough has doubled, press down gently to deflate; turn the dough out onto a work surface and divide into four equal pieces. With cupped palms, form each piece into a smooth, tight ball. Set the dough balls on a well-floured work surface. Press the dough rounds by hand to flatten; cover loosely with plastic wrap and let rest for about 15 minutes.

3. FOR THE TOPPING: Meanwhile, toss the tomatoes and table salt in a medium bowl; transfer to a colander and drain for 30 minutes (wipe out and reserve the bowl). Shake the colander to drain off the excess liquid; transfer the tomatoes to the now-empty bowl and set aside. Combine the cheeses in a second medium bowl and set aside.

4. Gently stretch the dough rounds into disks about ½ inch thick and 5 to 6 inches in diameter. Working with one piece at a time and keeping the rest covered, roll out each disk to ⅛-inch thickness, 9 to 10 inches in diameter, on a well-floured sheet of parchment paper, dusting with additional flour as needed to prevent sticking. (If the dough shrinks when rolled out, cover with plastic wrap and let rest until relaxed, 10 to 15 minutes.) Dust the surface of the rolled dough with flour and set aside. Repeat with the remaining dough, stacking the sheets of rolled dough on top of each other (with parchment in between) and covering the stack with plastic wrap; set aside until the grill is ready.

5. TO GRILL: Light a large chimney starter filled with charcoal (about 6 quarts) and allow to burn until the coals are partially covered with a layer of ash, about 20 minutes. Open the bottom grill vents. Arrange the coals evenly over three-quarters of the bottom of the grill, leaving one quadrant free of coals. Set the cooking grate in place, cover the grill with the lid, and heat the grill, about 5 minutes. Use a grill brush to scrape the cooking grate clean. Dip a wad of paper towels in vegetable oil; holding the wad with tongs, oil the cooking grate.

6. Lightly flour a pizza peel; invert one dough round onto the peel, gently stretching it as needed to retain its shape (do not stretch the dough too thin; thin spots will burn quickly). Peel off and discard the parchment; carefully slide the round onto the hotter side of the grill. Immediately repeat with another dough round. Cook until the tops are covered with bubbles (pierce larger bubbles with a paring knife) and the bottoms are grill-marked and charred in spots, 1 to 2 minutes; while the rounds cook, check the undersides and slide to a cooler area of the grill if browning too quickly. Transfer the crusts to a cutting board, browned sides up. Repeat with the two remaining dough rounds.

7. Brush two crusts generously with the garlic oil; top each evenly with one-quarter of the cheese mixture and one-quarter of the tomatoes. Return the pizzas to the grill and cover the grill with the lid; cook until the bottoms are well browned and the cheese is melted, 2 to 4 minutes, checking the bottoms frequently to prevent burning. Transfer the pizzas to a cutting board; repeat with the remaining two crusts. Sprinkle the pizzas with the basil and kosher salt to taste; cut into wedges and serve.

Grilled Tomato and Cheese Pizzas for a Gas Grill

Follow the recipe for Grilled Tomato and Cheese Pizzas for a Charcoal Grill through step 4. Turn all the burners to high, cover, and heat the grill with the lid down until very hot, about 15 minutes. Use a grill brush to scrape the cooking grate clean. Dip a wad of paper towels in vegetable oil; holding the wad with tongs, oil the cooking grate. Continue with the recipe from step 6, cooking the pizzas with the lid down in both steps 6 and 7 and increasing the cooking times in steps 6 and 7 by 1 to 2 minutes, if needed.

Spicy Garlic Oil
MAKES ENOUGH FOR 4 PIZZAS

⅓   cup extra-virgin olive oil
4   medium garlic cloves, minced or pressed through a
     garlic press (about 4 teaspoons)
½–¾ teaspoon red pepper flakes

Cook all the ingredients in a small saucepan over medium heat, stirring occasionally, until the garlic begins to sizzle, 2 to 3 minutes. Transfer to a small bowl.

TOMATO TART

WHY THIS RECIPE WORKS: Falling somewhere in between pizza and quiche, tomato and mozzarella tart shares the flavors of both but features unique problems. For starters, this is not fast food, as some sort of pastry crust is required. Second, the moisture in the tomatoes almost guarantees a soggy crust. Third, tomato tarts are often tasteless, despite their good looks, falling short on flavor. We wanted a recipe that could easily be made at home with a solid bottom crust and great vine-ripened flavor.

Frozen puff pastry was the solution to an easy crust, and prebaking it was a start—but only a start—to solving the problem of sogginess. Sealing the puff pastry shell with an egg wash helped. Yet even with these preventive measures, the tomato juice still found its way into the crust. To extract more moisture from the tomatoes before baking the tart, we sliced and salted them, then pressed them lightly between paper towels. This removed much of the moisture. But even with a layer of grated mozzarella cheese (whole-milk worked best) between tomatoes and crust, the tart shell still came out a bit soggy. Our breakthrough came when we added a layer of grated Parmesan cheese, which sealed the crust fully and repelled moisture. After a short stay in the oven, our tart had a crisp and sturdy crust, nutty flavor from the Parmesan, and rich flavors from the cheese and tomatoes.

Tomato and Mozzarella Tart

SERVES 4 TO 6

To keep the frozen dough from cracking, it's best to let it thaw slowly in the refrigerator overnight. For the best flavor, use authentic Parmesan cheese and very ripe, flavorful tomatoes. Fresh mozzarella will make the crust soggy, so be sure to use low-moisture, shrink-wrapped mozzarella.

1 (9 by 9½-inch) sheet frozen puff pastry, thawed (see note)
1 large egg, lightly beaten
1 ounce Parmesan cheese, grated (about ½ cup; see note)
½ pound plum tomatoes (2 medium), cored and sliced ¼ inch thick (see note)
½ teaspoon table salt
4 ounces whole-milk mozzarella cheese, shredded (about 1 cup; see note)
2 tablespoons extra-virgin olive oil
1 medium garlic clove, minced or pressed through a garlic press (about 1 teaspoon)
2 tablespoons minced fresh basil

1. Adjust an oven rack to the lowest position and heat the oven to 425 degrees. Line a large baking sheet with parchment paper. Lay the pastry in the center of the prepared baking sheet. Brush the pastry with the beaten egg. To form a rimmed crust, fold the long edges of the pastry over by ½ inch, then brush with the egg. Fold the short edges of the pastry over by ½ inch and brush with the egg. Use a paring knife to cut through the folded edges and corner of the pastry. Sprinkle the Parmesan evenly over the crust bottom. Poke the dough uniformly with a fork. Bake until golden brown and crisp, 15 to 20 minutes. Transfer to a wire rack to cool.

2. Meanwhile, spread the tomatoes over several layers of paper towels. Sprinkle with the salt and let drain for 30 minutes.

3. Sprinkle the mozzarella evenly over the crust bottom. Press excess moisture from the tomatoes, using additional

PREPARING THE TART

1. Fold the short edges of the pastry over by ½ inch and brush with egg. Then fold the long edges of the pastry over by ½ inch, making sure to keep the edges flush and square. Brush with egg.

2. Using a paring knife, cut through the folded edges and corners of the tart shell.

3. After sprinkling the bottom of the tart with the Parmesan, poke the dough repeatedly with a fork. Bake the pastry shell.

4. Sprinkle the mozzarella evenly over the crust and shingle the tomatoes attractively over the mozzarella.

paper towels. Following the photo, shingle the tomatoes evenly over the mozzarella. Whisk the olive oil and garlic together and drizzle over the tomatoes. Bake until the shell is deep golden, 10 to 15 minutes.

4. Cool on a wire rack for 5 minutes and then sprinkle with the basil. Slide the tart onto a cutting board, slice into pieces, and serve.

GARLIC BREAD

WHY THIS RECIPE WORKS: Garlic bread is a classic accompaniment to spaghetti and meatballs, baked ziti, and countless other Italian favorites. It seems so simple, yet it often goes so wrong. We wanted to banish greasy, bland, and bitter-tasting garlic bread forever in favor of crisp toasted bread imbued with sweet, nutty garlic flavor.

Starting with the bread, we chose a substantial loaf of football-shaped Italian bread, the best quality we could find, to give us generous slices. We cut it in half horizontally, so that the surfaces would crisp up in the oven. We tamed the garlic's harshness by toasting whole cloves, which turned them rich and mellow. We cut out the step of melting butter and simply spread it, after softening and mixing in the garlic, on the bread—not too much, so the bread wouldn't be greasy or soggy. The addition of some grated Parmesan cheese was nearly undetectable, but it added a deep and complex flavor. For baking, we found that leaving the bread unwrapped on a baking sheet gave us the crispy crust we wanted, and exposure to the oven's heat further mellowed the garlic.

Classic Garlic Bread

SERVES 6 TO 8

Plan to pull the garlic bread from the oven when you are ready to serve the other dishes—it is best served piping hot.

- 9–10 medium garlic cloves, unpeeled
- 6 tablespoons (¾ stick) unsalted butter, softened
- 2 tablespoons grated Parmesan cheese
- ½ teaspoon table salt
- 1 (1-pound) loaf high-quality Italian bread (preferably football-shaped), halved horizontally
  Ground black pepper

1. Adjust an oven rack to the middle position and heat the oven to 500 degrees. Meanwhile, toast the garlic cloves in a small skillet over medium heat, shaking the pan occasionally, until fragrant and the color of the cloves deepens slightly, about 8 minutes. When cool enough to handle, peel and mince the cloves (you should have about 3 tablespoons). Using a dinner fork, mash the garlic, butter, cheese, and salt in a small bowl until thoroughly combined.

2. Spread the cut sides of the loaf evenly with the butter mixture; season with pepper to taste. Transfer the loaf halves, buttered side up, onto a rimmed baking sheet;

bake, reversing the position of the baking sheet in the oven from front to back halfway through the baking time, until the surface of the bread is golden brown and toasted, 5 to 10 minutes. Cut each half into 2-inch slices; serve immediately.

CHEESY GARLIC BREAD

WHY THIS RECIPE WORKS: Garlic bread is a balancing act between the butter, garlic, and bread. Add cheese to the mix and things get complicated. We wanted cheese-topped garlic bread that was crisp on the outside but chewy within, buttery all the way through, and with no bitter garlic aftertaste.

Supermarket baguettes already have a chewy interior and crisp crust, so we started there. Grating the garlic cloves made for a smoother butter, and to tone down the garlic's harshness we sautéed it in butter with a little water (to prevent burning). We mixed the garlic into more softened butter, spread it on our split baguette, and wrapped the bread in foil. Baking it this way "steams" the bread and infuses it with garlic-butter flavor. To crisp the crust, we took the bread out of the foil and baked it a little longer. The final adornment was the cheese; rather than shredding several different kinds ourselves, we took a shortcut and used a prepackaged mixture of shredded Italian cheeses. The last step was to run it under the broiler, which gave us both melted cheese and an extra-crisp crust.

Cheesy Garlic Bread

SERVES 6 TO 8

The serrated edges on a bread knife can pull off the cheesy crust. To prevent this, place the finished garlic bread cheese side down on a cutting board. Slicing through the crust first (rather than the cheese) will keep the cheese in place. Shredded Italian cheese blend is sold in bags in the supermarket case near other packaged cheeses.

- 5 medium garlic cloves, peeled and grated
- 8 tablespoons (1 stick) unsalted butter, softened
- ½ teaspoon water
- ¼ teaspoon table salt
- ¼ teaspoon ground black pepper
- 1 (18 to 20-inch) baguette, sliced in half horizontally
- 1½ cups shredded Italian cheese blend (see note)

1. Adjust an oven rack to the lower-middle position and heat the oven to 400 degrees. Cook the garlic, 1 tablespoon of the butter, and the water in a small nonstick skillet over low heat, stirring occasionally, until straw-colored, 7 to 10 minutes.

2. Mix the hot garlic, remaining 7 tablespoons butter, the salt, and pepper in a bowl and spread on the cut sides of the bread. Sandwich the bread back together and wrap the loaf in foil. Place on a baking sheet and bake for 15 minutes.

3. Carefully unwrap the bread and place the halves, buttered sides up, on a baking sheet. Bake until just beginning to color, about 10 minutes. Remove from the oven and set the oven to broil.

4. Sprinkle the bread with the cheese. Broil until the cheese has melted and the bread is crisp, 1 to 2 minutes. Transfer the bread to a cutting board with the cheese side facing down. Cut into pieces and serve.

FRICO

WHY THIS RECIPE WORKS: As an accompaniment to cocktails or eaten just as a snack, frico is a simple, crisp wafer of flavorful cheese, usually Montasio, that has been melted and browned. We wanted to find the secret behind great frico, and then determine the best substitute for Montasio cheese, which can be difficult to find.

Cheese simply grated into a hot pan could turn into a sticky mess, but we found that using a nonstick skillet allowed us to cook the frico without adding butter or oil. We discovered that it was easy to turn the frico to the other side once the first side was browned if we first took the skillet off the heat; the slightly cooled cheese didn't stretch or tear when we flipped it. Turning the heat down to cook the second side gave the best results; a pan that was too hot turns the cheese bitter. Many recipes suggest Parmesan as a substitute for Montasio, but we found Asiago cheese to be a better stand-in—though the real thing is even better.

Frico

MAKES 8 LARGE WAFERS

Serve frico with drinks and a bowl of marinated olives or marinated sun-dried tomatoes. Frico is also good crumbled into a salad, crouton-style.

1 **pound Montasio or aged Asiago cheese, grated fine (about 8 cups)**

1. Sprinkle 2 ounces (about 1 cup) of the grated cheese over the bottom of a 10-inch nonstick skillet set over medium-high heat. Use a heat-resistant rubber spatula or a wooden spoon to tidy the lacy outer edges of the cheese. Cook, shaking the pan occasionally to ensure an even distribution of the cheese over the pan bottom, until the edges are lacy and toasted, about 4 minutes. Remove the pan from the heat and allow the cheese to set for about 30 seconds.

2. Using a fork on top and a heatproof spatula underneath, carefully flip the cheese wafer and return the pan to medium heat. Cook until the second side is golden brown, about 2 minutes. Slide the cheese wafer out of the pan and transfer to a plate. Repeat with the remaining cheese. Serve the frico within 1 hour.

PASTA E FAGIOLI

WHY THIS RECIPE WORKS: The American version of this hearty Italian bean-and-vegetable stew—sometimes called *pasta fazool*—often turns out bland, with mushy beans and pasta and too much tomato. And it can take hours to prepare. We wanted rich broth, perfectly cooked beans and pasta, and complex flavors—and we wanted to prepare it in a reasonable amount of time.

Substituting canned beans for dried would save the most preparation time, and we found cannellini beans to be the

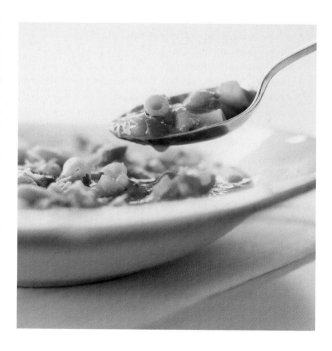

closest to the dried cranberry beans used in authentic recipes. We started to build deep flavor by sautéing pancetta (though bacon also works) and, for aromatics, onion, garlic, and celery. Tomatoes (diced worked better than crushed or sauce) went in next. A small amount of minced anchovies was unidentifiable but added complexity. Chicken broth diluted with water was our cooking liquid; chicken broth alone made the dish taste too much like chicken soup. A Parmesan rind added another layer of flavor. Last into the pot went the pasta. The flavors of our thick, hearty soup harmonized perfectly and, best of all, we had spent less than an hour at the stove.

Italian Pasta and Bean Soup (Pasta e Fagioli)

SERVES 8 TO 10

This soup does not hold well because the pasta absorbs the liquid, becomes mushy, and leaves the soup dry. You can, however, make the soup in two stages. Once the beans are simmered with the tomatoes, before the broth and water are added, the mixture can be cooled and refrigerated for up to 3 days. When ready to complete the soup, discard the Parmesan rind (otherwise it will become stringy), add the liquid, bring the soup to a boil, and proceed with the recipe.

- 1 tablespoon extra-virgin olive oil, plus extra for drizzling
- 3 ounces pancetta or bacon (about 3 slices), chopped fine
- 1 medium onion, minced
- 1 celery rib, chopped fine
- 4 medium garlic cloves, minced or pressed through a garlic press (about 4 teaspoons)
- 1 teaspoon dried oregano
- ¼ teaspoon red pepper flakes
- 3 anchovy fillets, minced to a paste (about 1½ teaspoons)
- 1 (28-ounce) can diced tomatoes
- 1 piece Parmesan cheese rind, about 5 inches by 2 inches
- 2 (15.5-ounce) cans cannellini beans, drained and rinsed
- 3½ cups low-sodium chicken broth
- 2½ cups water
  Table salt
- 8 ounces small pasta such as ditalini, tubetini, conchiglietti, or orzo
- 4 tablespoons chopped fresh parsley leaves
  Ground black pepper
  Grated Parmesan cheese, for serving

1. Heat the oil in a large Dutch oven over medium-high heat until shimmering. Add the pancetta and cook, stirring occasionally, until it begins to brown, 3 to 5 minutes. Add the onion and celery and cook, stirring occasionally, until the vegetables are softened, 5 to 7 minutes. Add the garlic, oregano, red pepper flakes, and anchovies and cook, stirring constantly, until fragrant, about 30 seconds. Add the tomatoes with their juice, scraping up any browned bits. Add the cheese rind and beans; bring to a boil, then reduce the heat to low and simmer to blend the flavors, 10 minutes. Add the chicken broth, water, and 1 teaspoon salt; increase the heat to high and bring to a boil. Add the pasta and cook until tender, about 10 minutes.

2. Discard the cheese rind. Off the heat, stir in 3 tablespoons of the parsley; season with salt and pepper to taste. Ladle the soup into individual bowls; drizzle each serving with olive oil and sprinkle with a portion of the remaining 1 tablespoon parsley. Serve immediately, passing the grated Parmesan separately.

HEARTY TUSCAN BEAN STEW

WHY THIS RECIPE WORKS: Unlike *Pasta e Fagioli*, where beans and pasta share the spotlight, Tuscan bean soup boasts creamy, buttery cannellini beans in the starring role. Ideally, the beans should have a uniformly tender texture, but too often the skins are tough and the insides mealy—or the beans turn mushy. We wanted to fix the bean problem and convert this Italian classic into a hearty, rustic stew for a deeply flavorful one-pot meal.

Since the beans are the centerpiece of this stew, we concentrated on cooking them perfectly. After testing a variety of soaking times, we settled on soaking the beans overnight, a method that consistently produced the most tender and evenly cooked beans. But none of the methods we tested properly softened the skins. The answer was to soak the beans in salted water. Brining the beans, rather than the conventional approach of soaking them in plain water and then cooking them in salt water, allowed the salt to soften the skins but kept it from penetrating inside, where it could make the beans mealy. Tests showed that gently cooking the beans in a 250-degree oven produced perfectly cooked beans that stayed intact. The final trick was to add the tomatoes toward the end of cooking, since their acid interfered with the softening process. To complete our stew, we looked for other traditional Tuscan flavors, including pancetta, kale, lots of garlic, and a sprig of rosemary. And to make it even more substantial, we served the stew on a slab of toasted country bread, drizzled with fruity extra-virgin olive oil.

Hearty Tuscan Bean Stew

SERVES 8

We prefer the creamier texture of beans soaked overnight for this recipe. If you're short on time, quick-soak them: Place the rinsed beans in a large heat-resistant bowl. Bring 2 quarts water and 3 tablespoons salt to a boil. Pour the water over the beans and let them sit for 1 hour. Drain and rinse the beans well before proceeding with step 2. If pancetta is unavailable, substitute 4 ounces bacon (about 4 slices).

Table salt
1 pound (about 2 cups) dried cannellini beans, picked over and rinsed
1 tablespoon extra-virgin olive oil, plus extra for drizzling
6 ounces pancetta or bacon, cut into ¼-inch pieces (see note)
1 large onion, chopped medium (about 1½ cups)
2 medium celery ribs, cut into ½-inch pieces (about ¾ cup)
2 medium carrots, peeled and cut into ½-inch pieces (about 1 cup)
8 medium garlic cloves, peeled and crushed
4 cups low-sodium chicken broth
3 cups water
2 bay leaves
1 bunch kale or collard greens (about 1 pound), stems trimmed and leaves chopped into 1-inch pieces (about 8 cups loosely packed)
1 (14.5-ounce) can diced tomatoes, drained
1 sprig fresh rosemary
Ground black pepper
8 slices country white bread, each 1¼ inches thick, broiled until golden brown on both sides and rubbed with a garlic clove (optional)

1. Dissolve 3 tablespoons salt in 4 quarts cold water in a large bowl or container. Add the beans and soak at room temperature for at least 8 hours or up to 24 hours. Drain the beans and rinse well.

2. Adjust an oven rack to the lower-middle position and heat the oven to 250 degrees. Heat the oil and pancetta in a large Dutch oven over medium heat. Cook, stirring occasionally, until the pancetta is lightly browned and the fat has rendered, 6 to 10 minutes. Add the onion, celery, and carrots. Cook, stirring occasionally, until the vegetables are softened and lightly browned, 10 to 16 minutes. Stir in the garlic and cook until fragrant, about 1 minute. Stir in the broth, water, bay leaves, and soaked beans. Increase the heat to high and bring the mixture to a simmer. Cover the pot, transfer it to the oven, and cook until the beans are almost tender (the very center of the beans will still be firm), 45 minutes to 1 hour.

3. Remove the pot from the oven and stir in the kale and tomatoes. Return the pot to the oven and continue to cook until the beans and greens are fully tender, 30 to 40 minutes longer.

4. Remove the pot from the oven and submerge the rosemary sprig in the stew. Cover and let stand for 15 minutes. Discard the bay leaves and rosemary sprig and season the stew with salt and pepper to taste. If desired, use the back of a spoon to press some beans against the side of the pot to thicken the stew. Serve over the toasted bread (if using) and drizzle with olive oil.

EGGPLANT PARMESAN

WHY THIS RECIPE WORKS: Frying the eggplant for this classic Italian dish not only is time-consuming but also can make the dish heavy and dull. In hopes of eliminating the grease as well as some of the prep time, we decided to cook the eggplant in the oven and see what other measures we could take to freshen up this Italian classic.

We salted and drained the eggplant slices to remove bitterness and improve the texture. A traditional bound breading—flour, egg, and fresh bread crumbs—worked best for giving the eggplant a crisp coating. Baking the eggplant on preheated and oiled baking sheets resulted in crisp, golden brown slices. While the eggplant was in the oven, we made a quick tomato sauce using garlic, red pepper flakes, basil, and canned diced tomatoes. We layered the sauce, eggplant, and mozzarella in a baking dish and left the top layer of eggplant mostly unsauced, so that it would crisp up in the oven. Our re-engineered eggplant Parmesan was lighter and fresher tasting, and a lot less work.

Eggplant Parmesan

SERVES 6 TO 8

Use kosher salt when salting the eggplant. The coarse grains don't dissolve as readily as the fine grains of regular table salt, so any excess can be easily wiped away. It's necessary to divide the eggplant into two batches when tossing it with the salt. To be time-efficient, use the 30 to 45 minutes during which the salted eggplant sits to prepare the breading.

EGGPLANT

- 2 pounds globe eggplant (2 medium eggplants), cut crosswise into ¼-inch-thick rounds
- 1 tablespoon kosher salt (see note)
- 8 slices high-quality white sandwich bread, torn into quarters
- 2 ounces Parmesan cheese, grated (about 1 cup) Table salt and ground black pepper
- 1 cup unbleached all-purpose flour
- 4 large eggs
- 6 tablespoons vegetable oil

TOMATO SAUCE

- 3 (14.5-ounce) cans diced tomatoes
- 2 tablespoons extra-virgin olive oil
- 4 medium garlic cloves, minced or pressed through a garlic press (about 4 teaspoons)
- ¼ teaspoon red pepper flakes
- ½ cup coarsely chopped fresh basil leaves Table salt and ground black pepper

- 8 ounces whole-milk or part-skim mozzarella cheese, shredded (about 2 cups)
- 1 ounce Parmesan cheese, grated (about ½ cup)
- 10 fresh basil leaves, torn, for garnish

1. FOR THE EGGPLANT: Toss half of the eggplant slices and 1½ teaspoons of the kosher salt in a large bowl until combined; transfer the salted eggplant to a large colander set over a bowl. Repeat with the remaining eggplant and kosher salt, placing the second batch on top of the first. Let stand until the eggplant releases about 2 tablespoons liquid, 30 to 45 minutes. Spread the eggplant slices on a triple thickness of paper towels; cover with another triple thickness of paper towels. Press firmly on each slice to remove as much liquid as possible, then wipe off the excess salt.

2. While the eggplant is draining, adjust the oven racks to the upper-middle and lower-middle positions, place a rimmed baking sheet on each rack, and heat the oven to 425 degrees. Process the bread in a food processor to fine, even crumbs, about 20 to 30 seconds. Transfer the crumbs to a pie plate and stir in the Parmesan, ¼ teaspoon table salt, and ½ teaspoon pepper; set aside. Wipe out the work-bowl (do not wash) and set aside.

3. Combine the flour and 1 teaspoon pepper in a large zipper-lock bag; shake to combine. Beat the eggs in a second pie plate. Place 8 to 10 eggplant slices in the bag with the flour; seal the bag and shake to coat the slices. Remove the slices, shaking off the excess flour, dip into the eggs, let the excess egg run off, then coat evenly with the bread-crumb mixture; set the breaded slices on a wire rack set over a baking sheet. Repeat with the remaining eggplant.

4. Remove the preheated baking sheets from the oven; add 3 tablespoons of the vegetable oil to each sheet, tilting to coat evenly with the oil. Place half of the breaded eggplant slices on each sheet in a single layer; bake until the eggplant is well browned and crisp, about 30 minutes, switching and rotating the baking sheets after 10 minutes, and flipping the eggplant slices with a wide spatula after 20 minutes. Do not turn off the oven.

5. FOR THE SAUCE: While the eggplant bakes, process 2 cans of the diced tomatoes in the food processor until almost smooth, about 5 seconds. Heat the olive oil, garlic, and red pepper flakes in a large heavy-bottomed saucepan over medium-high heat, stirring occasionally, until fragrant and the garlic is light golden, about 3 minutes; stir in the processed tomatoes and remaining can of diced tomatoes. Bring the sauce to a boil, then reduce the heat to medium-low and simmer, stirring occasionally, until slightly thickened and reduced, about 15 minutes (you should have about 4 cups). Stir in the basil and season with table salt and pepper to taste.

6. TO ASSEMBLE: Spread 1 cup of the tomato sauce in the bottom of a 13 by 9-inch baking dish. Layer in half of the eggplant slices, overlapping the slices to fit; distribute 1 cup more of the sauce over the eggplant; sprinkle with half of the mozzarella. Layer in the remaining eggplant and dot with 1 cup more of the sauce, leaving the majority of the eggplant exposed so it will remain crisp; sprinkle with the Parmesan and the remaining mozzarella. Bake until bubbling and the cheese is browned, 13 to 15 minutes. Cool for 10 minutes, scatter the basil over the top, and serve, passing the remaining tomato sauce separately.

POLENTA

WHY THIS RECIPE WORKS: A creamy mound of hot polenta can be a comforting dish, especially when served with a stew or saucy braise. Composed of little more than cornmeal and water, it should be easy to prepare. But often it's lumpy or gummy, and getting it right requires constant stirring. We wanted the smooth, creamy texture and great corn flavor of real polenta, but without the hassle.

It turns out that the type of cornmeal makes a difference in the end result, and we found that a medium-grind meal worked best. The traditional method of making polenta requires half an hour or more of constant stirring after the cornmeal is added to boiling salted water. Experimentation revealed that the way to avoid this continuous attention is very low heat. We added the cornmeal (very gradually, so it wouldn't seize up) to barely simmering water with the flame set as low as possible. With the cover on the pot to keep in moisture, the cornmeal had time to release its starches gradually and develop flavor, and we needed to stir it only every five minutes or so. Our polenta was smooth and creamy with lots of corn flavor, and we were able to serve it in half an hour without standing at the stove the whole time.

Basic Polenta

SERVES 4 TO 6

If you do not have a heavy-bottomed saucepan, you may want to use a flame tamer to manage the heat. A flame tamer can be purchased at most kitchen supply stores, or you can improvise one (see page 260). Use this polenta as the base for any stew or braise, especially osso buco (see page 309), or serve with a chunk of Gorgonzola cheese. Cooked leafy greens also make an excellent topping for soft polenta.

- 6 **cups water**
  Table salt
- 1½ **cups medium-grind cornmeal, preferably stone-ground**
- 3 **tablespoons unsalted butter, cut into large chunks**
  Ground black pepper

1. Bring the water to a rolling boil in a 4-quart heavy-bottomed saucepan over medium-high heat. Reduce the heat to the lowest possible setting, add 1½ teaspoons salt, and pour the cornmeal into the water in a very slow stream from a measuring cup, all the while whisking in a circular motion to prevent lumps.

2. Cover and cook, vigorously stirring the polenta with a wooden spoon for about 10 seconds once every 5 minutes and making sure to scrape clean the bottom and corners of the pot, until the polenta has lost its raw cornmeal taste and becomes soft and smooth, about 30 minutes. Stir in the butter, season with salt and pepper to taste, and serve immediately.

MUSHROOM RISOTTO

WHY THIS RECIPE WORKS: Earthy wild mushrooms added to a basic Italian risotto make a great main course. But the difficulty, not to mention the expense, of finding exotic fungi prompted us to try our hand at reproducing these flavors with supermarket mushrooms.

Cultivated mushrooms just don't have enough flavor for a dish like this, so we turned to aromatic dried porcini, which pack quite a flavor punch. But they need to be chopped, so for visual appeal and substantive texture we added fresh cremini. Because simmering the cremini in the rice-broth mixture would make them rubbery, we browned them in a separate skillet with some onion and garlic for added flavor, folding this mixture into the risotto only when the rice was done. We added extra wine to our basic risotto so that its acidity would balance the richness of the mushrooms, and used a decidedly un-Italian ingredient, soy sauce, to intensify the earthiness of the mushrooms and round out the flavors. Without relying on pricey fungi, we had created a risotto with the same exotic earthiness.

Mushroom Risotto

SERVES 4 TO 6

Cremini mushrooms are sometimes sold as baby bella mushrooms. If they're not available, button mushrooms make a fine, though somewhat less flavorful, substitute. Tie the thyme and parsley sprigs together with kitchen twine so they will be easy to retrieve from the pan.

- 2 bay leaves
- 6 sprigs fresh thyme (see note)
- 4 sprigs fresh parsley, plus 2 tablespoons minced parsley leaves (see note)
- 3½ cups low-sodium chicken broth
- 3½ cups water
- 1 ounce dried porcini mushrooms, rinsed in a mesh strainer under running water
- 2 teaspoons soy sauce
- 6 tablespoons (¾ stick) unsalted butter
- 1¼ pounds cremini mushrooms, wiped clean and cut into quarters if small or sixths if medium or large (see note)
- 2 medium onions, minced (about 2 cups)
  Table salt
- 3 medium garlic cloves, minced or pressed through a garlic press (about 1 tablespoon)
- 2⅛ cups Arborio rice
- 1 cup dry white wine or dry vermouth
- 2 ounces Parmesan cheese, grated fine (about 1 cup)
  Ground black pepper

1. Tie the bay leaves, thyme sprigs, and parsley sprigs together with kitchen twine. Bring the bundled herbs, chicken broth, water, porcini mushrooms, and soy sauce to a boil in a medium saucepan over medium-high heat; reduce the heat to medium-low and simmer until the dried mushrooms are softened and fully hydrated, about 15 minutes. Remove and discard the herb bundle and strain the broth through a fine-mesh strainer set over a medium bowl (you should have about 6½ cups strained liquid); return the liquid to the saucepan and keep warm over low heat. Finely mince the porcini and set aside.

2. Adjust an oven rack to the middle position and heat the oven to 200 degrees. Heat 2 tablespoons of the butter in a 12-inch nonstick skillet over medium-high heat. Add the cremini mushrooms, 1 cup of the onions, and ½ teaspoon salt; cook, stirring occasionally, until the moisture released by the mushrooms evaporates and the mushrooms are well browned, about 7 minutes. Stir in the garlic until fragrant, about 1 minute, then transfer the mushroom mixture to an ovensafe bowl and keep warm in the oven. Off the heat, add ¼ cup water to the now-empty skillet and

scrape with a wooden spoon to loosen any browned bits on the pan bottom; pour the liquid from the skillet into the saucepan with the broth.

3. Melt 3 tablespoons more butter in a large saucepan over medium heat. Add the remaining 1 cup onions and ¼ teaspoon salt; cook, stirring occasionally, until the onions are softened and translucent, about 9 minutes. Add the rice and cook, stirring frequently, until the edges of the grains are transparent, about 4 minutes. Add the wine and cook, stirring frequently, until the rice absorbs the wine. Add the minced porcini and 3½ cups of the broth and cook, stirring every 2 to 3 minutes, until the liquid is absorbed, 9 to 11 minutes. Stir in ½ cup more broth every 2 to 3 minutes until the rice is cooked through but the grains are still somewhat firm at the center, 10 to 12 minutes (the rice may not require all of the broth). Stir in the remaining 1 tablespoon butter, then stir in the mushroom mixture (and any accumulated juice), cheese, and reserved chopped parsley. Season with salt and pepper to taste; serve immediately in warmed bowls.

BUTTERNUT SQUASH RISOTTO

WHY THIS RECIPE WORKS: Butternut squash and risotto should make a perfect culinary couple, but too often the squash and rice never become properly intertwined. The squash is reduced to overly sweet orange blobs or the whole dish becomes a gluey squash paste. We wanted to find a way to integrate the flavor of the squash with the risotto but still preserve their individual personalities—to create a creamy, orange-tinged rice fully infused with deep (but not overly sweet) squash flavor.

We started with our basic risotto recipe, then addressed the squash. When added to the rice at the beginning, the squash ended up as squash paste; if we waited until the end, it never integrated properly with the rice. We decided to brown the diced squash in a skillet (oven-roasting made it too sweet) and set it aside while we sautéed the aromatics and toasted the rice. We added only half of the squash with the first addition of liquid. This squash broke down somewhat during cooking and infused the rice with its flavor; the remaining squash, added when the rice was finished, retained its shape and texture. Chicken broth cut with water was the basis of the liquid, but we simmered the squash seeds and fibers in it to intensify the squash flavor. And white wine balanced the squash's sweetness. This creamy risotto had deep squash flavor and pleasing textures.

Butternut Squash Risotto

SERVES 4 TO 6

Infusing the chicken broth with the squash's seeds and fibers helps to reinforce the earthy squash flavor without adding more squash. We found that a 2-pound squash often yields more than the 3½ cups in step 1; this can be added to the skillet along with the squash scrapings in step 2. To make this dish vegetarian, vegetable broth can be used instead of chicken broth, but the resulting risotto will have more pronounced sweetness.

- 2 tablespoons olive oil
- 1 medium butternut squash (about 2 pounds), peeled, seeded (reserve fibers and seeds), and cut into ½-inch cubes (about 3½ cups; see note)
- ¾ teaspoon table salt
- ¾ teaspoon ground black pepper
- 4 cups low-sodium chicken broth (see note)
- 1 cup water
- 4 tablespoons (½ stick) unsalted butter
- 2 small onions, minced (about 1½ cups)
- 2 medium garlic cloves, minced or pressed through a garlic press (about 2 teaspoons)
- 2 cups Arborio rice
- 1½ cups dry white wine
- 1½ ounces Parmesan cheese, grated fine (about ¾ cup)
- 2 tablespoons minced fresh sage leaves
- ¼ teaspoon grated nutmeg

1. Heat the oil in a 12-inch nonstick skillet over medium-high heat until shimmering but not smoking. Add the squash in an even layer and cook without stirring until golden brown, 4 to 5 minutes; stir in ¼ teaspoon of the salt and ¼ teaspoon of the pepper. Continue to cook, stirring occasionally, until the squash is tender and browned, about 5 minutes longer. Transfer the squash to a bowl and set aside.

2. Return the skillet to medium heat; add the reserved squash fibers and seeds and any leftover diced squash. Cook, stirring frequently to break up the fibers, until lightly browned, about 4 minutes. Transfer to a large saucepan and add the chicken broth and water; cover the saucepan and bring the mixture to a simmer over high heat, then reduce the heat to medium-low to maintain a bare simmer.

3. Melt 3 tablespoons of the butter in the now-empty skillet over medium heat; add the onions, garlic, remaining ½ teaspoon salt, and remaining ½ teaspoon pepper. Cook, stirring occasionally, until the onions are softened,

4 to 5 minutes. Add the rice to the skillet and cook, stirring frequently, until the grains are translucent around the edges, about 3 minutes. (To prevent the rice from spilling out of the pan, stir inward, from the edges of the pan toward the center, not in a circular motion.) Add the wine and cook, stirring frequently, until the liquid is fully absorbed, 4 to 5 minutes. Meanwhile, strain the hot broth through a fine-mesh strainer into a medium bowl, pressing on the solids to extract as much liquid as possible. Return the strained broth to the saucepan and discard the solids in the strainer; cover the saucepan and set over low heat to keep the broth hot.

4. When the wine is fully absorbed, add 3 cups of the hot broth and half of the reserved squash to the rice. Simmer, stirring every 3 to 4 minutes, until the liquid is absorbed and the bottom of the pan is almost dry, about 12 minutes.

5. Stir in ½ cup more of the hot broth and cook, stirring constantly, until absorbed, about 3 minutes; repeat with additional broth until the rice is cooked through but the grains are still somewhat firm at the center. Off the heat, stir in the remaining 1 tablespoon butter, the Parmesan, sage, and nutmeg; gently fold in the remaining cooked squash. If desired, add up to ¼ cup more broth to loosen the texture of the risotto. Serve immediately in warmed bowls.

CHICKEN MARSALA

WHY THIS RECIPE WORKS: Developed in Italy after a successful 19th-century marketing campaign to promote Marsala wine from Sicily, this combination of chicken and mushrooms in wine sauce has become an Italian restaurant staple. Too often, however, the chicken is dry, the mushrooms flabby, and the sauce nondescript. We felt a rescue was in order.

We browned chicken breasts in a skillet to start and kept them warm while we prepared the mushrooms and sauce. The mushrooms went into the skillet next, but the chicken drippings burned. Our solution was to sauté some pancetta before browning the mushrooms, which rendered additional fat as well as added meaty flavor. We preferred sweet (as opposed to dry) Marsala for its depth of flavor and smooth finish. Some lemon juice tempered the Marsala's sweetness, while a little garlic and tomato paste rounded out the flavors. Finally, butter, whisked into the sauce at the end, added a rich finish and beautiful sheen.

Chicken Marsala

SERVES 4

Our wine of choice for this dish is Sweet Marsala Fine, an imported wine that gives the sauce body, soft edges, and a smooth finish. To make slicing the chicken easier, freeze it for 15 minutes.

- 2 tablespoons vegetable oil
- 1 cup unbleached all-purpose flour
- 4 (5 to 6-ounce) boneless, skinless chicken breasts, tenderloins removed and breasts trimmed (see note)
  Table salt and ground black pepper
- 2½ ounces pancetta (about 3 slices), cut into pieces 1 inch long and ⅛ inch wide
- 8 ounces white mushrooms, wiped clean and sliced (about 2 cups)
- 1 medium garlic clove, minced or pressed through a garlic press (about 1 teaspoon)
- 1 teaspoon tomato paste
- 1½ cups sweet Marsala (see note)
- 1½ tablespoons juice from 1 lemon
- 4 tablespoons (½ stick) unsalted butter, cut into 4 pieces
- 2 tablespoons minced fresh parsley leaves

1. Adjust an oven rack to the lower-middle position, place a large ovensafe dinner plate on the oven rack, and heat the oven to 200 degrees. Heat the oil in a 12-inch skillet over medium-high heat until shimmering. Meanwhile, place the flour in a shallow baking dish or pie plate. Halve the chicken horizontally, then cover the chicken halves with plastic wrap and pound the cutlets to an even ¼-inch thickness. Pat the chicken breasts dry. Season both sides of the breasts with salt and pepper; working with one piece at a time, coat both sides with flour. Cooking the cutlets in two batches, place 4 floured cutlets in a single layer in the skillet and cook until golden brown, about 3 minutes. Using tongs, flip the cutlets and cook on the second side until golden brown and the meat feels firm when pressed with a finger, about 3 minutes longer. Transfer the chicken to the heated plate and return the plate to the oven while you cook the remaining cutlets.

2. Return the skillet to low heat and add the pancetta; sauté, stirring occasionally and scraping the pan bottom to loosen the browned bits, until the pancetta is brown and crisp, about 4 minutes. With a slotted spoon, transfer the pancetta to a paper towel–lined plate. Add the mushrooms and increase the heat to medium-high; sauté, stirring occasionally and scraping the pan bottom, until the liquid released by the mushrooms evaporates and the mushrooms begin to brown, about 8 minutes. Add the garlic, tomato paste, and cooked pancetta; sauté while stirring until the tomato paste begins to brown, about 1 minute. Off the heat, add the Marsala; return the pan to high heat and simmer vigorously, scraping the browned bits from the pan bottom, until the sauce is slightly syrupy and reduced to about 1¼ cups, about 5 minutes. Off the heat, add the lemon juice and any accumulated juices from the chicken; whisk in the butter 1 piece at a time. Season with salt and pepper to taste and stir in the parsley. Pour the sauce over the chicken and serve immediately.

LIGHTER CHICKEN PARMESAN

WHY THIS RECIPE WORKS: Crunchy fried chicken cutlets topped with cheese and tomato sauce, chicken Parmesan isn't exactly a dish for dieters. Not wanting to eliminate it as an option for healthy eating, we looked for a way to get the crispy coating without using all the oil.

Baking seemed to be the best alternative to frying. We toasted panko (ultracrisp Japanese-style bread crumbs) with a little oil for color and to give them "fried" flavor without the fat. Adopting the conventional breading technique of dipping the cutlets in flour (with garlic powder for flavor), then egg, then bread crumbs, we cut more calories by using only the egg whites. We baked the breasts on a wire rack until they were almost done, then topped them with tomato sauce and shredded low-fat mozzarella to finish. Leaving the breasts on the rack rather than putting them in a casserole dish ensured that they would stay crisp as they baked. Served with a little extra sauce and grated Parmesan on the side, these oven-baked chicken Parmesan cutlets were crisp and full of flavor. And with 310 calories and 8 grams of fat, they have one-third less calories and two-thirds less fat grams than traditional versions.

Lighter Chicken Parmesan

SERVES 6

If you are tight on time, you can substitute 2 cups of your favorite plain tomato sauce for the Simple Tomato Sauce. To make slicing the chicken easier, freeze it for 15 minutes.

- 1½ cups panko (Japanese-style bread crumbs)
- 1 tablespoon olive oil
- 1 ounce Parmesan cheese, grated (about ½ cup), plus extra for serving
- ½ cup unbleached all-purpose flour
- 1½ teaspoons garlic powder
  Table salt and ground black pepper
- 3 large egg whites
- 1 tablespoon water
- 3 (7 to 8-ounce) boneless, skinless chicken breasts, tenderloins removed and breasts trimmed (see note)
- 1 recipe Simple Tomato Sauce (recipe follows), warmed (see note)
- 3 ounces low-fat mozzarella cheese, shredded (about ¾ cup)
- 1 tablespoon minced fresh basil leaves

1. Adjust an oven rack to the middle position and heat the oven to 475 degrees. Combine the bread crumbs and oil in a 12-inch skillet and toast over medium heat, stirring often, until golden, about 10 minutes. Spread the bread crumbs in a shallow dish and cool slightly; when cool, stir in the Parmesan.

2. In a second shallow dish, combine the flour, garlic powder, 1 tablespoon salt, and ½ teaspoon pepper. In a third shallow dish, whisk the egg whites and water together.

3. Line a rimmed baking sheet with foil, place a wire rack over the sheet, and spray the rack with vegetable oil spray. Halve the chicken horizontally, then cover the chicken halves with plastic wrap and pound the cutlets to an even ¼-inch thickness. Pat the chicken dry with paper towels, then season with salt and pepper. Lightly dredge the cutlets in the flour, shaking off the excess. Using tongs, dip both sides of the cutlets into the egg whites and allow

the excess egg to drip back into the dish. Finally, coat both sides of the chicken with the bread crumbs. Press on the bread crumbs to make sure they adhere. Lay the chicken on the wire rack.

4. Spray the tops of the chicken with vegetable oil spray. Bake until the meat is no longer pink in the center and feels firm when pressed with a finger, about 15 minutes.

5. Remove the chicken from the oven. Spoon 2 tablespoons of the sauce onto the center of each cutlet and top the sauce with 2 tablespoons of the mozzarella. Return the chicken to the oven and continue to bake until the cheese has melted, about 5 minutes. Sprinkle with the basil and serve, passing the remaining sauce and Parmesan separately.

Simple Tomato Sauce

MAKES ABOUT 2 CUPS

This easy sauce also works well with pasta.

- 1 (28-ounce) can diced tomatoes
- 4 medium garlic cloves, minced or pressed through a garlic press (about 4 teaspoons)
- 1 tablespoon tomato paste
- 1 teaspoon olive oil
- ⅛ teaspoon red pepper flakes
- 1 tablespoon minced fresh basil leaves
  Table salt and ground black pepper

Pulse the tomatoes in a food processor until mostly smooth, about 10 pulses; set aside. Cook the garlic, tomato paste, oil, and red pepper flakes in a medium saucepan over medium heat until the tomato paste begins to brown, about 2 minutes. Stir in the pureed tomatoes and cook until the sauce is thickened and measures 2 cups, about 20 minutes. Off the heat, stir in the basil and season with salt and pepper to taste. Cover and set aside until needed.

CHICKEN PICCATA

WHY THIS RECIPE WORKS: Many recipes for chicken piccata are either bland or overcomplicated, with extra ingredients that ruin the dish's simplicity. Many recipes contain just a tablespoon of lemon juice and a teaspoon of capers, neither of which provides much flavor. But chicken piccata is one of those appealing Italian recipes that taste complex but are actually easy to prepare. Our goal was properly cooked chicken with a streamlined sauce that really tastes of lemons and capers.

Many recipes suggest breading cutlets for chicken piccata, but we found that flour alone was sufficient; there was no point building a crisp crust that would end up drenched in sauce. After browning the chicken and sautéing aromatics, we deglazed the pan with chicken broth alone; although wine is sometimes suggested, we found it to be too acidic for this dish. We simmered slices from half a lemon in the broth for a few minutes; this was easier than grating the zest. For maximum lemon flavor in the sauce, we used a full quarter-cup of lemon juice, added when the sauce was nearly done so as not to blunt its impact. Butter gave the sauce body and was preferable to flour, which made it overly thick. Plenty of capers and a bit of parsley finished our ultra-lemony piccata.

Chicken Piccata

SERVES 4

Because this sauce is so light, we find that each person should be served 1½ small cutlets. To make slicing the chicken easier, freeze it for 15 minutes.

- 2 large lemons
- 6 (5 to 6-ounce) boneless, skinless chicken breasts, tenderloins removed and breasts trimmed (see note)
  Table salt and ground black pepper
- ½ cup unbleached all-purpose flour
- 4 tablespoons vegetable oil
- 1 small shallot, minced (about 1 tablespoon), or 1 medium garlic clove, minced or pressed through a garlic press (about 1 teaspoon)
- 1 cup low-sodium chicken broth
- 2 tablespoons drained small capers
- 3 tablespoons cold unsalted butter
- 2 tablespoons minced fresh parsley leaves

1. Adjust an oven rack to the lower-middle position, set a large ovensafe plate on the rack, and heat the oven to 200 degrees.

2. Halve 1 lemon pole to pole. Trim the ends from one half and cut it crosswise into slices ⅛ to ¼ inch thick; set aside. Juice the remaining half and whole lemon to obtain ¼ cup juice; reserve.

3. Halve the chicken horizontally, then cover the chicken halves with plastic wrap and pound the cutlets to an even ¼-inch thickness. Sprinkle both sides of the cutlets generously with salt and pepper. Place the flour in a shallow baking dish or pie plate. Working with 1 cutlet at a time, coat with flour and shake to remove the excess.

4. Heat 2 tablespoons of the oil in a heavy-bottomed 12-inch skillet over medium-high heat until shimmering. Lay 3 chicken cutlets in the skillet. Cook the cutlets until lightly browned on the first side, 2 to 3 minutes. Flip the cutlets and cook until the second side is lightly browned, 2 to 3 minutes longer. Remove the pan from the heat and transfer the cutlets to the plate in the warm oven. Add the remaining 2 tablespoons oil to the now-empty skillet and heat until shimmering. Add the remaining 3 chicken cutlets and repeat.

5. Add the shallot or garlic to the now-empty skillet and return the skillet to medium heat. Sauté until fragrant, about 30 seconds for the shallot or 10 seconds for the garlic. Add the broth and lemon slices, increase the heat to high, and scrape the pan bottom with a wooden spoon or spatula to loosen the browned bits. Simmer until the liquid reduces to about ⅓ cup, about 4 minutes. Add the lemon juice and capers and simmer until the sauce reduces again to ⅓ cup, about 1 minute. Remove the pan from the heat and swirl in the butter until it melts and thickens the sauce. Stir in the parsley and season with salt and pepper to taste. Spoon the sauce over the chicken and serve immediately.

PARMESAN-CRUSTED CHICKEN BREASTS

WHY THIS RECIPE WORKS: With a short ingredient list of only chicken breasts and Parmesan cheese plus one or two binders such as eggs or flour, Parmesan-crusted chicken breasts should be straightforward. But we found pale, wet, and gummy baked versions as well as bitter and burnt pan-fried versions. We wanted moist and tender chicken coated with a thin, crispy-yet-chewy, waferlike sheath of Parmesan cheese.

A standard breading in which we merely substituted cheese for the bread crumbs and flour was disappointing; the cheese didn't provide the dry base to which the rest of the coating would stick. So we went back to flour, with a bit of Parmesan for flavor, and we left out the egg yolks to eliminate the eggy taste. For the outermost layer, shredding the cheese on the large holes of a box grater made a sturdier, more even crust, and a little flour added to this cheese helped the coating turn crisp. Pan-frying in a nonstick skillet prevented sticking, and keeping the heat no higher than medium browned the cheese without making it bitter. These cutlets were pale golden rather than deep golden brown, but the nutty, crisp Parmesan crust was everything we hoped it would be.

Parmesan-Crusted Chicken Cutlets

SERVES 4

To make slicing the chicken easier, freeze it for 15 minutes. Note that part of the Parmesan is grated on the smallest holes of a box grater (or rasp grater) and the remaining Parmesan is shredded on the largest holes of the box grater. We like the flavor that authentic Parmigiano-Reggiano lends to this recipe. A less-expensive cheese, such as Boar's Head Parmesan cheese, can also be used, but the resulting cheese crust will be slightly saltier and chewier. Although the portion size (one cutlet per person) might seem small, these cutlets are rather rich due to the cheese content. To make eight cutlets, double the ingredients and cook the chicken in four batches, transferring the cooked cutlets to a warm oven and wiping out the skillet after each batch.

2 (7 to 8-ounce) boneless, skinless chicken breasts, tenderloins removed and breasts trimmed (see note)
Table salt and ground black pepper
5 tablespoons unbleached all-purpose flour
¼ cup grated Parmesan cheese plus 6 ounces, shredded (about 2 cups; see note)
3 large egg whites
2 tablespoons minced fresh chives (optional)
4 teaspoons olive oil
Lemon wedges, for serving

1. Adjust an oven rack to the middle position and heat the oven to 200 degrees. Halve the chicken horizontally, then cover the chicken halves with plastic wrap and pound the cutlets to an even ¼-inch thickness. Pat the chicken dry with paper towels and season with salt and pepper.

2. Whisk ¼ cup of the flour and the ¼ cup grated Parmesan together in a shallow dish. Whisk the egg whites and chives (if using) in a medium bowl until slightly foamy. Combine the 2 cups shredded Parmesan and remaining 1 tablespoon flour in a second shallow dish. Working with 1 chicken cutlet at a time, dredge in the flour mixture, shaking off the excess, then coat with the egg white mixture, allowing the excess to drip off. Finally, coat with the shredded Parmesan mixture, pressing gently so that the cheese adheres. Place the coated cutlets in a single layer on a wire rack set over a rimmed baking sheet.

3. Heat 2 teaspoons of the oil in a 12-inch nonstick skillet over medium heat until shimmering. Add 2 of the cutlets and cook until pale golden brown on both sides, 4 to 6 minutes in total. (While the chicken is cooking, use a thin nonstick spatula to gently separate any cheesy edges that have melted together.) Transfer to a clean wire rack set over a rimmed baking sheet and keep warm in the oven. Wipe out the skillet with paper towels. Repeat with the remaining 2 teaspoons oil and chicken. Serve with the lemon wedges.

CHICKEN FRANCESE

WHY THIS RECIPE WORKS: This fast-fading star of red-sauce Italian restaurants often features a rubbery coating and a puckery lemon sauce. Yet this quick dinner still holds promise for the home cook. We wanted our chicken to have a rich, eggy coating that would remain soft and tender yet be sturdy enough to stand up to a silky, well-balanced lemon sauce.

We found that a first coating of flour was essential for getting the egg to stick, and a little milk added to the egg prevented it from turning rubbery. A final dip into flour made a soft, delicate veneer. We sautéed the cutlets in butter for its flavor, adding a little oil to keep the butter from burning, and kept them warm in the oven while we made our sauce. Fresh lemon juice with some vermouth and chicken broth gave us the bright, fresh citrus flavor we wanted; a little sautéed shallot balanced the lemon but didn't overpower it. To get the sauce to cling to the chicken without making it soggy, we made a roux with butter and flour. Our sauce was just right, but the chicken had dried out while waiting in the oven. Our solution was to make the sauce first, then cook the chicken and finish the sauce. We think this revitalized dish deserves a place in today's home kitchens.

Chicken Francese

SERVES 4

To make slicing the chicken easier, freeze it for 15 minutes. The sauce is very lemony—for less tartness, reduce the amount of lemon juice by about 1 tablespoon.

SAUCE

- 3 tablespoons unsalted butter
- 1 large shallot, minced (about 4 tablespoons)
- 1 tablespoon unbleached all-purpose flour
- 2¼ cups low-sodium chicken broth
- ½ cup dry vermouth or white wine
- ⅓ cup juice from 2 lemons (see note)
     Table salt and ground black pepper

CHICKEN

- 4 (5 to 6-ounce) boneless, skinless chicken breasts, tenderloins removed and breasts trimmed (see note)
     Table salt and ground black pepper
- 1 cup unbleached all-purpose flour
- 2 large eggs
- 2 tablespoons milk
- 2 tablespoons unsalted butter
- 2 tablespoons olive oil
- 2 tablespoons minced fresh parsley leaves

1. Adjust an oven rack to the middle position and heat the oven to 200 degrees.

2. FOR THE SAUCE: Melt 1 tablespoon of the butter in a medium saucepan over medium heat. Add the shallot and cook, stirring occasionally, until softened, about 2 minutes. Stir in the flour and cook until light golden brown, about 1 minute. Whisk in the broth, vermouth, and lemon juice and bring to a simmer. Cook, whisking occasionally, until the sauce measures 1½ cups, about 15 minutes. Strain the sauce through a fine-mesh strainer. Return the sauce to the saucepan and set aside, discarding the solids.

3. FOR THE CHICKEN: Halve the chicken horizontally, then cover the chicken halves with plastic wrap and pound the cutlets to an even ¼-inch thickness. Pat the chicken dry with paper towels and season with salt and pepper.

4. Combine the flour, 1 teaspoon salt, and ¼ teaspoon pepper in a shallow dish and whisk the eggs and milk together in a medium bowl. Working with 1 chicken cutlet at a time, dredge in the flour, shaking off the excess, then coat with the egg mixture, allowing the excess to drip off.

Finally, coat with the flour again, shaking off the excess. Place the coated chicken in a single layer on a wire rack set over a rimmed baking sheet.

5. Heat 1 tablespoon each of the butter and oil in a 12-inch nonstick skillet over medium-high heat. Add 4 of the cutlets and cook until lightly browned on one side, 2 to 3 minutes. Flip the chicken over and continue to cook until no longer pink and lightly browned on the second side, about 1 minute. Transfer the chicken to a clean wire rack set over a rimmed baking sheet and keep warm in the oven. Wipe out the skillet with paper towels. Add the remaining 1 tablespoon each of the butter and oil to the skillet and repeat with the remaining cutlets, then transfer to the oven. Wipe out the skillet with paper towels.

6. TO FINISH THE SAUCE AND SERVE: Transfer the sauce to the now-empty skillet and cook over medium-low heat until warmed, about 2 minutes. Whisk in the remaining 2 tablespoons butter, 1 tablespoon at a time, and season with salt and pepper to taste. Transfer 4 of the chicken cutlets to the skillet, turn to coat with the sauce, then transfer each serving (2 cutlets) to individual plates. Repeat with the remaining cutlets. Spoon 2 tablespoons of the sauce over each serving and sprinkle with the parsley. Serve, passing the remaining sauce separately.

CHICKEN SALTIMBOCCA

WHY THIS RECIPE WORKS: In its classic Italian form, saltimbocca is made with veal, prosciutto, and sage, but chicken is frequently substituted for the veal. The combination of flavors is meant to "jump in the mouth," as the name suggests. Preparing this dish can be complicated, but we wanted to streamline it and ensure that the flavors were well balanced.

Flouring only the chicken, rather than the chicken-prosciutto package, avoided gummy spots. The prosciutto is usually secured to the chicken with a toothpick, but we found that searing the prosciutto side of the chicken first worked as well; once browned, the two stuck together just fine. Prosciutto can overwhelm the other flavors in this dish, so it's important to use thin slices, but not so thin that they disintegrate during cooking. A single sage leaf is the usual garnish, but we wanted more sage flavor, so we sprinkled some minced fresh sage over the floured chicken before adding the prosciutto. (A single fried sage leaf is a pretty but optional garnish.) With a simple pan sauce of vermouth, lemon juice, butter, and parsley, our chicken saltimbocca was ready to serve and full of flavor.

Chicken Saltimbocca

SERVES 4

To make slicing the chicken easier, freeze it for 15 minutes. Although whole sage leaves make a beautiful presentation, they are optional and can be left out of step 3. Make sure to buy prosciutto that is thinly sliced, not shaved; also avoid slices that are too thick, as they won't stick to the chicken. The prosciutto slices should be large enough to fully cover one side of each cutlet.

- 4   (5 to 6-ounce) boneless, skinless chicken breasts, tenderloins removed and breasts trimmed (see note)
- ½   cup unbleached all-purpose flour
  Ground black pepper
- 1   tablespoon minced fresh sage leaves, plus 8 large leaves (optional; see note)
- 8   thin prosciutto slices (about 3 ounces; see note)
- 4   tablespoons olive oil
- 1¼   cups dry vermouth or white wine
- 2   teaspoons juice from 1 lemon
- 4   tablespoons (½ stick) unsalted butter, cut into 4 pieces and chilled
- 1   tablespoon minced fresh parsley leaves
  Table salt

1. Halve the chicken horizontally, then cover the chicken halves with plastic wrap and pound the cutlets to an even ¼-inch thickness.

2. Combine the flour and 1 teaspoon pepper in a shallow dish. Pat the chicken dry with paper towels. Dredge the chicken in the flour, shaking off any excess. Lay the cutlets flat and sprinkle evenly with the minced sage. Place 1 prosciutto slice on top of each cutlet, pressing lightly to adhere; set aside.

3. Heat 2 tablespoons of the oil in a 12-inch skillet over medium-high heat until shimmering. Add the sage leaves (if using) and cook until the leaves begin to change color and are fragrant, 15 to 20 seconds. Using a slotted spoon, transfer the sage to a paper towel–lined plate and set aside. Add 4 of the cutlets to the pan, prosciutto side down, and cook until lightly browned on one side, about 2 minutes. Flip the chicken over and continue to cook until no longer pink, 30 seconds to 1 minute. Transfer the chicken to a plate and tent loosely with foil. Add the remaining 2 tablespoons oil to the skillet and repeat with the remaining 4 cutlets. Transfer to the plate and tent loosely with foil while making the sauce.

4. Pour off the excess fat from the skillet. Stir in the vermouth, scraping up any browned bits, and simmer until reduced to about ⅓ cup, 5 to 7 minutes. Stir in the lemon juice. Turn the heat to low and whisk in the butter, 1 tablespoon at time. Off the heat, stir in the parsley and season with salt and pepper to taste. Spoon the sauce over the chicken, place a sage leaf (if using) on each cutlet, and serve.

ITALIAN BRAISED CHICKEN

WHY THIS RECIPE WORKS: Chicken *canzanese* is a regional Italian braised dish that transforms tough old birds into a moist and tender meal. Today's lean, mass-produced chickens, however, turn dried-out and bland when braised. We wanted old-fashioned results with a modern-day bird: tender, juicy chicken in an intensely flavored, well-developed sauce.

To start, we swapped out young, modern chickens for meaty chicken thighs that hold up especially well to braising. Next, we turned to the sauce. We browned diced prosciutto on the stovetop until it rendered enough fat to cook the garlic, which created a rich flavor base. Then we added white wine and chicken broth, and simmered them to concentrate flavors and burn off the raw alcohol flavor. We returned the chicken to the skillet and put it into the oven, uncovered to crisp the skin. To round out the flavors, we added a quick squeeze of lemon juice, a generous pat of butter, and a sprinkling of chopped rosemary.

Chicken Canzanese

SERVES 4 TO 6

When seasoning the dish at the end, be mindful that the prosciutto adds a fair amount of salt. It is important to use a piece of thickly sliced prosciutto in this recipe; thin strips will become tough and stringy. An equal amount of thickly sliced pancetta or bacon can be used in place of the prosciutto. Serve the chicken with boiled potatoes, noodles, or polenta.

    1 tablespoon olive oil
    2 ounces prosciutto (¼ inch thick), cut into ¼-inch
      cubes (see note)
    4 medium garlic cloves, sliced thin lengthwise
    3 pounds bone-in, skin-on chicken thighs (about
      8 thighs), trimmed
      Ground black pepper
    2 teaspoons unbleached all-purpose flour
    2 cups dry white wine
    1 cup low-sodium chicken broth
    4 whole cloves
    1 (4-inch) sprig fresh rosemary, leaves removed and
      minced fine (about ½ teaspoon), stem reserved
   12 whole fresh sage leaves
    2 bay leaves
¼–½ teaspoon red pepper flakes
    1 tablespoon juice from 1 lemon
    2 tablespoons unsalted butter
      Table salt

1. Adjust an oven rack to the lower-middle position and heat the oven to 325 degrees. Heat 1 teaspoon of the oil in a 12-inch heavy-bottomed ovensafe skillet over medium heat until shimmering. Add the prosciutto and cook, stirring frequently, until just starting to brown, about 3 minutes. Add the garlic slices and cook, stirring frequently, until the garlic is golden brown, about 1½ minutes. Using a slotted spoon, transfer the garlic and prosciutto to a small bowl and set aside. Do not rinse the pan.

2. Increase the heat to medium-high; add the remaining 2 teaspoons oil and heat until just smoking. Pat the chicken dry with paper towels and season with black pepper. Add the chicken, skin side down, and cook without moving until well browned, 5 to 8 minutes. Using tongs, turn the chicken and brown on the second side, about 5 minutes longer. Transfer the chicken to a large plate.

3. Remove all but 2 tablespoons fat from the pan. Sprinkle the flour over the fat and cook, stirring constantly, for 1 minute. Slowly add the wine and broth; bring to a simmer, scraping the bottom of the pan with a wooden spoon to loosen the browned bits. Cook until the liquid is slightly reduced, 3 minutes. Stir in the cloves, rosemary stem, sage leaves, bay leaves, red pepper flakes, and reserved prosciutto and garlic. Nestle the chicken into the liquid, skin side up (the skin should be above the surface of the liquid), and bake, uncovered, until the meat offers no resistance when poked with a fork but is not falling off the bones, about 1 hour 15 minutes. (Check the chicken after 15 minutes; the broth should be barely bubbling. If bubbling vigorously, reduce the oven temperature to 300 degrees.)

4. Using tongs, transfer the chicken to a serving platter and tent with foil. Remove and discard the sage leaves, rosemary stem, cloves, and bay leaves. Place the skillet over high heat and bring the sauce to a boil. Cook until the sauce is reduced to 1¼ cups, 2 to 5 minutes. Off the heat, stir in the minced rosemary, lemon juice, and butter. Season with salt and pepper to taste. Pour the sauce around the chicken and serve.

ITALIAN GRILLED CHICKEN

WHY THIS RECIPE WORKS: Anyone who has tried to grill a whole chicken knows that it's challenging at best, and the results are often inedible. Many cuisines have developed methods to overcome the problems of chicken cooked over a fire; the Italian way is to cook the chicken under bricks. This was one method we had to try.

One attempt to grill a butterflied chicken the Italian way was enough to let us know that we needed more than just bricks to make this recipe work. We thought of brining to keep the meat moist, but it produced burnt chicken when the liquid dripped into the fire. An alternative way to retain moisture in meat is salting; we rubbed the flesh under the skin with salt, mixed with garlic, red pepper flakes, and herbs for Italian flavor. With a modified two-level fire in the grill, we cooked the chicken under preheated bricks on the cooler side, skin side down, to firm up the flesh and release fat and liquid where the fire wouldn't cause flare-ups. We flipped the chicken and finished cooking it on the hot side; another flip and a few minutes without the bricks crisped up the skin. The combination of flipping and moving the chicken from the cool side to the hot side guaranteed even cooking, and the salting had kept the meat juicy. With a finishing embellishment of a quick vinaigrette, we had perfectly cooked chicken with zesty Italian flavor, and not a burnt piece in sight.

Italian-Style Charcoal-Grilled Chicken

SERVES 4

Use an oven mitt or dish towel to safely grip and maneuver the hot bricks. You will need two standard-size bricks for this recipe. Placing the bricks on the chicken while it cooks ensures that the skin will be evenly browned and well rendered—don't skip this step. A cast-iron skillet or other heavy pan can be used in place of the bricks.

⅓ cup extra-virgin olive oil
8 medium garlic cloves, minced or pressed through a garlic press (about 2½ tablespoons)
1 teaspoon finely grated zest plus 2 tablespoons juice from 1 lemon
Pinch crushed red pepper flakes
4 teaspoons chopped fresh thyme leaves
1 tablespoon chopped fresh rosemary leaves
1 (3¾ to 4¼-pound) whole chicken
Kosher salt
Ground black pepper
Vegetable oil for the cooking grate

1. Combine the olive oil, garlic, lemon zest, and red pepper flakes in a small saucepan. Bring to a simmer, stirring frequently, over medium-low heat, about 3 minutes. Once the mixture is simmering, add 3 teaspoons of the thyme and 2 teaspoons of the rosemary and cook for 30 seconds longer. Strain the mixture through a fine-mesh strainer set over a small bowl, pushing on the solids to extract the oil. Transfer the solids to a small bowl and cool; set the oil and solids aside.

2. Butterfly the chicken by cutting through the bones on either side of the backbone; discard the backbone. Flatten the breastbone and tuck the wings behind the back. Using your hands or the handle of a wooden spoon, loosen the skin over the breast and thighs and remove any excess fat. Combine 1 tablespoon salt and 1 teaspoon pepper in a small bowl. Mix 3 teaspoons of the salt mixture with the cooled garlic solids. Spread the salt-garlic mixture evenly under the skin over the chicken breast and thighs. Sprinkle the remaining 1 teaspoon salt mixture on the exposed meat of the bone side. Place the chicken, skin side up, on a wire rack set over a rimmed baking sheet and refrigerate for 1 to 2 hours.

3. Wrap two bricks tightly in aluminum foil. Light a large chimney starter filled three-quarters with charcoal (4½ quarts) and allow to burn until the coals are partially covered with a layer of gray ash, about 20 minutes. Build a modified two-level fire by arranging all the coals over one half of the grill, leaving the other half empty. Set the cooking grate in place, cover, and heat the grate until hot, about 5 minutes. Use a grill brush to scrape the cooking grate clean. Dip a wad of paper towels in vegetable oil; holding the wad with tongs, oil the cooking grate.

4. Place the chicken, skin side down, over the cooler side of the grill with the legs facing the fire, place the hot bricks lengthwise over each breast half, cover the grill, and cook until the skin is lightly browned and faint grill marks appear, 22 to 25 minutes. Remove the bricks from the chicken. Using tongs or a dish towel, grip the legs and flip the chicken (the chicken should release freely from the grill; use a thin metal spatula to loosen it if it sticks); transfer the chicken to the hot side of the grill, skin side up, with the breast facing the center of the grill. Place the bricks over the breast, cover the grill, and cook until the chicken is well browned, 12 to 15 minutes.

5. Remove the bricks, flip the chicken skin side down over the hot coals, and cook until the chicken skin is well crisped and the thickest part of the breast registers 160 to 165 degrees and the thickest part of the thigh registers 175 degrees on an instant-read thermometer, 5 to 10 minutes, moving the chicken as necessary to prevent flare-ups. Transfer the chicken to a carving board and let rest for 10 minutes. Whisk the lemon juice, the remaining 1 teaspoon thyme, and the remaining 1 teaspoon rosemary into the reserved oil; season with salt and pepper to taste. Carve the chicken and serve, passing the sauce separately.

Italian-Style Gas-Grilled Chicken

Follow the instructions for Italian-Style Charcoal-Grilled Chicken through step 2 and wrap two bricks tightly with aluminum foil. Turn all the burners to high, place the bricks on the cooking grate, and heat the grill with the lid down until very hot, about 15 minutes. Use a grill brush to scrape the cooking grate clean. Dip a wad of paper towels in vegetable oil; holding the wad with tongs, oil the cooking grate. Leave the primary burner on high and turn off the other burner(s). Proceed with the recipe from step 4, cooking with the lid down.

PORK CHOPS WITH VINEGAR AND PEPPERS

WHY THIS RECIPE WORKS: This Italian-American dish was devised when pork chops had plenty of fat to keep them juicy; the leaner pork we have today tends to dry out and ruin it. But the thought of succulent pork with a tangy vinegar and pepper sauce spurred us to search for a way to make this dish taste the way it should.

The first step was choosing the right chop to use. Bone-in rib chops of medium thickness had the best flavor, and the bone helped keep the meat juicy. Brining the chops in a solution of salt and sugar added moisture and flavor, and the sugar enhanced browning. Cooking the chops and then assembling a pan sauce of vinegar and peppers didn't give us the marriage of flavors the dish should have, but braising the chops in a vinegar sauce produced chalky meat. We discovered that browning the chops, removing them from the pan to build the sauce, then finishing everything together in the oven worked best to get the flavors of the sauce into the meat. We also ditched the jarred vinegar peppers, which are traditional, and made our own; they were far superior to any we'd found at the supermarket.

Pork Chops with Vinegar and Sweet Peppers
SERVES 4

We prefer natural to enhanced pork (pork that has been injected with a salt solution to increase moistness and flavor) for this recipe, though enhanced pork can be used. If using enhanced pork, skip the brining in step 1. To keep the chops from overcooking and becoming tough and dry, remove them from the oven when they are just shy of fully cooked; as they sit in the hot skillet, they will continue to cook with residual heat.

1   **cup sugar**
    Table salt and ground black pepper
4   **(8 to 10-ounce) bone-in rib loin pork chops,**
    ¾ to 1 inch thick, trimmed of excess fat (see note)
2   **tablespoons olive oil**
1   **medium onion, minced**
1   **medium red bell pepper, stemmed, seeded, and cut into ¼-inch-wide strips**
1   **medium yellow bell pepper, stemmed, seeded, and cut into ¼-inch-wide strips**
2   **anchovy fillets, minced (about 1 teaspoon)**
1   **medium sprig fresh rosemary**
2   **medium garlic cloves, minced or pressed through a garlic press (about 2 teaspoons)**
¾   **cup water**

½ **cup white wine vinegar, plus 2 tablespoons to finish the sauce (optional)**

2 **tablespoons cold unsalted butter**

2 **tablespoons chopped fresh parsley leaves**

1. Dissolve the sugar and ½ cup salt in 2 quarts water in a large container; add the pork chops and refrigerate for 30 minutes. Remove the chops from the brine, rinse, and pat dry with paper towels. Using a sharp knife, cut two slits, about 2 inches apart, through the outer layer of fat and silver skin of each chop (do not cut into the meat of the chops). Season the chops with ¾ teaspoon pepper and set aside.

2. Adjust an oven rack to the middle position and heat the oven to 400 degrees. Heat the oil in an oven-safe 12-inch skillet over medium-high heat until the oil begins to smoke; swirl the skillet to coat with the oil. Place the chops in the skillet; cook until well browned, 3 to 4 minutes, using a spoon or spatula to press down on the center of the chops to aid in browning. Using tongs, flip the chops and brown lightly on the second side, about 1 minute. Transfer the chops to a large plate; set aside.

3. Set the skillet over medium-high heat. Add the onion and cook, stirring occasionally, until just beginning to soften, about 2 minutes. Add the peppers, anchovies, and rosemary; cook, stirring frequently, until the peppers just begin to soften, about 4 minutes. Add the garlic; cook, stirring constantly, until fragrant, about 30 seconds. Add the water and ½ cup of the vinegar and bring to a boil, scraping up the browned bits with a wooden spoon. Reduce the heat to medium; simmer until the liquid is reduced to about ⅓ cup, 6 to 8 minutes. Off the heat, discard the rosemary.

4. Return the pork chops, browner side up, to the skillet; nestle the chops in the peppers, but do not cover them. Add any accumulated juices to the skillet; set the skillet in the oven and cook until the center of the chops registers 140 to 145 degrees on an instant-read thermometer, 8 to 12 minutes (begin checking the temperature after 6 minutes). Using potholders, carefully remove the skillet from the oven (the handle will be very hot) and cover the skillet with a lid or foil; let stand until the center of the chops registers 150 degrees, 5 to 7 minutes. Transfer the chops to a platter or individual plates. Swirl the butter into the sauce and the peppers in the skillet; taste and stir in the remaining 2 tablespoons vinegar (if using) and the parsley. Season with salt and pepper to taste, then pour or spoon the sauce and peppers over the chops. Serve immediately.

OSSO BUCO

WHY THIS RECIPE WORKS: Osso buco, veal shanks braised in a rich sauce until tender, is incredibly rich and hearty. We felt that this time-honored recipe shouldn't be altered much, but we hoped to identify the keys to flavor so that we could perfect it.

To serve one shank per person, we searched for medium-sized shanks, and tied them around the equator to keep the meat attached to the bone for an attractive presentation. Most recipes suggest flouring the veal before browning it, but we got better flavor when we seared the meat, liberally seasoned with just salt and pepper. Browning in two batches enabled us to deglaze the pan twice, thus enriching the sauce. Celery, onion, and carrots formed the basis of the sauce; for the liquid we used a combination of chicken broth, white wine, and canned tomatoes. The traditional garnish of gremolata—minced garlic, lemon, and parsley—required no changes; we stirred half into the sauce and sprinkled the rest over individual servings for a fresh burst of citrus flavor.

Osso Buco

SERVES 6

To keep the meat attached to the bone during the long simmering process, tie a piece of kitchen twine around the thickest portion of each shank before it is browned. Just before serving, taste the liquid and, if it seems too thin, simmer it on the stovetop as you remove the strings from the osso buco and arrange them in individual bowls. Serve with Basic Polenta (page 297).

OSSO BUCO

4 **tablespoons vegetable oil**

6 **(8 to 10-ounce) veal shanks, 1½ inches thick, patted dry with paper towels and tied with kitchen twine at 1½-inch intervals**

Table salt and ground black pepper

2½ **cups dry white wine**

2 **medium onions, cut into ½-inch pieces**

2 **medium carrots, cut into ½-inch pieces**

2 **medium celery ribs, cut into ½-inch pieces**

6 **medium garlic cloves, minced or pressed through a garlic press (about 2 tablespoons)**

2 **cups low-sodium chicken broth**

2 **small bay leaves**

1 **(14.5-ounce) can diced tomatoes, drained**

¼ cup minced fresh parsley leaves

3 medium garlic cloves, minced or pressed through a garlic press (about 1 tablespoon)

2 teaspoons grated zest from 1 lemon

1. FOR THE OSSO BUCO: Adjust an oven rack to the lower-middle position and heat the oven to 325 degrees. Heat 1 tablespoon of the oil in a large Dutch oven over medium-high heat until shimmering. Meanwhile, sprinkle both sides of the shanks generously with salt and pepper. Place 3 shanks in the pan and cook until they are golden brown on one side, about 5 minutes. Using tongs, flip the shanks and cook on the second side until golden brown, about 5 minutes longer. Transfer the shanks to a bowl and set aside. Off the heat, add ½ cup of the wine to the Dutch oven, scraping the pan bottom with a wooden spoon to loosen any browned bits. Pour the liquid into the bowl with the browned shanks. Return the pot to medium-high heat, add 1 tablespoon more oil, and heat until shimmering. Brown the remaining shanks, about 5 minutes for each side. Transfer the shanks to the bowl. Off the heat, add 1 cup more wine to the pot, scraping the bottom to loosen the browned bits. Pour the liquid into the bowl with the shanks.

2. Set the pot over medium heat. Add the remaining 2 tablespoons oil and heat until shimmering. Add the onions, carrots, celery, ¼ teaspoon salt, and ⅛ teaspoon pepper and cook, stirring occasionally, until soft and lightly browned, about 9 minutes. Stir in the garlic and cook until fragrant, about 30 seconds. Increase the heat to high and stir in the broth, remaining 1 cup wine, and bay leaves. Add the tomatoes; return the veal shanks to the pot along with any accumulated juices (the liquid should just cover the shanks). Bring the liquid to a simmer. Cover the pot and transfer the pot to the oven. Cook the shanks until the meat is easily pierced with a fork but not falling off the bone, about 2 hours. (At this point the osso buco can be refrigerated for up to 2 days. Bring to a simmer over medium-low heat.)

3. FOR THE GREMOLATA: Combine the parsley, garlic, and lemon zest in a small bowl. Stir half of the gremolata into the pot, reserving the rest for garnish. Season with salt and pepper to taste. Let the osso buco stand, uncovered, for 5 minutes.

4. Using tongs, remove the shanks from the pot, cut off and discard the twine, and place 1 veal shank in each of six bowls. Ladle some of the braising liquid over each shank and sprinkle each serving with the remaining gremolata. Serve immediately.

BEEF IN BAROLO

WHY THIS RECIPE WORKS: Italian pot roast is an inexpensive cut of beef braised in wine. But what a difference that wine makes. Full-bodied Barolo has been called the "wine of kings." It can be somewhat expensive, so this pot roast has to be special. We wanted tender meat in a rich, savory sauce that would do justice to the regal wine.

A chuck-eye roast won't dry out after a long braise, but it has a line of fat in the middle that we felt was out of place in this refined dish. Separating one roast into two smaller ones enabled us to discard most of this fat before cooking. We then tied the roasts together and browned them in fat rendered from pancetta, which added rich flavor. We browned aromatics, then poured a whole bottle of wine into the pot. The Barolo's bold flavor needed something to temper it, and we liked a can of diced tomatoes. When the meat was done, we reduced the sauce and strained out the vegetables. Dark, full-flavored, and lustrous, this sauce bestowed nobility on our humble cut of meat.

Beef Braised in Barolo

SERVES 6

Don't skip tying the roasts—it keeps them intact during the long cooking time. Purchase pancetta that is cut to order, about ¼ inch thick. If pancetta is not available, substitute an equal amount of salt pork (find the meatiest piece possible), cut it into ¼-inch cubes, and boil it in 3 cups of water for about 2 minutes to remove excess salt. After draining, use it as you would pancetta.

1 (3½-pound) boneless chuck-eye roast
  Table salt and ground black pepper

4 ounces pancetta (about 4 slices), cut into ¼-inch cubes (see note)

2 medium onions, chopped medium

2 medium carrots, chopped medium

2 medium celery ribs, chopped medium

1 tablespoon tomato paste

3 medium garlic cloves, minced or pressed through a garlic press (about 1 tablespoon)

1 tablespoon unbleached all-purpose flour

½ teaspoon sugar

1 (750-milliliter) bottle Barolo wine

1 (14.5-ounce) can diced tomatoes, drained

1 sprig fresh thyme plus 1 teaspoon minced thyme leaves

1 sprig fresh rosemary

10 sprigs fresh parsley

1. Adjust an oven rack to the middle position and heat the oven to 300 degrees. Pull the roast apart at its major seams (delineated by lines of fat) into two halves. Use a knife as necessary. With the knife, remove the large knobs of fat from each piece, leaving a thin layer of fat on the meat. Tie three pieces of kitchen twine around each piece of meat. Thoroughly pat the beef dry with paper towels; sprinkle generously with salt and pepper. Place the pancetta in a large Dutch oven; cook over medium heat, stirring occasionally, until browned and crisp, about 8 minutes. Using a slotted spoon, transfer the pancetta to a paper towel–lined plate and reserve. Pour off all but 2 tablespoons of fat; set the Dutch oven over medium-high heat and heat the fat until beginning to smoke. Add the beef to the pot and cook until well browned on all sides, about 8 minutes total. Transfer the beef to a large plate; set aside.

2. Reduce the heat to medium; add the onions, carrots, celery, and tomato paste to the pot and cook, stirring occasionally, until the vegetables begin to soften and brown, about 6 minutes. Add the garlic, flour, sugar, and reserved pancetta; cook, stirring constantly, until combined and fragrant, about 30 seconds. Add the wine and tomatoes, scraping the bottom of the pan with a wooden spoon to loosen the browned bits; add the thyme sprig, rosemary, and parsley. Return the roast and any accumulated juice to the pot; increase the heat to high and bring the liquid to a boil, then place a large sheet of foil over the pot and cover tightly with the lid. Set the pot in the oven and cook, using tongs to turn the beef every 45 minutes, until a dinner fork easily slips in and out of the meat, about 3 hours.

3. Transfer the beef to a carving board and tent with foil to keep warm. Allow the braising liquid to settle for about 5 minutes, then, using a wide shallow spoon, skim the fat off the surface. Add the minced thyme, bring the liquid to a boil over high heat, and cook, whisking vigorously to help the vegetables break down, until the mixture is thickened and reduced to about 3½ cups, about 18 minutes. Strain the liquid through a large fine-mesh strainer, pressing on the solids with a spatula to extract as much liquid as possible; you should have 1½ cups strained sauce (if necessary, return the strained sauce to the Dutch oven and reduce to 1½ cups). Discard the solids in the strainer. Season the sauce with salt and pepper to taste.

4. Remove the kitchen twine from the meat and discard. Using a chef's knife or carving knife, cut the meat against the grain into ½-inch-thick slices. Divide the meat among warmed bowls or plates; pour about ¼ cup sauce over each portion and serve immediately.

SHRIMP SCAMPI

WHY THIS RECIPE WORKS: Restaurant versions of shrimp scampi often run the gamut from boiled shrimp and tomato sauce on a bed of pasta to rubbery shrimp overloaded in butter or olive oil. We wanted lightly cooked, moist shrimp in a light garlic and lemon sauce.

A quick sauté in batches was all the shrimp needed to cook fully without becoming rubbery; we then set them aside to build the sauce. We cooked minced garlic briefly in butter, so as not to scorch it, then added lemon juice and vermouth for depth of flavor; the liquids also protected the garlic from burning. Additional butter thickened the sauce, and parsley and cayenne provided the finishing touches to this light, flavorful Italian favorite.

Shrimp Scampi

SERVES 4 TO 6

Serve the scampi with plenty of chewy bread to soak up the extra juices.

- 2 **tablespoons olive oil**
- 2 **pounds extra-large shrimp (21 to 25 per pound), peeled and deveined (see page 205)**
- 3 **tablespoons unsalted butter**
- 4 **medium garlic cloves, minced or pressed through a garlic press (about 4 teaspoons)**
- 2 **tablespoons juice from 1 lemon**
- 1 **tablespoon dry vermouth**
- 2 **tablespoons minced fresh parsley leaves**
  Pinch cayenne pepper
  Table salt and ground black pepper

1. Heat 1 tablespoon of the oil in a 12-inch skillet over high heat until shimmering. Add 1 pound of the shrimp and cook, stirring occasionally, until just opaque, about 1 minute; transfer to a medium bowl. Return the pan to high heat and repeat with the remaining 1 tablespoon oil and remaining 1 pound shrimp.

2. Return the skillet to medium-low heat; melt 1 tablespoon of the butter. Add the garlic and cook, stirring constantly, until fragrant, about 30 seconds. Off the heat, add the lemon juice and vermouth. Whisk in the remaining 2 tablespoons butter; add the parsley and cayenne, and season with salt and black pepper to taste. Return the shrimp and any accumulated juices to the skillet. Toss to combine; serve immediately.

CHAPTER 14

THE FLAIR OF THE FRENCH

Classic French
Onion Soup 314

Streamlined French
Onion Soup 315

French Potato Salad 316

French Onion and
Bacon Tart 317

Pissaladière 318

Summer Vegetable
Gratin 320

Simplified Potato
Galette 321

Pommes Anna 322

French Mashed
Potatoes with Cheese
and Garlic (Aligot) 323

Potatoes Lyonnaise 324

Quick Chicken
Fricassee 325

French-Style Stuffed
Chicken Breasts 326

Coq au Vin 328

Chicken with 40 Cloves
of Garlic 329

French Chicken
in a Pot 331

Chicken Provençal 332

Daube Provençal 333

Beef Burgundy 334

Slow-Cooker Beef
Burgundy 335

Simplified Cassoulet with
Pork and Kielbasa 337

Steak au Poivre with
Brandied Cream Sauce 338

Steak Frites 339

Steak Diane 341
    Sauce Base for
    Steak Diane

Fish Meunière with Browned
Butter and Lemon 343

CLASSIC FRENCH ONION SOUP

WHY THIS RECIPE WORKS: With too many onion soups, digging through a layer of congealed cheese unearths a disappointing broth that just doesn't taste like onions. The ideal French onion soup combines a satisfying broth redolent of sweet caramelized onions with a slice of toasted baguette and melted cheese. We wanted a fool-proof method for achieving extraordinarily deep flavor from the humble onion—the star of this classic soup.

The secret to a rich broth was to caramelize the onions fully. The good news is that caramelizing the onions, deglazing the pot, and then repeating this process dozens of times will keep ratcheting up the flavor. The bad news is what a laborious, hands-on process this proved to be. Fortunately, we found that if we first cooked the onions, covered, in a hot oven for two and a half hours, we only needed to deglaze the onions on the stovetop three or four times. Just one type of onion (yellow) was sufficient, but a combination of three different liquids (water, chicken broth, and beef broth) added maximum flavor. For the topping, we toasted the bread before floating it on the soup to ward off sogginess and added only a modest sprinkling of nutty Gruyère so the broth wasn't overpowered.

Classic French Onion Soup
SERVES 6

Sweet onions, such as Vidalia or Walla Walla, will make this dish overly sweet. Be patient when caramelizing the onions in step 2; the entire process takes 45 to 60 minutes. Use broiler-safe crocks and keep the rims of the bowls 4 to 5 inches from the heating element to obtain a proper gratinée of melted, bubbly cheese. If using ordinary soup bowls, sprinkle the toasted bread slices with Gruyère and return them to the broiler until the cheese melts, then float them on top of the soup. For the best flavor, make the soup a day or two in advance. Alternatively, the onions can be prepared through step 1, cooled in the pot, and refrigerated for up to 3 days before proceeding with the recipe.

SOUP
- 3 tablespoons unsalted butter, cut into 3 pieces
- 4 pounds onions (about 6 large), halved pole to pole and sliced lengthwise ¼ inch thick (see note)
  Table salt
- 2 cups water, plus extra for deglazing
- ½ cup dry sherry
- 4 cups low-sodium chicken broth
- 2 cups beef broth
- 6 sprigs fresh thyme, tied together with kitchen twine
- 1 bay leaf
  Ground black pepper

CHEESE CROUTONS
- 1 small baguette, cut on the bias into ½-inch slices
- 8 ounces Gruyère cheese, shredded (about 2 cups)

1. FOR THE SOUP: Adjust an oven rack to the lower-middle position and heat the oven to 400 degrees. Generously spray the inside of a large (at least 7-quart) Dutch oven with vegetable oil spray. Add the butter, onions, and 1 teaspoon salt to the pot. Cook, covered, for 1 hour (the onions will be moist and slightly reduced in volume). Remove the pot from the oven and stir the onions, scraping the bottom and sides of the pot. Return the pot to the oven with the lid slightly ajar and continue to cook until the onions are very soft and golden brown, 1½ to 1¾ hours longer, stirring the onions and scraping the bottom and sides of the pot after 1 hour.

2. Carefully remove the pot from the oven and place over medium-high heat. Cook the onions, stirring frequently and scraping the bottom and sides of the pot, until the liquid evaporates and the onions brown, 15 to 20 minutes, reducing the heat to medium if the onions are browning too quickly. Continue to cook, stirring frequently, until the pot bottom is coated with a dark crust, 6 to 8 minutes, adjusting the heat as necessary. (Scrape any browned bits that collect on the spoon back into the onions.) Stir in ¼ cup water, scraping the pot bottom to loosen the crust, and cook until the water evaporates and the pot bottom has formed another dark crust, 6 to 8 minutes. Repeat the process of deglazing

2 to 3 more times, until the onions are very dark brown. Stir in the sherry and cook, stirring frequently, until the sherry evaporates, about 5 minutes.

3. Stir in 2 cups water, the chicken broth, beef broth, thyme, bay leaf, and ½ teaspoon salt, scraping up any final bits of browned crust on the bottom and sides of the pot. Increase the heat to high and bring to a simmer. Reduce the heat to low, cover, and simmer for 30 minutes. Remove and discard the thyme and bay leaf, then season with salt and pepper to taste.

4. FOR THE CROUTONS: While the soup simmers, heat the oven to 400 degrees. Arrange the baguette slices in a single layer on a rimmed baking sheet and bake until dry, crisp, and golden at the edges, about 10 minutes. Set aside.

5. Adjust an oven rack 6 inches from the broiler element and heat the broiler. Set individual broiler-safe crocks on the baking sheet and fill each with about 1¾ cups of the soup. Top each bowl with one or two baguette slices (do not overlap the slices) and sprinkle evenly with the Gruyère. Broil until the cheese is melted and bubbly around the edges, 3 to 5 minutes. Cool for 5 minutes; serve.

STREAMLINED FRENCH ONION SOUP

WHY THIS RECIPE WORKS: Streamlined versions of onion soup often amount to a sad crock of flavorless onions floating in super-salty beef bouillon topped with an oily blob of cheese. Or it might be just the opposite: a weak and watery affair. We wanted to make a better onion soup—a dark, rich broth, intensely flavored by an abundance of seriously cooked onions, covered by a broth-soaked crouton with a cheesy, crusty top—and we wanted to make it in record time.

We cheated from the get-go and created a simple broth with store-bought beef and chicken broths and wine. Red onions were chosen for their subtle complexity and nuance, and for the maximum flavor they offered when caramelized. Parsley, thyme, and a bay leaf rounded out the flavors and imparted freshness. To prevent the croutons from getting too soggy, we placed them atop the soup, so only the bottom was submerged. For the cheese, we liked a combination of pungent Swiss cheese topped with subdued Asiago; their flavors added some punch to our speedy but still irresistible soup.

Streamlined French Onion Soup

SERVES 6

Tie the parsley and thyme sprigs together with kitchen twine so they will be easy to retrieve from the soup pot. Use broiler-safe crocks and keep the rims of the bowls 4 to 5 inches from the heating element to obtain a proper gratinée of melted, bubbly cheese. If using ordinary soup bowls, top the toasted bread slices with the cheeses as directed in step 3 and return them to the broiler until the cheese melts, then float them on top of the soup.

SOUP

- 2 tablespoons unsalted butter
- 3 pounds red onions (about 6 medium), halved pole to pole and sliced crosswise ⅛ inch thick
  Table salt
- 6 cups low-sodium chicken broth
- 1¾ cups beef broth
- ¼ cup dry red wine
- 2 sprigs fresh parsley (see note)
- 1 sprig fresh thyme (see note)
- 1 bay leaf
- 1 tablespoon balsamic vinegar
  Ground black pepper

CHEESE CROUTONS

- 1 small baguette, cut on the bias into ½-inch slices
- 4½ ounces thinly sliced Swiss cheese
- 1½ ounces Asiago cheese, grated (about ¾ cup)

1. FOR THE SOUP: Melt the butter in a large Dutch oven over medium-high heat. Add the onions and ½ teaspoon salt and cook, stirring frequently, until the onions are reduced and syrupy and the inside of the pot is coated with a deep brown crust, 30 to 35 minutes. Add the chicken and beef broths, red wine, parsley, thyme, and bay leaf, scraping the pot bottom with a wooden spoon to loosen the browned bits, and bring to a simmer. Simmer to blend the flavors, about 20 minutes; discard the herbs. Stir in the balsamic vinegar and season with salt and pepper to taste. (The cooled soup can be refrigerated in an airtight container for up to 2 days; return to a simmer before finishing the soup with the croutons and cheese.)

2. FOR THE CROUTONS: Adjust an oven rack to the upper-middle position and heat the oven to 350 degrees. Arrange the baguette slices on a rimmed baking sheet and bake, turning once, until lightly browned, about 15 minutes. Remove the bread from the oven, carefully adjust an oven rack 6 inches from the broiler element, and heat the broiler.

3. Set individual broiler-safe crocks on the baking sheet and fill each with about 1½ cups of the soup. Top each bowl with two baguette slices and divide the Swiss cheese slices, placing them in a single layer, if possible, on the bread; sprinkle with 2 tablespoons of the grated Asiago and broil until the cheese is browned and bubbly around the edges, 7 to 10 minutes. Cool for 5 minutes; serve.

FRENCH POTATO SALAD

WHY THIS RECIPE WORKS: French potato salad is served warm or at room temperature and is composed of sliced potatoes glistening with olive oil, white wine vinegar, and plenty of fresh herbs. We wanted a potato salad that was not only pleasing to the eye but to the palate as well. The potatoes should be tender but not mushy, and the flavor of the vinaigrette should penetrate the relatively bland potatoes but not be oily or dull.

We learned the hard way that to prevent torn skins and broken slices, we had to slice the potatoes before boiling them. To tone down the flavor of harsh garlic, we blanched it before mixing the vinaigrette. A little extra vinegar—more than we would normally call for in a vinaigrette—added a pleasing sharpness, while some reserved potato water added just the right amount of moisture and saltiness to the salad. Dijon mustard combined with strong herbs also perked things up. Tossing the vinaigrette with the cooked potatoes led to mangled, shabby slices, but pouring the vinaigrette over the warm potatoes on a sheet pan, then folding in the other ingredients, kept the potato slices intact.

French Potato Salad

SERVES 4 TO 6

If fresh chervil isn't available, substitute an additional ½ tablespoon minced parsley and an additional ½ teaspoon minced tarragon. For best flavor, serve the salad warm, but to make ahead, follow the recipe through step 2, cover with plastic wrap, and refrigerate. Before serving, bring the salad to room temperature, then add the shallot and herbs.

- 2 pounds red potatoes (about 6 medium or 18 small), scrubbed and sliced ¼ inch thick
- 2 tablespoons table salt
- 1 medium garlic clove, peeled and threaded on a skewer
- ¼ cup olive oil
- 1½ tablespoons champagne vinegar or white wine vinegar
- 2 teaspoons Dijon mustard
- ½ teaspoon ground black pepper
- 1 small shallot, minced (about 1 tablespoon)
- 1 tablespoon minced fresh chervil leaves (see note)
- 1 tablespoon minced fresh parsley leaves
- 1 tablespoon minced fresh chives
- 1 teaspoon minced fresh tarragon leaves

1. Place the potatoes, 6 cups cold water, and the salt in a large saucepan. Bring to a boil over high heat, then their pure onion flavor, and cooking more evenly. We liked bacon, which acted as a crisp foil to the creamy filling, but we found a traditional custard with the bacon to be simply too rich. To resolve the issue, we reduced the number of eggs and switched out the cream for half-and-half. And to ensure the bacon stayed crisp, we sprinkled it on top of the custard. We tried several classic crust recipes, looking for one that had the intense butteriness of traditional tart dough but could still be easily patted into a tart pan. We found that using a food processor to cut cold butter completely into the flour mixture required less ice water than a conventional crust, which kept the dough firm enough to press into the pan.

reduce the heat to medium. Lower the skewered garlic into the simmering water and blanch, about 45 seconds. Immediately run the garlic under cold tap water to stop the cooking process; remove the garlic from the skewer and set aside. Simmer the potatoes, uncovered, until tender but still firm (a paring knife can be slipped into and out of the center of a potato slice with no resistance), about 5 minutes. Drain the potatoes, reserving ¼ cup cooking water. Arrange the hot potatoes close together in a single layer on a rimmed baking sheet.

2. Press the garlic through a garlic press or mince by hand. Whisk the garlic, reserved potato cooking water, oil, vinegar, mustard, and pepper together in a small bowl until combined. Drizzle the dressing evenly over the warm potato slices; let stand for 10 minutes.

3. Meanwhile, toss the shallot and herbs gently together in a small bowl. Transfer the potatoes to a large serving bowl. Add the shallot-herb mixture and mix lightly with a rubber spatula to combine. Serve immediately.

FRENCH ONION TART

WHY THIS RECIPE WORKS: French onion tart is similar to quiche but delivers a more refined slice of pie, with more onions than custard. But re-creating this tart at home can produce a tough and crackery crust, which is doubly disappointing after spending long hours delicately cooking the onions, making the custard, and baking the whole thing together. We wanted to simplify the crust and shorten the overall preparation time.

We found that our onions would cook in half the usual time if we left the lid on the skillet throughout cooking. And covering the onions allowed them to cook entirely in their own juices, thereby becoming tender, retaining

French Onion and Bacon Tart

SERVES 6 TO 8

Either yellow or white onions work well in this recipe, but stay away from sweet onions, such as Vidalias, which will make the tart watery. Use a 9-inch tinned-steel tart pan; see page 721 for our recommended brand. This tart can be served hot or at room temperature and pairs well with a green salad as a main course.

CRUST

1¼ cups (6¼ ounces) unbleached all-purpose flour
1 tablespoon sugar
½ teaspoon table salt
8 tablespoons (1 stick) unsalted butter, cut into ½-inch cubes and chilled
2–3 tablespoons ice water

FILLING

4 ounces bacon (about 4 slices), halved lengthwise and cut crosswise into ¼-inch pieces
Vegetable oil, as needed
1½ pounds onions (about 3 medium), halved pole to pole and cut crosswise into ¼-inch slices (about 6 cups; see note)
¾ teaspoon table salt
1 sprig fresh thyme
2 large eggs
½ cup half-and-half
¼ teaspoon ground black pepper

1. FOR THE CRUST: Spray a 9-inch tart pan with a removable bottom with vegetable oil spray; set aside. Pulse the flour, sugar, and salt together in a food processor until combined, about 4 pulses. Scatter the butter pieces over the flour mixture and pulse until the mixture resembles coarse sand, about 15 pulses. Add 2 tablespoons of the ice water and continue to process until large clumps of dough form and no powdery bits remain, about 5 seconds. If the dough doesn't clump, add the remaining 1 tablespoon water and pulse to incorporate, about 4 pulses. Transfer the dough to the greased tart pan and, working outward from the center, pat the dough into an even layer, sealing any cracks. Working around the edge, press the dough firmly into the corners of the pan and up the sides, using your thumb to level off the top edge. Lay plastic wrap over the dough and smooth out any bumps or shallow areas. Place the tart shell on a plate and freeze for 30 minutes.

2. Adjust an oven rack to the middle position and heat the oven to 375 degrees. Place the frozen tart shell (still in the tart pan) on a rimmed baking sheet. Gently press a piece of extra-wide heavy-duty foil that has been sprayed with vegetable oil spray against the dough and over the edges of the tart pan. Fill the shell with pie weights and bake until the top edge of the dough just starts to color and the surface of dough under the foil no longer looks wet, about 30 minutes. Remove the tart shell from the oven and carefully remove the weights and foil. Return the baking sheet with the tart shell to the oven and continue to bake, uncovered, until golden brown, 5 to 10 minutes. Set the baking sheet with the tart shell on a wire rack to cool while making the filling. (Do not turn off the oven.)

3. FOR THE FILLING: While the crust is baking, cook the bacon in a 12-inch nonstick skillet over medium heat until browned and crisp, 8 to 10 minutes. Using a slotted spoon, transfer the bacon to a paper towel–lined plate; set aside. Pour off all but 2 tablespoons bacon fat from the skillet (or add vegetable oil if needed to make this amount).

4. Add the onions, salt, and thyme to the skillet. Cover and cook until the onions release their liquid and start to wilt, about 10 minutes. Reduce the heat to low and continue to cook, covered, until the onions are very soft, about 20 minutes, stirring once or twice (if after 15 minutes the onions look wet, remove the lid and continue to cook for another 5 minutes). Remove the pan from the heat and cool for 5 minutes.

5. Whisk the eggs, half-and-half, and pepper together in a large bowl. Remove the thyme from the onions; discard. Stir the onions into the egg mixture until just incorporated. Spread the onion mixture over the bottom of the baked crust and sprinkle the reserved bacon evenly on top.

6. Bake the tart on the baking sheet until the center of the tart feels firm to the touch, 20 to 25 minutes. Set the baking sheet with the tart on a wire rack and cool for at least 10 minutes. Remove the tart pan ring, gently slide a thin-bladed spatula between the pan bottom and crust to loosen, and slide the tart onto a serving plate. Cut into wedges and serve.

PISSALADIÈRE

WHY THIS RECIPE WORKS: *Pissaladière,* the classic olive, anchovy, and onion tart from Provence, is easy enough to prepare, but each ingredient must be handled carefully. We wanted to harmonize the onions, olives, and anchovies with a crisp crust to produce a tart worthy of the finest bakery in Nice.

We made the dough in a food processor and kneaded it as little as possible to create a pizza-like dough with a cracker-like exterior and a decently chewy crumb, a dough with the structure to stand up to the heavy toppings. Bread flour was our flour of choice as it has more protein than all-purpose flour, and that translates to a more substantial chew. Using a combination of high and low heat to cook the onions—starting the onions on high to release their juices and soften them, then turning the heat to medium-low to caramelize them—gave us perfectly browned and caramelized, but not burnt, onions. Adding a bit of water before spreading them on the crust kept them from clumping. We placed the onions on top of the chopped black olives, anchovies (also chopped; whole anchovies were too overpowering), and fresh thyme leaves to protect them from burning in the oven. Diehard fish lovers can add more anchovies as a garnish if desired.

Pissaladière

MAKES 2 TARTS, SERVING 6

For the best flavor, use high-quality oil-packed anchovies; in a tasting, Ortiz was our favorite brand (see page 735). If desired, you can slow down the dough's rising time by letting it rise in the refrigerator for 8 to 16 hours in step 1; let the refrigerated dough soften at room temperature for 30 minutes before using. The caramelized onions can also be made a day ahead and refrigerated.

DOUGH

- 2 cups (11 ounces) bread flour, plus extra for dusting the work surface
- 1 teaspoon instant or rapid-rise yeast
- 1 teaspoon table salt
- 1 tablespoon olive oil, plus extra for brushing the dough and greasing hands
- 1 cup warm water (110 degrees)

CARAMELIZED ONIONS

- 2 tablespoons olive oil
- 2 pounds onions (about 4 medium), halved and sliced ¼ inch thick
- 1 teaspoon brown sugar
- ½ teaspoon table salt
- 1 tablespoon water

OLIVES, ANCHOVIES, AND GARNISHES

- Olive oil
- ½ teaspoon ground black pepper
- ½ cup niçoise olives, pitted and chopped coarse
- 8 anchovy fillets, rinsed, patted dry, and chopped coarse (about 2 tablespoons), plus 12 fillets, rinsed and patted dry for garnish (optional; see note)
- 2 teaspoons minced fresh thyme leaves
- 1 teaspoon fennel seeds (optional)
- 1 tablespoon minced fresh parsley leaves (optional)

1. FOR THE DOUGH: Pulse the flour, yeast, and salt in a food processor (fitted with a dough blade, if possible) until combined, about 5 pulses. With the machine running, slowly add the oil, then the water, through the feed tube; continue to process until the dough forms a ball, about 15 seconds. Turn the dough out onto a lightly floured work surface and form it into a smooth, round ball. Place the dough in a large lightly oiled bowl and cover tightly with greased plastic wrap. Let rise in a warm place until doubled in volume, 1 to 1½ hours.

2. FOR THE CARAMELIZED ONIONS: While the dough is rising, heat the oil in a 12-inch nonstick skillet over medium-low heat until shimmering. Stir in the onions, sugar, and salt. Cover and cook, stirring occasionally, until the onions are softened and have released their juice, about 10 minutes. Remove the lid, increase the heat to medium-high, and continue to cook, stirring often, until the onions are deeply browned, 10 to 15 minutes. Off the heat, stir in the water, then transfer the onions to a bowl and set aside. Adjust the oven rack to the lowest position, set a baking stone on the rack, and heat the oven to 500 degrees. (Let the baking stone heat for at least 30 minutes but no longer than 1 hour.)

3. TO SHAPE, TOP, AND BAKE THE DOUGH: Turn the dough out onto a lightly floured work surface, divide it into two equal pieces, and cover with greased plastic wrap. Working with one piece at a time (keep the other piece covered), form each piece into a rough ball by gently pulling the edges of the dough together and pinching to seal. With floured hands, turn the dough ball seam side down. Cupping the dough with both hands, gently push the dough in a circular motion to form a taut ball. Repeat with the second piece. Brush each piece lightly with oil, cover with plastic wrap, and let rest for 10 minutes. Meanwhile, cut two 20-inch lengths of parchment paper and set aside.

4. Coat your fingers and palms generously with oil. Working with one piece of dough at a time, hold the dough up and gently stretch it to a 12-inch length. Place the dough on the parchment sheet and gently dimple the surface of the dough with your fingertips. Using your oiled palms, push and flatten the dough into a 14 by 8-inch oval. Brush the dough with oil and sprinkle with ¼ teaspoon of the pepper. Leaving a ½-inch border around the edge, sprinkle ¼ cup of the olives, 1 tablespoon of the chopped anchovies, and 1 teaspoon of the thyme evenly over the dough, then evenly scatter with half of the onions. Arrange 6 whole anchovy fillets (if using) on the tart and sprinkle with ½ teaspoon of the fennel seeds (if using). Slip the parchment with the tart onto a pizza peel (or inverted baking sheet), then slide it onto the hot baking stone. Bake until deep golden brown, 13 to 15 minutes. While the first tart bakes, shape and top the second tart.

5. Remove the first tart from the oven with a peel (or pull the parchment onto a baking sheet). Transfer the tart to a cutting board and slide the parchment out from under the tart; cool for 5 minutes. While the first tart cools, bake the second tart. Sprinkle with the parsley (if using) and cut each tart into 8 pieces before serving.

SUMMER VEGETABLE GRATIN

WHY THIS RECIPE WORKS: Layering summer's best vegetables into a gratin can lead to a memorable side dish—or a soggy mess. Juicy summer vegetables like zucchini and tomatoes can exude a torrent of liquid that washes away flavors and turns the dish squishy and soggy. We wanted a simple, Provençal-style vegetable gratin, where a golden brown, cheesy topping provides a rich contrast to the fresh, bright flavor of the vegetables.

To start, we chose our vegetables. The typical combination of tomatoes, zucchini, and summer squash won out (eggplant was too mushy and bell peppers took on a steamed flavor). To eliminate excess moisture, we baked the casserole uncovered, after salting the vegetables. Salting worked like a charm to both season and dry out the zucchini and summer squash, but proved insufficient to deal with all the tomato juice. While we could remove the watery jelly and seeds from the tomatoes, the jelly was crucial for full tomato flavor. We moved the tomatoes to the top gratin layer, which allowed them to roast and caramelize. The roasting not only eliminated moisture but also added flavor, especially when drizzled with an aromatic garlic-thyme oil. Finally, for more complexity, we added a layer of caramelized onions between the zucchini/squash and tomato layers and sprinkled the dish with Parmesan bread crumbs before baking.

Summer Vegetable Gratin

SERVES 6 TO 8

The success of this recipe depends on good-quality produce. Buy zucchini and summer squash of roughly the same diameter. We like the visual contrast zucchini and summer squash bring to the dish, but you can also use just one or the other. A similarly sized ovensafe gratin dish can be substituted for the 13 by 9-inch baking dish. Serve the gratin alongside grilled fish or meat, accompanied by bread to soak up any flavorful juices.

- 6 tablespoons extra-virgin olive oil
- 1 pound zucchini, ends trimmed and cut crosswise into ¼-inch-thick slices (see note)
- 1 pound yellow summer squash, ends trimmed and cut crosswise into ¼-inch-thick slices (see note)
- 2 teaspoons table salt
- 1½ pounds ripe tomatoes (3 to 4 large), cut into ¼-inch-thick slices
- 2 medium onions, halved pole to pole and sliced thin (about 3 cups)
- ¾ teaspoon ground black pepper
- 2 medium garlic cloves, minced or pressed through a garlic press (about 2 teaspoons)
- 1 tablespoon minced fresh thyme leaves
- 1 slice high-quality white sandwich bread, torn into quarters
- 2 ounces grated Parmesan cheese (about 1 cup)
- 2 medium shallots, minced (about 6 tablespoons)
- ¼ cup chopped fresh basil leaves

1. Adjust an oven rack to the upper-middle position and heat the oven to 400 degrees. Brush a 13 by 9-inch baking dish with 1 tablespoon of the oil; set aside.

2. Toss the zucchini and summer squash slices with 1 teaspoon of the salt in a large bowl; transfer to a colander set over a bowl. Let stand until the zucchini and squash release at least 3 tablespoons of liquid, about 45 minutes. Arrange the slices on a triple layer of paper towels; cover with another triple layer of paper towels. Firmly press each slice to remove as much liquid as possible.

3. Place the tomato slices in a single layer on a double layer of paper towels and sprinkle evenly with ½ teaspoon more salt; let stand for 30 minutes. Place a second double layer of paper towels on top of the tomatoes and press firmly to dry the tomatoes.

4. Meanwhile, heat 1 tablespoon more oil in a 12-inch nonstick skillet over medium heat until shimmering. Add the onions, the remaining ½ teaspoon salt, and ¼ teaspoon of the pepper; cook, stirring occasionally, until the onions are softened and dark golden brown, 20 to 25 minutes. Set the onions aside.

5. Combine the garlic, 3 tablespoons more oil, the remaining ½ teaspoon pepper, and the thyme in a small bowl. In a large bowl, toss the zucchini and summer squash in half of the oil mixture, then arrange in the greased baking dish. Arrange the caramelized onions in an even layer over the squash. Slightly overlap the tomato slices in a single layer on top of the onions. Spoon the remaining garlic-oil mixture evenly over the tomatoes. Bake until the vegetables are tender and the tomatoes are starting to brown on the edges, 40 to 45 minutes.

6. Meanwhile, process the bread in a food processor until finely ground, about 10 seconds. (You should have about 1 cup crumbs.) Combine the bread crumbs, remaining 1 tablespoon oil, the Parmesan, and shallots in a medium bowl. Remove the baking dish from the oven and increase the heat to 450 degrees. Sprinkle the breadcrumb mixture evenly on top of the tomatoes. Bake the gratin until bubbling and the cheese is lightly browned, 5 to 10 minutes. Sprinkle with the basil and cool for 10 minutes before serving.

SIMPLIFIED POTATO GALETTE

WHY THIS RECIPE WORKS: Pommes Anna, the classic French potato cake (or galette) in which thinly sliced potatoes are tossed with butter, tightly shingled in a skillet, and cooked slowly on the stovetop, delivers showstopping results, but it requires so much labor and time that we're willing to make it only once a year. We wanted a potato galette with a crisp, deeply bronzed crust encasing a creamy center that tastes of earthy potatoes and

sweet butter—and we wanted one we could make on a weeknight.

We started by neatly arranging just the first layer of potatoes in the skillet, then casually packed the rest of the potatoes into the pan; once the galette was inverted onto the plate, only the tidy layer was visible. We swapped the traditional cast-iron skillet for a nonstick pan and achieved superior browning by starting the galette on the stovetop, then transferring it to the bottom rack of the oven. For a galette that held together but wasn't gluey, we rinsed the potatoes to rid them of excess starch, then incorporated a little cornstarch for just the right amount of adhesion. And in lieu of occasionally tamping down on the galette during cooking as in traditional recipes, we simply filled a cake pan with pie weights and set it on the galette for a portion of the baking time.

Simplified Potato Galette
SERVES 6 TO 8

For the potato cake to hold together, it is important to slice the potatoes no more than ⅛ inch thick and to make sure the slices are thoroughly dried before assembling the cake. Use a mandoline slicer or the slicing attachment of a food processor to slice the potatoes uniformly thin. A pound of dried beans, rice, or coins can be substituted for the pie weights. You will need a 10-inch ovensafe nonstick skillet for this recipe.

- 2½ pounds Yukon Gold potatoes, sliced ⅛ inch thick
- 5 tablespoons unsalted butter, melted
- 1 tablespoon cornstarch
- 1½ teaspoons chopped fresh rosemary leaves (optional)
- 1 teaspoon table salt
- ½ teaspoon ground black pepper

1. Adjust an oven rack to the lowest position and heat the oven to 450 degrees. Place the potatoes in a large bowl and fill with cold water. Using your hands, swirl to remove excess starch, drain, then spread the potatoes onto kitchen towels and dry thoroughly.

2. Whisk 4 tablespoons of the butter, the cornstarch, rosemary (if using), salt, and pepper together in a large bowl. Add the dried potatoes and toss to thoroughly coat. Place the remaining 1 tablespoon butter in a 10-inch ovensafe nonstick skillet and swirl to coat. Place 1 potato slice in the center of the skillet, then overlap slices in a circle around the center slice, followed by an outer circle of overlapping slices. Gently place the remaining sliced potatoes on top of the first layer, arranging so they form an even thickness.

3. Place the skillet over medium-high heat and cook until sizzling and the potatoes around the edge of the skillet start to turn translucent, about 5 minutes. Spray a 12-inch square of aluminum foil with vegetable oil spray. Place the foil, sprayed side down, on top of the potatoes. Place a 9-inch cake pan on top of the foil and fill with 2 cups pie weights. Firmly press down on the cake pan to compress the potatoes. Transfer the skillet to the oven and bake for 20 minutes.

4. Remove the cake pan and the foil from the skillet. Continue to bake until the potatoes are tender when a paring knife is inserted in the center, 20 to 25 minutes. Return the skillet to the stovetop and cook over medium heat, gently shaking the pan, until the galette releases from the sides of the pan, 2 to 3 minutes.

5. Following the photos, invert the galette onto a cutting board. Using a serrated knife, gently cut into wedges and serve immediately.

NOTES FROM THE TEST KITCHEN

INVERTING A GALETTE

1. Using a spatula, loosen the galette and slide it out of the skillet onto a large plate.

2. Gently place a cutting board over the galette. Do not use an overly heavy board, which may crush the cake.

3. Flip the plate over so the board is on the bottom. Remove the plate, and the galette is ready to be sliced and served.

POMMES ANNA

WHY THIS RECIPE WORKS: Traditional *pommes Anna* is rarely seen on home or restaurant menus these days because it takes an inordinately long time to compose, and it is hard to remove cleanly from the pan, resulting in an unsatisfactory time-consuming and messy dish. We wanted a foolproof, elegant potato cake with a crisp, deep brown crust covering the soft, creamy potato layers within.

We used a nonstick skillet to ensure easy release of our potatoes. Most recipes for pommes Anna call for clarified butter, but we decided to cut down on time and waste (a good portion of the butter is lost with clarifying) and instead tossed the sliced potatoes with melted butter. To accelerate cooking, we arranged the potatoes in the skillet as it was heating on the stovetop; when we were done layering the slices, we pressed the potatoes with the bottom of a cake pan to compact them into a cohesive cake. To unmold, we simply inverted the potato cake onto a baking sheet and then slid it onto a serving dish.

Pommes Anna

SERVES 6 TO 8

Use a food processor fitted with a fine slicing disk or a mandoline to slice the potatoes, but do not slice them until you are ready to start assembling; see page 709 for our recommended mandoline. Remember to start timing when you begin arranging the potatoes in the skillet; they will need 30 minutes on the stovetop to brown properly no matter how quickly you arrange them.

> 3 **pounds russet or Yukon Gold potatoes (about**
> **6 medium), peeled and sliced ⅛ inch thick (see note)**
> 5 **tablespoons unsalted butter, melted**
> ¼ **cup vegetable oil or peanut oil**
> **Table salt and ground black pepper**

1. Adjust an oven rack to the lower-middle position and heat the oven to 450 degrees. Toss the potatoes with the butter to coat.

2. Heat the oil in an ovensafe 10-inch nonstick skillet over medium-low heat. Begin timing, and arrange the potato slices in the skillet, using the most attractive slices to form the bottom layer, by placing one slice in the center of the skillet and overlapping more slices in a circle around the center slice; form another circle of overlapping slices to cover the pan bottom. Season with ¼ teaspoon salt and pepper to taste. Arrange the second layer of potatoes, working in the opposite direction of the first layer; season with ¼ teaspoon salt and pepper to taste. Repeat, layering the potatoes in opposite directions and seasoning with ¼ teaspoon salt and pepper to taste, until no slices remain (broken or uneven slices can be pieced together to form a single slice; potatoes will mound in the center of the skillet). Continue to cook until 30 minutes elapse from when you began arranging the potatoes in the skillet.

3. Using the bottom of a 9-inch cake pan, press on the potatoes firmly to compact. Cover the skillet and place in the oven; bake until the potatoes begin to soften, about 15 minutes. Uncover and continue to bake until the potatoes are tender when pierced with the tip of a paring knife and the edge of the potatoes near the skillet is browned, about 10 minutes longer. Meanwhile, line a rimless baking sheet or an inverted rimmed baking sheet with foil and spray lightly with vegetable oil spray. Carefully drain off the excess fat from the potatoes by pressing the bottom of the cake pan against the potatoes while tilting the skillet. (Be sure to use heavy potholders.)

4. Set the baking sheet, foil side down, on top of the skillet. Using potholders, hold the baking sheet in place with one hand and carefully invert the skillet and baking sheet together. Lift the skillet off the potatoes; slide the potatoes from the baking sheet onto a platter. Cut into wedges and serve immediately.

FRENCH-STYLE MASHED POTATOES

WHY THIS RECIPE WORKS: *Aligot* is French cookery's intensely rich, cheesy take on mashed potatoes. These potatoes get their elastic, satiny texture through prolonged, vigorous stirring—which can easily go awry and lead to a gluey, sticky mess. We wanted to create cheesy, garlicky mashed potatoes with a smooth, elastic texture and the same signature stretch as the French original.

After making aligot with different potatoes, we found medium-starch Yukon Golds to be the clear winner, yielding a puree with a mild, buttery flavor and a light, creamy consistency. We boiled the potatoes, then used a food processor to "mash" them. Traditional aligot uses butter and crème fraîche to add flavor and creaminess and loosen the texture before mixing in the cheese. But crème fraîche isn't always easy to find, so we substituted whole milk, which provided depth without going overboard. For the cheese, a combination of mild

mozzarella and nutty Gruyère proved just right. As for the stirring, we needed to monitor the consistency closely: too much stirring and the aligot turned rubbery, too little and the cheese didn't marry with the potatoes for that essential elasticity.

French Mashed Potatoes with Cheese and Garlic (Aligot)

SERVES 6

The finished potatoes should have a smooth and slightly elastic texture. White cheddar can be substituted for the Gruyère. For richer, stretchier aligot, double the mozzarella.

- **2 pounds Yukon Gold potatoes (about 4 medium), peeled, cut into ½-inch-thick slices, rinsed well, and drained**
- **Table salt**
- **6 tablespoons (¾ stick) unsalted butter**
- **2 medium garlic cloves, minced or pressed through a garlic press (about 2 teaspoons)**
- **1–1½ cups whole milk**
- **4 ounces mozzarella cheese, shredded (about 1 cup; see note)**
- **4 ounces Gruyère cheese, shredded (about 1 cup; see note)**
- **Ground black pepper**

1. Place the potatoes and 1 tablespoon salt in a large saucepan; add water to cover by 1 inch. Partially cover the saucepan with a lid and bring to a boil over high heat. Reduce the heat to medium-low and simmer until the potatoes are tender and just break apart when poked with a fork, 12 to 17 minutes. Drain the potatoes and dry the saucepan.

2. Add the potatoes, butter, garlic, and 1½ teaspoons salt to a food processor. Pulse until the butter is melted and incorporated, about 10 pulses. Add 1 cup of the milk and continue to process until the potatoes are smooth and creamy, about 20 seconds, scraping down the sides of the workbowl halfway through.

3. Return the potato mixture to the saucepan and set over medium heat. Stir in the cheeses, 1 cup at a time, until incorporated. Continue to cook the potatoes, stirring vigorously, until the cheese is fully melted and the mixture is smooth and elastic, 3 to 5 minutes. If the mixture is difficult to stir and seems thick, stir in 2 tablespoons milk at a time (up to ½ cup) until the potatoes are loose and creamy. Season with salt and pepper to taste. Serve immediately.

POTATOES LYONNAISE

WHY THIS RECIPE WORKS: Originally conceived as a way to use up leftover boiled potatoes, *potatoes Lyonnaise* came to represent the best of classic French bistro cuisine: buttery, browned potato slices with strands of sweet, caramelized onion and fresh parsley—a simple yet complex skillet potato dish. Sadly, many versions are greasy and heavy rather than rich and complex. We wanted a return to the original elegant, buttery potato and onion dish—but one that didn't require leftover potatoes to make.

First, we had to choose the right potato. Yukon Golds beat out high-starch russets and low-starch Red Bliss. We precooked the potatoes in the microwave so that, once added to the skillet, they would cook through in the time they took to brown (without the microwave, the potatoes charred on the outside before cooking through). While the potatoes were in the microwave, we cooked the onions just long enough to release moisture and cook in their own juices. To finish the dish, we united the onions and potatoes in a brief sauté for the perfect melding of flavors. A sprinkling of minced parsley gave the dish a fresh taste and bright color.

Potatoes Lyonnaise

SERVES 4

Toss the potatoes halfway through the microwave session to prevent uneven cooking. If using a lightweight skillet, you will need to stir the potatoes more frequently to prevent burning.

- 3 tablespoons unsalted butter
- 1 large onion, halved pole to pole and sliced ¼ inch thick (about 3 cups)
- ½ teaspoon table salt
- 2 tablespoons water
- 1½ pounds Yukon Gold potatoes (about 3 medium), peeled and sliced crosswise into ¼-inch rounds
- ¼ teaspoon ground black pepper
- 1 tablespoon minced fresh parsley leaves

1. Melt 1 tablespoon of the butter in a 12-inch heavy nonstick skillet over medium-high heat. Add the onion and ¼ teaspoon of the salt and stir to coat; cook, stirring occasionally, until the onion begins to soften, about 3 minutes. Reduce the heat to medium and cook, covered, stirring occasionally, until the onion is light brown and soft, about 12 minutes longer, deglazing with the water when the pan gets dry, about halfway through the cooking time. Transfer to a bowl and cover. Do not wash the skillet.

2. While the onion cooks, microwave 1 tablespoon more butter on high power in a large microwave-safe bowl until melted, about 15 seconds. Add the potatoes to the bowl and toss to coat with the melted butter. Microwave on high power until the potatoes just start to turn tender, about 6 minutes, tossing halfway through the cooking time. Toss the potatoes again and set aside.

3. Melt the remaining 1 tablespoon butter in the now-empty skillet over medium-high heat. Add the potatoes and shake the skillet to distribute evenly. Cook, without stirring, until browned on the bottom, about 3 minutes. Using a spatula, stir the potatoes carefully and continue to cook, stirring every 2 to 3 minutes, until the potatoes are well browned and tender when pierced with the tip of a paring knife, 8 to 10 minutes more. Season with the remaining salt and the pepper.

4. Add the onion back to the skillet and stir to combine. Cook until the onion is heated through and the flavors have melded, 1 to 2 minutes. Transfer to a large plate, sprinkle with the parsley, and serve.

CHICKEN FRICASSEE

WHY THIS RECIPE WORKS: In search of a streamlined technique that would give this classic French braise weeknight potential and a brighter, more complex sauce, we replaced the bone-in chicken parts with the busy cook's favorite timesaver: boneless, skinless breasts and thighs. Then we found two ways to add back the richness that we'd lost by omitting the skin and bones: We browned the meat in a combination of butter and oil, and we browned the vegetables until they developed their own fond to serve as the base of the sauce. Increasing the amount of glutamate-rich mushrooms boosted the fricassee's meaty flavor, while finishing the sauce with sour cream added body and pleasant tang. Finally, whisking an egg yolk into the sour cream thickened the sauce and made it incredibly silky.

Quick Chicken Fricassee

SERVES 4 TO 6

Two tablespoons of chopped fresh parsley leaves may be substituted for the tarragon in this recipe.

2	pounds boneless, skinless chicken breasts and/or thighs, trimmed
	Table salt and ground black pepper
1	tablespoon unsalted butter
1	tablespoon olive oil
1	pound cremini mushrooms, trimmed and sliced ¼ inch thick
1	medium onion, chopped fine
¼	cup dry white wine
1	tablespoon unbleached all-purpose flour
1	medium garlic clove, minced or pressed through a garlic press (about 1 teaspoon)
1½	cups low-sodium chicken broth
⅓	cup sour cream
1	large egg yolk
2	teaspoons juice from 1 lemon
2	teaspoons minced fresh tarragon leaves
½	teaspoon freshly grated nutmeg

1. Pat the chicken dry with paper towels and season with 1 teaspoon salt and ½ teaspoon pepper. Heat the butter and oil in a 12-inch skillet over medium-high heat until the butter is melted. Place the chicken in a skillet and cook until browned, about 4 minutes. Using tongs, flip the chicken and cook until browned on the second side, about 4 minutes longer. Transfer the chicken to a large plate.

2. Add the mushrooms, onion, and wine to the now-empty skillet and cook, stirring occasionally, until the liquid has evaporated and the mushrooms are browned, 8 to 10 minutes. Add the flour and garlic; cook, stirring constantly, for 1 minute. Add the broth and bring the mixture to a boil, scraping up the browned bits from the bottom of the pan. Add the chicken and any accumulated juices to the skillet. Reduce the heat to medium-low, cover, and simmer until the breasts register 160 to 165 degrees and the thighs register 175 degrees on an instant-read thermometer, 5 to 10 minutes.

3. Transfer the chicken to a clean platter and tent loosely with foil. Whisk the sour cream and the egg yolk together in a medium bowl. Whisking constantly, slowly stir ½ cup of the hot sauce from the skillet into the sour cream mixture to temper. Stirring constantly, slowly pour the sour cream mixture into the simmering sauce. Stir in the lemon juice, tarragon and nutmeg; return to a simmer. Season with salt and pepper to taste, pour the sauce over the chicken, and serve.

STUFFED CHICKEN BREASTS

WHY THIS RECIPE WORKS: Most American cooks stuff chicken breasts with cheesy, bready fillings. French chefs, on the other hand, use a forcemeat stuffing to transform ordinary chicken breasts into a four-star affair. The French technique requires some serious labor, and includes skinning and boning a whole chicken, stuffing the breasts with the leg meat, and wrapping them up in the skin. We wanted to achieve the same flavorful package of chicken and filling—using a much simpler procedure.

Starting with boneless, skinless chicken breasts eliminated the need to bone a whole chicken. We mimicked a forcemeat stuffing by trimming a bit of meat from each chicken breast, and combining the meat with mushrooms, herbs, and leeks. Pureeing the meat trimmings created a cohesive filling that stayed put inside the chicken breasts.

Turning to the mechanics, we needed to create easy-to-roll rectangles of chicken breast to encase the stuffing. After butterflying the chicken breasts, we pounded them thin and trimmed them into a rectangular shape. The stuffing was easy to spread on the breasts, which we simply rolled up and tied with twine. Finally, we browned the chicken in a hot skillet and then added chicken broth and wine to braise the meat in the pan. Not only did the chicken stay tender when simmered, but the liquid served as a base for a simple yet intensely flavored pan sauce.

French-Style Stuffed Chicken Breasts
SERVES 4

To make slicing the chicken easier, freeze it for 15 minutes. If your chicken breasts come with the tenderloins attached, pull them off and reserve them to make the puree (along with the breast meat you will trim in step 1). Because the stuffing contains raw chicken, it is important to check its temperature in step 5.

CHICKEN AND STUFFING
- 4 (7 to 8-ounce) boneless, skinless chicken breasts, tenderloins removed and breasts trimmed (see note)
- 3 tablespoons vegetable oil
- 10 ounces white mushrooms, wiped clean and sliced thin
- 1 small leek, white part only, chopped and rinsed thoroughly (about 1 cup)
- 2 medium garlic cloves, minced or pressed through a garlic press (about 2 teaspoons)
- ½ teaspoon minced fresh thyme leaves
- 1 tablespoon juice from 1 lemon
- ½ cup dry white wine
- 1 tablespoon minced fresh parsley leaves
  Table salt and ground black pepper
- 1 cup low-sodium chicken broth

SAUCE
- 1 teaspoon Dijon mustard
- 2 tablespoons unsalted butter
  Table salt and ground black pepper

1. FOR THE CHICKEN AND STUFFING: Following the photos on page 327, butterfly the chicken horizontally, stopping ½ inch from the edges so the halves remain attached, then open up each breast, cover with plastic wrap, and pound the cutlets to an even ¼-inch thickness (each cutlet should measure about 8 by 6 inches). Trim about ½ inch from the long sides of the cutlets (1½ to 2 ounces of meat per cutlet, or a total of ½ cup from all 4 cutlets) to form rectangles that measure about 8 by 5 inches. Process all the trimmings in a food processor until smooth, about 20 seconds. Transfer the puree to a medium bowl and set aside. (Do not wash the food processor bowl.)

2. Heat 1 tablespoon of the oil in a 12-inch skillet over medium-high heat until shimmering. Add the mushrooms and cook, stirring occasionally, until all the moisture has evaporated and the mushrooms are golden brown, 8 to 11 minutes. Add 1 tablespoon more oil and the leek; continue to cook, stirring frequently, until softened, 2 to 4 minutes. Add the garlic and thyme and cook until fragrant, about 30 seconds. Add 1½ teaspoons of the lemon juice and cook until all the moisture has evaporated, about 30 seconds. Transfer the mixture to the bowl of the food processor. Return the pan to the heat, add the wine, and scrape the pan bottom to loosen any browned bits. Transfer the wine to a small bowl and set aside. Rinse and dry the skillet.

3. Pulse the mushroom mixture in the food processor until roughly chopped, about 5 pulses. Transfer the mushroom mixture to the bowl with the pureed chicken. Add 1½ teaspoons of the parsley, ¾ teaspoon salt, and ½ teaspoon pepper. Using a rubber spatula, fold together the stuffing ingredients until well combined (you should have about 1½ cups stuffing).

4. Spread one-quarter of the stuffing evenly over each cutlet with a rubber spatula, leaving a ¾-inch border along the short sides of the cutlet and a ¼-inch border along the long sides. Roll each breast up as tightly as possible without squeezing out the filling and place seam side down. Evenly space three pieces of kitchen twine (each about 12 inches long) beneath each breast and tie, trimming any excess.

5. Season the chicken with salt and pepper. Heat the remaining 1 tablespoon oil in the skillet over medium-high heat until just smoking. Add the chicken bundles and brown on all four sides, about 2 minutes per side. Add the broth and reserved wine to the pan and bring to a boil. Reduce the heat to low, cover the pan, and cook until the center of the chicken registers 160 to 165 degrees on an instant-read thermometer, 12 to 18 minutes. Transfer the chicken to a carving board and tent loosely with foil.

6. FOR THE SAUCE: While the chicken rests, whisk the mustard into the cooking liquid. Increase the heat to high and simmer, scraping the pan bottom to loosen the browned bits, until dark brown and reduced to ½ cup, 7 to 10 minutes. Off the heat, whisk in the butter and the remaining 1½ teaspoons parsley and 1½ teaspoons lemon juice; season with salt and pepper to taste. Remove the twine and cut each chicken bundle on the bias into six medallions. Spoon the sauce over the chicken and serve.

NOTES FROM THE TEST KITCHEN

STUFFING CHICKEN BREASTS

1. Slice each breast horizontally, stopping ½ inch from the edges so the halves remain attached.

2. Open up each breast, cover it with plastic wrap, and pound it to an even ¼-inch thickness.

3. Trim about ½ inch from the long side of each cutlet to form an 8 by 5-inch rectangle. Reserve the trimmings for the stuffing.

4. Spread the stuffing evenly over each cutlet, leaving a ¾-inch border along the short sides and a ¼-inch border along the long sides.

5. With the short side facing you, roll up each cutlet and secure it snugly with kitchen twine.

COQ AU VIN

WHY THIS RECIPE WORKS: Although conventional recipes for *coq au vin* take upwards of three hours to prepare, we felt that this rustic dish shouldn't be so time-consuming. After all, it's basically a chicken fricassee. We wanted to create a dish with tender, juicy chicken infused with the flavors of red wine, onions, mushrooms, and bacon in under two hours.

We decided to use chicken parts; this way, we could pick the parts we liked best. If using a mix of dark and white meat, we found it's essential to start the dark before the white, so that all the meat finishes cooking at the same time and nothing is overcooked or undercooked. To thicken the stewing liquid, we sprinkled flour over the sautéed vegetables and whisked in butter toward the end of cooking; the butter also provided a nice richness in the sauce. Chicken broth added a savory note to the sauce and gave it some body; an entire bottle of red wine provided a great base of flavor. Tomato paste was a fuss-free way to add extra depth and body to the sauce, while a sprinkling of crisp, salty bacon rounded out the acidity of the wine.

Coq au Vin

SERVES 4

Use any $10 bottle of fruity, medium-bodied red wine, such as Pinot Noir, Côtes du Rhône, or Zinfandel. If using both chicken breasts and thighs/drumsticks, we recommend cutting the breast pieces in half so that each person can have some white meat and dark meat. The breasts and thighs/drumsticks do not cook at the same rate; if using both, note that the breast pieces are added partway through the cooking time. Serve with egg noodles.

- 6 ounces thick-cut bacon (about 5 slices), chopped medium
  Vegetable oil, as needed
- 4 pounds bone-in, skin-on chicken pieces (split breasts cut in half, drumsticks, and/or thighs; see note)
  Table salt and ground black pepper
- 8 ounces (about 2 cups) frozen pearl onions
- 10 ounces white mushrooms, wiped clean and quartered
- 2 medium garlic cloves, minced or pressed through a garlic press (about 2 teaspoons)
- 1 tablespoon tomato paste
- 3 tablespoons unbleached all-purpose flour
- 1 (750-milliliter) bottle medium-bodied red wine (see note)
- 2½ cups low-sodium chicken broth
- 1 teaspoon minced fresh thyme leaves or ¼ teaspoon dried
- 2 bay leaves
- 2 tablespoons unsalted butter, cut into 2 pieces, chilled
- 2 tablespoons minced fresh parsley leaves

1. Fry the bacon in a large Dutch oven over medium heat until crisp, 5 to 7 minutes. Transfer the bacon to a paper towel–lined plate, leaving the fat in the pot (you should have about 2 tablespoons; if necessary, add vegetable oil to make this amount). Set aside.

2. Pat the chicken dry with paper towels and season with salt and pepper. Return the pot with the bacon fat to medium-high heat until shimmering. Brown half of the chicken on both sides, 5 to 8 minutes per side, reducing the heat if the pan begins to scorch. Transfer the chicken to a plate, leaving the fat in the pot. Return the pot to medium-high heat and repeat with the remaining chicken; transfer the chicken to the plate.

3. Pour off all but 1 tablespoon of the fat in the pot (or add vegetable oil if needed to make this amount). Add the onions and mushrooms and cook over medium heat, stirring occasionally, until lightly browned, about 10 minutes. Stir in the garlic and tomato paste and cook until fragrant, about 30 seconds. Stir in the flour and cook for 1 minute. Stir in the wine, broth, thyme, and bay leaves, scraping up any browned bits.

4. Nestle the chicken, along with any accumulated juices, into the pot and bring to a simmer. Cover, turn the heat to medium-low, and simmer until the chicken is tender and the thickest part of the breasts registers 160 to 165 degrees on an instant-read thermometer, about 20 minutes, or the thickest part of the thighs and drumsticks registers 175 degrees on an instant-read thermometer, about 1 hour. (If using both types of chicken, simmer the thighs and drumsticks for 40 minutes before adding the breasts.)

5. Transfer the chicken to a serving dish, tent loosely with foil, and let rest while finishing the sauce. Skim as much fat as possible off the surface of the sauce and return to a simmer until the sauce is thickened and measures about 2 cups, about 20 minutes. Off the heat, remove the bay leaves, whisk in the butter, and season with salt and pepper to taste. Pour the sauce over the chicken, sprinkle with the reserved bacon and the parsley, and serve.

CHICKEN WITH 40 CLOVES OF GARLIC

WHY THIS RECIPE WORKS: In most versions of chicken with 40 cloves of garlic, the garlic is soft and spreadable, but its flavor is spiritless. The chicken is tender, but the breast meat takes on a dry, chalky quality, and its flavor is washed out. We wanted to revisit this classic French dish to make it faster and better, so it would boast well-browned, full-flavored chicken, sweet and nutty garlic, and a savory sauce.

Using a cut-up chicken rather than a whole bird ensures that the meat cooks quickly and evenly. We roasted the garlic cloves first to caramelize them and develop their flavor, then added them to the braising liquid with the chicken. Cooking it all with a two-part pan-roasting/braising technique kept the chicken moist, and finishing the chicken under the broiler made the chicken skin crispy. Some shallots and herbs added flavor to the sauce, and several roasted garlic cloves, smashed into a paste, thickened and flavored the sauce. A few tablespoons of butter, swirled in before serving, added richness.

Chicken with 40 Cloves of Garlic
SERVES 4

If using a kosher chicken, skip the brining process and begin with step 2. Avoid heads of garlic that have begun to sprout (the green shoots will make the sauce taste bitter). Tie the rosemary and thyme sprigs together with kitchen twine so they will be easy to retrieve from the pan. Serve the dish with slices of crusty baguette; you can spread them with the roasted garlic cloves.

Table salt and ground black pepper
1 (3½ to 4-pound) chicken, cut into 8 pieces (4 breast pieces, 2 thighs, 2 drumsticks; see page 330) and trimmed
3 medium heads garlic (about 8 ounces), outer papery skins removed, cloves separated and unpeeled (see note)
2 medium shallots, peeled and quartered
1 tablespoon olive oil
¾ cup dry vermouth or dry white wine
¾ cup low-sodium chicken broth
2 sprigs fresh thyme (see note)
1 sprig fresh rosemary (see note)
1 bay leaf
2 tablespoons unsalted butter

1. Adjust an oven rack to the middle position and heat the oven to 400 degrees. Dissolve ¼ cup salt in 2 quarts cold water in a large container; submerge the chicken in the brine, cover with plastic wrap, and refrigerate for 30 minutes. Remove the chicken from the brine, rinse, and pat dry with paper towels. Season both sides of the chicken pieces with pepper.

2. Meanwhile, combine the garlic, shallots, 2 teaspoons of the olive oil, ½ teaspoon salt, and ¼ teaspoon pepper in a 9-inch pie plate; cover tightly with foil and roast until softened and beginning to brown, about 30 minutes, shaking the pan once halfway through cooking. Uncover, stir, and continue to roast, uncovered, until browned and fully tender, about 10 minutes longer, stirring once or twice. Remove from the oven and increase the oven temperature to 450 degrees.

3. Heat the remaining 1 teaspoon oil in a 12-inch ovensafe skillet over medium-high heat until smoking. Brown the chicken, skin side down, until golden, about 5 minutes; flip the chicken pieces and brown until golden on the second side, about 4 minutes longer. Transfer the chicken to a large plate and pour off the fat from

CUTTING UP A WHOLE CHICKEN

Buying chicken parts is convenient, but packages often contain pieces of varying sizes. Cutting up a whole chicken yourself isn't difficult and it will guarantee evenly sized pieces of meat.

1. Using a chef's knife, cut off the legs, one at a time, by severing the joint between the leg and the body.

2. Cut each leg into two pieces—the drumstick and thigh—by slicing through the joint that connects them (marked by a thick white line of fat).

3. Flip the chicken over and remove the wings by slicing through each wing joint.

4. Turn the chicken (now without its legs and wings) on its side and, using scissors, remove the back from the chicken breast.

5. Flip the breast skin side down and, using a chef's knife, cut it in half through the breast plate (marked by a thin white line of cartilage), then cut each piece in half again.

the skillet. Off the heat, add the vermouth, chicken broth, thyme, rosemary, and bay leaf to the pan, scraping up any browned bits. Set the skillet over medium heat, add the garlic mixture, and return the chicken, skin side up, to the pan, nestling the pieces on top of and between the garlic cloves. Place the skillet in the oven and roast until the thickest part of the breasts registers 160 to 165 degrees on an instant-read thermometer; remove the skillet from the oven.

4. Adjust an oven rack 6 inches from the broiler element and heat the broiler. Broil the chicken to crisp the skin, 3 to 5 minutes. Remove the skillet from the oven and transfer the chicken to a serving dish. Transfer 10 to 12 garlic cloves to a fine-mesh sieve and reserve. Using a slotted spoon, scatter the remaining garlic cloves and shallots around the chicken; discard the herbs. With a rubber spatula, push the reserved garlic cloves through the sieve and into a bowl; discard the skins. Add the garlic paste to the skillet and bring the liquid to a simmer over medium-high heat, whisking to incorporate the garlic. Whisk in the butter and season with salt and pepper to taste. Serve the chicken, passing the sauce separately.

FRENCH CHICKEN IN A POT

WHY THIS RECIPE WORKS: *Poulet en cocotte* (chicken in a pot) is a classic French specialty—at its best, it's a whole chicken baked with root vegetables in a covered pot that delivers incredibly tender and juicy meat. Sounds simple, but it's actually more challenging than throwing chicken in a pot with vegetables. One potential problem is too much moisture in the pot, which washes out the flavor; another pitfall is overcooking. We wanted chicken in a pot that delivered moist meat and satisfying flavor.

We removed the vegetables—the liquid they released made the pot too steamy—and cooked the chicken by itself (after browning it in a little oil to prevent it from sticking). We also tightly sealed the pot with foil before adding the lid. To keep the breast meat from drying out and becoming tough, we cooked the chicken very slowly. After developing the basic technique, we revisited the idea of vegetables, and found that a small amount of potently flavored aromatic vegetables could be added if they were lightly browned with the chicken to erase most of their moisture. Finally, defatting the liquid in the pot rewarded us with a richly flavored sauce.

French Chicken in a Pot

SERVES 4

The cooking times in the recipe are for a 4½ to 5-pound bird. A 3½ to 4½-pound chicken will take about an hour to cook, and a 5 to 6-pound bird will take close to 2 hours. We developed this recipe to work with a 5 to 8-quart Dutch oven with a tight-fitting lid. If using a 5-quart pot, do not cook a chicken larger than 5 pounds. If using a kosher chicken, reduce the amount of table salt to ½ teaspoon. If you choose not to serve the skin with the chicken, simply remove it before carving. The amount of sauce will vary depending on the size of the chicken; season it with about ¼ teaspoon lemon juice for every ¼ cup.

1 (4½ to 5-pound) whole chicken, giblets discarded, wings tucked under back (see note)
1 teaspoon table salt (see note)
¼ teaspoon ground black pepper
1 tablespoon olive oil
1 small onion, chopped medium
1 small celery rib, chopped medium
6 medium garlic cloves, peeled and trimmed
1 bay leaf
1 medium sprig fresh rosemary (optional)
½-1 teaspoon juice from 1 lemon (see note)

1. Adjust an oven rack to the lowest position and heat the oven to 250 degrees. Pat the chicken dry with paper towels and season with the salt and pepper.

2. Heat the oil in a large Dutch oven over medium heat until just smoking. Add the chicken, breast side down, and scatter the onion, celery, garlic cloves, bay leaf, and rosemary (if using) around the chicken. Cook until the breast is lightly browned, about 5 minutes. Flip the chicken breast side up and continue to cook until the chicken and vegetables are well browned, 6 to 8 minutes.

3. Off the heat, place a large sheet of foil over the pot and cover tightly with the lid. Transfer the pot to the oven and cook until the thickest part of the breast registers 160 to 165 degrees and the thickest part of the thighs registers 175 degrees on an instant-read thermometer, 1 hour and 20 minutes to 1 hour and 50 minutes.

4. Remove the pot from the oven. Transfer the chicken to a cutting board, tent loosely with foil, and let rest for 20 minutes. Strain the chicken juices from the pot into a fat separator, pressing on the solids to extract the liquid; discard the solids (you should have about ¾ cup juices). Let the liquid settle for 5 minutes, then pour into a saucepan and cook over low heat until hot. Carve the chicken, adding any accumulated juices to the saucepan. Season the sauce with lemon juice to taste (see note). Serve the chicken, passing the sauce separately.

CHICKEN PROVENÇAL

WHY THIS RECIPE WORKS: Chicken Provençal represents the best of rustic, peasant food—bone-in chicken is simmered all day in a tomatoey, garlicky herb broth. But all too often, this formula results in dry, rubbery chicken, watery or overly thick sauce, and dulled or muddied flavors. We wanted to rejuvenate this dish, and create a chicken dish that was meltingly tender, moist, and flavorful, napped in an aromatic, garlicky tomato sauce that we could mop up with a good loaf of crusty bread.

For the best flavor and most tender texture, we used bone-in chicken thighs and browned them in a sheer film of olive oil. Skinless thighs stuck to the pan, and skin-on thighs developed a flabby texture when braised later on. So we settled on a compromise—browning the thighs with the skin on (to develop rich flavor and leave browned bits in the pan), then ditching the skins prior to the braising (to avoid flab central). To keep the sauce from becoming greasy, we spooned off the excess fat left behind from browning the chicken, but kept enough to sauté our garlic and onion. Diced tomatoes, white wine, and chicken broth also went into the sauce. We then braised the chicken until it was meltingly tender. As for flavor enhancers, a small amount of niçoise olives added an essential brininess to the dish, and some minced anchovy made the sauce taste richer and fuller.

Chicken Provençal

SERVES 4

This dish is often served with rice or slices of crusty bread, but soft polenta is also a good accompaniment. Niçoise olives are the preferred olives here; the flavor of kalamatas and other types of brined or oil-cured olives is too potent.

8	(5 to 6-ounce) bone-in, skin-on chicken thighs, trimmed
	Table salt
1	tablespoon extra-virgin olive oil
1	small onion, minced
6	medium garlic cloves, minced or pressed through a garlic press (about 2 tablespoons)
1	anchovy fillet, minced (about ½ teaspoon)
⅛	teaspoon cayenne pepper
1	cup dry white wine
1	cup low-sodium chicken broth
1	(14.5-ounce) can diced tomatoes, drained
2½	tablespoons tomato paste
1½	tablespoons chopped fresh thyme leaves
1	teaspoon chopped fresh oregano leaves
1	teaspoon herbes de Provence (optional)
1	bay leaf
1½	teaspoons grated zest from 1 lemon
½	cup pitted niçoise olives (see note)
1	tablespoon chopped fresh parsley leaves

1. Adjust an oven rack to the lower-middle position and heat the oven to 300 degrees. Season both sides of the chicken thighs with salt. Heat 1 teaspoon of the oil in a large Dutch oven over medium-high heat until shimmering. Add 4 chicken thighs, skin side down, and cook, without moving, until the skin is crisp and well browned, about 5 minutes. Flip the chicken pieces and brown on the second side, about 5 minutes longer; transfer to a large plate. Repeat with the remaining 4 chicken thighs, then transfer them to the plate and set aside. Discard all but 1 tablespoon of fat from the pot.

2. Add the onion to the pot and cook, stirring occasionally, over medium heat until softened and browned, about 4 minutes. Add the garlic, anchovy, and cayenne; cook, stirring constantly, until fragrant, about 1 minute. Add the wine, scraping up any browned bits. Stir in the chicken broth, tomatoes, tomato paste, thyme, oregano, herbes de Provence (if using), and bay leaf. Remove and discard the skin from the chicken thighs, then submerge

the chicken pieces in the liquid and add the accumulated chicken juices to the pot. Increase the heat to high, bring to a simmer, cover, and set the pot in the oven; cook until the chicken offers no resistance when poked with a knife but is still clinging to the bones, about 1¼ hours.

3. Using a slotted spoon, transfer the chicken to a serving platter and tent loosely with foil. Discard the bay leaf. Set the pot over high heat, stir in 1 teaspoon of the lemon zest, bring to a boil, and cook, stirring occasionally, until slightly thickened and reduced to 2 cups, about 5 minutes. Stir in the olives and cook until heated through, about 1 minute. Combine the remaining ½ teaspoon zest and the parsley. Spoon the sauce over the chicken, drizzle the chicken with the remaining 2 teaspoons oil, sprinkle with the parsley mixture, and serve.

DAUBE PROVENÇAL

WHY THIS RECIPE WORKS: *Daube Provençal,* also known as *daube Niçoise,* has all the elements of the best French fare: tender beef, a luxurious sauce, and complex flavors. So why does it usually end up as beef stew with a few misplaced ingredients instead of being its own, coherent dish? We wanted to translate the flavors of Provence—olive oil, olives, garlic, wine, herbs, oranges, tomatoes, mushrooms, and anchovies—to an American home kitchen, and create a bold, brash, and full-flavored beef stew, with ingredients that married into a robust but unified dish.

We started with the test kitchen's reliable set of techniques to turn tough but flavorful beef into a tender stew: Brown the beef; add the aromatics; sprinkle some flour in the pan to thicken the braising liquid; deglaze with more cooking liquid; add the meat back to the pot; and finally, cover and cook slowly in the oven until tender. Technique established, we concentrated on selecting and managing the complex blend of ingredients that defines this dish. We chose briny niçoise olives, bright tomatoes, floral orange peel, and the regional flavors of thyme and bay leaf. A few anchovies added complexity without a fishy taste, and salt pork contributed rich body. A whole bottle of wine added bold flavor and needed just a little cooking to tame its raw bite. Finally, to keep the meat from drying out during the long braising time required to create a complex-tasting sauce, we cut it into relatively large 2-inch pieces.

Daube Provençal

SERVES 4 TO 6

Serve this French beef stew with egg noodles or boiled potatoes. If niçoise olives are not available, kalamata olives, though not authentic, can be substituted. Cabernet Sauvignon is our favorite wine for this recipe, but Côtes du Rhône and Zinfandel also work. Our favorite cut of beef for this recipe is chuck-eye roast, but any boneless roast from the chuck will work. Because the tomatoes are added just before serving, it is preferable to use canned whole tomatoes and dice them yourself—uncooked, they are more tender than canned diced tomatoes. Once the salt pork, thyme, and bay leaves are removed in step 4, the daube can be cooled and refrigerated in an airtight container for up to 4 days. Before reheating, skim the hardened fat from the surface, then continue with the recipe.

¾ ounce dried porcini mushrooms, rinsed

1 (3½-pound) boneless beef chuck-eye roast, trimmed and cut into 2-inch chunks (see note)

1½ teaspoons table salt

1 teaspoon ground black pepper

4 tablespoons olive oil

5 ounces salt pork, rind removed

2 medium onions, halved pole to pole and cut into ⅛-inch-thick slices (about 4 cups)

4 large carrots, peeled and cut into 1-inch-thick rounds (about 2 cups)

2 tablespoons tomato paste

4 medium garlic cloves, peeled and sliced thin

⅓ cup unbleached all-purpose flour

1 (750-milliliter) bottle bold red wine (see note)

1 cup low-sodium chicken broth

1 cup water

1 cup pitted niçoise olives, drained well (see note)

4 strips zest from 1 orange, each strip about 3 inches long, removed with a vegetable peeler, cleaned of white pith, and cut lengthwise into thin strips

2 anchovy fillets, minced (about 1 teaspoon)

5 sprigs fresh thyme, tied together with kitchen twine

2 bay leaves

1 (14.5-ounce) can whole tomatoes, drained and cut into ½-inch cubes (see note)

2 tablespoons minced fresh parsley leaves

1. Combine the mushrooms and 1 cup water in a small microwave-safe bowl; cover with plastic wrap, cut three vents for steam with a knife, and microwave on high power for 30 seconds. Let stand until the mushrooms soften, about 5 minutes. Lift the mushrooms from the liquid with a fork and chop into ½-inch pieces (you should have about 4 tablespoons). Strain the liquid through a fine-mesh strainer lined with a paper towel into a medium bowl. Set the mushrooms and liquid aside.

2. Adjust an oven rack to the lower-middle position and heat the oven to 325 degrees. Dry the beef thoroughly with paper towels, then season with the salt and pepper. Heat 2 tablespoons of the oil in a large heavy-bottomed Dutch oven over medium-high heat until just smoking; add half of the beef. Cook without moving the pieces until well browned, about 2 minutes on each side, for a total of 8 to 10 minutes, reducing the heat if the fat begins to smoke. Transfer the meat to a medium bowl. Repeat with the remaining 2 tablespoons oil and the remaining beef.

3. Reduce the heat to medium and add the salt pork, onions, carrots, tomato paste, and garlic to the now-empty pot; cook, stirring occasionally, until light brown, about 2 minutes. Stir in the flour and cook, stirring constantly, about 1 minute. Slowly add the wine, gently scraping up any browned bits. Add the broth, water, and beef with any accumulated juices. Increase the heat to medium-high and bring to a simmer. Add the mushrooms and their liquid, ½ cup of the olives, the orange zest, anchovies, thyme, and bay leaves, distributing evenly and arranging the beef so it is completely covered by the liquid; partially cover the pot and place in the oven. Cook until a fork inserted in the beef meets little resistance (the meat should not be falling apart), 2½ to 3 hours.

4. Discard the salt pork, thyme, and bay leaves. Add the tomatoes and the remaining ½ cup olives; warm over medium-high heat until heated through, about 1 minute. Cover the pot and allow the stew to settle, about 5 minutes. Using a spoon, skim the excess fat from the surface of the stew. Stir in the parsley and serve.

BEEF BURGUNDY

WHY THIS RECIPE WORKS: Leave it to the French to make beef stew into an elegant affair. Unfortunately, when translated to the home kitchen, classic, intensely flavorful beef burgundy, also known as *boeuf bourguignon*, tends to lose its appeal. We've seen too many versions of this rustic French dish with tough meat or a dull sauce and no flavor complexity. We wanted to bring this dish to its earthy, robust, warm potential: satisfyingly large chunks of tender meat draped with a velvety sauce brimming with the flavor of good Burgundy wine and studded with caramelized mushrooms and pearl onions.

We started by rendering salt pork until crisp, then browned large chunks of beef chuck roast in the rendered fat. For the braising liquid, a combination of chicken broth and water, enhanced with a small amount of dried porcini mushrooms and tomato paste, provided balanced, well-rounded flavor. Using anything less than a full bottle of red wine (preferably a Burgundy, but a good Pinot Noir will suffice) left the sauce lacking and unremarkable. We deglazed the pan twice, used a roux to thicken the sauce, and then added the wine. Wrapping the aromatic vegetables in cheesecloth made it easy to remove them from the braising liquid. While the liquid reduced to a velvety sauce, we simmered pearl onions then sautéed them briefly with mushrooms to create the perfect garnish for our rich, tender beef.

Beef Burgundy
SERVES 6

Thick-cut bacon can be substituted for the salt pork; cut the bacon crosswise into ¼-inch pieces and treat it just as you would the salt pork, but note that you will have no rind to include in the vegetable and herb pouch. Boiled potatoes are the traditional accompaniment, but mashed potatoes or buttered noodles are nice as well.

STEW

- 6 ounces salt pork, trimmed of rind and rind reserved, salt pork cut into ¼-inch pieces (see note)
- 2 medium onions, chopped coarse
- 2 medium carrots, chopped coarse
- 1 medium head garlic, cloves separated and crushed but unpeeled
- 10 sprigs fresh parsley, torn into pieces
- 6 sprigs fresh thyme
- 2 bay leaves, crumbled
- ½ teaspoon black peppercorns
- ½ ounce dried porcini mushrooms, rinsed (optional)
- 1 (4 to 4½-pound) boneless beef chuck-eye roast, trimmed and cut into 2-inch chunks
  Table salt and ground black pepper
- 2½ cups water
- 4 tablespoons (½ stick) unsalted butter, cut into 4 pieces
- ⅓ cup unbleached all-purpose flour
- 1¾ cups low-sodium chicken broth
- 1 (750-milliliter) bottle red Burgundy or Pinot Noir
- 1 teaspoon tomato paste
- 2 tablespoons brandy
- 3 tablespoons minced fresh parsley leaves

ONION AND MUSHROOM GARNISH

- 7 ounces (about 1¾ cups) frozen pearl onions
- ¾ cup water
- 1 tablespoon unsalted butter
- 1 tablespoon sugar
- ½ teaspoon table salt
- 10 ounces medium white mushrooms, wiped clean and halved

1. FOR THE STEW: Bring the salt pork, reserved salt pork rind, and 3 cups water to a boil in a medium saucepan over high heat. Boil for 2 minutes, then drain well.

2. Lay a double layer of cheesecloth (each piece should measure 22 by 8 inches) in a medium bowl, placing the sheets perpendicular to each other. Place the onions, carrots, garlic, parsley pieces, thyme, bay leaves, peppercorns, porcini mushrooms (if using), and salt pork rind in the cheesecloth-lined bowl. Gather together the edges of the cheesecloth and fasten them securely with kitchen twine; trim the excess cheesecloth with scissors if necessary. Set the pouch in a large ovensafe Dutch oven. Adjust the oven rack to the lower-middle position and heat the oven to 300 degrees.

3. Cook the salt pork in a 12-inch skillet over medium heat until lightly browned and crisp, about 12 minutes. With a slotted spoon, transfer the salt pork to the pot. Pour off and reserve all but 2 teaspoons of the fat from the skillet. Pat the beef dry with paper towels and season with salt and pepper. Add half of the beef to the skillet, increase the heat to high, and brown in a single layer, turning once or twice, until deep brown, about 7 minutes; transfer the browned beef to the pot. Add ½ cup of the water to the skillet and scrape the pan with a wooden spoon to loosen the browned bits; add the liquid to the pot.

4. Heat 2 teaspoons of the reserved pork fat in the skillet over high heat until smoking. Add the remaining beef in a single layer, turning once or twice, until deep brown, about 7 minutes; transfer the browned beef to the pot. Add ½ cup more water to the skillet and scrape the pan with a wooden spoon to loosen the browned bits; add the liquid to the pot.

5. Melt the butter in the skillet over medium heat. Whisk in the flour and cook, stirring constantly, until light brown, about 5 minutes. Gradually whisk in the chicken broth and the remaining 1½ cups water. Increase the heat to medium-high and bring to a simmer, stirring frequently, until thickened; add the mixture to the pot. Add 3 cups of the wine and the tomato paste to the pot and season with salt and pepper to taste; stir to combine. Set the pot over high heat and bring to a boil; cover and place in the oven. Cook until the meat is tender, 2½ to 3 hours.

6. Remove the pot from the oven and transfer the vegetable and herb pouch to a mesh strainer; set the strainer over the pot. Using the back of a spoon, press the liquid from the pouch into the pot; discard the pouch. With a slotted spoon, transfer the beef to a medium bowl; set aside. Let the pot contents settle for about 15 minutes, then skim off and discard the fat.

7. Bring the liquid in the pot to a boil over medium-high heat. Simmer, stirring occasionally, until thickened and reduced to about 3 cups, 15 to 25 minutes.

8. FOR THE ONION AND MUSHROOM GARNISH: Meanwhile, bring the pearl onions, ½ cup of the water, the butter, sugar, and ¼ teaspoon of the salt to a boil in a 10-inch skillet over high heat. Cover, reduce the heat to medium-low, and simmer, shaking the pan occasionally, until the onions are tender, about 5 minutes. Uncover, increase the heat to high, and simmer until all the liquid evaporates, about 3 minutes. Add the mushrooms and the remaining ¼ teaspoon salt. Cook, stirring occasionally, until the liquid released by the mushrooms evaporates and the vegetables are browned, about 5 minutes. Transfer the vegetables to a bowl and set aside. Add the remaining ¼ cup water to the skillet and scrape the pan with a wooden spoon to loosen the browned bits; add the liquid to the pot with the reducing sauce.

9. When the sauce has reduced, reduce the heat to medium-low and stir in the beef, the remaining 2 tablespoons wine, the brandy, and the mushrooms and onions (and any accumulated juices). Cover the pot and cook until heated through, 5 to 8 minutes. Season with salt and pepper to taste and serve, sprinkling individual servings with the parsley.

SLOW-COOKER BEEF BURGUNDY

WHY THIS RECIPE WORKS: Given the amount of simmering time required for classic Beef Burgundy (page 334), we thought this stew could be easily morphed into a slow-cooker version that would have the same tender beef chunks and rich, earthy sauce as the original.

For a long braise, chuck roast cut into pieces is the best choice. The usual first step in making a stew is to brown the meat, but we found that we could get the same meaty flavor base from browning only half the beef. We used rendered bacon fat instead of oil; the bacon would go back into the stew at the end, lending a smoky note. Sautéed carrots and onions went into the slow-cooker insert next, with plenty of garlic, thyme, and tomato paste to withstand the long cooking time. As our braising liquid, beef broth tasted tinny but chicken broth worked well. We mixed it with red wine and a surprising ingredient, soy sauce, which intensified the savory flavors in the stew as well as deepened its color. To enrich the sauce, we stirred in a small amount of tapioca, a common thickening agent, in place of flour. We prepared the traditional onion and mushroom garnish separately, when the stew was almost finished cooking, and folded it in. The final touch was more red wine, which we reduced first so that it wouldn't impart a sour alcoholic taste. This slow-cooker beef burgundy had everything we would expect from the refined French original.

Slow-Cooker Beef Burgundy

SERVES 6 TO 8

Make sure to use the low setting on your slow cooker; the stew will burn on the high setting. Don't spend a lot of money for the wine in this recipe—in our testing, we found that California Pinot Noir wines in the $6 to $20 price range worked just fine. Boiled potatoes are the traditional accompaniment, but mashed potatoes or buttered noodles are nice as well.

STEW

- 8   ounces (about 8 slices) bacon, cut into ¼-inch pieces
- 1   (4-pound) boneless beef chuck-eye roast, trimmed and cut into 1½-inch chunks
     Table salt and ground black pepper
- 1   large onion, minced

2   carrots, peeled and minced

8   medium garlic cloves, minced or pressed through a
    garlic press (about 2 tablespoons plus 2 teaspoons)

2   teaspoons chopped fresh thyme leaves

4   tablespoons tomato paste

2½ cups Pinot Noir (see note)

1½ cups low-sodium chicken broth

⅓   cup soy sauce

3   bay leaves

3   tablespoons Minute tapioca

3   tablespoons minced fresh parsley leaves

ONION AND MUSHROOM GARNISH

8   ounces (about 2 cups) frozen pearl onions

½   cup water

5   tablespoons unsalted butter

1   tablespoon sugar

10 ounces white mushrooms, wiped clean
    and quartered
    Table salt

1. FOR THE STEW: Cook the bacon in a 12-inch skillet over medium-high heat until crisp. Using a slotted spoon, transfer the bacon to a paper towel–lined plate and refrigerate. Pour half of the bacon fat into a small bowl; set the skillet with the remaining bacon fat aside.

2. Pat the beef dry with paper towels and season with salt and pepper; place half of the beef in a slow-cooker insert. Heat the skillet with the remaining bacon fat over medium-high heat until smoking. Cook the remaining beef in a single layer until deep brown on all sides, about 8 minutes. Transfer the browned beef to the slow-cooker insert.

3. Add the reserved bacon fat to the now-empty skillet and heat over medium-high heat until shimmering. Add the onion, carrots, and ¼ teaspoon salt and cook until the vegetables begin to brown, about 5 minutes. Add the garlic and thyme and cook until fragrant, about 30 seconds. Add the tomato paste and stir until beginning to brown, about 45 seconds. Transfer the mixture to the slow-cooker insert.

4. Return the now-empty skillet to high heat and add 1½ cups of the wine, the chicken broth, and soy sauce. Simmer, scraping up any browned bits, for about 1 minute. Transfer the wine mixture to the slow-cooker insert.

5. Stir the bay leaves and tapioca into the slow-cooker insert. Set the slow cooker on low, cover, and cook until the meat is fork-tender, about 9 hours.

MISE EN PLACE—A FRENCH PHRASE EVERY HOME COOK SHOULD KNOW

When Bridget, Julia, and Becky prepare recipes on TV they always have each ingredient prepared and measured into its own glass bowl. Yes, this looks nice on television, but our test cooks follow the same procedure when the cameras aren't rolling. This practice has a fancy French name—*mise en place*, which means "to put in place"—but the concept is really quite simple. Prepare your ingredients *before* you start cooking.

To stay organized from the get-go, the test cooks measure out the amounts required in their recipes and then individually label each ingredient with its corresponding quantity, such as 1 cup unbleached all-purpose flour, 2 large egg whites, 1 cup toasted chopped walnuts, and so on. (Note that some ingredients such as onions and garlic are best prepared just before cooking, rather than in advance.) The measured and labeled ingredients are then kept together, by recipe, on large baking sheets and stored. When the test cooks are ready to cook, they grab their prepped ingredients and are ready to go. Try mise en place at home—you'll find it useful not only in helping you keep on track when tackling an involved recipe (think labor-intensive holiday meals) but also for day-to-day cooking—prepping your ingredients the night before will allow you to walk in the door after work and get dinner on the table fast. And since you can focus on what's cooking (rather than preparing ingredients), you eliminate the risk that something will burn or overcook.

6. FOR THE ONION AND MUSHROOM GARNISH: Bring the pearl onions, water, butter, and sugar to a boil in a 12-inch skillet over high heat. Cover and simmer over medium-low heat until the onions are tender, about 5 minutes. Uncover, increase the heat to high, and cook until the liquid evaporates, about 3 minutes. Add the mushrooms and ¼ teaspoon salt and cook until the vegetables are browned and glazed, about 5 minutes.

7. When ready to serve, discard the bay leaves and stir in the onion and mushroom garnish and the reserved bacon. Bring the remaining 1 cup wine to a boil in a 12-inch skillet over high heat and simmer until reduced by half, about 5 minutes. Stir the reduced wine and parsley into the stew and season with salt and pepper to taste. Serve.

CASSOULET

WHY THIS RECIPE WORKS: Comforting and delectable as it is, cassoulet is just too much trouble for most cooks. It can take three days to make, and the ingredients can be both hard to find and difficult to prepare. We wanted to see if there was a way to streamline the preparation of this dish without compromising its essential character.

Instead of duck confit, which is difficult to find and time-consuming to prepare, we brined chicken thighs and cooked them in bacon fat to simulate the smoky flavor and moist texture of the confit. With our mock confit lined up, the other elements fell into place. We decided on the flavorful, fatty blade-end pork roast for stewing, dried beans instead of canned beans (canned beans were out because they fell apart during cooking), and smoky kielbasa for the sausage component (the classically correct French sausage was too hard to find). We cooked the beans with onion and garlic to season them, then added some crisp bacon to infuse them with a salty smokiness. Cooking the dish entirely on the stove at a slow simmer, with a quick finish to brown our homemade croutons, gave us a quick and easy cassoulet that was worthy of the name.

Simplified Cassoulet with Pork and Kielbasa

SERVES 8

This dish can be made without brining the chicken, but we recommend that you do so. To ensure the most time-efficient preparation of the cassoulet, while the chicken is brining and the beans are simmering, prepare the remaining ingredients. Look for dried flageolet beans in specialty food stores. You can substitute a boneless Boston butt for the boneless blade-end pork loin roast. Additional salt is not necessary because the brined chicken adds a good deal of it, but if you skip the brining step, add salt to taste before serving.

CHICKEN

- 1 cup sugar
- ½ cup table salt
- 10 (5 to 6-ounce) bone-in, skin-on chicken thighs, trimmed and skin removed (see note)

BEANS

- 1 pound dried flageolet or great Northern beans, picked over and rinsed (see note)
- 1 medium onion, peeled, plus 1 small onion, minced

- 1 medium head garlic, outer papery skin removed and top ½ inch sliced off, plus 2 medium garlic cloves, minced or pressed through a garlic press (about 2 teaspoons)
- 1 teaspoon table salt
  Ground black pepper
- 6 ounces (about 6 slices) bacon, cut into ¼-inch pieces
- 1 (1-pound) boneless blade-end pork loin roast, trimmed and cut into 1-inch pieces (see note)
- 1 (14.5-ounce) can diced tomatoes, drained
- 1 tablespoon tomato paste
- 1 large sprig fresh thyme
- 1 bay leaf
- ¼ teaspoon ground cloves
- 3½ cups low-sodium chicken broth
- 1½ cups dry white wine
- ½ pound kielbasa, halved lengthwise and cut into ¼-inch slices

CROUTONS

- 6 slices high-quality white sandwich bread, cut into ½-inch cubes
- 3 tablespoons unsalted butter, melted

1. FOR THE CHICKEN: Dissolve the sugar and salt in 1 quart cold water in a gallon-size zipper-lock bag. Add the chicken, pressing out as much air as possible, seal the bag, and refrigerate for 1 hour. Remove the chicken from the brine, rinse, and pat dry with paper towels. Refrigerate until ready to use.

2. FOR THE BEANS: Bring the beans, the peeled onion, head of garlic, salt, ¼ teaspoon pepper, and 8 cups water to a boil in a large Dutch oven over high heat. Cover, reduce the heat to medium-low, and simmer until the beans are almost tender, 1¼ to 1½ hours. Drain the beans; discard the onion and garlic.

3. While the beans are cooking, fry the bacon in a large Dutch oven over medium heat until just beginning to crisp and most of the fat has rendered, 5 to 6 minutes. Using a slotted spoon, add half of the bacon to the pot with the beans; transfer the remaining bacon to a paper towel–lined plate and set aside. Increase the heat to medium-high and add half of the chicken, skinned side down; cook until lightly browned, 4 to 5 minutes. Flip the chicken thighs and cook until lightly browned on the second side, 3 to 4 minutes longer. Transfer the chicken to a large plate; repeat with the remaining thighs and set aside. Pour off all but 2 tablespoons fat from the pot. Return the pot to medium heat; add the pork pieces and cook, stirring occasionally, until lightly browned, about 5 minutes.

WHY THE TEST KITCHEN IS FOND OF FOND AND WHY YOU SHOULD BE, TOO

Ever wonder how restaurants make rich sauces to accompany sautéed cutlets and steaks? Chances are it's a pan sauce, made with the delicious caramelized browned bits (called fond) that sit on the bottom of the pan after the meat has been sautéed or pan-seared.

Pan sauces are usually made by adding liquid (broth, wine, or juice) to the pan once the cooked cutlets or steaks have been transferred to a plate to rest. The liquid dissolves the fond (a process known as deglazing) and incorporates it into the sauce.

So what makes those browned bits so flavorful and so valuable? When meat or chicken browns, a process called the Maillard reaction occurs. This process is named after the French chemist who first described this reaction about 100 years ago. When the amino acids (or protein components) and natural sugars in meat are subjected to intense heat, like that found in a skillet, they begin to combine and form new compounds. These compounds in turn break down and form yet more new flavor compounds, and so on and so on, like rabbits multiplying. The browned bits left in the pan once the meat has been cooked are packed with complex flavors, which in turn are carried over to the pan sauce once the fond has been dissolved. And fond isn't limited to just pan sauces—we also rely on fond to flavor braises, as well as other dishes where meat is browned, such as soups and stews.

Add the minced onion and cook, stirring occasionally, until softened, 3 to 4 minutes. Add the minced garlic, tomatoes, tomato paste, thyme, bay leaf, cloves, and pepper to taste and cook until fragrant, about 1 minute. Stir in the chicken broth and wine, scraping up any browned bits. Submerge the chicken in the pot, adding any accumulated juices, increase the heat to high, and bring to a boil. Reduce the heat to low, cover, and simmer for 40 minutes. Uncover and continue to simmer until the chicken and pork are fully tender, 20 to 30 minutes more.

4. FOR THE CROUTONS: While the chicken is simmering, adjust an oven rack to the lower-middle position and heat the oven to 400 degrees. Toss the bread cubes with the melted butter and spread out over a rimmed baking sheet. Bake until light golden brown and crisp, 8 to 12 minutes. Cool to room temperature; set aside (do not turn off the oven).

5. Gently stir the kielbasa, drained beans, and reserved bacon into the pot with the chicken and pork; remove and discard the thyme and bay leaf and season with pepper to taste (see note). Sprinkle the croutons evenly over the surface and bake, uncovered, until the croutons are deep golden brown, about 15 minutes. Let stand for 10 minutes; serve.

STEAK AU POIVRE

WHY THIS RECIPE WORKS: Steak au poivre is often nothing more than uninspired skillet steak. We were after the real thing—a perfectly cooked steak with a well-seared crust of pungent, cracked peppercorns and a silky sauce.

The trick to successful steak au poivre is coating just one side of the steaks with peppercorns and cooking the steaks on the uncoated side as long as possible to promote browning and prevent scorching of the peppercorns. With the first side browned, the steaks can be flipped and cooked for less time on the peppered side. Pressing the steaks with a cake pan once they have been placed in the hot skillet ensures that the peppercorns stick. After the steaks were done to our liking, we made a simple pan sauce with a mixture of beef broth and chicken broth that we first reduced, then flavored with brandy and lemon juice. Cream made the sauce luxurious and gave it some substance; butter whisked in at the end brought silkiness.

Steak au Poivre with Brandied Cream Sauce

SERVES 4

To save time, crush the peppercorns and trim the steaks while the broth mixture simmers. Many pepper mills do not have a sufficiently coarse setting. In that case, crush peppercorns with the back of a heavy pan. See page 713 for information on our top-rated pepper mill.

- 4 **tablespoons (½ stick) unsalted butter**
- 1 **medium shallot, minced (about 3 tablespoons)**
- 1 **cup beef broth**
- ¾ **cup low-sodium chicken broth**
- 4 **(8 to 10-ounce) strip steaks, ¾ to 1 inch thick, trimmed**
  Table salt
- 4 **teaspoons black peppercorns, crushed (see note)**
- 1 **tablespoon vegetable oil**
- ¼ **cup plus 1 tablespoon brandy**
- ¼ **cup heavy cream**
- 1 **teaspoon juice from 1 lemon or 1 teaspoon champagne vinegar**

1. Melt 1 tablespoon of the butter in a 12-inch skillet over medium heat. Add the shallot and cook, stirring occasionally, until softened, about 2 minutes. Add the beef and chicken broths and bring to a boil over high heat; cook until reduced to ½ cup, about 8 minutes. Transfer the broth mixture to a small bowl; wipe out the skillet with paper towels.

2. Meanwhile, pat the steaks dry with paper towels and season with salt. Sprinkle one side of each steak with 1 teaspoon of the crushed peppercorns and press them into the steaks with your fingers to adhere.

3. Heat the oil in the skillet over medium-high heat until just smoking. Carefully lay the steaks in the skillet, peppered side up. Press on the steaks with the bottom of a cake pan and cook until well-browned on the first side, 3 to 5 minutes. Flip the steaks over and continue to cook, pressing again with the cake pan, until the center of the steaks registers 120 degrees on an instant-read thermometer for rare (3 minutes), 125 degrees for medium-rare (4 minutes), or 130 degrees for medium (5 minutes). Transfer the steaks to a plate, tent loosely with foil, and let rest while making the sauce.

4. Pour off any fat left in the pan and remove any stray peppercorns. Add the broth mixture, ¼ cup of the brandy, and the cream to the skillet and bring to a boil over high heat, scraping up any browned bits. Simmer until golden brown and thickened, about 5 minutes. Off the heat, whisk in the remaining 3 tablespoons butter, the remaining 1 tablespoon brandy, the lemon juice, and any accumulated meat juices from the plate; season with salt to taste. Spoon the sauce over the steaks and serve immediately.

STEAK FRITES

WHY THIS RECIPE WORKS: Too often, steak frites in American restaurants misses the mark. The fries are usually too soggy and the steak just isn't as flavorful as it should be. We wanted to re-create the steak frites of our Parisian dreams, with perfectly cooked steak and fries that are fluffy on the inside and crisp on the outside, even when bathed in juices from the meat.

For our fries, we liked high-starch russet potatoes and found that double-cooking, or a low-temperature "blanch" in oil followed by a high-temperature "fry," yielded the crispiest exterior and fluffiest interior. Cooking multiple small batches of fries ensured that the oil's temperature wouldn't plunge too much. Soaking the potatoes in cold water before they were cooked further improved their crispiness, and a "rest" between the first and second frying

allowed the fries to develop a thin coating of starch, which even further improved their crispiness. Tossing them with additional starch—in the form of cornstarch—made them perfect.

In France, steak frites is usually prepared with a cut called *entrecôte* (literally, "between the ribs"), which is a French cut you won't find in the States, but is actually quite similar to our rib-eye steak. Choosing the right size—or cutting them to fit—meant we could sear four steaks at once in a large skillet. Capped with a quick herb butter, the steaks tasted just like the bistro classic of our dreams.

Steak Frites

SERVES 4

Make sure to dry the potatoes well before tossing them with the cornstarch. For safety, use a Dutch oven with a capacity of at least 7 quarts. Use refined peanut oil (such as Planters) to fry the potatoes, not toasted peanut oil. A 12-inch skillet is essential for cooking four steaks at once. The recipe can be prepared through step 4 up to 2 hours in advance; shut off the heat under the oil, turning the heat back to medium when you start step 6. The ingredients can be halved to serve two—keep the oil amount the same and forgo blanching and frying the potatoes in batches.

HERB BUTTER

- 4 tablespoons (½ stick) unsalted butter, softened
- ½ shallot, minced (about 1 tablespoon)
- 1 tablespoon minced fresh parsley leaves
- 1 tablespoon minced fresh chives
- 1 medium garlic clove, minced or pressed through a garlic press (about 1 teaspoon)
- ¼ teaspoon table salt
- ¼ teaspoon ground black pepper

STEAK AND POTATOES

2½ **pounds russet potatoes (about 4 large), sides squared off, cut lengthwise into ¼ by ¼-inch fries (see note)**

2 **tablespoons cornstarch**

3 **quarts peanut oil (see note)**

1 **tablespoon vegetable oil**

2 **(1-pound) boneless rib-eye steaks, cut in half**

  Table salt and ground black pepper

1. FOR THE BUTTER: Combine all the ingredients in a medium bowl; set aside.

2. FOR THE POTATOES: Rinse the cut potatoes in a large bowl under cold running water until the water turns clear. Cover with cold water and refrigerate for at least 30 minutes or up to 12 hours.

3. Pour off the water, spread the potatoes onto clean kitchen towels, and thoroughly dry. Transfer the potatoes to a large bowl and toss with the cornstarch until evenly coated. Transfer the potatoes to a wire rack set over a rimmed baking sheet and let rest until a fine white coating forms, about 20 minutes.

4. Meanwhile, heat the peanut oil over medium heat to 325 degrees in a large, heavy-bottomed Dutch oven fitted with a clip-on candy thermometer.

5. Add half of the potatoes, a handful at a time, to the hot oil and increase the heat to high. Fry, stirring with a mesh spider or slotted spoon, until the potatoes start to turn from white to blond, 4 to 5 minutes. (The oil temperature will drop about 75 degrees during this frying.) Transfer the fries to a thick paper bag or paper towels. Return the oil to 325 degrees and repeat with the remaining potatoes. Reduce the heat to medium and let the fries cool while cooking the steaks, at least 10 minutes.

6. FOR THE STEAKS: Heat the vegetable oil in a 12-inch skillet over medium-high heat until smoking. Meanwhile, season the steaks with salt and pepper. Lay the steaks in the pan, leaving ¼ inch between them. Cook, without moving the steaks, until well browned, about 4 minutes. Flip the steaks and continue to cook until an instant-read thermometer inserted in the center registers 120 degrees for rare to medium-rare, 3 to 7 minutes. Transfer the steaks to a large plate, top with the herb butter, and tent loosely with foil; let rest while finishing the fries.

7. Increase the heat under the Dutch oven to high and heat the oil to 375 degrees. Add half of the fries, a handful at a time, and fry until golden brown and puffed, 2 to 3 minutes. Transfer to a thick paper bag or paper towels. Return the oil to 375 degrees and repeat with the remaining fries. Season the fries with salt to taste and serve immediately with the steaks.

NOTES FROM THE TEST KITCHEN

SQUARING THE SPUD

The best way to uniformly cut fries is to start by trimming a thin slice from each side of the potato. Once the potato is "squared," you can slice it into planks and then cut each plank into fries.

ONE STEAK BECOMES TWO

For steaks of the right thickness for Steak Frites (so they'll sear well without overcooking), it is necessary to buy two 1-pound steaks and cut them in half according to their thickness. If your steaks are 1¼ to 1¾ inches thick, cut them in half vertically into small, thick steaks. If your steaks are thicker than 1¾ inches, cut them in half horizontally into two thinner steaks.

THIN STEAK
Cut in half vertically.

THICK STEAK
Cut in half horizontally

STEAK DIANE

WHY THIS RECIPE WORKS: For a different spin on the usual pan-seared steaks, we turn to the French classic, steak Diane. But the demanding rich sauce is based on an all-day veal stock reduction—then the steaks still have to be cooked (if you have the energy, that is), and the sauce completed. We aimed to determine the right cut of steak, create a lighter, less labor-intensive sauce, and find a fool-proof method for cooking the meat.

For a rich sauce base that mimics the complexity of labor-intensive veal stock in a fraction of the time, we used a flavorful combination of sautéed tomato paste, aromatics such as garlic, onion, and carrots, both beef broth and chicken broth, red wine, peppercorns, and herbs. Omitting the traditional cream allowed the sauce to fully develop in intensity, and the inclusion of cognac gave the sauce a slightly sweet, complex flavor. For the meat, we selected strip steaks for great beefy flavor and ease of preparation. To brown the steaks evenly and develop enough fond (the flavorful browned meaty bits that cling to the pan and give pan sauces their rich, meaty flavor), we weighted the steaks with a heavy-bottomed skillet when cooking the second side.

Steak Diane

SERVES 4

If you prefer not to make the sauce base (recipe follows), mix ½ cup glace de viande with ¾ cup water and ¼ cup red wine and use this mixture in place of the base in step 2. Glace de viande is meat stock, in this case veal stock, that's been reduced to a thick syrup; we recommend Provimi Glace de Veau and CulinArte' Bonewerks Glace de Veau. Before preparing the sauce, read "Tips for Fearless Flambé" on page 342, or, if you do not wish to flambé, simmer the cognac in step 2 for 10 to 15 seconds for a slightly less sweet flavor profile.

STEAKS

- **4 (12-ounce) strip steaks, 1 to 1¼ inch thick, trimmed**
  Table salt and ground black pepper
- **2 tablespoons vegetable oil**

SAUCE

- **1 tablespoon vegetable oil**
- **1 small shallot, minced (about 1 tablespoon)**
- **¼ cup cognac**
- **1 recipe Sauce Base for Steak Diane (recipe follows; see note)**
- **2 teaspoons Dijon mustard**
- **2 tablespoons unsalted butter, chilled**
- **1 teaspoon Worcestershire sauce**
- **2 tablespoons minced fresh chives**
  Table salt and ground black pepper

1. FOR THE STEAKS: Cover the steaks with plastic wrap and use a meat pounder to pound them to an even ½-inch thickness; season them with salt and pepper. Heat 1 tablespoon of the oil in a 12-inch skillet over medium-high heat until smoking. Place 2 steaks in the skillet and cook until well browned, about 1½ minutes. Flip the steaks and weight with a heavy-bottomed pan; continue to cook until well browned on the second side, about 1½ minutes longer. Transfer the steaks to a plate and tent with foil. Add the remaining 1 tablespoon oil to the skillet and repeat with the remaining 2 steaks; transfer the second batch of steaks to the plate.

2. FOR THE SAUCE: Off the heat, add the oil and shallot to the skillet. Using the skillet's residual heat, cook, stirring frequently, until the shallot is slightly softened and browned, about 45 seconds. Add the cognac and let stand until the cognac warms slightly, about 10 seconds, then set the skillet over high heat. Wave a lit match over the skillet until the cognac ignites, shaking the skillet until the flames subside, then simmer the cognac until reduced to about 1 tablespoon, about 10 seconds. Add the sauce base and mustard and simmer until slightly thickened and reduced to 1 cup, 2 to 3 minutes. Whisk in the butter. Off the heat, add the Worcestershire sauce, any accumulated juices from the steaks, and 1 tablespoon of the chives. Season with salt and pepper to taste.

3. Serve immediately, spooning 2 tablespoons sauce and sprinkling a portion of the remaining 1 tablespoon chives over each steak, and passing the remaining sauce separately.

Sauce Base for Steak Diane

MAKES 1¼ CUPS

This recipe yields a sauce base that is an excellent facsimile of a demi-glace, a very labor-intensive and time-consuming classic French sauce base. Because the sauce base is very concentrated, make sure to use low-sodium chicken and beef broths; otherwise, the base may be unpalatably salty.

- **2 tablespoons vegetable oil**
- **4 teaspoons tomato paste**
- **2 small onions, chopped medium**
- **1 medium carrot, chopped medium**
- **4 medium garlic cloves, peeled**
- **¼ cup water**
- **4 teaspoons unbleached all-purpose flour**
- **1½ cups dry red wine**

TIPS FOR FEARLESS FLAMBÉ

Flambéing is more than just tableside theatrics: As dramatic as it looks, igniting alcohol actually helps develop a deeper, more complex flavor in sauces—thanks to flavor-boosting chemical reactions that occur only at the high temperatures reached in flambéing. But accomplishing this feat at home can be daunting. Here are some tips for successful—and safe—flambéing at home.

BE PREPARED: Turn off the exhaust fan, tie back long hair, and have a lid at the ready to smother flare-ups.

USE THE PROPER EQUIPMENT: A pan with flared sides (such as a skillet) rather than straight sides will allow more oxygen to mingle with the alcohol vapors, increasing the chance that you'll spark the desired flame. If possible, use long chimney matches, and light the alcohol with your arm extended to full length.

IGNITE WARM ALCOHOL: If the alcohol becomes too hot, the vapors can rise to dangerous heights, causing large flare-ups once lit. Inversely, if the alcohol is too cold, there won't be enough vapors to light at all. We found that heating alcohol to 100 degrees Fahrenheit (best achieved by adding alcohol to a hot pan off heat and letting it sit for five to 10 seconds) produced the most moderate, yet long-burning, flames.

IF A FLARE-UP SHOULD OCCUR: Simply slide the lid over the top of the skillet (coming in from the side of, rather than over, the flames) to put out the fire quickly. Let the alcohol cool down and start again.

IF THE ALCOHOL WON'T LIGHT: If the pan is full of other ingredients (as is the case in Crêpes Suzette, page 671), the potency of the alcohol can be diminished as it becomes incorporated. For a more foolproof flame, ignite the alcohol in a separate small skillet or saucepan; once the flame has burned off, add the reduced alcohol to the remaining ingredients.

3½ **cups low-sodium beef broth (see note)**
1¾ **cups low-sodium chicken broth (see note)**
2 **teaspoons black peppercorns**
8 **sprigs fresh thyme**
2 **bay leaves**

1. Heat the oil and tomato paste in a Dutch oven over medium-high heat and cook, stirring constantly, until the paste begins to brown, about 3 minutes. Add the onions, carrot, and garlic and cook, stirring frequently, until the mixture is reddish brown, about 2 minutes. Add 2 tablespoons of the water and continue to cook, stirring constantly, until the mixture is well browned, about 3 minutes, adding the remaining 2 tablespoons water as needed to prevent scorching. Add the flour and cook, stirring constantly, for about 1 minute. Add the wine, scraping up the browned bits on the bottom and sides of the pot; bring to a boil, stirring occasionally (the mixture will thicken slightly). Add the beef and chicken broths, peppercorns, thyme, and bay leaves; bring to a boil and cook, uncovered, occasionally scraping the bottom and sides of the pot with a spatula, until reduced to 2½ cups, 35 to 40 minutes.

2. Strain the mixture through a fine-mesh strainer, pressing on the solids to extract as much liquid as possible; you should have about 1¼ cups. (The sauce base can be refrigerated in an airtight container for up to 3 days.)

FISH MEUNIÈRE

WHY THIS RECIPE WORKS: Fish meunière typically features pale, soggy fillets in pools of greasy sauce—that is, if the fish doesn't stick to the pan or fall apart as it is plated. We wanted perfectly cooked fillets that were delicately crisp and golden brown on the outside and moist and flavorful on the inside, napped in a buttery yet light sauce.

Whole Dover sole is the most authentic choice, but it's also hard to come by and prohibitively expensive; either sole or flounder fillets are good stand-ins. To prevent the likelihood of overcooking the fish, the fillets need to be no less than ⅜ inch thick. The fillets must be patted dry before being seasoned with salt and pepper and dredged in flour (no need for eggs and bread crumbs). Using a nonstick skillet for pan-frying meant there was less chance for our fillets to fall apart; lubricating the pan with a mixture of oil and butter added extra insurance. Removing the pan from the heat just before the fish was cooked prevented the fish from being dry (the fish will continue to cook off the heat). Butter browned in a traditional skillet (so the changing color is easy to monitor) and brightened with lemon juice made the ideal accompaniment to our crispy, golden fillets.

Fish Meunière with Browned Butter and Lemon

SERVES 4

Try to purchase fillets that are of similar size, and avoid those that weigh less than 5 ounces because they will cook too quickly. When placing the fillets in the skillet, be sure to place them skinned side up so that the opposite side, which had bones, will brown first. To flip the fillets while cooking, use two spatulas; gently lift one side of the fillet with one spatula, then support the fillet with the other spatula and gently flip it so that the browned side faces up. A nonstick skillet ensures that the fillets will release from the pan, but for the sauce a traditional skillet is preferable because its light-colored surface will allow you to monitor the color of the butter as it browns.

FISH

- ½ cup unbleached all-purpose flour
- 4 (5 to 6-ounce) sole or flounder fillets, ⅜ inch thick (see note)
  Table salt and ground black pepper
- 2 tablespoons vegetable oil
- 2 tablespoons unsalted butter, cut into 2 pieces

BROWNED BUTTER

- 4 tablespoons (½ stick) unsalted butter, cut into 4 pieces
- 1 tablespoon chopped fresh parsley leaves
- 1½ tablespoons juice from 1 lemon
  Table salt
  Lemon wedges, for serving

1. FOR THE FISH: Adjust an oven rack to the lower-middle position, set four heatproof dinner plates on the rack, and heat the oven to 200 degrees. Place the flour in a large baking dish. Pat the fillets dry with paper towels and season with salt and pepper; let stand until the fillets are glistening with moisture, about 5 minutes. Coat both sides of the fillets with flour, shake off the excess, and place in a single layer on a rimmed baking sheet.

2. Heat 1 tablespoon of the oil in a 12-inch nonstick skillet over high heat until shimmering; add 1 tablespoon of the butter and swirl to coat the pan bottom. Carefully place 2 fillets, skinned side up, in the skillet. Immediately reduce the heat to medium-high and cook, without moving the fish, until the edges of the fillets are opaque and the bottoms are golden brown, about 3 minutes. Using two spatulas, gently flip the fillets and cook on the second side until the thickest part of the fillet easily separates into flakes when a toothpick is inserted, about 2 minutes longer. Transfer the fillets to two of the heated dinner plates, keeping them boned side up, and return the plates to the oven. Wipe out the skillet and repeat with the remaining 1 tablespoon oil, remaining 1 tablespoon butter, and the remaining fish fillets.

3. FOR THE BROWNED BUTTER: Melt the butter in a 10-inch traditional skillet over medium-high heat. Continue to cook, swirling the pan constantly, until the butter is golden brown and has a nutty aroma, 1 to 1½ minutes; remove the skillet from the heat. Remove the plates from the oven and sprinkle the fillets with the parsley. Add the lemon juice to the browned butter and season with salt to taste. Spoon the sauce over the fish and serve immediately, garnished with the lemon wedges.

SCOVILLE SCALE

Cherry | New Mexico Green | Anaheim | Poblano | Jalapeño | Banana | Serrano

CHAPTER 15

TEX-MEX TONIGHT

Fresh Margaritas   346

Sangria   346

Cheesy Nachos with
Guacamole and Salsa   347
  One-Minute Salsa

Chunky Guacamole   348

Quesadillas   349

Tortilla Soup   349

Black Bean Soup   351

Beef Empanadas   352

Beef Tacos   354
  Home-Fried Taco Shells

Steak Tacos   355
  Sweet and Spicy
  Pickled Onions

Chicken Fajitas   357

Steak Fajitas   358

Chicken Enchiladas with
Red Chili Sauce   359

Enchiladas Verdes   361

Spicy Mexican Shredded
Pork Tostadas   362

Mexican Pulled Pork
(Carnitas)   363

Mexican Rice   364

Beef Chili with Kidney
Beans   365

Chili Con Carne   366

White Chicken Chili   367

Huevos Rancheros   369
  Refried Beans

MARGARITAS

WHY THIS RECIPE WORKS: The typical margarita tends to be a slushy, headache-inducing concoction made with little more than ice, tequila, and artificially flavored corn syrup. We wanted a margarita with a balanced blend of fresh citrus flavors and tequila.

We found that the key was using the right proportions of alcohol and citrus juice—equal parts of each one. For a mellow, delicate flavor, we preferred reposado tequila, made from 100 percent blue agave, which is aged about 12 months. Unaged tequilas gave our margaritas a raw, harsh flavor. And those made with superpremium tequilas, which are aged up to 6 years, tasted smooth, but their distinct tannic taste dominated the cocktail. As for orange-flavored liqueurs, a lower-alcohol liqueur, such as triple sec, worked best. Mixes and bottled citrus juice had no place in our cocktail—instead we steeped lemon and lime zest in their own juice for a deep, refreshing citrus flavor. And with a bit of easy-to-dissolve superfine sugar and crushed ice, our margaritas were complete.

Fresh Margaritas
SERVES 4 TO 6

The longer the zest and juice mixture is allowed to steep, the more developed the citrus flavors will be in the finished margaritas. We recommend steeping for the full 24 hours, although the margaritas will still be great if the mixture is steeped for only the minimum 4 hours. If you're in a rush and want to serve margaritas immediately, omit the zest and skip the steeping process altogether. If you can't find superfine sugar, process an equal amount of regular sugar in a food processor for 30 seconds.

- 4 teaspoons grated zest plus ½ cup juice from 4 limes (see note)
- 4 teaspoons grated zest plus ½ cup juice from 3 lemons (see note)
- ¼ cup superfine sugar (see note)
  Pinch table salt
- 2 cups crushed ice
- 1 cup 100 percent agave tequila, preferably reposado
- 1 cup triple sec

1. Combine the lime zest and juice, lemon zest and juice, sugar, and salt in a large liquid measuring cup; cover with plastic wrap and refrigerate until the flavors meld, 4 to 24 hours.

2. Divide 1 cup of the crushed ice among 4 or 6 margarita or double old-fashioned glasses. Strain the juice mixture into a 1-quart pitcher or cocktail shaker. Add the tequila, triple sec, and the remaining 1 cup crushed ice; stir or shake until thoroughly combined and chilled, 20 to 60 seconds. Strain into the ice-filled glasses and serve immediately.

SANGRIA

WHY THIS RECIPE WORKS: Many people mistake sangria for an unruly collection of fruit awash in a sea of overly sweetened red wine. We wanted a robust, sweet-tart wine punch.

After trying a variety of red wines, we found that inexpensive wine works best. (Experts told us that the sugar and fruit called for in sangria throw off the balance of any wine used, so why spend a lot on something that was carefully crafted?) We experimented with untold varieties of fruit to put in our sangria and finally concluded that simpler is better. We preferred the straightforward tang of citrus in the form of oranges and lemons. And we discovered that the zest and pith as well as the fruit itself make an important contribution to flavor. Orange liqueur is standard in recipes for sangria, and after experimenting we found that here, as with the wine, cheaper was just fine, this time in the form of triple sec. Fortification with any other alcoholic beverage, from gin to port to brandy, simply gave the punch too much punch. What we wanted, and what we now had, was a light, refreshing drink.

Sangria
SERVES 4

Although this punch hails from Spain, it has become a mainstay on Mexican restaurant menus and pairs well with the country's spicy dishes. The longer sangria sits before drinking, the more smooth and mellow it will taste. A full day is best, but if that's impossible, give it an absolute minimum of two hours to sit. Use large, heavy, juicy oranges and lemons for the best flavor. If you can't find superfine sugar, process an equal amount of regular sugar in a food processor for 30 seconds. Doubling or tripling the recipe is fine, but you'll have to switch to a large punch bowl in place of the pitcher. An inexpensive Merlot is the best choice for this recipe.

2 large juice oranges, washed; one orange sliced,
   remaining orange juiced (see note)
1 large lemon, washed and sliced (see note)
¼ cup superfine sugar (see note)
1 (750-milliliter) bottle inexpensive, fruity,
   medium-bodied red wine, chilled (see note)
¼ cup triple sec

1. Add the sliced orange and lemon and the sugar to a
large pitcher. Mash the fruit gently with a wooden spoon
until the fruit releases some juice, but is not totally crushed,
and the sugar dissolves, about 1 minute. Stir in the orange
juice, wine, and triple sec; refrigerate for at least 2 hours
or up to 8 hours.

2. Before serving, add 6 to 8 ice cubes and stir briskly
to distribute the settled fruit and pulp; serve immediately.

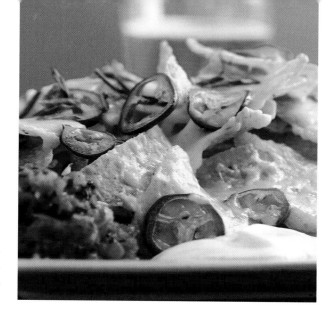

NACHOS

WHY THIS RECIPE WORKS: Prepackaged shredded cheese
and jars of premade salsa and guacamole transform
nachos from something delicious into bland fast food.
We wanted nachos with hot, crisp tortilla chips, plentiful
cheese and toppings, and the right amount of spicy heat.

To ensure that all of the chips would be cheesy and spicy,
we layered tortilla chips with a full pound of shredded
cheddar cheese and sliced jalapeños. Layering the jalapeños
with the cheese also helped the chiles stick to the chips. We
prepared a quick homemade salsa and chunky guacamole
to spoon around the edges of the hot nachos after they
came out of the oven. Spoonfuls of sour cream and a sprinkling of chopped fresh scallions provided final touches.
Served with lime wedges, this fresh take on nachos is light-
years beyond any fast-food version of the dish.

Cheesy Nachos with Guacamole and Salsa
SERVES 4 TO 6

8 ounces tortilla chips
1 pound cheddar cheese, shredded (about 4 cups)
2 large jalapeño chiles, sliced thin (about ¼ cup)
2 scallions, sliced thin
½ cup sour cream
1 recipe One-Minute Salsa (recipe follows)
1 recipe Chunky Guacamole (page 348)
   Lime wedges, for serving

Adjust an oven rack to the middle position and heat the
oven to 400 degrees. Spread half of the chips in an even
layer in a 13 by 9-inch baking dish. Sprinkle the chips
evenly with 2 cups of the cheese and half of the jalapeño
slices. Repeat with the remaining chips, cheese, and jalapeños. Bake until the cheese is melted, 7 to 10 minutes.
Remove the nachos from the oven and sprinkle with the
scallions. Along the edge of the baking dish, drop scoops
of the sour cream, salsa, and guacamole. Serve immediately, passing the lime wedges separately.

One-Minute Salsa
MAKES ABOUT 1 CUP

This quick salsa can be made with either fresh or canned
tomatoes. If you like, replace the jalapeño with ½ chipotle
chile in adobo sauce, minced.

2 tablespoons chopped red onion
2 tablespoons fresh cilantro leaves
2 teaspoons juice from 1 lime
½ small jalapeño chile, stemmed and seeded (about
   1½ teaspoons; see note)
1 small garlic clove, minced or pressed through a
   garlic press (about ½ teaspoon)
¼ teaspoon table salt
   Pinch ground black pepper
2 small ripe tomatoes, each cored and cut into eighths,
   or one (14.5-ounce) can diced tomatoes, drained

Pulse all the ingredients except the tomatoes in a food
processor until minced, about 5 pulses, scraping down the
sides of the workbowl as necessary. Add the tomatoes and
pulse until roughly chopped, about 2 pulses.

GUACAMOLE

WHY THIS RECIPE WORKS: Not only eaten as a party dip, guacamole is also the traditional accompaniment to several Mexican dishes. Unfortunately, it often has so many ingredients that the primary one—the avocado—becomes overshadowed by secondary ingredients. We wanted to get back to the basics of this dish, emphasizing the avocado.

Hass avocados, the dark, pebbly-skinned type, work best, and they must be ripe; they should yield slightly to a gentle squeeze. We wanted a chunky texture in our guacamole, so instead of mashing or pureeing the avocados we diced two of them and mashed one lightly. Combining the avocados gave the guacamole a chunky, cohesive texture. As for flavorings, just a bit of finely minced onion provided some bite but not overwhelming onion flavor. Lime juice was essential for its bright citrus flavor. Cumin, a jalapeño, and fresh cilantro rounded out the dip's flavors. Cool and creamy, our guacamole makes a perfect partner to a bowl of tortilla chips or a garnish to a variety of Mexican dishes.

Chunky Guacamole

MAKES 2½ TO 3 CUPS

To minimize the risk of discoloration, prepare the minced ingredients first so they are ready to mix with the avocados as soon as they are cut. Ripe avocados are essential here. To test for ripeness, try to flick the small stem off the end of the avocado. If it comes off easily and you can see green underneath it, the avocado is ripe. If it does not come off or if you see brown underneath after prying it off, the avocado is not ripe. If you like, garnish the guacamole with diced tomatoes and chopped cilantro just before serving.

> 3 medium, ripe avocados (see note)
> ¼ cup minced fresh cilantro leaves
> 2 tablespoons minced onion
> 1 small jalapeño chile, stemmed, seeded, and minced
> 1 medium garlic clove, minced or pressed through a garlic press (about 1 teaspoon)
> ½ teaspoon ground cumin (optional)
> Table salt
> 2 tablespoons juice from 1 lime

1. Halve 1 avocado, remove the pit, and scoop the flesh into a medium bowl. Mash the flesh lightly with the cilantro, onion, jalapeño, garlic, cumin (if using), and ¼ teaspoon salt with the tines of a fork until just combined.

2. Halve, pit, and cube the remaining 2 avocados. Add the cubes to the bowl with the mashed avocado mixture.

3. Sprinkle the lime juice over the diced avocado and mix the entire contents of the bowl lightly with a fork until combined but still chunky. Season with salt, if necessary, and serve. (The guacamole can be covered with plastic wrap, pressed directly onto the surface of the mixture, and refrigerated for up to 1 day. Return the guacamole to room temperature, removing the plastic wrap at the last moment, before serving.)

QUICK AND EASY QUESADILLAS

WHY THIS RECIPE WORKS: An authentic quesadilla is meant to be a quick snack, not an overstuffed tortilla with complicated fillings. We wanted a simple toasted tortilla, crisp and hot, filled with just the right amount of cheese.

We kept the tortillas crisp by lightly toasting them in a dry skillet. We then filled them with cheese and pickled jalapeños, lightly coated the tortillas with oil, and returned them to the skillet until they were well browned and the cheese was fully melted. Not yet satisfied that our recipe was speedy enough, we made the process even more convenient by switching to small 8-inch tortillas and folding them in half around the filling. This allowed us to cook two at one time in the same skillet, and the fold also kept our generous cheese filling from oozing out.

Quesadillas

MAKES 2 FOLDED 8-INCH QUESADILLAS

Cooling the quesadillas before cutting and serving them is important; straight from the skillet, the melted cheese will ooze out. Finished quesadillas can be held on a baking sheet in a 200-degree oven for up to 20 minutes.

- 2 (8-inch) flour tortillas
- 2 ounces Monterey Jack or cheddar cheese, shredded (about ½ cup)
- 1 tablespoon minced pickled jalapeños (optional)
  Vegetable oil for brushing the tortillas
  Kosher salt

1. Heat a 10-inch nonstick skillet over medium heat until hot, about 2 minutes. Place 1 tortilla in the skillet and toast until soft and puffed slightly at the edges, about 2 minutes. Flip the tortilla and toast until puffed and slightly browned, 1 to 2 minutes longer. Slip the tortilla onto a cutting board. Repeat to toast the second tortilla while assembling the first quesadilla. Sprinkle ¼ cup of the cheese and half of the jalapeños (if using) over half of the tortilla, leaving a ½-inch border around the edge. Fold the tortilla in half and press to flatten. Brush the top generously with oil, sprinkle lightly with salt, and set aside. Repeat to form the second quesadilla.

2. Place both quesadillas in the skillet, oiled sides down; cook over medium heat until crisp and well browned, 1 to 2 minutes. Brush the tops with oil and sprinkle lightly with salt. Flip the quesadillas and cook until the second sides are crisp, 1 to 2 minutes. Transfer the quesadillas to a cutting board; cool for 3 minutes, halve each quesadilla, and serve.

NOTES FROM THE TEST KITCHEN

COOKING QUESADILLAS

To cook two quesadillas at the same time, arrange the folded edges at the center of a 10-inch nonstick skillet.

TORTILLA SOUP

WHY THIS RECIPE WORKS: The classic method of making this flavorful Mexican soup is not only arduous, but it relies on a long list of ingredients, many of which are difficult, if not impossible, to find outside of specialty markets. We wanted to make an intensely and authentically flavored tortilla soup in less than one hour, using supermarket ingredients.

By breaking the soup down to its three classic components—the flavor base (tomatoes, garlic, onion, and chiles), the chicken stock, and the garnishes (including fried tortilla chips)—we found we could devise techniques and substitute ingredients that together make a compelling version of tortilla soup. We began achieving maximum flavor by composing a puree made from chipotle chiles, tomatoes, onions, garlic, jalapeños, and a cilantro/oregano substitute for the Mexican ingredient epazote, and then frying the puree in oil over high heat. We then added the puree to low-sodium canned chicken broth that we strained after poaching chicken in it and infusing it with onions, garlic, cilantro, and oregano. Addressing the garnish issue, we oven-toasted our lightly oiled tortilla strips instead of frying them and substituted sour cream and Monterey Jack cheese for the harder-to-find Mexican crema and cotija.

Tortilla Soup

SERVES 6

Despite its somewhat lengthy ingredient list, this recipe is very easy to prepare. If desired, the soup can be completed short of adding the shredded chicken to the pot at the end of step 3. Return the soup to a simmer over medium-high heat before proceeding. The tortilla strips and the garnishes are best prepared the day of serving.

TORTILLA STRIPS

8 (6-inch) corn tortillas, cut into ½-inch-wide strips
1 tablespoon vegetable oil
   Table salt

SOUP

2 bone-in, skin-on split chicken breasts (about 1½ pounds)
   or 4 bone-in, skin-on chicken thighs (about
   1¼ pounds), skin removed and trimmed
8 cups low-sodium chicken broth
1 very large white onion (about 1 pound), peeled and
   quartered
4 medium garlic cloves, peeled
2 sprigs fresh epazote or 8 to 10 sprigs fresh cilantro
   plus 1 sprig fresh oregano
   Table salt
2 medium tomatoes, cored and quartered
½ medium jalapeño chile
1 chipotle chile in adobo sauce, plus up to 1 tablespoon
   adobo sauce
1 tablespoon vegetable oil

GARNISHES

   Lime wedges
   Avocado, peeled, pitted, and diced fine
   (see page 348)
   Cotija cheese, crumbled, or Monterey Jack
   cheese, diced fine
   Fresh cilantro leaves
   Jalapeño chile, minced
   Crema Mexicana or sour cream

1. FOR THE TORTILLA STRIPS: Adjust an oven rack to the middle position and heat the oven to 425 degrees. Spread the tortilla strips on a rimmed baking sheet; drizzle with the oil and toss until evenly coated. Bake until the strips are deep golden brown and crisped, about 14 minutes, rotating the pan and shaking the strips (to redistribute) halfway through baking. Season the strips lightly with salt; transfer to a plate lined with several layers of paper towels.

2. FOR THE SOUP: While the tortilla strips bake, bring the chicken, broth, 2 of the onion quarters, 2 of the garlic cloves, the epazote, and ½ teaspoon salt to a boil over medium-high heat in a large saucepan; reduce the heat to low, cover, and simmer until the chicken is just cooked through, about 20 minutes. Using tongs, transfer the chicken to a large plate. Pour the broth through a fine-mesh strainer; discard the solids in the strainer. When cool enough to handle, shred the chicken into bite-size pieces; discard the bones.

3. Puree the tomatoes, remaining 2 onion quarters, remaining 2 garlic cloves, the jalapeño, chipotle chile, and 1 teaspoon of the adobo sauce in a food processor until smooth, about 20 seconds. Heat the oil in a Dutch oven over high heat until shimmering; add the tomato-onion puree and ⅛ teaspoon salt and cook, stirring frequently, until the mixture has darkened in color, about 10 minutes. Stir the strained broth into the tomato mixture, bring to a boil, then reduce the heat to low and simmer to blend the flavors, about 15 minutes. Taste the soup; if desired, add up to 2 teaspoons more adobo sauce. Add the shredded chicken and simmer until heated through, about 5 minutes. To serve, place portions of tortilla strips in the bottom of individual bowls and ladle the soup into the bowls; pass the garnishes separately.

BLACK BEAN SOUP

WHY THIS RECIPE WORKS: Making traditional black bean soup used to be an all-day affair. Generating full flavor required hours of simmering soaked beans with numerous ingredients, including parsnips, carrots, beef bones, and smoked ham hocks. But quicker versions developed for modern kitchens often produce watery, bland, and unattractive soups. We wanted a simplified procedure that would result in an attractive, dark-colored soup full of sweet, spicy, smoky flavors and brightened with fresh garnishes.

Though convenient, canned beans couldn't compare in flavor to dried, which imparted good flavor to the broth as they simmered, and we discovered that we didn't have to soak them. A touch of baking soda in the cooking water kept the beans from turning gray. Homemade stock would be time-consuming to prepare, so we focused on adding flavor to prepared broth. Ham steak provided the smoky pork flavor of the more conventional ham hock and more meat as well. We spiced up our aromatics—carrot, celery, onion, and garlic—with lots of cumin and some red pepper flakes. We wanted a chunky texture in our soup, so we pureed it only partially, thickening it further with a slurry of cornstarch and water. Some lime juice added brightness. The customary garnishes of sour cream, avocado, red onion, cilantro, and lime wedges topped our richly flavored but easy-to-make black bean soup.

Black Bean Soup

SERVES 6

Dried beans tend to cook unevenly, so be sure to taste several beans to determine their doneness in step 1. For efficiency, you can prepare the soup ingredients while the beans simmer and the garnishes while the soup simmers. Though you do not need to offer all of the garnishes listed below, do choose at least a couple; garnishes are essential for this soup, as they add not only flavor but texture and color as well. Leftover soup can be refrigerated in an airtight container for up to 3 days; reheat it in a saucepan over medium heat until hot, stirring in additional chicken broth if it has thickened beyond your liking.

BEANS

- 1 **pound (2 cups) dried black beans, rinsed and picked over**
- 4 **ounces ham steak, trimmed of rind**
- 2 **bay leaves**
- 5 **cups water**
- ⅛ **teaspoon baking soda**
- 1 **teaspoon table salt**

SOUP

- 3 **tablespoons olive oil**
- 2 **large onions, minced**
- 3 **celery ribs, chopped fine**
- 1 **large carrot, chopped**
- ½ **teaspoon table salt**
- 5–6 **medium garlic cloves, minced or pressed through a garlic press (about 2 tablespoons)**
- 1½ **tablespoons ground cumin**
- ½ **teaspoon red pepper flakes**
- 6 **cups low-sodium chicken broth**
- 2 **tablespoons cornstarch**
- 2 **tablespoons water**
- 2 **tablespoons juice from 1 lime**

GARNISHES

- **Lime wedges**
- **Minced fresh cilantro leaves**
- **Red onion, diced fine**
- **Avocado, peeled, pitted, and diced medium (see page 348)**
- **Sour cream**

1. FOR THE BEANS: Place the beans, ham, bay leaves, water, and baking soda in a large saucepan with a tight-fitting lid. Bring to a boil over medium-high heat; using a large spoon, skim the foam as it rises to the surface. Stir in the salt, reduce the heat to low, cover, and simmer briskly until the beans are tender, 1¼ to 1½ hours (if necessary, add 1 cup more water and continue to simmer until the beans are tender); do not drain the beans. Discard the bay leaves. Remove the ham steak (ham steak darkens to the color of the beans), cut it into ¼-inch cubes, and set aside.

2. FOR THE SOUP: Heat the oil in a large Dutch oven over medium-high heat until shimmering but not smoking; add the onions, celery, carrot, and salt and cook, stirring occasionally, until the vegetables are soft and lightly browned, 12 to 15 minutes. Reduce the heat to medium-low and add the garlic, cumin, and red pepper flakes; cook, stirring constantly, until fragrant, about 3 minutes. Stir in the beans, bean cooking liquid, and chicken broth. Increase the heat to medium-high and bring to a boil, then reduce the heat to low and simmer, uncovered, stirring occasionally, to blend the flavors, about 30 minutes.

3. TO FINISH THE SOUP: Ladle 1½ cups of the beans and 2 cups of the liquid into a food processor or blender, process until smooth, and return to the pot. Stir together the cornstarch and water in a small bowl until combined, then gradually stir half of the cornstarch mixture into the soup; bring to a boil over medium-high heat, stirring occasionally, to fully thicken. If the soup is still thinner than desired once boiling, stir the remaining cornstarch mixture to recombine and gradually stir the mixture into the soup; return to a boil to fully thicken. Off the heat, stir in the lime juice and reserved ham; ladle the soup into bowls and serve immediately, passing the garnishes separately.

BEEF EMPANADAS

WHY THIS RECIPE WORKS: In Latin America, crisp pastry pockets stuffed with spiced beef make a savory, light lunch. We wanted to streamline the process but still get an empanada hearty enough to take center stage at dinner, with a moist, savory filling encased in a tender crust.

To streamline the filling, we first enhanced packaged ground chuck with a milk-and-bread mixture known as a panade. As the meat and panade cook, the starches in the panade's bread absorb moisture from the milk and form a gel around the protein molecules, which lubricates the meat. But to intensify the meaty flavor, we replaced the milk with an equal amount of chicken broth. To round it out we added a hefty dose of aromatics. Finally, we threw in a handful of cilantro leaves and a splash of vinegar along with chopped hard-cooked eggs, raisins, and green olives.

For our crust, we made a few Latin-inspired changes to our Foolproof Double-Crust Pie Dough (page 683), a recipe that combines butter (for flavor) and shortening (for tenderness) with water and vodka for a dough that's both workable and tender (tequila can also be substituted for the vodka). We traded some of the flour for masa harina, the ground, dehydrated cornmeal used

to make Mexican tortillas and tamales. This provided nutty richness and rough-hewn texture. Finally, a quick brush of oil on the top of the empanadas gave us a shiny, crunchy crust, and preheating the baking sheet and drizzling it with oil ensured the underside of the crust got as crispy as the top.

Beef Empanadas

SERVES 4 TO 6

The alcohol in the dough is essential to the texture of the crust and imparts no flavor—do not omit it or substitute water. Masa harina can be found in the international aisle of the supermarket with other Latin foods or in the baking aisle with the flour. If you cannot find masa harina, replace it with additional all-purpose flour (for a total of 4 cups). See page 32 for instructions on how to hard-cook eggs.

FILLING
- 1 slice high-quality white sandwich bread, torn into quarters
- 2 tablespoons plus ½ cup low-sodium chicken broth
- 1 pound 85 percent lean ground beef
  Table salt and ground black pepper
- 1 tablespoon olive oil
- 2 medium onions, minced
- 4 medium garlic cloves, minced or pressed through a garlic press (about 4 teaspoons)
- 1 teaspoon ground cumin
- ¼ teaspoon cayenne pepper
- ⅛ teaspoon ground cloves
- ½ cup fresh cilantro leaves, chopped coarse
- 2 hard-cooked eggs (see note), chopped coarse
- ⅓ cup raisins, chopped coarse
- ¼ cup pitted green olives, chopped coarse
- 4 teaspoons cider vinegar

DOUGH
- 3 cups (15 ounces) unbleached all-purpose flour
- 1 cup (5 ounces) masa harina (see note)
- 1 tablespoon sugar
- 2 teaspoons table salt
- 12 tablespoons (1½ sticks) unsalted butter, cut into ½-inch pieces and chilled
- ½ cup cold vodka or tequila
- ½ cup cold water
- 5 tablespoons olive oil

1. FOR THE FILLING: Process the bread and 2 tablespoons of the chicken broth in a food processor until a paste forms, about 5 seconds, scraping down the sides of the bowl as necessary. Add the beef, ¾ teaspoon salt, and ½ teaspoon pepper and pulse until the mixture is well combined, 6 to 8 pulses.

2. Heat the oil in a 12-inch nonstick skillet over medium-high heat until shimmering. Add the onions and cook, stirring frequently, until beginning to brown, about 5 minutes. Stir in the garlic, cumin, cayenne, and cloves and cook until fragrant, about 1 minute. Add the beef mixture and cook, breaking the meat into 1-inch pieces with a wooden spoon, until browned, about 7 minutes. Add the remaining ½ cup chicken broth and simmer until the mixture is moist but not wet, 3 to 5 minutes. Transfer the mixture to a bowl and cool for 10 minutes. Stir in the cilantro, eggs, raisins, olives, and vinegar. Season with salt and pepper to taste and refrigerate until cool, about 1 hour.

3. FOR THE DOUGH: Pulse 1 cup of the flour, the masa harina, sugar, and salt in a food processor until combined, about 2 pulses. Add the butter and process until the mixture is homogeneous and the dough resembles wet sand, about 10 seconds. Add the remaining 2 cups flour and pulse until the mixture is evenly distributed around the bowl, 4 to 6 quick pulses. Empty the mixture into a medium bowl.

4. Sprinkle the vodka and water over the mixture. Using your hands, mix the dough until it forms a tacky mass that sticks together. Following the photo, divide the dough in half, then divide each half into six equal pieces. Transfer the dough pieces to a plate, cover with plastic wrap, and refrigerate until firm, about 45 minutes.

5. TO ASSEMBLE: Adjust the oven racks to the upper-middle and lower-middle positions, place 1 baking sheet on each rack, and heat the oven to 425 degrees. While the baking sheets are preheating, remove the dough from the refrigerator. Following the photos, roll each dough piece out on a lightly floured work surface into a 6-inch circle about ⅛ inch thick, covering each rolled-out dough round with plastic wrap while rolling out the remaining dough. Place about ⅓ cup of the filling in the center of each dough round. Brush the edges of each round with water and fold the dough over the filling. Trim any ragged edges, then crimp the edges of the empanadas shut using a fork.

6. Drizzle 2 tablespoons of the oil over the surface of each hot baking sheet, then return the sheets to the oven

NOTES FROM THE TEST KITCHEN

ASSEMBLING EMPANADAS

1. Divide the dough in half, then divide each half into six equal pieces.

2. Roll each piece of dough into a 6-inch round about ⅛ inch thick.

3. Place about ⅓ cup of the filling on each round, then brush the edges with water.

4. Fold the dough over the filling, then crimp the edges using a fork to seal.

for 2 minutes. Brush the empanadas with the remaining 1 tablespoon oil. Carefully place 6 empanadas on each baking sheet and cook until well browned and crisp, 25 to 30 minutes, switching and rotating the baking sheets halfway through baking. Cool the empanadas on a wire rack for 10 minutes before serving. (After step 5, the empanadas can be covered tightly with plastic wrap and refrigerated for up to 2 days.)

BEEF TACOS

WHY THIS RECIPE WORKS: Tacos made from supermarket kits are disappointing substitutes for the real thing. Easy as they may be to prepare, taco fillings made with store-bought spice mixes taste flat and stale, and the shells don't taste much different than the cardboard they're packaged in. We set out to develop a recipe for toasty, not greasy, taco shells filled with a boldly spiced beef mixture and fresh toppings.

Home-fried corn tortillas made superior homemade taco shells. For the filling, we seasoned lean ground beef with onions, garlic, and spices (chili powder, cumin, coriander, and oregano). To moisten and further flavor the beef filling, we added chicken broth, brown sugar, and vinegar. Spooned into our fresh, crisp taco shells and topped with tomatoes, lettuce, avocado, Monterey Jack, onion, and cilantro, these tacos have far better flavor than taco-kit versions.

NOTES FROM THE TEST KITCHEN

MAKING YOUR OWN TACO SHELLS

1. Using tongs to hold the tortilla, slip half of it into the hot oil. With a metal spatula in the other hand, submerge the half in the oil. Fry until just set, but not brown, about 30 seconds.

2. Flip the tortilla and, using tongs, hold the tortilla open about 2 inches while keeping the bottom submerged in the oil. Fry until golden brown, about 1½ minutes. Flip again and fry the other side until golden brown, about 30 seconds.

3. Transfer the shell, upside down, to the paper towel-lined baking sheet to drain. Repeat with the remaining tortillas, adjusting the heat as necessary to keep the oil between 350 and 375 degrees.

Beef Tacos

SERVES 4

Taco toppings are highly individual. We consider the ones listed below essential, but you might also want to consider diced avocado, sour cream, and chopped onion.

BEEF FILLING

- 2 teaspoons vegetable oil
- 1 small onion, minced
- 3 medium garlic cloves, minced or pressed through a garlic press (about 1 tablespoon)
- 2 tablespoons chili powder
- 1 teaspoon ground cumin
- 1 teaspoon ground coriander
- ½ teaspoon dried oregano
- ¼ teaspoon cayenne pepper
  Table salt
- 1 pound 90 percent lean ground beef
- ½ cup canned tomato sauce
- ½ cup low-sodium chicken broth
- 2 teaspoons vinegar, preferably cider vinegar
- 1 teaspoon brown sugar
  Ground black pepper

SHELLS AND TOPPINGS

- 8 Home-Fried Taco Shells (recipe follows)
  Shredded Monterey Jack cheese
  Shredded iceberg lettuce
  Diced tomatoes
  Chopped fresh cilantro leaves

1. FOR THE FILLING: Heat the oil in a medium skillet over medium heat until shimmering. Add the onion and cook, stirring occasionally, until softened, about 4 minutes. Add the garlic, spices, and ½ teaspoon salt; cook, stirring constantly, until fragrant, about 30 seconds. Add the ground beef and cook, breaking up the meat with a wooden spoon and scraping the pan bottom to prevent scorching, until the beef is no longer pink, about 5 minutes. Add the tomato sauce, broth, vinegar, and brown sugar; bring to a simmer. Reduce the heat to medium-low and simmer uncovered, stirring frequently and breaking up the meat so that no chunks remain, until the liquid has reduced and thickened (the mixture should not be completely dry), about 10 minutes. Season with salt and pepper to taste.

2. Using a wide, shallow spoon, divide the mixture evenly among the taco shells; place two tacos on each plate. Serve immediately, passing the toppings separately.

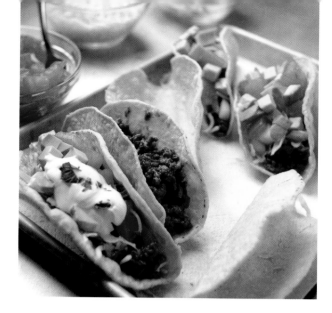

Home-Fried Taco Shells

MAKES 8 SHELLS

Fry the taco shells before you make the filling, then rewarm them in a 200-degree oven for about 10 minutes before serving.

¾ cup corn oil, vegetable oil, or canola oil
8 (6-inch) corn tortillas

1. Line a rimmed baking sheet with a double thickness of paper towels and set aside. Heat the oil in an 8-inch skillet over medium heat to 350 degrees, about 5 minutes (the oil should bubble when a small piece of tortilla is dropped in; the piece should rise to the surface in 2 seconds and be light golden brown in about 1 minute).

2. Following the photos on page 354, fry the tortillas. One at a time, place each fried taco shell on the prepared baking sheet (see note).

STEAK TACOS

WHY THIS RECIPE WORKS: Upscale steak tacos usually get their rich, beefy flavor from the grill, but cooking outdoors isn't always possible. We wanted an indoor cooking method that would always yield steak taco meat as tender, juicy, and rich-tasting as the grilled method.

We didn't want to wrap a pricey cut of beef in a taco, so we explored inexpensive cuts and chose flank steak for its good flavor and ready availability; when sliced against the grain, it can be just as tender as pricier cuts. To add flavor, we poked holes in the meat with a fork and rubbed it with a paste of oil, cilantro, jalapeño, garlic, and scallions; salt helped draw all the flavors into the steak and ensured juiciness. Pan-searing, with a sprinkling of sugar to enhance browning, gave us a crust that mimicked the char of the grill. To maximize this effect, we cut the steak into four long pieces, which gave us more sides to brown and turn crispy. For additional flavor, we tossed the cooked steak with some marinade that we had reserved and garnished the tacos simply with onion, cilantro, and lime wedges. In Mexico, steak tacos are often served with *curtido,* a relish of pickled vegetables; we devised a quick recipe for pickled onions to accompany our good-as-grilled steak tacos.

Steak Tacos

SERVES 4 TO 6

Our preferred method for warming tortillas is to place each one over the medium flame of a gas burner until slightly charred, about 30 seconds per side. We also like toasting them in a dry skillet over medium-high heat until softened and speckled with brown spots, 20 to 30 seconds per side. For a less spicy dish, remove some or all of the ribs and seeds from the jalapeños before chopping them for the marinade. In addition to the toppings suggested below, try serving the tacos with Sweet and Spicy Pickled Onions (recipe follows), thinly sliced radish or cucumber, or salsa.

MARINADE
½ cup packed fresh cilantro leaves
3 medium scallions, roughly chopped
1 medium jalapeño chile, stemmed and roughly chopped (see note)
3 medium garlic cloves, roughly chopped
½ teaspoon ground cumin
¼ cup vegetable oil
1 tablespoon juice from 1 lime

STEAK
1 (1½ to 1¾-pound) flank steak, trimmed and cut lengthwise (with the grain) into 4 equal pieces
1 tablespoon kosher salt or 1½ teaspoons table salt
½ teaspoon sugar
½ teaspoon ground black pepper
2 tablespoons vegetable oil

TACOS
12 (6-inch) corn tortillas, warmed (see note)
Fresh cilantro leaves
Minced white onion
Lime wedges

1. FOR THE MARINADE: Pulse the cilantro, scallions, jalapeño, garlic, and cumin in a food processor until finely chopped, 10 to 12 pulses, scraping down the sides of the workbowl as necessary. Add the oil and process until the mixture is smooth and resembles pesto, about 15 seconds, scraping down the sides as necessary. Transfer 2 tablespoons of the herb paste to a medium bowl; whisk in the lime juice and set aside.

2. FOR THE STEAK: Using a dinner fork, poke each piece of steak 10 to 12 times on each side. Place in a large baking dish; rub all sides of the steak pieces evenly with the salt and then coat with the remaining herb paste. Cover with plastic wrap and refrigerate for at least 30 minutes or up to 1 hour.

3. Scrape the herb paste off the steak and sprinkle all sides of the pieces evenly with the sugar and black pepper. Heat the oil in a 12-inch nonstick skillet over medium-high heat until smoking. Place the steak in the skillet and cook until well browned, about 3 minutes. Flip the steak and sear until the second side is well browned, 2 to 3 minutes. Using tongs, stand each piece on a cut side and cook, turning as necessary, until all cut sides are well browned and the internal steak temperature registers 125 to 130 degrees on an instant-read thermometer, 2 to 7 minutes. Transfer the steak to a cutting board and let rest for 5 minutes.

4. FOR THE TACOS: Slice the steak against the grain into ⅛-inch-thick pieces. Transfer the sliced steak to the bowl with the herb paste–lime juice mixture and toss to coat. Season with salt to taste. Spoon a small amount of the sliced steak into the center of each warm tortilla and serve immediately, passing the toppings separately.

Sweet and Spicy Pickled Onions

MAKES ABOUT 2 CUPS

The onions can be refrigerated, tightly covered, for up to 1 week.

- 1 **medium red onion, halved and sliced thin (about 1½ cups)**
- 1 **cup red wine vinegar**
- ⅓ **cup sugar**
- 2 **jalapeño chiles, stemmed, seeded, and cut into thin rings**
- ¼ **teaspoon table salt**

Place the onions in a medium heat-resistant bowl. Bring the vinegar, sugar, jalapeños, and salt to a simmer in a small saucepan over medium-high heat, stirring occasionally, until the sugar dissolves. Pour the vinegar mixture over the onions, cover loosely, and let cool to room temperature, about 30 minutes. Once cool, drain and discard the liquid.

CHICKEN FAJITAS

WHY THIS RECIPE WORKS: Too often, chicken fajitas need to be slathered with guacamole, sour cream, and salsa to compensate for the bland flavor of the main ingredients. We wanted to go back to the basics, creating a simple combination of smoky grilled vegetables and strips of chicken wrapped up in warm flour tortillas. The chicken and vegetables should be flavorful enough to make condiments unnecessary.

To boost the flavor of the chicken, we used a marinade of lime juice and oil. We added jalapeño and cilantro for some bright spice and herbal flavor, and a surprising addition—Worcestershire sauce—lent a subtle but complex savory note. We marinated the chicken only briefly, so the acid wouldn't turn the delicate chicken to mush. Bell peppers and onions are the customary vegetables, and we found that their sweet-bitter flavors contrasted well with the chicken. To prepare the vegetables for grilling, we quartered the peppers, so they'd lie flat on the grill, and cut the onion into thick rounds that would hold together during cooking. A two-level fire enabled us to grill the chicken and vegetables at the same time, the latter on the cooler part so they wouldn't burn. We saved some of the marinade to toss with everything at the end for a bright flavor burst; nestled in a warm tortilla, the smoky vegetables and well-seasoned chicken were so good on their own that we forgot all about toppings.

Chicken Fajitas for a Charcoal Grill

SERVES 4 TO 6

The chicken and vegetables in these fajitas are only mildly spicy. For more heat, include the jalapeño seeds and ribs when mincing. When you head outside to grill, bring along a clean kitchen towel or a large piece of foil in which to wrap the tortillas and keep them warm as they come off the grill. Although the chicken and vegetables have enough flavor to stand on their own, accompaniments (guacamole, salsa, sour cream, shredded cheddar or Monterey Jack cheese, and lime wedges) can be offered at the table. The chicken tenderloins can be reserved for another use or marinated and grilled along with the breasts.

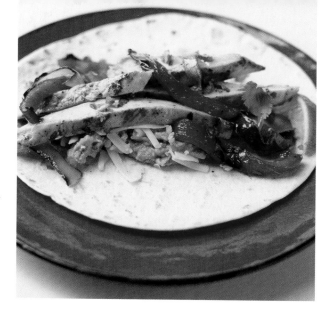

    6 tablespoons vegetable oil, plus extra for the
       cooking grate
    ⅓ cup juice from 3 to 4 limes
    3 medium garlic cloves, minced or pressed through
       a garlic press (about 1 tablespoon)
    1 tablespoon Worcestershire sauce
  1½ teaspoons brown sugar
    1 jalapeño chile, stemmed, seeded, and minced
       (see note)
  1½ tablespoons minced fresh cilantro leaves
       Table salt and ground black pepper
    3 (7 to 8-ounce) boneless, skinless chicken breasts,
       tenderloins removed (see note), and breasts trimmed
       and pounded to ½-inch thickness
    1 large red onion, peeled and cut into ½-inch-thick
       rounds (do not separate the rings)
    1 large red bell pepper, stemmed, seeded, and
       quartered
    1 large green bell pepper, stemmed, seeded,
       and quartered
 8–12 (6-inch) flour tortillas

1. In a medium bowl, whisk together 4 tablespoons of the oil, the lime juice, garlic, Worcestershire sauce, brown sugar, jalapeño, cilantro, 1 teaspoon salt, and ¾ teaspoon pepper. Reserve ¼ cup of the marinade in a small bowl; set aside. Add 1 teaspoon salt to the remaining marinade. Place the chicken in the marinade; cover with plastic wrap and refrigerate for 15 minutes. Brush both sides of the onion rounds and peppers with the remaining 2 tablespoons oil and season with salt and pepper.

2. Meanwhile, light a large chimney starter filled with charcoal (about 6 quarts) and allow to burn until the coals are partially covered with a layer of ash, about 20 minutes.

Build a two-level fire by arranging two-thirds of the coals evenly over half of the grill and arranging the remaining coals over the other half. Set the cooking grate in place, cover the grill, and heat the grate until hot, about 5 minutes. Use a grill brush to scrape the cooking grate clean. Dip a wad of paper towels in oil; holding the wad with tongs, oil the cooking grate.

3. Remove the chicken from the marinade and place the chicken, smooth side down, on the hotter side of the grill; discard the remaining marinade. Place the onion rounds and peppers (skin side down) on the cooler side of the grill. Cook the chicken until well browned, 4 to 5 minutes; using tongs, flip the chicken and continue grilling until the thickest part of the chicken registers 160 to 165 degrees on an instant-read thermometer, 4 to 5 minutes longer. Meanwhile, cook the peppers until spottily charred and crisp-tender, 8 to 10 minutes, turning once or twice as needed; cook the onions until tender and charred on both sides, 10 to 12 minutes, turning every 3 to 4 minutes. When the chicken and vegetables are done, transfer them to a large plate and tent with foil to keep warm.

4. Working in two or three batches, place the tortillas in a single layer on the cooler side of the now-empty grill and cook until warm and lightly browned, about 20 seconds per side (do not grill too long or the tortillas will become brittle). As the tortillas are done, wrap them in a kitchen towel or large sheet of foil.

5. Separate the onions into rings and place in a medium bowl; slice the bell peppers lengthwise into thin strips and place in the bowl with the onions. Add 2 tablespoons of the reserved unused marinade to the vegetables and toss well to combine. Slice the chicken into ¼-inch strips and toss with the remaining 2 tablespoons reserved marinade in another bowl; arrange the chicken and vegetables on a large platter and serve with the warmed tortillas.

Chicken Fajitas for a Gas Grill

1. Follow the recipe for Chicken Fajitas for a Charcoal Grill through step 1.

2. Turn all the burners to high and heat the grill, with the lid down, until very hot, about 15 minutes. Use a grill brush to scrape the cooking grate clean. Dip a wad of paper towels in the oil; holding the wad with tongs, oil the cooking grate. Leave one burner on high heat and turn the remaining burner(s) down to medium. Continue with the recipe from step 3, cooking the chicken and vegetables covered.

3. When the grill is empty, set all the burners to medium. Working in batches, if necessary, place the tortillas in a single layer on the cooking grate and grill until warm and lightly browned, about 20 seconds per side. As they are done, wrap the tortillas in a kitchen towel or large sheet of foil. Proceed with the recipe as directed in step 5.

STEAK FAJITAS

WHY THIS RECIPE WORKS: Steak fajitas were originally made with skirt steak, but the wider availability of flank steak has made it the cut of choice for this dish. Recipes for fajitas are fairly straightforward—grill the meat and vegetables and serve them in a warm tortilla. But too often, fajitas are lackluster or ruined by unnecessary complexity. We want fajitas that boasted flawless, flavorful meat with a rosy interior and browned crust.

Marinating is often recommended as a way to tenderize flank steak, but we learned that it's plenty tender without a marinade if sliced thin against the grain after being cooked. But we did want to add flavor. A long soak turned the meat mushy, but a squeeze of lime juice and a generous dose of salt and pepper just before grilling added all the extra flavor we wanted. The tried-and-true way of cooking flank steak—over high heat for a short period of time—required no changes. We found that the meat is juicier when allowed to rest after grilling, and that gave us time to grill the vegetables. Served in tortillas with freshly made guacamole, these fajitas delivered on all fronts.

Steak Fajitas for a Charcoal Grill

SERVES 8

The ingredients go on the grill in order as the fire dies down: steak over a medium-hot fire, vegetables over a medium fire, and tortillas around the edge of a medium to low fire just to warm them. Make sure to cover the grilled but unsliced flank steak with foil; it will take you at least 10 minutes to get the vegetables and tortillas ready.

Vegetable oil for the cooking grate
1 (2½-pound) flank steak, trimmed
¼ cup juice from 2 limes
Table salt and ground black pepper
1 very large onion, peeled and cut into ½-inch-thick rounds (do not separate the rings)
2 very large red or green bell peppers, stemmed, seeded, and quartered
16 (10 to 12-inch) flour tortillas
1 recipe Chunky Guacamole (page 348)

1. Light a large chimney starter filled with charcoal (about 6 quarts) and allow to burn until the coals are partially covered with a layer of ash, about 20 minutes. Build a single-level fire by arranging the coals evenly over the bottom of the grill. Set the cooking grate in place, cover the grill, and heat the grate until hot, about 5 minutes. Use a grill brush to scrape the cooking grate clean. Dip a wad of paper towels in oil; holding the wad with tongs, oil the cooking grate.

2. Generously sprinkle both sides of the steak with the lime juice and season with salt and pepper. Grill the steak over the coals until well seared and dark brown on one side, 5 to 7 minutes. Flip the steak using tongs; continue grilling on the other side until the interior of the meat is slightly less done than you want it to be when you eat it, 2 to 5 minutes more for medium-rare (depending on the heat of the fire and the thickness of the steak). Transfer the meat to a cutting board; cover loosely with foil, and let rest for 10 minutes.

3. While the meat rests, grill the onions and peppers, turning them occasionally, until the onions are lightly charred, about 6 minutes, and the peppers are streaked with grill marks, about 10 minutes. Remove the vegetables from the grill. Separate the onions into rings and slice the bell peppers lengthwise into thin strips; set aside. Arrange the tortillas around the edge of the grill; heat until just warmed, about 20 seconds per side. Wrap the tortillas in a towel to keep warm and place in a basket.

4. Slice the steak very thin on the bias against the grain; season with salt and pepper to taste. Arrange the sliced meat and the vegetables on a large platter; serve immediately with the tortillas and guacamole passed separately.

Steak Fajitas for a Gas Grill

Follow the recipe for Steak Fajitas for a Charcoal Grill. In step 1, turn all the burners to high and heat the grill, covered, until very hot, about 15 minutes. Scrape the cooking grate clean with a wire brush. Dip a wad of paper towels in oil; holding the wad with tongs, oil the cooking grate. Cook the steak in step 2 with the lid down for 4 to 6 minutes on the first side and 2 to 5 minutes on the second side. In step 3, adjust the burners to medium before grilling the vegetables.

NOTES FROM THE TEST KITCHEN

STEMMING AND SEEDING BELL PEPPERS

1. Slice ¼ inch from the top and bottom of each pepper and then gently remove the stem from the top lobe.

2. Pull the core out of the pepper. Make a slit down one side of the pepper and lay it flat, skin side down, in one long strip.

3. Slide a sharp knife along the inside of the pepper to remove all the ribs and seeds.

CHICKEN ENCHILADAS

WHY THIS RECIPE WORKS: Chicken enchiladas are a complete meal that offers a rich and complex combination of flavors, textures, and ingredients. The problem with preparing enchiladas at home is that traditional cooking methods require a whole day of preparation. We wanted a recipe for an Americanized version of chicken enchiladas that could be made in 90 minutes from start to finish.

To save time preparing the tortillas, we sprayed them with vegetable oil spray and warmed them on a baking sheet in the oven. We created a quick chili sauce with onions, garlic, spices, and tomato sauce, and to further enhance the sauce's flavor, we poached the chicken right in the sauce. This step also made for moist, flavorful meat. And cheddar cheese spiked with canned jalapeños and fresh cilantro made a rich, flavorful filling.

Chicken Enchiladas with Red Chili Sauce

SERVES 4 TO 5

Monterey Jack can be used instead of cheddar, or for a mellower flavor and creamier texture, try farmer's cheese. Be sure to cool the chicken before filling the tortillas; otherwise the hot filling will make the enchiladas soggy.

SAUCE AND FILLING

1½ tablespoons vegetable oil
1   medium onion, chopped fine
3   medium garlic cloves, minced or pressed through
    a garlic press (about 1 tablespoon)
3   tablespoons chili powder
2   teaspoons ground coriander
2   teaspoons ground cumin
2   teaspoons sugar
½   teaspoon table salt
12 ounces boneless, skinless chicken thighs
    (about 4 thighs), trimmed and cut into
    ¼-inch-wide strips
2   (8-ounce) cans tomato sauce
¾   cup water
8   ounces sharp cheddar cheese (see note), shredded
    (about 2 cups)
½   cup coarsely chopped fresh cilantro leaves
1   (4-ounce) can pickled jalapeño chiles, drained
    and chopped (about ¼ cup)

TORTILLAS AND TOPPINGS

  10 **(6-inch) corn tortillas**
     Vegetable oil spray
   3 **ounces sharp cheddar cheese (see note), shredded**
     (about ¾ cup)
  ¾ **cup sour cream**
   1 **medium, ripe avocado, diced medium**
     (see page 348)
   5 **romaine lettuce leaves, shredded**
     Lime wedges

1. FOR THE SAUCE AND FILLING: Heat the oil in a medium saucepan over medium-high heat until shimmering. Add the onion and cook, stirring occasionally, until softened and beginning to brown, about 5 minutes. Add the garlic, chili powder, coriander, cumin, sugar, and salt and cook, stirring constantly, until fragrant, about 30 seconds. Add the chicken and cook, stirring constantly, until coated with the spices, about 30 seconds. Add the tomato sauce and water, stir to separate the chicken pieces, and bring to a simmer. Reduce the heat to medium-low and simmer, uncovered, stirring occasionally, until the chicken is cooked through and the flavors have melded, about 8 minutes. Pour the mixture through a medium-mesh strainer into a medium bowl, pressing on the chicken and onions to extract as much sauce as possible; set the sauce aside. Transfer the chicken

mixture to a large plate; place in the freezer for 10 minutes to cool, then combine with the cheddar, cilantro, and jalapeños in a medium bowl.

2. Adjust the oven racks to the upper-middle and lower-middle positions and heat the oven to 300 degrees.

3. TO ASSEMBLE: Smear the bottom of a 13 by 9-inch baking dish with ¾ cup of the chili sauce. Place the tortillas in a single layer on two baking sheets. Spray both sides of the tortillas lightly with vegetable oil spray. Bake until the tortillas are soft and pliable, about 4 minutes. Transfer the warm tortillas to a work surface. Increase the oven temperature to 400 degrees. Spread ⅓ cup of the filling down the center of each tortilla. Roll each tortilla tightly by hand and place, seam side down, side by side on the sauce in the baking dish. Pour the remaining chili sauce over the top of the enchiladas. Use the back of a spoon to spread the sauce so it coats the top of each tortilla. Sprinkle the cheese down the center of the enchiladas.

4. TO BAKE: Cover the baking dish with foil. Bake the enchiladas on the lower-middle rack until heated through and the cheese is melted, 20 to 25 minutes. Uncover and serve immediately, passing the sour cream, avocado, lettuce, and lime wedges separately.

ENCHILADAS VERDES

WHY THIS RECIPE WORKS: We love the bright taste of enchiladas verdes. But too often the green chili sauce is watery and lacks good green chile flavor. We wanted to re-create the memorable enchiladas verdes found in good Mexican restaurants: moist, tender chicken and fresh, citrusy flavors wrapped in soft corn tortillas and topped with just the right amount of melted cheese.

The chicken was easy; we poached it in chicken broth enhanced with sautéed onion, garlic, and cumin. The green sauce is based on tomatillos and chiles. Jalapeños and serranos are good for adding heat to a dish, but we wanted a more complex herbal flavor and opted for poblanos. To get the characteristic char, which Mexican cooks achieve by roasting on a comal, we tossed the chiles and fresh tomatillos with a little oil and ran them under the broiler. Pulsed in a food processor and thinned with a bit of the broth left from poaching the chicken, the tomatillos and chiles formed a well-seasoned, chunky sauce. To enrich the filling, we liked pepper Jack cheese—and sprinkled more on top of the dish. To make the tortillas pliable and easy to roll, we picked up the same technique from our Chicken Enchiladas with Red Chili Sauce (page 359): We sprayed them with vegetable oil spray and baked them for a few minutes. The enchiladas required just a brief stint in the oven to heat through and melt the cheese. Garnished with sour cream, scallions, and radishes, these enchiladas may have the authentic restaurant version beat.

Enchiladas Verdes

SERVES 4 TO 6

You can substitute 3 (11-ounce) cans tomatillos, drained and rinsed, for the fresh ones in this recipe. Halve large tomatillos (more than 2 inches in diameter) and place them skin side up for broiling in step 2 to ensure even cooking and charring. If you can't find poblanos, substitute 4 large jalapeño chiles (with seeds and ribs removed). To increase the spiciness of the sauce, reserve some of the chiles' ribs and seeds and add them to the food processor in step 3.

ENCHILADAS

- 4 teaspoons vegetable oil
- 1 medium onion, chopped medium
- 3 medium garlic cloves, minced or pressed through a garlic press (about 1 tablespoon)
- ½ teaspoon ground cumin
- 1½ cups low-sodium chicken broth
- 1 pound boneless, skinless chicken breasts (2 to 3 breasts), trimmed
- 1½ pounds tomatillos (16 to 20 medium), husks and stems removed, rinsed well and dried (see note)
- 3 medium poblano chiles, halved lengthwise, stemmed, and seeded (see note)
- 1–2 teaspoons sugar
  Table salt and ground black pepper
- ½ cup coarsely chopped fresh cilantro leaves
- 8 ounces pepper Jack or Monterey Jack cheese, grated (about 2 cups)
- 12 (6-inch) corn tortillas

GARNISHES

- 2 medium scallions, sliced thin
  Thinly sliced radishes
  Sour cream

1. Adjust the oven racks to the middle and highest positions and heat the broiler. Heat 2 teaspoons of the oil in

a medium saucepan over medium heat until shimmering; add the onion and cook, stirring frequently, until golden, 6 to 8 minutes. Add 2 teaspoons of the garlic and the cumin; cook, stirring frequently, until fragrant, about 30 seconds. Decrease the heat to low and stir in the broth. Add the chicken, cover, and simmer until the thickest part of the chicken registers 160 to 165 degrees on an instant-read thermometer, 15 to 20 minutes, flipping the chicken halfway through cooking. Transfer the chicken to a large bowl; place in the refrigerator to cool, about 20 minutes. Remove ¼ cup liquid from the saucepan and set aside; discard the remaining liquid.

2. Meanwhile, toss the tomatillos and poblanos with the remaining 2 teaspoons oil; arrange on a rimmed baking sheet lined with foil, with the poblanos skin side up. Broil until the vegetables blacken and start to soften, 5 to 10 minutes, rotating the pan halfway through cooking. Cool for 10 minutes, then remove the skin from the poblanos (leave the tomatillo skins intact). Transfer the tomatillos and chiles to a food processor. Decrease the oven temperature to 350 degrees. Discard the foil from the baking sheet and set the baking sheet aside for warming the tortillas.

3. Add 1 teaspoon of the sugar, 1 teaspoon salt, the remaining 1 teaspoon garlic, and the reserved ¼ cup cooking liquid to the food processor; pulse until the sauce is somewhat chunky, about 8 pulses. Taste the sauce; season with salt and pepper to taste and adjust tartness by stirring in the remaining sugar, ½ teaspoon at a time. Set the sauce aside (you should have about 3 cups).

4. When the chicken is cool, pull into shreds using your hands or two forks, then chop into small bite-size pieces. Combine the chicken with the cilantro and 1½ cups of the cheese; season with salt to taste.

5. Smear the bottom of a 13 by 9-inch baking dish with

¾ cup of the tomatillo sauce. Place the tortillas in a single layer on two baking sheets. Spray both sides of the tortillas lightly with vegetable oil spray. Bake until the tortillas are soft and pliable, 2 to 4 minutes. Increase the oven temperature to 450 degrees. Place the warm tortillas on the work surface and spread ⅓ cup of the filling down the center of each tortilla. Roll each tortilla tightly by hand and place in the baking dish, seam side down. Pour the remaining tomatillo sauce over the top of the enchiladas. Use the back of a spoon to spread the sauce so that it coats the top of each tortilla. Sprinkle with the remaining ½ cup cheese and cover the baking dish with foil.

6. Bake the enchiladas on the middle oven rack until heated through and the cheese is melted, 15 to 20 minutes. Uncover, sprinkle with the scallions, and serve immediately, passing the radishes and sour cream separately.

SPICY MEXICAN SHREDDED PORK TOSTADAS

WHY THIS RECIPE WORKS: True Mexican shredded pork, or *tinga*, is a far cry from the bland burrito-joint version often found languishing on steam tables. We set out to perfect the methods that give tinga its characteristic crisp texture and smoky tomato flavor. We wanted tender, full-flavored Mexican shredded pork that we could serve atop crisp corn tortillas or spoon into taco shells.

We trimmed and cubed a Boston butt (chosen for its good marbling and little sinew), then simmered the pieces in water that we flavored with garlic, thyme, and onion. Once the pork was tender, we drained the meat (reserving some of the cooking liquid for the sauce) and returned it to the pot to shred. The meat was so tender, it fell apart with nothing more than the pressure of a potato masher. We then sautéed the meat in a hot frying pan along with the requisite additions of finely chopped onion and oregano. Minutes later, the pork had developed crackling edges crisp enough to survive the final step of simmering in tomato sauce. Unlike American barbecue with its sweet and tangy barbecue sauce, tinga relies on a complex smoke-flavored tomato sauce. For our version, we diluted canned tomato sauce with the reserved flavorful cooking liquid from the pork and added bay leaves for herbal complexity. And for tinga's all-important smokiness, we turned to ground chipotle powder, which is a little harder to find than the other option of canned chipotle chiles in adobo sauce, but has a deeper, more complex flavor.

Spicy Mexican Shredded Pork Tostadas

SERVES 4 TO 6

The trimmed pork should weigh about 1½ pounds. The shredded pork is traditionally served on tostadas (crisp fried corn tortillas), but you can also use the meat in tacos or burritos or simply served over rice. Make sure to buy tortillas made only with corn, lime, and salt—preservatives will compromise quality. We prefer the complex flavor of chipotle powder, but two minced canned chipotle chiles can be used in its place. The pork can be prepared through step 1 and refrigerated in an airtight container for up to 2 days. The tostadas can be made up to a day in advance and stored in an airtight container.

SHREDDED PORK

2 pounds boneless pork butt roast, trimmed of excess fat and cut into 1-inch pieces (see note)

2 medium onions, 1 quartered and 1 chopped fine

5 medium garlic cloves, 3 peeled and smashed and 2 minced or pressed through a garlic press (about 2 teaspoons)

4 sprigs fresh thyme

Table salt

2 tablespoons olive oil

½ teaspoon dried oregano

1 (14.5-ounce) can tomato sauce

1 tablespoon ground chipotle powder (see note)

2 bay leaves

TOSTADAS

¾ cup vegetable oil

12 (6-inch) corn tortillas (see note)

Table salt

GARNISHES

Queso fresco or feta cheese

Fresh cilantro leaves

Sour cream

Diced avocado

Lime wedges

1. FOR THE SHREDDED PORK: Bring the pork, quartered onion, smashed garlic cloves, thyme, 1 teaspoon salt, and 6 cups water to a simmer in a large saucepan over medium-high heat, skimming off any foam that rises to the surface. Reduce the heat to medium-low, partially cover, and cook until the pork is tender, 1¼ to 1½ hours. Drain the pork, reserving 1 cup cooking liquid. Discard the onion, garlic, and thyme. Return the pork to the saucepan and, using a potato masher, mash until shredded into rough ½-inch pieces; set aside.

2. Heat the olive oil in a 12-inch nonstick skillet over medium-high heat until shimmering. Add the shredded pork, chopped onion, and oregano; cook, stirring often, until the pork is well browned and crisp, 7 to 10 minutes. Add the minced garlic and cook until fragrant, about 30 seconds.

3. Stir in the tomato sauce, chipotle powder, reserved pork cooking liquid, and bay leaves; simmer until almost all the liquid has evaporated, 5 to 7 minutes. Remove and discard the bay leaves and season with salt to taste.

4. TO FRY THE TOSTADAS: Heat the vegetable oil in an 8-inch heavy-bottomed skillet over medium heat to 350 degrees. Using a fork, poke the center of each tortilla three or four times (to prevent puffing and allow for even cooking). Fry one at a time, holding a metal potato masher in the upright position on top of the tortilla to keep it submerged, until crisp and lightly browned, 45 to 60 seconds (no flipping is necessary). Drain on a paper towel–lined plate and season with salt to taste. Repeat with the remaining tortillas.

5. TO SERVE: Spoon a small amount of shredded pork onto the center of each tostada and serve, passing the garnishes separately.

MEXICAN PULLED PORK

WHY THIS RECIPE WORKS: Traditional *carnitas*, Mexico's version of pulled pork, is fried in gallons of lard or oil. The results are tasty, but who wants to deal with all that hot fat? We wanted restaurant-style carnitas—tender chunks of lightly crisped, caramelized pork, subtly accented with oregano and citrus—without the hassle of frying.

Our initial recipe for carnitas started by simmering the meat (taste tests proved boneless pork butt had the best flavor) in a seasoned broth in the oven and then sautéing it in some of the rendered fat. The flavor was OK, but too much of the pork flavor was lost when we discarded the cooking liquid. So we reduced the liquid on the stovetop (after the meat had been removed) to the consistency of a thick, syrupy glaze that was perfect for coating the meat. Broiled on a rack set over a baking sheet, the glazed meat developed a wonderfully rich flavor, and the rack allowed the excess fat to drip off. We emulated the flavor of the Mexican sour oranges used in authentic carnitas with a mixture of fresh lime and orange juices. Bay leaves and oregano provided aromatic notes, and cumin brought an earthiness that complemented the other flavors.

Mexican Pulled Pork (Carnitas)

SERVES 6

We like serving carnitas spooned into tacos, but you can also use it as a filling for tamales, enchiladas, and burritos.

PORK

1 (3½ to 4-pound) boneless pork butt, fat cap trimmed to ⅛ inch thick, cut into 2-inch chunks

1 small onion, peeled and halved

2 bay leaves

1 teaspoon dried oregano

1 teaspoon ground cumin
Table salt and ground black pepper
2 cups water
2 tablespoons juice from 1 lime
1 medium orange, halved

TORTILLAS AND GARNISHES
18 (6-inch) corn tortillas, warmed (see note on page 362)
Lime wedges
Minced white or red onion
Fresh cilantro leaves
Thinly sliced radishes
Sour cream

1. Adjust an oven rack to the lower-middle position and heat the oven to 300 degrees. Combine the pork, onion, bay leaves, oregano, cumin, 1 teaspoon salt, ½ teaspoon pepper, water, and lime juice in a large Dutch oven (the liquid should just barely cover the meat). Juice the orange into a medium bowl and remove any seeds (you should have about ⅓ cup juice). Add the juice and spent orange halves to the pot. Bring the mixture to a simmer over medium-high heat, stirring occasionally. Cover the pot and transfer it to the oven; cook until the meat is soft and falls apart when prodded with a fork, about 2 hours, flipping the pieces of meat once during cooking.

2. Remove the pot from the oven and turn the oven to broil. Using a slotted spoon, transfer the pork to a bowl; remove the orange halves, onion, and bay leaves from the cooking liquid and discard (do not skim the fat from the liquid). Place the pot over high heat (use caution, as the handles will be very hot) and simmer the liquid, stirring frequently, until thick and syrupy (a heatproof spatula should leave a wide trail when dragged through the glaze), 8 to 12 minutes. You should have about 1 cup reduced liquid.

3. Using two forks, pull each piece of pork in half. Fold in the reduced liquid; season with salt and pepper to taste. Spread the pork in an even layer on a wire rack set over a rimmed baking sheet or on a broiler pan (the meat should cover almost the entire surface of the rack or broiler pan). Place the baking sheet on the lower-middle oven rack and broil until the top of the meat is well browned (but not charred) and the edges are slightly crisp, 5 to 8 minutes. Using a wide metal spatula, flip the pieces of meat and continue to broil until the top is well browned and the edges are slightly crisp, 5 to 8 minutes longer. Serve immediately with the warm tortillas and garnishes.

MEXICAN RICE

WHY THIS RECIPE WORKS: Rice cooked the Mexican way is a flavorful pilaf-style dish, but we've had our share of soupy or greasy versions. We wanted tender rice infused with well-balanced fresh flavor.

Texture is the backbone of this dish. To keep the rice grains distinct, we found it important to rinse the rice of excess starch before cooking it. And sautéing the rice in vegetable oil before adding the cooking liquid produced superior grains. The best texture for the rice was achieved by properly balancing the grain-to-liquid ratio. We found that equal portions of chicken broth and fresh tomatoes were ideal for a flavorful liquid base, which we combined in a 2:1 ratio with the rice. To further guarantee the right flavor, color, and texture, we added a little tomato paste and stirred the rice midway through cooking to reincorporate the tomato mixture. The garlic and jalapeños, meanwhile, fared best sautéed and then combined with a raw puree of tomato and onion. More than a garnish, fresh cilantro, minced jalapeño, and squirt of fresh lime juice complemented the richer tones of the cooked tomatoes, garlic, and onions. Our rice was neither greasy nor soggy, and the fresh flavors and easy preparation made it a unique side dish for a weeknight dinner.

Mexican Rice
SERVES 6 TO 8
Because the spiciness of jalapeños varies from chile to chile, we try to control the heat by removing the ribs and seeds (the source of most of the heat) from those chiles that are cooked into the rice. It is important to use an ovensafe pot about 12 inches in diameter so that the rice cooks evenly and in the time indicated. The pot's depth is less important than its diameter; we've successfully used both a straight-sided sauté pan and a Dutch oven. Whichever type of pot you use, it should have a tight-fitting, ovensafe lid. Vegetable broth can be substituted for the chicken broth.

2 medium ripe tomatoes (about 12 ounces),
cored and quartered
1 medium onion, preferably white, peeled and quartered
3 medium jalapeño chiles (see note)
2 cups long-grain white rice

⅓   cup vegetable oil

4   medium garlic cloves, minced or pressed through a garlic press (about 4 teaspoons)

2   cups low-sodium chicken broth (see note)

1   tablespoon tomato paste

1½ teaspoons table salt

½   cup minced fresh cilantro leaves

Lime wedges, for serving

1. Adjust an oven rack to the middle position and heat the oven to 350 degrees. Process the tomatoes and onion in a food processor until smooth and thoroughly pureed, about 15 seconds, scraping down the bowl if necessary. Transfer the mixture to a liquid measuring cup; you should have 2 cups (if necessary, spoon off the excess so that the volume equals 2 cups). Remove the ribs and seeds from 2 of the jalapeños and discard; mince the flesh and set aside. Mince the remaining jalapeño, including the ribs and seeds; set aside.

2. Place the rice in a large fine-mesh strainer and rinse under cold running water until the water runs clear, about 1½ minutes. Shake the rice vigorously in the strainer to remove all excess water.

3. Heat the oil in a heavy-bottomed straight-sided 12-inch ovenproof sauté pan or Dutch oven with a tight-fitting lid over medium-high heat for 1 to 2 minutes. Drop

3 or 4 grains of rice into the oil; if the grains sizzle, the oil is ready. Add the rice and fry, stirring frequently, until the rice is light golden and translucent, 6 to 8 minutes. Reduce the heat to medium, add the garlic and seeded minced jalapeños, and cook, stirring constantly, until fragrant, about 1½ minutes. Stir in the pureed tomato mixture, chicken broth, tomato paste, and salt. Increase the heat to medium-high and bring to a boil. Cover the pan and transfer to the oven. Bake until the liquid is absorbed and the rice is tender, 30 to 35 minutes, stirring well after 15 minutes.

4. Stir in the cilantro and reserved minced jalapeño with seeds to taste. Serve immediately, passing the lime wedges separately.

BASIC CHILI

WHY THIS RECIPE WORKS: Many basic chili recipes yield a pot of underspiced, underflavored chili reminiscent of sloppy Joes. We wanted an easy recipe for a basic chili, made with supermarket staples, that would have some heat and great flavors—chili that would please almost everyone.

To start, we added the spices to the pan with the aromatics (bell peppers, onion, and lots of garlic) to get the most flavor, and used commercial chili powder with a boost from more cumin, oregano, cayenne, and coriander. For the meat, we found that 85 percent lean beef gave us full flavor. A combination of diced tomato and tomato puree gave our chili a well-balanced saucy backbone. We added quick-cooking canned red kidney beans with the tomatoes so that they heated through and absorbed flavor. For a rich, thick consistency, we cooked the chili with the lid on for half of the cooking time.

Beef Chili with Kidney Beans
SERVES 8 TO 10

Good choices for condiments include diced fresh tomatoes, diced avocado, sliced scallions, chopped red onion, chopped cilantro leaves, sour cream, and shredded Monterey Jack or cheddar cheese. If you are a fan of spicy food, consider using a little more of the red pepper flakes or cayenne—or both. The flavor of the chili improves with age; if possible, make it a day or up to 3 days in advance and reheat before serving. Leftovers can be frozen for up to 1 month.

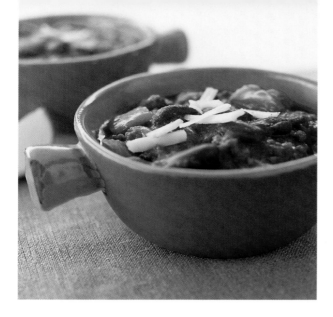

2 tablespoons vegetable oil

2 medium onions, minced (about 2 cups)

1 medium red bell pepper, stemmed, seeded, and cut into
   ½-inch dice

6 medium garlic cloves, minced or pressed through
   a garlic press (about 2 tablespoons)

¼ cup chili powder

1 tablespoon ground cumin

2 teaspoons ground coriander

1 teaspoon red pepper flakes (see note)

1 teaspoon dried oregano

½ teaspoon cayenne pepper (see note)

2 pounds 85 percent lean ground beef

2 (15-ounce) cans dark red kidney beans, drained
   and rinsed

1 (28-ounce) can diced tomatoes

1 (28-ounce) can tomato puree

   Table salt

   Lime wedges, for serving

1. Heat the oil in a large heavy-bottomed nonreactive Dutch oven over medium heat until shimmering but not smoking. Add the onions, bell pepper, garlic, chili powder, cumin, coriander, red pepper flakes, oregano, and cayenne and cook, stirring occasionally, until the vegetables are softened and beginning to brown, about 10 minutes. Increase the heat to medium-high and add half of the beef. Cook, breaking up the pieces with a wooden spoon, until no longer pink and just beginning to brown, 3 to 4 minutes. Add the remaining beef and cook, breaking up the pieces with a wooden spoon, until no longer pink, 3 to 4 minutes.

2. Add the beans, tomatoes with juice, tomato puree, and ½ teaspoon salt. Bring to a boil, then reduce the heat to low and simmer, covered, stirring occasionally, for 1 hour. Remove the lid and continue to simmer for

1 hour longer, stirring occasionally (if the chili begins to stick to the bottom of the pot, stir in ½ cup water and continue to simmer), until the beef is tender and the chili is dark, rich, and slightly thickened. Season with salt to taste. Serve with the lime wedges and condiments (see note), if desired.

CHILI CON CARNE

WHY THIS RECIPE WORKS: Real Texas chili, made with dried chiles rather than chili powder, should have exceptional chile flavor but not overpowering heat, a smooth, rich sauce, and hearty chunks of meat. We wanted to develop the ultimate version.

There are many types of dried chiles, and we chose a combination of ancho and New Mexican for a combination of earthy, fruity sweetness and crisp acidity. While chili powder works fine, we got the best flavor by toasting and grinding chiles ourselves. Chuck-eye is our favored cut of beef for stews and it seemed right for our chili. We cut the meat into 1-inch chunks, which gave the chili a hearty texture. Then, we browned the meat in fat rendered from bacon, which added a smoky depth to the dish. From among the many recommended liquids to use in chili con carne, we chose plain old water—everything else diluted or competed with the flavor of the chiles. Although many "authentic" recipes include neither tomatoes nor onions, we found both to be valuable additions. To thicken the chili, we mixed in some masa harina, which also imparted a subtle corn flavor.

Chili Con Carne

SERVES 6

To ensure the best chile flavor, we recommend toasting whole dried chiles and grinding them in a minichopper or spice-dedicated coffee grinder, all of which takes only 10 (very well-spent) minutes. Select dried chiles that are moist and pliant, like dried fruit. To toast and grind dried chiles: Place the chiles on a baking sheet in a 350-degree oven until fragrant and puffed, about 6 minutes. Cool, stem, and seed the pods, and tear them into pieces. Place pieces of the pods in a spice grinder and process until powdery, 30 to 45 seconds. For hotter chili, boost the heat with a pinch of cayenne pepper or a dash of hot sauce. Top with any of the following garnishes: chopped fresh cilantro leaves, minced white onion, diced avocado, shredded cheddar or Jack cheese, or sour cream.

3 medium ancho pods (about ½ ounce), toasted and ground (see note), or 3 tablespoons ancho chile powder

3 medium New Mexican pods (about ¾ ounce), toasted and ground (see note), or 3 tablespoons New Mexican chile powder

2 tablespoons cumin seeds, toasted in a dry skillet over medium heat until fragrant, about 4 minutes, and ground

2 teaspoons dried oregano, preferably Mexican

7½ cups water, plus extra for the masa harina or cornstarch

4 pounds beef chuck-eye roast, trimmed of excess fat and cut into 1-inch cubes
  Table salt

8 ounces bacon (about 8 slices), cut into ¼-inch pieces

1 medium onion, minced

5 medium garlic cloves, minced or pressed through a garlic press (about 5 teaspoons)

4–5 small jalapeño chiles, stemmed, seeded, and minced

1 cup canned crushed tomatoes or plain tomato sauce

2 tablespoons juice from 1 lime

5 tablespoons masa harina or 3 tablespoons cornstarch
  Ground black pepper

1. Mix the chili powders, cumin, and oregano in a small bowl and stir in ½ cup of the water to form a thick paste; set aside. Toss the beef cubes with 2 teaspoons salt in a large bowl; set aside.

2. Fry the bacon in a large Dutch oven over medium-low heat until the fat renders and the bacon crisps, about 10 minutes. Remove the bacon with a slotted spoon to a paper towel–lined plate; pour all but 2 teaspoons fat from the pot into a small bowl; set aside. Increase the heat to medium-high; sauté the meat in four batches until well browned on all sides, about 5 minutes per batch, adding 2 teaspoons more bacon fat to the pot each time as necessary. Set the browned meat aside in a large bowl.

3. Reduce the heat to medium and add 3 tablespoons more bacon fat to the now-empty pan. Add the onion and sauté until softened, 5 to 6 minutes. Add the garlic and jalapeños and sauté until fragrant, about 1 minute. Add the chili powder mixture and sauté until fragrant, 2 to 3 minutes. Add the reserved bacon and browned beef, the remaining 7 cups water, the crushed tomatoes, and lime juice. Bring to a simmer. Continue to cook at a steady simmer (lowering the heat as necessary) until the meat is tender and the juices are dark and rich and starting to thicken, about 2 hours.

4. Mix the masa harina with ⅔ cup water (or cornstarch with 3 tablespoons water) in a small bowl to form a smooth paste. Increase the heat to medium, stir in the paste, and simmer until thickened, 5 to 10 minutes. Season generously with salt and pepper to taste. Serve immediately or, for best flavor, cool slightly, cover, and refrigerate overnight or for up to 5 days. Reheat before serving.

WHITE CHICKEN CHILI

WHY THIS RECIPE WORKS: Chili made with chicken has become popular as a lighter, fresher alternative to the red kind. Though many recipes produce something more akin to chicken and bean soup, we thought there was potential to develop a rich stewlike chili with moist chicken, tender beans, and a complex flavor profile.

Ground chicken had a spongy texture and crumbly appearance, so we chose bone-in, skin-on breasts, later shredding the meat and discarding the skin and bones, and used the fat rendered from searing them to cook the aromatics. A single type of chile was one-dimensional; we used a combination of jalapeño, Anaheim, and poblano chiles, which have distinct characteristics that complement one another. Simply sautéing the chiles with the other aromatics left them flat-tasting and too crisp, so we covered the pot and cooked them longer to soften them and deepen their flavors. Canned cannellini beans circumvented the hassle of dried beans and tasted just as good. We tried thickening the chili with masa harina, which we had used for chili con carne, but the texture and flavor didn't work well here. Instead, we pureed some of the chili mixture, beans, and broth, which made the chili thicker without compromising its flavor. To finish, a minced raw jalapeño stirred in before serving provided a shot of fresh chile flavor.

White Chicken Chili

SERVES 6 TO 8

Adjust the heat in this dish by adding the minced ribs and seeds from the jalapeño as directed in step 6. If Anaheim chiles cannot be found, add an additional poblano and jalapeño to the chili. This dish can also be successfully made by substituting chicken thighs for the chicken breasts. If using thighs, increase the cooking time in step 4 to about 40 minutes or until the chicken registers 175 degrees on an instant-read thermometer. Serve the chili with sour cream, tortilla chips, and lime wedges.

    3 pounds bone-in, skin-on chicken breast halves,
       trimmed
       Table salt and ground black pepper
    1 tablespoon vegetable oil
    3 medium jalapeño chiles (see note)
    3 medium poblano chiles (see note), stemmed,
       seeded, and cut into large pieces
    3 medium Anaheim chiles (see note), stemmed,
       seeded, and cut into large pieces
    2 medium onions, cut into large pieces (about 2 cups)
    6 medium garlic cloves, minced or pressed through
       a garlic press (about 2 tablespoons)
    1 tablespoon ground cumin
 1½ teaspoons ground coriander
    2 (15-ounce) cans cannellini beans, drained and rinsed
    3 cups low-sodium chicken broth
 ¼ cup minced fresh cilantro leaves
    3 tablespoons juice from 2 limes
    4 scallions, white and light green parts sliced thin

1. Season the chicken liberally with salt and pepper. Heat the oil in a large Dutch oven over medium-high heat until just smoking. Add the chicken, skin side down, and cook without moving until the skin is golden brown, about 4 minutes. Using tongs, turn the chicken and lightly brown the other side, about 2 minutes. Transfer the chicken to a plate; remove and discard the skin.

2. While the chicken is browning, remove and discard the ribs and seeds from 2 of the jalapeños; mince the flesh. In a food processor, pulse half of the poblanos, Anaheims, and onions until the consistency of chunky salsa, 10 to 12 pulses, scraping down the sides of the workbowl halfway through. Transfer the mixture to a medium bowl. Repeat with the remaining poblanos, Anaheims, and onions; combine with the first batch (do not wash the food processor blade or workbowl).

3. Pour off all but 1 tablespoon of the fat from the Dutch oven (adding more vegetable oil if necessary) and reduce the heat to medium. Add the minced jalapeños, chile-onion mixture, garlic, cumin, coriander, and ¼ teaspoon salt. Cover and cook, stirring occasionally, until the vegetables soften, about 10 minutes. Remove the pot from the heat.

4. Transfer 1 cup of the cooked vegetable mixture to the now-empty food processor workbowl. Add 1 cup of the beans and 1 cup of the broth and process until

smooth, about 20 seconds. Add the vegetable-bean mixture, remaining 2 cups broth, and chicken breasts to the Dutch oven and bring to a boil over medium-high heat. Reduce the heat to medium-low and simmer, covered, stirring occasionally, until the chicken registers 160 degrees (175 degrees if using thighs) on an instant-read thermometer, 15 to 20 minutes (40 minutes if using thighs).

5. Using tongs, transfer the chicken to a large plate. Stir in the remaining beans and continue to simmer, uncovered, until the beans are heated through and the chili has thickened slightly, about 10 minutes.

6. Mince the remaining jalapeño, reserving and mincing the ribs and seeds (see note), and set aside. When cool enough to handle, shred the chicken into bite-size pieces, discarding the bones. Stir the shredded chicken, cilantro, lime juice, scallions, and minced jalapeño (with seeds if desired) into the chili and return to a simmer. Season with salt and pepper to taste and serve.

HUEVOS RANCHEROS

WHY THIS RECIPE WORKS: This Mexican egg dish was devised to use up leftover salsa and tortillas for a quick but filling "rancher-style" breakfast. What you get on this side of the border, however, is often spoiled with unnecessary ingredients and muddy flavors. We wanted to use readily available ingredients to produce as authentic a version of this dish as we could.

The salsa is a crucial element, and we know from experience that jarred salsa can't compare to freshly made, so we looked for ways to maximize the flavor of our supermarket tomatoes. We found that roasting plum tomatoes turned them more flavorful, and we thought roasting the onion and jalapeños improved their flavor as well. It was difficult to get fried eggs from the skillet onto the tortillas neatly (and without breaking the yolks), so we turned to poaching the eggs for a tidier presentation. We made things even easier by poaching them right in the simmering salsa, saving ourselves a pot to clean in the bargain. To pep up the supermarket tortillas, we brushed them with a little oil, sprinkled them with salt, and toasted them in the oven. Crisp tortillas, creamy eggs, and fiery salsa combined for a great American version of this Mexican classic.

Huevos Rancheros

SERVES 2 TO 4

To save time, make the salsa the day before and store it in the refrigerator. If you like, serve with Refried Beans (recipe follows).

- 3 jalapeño chiles, halved, seeds and ribs removed
- 1½ pounds ripe plum tomatoes (about 6 medium), cored and halved
- ½ medium onion, cut into ½-inch wedges
- 3 tablespoons vegetable oil
- 1 tablespoon tomato paste
- 2 medium garlic cloves, peeled
  Table salt
- ½ teaspoon ground cumin
- ⅛ teaspoon cayenne pepper
- 3 tablespoons minced fresh cilantro leaves
  Ground black pepper
- 1–2 tablespoons juice from 1 lime, plus an additional lime cut into wedges, for serving
- 4 (6-inch) corn tortillas
- 4 large eggs

1. FOR THE SALSA: Adjust an oven rack to the middle position and heat the oven to 375 degrees. Mince 1 jalapeño and set aside. In a medium bowl, combine the tomatoes, remaining 2 jalapeños, onion, 2 tablespoons of the oil, the tomato paste, garlic, 1 teaspoon salt, cumin, and cayenne; toss to mix thoroughly. Place the vegetables, cut side down, on a rimmed baking sheet. Roast until the tomatoes are tender and the skins begin to shrivel and brown, 35 to 45 minutes; cool on the baking sheet for 10 minutes. Increase the oven temperature to 450 degrees. Using tongs, transfer the roasted onion, garlic, and jalapeños to a food processor. Process until almost completely broken down, about 10 seconds, pausing halfway through to scrape down the sides of the workbowl with a rubber spatula. Add the tomatoes and process until the salsa is slightly chunky, about 15 seconds more. Add 2 tablespoons of the cilantro, and the reserved minced jalapeño, salt, pepper, and lime juice to taste.

2. FOR THE TORTILLAS: Brush both sides of each tortilla lightly with the remaining 1 tablespoon oil, sprinkle both sides with salt, and place on a clean baking sheet. Bake until the tops just begin to color, 5 to 7 minutes; flip the tortillas and continue to bake until golden brown, 2 to 3 minutes more.

3. FOR THE EGGS: Meanwhile, bring the salsa to a gentle simmer in a 12-inch nonstick skillet over medium heat. Remove from the heat and make four shallow wells in the salsa with the back of a large spoon. Break 1 egg into a cup, then carefully pour the egg into a well in the salsa; repeat with the remaining 3 eggs. Season each egg with salt and pepper, then cover the skillet and place over medium–low heat. Cook to the desired doneness: 4 to 5 minutes for runny yolks, 6 to 7 minutes for set yolks.

4. TO SERVE: Place the tortillas on serving plates; gently scoop one egg onto each tortilla. Spoon the salsa around each egg, covering the tortillas but leaving a portion of the eggs exposed. Sprinkle with the remaining 1 tablespoon cilantro and serve with the lime wedges.

Refried Beans

MAKES ABOUT 3 CUPS

- 2 (15-ounce) cans pinto beans, drained and rinsed
- ¾ cup low-sodium chicken broth
- ½ teaspoon table salt
- 3 ounces (about 3 slices) bacon, minced
- 1 small onion, minced (about ¾ cup)
- 1 large jalapeño chile, stemmed, seeded, and minced (about 2 tablespoons)
- ½ teaspoon ground cumin
- 2 medium garlic cloves, minced or pressed through a garlic press (about 2 teaspoons)
- 2 tablespoons minced fresh cilantro leaves
- 2 teaspoons juice from 1 lime

1. Process all but 1 cup of the beans, the broth, and salt in a food processor until smooth, about 15 seconds, scraping down the sides of the workbowl with a rubber spatula if necessary. Add the remaining beans and pulse until slightly chunky, about 10 pulses.

2. Cook the bacon in a 12-inch nonstick skillet over medium heat until the bacon just begins to brown and most of the fat has rendered, about 4 minutes; transfer to a small bowl lined with a strainer; discard the bacon and add 1 tablespoon bacon fat back to the skillet. Increase the heat to medium-high, add the onion, jalapeño, and cumin, and cook until softened and just starting to brown, 3 to 5 minutes. Stir in the garlic and cook until fragrant, about 30 seconds. Reduce the heat to medium, stir in the pureed beans, and cook until thick and creamy, 4 to 6 minutes. Off the heat, stir in the cilantro and lime juice and serve.

CHAPTER 16

LET'S DO TAKEOUT

Potstickers with Scallion Dipping Sauce 372

Shu Mai (Steamed Chinese Dumplings) 373

Shrimp Tempura 375

Thai Pork Lettuce Wraps 376

Beef Satay 377

   Spicy Peanut Dipping Sauce

Thai-Style Chicken Soup 378

Hot and Sour Soup 379

Sesame Noodles with Shredded Chicken 380

Fried Rice with Shrimp, Pork, and Shiitakes 381

Fried Rice with Peas and Bean Sprouts 381

   Basic White Rice

Indonesian-Style Fried Rice (Nasi Goreng) 382

   Faux Leftover Rice

Chicken Teriyaki 383

Orange-Flavored Chicken 384

Stir-Fried Chicken with Bok Choy and Crispy Noodle Cake 385

Stir-Fried Chicken and Zucchini with Ginger Sauce 387

Stir-Fried Shrimp, Asparagus, and Yellow Pepper with Lemon Sauce 388

Stir-Fried Tofu, Snow Peas, and Red Onion with Hot and Sour Sauce 388

Stir-Fried Beef and Broccoli with Oyster Sauce 389

Teriyaki Stir-Fried Beef with Green Beans and Shiitakes 390

Tangerine Stir-Fried Beef with Onion and Snow Peas 391

Stir-Fried Pork, Eggplant, and Onion with Garlic and Black Pepper 392

Stir-Fried Pork, Green Beans, and Red Bell Pepper with Gingery Oyster Sauce 393

Pork Lo Mein 394

Stir-Fried Shrimp with Snow Peas and Red Bell Pepper in Hot and Sour Sauce 395

Stir-Fried Shrimp with Garlicky Eggplant, Scallions, and Cashews 396

Kung Pao Shrimp 396

Stir-Fried Portobellos with Ginger-Oyster Sauce 397

Stir-Fried Portobellos with Sweet Chili-Garlic Sauce 398

Thai-Style Chicken with Basil 399

Thai Green Curry with Chicken, Broccoli, and Mushrooms 400

   Green Curry Paste

Thai Red Curry with Shrimp, Pineapple, and Peanuts 400

   Red Curry Paste

Stir-Fried Thai-Style Beef with Chiles and Shallots 402

Pad Thai 403

Thai Grilled Chicken with Spicy, Sweet, and Sour Dipping Sauce 404

Grilled Thai Beef Salad 405

Chicken Tikka Masala 406

Chicken Biryani 407

Indian Curry 408

Indian-Style Curry with Potatoes, Cauliflower, Peas, and Chickpeas 409

Indian-Style Curry with Sweet Potatoes, Eggplant, Green Beans, and Chickpeas 410

   Onion Relish

   Cilantro-Mint Chutney

Tandoori Chicken 411

PERFECT POTSTICKERS

WHY THIS RECIPE WORKS: Too often, potstickers are dense, flavorless meatballs wrapped in a doughy blanket. We wanted soft, savory pillows filled with tender ground meat and crunchy cabbage and spiked with a pleasing hit of garlic, ginger, and soy. And we weren't willing to make wrappers from scratch.

To lighten up the filling a bit, we increased the amount of cabbage, after first salting and draining it to get rid of excess moisture, and then added lightly beaten egg whites. For the wrappers, we found that store-bought gyoza-style wrappers and wonton wrappers both made terrific potstickers, although tasters preferred the slightly chewy texture of the gyoza-style. To keep the filling in place and the wrapper from puffing up and away from the meat during cooking, we found it best to fold each meat-filled wrapper into a half-moon, pinch the middle closed, then carefully press out any air while sealing the edges. Our final challenge was the cooking method. A sequence of browning, steaming, then cranking up the heat produced potstickers with a perfect balance of soft and crispy textures.

Potstickers with Scallion Dipping Sauce

MAKES 24 DUMPLINGS

We prefer to use gyoza wrappers. You can substitute won-ton wrappers, but the cooking time and recipe yield will vary. Potstickers are best served hot from the skillet; we recommend that you serve the first batch immediately, then cook the second batch.

SCALLION DIPPING SAUCE

- ¼ cup soy sauce
- 2 tablespoons rice vinegar
- 2 tablespoons mirin or sweet sherry
- 2 tablespoons water
- 1 teaspoon chili oil (optional)
- ½ teaspoon toasted sesame oil
- 1 scallion, minced

POTSTICKERS

- 12 ounces napa cabbage (½ medium head), cored and minced
- ¾ teaspoon table salt
- 12 ounces ground pork
- 4 scallions, minced
- 2 large egg whites, lightly beaten
- 4 teaspoons soy sauce
- 1½ teaspoons minced or grated fresh ginger
- 1 medium garlic clove, minced or pressed through a garlic press (about 1 teaspoon)
- ⅛ teaspoon ground black pepper
- 24 round gyoza wrappers (see note)
- 4 teaspoons peanut or vegetable oil

1. FOR THE SAUCE: Combine all the ingredients in a small bowl and set aside. (The sauce can be refrigerated in an airtight container for up to 24 hours.)

2. FOR THE FILLING: Toss the cabbage and salt together in a colander set over a bowl and let sit until the cabbage begins to wilt, about 20 minutes. Press the cabbage gently with a rubber spatula to squeeze out excess moisture, then transfer to a medium bowl. Stir the pork, scallions, egg whites, soy sauce, ginger, garlic, and pepper into the cabbage until combined. Cover and refrigerate until the mixture is cold, at least 30 minutes or up to 24 hours.

3. Working with 4 wrappers at a time (keep the remaining wrappers covered with plastic wrap), follow the photos on page 373 to fill, seal, and shape the dumplings using a generous 1 tablespoon of the chilled filling per dumpling. Transfer the dumplings to a baking sheet. (The filled dumplings can be refrigerated for up to 24 hours in a single layer on a baking sheet wrapped tightly with plastic wrap or frozen for up to 1 month. Once frozen, the dumplings can be transferred to a zipper-lock bag to save space in the freezer; do not thaw before cooking.)

4. Brush 2 teaspoons of the peanut oil over the bottom of a 12-inch nonstick skillet and arrange half of the dumplings in the skillet, with a flat side facing down (overlapping just slightly, if necessary). Place the skillet over medium-high heat and cook the dumplings, without moving, until golden brown on the bottom, about 5 minutes.

5. Reduce the heat to low, add ½ cup water, and cover immediately. Cook until most of the water is absorbed and the wrappers are slightly translucent, about 10 minutes. Uncover, increase the heat to medium-high, and cook, without stirring, until the dumpling bottoms are well browned and crisp, 3 to 4 minutes. Slide the dumplings from the skillet onto a paper towel–lined plate, browned side down, and let drain briefly.

6. Transfer the dumplings to a platter and serve with the sauce. Let the skillet cool until just warm, then wipe out the skillet with a wad of paper towels and repeat with the remaining peanut oil and dumplings.

NOTES FROM THE TEST KITCHEN

WRAPPING POTSTICKERS

The instructions below are for round wrappers, our preferred shape. If using square wrappers, fold diagonally into a triangle (step 2) and proceed with the recipe. For rectangular wrappers, fold in half lengthwise.

1. Place a rounded tablespoon of the filling in the center of each gyoza wrapper.

2. After moistening the edge of the wrapper, fold it in half to make a half-moon shape.

3. With your forefinger and thumb, pinch the dumpling closed, pressing out any air pockets.

4. Place the dumpling on its side and press gently to flatten the bottom.

SHU MAI

WHY THIS RECIPE WORKS: Every so often we'll land on an exemplary version of *shu mai* (steamed Chinese dumplings)—one that boasts a tender, thin skin and a moist, flavorful filling. Our goal was to replicate this version at home.

Our favorite restaurant dumplings rely on coarse-ground pork and shrimp. We started with the pork. To ensure proper flavor and texture, we chose to chop the pork (boneless country-style ribs) in a food processor rather than relying on supermarket ground pork. Supermarket ground pork is often inconsistent—some packages can be lean while others are riddled with fat, and one package can be almost pastelike while another might contain visible chunks of meat and fat. To prevent the meat from drying out during steaming, we mixed in a little powdered gelatin dissolved in soy sauce. As for the shrimp, we added that to the food processor, too. Dried shiitake mushrooms, minced cilantro, fresh ginger, and water chestnuts were just a few of the ingredients we relied on to round out our flavorful filling.

For our dumpling wrappers, we chose widely available egg roll skins and cut them into rounds with a biscuit cutter. Once we added the filling and gathered the edges of the wrappers up around each one, we steamed our dumplings in a steamer basket. Served with a hot chili sauce, our dumplings were full-flavored and virtually foolproof.

Shu Mai (Steamed Chinese Dumplings)
MAKES ABOUT 40 DUMPLINGS

Do not trim the excess fat from the spareribs, as the fat contributes flavor and moistness. Use any size shrimp except popcorn shrimp; there's no need to halve shrimp smaller than 26 to 30 per pound before processing. The dumplings may be frozen for up to 3 months; cook straight from the freezer for about an extra 5 minutes. Shu mai are traditionally served with a spicy chili oil (recipe follows), or use store-bought.

FILLING AND FORMING SHU MAI

1. Brush the edges of the dumpling wrapper lightly with water. Place a heaping tablespoon of filling in the center of each wrapper.

2. Pinch two opposing sides of the wrapper with your fingers. Rotate the dumpling 90 degrees, and, again, pinch the opposing sides of the wrapper with your fingers.

3. Continue to pinch the dumpling until you have eight equidistant pinches around the circumference of the dumpling.

4. Gather up the sides of the dumpling and squeeze gently at the top to create a "waist."

5. Hold the dumpling in your hand and gently but firmly pack the filling into the dumpling with a butter knife.

- 2 **tablespoons soy sauce**
- ½ **teaspoon unflavored powdered gelatin**
- 1 **pound boneless country-style pork spareribs, cut into 1-inch pieces (see note)**
- ½ **pound shrimp, peeled, deveined (see page 205), tails removed, and halved lengthwise (see note)**
- ¼ **cup chopped water chestnuts**
- 4 **dried shiitake mushroom caps (about ¾ ounce), soaked in hot water for 30 minutes, squeezed dry, and cut into ¼-inch dice**
- 2 **tablespoons cornstarch**
- 2 **tablespoons minced fresh cilantro leaves**
- 1 **tablespoon toasted sesame oil**
- 1 **tablespoon dry sherry or Chinese rice cooking wine (Shao Xing)**
- 1 **tablespoon rice wine vinegar**
- 2 **teaspoons sugar**
- 2 **teaspoons grated fresh ginger**
- ½ **teaspoon table salt**
- ½ **teaspoon ground black pepper**
- 1 **(1 pound) package 5½-inch square egg roll wrappers**
- ¼ **cup finely grated carrot (optional)**

1. Combine the soy sauce and gelatin in a small bowl. Set aside to allow the gelatin to bloom, about 5 minutes.

2. Meanwhile, place half of the pork in a food processor and pulse until coarsely ground into pieces that are about ⅛ inch, about 10 pulses; transfer to a large bowl. Add the shrimp and remaining pork to the food processor and pulse until coarsely chopped into pieces that are about ¼ inch, about 5 pulses. Transfer to the bowl with the coarsely ground pork. Stir in the soy sauce mixture, water chestnuts, mushrooms, cornstarch, cilantro, sesame oil, cooking wine, vinegar, sugar, ginger, salt, and pepper until well combined.

3. Line a large baking sheet with parchment paper. Divide the egg roll wrappers into three stacks (six to seven per stack). Using a 3-inch biscuit cutter, cut two 3-inch rounds from each stack of egg roll wrappers (you should have 40 to 42 rounds). Cover the rounds with moist paper towels to prevent drying.

4. Working with six rounds at a time, brush the edges of each round lightly with water. Place a heaping table-spoon of filling in the center of each round. Following the photos, form the dumplings by crimping the wrapper around the sides of the filling and leaving the top exposed. Transfer to the prepared baking sheet, cover with a damp kitchen towel, and repeat with the remaining wrappers and filling. Top the center of each dumpling with a pinch of grated carrot (if using).

5. Cut a piece of parchment paper slightly smaller than the diameter of a steamer basket and place in the basket. Poke about 20 small holes in the parchment to allow steam to pass through and lightly coat with vegetable oil spray. Place batches of the dumplings on the parchment, making sure they are not touching. Set the steamer basket over simmering water and cook, covered, until no longer pink, 8 to 10 minutes. Serve immediately with chili oil.

Chili Oil

MAKES ABOUT ½ CUP

- 1 tablespoon soy sauce
- 2 teaspoons sugar
- ½ teaspoon table salt
- ½ cup peanut oil
- ¼ cup red pepper flakes
- 2 medium garlic cloves, peeled

Combine the soy sauce, sugar, and salt in a small bowl; set aside. Heat the oil in a small saucepan over medium heat until just shimmering and it registers 300 degrees on an instant-read thermometer. Remove the pan from the heat and stir in the red pepper flakes, garlic, and soy mixture. Let cool to room temperature, stirring occasionally, about 1 hour. Discard the garlic before storing.

SHRIMP TEMPURA

WHY THIS RECIPE WORKS: A few preliminary attempts at making tempura made us see why some Japanese chefs devote their entire careers to this one technique. Success hinges almost entirely on the batter—which is maddeningly hard to get right. We wanted a recipe for perfectly cooked shrimp tempura—light, crisp, and so fresh-tasting that it barely seemed fried.

We settled on using the largest shrimp available, since it's easy to overcook small shrimp. Instead of a wok, we substituted a large Dutch oven, the test kitchen's preferred deep-frying vessel. Cooking the tempura in 400-degree oil also helped limit grease absorption. To prevent the batter from clumping on the inside curl of the shrimp, we made two shallow cuts on the underside of its flesh. For the batter, we replaced a bit of the flour with cornstarch to improve the structure and lightness. For a super tender coating, we used a combination of seltzer and vodka instead of the traditional tap water. Seltzer is a little more acidic than tap water and therefore slows down gluten development, while the vodka prevents the formation of gluten. Our tempura was now light and crisp with the essence of sweet, tender shrimp.

Shrimp Tempura

SERVES 8

Do not omit the vodka; it is critical for a crisp coating. For safety, use a Dutch oven with a capacity of at least 7 quarts. Be sure to begin mixing the batter when the oil reaches 385 degrees (the final temperature should reach 400 degrees). It is important to maintain a high oil temperature throughout cooking. If you are unable to find colossal shrimp (8 to 12 per pound), jumbo (16 to 20 per pound) or extra-large (21 to 25 per pound) may be substituted. Fry smaller shrimp in three batches, reducing the cooking time to 1½ to 2 minutes per batch.

- 3 quarts peanut or vegetable oil
- 1½ pounds colossal shrimp (8 to 12 per pound), peeled and deveined (see page 205), tails left on (see note)
- 1½ cups (7½ ounces) unbleached all-purpose flour
- ½ cup cornstarch
- 1 cup vodka (see note)
- 1 large egg
- 1 cup seltzer water
  Table salt
- 1 recipe Scallion Dipping Sauce (page 372)

1. Adjust an oven rack to the upper-middle position and heat the oven to 200 degrees. In a large, heavy Dutch oven fitted with a clip-on candy thermometer, heat the oil over high heat to 385 degrees, 18 to 22 minutes.

2. While the oil heats, make two shallow cuts about ¼ inch deep and 1 inch apart on the underside of each shrimp. Whisk the flour and cornstarch together in a large bowl. Whisk the vodka and egg together in a second large bowl, then whisk in the seltzer water.

3. When the oil reaches 385 degrees, whisk the vodka mixture into the bowl with the flour mixture until just combined (it is OK if small lumps remain). Submerge half of the shrimp in the batter. Using tongs, remove the shrimp from the batter one at a time, allowing the excess batter to drip off, and carefully place in the oil (the temperature should now be at 400 degrees). Fry, stirring with a chopstick or wooden skewer to prevent sticking, until light brown, 2 to 3 minutes. Using a slotted spoon, transfer the shrimp to a paper towel–lined plate and sprinkle with salt. Once the paper towels absorb the excess oil, transfer the shrimp to a wire rack set over a rimmed baking sheet and place in the oven to keep warm.

4. Return the oil to 400 degrees, about 4 minutes, then repeat with the remaining shrimp. Serve with the dipping sauce.

THAI PORK LETTUCE WRAPS

WHY THIS RECIPE WORKS: The classic Thai salad, *larb*, is made with finely chopped meat and nutty rice powder tossed with fresh herbs and a light dressing that embodies the cuisine's signature balance of sweet, sour, hot, and salty flavors. We aimed to develop a home-cook-friendly recipe.

Americanized recipes typically call for ground pork, but inconsistent results with supermarket ground pork inspired us to grind our own, using pork tenderloin and a food processor. To impart flavor and moisture to this lean cut, we marinated the meat in fish sauce. Toasted rice powder, which adds a nutty flavor and texture to the pork, can be found in Asian markets, but we found it was easier to just make our own by toasting rice until golden brown and grinding it in a mini food processor or mortar and pestle. As for the aromatic components, we found that the pungency of sliced shallots and the bright flavor of chopped mint and cilantro yielded a very flavorful salad without a trip to a specialty store. For serving, the pork is spooned into lettuce leaves and wrapped. We preferred the crisp spine, tender leaf, and mild taste of Bibb lettuce.

Thai Pork Lettuce Wraps

SERVES 6

We prefer natural pork in this recipe. If using enhanced pork (pork that has been injected with a salt solution to increase moistness and flavor), skip the marinating in step 1 and reduce the amount of fish sauce to 2 tablespoons, adding it all in step 4.

- 1 (1-pound) pork tenderloin, trimmed of silver skin and fat, cut into 1-inch chunks, and frozen for 20 minutes (see note)
- 2½ tablespoons fish sauce
- 1 tablespoon white rice
- ¼ cup low-sodium chicken broth
- 3 medium shallots, peeled and sliced into thin rings (about ½ cup)
- 3 tablespoons roughly chopped fresh mint leaves
- 3 tablespoons roughly chopped fresh cilantro leaves
- 3 tablespoons juice from 2 limes
- 2 teaspoons sugar
- ¼ teaspoon red pepper flakes
- 1 head Bibb lettuce, washed and dried, leaves separated and left whole

1. Pulse half of the pork in a food processor until coarsely chopped, about 6 pulses. Transfer the ground pork to a medium bowl and repeat with the remaining chunks. Stir 1 tablespoon of the fish sauce into the ground pork, cover, refrigerate, and let marinate for 15 minutes.

2. Toast the rice in a small skillet over medium-high heat, stirring constantly, until deep golden brown, about 5 minutes. Transfer to a small bowl and cool for 5 minutes. Grind the rice with a spice grinder, mini food processor, or mortar and pestle until it resembles fine meal, 10 to 30 seconds (you should have about 1 tablespoon rice powder).

3. Bring the broth to a simmer in a 12-inch nonstick skillet over medium-high heat. Add the pork and cook, stirring frequently, until about half of the pork is no longer pink, about 2 minutes. Sprinkle 1 teaspoon of the rice powder over the pork and continue to cook, stirring constantly, until the remaining pork is no longer pink, 1 to 1½ minutes longer. Transfer the pork to a large bowl and cool for 10 minutes.

4. Add the remaining 1½ tablespoons fish sauce, remaining 2 teaspoons rice powder, the shallots, mint, cilantro, lime juice, sugar, and red pepper flakes to the pork and toss to combine. Serve with the lettuce leaves, spooning the meat into the leaves at the table.

BEEF SATAY

WHY THIS RECIPE WORKS: This Southeast Asian street food should be simple enough, but more often than not it is tough, bland, and boring. We wanted tender meat that could easily be pulled apart into small bites right off the skewer, with great Southeast Asian flavors like garlic, chiles, and cilantro.

Choosing the right cut of meat proved to be more about texture than flavor. Flank steak was the winner. We used two techniques to slice it, first freezing the meat to firm it up enough to slice cleanly, then cutting the beef across the grain to keep it tender. Since the meat is so thin, cooking it was a breeze. Placing the skewered meat on a wire rack and cooking it 6 inches from the heating element proved just right. We found our marinade ingredients in the supermarket (Asian chili sauce is now commonly available) and added generous amounts of cilantro and garlic.

Beef Satay

SERVES 8 TO 10

Asian chili sauce, also called sriracha, is available in most supermarkets. Use 6-inch-long skewers for this recipe; you'll need about 24.

- ¼ **cup soy sauce**
- ¼ **cup peanut or vegetable oil**
- ¼ **cup packed dark brown sugar**
- ¼ **cup minced fresh cilantro leaves**
- 4 **scallions, sliced thin**
- 2 **tablespoons Asian chili sauce, or more to taste (see note)**
- 2 **medium garlic cloves, minced or pressed through a garlic press (about 2 teaspoons)**
- 1 **(1½-pound) flank steak, trimmed, halved lengthwise, frozen for 30 minutes, and sliced across the grain into ¼-inch-thick strips**
- 1 **recipe Spicy Peanut Dipping Sauce (recipe follows)**

1. Combine the soy sauce, oil, sugar, cilantro, scallions, chili sauce, and garlic in a large bowl. Stir in the beef, cover, and refrigerate for 1 hour.

2. Adjust an oven rack 6 inches from the heating element and heat the broiler.

3. Weave the meat onto 6-inch bamboo skewers (one piece per skewer). Lay the skewers on a wire rack set over a rimmed baking sheet and cover the skewer ends with foil. Broil the skewers until the meat is browned, 6 to 9 minutes, flipping the skewers over halfway through. Transfer the skewers to a serving platter and serve with the peanut sauce.

Spicy Peanut Dipping Sauce

MAKES ABOUT 1½ CUPS

This sauce can be refrigerated in an airtight container for up to 24 hours; bring to room temperature before serving.

- ½ **cup creamy peanut butter**
- ¼ **cup hot water**
- 2 **tablespoons juice from 1 lime**
- 2 **tablespoons Asian chili sauce**
- 1 **tablespoon soy sauce**
- 1 **tablespoon dark brown sugar**
- 1 **tablespoon chopped fresh cilantro leaves**
- 2 **scallions, sliced thin**
- 1 **medium garlic clove, minced or pressed through a garlic press (about 1 teaspoon)**

Whisk the peanut butter and hot water together in a small bowl until smooth. Stir in the remaining ingredients.

THAI-STYLE CHICKEN SOUP

WHY THIS RECIPE WORKS: Replicating the complex flavors of Thai chicken soup at home can be difficult, since it relies on such exotica as galangal, kaffir lime leaves, lemon grass, and bird's eye chiles. We wanted a plausibly authentic version of Thai chicken soup that could be prepared with more readily available (i.e., supermarket) substitutions.

We started by making a classic version of the soup, then substituting one ingredient at a time. We developed an acceptably rich and definitely chicken-flavored broth by using equal parts chicken broth and coconut milk (adding the coconut milk in two stages: at the beginning and just before serving). We couldn't fake the flavor of lemon grass, but it proved to be easy enough to find.

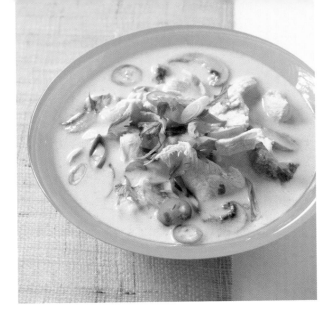

Our most exciting find was a "magic bullet" substitution: jarred red curry paste includes all the other exotic ingredients we were missing. Just adding a dollop at the very end of cooking and whisking it with pungent fish sauce and tart lime juice allowed all the classic flavors to come through loud and clear.

Thai-Style Chicken Soup

SERVES 6 TO 8

To make slicing the chicken easier, freeze it for 15 minutes. Although we prefer the richer, more complex flavor of regular coconut milk, light coconut milk can be substituted for one or both cans. For a spicier soup, add additional red curry paste to taste.

SOUP

- 1 teaspoon peanut or vegetable oil
- 3 stalks lemon grass, bottom 5 inches only, trimmed and sliced thin (see page 401)
- 3 large shallots, chopped coarse (about ¾ cup)
- 8 sprigs fresh cilantro, chopped coarse
- 3 tablespoons fish sauce
- 4 cups low-sodium chicken broth
- 2 (14-ounce) cans coconut milk (see note)
- 1 tablespoon sugar
- 8 ounces white mushrooms, wiped clean and sliced ¼ inch thick
- 1 pound boneless, skinless chicken breasts, trimmed, halved lengthwise, and cut on the bias into ⅛-inch pieces (see note)
- 3 tablespoons juice from 2 limes
- 2 teaspoons Thai red curry paste (see note)

GARNISH

- ½ cup loosely packed fresh cilantro leaves
- 2 Thai, serrano, or jalapeño chiles, seeds and ribs removed, chiles sliced thin
- 2 scallions, sliced thin on the bias
  Lime wedges, for serving

1. Heat the oil in a large saucepan over medium heat until just shimmering. Add the lemon grass, shallots, cilantro sprigs, and 1 tablespoon of the fish sauce and cook, stirring frequently, until just softened but not browned, 2 to 5 minutes.

2. Stir in the broth and 1 can of the coconut milk and bring to a simmer over high heat. Cover, reduce the heat to low, and simmer until the flavors have blended, about 10 minutes. Pour the broth through a fine-mesh strainer, discarding the solids in the strainer. (At this point, the soup can be refrigerated in an airtight container for up to 1 day.)

3. Return the strained soup to a clean saucepan and bring to a simmer over medium-high heat. Stir in the remaining can of coconut milk and the sugar and bring to a simmer. Reduce the heat to medium, add the mushrooms, and cook until just tender, 2 to 3 minutes. Add the chicken and cook, stirring constantly, until no longer pink, 1 to 3 minutes. Remove the soup from the heat.

4. Whisk the remaining 2 tablespoons fish sauce, the lime juice, and curry paste together, then stir into the soup. Ladle the soup into individual bowls and garnish with the cilantro, chiles, and scallions. Serve with the lime wedges.

HOT AND SOUR SOUP

WHY THIS RECIPE WORKS: Authentic versions of this soup have some hard-to-find ingredients such as mustard pickle, pig's-foot tendon, and dried sea cucumber—ingredients we couldn't find in the local grocery store. Using inventory only from our local supermarket, we wanted an authentic take on hot and sour soup, including spicy, bracing, pungent elements.

We created the "hot" side of the soup with two heat sources—distinctive, penetrating white pepper and a little chili oil. For the "sour" component, we preferred the traditional Chinese black vinegar, but found that a tablespoon each of balsamic and red wine vinegar made a suitable substitution. Cornstarch turned out to be a key ingredient: A cornstarch-based slurry thickened the soup;

adding cornstarch to the pork marinade gave the pork a protective sheath that kept it tender; and beating the egg with cornstarch before drizzling it into the thickened soup kept the egg light, wispy, and cohesive. Pork and tofu are the usual, easy-to-find additions to the broth, but we had to come up with substitutes for a few other classic ingredients, settling on fresh shiitakes in lieu of wood ear mushrooms and canned bamboo shoots instead of lily buds. Spicy, bracing, rich, and complex, this soup has all the flavor of the classic version.

Hot and Sour Soup

SERVES 6 TO 8

To make slicing the pork chop easier, freeze it for 15 minutes. We prefer the distinctive flavor of Chinese black vinegar; look for it in Asian supermarkets. If you can't find it, use 1 tablespoon red wine vinegar and 1 tablespoon balsamic vinegar. This soup is very spicy. For a less spicy soup, omit the chili oil altogether or add only 1 teaspoon.

- 7 ounces (½ block) extra-firm tofu
- ¼ cup soy sauce
- 3 tablespoons plus 1½ teaspoons cornstarch
- 1 teaspoon toasted sesame oil
- 1 (6-ounce) boneless center-cut pork chop (about ½ inch thick), trimmed and cut into 1-inch-long matchsticks (see note)
- 3 tablespoons plus 1 teaspoon water
- 1 large egg
- 6 cups low-sodium chicken broth
- 1 (5-ounce) can bamboo shoots, sliced into matchsticks (about 1 cup)
- 4 ounces shiitake mushrooms, stemmed, wiped clean, caps sliced ¼ inch thick
- 5 tablespoons Chinese black vinegar (see note)
- 2 teaspoons chili oil (see note)
- 1 teaspoon ground white pepper
- 3 scallions, sliced thin

1. Place the tofu in a pie plate, top with a heavy plate, and weigh down with two heavy cans. Set the tofu aside until it has released about ½ cup liquid, about 15 minutes. When drained, cut the tofu into ½-inch cubes and set aside.

2. Meanwhile, whisk 1 tablespoon of the soy sauce, 1 teaspoon of the cornstarch, and the sesame oil together in a medium bowl. Stir in the pork, cover, and let marinate for at least 10 minutes or up to 30 minutes.

3. Combine 3 tablespoons more cornstarch with 3 tablespoons of the water in a small bowl. Mix the remaining ½ teaspoon cornstarch with the remaining 1 teaspoon water in a second small bowl, then add the egg and beat with a fork until combined.

4. Bring the broth to a simmer in a large saucepan over medium-low heat. Add the bamboo shoots and mushrooms and simmer until the mushrooms are just tender, 2 to 3 minutes. Stir in the diced tofu and pork with its marinade and continue to simmer, stirring to separate any pieces of pork that stick together, until the pork is no longer pink, about 2 minutes.

5. Stir the cornstarch mixture to recombine, then add it to the soup, increase the heat to medium-high, and cook, stirring occasionally, until the soup thickens and turns translucent, about 1 minute. Stir in the remaining 3 tablespoons soy sauce, the vinegar, chili oil, and pepper and turn off the heat.

6. Without stirring the soup, use a soupspoon to slowly drizzle very thin streams of the egg mixture into the pot in a circular motion. Let the soup sit off the heat for 1 minute. Briefly return the soup to a simmer over medium-high heat, then remove from the heat immediately. Gently stir the soup once to evenly distribute the egg; ladle into individual bowls, sprinkle with the scallions, and serve.

COLD SESAME NOODLES

WHY THIS RECIPE WORKS: Cold noodles are underrated. Not as humble as they appear, these toothsome noodles tossed with shreds of tender chicken and fresh sesame sauce can be addicting if made properly. For this recipe, we set out to eliminate sticky noodles, gloppy sauce, and lackluster flavors.

We found that rinsing and tossing the noodles (either fresh Chinese noodles or dried spaghetti) with a little sesame oil after cooking prevents a rubbery texture and washes away much of their sticky starch. Boneless, skinless chicken breasts were the obvious choice for easy cooking and shredding, and broiling the meat helped retain the chicken's moisture and flavor. And for an authentic sauce, a combination of chunky peanut butter and freshly ground toasted sesame seeds was the best substitute for Asian sesame paste. After adding fresh garlic and ginger, as well as soy sauce, rice vinegar, hot sauce, and brown sugar, we achieved the perfect texture by thinning out the sauce with hot water.

Sesame Noodles with Shredded Chicken

SERVES 4 TO 6

Although our preference is for fresh Chinese noodles, we found that dried spaghetti works well, too. Because dried pasta swells so much more than fresh pasta during cooking, 12 ounces of dried spaghetti can replace 1 pound of fresh noodles.

- 5   tablespoons soy sauce
- ¼   cup sesame seeds, toasted
- ¼   cup chunky peanut butter
- 2   tablespoons rice vinegar
- 2   tablespoons light brown sugar
- 1   tablespoon minced or grated fresh ginger
- 2   medium garlic cloves, minced or pressed through a garlic press (about 2 teaspoons)
- 1   teaspoon hot sauce
       Hot water
- 1   pound fresh Chinese noodles or 12 ounces dried spaghetti (see note)
- 1   tablespoon table salt
- 2   tablespoons toasted sesame oil
- 1½ pounds boneless, skinless chicken breasts, trimmed
- 4   scallions, sliced thin on the bias
- 1   carrot, peeled and shredded

1. Process the soy sauce, 3 tablespoons of the sesame seeds, the peanut butter, vinegar, brown sugar, ginger, garlic, and hot sauce together in a blender or food processor until smooth, about 30 seconds. With the machine running, add hot water, 1 tablespoon at a time, until the sauce has the consistency of heavy cream (you should need about 5 tablespoons); set aside.

2. Position an oven rack 6 inches from the heating element and heat the broiler.

3. Bring 6 quarts water to a boil in a large pot. Add the noodles and salt and cook, stirring often, until tender, about 4 minutes for fresh and 10 minutes for dried. Drain the noodles, rinse them under cold running water until cold, then toss them with the sesame oil.

4. Set a wire rack over a foil-lined rimmed baking sheet and lightly coat the rack with vegetable oil spray. Lay the chicken on the rack and broil until lightly browned, 4 to 8 minutes. Flip the chicken over and continue to broil until the thickest part of the breast registers 160 to 165 degrees on an instant-read thermometer, 6 to 8 minutes longer. Transfer the chicken to a carving board and let rest for 5 minutes. Using two forks, shred the chicken into bite-size pieces and set aside.

5. Transfer the noodles to a large bowl, add the shredded chicken, sauce, scallions, and carrot and toss to combine. Divide the mixture among individual bowls, sprinkle with the remaining 1 tablespoon sesame seeds, and serve.

FRIED RICE

WHY THIS RECIPE WORKS: Fried rice is the perfect solution for leftover rice, but it often arrives in the bowl as a soggy mess of greasy rice doused in so much flavor-disguising soy sauce that you can hardly tell the vegetables from the chicken. We wanted fried rice with firm, separate grains, and we wanted a finished dish so clean and light that we could distinguish its many different flavors in every bite.

For fried rice that is light and flavorful rather than sodden and greasy, we found it essential to start with cold, dry rice (like leftover rice). Instead of gallons of soy sauce, we added a small amount in conjunction with complex oyster-flavored sauce to yield well-seasoned but not soggy rice. Cooking the vegetables and shrimp separately ensured that everything was cooked to perfection—no rubbery shrimp or mushy peas. And frying the rice in just a couple tablespoons of oil kept it from being greasy. Lastly, we finished the dish with tender vegetables including bean sprouts and a sprinkling of scallions.

Fried Rice with Shrimp, Pork, and Shiitakes
SERVES 4 TO 6

See the Basic White Rice recipe on page 382 for tips on preparing and cooling rice.

- ½ ounce (5 to 6 medium) dried shiitake mushrooms
- ¼ cup oyster-flavored sauce
- 1 tablespoon soy sauce
- 3 tablespoons plus 1½ teaspoons peanut or vegetable oil
- 2 large eggs, lightly beaten
- 8 ounces small shrimp (51 to 60 per pound), peeled and deveined (see page 205)
- 1 cup frozen peas, thawed
- 8 ounces sliced smoked ham, cut into ½-inch pieces
- 2 medium garlic cloves, minced or pressed through a garlic press (about 2 teaspoons)
- 5 cups cold cooked white rice, large clumps broken up with fingers (see note)
- 1 cup bean sprouts
- 5 scallions, sliced thin

1. Cover the dried shiitakes with 1 cup hot tap water in a small microwave-safe bowl. Cover the bowl with plastic wrap and microwave on high power for 30 seconds. Let sit until the mushrooms soften, about 5 minutes. Lift the mushrooms from the liquid with a fork. Trim the stems, slice into ¼-inch strips, and set aside.

2. Combine the oyster-flavored sauce and soy sauce in a small bowl and set aside.

3. Heat 1½ teaspoons of the oil in a 12-inch nonstick skillet over medium heat until shimmering. Add the eggs and cook, without stirring, until they just begin to set, about 20 seconds. Scramble and break into small pieces with a wooden spoon and continue to cook, stirring constantly, until the eggs are cooked through but not browned, about 1 minute longer. Transfer the eggs to a small bowl and set aside.

4. Add 1½ teaspoons more oil to the skillet and heat over medium heat until shimmering. Add the shrimp and cook, stirring constantly, until opaque and just cooked through, about 30 seconds. Transfer the shrimp to the bowl with the eggs and set aside.

5. Add the remaining 2½ tablespoons oil to the skillet and heat over medium heat until shimmering. Add the mushrooms, peas, and ham and cook, stirring constantly, for 1 minute. Stir in the garlic and cook until fragrant, about 30 seconds. Add the rice and oyster-flavored sauce mixture and cook, stirring constantly and breaking up any rice clumps, until the mixture is heated through, about 3 minutes. Stir in the eggs, shrimp, bean sprouts, and scallions and cook until heated through, about 1 minute. Serve.

Fried Rice with Peas and Bean Sprouts
SERVES 4 TO 6

See the Basic White Rice recipe (page 382) for tips on preparing and cooling rice.

- ¼ cup oyster-flavored sauce
- 1 tablespoon soy sauce
- 3 tablespoons peanut or vegetable oil
- 2 large eggs, lightly beaten
- 1 cup frozen peas, thawed
- 2 medium garlic cloves, minced or pressed through a garlic press (about 2 teaspoons)
- 5 cups cold cooked white rice, large clumps broken up with fingers (see note)
- 1 cup bean sprouts
- 5 scallions, sliced thin

1. Combine the oyster-flavored sauce and soy sauce in a small bowl and set aside.

2. Heat 1½ teaspoons of the oil in a 12-inch nonstick skillet over medium heat until shimmering. Add the eggs and cook, without stirring, until they just begin to set, about 20 seconds. Scramble and break into small pieces with a wooden spoon and continue to cook, stirring constantly, until the eggs are cooked through but not browned, about 1 minute longer. Transfer the eggs to a small bowl and set aside.

3. Add the remaining 2½ tablespoons oil to the skillet and heat over medium heat until shimmering. Add the peas and cook, stirring constantly, for 1 minute. Stir in the garlic and cook until fragrant, about 30 seconds. Add the rice and oyster-flavored sauce mixture and cook, stirring constantly and breaking up any rice clumps, until the mixture is heated through, about 3 minutes. Stir in the eggs, bean sprouts, and scallions and cook until heated through, about 1 minute. Serve.

Basic White Rice

MAKES ABOUT 5 CUPS

To rinse the rice, you can either place it in a fine-mesh strainer and rinse it under cool water or place it in a medium bowl and repeatedly fill the bowl with water while swishing the rice around, then drain off the water. In either case, you must rinse the rice until the water runs clear.

    3 cups water
    2 cups long-grain white rice, rinsed (see note)

1. Bring the water and rice to a boil in a large saucepan over high heat. Reduce the heat to low, cover, and cook until all the water has been absorbed, about 10 minutes. Remove the pot from the heat and let sit, covered, until the rice is tender, about 15 minutes.

2. Serve, or to make fried rice, spread the cooked rice out over a baking sheet and let cool to room temperature, about 30 minutes. (The rice can be refrigerated in an airtight container for up to 24 hours.)

INDONESIAN-STYLE FRIED RICE

WHY THIS RECIPE WORKS: Chinese takeout versions of fried rice are satisfying, to be sure, but frequently leave little to the imagination. We wanted to create a less heavy version of fried rice featuring the pungent, complex flavors of Indonesia—without heading to specialty markets for all of our ingredients. The primary source of this dish's flavor is chili paste, and we were happy to discover that the ingredients for this paste (staples like chiles, shallots, brown sugar, and soy sauce) are readily available at the average supermarket. To replicate the flavor of shrimp paste—another key but hard-to-find ingredient—we used a combination of fish sauce and chopped shrimp, which we added to the skillet with the chili paste. This dish requires chilled, firm rice, but most of us don't have leftover rice sitting in our fridge. For rice with the proper consistency, we cooked it in less water and then spread it out on a baking sheet to allow it to chill quickly in the fridge.

Indonesian-Style Fried Rice (Nasi Goreng)

SERVES 4 TO 6

If Thai chiles are unavailable, substitute two serranos or two medium jalapeños. Reduce the spiciness of this dish by removing the ribs and seeds from the chiles. This dish progresses very quickly at step 4; it's imperative that your ingredients are in place by then and ready to go. If desired, serve the rice with sliced cucumbers and tomato wedges.

     5 green or red Thai chiles, stemmed (see note)
     7 large shallots, peeled
     4 large garlic cloves, peeled
     2 tablespoons dark brown sugar
     2 tablespoons light or mild molasses
     2 tablespoons soy sauce
     2 tablespoons fish sauce
        Table salt
     4 large eggs
     ½ cup vegetable oil
     1 recipe Faux Leftover Rice (recipe follows)
    12 ounces extra-large shrimp (21 to 25 per pound), peeled, deveined (see page 205), tails removed, and cut crosswise into thirds
     4 large scallions, sliced thin
     2 limes, cut into wedges

1. Pulse the chiles, 4 of the shallots, and the garlic in a food processor until a coarse paste is formed, about 15 pulses, scraping down the sides of the bowl as necessary. Transfer the mixture to a small bowl and set aside. In a second small bowl, stir together the brown sugar, molasses, soy sauce, fish sauce, and 1¼ teaspoons salt. Whisk the eggs and ¼ teaspoon salt together in a medium bowl.

2. Thinly slice the remaining 3 shallots and place in a 12-inch nonstick skillet with the oil. Cook over medium heat, stirring constantly, until the shallots are golden and crisp, 6 to 10 minutes. Using a slotted spoon, transfer the shallots to a paper towel–lined plate and season with salt to taste. Pour off the oil and reserve. Wipe out the skillet with paper towels.

3. Heat 1 teaspoon of the reserved oil in the now-empty skillet over medium heat until shimmering. Add half of the eggs to the skillet, gently tilting the pan to evenly coat the bottom. Cover and cook until the bottom of the omelet is spotty golden brown and the top is just set, about 1½ minutes. Slide the omelet onto a cutting board and gently roll up into a tight log. Using a sharp knife, cut the log crosswise into 1-inch segments (leaving the segments rolled). Repeat with 1 teaspoon more reserved oil and the remaining egg.

4. Remove the rice from the refrigerator and break up any large clumps with your fingers. Heat 3 tablespoons more reserved oil in the now-empty skillet over medium heat until just shimmering. Add the chile mixture and cook until the mixture turns golden, 3 to 5 minutes. Add the shrimp, increase the heat to medium-high, and cook, stirring constantly, until the exterior of the shrimp is just opaque, about 2 minutes. Push the shrimp to the sides of the skillet to clear the center; stir the molasses mixture to recombine and pour into the center of the skillet. When the molasses mixture bubbles, add the rice and cook, stirring and folding constantly, until the shrimp is cooked, the rice is heated through, and the mixture is evenly coated, about 3 minutes. Stir in the scallions, remove from the heat, and transfer to a serving platter. Garnish with the egg segments, fried shallots, and lime wedges; serve immediately.

Faux Leftover Rice

MAKES 6 CUPS

To rinse the rice, place it in a fine-mesh strainer and rinse under cool water until the water runs clear.

- 2 tablespoons vegetable oil
- 2 cups jasmine or long-grain white rice, rinsed (see note)
- 2⅔ cups water

Heat the oil in a large saucepan over medium heat until shimmering. Add the rice and stir to coat the grains with oil, about 30 seconds. Add the water, increase the heat to high, and bring to a boil. Reduce the heat to low, cover, and simmer until all the liquid is absorbed, about 18 minutes. Off the heat, remove the lid and place a clean kitchen towel, folded in half, over the saucepan; replace the lid. Let stand until the rice is just tender, about 8 minutes. Spread the cooked rice onto a rimmed baking sheet, set on a wire rack, and cool for 10 minutes. Transfer to the refrigerator and chill for 20 minutes.

CHICKEN TERIYAKI

WHY THIS RECIPE WORKS: Too many chicken teriyaki recipes are lackluster—they can include everything from skewered chicken chunks shellacked in a corn-syrupy sauce to overmarinated, preformed chicken breast patties. They're a long way away from the simple recipe promised in the name "teriyaki"—meaning "to shine" (referring to the sauce) and meaning "to broil." We wanted a straightforward recipe that delivered the simple and authentic result of crisp and moist, sweet and salty, glazed chicken.

First, we decided against using breast meat. Bone-in, skin-on thighs stood up best to the salty profile of the teriyaki sauce. We set a weight on top of the chicken as it cooked (we used a heavy Dutch oven), which helped to brown a greater surface area of the chicken evenly, as well as to aid in pressing out most of the fat. We also found that a quick mixture of soy sauce, sugar, mirin, and a few other flavorings made an incredible teriyaki sauce that far surpassed any we could buy in a bottle.

Chicken Teriyaki

SERVES 4

A splatter screen (or an inverted large strainer or colander) is helpful for controlling the splatter that occurs when the second side of the chicken browns. There is a fair amount of soy sauce in this dish, so there is no need to salt it before serving. Serve with Basic White Rice (page 382).

- 8 (5 to 6-ounce) bone-in, skin-on chicken thighs, trimmed
  Ground black pepper
- 2 teaspoons peanut or vegetable oil
- ½ cup soy sauce
- ½ cup sugar

2 tablespoons mirin or sweet sherry
2 teaspoons minced or grated fresh ginger
1 medium garlic clove, minced or pressed through a
garlic press (about 1 teaspoon)
½ teaspoon cornstarch
⅛ teaspoon red pepper flakes

1. Pat the chicken thighs dry with paper towels and season with pepper. Heat the oil in a 12-inch nonstick skillet over medium-high heat until just smoking. Carefully lay the chicken in the skillet, skin side down. Weigh down the chicken with a heavy pot and cook until the skin is a deep mahogany brown and very crisp, 15 to 20 minutes. (The chicken should be moderately brown after 10 minutes. If it is very brown, reduce the heat; if it is still pale, increase the heat.)

2. Remove the weight and flip the chicken over. Reduce the heat to medium and continue to cook, without the weight, until the second side is brown and the thickest part of the thighs registers 175 degrees on an instant-read thermometer, about 10 minutes longer.

3. Meanwhile, whisk the soy sauce, sugar, mirin, ginger, garlic, cornstarch, and red pepper flakes together in a small bowl; set aside.

4. Transfer the chicken to a plate. Pour off all of the fat from the skillet. Whisk the soy mixture to recombine, then add to the skillet and return to medium heat. Return the chicken to the skillet, skin side up, and spoon the sauce over the top. Continue to simmer until the sauce is thick and glossy, about 2 minutes longer. Serve.

ORANGE-FLAVORED CHICKEN

WHY THIS RECIPE WORKS: Chinese takeout orange-flavored chicken is never as good as its name promises—too often the dish delivers ultrathick breading wrapped around scraps of greasy, gristly, tasteless chicken bathed in an "orange" sauce that tastes likes a mixture of corn syrup and orange food coloring. We wanted substantial, well-seasoned chicken chunks with a crisp, golden brown crust, and a sauce that offered a clear hit of fresh orange flavor with balanced sweet, sour, and spicy background notes.

We chose thigh meat over breast meat for its rich flavor and tendency to remain moist when deep-fried. We marinated the chicken in a mixture of soy sauce, garlic, ginger, sugar, vinegar, fresh orange juice, and chicken broth, reserving some marinade to become the base for the final sauce. Then, we created a tender/crisp coating

by dunking the marinated chicken first in egg white, then cornstarch. The egg white created a thin sheath of protein beneath the cornstarch that kept it dry, helping it to brown more readily than a wet, gluey coating would. A touch of baking soda helped the chicken pieces develop golden color during frying.

Orange-Flavored Chicken
SERVES 4

We prefer the flavor and texture of thigh meat for this recipe, though an equal amount of boneless, skinless chicken breasts can be used. Unless you have a taste for the incendiary, do not eat the whole chiles in the finished dish. Serve with Basic White Rice (page 382).

MARINADE AND SAUCE
¾ cup low-sodium chicken broth
¾ cup juice, 1½ teaspoons grated zest, and 8 strips peel
(each about 2 inches long by ½ inch wide) from
2 oranges
½ cup packed dark brown sugar
6 tablespoons distilled white vinegar
¼ cup soy sauce
3 medium garlic cloves, minced or pressed through a
garlic press (about 1 tablespoon)
1 tablespoon minced or grated fresh ginger
¼ teaspoon cayenne pepper
1½ pounds boneless, skinless chicken thighs, trimmed and
cut into 1½-inch pieces (see note)
2 tablespoons cold water
1 tablespoon plus 2 teaspoons cornstarch
8 small whole dried red chiles (optional; see note)

COATING AND FRYING OIL
3 large egg whites
1 cup cornstarch
½ teaspoon baking soda
¼ teaspoon cayenne pepper
3 cups peanut or vegetable oil

1. FOR THE MARINADE AND SAUCE: Whisk the broth, orange juice, grated zest, sugar, vinegar, soy sauce, garlic, ginger, and cayenne together in a large saucepan until the sugar is fully dissolved. Transfer ¾ cup of the mixture to a medium bowl and add the chicken. Let marinate for at least 10 minutes or up to 1 hour.

2. In a small bowl, stir the cold water and cornstarch together. Bring the remaining mixture in the saucepan to a simmer over high heat. Whisk the cornstarch mixture into the sauce, bring to a simmer, and cook, stirring occasionally, until thick and translucent, about 1 minute. Off the heat, stir in the orange peel and chiles (if using) and set aside. (The sauce should measure 1½ cups.)

3. FOR THE COATING: Using a fork, lightly beat the egg whites in a shallow dish until frothy. In a second shallow dish, whisk the cornstarch, baking soda, and cayenne together until combined. Drain the chicken and pat dry with paper towels. Place half of the chicken pieces in the egg whites and turn to coat. Transfer the chicken pieces to the cornstarch mixture and coat thoroughly. Place the dredged chicken pieces on a wire rack set over a baking sheet. Repeat with the remaining chicken pieces.

4. TO FRY THE CHICKEN: Heat the oil in a Dutch oven over high heat until the oil registers 350 degrees on an instant-read or deep-fry thermometer. Carefully place half of the chicken in the oil and fry until golden brown, about 5 minutes, turning each piece with tongs halfway through. Transfer the chicken pieces to a paper towel–lined plate. Return the oil to 350 degrees and repeat with the remaining chicken.

5. TO SERVE: Reheat the sauce over medium heat until simmering, about 2 minutes. Add the chicken and gently toss until evenly coated and heated through. Serve.

CHICKEN STIR-FRY WITH CRISPY NOODLE CAKE

WHY THIS RECIPE WORKS: Stir-fries are the quintessential weeknight dinner. And while a stir-fry served on top of rice is great, a pan-fried noodle cake—crispy and crunchy on the outside and tender and chewy in the middle—offers a welcome change of pace.

For the noodle cake, we had the most success with fresh Chinese egg noodles—they made for a cohesive cake with a crunchy exterior. A nonstick skillet was crucial—it kept the cake from sticking and falling apart and allowed us to use less oil so the cake wasn't greasy. We found the best way to flip the cake in the skillet was to slide it onto a plate, invert it onto another plate, and then slide it back in the pan to finish cooking. We kept the stir-fry simple; chicken and bok choy are a classic combination. A quick marinade gave our chicken welcome flavor, and a modified version of the Chinese technique called velveting prevented the chicken from drying out over high heat.

Stir-Fried Chicken with Bok Choy and Crispy Noodle Cake

SERVES 4

To make slicing the chicken easier, freeze it for 15 minutes. Fresh Chinese noodles are often kept in the produce section of the grocery store. If you can't find them, substitute an equal amount of fresh spaghetti.

SAUCE
- ¼ **cup low-sodium chicken broth**
- 2 **tablespoons soy sauce**
- 1 **tablespoon dry sherry**
- 1 **tablespoon oyster-flavored sauce**
- 1 **teaspoon sugar**
- 1 **teaspoon cornstarch**
- ¼ **teaspoon red pepper flakes**

NOODLE CAKE
- 1 **(9-ounce) package fresh Chinese noodles (see note)**
- 1 **teaspoon table salt**
- 2 **scallions, sliced thin**
- ¼ **cup peanut or vegetable oil**

CHICKEN AND VEGETABLES
- 1 **pound boneless, skinless chicken breasts, trimmed and sliced thin (see note)**
- 1 **tablespoon soy sauce**
- 1 **tablespoon dry sherry**
- 2 **tablespoons toasted sesame oil**
- 1 **tablespoon cornstarch**
- 1 **tablespoon unbleached all-purpose flour**
- 2 **tablespoons plus 2 teaspoons peanut or vegetable oil**

1 **tablespoon minced or grated fresh ginger**

1 **medium garlic clove, minced or pressed through a garlic press (about 1 teaspoon)**

1 **small head bok choy, stalks cut on the bias into ¼-inch pieces and greens cut into ½-inch strips**

1 **small red bell pepper, stemmed, seeded, and cut into ¼-inch strips**

1. FOR THE SAUCE: Combine all the ingredients in a small bowl and set aside.

2. FOR THE NOODLE CAKE: Bring 6 quarts water to a boil in a large pot. Add the noodles and salt and cook, stirring often, until almost tender, 2 to 3 minutes. Drain the noodles, then toss them with the scallions.

3. Heat 2 tablespoons of the peanut oil in a 12-inch non-stick skillet over medium heat until shimmering. Spread the noodles evenly across the bottom of the skillet and press with a spatula to flatten into a cake. Cook until crisp and golden brown, 5 to 8 minutes.

4. Slide the noodle cake onto a large plate. Add the remaining 2 tablespoons peanut oil to the skillet and swirl to coat. Invert the noodle cake onto a second plate and slide it, browned side up, back into the skillet. Cook until golden brown on the second side, 5 to 8 minutes.

5. Slide the noodle cake onto a cutting board and let sit for at least 5 minutes before slicing into wedges and serving. (The noodle cake can be transferred to a wire rack set over a baking sheet and kept warm in a 200-degree oven for up to 20 minutes.) Wipe out the skillet with a wad of paper towels.

6. FOR THE CHICKEN AND VEGETABLES: While the noodles boil, toss the chicken with the soy sauce and sherry in a medium bowl and let marinate for at least 10 minutes or up to 1 hour. In a large bowl, whisk the sesame oil, cornstarch, and flour together. In a small bowl, mix 1 teaspoon of the peanut oil, the ginger, and garlic together.

7. Stir the marinated chicken into the sesame oil–cornstarch mixture. Heat 2 teaspoons more peanut oil in the skillet over high heat until just smoking. Add half of the chicken, break up any clumps, then cook without stirring until the meat is browned at the edges, about 1 minute. Stir the chicken and continue to cook until cooked through, about 1 minute longer. Transfer the chicken to a clean bowl and cover with foil to keep warm. Repeat with 2 teaspoons more peanut oil and the remaining chicken.

8. Add the remaining 1 tablespoon peanut oil to the skillet and return to high heat until just smoking. Add the bok choy stalks and bell pepper and cook until lightly browned, 2 to 3 minutes.

BEHIND THE SCENES

STIR-FRIES AT HOME? THROW OUT YOUR WOK!

We love the theatrics of the kitchen. And few pans seem as fun to use as a wok—watching a Chinese cook stir-fry with a wok can be as exciting as catching a great drum solo at a rock concert. So imagine our disappointment when we realized woks simply don't perform as well as we thought. A wok's shape is the culprit. A wok's conical bottom is designed for a pit-style stove; the flames lick and engulf the pan, making most of the surface area hot even when food is added. But when you set a wok over a conventional stovetop, the heat becomes concentrated in the pan's bottom, and the larger surface area—the sides—simply doesn't heat as well. And when food is added to the wok, the pan's temperature drops. The results? Meat that steams instead of sears and vegetables that turn soggy, rather than crisp-tender.

What *does* work on a conventional stovetop? A large nonstick skillet. Its flat-bottom design allows more surface area to come in direct contact with the flat burner, delivering more heat over more parts than a wok—and enabling it to remain hot even after food is added.

To quantify their differences, we heated oil in a wok and a heavy 12-inch skillet over high heat on gas burners. Once the oil was smoking (at around 415 degrees), we added stir-fry ingredients to each pan. The wok's temperature plummeted dramatically, to 220 degrees at its center, rising only another 50 degrees over the course of cooking. The skillet's temperature dipped to 345 degrees, then recovered quickly, continuing to rise to almost 500 degrees. This higher heat translated to better browning and more flavor. The bottom line? Don't invest in a wok—use what you probably already have: a skillet. And if you want theatrics order some concert tickets.

9. Clear the center of the skillet, add the ginger mixture, and cook, mashing the mixture into the pan, until fragrant, 15 to 20 seconds. Stir the ginger mixture into the vegetables, then stir in the bok choy greens and cook until beginning to wilt, about 30 seconds.

10. Stir in the chicken with any accumulated juices. Whisk the sauce to recombine, then add to the skillet and cook, tossing constantly, until the sauce is thickened, about 30 seconds. Transfer to a serving platter and serve with the noodle cake.

STIR-FRIES MADE SIMPLE

WHY THIS RECIPE WORKS: A good stir-fry made with chicken, shrimp, or tofu is more difficult to prepare than a beef or pork stir-fry because these proteins, which have less fat, are often bland. Worse, they inevitably become dry and stringy or rubbery when cooked over high heat. We aimed to create stir-fry recipes that harmonized the flavors and textures of these lighter proteins with complementary vegetables and sauces.

These leaner proteins inspired us to create light, fresh-tasting stir-fries. We paired the chicken with zucchini, red bell pepper, and a zesty ginger sauce. And asparagus, yellow bell pepper, and a brightly flavored lemon sauce were a natural fit for the shrimp. Lastly, we selected a slightly more assertive hot and sour sauce, along with red onion and snow peas, to enhance the mild-flavored tofu. As with most of our stir-fries, we marinated the thinly sliced chicken and shrimp, and the cubes of tofu, in a combination of soy sauce and dry sherry to add flavor and moisture. After cooking the chicken, shrimp, or tofu and removing it from the pan, we stir-fried the vegetables in batches, quickly cooked the garlic and ginger (the classic stir-fry combination) in the center of the pan, and returned the protein to the pan along with the sauce. This final mixture needed less than a minute over medium heat to finish.

Stir-Fried Chicken and Zucchini with Ginger Sauce

SERVES 4

To make slicing the chicken easier, freeze it for 15 minutes. Serve with Basic White Rice (page 382).

SAUCE

- ¼ cup soy sauce
- 3 tablespoons minced or grated fresh ginger
- 2 tablespoons low-sodium chicken broth
- 1 tablespoon dry sherry
- ½ teaspoon sugar

CHICKEN AND VEGETABLES

- 12 ounces boneless, skinless chicken breasts, trimmed and sliced thin (see note)
- 1 tablespoon soy sauce

- 1 tablespoon dry sherry
- 2 tablespoons toasted sesame oil
- 1 tablespoon cornstarch
- 1 tablespoon unbleached all-purpose flour
- 2 tablespoons peanut or vegetable oil
- 1 tablespoon minced or grated fresh ginger
- 3 medium garlic cloves, minced or pressed through a garlic press (about 1 tablespoon)
- 2 scallions, white parts only, minced
- 2 carrots, peeled and cut into 2-inch-long matchsticks
- 1 red bell pepper, stemmed, seeded, and cut into ½-inch strips
- 1 medium zucchini, halved lengthwise and sliced ½ inch thick

1. FOR THE SAUCE: Combine all the ingredients in a small bowl and set aside.

2. FOR THE CHICKEN AND VEGETABLES: Toss the chicken with the soy sauce and sherry in a medium bowl and let marinate for at least 10 minutes or up to 1 hour. In a large bowl, whisk the sesame oil, cornstarch, and flour together. In a small bowl, mix 1 teaspoon of the peanut oil, the ginger, garlic, and scallions together.

3. Stir the marinated chicken into the sesame oil–cornstarch mixture. Heat 2 teaspoons more peanut oil in a 12-inch nonstick skillet over high heat until just smoking. Add the chicken, break up any clumps, then cook without stirring until the meat is browned at the edges, about 1 minute. Stir the chicken and continue to cook until cooked through, about 1 minute longer. Transfer the chicken to a clean bowl and cover with foil to keep warm.

4. Add the remaining 1 tablespoon peanut oil to the skillet and return to high heat until just smoking. Add the carrots and cook until beginning to soften, about 1 minute. Add the bell pepper and cook until spotty brown, about 1 minute. Add the zucchini and cook for 15 to 30 seconds, until just tender.

5. Clear the center of the skillet, add the ginger mixture, and cook, mashing the mixture into the pan, until fragrant, 15 to 20 seconds. Stir the ginger mixture into the vegetables.

6. Stir in the chicken with any accumulated juices. Whisk the sauce to recombine, then add to the skillet and cook, tossing constantly, until the sauce is thickened, about 30 seconds. Transfer to a serving platter and serve.

Stir-Fried Shrimp, Asparagus, and Yellow Pepper with Lemon Sauce

SERVES 4

One large lemon yields enough juice and zest for this sauce. Serve with Basic White Rice (page 382).

SAUCE

- 3 tablespoons juice plus ½ teaspoon zest from 1 lemon
- 2 tablespoons low-sodium chicken broth
- 1 tablespoon soy sauce
- 2 teaspoons sugar

SHRIMP AND VEGETABLES

- 1 pound medium shrimp (41 to 50 per pound), peeled and deveined (see page 205)
- 1 tablespoon soy sauce
- 1 tablespoon dry sherry
- 2 tablespoons plus 2 teaspoons peanut or vegetable oil
- 1 tablespoon minced or grated fresh ginger
- 3 garlic cloves, minced or pressed through a garlic press (about 1 tablespoon)
- 2 scallions, white parts only, minced
- 1 pound asparagus (1 bunch), tough ends trimmed, cut on the bias into 1-inch lengths
- ¼ cup water
- 1 yellow bell pepper, stemmed, seeded, and cut into ½-inch strips
  Table salt and ground black pepper
- ¼ cup chopped fresh cilantro leaves

1. FOR THE SAUCE: Combine all the ingredients in a small bowl and set aside.

2. FOR THE SHRIMP AND VEGETABLES: Toss the shrimp with the soy sauce and sherry in a medium bowl and let marinate for at least 10 minutes or up to 1 hour. In a small bowl, mix 1 teaspoon of the oil, the ginger, garlic, and scallions together.

3. Heat 2 teaspoons more oil in a 12-inch nonstick skillet over high heat until just smoking. Add the shrimp and cook without stirring until bright pink, about 1 minute. Stir the shrimp and continue to cook until cooked through, 15 to 30 seconds longer. Transfer the shrimp to a clean bowl and cover with foil to keep warm.

4. Add 1 tablespoon more oil to the skillet and return to high heat until just smoking. Add the asparagus and cook, stirring frequently, until spotty brown, about 2 minutes. Add the water, cover the pan, and lower the heat to medium. Cook the asparagus until crisp-tender, about 2 minutes. Transfer the asparagus to the bowl with the shrimp. Add the remaining 2 teaspoons oil to the skillet

and return to high heat until just smoking. Add the bell pepper and cook, stirring frequently, until spotty brown, about 1½ minutes.

5. Clear the center of the skillet, add the ginger mixture, and cook, mashing the mixture into the pan, until fragrant, 15 to 20 seconds. Stir the ginger mixture into the bell pepper.

6. Stir in the asparagus and shrimp with any accumulated juices. Whisk the sauce to recombine, then add to the skillet and cook, tossing constantly, until the sauce is thickened, about 30 seconds. Season with salt and pepper to taste. Transfer to a serving platter, sprinkle with the cilantro, and serve.

Stir-Fried Tofu, Snow Peas, and Red Onion with Hot and Sour Sauce

SERVES 4

Make sure to buy firm or extra-firm tofu; silken or soft tofu will crumble if stir-fried. To promote caramelization on the exterior of the tofu, turn the cubes as little as possible so that they have time to brown on several sides. For more heat, include the jalapeño seeds and ribs when mincing. Serve with Basic White Rice (page 382).

SAUCE

- 3 tablespoons cider vinegar
- 1 tablespoon low-sodium chicken broth
- 1 tablespoon soy sauce
- 2 teaspoons sugar

TOFU AND VEGETABLES

- 1 (14-ounce) block firm or extra-firm tofu, drained and cut into 1-inch cubes (see note)
- 1 tablespoon soy sauce
- 1 tablespoon dry sherry
- 2 tablespoons plus 1 teaspoon peanut or vegetable oil
- 1 tablespoon minced or grated fresh ginger
- 3 garlic cloves, minced or pressed through a garlic press (about 1 tablespoon)
- 2 scallions, white parts only, minced
- 1 jalapeño chile, seeds and ribs removed, chile minced (see note)
- 1 medium red onion, halved and sliced thin
- 1 pound snow peas, tips and strings removed
- 2 tablespoons water

1. FOR THE SAUCE: Combine all the ingredients in a small bowl and set aside.

2. FOR THE TOFU AND VEGETABLES: Toss the tofu with

the soy sauce and sherry in a medium bowl and let marinate for at least 10 minutes or up to 1 hour. In a small bowl, mix 1 teaspoon of the oil, the ginger, garlic, scallions, and jalapeño together.

3. Heat 1 tablespoon more oil in a 12-inch nonstick skillet over high heat until just smoking. Add the tofu and cook until golden brown on several sides, 2 to 3 minutes, turning as needed. Transfer the tofu to a clean bowl and cover with foil to keep warm.

4. Add the remaining 1 tablespoon oil to the skillet and return to high heat until just smoking. Add the onion and cook, stirring frequently, until beginning to brown, about 2 minutes. Add the snow peas and cook until spotty brown, about 2 minutes. Add the water, cover the pan, and lower the heat to medium. Cook the snow peas until crisp-tender, about 1 minute.

5. Clear the center of the skillet, add the ginger mixture, and cook, mashing the mixture into the pan, until fragrant, 15 to 20 seconds. Stir the ginger mixture into the vegetables.

6. Stir in the tofu. Whisk the sauce to recombine, then add to the skillet and cook, tossing constantly, until the sauce is thickened, about 30 seconds. Transfer to a serving platter and serve.

STIR-FRIED BEEF AND BROCCOLI

WHY THIS RECIPE WORKS: Order beef and broccoli in most Chinese restaurants, and you are served a pile of tough meat and overcooked army-issue broccoli. Worst of all is the thick-as-pudding brown sauce, which, aside from being flavored with burnt garlic, is otherwise tasteless. We set out to rescue this dish from the tyranny of third-rate Chinese restaurants.

For the meat, we found that flank steak offered the biggest beefy taste and slicing it thin made it tender. We cooked the beef in two batches over high heat to make sure it browned and didn't steam. Then we cooked the broccoli until crisp-tender using a combination of methods—sautéing and steaming—and added some red bell pepper for sweetness and color. For the sauce, we made a simple mixture of oyster-flavored sauce, chicken broth, dry sherry, sugar, and sesame oil, which we lightly thickened with cornstarch so it clung beautifully to the beef and vegetables. Now we had it: Every component of the dish—the beef, the broccoli, and sauce—was distinct and cooked to the best of its ability.

Stir-Fried Beef and Broccoli with Oyster Sauce
SERVES 4
To make slicing the flank steak easier, freeze it for 15 minutes. Serve with Basic White Rice (page 382).

SAUCE
- **5** tablespoons oyster-flavored sauce
- **2** tablespoons low-sodium chicken broth
- **1** tablespoon dry sherry
- **1** tablespoon light brown sugar
- **1** teaspoon toasted sesame oil
- **1** teaspoon cornstarch

BEEF AND BROCCOLI
- **1** (1-pound) flank steak, trimmed and cut into 2-inch-wide strips with the grain, then sliced across the grain into ⅛-inch-thick slices (see note)
- **3** tablespoons soy sauce
- **3** tablespoons peanut or vegetable oil
- **6** medium garlic cloves, minced or pressed through a garlic press (about 2 tablespoons)
- **1** tablespoon minced or grated fresh ginger
- **1¼** pounds broccoli, florets cut into 1-inch pieces, stems trimmed and sliced thin
- **⅓** cup water
- **1** small red bell pepper, stemmed, seeded, and cut into ½-inch pieces
- **3** scallions, sliced ½ inch thick on the bias

1. FOR THE SAUCE: Combine all the ingredients in a small bowl and set aside.

2. FOR THE BEEF AND BROCCOLI: Toss the beef with the soy sauce in a medium bowl and let marinate for at least 10 minutes or up to 1 hour. In a small bowl, mix 1 teaspoon of the peanut oil, the garlic, and ginger together.

3. Heat 2 teaspoons more peanut oil in a 12-inch nonstick skillet over high heat until just smoking. Add half of the beef, break up any clumps, then cook without stirring until the meat is browned at the edges, about 1 minute. Stir the beef and continue to cook until cooked through, about 1 minute longer. Transfer the beef to a clean bowl and cover with foil to keep warm. Repeat with 2 teaspoons more peanut oil and the remaining beef.

4. Add 1 tablespoon more peanut oil to the skillet and return to high heat until just smoking. Add the broccoli and cook for 30 seconds. Add the water, cover the pan, and lower the heat to medium. Cook the broccoli until crisp-tender, about 2 minutes. Transfer the broccoli to a paper towel–lined plate.

5. Add the remaining 1 teaspoon peanut oil to the skillet and return to high heat until just smoking. Add the bell pepper and cook, stirring frequently, until spotty brown, about 1½ minutes. Clear the center of the skillet, add the garlic mixture, and cook, mashing the mixture into the pan, until fragrant, 15 to 20 seconds. Stir the garlic mixture into the bell pepper.

6. Stir in the broccoli and beef with any accumulated juices. Whisk the sauce to recombine, then add to the skillet and cook, tossing constantly, until the sauce is thickened, about 30 seconds. Transfer to a serving platter, sprinkle with the scallions, and serve.

BEEF AND VEGETABLE STIR-FRIES

WHY THIS RECIPE WORKS: More often than not, beef and vegetable stir-fries consist of chewy, gray beef, surrounded by unevenly cooked vegetables, smothered in a gloppy sauce. We wanted browned, tender beef and crisp-tender vegetables coated in deep-flavored, silky sauces.

We chose flank steak for the best texture and flavor. We thinly sliced and marinated the steak in soy sauce and sugar and cooked it over high heat to achieve a good sear. We cooked the vegetables in batches for best texture. For one stir-fry, we paired the beef with green beans, shiitakes, and a teriyaki sauce. Next, we combined the beef with a tangerine sauce, snow peas, and onion. The sauces were lightly thickened with just 1 teaspoon of cornstarch, so they clung to the beef and vegetables but were not overly thick.

Teriyaki Stir-Fried Beef with Green Beans and Shiitakes

SERVES 4

To make slicing the flank steak easier, freeze it for 15 minutes. Serve with Basic White Rice (page 382).

SAUCE
- ½ cup low-sodium chicken broth
- 2 tablespoons soy sauce
- 2 tablespoons sugar
- 1 tablespoon mirin or sweet sherry
- 1 teaspoon cornstarch
- ¼ teaspoon red pepper flakes

BEEF AND VEGETABLES
- 12 ounces flank steak, trimmed and cut into 2-inch-wide strips with the grain, then sliced across the grain into ⅛-inch-thick slices (see note)
- 2 tablespoons soy sauce
- 1 teaspoon sugar
- 2 tablespoons peanut or vegetable oil
- 1 tablespoon minced or grated fresh ginger
- 3 medium garlic cloves, minced or pressed through a garlic press (about 1 tablespoon)
- 8 ounces shiitake mushrooms, stemmed, wiped clean, caps cut into 1-inch pieces
- 12 ounces green beans, ends trimmed, cut into 2-inch lengths (see photo)
- ¼ cup water
- 3 scallions, quartered lengthwise and cut into 1½-inch pieces

1. FOR THE SAUCE: Combine all the ingredients in a small bowl and set aside.

NOTES FROM THE TEST KITCHEN

TRIMMING GREEN BEANS QUICKLY

Line up several green beans in a row on a cutting board. Trim about ½ inch from each end, then cut the beans as directed in the recipe.

2. FOR THE BEEF AND VEGETABLES: Toss the beef with the soy sauce and sugar in a medium bowl and let marinate for at least 10 minutes or up to 1 hour. In a small bowl, mix 1 teaspoon of the oil, the ginger, and garlic together.

3. Heat 2 teaspoons more oil in a 12-inch nonstick skillet over high heat until just smoking. Add the beef, break up any clumps, then cook without stirring until the meat is browned at the edges, about 1 minute. Stir the beef and continue to cook until cooked through, about 1 minute longer. Transfer the beef to a clean bowl and cover with foil to keep warm.

4. Add the remaining 1 tablespoon oil to the skillet and return to high heat until just smoking. Add the mushrooms and cook until beginning to brown, about 2 minutes. Add the green beans and cook, stirring frequently, until spotty brown, 3 to 4 minutes. Add the water, cover the pan, and lower the heat to medium. Cook the green beans until crisp-tender, about 2 minutes.

5. Clear the center of the skillet, add the ginger mixture, and cook, mashing the mixture into the pan, until fragrant, 15 to 20 seconds. Stir the ginger mixture into the vegetables.

6. Stir in the beef with any accumulated juices. Whisk the sauce to recombine, then add to the skillet and cook, tossing constantly, until the sauce is thickened, about 30 seconds. Stir in the scallions. Transfer to a serving platter and serve.

Tangerine Stir-Fried Beef with Onion and Snow Peas

SERVES 4

To make slicing the flank steak easier, freeze it for 15 minutes. Two to 3 oranges can be substituted for the tangerines. Note that you should zest the tangerines before juicing them. Use the larger amount of red pepper flakes if you desire a spicier dish. If available, substitute 1 teaspoon toasted and ground Sichuan peppercorns for the red pepper flakes. Serve with Basic White Rice (page 382).

SAUCE

- ¾ cup juice from 3 to 4 tangerines (see note)
- 2 tablespoons soy sauce
- 1 tablespoon light brown sugar
- 1 teaspoon toasted sesame oil
- 1 teaspoon cornstarch

BEEF AND VEGETABLES

- 12 ounces flank steak, trimmed and cut into 2-inch-wide strips with the grain, then sliced across the grain into ⅛-inch-thick slices (see note)
- 2 tablespoons soy sauce
- 1 teaspoon light brown sugar
- 2 tablespoons peanut or vegetable oil
- 1 tablespoon minced or grated fresh ginger
- 3 medium garlic cloves, minced or pressed through a garlic press (about 1 tablespoon)
- 1 tablespoon Chinese black bean sauce
- 1 teaspoon grated zest from 1 tangerine (see note)
- ¼–½ teaspoon red pepper flakes (see note)
- 1 large onion, halved and cut into ½-inch wedges
- 10 ounces snow peas, tips and strings removed
- 2 tablespoons water

1. FOR THE SAUCE: Combine all the ingredients in a small bowl and set aside.

2. FOR THE BEEF AND VEGETABLES: Toss the beef with the soy sauce and sugar in a medium bowl and let marinate for at least 10 minutes or up to 1 hour. In a small bowl, mix 1 teaspoon of the peanut oil, the ginger, garlic, black bean sauce, tangerine zest, and red pepper flakes together.

3. Heat 2 teaspoons more peanut oil in a 12-inch nonstick skillet over high heat until just smoking. Add the beef, break up any clumps, then cook without stirring until the meat is browned at the edges, about 1 minute. Stir the beef and continue to cook until cooked through, about 1 minute longer. Transfer the beef to a clean bowl and cover with foil to keep warm.

4. Add the remaining 1 tablespoon peanut oil to the skillet and return to high heat until just smoking. Add the onion and cook, stirring frequently, until beginning to brown, about 2 minutes. Add the snow peas and cook until spotty brown, about 2 minutes. Add the water, cover the pan, and lower the heat to medium. Cook the snow peas until crisp-tender, about 1 minute.

5. Clear the center of the skillet, add the ginger mixture, and cook, mashing the mixture into the pan, until fragrant, 15 to 20 seconds. Stir the ginger mixture into the vegetables.

6. Stir in the beef with any accumulated juices. Whisk the sauce to recombine, then add to the skillet and cook, tossing constantly, until the sauce is thickened, about 30 seconds. Transfer to a serving platter and serve.

PORK AND VEGETABLE STIR-FRIES

WHY THIS RECIPE WORKS: Pork and vegetable stir-fries, homemade or ordered out, are usually nothing more than tough, tasteless pork and barely cooked vegetables in a thick, slithery sauce. We wanted to make pork and vegetable stir-fries that had tender, flavorful pork and perfectly cooked vegetables—dishes that would taste authentic but would not have epic ingredient lists.

We chose pork tenderloin for our stir-fry because it is so tender. Marinating improved the pork's flavor. As with most stir-fries, cooking quickly over high heat ensured browning. Because different vegetables cook at different rates, we batch-cooked the vegetables and added aromatics (like ginger and garlic) at the end so they would cook long enough to develop their flavors but not burn. For the sauce, we used chicken broth as the backbone and added an acid to brighten the flavors. As with our other stir-fries, cornstarch created a slightly thickened sauce that lightly cloaked the pork and vegetables.

Stir-Fried Pork, Eggplant, and Onion with Garlic and Black Pepper

SERVES 4

To make slicing the pork easier, freeze it for 15 minutes. This classic Thai stir-fry is not for those with timid palates. Serve with Basic White Rice (page 382).

SAUCE
- 2½ tablespoons soy sauce
- 2½ tablespoons fish sauce
- 2½ tablespoons light brown sugar
- 2 tablespoons low-sodium chicken broth
- 2 teaspoons juice from 1 lime
- 1 teaspoon cornstarch

PORK AND VEGETABLES
- 1 (12-ounce) pork tenderloin, trimmed of fat and silver skin and cut into ¼-inch strips (see note)
- 1 teaspoon soy sauce
- 1 teaspoon fish sauce
- 3 tablespoons peanut or vegetable oil
- 12 medium garlic cloves, minced or pressed through a garlic press (about ¼ cup)
- 2 teaspoons ground black pepper
- 1 medium eggplant (1 pound), cut into ¾-inch cubes
- 1 large onion, halved and cut into ¼-inch wedges
- ½ cup chopped fresh cilantro leaves

1. FOR THE SAUCE: Combine all the ingredients in a small bowl and set aside.

2. FOR THE PORK AND VEGETABLES: Toss the pork with the soy sauce and fish sauce in a medium bowl and let marinate for at least 10 minutes or up to 1 hour. In a small bowl, mix 2 teaspoons of the oil, the garlic, and pepper together.

3. Heat 2 teaspoons more oil in a 12-inch nonstick skillet over high heat until just smoking. Add the pork, break up any clumps, then cook without stirring until the meat is browned at the edges, about 1 minute. Stir the pork and continue to cook until cooked through, about 1 minute longer. Transfer the pork to a clean bowl and cover with foil to keep warm.

4. Add 1 tablespoon more oil to the skillet and return to high heat until just smoking. Add the eggplant and cook, stirring frequently, until browned and no longer spongy, about 5 minutes. Transfer the eggplant to the bowl with the pork. Add the remaining 2 teaspoons peanut oil to the skillet and return to high heat until just smoking. Add the onion and cook until beginning to brown and soften, about 2 minutes.

5. Clear the center of the skillet, add the garlic mixture, and cook, mashing the mixture into the pan, until fragrant, 15 to 20 seconds. Stir the garlic mixture into the onion.

6. Stir in the eggplant and pork with any accumulated juices. Whisk the sauce to recombine, then add to the skillet and cook, tossing constantly, until the sauce is thickened, about 30 seconds. Transfer to a serving platter, sprinkle with the cilantro, and serve.

Stir-Fried Pork, Green Beans, and Red Bell Pepper with Gingery Oyster Sauce

SERVES 4

To make slicing the pork easier, freeze it for 15 minutes. Serve with Basic White Rice (page 382).

SAUCE

⅓ cup low-sodium chicken broth
2½ tablespoons oyster-flavored sauce
1 tablespoon dry sherry
2 teaspoons toasted sesame oil
1 teaspoon rice vinegar
1 teaspoon cornstarch
¼ teaspoon ground white pepper

PORK AND VEGETABLES

1 (12-ounce) pork tenderloin, trimmed of fat and silver skin and cut into ¼-inch strips (see note)
2 teaspoons soy sauce
2 teaspoons dry sherry
3 tablespoons peanut or vegetable oil
2 tablespoons minced or grated fresh ginger
2 medium garlic cloves, minced or pressed through a garlic press (about 2 teaspoons)
12 ounces green beans, trimmed and cut on the bias into 2-inch lengths
¼ cup water
1 large red bell pepper, stemmed, seeded, and cut into ¾-inch squares
3 scallions, sliced thin on the bias

1. FOR THE SAUCE: Combine all the ingredients in a small bowl and set aside.

2. FOR THE PORK AND VEGETABLES: Toss the pork with the soy sauce and sherry in a medium bowl and let marinate for at least 10 minutes or up to 1 hour. In a small bowl, mix 2 teaspoons of the peanut oil, the ginger, and garlic together.

3. Heat 2 teaspoons more peanut oil in a 12-inch non-stick skillet over high heat until just smoking. Add the pork, break up any clumps, then cook without stirring until the meat is browned at the edges, about 1 minute. Stir the pork and continue to cook until cooked through, about 1 minute longer. Transfer the pork to a clean bowl and cover with foil to keep warm.

4. Add 1 tablespoon more peanut oil to the skillet and return to high heat until just smoking. Add the green beans and cook, stirring frequently, until spotty brown,

3 to 4 minutes. Add the water, cover the pan, and lower the heat to medium. Cook the green beans until crisp-tender, about 2 minutes. Transfer the green beans to the bowl with the pork. Add the remaining 2 teaspoons peanut oil to the skillet and return to high heat until just smoking. Add the bell pepper and cook until spotty brown, about 1½ minutes.

5. Clear the center of the skillet, add the ginger mixture, and cook, mashing the mixture into the pan, until fragrant, 15 to 20 seconds. Stir the ginger mixture into the bell pepper.

6. Stir in the green beans and pork with any accumulated juices. Whisk the sauce to recombine, then add to the skillet and cook, tossing constantly, until the sauce is thickened, about 30 seconds. Transfer to a serving platter, sprinkle with the scallions, and serve.

PORK LO MEIN

WHY THIS RECIPE WORKS: Ordinary takeout pork lo mein invariably disappoints, with greasy flavors and sodden vegetables. We wanted a dish representative of the best that a good Chinese home cook could turn out: chewy noodles tossed in a salty-sweet sauce and accented with bits of smoky, barbecued pork and still-crisp cabbage.

First we needed to tackle the char siu, preferably perfecting a stir-fried version since we were already stir-frying the vegetables. Country-style pork ribs won for best cut. Though fatty, these meaty ribs have the same rich flavor of pork shoulder—but don't need to be cooked for hours since they're naturally tender. To avoid an overly greasy dish, we trimmed the fat and cut the meat into thin strips that would allow our classic Chinese marinade to penetrate effectively. A few drops of liquid smoke mimicked char siu's characteristic smoky flavor. Turning to the noodles, only ones labeled "lo mein" at the Asian market won raves. Fortunately, dried linguine, cooked al dente, worked beautifully. For the vegetables, we opted for traditional choices—cabbage, scallions, and shiitake mushrooms—stir-frying them with garlic and fresh ginger. We used our meat marinade as a sauce base, with a little chicken broth and a teaspoon of cornstarch added for body. A splash of Asian chili-garlic sauce added a little kick.

Pork Lo Mein

SERVES 4

Use a cast-iron skillet for this recipe if you have one—it will help create the best sear on the pork. If boneless pork ribs are unavailable, substitute 1½ pounds bone-in country-style ribs, followed by the next-best option, pork tenderloin. Liquid smoke provides a flavor reminiscent of the Chinese barbecued pork traditional to this dish. It is important to cook the noodles at the last minute to avoid clumping.

    3 tablespoons soy sauce
    2 tablespoons oyster-flavored sauce
    2 tablespoons hoisin sauce
    1 tablespoon toasted sesame oil
    ¼ teaspoon Chinese five-spice powder
    1 pound boneless country-style pork ribs, trimmed of
       fat and gristle, sliced crosswise into ⅛-inch pieces
       (see note)
    ¼ teaspoon liquid smoke (optional; see note)
    ½ cup low-sodium chicken broth
    1 teaspoon cornstarch
    2 tablespoons plus 1 teaspoon peanut or vegetable oil
    2 teaspoons minced or grated fresh ginger
    2 medium garlic cloves, minced or pressed through a
       garlic press (about 2 teaspoons)
    ¼ cup Chinese rice cooking wine (Shao Xing) or dry sherry
    8 ounces shiitake mushrooms, stemmed, wiped clean, caps
       sliced ¼ inch thick
    2 bunches scallions, whites sliced thin, greens cut into
       1-inch pieces
    1 pound napa cabbage (1 small head), cored and cut into
       ½-inch strips
   12 ounces fresh Chinese noodles or 8 ounces dried linguine
    1 tablespoon Asian chili-garlic sauce

1. Whisk the soy sauce, oyster-flavored sauce, hoisin sauce, sesame oil, and five-spice powder together in a small bowl. Transfer 3 tablespoons of the mixture to a medium bowl and add the pork and liquid smoke (if using). Let marinate for at least 10 minutes or up to 1 hour. Whisk the broth and cornstarch into the remaining soy sauce mixture and set aside. In a small bowl, mix 1 teaspoon of the peanut oil, the ginger, and garlic together and set aside.

2. Heat 2 teaspoons more peanut oil in a 12-inch nonstick or cast-iron skillet over high heat until just smoking. Add half of the pork, break up any clumps, then cook without stirring until the meat is browned at the edges, about 1 minute. Stir the pork and continue to cook until cooked through, about 1 minute longer. Add 2 tablespoons of the wine to the skillet and cook, stirring constantly, until the liquid is reduced and the pork is well coated, 30 to 60 seconds. Transfer the pork to a clean bowl and cover with foil to keep warm. Repeat with 2 teaspoons more peanut oil, the remaining pork, and the remaining 2 tablespoons wine. Wipe out the skillet with a wad of paper towels.

3. Add 1 teaspoon more peanut oil to the skillet and return to high heat until just smoking. Add the mushrooms and cook, stirring occasionally, until light golden brown, 4 to 6 minutes. Add the scallion whites and greens and cook, stirring occasionally, until wilted, 2 to 3 minutes. Transfer the vegetables to the bowl with the pork.

4. Add the remaining 1 teaspoon peanut oil to the skillet and heat over high heat until just smoking. Add the cabbage and cook, stirring occasionally, until spotty brown, 3 to 5 minutes. Clear the center of the skillet, add the ginger mixture, and cook, mashing the mixture into the pan, until fragrant, 15 to 20 seconds. Stir the ginger mixture into the cabbage.

5. Stir in the vegetables and pork with any accumulated juices. Whisk the sauce to recombine, then add to the skillet and cook, tossing constantly, until the sauce is thickened, about 30 seconds.

6. Bring 6 quarts water to a boil in a large pot. Add the noodles and cook, stirring often, until tender, about 4 minutes for fresh and 10 minutes for dried. Drain the noodles and return them to the pot. Add the cooked stir-fry mixture and the chili-garlic sauce to the noodles and toss to combine. Transfer to a serving platter and serve.

SHRIMP STIR-FRIES

WHY THIS RECIPE WORKS: Stir-fries are typically cooked over high heat to sear the food and develop flavor. This works well with chicken, beef, and pork, but delicate shrimp turns to rubber when cooked this way. We wanted a stir-fry with plump, juicy, well-seasoned shrimp in a balanced, flavorful sauce.

To start, we wondered if browning was really necessary. Abandoning the high-heat method, we turned down the burner to medium-low and gently parcooked a batch of shrimp (marinated in oil, salt, and garlic for better flavor and texture), removed them from the skillet, then turned up the heat to sear the vegetables, sauté the aromatics, and finish cooking the shrimp with the sauce. This worked beautifully. Reversing the approach—cooking the veggies followed by the aromatics over high heat, then turning the heat down before adding the shrimp—made the process more efficient.

As for an assertive sauce, the heavily soy-based brews we turn to for meat stir-fries were runny and salty. Better suited to the shrimp (and more traditional in Chinese cuisine) were sweeter or spicier sauces flavored with garlic and chiles and reduced to a consistency that tightly adhered to the shellfish.

Stir-Fried Shrimp with Snow Peas and Red Bell Pepper in Hot and Sour Sauce

SERVES 4

Serve with Basic White Rice (page 382).

- 1 pound extra-large shrimp (21 to 25 per pound), peeled, deveined (see page 205), and tails removed
- 3 tablespoons vegetable oil
- 1 tablespoon minced or grated fresh ginger
- 2 medium garlic cloves, 1 minced or pressed through a garlic press (about 1 teaspoon), 1 sliced thin
- ½ teaspoon table salt
- 3 tablespoons sugar
- 3 tablespoons white vinegar
- 1 tablespoon Asian chili-garlic sauce
- 1 tablespoon dry sherry or Chinese rice cooking wine (Shao Xing)
- 1 tablespoon ketchup
- 2 teaspoons toasted sesame oil
- 2 teaspoons cornstarch
- 1 teaspoon soy sauce
- 1 large shallot, sliced thin (about ⅓ cup)

- ½ pound snow peas or sugar snap peas, tips snapped off and strings removed
- 1 medium red bell pepper, stemmed, seeded, and cut into ¾-inch dice

1. Combine the shrimp with 1 tablespoon of the vegetable oil, the ginger, minced garlic, and salt in a medium bowl. Let the shrimp marinate at room temperature for 30 minutes.

2. Meanwhile, whisk the sugar, vinegar, chili-garlic sauce, sherry, ketchup, sesame oil, cornstarch, and soy sauce in a small bowl. Combine the sliced garlic with the shallot in a second small bowl.

3. Heat 1 tablespoon more vegetable oil in a 12-inch nonstick skillet over high heat until just smoking. Add the snow peas and bell pepper and cook, stirring frequently, until the vegetables begin to brown, 1½ to 2 minutes. Transfer the vegetables to a medium bowl.

4. Add the remaining 1 tablespoon vegetable oil to the now-empty skillet and heat until just smoking. Add the garlic-shallot mixture and cook, stirring frequently, until just beginning to brown, about 30 seconds. Reduce the heat to medium-low, add the shrimp, and cook, stirring frequently, until the shrimp are light pink on both sides, 1 to 1½ minutes. Whisk the soy sauce mixture to recombine and add to the skillet; return to high heat and cook, stirring constantly, until the sauce is thickened and the shrimp are cooked through, 1 to 2 minutes. Return the vegetables to the skillet, toss to combine, and serve.

Stir-Fried Shrimp with Garlicky Eggplant, Scallions, and Cashews

SERVES 4

To make quick work of cutting the scallions, use sharp kitchen shears. Serve with Basic White Rice (page 382).

- 1 **pound extra-large shrimp (21 to 25 per pound), peeled, deveined (see page 205), and tails removed**
- 3 **tablespoons vegetable oil**
- 6 **medium garlic cloves, 1 minced or pressed through a garlic press (about 1 teaspoon), 5 sliced thin**
- ½ **teaspoon table salt**
- 2 **tablespoons soy sauce**
- 2 **tablespoons oyster-flavored sauce**
- 2 **tablespoons dry sherry or Chinese rice cooking wine (Shao Xing)**
- 2 **tablespoons sugar**
- 1 **tablespoon toasted sesame oil**
- 1 **tablespoon white vinegar**
- 2 **teaspoons cornstarch**
- ⅛ **teaspoon red pepper flakes**
- 6 **large scallions, greens cut into 1-inch pieces and whites sliced thin**
- ½ **cup unsalted cashews**
- 1 **medium eggplant (about ¾ pound), cut into ¾-inch dice**

1. Combine the shrimp with 1 tablespoon of the vegetable oil, the minced garlic, and salt in a medium bowl. Let the shrimp marinate at room temperature for 30 minutes.

2. Meanwhile, whisk the soy sauce, oyster-flavored sauce, sherry, sugar, sesame oil, vinegar, cornstarch, and red pepper flakes in a small bowl. Combine the sliced garlic with the scallion whites and cashews in a small bowl.

3. Heat 1 tablespoon more vegetable oil in a 12-inch nonstick skillet over high heat until just smoking. Add the eggplant and cook, stirring frequently, until lightly browned, 3 to 6 minutes. Add the scallion greens and continue to cook until the scallion greens begin to brown and the eggplant is fully tender, 1 to 2 minutes longer. Transfer the vegetables to a medium bowl.

4. Continue with the recipe for Stir-Fried Shrimp with Snow Peas and Red Bell Pepper in Hot and Sour Sauce from step 4, replacing the garlic-shallot mixture with the garlic-scallion-cashew mixture.

KUNG PAO SHRIMP

WHY THIS RECIPE WORKS: Kung pao is meant to have a fiery personality, but many restaurant versions are dismal, featuring tiny, tough shrimp drenched in a quart of pale, greasy, bland sauce. We wanted to make this classic Sichuan stir-fry at home, with large, tender shrimp, crunchy peanuts, and an assertive, well-balanced brown sauce.

For tender, flavorful shrimp, we stir-fried marinated extra-large shrimp for just a few seconds, then added small whole red chiles and whole unsalted roasted peanuts. For vegetables, we kept things simple and added just one diced red bell pepper (tasters found other vegetables to be superfluous) and the usual aromatics, garlic and ginger. We made a potently flavored, syrupy sauce using a mixture of chicken broth, rice vinegar, toasted sesame oil, oyster-flavored sauce, hoisin sauce, and cornstarch. Stirring in sliced scallions just before serving put the final touch on our dish. We no longer need to rely on dull, gloppy restaurant renditions of this Sichuan classic.

Kung Pao Shrimp

SERVES 4

Roasted unsalted cashews can be substituted for the peanuts. Unless you have a taste for the incendiary, do not eat the whole chiles in the finished dish. Serve with Basic White Rice (page 382).

SAUCE

- ¾ cup low-sodium chicken broth
- 1 tablespoon oyster-flavored sauce
- 1 tablespoon hoisin sauce
- 2 teaspoons rice vinegar
- 2 teaspoons toasted sesame oil
- 1½ teaspoons cornstarch

SHRIMP AND VEGETABLES

- 1 pound extra-large shrimp (21 to 25 per pound), peeled and deveined (see page 205)
- 1 tablespoon Chinese rice cooking wine (Shao Xing) or dry sherry
- 2 teaspoons soy sauce
- 2 tablespoons plus 1 teaspoon peanut or vegetable oil
- 3 medium garlic cloves, minced or pressed through a garlic press (about 1 tablespoon)
- 2 teaspoons minced or grated fresh ginger
- ½ cup unsalted roasted peanuts (see note)
- 6 small whole dried red chiles (see note)
- 1 red bell pepper, stemmed, seeded, and cut into ½-inch pieces
- 3 scallions, sliced thin

1. FOR THE SAUCE: Combine all the ingredients in a small bowl and set aside.

2. FOR THE SHRIMP AND VEGETABLES: Toss the shrimp with the rice cooking wine and soy sauce in a medium bowl and let marinate for at least 10 minutes or up to 1 hour. In a small bowl, mix 1 teaspoon of the peanut oil, the garlic, and ginger together.

3. Heat 1 tablespoon more peanut oil in a 12-inch nonstick skillet over high heat until just smoking. Add the shrimp and cook until barely opaque, 30 to 40 seconds, stirring halfway through. Add the peanuts and chiles and continue to cook until the shrimp are bright pink and the peanuts have darkened slightly, 30 to 40 seconds longer. Transfer the shrimp, peanuts, and chiles to a clean bowl and cover with foil to keep warm.

4. Add the remaining 1 tablespoon peanut oil to the skillet and return to high heat until just smoking. Add the bell pepper and cook, stirring frequently, until spotty brown, about 1½ minutes. Clear the center of the skillet, add the garlic mixture, and cook, mashing the mixture into the pan, until fragrant, 15 to 20 seconds. Stir the garlic mixture into the bell pepper.

5. Stir in the peanuts, chiles, and shrimp with any accumulated juices. Whisk the sauce to recombine, then add to the skillet and cook, tossing constantly, until the sauce is thickened, about 30 seconds. Stir in the scallions, transfer to a serving platter, and serve.

VEGETABLE STIR-FRIES

WHY THIS RECIPE WORKS: Without meat, vegetable stir-fries can feel more like a side dish than a dinner. We wanted to make a satisfying, filling stir-fry—without meat.

We chose meaty portobello mushrooms as the main vegetable. We found that removing the gills kept them from tasting leathery and raw. We tried cutting them in a variety of sizes and settled on 2-inch wedges, which felt the most substantial. We cooked the mushrooms over medium-high heat until browned and tender, then added a mixture of broth, soy sauce, and sugar and reduced it to a glaze—this provided an intense flavor boost. For this stir-fry, we bulked up the amount of vegetables in our traditional stir-fries, mixing carrots, snow peas, and napa cabbage. Finally, the sauce—a mixture of broth, oyster-flavored sauce, soy sauce, cornstarch, and sesame oil—and a heavy dose of ginger tied the dish together, giving the vegetables great flavor—and nobody missed the meat!

Stir-Fried Portobellos with Ginger-Oyster Sauce

SERVES 4

Serve with Basic White Rice (see page 382).

GLAZE

- ¼ cup low-sodium chicken or vegetable broth
- 2 tablespoons soy sauce
- 2 tablespoons sugar

SAUCE

- 1 cup low-sodium chicken or vegetable broth
- 3 tablespoons oyster-flavored sauce
- 1 tablespoon soy sauce
- 1 tablespoon cornstarch
- 2 teaspoons toasted sesame oil

VEGETABLES

- ¼ cup peanut or vegetable oil
- 4 teaspoons minced or grated fresh ginger
- 2 medium garlic cloves, minced or pressed through a garlic press (about 2 teaspoons)
- 6-8 portobello mushrooms (each 4 to 6 inches), stemmed, wiped clean, gills removed, and cut into 2-inch wedges
- 4 carrots, peeled and sliced ¼ inch thick on the bias
- ½ cup low-sodium chicken or vegetable broth
- 3 ounces snow peas, tips and strings removed
- 1 pound napa cabbage (1 small head), cored and cut into ¾-inch strips
- 1 tablespoon sesame seeds, toasted (optional)

1. FOR THE GLAZE: Combine all the ingredients in a small bowl and set aside.

2. FOR THE SAUCE: Combine all the ingredients in a small bowl and set aside.

3. FOR THE VEGETABLES: In a small bowl, mix 1 teaspoon of the peanut oil, the ginger, and garlic together.

4. Heat 3 tablespoons more peanut oil in a 12-inch nonstick skillet over medium-high heat until shimmering. Add the mushrooms and cook without stirring until browned on one side, 2 to 3 minutes. Using tongs, flip the mushrooms, reduce the heat to medium, and cook until the second sides are browned and the mushrooms are tender, about 5 minutes. Increase the heat to medium-high, add the glaze, and cook, stirring frequently, until the glaze is thick and the mushrooms are coated, 1 to 2 minutes. Transfer the mushrooms to a plate. Rinse the skillet clean and dry with a wad of paper towels.

5. Add 1 teaspoon more peanut oil to the skillet and return to high heat until just smoking. Add the carrots and cook, stirring frequently, until beginning to brown, 1 to 2 minutes. Add the broth, cover the pan, and lower the heat to medium. Cook the carrots until just tender, 2 to 3 minutes. Uncover and cook until the liquid evaporates, about 30 seconds. Transfer the carrots to the plate with the mushrooms.

6. Add the remaining 1 teaspoon peanut oil to the skillet and return to high heat until just smoking. Add the snow peas and cook until spotty brown, about 2 minutes. Add the cabbage and cook, stirring frequently, until wilted, about 2 minutes.

7. Clear the center of the skillet, add the ginger mixture, and cook, mashing the mixture into the pan, until fragrant, 15 to 20 seconds. Stir the ginger mixture into the vegetables.

8. Stir in the mushrooms and carrots. Whisk the sauce to recombine, then add to the skillet and cook, tossing constantly, until the sauce is thickened, 2 to 3 minutes. Transfer to a serving platter, sprinkle with the sesame seeds (if using), and serve.

Stir-Fried Portobellos with Sweet Chili-Garlic Sauce

Follow the recipe for Stir-Fried Portobellos with Ginger-Oyster Sauce, replacing the sugar in the glaze with 2 tablespoons honey. For the sauce, increase the soy sauce to 3 tablespoons, reduce the broth to ¾ cup, and replace the oyster-flavored sauce and toasted sesame oil with 2 tablespoons honey, 1 tablespoon rice vinegar, and 1 teaspoon Asian chili sauce. Increase the garlic to 4 cloves.

THAI CHICKEN WITH BASIL

WHY THIS RECIPE WORKS: In Thailand, street vendors have mastered an alternative to traditional Chinese high-heat stir-fry, using low flames to produce complex and flavorful dishes like chicken and basil—chopped pieces of moist chicken in a bright, basil-infused sauce. We set out to create our own version.

To start, we turned to the aromatics. Because Thai stir-fries are cooked over a lower temperature, the aromatics are added at the very beginning of cooking, where they infuse the oil with their flavors. To prevent scorching, we started our aromatics (garlic, chiles, and shallots) in a cold skillet.

It was too time-consuming to chop our chicken by hand, so we turned to the food processor. To ensure moist meat, we added fish sauce to the food processor when we ground the chicken, then rested the meat in the refrigerator—the fish sauce acted as a brine, seasoning the chicken and sealing in moisture. Next, we moved on to the sauce. For our sauce base, we liked Chinese-style oyster-flavored sauce brightened with a dash of white vinegar. We spiced up the flavor of the sauce by adding a reserved tablespoon of the raw garlic-chile mixture at the end of cooking. And for intense, bright basil flavor, we cooked a portion of chopped basil with the garlic, chile, and shallot mixture, and stirred in whole basil leaves just before serving.

Thai-Style Chicken with Basil

SERVES 4

Since tolerance for spiciness can vary, we've kept our recipe relatively mild. For a very mild version, remove the seeds and ribs from the chiles. If fresh Thai chiles are unavailable, substitute 2 serranos or 1 medium jalapeño. In Thailand, crushed red pepper and sugar are passed at the table, along with extra fish sauce and white vinegar. You do not need to wash the food processor bowl after step 1. Serve with Basic White Rice (page 382) and vegetables, if desired.

- 2 **cups tightly packed fresh basil leaves**
- 3 **garlic cloves, peeled**
- 6 **green or red Thai chiles, stemmed (see note)**
- 2 **tablespoons fish sauce, plus extra for serving**
- 1 **tablespoon oyster-flavored sauce**
- 1 **tablespoon sugar, plus extra for serving**
- 1 **teaspoon white vinegar, plus extra for serving**
- 1 **pound boneless, skinless chicken breasts, trimmed and cut into 2-inch pieces**
- 3 **shallots, peeled and sliced thin (about ¾ cup)**
- 2 **tablespoons vegetable oil**
  Red pepper flakes, for serving

1. Pulse 1 cup of the basil leaves, the garlic, and chiles in a food processor until chopped fine, 6 to 10 pulses, scraping down the sides of the bowl once during processing. Transfer 1 tablespoon of the basil mixture to a small bowl, stir in 1 tablespoon of the fish sauce, the oyster-flavored sauce, sugar, and vinegar and set aside. Transfer the remaining basil mixture to a 12-inch heavy-bottomed nonstick skillet.

2. Pulse the chicken and the remaining 1 tablespoon fish sauce in the food processor until the meat is chopped into ¼-inch pieces, 6 to 8 pulses. Transfer the chicken to a medium bowl and refrigerate for 15 minutes.

3. Stir the shallots and oil into the basil mixture in the skillet. Heat the mixture over medium-low heat (the mixture should start to sizzle after about 1½ minutes; if it doesn't, adjust the heat accordingly), stirring constantly, until the garlic and shallots are golden brown, 5 to 8 minutes.

4. Add the chicken, increase the heat to medium, and cook, stirring and breaking up the chicken with a potato masher or rubber spatula, until only traces of pink remain, 2 to 4 minutes. Add the reserved basil–fish sauce mixture and continue to cook, stirring constantly, until the chicken is no longer pink, about 1 minute. Stir in the remaining 1 cup basil leaves and cook, stirring constantly, until the basil is wilted, 30 to 60 seconds. Serve immediately, passing the extra fish sauce, sugar, vinegar, and red pepper flakes separately.

THAI CURRY

WHY THIS RECIPE WORKS: Like most Thai food, Thai curries embrace a delicate balance of tastes, textures, temperatures, and colors that come together to create a harmonious whole. Unlike Indian curries, Thai curries almost always contain coconut milk. Also, they tilt the spice balance towards fresh aromatics, which are added in the form of a paste. We wanted an authentic Thai red curry and green curry, perfumed with lemon grass, hot chiles, and coconut milk, both of which could be made easily by the home cook.

A food processor made quick work of blending together the curry pastes. For the green curry, we favored Thai green chiles (although serrano or jalapeño chiles make great substitutes), while the red curry was best with small dried red chiles and a fresh red jalapeño. Shallots, lemon grass, cilantro stems, garlic, ginger, coriander, and cumin rounded out the flavors of the pastes. And to approximate the flavor of kaffir lime leaves, we added grated lime zest. To make the curries, we skimmed the coconut cream off the coconut milk and cooked it with the curry paste—this gave our curries silky body and intense, rich flavor. We paired the green curry with chicken, broccoli, mushrooms, and bell pepper, and the red curry with shrimp, pineapple, and peanuts. All that we needed now was rice to soak up the flavorful sauce.

Thai Green Curry with Chicken, Broccoli, and Mushrooms

SERVES 4

To make slicing the chicken easier, freeze it for 15 minutes. Serve with Basic White Rice (page 382).

     2 (14-ounce) cans unsweetened coconut milk, not shaken
     1 recipe Green Curry Paste (recipe follows) or
        2 tablespoons store-bought green curry paste
     2 tablespoons fish sauce
     2 tablespoons brown sugar
  1½ pounds boneless, skinless chicken breasts, trimmed and
        sliced thin (see note)
        Table salt
     8 ounces broccoli (½ small bunch), florets cut into
        1-inch pieces
     4 ounces white mushrooms, wiped clean and quartered
     1 red bell pepper, stemmed, seeded, and cut into
        ¼-inch strips
     1 Thai chile, stemmed, seeded, and quartered lengthwise
        (optional)
     ½ cup loosely packed fresh basil leaves
     ½ cup loosely packed fresh mint leaves
     1 tablespoon juice from 1 lime

1. Carefully spoon off about 1 cup of the top layer of cream from one can of the coconut milk. Whisk the coconut cream and curry paste together in a large Dutch oven, bring to a simmer over high heat, and cook until almost all of the liquid evaporates, 5 to 7 minutes. Reduce the heat to medium-high and continue to cook, whisking constantly, until the cream separates into a puddle of colored oil and coconut solids, 3 to 8 minutes. Continue cooking until the curry paste is very aromatic, 1 to 2 minutes.

2. Whisk in the remaining coconut milk, the fish sauce, and sugar, bring to a simmer, and cook until the flavors meld and the sauce thickens, about 5 minutes. Season the chicken with salt, stir into the sauce, and cook until evenly coated, about 1 minute. Stir in the broccoli and mushrooms and cook until the vegetables are almost tender, about 5 minutes. Stir in the bell pepper and chile (if using) and cook until the bell pepper is crisp-tender, about 2 minutes. Off the heat, stir in the basil, mint, and lime juice. Serve.

Green Curry Paste

MAKES ABOUT ½ CUP

We strongly prefer the flavor of Thai chiles here; however, serrano and jalapeño chiles are decent substitutes. For more heat, include the chile seeds and ribs when chopping.

     ⅓ cup water
    12 fresh green Thai, serrano, or jalapeño chiles, seeds and
        ribs removed, chiles chopped coarse (see note)
     8 medium garlic cloves, peeled
     3 medium shallots, peeled and quartered
     2 stalks lemon grass, bottom 5 inches only, trimmed and
        sliced thin (see page 401)
     2 tablespoons grated zest from 2 limes
     2 tablespoons vegetable oil
     2 tablespoons minced fresh cilantro stems
     1 tablespoon minced or grated fresh ginger
     2 teaspoons ground coriander
     1 teaspoon ground cumin
     1 teaspoon table salt

Process all the ingredients in a food processor to a fine paste, about 3 minutes, scraping down the sides of the workbowl as needed.

Thai Red Curry with Shrimp, Pineapple, and Peanuts

SERVES 4

Roasted unsalted cashews can be substituted for the peanuts. For a more authentic appearance, leave the shells on the shrimp tails. Serve with Basic White Rice (page 382).

     2 (14-ounce) cans unsweetened coconut milk, not shaken
     1 recipe Red Curry Paste (recipe follows) or 2 tablespoons
        store-bought red curry paste
     2 tablespoons fish sauce
     2 tablespoons brown sugar
  1½ pounds medium shrimp (41 to 50 per pound), peeled
        and deveined (see page 205; see note)
        Table salt
     1 pound peeled and cored pineapple, cut into
        1-inch pieces
     4 ounces snow peas, tips and strings removed
     1 red bell pepper, stemmed, seeded, and cut into
        ¼-inch strips

1 Thai chile, stemmed, seeded, and quartered lengthwise (optional)

½ cup loosely packed fresh basil leaves

½ cup loosely packed fresh mint leaves

1 tablespoon juice from 1 lime

½ cup unsalted roasted peanuts, chopped coarse (see note)

1. Carefully spoon off about 1 cup of the top layer of cream from one can of the coconut milk. Whisk the coconut cream and curry paste together in a large Dutch oven, bring to a simmer over high heat, and cook until almost all of the liquid evaporates, 5 to 7 minutes. Reduce the heat to medium-high and continue to cook, whisking constantly, until the cream separates into a puddle of colored oil and coconut solids, 3 to 8 minutes. Continue cooking until the curry paste is very aromatic, 1 to 2 minutes.

2. Whisk in the remaining coconut milk, the fish sauce, and sugar, bring to a simmer, and cook until the flavors meld and the sauce thickens, about 5 minutes. Season the shrimp with salt, add them to the sauce with the pineapple, and cook, stirring occasionally, until the shrimp are almost opaque, about 4 minutes. Stir in the snow peas, bell pepper, and chile (if using) and cook until the vegetables are crisp-tender, about 2 minutes. Off the heat, stir in the basil, mint, and lime juice. Sprinkle with the peanuts and serve.

Red Curry Paste

MAKES ABOUT ½ CUP

If you can't find a red jalapeño chile, you can substitute a green jalapeño. For more heat, include the jalapeño seeds and ribs when chopping.

8 dried small red chiles, such as Thai, japonés, or de árbol

⅓ cup water

4 medium shallots, peeled and quartered

2 stalks lemon grass, bottom 5 inches only, trimmed and sliced thin (see photo)

6 medium garlic cloves, peeled

1 medium fresh red jalapeño chile, seeds and ribs removed, chile chopped coarse (see note)

2 tablespoons minced fresh cilantro stems

2 tablespoons vegetable oil

1 tablespoon grated zest from 1 lime

2 teaspoons ground coriander

1 teaspoon ground cumin

1 teaspoon minced or grated fresh ginger

1 teaspoon tomato paste

1 teaspoon table salt

1. Adjust an oven rack to the middle position and heat the oven to 350 degrees. Place the dried red chiles on a baking sheet and toast in the oven until fragrant and puffed, about 5 minutes. Remove the chiles from the oven and set aside to cool. When cool enough to handle, seed and stem the chiles, then break them into small pieces.

2. Process the chile pieces with the remaining ingredients in a food processor to a fine paste, about 3 minutes, scraping down the sides of the workbowl as needed.

NOTES FROM THE TEST KITCHEN

CUTTING LEMON GRASS

Because of its tough outer leaves, lemon grass can be difficult to slice or mince. We like this method, which relies on a sharp knife.

1. Trim all but the bottom 5 inches of the lemon grass stalk.

2. Remove the tough outer sheath from the trimmed lemon grass. If the lemon grass is particularly thick or tough, you may need to remove several layers to reveal the tender inner portion of the stalk.

3. TO SLICE: Thinly slice the trimmed and peeled lemon grass on a slight bias. **TO MINCE:** Cut the trimmed and peeled lemon grass in half lengthwise, then mince.

THAI CHILE BEEF

WHY THIS RECIPE WORKS: Most recipes for Thai chile beef require exotic ingredients and three hours of preparation—definitely not suitable for making midweek supper in an average American home kitchen. We wanted to create a sophisticated Thai chile beef recipe built around the traditional Thai flavors—spicy, sweet, sour, and salty—using readily available ingredients and requiring minimal cooking time.

A cheap and readily available cut—blade steak—won our taste test for its tenderness and very beefy flavor. We added the beef to our transformed stir-fry marinade—made with fish sauce for its briny flavor, white pepper for its spicy and almost gamy flavor, citrusy coriander, and a little light brown sugar for both sweetness and help in developing caramelization. With these elements, the beef only needed to marinate for 10 minutes to develop full flavor. We also wanted some heat and decided to use both a jalapeño and Asian chili-garlic paste (which added toasty garlicky flavors along with heat). More fish sauce, brown sugar, rice vinegar, fresh mint and cilantro, a few crunchy chopped peanuts, and a bright squirt of lime juice finished the dish.

Stir-Fried Thai-Style Beef with Chiles and Shallots
SERVES 4

To make slicing the blade steaks easier, freeze them for 15 minutes. If you cannot find blade steak, use flank steak; because flank steak requires less trimming, you will need only about 1¾ pounds. To cut a flank steak into the proper-sized slices for stir-frying, first cut the steak with the grain into 2-inch strips, then cut the strips against the grain into ⅛-inch-thick slices. Serve with Basic White Rice (page 382).

SAUCE
- 2 tablespoons fish sauce
- 2 tablespoons rice vinegar
- 2 tablespoons water
- 1 tablespoon light brown sugar
- 1 tablespoon Asian chili-garlic paste

BEEF AND VEGETABLES
- 2 pounds blade steaks, halved lengthwise, trimmed, and sliced into ⅛-inch-thick slices (see note)
- 1 tablespoon fish sauce
- 1 teaspoon light brown sugar
- ¾ teaspoon ground coriander
- ⅛ teaspoon ground white pepper
- 3 tablespoons peanut or vegetable oil
- 3 medium garlic cloves, minced or pressed through a garlic press (about 1 tablespoon)
- 3 serrano or jalapeño chiles, halved, seeds and ribs removed, chiles sliced thin
- 3 medium shallots, ends trimmed, peeled, quartered lengthwise, and layers separated
- ½ cup fresh mint leaves, large leaves torn into bite-size pieces
- ½ cup fresh cilantro leaves
- ⅓ cup unsalted roasted peanuts, chopped coarse
  Lime wedges, for serving

1. FOR THE SAUCE: Combine all the ingredients in a small bowl and set aside.

2. FOR THE BEEF AND VEGETABLES: Toss the beef with the fish sauce, sugar, coriander, and white pepper in a medium bowl and let marinate for at least 10 minutes or up to 1 hour. In a small bowl, mix 1 teaspoon of the oil and the garlic together.

3. Heat 2 teaspoons more oil in a 12-inch nonstick skillet over high heat until just smoking. Add one-third of the beef, break up any clumps, then cook without stirring until the meat is browned at the edges, about 1 minute. Stir the beef and continue to cook until cooked through, about 1 minute longer. Transfer the beef to a clean bowl and cover with foil to keep warm. Repeat with 4 teaspoons more oil and the remaining beef in two batches.

4. Add the remaining 2 teaspoons oil to the skillet and return to medium heat until shimmering. Add the chiles and shallots and cook until beginning to soften, 3 to 4 minutes. Clear the center of the skillet, add the garlic mixture, and cook, mashing the mixture into the pan, until fragrant, 15 to 20 seconds. Stir the garlic mixture into the shallots and chiles.

5. Stir in the beef with any accumulated juices. Whisk the sauce to recombine, then add to the skillet and cook, tossing constantly, until the sauce is thickened, about 30 seconds. Stir in the half of the mint and half of the cilantro. Transfer to a serving platter, sprinkle with the remaining mint, remaining cilantro, and peanuts, and serve with the lime wedges.

PAD THAI

WHY THIS RECIPE WORKS: Ordered out, pad thai suffers from indiscriminate amounts of sugar; slick, greasy noodles; or bloated, sticky, lifeless strands that clump together. We hoped to develop a pad thai with clean, fresh, not-too-sweet flavors, perfectly cooked noodles, and plenty of plump, juicy shrimp with tender bits of scrambled egg.

Soaking the rice sticks in boiling water for 10 minutes before stir-frying made for tender but not sticky noodles. We created the salty, sweet, sour, and spicy flavor profile of pad thai by combining fish sauce, sugar, ground chiles, and vinegar. For the fresh, bright, fruity taste that is essential to the dish, we used tamarind paste, which we soaked in hot water and passed through a fine-mesh strainer to make a smooth puree. Tossed with fresh and dried shrimp and eggs, and garnished with scallions, peanuts, and cilantro, this dish is an excellent rendition of the Thai classic.

Pad Thai

SERVES 4

Although pad thai cooks very quickly, the ingredient list is long, and everything must be prepared and within easy reach at the stovetop when you begin cooking. For maximum efficiency, use the time during which the tamarind and noodles soak to prepare the other ingredients. If tamarind paste is unavailable, substitute ⅓ cup lime juice and ⅓ cup water and use light brown sugar instead of granulated sugar.

SAUCE

- ¾ cup boiling water
- 2 tablespoons tamarind paste (see note)
- 3 tablespoons fish sauce
- 3 tablespoons sugar
- 2 tablespoons peanut or vegetable oil
- 1 tablespoon rice vinegar
- ¾ teaspoon cayenne pepper

NOODLES, SHRIMP, AND GARNISH

- 8 ounces dried rice stick noodles, ⅛ to ¼ inch wide
- 2 tablespoons peanut or vegetable oil
- 12 ounces medium shrimp (41 to 50 per pound), peeled and deveined (see page 205)
  Table salt
- 1 medium shallot, minced (about 2 tablespoons)
- 3 garlic cloves, minced or pressed through a garlic press (about 1 tablespoon)
- 2 large eggs, lightly beaten
- 2 tablespoons chopped Thai salted preserved radish (optional)
- 1 tablespoon dried shrimp, chopped fine (optional)
- 3 cups bean sprouts
- ½ cup unsalted roasted peanuts, chopped coarse
- 5 scallions, green parts only, sliced thin on the bias
- ¼ cup loosely packed fresh cilantro leaves (optional)
  Lime wedges, for serving

1. FOR THE SAUCE: Combine the water and tamarind paste in a small bowl and let sit until the tamarind is softened and mushy, 10 to 30 minutes. Mash the tamarind to break it up, then push it through a fine-mesh strainer into a medium bowl to remove the seeds and fibers and extract as much pulp as possible. Stir in the remaining sauce ingredients and set aside.

2. FOR THE NOODLES, SHRIMP, AND GARNISH: Bring 4 quarts water to a boil in a large pot. Remove the boiling water from the heat, add the rice noodles, and let sit, stirring occasionally, until almost tender, about 10 minutes. Drain the noodles and set aside.

3. Heat 1 tablespoon of the oil in a 12-inch nonstick skillet over high heat until just smoking. Add the shrimp, sprinkle with ⅛ teaspoon salt, and cook without stirring until bright pink, about 1 minute. Stir the shrimp and continue to cook until cooked through, 15 to 30 seconds longer. Transfer the shrimp to a clean bowl and cover with foil to keep warm.

4. Add the remaining 1 tablespoon oil to the skillet and return to medium heat until shimmering. Add the shallot and garlic and cook, stirring constantly, until light golden brown, about 1½ minutes. Stir in the eggs and cook, stirring constantly, until scrambled and barely moist, about 20 seconds.

5. Add the noodles and the salted radish and dried shrimp (if using) to the eggs and toss to combine. Add the sauce, increase the heat to high, and cook, tossing constantly, until the noodles are evenly coated, about 1 minute.

6. Add the cooked shrimp, bean sprouts, ¼ cup of the peanuts, and all but ¼ cup of the scallions and continue to cook, tossing constantly, until the noodles are tender, about 2½ minutes. (If not yet tender add 2 tablespoons water to the skillet and continue to cook until tender.) Transfer the noodles to a serving platter, sprinkle with the remaining ¼ cup peanuts, remaining ¼ cup scallions, and cilantro (if using) and serve with the lime wedges.

THAI GRILLED CHICKEN

WHY THIS RECIPE WORKS: This herb- and spice-rubbed chicken is served in small pieces and eaten as finger food, along with a sweet and spicy dipping sauce. We wanted to develop a recipe for Thai grilled chicken to offer a refreshing change of pace from typical barbecue fare.

After testing numerous rub combinations, we liked the simplest version, made only with cilantro, black pepper, lime juice, and garlic, accented with the earthy flavor of coriander and fresh ginger. To flavor the meat as well as the skin, we took some of the rub and placed it in a thick layer under the skin as well as on top of it. For perfectly cooked chicken, we made a modified two-level fire (one side of the grill holds all of the coals; the other side is empty), first browning the chicken directly over the coals and then moving it to the cool side of the grill to finish cooking. The true Thai flavors of this dish come through in the sauce, a classic combination of sweet and spicy. We found balance in a blend of sugar, lime juice, white vinegar, red pepper flakes, fish sauce, and garlic.

Thai Grilled Chicken with Spicy, Sweet, and Sour Dipping Sauce for a Charcoal Grill
SERVES 4

To help ensure that each breast finishes cooking at approximately the same time, buy pieces of similar size. Some of the rub is inevitably lost to the grill, but the chicken will still be flavorful.

CHICKEN AND BRINE
½ cup sugar
½ cup table salt
2 (1½-pound) bone-in, skin-on chicken breasts, split in half along the breast bone and trimmed of rib sections (see page 92)

SAUCE
⅓ cup sugar
¼ cup distilled white vinegar
¼ cup juice from 2 to 3 limes
2 tablespoons fish sauce
2 medium garlic cloves, minced or pressed through a garlic press (about 2 teaspoons)
1 teaspoon red pepper flakes

RUB
⅔ cup chopped fresh cilantro leaves
12 medium garlic cloves, minced or pressed through a garlic press (about ¼ cup)
¼ cup juice from 2 to 3 limes
2 tablespoons minced or grated fresh ginger
2 tablespoons ground black pepper
2 tablespoons ground coriander
2 tablespoons vegetable oil, plus extra for the cooking grate

1. FOR THE CHICKEN AND BRINE: Dissolve the sugar and salt in 2 quarts cold water in a large container. Submerge the chicken, cover with plastic wrap, and refrigerate for 1 hour. Rinse the chicken and pat dry with paper towels.

2. FOR THE SAUCE: Whisk all the ingredients together in a small bowl until the sugar dissolves and set aside.

3. FOR THE RUB: Combine all the ingredients in a small bowl.

4. Working with one chicken breast at a time, slide your fingers between the skin and meat to loosen the skin, taking care not to detach the skin. Rub about 2 tablespoons of the mixture under the skin, then rub an even layer of the rub mixture onto all exterior surfaces, including the bottom and sides.

5. TO GRILL THE CHICKEN: Light a large chimney starter filled with charcoal (about 6 quarts) and allow to burn until the coals are partially covered with a layer of ash, about 20 minutes. Build a modified two-level fire by arranging all the coals over one half of the grill, leaving the other half empty. Set the cooking grate in place, cover, and heat the grate until hot, about 5 minutes. Use a grill brush to scrape the cooking grate clean. Dip a wad of paper towels in oil; holding the wad with tongs, oil the cooking grate.

6. Cook the chicken on all sides over the hotter part of the grill until the skin is lightly browned and faint grill marks appear, 6 to 8 minutes. (If constant flare-ups occur, slide the chicken to the cooler side of the grill and mist the fire with water from a spray bottle.) Move the chicken, skin side down, to the cooler side of the grill, with the thicker sides of the breasts facing the coals. Cover the chicken loosely with foil, cover the grill, and continue to cook until the thickest part of the breasts registers 160 to 165 degrees on an instant-read thermometer, 20 to 30 minutes longer.

7. Transfer the chicken to a platter and let rest for 5 minutes. Serve, passing the sauce separately.

Thai Grilled Chicken for a Gas Grill

Follow the recipe for Thai Grilled Chicken with Spicy, Sweet, and Sour Dipping Sauce for a Charcoal Grill through step 4. Turn all the burners to high and heat the grill, with the lid down, until very hot, about 15 minutes. Use a grill brush to scrape the cooking grate clean. Dip a wad of paper towels in oil; holding the wad with tongs, oil the cooking grate. Leave the primary burner on high and turn off the other burner(s). Proceed with the recipe from step 6, increasing the browning time to 10 to 14 minutes.

GRILLED THAI BEEF SALAD

WHY THIS RECIPE WORKS: This traditional Thai salad features slices of deeply charred steak tossed with thinly sliced shallots and handfuls of torn mint and cilantro in a bright, bracing dressing. We started developing our own version at the grill, choosing flank steak for its generous marbling, beefy flavor, and moderate price. Grilling the steak over a modified two-level fire and flipping it just when moisture beaded on the surface yielded perfectly charred, juicy meat. Adding a fresh Thai chile and a mix of toasted cayenne and paprika gave the dressing a fruity, fiery heat. Toasted rice powder, a traditional Thai tableside condiment that gives the dressing fuller body and a subtle crunch, is not widely available here, but we found it easy enough to make our own by toasting rice in a skillet on the stovetop, then grinding it in a food processor, spice grinder, or even with a mortar and pestle.

Grilled Thai Beef Salad for a Charcoal Grill

SERVES 4 TO 6

If fresh Thai chiles are unavailable, substitute ½ serrano chile. Don't skip the toasted rice; it's integral to the texture and flavor of the dish. Any variety of white rice can be used. Toasted rice powder (kao kua) can also be found in many Asian markets; substitute 1 tablespoon rice powder for the white rice. Serve with Basic White Rice (page 382), if desired.

- 1 teaspoon paprika
- 1 teaspoon cayenne pepper
- 1 tablespoon white rice (see note)
- 3 tablespoons juice from 2 limes
- 2 tablespoons fish sauce
- 2 tablespoons water
- ½ teaspoon sugar
  Vegetable oil for the cooking grate
- 1 (1½-pound) flank steak, trimmed
  Table salt and coarsely ground white pepper
- 1 seedless English cucumber, sliced ¼ inch thick on bias
- 4 medium shallots, sliced thin
- 1½ cups fresh mint leaves, torn
- 1½ cups fresh cilantro leaves
- 1 Thai chile, stemmed, seeded, and sliced thin into rounds (see note)

1. Heat the paprika and cayenne in a small skillet over medium heat; cook, shaking the pan, until fragrant, about 1 minute. Transfer to a small bowl. Return the skillet to medium-high heat, add the rice and toast, stirring constantly, until deep golden brown, about 5 minutes. Transfer to a small bowl and let cool for 5 minutes. Grind the rice with a spice grinder, mini food processor, or mortar and pestle until it resembles a fine meal, 10 to 30 seconds (you should have about 1 tablespoon rice powder).

2. Whisk the lime juice, fish sauce, water, sugar, and ¼ teaspoon toasted paprika mixture in a large bowl and set aside.

3. Open the bottom vents completely. Light a large chimney starter filled with charcoal (about 6 quarts) and allow to burn until the coals are partially covered with a layer of ash, about 20 minutes. Build a modified two-level fire by arranging all the coals over one half of the grill, leaving the other half empty. Set the cooking grate in place, cover, and open the lid vents completely. Heat the grate until hot, about 5 minutes. Use a grill brush to scrape the cooking grate clean. Dip a wad of paper towels in oil; holding the wad with tongs, oil the cooking grate.

4. Season the steak with salt and white pepper. Place the steak on the grate over the hot part of grill and cook until beginning to char and beads of moisture appear on the outer edges of the meat, 5 to 6 minutes. Flip the steak and continue to cook on the second side until the meat registers 125 degrees on an instant-read thermometer, about 5 minutes longer. Transfer to a carving board, tent loosely with aluminum foil, and let rest for 10 minutes (or allow to cool to room temperature, about 1 hour).

5. Line a large platter with cucumber slices. Following the photos on page 147, slice the meat ¼ inch thick on the bias. Transfer the sliced steak to the bowl with the lime juice mixture, add the shallots, mint, cilantro, chile, and half of the rice powder, and toss to combine. Arrange the steak over the cucumber-lined platter. Serve, passing the remaining rice powder and toasted paprika mixture separately.

Grilled Thai Beef Salad for a Gas Grill

Follow the recipe for Grilled Thai Beef Salad for a Charcoal Grill through step 2. Turn all the burners to high and heat the grill, with the lid down, until very hot, about 15 minutes. Use a grill brush to scrape the cooking grate clean. Dip a wad of paper towels in oil; holding the wad with tongs, oil the cooking grate. Leave the primary burner on high and turn off the other burner(s). Proceed with the recipe from step 4.

CHICKEN TIKKA MASALA

WHY THIS RECIPE WORKS: Chicken tikka masala is arguably the single most popular Indian restaurant dish in the world. Turns out, it's not an authentic Indian dish—it was invented in a London curry house. Without historical roots, there is no definitive recipe. The variations we found had mushy or dry chicken and sauces that were unbearably rich and/or overspiced. We wanted an approachable method for producing moist, tender chunks of chicken in a rich, lightly spiced tomato sauce.

To season the chicken, we rubbed it with salt, coriander, cumin, and cayenne and refrigerated it for 30 to 60 minutes. Then we dipped it in yogurt mixed with oil, garlic, and ginger and broiled it. And since large pieces don't dry out as quickly as smaller ones under the broiler, we cooked the chicken breasts whole, cutting them into pieces only after cooking. While the chicken was cooking, we made the masala sauce. Masala means "hot

spice," and the ingredients in a masala sauce depend on the whim of the cook, although tomatoes and cream are always present. We added onions, ginger, garlic, chile, and a readily available commercial garam masala spice mixture. A little tomato paste and sugar gave our sauce color and sweetness.

Chicken Tikka Masala

SERVES 4 TO 6

This dish is best when prepared with whole-milk yogurt, but low-fat yogurt can be substituted. For more heat, include the chile seeds and ribs when mincing. Serve with Rice Pilaf (see page 497).

CHICKEN

 Table salt
½ teaspoon ground cumin
½ teaspoon ground coriander
¼ teaspoon cayenne pepper
2 pounds boneless, skinless chicken breasts, trimmed
1 cup plain whole-milk yogurt (see note)
2 tablespoons vegetable oil
1 tablespoon minced or grated fresh ginger
2 medium garlic cloves, minced or pressed through a garlic press (about 2 teaspoons)

SAUCE

3 tablespoons vegetable oil
1 medium onion, minced (about 1 cup)
1 tablespoon garam masala
1 tablespoon tomato paste
2 medium garlic cloves, minced or pressed through a garlic press (about 2 teaspoons)
2 teaspoons minced or grated fresh ginger
1 serrano chile, seeds and ribs removed, chile minced (see note)
1 (28-ounce) can crushed tomatoes
2 teaspoons sugar
 Table salt
⅔ cup heavy cream
¼ cup chopped fresh cilantro leaves

1. FOR THE CHICKEN: Combine ½ teaspoon salt, the cumin, coriander, and cayenne in a small bowl. Pat the chicken dry with paper towels and sprinkle with the spice mixture, pressing gently so the mixture adheres. Place the chicken on a plate, cover with plastic wrap, and refrigerate for 30 minutes or up to 1 hour. In a large bowl, whisk the yogurt, oil, ginger, and garlic together and set aside.

2. FOR THE SAUCE: Heat the oil in a large Dutch oven over medium heat until shimmering. Add the onion and cook, stirring frequently, until softened and light golden, 8 to 10 minutes. Stir in the garam masala, tomato paste, garlic, ginger, and serrano and cook, stirring frequently, until fragrant, about 3 minutes. Add the crushed tomatoes, sugar, and salt and bring to a boil. Reduce the heat to medium-low, cover, and simmer for 15 minutes, stirring occasionally. Stir in the cream and return to a simmer. Remove the pan from the heat and cover to keep warm. (The sauce can be refrigerated in an airtight container for up to 4 days and gently reheated before adding the hot chicken.)

3. TO COOK THE CHICKEN: While the sauce simmers, position an oven rack 6 inches from the heating element and heat the broiler. Line a rimmed baking sheet or broiler pan with foil and place a wire rack over the sheet.

4. Using tongs, dip the chicken into the yogurt mixture (the chicken should be coated with a thick layer of yogurt) and arrange on the wire rack. Discard the excess yogurt mixture. Broil the chicken until lightly charred and the thickest part of the breasts registers 160 to 165 degrees on an instant-read thermometer, 10 to 18 minutes, flipping the chicken halfway through.

5. Let the chicken rest for 5 minutes, then cut into 1-inch chunks and stir into the warm sauce (do not simmer the chicken in the sauce). Stir in the cilantro, season with salt to taste, and serve.

INDIAN-STYLE CHICKEN AND RICE

WHY THIS RECIPE WORKS: Chicken biryani is a complicated (and often greasy) "gourmet" Indian dish. Chicken and rice is a simple, but unremarkable, American one-pot meal. We wanted to find a happy medium between the two.

In biryani, long-grain basmati rice takes center stage, enriched with butter, saffron, and a variety of fresh herbs and pungent spices. Pieces of tender chicken and browned onions are layered with the rice and baked until the flavors have mingled. For our recipe, we browned bone-in, skin-on chicken thighs, then removed the skin and layered them with basmati rice, lots of caramelized onions, and just the right blend of spices. To get the most flavor out of the spices, we tied them into a cheesecloth bundle and simmered them in the rice cooking water—then we added some of that water to the biryani. For a finishing touch, we added saffron, currants, and plenty of ginger and chiles.

Chicken Biryani

SERVES 4

This recipe requires a 3½ to 4-quart saucepan about 8 inches in diameter. Do not use a large, wide Dutch oven, as it will adversely affect both the layering of the dish and the final cooking times. For more heat, add the jalapeño seeds and ribs when mincing.

YOGURT SAUCE

- 1   cup whole-milk or low-fat plain yogurt
- 2   tablespoons minced fresh cilantro leaves
- 2   tablespoons minced fresh mint leaves
- 1   medium garlic clove, minced or pressed through a garlic press (about 1 teaspoon)
     Table salt and ground black pepper

CHICKEN AND RICE

- 10   cardamom pods, preferably green, smashed with a chef's knife
- 1   cinnamon stick
- 1   (2-inch) piece fresh ginger, peeled, cut into ½-inch-thick coins, and smashed
- ½   teaspoon cumin seeds
- 3   quarts water
     Table salt and ground black pepper
- 4   (5 to 6-ounce) bone-in, skin-on chicken thighs, trimmed
- 3   tablespoons unsalted butter

2 medium onions, halved and sliced thin

2 jalapeño chiles, seeds and ribs removed, chiles minced (see note)

4 medium garlic cloves, minced or pressed through a garlic press (about 4 teaspoons)

1¼ cups basmati rice

½ teaspoon saffron threads, lightly crumbled

¼ cup dried currants or raisins

2 tablespoons chopped fresh cilantro leaves

2 tablespoons chopped fresh mint leaves

1. FOR THE YOGURT SAUCE: Combine all the ingredients in a small bowl, season with salt and pepper to taste, and set aside. (The sauce can be refrigerated in an airtight container for up to 2 days.)

2. FOR THE CHICKEN AND RICE: Wrap the cardamom pods, cinnamon stick, ginger, and cumin in a small piece of cheesecloth and secure with kitchen twine. In a 3½ to 4-quart heavy-bottomed saucepan about 8 inches in diameter, bring the spice bundle, water, and 1½ teaspoons salt to a boil over medium-high heat. Reduce the heat to medium and simmer, partially covered, until the spices have infused the water, at least 15 minutes (but no longer than 30 minutes).

3. Meanwhile, pat the chicken thighs dry with paper towels and season with salt and pepper. Melt the butter in a 12-inch nonstick skillet over medium-high heat. Add the onions and cook, stirring frequently, until soft and dark brown around the edges, 10 to 12 minutes. Stir in the jalapeños and garlic and cook, stirring frequently, until fragrant, about 2 minutes. Transfer the onion mixture to a bowl, season with salt, and set aside. Wipe out the skillet with a wad of paper towels.

4. Place the chicken, skin side down, in the skillet, return the skillet to medium-high heat, and cook until well browned on both sides, 8 to 10 minutes, flipping halfway through. Transfer the chicken to a plate and remove and discard the skin. Tent loosely with foil to keep warm.

5. If necessary, return the spice-infused water to a boil over high heat. Add the rice and cook, stirring occasionally, for 5 minutes. Drain the rice through a fine-mesh strainer, reserving ¾ cup of the cooking liquid; discard the spice bundle. Transfer the rice to a medium bowl and stir in the saffron and currants (the rice will turn splotchy yellow).

6. Spread half of the rice evenly in the bottom of the saucepan using a rubber spatula. Scatter half of the onion mixture over the rice, then place the chicken thighs, skinned side up, on top of the onions; add any accumulated chicken juices. Sprinkle evenly with the cilantro and mint, scatter the remaining onion mixture over the herbs, then

cover with the remaining rice. Pour the reserved ¾ cup cooking liquid evenly over the rice.

7. Cover the saucepan and cook over medium-low heat until the rice is tender and the chicken registers 175 degrees on an instant-read thermometer, about 30 minutes (if a large amount of steam is escaping from the pot, reduce the heat to low).

8. Run a heatproof rubber spatula around the inside rim of the saucepan to loosen any affixed rice. Using a large serving spoon, spoon the biryani into individual bowls, scooping from the bottom of the pot. Serve, passing the yogurt sauce separately.

INDIAN CURRY

WHY THIS RECIPE WORKS: For many home cooks Indian cooking is a mystery, full of exotic spices and unfamiliar, laborious cooking techniques. We hoped to create a complex but not heavy-flavored curry that wouldn't take all day to prepare.

Allowing the spices to cook completely provided the authentic, intense flavor we were after in our curry. We used a combination of whole spices—cinnamon sticks, cloves, green cardamom pods, black peppercorns, and a bay leaf—and toasted them in oil before adding aromatics, jalapeño, and ground spices. Instead of browning the meat (we chose lamb, but chicken thighs also work well), we simply stirred it into the pot along with crushed tomatoes and cooked the mixture until the liquid evaporated and the oil separated. This is a classic Indian technique that allows the spices to further develop their flavors in the oil, flavors which are then cooked into the meat (because it's not browned, it doesn't have a crust to inhibit its ability to absorb the flavors). We then added water and simmered the mixture until the meat was tender, then stirred in the spinach and channa dal (yellow split peas) and cooked the dish until all the ingredients were melded and tender.

Indian Curry

SERVES 4 TO 6

If desired, 1½ pounds boneless, skinless chicken thighs, trimmed and cut into ¾-inch chunks, can be substituted for the lamb. For more heat, add the jalapeño seeds and ribs when mincing. For a creamier curry, choose yogurt over the crushed tomatoes. Serve with Yogurt Sauce (page 407), Onion Relish (page 410), Cilantro-Mint Chutney (page 410), and Rice Pilaf (page 497).

SPICE BLEND

1½	cinnamon sticks
4	whole cloves
4	green cardamom pods
8	whole black peppercorns
1	bay leaf

CURRY

¼	cup vegetable oil
1	medium onion, halved and sliced thin
5	medium garlic cloves, minced or pressed through a garlic press (about 5 teaspoons)
1	tablespoon minced or grated fresh ginger
1	jalapeño chile, stemmed and halved lengthwise, seeds and ribs removed (see note)
2	teaspoons ground cumin
2	teaspoons ground coriander
1	teaspoon ground turmeric
	Table salt
1½	pounds boneless leg of lamb, trimmed and cut into ¾-inch cubes (see note)
⅔	cup crushed tomatoes or ½ cup plain low-fat yogurt (see note)
2	cups water
1½	pounds spinach, stemmed, washed, and chopped coarse (optional)
½	cup channa dal (yellow split peas)
¼	cup chopped fresh cilantro leaves

1. FOR THE SPICE BLEND: Combine all the ingredients in a small bowl and set aside.

2. FOR THE CURRY: Heat the oil in a Dutch oven over medium heat until shimmering. Add the spice blend and cook, stirring frequently, until the cinnamon stick unfurls and the cloves pop, about 5 seconds. Add the onion and cook, stirring occasionally, until softened, 5 to 7 minutes. Stir in the garlic, ginger, jalapeño, cumin, coriander, turmeric, and ½ teaspoon salt and cook until fragrant, about 30 seconds.

3. Stir in the lamb and the tomatoes. Bring to a simmer and cook, stirring frequently, until the liquid evaporates and the oil separates and turns orange, 5 to 7 minutes. Continue to cook until the spices are sizzling, about 30 seconds longer.

4. Stir in the water and bring to a simmer over medium heat. Reduce the heat to medium-low, cover, and cook until the lamb is almost tender, about 40 minutes.

5. Stir in the spinach (if using) and channa dal and cook until the channa dal are tender, about 15 minutes. Season with salt to taste, stir in the cilantro, and serve.

VEGETABLE CURRY

WHY THIS RECIPE WORKS: Vegetable curries can be complicated affairs, with lengthy ingredient lists and fussy techniques meant to compensate for the lack of meat. We wanted a curry we could make on a weeknight in less than an hour—without sacrificing flavor or overloading the dish with spices.

Although initially reluctant to use store-bought curry powder, we found that toasting the curry powder in a skillet turned it into a flavor powerhouse. Further experimentation proved that adding a few pinches of garam masala added even more spice flavor. To build the rest of our flavor base we started with a generous amount of sautéed onion, vegetable oil, garlic, ginger, fresh chile, and tomato paste for sweetness. When we chose our vegetables (chickpeas and potatoes for heartiness and cauliflower and peas for texture and color), we found that sautéing the spices and main ingredients together enhanced and melded the flavors. Finally, we rounded out our sauce with a combination of water, pureed canned tomatoes, and a splash of heavy cream or coconut milk.

Indian-Style Curry with Potatoes, Cauliflower, Peas, and Chickpeas

SERVES 4 TO 6

This curry is moderately spicy when made with one chile. For more heat, include the chile seeds and ribs when mincing. Serve with Yogurt Sauce (page 407), Onion Relish (page 410), Cilantro-Mint Chutney (page 410), and Rice Pilaf (page 497).

2	tablespoons sweet or mild curry powder
1½	teaspoons garam masala
4	tablespoons vegetable oil

3 medium garlic cloves, minced or pressed through a garlic press (about 1 tablespoon)
1 tablespoon minced or grated fresh ginger
1 serrano chile, seeds and ribs removed, chile minced (see note)
1 tablespoon tomato paste
1 (14.5-ounce) can diced tomatoes
2 medium onions, minced (about 2 cups)
12 ounces red potatoes (about 2 medium), scrubbed and cut into ½-inch pieces
1¼ pounds cauliflower (½ medium head), trimmed, cored, and cut into 1-inch florets
1¼ cups water
1 (15-ounce) can chickpeas, drained and rinsed
Table salt
1½ cups frozen peas
¼ cup heavy cream or coconut milk

CONDIMENTS
Onion Relish (recipe follows)
Cilantro-Mint Chutney (recipe follows) or mango chutney

1. Toast the curry powder and garam masala in a small skillet over medium-high heat, stirring constantly, until the spices darken slightly and become fragrant, about 1 minute. Transfer the spices to a small bowl and set aside. In a separate small bowl, stir 1 tablespoon of the oil, the garlic, ginger, serrano, and tomato paste together. Pulse the tomatoes with their juice in a food processor until coarsely chopped, 3 to 4 pulses.

2. Heat the remaining 3 tablespoons oil in a large Dutch oven over medium-high heat until shimmering. Add the onions and potatoes and cook, stirring occasionally, until the onions are caramelized and the potatoes are golden brown around the edges, about 10 minutes. (Reduce the heat to medium if the onions darken too quickly.)

3. Reduce the heat to medium. Clear the center of the pot, add the garlic mixture, and cook, mashing the mixture into the pan, until fragrant, 15 to 20 seconds. Stir the garlic mixture into the vegetables. Add the toasted spices and cook, stirring constantly, for 1 minute longer. Add the cauliflower and cook, stirring constantly, until the spices coat the florets, about 2 minutes longer.

4. Add the tomatoes, water, chickpeas, and 1 teaspoon salt, scraping up any browned bits. Bring to a boil over medium-high heat. Cover, reduce the heat to medium, and cook, stirring occasionally, until the vegetables are tender, 10 to 15 minutes. Stir in the peas and cream and

continue to cook until heated through, about 2 minutes longer. Season with salt to taste and serve, passing the condiments separately.

Indian-Style Curry with Sweet Potatoes, Eggplant, Green Beans, and Chickpeas

Follow the recipe for Indian-Style Curry with Potatoes, Cauliflower, Peas, and Chickpeas, substituting 12 ounces sweet potato (1 medium), peeled and cut into ½-inch pieces, for the red potatoes. Substitute 8 ounces green beans, trimmed and cut into 1-inch pieces, and 1 medium eggplant (1 pound), cut into ½-inch pieces, for the cauliflower. Omit the peas.

Onion Relish
MAKES ABOUT 1 CUP

If using a regular yellow onion, increase the sugar to 1 teaspoon. This relish can be refrigerated in an airtight container for up to 24 hours.

1 medium Vidalia onion, minced (about 1 cup; see note)
1 tablespoon juice from 1 lime
½ teaspoon sweet paprika
½ teaspoon sugar
⅛ teaspoon table salt
Pinch cayenne pepper

Combine all the ingredients in a small bowl.

Cilantro-Mint Chutney
MAKES ABOUT 1 CUP

This chutney can be refrigerated in an airtight container for up to 24 hours.

2 cups packed fresh cilantro leaves
1 cup packed fresh mint leaves
⅓ cup plain yogurt
¼ cup minced onion
1 tablespoon juice from 1 lime
1½ teaspoons sugar
½ teaspoon ground cumin
¼ teaspoon table salt

Process all the ingredients together in a food processor until smooth, about 20 seconds, scraping down the sides of the workbowl as needed.

2 tablespoons vegetable oil

6 medium garlic cloves, minced or pressed through a
garlic press (about 2 tablespoons)

2 tablespoons minced or grated fresh ginger

1 tablespoon garam masala

2 teaspoons ground cumin

2 teaspoons chili powder

1 cup plain whole-milk yogurt (see note)

¼ cup juice from 2 limes, plus 1 lime, cut into wedges
(for serving)

2 teaspoons table salt

3 pounds bone-in, skin-on chicken pieces (split breasts cut
in half, drumsticks, and/or thighs), trimmed and skin
removed

TANDOORI CHICKEN

WHY THIS RECIPE WORKS: We weren't going to let a 24-hour marinade or the lack of a 900-degree oven keep us from turning this great Indian classic into an easy weeknight dinner. We set out to reinvent this traditional dish as a recipe that could be made year-round in the oven.

Traditional tandoors produce moist, smoky meat because the fierce heat allows protein molecules on the meat's surface to cross-link and contract, trapping moisture inside. Juices fall on the coals along with rendered fat, creating smoke that flavors the food. Trying to mimic the tandoor by cooking chicken in a very hot oven gave us disappointing results. Instead we turned to a technique we use to preserve the juiciness of thick-cut steaks. We baked the chicken in a low-temperature oven until almost done, then gave it a quick broil to char the exterior. To get flavor into the meat, we turned to a salt-spice rub made with garam masala, cumin, and chili powder bloomed in oil with ginger and garlic. We massaged the rub into chicken pieces to lock in juices and infuse flavor, then left them to sit. Following a dunk in yogurt flavored with the same spice mix, the chicken was ready for the oven. The results? Juicy, lightly charred, well-seasoned meat with just the right degree of tenderness.

Tandoori Chicken

SERVES 4

We prefer this dish with whole-milk yogurt, but low-fat yogurt can be substituted. It is important to remove the chicken from the oven before switching to the broiler setting to allow the heating element to come up to temperature. Serve with Yogurt Sauce (page 407), Onion Relish (page 410), Cilantro-Mint Chutney (page 410), and Rice Pilaf (page 497).

1. Heat the oil in an 8-inch skillet over medium heat until shimmering. Add the garlic and ginger and cook until fragrant, about 1 minute. Stir in the garam masala, cumin, and chili powder and cook until fragrant, about 30 seconds. Transfer half of the garlic-spice mixture to a medium bowl, stir in the yogurt and 2 tablespoons of the lime juice, and set aside. 2. In a large bowl, combine the remaining garlic-spice mixture, remaining 2 tablespoons lime juice, and salt. Using a sharp knife, lightly score the skin side of each piece of chicken, making two or three shallow cuts about 1 inch apart and about ⅛ inch deep. Transfer the chicken to the bowl and gently rub with the salt-spice mixture until evenly coated. Let sit at room temperature for 30 minutes.

3. Adjust an oven rack to the upper-middle position (about 6 inches from the heating element) and heat the oven to 325 degrees. Set a wire rack over a foil-lined rimmed baking sheet or broiler pan bottom.

4. Pour the yogurt mixture over the chicken and toss until the chicken is evenly coated with a thick layer. Arrange the chicken pieces, scored side down, on the prepared wire rack. Discard the excess yogurt mixture. Bake the chicken until an instant-read thermometer inserted into the thickest part of the chicken registers 125 degrees for breasts and 130 degrees for legs and thighs, 15 to 25 minutes. (Smaller pieces may cook faster than larger pieces.) Transfer the chicken to a plate.

5. Turn the oven to broil and heat for 10 minutes. Flip the chicken pieces scored side up and broil until lightly charred in spots and the thickest part of the breasts registers 165 degrees and the thickest part of the legs and thighs registers 175 degrees, 8 to 15 minutes.

6. Transfer the chicken to a serving platter, tent loosely with foil, and let rest for 5 minutes. Serve with the lime wedges.

CHAPTER 17

IT'S GRILL TIME!

Grilled Bone-In Chicken Breasts 414

    Orange-Chipotle Glaze

    Soy-Ginger Glaze

Grilled Stuffed Chicken Breasts with Prosciutto and Fontina 416

Smoked Chicken 417

Barbecued Pulled Chicken 418

Barbecued Pulled Chicken for a Crowd 419

Grill-Roasted Beer Can Chicken 420

    Spice Rub

Grill-Roasted Cornish Game Hens 422

Grilled Hamburgers 424

Grilled Cheeseburgers 424

Well-Done Grilled Hamburgers 424

Well-Done Grilled Bacon Cheeseburgers 425

Grilled Marinated Flank Steak 426

    Garlic-Shallot-Rosemary Wet Paste Marinade

    Garlic-Ginger-Sesame Wet Paste Marinade

    Garlic-Chile Wet Paste Marinade

Grilled Stuffed Flank Steak 427

Grilled Stuffed Flank Steak with Spinach and Pine Nuts 428

Grilled Steak Tips 429

    Southwestern Marinade

    Garlic, Ginger, and Soy Marinade

Grilled Steaks 430

    Roasted Red Pepper and Smoked Paprika Butter

    Lemon, Garlic, and Parsley Butter

Grilled Argentine Steaks with Chimichurri Sauce 432

Inexpensive Grill-Roasted Beef with Garlic and Rosemary 433

Grill-Roasted Beef Tenderloin 434

    Salsa Verde

Barbecued Beef Brisket 436

    Spicy Chili Rub

Grilled Pork Chops 438

    Basic Spice Rub for Pork Chops

Grill-Smoked Pork Chops 439

Grilled Stuffed Pork Tenderloin 441

    Olive and Sun-Dried Tomato Stuffing

Grilled Pork Loin with Apple-Cranberry Filling 442

Grill-Roasted Pork Loin 444

    Chili-Mustard Spice Rub

Grill-Roasted Bone-In Pork Rib Roast 445

    Orange Salsa with Cuban Flavors

Barbecued Pulled Pork 446

    Dry Rub for Barbecue

    Eastern North Carolina Barbecue Sauce

    Mid–South Carolina Mustard Sauce

Kansas City Sticky Ribs 448

    Kansas City Barbecue Sauce

    Smoky Kansas City Barbecue Beans

Memphis-Style Barbecued Spareribs 451

Oven-Barbecued Spareribs 452

    Quick Barbecue Sauce

Barbecued Baby Back Ribs 453

Texas-Style Barbecued Beef Ribs 455

    Barbecue Sauce for Texas-Style Beef Ribs

Grilled Beef Kebabs with Lemon and Rosemary Marinade 456

Grilled Shish Kebabs 458

    Warm-Spiced Parsley Marinade with Ginger

    Garlic and Cilantro Marinade with Garam Masala

Grilled Rack of Lamb 459

Grilled Salmon Fillets 460

    Almond Vinaigrette

    Olive Vinaigrette

Grilled Glazed Salmon 462

    Orange-Sesame Glaze

    Spicy Apple Glaze

Barbecued Salmon 463

    Horseradish Cream Sauce with Chives

    Mustard-Dill Sauce

Grilled Tuna Steaks with Red Wine Vinegar and Mustard Vinaigrette 465

Grilled Blackened Red Snapper 466

    Rémoulade

    Pineapple and Cucumber Salsa with Mint

Grilled Sea Scallops 468

    Chile-Lime Vinaigrette

    Basil Vinaigrette

Grilled Shrimp Skewers 469

    Spicy Lemon-Garlic Sauce

    Fresh Tomato Sauce with Feta and Olives

Mexican-Style Grilled Corn 471

Grilled Potatoes with Garlic and Rosemary 472

Grilled Baba Ghanoush 473

GRILLED BONE-IN CHICKEN

WHY THIS RECIPE WORKS: Grilled chicken breasts aren't all that easy to get right. Burnt, limp skin and sooty, parched meat are too often the reality. The perfectly grilled chicken breast should boast tender and succulent meat and crisp skin.

Brining the chicken breasts for an hour or so before grilling helped ensure juicy, seasoned meat throughout, but consistency was an issue. We needed to focus on developing a precise grilling technique to minimize temperature fluctuation, thereby ensuring perfect meat every time. To do so, we created a sort of oven within an oven by covering the chicken with a piece of foil before closing the lid. This approach, combined with cooking the breasts skin side down on the cooler half of a modified two-level fire, finished cooking all six of the chicken breasts simultaneously. But we had one remaining problem: flabby skin. To solve it, we revised our plan and developed a three-step dance: We cooked the chicken on all sides over the hotter part of the grill until lightly browned; moved it to the cooler half and covered it with foil; and finished the breasts on the hotter side, cooking on both sides until the skin was brown and crisp.

Charcoal-Grilled Bone-In Chicken Breasts

SERVES 6

To help ensure that each breast finishes cooking at approximately the same time, buy pieces of similar size. Barbecue sauce can replace the optional glaze in step 4.

⅓ cup table salt
3 (1½-pound) bone-in, skin-on chicken breasts, split in half along breast bone and trimmed of rib sections (see page 92; see note)
  Ground black pepper
  Vegetable oil for the cooking grate
1 recipe glaze (recipes follow; optional; see note)

1. Dissolve the salt in 2 quarts cold water in a large container. Submerge the chicken in the brine, cover with plastic wrap, and refrigerate for 1 hour. Rinse the chicken under running water and pat dry with paper towels. Season the chicken with pepper.

2. Meanwhile, light a large chimney starter filled with charcoal (about 6 quarts) and allow to burn until the coals are partially covered with a thin layer of ash, about 20 minutes. Build a modified two-level fire by arranging all the coals over one half of the grill, leaving the other half empty. Set the cooking grate in place, cover, and heat the grate until hot, about 5 minutes. Use a grill brush to scrape the cooking grate clean. Dip a wad of paper towels in oil; holding the wad with tongs, oil the cooking grate.

3. Cook the chicken on all sides over the hotter part of the grill until the skin is lightly browned and faint grill marks appear, 6 to 8 minutes. (If constant flare-ups occur, slide the chicken to the cooler side of the grill and mist the fire with water from a spray bottle.) Move the chicken, skin side down, to the cooler side of the grill, with the thicker sides of the breasts facing the coals. Cover loosely with foil, cover the grill, and continue to cook until the thickest part of the breast registers 150 degrees on an instant-read thermometer, 15 to 25 minutes longer.

4. Brush the bone side of the chicken with glaze (if using). Move the chicken, bone side down, to the hotter side of the grill and cook until browned, 4 to 6 minutes. Brush the skin side of the chicken with glaze, turn the chicken over, and continue to cook until browned and the thickest part of the breast registers 160 to 165 degrees, 2 to 3 minutes longer. Transfer the chicken to a plate and let rest, tented with foil, for 5 minutes. Serve, passing the remaining glaze separately.

Gas-Grilled Bone-In Chicken Breasts

Follow the recipe for Charcoal-Grilled Bone-In Chicken Breasts through step 1. Turn all the burners to high and heat the grill, with the lid down, until very hot, about 15 minutes. Use a grill brush to scrape the cooking grate clean. Dip a wad of paper towels in oil; holding the wad with tongs, oil the cooking grate. Leave the primary burner on high and turn off the other burner(s). Proceed with the recipe from step 3, increasing the browning time in step 3 to 10 to 14 minutes.

Orange-Chipotle Glaze

MAKES ABOUT ¾ CUP

If you prefer more heat in this glaze, use the greater amount of chipotle chiles given.

- ⅔ cup juice plus 1 teaspoon grated zest from 2 oranges
- 1 small shallot, minced (about 1 tablespoon)
- 1–2 tablespoons minced chipotle chiles in adobo sauce (see note)
- 2 teaspoons minced fresh thyme leaves
- 1 tablespoon light molasses
- ¾ teaspoon cornstarch
  Table salt

Combine the juice, zest, shallot, chipotles, and thyme in a small saucepan; whisk in the molasses and cornstarch. Simmer the mixture over medium heat until thickened, about 5 minutes. Season with salt to taste. Reserve half of the glaze for serving and use the other half for brushing on the chicken in step 4.

Soy-Ginger Glaze

MAKES ABOUT 1 CUP

Reduce the amount of salt in the brine to ¼ cup when using this glaze.

- ⅓ cup water
- ¼ cup soy sauce
- 2 tablespoons mirin
- 1 tablespoon minced or grated fresh ginger
- 2 medium garlic cloves, minced or pressed through a garlic press (about 2 teaspoons)
- 3 tablespoons sugar
- ¾ teaspoon cornstarch
- 2 scallions, minced

Combine the water, soy sauce, mirin, ginger, and garlic in a small saucepan; whisk in the sugar and cornstarch. Simmer the mixture over medium heat until thickened, about 5 minutes; stir in the scallions. Reserve half of the glaze for serving and use the other half for brushing on the chicken in step 4.

BEHIND THE SCENES

LIGHT MY FIRE

Don't even think of using lighter fluid to light your charcoal. Sometimes we've found that we can taste the fluid residually on grilled food—and who wants that? Electric starters are fine, but most people don't have an electrical outlet near their grill. Where does that leave you? A chimney starter. A chimney starter is a metal cylinder with a heatproof handle. Simply dump in the charcoal, light, and wait until the coals are partially covered with a layer of ash. At this point the hot coals can be poured into the grill and arranged as necessary. One thing to keep in mind when buying a chimney starter is the charcoal capacity. We like a large chimney that holds about 6 quarts of charcoal briquettes— just the right amount for grilling most foods in a large kettle grill.

GRILLED STUFFED CHICKEN BREASTS

WHY THIS RECIPE WORKS: Chicken cordon bleu solves the problem of dry, mild-flavored chicken breasts with a flavorful stuffing of sharp, nutty melted cheese and salty sliced ham. We wanted to bring this concept to the grill, but leaky cheese can cause flare-ups as it drips from the chicken and into the coals. We wanted great grilled chicken breasts with a flavorful stuffing that stayed put.

Off the bat, we knew we wanted a strongly flavored stuffing for our chicken to stand up to the grill's smoke. We settled on more flavorful prosciutto and fontina cheese rather than the usual deli ham and Swiss cheese. And we chose bone-in, skin-on breasts since the skin acts as a natural protector of the meat. We butterflied the breasts—cutting them horizontally nearly halfway through so the meat opened like a book. We placed prosciutto-wrapped fontina inside, folded over the breast to enclose it and tied each breast up with kitchen twine. Encasing the fontina in prosciutto rather than layering it on top, prevented the cheese from leaking. We also chose to add a simple compound butter enlivened by shallots and tarragon for additional moisture and flavor.

ASSEMBLING STUFFED CHICKEN BREASTS FOR GRILLING

1. Starting on the thick side closest to the breastbone, cut a horizontal pocket in each breast, stopping ½ inch from the edge.

2. Spread an equal portion of compound butter inside each breast.

3. Place one prosciutto-wrapped piece of cheese inside each breast and fold the breast over to enclose.

4. Tie each breast with three 12-inch pieces of kitchen twine at even intervals.

CARVING STUFFED CHICKEN BREASTS

Insert the tip of a boning knife into the chicken breast just above the breastbone. While gently lifting the breast meat away from the rib cage, simultaneously cut with the tip of the knife against the ribs, following the contour, to separate the meat.

Cooking the stuffed breasts over a modified two-level fire (in which all the coals are banked on one side of the grill) allowed us to first sear the breasts over the hot coals for color and flavor, then finish cooking them over more moderate indirect heat. These boneless stuffed chicken breasts were so good, we could enjoy them straight through the grilling season.

Charcoal-Grilled Stuffed Chicken Breasts with Prosciutto and Fontina

SERVES 4

You can serve the chicken on the bone, but we prefer to carve it off and slice it before serving.

- 4 (12-ounce) bone-in, skin-on chicken breast halves, trimmed
  Table salt and ground black pepper
  Vegetable oil for the cooking grate
- 4 tablespoons (½ stick) unsalted butter, softened
- 1 medium shallot, minced (about 3 tablespoons)
- 4 teaspoons chopped fresh tarragon leaves
- 2 ounces fontina cheese, rind removed, cut into four 3 by ½-inch sticks
- 4 thin slices prosciutto (about 2 ounces)

1. Following the photos and starting on the thick side of the breast, closest to the breastbone, slice each breast half horizontally, stopping ½ inch from the edge so the halves remain attached. Dissolve 3 tablespoons salt in 1 quart cold water in a large container. Add the breasts, cover with plastic wrap, and refrigerate for 30 minutes.

2. Light a large chimney starter filled with charcoal (about 6 quarts) and allow to burn until the coals are partially covered with a thin layer of ash, about 20 minutes. Build a modified two-level fire by arranging all the coals over one half of the grill, leaving the other half empty. Set the cooking grate over the coals, cover the grill, and heat the grate until hot, about 5 minutes. Use a grill brush to scrape the cooking grate clean. Dip a wad of paper towels in oil; holding the wad with tongs, oil the cooking grate.

3. Meanwhile, combine the butter, shallot, and tarragon in a small bowl. Roll each piece of cheese in 1 slice prosciutto. Remove the breasts from the brine, dry them thoroughly inside and out with paper towels, and season them inside and out with pepper. Spread an equal amount of the butter mixture inside each breast. Place 1 prosciutto-wrapped piece of cheese inside each breast and fold the breast over to enclose. Evenly space three pieces of kitchen twine (each about 12 inches long) beneath each breast and tie, trimming any excess.

4. Place the chicken breasts, skin side down, over the hot part of the grill and cook until well browned, 3 to 5 minutes. Flip the chicken and cook until the second side is just opaque, about 2 minutes. Move the chicken, skin side up, to the cool side of the grill, with the thicker side of the breasts facing the fire. Cover the grill and continue to cook until an instant-read thermometer inserted into the thickest part of the stuffing registers 160 to 165 degrees, 25 to 30 minutes. Transfer the chicken to a carving board and let rest, tented with foil, for 10 minutes. Remove the twine, then carve the breast meat from the bone following the photo on page 416. Carve into ½-inch-thick slices and serve.

Gas-Grilled Stuffed Chicken Breasts with Prosciutto and Fontina

Follow the recipe for Charcoal-Grilled Stuffed Chicken Breasts with Prosciutto and Fontina through step 1. Turn all the burners to high and heat the grill, with the lid down, until very hot, about 15 minutes. Use a grill brush to scrape the cooking grate clean. Dip a wad of paper towels in oil; holding the wad with tongs, oil the cooking grate. Leave the primary burner (the burner that will remain on during grilling) on high and turn off the other burner(s). Proceed with the recipe from step 3, cooking the chicken with the lid closed and increasing the cooking time on the cooler side of the grill to 30 to 40 minutes.

SMOKED CHICKEN

WHY THIS RECIPE WORKS: When done right, smoking produces chicken with moist, tender, pleasantly smoky meat and an attractively browned exterior. But smoking a chicken is no easy feat—if the heat level isn't just right, the delicate breast meat inevitably dries out, and with too much exposure to the smoke, the flavor of the chicken becomes harsh and bitter. Brining the bird ensured the meat would remain moist, and building a slow-burning moderate fire (by piling lit coals on top of unlit coals) allowed us to extend the life of the fire without having to tend to it. A pan of water underneath the chicken helped control the level of heat. Using chicken parts (rather than a whole bird) allowed each piece to be infused with smoke flavor. Finally, we discovered that using wood chunks and smoking the chicken for only half of the cooking time produced chicken with a pleasant—not overpowering—smoke flavor.

Smoked Chicken for a Charcoal Grill
SERVES 6 TO 8

Avoid mesquite wood chunks for this recipe; we find that the meat can turn bitter if they smolder too long. You will need a 13 by 19-inch disposable aluminum pan for this recipe.

- 1 **cup table salt**
- 1 **cup sugar**
- 6 **pounds bone-in chicken parts (breasts, thighs, and drumsticks), trimmed**
- 3 **tablespoons vegetable oil, plus extra for the cooking grate**
  Ground black pepper
- 2 **(3-inch) wood chunks**

1. Dissolve the salt and sugar in 4 quarts cold water in a large container. Submerge the chicken in the brine, cover, and refrigerate for 30 minutes to 1 hour. Remove the chicken from the brine and pat dry with paper towels. Brush both sides of the chicken with oil and season with pepper. Soak the wood chunks in cold water to cover for 30 minutes; drain.

2. Open the bottom grill vents halfway. Place a 13 by 9-inch disposable aluminum pan filled with 2 cups water on 1 side of the grill and 2 quarts unlit charcoal against the empty side of the grill. Light a large chimney starter filled halfway with charcoal (about 3 quarts) and allow to burn until the top coals are partially covered with ash, about 20 minutes. Build a single-banked fire by banking the coals over half of the grill on top of the unlit charcoal. Place the wood chunks on top of the coals. Set the cooking grate in place, cover, and open the lid vents halfway. Heat the grill until hot and the wood chunks begin to smoke, about 5 minutes. Use a grill brush to scrape the cooking grate clean. Dip a wad of paper towels in oil; holding the wad with tongs, oil the cooking grate.

3. Place the chicken, skin side up, as far away from the fire as possible with the thighs closest to the fire and the breasts furthest away. Cover, positioning the lid vents over the chicken, and cook until the breasts register 160 degrees and the thighs/drumsticks register 175 degrees on an instant-read thermometer, 1¼ to 1½ hours.

4. Transfer the chicken to a cutting board, tent loosely with foil, and let rest for 5 to 10 minutes before serving.

Smoked Chicken for a Gas Grill

You will need a disposable aluminum pie plate for this recipe.

Follow the recipe for Smoked Chicken for a Charcoal Grill through step 1, substituting 3 cups wood chips for the wood chunks. Soak half the chips in cold water to cover for 30 minutes; drain. Use a large piece of heavy-duty aluminum foil to wrap the soaked chips into a foil packet and cut several vent holes in the top. Wrap the unsoaked chips in a second foil packet and cut several vent holes in the top. Place the wood chip packets directly on the primary burner. Place a disposable aluminum pie plate with 2 cups water on the other burner(s). Turn all the burners to high and heat the grill, with the lid down, until very hot and the chips are smoking, about 15 minutes. Use a grill brush to scrape the cooking grate clean. Dip a wad of paper towels in oil; holding the wad with tongs, oil the cooking grate. Proceed with the recipe from step 3, cooking with the lid down.

BARBECUED PULLED CHICKEN

WHY THIS RECIPE WORKS: Made-from-scratch barbecued pulled chicken sandwiches often rely on boneless chicken breasts and bottled barbecue sauce. The result is a sandwich with no smoke, tough meat, and artificial flavor. We wanted to take pulled chicken sandwiches seriously—using tender, smoky meat pulled off the bone in moist, soft shreds and then tossed with a tangy, sweet sauce—but we didn't want to take all day to make them. We chose whole chicken legs for great flavor, low cost, and resistance to overcooking. The legs cooked gently but thoroughly over indirect heat, absorbing plenty of smoke flavor along the way. Cooking the chicken to a higher-than-usual temperature also dissolves connective tissue and renders more fat, making the meat tender and less greasy. Once the chicken finished cooking, we hand-shredded half and machine-processed the other

half to produce the perfect texture—one similar to pulled pork. The chicken then just had to be combined with a thin but tangy barbecue sauce to become truly bun-worthy.

Barbecued Pulled Chicken for a Charcoal Grill
SERVES 6 TO 8

Chicken leg quarters consist of drumsticks attached to thighs; often also attached are backbone sections that must be trimmed away. To do this, carefully grasp the leg and bend the backbone section to pop out the joint; using a sharp boning knife, cut the backbone section from the leg. When trimming the fat from the chicken legs, try to leave the excess skin intact, as it will keep the meat moist on the grill. You will need a 16 by 12-inch disposable aluminum pan for this recipe. We prefer to use hickory or mesquite wood chunks with this dish.

If you would like to hold the dish once the chicken and sauce are combined and heated through, transfer the mixture to a 13 by 9-inch glass baking dish, cover with foil, and place in a 250-degree oven for up to an hour. Serve the pulled chicken on hamburger rolls or sandwich bread, along with pickles and coleslaw.

2	(3-inch) wood chunks (see note)
1	tablespoon vegetable oil, plus extra for the cooking grate
8	bone-in, skin-on chicken leg quarters (about 7 pounds), trimmed (see note)
	Table salt and ground black pepper
1	large onion, peeled and quartered
¼	cup water
1½	cups ketchup
1½	cups apple cider
¼	cup molasses
3	tablespoons Worcestershire sauce
3	tablespoons Dijon mustard
4	tablespoons apple cider vinegar
2	medium garlic cloves, minced or pressed through a garlic press (about 2 teaspoons)
1½	tablespoons chili powder
½	teaspoon cayenne pepper
	Hot sauce

1. Soak the wood chunks in cold water to cover for 1 hour; drain.

2. Light a large chimney starter filled three-quarters with charcoal (about 4½ quarts) and allow to burn until the coals are partially covered with a layer of ash, about 20 minutes. Open the bottom grill vents completely.

Place a 16 by 12-inch disposable aluminum pan in the center of the grill. Build a double-banked fire by banking half the coals into a pile on each side of the pan. Place one wood chunk on top of one of the coal piles. Set the cooking grate in place, cover, and heat the grate until hot, about 5 minutes. Use a grill brush to scrape the cooking grate clean. Dip a wad of paper towels in oil; holding the wad with tongs, oil the cooking grate.

3. Pat the chicken dry with paper towels and season with salt and black pepper. Place the chicken, skin side up, in a single layer in the center of the grill over the pan. Cover and cook, rotating the chicken pieces halfway through (do not flip the chicken over) and adding the remaining wood chunk to either pile of coals, until the thickest part of the thigh registers about 185 degrees on an instant-read thermometer, 1 to 1¼ hours. Transfer the chicken to a carving board, tent loosely with foil, and let rest until cool enough to handle.

4. While the chicken is cooking or cooling, puree the onion and water in a food processor until the mixture resembles slush, about 30 seconds. Pass the mixture through a fine-mesh strainer into a liquid measuring cup, pressing on the solids with a rubber spatula (you should have ¾ cup strained onion juice). Discard the solids in the strainer.

5. Whisk the onion juice, ketchup, cider, molasses, Worcestershire sauce, mustard, ½ teaspoon black pepper, and 3 tablespoons of the cider vinegar together in a medium bowl. Heat 1 tablespoon oil in a large saucepan over medium heat until shimmering; add the garlic, chili powder, and cayenne and cook until fragrant, about 30 seconds. Stir in the ketchup mixture and bring to a boil over medium-high heat; reduce the heat to medium-low and simmer, uncovered, until the sauce is slightly thickened, about 15 minutes (you should have about 4 cups of sauce). Transfer 2 cups of the sauce to a serving bowl; leave the remaining sauce in the saucepan.

6. Remove and discard the skin from the chicken legs. Using your fingers, pull the meat off the bones, separating the larger pieces (which should fall off the bones easily) from the smaller, drier pieces into two equal piles.

7. Pulse the smaller chicken pieces in a food processor until just coarsely chopped, 3 to 4 pulses, stirring the chicken with a rubber spatula after each pulse. Add the chicken to the sauce in the saucepan. Using your fingers or two forks, pull the larger chicken pieces into long shreds and add to the saucepan. Stir in the remaining 1 tablespoon cider vinegar; cover the saucepan and heat the chicken over medium-low heat, stirring occasionally, until heated through, about 10 minutes. Add hot sauce to taste and serve, passing the remaining sauce separately.

Barbecued Pulled Chicken for a Gas Grill

You will need a disposable aluminum pie plate for this recipe.

1. Substitute 2 cups wood chips for the wood chunks and soak them in cold water to cover for 30 minutes; drain. Place the chips in a small disposable aluminum pie plate; place the pan on top of the primary burner. Turn all the burners to high and heat the grill, with the lid down, until very hot and the chips are smoking, about 15 minutes. (If the chips ignite, use a water-filled spray bottle to extinguish them.) Use a grill brush to scrape the cooking grate clean. Dip a wad of paper towels in oil; holding the wad with tongs, oil the cooking grate. Leave the primary burner on high and turn off the other burner(s).

2. Follow the recipe for Barbecued Pulled Chicken for a Charcoal Grill from step 3, placing the chicken, skin side up, in a single layer on the cooler side of the grill. Proceed as directed, omitting the wood chunks and disposable aluminum pan and extending the cooking time in step 3 to 1¼ to 1½ hours.

Barbecued Pulled Chicken for a Crowd

This technique works well on a charcoal grill but not so well on a gas grill. If your gas grill is large and can accommodate more than 8 legs, follow the recipe above, adding as many legs as will comfortably fit in a single layer. You may need to increase the cooking time.

Follow the recipe for Barbecued Pulled Chicken for a Charcoal Grill, lighting a large chimney starter filled with charcoal (about 6 quarts), using 12 chicken legs. Following the photo, slot them into a V-shaped roasting rack set on top of the cooking grate over a 16 by 12-inch disposable aluminum pan. Increase the cooking time in step 3 to 1½ to 1¾ hours. In step 5, remove only 1 cup of sauce from the saucepan. In step 7, pulse the chicken in a food processor in two batches.

NOTES FROM THE TEST KITCHEN

BARBECUED PULLED CHICKEN FOR A CROWD

To make barbecued pulled chicken for a crowd, we found that a roasting rack, with six slots, was the perfect tool for the job. By sliding two legs into each slot, a total of 12 legs fit (and finish cooking) at once—plenty to feed a hungry crowd.

NAKED ROAST CHICKEN AND OTHER WACKY RECIPE TESTS

Our test cooks will do almost anything in pursuit of the perfect recipe. No idea is too silly or odd to try—not if it will make a recipe better. Here are some notable recipe tests performed over the years. Each one was deemed promising but ultimately never worked.

• Removing the skin from a chicken before it goes into the oven, pulling the skin taut with toothpicks, and then roasting the skin separately from the chicken pieces to maximize crispness. Too Hannibal Lecter.

• Cooking a roast beef in a 130-degree oven for 24 hours to maximize juiciness. Most ovens don't operate at such a low temperature, and it's probably just as well; this is a perfect recipe for food-borne illness.

• Rubbing the skin off every single chickpea to make extra-smooth hummus. Peeling chickpeas? What were we thinking?!

• Flipping a steak every 4 seconds—for a total of 176 flips over the course of the 11-minute cooking time—to ensure absolutely even heat distribution. Only cooks with Olympic aspirations need to try this.

• Attaching a still (yes, like you might devise to make moonshine) to a covered grill to make our own liquid smoke. The cost for 1 teaspoon of liquid smoke? Fifty bucks. And it didn't taste very good. Plus, this odd setup looked just a little suspicious (read: illegal) to our neighbors.

BEER CAN CHICKEN

WHY THIS RECIPE WORKS: We wanted to know if the curious cooking method of grill-roasting chicken over a can of beer really worked. To earn our approval, this technique would have to produce a tender, juicy, and deeply seasoned bird.

We found that beer can chicken is the real deal—why? The beer in the open can simmers and turns to steam as the chicken roasts, which makes the meat remarkably juicy and rich-textured, similar to braised chicken. As an added bonus, the dry heat of the grill crisps the skin and renders the fat away. To perfect the technique, we added a few hardwood chunks to the fire for smoky flavor. The best grilling setup (for a charcoal grill) proved to be banking the lit coals on either side of the grill and propping the chicken up on an open can of beer on the grill in the center, using the bird's drumsticks to form a tripod.

Finally, we found we didn't have to spend money on an expensive beer—the beer flavor wasn't really detectable in the chicken, so a cheap brew worked just fine (so does lemonade, which proved an acceptable substitute for the beer).

Grill-Roasted Beer Can Chicken for a Charcoal Grill

SERVES 4

Using the right amount of charcoal is crucial here; using too much charcoal will burn the chicken, while using too little will extend the cooking time substantially. The temperature inside the grill should be about 375 degrees at the outset and will fall to about 300 by the time the chicken is done. For added accuracy, place a grill thermometer in the lid vents as the chicken cooks. If you prefer, use lemonade instead of beer; fill an empty 12-ounce soda or beer can with 10 ounces (1¼ cups) of lemonade and proceed as directed. You will need a 13 by 9-inch disposable aluminum pan for this recipe.

- 2 (3-inch) wood chunks or 2 cups wood chips
- 1 (12-ounce) can beer (see note)
- 2 bay leaves
- 1 (3½-pound) whole chicken
- 3 tablespoons Spice Rub (recipe follows)
  Vegetable oil for the cooking grate

1. Soak the wood chunks or chips in cold water to cover for 1 hour and drain. If using wood chips, divide them between two 18-inch squares of foil, fold in the sides of each piece of foil and seal to make two packets, and use a fork to poke about six holes in each packet to allow smoke to escape.

2. Open the beer can and pour out (or drink) about ¼ cup. With a church key can opener, punch two more large holes in the top of the can (for a total of three holes). Crumble the bay leaves into the beer. Pat the chicken dry with paper towels and massage the spice rub all over the chicken, inside and out. Gently lift up the skin over the breast and rub the spice rub directly onto the meat. Using a skewer, poke the skin all over. Slide the chicken over the beer can so that the drumsticks reach down to the bottom of the can and the chicken stands upright; set aside at room temperature.

3. Light a large chimney starter filled two-thirds with charcoal (about 4 quarts) and allow to burn until the coals are partially covered with a layer of ash, about 20 minutes.

4. Place a 13 by 9-inch disposable aluminum pan in the center of the grill. Build a double-banked fire by banking half the coals into a pile on each side of the pan. Place one soaked wood chunk (or one foil packet) on top of each coal pile. Set the cooking grate in place, cover, and heat the grate until hot, about 5 minutes. Use a grill brush to scrape the cooking grate clean. Dip a wad of paper towels in oil; holding the wad with tongs, oil the cooking grate.

5. Place the chicken (with the can) in the center of the cooking grate with the wings facing the coals (the ends of the drumsticks will help steady the bird). Cover and cook until the thickest part of the breast registers 160 to 165 degrees and the thickest part of the thigh registers 175 degrees on an instant-read thermometer, 65 to 85 minutes.

6. With a large wad of paper towels in each hand, transfer the chicken to a platter or tray, making sure to keep the can upright; let rest for 15 minutes. Carefully lift the chicken off the can and onto a cutting board. Discard the remaining beer and can. Carve the chicken and serve.

Grill-Roasted Beer Can Chicken for a Gas Grill

Be sure not to open the lid of the gas grill too often during cooking; the temperature of the grill will drop significantly each time you open it. You will need a disposable aluminum pie plate for this recipe.

1. Soak 2 cups wood chips in cold water to cover for 30 minutes and drain. Place the wood chips in a disposable aluminum pie plate; place the pie plate on top of the primary burner (the burner that will remain on during cooking). Turn all the burners to high and heat the grill with the lid down until very hot and the chips are smoking heavily, about 15 minutes.

2. Meanwhile, follow the recipe for Grill-Roasted Beer Can Chicken for a Charcoal Grill from step 2. Carefully open the grill (there may be some smoke) and use a grill brush to scrape the cooking grate clean. Dip a wad of paper towels in oil; holding the wad with tongs, oil the cooking grate. Turn the primary burner down to medium and turn off the other burner(s). Position the chicken over the cool part of the grill with a wing side facing the primary burner. Cover and cook for 35 minutes. (The temperature inside the grill should be 325 to 350 degrees; adjust the lit burner as necessary.) Rotate the chicken so that the drumstick and wing that were facing away from the lit burner are now facing toward it. Cover and continue to cook until the thickest part of the breast registers 160 to 165 degrees and the thickest part of the thigh registers 175 degrees on an instant-read thermometer, 25 to 40 minutes longer; proceed as directed in step 6.

Spice Rub

MAKES 1 CUP

- ½ cup sweet paprika
- 2 tablespoons kosher salt
- 2 tablespoons garlic powder
- 1 tablespoon dried thyme
- 2 teaspoons ground celery seed
- 2 teaspoons ground black pepper
- 2 teaspoons cayenne pepper

Combine all the ingredients in a small bowl. (Extra rub can be stored in an airtight container for up to 2 months.)

GRILLED CORNISH GAME HENS

WHY THIS RECIPE WORKS: Grilled Cornish game hens provide an attractive, elegant alternative to grilled chicken. We wanted to develop a foolproof technique that would deliver smoky notes, really crisp skin, and juicy meat infused with great grilled flavor.

We found that by butterflying the birds we could keep all of the skin on one side, which meant it crisped more quickly when placed facing the coals. Butterflying also produced a uniformly thick bird, which promoted even cooking. We needed to secure the legs to the body to keep the skin from tearing, so we developed a special skewering procedure that stabilized the legs, made it easier to fit the birds on the cooking grate, and created a restaurant-worthy presentation. A seven-ingredient rub gave the hens a sweet and savory complexity and helped crisp the skin even further, giving it a rich mahogany hue. Our quick glaze of ketchup, brown sugar, and soy sauce provided the crowning touch.

NOTES FROM THE TEST KITCHEN

SKEWERING GAME HENS

1. Insert a flat metal skewer ½ inch from the end of a drumstick through the skin and meat and out the other side.

2. Turn the leg so that the end of the drumstick faces the wing, then insert the tip of the skewer into the meaty section of the thigh under the bone.

3. Press the skewer all the way through the breast and second thigh. Fold the end of the drumstick toward the wing and insert the skewer ½ inch from the end.

4. Press the skewer so that the blunt end rests against the bird and stretch the skin tight over the legs, thighs, and breast halves.

Grill-Roasted Cornish Game Hens for a Charcoal Grill

SERVES 4

Butterflying a Cornish game hen is similar to butterflying a chicken or turkey (see page 102 and page 121). Use poultry shears to cut out and remove the backbone, then make a ¼-inch cut in the breastbone to separate the breast halves and lightly press down to flatten the bird. Finally, with the skin facing up, fold the wingtips behind the bird to secure them.

If your hens weigh 1½ to 2 pounds, cook three instead of four, brine them for an extra 15 minutes, and extend the cooking time in step 5 by 10 to 15 minutes. Thaw frozen game hens in the refrigerator for 24 to 36 hours before brining. To add smoke flavor to the hens, use the optional wood chunks. Note that you will need a 16 by 12-inch disposable aluminum pan and four 8 to 10-inch flat metal skewers to secure the hens.

HENS

1 cup table salt
4 (1¼ to 1½-pound) Cornish game hens, butterflied (see note)
2 tablespoons brown sugar
1 tablespoon paprika
2 teaspoons garlic powder
2 teaspoons chili powder
1 teaspoon ground black pepper
1 teaspoon ground coriander
⅛ teaspoon cayenne pepper
4 (3-inch) wood chunks (optional; see note)
Vegetable oil for the cooking grate

BARBECUE GLAZE

½ cup ketchup
2 tablespoons brown sugar
1 tablespoon soy sauce
1 tablespoon distilled white vinegar
1 tablespoon yellow mustard
1 medium garlic clove, minced or pressed through a garlic press (about 1 teaspoon)

1. FOR THE HENS: Dissolve the salt in 4 quarts cold water in a large container. Submerge the hens in the brine, cover with plastic wrap, and refrigerate for 1 hour.

2. While the hens brine, combine the sugar and spices in a small bowl. If using the wood chunks, soak them in cold water to cover for 1 hour; drain. Remove the birds from the brine and rinse inside and out under running water; pat dry with paper towels. Following the photos on page 422, use an 8 to 10-inch flat metal skewer to secure each hen. Rub the hens evenly with the spice mixture and refrigerate while preparing the grill.

3. FOR THE GLAZE: Combine all the ingredients in a small saucepan and cook over medium heat, stirring occasionally, until thick and slightly reduced, about 5 minutes. Set aside.

4. Light a large chimney starter filled with charcoal (about 6 quarts) and allow to burn until the coals are partially covered with a layer of ash, about 20 minutes. Place a 16 by 12-inch disposable aluminum pan in the center of the grill. Build a double-banked fire by banking half of the coals into a pile on each side of the pan. Place two soaked wood chunks (if using) on each pile of coals. Set the cooking grate in place, cover, and heat the grate until hot, about 5 minutes. Use a grill brush to scrape the cooking grate clean. Dip a wad of paper towels in oil; holding the wad with tongs, oil the cooking grate.

5. Place the hens, skin side down, on the center of the grill over the pan. Open the grill lid vents completely and cover, positioning the vents over the hens. Cook the hens until the thickest part of the thigh registers 160 to 165 degrees on an instant-read thermometer, 20 to 30 minutes.

6. Using tongs, move the birds to the hot sides of the grill (2 hens per side). Cover and continue to cook until browned, about 5 minutes. Brush the birds with half of the glaze; flip and cook for 2 minutes. Brush the remaining glaze over the hens; flip and continue to cook until the thickest part of the breast registers 160 to 165 degrees and the thickest part of the thigh registers 175 degrees, 1 to 3 minutes longer.

7. Transfer the hens to a cutting board and let rest for 10 minutes. Cut in half through the breastbone and serve immediately.

Grill-Roasted Cornish Game Hens for a Gas Grill

If using the optional wood chips for a smoky flavor, you will need a disposable aluminum pie plate for this recipe.

1. Follow the recipe for Grill-Roasted Cornish Game Hens for a Charcoal Grill through step 3, substituting 1 cup wood chips for the wood chunks and soaking them in cold water to cover for 30 minutes. Drain the chips and place in a disposable aluminum pie plate; set the pie plate on one burner. Turn all the burners to high and heat the grill, with the lid down, until very hot and the chips are smoking, about 15 minutes (if the chips ignite, use a water-filled spray bottle to extinguish). Use a grill brush to scrape the cooking grate clean. Dip a wad of paper towels in oil; holding the wad with tongs, oil the cooking grate. Turn all the burners to medium.

2. Place the hens, skin side down, on the cooking grate. Cover and cook until the skin is deeply browned and has grill marks, 10 to 15 minutes. (If the grill has hot spots, you might have to move the hens on the grill.) Using tongs, flip the birds; cover and continue to cook until the thickest part of the thigh registers 160 to 165 degrees on an instant-read thermometer, 10 to 15 minutes more.

3. Brush the birds with half of the glaze. Using tongs, flip the birds and cook until deeply browned, 2 to 3 minutes. Brush the remaining glaze over the hens; flip and continue to cook until deeply browned and the thickest part of the breast registers 160 to 165 degrees and the thickest part of the thigh registers 175 degrees, 2 to 3 minutes more.

4. Transfer the hens to a carving board and let rest for 10 minutes. Cut in half through the breastbone and serve immediately.

GRILLED HAMBURGERS

WHY THIS RECIPE WORKS: Burgers often come off the grill tough, dry, and bulging in the middle. We wanted a moist and juicy burger, with a texture that is tender and cohesive, not dense and heavy. Just as important, we wanted a flavorful, deeply caramelized reddish brown crust with an even surface capable of holding as many condiments as we could pile on.

Ground chuck gave us the most robustly flavored burgers when pitted head to head against burgers made from other cuts of ground beef. We selected meat with a ratio of 20 percent fat to 80 percent lean; more fat than that, and the burgers were too greasy. Burgers made with less fat lacked in juiciness and moisture. We formed the meat into 6-ounce patties that were fairly thick, with a depression in the middle. Rounds of testing taught us that indenting the center of each burger ensured that the patties would come off the grill with an even thickness instead of puffed up like a tennis ball. Cooking the burgers over the fire for just a few minutes kept them tender, and lightly oiling the cooking grate prevented them from sticking.

Charcoal-Grilled Hamburgers

SERVES 4

For those who like their burgers well-done, we found that poking a small hole in the center of the patty before cooking helped the center to cook through before the edges dried out.

    Vegetable oil for the cooking grate
1½ pounds 80 percent lean ground chuck
1 teaspoon table salt
½ teaspoon ground black pepper
4 buns or rolls

1. Light a large chimney starter filled with charcoal (about 6 quarts) and allow to burn until the coals are partially covered with a layer of ash, about 20 minutes. Build a single-level fire by arranging the coals evenly over the bottom of the grill. Set the cooking grate in place, cover, and heat the grate until hot, about 5 minutes. Use a grill brush to scrape the cooking grate clean. Dip a wad of paper towels in oil; holding the wad with tongs, oil the cooking grate.

2. Meanwhile, using your hands, gently break up the meat, season with the salt and pepper, and toss lightly to distribute. Divide the meat into four equal portions. Gently toss one portion of meat back and forth between your hands to form a loose ball. Gently flatten into a ¾-inch-thick patty that measures about 4½ inches in diameter. Press the center of the patty down with your fingertips until it is about ½ inch thick, creating a slight depression in each patty. Repeat with the remaining portions of meat.

3. Grill the burgers, uncovered, until well seared on the first side, about 2½ minutes. Using a wide metal spatula, flip the burgers and continue grilling, about 2 minutes for rare, 2½ minutes for medium-rare, 3 minutes for medium, or 4 minutes for well-done. While the burgers grill, toast the buns on the cooler side of the grill. Serve on buns with desired toppings.

Gas-Grilled Hamburgers

Turn all the burners to high and heat the grill, with the lid down, until very hot, about 15 minutes. Use a grill brush to scrape the cooking grate clean. Dip a wad of paper towels in oil; holding the wad with tongs, oil the cooking grate. Follow the recipe for Charcoal-Grilled Hamburgers, proceeding from step 2. In step 3, grill the burgers on the first side for 3 minutes and increase the cooking times on the second side by 1 minute.

Grilled Cheeseburgers

Since the cheese is evenly distributed in these burgers, just a little goes a long way.

Follow the recipe for Charcoal- or Gas-Grilled Hamburgers, sprinkling 3 ounces cheddar, Swiss, or Monterey Jack cheese, shredded (about ¾ cup), or 3 ounces blue cheese, crumbled (about ¾ cup), over the meat with the salt and pepper in step 2.

WELL-DONE BURGERS

WHY THIS RECIPE WORKS: We know that many backyard cooks grill their burgers to medium-well and beyond, but we aren't willing to accept the usual outcome of tough, desiccated hockey pucks with no beefy flavor. We wanted to work with supermarket ground beef to produce a tender and moist-as-can-be burger, with perfect grill marks and all, even when well-done.

Taste tests proved that well-done burgers made with 80 percent lean chuck were noticeably moister than burgers made from leaner beef, but they still weren't juicy enough. Because we couldn't force the meat to retain moisture, we opted to pack the patties with a panade, a paste made from bread and milk that's often used to keep meat loaf and meatballs moist. To punch up the flavor, we also added minced garlic and tangy steak sauce. To keep our burgers from puffing up the way most burgers do, we made use of a previous test kitchen discovery: If you make a slight depression in the center of the patty, it will puff slightly as it cooks and level out to form a flat top.

Well-Done Charcoal-Grilled Hamburgers

SERVES 4

Adding bread and milk to the beef creates burgers that are juicy and tender even when well-done. For cheeseburgers, follow the optional instructions below.

    Vegetable oil for the cooking grate
1 large slice high-quality white sandwich bread, crust removed and discarded, bread cut into ¼-inch pieces (about ½ cup)
2 tablespoons whole milk
2 teaspoons steak sauce, such as A-1
1 medium garlic clove, minced or pressed through a garlic press (about 1 teaspoon)
¾ teaspoon table salt

¾ teaspoon ground black pepper

1½ pounds 80 percent lean ground chuck

6 ounces sliced cheese (optional)

4 buns or rolls

1. Light a large chimney starter filled with charcoal (about 6 quarts) and allow to burn until the coals are partially covered with a layer of ash, about 20 minutes. Open the bottom grill vents. Build a modified two-level fire by arranging the coals over half of the grill, leaving the other half empty. Set the cooking grate in place, cover the grill, and heat the grate until hot, about 5 minutes. Use a grill brush to scrape the cooking grate clean. Dip a wad of paper towels in oil; holding the wad with tongs, oil the cooking grate.

2. Meanwhile, mash the bread and milk in a large bowl with a fork until homogeneous (you should have about ¼ cup). Stir in the steak sauce, garlic, salt, and pepper.

3. Break up the beef into small pieces over the bread mixture. Using a fork or your hands, lightly mix together until the mixture forms a cohesive mass. Divide the meat into four equal portions. Gently toss one portion of meat back and forth between your hands to form a loose ball. Gently flatten into a ¾-inch-thick patty that measures about 4½ inches in diameter. Press the center of the patty down with your fingertips until it is about ½ inch thick, creating a slight depression in each patty. Repeat with the remaining portions of meat.

4. Grill the burgers on the hot side of the grill, uncovered, until well seared on the first side, 2 to 4 minutes. Using a wide metal spatula, flip the burgers and continue grilling, about 3 minutes for medium-well or 4 minutes for well-done. (Add the cheese, if using, about 2 minutes before reaching the desired doneness, covering the burgers with a disposable aluminum pan to melt the cheese.) While the burgers grill, toast the buns on the cooler side of the grill. Serve the burgers on the buns with desired toppings.

Well-Done Gas-Grilled Hamburgers

Turn all the burners to high and heat the grill, with the lid down, until very hot, about 15 minutes. Use a grill brush to scrape the cooking grate clean. Dip a wad of paper towels in oil; holding the wad with tongs, oil the cooking grate. Leave the primary burner on high and turn the other burner(s) to low. Follow the recipe for Well-Done Charcoal-Grilled Hamburgers from step 2, grilling the patties with the lid down.

Well-Done Grilled Bacon Cheeseburgers

Most bacon burgers simply top the burgers with bacon. The test kitchen goes a step further, adding bacon fat to the ground beef, which adds juiciness and unmistakable bacon flavor throughout the burger.

Cook 8 ounces bacon (about 8 slices) in a medium skillet over medium heat until crisp, 7 to 9 minutes. Transfer the bacon to a paper towel–lined plate; set aside. Measure 2 tablespoons bacon fat into a heatproof bowl; refrigerate until just warm. Follow the recipe for Well-Done Charcoal- or Gas-Grilled Hamburgers, including the optional cheese, adding the reserved bacon fat to the beef mixture in step 3, and topping each finished burger with 2 strips of bacon just before serving.

GRILLED FLANK STEAK

WHY THIS RECIPE WORKS: A common way to prepare flank steak is to marinate it in a bottle of Italian-style salad dressing. But while the resulting flavor can be interesting, the acid in the vinegar can ruin the texture, making the exterior mushy and gray. We wanted to develop a fresh, Mediterranean-style marinade without acid—a marinade that would really boost flavor without over-tenderizing the meat.

We turned to the optimal method for cooking a flank steak—use a two-level fire (which lets you move the thin part of the steak to the cooler side of the grill once it is done), cook the steak only to medium-rare to keep it from getting tough, and let the steak rest before slicing to reduce the loss of juices. Now we could concentrate on developing and applying an acid-free marinade.

Because fat carries flavor so well, we knew oil would be a key ingredient—the challenge was to infuse Mediterranean flavors (garlic, shallots, and rosemary) into the oil and then into the steak. We developed two key steps. First, we minced the aromatics and combined them with the oil in a blender to create a marinade paste. Next, we invented a novel "marinating" technique—prick the steak all over with a fork, rub it first with salt and then with the marinade paste, then let it sit for up to 24 hours. After marinating, the paste is wiped off to prevent burning, and the steak is ready for the grill. Our technique was so successful, we were free to create two more marinades—one with Asian flavors, and the other with a smoky-spicy kick.

Charcoal-Grilled Marinated Flank Steak

SERVES 4 TO 6

Flank steaks smaller or larger than 2 pounds can be used, but adjust the amount of salt and pepper accordingly. We prefer flank steak cooked medium-rare or medium. To keep the steak juicy, allow it to rest before slicing it.

- 1 (2-pound) whole flank steak, trimmed (see note)
- 1 teaspoon table salt (see note)
- 1 recipe wet paste marinade (recipes follow)
  Vegetable oil for the cooking grate
- ¼ teaspoon ground black pepper (see note)

1. Pat the steak dry with paper towels and plate it on a rimmed baking sheet or in a large baking dish. Using a dinner fork, prick the steak about 20 times on each side. Rub both sides of the steak evenly with the salt, and then with the paste. Cover with plastic wrap and refrigerate for at least 1 hour or up to 24 hours.

2. Light a large chimney starter filled with charcoal (about 6 quarts) and allow to burn until the coals are partially covered with a layer of ash, about 20 minutes. Open the bottom grill vents. Build a two-level fire by arranging two-thirds of the coals evenly over half of the grill and arranging the remaining coals over the other half. Set the cooking grate in place, cover the grill, and heat the grate until hot, about 5 minutes. Use a grill brush to scrape the cooking grate clean. Dip a wad of paper towels in oil; holding the wad with tongs, oil the cooking grate.

3. Using paper towels, wipe the paste off the steak; season both sides with the pepper. Grill the steak directly over the coals until well browned, 4 to 6 minutes. Using tongs, flip the steak; grill until the second side is well browned and an instant-read thermometer inserted into the steak reads 125 degrees for medium-rare and 135 degrees for

medium, 3 to 6 minutes; if the exterior of the meat is browned but the meat is not yet cooked through, move the steak to the cooler side of the grill and continue to grill to the desired doneness. Transfer the steak to a carving board.

4. Tent the steak loosely with foil; let rest for 5 to 10 minutes. Using a sharp chef's knife or carving knife, slice the steak about ¼ inch thick against the grain and on the bias. Serve immediately.

Gas-Grilled Marinated Flank Steak

Follow the recipe for Charcoal-Grilled Marinated Flank Steak through step 1. Turn all the burners to high and heat the grill, with the lid down, until very hot, about 15 minutes. Use a grill brush to scrape the cooking grate clean. Dip a wad of paper towels in oil; holding the wad with tongs, oil the cooking grate. Leave all the burners on high. Proceed with the recipe from step 3, cooking with the lid down. If the meat is significantly underdone when tested with a paring knife, turn off one burner and position the steak so that the thinner side is over the cool part of the grill and the thicker side is over the hot part of the grill.

Garlic-Shallot-Rosemary Wet Paste Marinade

MAKES ENOUGH FOR 1 FLANK STEAK

- 6 tablespoons olive oil
- 1 medium shallot, minced (about 3 tablespoons)
- 6 medium garlic cloves, minced or pressed through a garlic press (about 2 tablespoons)
- 2 tablespoons minced fresh rosemary leaves

Puree all of the ingredients in a blender until smooth, scraping down the sides of the blender jar as needed.

Garlic-Ginger-Sesame Wet Paste Marinade

MAKES ENOUGH FOR 1 FLANK STEAK

- ¼ cup toasted sesame oil
- 3 tablespoons minced or grated fresh ginger
- 2 tablespoons vegetable oil
- 2 scallions, minced
- 3 medium garlic cloves, minced or pressed through a garlic press (about 1 tablespoon)

Puree all of the ingredients in a blender until smooth, scraping down the sides of the blender jar as needed.

Garlic-Chile Wet Paste Marinade

MAKES ENOUGH FOR 1 FLANK STEAK

- 6 tablespoons vegetable oil
- 6 medium garlic cloves, minced or pressed through a garlic press (about 2 tablespoons)
- 2 scallions, minced
- 1 tablespoon minced chipotle chiles in adobo sauce
- 1 medium jalapeño chile, minced

Puree all of the ingredients in a blender until smooth, scraping down the sides of the blender jar as needed.

GRILLED STUFFED FLANK STEAK

WHY THIS RECIPE WORKS: Stuffed steak originated with Italian-American cooking as a way to transform an inexpensive steak into something more exciting and colorful. But when we tried a few of the premade stuffed "pinwheels" from our local grocery store, both the stuffing and the cheese tried to make a run for it, with the cheese oozing out all over the grill, and the stuffing—which can include prosciutto, nuts, or spinach, among other things—falling out onto the grill in big clumps. We were sure we could turn this dish into an easy dinner, with tender beef and a juicy, flavorful filling that stayed in place.

Thanks to its uniform shape and good beefy taste, flank steak was clearly the best bet. To guarantee the filling stayed in place, we butterflied and pounded the steak, so we were starting with the flattest and widest surface possible. As for the filling, we eliminated bread crumbs from consideration—after grilling, they contributed a taste of burnt toast. The classic Italian-American combo of prosciutto and provolone won raves for its salty savor and the way the dry cheese melted inside the pinwheel yet turned crisp where exposed to the grill. To prevent the meat from shrinking on the grill, and squeezing the centers of the pinwheels, we rolled up our flank steak, tied it with twine, and skewered it at 1-inch intervals before slicing and grilling. The twine kept the steak from unraveling, while the skewers prevented the meat from shrinking. Finally, we had stuffing that stayed stuffed and rich, smoky beef.

Grilled Stuffed Flank Steak for a Charcoal Grill

SERVES 4 TO 6

Look for a flank steak measuring approximately 8 by 6 inches, with the grain running the long way. Depending on the steak's size, you may have more or less than eight slices of meat at the end of step 2. You will need both wooden skewers and kitchen twine for this recipe.

- 2 tablespoons olive oil, plus extra for the cooking grate
- 1 small shallot, minced (about 1 tablespoon)
- 2 tablespoons finely minced fresh parsley leaves
- 2 medium garlic cloves, minced or pressed through a garlic press (about 2 teaspoons)
- 1 teaspoon finely minced fresh sage leaves
- 1 (2 to 2½-pound) flank steak, trimmed (see note)
- 4 ounces thinly sliced prosciutto
- 4 ounces thinly sliced provolone cheese
  Table salt and ground black pepper

1. Combine the oil, shallot, parsley, garlic, and sage in a small bowl. Following the photos on page 428, butterfly and pound the flank steak into a rough rectangle. Spread the herb mixture evenly over the opened side of the steak. Lay the prosciutto evenly over the steak, leaving a 2-inch border along the top edge. Cover the prosciutto with an even layer of cheese, leaving a 2-inch border along the top edge. Starting from the short edge, roll the beef into a tight log and place on the cutting board seam side down.

2. Soak 8 to 12 wooden skewers in warm water to cover (you will need one skewer per inch of rolled steak length) for 30 minutes; set aside. Starting ½ inch from the end of the rolled steak, evenly space eight to twelve 14-inch pieces of kitchen twine at 1-inch intervals underneath the steak. Tie the middle string first, then, working from the outer strings toward the center, tightly tie the roll and turn

HOW TO BUTTERFLY AND STUFF FLANK STEAK

1. Lay the flank steak on the edge of a cutting board. Slice the steak horizontally, making sure to leave a ½-inch "hinge" along the top edge.

2. Open up the steak, cover with plastic wrap, and pound it to a 12 by 8-inch rectangle of even thickness.

3. Leaving the steak in place with the grain still running perpendicular to the edge of the cutting board, rub the steak evenly with the herb mixture, and layer it with the prosciutto and cheese, leaving a 2-inch border along the top edge.

4. Roll the steak away from you into a tight log, then tie it at even 1-inch intervals. Skewer the meat directly through each string, making sure to insert the skewer through the seam in the roll to prevent the beef from unraveling during cooking.

5. Slice the beef into 1-inch-thick pinwheels. Each spiral should be held together with a skewer and a piece of twine.

the tied steak 90 degrees so the seam is facing you. Dry the skewers and skewer the beef directly through the outer flap of steak near the seam through each piece of string, allowing the skewers to extend ½ inch on the other side. Using a chef's knife, slice the roll between each piece of twine into 1-inch-thick pinwheels. Season the pinwheels with salt and pepper.

3. Light a large chimney starter three-quarters full with charcoal (about 4½ quarts) and allow to burn until the coals are partially covered with a layer of ash, about 20 minutes. Build a modified two-level fire by arranging all the coals over half of the grill, leaving the other half empty. Set the cooking grate in place, cover, and heat the grate until hot, about 5 minutes. Use a grill brush to scrape the cooking grate clean. Dip a wad of paper towels in oil; holding the wad with tongs, oil the cooking grate.

4. Grill the pinwheels directly over the hot side of the grill until well browned, 3 to 6 minutes. Using tongs, flip the pinwheels; grill until the second side is well browned, 3 to 5 minutes longer. Transfer the pinwheels to the cooler side of the grill, cover, and continue to cook until the center of the pinwheels registers 125 degrees on an instant-read thermometer, 1 to 4 minutes (slightly thinner pinwheels may not need time on the cooler side of the grill). Transfer the pinwheels to a large plate, tent loosely with foil, and let rest for 5 minutes. Remove and discard the skewers and string and serve immediately.

Grilled Stuffed Flank Steak for a Gas Grill

Follow the recipe for Grilled Stuffed Flank Steak for a Charcoal Grill through step 2. Turn all the burners to high and heat the grill, with the lid down, until very hot, about 15 minutes. Use a grill brush to scrape the cooking grate clean. Dip a wad of paper towels in oil; holding the wad with tongs, oil the cooking grate. Leave the primary burner on high and turn the other burner(s) off. Proceed as directed in step 4.

Grilled Stuffed Flank Steak with Spinach and Pine Nuts

Combine 4 ounces washed, chopped spinach, ½ teaspoon ground black pepper, ½ teaspoon table salt, and 1 tablespoon water in a medium microwave-safe bowl. Cover and microwave on high power until the spinach is wilted and decreased in volume by half, 3 to 4 minutes. Allow to cool completely, then stir in ¼ cup toasted pine nuts. Follow the recipe for Grilled Stuffed Flank Steak for a Charcoal or Gas Grill, replacing the prosciutto with the spinach mixture in step 1.

STEAK TIPS

WHY THIS RECIPE WORKS: Steak tips have long been the darling of all-you-can-eat restaurant chains where quantity takes precedence over quality. If they're not mushy, they land on the table tough and dry. We wanted to improve this classic bar food and instill it with deep flavor and a tender texture.

To stay true to the inexpensive nature of this dish, we set our sights on finding the best affordable (read: cheap) cut of meat that would stay tender and moist during a brief stint on the grill. The best cut, we found, is what butchers call flap meat. To tenderize and flavor the meat, we used a soy sauce–based marinade and let the meat marinate for at least an hour—just the right amount of time to allow the thicker parts of the meat to become tender while preventing the thinner sections from becoming too salty. Grilling the tips over a two-level fire, which has hotter and cooler areas, helps to cook this often unevenly shaped cut evenly. We let the meat rest for five minutes after grilling to ensure juicy meat, then sliced it thin so the meat would be tender and flavorful. Lime or orange wedges provided a bright acidic counterpoint to the steak tips.

Charcoal-Grilled Steak Tips

SERVES 4 TO 6

A two-level fire allows you to brown the steak over the hot side of the grill, then move it to the cooler side if it is not yet cooked through. If your steak is thin, however, you may not need to use the cooler side of the grill. The times in the recipe below are for relatively even, 1-inch-thick steak tips. When grilling, bear in mind that even those tasters who usually prefer rare beef preferred steak tips cooked medium-rare to medium because the texture is firmer and not quite so chewy. Serve lime wedges with the Southwestern-marinated tips and orange wedges with the tips marinated in garlic, ginger, and soy sauce.

- 1 recipe marinade (recipes follow)
- 2 pounds flap meat sirloin steak tips, trimmed
  Vegetable oil for the cooking grate
  Lime or orange wedges, for serving (see note)

1. Combine the marinade and meat in a gallon-size zipper-lock bag, seal the bag, and refrigerate for 1 hour, flipping the bag once halfway through the marinating time.

2. About halfway through the marinating time, light a large chimney starter filled with charcoal (about 6 quarts)

and allow to burn until the coals are partially covered with a layer of ash, about 20 minutes. Build a two-level fire by arranging two-thirds of the coals evenly over half of the grill and arranging the remaining coals over the other half. Set the cooking grate in place, cover the grill, and heat the grate until hot, about 5 minutes. Use a grill brush to scrape the cooking grate clean. Dip a wad of paper towels in oil; holding the wad with tongs, oil the cooking grate.

3. Remove the steak tips from the marinade and pat dry with paper towels. Grill, uncovered, until well seared and dark brown on the first side, about 4 minutes. Using tongs, flip the steak tips and grill until the second side is well seared and an instant-read thermometer inserted into the center of the steak reads 130 degrees for medium-rare (4 to 5 minutes) or 135 degrees for medium (6 to 8 minutes); if the exterior of the meat is browned but the steak is not yet cooked through, move the steak tips to the cooler side of the grill and continue to grill to the desired doneness.

4. Transfer the steak tips to a cutting board, tent loosely with foil, and let rest for 5 minutes. Slice the steak tips very thin on the bias; serve immediately with the lime or orange wedges.

Gas-Grilled Steak Tips

Follow the recipe for Charcoal-Grilled Steak Tips through step 1. When about 15 minutes of marinating time remain, turn all the burners to high and heat the grill, with the lid down, until very hot, about 15 minutes. Use a grill brush to scrape the cooking grate clean. Dip a wad of paper towels in oil; holding the wad with tongs, oil the cooking grate. Leave all the burners on high. Proceed with the recipe from step 3, grilling the steak tips covered.

Southwestern Marinade

MAKES ABOUT ¾ CUP

- ⅓ cup soy sauce
- ⅓ cup vegetable oil
- 3 medium garlic cloves, minced or pressed through a garlic press (about 1 tablespoon)
- 1 tablespoon dark brown sugar
- 1 tablespoon tomato paste
- 1 tablespoon chili powder
- 2 teaspoons ground cumin
- ¼ teaspoon cayenne pepper

Mix all the ingredients together in a small bowl.

Garlic, Ginger, and Soy Marinade
MAKES ABOUT ⅔ CUP

⅓ cup soy sauce
3 tablespoons vegetable oil
3 tablespoons toasted sesame oil
3 medium garlic cloves, minced or pressed through a garlic press (about 1 tablespoon)
2 tablespoons dark brown sugar
1 tablespoon minced or grated fresh ginger
2 teaspoons grated zest from 1 orange
½ teaspoon red pepper flakes
1 scallion, sliced thin

Mix all the ingredients together in a small bowl.

GRILLED STEAKS

WHY THIS RECIPE WORKS: Grilled steaks have many tempting qualities—rich, beefy flavor, a thick, caramelized crust, and almost zero cleanup or prep for the cook. But the occasional small bonfire caused by the rendered fat can leave pricey cuts of meat charred and tasting like the inside of a smokestack. We wanted to develop a surefire technique for grilling the three most popular premium steaks—strip, rib eye, and filet mignon—so they would turn out juicy and tender every time.

To get the crust we wanted, a very hot fire was essential. But we quickly learned we couldn't cook a thick steak over consistently high heat without either burning the steak or causing the fat to drip down onto the charcoal and ignite. The solution was to cook these premium steaks over a two-level fire, searing them first over high heat and then moving them to the cooler part of the grill to cook through. For the strip and rib-eye steaks, lightly oiling the cooking grate was enough to get them going and keep them from sticking, but the lean filets mignons required a bit of olive oil to encourage browning. Otherwise, we didn't fuss with our steaks before cooking them—a light seasoning with salt and pepper was sufficient.

To add a little richness to the filets mignons, we made two compound butters, one with smoked paprika and roasted red peppers, the other with lemon, parsley, and garlic—perfect for melting down the sides of the still-warm steaks.

Charcoal-Grilled Strip or Rib Steaks
SERVES 4

If your guests are more likely to eat only an 8-ounce steak, grill two 1-pound steaks, slice them, and serve half-steak portions. The most accurate way to judge doneness is to stick an instant-read thermometer through the side of the steak deep into the meat, so that most of the shaft is embedded in the steak.

Vegetable oil for the cooking grate
4 (12 to 16-ounce) strip or rib steaks, 1¼ to 1½ inches thick (see note)
Table salt and ground black pepper

1. Light a large chimney starter filled with charcoal (about 6 quarts) and allow to burn until the coals are partially covered with a layer of ash, about 20 minutes. Build a two-level fire by arranging two-thirds of the coals evenly over half of the grill and arranging the remaining coals over the other half. Set the cooking grate in place, cover the grill, and heat the grate until hot, about 5 minutes. Use a grill brush to scrape the cooking grate clean. Dip a wad of paper towels in oil; holding the wad with tongs, oil the cooking grate.

2. Meanwhile, pat the steaks dry with paper towels and season both sides of the steaks with salt and pepper. Grill the steaks, uncovered, over the hotter part of the grill until well browned on one side, 2 to 3 minutes. Flip the steaks and cook until well browned on the other side, 2 to 3 minutes. (Small flare-ups may occur; if flames become constant, slide the steaks to the cooler side of the grill and mist the fire with water from a spray bottle.)

3. Move the steaks to the cooler side of the grill. Continue cooking, uncovered, until an instant-read thermometer inserted into the center of the steaks registers 120 degrees for rare (5 to 6 minutes), 125 degrees for medium-rare (6 to 7 minutes), or 135 degrees for medium (7 to 8 minutes).

4. Remove the steaks from the grill and let rest for 5 minutes. Serve immediately.

Gas-Grilled Strip or Rib Steaks

Depending on the heat output of your gas grill, you may need to cook the steaks on the cooler side of the grill for an extra minute or two.

Turn all the burners to high and heat the grill, with the lid down, until very hot, about 15 minutes. Use a grill brush to scrape the cooking grate clean. Dip a wad of paper towels in oil; holding the wad with tongs, oil the cooking grate. Leave the primary burner on high and turn the other burner(s) to medium. Follow the recipe for Charcoal-Grilled Strip or Rib Steaks from step 2.

Charcoal-Grilled Filets Mignons

SERVES 4

Filet mignon steaks are cut from the tenderloin, which is, as the name indicates, an extremely tender portion of meat. Though tender, the steaks are not very rich. To prevent the steaks from drying out on the grill and to encourage browning, we found it helpful to lightly rub each steak with a little oil before grilling. We suggest drizzling the grilled steaks with olive oil and serving them with lemon wedges, or serving the steaks with one of our flavored butters (recipes follow).

Vegetable oil for the cooking grate
4 (7 to 8-ounce) center-cut filets mignons, 1½ to 2 inches thick
4 teaspoons olive oil
Table salt and ground black pepper

1. Light a large chimney starter filled with charcoal (about 6 quarts) and allow to burn until the coals are partially covered with a layer of ash, about 20 minutes. Build a two-level fire by arranging two-thirds of the coals evenly over half of the grill and arranging the remaining coals over the other half. Set the cooking grate in place, cover the grill, and heat the grate until hot, about 5 minutes. Use a grill brush to scrape the cooking grate clean. Dip a wad of paper towels in vegetable oil; holding the wad with tongs, oil the cooking grate.

2. Meanwhile, pat the steaks dry with paper towels and lightly rub them with the olive oil; season both sides of the steaks with salt and pepper. Grill the steaks, uncovered, on the hotter side of the grill until well browned on one side, 2 to 3 minutes. Flip the steaks and cook until well browned on the second side, 2 to 3 minutes.

3. Move the steaks to the cooler side of the grill. Continue cooking, uncovered, until the center of the steaks registers 120 degrees for rare (about 6 minutes), 125 degrees for medium-rare (7 to 8 minutes), or 135 degrees for medium (about 9 minutes) on an instant-read thermometer.

4. Remove the steaks from the grill and let rest for 5 minutes. Serve immediately.

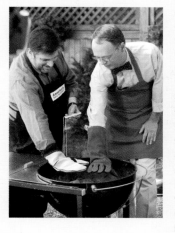
Gas-Grilled Filets Mignons

Depending on the heat output of your gas grill, you may need to cook the steaks on the cooler side of the grill for an extra minute or two.

Turn all the burners to high and heat the grill, with the lid down, until very hot, about 15 minutes. Use a grill brush to scrape the cooking grate clean. Dip a wad of paper towels in vegetable oil; holding the wad with tongs, oil the cooking grate. Leave the primary burner on high and turn the other burner(s) to medium. Follow the recipe for Charcoal-Grilled Filets Mignons from step 2.

Roasted Red Pepper and Smoked Paprika Butter

MAKES ¼ CUP

- 4 tablespoons (½ stick) unsalted butter, softened
- 2 tablespoons finely minced jarred roasted red peppers
- 1 tablespoon minced fresh thyme leaves
- ¾ teaspoon smoked paprika
- ½ teaspoon table salt
  Ground black pepper

Combine all the ingredients and pepper to taste in a small bowl and mix until smooth. While the steaks are resting, spoon 1 tablespoon of the butter on each one.

Lemon, Garlic, and Parsley Butter

MAKES ¼ CUP

- 4 tablespoons (½ stick) unsalted butter, softened
- 1 tablespoon minced fresh parsley leaves
- 1 medium garlic clove, minced or pressed through a garlic press (about 1 teaspoon)
- ½ teaspoon grated zest from 1 lemon
- ½ teaspoon table salt
  Ground black pepper

Combine all the ingredients and pepper to taste in a small bowl and mix until smooth. While the steaks are resting, spoon 1 tablespoon of the butter on each one.

GRILLED ARGENTINE STEAKS

WHY THIS RECIPE WORKS: In Argentina, large 2-pound steaks are grilled low and slow over hardwood logs, not charcoal (and never over gas), which imbues them with a smokiness that is subtler and more complex that the typical "barbecue" flavor one comes to expect of grilled meat here in the States. With the piquant parsley, garlic, and olive oil sauce known as chimichurri served alongside, it's a world favorite. We wanted to duplicate the Argentinean method with American supermarket steaks and a kettle grill. For our choice of steak, we selected well-marbled New York strip steak for its big beefy flavor and meaty chew. To mimic a wood fire, we added unsoaked wood chunks to the perimeter of our grill fire. Setting the lid down on the grill for the first few minutes of cooking helped to quickly trap smoke flavor. To get a deep brown

char on the meat without overcooking it, we used two strategies. First, we rubbed the meat with a mixture of salt and cornstarch. Salt seasons the meat and draws out moisture, as does cornstarch. Then we moved the steaks into the freezer for 30 minutes. The inside of a freezer is so dry that it often robs unprotected food of its moisture. In this instance, this was a good thing. Par-frozen steaks browned within moments of hitting the grill. Even better, these partially frozen steaks could stand about five more minutes of fire, adding up to more char and more flavor. To finish, garlicky chimichurri sauce cut through the rich, unctuous qualities of our great grilled steak.

Charcoal-Grilled Argentine Steaks with Chimichurri Sauce

SERVES 6 TO 8

The chimichurri sauce can be made up to 3 days in advance. Our preferred steak for this recipe is strip steak, also known as New York strip. A less expensive alternative is a boneless shell sirloin steak (or top sirloin steak). We prefer oak wood chunks, but other types can be used. Flipping three times during cooking allows for even cooking and limits flare-ups.

CHIMICHURRI SAUCE

- ¼ cup hot water
- 2 teaspoons dried oregano
- 2 teaspoons kosher salt
- 1⅓ cups loosely packed fresh parsley leaves
- ⅔ cup loosely packed fresh cilantro leaves
- 6 medium garlic cloves, minced or pressed through a garlic press (about 2 tablespoons)
- ½ teaspoon red pepper flakes
- ¼ cup red wine vinegar
- ½ cup extra-virgin olive oil

STEAK

- 1 tablespoon cornstarch
- 2 tablespoons kosher salt
- 4 (1-pound) boneless strip steaks, 1½ inches thick (see note)
- 4 (2-inch) unsoaked wood chunks (see note)
  Ground black pepper
  Vegetable oil for the cooking grate

1. FOR THE SAUCE: Combine the hot water, oregano, and salt in a small bowl; let stand for 5 minutes to soften the oregano. Pulse the parsley, cilantro, garlic, and red pepper flakes in a food processor until coarsely chopped, about 10 pulses. Add the water mixture and the vinegar and pulse briefly to combine. Transfer the mixture to a medium bowl and slowly whisk in the oil until incorporated and the mixture is emulsified. Cover with plastic wrap and let stand at room temperature for at least 1 hour (if preparing the sauce in advance, refrigerate and bring to room temperature before using).

2. FOR THE STEAK: Combine the cornstarch and salt in a small bowl. Pat the steaks dry with paper towels and place on a wire rack set over a rimmed baking sheet. Rub the entire surface of the steaks with the cornstarch mixture and place the steaks, uncovered, in a freezer until very firm, about 30 minutes.

3. Light a large chimney starter filled with charcoal (about 6 quarts) and allow to burn until the coals are partially covered with a thin layer of ash, about 20 minutes. Build a single-level fire by arranging the coals evenly over the bottom of the grill and place the wood chunks directly on the coals, spacing them evenly around the perimeter of the grill. Set the cooking grate in place, cover, and heat the grate until hot, about 5 minutes. Use a grill brush to scrape the cooking grate clean. Dip a wad of paper towels in vegetable oil; holding the wad with tongs, oil the cooking grate.

4. Season the steaks with black pepper. Place the steaks on the grill, cover, and cook until the steaks begin to char, 2 to 3 minutes. Uncover the grill, flip the steaks, and cook on the second side until beginning to char, 2 to 3 minutes. Flip again and cook the first side until well charred, 2 to 3 minutes. Flip one last time and continue to cook until the second side is well charred and the center of the steak registers 115 degrees for rare (about 2 minutes) or 120 degrees for medium-rare (about 4 minutes) on an instant-read thermometer. Transfer to a large plate and let rest, loosely tented with foil, for 10 minutes. Slice and serve, passing the chimichurri sauce separately.

Gas-Grilled Argentine Steaks with Chimichurri Sauce

You will need a disposable 9-inch aluminum pie plate to hold the wood chunks in this variation.

Follow the recipe for Charcoal-Grilled Argentine Steaks with Chimichurri Sauce through step 2. Turn all the burners to high and heat the grill, with the lid down, until very hot, about 15 minutes. Place the wood chunks in a perforated disposable 9-inch aluminum pie plate and set on the cooking grate. Close the lid and heat until the wood chunks begin to smoke, about 5 minutes. Use a grill brush to scrape the cooking grate clean. Dip a wad of paper towels in vegetable oil; holding the wad with tongs, oil the cooking grate. Proceed with the recipe from step 4, cooking the steaks alongside the pie plate.

INEXPENSIVE GRILLED ROAST BEEF

WHY THIS RECIPE WORKS: Trying to grill an uneven piece of meat usually results in a fibrous, chewy, and woefully dry roast. We wanted to turn an inexpensive cut of meat into a juicy, evenly cooked roast with a substantial, well-seasoned garlic-rosemary crust.

After extensively testing five "cheap" roast beef options and subjecting each to a 24-hour salt rub, we settled on top sirloin, a beefy, relatively tender cut from the back half of the cow. To grill our roast, we set up a fire in which the coals cover one-third of the grill. In effect, this created hot zones for searing and cooler zones for gentler, indirect cooking. To prevent the meat from cooking too quickly, we placed the roast inside a disposable aluminum pan on the cooler side of the grill after searing it. Poking a few escape channels in the bottom of the aluminum allowed any liquid to drain away, preserving the meat's sear. We also found that cutting the roast into thin slices made the meat taste even more tender.

Inexpensive Grill-Roasted Beef with Garlic and Rosemary for a Charcoal Grill
SERVES 6 TO 8

A pair of kitchen shears works well for punching the holes in the aluminum pan. Start this recipe the day before you plan to grill so the salt rub has time to flavor and tenderize the meat. You will need a 13 by 9-inch disposable aluminum pan for this recipe.

6 medium garlic cloves, minced or pressed through a garlic press (about 2 tablespoons)

2 tablespoons minced fresh rosemary leaves

1 tablespoon ground black pepper

4 teaspoons kosher salt

1 (3 to 4-pound) top sirloin roast

Vegetable oil for the cooking grate

1. Combine the garlic, rosemary, pepper, and salt in a small bowl. Sprinkle all sides of the roast evenly with the salt mixture, wrap with plastic wrap, and refrigerate for 18 to 24 hours.

2. Open the bottom grill vents fully. Light a large chimney starter filled halfway with charcoal (about 3 quarts) and allow to burn until the coals are partially covered with a layer of ash, about 20 minutes. Arrange all the coals over one-third of the grill. Set the cooking grate over the coals, cover the grill, and heat the grate until hot, about 5 minutes. Use a grill brush to scrape the cooking grate clean. Dip a wad of paper towels in oil; holding the wad with tongs, oil the cooking grate.

3. Place the roast over the hot part of the grill and cook until well browned on all sides, about 10 minutes. Meanwhile, punch fifteen ¼-inch holes in the center of a 13 by 9-inch disposable aluminum pan in an area roughly the same size as the roast. Once browned, place the beef in the pan over the holes and transfer the pan to the cool side of the grill. Open the lid vents halfway and cover the grill, positioning the vents over the meat.

4. Cook the roast, rotating the pan 180 degrees halfway through cooking and removing the lid as seldom as possible, until the thickest part of the meat registers 125 degrees for medium-rare (40 minutes) or 130 degrees for medium (60 minutes) on an instant-read thermometer. Transfer the meat to a wire rack set on a rimmed baking sheet, tent loosely with foil, and let rest for 20 minutes. Transfer the meat to a carving board and cut across the grain into thin slices. Serve immediately.

Inexpensive Grill-Roasted Beef with Garlic and Rosemary for a Gas Grill

Follow the recipe for Inexpensive Grill-Roasted Beef with Garlic and Rosemary for a Charcoal Grill through step 1. Turn all the burners to high and heat the grill, with the lid down, until very hot, about 15 minutes. Use a grill brush to scrape the cooking grate clean. Dip a wad of paper towels in oil; holding the wad with tongs, oil the cooking grate. Proceed with the recipe from step 3, reducing the primary burner (the burner that will remain on during grill-roasting) to medium and turning off the other burner(s) and cooking with the lid down.

GRILL-ROASTED BEEF TENDERLOIN

WHY THIS RECIPE WORKS: Grilled tenderloin sounds appealing, but with a whole tenderloin going for as much as $100, uneven cooking, bland flavor, and a tough outer crust just don't cut it. We wanted it cheaper and better. At its peak, tenderloin should be an even, rosy pink throughout, have a browned, crusty exterior, and boast a well-seasoned, grilled flavor.

In need of an affordable alternative to butcher prices, we found that beef at wholesale clubs was far more wallet-friendly. Though these tenderloins needed some home butchering, they were well worth the modest time and effort it took to trim them. Flavor-enhancement came next through just an hour of salting the meat, wrapping it in plastic wrap, and letting it rest on the countertop before hitting the hot coals. Tucking the narrow tip end of the tenderloin under and tying it securely gave the tenderloin a more consistent thickness that allowed it to cook through more evenly on the grill. Direct fire was too hot for the roast to endure throughout the cooking stages, so after briefly searing the meat over the coals, we moved it away from the coals (and soaked wood chips that had been added to amplify the smoky flavor) for grill-roasting via indirect heat. Removing it from the grill while still rare, we let the meat rest before slicing to ensure the meat stayed juicy.

Grill-Roasted Beef Tenderloin for a Charcoal Grill

SERVES 10 TO 12

Beef tenderloins purchased from wholesale clubs require a good amount of trimming before cooking. At the grocery store, however, you may have the option of having the butcher trim it for you. Once trimmed, and with the butt tenderloin still attached (the butt tenderloin is the lobe attached to the large end of the roast), the roast should weigh 4½ to 5 pounds. If you purchase an already-trimmed tenderloin without the butt tenderloin attached, begin checking for doneness about 5 minutes early. If you prefer your tenderloin without a smoky flavor, you may opt not to use wood chips or chunks. Serve as is or with Salsa Verde (recipe follows).

1 (6-pound) beef tenderloin, trimmed of fat and silver skin, tail end tucked and tied with kitchen twine at 2-inch intervals (see note)

¾ tablespoon table salt

2 (2-inch) wood chunks (optional; see note)
   Vegetable oil for the cooking grate

2 tablespoons olive oil

1 tablespoon ground black pepper

1. About 1 hour prior to grilling, set the tenderloin on a cutting board and rub with the salt. Cover loosely with plastic wrap and let stand at room temperature. If using, soak the wood chunks in cold water to cover for 1 hour; drain.

2. About 30 minutes prior to grilling, light a large chimney starter filled with charcoal (about 6 quarts) and allow to burn until the coals are partially covered with a layer of ash, about 20 minutes. Build a modified two-level fire by arranging all the coals over half of the grill, leaving the other half empty; set the wood chunks (if using) on the coals and open the bottom grill vents. Set the cooking grate in place, cover, and heat the grate until hot, about 5 minutes. Use a grill brush to scrape the cooking grate clean. Dip a wad of paper towels in vegetable oil; holding the wad with tongs, oil the cooking grate.

3. Uncover the tenderloin, coat with the olive oil, and season with the pepper. Place the tenderloin on the hot side of the grill directly over the coals. Cook until well browned, about 2 minutes, then rotate one quarter-turn and repeat until all sides are well browned, a total of 8 minutes. Move the tenderloin to the cooler side of the grill and cover, positioning the lid vents over the tenderloin. Cook until the thickest part of the tenderloin registers 120 degrees for rare (16 to 20 minutes) or 125 degrees for medium-rare (20 to 25 minutes) on an instant-read thermometer.

4. Transfer the tenderloin to a cutting board, tent loosely with foil, and let rest for 10 to 15 minutes. Cut into ½-inch-thick slices and serve.

Grill-Roasted Beef Tenderloin for a Gas Grill

You will need a disposable aluminum pie plate for this recipe.

1. Follow step 1 of the recipe for Grill-Roasted Beef Tenderloin for a Charcoal Grill, substituting 2 cups wood chips for the wood chunks and soaking them for 30 minutes. Drain the chips, place in a disposable aluminum pie plate, and cover with heavy-duty foil; poke six holes in the foil and set aside.

2. About 20 minutes prior to grilling, place the pie plate on top of the primary burner (the burner that will remain on during cooking). Turn all the burners to high and heat the grill, with the lid down, until very hot and the chips are smoking heavily, about 20 minutes (if the chips ignite, extinguish the flames with water from a spray bottle). Use a grill brush to scrape the cooking grate clean. Dip a wad of paper towels in oil; holding the wad with tongs, oil the cooking grate.

3. Uncover the tenderloin, coat with the olive oil, and season all sides with the pepper. Place the tenderloin on the side of the grate opposite the primary burner. Grill the tenderloin over the burner(s) without wood chips until well browned, 2 to 3 minutes, then rotate one quarter-turn and repeat until all sides are well browned, for a total of 8 to 12 minutes. Turn off all burner(s) except the primary burner [the tenderloin should be positioned over the extinguished burners(s)]. Cover and cook until the thickest part of the tenderloin registers 120 degrees for rare (16 to 20 minutes) or 125 degrees for medium-rare (20 to 25 minutes) on an instant-read thermometer.

4. Transfer the tenderloin to a cutting board, tent loosely with foil, and let rest for 10 to 15 minutes. Cut into ½-inch-thick slices and serve.

Salsa Verde

MAKES 1½ CUPS

Toasting the bread rids it of excess moisture that might otherwise make a gummy sauce. Salsa verde is excellent with Grill-Roasted Beef Tenderloin (page 434) and other roasted meats, but it can also be used as a garnish for fish or poultry or as a condiment on sandwiches. It can be refrigerated in an airtight container for up to 2 days; before serving, bring the sauce to room temperature and stir it to recombine.

2 slices high-quality white sandwich bread, lightly toasted and cut into ½-inch pieces (about 1½ cups; see note)

1 cup extra-virgin olive oil

¼ cup juice from 2 lemons

4 cups lightly packed flat-leaf parsley leaves, washed and dried thoroughly

¼ cup capers, drained

4 anchovy fillets

1 medium garlic clove, minced or pressed through a garlic press (about 1 teaspoon)

¼ teaspoon table salt

Process the bread, oil, and lemon juice in a food processor until smooth, about 10 seconds. Add the parsley, capers, anchovies, garlic, and salt. Pulse until the mixture is finely chopped (the mixture should not be smooth), about 5 pulses, scraping down the sides of the workbowl with a rubber spatula once. Transfer the mixture to a small bowl and serve.

BARBECUED BRISKET

WHY THIS RECIPE WORKS: The main reason it's so hard to cook brisket is that it starts out as a very tough cut of meat. It's also big, sometimes weighing upward of 13 pounds, which is why most butchers separate it into two cuts: the "point" (the fattier of the two pieces) and the "flat" (which is leaner and also a little tougher). Slow-cooking for as many as six to 12 hours at a low temperature tends to be the norm for cooking brisket, but we wanted to jump-start the cooking on the grill, to give us tender, smoky meat.

We didn't get the total cooking time below six hours, but we did make the job easier using the grill. First, we cooked the meat over the grill for two hours to let in those all-important smoky flavors; barbecuing the brisket fat side up allowed the fat to melt slowly over the meat. Then we moved it to the oven to cook for a few more hours unattended. For flavor, we turned to a dry rub; typical barbecuing methods like basting the meat or setting a pan of liquid on the cooking grate to create a moist environment just didn't work. Our grill-to-oven approach, although unconventional, gave us fork-tender meat with real barbecue flavor in about half the time it would take to cook the meat entirely on the grill.

Charcoal-Grilled Barbecued Beef Brisket
SERVES 18 TO 24

Cooking a whole brisket, which weighs about 10 pounds, may seem like overkill. However, the process is easy, and the leftovers keep well in the refrigerator for up to 4 days. (Leave leftover brisket unsliced, and reheat the foil-wrapped meat in a 300-degree oven until warm.) Still, if you don't want to bother with a big piece of meat or if your grill has fewer than 400 square inches of cooking space, barbecuing brisket for less than a crowd is easy to do. Simply ask your butcher for either the point or flat portion of the brisket, each of which weighs about half as much as a whole brisket. Then follow this recipe, reducing the spice rub by half and barbecuing for just one hour and 30 minutes. Wrap the meat tightly in foil and reduce the time in the oven to two hours. No matter how large or small a piece you cook, it's a good idea to save the juices the meat gives off while in the oven to enrich the barbecue sauce. Hickory and mesquite are both traditional wood choices with brisket.

1 recipe Spicy Chili Rub (recipe follows)

1 (9 to 11-pound) whole beef brisket, fat trimmed to ¼-inch thickness (see note)

2 (3-inch) wood chunks (see note)
Vegetable oil for the cooking grate

3 cups store-bought barbecue sauce

1. Apply the dry rub liberally to all sides of the meat, patting it on firmly to make sure the spices adhere and completely cover the meat. Wrap the brisket tightly in plastic wrap and refrigerate for 2 hours. (For stronger flavor, refrigerate for up to 2 days.)

2. About 1 hour prior to cooking, remove the brisket from the refrigerator, unwrap, and let it come up to room temperature. Soak the wood chunks in cold water to cover for 1 hour and drain.

3. Meanwhile, light a large chimney starter filled halfway with charcoal (about 3 quarts) and allow to burn until the coals are partially covered with a layer of ash, about 20 minutes. Build a single-banked fire by banking the coals over half of the grill, piling them up two or three coals high, leaving the other half empty. Open the bottom grill vents. Place the wood chunks on top of the charcoal. Set the cooking grate in place, open the grill lid vents completely, and cover the grill, turning the lid so that the vents are opposite the wood chunks to draw smoke through the grill. Heat the grate until hot, about 5 minutes. Use a grill brush to scrape the cooking grate clean. Dip a wad

of paper towels in oil; holding the wad with tongs, oil the cooking grate.

4. Position the brisket, fat side up, on the side of the grill opposite the fire. Cook, without removing the lid, for 2 hours. (The temperature inside the grill should be about 350 degrees and will fall to 250 degrees after 2 hours.)

5. Adjust an oven rack to the middle position and heat the oven to 300 degrees. Attach two pieces of heavy-duty foil, 4 feet long, by folding the long edges together two or three times, crimping tightly to seal well, to form an approximately 4 by 3-foot rectangle. Position the brisket lengthwise in the center of the foil. Bring the short edges over the brisket and fold down, crimping tightly to seal. Repeat with the long sides of the foil to seal the brisket completely. Place the brisket on a rimmed baking sheet. Bake until the meat is fork-tender, 3 to 3½ hours.

6. Remove the brisket from the oven, loosen the foil at one end to release steam, and let rest for 30 minutes. If you like, drain the juices into a bowl and defat in a gravy skimmer.

7. Unwrap the brisket and place it on a carving board. Separate the meat into two sections and carve it on the bias across the grain into long, thin slices. Serve with plain barbecue sauce or with barbecue sauce that has been flavored with up to 1 cup of the defatted brisket juices.

Gas-Grilled Barbecued Beef Brisket

You will need a pretty large grill to cook a whole brisket. If your grill has fewer than 400 square inches of cooking space, barbecue either the point or flat end, each of which weighs about half as much as a whole brisket. Follow the directions in the note on page 436 for cooking a smaller piece of brisket. You will need a disposable aluminum pie plate for this recipe.

Follow the recipe for Charcoal-Grilled Barbecued Beef Brisket through step 2, substituting 2 cups wood chips for the wood chunks and soaking them for 30 minutes in cold water to cover. Drain the chips and place them in a disposable aluminum pie plate. Place the pie plate on top of the primary burner (the burner that will remain on during cooking). Turn all the burners to high and heat the grill with the lid down, until very hot and the chips are smoking heavily, about 20 minutes. Use a grill brush to scrape the cooking grate clean. Dip a wad of paper towels in oil; holding the wad with tongs, oil the cooking grate. Turn the primary burner to medium

and turn off the other burner(s). Position the brisket, fat side up, over the cooler part of the grill. Cover and cook for 2 hours. (The temperature inside the grill should be 275 degrees; adjust the lit burner as necessary.) Proceed as directed from step 5.

Spicy Chili Rub

MAKES ABOUT 1 CUP

If you cannot abide spicy food, reduce or eliminate the cayenne.

- 4 **tablespoons paprika**
- 2 **tablespoons chili powder**
- 2 **tablespoons ground cumin**
- 2 **tablespoons dark brown sugar**
- 2 **tablespoons table salt**
- 1 **tablespoon ground oregano**
- 1 **tablespoon granulated sugar**
- 1 **tablespoon ground black pepper**
- 1 **tablespoon ground white pepper**
- 2 **teaspoons cayenne pepper (see note)**

Combine all the ingredients in a small bowl. (The rub can be stored in an airtight container at room temperature for up to a month.)

GRILLED PORK CHOPS

WHY THIS RECIPE WORKS: Too many grilled pork chops are burnt on the outside and raw on the inside. And even if they are cooked evenly, they can still be tough and bland. We wanted great-looking and great-tasting chops with a perfectly grilled, crisp crust and juicy, flavorful meat. What's more, we wanted our chops plump and meaty, not thin and tough.

We started with the right chops—tender and flavorful bone-in rib loin or center-cut loin chops worked best—and brined them to pump up their flavor and lock in moisture. To brown the pork chops, only a really hot fire would do. But keeping them over high heat long enough to cook through dried them out. So we grilled the chops over a two-level fire, with one side of the grill intensely hot to sear the chops, and the other only moderately hot to allow the chops to cook through without burning the exterior. So they wouldn't overcook, we pulled the chops from the grill when they were just underdone, then we covered them with a foil pan, and let the chops rest until the temperature rose to serving temperature and the juices were redistributed in the meat. A spice rub, made with potent spices and applied before grilling, added big flavor and gave our chops a nice crust.

Charcoal-Grilled Pork Chops

SERVES 4

We prefer natural to enhanced pork (pork that has been injected with a salt solution to increase moistness and flavor) for this recipe, though enhanced pork can be used. If using enhanced pork, skip the brining in step 1. Rib loin chops are our top choice for their big flavor and juiciness. Spice rubs add a lot of flavor for very little effort, but the chops can also be seasoned with pepper alone just before grilling. You will need a 13 by 9-inch disposable aluminum pan to cover the chops and help them finish cooking through.

- 6 **tablespoons table salt**
- 6 **tablespoons sugar**
- 4 **(12-ounce) bone-in rib loin pork chops or center-cut loin pork chops, about 1½ inches thick (see note)**
- 1 **recipe Basic Spice Rub for Pork Chops (recipe follows) or ground black pepper (see note)**
  Vegetable oil for the cooking grate

1. Dissolve the salt and sugar in 3 quarts cold water in a large bowl or container. Submerge the chops in the brine, cover with plastic wrap, and refrigerate for 1 hour. Remove the chops from the brine, rinse under running water, and pat dry with paper towels. Coat the chops with the spice rub or season generously with pepper.

2. Light a large chimney starter filled with charcoal (about 6 quarts) and allow to burn until the coals are partially covered with a layer of ash, about 20 minutes. Build a two-level fire by arranging two-thirds of the coals evenly over half of the grill and arranging the remaining coals over the other half. Set the cooking grate in place, cover the grill, and heat the grate until hot, about 5 minutes. Use a grill brush to scrape the cooking grate clean. Dip a wad of paper towels in oil; holding the wad with tongs, oil the cooking grate.

3. Grill the chops, uncovered, on the hotter side of the grill until browned on each side, 2½ to 3 minutes per side. Move the chops to the cooler side of the grill and cover with a large disposable aluminum pan. Continue to cook, turning once, until the center of the chops registers 140 to 145 degrees on an instant-read thermometer, 7 to 9 minutes longer. Transfer the chops to a platter, tent loosely with foil, and let rest until the temperature registers 150 degrees, about 5 minutes. Serve immediately.

Gas-Grilled Pork Chops

We prefer natural to enhanced pork (pork that has been injected with a salt solution to increase moistness and flavor) for this recipe, though enhanced pork can be used. If using enhanced pork, skip the brining in step 1.

Follow the recipe for Charcoal-Grilled Pork Chops through step 1. Turn all the burners to high and heat the grill, with the lid down, until very hot, about 15 minutes. Use a grill brush to scrape the cooking grate clean. Dip a wad of paper towels in oil; holding the wad with tongs, oil the cooking grate. Leave the primary burner on high and turn the other burner(s) off. Place the chops on the hotter side of the grill, cover, and cook until browned on each side, 3 to 4 minutes per side. Move the chops to the cooler side of the grill. Cover and continue to cook, turning once, until the center of the chops registers 140 to 145 degrees on an instant-read thermometer, 7 to 9 minutes longer. Transfer the chops to a platter, tent loosely with foil, and let rest until the temperature registers 150 degrees, about 5 minutes. Serve immediately.

Basic Spice Rub for Pork Chops

MAKES ¼ CUP

- 1 **tablespoon ground cumin**
- 1 **tablespoon chili powder**
- 1 **tablespoon curry powder**
- 1 **teaspoon ground black pepper**
- 2 **teaspoons brown sugar**

Combine all the ingredients in a small bowl.

GRILL-SMOKED PORK CHOPS

WHY THIS RECIPE WORKS: Getting good smoke flavor and a charred crust is an elusive grilling goal. Smokiness generally requires a lengthy exposure to a slow fire, while a charred crust requires a blast of high heat to quickly sear the exterior of the meat before the interior turns dry and leathery. We wanted chops that had it all: charred crust, rosy-pink, ultra-moist meat, and true smoke flavor throughout.

We decided to employ a technique we had perfected for Pan-Seared Thick-Cut Pork Chops (page 152): reversing the cooking by starting low and finishing with

a quick sear. To reap the benefits of both high and low heat, we used a double-banked fire (made by placing a disposable aluminum pan between two mounds of coals) and started our chops under cover on the cooler center of the grill, allowing the smoke to do its job for about 25 minutes. We then applied a few coats of sauce and finished by searing them, uncovered, over hot coals.

As for arranging the chops on the grill, we found it best to rest each chop on its bone instead of laying it flat. To keep them from toppling over, we speared the chops together with skewers, making sure to leave a good inch between each one to allow smoke to circulate, then stood them upright in the center of the grill with bone, not meat, touching the grill. This allowed us to keep the chops over the fire for a full 30 minutes, after which we removed the skewers, applied the glaze, and finished the chops over hot coals for that crusty char.

Grill-Smoked Pork Chops for a Charcoal Grill

SERVES 4

Buy chops of the same thickness so they will cook uniformly. We prefer natural pork to enhanced pork (pork that has been injected with a salt solution to increase moistness and flavor) for this recipe, though enhanced pork can be used. If using enhanced pork, do not sprinkle with salt in step 3. Use the large holes on a box grater to grate the onions. Although we prefer hickory wood chips, any variety of chips will work, except mesquite. You will need a 13 by 9-inch disposable aluminum pan and skewers for this recipe.

SAUCE

- ½ **cup ketchup**
- ¼ **cup light or mild molasses**
- 2 **tablespoons grated onion (see note)**
- 2 **tablespoons Worcestershire sauce**
- 2 **tablespoons Dijon mustard**
- 2 **tablespoons cider vinegar**
- 1 **tablespoon brown sugar**

CHOPS

- 2 **cups wood chips (see note)**
- 4 **(12-ounce) bone-in rib loin pork chops, 1½ inches thick (see note)**
- 4 **teaspoons kosher salt**
- 2 **teaspoons ground black pepper**

1. FOR THE SAUCE: Bring all the ingredients to a simmer in a small saucepan over medium heat; cook, stirring occasionally, until the sauce reaches a ketchup-like consistency and is reduced to about 1 cup, 5 to 7 minutes. Transfer ½ cup of the sauce to a small bowl and set aside to serve with the cooked chops.

2. FOR THE CHOPS: Soak the wood chips in cold water to cover for 30 minutes; drain. Light a large chimney starter filled with charcoal (about 6 quarts) and allow to burn until the coals are partially covered with a thin layer of ash, about 20 minutes. Place a 13 by 9-inch disposable aluminum pan in the center of the grill. Empty the coals into the grill, creating equal-size piles on each side of the pan. Sprinkle 1 cup of the soaked wood chips on each charcoal pile, set the cooking grate over the coals, cover the grill, and heat the grate until hot and the chips are smoking, about 5 minutes. Use a grill brush to scrape the cooking grate clean.

3. While the grill is heating, pat the chops dry with paper towels. Following the photo on page 156, use a sharp knife to cut two slits about 1 inch apart through the outer layer of fat and connective tissue to prevent buckling. Sprinkle the entire surface of each chop with 1 teaspoon salt and ½ teaspoon pepper. Following the photos, place the chops side by side, facing in the same direction, on a cutting board with the curved rib bone facing down. Pass two skewers through the loin muscle of each chop, close to the bone, about 1 inch from each end. Once the chops have been threaded onto the skewers, pull them apart to create a 1-inch space between each.

4. Place the skewered chops, bone side down, in the center of the grill on the cooking grate, over the aluminum pan. Cover the grill and cook until an instant-read thermometer inserted into the center of a pork chop, but away from any bone, registers 120 degrees, 28 to 32 minutes.

5. Remove the skewers from the chops; tip the chops onto a flat side and brush the surface with 1 tablespoon of the sauce. Transfer the chops, sauce side down, to the hotter parts of the grill (2 on each side) and cook, uncovered, until browned, 2 to 4 minutes. Brush the top of each chop with 1 tablespoon more sauce; flip and continue to cook on the second side until browned and an instant-read thermometer inserted into the center of a pork chop, but away from any bone, registers 140 to 145 degrees, 2 to 4 minutes longer. Remove the chops from the grill and allow to rest, tented with foil, for 5 minutes. Serve, passing the ½ cup reserved sauce separately.

Grill-Smoked Pork Chops for a Gas Grill

You will need a 9-inch disposable aluminum pie plate and skewers for this recipe.

Follow the recipe for Grill-Smoked Pork Chops for a Charcoal Grill through step 1. Place the soaked wood chips in a 9-inch disposable aluminum pie plate and place the plate on the primary burner (the burner that will remain on during barbecuing), then reposition the cooking grate(s). Turn all the burners to high and heat, with the lid down, until hot and the chips are smoking, about 15 minutes. (If the chips ignite, use a water-filled spray bottle to extinguish.) Use a grill brush to scrape the cooking grate clean. Proceed with the recipe from step 3, leaving the primary burner on high, turning off the other burner(s), and cooking with the lid down. Cook the chops on the cooler side of the grill to an internal temperature of 110 degrees, 20 to 25 minutes, and increase the browning time on the hotter side of the grill to 4 to 7 minutes per side.

NOTES FROM THE TEST KITCHEN

SKEWERING PORK CHOPS FOR THE GRILL

1. Pass two skewers through the loin muscle of each chop to provide stability when standing on the grill.

2. Stand the skewered chops, bone side down, on the cooking grate in the center of the grill so smoke can reach all sides.

GRILLED STUFFED PORK TENDERLOIN

WHY THIS RECIPE WORKS: Pork tenderloin has many advantages that make it an ideal candidate for the grill: It's quick cooking, is extremely tender, and has a uniform shape that allows for even cooking. But this cut is also mild and lean, making it prone to drying out. Stuffing this roast solves these problems by adding flavor and moisture. For more surface area for the filling and to help prevent leaks, we pound, fill, then roll the tenderloins. And for our flavor filling, we pulsed bold ingredients—such as olives, sun-dried tomatoes, and porcini mushrooms—in a food processor to produce an intense paste that didn't ooze out. When it came time to fire up the grill, we found that a two-level fire, with the coals spread over half the grill, allowed the pork to cook evenly without drying out. Our last touch was a sprinkling of sugar on the exterior of each tenderloin, which boosted browning significantly.

Charcoal-Grilled Stuffed Pork Tenderloin
SERVES 4 TO 6

- 4 teaspoons packed dark brown sugar
  Kosher salt and ground black pepper
- 2 (1¼ to 1½-pound) pork tenderloins, trimmed
- 1 recipe Olive and Sun-Dried Tomato Stuffing
  (recipe follows)
- 1 cup baby spinach
  Vegetable oil for the cooking grate
- 2 tablespoons olive oil

1. Combine the sugar, 2 teaspoons salt, and 1 teaspoon pepper in a bowl. Cut each tenderloin in half horizontally, stopping ½ inch away from the edge so the halves remain attached. Open up the tenderloins, cover with plastic wrap, and pound to an even ¼-inch thickness. Trim any ragged edges to create a rough rectangle about 10 inches by 6 inches. Sprinkle the interior of each tenderloin with ⅛ teaspoon salt and ⅛ teaspoon pepper.

2. With the long side of the pork facing you, spread half of the stuffing mixture over the bottom half of one tenderloin followed by ½ cup of the spinach. Roll away from you into a tight cylinder, taking care not to squeeze the stuffing out the ends. Position the tenderloin seam side down, evenly space 5 pieces of kitchen twine underneath, and tie.

Repeat with the remaining tenderloin, stuffing, and spinach.

3. Light a large chimney starter filled with charcoal (about 6 quarts) and allow to burn until the top coals are partially covered with ash, about 20 minutes. Build a modified two-level fire by arranging the coals over half of the grill, leaving the other half empty. Set the cooking grate in place, cover, and heat the grill until hot, about 5 minutes. Use a grill brush to scrape the cooking grate clean. Dip a wad of paper towels in vegetable oil; holding the wad with tongs, oil the cooking grate.

4. Coat the pork with the olive oil, then rub the entire surface with the brown sugar mixture. Place the pork on the cooler side of grill, cover, and cook until the center of the stuffing registers 140 degrees on an instant-read thermometer, 25 to 30 minutes, rotating the pork once halfway through cooking.

5. Transfer the pork to a carving board, tent loosely with foil, and let rest for 5 to 10 minutes. Remove the twine, slice the pork into ½-inch-thick slices, and serve.

Gas-Grilled Stuffed Pork Tenderloin

Follow the recipe for Charcoal-Grilled Stuffed Pork Tenderloin through step 2. Turn all the burners to high and heat the grill, with the lid down, until very hot, about 15 minutes. Use a grill brush to scrape the cooking grate clean. Dip a wad of paper towels in vegetable oil; holding the wad with tongs, oil the cooking grate. Proceed with the recipe from step 4, cooking with the lid down.

Olive and Sun-Dried Tomato Stuffing
MAKES ABOUT 1 CUP, ENOUGH FOR 2 TENDERLOINS

- ½ cup pitted kalamata olives
- ½ cup oil-packed sun-dried tomatoes, rinsed and chopped coarse
- 4 anchovy fillets
- 2 medium garlic cloves, minced or pressed through a garlic press (about 2 teaspoons)
- 1 teaspoon minced fresh thyme leaves
- 1 teaspoon grated zest from 1 lemon
  Table salt and ground black pepper

Pulse all the ingredients except the salt and pepper in a food processor until coarsely chopped, 5 to 10 pulses; season with salt and pepper to taste.

GRILLED STUFFED PORK LOIN

WHY THIS RECIPE WORKS: Center-cut pork loin is an especially lean cut, making it difficult to cook without drying out. We wanted to cook our pork loin on the grill but keep it moist using an approach other than traditional brines or sauces. We decided to use a moist, well-seasoned stuffing (and careful cooking) so our grilled pork loin would be juicy and flavorful.

We bought a short and wide roast, more square than cylindrical. This shape only required four straight, short cuts to open to a long, flat sheet that was easy to fill and roll up. The best stuffing required both a deep flavor to counter the pork's rather bland taste and a texture thick enough to stay put. Poaching apples and cranberries in a blend of apple cider, apple cider vinegar, and spices developed a filling with the dense, chewy consistency we wanted. And this process had an added bonus—we had ample poaching liquid left, which could be reduced to a glaze. We had already decided not to give the loin a preliminary sear, which can create a tough exterior, but found we missed the brown color that searing produces. Rolling the loin in our glaze gave it a beautifully burnished finish.

Charcoal-Grilled Pork Loin with Apple-Cranberry Filling

SERVES 6

This recipe is best prepared with a loin that is 7 to 8 inches long and 4 to 5 inches wide. To make cutting the pork easier, freeze it for 30 minutes. If mustard seeds are unavailable, stir an equal amount of whole grain mustard into the filling after the apples have been processed. Use more or less cayenne, depending on how spicy you'd like the stuffing. The pork loin can be stuffed and tied a day ahead of time, but don't season the exterior until you are ready to grill.

FILLING

- 1½ cups packed dried apples
- 1 cup apple cider
- ¾ cup packed light brown sugar
- ½ cup cider vinegar
- ½ cup packed dried cranberries
- 1 large shallot, halved lengthwise and sliced thin crosswise (about ¼ cup)
- 1 tablespoon minced or grated fresh ginger
- 1 tablespoon yellow mustard seeds (see note)
- ½ teaspoon ground allspice
- ⅛–¼ teaspoon cayenne pepper (see note)

PORK

- 2 (3-inch) wood chunks
- 1 (2½-pound) boneless center-cut pork loin roast (see note)
- Table salt and ground black pepper
- Vegetable oil for the cooking grate

1. FOR THE FILLING: Bring all of the ingredients to a simmer in a medium saucepan over medium-high heat. Cover, reduce the heat to low, and cook until the apples are very soft, about 20 minutes. Pour the mixture through a fine-mesh strainer set over a bowl, pressing with the back of a spoon to extract as much liquid as possible. Return the liquid to the saucepan and simmer over medium-high heat until reduced to ⅓ cup, about 5 minutes; reserve the glaze. Meanwhile, pulse the apple mixture in a food processor until uniformly coarsely chopped, about 15 pulses. Transfer the filling to a bowl and refrigerate while preparing the pork.

2. FOR THE PORK: Soak the wood chunks in cold water to cover for 1 hour. Meanwhile, following the photos on page 443, cut the meat to an even ½-inch thickness. Season with salt and spread the apple filling in an even layer, leaving a ½-inch border. Roll tightly and tie with kitchen twine at 1-inch intervals. Season with salt and pepper.

3. Light a large chimney starter filled three-quarters with charcoal (about 4½ quarts) and allow to burn until the coals are partially covered with a layer of ash, about 20 minutes. Build a modified two-level fire by arranging all the coals over half of the grill, leaving the other half empty. Drain the wood chunks and place on the coals. Open the bottom grill vents completely. Set the cooking grate in place, cover, and heat the grate until hot, about 5 minutes. Use a grill brush to scrape the cooking grate clean. Dip a wad of paper towels in oil; holding the wad with tongs, oil the cooking grate.

4. Place the roast, fat side up, on the cool side of the grill. Cover the grill and position the vent, halfway open, over the roast to draw the smoke through the grill. Cook until the thickest part of the roast registers 130 to 135 degrees on an instant-read thermometer, 55 to 70 minutes, flipping the roast once halfway through the cooking time. Brush the roast with half of the reserved glaze; flip and brush with the remaining glaze. (You may need to reheat the glaze briefly to make it spreadable.) Continue to cook until the glaze is glossy and sticky, about 5 minutes longer.

5. Transfer the roast to a carving board, tent loosely with foil, and let rest until the center registers 150 degrees, about 15 minutes. Cut into ½-inch-thick slices, removing the twine as you cut. Serve immediately.

Gas-Grilled Pork Loin with Apple-Cranberry Filling

You will need a disposable aluminum pie plate for this recipe.

Follow the recipe for Charcoal-Grilled Pork Loin with Apple-Cranberry Filling through step 2, substituting 2 cups wood chips for the wood chunks and soaking them in cold water to cover for 30 minutes. Drain the chips and place in a disposable aluminum pie plate. About 20 minutes prior to grilling, place the pie plate on top of the primary burner (the burner that will remain on during cooking). Turn all the burners to high and heat the grill with the lid down, until very hot and the chips are smoking, about 15 minutes. Use a grill brush to scrape the cooking grate clean. Dip a wad of paper towels in oil; holding the wad with tongs, oil the cooking grate. Turn off all the burner(s) except the primary burner. Place the roast, fat side up, on the side opposite the primary burner and proceed with the recipe from step 4.

HOW TO STUFF A PORK LOIN

1. Position the roast fat side up. Insert a knife ½ inch from the bottom of the roast and cut horizontally, stopping ½ inch before the edge. Open up this flap.

2. Cut through the thicker half of the roast about ½ inch from the bottom, stopping about ½ inch before the edge. Open up this flap.

3. Repeat until the pork loin is an even ½-inch thickness throughout. If uneven, cover with plastic wrap and use a meat pounder to even out.

4. With the long side of the meat facing you, season the meat and spread the filling, leaving a ½-inch border on all sides.

5. Starting from the short side, roll the pork loin tightly then tie the roast with kitchen twine at 1-inch intervals.

GRILL-ROASTED PORK LOIN

WHY THIS RECIPE WORKS: When we're looking to dress up an outdoor dinner—and offer guests more than burgers or grilled chicken—we like to serve a juicy, crisp-crusted pork loin. But because the roasts available at the supermarket nowadays are so incredibly lean, this cut of meat can dry out considerably when cooked with the dry heat of the grill. We planned to bring back the juiciness and produce a succulent roast with a deep brown crust and aromatic, smoke-flavored meat.

First, we chose the best cut. Our top choice—the blade-end roast—was moist and flavorful and was the hands-down winner over center-cut, sirloin, and tenderloin roasts. Brining ensured that our finished roast met with rave reviews from testers and stayed juicy and moist, and a generous coating of black pepper—or our own spicy rub—provided ample flavoring. We then used a two-step grilling process, searing the roast directly over hot coals for a nice crust and finishing it over indirect heat, so as not to overcook it. The final step was removing the roast from the grill when the internal temperature was just shy of done, then allowing it to rest until the temperature rose and the meat was juicy and tender.

Grill-Roasted Pork Loin for a Charcoal Grill
SERVES 4 TO 6

We prefer natural to enhanced pork (pork that has been injected with a salt solution to increase moistness and flavor) for this recipe, though enhanced pork can be used. If using enhanced pork, skip the brining in step 1. Instead, simply add 1 tablespoon table salt to the black pepper seasoning.

With minor recipe adjustments, a roast larger than the one called for can be cooked using the same method. For each additional pound of meat over 3 pounds (do not use a roast larger than 6 pounds), increase the salt in the brine by ¼ cup and the water by 1 quart; also increase the olive oil and pepper by 1 teaspoon each (if using a spice rub, increase the recipe by one third). Because the cooking time depends more on the diameter of the loin than on its length, the cooking time for a larger roast will not increase significantly. After rotating the roast in step 5, begin checking the internal temperature after 30 minutes of cooking.

¾ cup table salt (see note)
1 (2½ to 3-pound) boneless blade-end pork loin roast, tied with kitchen twine at 1½-inch intervals (see note)
2 tablespoons olive oil
1 tablespoon ground black pepper or 1 recipe Chili-Mustard Spice Rub (recipe follows)
2 (3-inch) wood chunks
Vegetable oil for the cooking grate

1. Dissolve the salt in 3 quarts water in a large container; submerge the roast, cover with plastic wrap, and refrigerate for 3 to 4 hours. Remove the roast from the brine, rinse under running water, and pat dry with paper towels.

2. Rub the roast with the olive oil, season with the pepper, and press the pepper into the meat. Let stand at room temperature for 1 hour.

3. Meanwhile, soak the wood chunks in cold water to cover for 1 hour; drain. About 25 minutes prior to grilling, open the bottom grill vents. Light a large chimney starter filled three-quarters with charcoal (about 4½ quarts) and allow to burn until the coals are partially covered with a layer of ash, about 20 minutes. Build a modified two-level fire by arranging all the coals over half of the grill, leaving the other half empty. Place the wood chunks on top of the coals. Set the cooking grate in place, cover, and heat the grate until hot, about 5 minutes. Use a grill brush to scrape the cooking grate clean. Dip a wad of paper towels in vegetable oil; holding the wad with tongs, oil the cooking grate.

4. Grill the pork on the hot side of the grill until browned, about 2 minutes; using tongs, rotate one quarter-turn and repeat until all the sides are well browned, about 8 minutes total. Move the loin to the cooler side of the grill, positioning the roast parallel with and as close as possible to the fire. Open the grill lid vents halfway; cover the grill, turning the lid so that the vents are opposite the fire and draw smoke through the grill, and cook for 20 minutes. (The temperature inside the grill should be about 425 degrees.)

5. Uncover and rotate the roast 180 degrees so that the side facing the fire now faces away. Cover and continue to cook until the thickest part of the roast registers 140 to 145 degrees on an instant-read thermometer, 10 to 30 minutes longer, depending on the thickness.

6. Transfer the roast to a carving board, tent loosely with foil, and let rest until the temperature registers 150 degrees, about 15 minutes. Remove the twine, cut the roast into ½-inch-thick slices, and serve.

Grill-Roasted Pork Loin for a Gas Grill

You will need a disposable aluminum pie plate for this recipe.

1. Follow the recipe for Grill-Roasted Pork Loin for a Charcoal Grill through step 2. Substitute 2 cups wood chips for the wood chunks and soak them in cold water to cover for 30 minutes; drain. Place the chips in a disposable aluminum pie plate.

2. About 20 minutes prior to grilling, place the pie plate on top of the primary burner (the burner that will remain on during cooking). Turn all the burners to high and heat the grill with the lid down, until very hot and the chips are smoking, about 15 minutes (if the chips ignite, extinguish the flames with water from a spray bottle). Use a grill brush to scrape the cooking grate clean. Dip a wad of paper towels in vegetable oil; holding the wad with tongs, oil the cooking grate.

3. Continue with the recipe from step 4, turning off all the burner(s) except the primary burner after browning the pork.

Chili-Mustard Spice Rub
MAKES ABOUT 2 TABLESPOONS

This rub packs some heat, so use the lesser amount of cayenne if you want a milder rub.

2 teaspoons chili powder
2 teaspoons dry mustard
1 teaspoon ground cumin
½–1 teaspoon cayenne pepper (see note)

Combine all the ingredients in a small bowl.

GRILLED BONE-IN PORK ROAST

WHY THIS RECIPE WORKS: Grilling a bulky cut of meat like a pork roast may sound difficult, but we found that a tender, quick-cooking center-cut rib roast and a simple salt rub were all that we needed for a juicy grilled roast with a thick mahogany crust. We grilled it over indirect heat (on the cooler side of the grill) so it could cook through slowly, adding a single soaked wood chunk to the fire for a subtle tinge of smoke flavor. After little more than an hour on the grill, our roast was tender and juicy, with plenty of rich, deep flavor. For the perfect counterpoint to the roast's richness, we whipped up a fresh orange salsa with bright citrus and fresh herbs, jalapeño, and a warm touch of cumin.

Charcoal Grill–Roasted Bone-In Pork Rib Roast
SERVES 6 TO 8

If you buy a blade-end roast (sometimes called a "rib-end roast"), tie it into a uniform shape with kitchen twine at 1-inch intervals; this step is unnecessary with a center-cut roast. For easier carving, ask the butcher to remove the tip of the chine bone and to cut the remainder of the chine bone between each rib.

1 (4 to 5-pound) center-cut rib or blade-end bone-in pork roast, tip of chine bone removed, fat trimmed to ¼-inch thickness (see note)
4 teaspoons kosher salt
1 (3-inch) wood chunk
Vegetable oil for the cooking grate
1½ teaspoons ground black pepper
1 recipe Orange Salsa with Cuban Flavors (optional; recipe follows)

1. Pat the roast dry with paper towels. Using a sharp knife, cut slits in the surface fat layer, spaced 1 inch apart, in a crosshatch pattern, being careful not to cut into the meat. Season the roast with the salt. Wrap with plastic wrap and refrigerate for at least 6 hours or up to 24 hours. Soak the wood chunk in cold water to cover for 1 hour; drain.

2. Open the bottom vents halfway. Light a large chimney starter filled with charcoal (about 6 quarts) and allow to burn until the top coals are partially covered with ash, about 20 minutes. Build a single-banked fire by banking the coals over half of the grill, leaving the other half empty. Place the wood chunk on the pile of coals. Set the cooking grate in place, cover, and open the lid vents halfway. Heat the grill until hot and the wood chips are smoking, about 5 minutes. Use a grill brush to scrape the cooking grate clean. Dip a wad of paper towels in oil; holding the wad with tongs, oil the cooking grate.

3. Unwrap the roast and season with the pepper. Place the roast on the grate with the meat near, but not over, the coals and flames and the bones facing away from the coals and flames. Cover, positioning the lid vents over the meat, and cook until the meat registers 140 degrees on an instant-read thermometer, 1¼ to 1½ hours.

4. Transfer the roast to a carving board, tent loosely with aluminum foil, and let rest for 30 minutes. Carve into thick slices by cutting between the ribs. Serve, passing the salsa separately.

Gas Grilled–Roasted Bone-In Pork Rib Roast

Follow the recipe for Charcoal Grill–Roasted Bone-In Pork Rib Roast through step 1, substituting 1 cup wood chips for the wood chunk. Soak the wood chips in cold water to cover for 15 minutes; drain. Using a large piece of heavy-duty aluminum foil, wrap the soaked chips in a foil packet and cut several vent holes in the top. Place the wood chip packet over the primary burner. Turn all the burners to high and heat the grill, with the lid down, until very hot and the wood chips are smoking, about 15 minutes. Use a grill brush to scrape the cooking grate clean. Dip a wad of paper towels in oil; holding the wad with tongs, oil the cooking grate. Proceed with the recipe from step 3, cooking with the lid down and adjusting the primary burner as needed during cooking to maintain the grill temperature around 350 degrees.

Orange Salsa with Cuban Flavors

MAKES ABOUT 2½ CUPS
To make this salsa spicier, add the reserved chile seeds.

- ½ teaspoon grated zest from 1 orange, plus 5 oranges peeled and segmented; each segment quartered crosswise
- ½ cup minced red onion
- 1 jalapeño chile, stemmed, seeds reserved, and minced (see note)
- 2 tablespoons juice from 1 lime
- 2 tablespoons minced fresh parsley leaves
- 1 tablespoon extra-virgin olive oil
- 2 teaspoons packed brown sugar

- 1½ teaspoons distilled white vinegar
- 1½ teaspoons minced fresh oregano leaves
- 1 medium garlic clove, minced or pressed through a garlic press (about 1 teaspoon)
- ½ teaspoon ground cumin
- ½ teaspoon table salt
- ½ teaspoon ground black pepper

Combine all the ingredients in a medium bowl.

PULLED PORK

WHY THIS RECIPE WORKS: Pulled pork is classic summertime party food: slow-cooked pork roast, shredded and seasoned, served on the most basic of hamburger buns (or sliced white bread), with just enough of your favorite barbecue sauce, a couple of dill pickle chips, and a topping of coleslaw. However, many barbecue procedures demand the regular attention of the cook for eight hours or more. We wanted to find a way to make moist, fork-tender pulled pork without the marathon cooking time and constant attention to the grill.

After testing shoulder roasts (also called Boston butt), fresh ham, and picnic roasts, we determined that the shoulder roast, which has the most fat, retained the most moisture and flavor during a long, slow cook. We massaged a spicy chili rub into the meat, then wrapped the roast in plastic wrap and refrigerated it for at least three hours to "marinate." The roast is first cooked on the grill to absorb smoky flavor (from wood chips—no smoker required), then finished in the oven. Finally, we let the pork rest in a paper bag so the meat would steam and any remaining collagen would break down, allowing the flavorful juices to be reabsorbed. We also developed a pair of sauce recipes to please barbecue fans with different tastes.

Barbecued Pulled Pork for a Charcoal Grill

SERVES 8
Pulled pork can be made with a fresh ham or picnic roast, although our preference is for Boston butt. If using a fresh ham or picnic roast, remove the skin by cutting through it with the tip of a chef's knife; slide the blade just under the skin and work around to loosen it while pulling it off with your other hand. Boston butt, or shoulder roast, does not need to be trimmed. Preparing pulled pork requires little effort but lots of time. Plan on 10 hours from start to finish: three hours with the spice rub, one hour to come to room temperature, three hours on the grill, two hours

in the oven, and one hour to rest. Wood chunks help flavor the meat; hickory is the traditional choice with pork, although mesquite can be used if desired. Serve the pulled pork on plain white bread or warmed buns with the classic accompaniments of dill pickle chips and coleslaw. You will need a 13 by 9-inch disposable aluminum pan as well as heavy-duty aluminum foil and a brown paper grocery bag for this recipe.

¾ cup Dry Rub for Barbecue (recipe follows)
1 (6 to 8-pound) bone-in pork roast, preferably Boston butt (see note)
4 (3-inch) wood chunks (see note)
   Vegetable oil for the cooking grate
2 cups barbecue sauce (recipes follow)

1. Massage the dry rub into the meat. Wrap the meat tightly in a double layer of plastic wrap and refrigerate for at least 3 hours. (For stronger flavor, the roast can be refrigerated for up to 3 days.)

2. At least 1 hour prior to cooking, remove the roast from the refrigerator, unwrap, and let it come to room temperature. Soak the wood chunks in cold water to cover for 1 hour and drain.

3. Meanwhile, light a large chimney starter filled halfway with charcoal (about 3 quarts) and allow to burn until the coals are partially covered with a layer of ash. Build a modified two-level fire by arranging all the coals over half of the grill, leaving the other half empty. Open the bottom grill vents completely. Place the wood chunks on the coals. Set the cooking grate in place, cover, and heat the grate until hot, about 5 minutes. Use a grill brush to scrape the cooking grate clean. Dip a wad of paper towels in oil; holding the wad with tongs, oil the cooking grate.

4. Set the unwrapped roast in a 13 by 9-inch disposable aluminum pan and place it on the grate opposite the coals. Open the grill lid vents three-quarters of the way and cover, turning the lid so that the vents are opposite the wood chunks to draw smoke through the grill. Cook, adding about eight briquettes every hour or so to maintain an average temperature of 275 degrees, for 3 hours.

5. Adjust an oven rack to the middle position and heat the oven to 325 degrees. Wrap the pan holding the roast with heavy-duty foil to cover completely. Place the pan in the oven and cook until the meat is fork-tender, about 2 hours.

6. Carefully slide the foil-wrapped pan with the roast into a brown paper bag. Crimp the end shut. Let rest for 1 hour.

7. Transfer the roast to a carving board and unwrap. When cool enough to handle, separate the roast into muscle sections, removing the fat, if desired, and tearing the meat into shreds with your fingers. Place the shredded meat in a large bowl. Toss with 1 cup of the barbecue sauce, adding more to taste. Serve, passing the remaining sauce separately.

Barbecued Pulled Pork for a Gas Grill

You will need a disposable aluminum pie plate as well as a 10 by 8-inch disposable aluminum pan for this recipe.

1. Follow the recipe for Barbecued Pulled Pork for a Charcoal Grill through step 2, substituting 4 cups wood chips for the wood chunks and soaking them in cold water to cover for 30 minutes. Drain the chips and place in a disposable aluminum pie plate.

2. Place the pie plate on the primary burner (the burner that will remain on during cooking). Turn all the burners to high and heat the grill with the lid down, until very hot and the chips are smoking heavily, about 20 minutes (if the chips ignite, use a water-filled spray bottle to extinguish). Use a grill brush to scrape the cooking grate clean. Dip a wad of paper towels in oil; holding the wad with tongs, oil the cooking grate. Turn the primary burner down to medium and turn off the other burner(s). Set the unwrapped roast in a 10 by 8-inch disposable aluminum pan, position the pan over the cooler side of the grill, close the lid, and cook for 3 hours. (The temperature inside the grill should be 275 degrees; adjust the lit burner as necessary.) Proceed as directed from step 5 of the recipe.

Dry Rub for Barbecue

MAKES ABOUT 1 CUP

You can adjust the proportions of spices in this all-purpose rub or add or subtract a spice, as you wish. For instance, if you don't like spicy foods, reduce the cayenne. Or, if you are using hot chili powder, eliminate the cayenne entirely.

4 tablespoons sweet paprika
2 tablespoons chili powder
2 tablespoons ground cumin
2 tablespoons dark brown sugar
2 tablespoons table salt
1 tablespoon dried oregano
1 tablespoon granulated sugar
1 tablespoon ground black pepper
1 tablespoon ground white pepper
1–2 teaspoons cayenne pepper

Combine all the ingredients in a small bowl.

Eastern North Carolina Barbecue Sauce

MAKES ABOUT 2 CUPS

- 1 cup distilled white vinegar
- 1 cup cider vinegar
- 1 tablespoon sugar
- 1 tablespoon red pepper flakes
- 1 tablespoon hot sauce
  Table salt and ground black pepper

Mix all the ingredients with salt and pepper to taste together in a medium bowl. (The sauce can be refrigerated in an airtight container for up to 4 days.)

Mid-South Carolina Mustard Sauce

MAKES ABOUT 2½ CUPS

- 1 cup cider vinegar
- 1 cup vegetable oil
- 6 tablespoons Dijon mustard
- 2 tablespoons maple syrup or honey
- 4 teaspoons Worcestershire sauce
- 2 teaspoons table salt
- 1 teaspoon hot sauce
  Ground black pepper

Mix all the ingredients with pepper to taste together in a medium bowl. (The sauce can be refrigerated in an airtight container for up to 4 days.)

KANSAS CITY RIBS

WHY THIS RECIPE WORKS: Kansas City ribs are slow-smoked pork ribs slathered in a sauce so thick, sweet, and sticky that you need a case of wet naps to get your hands clean after eating them. But authentic ribs can take all day to prepare. We knew we could come up with a faster method for Kansas City ribs—one that would produce the same fall-off-the-bone, tender smoky meat of the long-cooked original recipe.

We quickly learned that spareribs, which are well marbled with fat, produce moist, tender ribs, but some racks are so big they barely fit on the grill. We turned to a more manageable cut, referred to as "St. Louis" ribs, which is a narrower, rectangular rack that offers all the taste of whole spareribs without any of the trouble. A spice rub added flavor and encouraged a savory crust on the meat.

We barbecued the ribs, covered with foil, over indirect heat for four hours—the foil traps some of the steam over the meat, so that it cooks up tender, not dry. Using wood chips on the grill imparts the meat with great smoky flavor. For sticky, saucy ribs, we brushed the ribs all over with barbecue sauce during the last hour of cooking, then cooked them until they were tender and falling off the bone.

Kansas City Sticky Ribs for a Charcoal Grill

SERVES 4 TO 6

Buy St. Louis–style racks, which are more manageable than untrimmed pork ribs. If you can find only whole spareribs, use the biggest grill possible and be prepared to increase the cooking time significantly. We prefer our sauce recipe but store-bought works, too. You will need a 13 by 9-inch disposable aluminum pan for this recipe. Serve with Smoky Kansas City Barbecue Beans (recipe follows).

- 3 tablespoons paprika
- 2 tablespoons light brown sugar
- 1 tablespoon ground black pepper
- 1 tablespoon table salt
- ¼ teaspoon cayenne pepper
- 2 full racks pork spareribs, preferably St. Louis cut, trimmed of large pieces of excess fat and membrane removed (see note and step 1 on page 452)
- 2 cups wood chips
  Vegetable oil for the cooking grate
- 2 cups Kansas City Barbecue Sauce (see note; recipe follows)

1. Combine the paprika, sugar, black pepper, salt, and cayenne in a small bowl. Pat the rib racks dry with paper towels and massage the spice rub into both sides.

2. Soak the wood chips in cold water to cover for 30 minutes; drain. Open the bottom grill vents. Light a large chimney starter filled three-quarters with charcoal (about 4½ quarts) and allow to burn until the coals are partially covered with a layer of ash, about 20 minutes. Arrange a 13 by 9-inch disposable aluminum pan on one side of the grill and build a single-banked fire by steeply banking all the coals on the opposite side. Sprinkle 1 cup of the wood chips over the coals. Set the cooking grate in place, cover, and heat the grate until hot, about 5 minutes. Use a grill brush to scrape the cooking grate clean. Dip a wad of paper towels in oil; holding the wad with tongs, oil the cooking grate. Place the ribs over the pan.

3. Place a sheet of foil on top of the ribs and cover the grill, positioning the lid vents, three-quarters open, directly over the ribs. Cook until the coals are almost spent, about 2 hours, turning and rotating the ribs once halfway through the cooking time.

4. About 20 minutes before the coals are spent, light the chimney starter filled again three-quarters with charcoal (about 4½ quarts) and allow to burn until the coals are partially covered with a layer of ash, about 20 minutes. Place the hot coals from the chimney on top of the spent coals and sprinkle the remaining 1 cup wood chips over the coals. Turn and rotate the ribs and cook, covered, about 1 hour. Brush the ribs on both sides with the sauce, wrap tightly with foil, and cook until tender, about 1 hour.

5. Transfer the ribs (still in the foil) to a cutting board and let rest for 30 minutes. Unwrap the ribs and brush with additional barbecue sauce. Slice the ribs between the bones and serve with the remaining sauce.

Kansas City Sticky Ribs for a Gas Grill

You will need a disposable aluminum pie plate for this recipe.

Follow step 1 of Kansas City Sticky Ribs for a Charcoal Grill. Soak the wood chips in cold water to cover for 30 minutes; drain. Place the wood chips in a disposable aluminum pie plate. Place the pie plate on top of the primary burner (the burner that will remain on during cooking). Turn all the burners to high and heat the grill, with the lid down, until very hot and the chips are smoking heavily, about 20 minutes. Use a grill brush to scrape the cooking grate clean. Dip a wad of paper towels in oil; holding the wad with tongs, oil the cooking grate. Turn the primary burner to medium and turn off the other burner(s). (The temperature inside the grill should be about 275 degrees; adjust the lit burner as necessary.) Place the ribs on the cooler part of the grill and cook as directed, omitting the disposable aluminum pan, in step 3. Brush the ribs and wrap in foil as directed in step 4, then continue as directed.

Easiest Kansas City Sticky Ribs

Not keen on tending a grill for four hours? Our ribs will taste good even if they spend the last two hours of cooking in your oven.

Follow the recipe for Kansas City Sticky Ribs for a Gas or Charcoal Grill through step 3. Wrap the ribs tightly in foil, place on a rimmed baking sheet, and bake in a 250-degree oven for 1 hour. Remove from the oven, brush both sides with the barbecue sauce, rewrap with foil, and bake until tender, about 1 hour. Proceed as directed in step 5.

Kansas City Barbecue Sauce

MAKES ABOUT 4 CUPS

Kansas City barbecue sauce is a sweet, smoky, sticky, and thick tomato-based sauce. This style of sauce is the model for most bottled brands, including KC Masterpiece. We like our barbecue sauce extra-thick. If you like a thinner, smoother texture, the sauce can be strained after it has finished cooking.

- **2** teaspoons vegetable oil
- **1** medium onion, minced
- **4** cups low-sodium chicken broth
- **1** cup root beer
- **1** cup cider vinegar
- **1** cup dark corn syrup
- **½** cup molasses
- **½** cup tomato paste
- **½** cup ketchup
- **2** tablespoons brown mustard
- **1** tablespoon hot sauce
- **½** teaspoon garlic powder
- **¼** teaspoon liquid smoke (optional)

Heat the oil in a saucepan over medium-high heat until shimmering. Add the onion and cook until softened, about 5 minutes. Whisk in the remaining ingredients, except for the liquid smoke, and bring to a boil. Reduce the heat to medium and simmer until the mixture is thick and has reduced to 4 cups, about 1 hour. Stir in the liquid smoke, if using. (The sauce can be refrigerated in an airtight container for up to 1 week.)

Smoky Kansas City Barbecue Beans
SERVES 4 TO 6

This recipe is meant for a charcoal grill. If you're cooking on a gas grill, omit step 3 and finish cooking the beans in a 300-degree oven for 2 to 2½ hours. We prefer our sauce recipe but store-bought works, too. You will need a 13 by 9-inch disposable aluminum pan for this recipe.

- 4 ounces (about 4 slices) bacon, chopped fine
- 1 medium onion, minced
- 4 medium garlic cloves, minced or pressed through a garlic press (about 4 teaspoons)
- 1 pound dried pinto beans, picked over, rinsed, and soaked overnight
- 6 cups water
- 1 cup Kansas City Barbecue Sauce (see note; see page 449)
- ⅓ cup packed light brown sugar
- 2 tablespoons brown mustard
- 1 teaspoon hot sauce
  Table salt

NOTES FROM THE TEST KITCHEN

MAKING BEANS ON THE GRILL
Our barbecue beans finish cooking on the grill, where they pick up smoke and pork flavors. Here's how to let the flavors in and keep the grease out.

1. Transfer the precooked beans to a 13 by 9-inch disposable aluminum pan. Wrap tightly in foil and poke several holes in the foil so that the juices from the ribs can flavor the beans.

2. When you're ready to add more coals, nestle the beans in the pan already on the bottom of the grill. Replace the cooking grate, making sure to position the ribs directly above the beans.

---

1. Cook the bacon in a Dutch oven over medium heat until beginning to crisp, about 5 minutes. Add the onion and cook until softened, about 5 minutes. Add the garlic and cook until fragrant, about 30 seconds. Add the beans and water and bring to a simmer. Reduce the heat to medium-low, cover, and cook until the beans are just softened, about 1 hour.

2. Stir in ½ cup of the barbecue sauce, the brown sugar, mustard, hot sauce, and 2 teaspoons salt and simmer, uncovered, over medium-low heat until the beans are tender and the sauce is slightly thickened, about 1 hour. (If the mixture becomes too thick, add water.) Transfer the beans to a 13 by 9-inch disposable aluminum pan and wrap tightly with aluminum foil. Using a paring knife or skewer, poke holes in the foil.

3. In step 4 of Kansas City Sticky Ribs for a Charcoal Grill on page 448, when new coals are added, nestle the pan with the beans inside the disposable pan already in the grill. Replace the cooking grate and position the ribs directly above the beans. Cover the grill and cook until the beans are smoky and completely tender, about 2 hours. Discard the foil, stir in the remaining ½ cup barbecue sauce, and season with salt to taste. Serve.

MEMPHIS DRY RUBBED PORK RIBS

WHY THIS RECIPE WORKS: Memphis pit masters pride themselves on their all-day barbecued pork ribs with a dark bark-like crust and distinctive chew. Up for a challenge, we decided to come up with our own version, but one that wouldn't involve tending a grill all day.

After failing to grill the ribs in a reasonable amount of time (less than seven hours), we opted for a grill-to-oven approach. We started first with the grill. For a fire that would maintain the key amount of indirect heat (roughly 250 to 275 degrees), we turned to a modified two-level fire where the hot coals are arranged over half the grill. To avoid the constant dance of lifting the lid to add more charcoal to keep the heat stabilized, we mounded coals we'd burned for 15 minutes in a chimney starter on top of unlit coals—a trick that would allow us to extend the life of the flame without opening the grill. In addition, we stowed a pan of water underneath the cooking grate on the cooler side of the grill, where it would absorb heat and work to keep the temperature stable, as well as help keep the meat moister. Then we transferred the ribs to a wire rack set over a rimmed baking sheet and cooked them in a moderate oven until tender and thick-crusted.

We even mimicked our grill setup by pouring 1½ cups water into the rimmed baking sheet. In all, we'd shaved more than three hours off of our shortest recipe.

Finally, because dry rub ribs are more exacting and have a very small window during which they are perfectly cooked (compared to the more forgiving wet ribs), we used an instant-read thermometer—once the thickest section of the ribs reached 195 degrees, the meat was tender and boasted a satisfying chew.

Memphis-Style Barbecued Spareribs for a Charcoal Grill

SERVES 4 TO 6

Pouring lit briquettes over unlit briquettes provides the low, steady heat necessary for effective smoking. To maintain a constant temperature, manipulate the upper and lower vents of your grill and do not remove the lid any more than necessary. For less spiciness, reduce the cayenne to ½ teaspoon. You will need a 13 by 9-inch disposable aluminum pan for this recipe.

RUB

- 2 tablespoons sweet paprika
- 2 tablespoons light brown sugar
- 1 tablespoon table salt
- 2 teaspoons chili powder
- 1½ teaspoons ground black pepper
- 1½ teaspoons garlic powder
- 1½ teaspoons onion powder
- 1½ teaspoons cayenne pepper (see note)
- ½ teaspoon dried thyme

RIBS

- 2 racks St. Louis-style spareribs, 2½ to 3 pounds each
- ½ cup wood chips
- ½ cup apple juice
- 3 tablespoons apple cider vinegar

1. Combine the rub ingredients in a small bowl. Place the racks on a rimmed baking sheet; sprinkle the rub on both sides of each rack, rubbing and pressing to adhere. Set the racks aside while preparing the grill.

2. Soak the wood chips in cold water to cover for 30 minutes; drain. Combine the apple juice and vinegar in a small bowl; set aside. Open the top and bottom vents halfway and arrange 15 unlit charcoal briquettes evenly on one side of the grill. Place a 13 by 9-inch disposable aluminum pan filled with 1 inch of water on the other side of the grill. Light a large chimney starter filled one-third with charcoal (about 33 briquettes) and allow to burn until the coals are

half coated with a thin layer of ash, about 15 minutes. Empty the coals into the grill on top of the unlit briquettes to cover half of the grill. Sprinkle the soaked wood chips over the coals. Set the cooking grate over the coals, cover the grill, and heat the grate until hot, about 5 minutes. Use a grill brush to scrape the cooking grate clean.

3. Place the ribs, meat side down, on the grate over the water pan. Cover the grill, positioning the top vent over the ribs to draw smoke through the grill. Cook the ribs for 45 minutes, adjusting the vents to keep the temperature inside the grill at 250 to 275 degrees. Flip the ribs meat side up, turn 180 degrees, and switch their positions so that the rack that was nearest the fire is on the outside. Brush each rack with 2 tablespoons of the apple juice mixture; cover the grill and cook another for 45 minutes. About 15 minutes before removing the ribs from the grill, adjust an oven rack to the middle position and heat the oven to 300 degrees.

4. Transfer the ribs, meat side up, to a wire rack set over a rimmed baking sheet; pour 1½ cups water into the bottom of the baking sheet. Brush the top of each rack with 2 tablespoons more apple juice mixture; roast for 1 hour. Brush the ribs with the remaining apple juice mixture and continue to roast until the meat is tender but not falling off the bone and the thickest part of the roast registers 195 to 200 degrees on an instant-read thermometer. Transfer the ribs to a carving board, tent loosely with foil, and let rest for 15 minutes. Cut the ribs between the bones to separate and serve.

Memphis-Style Barbecued Spareribs for a Gas Grill

If using a small two-burner gas grill, it may be necessary to cut each rack in half crosswise between the bones and use a foil shield to protect the ribs from the direct heat of the primary burner: Place a 24-inch length of heavy-duty foil down the center of the grill. Place the halved racks over the cool side of the grill, perpendicular to the cooking grates, so that they cover about half of the foil. Lift up the foil to shield the ribs. You will need two 9-inch disposable aluminum pie plates for this recipe.

Follow the recipe for Memphis-Style Barbecued Spareribs for a Charcoal Grill through step 1, increasing the amount of wood chips to ¾ cup. Place the soaked chips in a 9-inch disposable aluminum pie plate with ¼ cup of water and set on the primary burner of a gas grill. Place a second 9-inch disposable aluminum pie plate filled with 1 inch of water on the other burner(s). Set the cooking grates over the burners. Turn all the burners to high and heat the grill, with the lid down, until very hot, about 15 minutes. Turn the primary burner to medium-high and turn off the other burner(s). Use a grill brush to scrape the grate clean. Proceed with the recipe from step 3, maintaining a grill temperature of 250 to 275 degrees by adjusting the heat of the primary burner.

RAINY DAY BARBECUED RIBS

WHY THIS RECIPE WORKS: When the craving for barbecued ribs strikes in the dead of winter, you're out of luck unless you visit the local rib joint. There are recipes for oven barbecuing, but the smoke-flavored sauce they use is no substitute for actual smoke. We wanted the real thing, but prepared indoors.

St. Louis–style ribs, trimmed of skirt meat and excess cartilage, work best here. We started with a spice rub as we would for grilling, and found that a thin coating of mustard, ketchup, and garlic helped the rub adhere. We tried wood chips in a stovetop smoker, but we had difficulty fitting the ribs in the pan, and it's hard to find wood chips in wintertime—however, the smoke-filled kitchen was the clincher. We gave up on wood chips and instead borrowed a Chinese cooking method of smoking over tea leaves. Lapsang Souchong tea, which has a smoky flavor, worked perfectly when ground fine. Chilling the ribs first helped prevent toughening in the oven's initial high heat. Apple juice, a common ingredient in barbecue "mops," added moisture and more flavor. And running the ribs under the broiler at the end browned and crisped them. These tender, smoky, and spicy ribs taste amazingly like those barbecued on the grill, but can be made any time of the year.

Oven-Barbecued Spareribs
SERVES 4

To make this recipe, you will need a baking stone, a sturdy baking sheet with a 1-inch rim, and a wire rack that fits inside it. It's fine if the ribs overlap slightly on the rack. In step 1, removing the surface fat keeps the ribs from being too greasy. And removing the membrane from the ribs allows the smoke to penetrate both sides of the racks and also makes the ribs easier to eat. Note that the ribs must be coated with the rub and refrigerated at least 8 hours or up to 24 hours ahead of cooking. Be careful when opening the crimped foil to add the juice, as hot steam and smoke will billow out. If desired, serve the ribs with Quick Barbecue Sauce (recipe follows) or your favorite store-bought brand (and for information on the test kitchen favorite, Bull's-Eye Original, see page 735).

RIBS
- 2 (2½ to 3-pound) racks St. Louis–style spareribs
- ¼ cup finely ground Lapsang Souchong tea (from about 10 tea bags, or ½ cup loose tea leaves ground to a powder in a spice grinder)
- ½ cup apple juice

RUB
- 6 tablespoons yellow mustard
- 2 tablespoons ketchup
- 3 medium garlic cloves, minced or pressed through a garlic press (about 1 tablespoon)
- 3 tablespoons brown sugar
- 1 tablespoon sweet paprika
- 1 tablespoon chili powder
- 2 teaspoons ground black pepper
- ¾ teaspoon table salt
- ½ teaspoon cayenne pepper

1. FOR THE RIBS: Using a sharp knife, trim any surface fat from both racks. To remove the membrane (the thin white sheath that lines the concave side of the rack), insert a spoon handle between the membrane and the ribs of one rack to loosen slightly. Using a paper towel, grasp the loosened membrane and pull away gently to remove. Repeat with the second rack.

2. FOR THE RUB: Combine the mustard, ketchup, and garlic in a small bowl; combine the sugar, paprika, chili powder, black pepper, salt, and cayenne in a separate small bowl. Spread the mustard mixture in a thin, even layer over both sides of the ribs and coat both sides with the spice mixture, then wrap the ribs in plastic wrap and refrigerate for at least 8 hours or up to 24 hours.

3. Transfer the ribs from the refrigerator to the freezer for 45 minutes. Adjust one oven rack to the lowest position and the second rack to the upper-middle position (at least 5 inches below the broiler). Place the baking stone on the lower rack and heat the oven to 500 degrees. Sprinkle the ground tea evenly over the bottom of the rimmed baking sheet and set the wire rack on the sheet. Place the ribs, meat side up, on the rack and cover with heavy-duty foil, crimping the edges tightly to seal. Set the baking sheet with the ribs directly on the stone and roast for 30 minutes, then reduce the oven temperature to 250 degrees, leaving the oven door open for 1 minute to cool. While the oven is open, carefully open one corner of the foil and pour the apple juice into the bottom of the baking sheet; reseal the foil. Continue to roast until the meat is very tender and begins to pull away from the bones, about 1½ hours. (Begin to check the ribs after 1 hour; leave loosely covered with foil for the remaining cooking time.)

4. Remove the foil, carefully flip the racks bone side up, and place the baking sheet on the upper-middle oven rack. Turn on the broiler and cook the ribs until well browned and crispy in spots, 5 to 10 minutes. Flip the ribs meat side up and cook until well browned and crispy, 5 to 7 minutes more. Cool for at least 10 minutes before cutting into individual ribs. Serve with barbecue sauce, if desired.

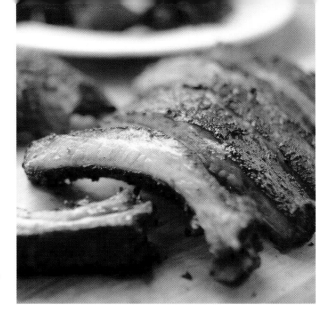

Quick Barbecue Sauce

MAKES ABOUT 1½ CUPS

Classic barbecue sauce must simmer for a long time for the whole tomatoes in it to break down. However, we found that starting with ketchup can shorten the process.

> 1 medium onion, peeled and quartered
> ¼ cup water
> 1 cup ketchup
> 5 tablespoons molasses
> 2 tablespoons cider vinegar
> 2 tablespoons Worcestershire sauce
> 2 tablespoons Dijon mustard
> 1½ teaspoons liquid smoke (optional)
> 1 teaspoon hot sauce
> ¼ teaspoon ground black pepper
> 2 tablespoons vegetable oil
> 1 medium garlic clove, minced or pressed through a garlic press (about 1 teaspoon)
> 1 teaspoon chili powder
> ¼ teaspoon cayenne pepper

1. Process the onion with the water in a food processor until pureed and the mixture resembles slush, about 30 seconds. Strain the mixture through a fine-mesh strainer into a liquid measuring cup, pressing on the solids with a rubber spatula to obtain ½ cup juice. Discard the solids.

2. Whisk the onion juice, ketchup, molasses, vinegar, Worcestershire sauce, mustard, liquid smoke (if using), hot sauce, and black pepper together in a medium bowl.

3. Heat the oil in a large nonreactive saucepan over medium heat until shimmering but not smoking. Add the garlic, chili powder, and cayenne and cook until fragrant, about 30 seconds. Whisk in the ketchup mixture and bring to a boil; reduce the heat to medium-low and simmer gently, uncovered, until the flavors meld and the sauce is thickened, about 25 minutes. Cool the sauce to room temperature before using. (The sauce can be refrigerated in an airtight container for up to 1 week.)

BARBECUED BABY BACK RIBS

WHY THIS RECIPE WORKS: Dry, flavorless ribs are a true culinary disaster. More often than not, baby back ribs cooked at home come out tasting like dry shoe leather on a bone. We wanted ribs that were juicy, tender, and fully seasoned, with an intense smokiness, ribs that would be well worth the time, money, and effort.

Meaty ribs—racks as close to 2 pounds as possible—provided substantial, satisfying portions. For ribs that are so good and moist they don't even need barbecue sauce, they must be brined first—we used a salt, sugar, and water solution—then rubbed with a spice mix before barbecuing. Chili powder, cayenne pepper, cumin, and dark brown sugar formed a nice, crisp crust on the ribs and provided the best balance of sweet and spicy. For even more flavor, we piled wood chunks on top of the coals before barbecuing and used the "low and slow" cooking method: Barbecue the ribs for a few hours on the cool side of the grill, then add fresh briquettes to the coals and continue to cook for another hour or two. This extended amount of time on the grill made for tender baby back ribs with an intensely smoky flavor.

Barbecued Baby Back Ribs for a Charcoal Grill

SERVES 4

For a more potent spice flavor, you can brine and dry the ribs as directed, then coat them with the spice rub and refrigerate them overnight, wrapped tightly in plastic wrap, before grilling.

> Table salt
> ½ cup sugar
> 2 (2-pound) racks baby back or loin back ribs, membrane removed

2   (3-inch) wood chunks
1   tablespoon plus ½ teaspoon sweet paprika
1¾ teaspoons ground cumin
1½ teaspoons chili powder
1½ teaspoons dark brown sugar
¾   teaspoon dried oregano
¾   teaspoon ground black pepper
1   teaspoon ground white pepper
½   teaspoon cayenne pepper
    Vegetable oil for the cooking grate

1. Dissolve ½ cup salt and the sugar in 4 quarts cold water in a large bowl or container. Submerge the ribs in the brine, cover with plastic wrap, and refrigerate for 1 hour. Remove the ribs from the brine, rinse under running water, and pat dry with paper towels. Soak the wood chunks in cold water to cover for 1 hour; drain.

2. Combine the paprika, cumin, chili powder, brown sugar, ¾ teaspoon salt, oregano, black pepper, white pepper, and cayenne in a small bowl. Rub each rack with 1 tablespoon of the spice rub and refrigerate for 30 minutes.

3. Light a large chimney starter filled three-quarters with charcoal (about 4½ quarts) and allow to burn until the coals are partially covered with a layer of ash, about 20 minutes. Build a modified two-level fire by arranging all the coals over half of the grill, leaving the other half empty. Place the wood chunks on top of the coals. Open the bottom grill vents. Set the cooking grate in place, cover, and heat the grate until hot, about 5 minutes. Use a grill brush to scrape the cooking grate clean. Dip a wad of paper towels in oil; holding the wad with tongs, oil the cooking grate.

4. Place the ribs on the cooler side of the grill parallel to the fire. Cover the grill so that the vents are opposite the fire and draw smoke through the grill (the temperature inside the grill should be about 350 degrees, but will start to fall). Cook, flipping the rib racks, switching their position so the rack that was nearest the fire is on the outside, and turning the racks 180 degrees every 30 minutes, for about 2 hours (the temperature inside the grill should be about 250 degrees); add 10 fresh briquettes to the coals. Continue to cook (the temperature inside the grill should be 275 to 300 degrees), flipping, switching, and rotating the ribs every 30 minutes, until the meat easily pulls away from the bone, 1½ to 2 hours longer. Transfer the ribs to a carving board, slice between the bones, and serve.

Barbecued Baby Back Ribs for a Gas Grill

Barbecued Baby Back Ribs for a Gas Grill

You will need a disposable aluminum pie plate for this recipe.

1. Follow the recipe for Barbecued Baby Back Ribs for a Charcoal Grill through step 2, substituting 2 cups wood chips for the wood chunks. Soak the wood chips in cold water to cover for 30 minutes; drain. Place the chips in a disposable aluminum pie plate and place the pie plate on top of the primary burner (the burner that will remain on during cooking). Turn all the burners to high and heat the grill with the lid down, until very hot and the chips are smoking heavily, about 20 minutes (if the chips ignite, extinguish the flames with water from a spray bottle). Use a grill brush to scrape the cooking grate clean. Dip a wad of paper towels in oil; holding the wad with tongs, oil the cooking grate. Turn off all the burner(s) except the primary burner.

2. Place the ribs on the cooler side of the grill and cover (the temperature inside the grill should be about 275 degrees; adjust the lit burner as necessary). Cook until the meat easily pulls away from bone, flipping the racks, switching their position so that the rack that was nearest the fire is on the outside, and turning the racks 180 degrees every 30 minutes, about 4 hours. Transfer the ribs to a carving board, slice between the bones, and serve.

TEXAS BEEF RIBS

WHY THIS RECIPE WORKS: In Texas, good beef ribs are all about intense meat flavor—not just smoke and spice. The barbecue chefs we've met get this flavor just right, thanks to the assistance of massive electric smokers with automated temperature controls. But can a backyard cook replicate this Lone Star classic without the help of special equipment? We were looking for a recipe that would yield potent meat flavor with a bit of honest Texas chew—on our conventional-size grill.

We began by debating whether to trim the fatty membrane that runs along the back side of the ribs. Surprisingly, the juiciest meat with the most flavor was accomplished by the path of least resistance: simply leaving the membrane in place. The fat not only bastes the ribs as they cook but also renders to a crisp, bacon-like texture. A simple mixture of salt, pepper, cayenne, and chili powder rubbed into each rack was all that it took to bring out the flavor of the meat. To turn our grill into a backyard smoker, we made a slow, even fire with a single pile of coals on one side of the grill and kept the temperature in the range of 250 to 300 degrees. A couple of hours of slow cooking were enough to render some of the fat and make the ribs juicy, tender, and slightly toothy. When cooked any longer, as is the case with pork ribs, the meat disintegrates into messy shreds, taking on a sticky, pot-roasted sort of texture that any real Texan would immediately reject.

For real Texas-style barbecue sauce to pair with our ribs, we pulled together the usual ingredients—vinegar, onion, and molasses, to name a few—with dry mustard and chipotle chiles for spiciness. Savory Worcestershire sauce added depth while tomato juice (in place of ketchup) provided tangy flavor and helped thin the sauce out.

Texas-Style Barbecued Beef Ribs for a Charcoal Grill

SERVES 4

It is important to use beef ribs with a decent amount of meat, not bony scraps; otherwise, the rewards of making this recipe are few. For the wood chunks, use any type of wood but mesquite, which can have an overpowering smokiness. Except when adding coals, do not lift the grill lid, which will allow both smoke and heat to escape.

    4   teaspoons chili powder
    2   teaspoons table salt
  1½   teaspoons ground black pepper
    ½   teaspoon cayenne pepper
  3–4   beef rib slabs (3 to 4 ribs per slab, about 5 pounds
        total; see note)
    2   (3-inch) wood chunks (see note)
        Vegetable oil for the cooking grate
    1   recipe Barbecue Sauce for Texas-Style Beef Ribs
        (recipe follows)

1. Combine the chili powder, salt, black pepper, and cayenne in a small bowl; rub the ribs evenly with the spice mixture and let stand at room temperature for 1 hour.

2. Meanwhile, soak the wood chunks in cold water to cover for 1 hour; drain. About 20 minutes prior to grilling, open the bottom grill vents. Light a large chimney starter filled one-third with charcoal (about 2 quarts) and allow to burn until the coals are partially covered with a layer of ash, about 10 minutes. Build a single-banked fire by steeply banking all the coals on one side of the grill. Place one wood chunk on top of the coals. Set the cooking grate in place, cover, opening the lid vents so they are two-thirds open, and heat the grate until hot, about 5 minutes. Use a grill brush to scrape the cooking grate clean. Dip a wad of paper towels in oil; holding the wad with tongs, oil the cooking grate.

3. Place the ribs, meat side down, on the cooler side of the grill (they may overlap slightly); cover, positioning the lid so that the vents are directly above the ribs. (The temperature inside the grill should be about 300 degrees.) Cook until the grill temperature drops to about 250 degrees, about 1 hour. (If necessary, add five additional briquettes to maintain the temperature above 250 degrees during the first hour of cooking.)

4. After 1 hour, add 20 more briquettes and the remaining wood chunk to the coals. Using tongs, flip the ribs meat side up and rotate the racks. Cover the grill, positioning the lid so that the vents are opposite the wood chunk. Continue to cook until a fork can be inserted into and removed from the meat with some resistance and the meat begins to pull away from the bone and shrinks ½ to 1 inch up the bone, 1¼ to 1¾ hours longer. Transfer the ribs to a carving board and let rest for 5 minutes. Slice between the bones and serve, passing the sauce separately.

Texas-Style Barbecued Beef Ribs for a Gas Grill

You will need a disposable aluminum pie plate for this recipe. Try to maintain a 250 to 300-degree grill temperature by adjusting the lit burner.

1. Follow the recipe for Texas-Style Barbecued Beef Ribs for a Charcoal Grill through step 1.

2. Substitute 3 cups wood chips for the wood chunks. Soak the chips in cold water to cover for 30 minutes; drain. Place the chips in a disposable aluminum pie plate; set the pie plate on top of the primary burner (the burner that will remain on during cooking). Turn all the burners to high and heat the grill, with the lid down, until very hot and the chips are smoking heavily, about 20 minutes (if the chips ignite, extinguish the flames with water from a spray bottle). Use a grill brush to scrape the cooking grate clean. Dip a wad of paper towels in oil; holding the wad with tongs, oil the cooking grate. Turn off all the burner(s) except the primary burner. Place the ribs, meat side down, on the cooler side of the grill. Cover and cook for 1¼ hours (the temperature inside the grill should be 250 to 300 degrees; adjust the lit burner as necessary).

3. Using tongs, flip the ribs meat side up and rotate the racks. Cover and continue to cook until a fork can be inserted into and removed from the meat with little resistance and the meat shrinks ½ to 1 inch up the bone, 1 to 1½ hours longer. Transfer the ribs to a carving board and let rest for 5 minutes. Slice between the bones and serve, passing the sauce separately.

Barbecue Sauce for Texas-Style Beef Ribs

MAKES 1¾ CUPS

This is a simple, vinegary dipping sauce quite unlike the sweet, thick barbecue sauces found in the supermarket.

- 2 **tablespoons unsalted butter**
- ¼ **cup minced onion**
- 1½ **teaspoons chili powder**
- 1 **medium garlic clove, minced or pressed through a garlic press (about 1 teaspoon)**
- 2 **cups tomato juice**
- ¾ **cup distilled white vinegar**
- 2 **tablespoons Worcestershire sauce**
- 2 **tablespoons mild or dark (not blackstrap) molasses**
- ½ **teaspoon dry mustard mixed with 1 tablespoon water**
- 1½ **teaspoons table salt**
- 1 **teaspoon minced chipotle chiles in adobo sauce**
- ¼ **teaspoon ground black pepper**

Melt the butter in a small saucepan over medium heat. Add the onion and cook, stirring occasionally, until softened, 2 to 3 minutes. Add the chili powder and garlic and cook, stirring constantly, until fragrant, about 20 seconds. Add the tomato juice, ½ cup of the vinegar, the Worcestershire sauce, molasses, mustard, salt, and chipotles. Bring to a simmer over high heat, then reduce the heat to medium and continue to simmer, stirring occasionally, until the sauce is slightly thickened and reduced to 1½ cups, 30 to 40 minutes. Off the heat, stir in the pepper and remaining ¼ cup vinegar. Cool to room temperature before serving. (The sauce can be refrigerated in an airtight container for up to 4 days; bring to room temperature before serving.)

BEEF KEBABS

WHY THIS RECIPE WORKS: Most beef kebabs are disappointing, with overcooked meat and vegetables that are either raw or mushy. We wanted to develop a foolproof approach to creating meaty kebabs that looked and tasted like the real thing: chunks of beef with a thick, caramelized char on the outside and a juicy, pink interior, all thoroughly seasoned by a marinade and paired with nicely browned, tender-firm vegetables. For the meat, we chose well-marbled steak tips for their beefy flavor and tender texture. For the marinade, we included salt for moisture, oil for flavor, and sugar for browning. For even more depth, we used tomato paste, a host of seasonings and herbs, and beef broth. We settled on three grill favorites for the vegetables: peppers, onions, and zucchini. Grilling the beef kebabs and vegetables on separate skewers and building a fire that has hotter and cooler areas allowed us to cook the vegetables over a lower temperature while the beef seared over the hotter area.

Charcoal-Grilled Beef Kebabs with Lemon and Rosemary Marinade

SERVES 4 TO 6

If you can't find sirloin steak tips, sometimes labeled "flap meat," substitute 2½ pounds blade steak; if using, cut each steak in half to remove the gristle. You will need four 12-inch metal skewers for this recipe. If you have long, thin pieces of meat, roll or fold them into approximate 2-inch cubes before skewering.

MARINADE

- 1 medium onion, chopped medium
- ⅓ cup beef broth
- ⅓ cup vegetable oil
- 3 tablespoons tomato paste
- 6 medium garlic cloves, chopped
- 2 tablespoons chopped fresh rosemary leaves
- 2 teaspoons grated zest from 1 lemon
- 2 teaspoons table salt
- 1½ teaspoons sugar
- ¾ teaspoon ground black pepper

BEEF AND VEGETABLES

- 2 pounds sirloin steak tips, trimmed and cut into 2-inch chunks (see note)
- 1 large zucchini or summer squash, halved lengthwise and sliced 1 inch thick
- 1 large red or green bell pepper, stemmed, seeded, and cut into 1½-inch pieces
- 1 large red or sweet onion, peeled, halved lengthwise, each half cut into 4 wedges and each wedge cut crosswise into thirds
  Vegetable oil for the cooking grate

1. FOR THE MARINADE: Process all the ingredients in a blender until smooth, about 45 seconds. Transfer ¾ cup of the marinade to a large bowl and set aside.

2. FOR THE BEEF AND VEGETABLES: Place the remaining marinade and the beef in a 1-gallon zipper-lock bag and toss to coat; press out as much air as possible and seal the bag. Refrigerate for at least 1 to 2 hours, flipping the bag every 30 minutes.

3. Add the zucchini, bell pepper, and onion to the bowl with the reserved marinade and toss to coat. Cover and let sit at room temperature for at least 30 minutes.

4. Remove the beef from the bag and pat dry with paper towels. Thread the beef tightly onto two 12-inch metal skewers. Thread the vegetables onto two 12-inch metal skewers, in an alternating pattern of zucchini, bell pepper, and onion.

5. Open the bottom vents completely. Light a large chimney starter mounded with charcoal (about 7 quarts) and allow to burn until the top coals are partially covered with ash, about 20 minutes. Build a single-level fire by arranging all of the coals evenly over the center of the grill, leaving a 2-inch gap between the grill wall and the charcoal. Set the cooking grate in place, cover, and open the lid vents completely. Heat the grill until hot, about 5 minutes. Use a grill brush to scrape the cooking grate clean. Dip a wad of paper towels in oil; holding the wad with tongs, oil the cooking grate.

6. Place the vegetable skewers on the grill near the edge of the coals and cook, turning the kebabs every 4 to 5 minutes, until tender and lightly charred, 17 to 21 minutes. Transfer the skewers to a serving platter and tent loosely with aluminum foil.

7. Meanwhile, place the meat skewers on the center of the grill and cook, turning the kebabs every 3 to 4 minutes, until well browned and the beef registers 120 to 125 degrees (for medium-rare) or 130 to 135 degrees (for medium) on an instant-read thermometer, 12 to 16 minutes. Transfer the meat skewers to the platter with the vegetable skewers, tent loosely with foil, and let rest for 5 to 10 minutes before serving.

Gas-Grilled Beef Kebabs with Lemon and Rosemary Marinade

Follow the recipe for Charcoal-Grilled Beef Kebabs with Lemon and Rosemary Marinade through step 4. Turn all the burners to high and heat the grill, with the lid down, until very hot, about 15 minutes. Use a grill brush to scrape the cooking grate clean. Dip a wad of paper towels in oil; holding the wad with tongs, oil the cooking grate. Proceed with the recipe from step 6, cooking with the lid down.

SHISH KEBABS

WHY THIS RECIPE WORKS: Kebabs, for all their popularity and convenience, are usually over- or undercooked, with vegetables and meat that are either burnt or raw and falling off the skewer. But kebabs are so simple, they should be a go-to grilling recipe for most home cooks; they're easy to put together and take little time on the grill, thanks to the vegetables and meat already being in bite-size pieces. We decided to revisit the kebab, grabbed some metal skewers, and headed to our grill, in search of perfectly cooked lamb and crisp, slightly charred vegetables.

To avoid the raw lamb and charred vegetables that cooking on skewers often delivers, we cut the meat (boneless leg of lamb, trimmed of fat and silver skin) into 1-inch cubes and narrowed the vegetable field. Onions and peppers were the vegetable combination most preferred by tasters; they aren't incredibly watery like tomatoes, which were out from the beginning, and they cooked at the same rate as the meat. Marinating the meat for 2 hours added extra flavor; for the marinades, we used fruity, sweet, and spicy ingredients that stood up well to the hearty lamb.

Charcoal-Grilled Shish Kebabs

SERVES 6

Cutting up the onion so the pieces will stay together on skewers is a little tricky; we recommend the following method: Trim away the stem and root end and cut the onion into quarters. Peel the three outer layers of the onion away from the inner core. Working with the outer layers only, cut each quarter—from pole to pole—into three strips of equal width. Cut each of the 12 strips crosswise into three pieces, for 36 small stacks of three layers each. You will need 12 metal skewers for this recipe.

- 1 recipe marinade (recipes follow)
- 1 (2¼-pound) shank end boneless leg of lamb, trimmed of fat and silver skin, cut into 1-inch pieces
  Vegetable oil for the cooking grate
- 1 large red onion, cut into 36 stacks of three ¾-inch pieces (see note)
- 3 medium bell peppers, 1 red, 1 yellow, and 1 orange, cut into twenty-four 1-inch pieces
  Lemon or lime wedges (optional)

1. Toss the marinade and lamb in a gallon-size zipper-lock bag or a large bowl; seal the bag, or cover the bowl with plastic wrap, and refrigerate for at least 2 hours or up to 24 hours.

2. Light a large chimney starter filled with charcoal (about 6 quarts) and allow to burn until the coals are partially covered with a layer of ash, about 20 minutes. Build a single-level fire by spreading all the coals evenly over the bottom of the grill. Set the cooking grate in place, cover the grill, and heat the grate until hot, about 5 minutes. Use a grill brush to scrape the cooking grate clean. Dip a wad of paper towels in oil; holding the wad with tongs, oil the cooking grate.

3. Meanwhile, starting and ending with the meat, thread 4 pieces of meat, 3 pieces of onion (three 3-layer stacks), and 6 pieces of pepper in mixed order on 12 metal skewers.

4. Grill the kebabs, uncovered, until the meat is well browned and grill marks appear, about 7 minutes for medium-rare or about 8 minutes for medium, turning each kebab one-quarter turn every 1¾ minutes to brown all sides. Transfer the kebabs to a serving platter, tent loosely with foil, and let rest for 5 minutes. Squeeze the lemon or lime wedges over the kebabs (if using), and serve.

Gas-Grilled Shish Kebabs

Follow the recipe for Charcoal-Grilled Shish Kebabs through step 1. Turn all the burners to high and heat the grill, with the lid down, until very hot, about 15 minutes.

Use a grill brush to scrape the cooking grate clean. Dip a wad of paper towels in oil; holding the wad with tongs, oil the cooking grate. Starting and ending with the meat, thread 4 pieces of meat, 3 pieces of onion (three 3-layer stacks), and 6 pieces of pepper in mixed order on 12 metal skewers. Grill the kebabs, covered, until the meat is well browned and grill marks appear, about 8 minutes for medium-rare or about 9 minutes for medium, turning each kebab one quarter-turn every 2 minutes to brown all sides. Transfer the kebabs to a serving platter, tent loosely with foil, and let rest for 5 minutes. Squeeze the lemon or lime wedges over the kebabs (if using), and serve.

Warm-Spiced Parsley Marinade with Ginger

MAKES ABOUT ¾ CUP

- ½ cup olive oil
- ½ cup packed fresh parsley leaves
- 1 jalapeño chile, seeded and chopped coarse
- 2 tablespoons minced or grated fresh ginger
- 3 medium garlic cloves, peeled
- 1 teaspoon ground cumin
- 1 teaspoon ground cardamom
- 1 teaspoon ground cinnamon
- 1 teaspoon table salt
- ⅛ teaspoon ground black pepper

Process all the ingredients in a food processor until smooth, about 1 minute, scraping down the sides of the workbowl as necessary.

Garlic and Cilantro Marinade with Garam Masala

MAKES ABOUT ¾ CUP

- ½ cup olive oil
- ½ cup packed fresh cilantro leaves
- ¼ cup raisins
- 1½ tablespoons juice from 1 lemon
- 3 medium garlic cloves, peeled
- 1 teaspoon table salt
- ½ teaspoon garam masala
- ⅛ teaspoon ground black pepper

Process all the ingredients in a food processor until smooth, about 1 minute, scraping down the sides of the workbowl as necessary.

GRILLED RACK OF LAMB

WHY THIS RECIPE WORKS: With its juicy, pink meat, rich crust, and classic stand-up-straight presentation, rack of lamb is a bona fide showstopper—and it has the price tag to prove it. But grill this piece of meat improperly and you've made a very costly mistake. That's why we wanted to come up with a foolproof technique for grilling rack of lamb—one that would deliver a great crust and flavorful, tender meat, every time.

Our first challenge was choosing just the right cut. While the racks from butcher shops and high-end specialty stores cost more than those from the supermarket, they come already trimmed. And once we trimmed all the excess fat from our supermarket samples, we found this meat wasn't actually much cheaper. However, even the trimmed lamb needed additional butchering, both to remove the "cap" of fat that creates meat-scorching flare-ups and to trim away any excess meat and fat. (For perfect grilling results, we needed fairly lean racks of uniform thickness.)

To cook the lamb evenly as well as to effectively render its fat, we placed a disposable aluminum pan in the middle of the grill and heaped a small pile of coals on either side of the pan. Placing the lamb in the middle of the grill, over the pan, ensured the pan would catch the rendering fat, preventing flare-ups. A wet rub (garlic, rosemary, thyme, and olive oil) was the best way to flavor the meat—marinades turned the lamb mushy and dry rubs simply didn't work with our grilling method. For a rich crust that wasn't charred, we applied the wet rub during the last few minutes of grilling, keeping the surface crisp.

Charcoal-Grilled Rack of Lamb

SERVES 4

We prefer the milder taste and bigger size of domestic lamb, but you may substitute imported lamb from New Zealand or Australia. Since imported racks are generally smaller, follow the shorter cooking times given in the recipe. Most lamb is sold frenched (meaning part of each rib bone is exposed), but chances are there will still be some extra fat between the bones. Remove the majority of this fat, leaving an inch at the top of the small eye of meat. Also, make sure that the chine bone (along the bottom of the rack) has been removed to ensure that it will be easy to cut between the ribs after cooking. Ask the butcher to do it; it's very hard to cut off at home. You will need a 13 by 9-inch disposable aluminum pan for this recipe.

Vegetable oil for the cooking grate
4 teaspoons olive oil
4 teaspoons chopped fresh rosemary leaves
2 teaspoons chopped fresh thyme leaves
2 medium garlic cloves, minced or pressed through a garlic press (about 2 teaspoons)
2 (1½-pound) racks of lamb, rib bones frenched, meat trimmed of all excess fat (see note; see page 460)
Table salt and ground black pepper

1. Light a large chimney starter filled with charcoal (about 6 quarts) and allow to burn until the coals are partially covered with a layer of ash, about 20 minutes. Place a 13 by 9-inch disposable aluminum pan in the center of the grill. Build a double-banked fire by banking half of the coals into a pile on each side of the pan. Set the cooking grate in place, cover, and heat the grate until hot, about 5 minutes. Use a grill brush to scrape the cooking grate clean. Dip a wad of paper towels in vegetable oil; holding the wad with tongs, oil the cooking grate.

2. Combine 3 teaspoons of the olive oil, the rosemary, thyme, and garlic in a small bowl; set aside. Rub the lamb with the remaining 1 teaspoon olive oil and season generously with salt and pepper. Place the racks, bone side up, on the center of the grill over the pan, with the meaty side of the racks very close to, but not quite over, the coals. Cover and grill until the meat is lightly browned, faint grill marks appear, and the fat has begun to render, 8 to 10 minutes.

3. Flip the racks over, bone side down, and move to the hotter sides of the grill. Grill, without moving, until well browned, 3 to 4 minutes. Brush the racks with the rosemary mixture. Flip the racks bone side up and continue to grill over the hotter parts of the grill until well browned, 3 to 4 minutes. Stand the racks up and lean them against each other; continue to grill over one side of the hotter part of the grill until the bottoms are well browned and the center of the racks registers 120 degrees

TRIMMING FAT FROM RACK OF LAMB

Use a boning or paring knife to cut away any thick portions of fat until a thin layer remains.

for medium-rare or 125 degrees for medium on an instant-read thermometer inserted from the side of a rack into the center, but away from any bones, 3 to 8 minutes longer.

4. Transfer the lamb to a carving board, tent loosely with foil, and let rest for 15 minutes. Cut between each rib to separate the chops and serve immediately.

Gas-Grilled Rack of Lamb

Follow the recipe for Charcoal-Grilled Rack of Lamb, turning all the burners to high and heating the grill, with the lid down, until very hot, about 15 minutes. Use a grill brush to scrape the cooking grate clean. Dip a wad of paper towels in vegetable oil; holding the wad with tongs, oil the cooking grate. Proceed with the recipe from step 2, leaving the primary burner on high and turning off the other burner(s). Grill the lamb on the cooler side of the grill, omitting the disposable pan, with the lid down and proceed as directed.

GRILLED SALMON FILLETS

WHY THIS RECIPE WORKS: Cooking delicate salmon can be tricky. Even using a nonstick skillet, it's still easy to break the occasional fillet. Introduce that same fillet to a grill, and you've got a real challenge. We wanted grilled salmon with a tender interior and crisp skin, and with each fillet perfectly intact.

Part of the solution lay in a procedure we developed to clean the grill thoroughly: Place an overturned disposable aluminum pan over the grate as the grill warms up, trapping hot air and superheating the grate. Just like in a self-cleaning oven, the high heat causes grease and debris to disintegrate. By replacing the disposable pan with foil pressed against the grate,

we bumped the temperature up higher, making the technique even more effective. We chose thicker salmon fillets, which could stand the heat of the grill for a little while longer before the first turn. To prevent the fish from sticking, we dried the fish's exterior by wrapping it in kitchen towels and "seasoned" our cooking grate by brushing it over and over with multiple layers of oil until it developed a dark, shiny coating. After laying the fillets on the grate, we easily flipped each fillet without even the tiniest bit of sticking.

Charcoal-Grilled Salmon Fillets
SERVES 4

This recipe works best with salmon fillets but can be used with any thick, firm-fleshed white fish, including red snapper, grouper, halibut, and sea bass (cook white fish to 140 degrees, up to two minutes longer per side). If you are using skinless fillets, treat the skinned side of each as if it were the skin side. If your fillets are thicker than 1 inch, increase the cooking time on the second side in step 3 until the center of the fillet registers 125 degrees (or 140 degrees for white fish). If desired, serve with Olive Vinaigrette or Almond Vinaigrette (recipes follow).

   1 **(1½ to 2-pound) skin-on salmon fillet, about 1 inch thick at the thickest part (see note)**
      Vegetable oil for the fish and cooking grate
      Table salt and ground black pepper
      Lemon wedges, for serving

1. Remove any whitish fat from the belly of the fillet and cut it into four equal pieces. Place the fillets, skin side up, on a rimmed baking sheet, or large plate, lined with a clean kitchen towel. Place a second clean kitchen towel on top of the fillets and press down to blot the liquid. Refrigerate the fish, wrapped in towels, while preparing the grill, at least 20 minutes.

2. Meanwhile, light a large chimney starter filled three-quarters with charcoal (about 4½ quarts) and allow to burn until the coals are partially covered with a layer of ash, about 20 minutes. Open the bottom grill vents. Build a modified two-level fire by arranging the coals over half of the grill, leaving the other half empty. Set the cooking grate in place, cover the grill, and heat the grate until hot, about 5 minutes. Use a grill brush to scrape the cooking grate clean. Dip a wad of paper towels in oil; holding the wad with tongs, oil the cooking grate. Continue to wipe the grate with oiled paper towels, re-dipping towels in the oil between applications, until the cooking grate is black and glossy, 5 to 10 times.

3. Brush both sides of the fish with a thin coat of oil and season with salt and pepper. Place the fish, skin side down, on the grill diagonal to the grate and directly over the coals, and cook, covered, without moving until the skin side is brown, well marked, and crisp, 3 to 5 minutes. (Try lifting the fish gently with a spatula after 3 minutes; if it doesn't cleanly lift off the grill, continue to cook, checking at 30-second intervals until it releases.) Flip the fish to the second side and cook, covered, until the center of each fillet is opaque and registers 125 degrees on an instant-read thermometer, 2 to 6 minutes longer. Serve immediately with the lemon wedges.

Gas-Grilled Salmon Fillets

Follow the recipe for Charcoal-Grilled Salmon Fillets through step 1. While the fish dries, turn all the burners to high and heat the grill, with the lid down, until very hot, about 15 minutes. Use a grill brush to scrape the cooking grate clean. Dip a wad of paper towels in oil; holding the wad with tongs, oil the cooking grate. Continue to wipe the grate with oiled paper towels, re-dipping towels in the oil between applications, until the cooking grate is black and glossy, 5 to 10 times. Proceed with the recipe from step 3. Immediately reduce the heat to medium after placing the fish on the grill and continue with the recipe, grilling the fish with the lid down.

Almond Vinaigrette

MAKES ABOUT ½ CUP, ENOUGH FOR 4 PIECES OF GRILLED SALMON

⅓ cup almonds, toasted
1 small shallot, minced (about 1 tablespoon)
4 teaspoons white wine vinegar
2 teaspoons honey
1 teaspoon Dijon mustard
⅓ cup extra-virgin olive oil
1 tablespoon cold water
1 tablespoon chopped fresh tarragon leaves
Table salt and ground black pepper

Place the almonds in a zipper-lock bag and, using a rolling pin or the bottom of a skillet, pound until pieces no larger than ½ inch remain. Combine the pounded almonds, shallot, vinegar, honey, and mustard in a medium bowl. Whisking constantly, slowly drizzle

in the oil until a smooth emulsion forms. Add the water and tarragon and whisk to combine, then season with salt and pepper to taste. Rewhisk before serving with the salmon.

Olive Vinaigrette

MAKES ABOUT ½ CUP, ENOUGH FOR 4 PIECES OF GRILLED SALMON

½ cup pitted green or kalamata olives, coarsely chopped
¼ cup extra-virgin olive oil
2 tablespoons chopped fresh parsley leaves
1 small shallot, minced (about 1 tablespoon)
2 teaspoons juice from 1 lemon
Table salt and ground black pepper

Combine all the ingredients in a medium bowl and season with salt and pepper to taste. Rewhisk before serving with the grilled salmon.

GRILLED GLAZED SALMON

WHY THIS RECIPE WORKS: A burnt, stuck-to-the-grill crust and flavorless interior are too often the reality of glazed salmon. But truly great glazed salmon right off the grill is a thing of beauty—the sweet glaze not only forms a glossy, deeply caramelized crust, but it also permeates the flesh, making the last bite of fish every bit as good as the first. This was the salmon that we wanted to re-create—sweet, crisp, moist, and flavorful.

Our recipe coup came early on in development—we realized that the best way to prevent the glazed salmon from sticking to the cooking grate was by not letting it touch the grate at all. We grilled the salmon fillets in individual aluminum trays set over the grill. There was no need for special equipment—we simply folded heavy-duty foil into 7 by 5-inch trays. This way, the fish still picked up great smoky flavor, but didn't stick to the cooking grate. Jelly was the best base ingredient for a sweet and sticky glaze. For the deepest flavor, we brushed some glaze over the fish toward the end of grilling, so it caramelized, and spooned the remaining glaze, enriched with butter, over the fish just before serving.

Charcoal-Grilled Glazed Salmon

SERVES 4

Use any brand of heavy-duty aluminum foil to make the grill trays, but be sure to spray the foil with vegetable oil spray. Alternatively, you can use Reynolds Wrap nonstick aluminum foil and skip the spray.

½   cup jalapeño jelly
½   cup packed fresh cilantro leaves and stems
1   teaspoon grated zest and 2 tablespoons juice
    from 1 large lime
2   medium garlic cloves, minced or pressed through a
    garlic press (about 2 teaspoons)
2   scallions, chopped coarse
2   tablespoons unsalted butter
    Vegetable oil for the cooking grate
1   (1½ to 2-pound) skin-on salmon fillet, about 1½ inches
    thick at the thickest part, skin removed (see page 195)
    Table salt and ground black pepper

1. Process the jelly, cilantro, lime zest and juice, garlic, and scallions in a food processor or blender until smooth. Heat the glaze in a small saucepan over medium heat until just bubbling, 2 to 3 minutes. Remove from the heat and transfer ¼ cup of the glaze to a small bowl to cool slightly. Stir the butter into the glaze remaining in the saucepan, cover, and set aside.

2. Light a large chimney starter filled with charcoal (about 6 quarts) and allow to burn until the coals are partially covered with a layer of ash, about 20 minutes. Build a three-quarter fire by evenly arranging the coals over three-quarters of the grill. Set the cooking grate in place, cover the grill, and heat the grate until hot, about 5 minutes. Use a grill brush to scrape the cooking grate clean.

3. Following the photo on page 463, use heavy-duty foil to make four 7 by 5-inch trays. Coat the trays with vegetable oil spray. Remove any whitish fat from the belly of the fillet and cut it into four equal pieces. Season the salmon with salt and pepper, brush each side of each fillet with ½ tablespoon reserved glaze (without the butter), and place the fillets, skinned side up, on the trays.

4. Place the trays with the salmon over the hot side of the grill and grill until the glaze forms a golden brown crust, 6 to 8 minutes. (Move the fillets to the cooler part of the grill if they darken too soon.) Using tongs, flip the salmon and cook for 1 minute. Spoon half of the buttered glaze on the salmon and cook until the center of each fillet is just translucent, about 1 minute. Transfer the salmon to a platter, spoon the remaining buttered glaze over the top, and serve.

Gas-Grilled Glazed Salmon

Follow the recipe for Charcoal-Grilled Glazed Salmon through step 1. Turn all the burners to high and heat the grill, with the lid down, until very hot, about 15 minutes. Use a grill brush to scrape the cooking grate clean. Proceed with the recipe from step 3, leaving the burners on high and cooking with the lid down.

MAKING A FOIL TRAY

Cut out four rectangles of heavy-duty aluminum foil and crimp the edges until each tray measures 7 by 5 inches.

Grilled Salmon with Orange-Sesame Glaze

Follow the recipe for Charcoal- or Gas-Grilled Glazed Salmon, replacing the lime zest and juice with lemon zest and juice, and replacing the jalapeño jelly with orange marmalade. Puree 2 tablespoons oyster-flavored sauce and 1 teaspoon toasted sesame oil with the other glaze ingredients. Add 1 teaspoon toasted sesame seeds along with the butter.

Grilled Salmon with Spicy Apple Glaze

Follow the recipe for Charcoal- or Gas-Grilled Glazed Salmon, replacing the lime zest and juice with 2 tablespoons cider vinegar and replacing the jalapeño jelly with apple jelly. Puree ½ teaspoon red pepper flakes with the other glaze ingredients.

BARBECUED SALMON

WHY THIS RECIPE WORKS: Store-bought smoked salmon is inconsistent in quality and also incredibly expensive—up to $8 for just 4 ounces. We wanted to create our own easy recipe for this dish that's often reserved for weekend brunch, and make moist (but not too moist), nicely crusted salmon with a hint of smoked flavor in any covered grill—in just two hours.

Surprisingly, impatience turned out to be the key to our success. Instead of the traditional cold-smoking technique, which keeps the salmon moist but lacks flavor, we developed a "hot-smoked" method, and kept the salmon moist by brining. We achieved full smoked salmon flavor on the grill using a whole side of salmon. To get a firm but not overly dry texture, complemented by a strong

hit of smoke and wood, we slow-cooked the salmon for more than an hour over a modified two-level fire, with wood chunks on the coals, but kept the fish on the cooler part of the grill the whole time. Using two spatulas to transfer the cooked fish from the grill prevented it from falling apart, and cutting through the pink flesh, not the skin, to divide individual portions kept the meat intact while leaving the skin behind.

Barbecued Salmon for a Charcoal Grill

SERVES 4 TO 6

The cooking grate must be hot and thoroughly clean before you place the salmon on it; otherwise the fish might stick. Use foil or the back of a large rimmed baking sheet to get the fish onto the grill. Alder wood is our first choice for this recipe, but hickory works fine, too. If desired, serve the salmon with Horseradish Cream Sauce with Chives or Mustard-Dill Sauce (recipes follow).

1   **cup sugar**
½   **cup table salt**
1   **(2½-pound) skin-on salmon fillet**
2   **(3-inch) wood chunks (see note)**
2   **tablespoons vegetable oil, plus extra for the cooking grate**
1½   **teaspoons sweet paprika**
1   **teaspoon ground white pepper**

1. Dissolve the sugar and salt in 7 cups cold water in a gallon-size zipper-lock bag. Add the salmon, seal the bag, and refrigerate for 3 hours.

2. Meanwhile, soak the wood chunks in cold water to cover for 1 hour; drain and set aside.

3. Remove the salmon from the brine and pat dry with paper towels. Place the fillet, skin side down, on a 30-inch sheet of heavy-duty foil. Rub both sides of the fillet with the oil. Season the flesh side of the fillet with the paprika and pepper.

4. Meanwhile, light a large chimney starter filled halfway with charcoal (about 3 quarts) and allow to burn until the coals are partially covered with a layer of ash, about 10 minutes. Build a modified two-level fire by arranging all the coals over half of the grill, leaving the other half empty; set the wood chunks on the coals and open the bottom grill vents. Set the cooking grate in place, cover, and heat the grate until hot, about 5 minutes. Use a grill brush to scrape the cooking grate clean. Dip a wad of paper towels in oil; holding the wad with tongs, oil the cooking grate.

5. Slide the salmon onto the grill opposite the fire so that the long side of the fillet is perpendicular to the grill grate. Cover, turning the lid so that the vents are opposite the wood chunks to draw smoke through the grill. Cook until heavily flavored with smoke, about 1½ hours. (The temperature inside the grill should be about 350 degrees and will fall to 250 degrees.)

6. Use two spatulas to remove the salmon from the grill. Serve hot or at room temperature, cutting through the flesh but not the skin to divide the salmon into individual portions, leaving the skin behind.

Barbecued Salmon for a Gas Grill

You will need a disposable aluminum pie plate for this recipe. Keep a close eye on the temperature of the grill; it should remain around 275 degrees.

Follow the recipe for Barbecued Salmon for a Charcoal Grill through step 3, substituting 2 cups wood chips for the wood chunks. Soak the wood chips in cold water to cover for 30 minutes, then drain. Place the wood chips in a disposable aluminum pie plate; set the pie plate on the primary burner (the burner that will remain on during cooking). Turn all the burners to high and heat the grill with the lid down until very hot and the chips are smoking heavily, about 20 minutes. (If the chips ignite, extinguish the flames with water from a spray bottle.) Use a grill brush to scrape the cooking grate clean. Dip a wad of paper towels in oil; holding the wad with tongs, oil the cooking grate. Leave the primary burner on high and turn the other burner(s) off. Slide the salmon onto the grill as directed in step 5 and proceed with the recipe.

Horseradish Cream Sauce with Chives

MAKES ABOUT 1 CUP

Horseradish and crème fraîche are natural partners to the smoky salmon.

- 1 cup crème fraîche or sour cream
- 2 tablespoons prepared horseradish
- 2 tablespoons minced fresh chives
  Pinch table salt

Combine the ingredients in a small bowl. (The sauce can be refrigerated in an airtight container for up to 1 day.)

Mustard-Dill Sauce

MAKES ABOUT 1 CUP

Use Dijon, honey, or grainy mustard, as desired. Depending on your choice of mustard, this sauce can be fairly hot.

- 1 cup mustard (see note)
- ¼ cup minced fresh dill

Combine the ingredients in a small bowl. (The sauce can be refrigerated in an airtight container for up to 1 day.)

FOOLPROOF GRILLED TUNA

WHY THIS RECIPE WORKS: Most grilled tuna steaks are either rare in the center with no char or have a great sear enveloping a dry, mealy interior. We wanted a thick layer of hot, grilled tuna with an intense smoky char wrapped around a cool, delicately flavored, tender, and moist center.

We began by selecting tuna steaks that were thick enough to stay on the grill long enough to achieve a decent crust without overcooking. Our initial test of cooking methods proved that using direct heat with a hot fire and getting the tuna on and off the grill as quickly as possible worked well. We started by covering the grill with aluminum foil while it preheated so it became ultra-hot for a clean release for the fish, which can often stick to the cooking grate. For the charred flavor we were after, we turned to an ingredient that can enhance browning—oil. Oil helps to distribute heat evenly over the surface of the fish, including those areas not actually touching the cooking grate, and it adds a little fat to lean tuna, which keeps the exterior from getting too dry and stringy. But oil alone didn't infuse our fish with grill flavor. We discovered that to moisten the tuna's flesh, the oil needs to penetrate the meat's tiny muscle fibers. Instead, we turned to a vinaigrette. The dressing (and its oil) clung to the fish, moistening its exterior and solving the problem of dry flesh. To improve browning we added honey to our vinaigrette. The sugars caramelized quickly on the grill, helping deliver a perfectly browned crust on our tuna steaks.

Charcoal-Grilled Tuna Steaks with Red Wine Vinegar and Mustard Vinaigrette

SERVES 6

We prefer our tuna served rare or medium-rare. If you like your fish cooked medium, observe the timing for medium-rare, then tent the steaks loosely with foil for 5 minutes before serving. To achieve a nicely grilled exterior and a rare center, it is important to use fish steaks that are at least 1 inch thick.

> Vegetable oil for the cooking grate
> 3 tablespoons plus 1 teaspoon red wine vinegar
> Table salt
> 2 tablespoons Dijon mustard
> 2 teaspoons honey
> 2 tablespoons chopped fresh thyme or rosemary leaves
> ¾ cup olive oil
> 6 (8-ounce) tuna steaks, 1 inch thick (see note)
> Ground black pepper

1. Light a large chimney starter filled with charcoal (about 6 quarts) and allow to burn until the coals are partially covered with a thin layer of ash, about 20 minutes. Build a modified two-level fire by arranging all the coals over one half of the grill, leaving the other half empty. Set the cooking grate in place, cover the grill, and heat the grate until hot, about 5 minutes. Use a grill brush to scrape the cooking grate clean. Dip a wad of paper towels in vegetable oil; holding the wad with tongs, oil the cooking grate. Continue to wipe the grate with oiled paper towels, redipping the towels in oil between applications, until the grate is black and glossy, 5 to 10 times.

2. While the grill heats, whisk the vinegar, ½ teaspoon salt, mustard, honey, and thyme together in a large bowl.

While whisking constantly, slowly drizzle the oil into the vinegar mixture until lightly thickened and emulsified. Measure out ¾ cup of the vinaigrette and set aside for cooking the fish. Reserve the remaining vinaigrette for serving.

3. Brush both sides of the fish liberally with the vinaigrette and season with salt and pepper. Grill the fish without moving until grill marks form and the underside is opaque, about 1½ minutes. Carefully flip, cooking until grill marks form on the second side, about 1½ minutes longer for rare (opaque at the perimeter and translucent red at the center when checked with the tip of a paring knife) or 3 minutes for medium-rare (opaque at the perimeter and reddish pink at the center). Transfer to a large plate and serve immediately, passing the reserved vinaigrette.

Gas-Grilled Tuna Steaks with Red Wine Vinegar and Mustard Vinaigrette

Turn all the burners to high and heat the grill, with the lid down, until very hot, about 15 minutes. Follow the recipe for Charcoal-Grilled Tuna Steaks with Red Wine Vinegar and Mustard Vinaigrette, oiling the cooking grate as directed in step 1. Continue with the recipe from step 2, leaving the burners on high and cooking with the lid down.

BLACKENED SNAPPER

WHY THIS RECIPE WORKS: Blackened fish is usually prepared in a cast-iron skillet, but it can lead to one smoky kitchen. We thought we'd solve this issue by throwing our fish on the barbie (it works for more than just shrimp, right?). Unfortunately, this move created a host of other problems, including fish stuck to the grate, the outside of the fish being way overdone by the time the flesh had cooked through, and the skin-on fillets curling midway through cooking. We were done with the smoke—and were ready for our fillets to have a dark brown, crusty, sweet-smoky, toasted spice exterior, providing a rich contrast to the moist, mild-flavored fish inside.

The curling problem was easy to fix. We simply needed to score the skin. The sticking solution proved more difficult, but the answer turned out to be a trick that we'd used before to grill salmon fillets (see page 462)—setting a big piece of heavy-duty foil on the grill. By placing a large piece of foil over the grate while it preheated, we made the grill superhot. This heat incinerated all the nasty gunk on the grate and gave us a really clean surface on which to cook the fish; oiling the grate with a heavy hand didn't hurt, either. Finally, to give the fish its flavorful "blackened but not burned" coating, we bloomed our spice mixture in melted butter, allowed it to cool, and then applied the coating to the fish. Once on the grill, the spice crust acquired the proper depth and richness while the fish cooked through.

Charcoal-Grilled Blackened Red Snapper

SERVES 4

If using fillets that are ½ inch or thinner, reduce the cooking time to 3 minutes per side. If using fillets that are 1 inch or thicker, increase the cooking time on the second side by 2 minutes, moving the fish to the cooler side of the grill after the second side has browned. If you cannot find red snapper, substitute striped bass, halibut, or catfish. Making the slashes in the skin requires a sharp knife. If your knife isn't sharp enough, try cutting through the skin with a serrated knife. However, cut in one direction (don't saw) and be careful to not cut into the flesh. If you choose not to eat the skin, be sure to remove it after cooking rather than beforehand. Serve the fish with lemon wedges, Rémoulade, or Pineapple and Cucumber Salsa with Mint (recipes follow).

- 2 tablespoons sweet paprika
- 2 teaspoons onion powder
- 2 teaspoons garlic powder
- ¾ teaspoon ground coriander
- ¾ teaspoon table salt
- ¼ teaspoon cayenne pepper
- ¼ teaspoon ground black pepper
- ¼ teaspoon ground white pepper
- 3 tablespoons unsalted butter
  Vegetable oil for the cooking grate
- 4 (6 to 8-ounce) red snapper fillets, ¾ inch thick (see note)

1. Combine the paprika, onion powder, garlic powder, coriander, salt, cayenne, and peppers in a small bowl. Melt the butter in a 10-inch skillet over medium heat. Stir in the spice mixture and cook, stirring frequently, until fragrant and the spices turn a dark rust color, 2 to 3 minutes. Transfer the mixture to a pie plate and cool, stirring occasionally, to room temperature, about 10 minutes. Once cooled, use a fork to break up any large clumps.

2. Light a large chimney starter filled three-quarters with charcoal (about 4½ quarts) and allow to burn until the coals are partially covered with a layer of ash, about 20 minutes. Build a modified two-level fire by arranging the coals over half of the grill, leaving the other half empty. Set the cooking grate in place, cover the grill, and heat the grate until hot, about 5 minutes. Use a grill brush to scrape the cooking grate clean. Dip a wad of paper towels in oil; holding the wad with tongs, oil the cooking grate. Continue to wipe the grate with oiled paper towels, re-dipping towels in the oil between applications, until the cooking grate is black and glossy, 5 to 10 times.

3. Meanwhile, pat the fillets dry on both sides with paper towels. Using a sharp knife, make shallow diagonal slashes every inch along the skin side of the fish, being careful not to cut into the flesh. Place the fillets, skin side up, on a rimmed baking sheet or a large plate. Using your fingers, rub the spice mixture in a thin, even layer on the top and sides of the fish. Flip the fillets over and repeat on the other side (you should use all of the spice mixture).

4. Place the fish lengthwise so it is perpendicular to the grill grate, skin side down, on the hot side of the grill. Grill, uncovered, until the skin is very dark brown and crisp, 3 to 4 minutes. Using a thin metal spatula, carefully flip the fish and continue to grill until dark brown and beginning to flake and the center is opaque but still moist, about 5 minutes longer. Serve immediately.

Gas-Grilled Blackened Red Snapper

Follow the recipe for Charcoal-Grilled Blackened Red Snapper, skipping step 2. Turn all the burners to high and heat the grill, with the lid down, until very hot, about 15 minutes. Use a grill brush to scrape the cooking grate clean. Dip a wad of paper towels in oil; holding the wad with tongs, oil the cooking grate. Continue to wipe the grate with oiled paper towels, re-dipping towels in the oil between applications, until the cooking grate is black and glossy, 5 to 10 times. Proceed with the recipe from step 3, leaving the burners on high and cooking with the lid up.

Rémoulade

MAKES ABOUT ½ CUP

The rémoulade can be refrigerated for up to three days.

- ½ cup mayonnaise
- 1½ teaspoons sweet pickle relish
- 1 teaspoon hot sauce
- 1 teaspoon juice from 1 lemon
- 1 teaspoon minced fresh parsley leaves
- ½ teaspoon capers, drained and rinsed
- ½ teaspoon Dijon mustard
- 1 small garlic clove, minced or pressed through a garlic press (about ½ teaspoon)
- Table salt and ground black pepper

Pulse the mayonnaise, relish, hot sauce, lemon juice, parsley, capers, mustard, and garlic in a food processor until well combined but not smooth, about 10 pulses. Season with salt and pepper to taste. Transfer to a serving bowl.

Pineapple and Cucumber Salsa with Mint

MAKES ABOUT 3 CUPS

This salsa can be made spicier by mincing and adding the seeds and ribs from the chile.

- ½ large pineapple, peeled, cored, and cut into ¼-inch pieces (about 2 cups)
- ½ medium cucumber, peeled, seeded, and cut into ¼-inch pieces (about 1 cup))
- 1 medium serrano chile, seeds and ribs removed, chile minced (about 2 tablespoons; see note)
- 2 tablespoons chopped fresh mint leaves
- 1 small shallot, minced (about 1 tablespoon
- 1–2 tablespoons juice from 1 lime
- ½ teaspoon minced or grated fresh ginger
- Table salt
- Sugar

Combine the pineapple, cucumber, chile, mint, shallot, 1 tablespoon of the lime juice, the ginger, and ½ teaspoon salt in a medium bowl; let stand at room temperature for 15 to 30 minutes. Season with additional lime juice and salt to taste, and add sugar as needed if the pineapple is tart; transfer to a serving bowl.

GRILLED SEA SCALLOPS

WHY THIS RECIPE WORKS: In theory, the blazing-hot fire of a grill is perfect for cooking scallops with an extra-crisp crust and moist interior, but in practice they're usually rubbery and overcooked by the time they develop a good sear—and they inevitably stick to the grate. For great grilled scallops, we needed to figure out how to build the biggest fire possible. The solution was a disposable aluminum pan—it allowed us to corral the coals in just the center of the grill for a tall, even, super-hot fire that gave us scallops with impressive char and juicy centers. Drying the scallops with kitchen towels before cooking helped ensure browning, and threading them onto two side-by-side skewers made them easy to flip all at once. To combat the problem of sticking, we lightly coated the scallops in a mixture of flour, cornstarch, oil, and sugar. With this simple coating, our scallops were crisp-crusted, moist and tender within, and they came off the grill without hesitation. To complement the scallops, a chile-lime vinaigrette contributes both brightness and heat, or a basil vinaigrette adds a light, summery flavor.

Charcoal-Grilled Sea Scallops

SERVES 4

We recommend buying "dry" scallops, those without chemical additives. Dry scallops will look ivory or pinkish and feel tacky; wet scallops look bright white and feel slippery. If using wet scallops, soak them in a solution of 1 quart water, ¼ cup juice from 2 lemons, and 2 tablespoons table salt for 30 minutes before step 1, and do not season with salt in step 3. Double-skewering the scallops makes flipping easier. To skewer, thread 4 to 6 scallops onto one skewer and then place a second skewer through the scallops parallel to and about ¼ inch from the first. You will need eight to twelve 12-inch metal skewers for this recipe. You will also need a deep (at least 2¾ inches) disposable 13 by 9-inch aluminum pan.

- 1½ pounds large dry sea scallops, tendons removed (see note)
- 2 tablespoons vegetable oil, plus more for the cooking grate
- 1 tablespoon unbleached all-purpose flour
- 1 teaspoon cornstarch
- 1 teaspoon sugar
- Table salt and ground black pepper
- Lemon wedges, for serving
- 1 recipe vinaigrette (optional; recipes follow)

1. Place the scallops on a rimmed baking sheet lined with a clean kitchen towel. Place a second clean kitchen towel on top of the scallops and press gently on the towel to blot liquid. Let the scallops sit at room temperature, covered with the towel, for 10 minutes. With the scallops on a work surface, thread them onto doubled skewers so that the flat sides will directly touch the cooking grate, 4 to 6 scallops per doubled skewer. Return the skewered scallops to the towel-lined baking sheet; refrigerate, covered with the second towel, while preparing the grill.

2. Light a large chimney starter mounded with charcoal (about 7 quarts) and allow to burn until the top coals are partially covered with ash, about 20 minutes. Build a concentrated fire by poking 12 holes in the bottom of a 13 by 9-inch disposable aluminum pan with a skewer, placing the pan in the center of the grill, and emptying the coals into the pan.

3. While the grill is heating, whisk the oil, flour, cornstarch, and sugar together in a small bowl. Remove the towels from the scallops. Brush both sides of the skewered scallops with the oil mixture and season with salt and pepper.

4. Use a grill brush to scrape the cooking grate clean. Dip a wad of paper towels in oil; holding the wad with tongs, repeatedly brush the grate with well-oiled paper towels until the grate is black and glossy, 5 to 10 times. Place the skewered scallops directly over the hot coals. Cook without moving the scallops until lightly browned, 2½ to 4 minutes. Carefully flip the skewers and continue to cook until the second side is browned, the sides of the scallops are firm, and the centers are opaque, 2 to 4 minutes longer. Serve immediately with the lemon wedges and vinaigrette (if using).

Gas-Grilled Sea Scallops

Follow step 1 of the recipe for Charcoal-Grilled Sea Scallops. Turn all burners to high and heat the grill, with the lid down, until very hot, about 15 minutes. Proceed with the recipe from step 3, cooking with the lid down.

Chile-Lime Vinaigrette

MAKES ABOUT 1 CUP; ENOUGH FOR 1 RECIPE GRILLED SEA SCALLOPS

- 3 tablespoons plus 1 teaspoon juice from 2 limes
- 2 tablespoons honey
- 1 tablespoon sriracha sauce
- 2 teaspoons fish sauce
- ½ cup vegetable oil

Whisk the lime juice and zest, honey, sriracha sauce, and fish sauce until combined. Whisking constantly, slowly drizzle in the oil until emulsified.

Basil Vinaigrette

MAKES ABOUT 1 CUP; ENOUGH FOR 1 RECIPE GRILLED SEA SCALLOPS

- 1 cup packed fresh basil leaves
- 3 tablespoons minced fresh chives
- 2 tablespoons champagne vinegar
- 2 medium garlic cloves, minced or pressed through a garlic press (about 2 teaspoons)
- 2 teaspoons sugar
- 1 teaspoon table salt
- ½ teaspoon ground black pepper
- ⅔ cup vegetable oil

Pulse the basil, chives, vinegar, garlic, sugar, salt, and pepper in a blender until roughly chopped, 5 to 7 pulses. With the blender running, slowly drizzle in the oil until emulsified, about 1 minute, scraping down the blender jar as necessary.

GRILLED SHRIMP

WHY THIS RECIPE WORKS: Really great grilled shrimp—tender, moist, and flavorful—are hard to come by. Usually, they're overcooked and rubbery, giving the jaws a work-out, thanks to their quick cooking time and the high temperature of the grill. Grilling shrimp in their shells can guarantee juiciness, but the seasoning tends to be lost when the shells are pulled off. We wanted tender, juicy, boldly seasoned grilled shrimp, with the flavor in the shrimp and not on our fingers.

Our decision to go with peeled shrimp for this recipe meant we had to revisit how we traditionally grilled shrimp. First we eliminated brining, which created waterlogged shrimp and hindered caramelization. Then we set the shrimp over a screaming-hot fire. This worked well with jumbo shrimp, but smaller shrimp overcooked before charring. With jumbo shrimp costing as much as $25 per pound, we decided against them. They did give us an idea, though. For our next step, we created faux jumbo shrimp by cramming a skewer with several normal-sized shrimp pressed tightly together. Our final revision was to take the shrimp off the fire before they were completely cooked (but after they had picked up attractive grill marks). We finished cooking them in a heated sauce waiting on the cool side of the grill; this final simmer gave them tons of flavor.

Charcoal-Grilled Shrimp Skewers
SERVES 4

The shrimp and sauce (recipes follow) finish cooking together on the grill, so prepare the sauce ingredients while the coals are heating. To fit all of the shrimp on the cooking grate at once, you'll need three 14-inch metal skewers. Serve with grilled bread.

1½   **pounds extra-large shrimp (21 to 25 per pound), peeled and deveined (see page 205)**
2–3 **tablespoons olive oil for brushing the shrimp**
      Table salt and ground black pepper
¼   **teaspoon sugar**
      Vegetable oil for the cooking grate
1   **recipe Spicy Lemon-Garlic Sauce or Fresh Tomato Sauce with Feta and Olives (recipes follow)**
      Lemon wedges, for serving

1. Pat the shrimp dry with paper towels. Thread the shrimp onto three skewers, alternating direction of heads and tails. Brush both sides of the shrimp with the olive oil and season lightly with salt and pepper. Sprinkle one side of each skewer evenly with the sugar.

2. Light a large chimney starter filled with charcoal (about 6 quarts) and allow to burn until the coals are partially covered with a layer of ash, about 20 minutes. Open the bottom vent on the grill. Build a modified two-level fire by arranging the coals over half of the grill, leaving the other half empty. Set the cooking grate in place, cover the grill, and heat the grate until hot, about 5 minutes. Use a grill brush to scrape the cooking grate clean. Dip a wad of paper towels in vegetable oil; holding the wad with tongs, oil the cooking grate.

3. Set the disposable pan with the sauce ingredients on the hot side of the grill and cook, stirring occasionally, until hot, about 1½ minutes; transfer the pan to the cooler side of the grill. Place the shrimp skewers, sugared sides down, on the hot side of the grill and use tongs to push the shrimp together on the skewers if they have separated. Grill the shrimp, uncovered, until lightly charred, 4 to 5 minutes. Using tongs, flip and grill until the second side is pink and slightly translucent, 1 to 2 minutes longer.

4. Using a potholder or oven mitt, carefully lift each skewer from the grill and use tongs to slide the shrimp off

---

NOTES FROM THE TEST KITCHEN

ARRANGING SHRIMP ON A SKEWER

Pass the skewer through the center of each shrimp. As you add shrimp to the skewer, alternate the directions of the heads and tails for a compact arrangement of shrimp. The shrimp should fit snugly against one another.

the skewers into the pan with the sauce. Toss the shrimp and sauce to combine and transfer the pan to the hot side of the grill; cook, stirring, until the shrimp are opaque and fully cooked, about 30 seconds. Remove from the grill, add the remaining sauce ingredients, and toss to combine. Transfer to a serving platter and serve immediately with the lemon wedges.

Gas-Grilled Shrimp Skewers

Follow step 1 of the recipe for Charcoal-Grilled Shrimp Skewers. Turn all the burners to high and heat the grill, with the lid down, until very hot, about 15 minutes. Use a grill brush to scrape the cooking grate clean. Dip a wad of paper towels in vegetable oil; holding the wad with tongs, oil the cooking grate. Proceed with step 3 of the recipe, setting the sauce aside off the heat once hot and grilling the shrimp with the lid down, checking occasionally to make sure they're not burning (the timing may be a few minutes longer than in the charcoal grill recipe).

Spicy Lemon-Garlic Sauce

MAKES ABOUT ½ CUP

You will need a 10-inch disposable aluminum pan or pie plate for this recipe.

- 4 tablespoons (½ stick) unsalted butter, cut into 4 pieces
- 4 tablespoons juice from 2 lemons
- 3 medium garlic cloves, minced or pressed through a garlic press (about 1 tablespoon)
- ½ teaspoon red pepper flakes
- ⅛ teaspoon table salt
- ⅓ cup minced fresh parsley leaves

Combine the butter, lemon juice, garlic, red pepper flakes, and salt in a 10-inch disposable aluminum pan or pie plate. Cook over the hot side of the grill, stirring occasionally, until the butter melts, about 1½ minutes; transfer to the cooler side of the grill (if using a charcoal grill) or set aside off the heat (if using a gas grill). Proceed to grill the shrimp, adding the parsley just before serving.

Fresh Tomato Sauce with Feta and Olives

MAKES ABOUT ½ CUP

You will need a 10-inch disposable aluminum pan or pie plate for this recipe.

- 4 tablespoons extra-virgin olive oil
- 1 large ripe tomato, cored, seeded, and minced
- 1 tablespoon minced fresh oregano leaves
- ⅛ teaspoon salt
- 4 ounces feta cheese, crumbled into ¼-inch pieces (about 1 cup)
- ⅓ cup pitted kalamata olives, chopped fine
- 2 tablespoons juice from 1 lemon
- 3 scallions, sliced very thin

Combine the oil, tomato, oregano, and salt in a 10-inch disposable aluminum pan or pie plate. Cook over the hot side of the grill, stirring occasionally, until hot, about 1½ minutes; transfer to the cooler side of the grill (if using a charcoal grill) or set aside off the heat (if using a gas grill). Proceed to grill the shrimp, adding the feta, olives, lemon juice, and scallions just before serving.

GRILLED CORN

WHY THIS RECIPE WORKS: In Mexico, street vendors add kick to grilled corn by slathering it with a creamy, spicy sauce. The corn takes on an irresistibly sweet, smoky, charred flavor, which is heightened by the lime juice and chili powder in the cheesy sauce. We wanted to develop our own rendition of this south-of-the-border street fare.

To cook the corn, we ditched the husks, coated the ears with oil to prevent sticking, and grilled them directly on the grate. Over a single-level fire, the corn emerged nicely smoky but insufficiently charred, so we pushed all the coals to one side to create a modified two-level fire, allowing the ears to cook closer to the coals.

The traditional base for the sauce is *crema*, a thick, soured Mexican cream. But given its spotty availability in supermarkets, we replaced the crema with a combination of mayonnaise (for richness) and sour cream (for tanginess). Most recipes call for *queso fresco* or *Cotija*, but these cheeses can be hard to find. Pecorino Romano made a good substitute. We included the usual seasonings of chopped cilantro, lime juice, minced garlic, and chili powder. To provide more depth, we added some chili powder to the oil used for coating the corn; once heated on the grill, the chili powder bloomed with a full flavor that penetrated the corn kernels.

powder, the black pepper, and cayenne (if using) in a large bowl; set aside. In a second large bowl, combine the oil, salt, and remaining ½ teaspoon chili powder; add the corn and toss to coat evenly.

3. Grill the corn until lightly charred on all sides, 7 to 12 minutes total. Place the corn in the bowl with the cheese mixture; toss to coat evenly. Serve immediately.

Mexican-Style Gas-Grilled Corn

Turn all the burners to high and heat the grill, with the lid down, until very hot, about 15 minutes. Use a grill brush to scrape the cooking grate clean. Dip a wad of paper towels in vegetable oil; holding the wad with tongs, oil the cooking grate. Follow the recipe for Mexican-Style Charcoal-Grilled Corn from step 2, leaving the burners on high and cooking the corn with the lid down.

GRILLED POTATOES

WHY THIS RECIPE WORKS: Grilled potatoes are a summer classic, but we wanted to put a new spin on our grilled potatoes by adding rosemary and garlic for a heartier, more savory side. Unfortunately, we found it harder than it sounded to add garlic and rosemary flavors to plain grilled potatoes. Coating the potatoes with oil, garlic, and rosemary produced burnt, bitter garlic and charred rosemary. If we tossed the potatoes in garlic oil after cooking, the raw garlic was too harsh. We wanted potent garlic and rosemary flavors in our potatoes, without bitterness and charring.

We learned that we needed to introduce the potatoes to the garlic-oil mixture not once, but three times. Before cooking, we pierced the potatoes, skewered them, seasoned them with salt, brushed on a garlic-rosemary oil, and precooked them in the microwave. Then, before grilling, we brushed them again with the infused oil. After grilling, we tossed them with the garlic and rosemary oil yet again. We finally had it—tender grilled potatoes infused with the smoky flavor of the grill and enlivened with the bold flavors of garlic and rosemary.

Mexican-Style Charcoal-Grilled Corn

SERVES 6

If you can find queso fresco or Cotija, use either in place of the Pecorino Romano. If you prefer the corn spicy, add the optional cayenne pepper.

- 4 teaspoons vegetable oil plus extra for the cooking grate
- 1½ ounces Pecorino Romano, grated (about ½ cup)
- ¼ cup mayonnaise
- 3 tablespoons sour cream
- 3 tablespoons minced fresh cilantro leaves
- 4 teaspoons juice from 1 lime
- 1 medium garlic clove, minced or pressed through a garlic press (about 1 teaspoon)
- ¾ teaspoon chili powder
- ¼ teaspoon ground black pepper
- ¼ teaspoon cayenne pepper (optional; see note)
- ¼ teaspoon table salt
- 6 large ears corn, husks and silk removed

1. Light a large chimney starter filled with charcoal (about 6 quarts) and allow to burn until the coals are partially covered with a layer of ash, about 20 minutes. Build a modified two-level fire by arranging all the coals over half of the grill, leaving the other half empty. Set the cooking grate in place, cover, and heat the grate until hot, about 5 minutes. Use a grill brush to scrape the cooking grate clean. Dip a wad of paper towels in vegetable oil; holding the wad with tongs, oil the cooking grate.

2. Meanwhile, combine the cheese, mayonnaise, sour cream, cilantro, lime juice, garlic, ¼ teaspoon of the chili

Charcoal-Grilled Potatoes with Garlic and Rosemary

SERVES 4

This recipe allows you to grill an entrée while the hot coals burn down in step 1. Once that item is done, start grilling the potatoes. This recipe works best with small potatoes that are about 1½ inches in diameter. If using medium potatoes, 2 to 3 inches in diameter, cut them into quarters. If the potatoes are larger than 3 inches in diameter, cut each potato into eighths. Since the potatoes are cooked in the microwave, use wooden skewers. You will need a 13 by 9-inch disposable aluminum pan for this recipe.

Vegetable oil for the cooking grate
¼ cup olive oil
9 medium garlic cloves, minced or pressed through a garlic press (about 3 tablespoons)
1 teaspoon chopped fresh rosemary leaves
Table salt
2 pounds small red potatoes (about 18), scrubbed, halved, and skewered (see note)
Ground black pepper
2 tablespoons chopped fresh chives

1. Light a large chimney starter filled with charcoal (about 6 quarts) and allow to burn until the coals are partially covered with a layer of ash, about 20 minutes. Open the bottom vent on the grill. Build a two-level fire by arranging two-thirds of the coals evenly over half of the grill and arranging the remaining coals over the other half. Set the cooking grate in place, cover the grill, and heat the grate until hot, about 5 minutes. Remove the lid and let the coals burn until the fire on the hotter part of the grill is medium (you can hold your hand 5 inches above the grate for 5 to 6 seconds), about 10 minutes. Use a grill brush to scrape the cooking grate clean. Dip a wad of paper towels in vegetable oil; holding the wad with tongs, oil the cooking grate.

2. Meanwhile, heat the olive oil, garlic, rosemary, and ½ teaspoon salt in a small skillet over medium heat until sizzling, about 3 minutes. Reduce the heat to medium-low and continue to cook until the garlic is light blond, about 3 minutes. Pour the mixture through a fine-mesh strainer into a small bowl; press on the solids. Measure 1 tablespoon of the solids and 1 tablespoon of the oil into a large bowl and set aside. Discard the remaining solids but reserve the remaining oil.

3. Following the photo, skewer the potatoes, then place them in a single layer on a large microwave-safe plate and poke each potato several times with a skewer. Brush with 1 tablespoon of the reserved strained oil and season liberally with salt. Microwave on high power until the potatoes offer slight resistance when pierced with the tip of a paring knife, about 8 minutes, turning them halfway through the cooking time. Transfer the potatoes to a baking sheet coated with 1 tablespoon more strained oil. Brush the potatoes with the remaining 1 tablespoon strained oil; season with salt and pepper to taste.

4. Place the potatoes on the hotter side of the grill. Cook, turning once, until grill marks appear, about 4 minutes. Move the potatoes to the cooler side of the grill; cover with the disposable aluminum pan and continue to cook until a paring knife slips in and out of the potatoes easily, 5 to 8 minutes longer. Remove the potatoes from the skewers and transfer to the bowl with the reserved garlic-oil mixture; add the chives and toss until thoroughly coated. Serve immediately.

NOTES FROM THE TEST KITCHEN

SKEWERING POTATOES FOR THE GRILL

Place a potato half, cut side down, on the work surface and pierce through the center with a skewer. Repeat, holding the already-skewered potatoes for better leverage.

Gas-Grilled Potatoes with Garlic and Rosemary

Turn all the burners to high and heat the grill, with the lid down, until very hot, about 15 minutes. Use a grill brush to scrape the cooking grate clean. Dip a wad of paper towels in vegetable oil; holding the wad with tongs, oil the cooking grate. Leave the primary burner on high and reduce the other burner(s) to medium. Follow the recipe for Charcoal-Grilled Potatoes with Garlic and Rosemary from step 2, grilling the potatoes with the lid down and omitting the disposable aluminum pan.

BABA GHANOUSH

WHY THIS RECIPE WORKS: Baba ghanoush often appears on the appetizer table as a gray, bitter, watery mass of eggplant puree. We were after a dip that had realized its potential—full of smoky eggplant flavor and brightened with garlic and lemon juice. And one certain way to produce this creation was to start off by grilling our eggplant.

For the best flavor, it's imperative to start out with firm, shiny, and unblemished eggplants. To achieve a deep smoky flavor, we grilled the eggplants directly over a hot fire until they were wrinkled and soft. So the eggplant wouldn't burst over the heat, we had to poke the entire surface with a fork. To avoid a watery texture and any bitterness, we drained the pulp of excess fluid, but didn't bother spending time deseeding the eggplants. We processed the pulp with a modest amount of garlic, tahini paste, and lemon juice for the creaminess and bright flavor that traditional baba ghanoush is known for.

Charcoal-Grilled Baba Ghanoush
MAKES ABOUT 2 CUPS

We prefer to serve baba ghanoush only lightly chilled. If yours is cold, let it stand at room temperature for about 20 minutes before serving. Baba ghanoush does not keep well, so plan to make it the day you want to serve it. Pita bread, black olives, tomato wedges, and cucumber slices are nice accompaniments.

Vegetable oil for the cooking grate
2 pounds eggplant (about 2 large globe eggplants, 5 medium Italian eggplants, or 12 medium Japanese eggplants), each eggplant poked uniformly over the entire surface with a fork

2 tablespoons tahini paste
1 tablespoon juice from 1 lemon
1 small garlic clove, minced or pressed through a garlic press (about ½ teaspoon)
Table salt and ground black pepper
1 tablespoon extra-virgin olive oil
2 teaspoons chopped fresh parsley leaves

1. Light a large chimney starter filled with charcoal (about 6 quarts) and allow to burn until the coals are partially covered with a layer of ash, about 20 minutes. Build a single-level fire by arranging the coals evenly over the bottom of the grill; arrange an additional chimney starter of unlit charcoal (about 6 quarts) over the lit coals. Set the cooking grate in place, cover, and heat the grate until hot, about 5 minutes. Use a grill brush to scrape the cooking grate clean. Dip a wad of paper towels in vegetable oil; holding the wad with tongs, oil the cooking grate.

2. Place the eggplants on the grill and cook until the skins darken and wrinkle on all sides and the eggplants are uniformly soft when pressed with tongs, about 25 minutes for large globe eggplants, 20 minutes for Italian eggplants, and 15 minutes for Japanese eggplants, turning every 5 minutes and reversing the direction of the eggplants on the grill with each turn. Transfer the eggplants to a rimmed baking sheet and cool for 5 minutes.

3. Set a small colander over a bowl. Trim the top and bottom off each eggplant. Slice the eggplants lengthwise and use a spoon to scoop the hot pulp from the skins and place the pulp in the colander (you should have about 2 cups packed pulp); discard the skins. Let the pulp drain for 3 minutes.

4. Pulse the pulp, tahini, lemon juice, garlic, ¼ teaspoon salt, and ¼ teaspoon pepper in a food processor until coarse, about eight pulses. Season with salt and pepper to taste; transfer to a serving bowl, cover with plastic wrap pressed against the surface of the dip, and refrigerate for 1 hour. Use a spoon to make a trough in the center of the dip and spoon the olive oil into it; sprinkle with the parsley and serve.

Gas-Grilled Baba Ghanoush

Turn all the burners to high and heat the grill, with the lid down, until very hot, about 15 minutes. Use a grill brush to scrape the cooking grate clean. Dip a wad of paper towels in vegetable oil; holding the wad with tongs, oil the cooking grate. Follow the recipe for Charcoal-Grilled Baba Ghanoush from step 2.

CHAPTER 18

SIDES OF PLENTY

Simple Applesauce   476

Broiled Asparagus   476

Pan-Roasted
Asparagus   477

Roasted Broccoli   477

   Roasted Broccoli
   with Garlic

Roasted Carrots   478

   Roasted Carrots and
   Fennel with Toasted
   Almonds and Lemon

   Roasted Carrots and
   Parsnips with Rosemary

Quick Roasted
Baby Carrots   479

Glazed Carrots   479

Corn Fritters   480

Boston Baked Beans   481

Blanched Green Beans   481

Green Beans with Sautéed
Shallots and Vermouth   482

Green Beans with Toasted
Hazelnuts and Brown
Butter   482

Green Beans
Amandine   482

Roasted Green Beans   483

Sautéed Garlic-Lemon
Spinach   483

Sautéed Baby Spinach
with Almonds and
Golden Raisins   484

Creamy Herbed
Spinach Dip   485

Quick-Cooked
Tough Greens   485

Simple Sautéed Swiss
Chard   486

Smashed Potatoes   486

Classic Mashed
Potatoes   487

Garlic and Olive Oil
Mashed Potatoes   488

Creamy Mashed
Potatoes   489

Mashed Potatoes and
Root Vegetables   489

Fluffy Mashed
Potatoes   490

Buttermilk Mashed
Potatoes   491

Crispy Roasted
Potatoes   491

Skillet-Roasted
Potatoes   492

Salt-Baked Potatoes with
Roasted Garlic and
Rosemary Butter   493

   Salt-Baked Potatoes
   with Roasted Shallot and
   Thyme Butter

Scalloped Potatoes   493

Twice-Baked
Potatoes   494

Crispy Smashed
Potatoes   495

Mashed Sweet
Potatoes   496

Quick Roasted Acorn
Squash with Brown
Sugar   497

Rice Pilaf   497

Wild Rice Pilaf with Pecans
and Dried Cranberries   498

Almost Hands-Free
Risotto with Parmesan and
Herbs   499

Simple Couscous   500

   Couscous with Dates
   and Pistachios

   Couscous with Dried
   Cherries and Pecans

   Couscous with Carrots,
   Raisins, and Pine Nuts

   Couscous with Shallots,
   Garlic, and Almonds

No-Fuss Creamy Parmesan
Polenta   500

Spiced Pecans with
Rum Glaze   501

SIMPLE APPLESAUCE

WHY THIS RECIPE WORKS: Applesauce should taste like apples, but all too often the tart, sweet, and fruity nuances of fresh apple flavor are overpowered by sweeteners and spices, and the sauce ends up tasting like bad pie filling. The texture, too, can vary from dry and chunky to loose and thin. We wanted a smooth, thick sauce that showcases fresh apple flavor without too much sweetness or spice—the perfect partner to pork chops or as a snack.

The first step was to find the right variety of apple. We began by gathering 18 varieties and making each into applesauce. We found that Jonagold, Jonathan, Pink Lady, and Macoun varieties all produce a sauce with a pleasing balance of tart and sweet. We tried blending varieties in combination with each other, but concluded that single-variety sauces had purer, stronger character. Cooking the apples with their skins on saved us the step of peeling and enhanced the flavor of the sauce. Processing the cooked apples through a food mill, not a food processor or blender, removed the skins and produced a sauce with the silky-smooth, thick texture we were after. Adding a little water, sugar, and a pinch of salt—and no spices—resulted in a perfectly sweetened sauce that tasted first and foremost of apples.

Simple Applesauce
MAKES ABOUT 3½ CUPS

If you do not own a food mill or prefer applesauce with a coarse texture, peel the apples before coring and cutting them and, after cooking, mash them against the side of the pot with a wooden spoon or against the bottom of the pot with a potato masher. Applesauce made with out-of-season apples may be somewhat drier than sauce made with peak-season apples, so it's likely that in step 2 of the recipe you will need to add more water to adjust the texture. If you double the recipe, the apples will need 10 to 15 minutes of extra cooking time.

    4   pounds apples (about 10 medium), preferably Jonagold, Pink Lady, Jonathan, or Macoun, unpeeled, cored, and cut into rough 1½-inch pieces (see note)
    1   cup water, plus more as needed
    ¼   cup sugar, plus more to taste
        Pinch table salt

1. Toss the apples, water, sugar, and salt in a large Dutch oven. Cover the pot and cook the apples over medium-high heat until they begin to break down, 15 to 20 minutes, checking and stirring occasionally with a wooden spoon to break up any large chunks.

2. Process the cooked apples through a food mill fitted with the medium disk. Season with extra sugar to taste or add water to adjust the consistency as desired. Serve hot, warm, at room temperature, or chilled.

BROILED ASPARAGUS

WHY THIS RECIPE WORKS: Broiling can intensify the flavor of asparagus, turning it sweet and nutty. But getting the asparagus to cook through evenly can be tricky. We wanted a foolproof broiling method for turning out browned, tender spears every time.

To start, we found that with thicker asparagus, the exterior began to char before the interior of the spears became fully tender. When we used thinner spears, however, the interior was tender by the time the exterior was browned. Keeping the spears about four inches away from the broiling element allowed them to caramelize properly without charring. To encourage browning, we tossed the asparagus with olive oil before broiling. Shaking the pan with the asparagus as it cooked ensured that the spears cooked evenly. The intense dry heat of the broiler concentrated the flavor of the asparagus, and the exterior caramelization made the spears especially sweet.

Broiled Asparagus
SERVES 6

Broilers vary significantly in intensity, thus the wide range of cooking times in this recipe. Choose asparagus no thicker than ½ inch near the base for this recipe.

    2   pounds thin asparagus (about 2 bunches), tough ends trimmed (see page 251; see note)
    1   tablespoon olive oil
        Table salt and ground black pepper

Adjust an oven rack to the highest position (about 4 inches from the heating element) and heat the broiler. Toss the asparagus with the oil and salt and pepper to taste, then lay the spears in a single layer on a rimmed baking sheet. Broil, shaking the pan halfway through cooking to turn the spears, until the asparagus is tender and lightly browned, 6 to 10 minutes. Serve hot or warm.

PAN-ROASTED ASPARAGUS

WHY THIS RECIPE WORKS: Recipes for pan-roasted asparagus promise ease and flavor, but the results are usually disappointing: limp, greasy, and shriveled spears. We wanted a simple stovetop method that would deliver crisp, nicely browned spears.

We quickly learned to choose thick spears because thinner spears overcooked too quickly. Taking a cue from restaurant chefs who blanch asparagus first, we developed a method to lightly steam and then brown the asparagus in the same skillet. For both flavor and browning, we used olive oil and butter. Positioning half the spears in one direction and the other half in the opposite direction ensured a better fit in the pan. Browning just one side of the asparagus provided a contrast in texture and guaranteed that the asparagus were firm and tender, never limp.

Pan-Roasted Asparagus

SERVES 3 TO 4

This recipe works best with asparagus that is at least ½ inch thick near the base. If using thinner spears, reduce the covered cooking time to 3 minutes and the uncovered cooking time to 5 minutes. Do not use pencil-thin asparagus; it cannot withstand the heat and overcooks too easily.

- 1 tablespoon olive oil
- 1 tablespoon unsalted butter
- 2 pounds thick asparagus (about 2 bunches), tough ends trimmed (see page 251; see note)
-    Table salt and ground black pepper
- ½ lemon (optional)

1. Heat the oil and butter in a 12-inch skillet over medium-high heat. When the butter has melted, add half of the asparagus to the skillet with the tips pointed in one direction; add the remaining asparagus with the tips pointed in the opposite direction. Using tongs, distribute the spears in an even layer (the spears will not quite fit into a single layer); cover and cook until the asparagus is bright green and still crisp, about 5 minutes.

2. Uncover and increase the heat to high; season the asparagus with salt and pepper to taste. Cook until the spears are tender and well browned along one side, 5 to 7 minutes, using the tongs to occasionally move the spears from the center of the pan to the edge of the pan to ensure all are browned. Transfer the asparagus to a dish, season with salt and pepper to taste, and squeeze the lemon half (if using) over the spears. Serve.

ROASTED BROCCOLI

WHY THIS RECIPE WORKS: Roasting can concentrate flavor to turn dull vegetables into something great, but roasting broccoli usually makes for spotty browning and charred, bitter florets. We wanted to figure out how to roast broccoli so that it turned out perfectly browned and deeply flavorful every time.

To ensure that the broccoli would brown evenly, we cut the crown into uniform wedges that lay flat on the baking sheet, increasing contact with the pan. To promote even cooking of the stem, we sliced away the exterior and cut the stalk into rectangular pieces slightly smaller than the more delicate wedges. After trial and error, we discovered that preheating the baking sheet helped the broccoli cook faster, crisping but not charring the florets, while a very hot oven delivered the best browning. Sprinkling a little sugar over the broccoli along with the salt and pepper helped it brown even more deeply. We finally had roasted broccoli with crispy-tipped florets and sweet, browned stems.

Roasted Broccoli

SERVES 4

It is important to trim away the outer peel from the broccoli stalks; otherwise they will turn tough when cooked.

1¾ **pounds broccoli (about 1 large bunch)**
  3 **tablespoons extra-virgin olive oil**
  ½ **teaspoon table salt**
  ½ **teaspoon sugar**
     Ground black pepper
     Lemon wedges, for serving

1. Adjust an oven rack to the lowest position, place a large rimmed baking sheet on the rack, and heat the oven to 500 degrees. Cut the broccoli at the juncture of the florets and stems; remove the outer peel from the stalk. Cut the stalk into 2 to 3-inch lengths and each length into ½-inch-thick pieces. Cut the crowns into four wedges (if 3 to 4 inches in diameter) or six wedges (if 4 to 5 inches in diameter). Place the broccoli in a large bowl; drizzle with the oil and toss well until evenly coated. Season with the salt, sugar, and pepper to taste and toss to combine.

2. Carefully remove the baking sheet from the oven. Working quickly, transfer the broccoli to the baking sheet and spread into an even layer, placing the flat sides down. Return the baking sheet to the oven and roast until the stalks are well browned and tender and the florets are lightly browned, 9 to 11 minutes. Transfer to a dish and serve with the lemon wedges.

Roasted Broccoli with Garlic

Follow the recipe for Roasted Broccoli, adding 1 garlic clove, minced or pressed through a garlic press, to the oil before drizzling it over the broccoli in step 1.

ROASTED CARROTS

WHY THIS RECIPE WORKS: Roasting carrots draws out their natural sugars and intensifies their flavor, but too often carrots shrivel up and turn jerky-like under the high heat of the oven. We wanted roasted carrots with a pleasingly al dente chew and earthy, sweet flavor.

To compensate for the oven's arid heat, we tried adding liquid to the roasting pan. While our carrots turned out moist, they weren't browned and lacked the intense roasted flavor we wanted. Our science editor then explained that no additional moisture was necessary. While a carrot's hard, woody structure doesn't suggest it, the average carrot is actually 87.5 percent water by weight. For our next test we tossed the carrots with melted butter, spread them onto a baking sheet, and covered the sheet tightly with foil. We roasted the carrots, covered, just until softened, then we removed the foil and continued to roast them to draw out their moisture and brown them. The result? Rich-tasting, tender carrots with a nutty flavor. Best of all, the technique worked just as well when we paired the carrots with other roasted root vegetables: parsnips, fennel, and shallots.

Roasted Carrots

SERVES 4 TO 6
Most bagged carrots come in a variety of sizes and must be cut lengthwise for evenly cooked results. After halving the carrots crosswise, leave small (less than ½ inch in diameter) pieces whole; halve medium pieces (½ to 1-inch diameter), and quarter large pieces (over 1 inch).

1½ **pounds carrots, peeled, halved crosswise, and cut**
     lengthwise if necessary (see note)
  2 **tablespoons unsalted butter, melted**
     Table salt and ground black pepper

1. Adjust an oven rack to the middle position and heat the oven to 425 degrees. Line a large rimmed baking sheet with parchment or aluminum foil. In a large bowl, combine the carrots with the butter, ½ teaspoon salt, and ¼ teaspoon pepper; toss to coat. Transfer the carrots to the prepared baking sheet and spread in a single layer.

2. Cover the baking sheet tightly with foil and roast for 15 minutes. Remove the foil and continue to roast, stirring twice, until well-browned and tender, 30 to 35 minutes. Transfer to a serving platter, season with salt and pepper to taste, and serve.

Roasted Carrots and Fennel with Toasted Almonds and Lemon

Follow the recipe for Roasted Carrots, reducing the amount of carrots to 1 pound. Add ½ large fennel bulb, cored and sliced ½ inch thick, to the bowl with the carrots and roast as directed. Toss the roasted vegetables with ¼ cup toasted sliced almonds, 1 teaspoon juice from 1 lemon, and 2 teaspoons chopped fresh parsley leaves before serving in step 2.

Roasted Carrots and Parsnips with Rosemary

Follow the recipe for Roasted Carrots, reducing the amount of carrots to 1 pound. Add ½ pound peeled parsnips, cut like the carrots, and 1 teaspoon chopped fresh rosemary leaves to the bowl with the carrots and roast as directed. Toss the roasted vegetables with 2 teaspoons chopped fresh parsley leaves before serving in step 2.

QUICK ROASTED BABY CARROTS

WHY THIS RECIPE WORKS: Roasted carrots frequently end up either undercooked, with a bitter, hard center or, at the other end of the spectrum, are subjected to such intense heat that they become wan, limp, and utterly unpalatable. We wanted to release the sweetness from the carrots, yielding a caramelized exterior and a creamy, tender interior.

Roasting prepared baby carrots saved us time, because they require no cleaning or cutting. The flavor of the carrots needed a little help; plain olive oil with a little salt worked well—it neither masked the carrots' flavor nor changed their texture. Roasting the carrots uncovered at a high temperature created the caramelized exterior we were after, and using the bottom of a broiler pan prevented them from burning. We were now able to produce perfectly cooked, deeply flavorful roasted carrots in just 20 minutes.

Quick Roasted Baby Carrots

SERVES 8

When buying carrots, inspect the bag carefully for pockets of water. Bags taken from the top of the supermarket's pile are often waterlogged. This not only makes carrots mealy, it also prevents them from caramelizing properly.

2 pounds baby carrots (two 16-ounce bags; see note)
2 tablespoons olive oil
½ teaspoon table salt

Adjust an oven rack to the middle position and heat the oven to 475 degrees. Toss the carrots, oil, and salt in a broiler pan bottom. Spread into a single layer and roast for 12 minutes. Shake the pan to toss the carrots; continue roasting about 8 minutes longer, shaking the pan twice more, until the carrots are browned and tender. Serve.

GLAZED CARROTS

WHY THIS RECIPE WORKS: Glazing is probably the most popular way to prepare carrots, but they often turn out saccharine, with a limp and soggy or undercooked and fibrous texture. We wanted fully tender, well-seasoned carrots with a glossy and clingy—yet modest—glaze.

Peeling regular bagged carrots and cutting them on the bias yielded uniform ovals that cooked evenly. We cooked and glazed the carrots in one single operation, starting by cooking the sliced carrots in a covered skillet with chicken broth, salt, and sugar. After the carrots were cooked until almost tender, we removed the lid and turned up the heat to reduce the liquid. Finally, a little butter and a bit more sugar added to the skillet resulted in a pale amber glaze with light caramel flavor. A sprinkle of fresh lemon juice gave the dish sparkle, and a pinch of freshly ground black pepper provided depth.

Glazed Carrots

SERVES 4

We like to use a nonstick skillet here for easy cleanup, but any 12-inch skillet with a cover will work.

1 pound carrots (about 6 medium), peeled and sliced
   ¼ inch thick on the bias
½ cup low-sodium chicken broth
3 tablespoons sugar
½ teaspoon table salt
1 tablespoon unsalted butter, cut into 4 pieces
2 teaspoons juice from 1 lemon
   Ground black pepper

1. Bring the carrots, broth, 1 tablespoon of the sugar, and the salt to a boil in a 12-inch nonstick skillet, covered, over medium-high heat. Reduce the heat to medium and simmer, stirring occasionally, until the carrots are almost tender when poked with the tip of a paring knife, about 5 minutes. Uncover, increase the heat to high, and simmer rapidly, stirring occasionally, until the liquid is reduced to about 2 tablespoons, 1 to 2 minutes.

2. Add the remaining 2 tablespoons sugar and the butter to the skillet. Toss the carrots to coat and cook, stirring frequently, until the carrots are completely tender and the glaze is light gold, about 3 minutes. Off the heat, add the lemon juice and toss to coat. Transfer the carrots to a dish, scraping the glaze from the pan into the dish. Season with pepper to taste and serve.

CORN FRITTERS

WHY THIS RECIPE WORKS: Good corn fritters should be light—creamy in the middle and crisp on the outside. This is rarely the case, however; most corn fritters have little corn flavor and cook up dense and greasy. We wanted to make perfect corn fritters—light, crisp, and packed with fresh corn flavor.

We found that combining whole corn kernels and grated kernels worked best for visual appeal, textural contrast, and fullest corn flavor. Running the back of a knife over the cobs from which the corn had been grated helped us extract the flavorful pulp. Equal amounts of flour and cornmeal bound the mixture together without making the fritters heavy and kept the corn flavor strong. A bit of heavy cream added welcome richness. For pan-frying the cakes, vegetable oil was the cooking medium of choice for its high smoke point and neutral flavor, which didn't overpower the corn. Keeping the oil hot helped the fritters brown quickly.

Corn Fritters

MAKES TWELVE 2-INCH FRITTERS

Serve these fritters with hot sauce, salsa, or even maple syrup.

  4 ears corn, husks and silk removed
  1 large egg, lightly beaten
  3 tablespoons unbleached all-purpose flour
  3 tablespoons cornmeal
  2 tablespoons heavy cream
  1 small shallot, minced (about 1 tablespoon)
  ½ teaspoon table salt
     Pinch cayenne pepper
  ¼ cup vegetable oil, plus more as needed

1. Stand the corn upright inside a large bowl and, using a paring knife, carefully cut the kernels from 2 ears of the corn; you should have about 1 cup. Transfer the kernels to a medium bowl. Use the back of a butter knife to scrape off any pulp remaining on the cobs and transfer it to the bowl. Grate the kernels from the remaining 2 ears of corn on the large holes of a box grater, then firmly scrape off any pulp remaining on the cobs with the back of a butter knife; you should have a generous cup of kernels and pulp. Transfer the grated kernels and pulp to the bowl with the cut kernels.

2. Mix the egg, flour, cornmeal, cream, shallot, salt, and cayenne into the corn mixture to form a thick batter.

3. Heat the oil in a 12-inch skillet over medium-high heat until almost smoking, about 2 minutes. Drop heaping tablespoons of batter into the oil (half the batter, or six fritters, should fit into the pan at once). Fry until golden brown, about 1 minute. Using a thin metal spatula, turn the fritters and fry until the second side is golden brown, about 1 minute longer. Transfer the fritters to a paper towel–lined plate. Repeat with the remaining batter, adding more oil to the skillet if necessary. Serve.

BOSTON BAKED BEANS

WHY THIS RECIPE WORKS: Boston baked beans are both sweet and savory, a unique combination of the simplest ingredients, unified and refined during a long simmer. Unfortunately, recipes with lengthy lists of untraditional ingredients and mushy beans abound. We wanted tender beans in a thick, smoky, slightly sweet sauce.

For depth of flavor, we started by browning a combination of salt pork and bacon in a Dutch oven. Small white beans were preferred for their creamy texture and ability to remain intact during the long simmer. Mild molasses provided just the right amount of sweetness, while brown mustard and cider vinegar added welcome notes of spice and tanginess. We removed the lid for the last hour of cooking to reduce the sauce to a syrupy, intensified consistency that perfectly napped the beans.

Boston Baked Beans

SERVES 4 TO 6

The beans can be made ahead. After cooking, cool them to room temperature and refrigerate in an airtight container for up to 4 days.

- 4 ounces salt pork, trimmed of rind and cut into ½-inch cubes
- 2 ounces (about 2 slices) bacon, cut into ¼-inch pieces
- 1 medium onion, minced
- 9 cups water
- 1 pound (2 cups) dried small white beans, rinsed and picked over
- ½ cup plus 1 tablespoon mild molasses
- 1½ tablespoons prepared brown mustard, such as Gulden's
- Table salt
- 1 teaspoon cider vinegar
- Ground black pepper

1. Adjust an oven rack to the lower-middle position and heat the oven to 300 degrees. Place the salt pork and bacon in a large Dutch oven; cook over medium heat, stirring occasionally, until lightly browned and most of the fat is rendered, about 7 minutes. Add the onion and continue to cook, stirring occasionally, until the onion is softened, 5 to 7 minutes. Add the water, beans, ½ cup of the molasses, the mustard, and 1¼ teaspoons salt; increase the heat to medium-high and bring to a boil. Cover the pot and place in the oven.

2. Bake until the beans are tender, about 4 hours, stirring once after 2 hours. Remove the lid and continue to bake until the liquid has thickened to a syrupy consistency, 1 to 1½ hours longer. Remove the beans from the oven; stir in the remaining 1 tablespoon molasses, the vinegar, and salt and pepper to taste. Serve.

BLANCHED GREEN BEANS

WHY THIS RECIPE WORKS: Most vegetable side dishes require last-minute preparation, but green beans are an ideal side dish that can be prepared largely beforehand without sacrificing texture or flavor. We wanted a foolproof way of cooking beans ahead of time and then simply reheating and seasoning them just before serving.

The easiest way to do this was to blanch the beans in salted water, shock them in ice water to stop the cooking process, and then towel-dry and refrigerate them until needed—a process that could be completed up to three days before serving. To serve, we reheated the beans in a skillet with a little water and flavored them with a butter sauce. The small amount of water came to a boil quickly and evaporated almost completely, helping to heat the beans in just a minute or two for a quick and flavorful side dish.

Blanched Green Beans

SERVES 4

Blanched and cooled beans can be refrigerated in a zipper-lock bag for up to 3 days. To blanch, dress, and serve the beans without holding them first, increase the blanching time to 5 to 6 minutes and don't bother shocking them in ice water. Instead, quickly arrange the warm, drained beans on a serving platter and top them with the sauce you've prepared as the beans blanch (recipes follow).

- 1 teaspoon table salt
- 1 pound green beans, trimmed

Bring 2½ quarts water to a boil in a large saucepan over high heat; add the salt and green beans, return to a boil, and cook until the beans are bright green and crisp-tender, 3 to 4 minutes. Drain the beans and transfer them immediately to a large bowl filled with ice water. When the beans have cooled to room temperature, drain again and dry thoroughly with paper towels. Set aside (or refrigerate) until needed.

Green Beans with Sautéed Shallots and Vermouth

- 4 tablespoons (½ stick) unsalted butter
- 4 large shallots, sliced thin (about 1 cup)
- 1 recipe Blanched Green Beans
  Table salt and ground black pepper
- 2 tablespoons dry vermouth

1. Melt 2 tablespoons of the butter in a small skillet over medium heat. Add the shallots and cook, stirring frequently, until golden brown, fragrant, and just crisp around the edges, about 10 minutes. Set the skillet aside, off the heat.

2. Heat ¼ cup water and the beans in a 12-inch skillet over high heat; cook, tossing frequently, until warmed through, 1 to 2 minutes. Season with salt and pepper to taste and arrange on a warm platter.

3. Meanwhile, return the skillet with the shallots to high heat, stir in the vermouth, and bring to a simmer. Whisk in the remaining 2 tablespoons butter, 1 tablespoon at a time, and season with salt and pepper to taste. Top the beans with the shallots and sauce and serve.

Green Beans with Toasted Hazelnuts and Brown Butter

Use a light-colored traditional saucepan instead of a darker nonstick saucepan for this recipe to easily monitor the butter's browning.

- 4 tablespoons (½ stick) unsalted butter
- ½ cup hazelnuts, toasted and chopped fine
  Table salt and ground black pepper
- 1 recipe Blanched Green Beans

1. Melt the butter in a small saucepan over medium heat and cook, swirling frequently, until brown and fragrant, 4 to 5 minutes. Add the hazelnuts and cook, stirring constantly, until fragrant, about 1 minute. Season with salt and pepper to taste.

2. Meanwhile, heat ¼ cup water and the beans in a 12-inch skillet over high heat; cook, tossing frequently, until warmed through, 1 to 2 minutes. Season with salt and pepper to taste and arrange on a warm platter. Top the beans with the hazelnuts and butter and serve.

GREEN BEANS AMANDINE

WHY THIS RECIPE WORKS: A simple dish of green beans tossed with toasted almonds and a light lemon-butter sauce, green beans amandine is refined yet not intimidating. Unfortunately, recipes too often yield limp beans swimming in pools of overly acidic sauce, with soft, pale almonds thrown on as an afterthought. We wanted to revive this side dish with tender green beans, crisp almonds, and a balanced sauce.

For maximum flavor, we toasted the almonds then added some butter to the skillet and allowed it to brown for further nuttiness. Adding some lemon juice off the heat brightened our sauce considerably. After steaming the green beans in a little water in a covered skillet until they were crisp-tender, we tossed them with our sauce for a simple, flavorful take on this classic side.

Green Beans Amandine

SERVES 8

Use a light-colored traditional skillet instead of a darker nonstick skillet for this recipe to easily monitor the butter's browning.

- ⅓ cup sliced almonds
- 3 tablespoons unsalted butter, cut into pieces
- 2 teaspoons juice from 1 lemon
- 2 pounds green beans, trimmed
  Table salt

1. Toast the almonds in a large skillet over medium-low heat, stirring often, until just golden, about 6 minutes. Add the butter and cook, stirring constantly, until the butter is golden brown and has a nutty aroma, about 3 minutes. Transfer the almond mixture to a bowl and stir in the lemon juice.

2. Add the beans, ½ cup water, and ½ teaspoon salt to the now-empty skillet. Cover and cook over medium-low heat, stirring occasionally, until the beans are nearly tender, 8 to 10 minutes. Remove the lid and cook over medium-high heat until the liquid evaporates, 3 to 5 minutes. Off the heat, add the reserved almond mixture to the skillet and toss to combine. Season with salt to taste and serve.

ROASTED GREEN BEANS

WHY THIS RECIPE WORKS: Mature supermarket green beans are often tough and dull, needing special treatment to become tender and flavorful. Braising works, but the stovetop can get awfully crowded as dinnertime approaches. Roasting is a great option for many vegetables, and we wanted to find out if this technique could help transform older green beans, giving them a flavor comparable to sweet, fresh-picked beans.

A remarkably simple test produced outstanding results: Beans roasted in a 450-degree oven with only oil, salt, and pepper transformed aged specimens into deeply caramelized, full-flavored beans. Just 20 minutes of roasting reversed the aging process (converting starch back to sugar) and encouraged flavorful browning. Just 1 tablespoon of oil was enough to lend flavor and moisture without making the beans greasy. Lining the pan with foil prevented scorching and made for easy cleanup.

Roasted Green Beans

SERVES 4

Lining the baking sheet with foil makes for easy cleanup.

- 1 **pound green beans, trimmed**
- 1 **tablespoon olive oil**
  Table salt and ground black pepper

1. Adjust an oven rack to the middle position and heat the oven to 450 degrees. Line a large rimmed baking sheet with foil; spread the beans on the baking sheet. Drizzle with the oil; using your hands, toss to coat evenly. Sprinkle with ½ teaspoon salt, toss to coat, and distribute in an even layer. Roast for 10 minutes.

2. Remove the baking sheet from the oven. Using tongs, redistribute the beans. Continue roasting until the beans are dark golden brown in spots and have started to shrivel, 10 to 12 minutes longer. Season with salt and pepper to taste and serve.

SPINACH WITH GARLIC AND LEMON

WHY THIS RECIPE WORKS: Overcooked spinach, bitter burnt garlic, and pallid lemon flavor are all too often the hallmarks of this simple side dish. Instead, we sought tender sautéed spinach, seasoned with a perfect balance of garlic and lemon.

We preferred the hearty flavor and texture of curly-leaf spinach in this classic dish. We cooked the spinach in extra-virgin olive oil with slivered garlic (lightly browned in the pan before the spinach was added), which gave the spinach a sweet nuttiness. Once the spinach was cooked, we used tongs to squeeze the spinach in a colander over the sink to get rid of all the excess moisture. As for seasoning, a squeeze of lemon juice and some grated lemon zest, as well as a pinch of red pepper flakes gave the spinach some gentle heat. And finally, a drizzle of extra-virgin olive oil boosted the fruitiness of the dish.

Sautéed Garlic-Lemon Spinach

SERVES 4

The amount of spinach may seem excessive, but the spinach wilts considerably with cooking. We like to use a salad spinner to wash and dry the spinach.

- 2 **tablespoons extra-virgin olive oil, plus 1 teaspoon for drizzling**
- 4 **medium garlic cloves, sliced thin crosswise (about 4 teaspoons)**
- 3 **(10-ounce) bags curly-leaf spinach, stems removed, leaves washed and dried (see note)**
  Table salt
  Pinch red pepper flakes
- ½ **teaspoon grated zest plus 2 teaspoons juice from 1 lemon**

1. Heat 2 tablespoons of the oil and the garlic in a large Dutch oven over medium-high heat until shimmering; cook until the garlic is light golden brown, shaking the pan back and forth when the garlic begins to sizzle, about 3 minutes. Add the spinach by the handful, using tongs to stir and coat the spinach with the oil.

2. Once all the spinach is added, sprinkle ¼ teaspoon salt, the red pepper flakes, and lemon zest over the top and continue stirring with the tongs until the spinach is uniformly wilted and glossy, about 2 minutes. Using the tongs, transfer the spinach to a colander set in a sink and gently squeeze the spinach with the tongs to release the excess liquid. Return the spinach to the Dutch oven; sprinkle with the lemon juice and stir to coat. Drizzle with the remaining 1 teaspoon olive oil and season with salt to taste. Serve.

SAUTÉED BABY SPINACH

WHY THIS RECIPE WORKS: Baby spinach is convenient—no stems to remove or grit to rinse out—but cooking often turns this tender green into a watery, mushy mess. We were determined to find a method for cooking baby spinach that would give us a worthwhile side dish.

Wilting, blanching, and steaming proved to be unsuccessful in removing excess water from baby spinach, but parcooking the spinach in the microwave with a little water added to the bowl worked great. After three minutes, the spinach had softened and shrunk to half its size, thanks to the release of a great deal of liquid. But there was still more water to remove. We found that pressing the spinach against the colander before roughly chopping it on a cutting board and then pressing it again removed any remaining excess liquid. The spinach was now tender, sweet, and ready to be combined with complementary ingredients. Pairing almonds and raisins introduced bold flavors and textures that enlivened this quick-cooking green.

Sautéed Baby Spinach with Almonds and Golden Raisins
SERVES 4

If you don't have a microwave-safe bowl large enough to accommodate the entire amount of spinach, cook it in a smaller bowl in two batches. Reduce the amount of water to 2 tablespoons per batch and cook each batch for about 1½ minutes.

- 3 (6-ounce) bags baby spinach (about 18 cups)
- ¼ cup water
- 2 tablespoons extra-virgin olive oil, plus 2 teaspoons for drizzling
- ½ cup golden raisins
- 4 medium garlic cloves, sliced thin crosswise (about 4 teaspoons)
- ¼ teaspoon red pepper flakes
  Table salt
- 2 teaspoons sherry vinegar
- ⅓ cup slivered almonds, toasted

1. Place the spinach and water in a large microwave-safe bowl. Cover the bowl with a large microwave-safe dinner plate (the plate should completely cover the bowl and not rest on the spinach). Microwave on high power until the spinach is wilted and decreased in volume by half, 3 to 4 minutes. Using potholders, remove the bowl from the microwave and keep covered for 1 minute. Carefully remove the plate and transfer the spinach to a colander set in the sink. Using the back of a rubber spatula, gently press the spinach against the colander to release excess liquid. Transfer the spinach to a cutting board and roughly chop. Return to the colander and press a second time.

2. Heat 2 tablespoons of the oil, the raisins, garlic, and red pepper flakes in a 10-inch skillet over medium-high heat. Cook, stirring constantly, until the garlic is light golden brown and beginning to sizzle, 3 to 6 minutes. Add the spinach to the skillet, using tongs to stir and coat with the oil. Sprinkle with ¼ teaspoon salt and continue stirring with the tongs until the spinach is uniformly wilted and glossy, about 2 minutes. Sprinkle with the vinegar and almonds; stir to combine. Drizzle with the remaining 2 teaspoons oil and season with salt to taste. Serve.

CREAMY HERBED SPINACH DIP

WHY THIS RECIPE WORKS: Spinach dip made with sour cream and soup mixes are flat, overly salty, and stale tasting. We wanted to ditch the mix and create a rich, thick, and creamy spinach dip brimming with big, bold flavors.

We were surprised to discover that frozen spinach actually made a better-tasting dip with a vibrant, more intense flavor than one made with fresh spinach. We used a food processor to chop the spinach and then enriched it with sour cream, mayonnaise, and a mixture of fresh herbs and seasonings. The only problem was that our dip, which took just about 15 minutes to make, took almost two hours to chill. Fortunately the solution turned out to be a simple one. Instead of thawing the spinach completely, we only partially thawed it, allowing the chunks of icy spinach to thoroughly cool the dip as they broke down in the food processor. This dip is fresh-tasting, quick to make, and ready to serve immediately.

Creamy Herbed Spinach Dip

MAKES ABOUT 1½ CUPS

Partial thawing of the spinach produces a cold dip that can be served without further chilling. Instead of microwaving, the frozen spinach can also be thawed at room temperature for 1½ hours, then squeezed of excess liquid. The garlic must be minced or pressed before going into the food processor; otherwise, the dip will contain large chunks of garlic.

1 (10-ounce) box frozen chopped spinach
½ cup sour cream
½ cup mayonnaise
3 scallions, white parts only, sliced thin
½ cup packed fresh parsley leaves
1 tablespoon minced fresh dill
1 small garlic clove, minced or pressed through a garlic press (about ½ teaspoon; see note)
½ teaspoon table salt
¼ teaspoon ground black pepper
¼ teaspoon hot sauce
½ red bell pepper, chopped fine

1. Thaw the spinach in a microwave for 3 minutes at 40 percent power. (The edges should be thawed but not warm; the center should be soft enough to be broken into icy chunks.) Squeeze the partially frozen spinach to remove excess water.

2. Process the spinach, sour cream, mayonnaise, scallions, parsley, dill, garlic, salt, pepper, and hot sauce in a food processor until smooth and creamy, about 30 seconds. Transfer the mixture to a bowl and stir in the bell pepper; serve. (The dip can be covered with plastic wrap and refrigerated for up to 2 days.)

QUICK-COOKED TOUGH GREENS

WHY THIS RECIPE WORKS: Unlike tender greens, tougher greens such as kale, mustard, turnip, and collard greens don't have enough moisture to be wilted in a hot pan; they'll simply scorch before they wilt. Their flavor is much more assertive, even peppery in some cases, and can be overwhelming. We wanted a technique for cooking Southern-style greens that would mellow their assertive bite and render them tender—while still retaining just the right amount of chew.

Because they are relatively dry, these greens required the addition of some liquid as they cooked. Steaming the greens produced a texture tasters liked, but it didn't help tame their bitter flavor. Shallow blanching removed enough bitterness to make these assertive greens palatable, but didn't rob them of their character. After blanching the greens, we drained and then briefly cooked them with a little garlic and red pepper flakes for a spicy kick. To prevent them from becoming too dry, we added a little chicken broth to the pan for moistness and extra flavor.

Quick-Cooked Tough Greens

SERVES 4

Shallow-blanched greens should be shocked in cold water to stop the cooking process, drained, and then braised. Shocked and drained greens can be held for up to an hour before being braised.

Table salt
2 pounds assertive greens, such as kale, collards, or mustard, stemmed, washed in several changes of cold water, and chopped coarse
3 tablespoons extra-virgin olive oil
3 medium garlic cloves, sliced thin crosswise (about 3 teaspoons)
Red pepper flakes
⅓–½ cup low-sodium chicken broth
Lemon wedges, for serving

1. Bring 2 quarts water to a boil in a large pot. Add 1½ teaspoons salt and the greens and stir until wilted, 1 to 2 minutes. Cover and cook until the greens are just tender, about 7 minutes. Drain the greens and pour them into a large bowl filled with ice water. Working with a handful of greens at a time, thoroughly squeeze them dry.

2. Heat the oil, garlic, and ¼ teaspoon red pepper flakes in a large skillet over medium heat until the garlic starts to sizzle, about 1 minute. Add the greens and toss to coat with the oil. Add ⅓ cup of the broth, cover, and cook over medium-high heat, adding more broth if necessary, until the greens are tender and juicy and most of the broth has been absorbed, about 5 minutes. Season with salt and additional red pepper flakes to taste. Serve with the lemon wedges.

SAUTÉED SWISS CHARD

WHY THIS RECIPE WORKS: Swiss chard, like spinach, is delicate and has an earthy flavor that mellows once cooked. A thick stalk runs through the center of each leaf, however, and can make cooking the greens a challenge. We set out to find a simple method for preparing Swiss chard—one that would yield tender, evenly cooked greens (both stalks and leaves) with deep flavor.

After testing blanching, steaming, microwaving, and wilting, the simplest, most straightforward method of cooking proved to be wilting our greens on the stovetop. First, however, we separated the leaves from the stalks and tossed the stalks, wet from washing, into the pan first. We added garlic for flavor, then added the leaves, covered the pan, and cooked, stirring occasionally, until the greens were wilted by the steam created by their own liquid. We then found that we got even better results when combining this technique with sautéing. To do this, we heated oil in the pan, then proceeded as before, adding the stalks before the leaves. Once the leaves wilted, we removed the lid, seasoned with salt and pepper, and sautéed the greens over high heat until all the liquid evaporated.

Simple Sautéed Swiss Chard

SERVES 4

A thick stalk runs through each Swiss chard leaf, so the leaf must be cut away from it.

- 3 tablespoons extra-virgin olive oil
- 2 pounds Swiss chard, stemmed, washed in several changes of cold water, stalks chopped medium and leaves chopped coarse
- 2 medium garlic cloves, minced or pressed through a garlic press (about 2 teaspoons)
  Table salt and ground black pepper
  Lemon wedges, for serving

1. Heat the oil in a large Dutch oven over medium heat until shimmering. Add the chard stalks and cook, stirring occasionally, until just tender, about 5 minutes. Add the garlic and cook until fragrant, about 30 seconds. Add the chard leaves, cover, increase the heat to medium-high, and cook, stirring occasionally, until the greens completely wilt, 2 to 3 minutes.

2. Uncover and season with salt and pepper to taste. Cook over high heat until the liquid evaporates, about 2 minutes. Serve with the lemon wedges.

SMASHED POTATOES

WHY THIS RECIPE WORKS: Bold flavors and a rustic, chunky texture make smashed potatoes a satisfying side dish, one that pairs well with everything from grilled steak to roast chicken. But good smashed potatoes are hard to find. We were after a good contrast of textures, with the rich, creamy puree of mashed potatoes accented by chunks of potato and skins.

Testing revealed that low-starch, high-moisture red potatoes were the best choice for this dish. Their compact structure held up well under pressure, maintaining its integrity. The thin skins were pleasantly tender and paired nicely with the chunky potatoes. Cooked whole in salted water with a bay leaf, the potatoes became lightly seasoned while also retaining their naturally creamy texture, as the skins protected the potato flesh from the water. For the best chunky texture, we smashed the potatoes with a rubber spatula or the back of a wooden spoon. Cream cheese and butter lent tang, richness, and body to the dish, and stirring in a little of the potato cooking water added enough moisture to the smash to give it a unified and creamy consistency without diluting the potato flavor. Seasoned with salt, freshly ground black pepper, and a sprinkling of chopped chives for bright flavor and color, these potatoes are a quick, no-fuss side dish to complement any casual dinner.

Smashed Potatoes

SERVES 4

Try to get potatoes of equal size; if that's not possible, test the larger potatoes for doneness (use a paring knife). If only large potatoes are available, increase the cooking time by about 10 minutes.

- 2 pounds red potatoes (about 12 small), scrubbed
  Table salt
- 1 bay leaf
- 4 tablespoons (½ stick) unsalted butter, melted
- 4 ounces cream cheese, at room temperature
- 3 tablespoons minced fresh chives (optional)
  Ground black pepper

1. Place the potatoes in a large saucepan and add cold water to cover by 1 inch; add 1 teaspoon salt and the bay leaf. Bring to a boil over high heat, then reduce the heat to medium-low and simmer gently until a paring knife can be inserted into the potatoes with no resistance, 35 to 45 minutes. Reserve ½ cup of the cooking water, then drain the potatoes. Return the potatoes to the pot, discard the bay leaf, and allow the potatoes to stand in the pot, uncovered, until the surfaces are dry, about 5 minutes.

2. While the potatoes dry, whisk the melted butter and softened cream cheese in a medium bowl until smooth and fully incorporated. Add ¼ cup of the reserved cooking water, the chives (if using), ½ teaspoon pepper, and ½ teaspoon salt. Using a rubber spatula or the back of a wooden spoon, smash the potatoes just enough to break the skins. Fold in the butter–cream cheese mixture until most of the liquid has been absorbed and chunks of potatoes remain. Add more cooking water as needed, 1 tablespoon at a time, until the potatoes are slightly looser than desired (the potatoes will thicken slightly with standing). Season with salt and pepper to taste and serve.

CLASSIC MASHED POTATOES

WHY THIS RECIPE WORKS: Many people would never consider consulting a recipe when making mashed potatoes, instead adding chunks of butter and spurts of cream until their conscience tells them to stop. Little wonder then that mashed potatoes made this way are consistent only in their mediocrity. We wanted mashed potatoes that were perfectly smooth and creamy, with great potato flavor and plenty of buttery richness every time.

We began by selecting russet potatoes for their high starch content. Through trial and error, we learned to boil them whole and unpeeled—this method yielded mashed potatoes that were rich, earthy, and sweet. We used a food mill or ricer for the smoothest texture imaginable, but a potato masher can be used if you prefer your potatoes a little chunky. For smooth, velvety potatoes, we added melted butter first and then half-and-half. Melting, rather than merely softening, the butter enables it to coat the starch molecules quickly and easily, so the potatoes turn out creamy and light.

Classic Mashed Potatoes

SERVES 4

Russet potatoes make fluffier mashed potatoes, but Yukon Golds have an appealing buttery flavor and can be used. This recipe yields smooth mashed potatoes. If you don't mind lumps, use a potato masher.

BEHIND THE SCENES

ADAM'S EQUIPMENT HALL OF SHAME

Adam and the equipment testing team have spent thousands of hours over the past decade separating the good from the bad— and once in a while they come across gadgets and equipment that perform so poorly, they deserve special mention.

QUESADILLA MAKER: If we're going to shell out money for a gadget devoted to just one dish, it better be awfully good. This quesadilla maker, however, severely limits the amount of cheese that can be sandwiched between the tortillas. So, uh, what's the point? Unless you're on a diet, use a skillet instead.

SHRIMP BUTLER: Although this gadget is supposed to peel and devein shrimp, it only accomplishes the task partway by slitting the shell to reveal the vein. Even worse, we found that the shrimp sometimes became mangled in the machine. And since our testing, shrimp is now often sold deveined and slit for easy peeling, so a "butler" for a shrimp is no longer necessary.

THERMOMETER FORK: Ouch! Put away your thermo fork and grab an instant-read thermometer and pair of tongs instead (see our recommended brands on pages 718 and 712). Thermometer forks are designed to enable the user to move the food being cooked on the grill and take its temperature at the same time. We found this gadget awkward to use, especially when trying to flip or turn meat for even browning.

ALLIGATOR CHOPPER: This gadget claims to deliver perfectly cubed onions and elegant batons of carrots, bell peppers, or apples with one punch of the handheld chopper blades against its platform base. But too often, we found ourselves cautiously extracting suspended vegetables from the blade. We'll stick to chopping veggies the old-fashioned way—with a sharp knife and cutting board.

BANANA HANGER: Supermarkets often suspend unripe bananas from tall poles covered with small hooks. Banana hangers miniaturize this idea for the home kitchen. Sounds good, but we found no difference in the ripening time between hanging bananas . . . and simply setting them on the counter.

2 pounds russet potatoes (about 4 medium), scrubbed
   (see note)
8 tablespoons (1 stick) unsalted butter, melted
1 cup half-and-half, warmed
1½ teaspoons table salt
   Ground black pepper

1. Place the potatoes in a large saucepan and add cold water to cover by 1 inch. Bring to a boil over high heat, reduce the heat to medium-low, and simmer until the potatoes are just tender when pricked with a fork, 20 to 30 minutes. Drain the potatoes.

2. Set a ricer or food mill over the now-empty saucepan. Using a potholder (to hold the potatoes) and a paring knife, peel the skins from the potatoes. Working in batches, cut the peeled potatoes into large chunks and press or mill into the saucepan.

3. Stir in the butter until incorporated. Gently whisk in the half-and-half, and season with the salt and pepper to taste. Serve.

GARLIC AND OLIVE OIL MASHED POTATOES

WHY THIS RECIPE WORKS: The Mediterranean approach of flavoring mashed potatoes with olive oil and garlic is an appealing one, but it's not as simple as replacing the dairy with oil: olive oil can turn the texture pasty and garlic can be harsh and overpowering. We wanted to translate these bold flavors into a light and creamy mashed potato side dish that would partner well with simple grilled meats or fish.

We chose to use russets in this dish for their light, fluffy texture. We first simmered the potatoes and then put the drained, peeled, still-hot potatoes through a ricer or food mill for a smooth texture. We created a mild flavor base by slowly cooking minced garlic in oil, then heightened the garlic flavor a bit by adding just a little garlic, mashed to a paste. Fruity extra-virgin olive oil and a splash of fresh lemon juice brightened the final dish.

Garlic and Olive Oil Mashed Potatoes
SERVES 6

As this dish is denser and more intensely flavored than traditional mashed potatoes, our suggested serving size is smaller than you might expect.

2 pounds russet potatoes (about 4 medium), scrubbed
5 medium garlic cloves, minced or pressed through a
   garlic press (about 5 teaspoons)
2⅛ teaspoons table salt
½ cup plus 2 tablespoons extra-virgin olive oil
½ teaspoon ground black pepper
2 teaspoons juice from 1 lemon

1. Place the potatoes in a large saucepan and add cold water to cover by 1 inch. Bring to a boil over high heat; reduce the heat to medium-low and cook at a bare simmer until just tender (the potatoes will offer very little resistance when poked with a paring knife), 40 to 45 minutes.

2. Meanwhile, place 1 teaspoon of the garlic on a cutting board and sprinkle with ⅛ teaspoon of the salt. Using the flat side of a chef's knife, drag the garlic and salt back and forth across the cutting board in small circular motions until the garlic is ground into a smooth paste. Transfer to a medium bowl and set aside.

3. Place the remaining 4 teaspoons garlic in a small saucepan with ¼ cup of the oil and cook over low heat, stirring constantly, until the garlic begins to sizzle and is soft, fragrant, and golden, about 5 minutes. Transfer the oil and garlic to the bowl with the raw garlic paste.

4. Drain the cooked potatoes; set a ricer or food mill over the now-empty saucepan. Using a potholder (to hold the potatoes) and a paring knife, peel the skins from the potatoes. Working in batches, cut the peeled potatoes into large chunks and press or mill into the saucepan.

5. Add the remaining 2 teaspoons salt, the pepper, lemon juice, and remaining 6 tablespoons oil to the bowl with the cooked garlic and oil and whisk to combine. Fold the mixture into the potatoes and serve.

ULTIMATE CREAMY MASHED POTATOES

WHY THIS RECIPE WORKS: Sometimes we want a luxurious mash, one that is silky smooth and loaded with cream and butter. But there's a fine line between creamy and gluey. We wanted lush, creamy mashed potatoes, with so much richness and flavor they can stand on their own—no gravy necessary.

For a creamier, substantial mash, we found that Yukon Golds were perfect—creamier than russets but not as heavy as red potatoes. Slicing the peeled potatoes into rounds and then rinsing away the surface starch before boiling helped intensify their creamy texture without making them gluey. Setting the boiled and drained potatoes in their pot over a low flame helped further evaporate any excess moisture. Using 1½ sticks of butter and 1½ cups of heavy cream gives these potatoes luxurious flavor and richness without making the mash too thin. We found that melting the butter and warming the cream before adding them to the potatoes ensured that the finished dish arrived at the table piping hot.

Creamy Mashed Potatoes

SERVES 8 TO 10

This recipe can be cut in half, if desired.

- 4 **pounds Yukon Gold potatoes (about 8 medium), scrubbed, peeled, and sliced ¾ inch thick**
- 1½ **cups heavy cream**
- 12 **tablespoons (1½ sticks) unsalted butter, cut into 6 pieces**
- 2 **teaspoons table salt**

1. Place the potatoes in a colander and rinse under cool running water, tossing with your hands, for 30 seconds. Transfer the potatoes to a large Dutch oven, add cold water to cover by 1 inch, and bring to a boil over high heat. Reduce the heat to medium and boil until the potatoes are tender, 20 to 25 minutes.

2. Meanwhile, heat the heavy cream and butter in a small saucepan over medium heat until the butter is melted, about 5 minutes. Set aside and keep warm.

3. Drain the potatoes and return to the Dutch oven. Stir over low heat until the potatoes are thoroughly dried, 1 to 2 minutes. Set a ricer or food mill over a large bowl and press or mill the potatoes into the bowl. Gently fold in the warm cream mixture and salt with a rubber spatula until the cream is absorbed and the potatoes are thick and creamy. Serve.

MASHED POTATOES AND ROOT VEGETABLES

WHY THIS RECIPE WORKS: Root vegetables like carrots, parsnips, turnips, and celery root can add an earthy, intriguing flavor to mashed potatoes, but because root vegetables and potatoes have different starch levels and water content, treating them the same way creates a bad mash. We wanted a potato and root vegetable mash with a creamy consistency and a balanced flavor that highlights the natural earthiness of these humble root cellar favorites.

We found that a 1:3 ratio of root vegetables to potatoes provided an optimal consistency, although the root vegetable flavor was barely recognizable. Caramelizing the root vegetables first in a little butter helped bring out their natural earthy sweetness; this step also boosted the flavor of the overall dish. To use just one pot, we first sautéed the root vegetables in butter until caramelized and then added the potatoes with a little chicken broth. This gave us great flavor, but the mash had a gluey texture. The answer was to remove the starch from the potatoes by rinsing the peeled, sliced potatoes in several changes of water ahead of time.

Mashed Potatoes and Root Vegetables

SERVES 4

Russet potatoes will yield a slightly fluffier, less creamy mash, but they can be used in place of the Yukon Gold potatoes if desired. Rinsing the potatoes in several changes of water reduces the amount of starch and prevents the mashed potatoes from becoming gluey. It is important to cut the potatoes and root vegetables into even-sized pieces so they cook at the same rate. This recipe can be doubled and cooked in a large Dutch oven. If doubling, increase the cooking time in step 2 to 40 minutes.

- 4 **tablespoons (½ stick) unsalted butter**
- 8 **ounces carrots, parsnips, turnips, or celery root, peeled; carrots or parsnips cut into ¼-inch-thick half-moons; turnips or celery root cut into ½-inch dice (about 1½ cups)**
- 1½ **pounds Yukon Gold potatoes (about 3 medium), peeled, quartered lengthwise, and cut crosswise into ¼-inch-thick slices; rinsed well in 3 to 4 changes of cold water and drained well (see note)**
- ⅓ **cup low-sodium chicken broth**
  Table salt
- ¾ **cup half-and-half, warmed**
- 3 **tablespoons minced fresh chives**
  Ground black pepper

1. Melt the butter in a large saucepan over medium heat. Add the root vegetables and cook, stirring occasionally, until the butter is browned and the vegetables are dark brown and caramelized, 10 to 12 minutes. (If after 4 minutes the vegetables have not started to brown, increase the heat to medium-high.)

2. Add the potatoes, broth, and ¾ teaspoon salt and stir to combine. Cook, covered, over low heat (the broth should simmer gently; do not boil), stirring occasionally, until the potatoes fall apart easily when poked with a fork and all the liquid has been absorbed, 25 to 30 minutes. (If the liquid does not gently simmer after a few minutes, increase the heat to medium-low.) Remove the pan from the heat; remove the lid and allow the steam to escape for 2 minutes.

3. Gently mash the potatoes and root vegetables in the saucepan with a potato masher (do not mash vigorously). Gently fold in the half-and-half and chives. Season with salt and pepper to taste and serve.

FLUFFY MASHED POTATOES

WHY THIS RECIPE WORKS: In Classic Mashed Potatoes (page 487), we boil potatoes in their jackets for earthy potato flavor (and peel them while they're still hot). We don't mind this somewhat inconvenient method when we've got time to spare, but thought an easier alternative was in order.

Cooking potatoes in their skins preserves their earthy flavor and keeps the starch granules from absorbing too much water, thereby preventing gluey mashed potatoes. To give peeled potatoes the same protection, we made two alterations to our usual technique. Steaming rather than boiling the potatoes exposed the potato pieces to less water, reducing the chance of the granules swelling to the point of bursting. When they were cooked partway, we rinsed them under cold water to rid them of free amylose, the substance that results in gluey mashed potatoes, and returned them to the steamer to finish cooking. Because potatoes cooked this way are so full of rich potato flavor, we were able to use less butter and substitute whole milk for cream.

Fluffy Mashed Potatoes
SERVES 4

This recipe works best with either a metal colander that sits easily in a Dutch oven or a large pasta pot with a steamer insert. To prevent excess evaporation, it is important for the lid to fit as snugly as possible over the colander or steamer. For the lightest, fluffiest texture, use a ricer. A food mill is the next best alternative. Russets will also work in this recipe, but avoid red potatoes.

> 2 pounds Yukon Gold potatoes (about 4 medium), peeled, cut into 1-inch chunks, rinsed well, and drained (see note)
> 4 tablespoons (½ stick) unsalted butter, melted
> Table salt
> ⅔ cup whole milk, warmed
> Ground black pepper

1. Place a metal colander or steamer insert in a large pot or Dutch oven. Add enough water to barely reach the bottom of the colander. Bring the water to a boil over high heat. Add the potatoes, cover, and reduce the heat to medium-high. Cook the potatoes for 10 minutes. Transfer the colander to the sink and rinse the potatoes under cold water until no longer hot, 1 to 2 minutes. Return the colander and potatoes to the pot, cover, and continue to cook until the potatoes are soft and the tip of a paring knife inserted into the potatoes meets no resistance, 10 to 15 minutes longer. Drain the potatoes.

2. Set a ricer or food mill over the now-empty pot. Working in batches, transfer the potatoes to the hopper and process or mill, removing any potatoes stuck to the bottom. Using a rubber spatula, stir in the butter and ½ teaspoon salt until incorporated. Stir in the milk until incorporated. Season with salt and pepper to taste and serve.

BUTTERMILK MASHED POTATOES

WHY THIS RECIPE WORKS: Merely replacing butter and cream with buttermilk to create tangy, creamy buttermilk mashed potatoes doesn't work—the finished potatoes are curdled, crumbly, chalky, and dry. We wanted easy mashed potatoes with buttermilk's trademark distinctive tang, but we didn't want to sacrifice texture to get them.

Many recipes for buttermilk mashed potatoes remove so much butter that the potatoes taste lean and lack creaminess. We started by restoring just enough butter to save our mashed potatoes from this fate. We then tackled the curdling problem. Buttermilk curdles at 160 degrees, a temperature reached almost instantly when the cold liquid hits steaming-hot potatoes. By adding the butter, melted, to room-temperature buttermilk, we coated the proteins in the buttermilk and protected them from the heat shock that causes curdling. We also simplified the recipe by choosing peeled and cut Yukon Gold potatoes rather than using unpeeled russets (our usual choice for mashed potatoes). Because Yukon Golds have less starch and are less absorbent than russets, they don't become soggy and thinned out when simmered without their jackets.

Buttermilk Mashed Potatoes
SERVES 4

To achieve the proper texture, it is important to cook the potatoes thoroughly; they are done if they break apart when a knife is inserted and gently wiggled. Buttermilk substitutes like clabbered milk do not produce sufficiently tangy potatoes. To reduce the likelihood of curdling, the buttermilk must be brought to room temperature and mixed with cooled melted butter.

- 2 pounds Yukon Gold potatoes (about 4 medium), peeled and cut into 1-inch chunks
  Table salt
- 6 tablespoons (¾ stick) unsalted butter, melted and cooled (see note)
- ⅔ cup buttermilk, room temperature (see note)
  Ground black pepper

1. Place the potatoes in a large saucepan and add cold water to cover by 1 inch; add 1 tablespoon salt. Bring to a boil over high heat, then reduce the heat to medium and simmer until the potatoes break apart very easily when a paring knife is inserted, about 18 minutes. Drain the potatoes briefly, then immediately return them to the saucepan set on the still-hot (but off) burner.

2. Using a potato masher, mash the potatoes until a few small lumps remain. Gently mix the melted butter and buttermilk in a small bowl until combined. Add the buttermilk mixture to the potatoes; using a rubber spatula, fold gently until just incorporated. Season with salt and pepper to taste and serve.

ULTIMATE ROASTED POTATOES

WHY THIS RECIPE WORKS: The aroma of roasting potatoes draws everyone into the kitchen come meal time. Too often, though, the potatoes turn out brown and leathery with a mealy interior, or worse, soft with no crisp crust at all. We wanted oven-roasted potatoes that had a crisp crust with a silky interior.

We tested using different potatoes and found that we liked Yukon Golds best. Parcooking the potatoes before subjecting them to high oven temperatures helped them develop a somewhat crisper exterior, but the browning was uneven and they still weren't crispy enough. When we switched from cubing the potatoes to slicing them thick, we created more surface area for crisping but enough heft for a creamy interior. As an added bonus, with only two surfaces to cook, we now only had to flip the potatoes once halfway through roasting. We boiled the potatoes very briefly before roasting to prevent them from breaking up on the baking sheet, and we tossed the precooked potatoes with some olive oil to rough up the exteriors and increase crispiness.

Crispy Roasted Potatoes
SERVES 4 TO 6

Note that the potatoes should be just undercooked when removed from the boiling water—this helps ensure that they will roast up crispy.

- 2½ pounds Yukon Gold potatoes (about 5 medium), rinsed and cut into ½-inch-thick slices
  Table salt
- 5 tablespoons olive oil
  Ground black pepper

1. Adjust an oven rack to the lowest position, place a rimmed baking sheet on the rack, and heat the oven to 450 degrees. Place the potatoes and 1 tablespoon salt in a Dutch oven; add cold water to cover by 1 inch. Bring to a boil over high heat; reduce the heat and gently simmer until the exterior of a potato has softened, but the center offers resistance when pierced with a paring knife, about 5 minutes. Drain the potatoes well, and transfer to a large bowl. Drizzle with 2 tablespoons of the oil and sprinkle with ½ teaspoon salt; using a rubber spatula, toss to combine. Drizzle with 2 tablespoons more oil and ½ teaspoon more salt; continue to toss until the exteriors of the potato slices are coated with a starchy paste.

2. Working quickly, remove the baking sheet from the oven and drizzle the remaining 1 tablespoon oil over the surface. Carefully transfer the potatoes to the baking sheet and spread them into an even layer (skin side up for the end pieces). Bake until the bottoms of the potatoes are golden brown and crisp, 15 to 25 minutes, rotating the baking sheet after 10 minutes.

3. Remove the baking sheet from the oven and, using a metal spatula and tongs, loosen the potatoes from the pan and carefully flip each slice. Continue to roast until the second side is golden and crisp, 10 to 20 minutes longer, rotating the pan as needed to ensure the potatoes brown evenly. Season with salt and pepper to taste and serve.

SKILLET-ROASTED POTATOES

WHY THIS RECIPE WORKS: Skillet-roasted potatoes often cook up unevenly, with a mixture of scorched and pallid potatoes. We wanted to be able to make truly outstanding skillet-roasted potatoes, as good as oven-roasted—extra-crisp on the outside and moist and creamy on the inside, evenly browned, and never greasy. This would be the recipe we'd turn to when we craved roasted potatoes but there was no room in the oven for the conventional kind.

The solution turned out to be choosing the right potato and cutting it uniformly. Red Bliss potatoes, cut in half if small or quartered if medium, offered a great crust and a moist interior, thanks to their high moisture content. We rinsed the cut potatoes to remove surface starch, which otherwise caused the potatoes to stick to the pan and inhibited browning. Olive oil added flavor and richness to the dish. The winning cooking technique was to first brown the potatoes over high heat, then cover and finish cooking over low heat. This allowed the insides to cook through while the outsides stayed crisp.

Skillet-Roasted Potatoes
SERVES 3 TO 4

Small and medium potatoes can be used in this recipe, but they must be cut differently. Small potatoes (1½ to 2 inches in diameter) should be cut in half and medium potatoes (2 to 3 inches in diameter) should be cut into quarters to create ¾ to 1-inch chunks. Large potatoes should not be used because the cut pieces will be uneven and won't cook at the same rate. For even cooking and proper browning, the potatoes must be cooked in a single layer and should not be crowded in the pan.

1½ pounds small or medium red potatoes (about 9 small or 4 to 5 medium), scrubbed, halved if small, quartered if medium (see note)
2 tablespoons olive oil
¾ teaspoon table salt
¾ teaspoon ground black pepper

1. Rinse the potatoes in cold water and drain well; spread on a clean kitchen towel and thoroughly pat dry.

2. Heat the oil in a 12-inch skillet over medium-high heat until shimmering. Add the potatoes, cut side down, in a single layer. Cook, without stirring, until the potatoes are golden brown (the oil should sizzle but not smoke), 5 to 7 minutes. Using tongs, turn the potatoes skin side down if halved or second cut side down if quartered. Cook, without stirring, until the potatoes are deep golden brown, 5 to 6 minutes longer. Stir the potatoes, then redistribute in a single layer. Reduce the heat to medium-low, cover, and cook until the potatoes are tender (a paring knife can be inserted into the potatoes with no resistance), 6 to 9 minutes.

3. When the potatoes are tender, sprinkle with the salt and pepper and toss gently to combine; serve.

SALT-BAKED POTATOES

WHY THIS RECIPE WORKS: Let's be honest: Sometimes baked potatoes could use a flavor boost. And instead of light and fluffy, most often they are dense and crumbly. The technique of salt-baking potatoes promises to remedy these problems. We tried burying potatoes under a mound of salt, cooking them on a bed of salt, covering them with foil, and making a salt crust on the potatoes with the help of an egg wash. All were good, but the bed of salt was the best. Moisture that escaped the potatoes during baking was trapped in the enclosed pan, then absorbed by the salt, and eventually reabsorbed by the potatoes, making their skins tender and their flesh light and fluffy. All we needed to do was fine-tune the variables. A hot oven and uncovering the potatoes toward the end of cooking ensured dry, crisp skin. A 13 by 9-inch baking dish provided plenty of space so we didn't crowd the potatoes, and 2½ cups of salt allowed us to thoroughly cover the bottom of the pan. A little rosemary and garlic added to the pan was all the flavor these spuds needed.

Salt-Baked Potatoes with Roasted Garlic and Rosemary Butter

SERVES 4

Kosher salt or table salt can be used in this recipe. The salt may be sifted through a strainer to remove any solid bits and reused for this recipe. These potatoes can be prepared without the roast garlic butter and topped with your favorite potato toppings such as sour cream, chives, crumbled bacon, or shredded cheese.

- 2½ cups plus ⅛ teaspoon salt
- 4 medium russet potatoes (about 8 ounces each), well scrubbed and dried
- 2 sprigs fresh rosemary plus ¼ teaspoon minced leaves
- 1 whole garlic head, outer papery skin removed and top quarter of head cut off and discarded
- 4 teaspoons olive oil
- 4 tablespoons (½ stick) unsalted butter, softened

1. Adjust an oven rack to the middle position and heat the oven to 450 degrees. Spread the salt into an even layer in a 13 by 9-inch baking dish. Gently nestle the potatoes in the salt, broad side down, leaving space between each potato. Add the rosemary sprigs and the garlic, cut side up, to the baking dish. Cover the baking dish with aluminum foil and crimp the edges to tightly seal. Bake for 1 hour and 15 minutes; remove the pan from the oven. Increase the oven temperature to 500 degrees.

2. Carefully remove the foil. Remove the garlic head from the baking dish and set aside to cool. Brush the exposed portion of each potato with 1 teaspoon oil. Return the uncovered baking dish to the oven and continue to bake until the potatoes are tender and the skins are glossy, 15 to 20 minutes.

3. Meanwhile, once the garlic is cool enough to handle, squeeze the root end until the cloves slip out of their skins. Using a fork, mash the garlic, butter, minced rosemary, and remaining ⅛ teaspoon salt to a smooth paste. Remove any clumped salt from the potatoes (holding the potatoes with a kitchen mitt if necessary), split lengthwise, top with a portion of the butter and serve immediately.

Salt-Baked Potatoes with Roasted Shallot and Thyme Butter

Follow the recipe for Salt-Baked Potatoes with Roasted Garlic and Rosemary Butter, substituting 5 crumbled bay leaves for the rosemary sprigs and 1 teaspoon chopped fresh thyme leaves for the chopped rosemary. Substitute 2 medium shallots for the garlic head.

SCALLOPED POTATOES

WHY THIS RECIPE WORKS: Thinly sliced potatoes layered with cream and baked until they are bubbling and browned are a classic accompaniment to baked ham or roast beef. But scalloped potatoes can occupy the oven for over two hours and still produce unevenly cooked potatoes in a heavy, curdled sauce. We wanted to minimize the cooking time while turning out layers of thinly sliced, tender potatoes, a creamy sauce, and a nicely browned, cheesy crust.

We tried using flour to thicken the sauce, but this produced a thick, pasty sauce. Instead we relied on heavy cream lightened with whole milk. To cut the cooking time, we simmered the potatoes briefly in the cream in a covered pot, before transferring the mixture to a baking dish and finishing the potatoes in the oven. We found russet potatoes had the best texture and flavor, and we sliced them thin so they formed neat layers.

Scalloped Potatoes

SERVES 8 TO 10

For the fastest and most consistent results, slice the potatoes in a food processor or on a mandoline or V-slicer.

- 2 tablespoons unsalted butter
- 1 small onion, minced
- 2 medium garlic cloves, minced or pressed through a garlic press (about 2 teaspoons)
- 4 pounds russet potatoes (about 8 medium), peeled and cut into ⅛-inch-thick slices (see note)
- 3 cups heavy cream
- 1 cup whole milk
- 4 sprigs fresh thyme
- 2 bay leaves
- 2 teaspoons table salt
- ½ teaspoon ground black pepper
- 4 ounces cheddar cheese, shredded (about 1 cup)

KEEPING A SHARP EDGE

With three dozen test cooks, editors, and cookware specialists working side by side in the test kitchen, we take knife care very seriously. Simply put, a dull knife is a dangerous knife. Here's why: The duller the blade, the more work it takes to do the job—and the easier it is for the blade to slip and miss the mark (slippery ingredients like onions are the worst offenders), quickly sending the knife toward your hand. With a sharp knife, the blade does the work—and the razor-like edge is far less likely to slip.

To determine if your knife is sharp, put it to a simple test. Hold a folded, but not creased, sheet of newspaper by one end. Lay the blade against the top edge at an angle and slice outward. If the knife fails to slice cleanly, try running the blade over a sharpening steel. A sharpening steel is a tune-up device, not a knife sharpener. Just a few minutes of cutting can knock the edge of a knife out of alignment and running the blade over the sharpening steel can reset the edge. That said, if your knife still fails to slice cleanly after using a steel, it means the edge is worn down and needs proper sharpening.

To sharpen your knife, you have three choices. You can send it out to a professional for sharpening, you can use a whetstone (tricky for anyone but a professional), or—the most convenient option—you can use an electric or manual sharpener. See page 709 for information on our top-rated sharpeners.

1. Adjust an oven rack to the middle position and heat the oven to 350 degrees. Melt the butter in a large Dutch oven over medium-high heat. Add the onion and cook until softened and lightly browned, 5 to 7 minutes. Add the garlic and cook until fragrant, about 30 seconds. Add the potatoes, cream, milk, thyme, bay leaves, salt, and pepper, and bring to a simmer. Cover, adjusting the heat as necessary to maintain a light simmer, and cook until the potatoes are almost tender (a paring knife can be slipped into and out of the center of a potato slice with some resistance), about 15 minutes.

2. Remove and discard the thyme sprigs and bay leaves. Transfer the potato mixture to a 3-quart gratin dish and sprinkle with the cheese. Bake until the cream has thickened and is bubbling around the sides, and the top is golden brown, about 20 minutes. Cool for 5 minutes before serving.

TWICE-BAKED POTATOES

WHY THIS RECIPE WORKS: Twice-baked potatoes are not difficult to make, but the process can be time-consuming, and too many versions of this dish feature rubbery, chewy skins filled with pasty, bland fillings. We wanted to perfect the process—from baking the potatoes and readying the shells to preparing the filling and finishing the potatoes in the oven—and have twice-baked potatoes with slightly crisp, chewy skins and a rich, creamy filling.

We had a head start, having already perfected a recipe for baked potatoes. Starting there, we oiled the potatoes before baking for a crisp skin, and we let the baked potatoes cool slightly before slicing them open and removing the flesh. We found that we could prevent the hollowed-out shells from turning soggy by keeping them in the oven while making the filling. And for the filling we found it best to combine the potato with tangy dairy ingredients—sour cream and buttermilk were ideal—a small amount of butter, and sharp cheddar cheese for its bold flavor. For a perfect finish, we placed the filled potatoes under the broiler, where they turned brown and crisp.

Twice-Baked Potatoes
SERVES 6 TO 8

Most potatoes have two relatively flat, blunt sides and two curved sides. Halve the baked potatoes lengthwise so the blunt sides are down once the shells are stuffed, making the potatoes much more stable in the pan during final baking. To vary the flavor a bit, try substituting other types of cheese, such as Gruyère, fontina, or feta, for the cheddar. Yukon Gold potatoes can be substituted for the russets.

    4   medium russet potatoes (about 8 ounces each),
         scrubbed, dried, and rubbed lightly with vegetable oil
         (see note)
    4   ounces sharp cheddar cheese, shredded (about 1 cup;
         see note)
    ½   cup sour cream
    ½   cup buttermilk
    2   tablespoons unsalted butter, softened
    3   scallions, sliced thin
    ½   teaspoon table salt
         Ground black pepper

1. Adjust an oven rack to the upper-middle position and heat the oven to 400 degrees. Bake the potatoes on a foil-lined baking sheet until the skin is crisp and deep brown and a skewer easily pierces the flesh, about 1 hour.

Transfer the potatoes to a wire rack and cool slightly, about 10 minutes. (Leave the oven on.)

2. Using an oven mitt or folded kitchen towel to handle the hot potatoes, cut each potato in half so that the long, blunt sides rest on the work surface. Using a small spoon, scoop the flesh from each half into a medium bowl, leaving a ⅛ to ¼-inch thickness of the flesh in each shell. Arrange the shells on the foil-lined baking sheet and return to the oven until dry and slightly crisp, about 10 minutes. Meanwhile, mash the potato flesh with a fork until smooth. Stir in the remaining ingredients, including pepper to taste, until well combined.

3. Remove the shells from the oven and increase the oven setting to broil. Holding the shells steady on the pan with an oven mitt or towel-protected hand, spoon the mixture into the crisped shells, mounding it slightly at the center, and return the potatoes to the oven. Broil until spotty brown and crisp on top, 10 to 15 minutes. Cool for 10 minutes and serve warm.

CRISPY SMASHED POTATOES

WHY THIS RECIPE WORKS: Crispy smashed potatoes are the best of both worlds, delivering mashed potato creaminess with the crackling crisp crust of roasted potatoes. The technique looked simple and straightforward. Skin-on spuds are parcooked in seasoned water, drained, and squashed just shy of an inch thick. Then the potatoes are oiled, and cooked hot enough (either pan-fried on the stovetop or spread out on a baking sheet in the oven) to render the roughened edges and torn skin browned and crispy and the interior flesh creamy and sweet. But parcooking the potatoes (waxy, thin-skinned Red Bliss) in water diluted their flavor, so they tasted flat, rather than rich and earthy.

To fix the flavor problem and streamline the cooking method, we turned to one pan to get the job done—a baking sheet. A baking sheet's roomy cooking surface allowed us to easily prepare potatoes for four at once rather than panfrying them in fussy batches. To soften the potatoes, we spread them out on the baking sheet, added a little water, covered the pan with foil, and baked them until tender. To smash all the potatoes at once, we used a second baking sheet, which we simply pressed evenly and firmly on top of the pan of parcooked potatoes. To crisp the potatoes we opted for olive oil to coat the baking sheet and to drizzle over the broken spuds. The result? A welcome addition to the potato rotation: browned and crunchy potato patties, full of deep, earthy flavor.

Crispy Smashed Potatoes
SERVES 4 TO 6

This recipe is designed to work with potatoes that are 1½ to 2 inches in diameter. Do not attempt it with potatoes that are over 2 inches. Remove the potatoes from the baking sheet as soon as they are done browning—they will toughen if left on the baking sheet for too long. A potato masher can also be used to "smash" the potatoes.

- **2 pounds small Red Bliss potatoes (about 18), scrubbed (see note)**
- **6 tablespoons extra-virgin olive oil**
- **1 teaspoon chopped fresh thyme leaves**
  Kosher salt and ground black pepper

1. Adjust the oven racks to the top and bottom positions and heat the oven to 500 degrees. Spread the potatoes on a rimmed baking sheet, pour ¾ cup water into the baking sheet, and wrap tightly with aluminum foil. Cook on the bottom rack until a skewer or paring knife slips in and out of the potatoes easily, 25 to 30 minutes (poke the skewer through the foil to test). Remove the foil and cool for 10 minutes. If any water remains on the pan, blot dry with a paper towel.

2. Drizzle 3 tablespoons of the oil over the potatoes and roll to coat. Space the potatoes evenly on the baking sheet. Following the photos on page 496, place a second baking sheet on top; press down uniformly on the baking sheet

MAKING CRISPY SMASHED POTATOES

You can smash each potato by hand with a potato masher, but we found that a baking sheet smashes the potatoes all at once.

1. After rolling the cooled, oven-steamed potatoes in olive oil, space the potatoes evenly on the baking sheet and place a second baking sheet on top; press down uniformly on the baking sheet until the potatoes are roughly ⅓ to ½ inch thick.

2. Sprinkle the smashed potatoes with the thyme leaves and season generously with salt and pepper; drizzle evenly with the remaining 3 tablespoons oil. Roast as directed.

until the potatoes are roughly ⅓ to ½ inch thick. Sprinkle with the thyme leaves and season generously with salt and pepper; drizzle evenly with the remaining 3 tablespoons oil. Roast the potatoes on the top rack for 15 minutes. Transfer the potatoes to the bottom rack and continue to roast until well browned, 20 to 30 minutes longer. Serve immediately.

MASHED SWEET POTATOES

WHY THIS RECIPE WORKS: Mashed sweet potatoes often turn out overly thick and gluey or, at the other extreme, sloppy and loose. We wanted a recipe that would push sweet potatoes' deep, earthy sweetness to the fore and that would produce a silky puree with enough body to hold its shape on a fork.

We braised the sweet potatoes in a mixture of butter and heavy cream to impart a smooth richness. Adding a little salt brought out the sweet potatoes' delicate flavor, and just a teaspoon of sugar bolstered their sweetness. Once the potatoes were tender, we mashed them in the saucepan with a potato masher. We skipped the typical pumpkin pie seasoning and instead let the simple sweet potato flavor shine through.

Mashed Sweet Potatoes

SERVES 4

Cutting the sweet potatoes into slices of even thickness is important so that they cook at the same rate. The potatoes are best served immediately, but they can be covered tightly with plastic wrap and kept warm for 30 minutes. This recipe can be doubled and prepared in a Dutch oven; the cooking time will need to be doubled as well.

- 4 tablespoons (½ stick) unsalted butter, cut into 4 pieces
- 2 tablespoons heavy cream
- 1 teaspoon sugar
- ½ teaspoon table salt
- 2 pounds sweet potatoes (2 to 3 medium), peeled, quartered lengthwise, and cut crosswise into ¼-inch-thick slices (see note)
  Ground black pepper

1. Melt the butter in a large saucepan over low heat. Stir in the cream, sugar, and salt; add the sweet potatoes and cook, covered, stirring occasionally, until the potatoes fall apart when poked with a fork, 35 to 45 minutes.

2. Off the heat, mash the sweet potatoes in the saucepan with a potato masher or transfer the mixture to a food mill and process into a warmed serving bowl. Season with pepper to taste and serve.

ACORN SQUASH

WHY THIS RECIPE WORKS: Cooked properly, acorn squash develops a sweet, almost nutty flavor and moist, smooth flesh—a result that should not take hours. But after what seems like eons in the oven, acorn squash often lands on the table with little flavor and a mealy, stringy texture. We wanted the flavor of better, slow-roasted acorn squash in a fraction of the time.

To our astonishment, microwaving was the ideal cooking method, presenting a squash that was tender and silky smooth, with nary a trace of dryness or stringiness. Microwaved on high power for 20 minutes, the squash was perfectly cooked. It was best to halve and seed the squash before cooking; whole pierced squash cooked unevenly. Last, we learned that when added before cooking, salt seemed to better permeate the squash. Filling in the only remaining gap, equal portions of butter and dark brown sugar gave the squash ample, but not excessive, and offers no resistance when pierced with a paring knife, 15 to 25 minutes. Using potholders, remove the baking dish or bowl from the microwave and set on a clean, dry surface (avoid damp or cold surfaces).

2. While the squash is cooking, adjust an oven rack to the highest position (about 6 inches from the broiler element) and heat the broiler. Melt the butter, brown sugar, and ⅛ teaspoon salt in a small saucepan over low heat, whisking occasionally, until combined.

3. When the squash is cooked, carefully pull back the plastic wrap from the side farthest from you. Using tongs, transfer the cooked squash halves, cut side up, to a rimmed baking sheet. Spoon a portion of the butter-sugar mixture onto each squash half. Broil until brown and caramelized, 5 to 8 minutes, rotating the baking sheet halfway through the cooking time and removing the squash halves as they are done. Set the squash halves on individual plates and serve immediately.

sweetness. And for a smooth, cohesive filling mixture, combining the butter and sugar with a pinch of salt and briefly broiling the final product eliminated the nagging sticky glaze problem. Finishing the squash under the broiler also gave it a welcome roasted texture and great caramelized flavor.

Quick Roasted Acorn Squash with Brown Sugar
SERVES 4

Squash smaller than 1½ pounds will likely cook a little faster than the recipe indicates, so begin checking for doneness a few minutes early. Likewise, larger squash will take slightly longer to cook. However, keep in mind that the cooking time is largely dependent on the microwave. If microwaving the squash in Pyrex, the manufacturer recommends adding water to the dish (or bowl) prior to cooking. To avoid a steam burn when uncovering the cooked squash, peel back the plastic wrap very carefully, starting from the side that is farthest away from you.

- 2 **acorn squash (about 1½ pounds each), halved pole to pole and seeded (see note)**
  Table salt
- 3 **tablespoons unsalted butter**
- 3 **tablespoons dark brown sugar**

1. Sprinkle the squash halves with salt and place the halves, cut side down, in a 13 by 9-inch microwave-safe baking dish or arrange the halves in a large (4-quart) microwave-safe bowl so that the cut sides face out. (If using Pyrex, add ¼ cup water to the dish or bowl.) Cover tightly with plastic wrap, using multiple sheets, if necessary; with a paring knife, poke four steam vents in the wrap. Microwave on high power until the squash is very tender

RICE PILAF

WHY THIS RECIPE WORKS: To make rice pilaf, rice is toasted or browned in fat to build flavor before being cooked through in liquid. The result should be rice that is fragrant, fluffy, and tender. Traditional recipes insist that for a truly great pilaf you must soak or at least repeatedly rinse the rice before cooking. We wondered if there was more to making perfect rice pilaf than this.

The variables included the kind of rice to use, the ratio of rice to cooking water, and whether or not to soak the rice before cooking. Testing revealed that using basmati rice was preferable, as was using a lower amount of water than is traditional for cooking rice. The step of rinsing the rice was also important for grains that were more tender, with a slightly shinier, smoother appearance. We also sautéed the rice in plenty of butter before adding the water. After the rice was cooked, we covered it with a kitchen towel and a lid and let it steam off the heat.

Rice Pilaf
SERVES 4

If you like, olive oil can be substituted for the butter depending on what you are serving with the pilaf. For the most evenly cooked rice, use a wide-bottomed saucepan with a tight-fitting lid.

1½ cups basmati or long-grain rice
2½ cups water
1½ teaspoons table salt
    Pinch ground black pepper
 3 tablespoons unsalted butter (see note)
 1 small onion, minced (about ½ cup)

1. Place the rice in a medium bowl and add enough water to cover by 2 inches; using your hands, gently swish the grains to release the excess starch. Carefully pour off the water, leaving the rice in the bowl. Repeat four to five times, until the water runs almost clear. Using a colander or fine-mesh strainer, drain the rice; place the colander over a bowl and set aside.

2. Bring the water to a boil, covered, in a small saucepan over medium-high heat. Add the salt and pepper; cover to keep hot. Meanwhile, melt the butter in a large saucepan over medium heat; add the onion and cook until softened but not browned, about 4 minutes. Stir in the rice until coated with the butter; cook until the edges of the rice grains begin to turn translucent, about 3 minutes. Stir the hot seasoned water into the rice; return to a boil, then reduce the heat to low, cover, and simmer until all the liquid is absorbed, 16 to 18 minutes. Off the heat, remove the lid and place a clean kitchen towel folded in half over the saucepan; replace the lid. Let stand for 10 minutes; fluff the rice with a fork and serve.

WILD RICE

WHY THIS RECIPE WORKS: Sometimes wild rice turns out undercooked and difficult to chew, other times the rice is overcooked and gluey. We wanted to figure out how to turn out properly cooked wild rice every time.

Through trial and error, we learned to simmer the rice slowly in plenty of liquid, making sure to stop the cooking process at just the right moment by checking it for doneness every couple of minutes past the 35-minute mark. For a simmering liquid, we used chicken broth— its mild yet rich profile tempered the rice's muddy flavor to a pleasant earthiness and affirmed its subdued nuttiness. To further tame the strong flavor of the wild rice, we added some white rice to the mixture, then added onions, carrots, dried cranberries, and toasted pecans for a winning pilaf.

Wild Rice Pilaf with Pecans and Dried Cranberries

SERVES 6 TO 8

Wild rice quickly goes from tough to pasty, so begin testing the rice at the 35-minute mark and drain the rice as soon as it is tender.

1¾ cups low-sodium chicken broth
2½ cups water
 2 bay leaves
 8 sprigs fresh thyme, divided into 2 bundles, each tied together with kitchen twine
 1 cup wild rice, rinsed well in a strainer
1½ cups long-grain white rice
 3 tablespoons unsalted butter
 1 medium onion, minced
 2 carrots, peeled and chopped fine
    Table salt
¾ cup sweetened or unsweetened dried cranberries
¾ cup pecans, toasted and chopped coarse
1½ tablespoons minced fresh parsley leaves
    Ground black pepper

1. Bring the chicken broth, ¼ cup of the water, the bay leaves, and 1 bundle of the thyme to a boil in a medium saucepan over medium-high heat. Add the wild rice, cover, and reduce the heat to low; simmer until the rice is plump and tender and has absorbed most of the liquid, 35 to 45 minutes. Drain the rice in a fine-mesh strainer. Return the rice to the saucepan; cover to keep warm and set aside.

2. While the wild rice is cooking, place the white rice in a medium bowl and add water to cover by 2 inches; gently swish the grains to release excess starch. Carefully pour off the water, leaving the rice in the bowl. Repeat four to five times, until the water runs almost clear. Drain the rice in a fine-mesh strainer.

3. Melt the butter in a medium saucepan over medium-high heat. Add the onion, carrots, and 1 teaspoon salt; cook, stirring frequently, until softened but not browned, about 4 minutes. Stir in the rinsed white rice until coated with the butter; cook, stirring frequently, until the grains begin to turn translucent, about 3 minutes. Meanwhile, bring the remaining 2¼ cups water to a boil in a small saucepan or a microwave. Add the boiling water and the second thyme bundle to the white rice; return to a boil, then reduce the heat to low, sprinkle the cranberries evenly over the rice, and cover. Simmer until all of the liquid is absorbed, 16 to 18 minutes. Off the heat, fluff the rice with a fork and discard the bay leaves and thyme bundles.

4. Combine the wild rice, white rice mixture, pecans, and parsley in a large bowl; toss with a rubber spatula until the ingredients are evenly mixed. Season with salt and pepper to taste and serve.

ALMOST HANDS-FREE RISOTTO

WHY THIS RECIPE WORKS: Classic risotto can demand half an hour of stovetop tedium for the best creamy results. Our goal was five minutes of stirring, tops.

First, we chose to cook our risotto in a Dutch oven, rather than a saucepan. A Dutch oven's thick, heavy bottom, deep sides, and tight-fitting lid are made to trap and distribute heat as evenly as possible. Typical recipes dictate adding the broth in small increments after the wine has been absorbed (and stirring constantly after each addition), but we added most of the broth at once. Then we covered the pan and simmered the rice until almost all the broth had been absorbed, stirring just twice during this time. After adding the second and final addition of broth, we stirred the pot for just a few minutes to ensure the bottom didn't cook more quickly than the top and turned off the heat. Without sitting over a direct flame, the sauce turned out perfectly creamy and the rice was thickened, velvety, and just barely chewy. To finish, we simply stirred in butter, herbs, and a squeeze of lemon juice to brighten the flavors.

Almost Hands-Free Risotto with Parmesan and Herbs

SERVES 6

This more hands-off method does require precise timing, so we strongly recommend using a timer. The consistency of risotto is largely a matter of personal taste; if you prefer a brothy risotto, add extra broth in step 4. This makes a great side dish for braised meats.

- 5 cups low-sodium chicken broth
- 1½ cups water
- 4 tablespoons (½ stick) unsalted butter
- 1 large onion, minced
  Table salt
- 1 medium garlic clove, minced or pressed through a garlic press (about 1 teaspoon)
- 2 cups Arborio rice
- 1 cup dry white wine

- 2 ounces Parmesan cheese, grated (about 1 cup)
- 1 teaspoon juice from 1 lemon
- 2 tablespoons chopped fresh parsley leaves
- 2 tablespoons chopped fresh chives
  Ground black pepper

1. Bring the broth and water to a boil in a large saucepan over high heat. Reduce the heat to medium-low to maintain a gentle simmer.

2. Heat 2 tablespoons of the butter in a large Dutch oven over medium heat. When the butter has melted, add the onion and ¾ teaspoon salt. Cook, stirring frequently, until the onion is softened but not browned, 5 to 7 minutes. Add the garlic and stir until fragrant, about 30 seconds. Add the rice and cook, stirring frequently, until the grains are translucent around the edges, about 3 minutes.

3. Add the wine and cook, stirring constantly, until fully absorbed, 2 to 3 minutes. Stir 5 cups of the warm broth mixture into the rice, reduce the heat to medium-low, cover, and simmer until almost all the liquid has been absorbed and the rice is just al dente, 16 to 19 minutes, stirring twice during cooking.

4. Add ¾ cup more broth mixture and stir gently and constantly until the risotto becomes creamy, about 3 minutes. Stir in the Parmesan. Remove the pot from the heat, cover, and let stand for 5 minutes. Stir in the remaining 2 tablespoons butter, the lemon juice, parsley, and chives. Season with salt and pepper to taste. If desired, add up to ½ cup remaining broth mixture to loosen the texture of the risotto. Serve immediately.

COUSCOUS

WHY THIS RECIPE WORKS: Although couscous traditionally serves as a sauce absorber under North African-style stews and braises, it can work equally well as a lighter, quicker alternative to everyday side dishes like rice pilaf. We wanted to develop a classic version as convenient as the box kind but much fresher tasting, as well as a handful of variations with a few flavorful add-ins. The box instructions—measure and boil water, stir in couscous, cover and let stand off heat for five minutes—gave us bland, clumpy grains. Toasting the couscous grains in butter deepened their flavor and helped them cook up fluffy and separate. And to bump up the flavor even further, we replaced half of the water with chicken broth. For our enriched variations, dried fruit, nuts, and citrus juice added textural interest and sweet, bright notes.

Simple Couscous

SERVES 4 TO 6

- **2 tablespoons unsalted butter**
- **2 cups couscous**
- **1 cup water**
- **1 cup low-sodium chicken broth**
- **1 teaspoon table salt**
  Ground black pepper

Melt the butter in a medium saucepan over medium-high heat. Add the couscous and cook, stirring frequently, until the grains are just beginning to brown, about 5 minutes. Add the water, broth, and salt and stir briefly to combine. Cover and remove the pan from the heat. Let stand until the grains are tender, about 7 minutes. Uncover and fluff the grains with a fork. Season with pepper to taste and serve.

Couscous with Dates and Pistachios

Follow the recipe for Simple Couscous, increasing the butter to 3 tablespoons and adding ½ cup chopped dates, 1 tablespoon grated fresh ginger, and ½ teaspoon ground cardamom to the saucepan with the couscous. Increase the amount of water to 1¼ cups. Stir ¾ cup coarsely chopped toasted pistachios, 3 tablespoons minced fresh cilantro leaves, and 2 teaspoons juice from 1 lemon into the couscous before serving.

Couscous with Dried Cherries and Pecans

Follow the recipe for Simple Couscous, increasing the butter to 3 tablespoons and adding ½ cup coarsely chopped dried cherries, 2 minced garlic cloves, ¾ teaspoon garam masala, and ⅛ teaspoon cayenne pepper to the saucepan with the couscous. Increase the amount of water to 1¼ cups. Stir ¾ cup coarsely chopped toasted pecans, 2 thinly sliced scallions, and 2 teaspoons juice from 1 lemon into the couscous before serving.

Couscous with Carrots, Raisins, and Pine Nuts

Follow the recipe for Simple Couscous, increasing the butter to 3 tablespoons. Once the foaming subsides, add 2 grated carrots and ½ teaspoon ground cinnamon; cook, stirring frequently, until the carrot softens, about 2 minutes. Continue with the recipe, adding ½ cup raisins to the saucepan with the couscous and increasing the water to 1¼ cups. Stir ¾ cup toasted pine nuts, 3 tablespoons minced fresh cilantro leaves, ½ teaspoon grated orange zest, and 1 tablespoon orange juice into the couscous before serving.

Couscous with Shallots, Garlic, and Almonds

Follow the recipe for Simple Couscous, increasing the butter to 3 tablespoons. Once the foaming subsides, add 3 thinly sliced shallots and cook, stirring frequently, until softened and lightly browned, about 5 minutes. Add 1 minced garlic clove and cook until fragrant, about 30 seconds. Continue with recipe, stirring ¾ cup toasted sliced almonds, ¾ cup minced fresh parsley, and ½ teaspoon grated zest and 2 teaspoons juice from 1 lemon into the couscous before serving.

NO-FUSS CREAMY POLENTA

WHY THIS RECIPE WORKS: If you don't stir polenta almost constantly, it forms intractable lumps. We wanted creamy, smooth polenta with rich corn flavor, but we wanted to find a way around the fussy process.

The prospect of stirring continuously for an hour made our arms ache, so we set out to find a way to give the water a head start on penetrating the cornmeal (we prefer the soft texture and nutty flavor of degerminated cornmeal in polenta). Our research led us to consider the similarities between cooking dried beans and dried corn. With beans, water has to penetrate the hard outer skin to gelatinize the starch within. In a corn kernel, the water has to penetrate the endosperm. To soften bean skins and speed up cooking, baking soda is sometimes added to the cooking liquid. Sure enough, a pinch was all it took to cut the cooking time in half without affecting the texture or flavor. Baking soda also helped the granules break down and release their starch in a uniform way, so we could virtually eliminate the stirring if we covered the pot and adjusted the heat to low. Parmesan cheese and butter stirred in at the last minute finishes our polenta, which is satisfying and rich.

No-Fuss Creamy Parmesan Polenta

SERVES 6 TO 8

Coarse-ground degerminated cornmeal such as yellow grits (with grains the size of couscous) works best in this recipe. Avoid instant and quick-cooking products, as well as whole grain, stone-ground, and regular cornmeal. Do not omit the baking soda—it reduces the cooking time and makes for a creamier polenta. The polenta should do little more than release wisps of steam. If it bubbles or sputters even slightly after the first 10 minutes, the heat is too high and you may need a flame tamer. A flame tamer can be purchased at most kitchen supply stores, or you can improvise your own (see page 260). For a main course, serve the polenta with a wedge of rich cheese, meat sauce, or cooked leafy greens. Served plain, the polenta makes a great accompaniment to stews and braises.

- 7½ cups water
- 1½ teaspoons table salt
- Pinch baking soda (see note)
- 1½ cups coarse-ground cornmeal (see note)
- 4 ounces Parmesan cheese, grated (about 2 cups), plus extra for serving
- 2 tablespoons unsalted butter
- Ground black pepper

1. Bring the water to a boil in a heavy-bottomed 4-quart saucepan over medium-high heat. Stir in the salt and baking soda. Slowly pour the cornmeal into the water in a steady stream, while stirring back and forth with a wooden spoon or rubber spatula. Bring the mixture to a boil, stirring constantly, about 1 minute. Reduce the heat to the lowest possible setting and cover.

2. After 5 minutes, whisk the polenta to smooth out any lumps that may have formed, about 15 seconds. (Make sure to scrape the sides and bottom of the pan.) Cover and continue to cook, without stirring, until the grains of polenta are tender but slightly al dente, about 25 minutes longer. (The polenta should be loose and barely hold its shape; it will continue to thicken as it cools.)

3. Remove from the heat, stir in the Parmesan and butter, and season with pepper to taste. Let stand, covered, for 5 minutes. Serve, passing extra Parmesan separately.

SPICED PECANS WITH RUM GLAZE

WHY THIS RECIPE WORKS: Most spiced nuts are made with a heavily sugared syrup that causes the nuts to clump awkwardly and leaves your hands in a sticky mess. We wanted to get maximum flavor and balanced sweetness with minimum mess.

We tried two popular methods—boiling the nuts in syrup and tossing them in butter—and eliminated both

straight off. The former made the nuts sticky, and the latter dulled their flavor. A third method, coating the nuts with an egg white mixture, pretty much overwhelmed them with a candy-like coating. What finally worked was a light glaze made from very small amounts of liquid (we like either rum or water), sugar, and butter, which left the nuts just tacky enough to pick up an even, light coating of dry spices.

Spiced Pecans with Rum Glaze

MAKES ABOUT 2 CUPS

The spiced nuts can be stored in an airtight container at room temperature for up to 5 days.

- 2 cups raw pecan halves

SPICE MIX
- 2 tablespoons sugar
- ¾ teaspoon table salt
- ½ teaspoon ground cinnamon
- ⅛ teaspoon ground cloves
- ⅛ teaspoon ground allspice

RUM GLAZE
- 1 tablespoon rum, preferably dark, or water
- 1 tablespoon unsalted butter
- 2 teaspoons vanilla extract
- 1 teaspoon light or dark brown sugar

1. Adjust an oven rack to the middle position and heat the oven to 350 degrees. Line a rimmed baking sheet with parchment paper and spread the pecans on it in an even layer; toast until fragrant and the color deepens slightly, about 8 minutes, rotating the sheet halfway through the baking time. Transfer the baking sheet with the nuts to a wire rack.

2. FOR THE SPICE MIX: While the nuts are toasting, combine all the spice mix ingredients in a medium bowl; set aside.

3. FOR THE RUM GLAZE: Bring the rum glaze ingredients to a boil in a medium saucepan over medium-high heat, whisking constantly. Stir in the pecans and cook, stirring constantly with a wooden spoon, until almost all the liquid has evaporated, about 1½ minutes.

4. Transfer the glazed pecans to the bowl with the spice mix; toss well to coat. Return the glazed spiced pecans to the parchment-lined baking sheet to cool before serving.

CHAPTER 19

COME FOR BRUNCH

Fluffy Scrambled Eggs 504

Rich and Creamy
Scrambled Eggs 504

Scrambled Eggs with
Bacon, Onion, and Pepper
Jack Cheese 505

Scrambled Eggs with
Sausage, Sweet Pepper, and
Cheddar Cheese 506

Fried Eggs 507

Poached Eggs 507

Diner-Style Home
Fries 508

Oven-Fried Bacon 509

Family-Sized Cheese
Omelet 509

Denver Omelets 510
  Filling for Denver Omelets

French Omelets 511

Spanish Tortilla with
Roasted Red Peppers and
Peas 513

Spanish Tortilla with
Chorizo and Scallions 513
  Garlic Mayonnaise

Asparagus, Ham, and
Gruyère Frittata 514

Leek, Prosciutto, and Goat
Cheese Frittata 514

Quiche Lorraine 515

Breakfast Strata with
Spinach and Gruyère 516

Breakfast Strata with
Sausage, Mushrooms, and
Monterey Jack 517

Blueberry Pancakes 518

German Apple
Pancake 518
  Caramel Sauce

Buttermilk Waffles 520

Easy Buttermilk
Waffles 520

French Toast 521

Ultimate Banana
Bread 522

Classic Banana Bread 523

Cream Scones 524

Blueberry Scones 525

Oatmeal Scones 527

Glazed Maple-Pecan
Oatmeal Scones 527

Croissants 528

Blueberry Muffins 531

Bran Muffins 532

Corn Muffins 533

Corn and Apricot Muffins
with Orange Essence 534

Cranberry-Pecan
Muffins 534

New York–Style Crumb
Cake 535

Blueberry Boy Bait 536

Quick Cinnamon Buns with
Buttermilk Icing 537

Sticky Buns with
Pecans 538

Sour Cream Coffee Cake
with Brown Sugar–Pecan
Streusel 540

Cream Cheese Coffee
Cake 541

Strawberries and Grapes
with Balsamic and Red
Wine Reduction 543

Nectarines, Blueberries,
and Raspberries with
Champagne-Cardamom
Reduction 543

Honeydew, Mango, and
Blueberries with Lime-
Ginger Reduction 543

FLUFFY SCRAMBLED EGGS

WHY THIS RECIPE WORKS: Sometimes the simplest things can be the hardest to get right. Scrambled eggs are a good example. Seemingly easy to make, they can easily go wrong, and overcooking is probably the most common problem. We wanted scrambled eggs that turn out of the pan into a mound of large, soft curds—cooked enough to hold their shape but soft enough to eat with a spoon.

We learned that beating the eggs too much before cooking them can result in toughness, so we whisked our eggs just until they were combined. Milk is better than water as an addition to scrambled eggs; the sugar, proteins, and fat in milk help create large curds, which trap steam for that pillowy texture we were after. A non-stick skillet is a must to prevent sticking, and pan size matters as well; if the skillet is too large, the eggs spread out in too thin a layer and overcook. Getting the pan hot is crucial for moist, puffy curds, and constant gentle stirring—really more like pushing and folding—prevents overcooking. Cooked on the stove until they were almost done, which took only a couple of minutes, these eggs finished cooking on the way to the table, remaining moist and meltingly soft.

Fluffy Scrambled Eggs
SERVES 4

These eggs cook very quickly, so it's important to be ready to eat before you start to cook them.

- 8 large eggs
- ½ cup milk
- ½ teaspoon table salt
  Pinch ground black pepper
- 1 tablespoon unsalted butter

1. Whisk the eggs, milk, salt, and pepper together in a medium bowl until any streaks are gone and the color is pure yellow.

2. Melt the butter in a 10-inch nonstick skillet over high heat, swirling to coat the pan. Add the eggs and, using a heatproof rubber spatula, cook while gently pushing, lifting, and folding them from one side of the pan to the other as they form curds. Continue until the eggs are nicely clumped into a single mound but remain shiny and wet, 1½ to 2 minutes. Serve.

RICH AND CREAMY SCRAMBLED EGGS

WHY THIS RECIPE WORKS: Scrambled eggs often end up as either tough, dry slabs or pebbly, runny curds. We wanted foolproof scrambled eggs with fluffy, moist curds so creamy and light that they practically dissolved on the tongue. The first step was to add salt to the uncooked eggs; salt dissolves some of the egg proteins so they are unable to bond when cooked, creating more tender curds. Beating the eggs until just combined, using the gentler action of a fork rather than a whisk, ensured our scramble didn't turn tough. For the intense creaminess we were after, we chose half-and-half over milk; it produced rich, clean-tasting curds that were both fluffy and stable. To replicate the richer flavor of farm-fresh eggs, we added extra yolks. Finally, when it came to the cooking process, we started the eggs on medium-high heat to create puffy curds, then finished them over low heat so they wouldn't overcook. Swapping out our 12-inch skillet for a 10-inch pan kept the eggs in a thicker layer, trapping more steam and producing heartier curds.

Rich and Creamy Scrambled Eggs
SERVES 4

It's important to follow the visual cues in this recipe, as pan thickness will affect cooking times. If using an electric stove, heat one burner on low heat and a second on medium-high heat; move the skillet between burners when it's time to adjust the heat. If you don't have half-and-half, substitute 8 teaspoons of whole milk and 4 teaspoons of heavy cream. To dress up the dish, add

2 tablespoons of chopped parsley, chives, basil, or cilantro or 1 tablespoon of dill or tarragon to the eggs after reducing the heat to low.

- 8 large whole eggs
- 2 large yolks
- ¼ cup half-and-half
  Table salt and ground black pepper
- 1 tablespoon unsalted butter, chilled

1. Beat the eggs, yolks, half-and-half, ⅜ teaspoon salt, and ¼ teaspoon pepper with a fork until the eggs are thoroughly combined and the color is pure yellow; do not overbeat.

2. Heat the butter in a 10-inch nonstick skillet over medium-high heat until fully melted (the butter should not brown), swirling to coat the pan. Add the egg mixture and, using a heatproof rubber spatula, constantly and firmly scrape along the bottom and the sides of the skillet until the eggs begin to clump and the spatula just leaves a trail on the bottom of the pan, 1½ to 2½ minutes. Reduce the heat to low and gently but constantly fold the eggs until clumped and just slightly wet, 30 to 60 seconds. Immediately transfer the eggs to warmed plates and season with salt to taste. Serve immediately.

Rich and Creamy Scrambled Eggs for Two

Follow the recipe for Rich and Creamy Scrambled Eggs, reducing the whole eggs to 4, the yolks to 1, the half-and-half to 2 tablespoons, and the salt and pepper to ⅛ teaspoon each. In step 2, reduce the butter to ½ tablespoon. Cook the eggs in an 8-inch skillet for 45 to 75 seconds over medium-high heat, then for 30 to 60 seconds over low heat.

NOTES FROM THE TEST KITCHEN

GETTING THE TIMING RIGHT

When your spatula just leaves a trail through the eggs, that's your cue in our dual-heat method to turn the dial from medium-high to low.

HEARTY SCRAMBLED EGGS

WHY THIS RECIPE WORKS: Having perfected the technique for cooking scrambled eggs, we figured that we could make a heartier dish by simply adding other ingredients. But even a sprinkling of some sausage or vegetables discolored the eggs and made them watery; clearly, there was more to hearty scrambled eggs than we first thought.

Experimenting with the temperature of the ingredients, adding binders, and eliminating the milk demonstrated that none of these was the issue. We had been starting our heartier eggs by sautéing onions in the skillet, then adding the eggs; we tried removing the onions after sautéing and wiping out the skillet, then cooking the eggs. This method of cooking in stages—sautéing the aromatics and removing them, cooking the eggs, then folding in all the other ingredients off the heat—prevented discoloration and helped with the wateriness. Lowering the heat to medium made the texture of the eggs somewhat more substantial, but we were able to get rid of the last bit of wateriness when we substituted a smaller amount of half-and-half—with its higher-fat, lower-water content—for the milk. Breakfast meats, crunchy vegetables, and dry leafy greens were successful additions to these eggs, so long as we avoided any that were moisture-laden. These eggs were not as fluffy as eggs without adornment, but the difference was imperceptible once we added meats and vegetables—and there were no watery puddles on the plate.

Scrambled Eggs with Bacon, Onion, and Pepper Jack Cheese

SERVES 4 TO 6

Note that you'll need to reserve 2 teaspoons of bacon fat to sauté the onion. After removing the cooked bacon from the skillet, be sure to drain it well on paper towels; otherwise, the eggs will be greasy.

- 12 large eggs
- 6 tablespoons half-and-half
- ¾ teaspoon table salt
- ¼ teaspoon ground black pepper
- 4 ounces bacon (about 4 slices), halved lengthwise, then cut crosswise into ½-inch pieces
- 1 medium onion, chopped medium
- 1 tablespoon unsalted butter
- 1½ ounces pepper Jack or Monterey Jack cheese, shredded (about ⅓ cup)
- 1 teaspoon minced fresh parsley leaves (optional)

HELP! MY RECIPE DOESN'T WORK!

It happens—even in America's Test Kitchen. Once in a while, we get a call from a viewer or reader that a recipe isn't working for them. And every time, our hearts sink. What did we do wrong? We not only test our recipes very carefully (as many as 100 times), but we also have our recipes vetted by a professional cook, and THEN we send them out to home cooks to test-drive our recipes. So why do recipes sometimes fail? The answers fall into three broad categories: substitutions, flawed equipment, or ingredient variables.

Substitutions are common (everyone does it), but if you decide to replace a key ingredient or piece of equipment, all bets are off. If you're on a diet, don't try making our crème brûlée with milk rather than cream. And don't sear four steaks in a 10-inch skillet when the recipe calls for a 12-inch pan—that is, unless you want them to taste steamed and bland. Our advice: Make the recipe once as it's written, then improvise.

Flawed equipment is harder to predict and control. Many home ovens are not properly calibrated and an oven that runs hot by 50 degrees (which is fairly common in home kitchens) will ruin many recipes. Always, always pay attention to the visual clues in our recipes, not the clock. And invest in an oven thermometer. It's cheap and will save you much frustration when cooking.

Ingredient variables are the hardest thing for us (or you) to control. Produce varies in sweetness and moisture content. The same cut of meat can have more or less fat. And brands of manufactured products are not all the same. In fact, we had trouble with a chocolate frosting recipe several years ago and realized that our recipe worked with the test kitchen's top-rated bittersweet chocolate (with 60 percent cacao) but failed when readers tried to use gourmet brands with a higher cacao content. We test all of our recipes with the ingredients that have won our blind taste tests (see pages 735 through 755). We suggest you do the same. Not only will your food taste better, but sometimes choosing the right brand can make the difference between a successful recipe and a failed one.

1. Whisk the eggs, half-and-half, salt, and pepper together in a medium bowl.

2. Cook the bacon in a 12-inch nonstick skillet over medium heat, stirring occasionally, until browned, 4 to 5 minutes. Using a slotted spoon, transfer the bacon to a paper towel–lined plate; discard all but 2 teaspoons bacon fat. Add the onion to the skillet and cook, stirring occasionally, until lightly browned, 2 to 4 minutes; transfer the onion to a second plate.

3. Thoroughly wipe out the skillet with paper towels, add the butter, and melt over medium heat, swirling to coat the pan. Add the eggs and, using a heatproof rubber spatula, cook while gently pushing, lifting, and folding them from one side of the pan to the other as they form curds. Cook until large curds form but the eggs are still very moist, 2 to 3 minutes. Off the heat, gently fold in the onion, pepper Jack, and half of the bacon until evenly distributed; if the eggs are still underdone, return the skillet to medium heat for no longer than 30 seconds. Divide the eggs among individual plates, sprinkle with the remaining bacon and parsley (if using), and serve.

Scrambled Eggs with Sausage, Sweet Pepper, and Cheddar Cheese

SERVES 4 TO 6

We prefer sweet Italian sausage here, especially for breakfast, but you can certainly use spicy sausage, if desired.

- 12 large eggs
- 6 tablespoons half-and-half
- ¾ teaspoon table salt
- ¼ teaspoon ground black pepper
- 1 teaspoon vegetable oil
- 8 ounces sweet Italian sausage, casings removed, sausage crumbled into ½-inch pieces (see note)
- 1 red bell pepper, stemmed, seeded, and cut into ½-inch cubes
- 3 scallions, white and green parts separated, both sliced thin on the bias
- 1 tablespoon unsalted butter
- 1½ ounces sharp cheddar cheese, shredded (about ⅓ cup)

1. Whisk the eggs, half-and-half, salt, and pepper together in a medium bowl.

2. Heat the oil in a 12-inch nonstick skillet over medium heat until shimmering. Add the sausage and cook until beginning to brown but still pink in the center, about 2 minutes. Add the bell pepper and scallion whites;

continue to cook, stirring occasionally, until the sausage is cooked through and the pepper is beginning to brown, about 3 minutes. Spread the mixture in a single layer on a medium plate; set aside.

3. Thoroughly wipe out the skillet with paper towels, add the butter, and melt over medium heat, swirling to coat the pan. Add the eggs and, using a heatproof rubber spatula, cook while gently pushing, lifting, and folding them from one side of the pan to the other as they form curds. Cook the eggs until large curds form but the eggs are still very moist, 2 to 3 minutes. Off the heat, gently fold in the sausage mixture and cheddar until evenly distributed; if the eggs are still underdone, return the skillet to medium heat for no longer than 30 seconds. Divide the eggs among individual plates, sprinkle with the scallion greens, and serve.

FRIED EGGS

WHY THIS RECIPE WORKS: Anyone can make fried eggs, but rare are the cooks who can make them perfectly every time. Eggs stick to the pan, yolks break, and over- or undercooked eggs seem to be the norm. We decided to eliminate the guesswork and figure out the best and easiest way to fry the perfect egg every time. For us, this meant a firm white and a yolk that is thick yet still runny.

We discovered that the first thing to do when about to fry an egg is to reach for a nonstick pan; there is no point in frying eggs in anything else. The initial heat setting is also important. A five-minute preheating of the pan over a very low fire puts it at just the right temperature to receive the eggs. Cover the pan as soon as the eggs are added and cook just a couple of minutes for evenly cooked whites and a yolk that is perfectly set up.

Fried Eggs
MAKES 2

Since burners vary, it may take an egg or two before you determine the ideal heat setting for frying eggs on your stovetop. Adjust the heat as necessary.

- **2   large eggs**
- **1½ teaspoons unsalted butter, chilled**
- **Table salt and ground black pepper**

1. Heat an 8-inch nonstick skillet over low heat for 5 minutes. Meanwhile, crack each egg into a cup or small bowl (1 egg per cup). Add the butter to the skillet and melt, swirling to coat the pan.

2. Working quickly, pour 1 egg on one side of the pan and the remaining egg on the other side. Sprinkle the eggs with salt and pepper; cover and cook for about 2 minutes for runny yolks, 2½ minutes for soft but set yolks, and 3 minutes for firmly set yolks. Slide the eggs onto a plate and serve.

POACHED EGGS

WHY THIS RECIPE WORKS: A poached egg should be a neat-looking pouch of tender egg, evenly cooked all the way through, with a yolk that is barely runny. But boiling water can agitate the eggs until they are a ragged mess; we needed to figure out how to cook these eggs gently.

Our first thought was to examine the type of pan used. Most recipes require a deep saucepan, but we found that a shallow pan—a skillet—was far better: The water boiled faster, and the egg hit bottom sooner, and thus more gently, so that it could solidify before becoming stringy. A touch of vinegar lowered the boiling point of the water so that we were able to cook the eggs over more gentle heat. Our most important discovery turned out to be the importance of cooking eggs in still, not bubbling, water—as long as it was hot enough. With this in mind, we covered the skillet and turned off the heat after adding the eggs to the boiling water, allowing the residual heat to cook the eggs through. Without bubbling water to tear them apart, our poached eggs came out of the pan perfectly shaped—and cooked—with no feathery whites in sight.

Poached Eggs
MAKES 4

To get four eggs into boiling water at the same time, crack each into a small cup with a handle. Holding two cups in each hand, lower the lip of each cup just into the water and then tip the eggs into the pan.

- **Table salt**
- **2   tablespoons distilled white vinegar**
- **4   large eggs, each cracked into a small handled cup (see note)**
- **Ground black pepper**

1. Fill an 8 to 10-inch nonstick skillet nearly to the rim with water, add 1 teaspoon salt and the vinegar, and bring the mixture to a boil over high heat.

2. Lower the lip of each cup just into the water; tip the eggs into the boiling water, cover, and immediately remove the pan from the heat. Poach the eggs for 4 minutes for medium-firm yolks. (For firmer yolks, poach for 4½ minutes; for looser yolks, poach for 3 minutes.)

3. With a slotted spoon, carefully lift and drain each egg over the skillet. Season with salt and pepper to taste and serve.

HOME FRIES

WHY THIS RECIPE WORKS: Whether made at home or eaten out, home fries frequently suffer from the same problems: greasy or undercooked potatoes, and bland or too-spicy flavors. We wanted to develop a recipe that produced potatoes with a crisp, deep golden brown crust and a tender, moist interior.

We started with the type of potato and determined that medium-starch Yukon Golds beat out russets and reds, remaining moist even when crisped on the outside. Attempts to cook raw diced potato in the skillet ended in failure; precooking was the way to go. But leftover potatoes tasted like—leftovers. We tried baking, boiling, and dicing the potatoes before frying them, but they overcooked, turning to mush and sticking to the pan. What finally worked was parcooking the potatoes—placing them in water and bringing them just to a boil, then immediately draining them before frying. This approach gave the interior of the potatoes a head start in the cooking process, but the potatoes weren't in the water long enough to absorb much liquid. The result: firm cubes of potato with crisp, browned exteriors. A combination of butter (for its rich flavor) and oil (for its higher smoke point) worked best for frying. Onion is the perfect foil for these potatoes; we cooked it in the skillet before adding the potatoes.

Diner-Style Home Fries

SERVES 2 TO 3

If doubling this recipe, cook two batches of home fries separately. While making the second batch, keep the first batch hot and crisp by spreading the fries on a baking sheet placed in a 300-degree oven.

2½ tablespoons corn oil or peanut oil
1 medium onion, minced
1 pound (2 medium) Yukon Gold potatoes, scrubbed and cut into ½-inch cubes
   Table salt
1 tablespoon unsalted butter
1 teaspoon paprika (optional)
1 tablespoon minced fresh parsley leaves (optional)
   Ground black pepper

1. Heat 1 tablespoon of the oil in a 12-inch skillet over medium-high heat until shimmering. Add the onion and cook, stirring frequently, until browned, 8 to 10 minutes. Transfer the onion to a small bowl and set aside.

2. Meanwhile, place the potatoes in a large saucepan, cover with ½ inch of water, add 1 teaspoon salt, and bring to a boil over high heat. As soon as the water begins to boil, drain the potatoes thoroughly in a colander.

3. Heat the butter and the remaining 1½ tablespoons oil in the now-empty skillet over medium-high heat. Add the potatoes and shake the skillet to evenly distribute the potatoes in a single layer, making sure that one side of each piece is touching the surface of the skillet. Cook without stirring until one side of the potatoes is golden brown, 4 to 5 minutes, then carefully turn the potatoes, making sure the potatoes remain in a single layer. Repeat the process until the potatoes are tender and browned on most sides, turning three or four times, 10 to 15 minutes longer. Add the onions, paprika (if using), parsley (if using), ¼ teaspoon salt, and pepper to taste; serve.

BACON

WHY THIS RECIPE WORKS: A couple of strips of crisp bacon are always a welcome accompaniment to a plate of eggs, but bacon requires frequent monitoring when cooked on the stovetop, and the grease can be messy. The microwave produces unevenly cooked and flavorless strips, so we looked to the oven for an easier way to cook bacon.

Bacon renders its fat while cooking, of course, so it was important to choose a pan that would contain it; a rimmed baking sheet worked just fine, and as a bonus it enabled us to cook more strips at the same time. We didn't have to turn the bacon because the heat of the oven cooked it evenly, though rotating the baking sheet front to back halfway through ensured even cooking. In comparison to the results from stovetop frying, bacon cooked in the oven wasn't quite as crisp, but it was certainly crisp enough, and it had the same great meaty flavor. Although preheating the oven and draining the bacon after cooking takes a little extra time, the payoff is that you don't have to stand at the stove while the bacon is in the oven—or deal with grease splattered on your stovetop.

Oven-Fried Bacon
SERVES 4 TO 6

A large rimmed baking sheet is important here to contain the rendered bacon fat. If cooking more than one tray of bacon, switch their oven positions once about halfway through cooking. You can use thin- or thick-cut bacon here, though the cooking times will vary.

12 slices bacon (see note)

Adjust an oven rack to the middle position and heat the oven to 400 degrees. Arrange the bacon slices on a rimmed baking sheet. Cook until the fat begins to render, 5 to 6 minutes; rotate the pan. Continue cooking until the bacon is crisp and browned, 5 to 6 minutes longer for thin-cut bacon, 8 to 10 minutes for thick-cut. Transfer the bacon to a paper towel–lined plate, drain, and serve.

FAMILY-SIZED OMELET

WHY THIS RECIPE WORKS: An omelet is a great breakfast or brunch dish, but cooking omelets one at a time for more than a couple of people is just not practical. We wanted to find a way to make an omelet that was big enough to serve four people. We wanted it to have tender, not rubbery, eggs and a rich, cheesy filling.

Flipping a huge eight-egg omelet was clearly not going to work, so we had to find a way to cook the top of the omelet as well as the bottom. Cooking the eggs longer over lower heat resulted in an unpleasant texture. Broiling to cook the top of the eggs worked, but it dried out the omelet, and we wanted it to be creamy. Then we had the idea of covering the pan after the bottom of the eggs was set but the top was still runny, which worked like a charm. The lid trapped the heat and moisture to steam the top of the omelet, and it partially melted the cheese as well. Now we had a perfectly cooked omelet for four, with tender eggs and bits of melted cheese in every bite.

HOW TO MAKE AN OVERSIZED OMELET

1. Pull the cooked edges of the egg toward the center of the pan and allow the raw egg to run to the edges.

2. When the omelet is set on the bottom but still very runny on the top, cover the skillet and reduce the heat to low.

3. After the top of the omelet begins to set, sprinkle with the cheese and let the omelet rest off the heat, covered, until the cheese has partially melted.

4. After using a heatproof rubber spatula to slide half of the omelet out onto a platter, tilt the skillet so that the omelet folds over onto itself to make the traditional half-moon shape.

Family-Sized Cheese Omelet
SERVES 4

Monterey Jack, colby, or any other good melting cheese can be substituted for the cheddar.

- **8 large eggs**
- **½ teaspoon table salt**
- **⅛ teaspoon ground black pepper**
- **2 tablespoons unsalted butter**
- **3 ounces cheddar cheese, shredded (about ¾ cup; see note)**

1. Whisk the eggs, salt, and pepper together in a medium bowl. Melt the butter in a 12-inch nonstick skillet over medium heat, swirling to coat the pan.

2. Add the eggs and cook, stirring gently in a circular motion, until the mixture is slightly thickened, about 1 minute. Following the photos on page 509, use a heatproof rubber spatula to pull the cooked edges of the egg toward the center of the pan, tilting the pan so the uncooked egg runs to the cleared edge of the pan. Repeat until the bottom of the omelet is just set but the top is still runny, about 1 minute. Cover the skillet, reduce the heat to low, and cook until the top of the omelet begins to set but is still moist, about 5 minutes.

3. Remove the pan from the heat. Sprinkle the cheddar evenly over the eggs, cover, and let sit until the cheese partially melts, about 1 minute. Slide half of the omelet onto a warmed platter using the spatula, then tilt the skillet so the remaining omelet flips over onto itself, forming a half-moon shape. Cut into wedges and serve.

DENVER OMELET

WHY THIS RECIPE WORKS: A substantial Denver omelet has become a breakfast feature in American restaurants and diners. Filled with ham and lots of vegetables in addition to cheese, it's a meal in itself. But it's hard to get the vegetables cooked without overcooking the eggs.

Cooking the filling separately, before the eggs, seemed to be the best way to avoid undercooked vegetables. In addition to the standard onion and green bell pepper, we also included red bell pepper, which made for a more colorful filling. Instead of julienning the vegetables, we finely chopped them; this made our filling easier to eat, and the peppers' skin was less intrusive. Ham steak was the easiest kind of ham to dice; it also imparted a welcome smoky flavor to the rest of the filling. For more complexity of flavor, we included garlic and parsley, which are unusual in a Denver omelet, and a dash of hot sauce livened things up without adding too much spiciness. We cooked the eggs according to our tried-and-true method, with some dairy (we used a little heavy cream, but milk worked as well) to keep the eggs from drying out, and added the warm filling just before folding the omelet onto a plate. Both components—eggs and filling—were perfectly cooked.

Denver Omelets

SERVES 2

You can make one omelet after another in the same pan, although you may need to reduce the heat. Refer to the photos for "How to Make an Oversized Omelet" on page 509—the steps are similar to the ones used here.

- 6 large eggs
- 2 tablespoons heavy cream or milk
- ½ teaspoon table salt
- ¼ teaspoon ground black pepper
- 2 tablespoons unsalted butter
- 4 ounces Monterey Jack cheese, shredded (about 1 cup)
- 1 recipe Filling for Denver Omelets (recipe follows)

1. Whisk together 3 of the eggs, 1 tablespoon of the cream, ¼ teaspoon of the salt, and ⅛ teaspoon of the pepper in a small bowl until thoroughly combined.

2. Melt 1 tablespoon of the butter in a 10-inch non-stick skillet over medium-high heat until it just begins to brown, swirling to coat the pan. Add the eggs to the skillet and cook until the edges begin to set, 2 to 3 seconds, then, with a heatproof rubber spatula, stir in a circular motion until slightly thickened, about 10 seconds. Use the spatula to pull the cooked edges into the center, then tilt the pan to one side so that the uncooked egg runs to the edge of the pan. Repeat until the omelet is just set but still moist on the surface, 1 to 2 minutes.

3. Sprinkle ½ cup of the cheese evenly over the eggs and allow to partially melt, 15 to 20 seconds. With the handle of the pan facing you, spoon half the filling over the left side of the omelet. Following step 4 on page 509, slide the filling-topped half of the omelet onto a warmed plate using the spatula, then tilt the skillet so the remaining omelet folds over the filling in a half-moon shape; set aside. Repeat the instructions for the second omelet. Serve.

Filling for Denver Omelets

MAKES ENOUGH TO FILL 2 OMELETS

A ham steak is our top choice for this recipe, although canned ham and sliced deli ham will work. (If using sliced deli ham, add it with the garlic, parsley, and hot sauce.)

    1 tablespoon unsalted butter
    ½ red bell pepper, stemmed, seeded, and chopped fine
    ½ green bell pepper, stemmed, seeded, and chopped fine
    1 small onion, minced
    ¼ teaspoon table salt
    4 ounces ham steak, diced (about 1 cup; see note)
    1 tablespoon minced fresh parsley leaves
    1 garlic clove, minced or pressed through a garlic press
       (about 1 teaspoon)
    ½ teaspoon hot sauce

Melt the butter in a 10-inch nonstick skillet over medium-high heat. Add the peppers, onion, and salt and cook, stirring occasionally, until the onion begins to soften, 5 to 7 minutes. Add the ham and cook until the peppers begin to brown, about 2 minutes. Add the parsley, garlic, and hot sauce and cook for 30 seconds. Transfer to a small bowl and cover to keep warm.

FRENCH OMELET

WHY THIS RECIPE WORKS: In contrast to half-moon diner-style omelets, the French omelet is a pristine rolled affair. The temperature of the pan must be just right, the eggs beaten just so, and hand movements must be swift. We decided to ditch the stuffy attitude and come up with a foolproof method for making the ideal French omelet—unblemished golden yellow with an ultra-creamy texture, rolled around minimal filling.

The classic method requires a black carbon steel omelet pan and a fork, but a nonstick skillet worked fine here. Instead of a fork, which scraped our nonstick pans, bamboo skewers and wooden chopsticks gave us small curds with a silky texture. Preheating the pan for 10 minutes over low heat eliminated any hot spots. For creaminess, we added very cold butter, which dispersed evenly and fused with the eggs for a moist, rich omelet. To keep the omelet light, we found the perfect number of strokes; excessive beating unravels egg proteins, leading to denseness. We tried different heat levels, but even at medium heat, the omelet cooked so quickly it was hard to judge when it was done, so we turned off the heat when it was

still runny and covered it to finish cooking. Finally, for an easy rolling method, we slid the omelet onto a paper towel and used the towel to roll the omelet into the sought-after cylinder.

French Omelets

SERVES 2

Because making these omelets is such a quick process, make sure to have all your ingredients and equipment at the ready. If you don't have skewers or chopsticks to stir the eggs in step 3, use the handle of a wooden spoon. Warm the plates in a 200-degree oven.

    2 tablespoons unsalted butter, cut into 2 pieces
    ½ teaspoon vegetable oil
    6 large eggs, chilled
       Table salt and ground black pepper
    2 tablespoons shredded Gruyère cheese
    4 teaspoons minced fresh chives

1. Cut 1 tablespoon of the butter in half. Cut the remaining 1 tablespoon butter into small pieces, transfer to a small bowl, and place in the freezer while preparing the eggs and the skillet, at least 10 minutes. Meanwhile, heat the oil in an 8-inch nonstick skillet over low heat for 10 minutes.

2. Crack 2 of the eggs into a medium bowl and separate a third egg; reserve the white for another use and add the yolk to the bowl. Add ⅛ teaspoon salt and a pinch of pepper. Break the yolks with a fork, then beat the eggs at a moderate pace, about 80 strokes, until the yolks and whites are well combined. Stir in half of the frozen butter cubes.

3. When the skillet is fully heated, use paper towels to wipe out the oil, leaving a thin film on the bottom and sides of the skillet. Add half of the reserved 1 tablespoon butter to the skillet and heat until melted. Swirl the butter to coat the skillet, add the egg mixture, and increase the heat to medium-high. Following the photos, use two chopsticks or wooden skewers to scramble the eggs using a quick circular motion to move around the skillet, scraping the cooked

NOTES FROM THE TEST KITCHEN

MAKING A FRENCH OMELET

1. Add the beaten egg mixture to the skillet and stir with chopsticks to produce small curds, which result in a silkier texture.

2. Turn off the heat while the eggs are still runny; smooth with a spatula into an even layer.

3. After sprinkling with the cheese and chives, cover so the residual heat gently finishes cooking the omelet.

4. Slide the finished omelet onto a paper towel–lined plate. Use the paper towel to lift the omelet and roll it up.

egg from the side of the skillet as you go, until the eggs are almost cooked but still slightly runny, 45 to 90 seconds. Turn off the heat (remove the skillet from the heat if using an electric burner) and smooth the eggs into an even layer using a heatproof rubber spatula. Sprinkle the omelet with 1 tablespoon of the Gruyère and 2 teaspoons of the chives. Cover the skillet with a tight-fitting lid and let sit, 1 minute for a runnier omelet and 2 minutes for a firmer omelet.

4. Heat the skillet over low heat for 20 seconds, uncover, and, using a heatproof rubber spatula, loosen the edges of the omelet from the skillet. Place a folded square of paper towel onto a warmed plate and slide the omelet out of the skillet onto the paper towel so that the omelet lies flat on the plate and hangs about 1 inch off the paper towel. Roll the omelet into a neat cylinder and set aside. Return the skillet to low heat and heat for 2 minutes before repeating the instructions for the second omelet starting with step 2. Serve.

SPANISH TORTILLA

WHY THIS RECIPE WORKS: This classic Spanish omelet is immensely appealing, but can be greasy, dense, and heavy if prepared incorrectly. Typical recipes call for up to 4 cups of extra-virgin olive oil to cook the potatoes, which can lead to an overly oily—and expensive—tortilla. We wanted an intensely rich, velvety, melt-in-your-mouth egg-and-potato omelet—that didn't require using a quart of oil.

We first stuck with the traditional volume of olive oil until we could determine the proper type and ratio of ingredients. We chose starchy russet potatoes, thinly sliced, and standard yellow onions, which had a sweet, mellow flavor. We also settled on the perfect ratio of eggs to potatoes that allowed the tortilla to set firm and tender, with the eggs and potatoes melding into one another. Next we set out to reduce the amount of oil. Unfortunately, with less oil in the pan, half the potatoes were frying, while the other half were steaming. We started over with slightly firmer, less starchy Yukon Golds. With a fraction of the oil in the skillet, they were a winner: starchy enough to become meltingly tender as they cooked, but sturdy enough to stir and flip halfway through cooking with few breaks. Finally, we had to determine the best way to flip the omelet. To do this, we simply slid the tortilla out of the pan and onto one plate. Then, placing another plate upside down over the tortilla, we easily flipped the whole thing and slid the tortilla back in the pan, making a once-messy task easy and foolproof.

Spanish Tortilla with Roasted Red Peppers and Peas

SERVES 4 TO 6

Spanish tortillas are often served warm or at room temperature with olives, pickles, and Garlic Mayonnaise (recipe follows) as an appetizer. They may also be served with a salad as a light entrée. For the most traditional tortilla, omit the roasted red peppers and peas. See page 747 for our top-rated extra-virgin olive oil.

- 6 tablespoons plus 1 teaspoon extra-virgin olive oil (see note)
- 1½ pounds (3 to 4 medium) Yukon Gold potatoes, peeled, quartered, and cut into ⅛-inch-thick slices
- 1 small onion, halved and sliced thin
- 1 teaspoon table salt
- ¼ teaspoon ground black pepper
- 8 large eggs
- ½ cup jarred roasted red peppers, rinsed, dried, and cut into ½-inch pieces
- ½ cup frozen peas, thawed
  Garlic Mayonnaise (optional; recipe follows)

1. Toss 4 tablespoons of the oil, the potatoes, onion, ½ teaspoon of the salt, and the pepper in a large bowl until the potato slices are thoroughly separated and coated in oil. Heat 2 tablespoons more oil in a 10-inch nonstick skillet over medium-high heat until shimmering. Reduce the heat to medium-low, add the potato mixture to the skillet, and set the bowl aside (do not rinse). Cover and cook, stirring occasionally with a heatproof rubber spatula, until the potatoes offer no resistance when poked with a paring knife, 22 to 28 minutes (some potato slices may break into smaller pieces).

2. Meanwhile, whisk the eggs and remaining ½ teaspoon salt in the reserved bowl until just combined. Using a heatproof rubber spatula, fold the hot potato mixture, red peppers, and peas into the eggs until combined, making sure to scrape all the potato mixture out of the skillet. Return the skillet to medium-high heat, add the remaining 1 teaspoon oil, and heat until just beginning to smoke. Add the egg-potato mixture and cook, shaking the pan and folding the mixture constantly for 15 seconds; smooth the top of the mixture with a heatproof rubber spatula. Reduce the heat to medium, cover, and cook, gently shaking the pan every 30 seconds, until the bottom is golden brown and the top is lightly set, about 2 minutes.

3. Using a heatproof rubber spatula, loosen the tortilla from the pan, shaking it back and forth until the tortilla slides around. Slide the tortilla onto a large plate. Invert the tortilla onto a second large plate and slide it, browned side up, back into the skillet. Tuck the edges of the tortilla into the skillet. Return the pan to medium heat and continue to cook, gently shaking the pan every 30 seconds, until the second side is golden brown, about 2 minutes longer. Slide the tortilla onto a cutting board; cool for at least 15 minutes. Cut the tortilla into cubes or wedges and serve with Garlic Mayonnaise (if using).

Spanish Tortilla with Chorizo and Scallions

Use a cured, Spanish-style chorizo for this recipe. Portuguese linguiça is a suitable substitute.

Follow the recipe for Spanish Tortilla with Roasted Red Peppers and Peas, omitting the roasted red peppers and peas. In step 1, heat 4 ounces Spanish-style chorizo, cut into ¼-inch pieces, with 1 tablespoon oil (reduced from 2 tablespoons) in a 10-inch nonstick skillet over medium-high heat, stirring occasionally, until the chorizo is browned and the fat has rendered, about 5 minutes. Proceed with the recipe as directed, adding the potato mixture to the skillet with the chorizo and rendered fat and folding 4 thinly sliced scallions into the eggs in step 2.

Garlic Mayonnaise

MAKES ABOUT 1¼ CUPS

- 2 large egg yolks
- 2 teaspoons Dijon mustard
- 2 teaspoons juice from 1 lemon
- 1 medium garlic clove, minced or pressed through a garlic press (about 1 teaspoon)
- ¾ cup vegetable oil
- 1 tablespoon water
- ¼ cup extra-virgin olive oil
- ½ teaspoon table salt
- ¼ teaspoon ground black pepper

Process the yolks, mustard, lemon juice, and garlic in a food processor until combined, about 10 seconds. With the machine running, slowly drizzle in the vegetable oil, about 1 minute. Transfer the mixture to a medium bowl and whisk in the water. Whisking constantly, slowly drizzle in the olive oil, about 30 seconds. Whisk in the salt and pepper. (The mayonnaise can be refrigerated in an airtight container for up to 4 days.)

THICK AND HEARTY FRITTATAS

WHY THIS RECIPE WORKS: A frittata loaded with meat and vegetables often ends up dry, overstuffed, and overcooked. We wanted a frittata big enough to make a substantial meal for 6 to 8 people—with a pleasing balance of egg to filling, firm yet moist eggs, and a lightly browned crust.

We started with an even dozen eggs, which we found required 3 cups of cooked vegetables and meat to create the best balance of filling to eggs. When we chose our fillings, we needed to be a little selective about the cheese— Gruyère and goat cheese both had just the right amount of moisture. Most any vegetable or meat can be added to a frittata, with two caveats: The food must be cut into small pieces, and it must be precooked to drive off excess moisture and fat. A little half-and-half added a touch of creaminess. Given the large number of eggs, we discovered we had to shorten the time the frittata spent on the stovetop so the bottom wouldn't scorch by the time the eggs were properly cooked. We solved the problem by starting the eggs on medium heat, and stirring them so they could cook quickly yet evenly. With the eggs still on the wet side, we slid the skillet under the broiler until the top had puffed and browned, but removed it while the eggs in the center were still slightly wet and runny, allowing the residual heat to finish the cooking.

Asparagus, Ham, and Gruyère Frittata

SERVES 6 TO 8

A 12-inch ovensafe nonstick skillet is necessary for this recipe. Because broilers vary so much in intensity, watch the frittata carefully as it cooks.

    12 large eggs
    3   tablespoons half-and-half
    ½   teaspoon table salt
    ¼   teaspoon ground black pepper
    2   teaspoons olive oil

    8   ounces asparagus, tough ends trimmed, spears cut
        on the bias into ¼-inch pieces
    4   ounces ¼-inch-thick deli ham, cut into ½-inch cubes
        (about ¾ cup)
    1   medium shallot, minced (about 3 tablespoons)
    3   ounces Gruyère cheese, cut into ¼-inch cubes
        (about ¾ cup)

1. Adjust an oven rack about 5 inches from the broiler element and heat the broiler. Whisk the eggs, half-and-half, salt, and pepper together in a medium bowl. Set aside.

2. Heat the oil in a 12-inch ovensafe nonstick skillet over medium heat until shimmering; add the asparagus and cook, stirring occasionally, until lightly browned and almost tender, about 3 minutes. Add the ham and shallot and cook until the shallot softens, about 2 minutes.

3. Stir the Gruyère into the eggs; add the egg mixture to the skillet and cook, using a heatproof rubber spatula to stir and scrape the bottom of the skillet, until large curds form and the spatula begins to leave a wake but the eggs are still very wet, about 2 minutes. Shake the skillet to distribute the eggs evenly and cook without stirring to let the bottom set, about 30 seconds.

4. Slide the skillet under the broiler and cook until the surface is puffed and spotty brown, yet the center remains slightly wet and runny when cut into with a paring knife, 3 to 4 minutes. Using a potholder (the skillet handle will be hot), remove the skillet from the oven and let stand for 5 minutes to finish cooking; using the spatula, loosen the frittata from the skillet and slide it onto a platter or cutting board. Cut into wedges and serve.

Leek, Prosciutto, and Goat Cheese Frittata

SERVES 6 TO 8

A 12-inch ovensafe nonstick skillet is necessary for this recipe. The goat cheese will crumble more easily if it is chilled.

    12 large eggs
    3   tablespoons half-and-half
        Table salt and ground black pepper
    2   tablespoons unsalted butter
    2   small leeks, white and light green parts only, halved
        lengthwise, sliced thin, and rinsed thoroughly
        (about 3 cups)
    3   ounces very thinly sliced prosciutto, cut into
        ½-inch-wide strips
    ¼   cup chopped fresh basil leaves
    4   ounces goat cheese, crumbled (about 1 cup; see note)

1. Adjust an oven rack about 5 inches from the broiler element and heat the broiler. Whisk the eggs, half-and-half, ½ teaspoon salt, and ¼ teaspoon pepper together in a medium bowl. Set aside.

2. Melt the butter in a 12-inch ovensafe nonstick skillet over medium heat. Add the leeks and ¼ teaspoon salt; reduce the heat to low and cook, covered, stirring occasionally, until softened, 8 to 10 minutes.

3. Stir the prosciutto, basil, and ½ cup of the goat cheese into the eggs; add the egg mixture to the skillet and cook, using a heatproof rubber spatula to stir and scrape the bottom of the skillet, until large curds form and the spatula begins to leave a wake but the eggs are still very wet, about 2 minutes. Shake the skillet to distribute the eggs evenly and cook without stirring to let the bottom set, about 30 seconds.

4. Distribute the remaining ½ cup goat cheese evenly over the frittata. Slide the skillet under the broiler and cook until the surface is puffed and spotty brown, yet the center remains slightly wet and runny when cut into with a paring knife, 3 to 4 minutes. Using a potholder (the skillet handle will be hot), remove the skillet from the oven and let stand for 5 minutes to finish cooking; using the spatula, loosen the frittata from the skillet and slide it onto a platter or cutting board. Cut into wedges and serve.

QUICHE

WHY THIS RECIPE WORKS: A really good quiche should have a smooth, creamy custard in a tender pastry crust. The custard should be rich, but not overwhelmingly so, and moist, not dried out. We aimed to find a way to make this perfect pie.

We experimented with multiple combinations of egg and dairy to find the one that would provide just the right balance of richness and lightness. Eggs alone were not rich enough; whole eggs plus yolks provided the degree of richness we wanted. For the dairy component, we found that equal parts of milk and heavy cream worked best. This custard was creamy and smooth. After layering bacon and Gruyère over the bottom of the pie shell—for a classic quiche Lorraine—we poured the custard on top and baked the quiche until it was puffed and set around the edges but still jiggled in the center; the residual heat finished cooking the center without turning the top into a rubbery skin. Before serving the quiche, we let it cool on a wire rack, which is a small but important step; this allows air to circulate under the crust and prevents it from becoming soggy.

Quiche Lorraine

SERVES 8

The center of the quiche will be surprisingly soft when it comes out of the oven, but the filling will continue to set (and sink somewhat) as it cools. If the pie shell has been previously baked and cooled, place it in the heating oven for about five minutes to warm it, making sure that it does not burn.

- 1 recipe Basic Single-Crust Pie Dough (page 681), fitted into a 9-inch pie plate and chilled
- 8 ounces bacon (about 8 slices), cut into ½-inch pieces
- 2 large whole eggs plus 2 large egg yolks
- 1 cup whole milk
- 1 cup heavy cream
- ½ teaspoon table salt
- ½ teaspoon ground white pepper
  Pinch freshly grated nutmeg
- 4 ounces Gruyère cheese, shredded (about 1 cup)

1. Adjust an oven rack to the middle position and heat the oven to 375 degrees. Following the photos on page 694, line the chilled crust with a double layer of foil and fill with pie weights. Bake until the pie dough looks dry and is light in color, 25 to 30 minutes. Transfer the pie plate to a wire rack and remove the weights and foil.

2. Cook the bacon in a 12-inch nonstick skillet over medium heat until crisp, about 5 minutes. Using a slotted spoon, transfer the bacon to a paper towel–lined plate. Whisk the remaining ingredients except the Gruyère together in a medium bowl.

3. Spread the Gruyère and bacon evenly over the bottom of the warm pie shell and set the shell on the oven rack. Pour the custard mixture into the pie shell (it should come to about ½ inch below the crust's rim). Bake until light golden brown and a knife blade inserted about 1 inch from the edge comes out clean and the center feels set but still soft, 32 to 35 minutes. Transfer the quiche to a wire rack and cool. Serve warm or at room temperature.

BREAKFAST STRATA

WHY THIS RECIPE WORKS: A classic breakfast dish, strata is easy to prepare, presents a variety of flavors, can feed a crowd and, perhaps best of all, can and indeed should be made ahead of time. Too often, though, it is overloaded with fillings; we wanted a savory bread pudding with a balanced, well-seasoned filling.

Recipes recommend all kinds of bread to use; we liked supermarket French or Italian loaves, which were neutral in flavor but had a sturdy texture. Rather than cubing the bread, which is often recommended, we sliced it to retain the layered quality of the dish and let the slices dry slightly (stale bread held up better than fresh). We used whole eggs and half-and-half for the custard, with a tad more dairy than eggs, and increased the amount of custard to saturate the bread more fully. A surprisingly successful addition to the custard was white wine, which we reduced to evaporate the alcohol; it brightened all the flavors. A key to ensuring cohesiveness in the strata was weighting it while it rested for at least one hour; this way, every piece of bread absorbed some custard. We kept our fillings minimal so they wouldn't overwhelm the bread and custard, and we sautéed the filling ingredients before adding them to the casserole to keep moisture from turning the dish watery.

Breakfast Strata with Spinach and Gruyère

SERVES 6

To weigh down the assembled strata, use two 1-pound boxes of sugar, laid side by side over the plastic-covered surface. To double this recipe, use a 13 by 9-inch baking dish greased with 1½ tablespoons butter and increase the baking time in step 5 to 1 hour and 20 minutes.

- 8–10 (½-inch-thick) slices supermarket French or Italian bread
- 5 tablespoons unsalted butter, softened
- 4 medium shallots, minced (about ½ cup)
- 1 (10-ounce) package frozen chopped spinach, thawed and squeezed dry
- Table salt and ground black pepper
- ½ cup dry white wine
- 6 ounces Gruyère cheese, shredded (about 1½ cups)
- 6 large eggs
- 1¾ cups half-and-half

1. Adjust an oven rack to the middle position and heat the oven to 225 degrees. Arrange the bread in a single layer on a large baking sheet and bake until dry and crisp, about 40 minutes, turning the slices over halfway through the baking time. (Alternatively, leave the slices out overnight to dry.) Let the bread cool completely, then spread butter evenly over one side of each bread slice, using 2 tablespoons of the butter; set aside.

2. Heat 2 tablespoons more butter in a medium non-stick skillet over medium heat. Add the shallots and cook until softened, about 3 minutes; add the spinach and salt and pepper to taste and cook until the spinach is warm, about 2 minutes. Transfer to a medium bowl and set aside. Add the wine to the skillet, increase the heat to medium-high, and simmer until reduced to ¼ cup, 2 to 3 minutes; set aside.

3. Butter an 8-inch square baking dish with the remaining 1 tablespoon butter; arrange half of the bread slices, buttered-side up, in a single layer in the dish. Sprinkle half of the spinach mixture, then ½ cup of the shredded Gruyère, evenly over the bread slices. Arrange the remaining bread slices in a single layer over the cheese; sprinkle the remaining spinach mixture and ½ cup more Gruyère evenly over the bread. Whisk the eggs in a medium bowl until combined; whisk in the reduced wine, half-and-half, 1 teaspoon salt, and a pinch of pepper. Pour the egg mixture evenly over the bread layers.

4. Wrap the strata tightly with plastic wrap, pressing the wrap against the surface of the strata. Weigh the strata down (see note), and refrigerate for at least 1 hour or up to 24 hours.

5. Remove the dish from the refrigerator and let stand at room temperature for 20 minutes. Meanwhile, adjust an oven rack to the middle position and heat the oven to 325 degrees. Uncover the strata and sprinkle the remaining ½ cup Gruyère evenly over the surface; bake until both edges and center are puffed and the edges have pulled away slightly from the sides of the dish, 50 to 55 minutes. Cool on a wire rack for 5 minutes and serve.

Breakfast Strata with Sausage, Mushrooms, and Monterey Jack

To double this recipe, use a 13 by 9-inch baking dish greased with 1½ tablespoons butter and increase the baking time in step 5 to 1 hour and 20 minutes.

8–10	(½-inch-thick) slices supermarket French or Italian bread
3	tablespoons unsalted butter, softened
8	ounces bulk breakfast sausage, crumbled
3	medium shallots, minced (about 6 tablespoons)
8	ounces white mushrooms, wiped clean and quartered
	Table salt and ground black pepper
½	cup dry white wine
6	ounces Monterey Jack cheese, shredded (about 1½ cups)
6	large eggs
1¾	cups half-and-half
2	tablespoons minced fresh parsley leaves

Follow the recipe for Breakfast Strata with Spinach and Gruyère through step 1. Fry the sausage in a medium nonstick skillet over medium heat, breaking the sausage apart with a wooden spoon, until it loses its raw color and begins to brown, about 4 minutes; add the shallots and cook, stirring frequently, until softened, about 3 minutes. Add the mushrooms to the skillet and cook until the mushrooms no longer release liquid, about 6 minutes; transfer to a medium bowl and season with salt and pepper to taste. Reduce the wine as directed in step 2; continue with the recipe from step 3, adding the parsley to the egg mixture along with the salt and pepper and substituting the sausage mixture for the spinach and the Monterey Jack for the Gruyère.

BLUEBERRY PANCAKES

WHY THIS RECIPE WORKS: Blueberry pancakes sound appetizing, but they are often tough and rubbery or dense and soggy. And they inevitably take on an unappealing blue-gray hue. We wanted pancakes that cooked up light and fluffy and were studded with sweet, tangy bursts of summer's best berry.

Starting with the pancakes themselves, we determined that unbleached flour, sugar, a little salt, and both baking powder and baking soda were essential for the dry ingredients. One egg added just enough structure and richness without making the pancakes overly eggy. Buttermilk was the preferred dairy component, but since our ground rules were to use only what most home cooks would be likely to have on hand, we searched for a substitute. Lemon juice thickens milk almost to the consistency of buttermilk and adds a similar tang that tasters actually preferred. Some melted butter added to the mix prevented our pancakes from being dry and bland. Mixing the batter too strenuously leads to tough pancakes; it's time to stop mixing when there are still a few lumps and streaks of flour. Once we had great-tasting pancakes, we turned to the blueberries. Stirring them into the batter would obviously lead to smashing and those blue-gray streaks, so rather than incorporating the berries, we simply dropped some onto the batter after we'd ladled it into the skillet.

Smaller wild berries are sweeter than the larger ones, but frozen berries work as well as fresh, which means we can have great blueberry pancakes any time of the year.

Blueberry Pancakes

MAKES ABOUT SIXTEEN 4-INCH PANCAKES, SERVING 4 TO 6

To make sure that frozen berries do not bleed, rinse them under cool water in a mesh strainer until the water runs clear, and then spread them on a paper towel–lined plate to dry. If you have buttermilk on hand, use 2 cups instead of the milk and lemon juice. To keep pancakes warm while cooking the remaining batter, hold them in a 200-degree oven on a greased rack set over a baking sheet.

- 2 cups milk (see note)
- 1 tablespoon juice from 1 lemon (see note)
- 2 cups (10 ounces) unbleached all-purpose flour
- 2 tablespoons sugar
- 2 teaspoons baking powder
- ½ teaspoon baking soda
- ½ teaspoon table salt
- 1 large egg
- 3 tablespoons unsalted butter, melted and cooled slightly
- 1–2 teaspoons vegetable oil
- 1 cup fresh or frozen blueberries, preferably wild, rinsed and dried (see note)

1. Whisk the milk and lemon juice together in a medium bowl or large measuring cup; set aside to thicken while preparing the other ingredients. Whisk the flour, sugar, baking powder, baking soda, and salt together in a medium bowl.

2. Whisk the egg and melted butter into the milk until combined. Make a well in the center of the dry ingredients in the bowl; pour in the milk mixture and whisk very gently until just combined (a few lumps should remain). Do not overmix.

3. Heat a 12-inch nonstick skillet over medium heat for 3 to 5 minutes; add 1 teaspoon of the oil and brush to coat the skillet bottom evenly. Pour ¼ cup batter onto three spots on the skillet; sprinkle 1 tablespoon of the blueberries over each pancake. Cook the pancakes until large bubbles begin to appear, 1½ to 2 minutes. Using a thin-bladed spatula, flip the pancakes and cook until golden brown on the second side, 1 to 1½ minutes longer. Serve and repeat with the remaining batter, using the remaining 1 teaspoon vegetable oil if necessary.

GERMAN APPLE PANCAKE

WHY THIS RECIPE WORKS: More akin to popovers than American pancakes, German apple pancakes are golden and puffed outside, custardy inside, with sweet apples baked right in. The dish suffers from many of the same problems as popovers, too: not enough rise, dense texture, and a too-eggy flavor. We wanted to solve these problems and get this pancake just right.

Flour and eggs are the basis of the batter; half-and-half for the dairy component imparted richness and a light texture. Sugar, salt, and vanilla completed the batter. Steam, not leavening, is what puffs the pancake, so to get the maximum rise we needed to find the right oven temperature. A very hot oven burned the exterior of the pancake; preheating the oven to a high temperature as well as preheating the pan, then lowering the temperature when the pancake went in, proved the ideal method. Granny Smith apples were our top pick if you like a little tartness; otherwise Braeburns are a good choice for their sweetness. We cooked apples with brown sugar rather than granulated for a deeper flavor, along with butter, cinnamon, and a bright touch of lemon juice. To keep the apples from being pushed out of the pan when the pancake rose, we first poured the batter around the edge of the skillet, then over the apples. Our pancake puffed spectacularly, and when we served it, every bite contained warm, tender apples.

German Apple Pancake

SERVES 4

A 10-inch ovensafe skillet is necessary for this recipe; we highly recommend using a nonstick skillet for the sake of easy cleanup, but a regular skillet will work. If you prefer tart apples, use Granny Smiths; if you prefer sweet ones, use Braeburns.

- ½ cup (2½ ounces) unbleached all-purpose flour
- 1 tablespoon granulated sugar
- ½ teaspoon table salt
- 2 large eggs
- ⅔ cup half-and-half
- 1 teaspoon vanilla extract
- 2 tablespoons unsalted butter
- 1¼ pounds Granny Smith or Braeburn apples (3 to 4 large apples), peeled, quartered, cored, and cut into ½-inch-thick slices (see note)
- ¼ cup packed (1¾ ounces) light or dark brown sugar

¼ teaspoon ground cinnamon

1 teaspoon juice from 1 lemon

Confectioners' sugar, for dusting

Maple syrup or Caramel Sauce (recipe follows),
for serving

1. Adjust an oven rack to the upper-middle position and heat the oven to 500 degrees.

2. Whisk the flour, granulated sugar, and salt together in a medium bowl. In a second medium bowl, whisk the eggs, half-and-half, and vanilla together until combined. Add the liquid ingredients to the dry ingredients and whisk until no lumps remain, about 20 seconds; set the batter aside.

3. Melt the butter in a 10-inch ovensafe nonstick skillet over medium-high heat. Add the apples, brown sugar, and cinnamon; cook, stirring frequently with a heatproof rubber spatula, until the apples are golden brown, about 10 minutes. Off the heat, stir in the lemon juice.

4. Working quickly, pour the batter around the edge of the pan and then over the apples. Place the skillet in the oven and immediately reduce the oven temperature to 425 degrees. Bake until the pancake edges are brown and puffy and have risen above the edges of the skillet, about 18 minutes.

5. Using a potholder (the skillet handle will be hot), remove the skillet from the oven and loosen the pancake edges with a heatproof rubber spatula; invert the pancake onto a platter. Dust with confectioners' sugar, cut into wedges, and serve with maple syrup or Caramel Sauce.

Caramel Sauce

MAKES ABOUT 1½ CUPS

Cooking the sugar with some water in a covered pot helps trap moisture and ensures that the sugar will dissolve. When the hot cream mixture is added in step 3, the hot sugar syrup will bubble vigorously (and dangerously), so don't use a smaller saucepan. If you make the caramel sauce ahead, reheat it in the microwave or a small saucepan over low heat until warm and fluid.

½ cup water

1 cup (7 ounces) sugar

1 cup heavy cream

⅛ teaspoon table salt

½ teaspoon vanilla extract

½ teaspoon juice from 1 lemon

1. Place the water in a 2-quart saucepan; pour the sugar into the center of the pan, taking care not to let the sugar crystals stick to the sides of the pan. Cover and bring the mixture to a boil over high heat; once the mixture is boiling, uncover the pan and continue to boil until the sugar syrup is thick and straw-colored and registers 300 degrees on an instant-read thermometer, about 7 minutes. Reduce the heat to medium and continue to cook until the syrup is deep amber and registers 350 degrees, 1 to 2 minutes.

2. Meanwhile, bring the cream and salt to a simmer in a small saucepan over high heat (if the cream boils before the sugar syrup reaches a deep amber color, remove the cream from the heat and cover to keep warm).

3. Remove the pan with the sugar syrup from the heat; very carefully pour about one-quarter of the hot cream into it (the mixture will bubble vigorously), and let the bubbling subside. Add the remaining cream, the vanilla, and lemon juice; whisk until the sauce is smooth. (The sauce can be cooled and refrigerated in an airtight container for up to 2 weeks.)

WAFFLES

WHY THIS RECIPE WORKS: You cannot simply put pancake batter in a waffle iron and make waffles; waffles should be moist and fluffy inside and crisp and brown outside—more like a soufflé with a crust than a pancake. We wanted to find the way to achieve this archetypal waffle.

Thick batter is the secret of the crisp exterior and custardy interior of a waffle, so we used a higher proportion of flour to liquid than that of standard recipes. With buttermilk (and buttermilk makes the best-tasting waffles) there's no need for baking powder, and we found that eliminating it also helped crisp up the waffles. A small amount of cornmeal added a pleasing crunch. Separating the egg and folding the whipped white into the batter was a definite improvement; we could see the pockets of air when we cut into a waffle made this way. Like pancakes, waffles turn tough when the batter is overmixed, so we used a light hand, adding the liquid gradually and using more of a folding motion to mix. Cooked to a medium toasty brown, these waffles were everything we wanted them to be.

Buttermilk Waffles

MAKES 3 TO 4 WAFFLES, DEPENDING ON THE SIZE OF THE IRON

The secret to great waffles is a thick batter, so don't expect a pourable batter. The optional dash of cornmeal adds a pleasant crunch to the finished waffle. This recipe can be doubled or tripled. Make toaster waffles out of leftover batter—undercook the waffles a bit, cool them on a wire rack, wrap them in plastic wrap, and freeze. Pop them in the toaster for a quick breakfast. The waffles are best served fresh from the iron but can be held in an oven until all of the batter is used. As you make the waffles, place them on a wire rack set in a rimmed baking sheet, cover them with a clean kitchen towel, and place the baking sheet in a 200-degree oven.

- 1 cup (5 ounces) unbleached all-purpose flour
- 1 tablespoon cornmeal (optional; see note)
- ½ teaspoon table salt
- ¼ teaspoon baking soda
- ⅞ cup buttermilk
- 1 large egg, separated
- 2 tablespoons unsalted butter, melted and cooled

1. Following the manufacturer's instructions, heat a waffle iron. Whisk the flour, cornmeal (if using), salt, and baking soda together in a medium bowl. In a separate medium bowl, whisk the buttermilk, egg yolk, and melted butter together.

2. Beat the egg white with an electric mixer on medium-low speed until foamy, about 1 minute. Increase the speed to medium-high and whip the whites to stiff peaks, 2 to 4 minutes.

3. Add the liquid ingredients to the dry ingredients in a thin, steady stream while mixing gently with a rubber spatula. (Do not add the liquid faster than you can incorporate it into the batter.) Toward the end of mixing, use a folding motion to incorporate the ingredients. Gently fold the egg white into the batter.

4. Spread an appropriate amount of batter onto the waffle iron. Following the manufacturer's instructions, cook the waffle until golden brown, 2 to 5 minutes. Serve.

EASY BUTTERMILK WAFFLES

WHY THIS RECIPE WORKS: Most waffle recipes are merely repurposed pancake recipes that rely on butter and maple syrup to mask the mediocre results. And even those designed specifically for a waffle iron are often time-consuming affairs. We wanted waffles with a crisp, golden-brown, dimpled crust surrounding a moist, fluffy interior. And for rushed morning schedules, we wanted this recipe to require little more than measuring out some flour and cracking an egg.

To get crisp, the exterior of a waffle must first become dry, and the moist steam racing past the crisping waffle as it cooked was slowing down the process. We needed a drier batter with much more leavening oomph. To do this, we took a cue from a Japanese cooking technique, tempura. In tempura batters, seltzer or club soda is often used in place of still water. The tiny bubbles of carbon dioxide released from the water inflate the batter the same way as a chemical leavener—minus the metallic taste that baking soda and powder sometimes impart. We replaced the buttermilk in our pancake recipe with a mixture of seltzer and powdered buttermilk. The resulting waffles were incredibly light, but not as crisp as we wanted. For better texture, we replaced the melted butter in the recipe with oil—melted butter, which is partly water, had been imparting moisture to the waffles, preventing them from crisping. Best of all, tasters didn't notice the swap, just the excellent flavor and wonderfully crisp texture.

Easy Buttermilk Waffles

MAKES ABOUT EIGHT 7-INCH ROUND WAFFLES

While the waffles can be eaten directly from the waffle iron, they will have a crispier exterior if rested in a warm oven for 10 minutes. Buttermilk powder is available in most supermarkets and is generally located near the dried milk products or in the baking aisle (leftover powder can be kept in the refrigerator for up to a year). Seltzer or club soda gives these waffles their light texture; use a freshly opened container for maximum lift. Avoid Perrier, which is not bubbly enough. Serve with butter and warm maple syrup.

- **2** **cups (10 ounces) unbleached all-purpose flour**
- **½** **cup dried buttermilk powder (see note)**
- **1** **tablespoon sugar**
- **¾** **teaspoon table salt**
- **½** **teaspoon baking soda**
- **½** **cup sour cream**
- **2** **large eggs**
- **¼** **cup vegetable oil**
- **¼** **teaspoon vanilla extract**
- **1¼** **cups unflavored seltzer water or club soda (see note)**

1. Adjust an oven rack to the middle position and heat the oven to 250 degrees. Set a wire rack over a rimmed baking sheet and place the baking sheet in the oven. Whisk the flour, buttermilk powder, sugar, salt, and baking soda in a large bowl to combine. Whisk the sour cream, eggs, oil, and vanilla in a medium bowl to combine. Gently stir the seltzer into the wet ingredients. Make a well in the center of the dry ingredients and pour in the wet ingredients. Gently stir until just combined. The batter should remain slightly lumpy with streaks of flour.

2. Heat a waffle iron and bake the waffles according to the manufacturer's instructions (use about ⅓ cup for a 7-inch round iron). Transfer the waffles to the rack in the warm oven and hold for up to 10 minutes before serving.

FRENCH TOAST

WHY THIS RECIPE WORKS: When it comes to French toast, the results are rarely worth the trouble. The bread is soggy, too eggy, or just plain bland. We wanted to come up with French toast that's crisp on the outside and soft and puffy on the inside, with rich, custard-like flavor every time.

We first focused on determining which type of bread fared best in a typical batter made with milk and eggs. Tasters eliminated French and Italian breads for being chewy. We then turned to white sandwich bread, which comes in two kinds: regular and hearty. Regular bread was gloppy both inside and out. Hearty bread crisped up nicely on the outside, but still had mushiness. Drying out

the bread in a low oven, however, produced French toast that was crisp on the outside and velvety on the inside. As for flavor, tasters thought the French toast tasted overly eggy. We recalled a recipe that required bread dipped in milk mixed with just yolks, versus whole eggs. The yolks-only soaking liquid made a huge difference, turning the taste rich and custardlike. Research revealed that most of the flavor in eggs comes not from the yolk but from the sulfur compounds in the whites, so problem solved. For flavorings, we settled on cinnamon, vanilla, and brown sugar. For nutty butter flavor, we incorporated melted butter into the soaking liquid, warming the milk first to prevent the butter from solidifying. A final bonus—the recipe works just as well with challah.

French Toast
SERVES 4

For best results, choose a good challah or a firm sandwich bread, such as Arnold Country Classics White or Pepperidge Farm Farmhouse Hearty White. Thomas' English Muffin Toasting Bread also works well. To prevent the butter from clumping during mixing, warm the milk in a microwave or small saucepan until warm to the touch (about 80 degrees). The French toast can be cooked all at once on an electric griddle, but may take an extra 2 to 3 minutes per side. Set the griddle temperature to 350 degrees and use the entire amount of butter for cooking. Serve with warm maple syrup.

8 large slices high-quality hearty white sandwich bread or challah (see note)
1½ cups whole milk, warmed (see note)
3 large egg yolks
3 tablespoons light brown sugar
½ teaspoon ground cinnamon
2 tablespoons unsalted butter, melted, plus 2 tablespoons for cooking
¼ teaspoon table salt
1 tablespoon vanilla extract

1. Adjust an oven rack to the middle position and heat the oven to 300 degrees. Place the bread on a wire rack set over a rimmed baking sheet. Bake the bread until almost dry throughout (the center should remain slightly moist), about 16 minutes, flipping the slices halfway through cooking. Remove the bread from the rack and let cool for 5 minutes. Return the baking sheet with the wire rack to the oven and reduce the temperature to 200 degrees.

2. Whisk the milk, egg yolks, sugar, cinnamon, 2 tablespoons melted butter, salt, and vanilla in a large bowl until well blended. Transfer the mixture to a 13 by 9-inch baking pan.

3. Soak the bread in the milk mixture until saturated but not falling apart, 20 seconds per side. Using a firm slotted spatula, pick up a bread slice and allow the excess milk mixture to drip off; repeat with the remaining slices. Place the soaked bread on another baking sheet or platter.

4. Heat ½ tablespoon of the butter in a 12-inch skillet over medium-low heat. When the foaming subsides, use a slotted spatula to transfer 2 slices of the soaked bread to the skillet and cook until golden brown, 3 to 4 minutes. Flip and continue to cook until the second side is golden brown, 3 to 4 minutes longer. (If the toast is cooking too quickly, reduce the heat slightly.) Transfer to the baking sheet in the oven. Wipe out the skillet with paper towels. Repeat cooking with the remaining bread, 2 pieces at a time, adding ½ tablespoon more butter for each batch. Serve warm.

ULTIMATE BANANA BREAD

WHY THIS RECIPE WORKS: Recipes for ultimate banana bread abound, but because they include an overload of bananas for flavor, the bread's texture is often soggy. We wanted a moist, not mushy, loaf that tasted of banana through and through.

To impart lots of banana flavor, we needed to use a generous amount of bananas, but we needed to rid them of excess moisture. We turned to the microwave to help us out. We piled as many bananas in a bowl as we dared and zapped them in the microwave. Then we drained the now-pulpy fruit and mixed the fruit into a batter. We didn't want to toss the flavorful liquid, so we reduced it and added it into the batter as well. Like a mock extract, our reduction infused the bread with ripe, intensely fruity banana flavor.

With the flavor problem solved, a few minor tweaks completed the recipe: We exchanged the granulated sugar for light brown sugar, finding that the latter's molasses notes better complemented the bananas. Swapping out the oil for the nutty richness of butter improved the loaf further. We also added toasted walnuts to the batter, finding that their crunch provided a pleasing contrast to the rich, moist crumb. Wondering if the crust might benefit from a little embellishment, we sliced a banana and shingled it on top of the batter. A final sprinkle of sugar helped the banana slices caramelize and gave this deeply flavored loaf an enticingly crisp, crunchy top.

Ultimate Banana Bread
MAKES ONE 9-INCH LOAF
Be sure to use very ripe, heavily speckled (or even black) bananas in this recipe. This recipe can be made using five thawed frozen bananas; since they release a lot of liquid naturally, they can bypass the microwaving in step 2 and go directly into the fine-mesh strainer. Do not use a thawed frozen banana in step 4; it will be too soft to slice. Instead, simply sprinkle the top of the loaf with sugar. The test kitchen's preferred loaf pan measures 8½ by 4½ inches; if you use a 9 by 5-inch loaf pan, start checking for doneness 5 minutes earlier than advised in the recipe. The texture is best when the loaf is eaten fresh, but it can be cooled completely and stored, covered tightly with plastic wrap, for up to 3 days.

1¾ **cups (8¾ ounces) unbleached all-purpose flour**

1 **teaspoon baking soda**

½ **teaspoon table salt**

6 **large very ripe bananas (about 2¼ pounds), peeled (see note)**

8 **tablespoons (1 stick) unsalted butter, melted and cooled slightly**

2 **large eggs**

¾ **cup packed (5¼ ounces) light brown sugar**

1 **teaspoon vanilla extract**

½ **cup walnuts, toasted and chopped coarse (optional)**

2 **teaspoons granulated sugar**

1. Adjust an oven rack to the middle position and heat the oven to 350 degrees. Spray an 8½ by 4½-inch loaf pan with vegetable oil spray. Whisk the flour, baking soda, and salt together in a large bowl.

2. Place 5 of the bananas in a microwave-safe bowl; cover with plastic wrap and cut several steam vents in the plastic with a paring knife. Microwave on high power until the bananas are soft and have released their liquid, about 5 minutes. Transfer the bananas to a fine-mesh strainer placed over a medium bowl and allow to drain, stirring occasionally, for 15 minutes (you should have ½ to ¾ cup liquid).

3. Transfer the liquid to a medium saucepan and cook over medium-high heat until reduced to ¼ cup, about 5 minutes. Remove the pan from the heat, stir the reduced liquid into the bananas, and mash them with a potato masher until fairly smooth. Whisk in the butter, eggs, brown sugar, and vanilla.

4. Pour the banana mixture into the flour mixture and stir until just combined with some streaks of flour remaining. Gently fold in the walnuts (if using). Scrape the batter into the prepared pan. Slice the remaining banana diagonally into ¼-inch-thick slices. Following the photo, shingle the banana slices on top of either side of

the loaf, leaving a 1½-inch-wide space down the center to ensure even rise. Sprinkle the granulated sugar evenly over the loaf.

5. Bake until a toothpick inserted in the center of the loaf comes out clean, 55 to 75 minutes. Cool the bread in the pan on a wire rack for 15 minutes, then remove the loaf from the pan and continue to cool on a wire rack. Serve warm or at room temperature.

CLASSIC BANANA BREAD

WHY THIS RECIPE WORKS: Overripe bananas are a good excuse to make banana bread, but the loaf can be dry, heavy, and bland. We wanted a banana bread with deep banana flavor, plenty of moisture, and a nice, light texture.

Very ripe, darkly speckled bananas contributed moisture as well as flavor to this bread (they're sweeter, too); unripe ones did not work. Pureeing the bananas kept the bread from rising well, so instead we mashed them thoroughly by hand. For additional moisture we included yogurt, which contributed a nice tang without masking the flavor of the bananas. The quick-bread method of mixing—melting the butter and folding the wet ingredients into the dry ones—produced a golden brown loaf and delicate texture; when we tried creaming the butter and sugar first, the bread came out more like butter cake and wasn't as golden brown. However, we found it was important not to overmix the batter; overly vigorous stirring developed excess gluten that turned the loaf tough and dense.

Classic Banana Bread

MAKES ONE 9-INCH LOAF

For best flavor, use bananas that are very ripe.

2 **cups (10 ounces) unbleached all-purpose flour**

¾ **cup (5¼ ounces) sugar**

¾ **teaspoon baking soda**

½ **teaspoon table salt**

3 **very ripe bananas, mashed well (about 1½ cups)**

¼ **cup plain yogurt**

2 **large eggs, lightly beaten**

6 **tablespoons (¾ stick) unsalted butter, melted and cooled**

1 **teaspoon vanilla extract**

1¼ **cup walnuts, toasted and chopped coarse**

NOTES FROM THE TEST KITCHEN

SHINGLING THE LOAF

Layering thin bananas slices on either side of the loaf adds even more banana flavor to our bread (and brings the total number of bananas in the recipe to six). To ensure an even rise, leave a 1½-inch-wide space down the center.

1. Adjust an oven rack to the lower-middle position and heat the oven to 350 degrees. Grease and flour a 9 by 5-inch loaf pan; set aside.

2. Whisk the flour, sugar, baking soda, and salt together in a large bowl; set aside.

3. Mix the mashed bananas, yogurt, eggs, butter, and vanilla together with a wooden spoon in a medium bowl. Lightly fold the banana mixture into the dry ingredients with a rubber spatula until just combined and the batter looks thick and chunky. Fold in the walnuts. Scrape the batter into the prepared loaf pan and smooth the surface with a rubber spatula.

4. Bake until the loaf is golden brown and a toothpick inserted in the center comes out clean, about 55 minutes. Cool in the pan for 5 minutes, then transfer to a wire rack. Serve warm or at room temperature.

CREAM SCONES

WHY THIS RECIPE WORKS: British-style scones, or cream scones, are a far cry from humongous American coffeehouse creations. Cream scones are delicate and light, much like a biscuit. We set out to perfect a technique for making these tea-time (or breakfast) favorites.

Experimentation with different kinds of flour revealed that all-purpose is the best choice for scones, and even better, for maximum tenderness, is a lower-protein brand of flour. Butter was important for flavor, but only a modest amount or the scones would practically melt in the oven. Cream won out over buttermilk and whole milk for the liquid; it made our scones rich and kept them tender. As a nod to American taste, we increased the amount of sugar from that used in traditional recipes, but only slightly to keep them from being too sweet. The discovery that the food processor did a great job of cutting the butter into the flour was a boon, making it even easier to make these treats. Our British-style cream scones were just right served with a bit of jam.

Cream Scones

MAKES 8 SCONES

Use a low-protein all-purpose flour, such as Gold Medal or Pillsbury. The easiest and most reliable approach to mixing the butter into the dry ingredients is to use a food processor fitted with the metal blade. If you want a light glaze on the scones, brush the tops of the scones with 1 tablespoon heavy cream and then sprinkle them with 1 tablespoon sugar just before you put them in the oven.

Resist the urge to eat the scones hot out of the oven. Letting them cool for at least 10 minutes firms them up and improves their texture.

- 2 cups (10 ounces) unbleached all-purpose flour (see note)
- 3 tablespoons sugar
- 1 tablespoon baking powder
- ½ teaspoon table salt
- 5 tablespoons unsalted butter, chilled and cut into ¼-inch cubes
- ½ cup currants
- 1 cup heavy cream

1. Adjust an oven rack to the middle position and heat the oven to 425 degrees.

2. Place the flour, sugar, baking powder, and salt in a food processor and pulse to combine, about 6 pulses.

3. Scatter the butter evenly over the top and continue to pulse until the mixture resembles coarse cornmeal with a few slightly larger butter lumps, about 12 more pulses. Transfer the mixture to a large bowl and stir in the currants. Stir in the heavy cream with a rubber spatula until a dough begins to form, about 30 seconds.

4. Transfer the dough and any dry, floury bits to a work surface and knead the dough by hand just until it comes together into a rough, slightly sticky ball, 5 to 10 seconds. Cut the dough into eight wedges. Place the wedges on an ungreased baking sheet. (The baking sheet can be covered in plastic wrap and refrigerated for up to 2 hours.)

5. Bake until the scone tops are light brown, 12 to 15 minutes. Cool on a wire rack for at least 10 minutes. Serve warm or at room temperature.

BLUEBERRY SCONES

WHY THIS RECIPE WORKS: Berry scones can be a treat—moist, sweet berries throughout a tender, light biscuit, but more often the berries weigh down the scone and impart little flavor. We wanted a rich, flaky scone studded with sweet, juicy blueberries.

Starting with traditional scone recipes, we increased the amounts of sugar and butter to add sweetness and richness to our scones. A combination of sour cream and milk lent both richness and tang. But now our scones were heavier than we wanted. We found two ways to lighten them. First, we borrowed a technique from puff pastry, where the dough is turned, rolled, and folded multiple times to create layers that are forced apart by steam when baked, and added a few quick folds to our scone dough. Then, to ensure that the butter would stay as cold and solid as possible while baking, we froze the butter and grated it into the dry ingredients using a box grater. Both tricks made for lighter, flakier scones. Adding the blueberries was a challenge. If we put them into the dry ingredients, they got mashed when we mixed the dough; when we added them to the already-mixed dough, we ruined our pockets of butter when we worked the berries in. The solution was pressing the berries into the dough, rolling the dough into a log, then pressing the log into a rectangle and cutting the scones. We had successfully transformed the scone into a fruit-filled, rich yet light treat.

Blueberry Scones

MAKES 8 SCONES

It is important to work the dough as little as possible—work quickly and knead and fold the dough only the number of times called for. The butter should be frozen solid before grating. If your kitchen is hot and humid, chill the flour mixture and bowls before use. The recipe calls for two whole sticks of butter, but only 10 tablespoons are actually used (see step 1). If fresh berries are unavailable, an equal amount of frozen berries, unthawed, can be substituted. An equal amount of raspberries, blackberries, or strawberries can also be used in place of the blueberries. Cut larger berries into ¼ to ½-inch pieces before incorporating. Refrigerate or freeze leftover scones, wrapped in foil, in an airtight container. To serve, remove the foil and place the scones on a baking sheet in a 375-degree oven. Heat until warmed through and recrisped, 8 to 10 minutes if refrigerated, 16 to 20 minutes if frozen.

- 16   **tablespoons (2 sticks) unsalted butter, frozen whole (see note)**
- 1½   **cups (about 7½ ounces) fresh blueberries, picked over (see note)**
- ½   **cup whole milk**
- ½   **cup sour cream**
- 2   **cups (10 ounces) unbleached all-purpose flour, plus extra for the work surface**
- ½   **cup (3½ ounces) sugar, plus 1 tablespoon for sprinkling**
- 2   **teaspoons baking powder**
- ½   **teaspoon table salt**
- ¼   **teaspoon baking soda**
- 1   **teaspoon grated zest from 1 lemon**

1. Adjust an oven rack to the middle position and heat the oven to 425 degrees. Score and remove half of the wrapper from each stick of frozen butter. Grate the unwrapped ends on the large holes of a box grater (you should grate a total of 8 tablespoons). Place the grated butter in the freezer until needed. Melt 2 tablespoons of the remaining ungrated butter and set aside. Save the remaining 6 tablespoons butter for another use. Place the blueberries in the freezer until needed.

2. Whisk the milk and sour cream together in a medium bowl; refrigerate until needed. Whisk the flour, ½ cup of the sugar, the baking powder, salt, baking soda, and lemon zest together in a medium bowl. Add the frozen butter to the flour mixture and toss with your fingers until the butter is thoroughly coated.

3. Add the milk mixture to the flour mixture; fold with a rubber spatula until just combined. Using the spatula, transfer the dough to a liberally floured work surface. Dust the surface of the dough with flour; with floured hands, knead the dough six to eight times, until it just holds together in a ragged ball, adding flour as needed to prevent sticking.

4. Roll the dough into an approximate 12-inch square. Following the photos on page 526, fold the dough into thirds like a business letter, using a bench scraper or metal spatula to release the dough if it sticks to the work surface. Lift the short ends of the dough and fold into thirds again

FOLDING AND SHAPING THE SCONES

1. Start by folding the dough into thirds (like a business letter). Then fold in the ends of the dough to form a 4-inch square. Chill the dough.

2. Reroll the dough into a 12-inch square. Press the berries into the dough.

3. Roll the dough into a jellyroll-like log to incorporate the blueberries.

4. Lay the log seam side down and press into an even 12 by 4-inch rectangle.

5. Cut the dough into eight triangular pieces.

to form an approximate 4-inch square. Transfer the dough to a plate lightly dusted with flour and chill in the freezer for 5 minutes.

5. Transfer the dough to a floured work surface and roll into an approximate 12-inch square again. Sprinkle the blueberries evenly over the surface of the dough, then press down so they are slightly embedded in the dough. Using a bench scraper or a thin metal spatula, loosen the dough from the work surface. Roll the dough, pressing to form a tight log. Lay the log seam side down and press it into a 12 by 4-inch rectangle. Using a sharp, floured knife, cut the rectangle crosswise into four equal rectangles. Cut each rectangle diagonally to form two triangles and transfer to a parchment-lined baking sheet.

6. Brush the tops of the scones with the melted butter and sprinkle with the remaining 1 tablespoon sugar. Bake until the tops and bottoms are golden brown, 18 to 25 minutes. Transfer to a wire rack and cool for 10 minutes before serving.

OATMEAL SCONES

WHY THIS RECIPE WORKS: The oatmeal scones served in a typical coffeehouse are so dry and leaden that they seem like a ploy to get people to buy more coffee to wash them down. We wanted rich toasted oat flavor in a tender, flaky, not-too-sweet scone.

Whole rolled oats and quick oats performed better than instant and steel-cut oats. The rolled oats had a deeper oat flavor, but the quick-cooking oats made scones with a softer texture; either type will work. Toasting the oats brought out their nutty flavor. We used a minimal amount of sugar and baking powder, but plenty of cold butter. A mixture of milk and heavy cream added richness without making the scones too heavy. An egg proved to be the ultimate touch of richness. Cutting the cold butter into the flour, instead of using melted butter, resulted in a lighter texture; we were careful not to overmix the dough, which toughened the scones. A very hot oven made the scones rise spectacularly and also gave them a craggy appearance; the high heat meant less time in the oven and therefore less time to dry out. You won't need a gallon of coffee to wash down these light, oaty scones.

Oatmeal Scones

MAKES 8 SCONES

Half-and-half is a suitable substitute for the milk-cream combination.

- 1½ cups (4½ ounces) old-fashioned oats or quick oats
- ¼ cup whole milk (see note)
- ¼ cup heavy cream (see note)
- 1 large egg
- 1½ cups (7½ ounces) unbleached all-purpose flour
- ⅓ cup (2⅓ ounces) sugar, plus 1 tablespoon for sprinkling
- 2 teaspoons baking powder
- ½ teaspoon table salt
- 10 tablespoons (1¼ sticks) unsalted butter, chilled and cut into ½-inch cubes

1. Adjust an oven rack to the middle position and heat the oven to 375 degrees. Spread the oats evenly on a rimmed baking sheet and toast in the oven until fragrant and lightly browned, 7 to 9 minutes; cool the oats on the baking sheet on a wire rack. Increase the oven temperature to 450 degrees. Line a second baking sheet with parchment paper. When the oats are cooled, measure out 2 tablespoons (for dusting the work surface and the dough) and set aside.

2. Whisk the milk, cream, and egg together in a large measuring cup; remove 1 tablespoon of the mixture and reserve for glazing.

3. Pulse the flour, ⅓ cup of the sugar, the baking powder, and salt in a food processor until combined, about 4 pulses. Scatter the cold butter evenly over the dry ingredients and pulse until the mixture resembles coarse cornmeal, about 12 pulses. Transfer the mixture to a medium bowl and stir in the cooled oats. Using a

rubber spatula, fold in the liquid ingredients until large clumps form. Mix the dough by hand in the bowl until the dough forms a cohesive mass.

4. Dust a work surface with half of the reserved oats, turn the dough out onto the work surface, and dust the top with the remaining oats. Gently pat into a 7-inch circle about 1 inch thick. Using a bench scraper or chef's knife, cut the dough into eight wedges and set on the prepared baking sheet, spacing the scones about 2 inches apart. Brush the surfaces with the reserved egg mixture and sprinkle with the remaining 1 tablespoon sugar. Bake until golden brown, 12 to 14 minutes; cool the scones on the baking sheet on a wire rack for 5 minutes, then transfer the scones to the rack and cool to room temperature, about 30 minutes. Serve.

Glazed Maple-Pecan Oatmeal Scones

Follow the recipe for Oatmeal Scones, toasting ½ cup chopped pecans with the oats, whisking ¼ cup maple syrup into the milk mixture, and omitting the sugar. When the scones are cooled, whisk 3 tablespoons maple syrup and ½ cup confectioners' sugar together in a small bowl until combined; drizzle the glaze over the scones.

CROISSANTS

WHY THIS RECIPE WORKS: We wanted to create an approachable croissant recipe for home bakers—one that would deliver authentic flavor. The layered structure that characterizes croissants is formed through a process called lamination. First, a basic dough of flour, water, yeast, sugar, salt, and a small amount of butter is made. Then a larger amount of butter is formed into a block and encased in the relatively lean dough. This dough and butter package is rolled out and folded multiple times (each is called a "turn") to form paper-thin layers of dough separated by even thinner layers of butter. Once baked, it's these layers that make croissants so flaky and decadent. To start, we found that more turns didn't necessarily produce more layers; we stopped at three turns, as any more produced a homogeneous bready texture. As for the star ingredient, butter, we found that great croissants demanded higher-fat European-style butter. And one essential tip we discovered during our recipe development was to give the dough a 30-minute quick freeze to firm it to the consistency of the butter, thus ensuring perfectly distinct layers.

Croissants

MAKES 22 CROISSANTS

These croissants take at least 10 hours to make from start to finish, but the process can be spread over 2 days. European-style cultured butters have a higher butterfat content, which makes it easier to fold them into the dough. (Our favorite is from Plugrá.) Any brand of all-purpose flour will produce acceptable croissants, but we recommend using King Arthur All-Purpose Flour, which has a slightly higher protein content. Do not attempt to make these croissants in a room that is warmer than 80 degrees. If at any time during rolling the dough retracts, dust it lightly with flour, fold it loosely, cover it, and return it to the freezer to rest for 10 to 15 minutes. This recipe makes 22 croissants, but only 12 are baked. Shaped croissants can be evenly spaced 1 inch apart on a parchment-lined baking sheet, wrapped with plastic wrap, and frozen until solid, about 2 hours. Once frozen, transfer the croissants from the baking sheet to a zipper-lock bag. Croissants can be kept frozen for up to 2 months. Bake frozen croissants as directed from step 8, increasing the rising time by 1 to 2 hours.

24 tablespoons European-style unsalted butter, very cold, plus 3 tablespoons unsalted butter at room temperature (see note)

1¾ cups whole milk

4 teaspoons instant or rapid-rise yeast

4¼ cups (21¼ ounces) unbleached all-purpose flour (see note)

¼ cup (1¾ ounces) sugar

Table salt

1 large egg

1 teaspoon cold water

1. Melt 3 tablespoons of the butter in a medium saucepan over low heat. Remove from the heat and immediately stir in the milk (the temperature should be lower than 90 degrees). Whisk in yeast; transfer the milk mixture to the bowl of a stand mixer. Add the flour, sugar, and 2 teaspoons salt. Using the mixer's dough hook, knead on low speed until a cohesive dough forms, 2 to 3 minutes. Increase the speed to medium-low and knead for 1 minute. Remove the bowl from the mixer, remove the dough hook, and cover the bowl with plastic wrap. Let the dough rest at room temperature for 30 minutes.

2. Transfer the dough to a parchment paper–lined baking sheet and shape into a 10 by 7-inch rectangle about 1 inch thick. Wrap tightly with plastic and refrigerate for 2 hours.

3. TO MAKE THE BUTTER BLOCK: While the dough chills, fold a 24-inch length of parchment in half to create a 12-inch rectangle. Following the photos on page 529, fold over 3 open sides of the rectangle to form an 8-inch square with enclosed sides. Crease the folds firmly. Place the cold butter directly on the work surface and beat with a rolling pin for about 60 seconds until the butter is just pliable, but not warm, folding the butter in on itself using a bench scraper. Beat into a rough 6-inch square. Unfold the parchment envelope. Using the bench scraper, transfer the butter to the center of the parchment square, re-folding at the creases to enclose. Turn the packet over so that the flaps are underneath and gently roll the butter packet until the butter fills the parchment square, taking care to achieve an even thickness. Refrigerate for at least 45 minutes.

4. TO LAMINATE THE DOUGH: Transfer the dough to the freezer. After 30 minutes, transfer the dough to a lightly floured work surface and roll into a 17 by 8-inch rectangle with the long side of the rectangle parallel to the edge of the work surface. Following the photos on page 529, unwrap the butter and place it in the center of the dough so that the butter and dough are flush at the top and bottom. Fold 2 sides of the dough over the butter square so they meet in the center. Press the seam together. With the rolling pin, press firmly on each open end of the packet. Roll out the dough, perpendicular to the edge of the work surface, until it is 24 inches long and 8 inches wide. Bring the bottom third of the dough up, then fold the upper third over it, folding like a business letter into an 8-inch square. Turn the dough 90 degrees counterclockwise. Roll out the dough again, perpendicular to the edge of the work surface, into a 24 by 8-inch rectangle and fold into thirds. Place the dough on the baking sheet, wrap tightly with plastic wrap, and return to the freezer for 30 minutes.

5. Transfer the dough to a lightly floured work surface so that the top flap of the dough is facing right. Roll once more, perpendicular to the edge of the work surface, into a 24 by 8-inch rectangle and fold into thirds. Place the dough on the baking sheet, wrap tightly with plastic wrap, and refrigerate for 2 hours.

6. Transfer the dough to the freezer. After 30 minutes, transfer to a lightly floured work surface and roll into an 18 by 16-inch rectangle with the long side of the rectangle parallel to the edge of the work surface. Fold the upper half of the dough over the lower half. Using a ruler, mark the dough at 3-inch intervals along the bottom edge with a bench scraper (you should have 5 marks). Move the ruler to the top of the dough, measure in 1½ inches from the left, then use this mark to measure out 3-inch intervals (you should have 6 marks). Starting at the lower left corner, use a pizza wheel or knife to cut the dough into triangles from mark to mark. You will have 12 single triangles and 5 double triangles; discard any scraps. Unfold the double triangles and cut into 10 single triangles (making 22 equal-size triangles in total). If the dough begins to soften, return to the freezer for 10 minutes.

7. TO SHAPE THE CROISSANTS: Position 1 triangle on the work surface. (Keep the remaining triangles covered with plastic while shaping.) Following the photos on page 530, cut a ½-inch slit in the center of the short end of the triangle. Grasp the triangle by 2 corners on either side of the slit and stretch gently, then grasp the bottom point and stretch. Fold both sides of the slit down. Positioning your palms on the folds, roll partway toward the point. Gently stretch the point again; continue to roll, tucking the point underneath. Curve the ends gently toward one another to create a crescent shape. Repeat with the remaining triangles.

8. Place 12 croissants on 2 parchment-lined baking sheets, leaving at least 2½ inches between the croissants, 6 croissants per sheet. Lightly wrap the baking sheets with plastic, leaving room for the croissants to expand. Let stand at room temperature until nearly doubled in size, 2½ to 3 hours. (Shaped croissants can be refrigerated on trays for up to 18 hours. Remove from the refrigerator to rise and add at least 30 minutes to the rising time.)

NOTES FROM THE TEST KITCHEN

MAKING THE BUTTER BLOCK

1. Fold a 24-inch length of parchment in half to create a 12-inch rectangle. Fold over 3 open sides of the rectangle to form an 8-inch enclosed square. Crease the folds firmly.

2. Using a rolling pin, beat the butter until it is just pliable, then fold the butter in on itself using a bench scraper. Beat the butter into a rough 6-inch square.

3. Unfold the envelope and, using a bench scraper, transfer the butter to the parchment, re-folding at the creases to enclose. Turn the packet over; gently roll the butter to fill the parchment square, taking care to achieve an even thickness.

LAMINATING THE DOUGH

1. Roll the dough into a 17 by 8-inch rectangle. Unwrap the butter and place in the center of the dough so that the edges of the butter and dough are flush at the top and bottom. Fold two sides of the dough over the butter so they meet in the center of the butter square.

2. Using your fingertips, press the seam together. Using a rolling pin, press firmly on each open end of the packet. Roll the dough out lengthwise until it is 24 inches long and 8 inches wide.

3. Starting at the bottom of the dough, fold it into thirds. Turn the dough 90 degrees; roll and fold again. Place it on a baking sheet, wrap with plastic wrap, and return to the freezer for 30 minutes. Roll and fold into thirds one more time.

SHAPING THE CROISSANTS

1. Transfer the dough from the freezer to a lightly floured work surface and roll it into an 18 by 12-inch rectangle. (If it begins to retract, fold it into thirds, wrap it, and return it to the freezer for 10 to 15 minutes.) Fold the upper half of the dough over the lower half.

2. Using a ruler, mark the dough at 3-inch intervals along the bottom edge. Move the ruler to the top of the dough, measure in 1½ inches from the left, then use this mark to measure out 3-inch intervals.

3. Using a sharp pizza wheel or knife, cut the dough into triangles from mark to mark; discard any scraps.

4. You should have 12 single triangles and 5 double triangles. Unfold the double triangles and cut in half to form 10 single triangles (making 22 triangles in all).

5. Cut a ½-inch slit in the center of the short end of a triangle. If the dough begins to soften, return it to the freezer for 10 minutes.

6. Grasp the triangle by the 2 corners on either side of the slit and stretch gently, then grasp the point and stretch.

7. Place the triangle on the work surface so the point is facing toward you. Fold both sides of the slit down.

8. Positioning your palms on the folds, roll partway toward the point.

9. Gently grasp the point with one hand and stretch again. Resume rolling, tucking the point underneath.

10. Curve the ends gently toward one another to form a crescent shape. Repeat with the remaining triangles.

9. After the croissants have been rising for 2 hours, adjust the oven racks to the upper-middle and lower-middle positions and heat the oven to 425 degrees. In a small bowl, whisk together the egg, water, and a pinch of salt. Brush the croissants with the egg wash using a pastry brush. Place the croissants in the oven and reduce the temperature to 400 degrees. Bake for 12 minutes then switch and rotate the baking sheets. Continue to bake until deep golden brown, 8 to 12 minutes longer. Transfer the croissants to a wire rack and allow to cool until just warm, about 15 minutes. Serve warm or at room temperature.

BLUEBERRY MUFFINS

WHY THIS RECIPE WORKS: Blueberry muffins should be packed with blueberry flavor and boast a moist crumb. But too often, the blueberry flavor is fleeting, thanks to the fact that the berries in the produce aisle have suffered from long-distance shipping. We wanted blueberry muffins that would taste great with blueberries of any origin, even the watery supermarket kind.

To intensify the blueberry in our muffins, we tried combining blueberry jam with fresh supermarket blueberries. The muffins baked up with a pretty blue filling, but tasters thought the jam made them too sweet. To solve this, we made our own fresh, low-sugar berry jam by simmering fresh blueberries on the stovetop with a bit of sugar. Adding our cooled homemade jam to the batter along with fresh, uncooked berries gave us the best of both worlds: intense blueberry flavor and the liquid burst that only fresh berries could provide.

As for the muffin base, we found that the quick-bread method—whisking together eggs and sugar before adding milk and melted butter, and then gently folding in the dry ingredients—produced a hearty, substantial crumb that could support a generous amount of fruit. We found that an equal amount of butter and oil gave us just the right combination of buttery flavor and moist, tender texture. To make the muffins even richer, we swapped the whole milk for buttermilk. Finally, for a nice crunch, we sprinkled lemon-scented sugar on top of the batter just before baking.

Blueberry Muffins

MAKES 12 MUFFINS

For finely grated lemon zest, use a rasp grater.

LEMON-SUGAR TOPPING
- ⅓ cup (2⅓ ounces) sugar
- 1½ teaspoons finely grated zest from 1 lemon (see note)

MUFFINS
- 2 cups (about 10 ounces) fresh blueberries, picked over
- 1 teaspoon plus 1⅛ cups (8 ounces) sugar
- 2½ cups (12½ ounces) unbleached all-purpose flour
- 2½ teaspoons baking powder
- 1 teaspoon table salt
- 2 large eggs
- 4 tablespoons (½ stick) unsalted butter, melted and cooled slightly
- 4 tablespoons vegetable oil
- 1 cup buttermilk
- 1½ teaspoons vanilla extract

1. FOR THE TOPPING: Stir the sugar and lemon zest together in a small bowl until combined and set aside.

2. FOR THE MUFFINS: Adjust an oven rack to the upper-middle position and heat the oven to 425 degrees. Spray a standard-size muffin pan with vegetable oil spray. Bring 1 cup of the blueberries and 1 teaspoon of the sugar to a simmer in a small saucepan over medium heat. Cook, mashing the berries with a spoon several times and stirring frequently, until the berries have broken down and the mixture is thickened and reduced to ¼ cup, about 6 minutes. Transfer to a small bowl and cool to room temperature, 10 to 15 minutes.

3. Whisk the flour, baking powder, and salt together in a large bowl. Whisk the remaining 1⅛ cups sugar and the eggs together in a medium bowl until thick and homogeneous, about 45 seconds. Slowly whisk in the butter and oil until combined. Whisk in the buttermilk and vanilla until combined. Using a rubber spatula, fold the egg mixture and remaining 1 cup blueberries into the flour mixture until just moistened. (The batter will be very lumpy with a few spots of dry flour; do not overmix.)

4. Using a ⅓-cup measure or an ice cream scoop, divide the batter equally among the prepared muffin cups (the batter should completely fill the cups and mound slightly). Following the photos, spoon 1 teaspoon of the cooked berry mixture into the center of each mound of batter. Using a chopstick or skewer, gently swirl the berry filling into the batter using a figure-eight motion. Sprinkle the lemon sugar evenly over the muffins.

5. Bake until the muffin tops are golden and just firm, 17 to 19 minutes, rotating the pan halfway through baking. Cool the muffins in the pan for 5 minutes, then transfer them to a wire rack and cool for 5 minutes before serving.

NOTES FROM THE TEST KITCHEN

SWIRLING JAM INTO BLUEBERRY MUFFINS

1. Place 1 teaspoon of cooled berry jam in the center of each batter-filled cup, pushing it below the surface.

2. Using a chopstick, swirl the jam into the batter following a figure-eight pattern.

BRAN MUFFINS

WHY THIS RECIPE WORKS: We've made bran muffins with unprocessed wheat bran, so we know how they're supposed to look and taste. But there are so many bran cereals at the supermarket with a muffin recipe on the box that we wondered if we could achieve the same thing without a special trip to the natural foods store.

Twig-style cereal worked better than flakes, but soaking the twigs in milk, as most recipes recommend, left our muffins dense and heavy—they were soaking up all the moisture. Instead, we stirred together the wet ingredients first and then added the cereal; grinding half of the twigs in the food processor and leaving the rest whole gave us the rustic texture we wanted, and the cereal softened in just a few minutes. Whole-milk yogurt added needed moisture to the batter. Molasses and brown sugar reinforced the earthy bran flavor. To improve the texture, we swapped baking soda for baking powder and used one egg plus a yolk—two eggs made the muffins too springy. To ensure that they would soften fully, we plumped the raisins in water in the microwave. These muffins were tender and moist, rustic but not dense, with hearty bran flavor—and all the ingredients came from the supermarket.

Bran Muffins

MAKES 12 MUFFINS

The test kitchen prefers Kellogg's All-Bran Original cereal in this recipe. Dried cranberries or dried cherries may be substituted for the raisins. Low-fat or nonfat yogurt can be substituted for whole-milk yogurt, though the muffins will be slightly less flavorful.

- 1 cup raisins (see note)
- 1 teaspoon water
- 2¼ cups (5 ounces) All-Bran Original cereal (see note)
- 1¼ cups (6¼ ounces) unbleached all-purpose flour
- ½ cup (2½ ounces) whole wheat flour
- 2 teaspoons baking soda
- ½ teaspoon table salt
- 1 large whole egg plus 1 large egg yolk
- ⅔ cup packed (4⅔ ounces) light brown sugar
- 3 tablespoons mild or light molasses
- 1 teaspoon vanilla extract
- 6 tablespoons (¾ stick) unsalted butter, melted and cooled
- 1¾ cups plain whole-milk yogurt (see note)

1. Adjust an oven rack to the middle position and heat the oven to 400 degrees. Spray a standard-size muffin pan with vegetable oil spray. Combine the raisins and water in a small microwave-safe bowl, cover with plastic wrap, cut several steam vents in the plastic with a paring knife, and microwave on high power for 30 seconds. Let stand, covered, until the raisins are softened and plump, about 5 minutes. Transfer the raisins to a paper towel–lined plate to cool.

2. Process half of the bran cereal in a food processor until finely ground, about 1 minute. Whisk the flours, baking soda, and salt in a large bowl to combine; set aside. Whisk the egg and egg yolk together in a medium bowl until well combined and light-colored, about 20 seconds. Add the sugar, molasses, and vanilla; whisk until the mixture is thick, about 30 seconds. Add the melted butter and whisk to combine; add the yogurt and whisk to combine. Stir in the processed cereal and unprocessed cereal; let the mixture sit until the cereal is evenly moistened (there will still be some small lumps), about 5 minutes.

3. Add the wet ingredients to the dry ingredients and gently mix with a rubber spatula until the batter is combined and evenly moistened. Do not overmix. Gently fold the raisins into the batter. Using a ⅓-cup measure or an ice cream scoop, divide the batter evenly among the prepared muffin cups, dropping the batter to form mounds. Do not level or flatten the surfaces of the mounds.

4. Bake until the muffins are dark golden and a toothpick inserted into the center of a muffin comes out with a few crumbs attached, 16 to 20 minutes, rotating the pan halfway through the baking time. Cool the muffins in the pan for 5 minutes, then transfer to a wire rack and cool for 10 minutes before serving.

CORN MUFFINS

WHY THIS RECIPE WORKS: A corn muffin shouldn't be as sweet and fluffy as a cupcake, nor should it be dense and "corny" like corn bread. It should taste like corn, but not overpoweringly, and should be moist with a tender crumb and a crunchy top. Our mission was to come up with a recipe for these seemingly simple muffins that struck just the right balance in both texture and flavor.

The cornmeal itself proved to be an important factor, and degerminated meal just didn't have enough corn flavor. A fine-ground, whole grain meal provided better flavor and texture. Our first batches of muffins were too dry, so we experimented with various ways to add moisture; butter, sour cream, and milk provided the moisture, fat (for richness), and acidity (for its tenderizing effect) that we wanted. We tried mixing the ingredients with both the quick-bread and creaming methods; not only was the former the easier way to go, but it also resulted in less airy, cakey muffins. We got our crunchy top from a 400-degree oven. All in all, we'd resolved all of our issues with corn muffins; these were subtly sweet, rich but not dense, and with a texture that was neither cake nor corn bread.

Corn Muffins

MAKES 12 MUFFINS

Whole grain cornmeal has a fuller flavor than regular cornmeal milled from degerminated corn. To determine what kind of cornmeal a package contains, look closely at the label.

 2 **cups (10 ounces) unbleached all-purpose flour**
 1 **cup (5 ounces) fine-ground, whole grain yellow cornmeal (see note)**
1½ **teaspoons baking powder**
 1 **teaspoon baking soda**
 ½ **teaspoon table salt**
 2 **large eggs**
 ¾ **cup (5¼ ounces) sugar**
 8 **tablespoons (1 stick) unsalted butter, melted**
 ¾ **cup sour cream**
 ½ **cup milk**

1. Adjust an oven rack to the middle position and heat the oven to 400 degrees. Spray a standard-size muffin pan with vegetable oil spray.

2. Whisk the flour, cornmeal, baking powder, baking soda, and salt together in a medium bowl; set aside. Whisk the eggs in a second medium bowl. Add the sugar to the eggs; whisk vigorously until thick and homogeneous, about 30 seconds; add the melted butter in three additions, whisking to combine after each addition. Add half of the sour cream and half of the milk and whisk to combine; whisk in the remaining sour cream and milk until combined. Add the wet ingredients to the dry ingredients; mix gently with a rubber spatula until the batter is just combined and evenly moistened. Do not overmix. Using a ⅓-cup measure or ice cream scoop, divide the batter evenly among the prepared muffin cups, dropping the batter to form mounds. Do not level or flatten the surface of the mounds.

3. Bake until the muffins are light golden brown and a skewer inserted into the center of the muffins comes out clean, about 18 minutes, rotating the pan halfway through the baking time. Cool the muffins in the pan for 5 minutes, then transfer to a wire rack and cool for 10 minutes before serving.

Corn and Apricot Muffins with Orange Essence

1. In a food processor, process ⅔ cup granulated sugar and 1½ teaspoons grated orange zest until pale orange, about 10 seconds. Transfer to a small bowl and set aside.

2. In a food processor, pulse 1½ cups (10 ounces) dried apricots for 10 pulses, until chopped fine. Transfer to a medium microwave-safe bowl; add ⅔ cup orange juice to the apricots, cover the bowl tightly with plastic wrap, and microwave on high power until simmering, about 1 minute. Let the apricots stand, covered, until softened and plump, about 5 minutes. Strain the apricots and discard the juice.

3. Follow the recipe for Corn Muffins, substituting ¼ cup packed dark brown sugar for an equal amount of the granulated sugar and stirring ½ teaspoon grated orange zest and the strained apricots into the wet ingredients before adding them to the dry ingredients. Before baking, sprinkle a portion of the orange sugar over each mound of batter. Cool the muffins in the pan for 5 minutes, then gently lift them out using the tip of a paring knife. Cool on a wire rack for 10 minutes before serving.

CRANBERRY-NUT MUFFINS

WHY THIS RECIPE WORKS: Cranberry-nut muffins can make a quick and hearty breakfast, but all too often they are dense and leaden, with an overwhelming sour berry flavor and soggy nuts distributed haphazardly throughout. We wanted a moist, substantial muffin accented—but not overtaken—by tart cranberries and toasted, crunchy nuts. Hand mixing the batter was quick and gave our muffins enough structure to accommodate the fruit and nuts. Grinding some of the nuts and using them in place of some of the flour added complexity and nutty flavor throughout. Chopping the berries and tossing them with a little sugar toned down their tartness. Finally, adding a streusel topping added back the crunch lost from grinding up the nuts.

Cranberry-Pecan Muffins
MAKES 12 MUFFINS

If fresh cranberries aren't available, substitute frozen cranberries. Before using, place the cranberries in a microwave-safe bowl and microwave on high power until the cranberries are partially thawed, 30 to 45 seconds. Do not overthaw the cranberries.

STREUSEL TOPPING
- 3 tablespoons unbleached all-purpose flour
- 1 tablespoon packed light brown sugar
- 1 tablespoon plus 1 teaspoon granulated sugar
  Table salt
- 2 tablespoons unsalted butter, cut into ½-inch pieces, softened
- ½ cup pecan halves

MUFFINS
- 1⅔ cups (6⅔ ounces) unbleached all-purpose flour
- 1½ teaspoons baking powder
- 1 teaspoon table salt
- 1¼ cups pecan halves, toasted and cooled
- 1 cup plus 1 tablespoon (7½ ounces) granulated sugar
- 2 large eggs
- 6 tablespoons (¾ stick) unsalted butter, melted and cooled
- ½ cup whole milk
- 2 cups fresh cranberries
- 1 tablespoon confectioners' sugar

1. Adjust an oven rack to the upper-middle position and heat the oven to 425 degrees. Spray a 12-cup muffin tin with vegetable oil spray.

2. FOR THE STREUSEL: Pulse the flour, brown sugar, granulated sugar, a pinch of salt, and the butter in a food processor until the mixture resembles coarse sand, 4 to 5 pulses. Add the pecans and pulse until the pecans are chopped coarse, about 4 pulses. Transfer to a small bowl; set aside.

3. FOR THE MUFFINS: Whisk the flour, baking powder, and ¾ teaspoon of the salt together in a bowl; set aside.

4. Process the toasted pecans and granulated sugar until the mixture resembles coarse sand, 10 to 15 seconds. Transfer to a large bowl and whisk in the eggs, butter, and milk until combined. Whisk the flour mixture into the egg mixture until just moistened and no streaks of flour remain. Set the batter aside for 30 minutes to thicken.

5. Pulse the cranberries, remaining ¼ teaspoon salt, and confectioners' sugar in the food processor until very coarsely chopped, 4 to 5 pulses. Using a rubber spatula, fold the cranberries into the batter. Using an ice cream scoop or large spoon, divide the batter equally among the prepared muffin cups (the batter should completely fill the cups and mound slightly). Evenly sprinkle the streusel topping over the muffins, gently pressing into the batter to adhere. Bake until the muffin tops are golden and just firm, 17 to 18 minutes, rotating the muffin tin halfway through baking. Cool the muffins in the muffin tin on a wire rack for 10 minutes. Remove the muffins from the tin and cool for 10 minutes before serving.

CRUMB CAKE

WHY THIS RECIPE WORKS: The original crumb cake was brought to New York by German immigrants; sadly, the bakery-fresh versions have all but disappeared, and most people know only the commercially baked (and preservative-laden) type. We wanted a recipe closer to the original version that could be made at home.

Most modern recipes use butter cake rather than the traditional yeast dough, which made our job that much easier. The essence of this cake is the balance between the tender, buttery cake and the thick, lightly spiced crumb topping. Starting with our favorite yellow cake recipe, we realized we needed to reduce the amount of butter or the richness would be overwhelming. We compensated for the resulting dryness by substituting buttermilk for milk, which also helped make the cake sturdy enough to support the crumbs, and we left out an egg white so the cake wouldn't be rubbery. We wanted our crumb topping to be soft and cookie-like, not a crunchy streusel, so we mixed granulated and brown sugars and melted the butter for a dough-like consistency, flavoring the mixture only with cinnamon.

Broken into little pieces and sprinkled over the cake batter, our topping held together during baking and made a thick layer of moist crumbs with golden edges that didn't sink into the cake.

New York–Style Crumb Cake
SERVES 8 TO 10

Don't be tempted to substitute all-purpose flour for the cake flour; doing so will make a dry, tough cake. If you can't find buttermilk, you can use an equal amount of plain low-fat yogurt, but do not substitute powdered buttermilk because it will make a sunken cake. When topping the cake, take care to not push the crumbs into the batter. This recipe can be easily doubled and baked in a 13 by 9-inch baking dish. If doubling, increase the baking time to about 45 minutes.

CRUMB TOPPING
- ⅓ cup (2⅔ ounces) granulated sugar
- ⅓ cup packed (2⅓ ounces) dark brown sugar
- ¾ teaspoon ground cinnamon
- ⅛ teaspoon table salt
- 8 tablespoons (1 stick) unsalted butter, melted and still warm
- 1¾ cups (7 ounces) cake flour (see note)

CAKE
- 1¼ cups (5 ounces) cake flour (see note)
- ½ cup (3½ ounces) granulated sugar
- ¼ teaspoon baking soda
- ¼ teaspoon table salt
- 6 tablespoons (¾ stick) unsalted butter, cut into 6 pieces, softened but still cool
- 1 large whole egg plus 1 large egg yolk
- ⅓ cup buttermilk (see note)
- 1 teaspoon vanilla extract
  Confectioners' sugar, for dusting

1. FOR THE CRUMB TOPPING: Whisk the sugars, cinnamon, salt, and butter together in a medium bowl to combine. Add the flour and stir with a rubber spatula or wooden spoon until the mixture resembles a thick, cohesive dough; set aside to cool to room temperature, 10 to 15 minutes.

2. FOR THE CAKE: Adjust an oven rack to the upper-middle position and heat the oven to 325 degrees. Cut a 16-inch length of parchment paper or aluminum foil and fold lengthwise to a 7-inch width. Spray an 8-inch square baking dish with vegetable oil spray and fit the parchment into the dish, pushing it into the corners and up the sides; allow the excess to overhang the edges of the dish.

3. In the bowl of a stand mixer fitted with the paddle attachment, mix the flour, sugar, baking soda, and salt on low speed to combine. With the mixer running at low speed, add the butter one piece at a time; continue beating until the mixture resembles moist crumbs, with no visible butter chunks remaining, 1 to 2 minutes. Add the egg, egg yolk, buttermilk, and vanilla; beat on medium-high speed until light and fluffy, about 1 minute, scraping once if necessary.

4. Transfer the batter to the prepared baking pan; using a rubber spatula, spread the batter into an even layer. Break apart the crumb topping into large pea-size pieces, rolling them between your thumb and forefinger to form crumbs, and spread in an even layer over the batter, beginning with the edges and then working toward the center. Bake until the crumbs are golden and a wooden skewer inserted into the center of the cake comes out clean, 35 to 40 minutes. Cool on a wire rack for at least 30 minutes. Remove the cake from the pan by lifting the parchment overhang. Dust with confectioners' sugar before serving.

BLUEBERRY BOY BAIT

WHY THIS RECIPE WORKS: This coffee cake, a moist cake with blueberries and a light streusel topping, is so called because the girl who created it for the Pillsbury Grand National Baking Contest said that teenage boys found it irresistible. We tracked down a version of the contest-winning recipe and decided to see if we could improve it.

The original recipe called for shortening and granulated sugar. We swapped butter for the shortening and brown sugar for some of the granulated sugar. Both exchanges resulted in richer, deeper flavor in the cake. We doubled the amount of blueberries; half went into the cake batter and the other half on top. An extra egg in the

cake batter firmed up the structure so that the extra fruit wouldn't make the cake mushy. The topping couldn't be simpler: in addition to the blueberries, just sugar and cinnamon instead of a streusel, which baked into a light, crisp, sweet coating. If the quick disappearance of this cake is any indication, it's not only teenage boys who can't refuse a second piece.

Blueberry Boy Bait

SERVES 12

If using frozen blueberries, do not let them thaw, as they will turn the batter a blue-green color.

CAKE

- 2 cups (10 ounces) plus 1 teaspoon unbleached all-purpose flour
- 1 tablespoon baking powder
- 1 teaspoon table salt
- 16 tablespoons (2 sticks) unsalted butter, softened
- ¾ cup packed (5¼ ounces) light brown sugar
- ½ cup (3½ ounces) granulated sugar
- 3 large eggs
- 1 cup whole milk
- ½ cup blueberries, fresh or frozen (see note)

TOPPING

- ½ cup blueberries, fresh or frozen (see note)
- ¼ cup (1¾ ounces) granulated sugar
- ½ teaspoon ground cinnamon

1. FOR THE CAKE: Adjust an oven rack to the middle position and heat the oven to 350 degrees. Grease and flour a 13 by 9-inch baking pan.

2. Whisk 2 cups of the flour, the baking powder, and salt together in a medium bowl. With an electric mixer, beat the butter and sugars on medium-high speed until fluffy, about 2 minutes. Add the eggs, one at a time, beating until just incorporated. Reduce the speed to medium and beat in one-third of the flour mixture until incorporated; beat in ½ cup of the milk. Beat in half of the remaining flour mixture, then the remaining ½ cup milk, and finally the remaining flour mixture. Toss the blueberries in a small bowl with the remaining 1 teaspoon flour. Using a rubber spatula, gently fold in the blueberries. Spread the batter into the prepared pan.

3. FOR THE TOPPING: Scatter the blueberries over the top of the batter. Stir the sugar and cinnamon together in a small bowl and sprinkle over the batter. Bake until a toothpick inserted in the center of the cake comes out clean, 45 to 50 minutes. Cool in the pan for 20 minutes, then turn out and place on a serving platter (topping side up). Serve warm or at room temperature. (The cake can be stored in an airtight container at room temperature for up to 3 days.)

CINNAMON BUNS

WHY THIS RECIPE WORKS: A tender, fluffy bun with a sweet cinnamon filling and rich glaze is a brunch treat no one will turn down. Most recipes, though, require yeast, which makes cinnamon buns time-consuming to make. We went into the kitchen to find a shortcut to good-tasting homemade cinnamon buns.

Eliminating the yeast would reduce the prep time substantially, so we started with the assumption that our leavener would be baking powder. A cream biscuit recipe, which could be mixed all in one bowl, was our starting point; buttermilk rather than cream (plus baking soda to balance the acidity of the buttermilk) made the interior of the buns light and airy. A small amount of melted butter restored some of the richness we had lost by eliminating the cream. A brief kneading ensured that the rolls would rise in the oven. We patted out the dough rather than rolling it and covered it with the filling of brown and granulated sugars, cinnamon, cloves, and salt, with melted butter to help the mixture adhere to the dough. We rolled up the dough, cut the buns, and put them in a nonstick cake pan to bake. When they were done, we topped the buns with a quick glaze of confectioners' sugar, buttermilk, and cream cheese. These cinnamon buns were on the table in less than a quarter of the time it would have taken for yeast buns—and they were just as tasty.

Quick Cinnamon Buns with Buttermilk Icing
MAKES 8 BUNS

Melted butter is used in both the filling and the dough and to grease the pan; melt the total amount (8 tablespoons) at once and measure it out as you need it. The buns are best eaten warm, but they will hold for up to 2 hours.

1 tablespoon unsalted butter, melted, for the pan (see note)

CINNAMON-SUGAR FILLING
¾ cup packed (5¼ ounces) dark brown sugar
¼ cup (1¾ ounces) granulated sugar
2 teaspoons ground cinnamon
⅛ teaspoon ground cloves
⅛ teaspoon table salt
1 tablespoon unsalted butter, melted (see note)

BISCUIT DOUGH
2½ cups (12½ ounces) unbleached all-purpose flour, plus extra for the work surface
2 tablespoons granulated sugar
1¼ teaspoons baking powder
½ teaspoon baking soda
½ teaspoon table salt
1¼ cups buttermilk
6 tablespoons (¾ stick) unsalted butter, melted (see note)

ICING
- 2 tablespoons cream cheese, softened
- 2 tablespoons buttermilk
- 1 cup (4 ounces) confectioners' sugar

1. Adjust an oven rack to the upper-middle position and heat the oven to 425 degrees. Pour 1 tablespoon of the melted butter into a 9-inch nonstick cake pan; brush to coat the pan. Spray a wire rack with vegetable oil spray and set aside.

2. FOR THE CINNAMON-SUGAR FILLING: Combine the sugars, spices, and salt in a small bowl. Add the melted butter and stir with a fork or your fingers until the mixture resembles wet sand; set the filling mixture aside.

3. FOR THE BISCUIT DOUGH: Whisk the flour, sugar, baking powder, baking soda, and salt together in a large bowl. Whisk the buttermilk and 2 tablespoons of the melted butter together in a measuring cup or small bowl. Add the liquid to the dry ingredients and stir with a wooden spoon until the liquid is absorbed (the dough will look very shaggy), about 30 seconds. Transfer the dough to a lightly floured work surface and knead until just smooth and no longer shaggy.

4. Pat the dough with your hands into a 12 by 9-inch rectangle. Brush the dough with 2 tablespoons more melted butter. Sprinkle evenly with the filling, leaving a ½-inch border of plain dough around the edges. Press the filling firmly into the dough. Using a bench scraper or metal spatula, loosen the dough from the work surface. Starting at a long side, roll the dough, pressing lightly, to form a tight log. Pinch the seam to seal. Roll the log seam side down and cut it evenly into eight pieces. With your hand, slightly flatten each piece of dough to seal the open edges and keep the filling in place. Place one roll in the center of the prepared pan, then place the remaining seven rolls around the perimeter of the pan. Brush with the remaining 2 tablespoons melted butter.

5. Bake until the edges are golden brown, 23 to 25 minutes. Use an offset metal spatula to loosen the buns from the pan. Wearing an oven mitt, place a large plate over the pan and invert the buns onto a plate. Place the greased wire rack over the plate and invert the buns onto the rack. Cool for 5 minutes.

6. FOR THE ICING: While the buns are cooling, line a rimmed baking sheet with parchment paper; set the rack with the buns over the baking sheet. Whisk the cream cheese and buttermilk together in a large nonreactive bowl until thick and smooth (the mixture will look like cottage cheese at first). Sift the confectioners' sugar over the mixture; whisk until a smooth glaze forms, about 30 seconds. Spoon the glaze evenly over the buns and serve.

STICKY BUNS

WHY THIS RECIPE WORKS: Sticky buns are often too sweet, too big, too rich—just too much. We wanted a bun that was neither dense nor bready, but tender and feathery. The sticky glaze should be gently chewy and gooey; the flavor should be warm and spicy, buttery and sweet—but just enough so that devouring one isn't a feat.

To keep the sticky bun glaze from hardening into a taffy-like shell, we hit on the idea of including cream, which kept the glaze supple. The yeast dough for these buns should be rich, so we added buttermilk, which gave the buns a complex flavor and a little acidity that balanced the sweetness. Butter and eggs enriched the dough further. After the first rise, we spread the filling—dark brown sugar, cinnamon, cloves, and butter—over the dough, rolled it, cut the individual buns, and laid them in the pan with the caramel to rise once more before being baked. We found that setting the pan (a metal nonstick pan was preferable) on a baking stone in the oven ensured that the bottoms of the buns (which would end up on top) baked completely. We wanted pecans in our sticky buns, too, but they lost their crunch when we put them into the filling or the topping. To preserve their crispness, we topped the rolls with the toasted nuts in a lightly sweetened glaze before serving.

Sticky Buns with Pecans

MAKES 12 BUNS

This recipe has four components: the dough that is shaped into buns, the filling that creates the swirl in the shaped buns, the caramel glaze that bakes in the bottom of the baking dish along with the buns, and the pecan topping that garnishes the buns once they're baked. Although the ingredient list may look long, note that many ingredients are repeated. Leftover sticky buns can be wrapped in foil or plastic wrap and refrigerated for up to 3 days, but they should be warmed through before serving. They reheat quickly in a microwave oven (for two buns, about 2 minutes at 50 percent power works well).

DOUGH
- 3 large eggs, at room temperature
- ¾ cup buttermilk, at room temperature
- ¼ cup (1¾ ounces) granulated sugar
- 1¼ teaspoons table salt
- 2¼ teaspoons (1 envelope) instant or rapid-rise yeast
- 4¼ cups (21¼ ounces) unbleached all-purpose flour, plus extra for the work surface
- 6 tablespoons (¾ stick) unsalted butter, melted and still warm

CARAMEL GLAZE

- ¾ cup packed (5¼ ounces) light brown sugar
- 6 tablespoons (¾ stick) unsalted butter
- 3 tablespoons light or dark corn syrup
- 2 tablespoons heavy cream
-   Pinch table salt

CINNAMON-SUGAR FILLING

- ¾ cup packed (5¼ ounces) light brown sugar
- 2 teaspoons ground cinnamon
- ¼ teaspoon ground cloves
-   Pinch table salt
- 1 tablespoon unsalted butter, melted

PECAN TOPPING

- ¼ cup packed (1¾ ounces) light brown sugar
- 3 tablespoons light or dark corn syrup
- 3 tablespoons unsalted butter
-   Pinch table salt
- ¾ cup (3 ounces) pecans, toasted in a small, dry skillet over medium heat until fragrant and browned, about 5 minutes, then cooled and chopped coarse
- 1 teaspoon vanilla extract

1. FOR THE DOUGH: In the bowl of a stand mixer, whisk the eggs to combine; add the buttermilk and whisk to combine. Whisk in the granulated sugar, salt, and yeast. Add about 2 cups of the flour and the butter; stir with a wooden spoon or rubber spatula until evenly moistened and combined. Add all but about ¼ cup of the remaining flour and knead with the dough hook at low speed for 5 minutes. Check the consistency of the dough (it should feel soft and moist but should not be wet and sticky; add more flour, if necessary); knead at low speed 5 minutes longer (the dough should clear the sides of the bowl but stick to the bottom). Turn the dough out onto a lightly floured work surface; knead by hand for about 1 minute to ensure that the dough is uniform (the dough should not stick to the work surface during hand kneading; if it does, knead in additional flour 1 tablespoon at a time).

2. Lightly spray a large bowl or plastic container with vegetable oil spray. Transfer the dough to the bowl, spray the dough lightly with vegetable oil spray, then cover the bowl tightly with plastic wrap and set in a warm, draft-free spot until doubled in volume, 2 to 2½ hours.

3. FOR THE CARAMEL GLAZE: Meanwhile, combine all the glaze ingredients in a small saucepan; cook over medium heat, whisking occasionally, until the butter is melted and the mixture is thoroughly combined. Pour the mixture into a nonstick metal 13 by 9-inch baking dish; using a rubber spatula, spread the mixture to cover the surface of the baking dish; set the baking dish aside.

4. FOR THE FILLING: Combine the brown sugar, cinnamon, cloves, and salt in a small bowl and mix until thoroughly combined, using your fingers to break up any sugar lumps; set aside.

5. TO ASSEMBLE AND BAKE THE BUNS: Turn the dough out onto a lightly floured work surface. Gently shape the dough into a rough rectangle with a long side nearest you. Lightly flour the dough and roll to a 16 by 12-inch rectangle. Brush the dough with the melted butter, leaving a ½-inch border along the top edge; brush the sides of the baking dish with the butter remaining on the brush. Sprinkle the filling mixture over the dough, leaving a ¾-inch border along the top edge; smooth the filling in an even layer with your hand, then gently press the mixture into the dough to adhere. Beginning with the long edge nearest you, roll the dough into a taut cylinder. Firmly pinch the seam to seal and roll the cylinder seam side down. Very gently stretch to form a cylinder of even diameter and 18-inch length; push the ends in to create an even thickness. Using a serrated knife and gentle sawing motion, slice the cylinder in half, then slice each half in half again to create evenly sized quarters. Slice each quarter evenly into thirds, yielding 12 buns (the end pieces may be slightly smaller).

6. Arrange the buns cut side down in the prepared baking dish; cover tightly with plastic wrap and set in a warm, draft-free spot until puffy and pressed against one another, about 1½ hours. Meanwhile, adjust an oven rack to the lowest position, place a baking stone on the rack, and heat the oven to 350 degrees.

7. Place the baking pan on the baking stone; bake until golden brown and the center of the dough registers 180 degrees on an instant-read thermometer, 25 to 30 minutes. Cool on a wire rack for 10 minutes; invert onto a rimmed baking sheet, large rectangular platter, or cutting board. With a rubber spatula, scrape any glaze remaining in the baking pan onto the buns; cool while making the pecan topping.

8. FOR THE PECAN TOPPING: Combine the brown sugar, corn syrup, butter, and salt in a small saucepan and bring to a simmer over medium heat, whisking occasionally to thoroughly combine. Off the heat, stir in the pecans and vanilla until the pecans are evenly coated. Using a soupspoon, spoon a heaping tablespoon of nuts and topping over the center of each sticky bun. Continue to cool until the sticky buns are warm, 15 to 20 minutes. Pull apart or use a serrated knife to cut apart the sticky buns; serve.

SOUR CREAM COFFEE CAKE

WHY THIS RECIPE WORKS: Sour cream coffee cakes should be buttery and rich. But some recipes yield a heavy cake that borders on greasy. We wanted a pleasantly rich cake with lots of streusel on top and throughout.

All-purpose flour gave us a better texture than the cake flour specified in many recipes. For richness, we used plenty of butter, sour cream, and eggs; the eggs also contributed to the tight crumb we wanted. Baking powder and baking soda were necessary to make this hefty batter rise. Rather than creaming the butter and sugar, which made the cake too light and airy, we cut softened butter and some of the sour cream into the dry ingredients, then added the eggs and the rest of the sour cream. In addition to the streusel in the middle of the cake, we wanted more on top, so we started with a mixture of brown and granulated sugars and added a big hit of cinnamon and some flour (to keep the streusel from congealing). We then divided the mixture—some for the interior streusel layers, which we sweetened further with more brown sugar, and the rest for the topping. To the latter, we added pecans and butter; the nuts toasted as the cake baked, so we didn't have to toast them first. With two layers of streusel in our moist, rich cake and another layer on top with toasty, crunchy nuts, this was a coffee cake worth getting up for.

Sour Cream Coffee Cake with Brown Sugar–Pecan Streusel

SERVES 12 TO 16

A 10-inch tube pan is best for this recipe.

STREUSEL

- ¾ cup (3¾ ounces) unbleached all-purpose flour
- ¾ cup (5¼ ounces) granulated sugar
- ½ cup packed (3½ ounces) dark brown sugar
- 2 tablespoons ground cinnamon
- 1 cup pecans, chopped
- 2 tablespoons unsalted butter, chilled and cut into 2 pieces

CAKE

- 12 tablespoons (1½ sticks) unsalted butter, softened but still cool, cut into ½-inch cubes, plus 2 tablespoons softened butter, for greasing the pan
- 4 large eggs
- 1½ cups sour cream
- 1 tablespoon vanilla extract
- 2¼ cups (11½ ounces) unbleached all-purpose flour
- 1¼ cups (8¾ ounces) granulated sugar
- 1 tablespoon baking powder
- ¾ teaspoon baking soda
- ¾ teaspoon table salt

1. FOR THE STREUSEL: In a food processor, process the flour, granulated sugar, ¼ cup of the brown sugar, and the cinnamon until combined, about 15 seconds. Transfer 1¼ cups of the flour-sugar mixture to a small bowl; stir in the remaining ¼ cup brown sugar and set aside to use for the streusel filling. Add the pecans and butter to the flour-sugar mixture in the food processor; pulse until the nuts and butter resemble small pebbly pieces, about 10 pulses; set aside.

2. FOR THE CAKE: Adjust an oven rack to the lowest position and heat the oven to 350 degrees. Grease a 10-cup tube pan with 2 tablespoons of the softened butter. Whisk the eggs, 1 cup of the sour cream, and the vanilla together in a medium bowl until combined.

3. Mix the flour, granulated sugar, baking powder, baking soda, and salt in the bowl of a stand mixer on low speed until combined, about 30 seconds. Add the remaining 12 tablespoons butter and remaining ½ cup sour cream; mix on low speed until the dry ingredients are moistened and the mixture resembles wet sand, with a few large butter pieces remaining, about 1½ minutes. Increase the speed to medium and beat until the batter comes together, about 10 seconds, scraping down the sides of the bowl with a rubber spatula as necessary. Lower the speed to medium-low and gradually add the egg mixture in three additions, beating for 20 seconds after each addition and scraping down the sides of the bowl as necessary. Increase the speed to medium-high and beat until the batter is light and fluffy, about 1 minute.

4. Using a rubber spatula, spread 2 cups of the batter in the bottom of the prepared pan, smoothing the surface. Sprinkle evenly with ¾ cup of the streusel filling without butter or nuts. Repeat with 2 cups more batter and the remaining ¾ cup streusel filling without butter or nuts. Spread the remaining batter over, then sprinkle with the streusel topping with butter and nuts.

5. Bake until the cake feels firm to the touch and a long toothpick or skewer inserted into the center comes out clean (bits of sugar from the streusel may cling to the tester), 50 to 60 minutes. Cool the cake in the pan on a wire rack for 30 minutes. Invert the cake onto a rimmed baking sheet (the cake will be streusel side down); remove the tube pan, place a wire rack on top of the cake, and reinvert the cake streusel side up. Cool to room temperature, about 2 hours. Cut into wedges and serve. (The cake can be wrapped in foil and stored at room temperature for up to 5 days.)

CREAM CHEESE COFFEE CAKE

WHY THIS RECIPE WORKS: This brunch staple is fraught with pitfalls—from dry, bland cake to lackluster fillings that sink to the bottom as they cook. We wanted a rich, moist cake with a texture that could support a tangy swirl of cream cheese filling.

We assembled a batter of flour, granulated sugar, salt, butter, eggs, whole milk, and baking powder and settled on a straightforward creaming method: Beat softened butter with sugar, then add the eggs, milk, and dry ingredients. The resulting cake was full of flavor and capable of supporting our cheese filling—but it was also a bit dry. To add moisture, we replaced the milk with rich sour cream, added baking soda, and upped the amount of butter. Our cake now had a lush texture as well as subtle acidity— a perfect backdrop for the cheese filling.

For the filling, we settled on a base mixture of softened cream cheese and sugar and added lemon juice to cut the richness and a hint of vanilla extract for depth of flavor. To prevent graininess, we incorporated some of the cake batter into the cheese. The filling not only stayed creamy, but it fused to the cake during baking, eliminating gaps that had afflicted our earlier tests. For a topping, we decided upon a crisp yet delicate coating of sliced almonds, sugar, and lemon zest. As it baked, the topping formed a glistening, crackly crust on our now-perfect coffee cake.

Cream Cheese Coffee Cake

SERVES 12 TO 16

Leftovers should be stored in the refrigerator, covered tightly with plastic wrap. For optimal texture, allow the cake to return to room temperature before serving.

LEMON SUGAR–ALMOND TOPPING

- ¼ cup (1¾ ounces) sugar
- 1½ teaspoons finely grated zest from 1 lemon
- ½ cup sliced almonds

CAKE

- 2¼ cups (11¼ ounces) unbleached all-purpose flour
- 1⅛ teaspoons baking powder
- 1⅛ teaspoons baking soda
- 1 teaspoon table salt
- 10 tablespoons (1¼ sticks) unsalted butter, softened but still cool
- 1 cup (7 ounces) plus 7 tablespoons sugar
- 1 tablespoon finely grated zest plus 4 teaspoons juice from 1 to 2 lemons
- 4 large eggs
- 5 teaspoons vanilla extract
- 1¼ cups sour cream
- 8 ounces cream cheese, softened

1. FOR THE TOPPING: Adjust an oven rack to the middle position and heat the oven to 350 degrees. Stir together the sugar and lemon zest in a small bowl until combined and the sugar is moistened. Stir in the almonds; set aside.

2. FOR THE CAKE: Spray a 10-inch tube pan with vegetable oil spray. Whisk the flour, baking powder, baking soda, and salt together in a medium bowl; set aside. In a stand mixer fitted with the paddle attachment, beat the butter, 1 cup plus 2 tablespoons of the sugar, and the lemon zest at medium speed until light and fluffy, about 3 minutes, scraping down the sides and bottom of the bowl with a rubber spatula. Add the eggs one at a time, beating well after each addition, about 20 seconds, and scraping down the beater and sides of the bowl as necessary. Add 4 teaspoons of the vanilla and mix to combine. Reduce the speed to low and add one-third of the flour mixture, followed by half of the sour cream, mixing until incorporated after each addition, 5 to 10 seconds. Repeat, using half of the remaining flour mixture and all of the remaining sour cream. Scrape the bowl and add the remaining flour mixture; mix at low speed until the batter is thoroughly combined, about 10 seconds. Remove the bowl from the mixer and fold the batter once or twice with a rubber spatula to incorporate any remaining flour.

3. Reserve 1¼ cups of the batter and set aside. Spoon the remaining batter into the prepared pan and smooth the top. Return the now-empty bowl to the mixer and beat the cream cheese, remaining 5 tablespoons sugar, lemon juice, and remaining 1 teaspoon vanilla on medium speed until smooth and slightly lightened, about 1 minute. Add ¼ cup of the reserved batter and mix until incorporated.

MAKING CREAM CHEESE COFFEE CAKE

1. Reserve 1¼ cups of the batter, then fill the pan with the remaining batter; smooth the top.

2. Beat ¼ cup of the reserved batter with the filling ingredients; spoon the filling evenly over the batter.

3. Top the filling with the remaining 1 cup reserved batter; smooth the top.

4. Using a figure-8 motion, swirl the filling into the batter. Tap the pan on the counter.

5. Sprinkle the lemon sugar–almond topping onto the batter, then gently press to adhere.

Spoon the cheese filling mixture evenly over the batter, keeping the filling about 1 inch from the edges of the pan; smooth the top. Spread the remaining 1 cup reserved batter over the filling and smooth the top. With a butter knife or offset spatula, gently swirl the filling into the batter using a figure-eight motion, being careful not to drag the filling to the bottom or edges of the pan. Firmly tap the pan on the counter two or three times to dislodge any bubbles. Sprinkle the lemon sugar–almond topping evenly over the batter and gently press into the batter to adhere.

4. Bake until the top is golden and just firm and a long skewer inserted into the cake comes out clean (a skewer will be wet if inserted into the cheese filling), 45 to 50 minutes. Remove the pan from the oven and firmly tap on the counter two or three times (the top of the cake may sink slightly). Cool the cake in the pan on a wire rack for 1 hour. Gently invert the cake onto a rimmed baking sheet (the cake will be topping side down); remove the tube pan, place a wire rack on top of the cake, and invert the cake sugar side up. Cool to room temperature, about 1½ hours, before serving.

FRUIT SALAD

WHY THIS RECIPE WORKS: A bowl of cut-up fresh fruit is a nice complement to the sweets and heavier egg dishes at a brunch, but it can be a little boring without additional flavors. Yogurt-based sauces mask the fresh flavors (not to mention the colors) of the fruit, and sweet syrups make the fruit too much like a dessert. We were looking for a lighter, more flavorful alternative.

We adapted a French dressing called a *gastrique*, a reduction of an acidic liquid with sugar that usually accompanies savory dishes made with fruit. It's a simple technique, and our experiments with reducing different types of acid—wine, citrus juice, and balsamic vinegar—were an unqualified success. We were able to use additional flavorings in the basic dressing, such as spices, extracts, and citrus zests, that would complement the flavors of different types of fruit. Served at room temperature or chilled, fresh fruit bathed in a light but sweet-tart dressing is not only delicious but easy to make, too.

Strawberries and Grapes with Balsamic and Red Wine Reduction

MAKES ABOUT 6 CUPS

An inexpensive balsamic vinegar is fine for use in this recipe. Save high-quality vinegar for other preparations in which the vinegar is not cooked.

- ¾ cup balsamic vinegar (see note)
- ¼ cup dry red wine
- ¼ cup sugar
- Pinch table salt
- 1 tablespoon grated zest plus 1 tablespoon juice from 1 lemon
- ¼ teaspoon vanilla extract
- 3 whole cloves
- 1 quart strawberries, hulled and halved lengthwise (about 4 cups)
- 9 ounces large seedless red or black grapes, each grape halved pole to pole (about 2 cups)

1. Simmer the vinegar, wine, sugar, and salt in a small saucepan over high heat until syrupy and reduced to ¼ cup, about 15 minutes. Off the heat, stir in the lemon zest and juice, vanilla, and cloves; steep for 1 minute to blend the flavors and strain.

2. Combine the strawberries and grapes in a medium bowl; pour the warm dressing over the fruit and toss to coat. Serve at room temperature, or cover with plastic wrap, refrigerate for up to 4 hours, and serve chilled.

Nectarines, Blueberries, and Raspberries with Champagne-Cardamom Reduction

MAKES ABOUT 6 CUPS

Dry white wine can be substituted for the champagne.

- 1 cup champagne (see note)
- ¼ cup sugar
- Pinch table salt
- 1 tablespoon grated zest plus 1 tablespoon juice from 1 lemon
- 5 cardamom pods, crushed
- 3 medium nectarines (about 18 ounces), cut into ½-inch wedges (about 3 cups)
- 1 pint blueberries
- ½ pint raspberries

1. Simmer the champagne, sugar, and salt in a small saucepan over high heat until syrupy, honey-colored, and reduced to ¼ cup, about 15 minutes. Off the heat, stir in the lemon zest and juice and cardamom; steep for 1 minute to blend the flavors and strain.

2. Combine the nectarines, blueberries, and raspberries in a medium bowl; pour the warm dressing over the fruit and toss to coat. Serve at room temperature, or cover with plastic wrap, refrigerate for up to 4 hours, and serve chilled.

Honeydew, Mango, and Blueberries with Lime-Ginger Reduction

MAKES ABOUT 6 CUPS

Be sure to zest one of the limes before juicing. Cantaloupe can be used in place of honeydew, although the color contrast with the mango won't be as vivid.

- 1 cup juice plus 1 tablespoon grated zest from 8 limes (see note)
- ¼ cup sugar
- Pinch table salt
- 1 (1-inch) piece fresh ginger, peeled and minced (about 1 tablespoon)
- 1 tablespoon juice from 1 lemon
- ½ small honeydew melon (see note), seeds and rind removed, cut into 1-inch pieces (about 2 cups)
- 1 mango (about 10 ounces), peeled and cut into ½-inch pieces (about 1½ cups)
- 1 pint blueberries

1. Simmer the lime juice, sugar, and salt in a small saucepan over high heat until syrupy, honey-colored, and reduced to ¼ cup, about 15 minutes. Off the heat, stir in the lime zest, ginger, and lemon juice; steep for 1 minute to blend the flavors and strain.

2. Combine the melon, mango, and blueberries in a medium bowl; pour the warm dressing over the fruit and toss to coat. Serve at room temperature, or cover with plastic wrap, refrigerate for up to 4 hours, and serve chilled.

CHAPTER 20

PLEASE PASS THE BREAD

Cream Biscuits   546

Cream Biscuits with Fresh Herbs   546

Cheddar Biscuits   546

Best Drop Biscuits   547

Rustic Dinner Rolls   547

Irish Soda Bread   549

Whole Wheat Soda Bread   549

Quick Cheese Bread   549

Quick Cheese Bread with Bacon, Onion, and Gruyère   550

All-Purpose Corn Bread   550

Spicy Jalapeño-Cheddar Corn Bread   551

Southern Corn Bread   552

Rustic Country Bread   552

Almost No-Knead Bread   553

Ciabatta   555

Best Whole Wheat Sandwich Bread   557

Multigrain Bread   559

CREAM BISCUITS

WHY THIS RECIPE WORKS: With a high rise, light texture, and rich flavor, fresh-from-the-oven biscuits tend to disappear quicker than cookies in the test kitchen. So it's a shame that many prospective bakers pass them up, just because the recipe calls for the strenuous step of cutting butter into flour, or the messy move of rolling out dough time and again to get every last piece into a round for the baking sheet. We wanted to make great biscuits that cut out these extra steps and used a basic combination of heavy cream, flour, baking powder, and salt.

Instead of cutting butter into flour, we included a generous amount of heavy cream in our biscuits, which gave them a lighter and more tender texture. Kneading for just 30 seconds was enough to get our dough smooth and uniform. We used an extra bit of cream to soak up all the last bits of flour in the bowl, ensuring that nothing was wasted. To enhance the light flavor of our biscuits, we added a small amount of sugar. All there was left to do was shape them, then pop them into the oven immediately to keep them from spreading. Although it is easy enough to pat out this dough and cut it into rounds with a biscuit cutter, we devised a second strategy of simply pressing the dough into an 8-inch cake pan, turning out the dough, and then slicing it into wedges.

Cream Biscuits

MAKES 8 BISCUITS

Bake the biscuits immediately after cutting them; letting them stand for any length of time can decrease the leavening power and thereby prevent the biscuits from rising properly in the oven.

- 2 cups (10 ounces) unbleached all-purpose flour, plus extra for the work surface
- 2 teaspoons sugar
- 1 teaspoon baking powder
- ½ teaspoon table salt
- 1½ cups heavy cream

1. Adjust an oven rack to the upper-middle position and heat the oven to 425 degrees. Line a large rimmed baking sheet with parchment paper. Whisk the flour, sugar, baking powder, and salt together in a medium bowl.

2. Add 1¼ cups of the cream to the flour mixture and stir with a wooden spoon until a dough forms, about 30 seconds. Transfer the dough to a lightly floured work surface, leaving all dry, floury bits behind in the bowl. Add the remaining ¼ cup cream, 1 tablespoon at a time, to the

bowl, mixing with a wooden spoon after each addition, until all the loose flour is just moistened; add these moistened bits to the dough. Knead the dough briefly just until smooth, about 30 seconds.

3. Pat the dough into a ¾-inch-thick circle or press it into an 8-inch cake pan and turn it out onto a lightly floured surface. Cut the biscuits into rounds using a 2½-inch biscuit cutter or into eight wedges using a knife. Place the rounds or wedges onto the prepared baking sheet and bake until golden brown, about 15 minutes. Serve immediately.

Cream Biscuits with Fresh Herbs

Use the herb of your choice in this variation.

Follow the recipe for Cream Biscuits, adding 2 tablespoons minced fresh herbs to the flour mixture in step 1. Proceed as directed.

Cheddar Biscuits

Follow the recipe for Cream Biscuits, adding 2 ounces sharp cheddar cheese, shredded (about ½ cup), to the flour mixture in step 1. Proceed as directed, increasing the baking time to 18 minutes.

BEST DROP BISCUITS

WHY THIS RECIPE WORKS: Drop biscuits have many things going for them: a crisp outer crust, a tender, flaky interior, and a simple, no-nonsense method. There's only one problem—they're often not very good. Too many are dense, gummy, and doughy or, on the flip side, lean and dry. Drop biscuits should, by nature, be simple to make and tender. We wanted a biscuit that could be easily broken apart and eaten piece by buttery piece.

Identifying the best ingredients was the first task. While oil-based biscuits are easy to work with, they lack flavor, so butter is a must. Replacing the usual milk with buttermilk helped heighten flavor; the biscuits now had a rich, buttery tang and were crisper on the exterior and fluffier on the interior. Choosing the right leavener was also important. We needed a substantial amount, but too much baking powder left a metallic taste. Since we'd added buttermilk, we could replace some of the baking powder with baking soda (buttermilk provides the acid that soda needs to act), which gave us the rise we needed, without the metallic bitterness. Once the ingredients had been identified, we were left with only one problem.

greased ¼-cup measuring cup, scoop a level amount of batter and drop onto the prepared baking sheet. Repeat with the remaining batter, spacing the biscuits about 1½ inches apart. Bake until the tops are golden brown and crisp, 12 to 14 minutes.

3. Brush the biscuit tops with the remaining 2 tablespoons melted butter. Transfer to a wire rack and cool for 5 minutes before serving.

RUSTIC DINNER ROLLS

WHY THIS RECIPE WORKS: The remarkably crisp crust of European-style dinner rolls is what keeps these rolls in the domain of professionals, who typically rely on a steam-injected oven to expose the developing crust to moisture. We wanted to create a reliable recipe for rustic dinner rolls with a crisp crust and chewy crumb that looked—and tasted—like they came from an artisanal bakery.

We baked our first batch using bread flour, but when we broke the rolls open, we found a dense, bland crumb beneath a leathery crust. The flavor was easy to improve—we replaced a few tablespoons of bread flour with whole wheat flour, which contributed earthiness, while honey added sweetness. A little extra yeast improved the crumb slightly, but not enough; making the dough wetter was the fix. Lots of water in the dough created more steam bubbles during baking, which produced an airier crumb. Giving the dough a couple of turns also encouraged the yeast to produce more carbon dioxide, creating more bubbles and a lighter crumb.

As for baking, we came up with a two-step baking process to mimic a steam-injected oven: First, we misted the rolls with water before baking them for an even crisper crust. We then partially baked them in a cake pan at a high temperature to help set their shape. Halfway through baking, we removed the cake pan from the oven, lowered the temperature, pulled the rolls apart, and returned them to the oven spaced out on a baking sheet for uniformly golden rolls with the crust and crumb we were looking for.

Properly combining the butter and buttermilk requires that both ingredients be at just the right temperature; if they aren't, the melted butter clumps in the buttermilk. But when we had trouble avoiding this, we made a batch with lumpy buttermilk anyway. The result was a surprisingly better biscuit, slightly higher and with better texture. The water in the lumps of butter (butter is 20 percent water) had turned to steam in the oven, helping create additional height.

Best Drop Biscuits

MAKES 12 BISCUITS

A ¼-cup (#16) portion scoop can be used to portion the batter. To refresh day-old biscuits, heat them in a 300-degree oven for 10 minutes.

    2 cups (10 ounces) unbleached all-purpose flour
    2 teaspoons baking powder
    1 teaspoon sugar
    ¾ teaspoon table salt
    ½ teaspoon baking soda
    1 cup buttermilk, chilled
    8 tablespoons (1 stick) unsalted butter, melted and
       cooled slightly, plus 2 tablespoons melted butter
       for brushing the biscuits

1. Adjust an oven rack to the middle position and heat the oven to 475 degrees. Line a large rimmed baking sheet with parchment paper. Whisk the flour, baking powder, sugar, salt, and baking soda together in a large bowl. Combine the buttermilk and 8 tablespoons of the melted butter in a medium bowl, stirring until the butter forms small clumps.

2. Add the buttermilk mixture to the dry ingredients and stir with a rubber spatula until just incorporated and the batter pulls away from the sides of the bowl. Using a

Rustic Dinner Rolls

MAKES 16 ROLLS

Because this dough is sticky, keep your hands well floured when handling it. Use a spray bottle to mist the rolls with water. The rolls will keep for up to 2 days at room temperature stored in a zipper-lock bag. To recrisp the crust, place the rolls in a 450-degree oven for 6 to 8 minutes.

The rolls will keep frozen for several months wrapped in foil and placed in a large zipper-lock freezer bag. Thaw the rolls at room temperature and recrisp using the instructions above.

1½ **cups plus 1 tablespoon water, at room temperature**
2 **teaspoons honey**
1½ **teaspoons instant or rapid-rise yeast**
3 **cups plus 1 tablespoon (16½ ounces) bread flour, plus extra for the dough and work surface**
3 **tablespoons whole wheat flour**
1½ **teaspoons table salt**

1. Whisk the water, honey, and yeast in the bowl of a stand mixer until well combined, making sure no honey sticks to the bottom of the bowl. Add the flours and mix on low speed with the dough hook until a cohesive dough is formed, about 3 minutes. Cover the bowl with plastic wrap and let sit at room temperature for 30 minutes.

2. Remove the plastic wrap and sprinkle the salt evenly over the dough. Knead on low speed for 5 minutes. (If the dough creeps up on the attachment, stop the mixer and scrape it down.) Increase the speed to medium and continue to knead until the dough is smooth and slightly tacky, about 1 minute. If the dough is very sticky, add 1 to 2 tablespoons flour and continue mixing for 1 minute. Lightly oil a medium bowl; transfer the dough to the bowl and cover with plastic wrap. Let the dough rise in a warm, draft-free place until doubled in size, about 1 hour.

3. Fold the dough over itself; rotate the bowl a quarter turn and fold again. Rotate the bowl again and fold once more. Cover with plastic wrap and let rise for 30 minutes. Repeat the folding, replace the plastic wrap, and let the dough rise until doubled in size, about 30 minutes. Spray two 9-inch round cake pans with vegetable oil spray and set aside.

4. Transfer the dough to a floured work surface and sprinkle the top with more flour. Using a bench scraper, cut the dough in half and gently stretch each half into a 16-inch log. Divide each log into quarters, then each quarter into two pieces (you should have 16 pieces total), and dust the top of each piece with more flour. With floured hands, gently pick up each piece and roll it in your palms to coat with flour, shaking off the excess, and place in the prepared cake pan. Arrange eight dough pieces in each cake pan, placing one piece in the middle and the others around it, with the long side of each piece running from the center of the pan to the edge and making sure the cut side faces up. Loosely cover the cake pans with plastic wrap and let the rolls rise until doubled in size, about 30 minutes (the dough is ready when it springs

back slowly when pressed lightly with a knuckle). Thirty minutes before baking, adjust an oven rack to the middle position and heat the oven to 500 degrees.

5. Remove the plastic wrap from the cake pans, spray the rolls lightly with water, and place in the oven. Bake until the tops of the rolls are brown, 10 minutes, then remove them from the oven. Reduce the oven temperature to 400 degrees; using kitchen towels or oven mitts, invert the rolls from both cake pans onto a rimmed baking sheet. When the rolls are cool enough to handle, turn them right side up, pull apart, and space evenly on the baking sheet. Continue to bake until the rolls develop a deep golden brown crust and sound hollow when tapped on the bottom, 10 to 15 minutes, rotating the baking sheet halfway through baking. Transfer the rolls to a wire rack and cool to room temperature, about 1 hour.

IRISH SODA BREAD

WHY THIS RECIPE WORKS: Authentic Irish soda bread has a tender, dense crumb and a rough-textured, thick crust—definitely a departure from the more common Americanized soda bread, which is closer to a supersized scone. We wanted to try our hand at the authentic version of this bread, which relies on a simple ingredient list of flour, baking soda, salt, and buttermilk.

Our first tests focused on flour. A loaf made with all-purpose flour produced a doughy, heavy bread with an overly thick crust. To soften the crumb, we added some cake flour to the mix, and this made a difference. (It also made historical sense. Because of Ireland's climate, the wheat grown there is a soft, low-protein variety more similar to cake flour than to American all-purpose, which is relatively high in protein.) A version made with all cake flour, however, was heavy and compact. A ratio of 3 parts all-purpose flour to 1 part cake flour proved best. With only the four basic ingredients of flour, buttermilk, baking soda, and salt, our bread was lacking in flavor and still a little tough; we turned to sugar and butter. Traditionally, very small amounts of butter and sugar are sometimes added to Irish soda bread, so we felt justified in using a minuscule amount of each. The sugar added flavor without making the bread sweet, and the butter softened the dough just enough without making it overly rich.

Irish Soda Bread

MAKES 1 LOAF

If you do not have a cast-iron skillet, the bread can be baked on a baking sheet, although the crust won't be quite as crunchy. Soda bread is best eaten on the day it is baked but does keep well covered and stored at room temperature for a couple of days, after which time it will become dry.

- 3 cups (15 ounces) unbleached all-purpose flour
- 1 cup (4 ounces) cake flour
- 2 tablespoons sugar
- 1½ teaspoons baking soda
- 1½ teaspoons cream of tartar
- 1½ teaspoons table salt
- 2 tablespoons unsalted butter, softened, plus 1 tablespoon melted butter for brushing the loaf (optional)
- 1¾ cups buttermilk

1. Adjust an oven rack to the middle position and heat the oven to 400 degrees. Whisk the flours, sugar, baking soda, cream of tartar, and salt together in a large bowl. Add the softened butter and rub it into the flour using your fingers until it is completely incorporated. Make a well in the center of the flour mixture and add 1½ cups of the buttermilk. Work the buttermilk into the flour mixture using a fork until the dough comes together in large clumps and there is no dry flour in the bottom of the bowl, adding up to ¼ cup more buttermilk, 1 tablespoon at a time, until all the loose flour is just moistened. Turn the dough onto a lightly floured work surface and pat together to form a 6-inch round. The dough will be scrappy and uneven.

2. Place the dough in a 12-inch cast-iron skillet. Score a deep cross, about 5 inches long and ¾ inch deep, on the top of the loaf and place in the oven. Bake until nicely browned and a knife inserted in the center of the loaf comes out clean, 40 to 45 minutes. Remove from the oven and brush with the melted butter (if using). Cool for at least 30 minutes before slicing.

Whole Wheat Soda Bread

This variation is known as brown bread in Ireland. The dough will be sticky and you may need to add a small amount of flour as you mix it.

Follow the recipe for Irish Soda Bread, reducing the unbleached all-purpose flour to 1½ cups (7½ ounces) and the cake flour to ½ cup (2 ounces) and increasing the sugar to 3 tablespoons. Add 1½ cups (8¼ ounces) whole wheat flour and ½ cup toasted wheat germ with the flours, sugar, baking soda, cream of tartar, and salt in step 1.

QUICK CHEESE BREAD

WHY THIS RECIPE WORKS: Run-of-the-mill cheese bread is at once dry and greasy, with almost no cheese flavor. Unlike pizza, wherein bread dough is merely topped with cheese, a true cheese bread makes equal partners of the two components. We wanted to make the most of this relationship and create a rich, moist loaf topped with a bold, cheesy crust.

We started with all-purpose flour and added whole milk and sour cream for a clean, creamy flavor and rich, moist texture. Just a few tablespoons of butter added enough richness without greasiness, and using less fat made the texture heartier and less cake-like. A single egg gave rise and structure without an overly eggy flavor. As for cheese, small chunks (rather than shreds) of Asiago or cheddar mixed into the dough offered rich, cheesy pockets throughout the bread; a moderate amount added plenty of flavor without weighing down the bread. For added cheesy flavor and a crisp, browned crust, we coated the pan and sprinkled the top of the loaf with shredded Parmesan.

Quick Cheese Bread

MAKES ONE 8-INCH LOAF

If using Asiago, choose a mild supermarket cheese that yields to pressure when pressed. Aged Asiago that is as firm as Parmesan is too sharp and piquant for this bread. If, when testing the bread for doneness, the toothpick comes out with what looks like uncooked batter clinging to it, try again in a different, but still central, spot; if the toothpick hits a pocket of cheese, it may give a false indication.

Quick Cheese Bread with Bacon, Onion, and Gruyère

Cook 5 ounces (about 5 slices) bacon, cut into ½-inch pieces, in a 10-inch nonstick skillet over medium heat, stirring occasionally, until crisp, about 8 minutes. Using a slotted spoon, transfer the bacon to a paper towel–lined plate and pour off all but 3 tablespoons fat from the skillet. Add ½ cup minced onion to the skillet and cook, stirring frequently, until softened, about 3 minutes; set the skillet with the onion aside. Follow the recipe for Quick Cheese Bread, substituting Gruyère for the cheddar, adding the bacon and onion to the flour mixture with the cheese, and omitting the butter.

- 3 ounces Parmesan cheese, shredded on the large holes of a box grater (about 1 cup)
- 3 cups (15 ounces) unbleached all-purpose flour
- 1 tablespoon baking powder
- 1 teaspoon table salt
- ¼ teaspoon cayenne pepper
- ⅛ teaspoon ground black pepper
- 4 ounces extra-sharp cheddar cheese, cut into ½-inch cubes, or mild Asiago (see note), crumbled into ¼ to ½-inch pieces (about 1 cup)
- 1¼ cups whole milk
- 3 tablespoons unsalted butter, melted
- 1 large egg, lightly beaten
- ¾ cup sour cream

1. Adjust an oven rack to the middle position and heat the oven to 350 degrees. Spray an 8½ by 4½-inch loaf pan with vegetable oil spray; sprinkle ½ cup of the Parmesan evenly over the bottom of the pan.

2. Whisk the flour, baking powder, salt, cayenne, and black pepper together in a large bowl. Using a rubber spatula, mix in the cheddar, breaking up clumps. Whisk the milk, melted butter, egg, and sour cream together in a medium bowl. Using a rubber spatula, gently fold the wet ingredients into the dry ingredients until just combined (the batter will be heavy and thick); do not overmix. Scrape the batter into the prepared loaf pan; smooth the surface with a rubber spatula. Sprinkle the remaining ½ cup Parmesan evenly over the surface.

3. Bake until deep golden brown and a toothpick inserted in the center comes out clean, 45 to 50 minutes. Cool on a wire rack for 5 minutes; invert the loaf onto the wire rack, then turn right side up and continue to cool until warm, about 45 minutes. Cut into slices and serve.

ALL-PURPOSE CORN BREAD

WHY THIS RECIPE WORKS: Corn bread can be sweet and cakey (the Northern version) or savory and light (the Southern version). We wanted a combination of the two. And most important, we wanted our corn bread to be bursting with corn flavor.

The secret to corn bread with real corn flavor was pretty simple: Use corn, not just cornmeal. While fresh corn was best, frozen was nearly as good, and pureeing the kernels in a food processor made them easy to use while eliminating tough, chewy kernels. For flavoring, buttermilk provided a tangy flavor, while light brown sugar enhanced the naturally sweet flavor of the corn. We couldn't assume everyone would own the cast-iron skillet in which Southern corn breads traditionally get their thick crust, so we compensated by baking the bread at a higher than conventional temperature, producing a crunchy crust full of toasted corn flavor.

All-Purpose Corn Bread
MAKES ONE 8-INCH SQUARE

Before preparing the baking dish or any of the other ingredients, measure out the frozen corn kernels and let them stand at room temperature until thawed. When corn is in season, fresh cooked kernels can be substituted for the frozen corn. This recipe was developed with Quaker yellow cornmeal; a stone-ground whole grain cornmeal will work but will yield a drier and less tender corn bread. We prefer a Pyrex glass baking dish because it yields a nice golden brown crust, but a metal baking dish (nonstick or traditional) will also work. The corn bread is best served warm; leftovers can be wrapped in foil and reheated in a 350-degree oven for 10 to 15 minutes.

1½ cups (7½ ounces) unbleached all-purpose flour
1 cup (about 5 ounces) yellow cornmeal (see note)
2 teaspoons baking powder
¾ teaspoon table salt
¼ teaspoon baking soda
1 cup buttermilk
¾ cup frozen corn kernels, thawed (see note)
¼ cup packed (1¾ ounces) light brown sugar
2 large eggs
8 tablespoons (1 stick) unsalted butter, melted and cooled slightly

1. Adjust an oven rack to the middle position and heat the oven to 400 degrees. Spray an 8-inch square baking dish with vegetable oil spray. Whisk the flour, cornmeal, baking powder, salt, and baking soda together in a medium bowl until combined; set aside.

2. Process the buttermilk, thawed corn kernels, and brown sugar in a food processor or blender until combined, about 5 seconds. Add the eggs and process until well combined (corn lumps will remain), about 5 seconds longer.

3. Using a rubber spatula, make a well in the center of the dry ingredients; pour the wet ingredients into the well. Begin folding the dry ingredients into the wet, giving the mixture only a few turns to barely combine; add the melted butter and continue folding until the dry ingredients are just moistened. Pour the batter into the prepared baking dish; smooth the surface with a rubber spatula. Bake until deep golden brown and a toothpick inserted in the center comes out clean, 25 to 35 minutes. Cool on a wire rack for 10 minutes; invert the corn bread onto the wire rack, then turn right side up and continue to cool until warm, about 10 minutes longer. Cut into pieces and serve.

Spicy Jalapeño-Cheddar Corn Bread

Follow the recipe for All-Purpose Corn Bread, reducing the table salt to ½ teaspoon; add ⅜ teaspoon cayenne pepper, 1 medium jalapeño chile, seeds and ribs removed, minced, and 2 ounces sharp cheddar cheese, shredded (about ½ cup), to the flour mixture in step 1 and toss well to combine. Reduce the brown sugar to 2 tablespoons and sprinkle 2 ounces more sharp cheddar, shredded (about ½ cup), over the batter in the baking dish just before baking.

BEHIND THE SCENES

WEIGHING IN ON WEIGHTS AND MEASURES

Variations in measurement can have a significant effect on baked goods. To prove this point, we asked 10 home cook volunteers to measure out 1 cup of flour and 3 tablespoons of water. The weights of the measured flour and water varied by as much as 20 percent! From these findings, we recommend three things to guarantee more consistent results from your baked goods:

WEIGH FLOUR: Don't rely on cup measurements alone. (One cup of all-purpose flour weighs 5 ounces; 1 cup of bread or whole wheat flour weighs 5½ ounces; and 1 cup of cake flour weighs 4 ounces.)

USE THE RIGHT MEASURING CUP: Liquid measurements should be made in a liquid cup measure (not a dry cup measure). To measure accurately, place the cup on a level surface and bring your eyes down to the level of the measurement markings. Add liquid until the bottom of the curved top surface of the liquid (called the meniscus)—not the edges of the surface, which can cling and ride up the walls of the measuring cup—is level with the measurement marking.

BE PRECISE: When measuring tablespoon or teaspoon amounts of liquid, make sure that the teaspoon is completely filled and that there is no excess liquid clinging to the bottom of the spoon after pouring.

SOUTHERN CORN BREAD

WHY THIS RECIPE WORKS: Classic Southern corn bread is made in a ripping hot skillet greased with bacon fat, which causes it to develop a thin, crispy crust as the bread bakes. The resulting bread is moist and tender, with the aroma of toasted corn and the subtle flavor of dairy. Traditionally, Southern-style corn bread is made from white cornmeal and has only trace amounts of sugar and flour. We wanted to perfect the proportions of ingredients and come up with our own crusty, savory Southern-style corn bread baked in a cast-iron skillet.

Departing from tradition, we chose yellow cornmeal over white—corn breads made with yellow cornmeal consistently had a more potent corn flavor than those made with white cornmeal. We chose a rustic method to incorporate the cornmeal—combining part of the cornmeal with boiling water to create a cornmeal "mush." Corn bread that started with some mush had the most corn flavor, and it also produced a fine, moist crumb. We then stirred the buttermilk and egg into the mush before adding the remaining cornmeal and other dry ingredients. As for sugar, a small amount enhanced the natural sweetness of the corn. Finally, we poured the batter into a hot, greased cast-iron skillet to bake until crusty and fragrant.

Southern Corn Bread
MAKES ONE 8-INCH LOAF

Cornmeal mush of just the right texture is essential to this bread. Make sure that the water is at a rapid boil when it is added to the cornmeal. And for an accurate measurement of boiling water, bring a kettle of water to a boil, then measure out the desired amount. Though we prefer to make corn bread in a preheated cast-iron skillet, a 9-inch round cake pan or 9-inch square baking pan, greased lightly with butter and not preheated, will also produce acceptable results if you double the recipe and bake the bread for 25 minutes. For our top-rated cast-iron skillet, see page 710.

- 4 teaspoons bacon drippings or vegetable oil
- 1 cup (about 5 ounces) yellow cornmeal, preferably stone-ground
- 2 teaspoons sugar
- 1 teaspoon baking powder
- ½ teaspoon table salt
- ¼ teaspoon baking soda
- ⅓ cup boiling water (see note)
- ¾ cup buttermilk
- 1 large egg, lightly beaten

1. Adjust an oven rack to the lower-middle position and heat the oven to 450 degrees. Add the bacon drippings to an 8-inch cast-iron skillet and place the skillet in the heating oven.

2. Place ⅓ cup of the cornmeal in a medium bowl. Whisk the remaining ⅔ cup cornmeal, the sugar, baking powder, salt, and baking soda together in a small bowl; set aside.

3. Add the boiling water to the ⅓ cup cornmeal and stir to make a stiff mush. Whisk in the buttermilk gradually, breaking up lumps until smooth, then whisk in the egg. When the oven is preheated and the skillet is very hot, add the dry ingredients to the cornmeal mush and stir until just moistened. Carefully remove the skillet from the oven.

Pour the hot bacon fat from the pan into the batter and stir to incorporate, then quickly pour the batter into the heated skillet. Bake until golden brown, about 20 minutes. Remove from the oven and immediately turn the corn bread onto a wire rack. Cool for 5 minutes; serve.

RUSTIC COUNTRY BREAD

WHY THIS RECIPE WORKS: Authentic rustic country bread should be made with little more than flour, water, yeast, and salt. We aimed to develop a reliable recipe for a big, crusty, pleasant loaf—one without shortcuts—made the old-fashioned way.

We decided to focus our tests around using a sponge starter—a mixture of flour, water, and yeast, left to ferment and then combined with additional flour, water, and other ingredients. A sponge starter gave our bread a complex flavor that yeast alone could not provide. We soon learned that bread with a high water content produces a chewier texture. So we ended up working with a wet dough, to which we could add more flour if necessary. This wet dough was tricky to work with but resulted in a bread with a texture so rough, chewy, and substantial that it was a meal all by itself. For a finishing touch, we added whole wheat and rye flours to the ingredients to enhance this bread's full flavor.

Rustic Country Bread
MAKES 1 ROUND LOAF

Because of its high water content, the bread will be gummy if pulled from the oven too soon. To ensure the bread's doneness, make sure its internal temperature reads 210 degrees by inserting an instant-read thermometer into the side or bottom of the loaf. Also look at the crust—it should be very dark brown, almost black. Leftover bread can be wrapped in a double layer of plastic wrap and stored at room temperature for up to 3 days; wrapped with an additional layer of aluminum foil, the bread can be frozen for up to one month. To recrisp the crust, place the unwrapped bread in a 450-degree oven for 10 minutes (frozen bread should be thawed at room temperature before recrisping).

SPONGE
- 1 cup water, at room temperature
- ½ teaspoon instant or rapid-rise yeast
- 1 cup (5½ ounces) bread flour
- 1 cup (5½ ounces) whole wheat flour

DOUGH

- 3–3½ cups (16½ to 19¼ ounces) bread flour, plus extra for the dough and work surface
- ½ cup (2¾ ounces) rye flour
- 1⅓ cups water, at room temperature
- 2 tablespoons honey
- 2 teaspoons table salt

1. FOR THE SPONGE: Combine the water and yeast in a medium bowl and stir until the yeast is dissolved. Add the flours and stir with a rubber spatula to create a stiff, wet dough. Cover the bowl with plastic wrap and let sit at room temperature for at least 5 hours or up to 24 hours. (The sponge can be refrigerated for up to 24 hours; return to room temperature before continuing with the recipe.)

2. FOR THE DOUGH: Using a rubber spatula, combine 3 cups of the bread flour, the rye flour, water, honey, and sponge in the bowl of a stand mixer. Knead the dough on low speed with the dough hook until smooth, about 15 minutes, adding the salt during the final 3 minutes. If more flour is needed, add the remaining ½ cup bread flour, 1 tablespoon at a time, until the dough clears the sides of the bowl but sticks to the bottom. Lightly oil a large bowl; transfer the dough to the bowl and cover with plastic wrap. Let the dough rise until tripled in size, about 2 hours.

3. Transfer the dough to a lightly floured work surface. Flour the top of the dough. With floured hands, shape the dough into a round by pulling the edges into the middle and gathering it loosely together. Transfer the dough, seam side down, to an inverted baking sheet lined with parchment paper. Cover with plastic wrap and let rise until almost doubled in size, about 45 minutes. (The dough should barely spring back when poked with a knuckle.)

4. Meanwhile, adjust an oven rack to the lower-middle position, place a baking stone on the rack, and heat the oven to 450 degrees at least 30 minutes before baking.

5. Use a razor blade or sharp knife to cut three slashes on the top of the dough. With scissors, trim the excess parchment around the dough. Lightly spray the dough with water.

6. Carefully slide the parchment with the dough onto the baking stone using a jerking motion. Bake until the crust is very dark brown and the center registers 210 degrees on an instant-read thermometer, 35 to 40 minutes, rotating the bread halfway through baking (see note). Turn the oven off, open the oven door, and let the bread remain in the oven 10 minutes longer. Remove from the oven, transfer to a wire rack, and cool to room temperature, about 2 hours.

ALMOST NO-KNEAD BREAD

WHY THIS RECIPE WORKS: The no-knead method of bread making first came to our attention in an article on baker Jim Lahey in the *New York Times.* The article claimed that Lahey's method produces artisanal-style loaves with minimum effort. Lahey uses two approaches to replace kneading (the mechanical process that forms gluten, which gives bread structure): a very high hydration level (85 percent—meaning that for every 10 ounces of flour, there are 8.5 ounces of water) and a 12-hour autolysis period that allows the flour to hydrate and rest before the dough is kneaded. After the dough is briefly kneaded, it is placed in a preheated Dutch oven to bake; the Dutch oven creates a humid environment that gives the loaf a dramatic open crumb structure and crisp crust.

However, as we baked loaf after loaf, we found two big problems: The dough deflated when carried to the pot, causing misshapen loaves, and it lacked flavor. To give the dough more strength, we lowered the hydration and gave the bread the bare minimum of kneading time (under a minute) to compensate. We also figured out a way to transfer the bread without doing any harm to the shape of the loaf—using a parchment paper sling. To solve the lack of flavor, we needed to introduce two elements that a starter adds to artisan breads: an acidic tang with vinegar and a shot of yeasty flavor with beer.

Almost No-Knead Bread

MAKES 1 ROUND LOAF

An enameled cast-iron Dutch oven with a tight-fitting lid yields best results, but the recipe also works in a regular cast-iron Dutch oven or heavy stockpot. Use a mild-flavored lager, such as Budweiser (mild nonalcoholic lager also works). The bread is best eaten the day it is baked but it will keep wrapped in a double layer of plastic wrap and stored at room temperature for up to 2 days. To recrisp the crust, place the unwrapped bread in a 450-degree oven for 6 to 8 minutes.

- 3 cups (15 ounces) unbleached all-purpose flour, plus extra for the work surface
- 1½ teaspoons table salt
- ¼ teaspoon instant or rapid-rise yeast
- ¾ cup plus 2 tablespoons water, at room temperature
- 6 tablespoons mild-flavored lager, at room temperature (see note)
- 1 tablespoon distilled white vinegar

MAKING ALMOST NO-KNEAD BREAD

1. Mix the dough by stirring the wet ingredients into the dry ingredients with a rubber spatula, then leave the dough to rest for 8 to 18 hours.

2. Turn the dough out onto a lightly floured surface and knead the dough 10 to 15 times.

3. After kneading the dough, shape it into a ball by pulling the edges into the middle.

4. Allow the dough to rise for 2 hours in a parchment paper-lined skillet.

5. Once the dough has risen, use the paper's edges to lift the dough and lower it into the preheated Dutch oven. The bread remains on the parchment as it bakes.

1. Whisk the flour, salt, and yeast together in a large bowl. Add the water, beer, and vinegar. Using a rubber spatula, fold the mixture, scraping up the dry flour from the bottom of the bowl, until a shaggy ball forms. Cover the bowl with plastic wrap and let sit at room temperature for 8 to 18 hours.

2. Lay an 18 by 12-inch sheet of parchment paper inside a 10-inch skillet and spray with vegetable oil spray. Transfer the dough to a lightly floured work surface and knead 10 to 15 times. Shape the dough into a ball by pulling the edges into the middle. Transfer the dough, seam side down, to the parchment-lined skillet and spray the surface of the dough with vegetable oil spray. Cover loosely with plastic wrap and let rise at room temperature until the dough has doubled in size and does not readily spring back when poked with a knuckle, about 2 hours.

3. Thirty minutes before baking, adjust an oven rack to the lowest position, place a 6 to 8-quart heavy-bottomed Dutch oven (with a lid) on the rack, and heat the oven to 500 degrees. Lightly flour the top of the dough and, using a razor blade or sharp knife, make one 6-inch-long, ½-inch-deep slit along the top of the dough. Carefully remove the pot from the oven and remove the lid. Pick up the dough by lifting the parchment overhang and lower into the pot (let any excess parchment hang over the pot edge). Cover the pot and place in the oven. Reduce the oven temperature to 425 degrees and bake, covered, for 30 minutes. Remove the lid and continue to bake until the loaf is deep brown and the center registers 210 degrees on an instant-read thermometer, 20 to 30 minutes longer. Carefully remove the bread from the pot; transfer to a wire rack and cool to room temperature, about 2 hours, before serving.

CIABATTA

WHY THIS RECIPE WORKS: Unless your source is an artisanal bakery, most loaves of ciabatta available just aren't any good. Some lack flavor, others are too flat, and still others have holes so big there's hardly any bread. Ideally, this Italian loaf should boast a crisp, flavorful crust, a full and tangy flavor, and a chewy, open crumb. Uninterested in yet another lackluster loaf from the supermarket, we decided to make our own.

We started with the flour selection—whole wheat, bread, or all-purpose? We preferred all-purpose, which is made from both hard and soft wheat and has less protein than bread flour, producing loaves with a more open, springy texture. The next step was to build flavor through the sponge (or *biga* in Italian), which we also used in our Rustic Country Bread (page 552). As it ferments, the yeast in the biga produces lactic and acetic acids as by-products, which give the bread its characteristic sourness. Kneading the sponge and remaining dough ingredients in a stand mixer for only a few minutes produced loaves that spread out instead of rising, so we turned to a combination of kneading and folding the dough over itself a few times before letting it rest. This two-step process gives the dough structure but also supports oversized holes. Adding a small amount of milk, which contains a protein that slightly weakens the gluten strands, remedied the problem and took down the size of those big bubbles.

To avoid extra handling of the dough, we formed the loaves, then moved them to parchment paper and slid the parchment onto the baking surface after another rest. We opted to bake the loaves at a cooler temperature than 500 degrees (as most recipes recommend). A final enhancement was to spray the loaves with water in the first minutes of baking for a crisper crust and loaves that rose a bit higher.

Ciabatta

MAKES 2 LOAVES

As you make this bread, keep in mind that the dough is wet and very sticky. The key to manipulating it is working quickly and gently; rough handling will result in flat, tough loaves. When possible, use a large rubber spatula or bowl scraper to move the dough. If you have to use your hands, make sure they are well floured. Because the dough is so sticky, it must be prepared in a stand mixer. If you don't have a baking stone, bake the bread on an overturned and preheated rimmed baking sheet set on the lowest oven rack. Leftover bread can be wrapped in a double layer of plastic wrap and stored at room temperature for up to 3 days; wrapped with an additional layer of aluminum foil, the bread can be frozen for up to 1 month. To recrisp the crust, place the unwrapped bread in a 450-degree oven for 6 to 8 minutes (frozen bread should be thawed at room temperature before recrisping).

SPONGE

- 1 cup (5 ounces) unbleached all-purpose flour
- ⅛ teaspoon instant or rapid-rise yeast
- ½ cup water, at room temperature

DOUGH

- 2 cups (10 ounces) unbleached all-purpose flour, plus extra for the dough and work surface
- 1½ teaspoons table salt
- ½ teaspoon instant or rapid-rise yeast
- ¾ cup water, at room temperature
- ¼ cup milk, at room temperature

1. FOR THE SPONGE: Combine the flour, yeast, and water in a medium bowl and stir with a wooden spoon until a uniform mass forms, about 1 minute. Cover the bowl tightly with plastic wrap and let stand at room temperature (about 70 degrees) for at least 8 hours or up to 24 hours.

2. FOR THE DOUGH: Place the sponge and dough ingredients in the bowl of a stand mixer fitted with the paddle attachment. Mix on low speed until roughly combined and a shaggy dough forms, about 1 minute; scrape down the sides of the bowl as necessary. Increase the speed to medium-low and continue mixing until the dough becomes a uniform mass that collects on the paddle and pulls away from the sides of the bowl, 4 to 6 minutes. Change to the dough hook and knead the bread on medium speed until smooth and shiny (the dough will be very sticky), about 10 minutes. (If the dough creeps up on the attachment, stop the mixer and scrape it down.) Transfer the dough to a large bowl and cover tightly with plastic wrap. Let the dough rise at room temperature until doubled in size, about 1 hour. (The dough should barely spring back when poked with a knuckle.)

3. Spray a rubber spatula or bowl scraper with vegetable oil spray; fold the partially risen dough over itself by gently lifting and folding the edge of the dough toward the middle. Turn the bowl 90 degrees; fold again. Turn the bowl and fold the dough six more times (for a total of eight turns). Cover with plastic wrap and let rise for 30 minutes. Repeat folding, replace the plastic wrap, and let rise until doubled in size, about 30 minutes longer. Meanwhile, adjust an oven rack to the lower-middle position, place a baking stone on the rack, and heat the oven to 450 degrees at least 30 minutes before baking.

MAKING CIABATTA

1. After mixing the dough and allowing it to rest, turn the partially risen dough by folding it in on itself to gently encourage more gluten development. Let it rest again, then repeat this step.

2. Transfer the dough to a lightly floured surface and halve it with a bench scraper.

3. Press each half into a rough 12 by 6-inch rectangle.

4. Fold each dough half like a business letter into a 7 by 4-inch loaf. Transfer each loaf, seam side down, to sheets of parchment, dust with flour, and cover with plastic wrap. Let rest for 30 minutes.

5. Use floured fingertips to evenly poke the entire surface of each loaf to form a 10 by 6-inch rectangle; spray the loaves lightly with water. Transfer the loaves, parchment and all, onto the hot baking stone and bake.

4. Cut two 12 by 6-inch pieces of parchment paper and liberally dust with flour. Transfer the dough to a floured work surface, being careful not to deflate it completely. Liberally flour the top of the dough and divide it in half with a bench scraper. Turn one piece of dough cut side up and dust with flour. Following the photos, with well-floured hands, press the dough into a rough 12 by 6-inch shape. Fold the shorter sides of the dough toward the center, overlapping them like a business letter to form a 7 by 4-inch loaf. Repeat with the second dough piece. Gently transfer each loaf, seam side down, to the parchment sheets, dust with flour, and cover with plastic wrap. Let the loaves sit at room temperature for 30 minutes (the surface of the loaves will develop small bubbles).

5. Slide the parchment with the loaves onto an inverted rimmed baking sheet or pizza peel. Using floured fingertips, evenly poke the entire surface of each loaf to form a 10 by 6-inch rectangle; spray the loaves lightly with water. Carefully slide the parchment with the loaves onto the baking stone using a jerking motion. Bake, spraying the loaves with water twice more during the first 5 minutes of baking time, until the crust is a deep golden brown and the center of the loaves registers 210 degrees on an instant-read thermometer, 22 to 27 minutes. Transfer to a wire rack, discard the parchment, and cool the loaves to room temperature, about 1 hour, before slicing and serving.

WHOLE WHEAT SANDWICH BREAD

WHY THIS RECIPE WORKS: Most whole wheat bread recipes turn out either squat bricks or white bread in disguise. We wanted a nutty, hearty, light-textured sandwich loaf that really tasted like wheat. We started with a good white-flour recipe and worked our way backward to "unrefine" it. We made a series of white bread loaves, replacing different amounts of all-purpose flour with whole wheat to find the highest percentage of whole wheat flour that we could use before the texture suffered, landing on 60 percent. To bump the amount of whole wheat up even more, we substituted protein-rich bread flour for the all-purpose flour. Next, we soaked the flour overnight in milk, with some wheat germ for added flavor. This softened the grain's fiber, kept the dough moist, and coaxed out some sweetness. Finally, we turned to a sponge, a mixture of flour, water, and yeast left to sit overnight to develop a full range of flavor in our loaf. Adding honey lent complexity and swapping out some of the butter in our dough for vegetable oil cut the richness.

Best Whole Wheat Sandwich Bread

MAKES TWO 8-INCH LOAVES

If you don't have a stand mixer, you can mix the dough by hand following the instructions on page 558. If you don't have a baking stone, bake the bread on an overturned and preheated rimmed baking sheet set on the lowest oven rack. The bread can be wrapped in a double layer of plastic wrap and stored at room temperature for up to 3 days. Wrapped with an additional layer of aluminum foil, the bread can be frozen for up to 1 month.

SPONGE

- **2 cups (11 ounces) bread flour**
- **1 cup water, heated to 110 degrees**
- **½ teaspoon instant or rapid-rise yeast**

SOAKER

- **3 cups (16½ ounces) whole wheat flour**
- **½ cup wheat germ**
- **2 cups whole milk**

DOUGH

- **6 tablespoons unsalted butter, softened**
- **¼ cup honey**
- **2 tablespoons instant or rapid-rise yeast**
- **2 tablespoons vegetable oil**
- **4 teaspoons table salt**

1. FOR THE SPONGE: Combine the flour, water, and yeast in a large bowl and stir with a wooden spoon until a uniform mass forms and no dry flour remains, about 1 minute. Cover the bowl tightly with plastic wrap and let sit at room temperature for at least 8 hours or up to 24 hours.

2. FOR THE SOAKER: Combine the flour, wheat germ, and milk in a separate large bowl and stir with a wooden spoon until a shaggy mass forms, about 1 minute. Transfer the dough to a lightly floured work surface and knead by hand until smooth, 2 to 3 minutes. Return the soaker to the bowl, cover tightly with plastic wrap, and refrigerate for at least 8 hours or up to 24 hours.

3. FOR THE DOUGH: Tear the soaker apart into 1-inch pieces and place in the bowl of a stand mixer fitted with the dough hook. Add the sponge, butter, honey, yeast, oil, and salt and mix on low speed until a cohesive mass starts to form, about 2 minutes. Increase the speed to medium and knead until the dough is smooth and elastic, 8 to 10 minutes. Transfer the dough to a lightly floured work surface and knead by hand to form a smooth, round ball, about 1 minute. Place the dough in a large, lightly greased bowl. Cover tightly with plastic wrap and let rise at room temperature for 45 minutes.

NOTES FROM THE TEST KITCHEN

FOLDING AND FORMING THE LOAVES

1. Deflate the center of the dough, then fold it in on itself. Turn the bowl 90 degrees; fold again. Repeat for a total of 8 folds. Let rise for 45 minutes.

2. Halve the dough and pat each portion into an 8 by 17-inch rectangle, with the short side facing you.

3. Roll each sheet toward you into a tight cylinder. Keep the roll taut by tucking it under itself as you go. Pinch the seams to seal.

4. Place each loaf seam side down in the prepared loaf pans. Let the dough rise until almost doubled in size, 60 to 90 minutes.

5. Using a knife, make a shallow slash down the center of each loaf to stop the bread from tearing when it rises. Bake for 40 to 50 minutes.

4. Gently press down on the center of the dough to deflate. Spray a rubber spatula or bowl scraper with vegetable oil spray; fold the partially risen dough over itself by gently lifting and folding the edge of the dough toward the middle. Turn the bowl 90 degrees; fold again. Turn the bowl and fold the dough 6 more times (for a total of 8 folds). Cover tightly with plastic wrap and allow to rise at room temperature until doubled in size, about 45 minutes.

5. Grease two 8½ by 4½-inch loaf pans. Transfer the dough to a well-floured work surface and divide in half. Press 1 piece of the dough into a 17 by 8-inch rectangle, with the short side facing you. Roll the dough toward you into a firm cylinder, keeping the roll taut by tucking it under itself as you go. Turn the loaf seam side up and pinch it closed. Place the loaf seam side down in a prepared pan, pressing gently into the corners. Repeat with the second piece of dough. Cover the loaves loosely with greased plastic wrap and let rise at room temperature until nearly doubled in size, 1 to 1½ hours (the top of the loaves should rise about 1 inch over the lip of the pan).

6. Thirty minutes before baking, adjust the oven racks to the middle and lowest positions, place a baking stone on the middle rack, place an empty loaf pan or other heatproof pan on the bottom rack, and heat the oven to 400 degrees. Bring 2 cups water to boil on the stovetop.

7. Using a sharp serrated knife or a single-edge razor blade, make one ¼-inch-deep slash lengthwise down the center of each loaf. Working quickly, pour the boiling water into the empty loaf pan in the oven and set the loaves on the baking stone. Reduce the oven temperature to 350 degrees. Bake until the crust is dark brown and the loaves register 200 degrees on an instant-read thermometer, 40 to 50 minutes, rotating the loaves front to back and side to side halfway through baking. Transfer the pans to a wire rack and let cool for 5 minutes. Remove the loaves from the pans, return to the rack, and let cool to room temperature, about 2 hours, before slicing and serving.

MULTIGRAIN BREAD

WHY THIS RECIPE WORKS: Although multigrain bread often has great flavor, the quantity of ingredients weighs it down so much that the loaf becomes as dense and as heavy as a brick. On the other end of the spectrum are loaves with a nice, light sandwich-style texture but so little grain that they're hard to distinguish from plain old white bread. We wanted a multigrain bread with both great flavor and balanced texture.

Our first challenge was to develop more gluten (a protein made when flour and water are mixed and that gives baked goods structure) in the dough, as early tests showed that the whole grains were impeding its development. Because the protein content of any flour is an indicator of how much gluten it will produce, we thought first to switch out all-purpose flour for higher-protein bread flour, but this move only made the bread chewier, not less dense. The solution was twofold: long kneading preceded by an autolyse, a resting period just after the initial mixing of water and flour that gives flour time to hydrate. This combination also made the dough less tacky and therefore easier to work with. The result was a loaf that baked up light yet chewy, without being tough. To incorporate grains into the bread, we hit upon a convenient, one-stop-shopping alternative: packaged seven-grain hot cereal. To soften the grains, we made a thick porridge with the cereal before adding it to the dough. A final step of rolling the shaped loaves in oats yielded a finished, professional look.

Multigrain Bread

MAKES TWO 8-INCH LOAVES

Don't confuse seven-grain hot cereal mix with boxed, cold breakfast cereals that may also be labeled "seven-grain." Our favorite brands of seven-grain mix are Bob's Red Mill and Arrowhead Mills. Leftover bread can be wrapped in a double layer of plastic wrap and stored at room temperature for up to 3 days; wrapped with an additional layer of aluminum foil, the bread can be frozen for up to 1 month. For an accurate measurement of boiling water, bring a kettle of water to a boil, then measure out the desired amount. See page 720 for information on our top-rated loaf pan.

- 1¼ cups (6¼ ounces) seven-grain hot cereal mix (see note)
- 2½ cups boiling water (see note)
- 3 cups (15 ounces) unbleached all-purpose flour, plus extra for the dough and work surface
- 1½ cups (8¼ ounces) whole wheat flour
- ¼ cup honey
- 4 tablespoons (½ stick) unsalted butter, melted and cooled slightly
- 1 envelope (2¼ teaspoons) instant or rapid-rise yeast
- 1 tablespoon table salt
- ¾ cup unsalted pumpkin seeds or sunflower seeds
- ½ cup old-fashioned rolled oats or quick oats

1. Place the cereal mix in the bowl of a stand mixer and pour the boiling water over it; let stand, stirring occasionally, until the mixture cools to 100 degrees and resembles thick porridge, about 1 hour. Whisk the flours together in a medium bowl.

2. Once the grain mixture has cooled, add the honey, melted butter, and yeast and stir to combine. Attach the bowl to a stand mixer fitted with the dough hook. With the mixer running on low speed, add the flours, ½ cup at a time, and knead until the dough forms a ball, 1½ to 2 minutes; cover the bowl with plastic wrap and let the dough rest for 20 minutes. Add the salt and knead on medium-low speed until the dough clears the sides of the bowl, 3 to 4 minutes (if it does not clear the sides, add 2 to 3 tablespoons additional all-purpose flour and continue mixing); continue to knead the dough for 5 more minutes. Add the seeds and knead for another 15 seconds. Transfer the dough to a floured work surface and knead by hand until the seeds are dispersed evenly and the dough forms a smooth, taut ball. Place the dough in a greased container with a 4-quart capacity; cover with plastic wrap and allow to rise until doubled in size, 45 to 60 minutes.

3. Adjust an oven rack to the middle position and heat the oven to 375 degrees. Spray two 8½ by 5½-inch loaf pans with vegetable oil spray. Transfer the dough to a lightly floured work surface and pat into a 12 by 9-inch rectangle; cut the dough in half crosswise with a knife or bench scraper. With a short side facing you, starting at the farthest end, roll one dough piece into a log, keeping the roll taut by tucking it under itself as you go. Seal the loaf by pinching the seam together gently with your thumb and forefinger; repeat with the remaining dough. Spray the loaves lightly with water or vegetable oil spray. Roll each dough log in oats to coat evenly and place, seam side down, in the greased loaf pans, pressing gently into the corners; cover lightly with plastic wrap and let rise until almost doubled in size, 30 to 40 minutes. (The dough should barely spring back when poked with a knuckle.) Bake until the center of the loaves registers 200 degrees on an instant-read thermometer, 35 to 40 minutes. Remove the loaves from the pans and cool on a wire rack before slicing, about 3 hours.

CHAPTER 21

COOKIE JAR FAVORITES

Chewy Sugar Cookies   562

Brown Sugar Cookies   563

Molasses Spice
Cookies   564

Molasses Spice Cookies
with Dark Rum Glaze   565

Classic Chocolate Chip
Cookies   565

Thick and Chewy Chocolate
Chip Cookies   566

Thin and Crispy Chocolate
Chip Cookies   567

Chocolate Cookies   568

Thick and Chewy Double-
Chocolate Cookies   569

Thick and Chewy Triple-
Chocolate Cookies   569

Peanut Butter
Cookies   570

Chocolate-Chunk Oatmeal
Cookies with Pecans and
Dried Cherries   571

Big and Chewy Oatmeal-
Raisin Cookies   572

Big and Chewy Oatmeal-
Date Cookies   572

Thin and Crispy Oatmeal
Cookies   573

Salty Thin and Crispy
Oatmeal Cookies   573

Triple-Coconut
Macaroons   574

Chocolate-Dipped Triple-
Coconut Macaroons   574

Spritz Cookies   575

Spritz Cookies with
Lemon Essence   576

Almond Spritz Cookies   576

Sablés (French
Butter Cookies)   576

Chocolate Sablés   578

Black and White Spiral
Cookies   578

Chocolate Sandwich
Cookies   578

Vanilla Pretzel Cookies   578

Glazed Butter Cookies   578

Jam Sandwiches   579

Lime-Glazed Coconut
Snowballs   580

Chocolate-Cherry
Bar Cookies with
Hazelnuts   580

Best Shortbread   582

Pecan or Walnut Crescent
Cookies   583

Almond or Hazelnut
Crescent Cookies   583

Meringue Cookies   584

Chocolate Meringue
Cookies   584

Toasted Almond Meringue
Cookies   584

Blondies   585

Congo Bars   585

Classic Brownies   585

Chewy Brownies   587

Fudgy Triple-Chocolate
Brownies   588

Triple-Chocolate
Espresso Brownies   588

Fudgy Low-Fat
Brownies   589

Raspberry Squares   590

Key Lime Bars   591

Triple Citrus Bars   591

CHEWY SUGAR COOKIES

WHY THIS RECIPE WORKS: Traditional recipes for sugar cookies require obsessive attention to detail. The butter must be at precisely the right temperature and it must be creamed to the proper degree of airiness. Slight variations in measures can result in cookies that spread or cookies that become brittle and hard upon cooling. We didn't want a cookie that depended on such a finicky process, we wanted an approachable recipe for great sugar cookies that anyone could make anytime. We melted the butter so our sugar cookie dough could easily be mixed together with a spoon—no more fussy creaming. Replacing a portion of the melted butter with vegetable oil ensured a chewy cookie without affecting flavor. And incorporating an unusual addition, cream cheese, into the cookie dough kept our cookies tender, while the slight tang of the cream cheese made for a rich, not-too-sweet cookie.

Chewy Sugar Cookies

MAKES ABOUT 24 COOKIES

The final dough will be slightly softer than most cookie doughs. For best results, handle the dough as briefly and gently as possible when shaping the cookies. Overworking the dough will result in flatter cookies.

- 2¼ cups (11¼ ounces) unbleached all-purpose flour
- 1 teaspoon baking powder
- ½ teaspoon baking soda
- ½ teaspoon table salt
- 1½ cups (10½ ounces) sugar, plus ⅓ cup for rolling
- 2 ounces cream cheese, cut into 8 pieces
- 6 tablespoons (¾ stick) unsalted butter, melted and still warm
- ⅓ cup vegetable oil
- 1 large egg
- 1 tablespoon whole milk
- 2 teaspoons vanilla extract

1. Adjust an oven rack to the middle position and heat the oven to 350 degrees. Line two large rimmed baking sheets with parchment paper. Whisk the flour, baking powder, baking soda, and salt together in a medium bowl. Set aside.

2. Place 1½ cups of the sugar and the cream cheese in a large bowl. Place the remaining ⅓ cup sugar in a shallow baking dish or pie plate and set aside. Pour the warm butter over the sugar and cream cheese and whisk to combine (some small lumps of cream cheese will remain but will smooth out later). Whisk in the oil until incorporated. Add the egg, milk, and vanilla; continue to whisk until smooth. Add the flour mixture and mix with a rubber spatula until a soft homogeneous dough forms.

3. Divide the dough into 24 equal pieces, about 2 tablespoons each. Using your hands, roll each piece of dough into a ball (see note). Working in batches, roll the balls in sugar to coat and set on the prepared baking sheet, 12 dough balls per sheet. Using the bottom of a drinking glass, flatten the dough balls until 2 inches in diameter. Sprinkle the tops of the cookies evenly with the remaining sugar, using 2 teaspoons for each sheet. (Discard the remaining sugar.)

4. Bake the cookies, one sheet at a time, until the edges are set and beginning to brown, 11 to 13 minutes, rotating the sheet after 7 minutes. Cool the cookies on the baking sheet for 5 minutes; using a wide metal spatula, transfer the cookies to a wire rack and cool to room temperature.

BROWN SUGAR COOKIES

WHY THIS RECIPE WORKS: Simple sugar cookies, while classic, can seem too simple—even dull—at times. We wanted to turn up the volume on the sugar cookie by switching out the granulated sugar in favor of brown sugar. We had a clear vision of this cookie. It would be oversized, with a crackling crisp exterior and a chewy interior. And, like Mick Jagger, this cookie would scream "brown sugar."

We wanted butter for optimal flavor, but the traditional creaming method (creaming softened butter with sugar until fluffy, beating in an egg, and then adding the dry ingredients) gave us cakey and tender cookies. Cutting the butter into the flour produced crumbly cookies. What worked was first melting the butter. We then tweaked the amount of eggs, dark brown sugar, flour, and leavener to give us a good cookie, but we wanted even more brown sugar flavor. We made progress by rolling the dough balls in a combination of brown and granulated sugar and adding a healthy amount of vanilla and table salt. But our biggest success came from an unlikely refinement. Browning the melted butter added a complex nuttiness that made a substantial difference.

Brown Sugar Cookies

MAKES ABOUT 24 COOKIES

Avoid using a nonstick skillet to brown the butter. The dark color of the nonstick coating makes it difficult to gauge when the butter is sufficiently browned. Use fresh brown sugar, as hardened brown sugar will make the cookies too dry. Achieving the proper texture—crisp at the edges and chewy in the middle—is critical to this recipe. Because the cookies are so dark, it's hard to judge doneness by color. Instead, gently press halfway between the edge and center of the cookie. When it's done, it will form an indentation with slight resistance. Check early and err on the side of underdone.

- 14 **tablespoons (1¾ sticks) unsalted butter**
- 2 **cups packed (14 ounces) dark brown sugar (see note)**
- ¼ **cup (1¾ ounces) granulated sugar**
- 2 **cups plus 2 tablespoons (about 10⅔ ounces) unbleached all-purpose flour**
- ½ **teaspoon baking soda**
- ¼ **teaspoon baking powder**
- ½ **teaspoon table salt**
- 1 **large whole egg**
- 1 **large egg yolk**
- 1 **tablespoon vanilla extract**

1. Melt 10 tablespoons of the butter in a 10-inch skillet over medium-high heat, about 2 minutes. Continue to cook, swirling the pan constantly until the butter is dark golden brown and has a nutty aroma, 1 to 3 minutes. Transfer the browned butter to a large heatproof bowl. Stir the remaining 4 tablespoons butter into the hot butter to melt; set aside for 15 minutes.

2. Meanwhile, adjust an oven rack to the middle position and heat the oven to 350 degrees. Line two large baking sheets with parchment paper. In a shallow baking dish or pie plate, mix ¼ cup of the brown sugar and the granulated sugar, rubbing the mixture between your fingers until well combined; set aside. Whisk the flour, baking soda, and baking powder together in a medium bowl; set aside.

3. Add the remaining 1¾ cups brown sugar and the salt to the bowl with the cooled butter; mix until no sugar lumps remain, about 30 seconds. Scrape down the bowl with a rubber spatula; add the whole egg, egg yolk, and vanilla and mix until fully incorporated, about 30 seconds. Scrape down the bowl. Add the flour mixture and mix until just combined, about 1 minute. Give the dough a final stir to ensure that no flour pockets remain and the ingredients are evenly distributed.

4. Divide the dough into 24 portions, each about 2 tablespoons, rolling them between your hands into balls about 1½ inches in diameter. Working in batches, drop 12 dough balls into the baking dish with the sugar mixture and toss to coat. Set the dough balls on the prepared baking sheet, spacing them about 2 inches apart; repeat with the second batch of 12.

5. Bake one sheet at a time until the cookies are browned and still puffy and the edges have begun to set but the centers are still soft (the cookies will look raw between the cracks and seem underdone), 12 to 14 minutes, rotating the baking sheet halfway through the baking time. Do not overbake.

6. Cool the cookies on the baking sheet for 5 minutes; using a wide metal spatula, transfer the cookies to a wire rack and cool to room temperature.

MOLASSES SPICE COOKIES

WHY THIS RECIPE WORKS: Molasses spice cookies are often miserable specimens, no more than flat, tasteless cardboard rounds of gingerbread. They can be dry and cakey without the requisite chew; others are timidly flavored with molasses and scantily spiced. We wanted to create the ultimate molasses spice cookie—soft, chewy, and gently spiced with deep, dark molasses flavor. We also wanted it to have the traditional cracks and crinkles so characteristic of these charming cookies.

We started with all-purpose flour and butter for full, rich flavor. Using just the right amount of molasses and brown sugar and flavoring the cookies with a combination of vanilla, ginger, cinnamon, cloves, black pepper, and allspice gave these spiced cookies the warm tingle that we were after. We found that to keep the cookies mild, using a light or mild molasses was imperative; but if it's a stronger flavor you want, dark molasses is in order. We pulled the cookies from the oven when they still looked a bit underdone; residual heat finished the baking and kept the cookies chewy and moist.

Molasses Spice Cookies

MAKES ABOUT 22 COOKIES

For best flavor, make sure that your spices are fresh. Light or mild molasses gives the cookies a milder flavor; for a stronger flavor, use dark molasses. Either way, measure molasses in a liquid measure. If you find that the dough sticks to your palms as you shape the balls, moisten your hands occasionally in a bowl filled with cold tap water and shake off the excess. Bake the cookies one sheet at a time; if baked two sheets at a time, the cookies started on the bottom rack won't develop attractive crackly tops. Remove the cookies from the oven when they still look slightly raw and underbaked.

⅓ cup (2⅓ ounces) granulated sugar, plus ½ cup for coating
2¼ cups (11¼ ounces) unbleached all-purpose flour
1 teaspoon baking soda
1½ teaspoons ground cinnamon
1½ teaspoons ground ginger
½ teaspoon ground cloves
¼ teaspoon ground allspice
¼ teaspoon ground black pepper
¼ teaspoon table salt
12 tablespoons (1½ sticks) unsalted butter, softened
⅓ cup packed (2⅓ ounces) dark brown sugar
1 large egg yolk
1 teaspoon vanilla extract
½ cup light or dark molasses (see note)

1. Adjust an oven rack to the middle position and heat the oven to 375 degrees. Line two large baking sheets with parchment paper. Place ½ cup of the granulated sugar in a shallow baking dish or pie plate; set aside.

2. Whisk the flour, baking soda, spices, and salt together in a medium bowl; set aside.

3. In a stand mixer fitted with the paddle attachment, beat the butter, brown sugar, and remaining ⅓ cup granulated sugar on medium-high speed until light and fluffy, about 3 minutes. Decrease the speed to medium-low and add the egg yolk and vanilla; increase the speed to medium and beat until incorporated, about 20 seconds. Decrease the speed to medium-low and add the molasses; beat until fully incorporated, about 20 seconds, scraping down the bowl once with a rubber spatula. Decrease the speed to low and add the flour mixture; beat until just incorporated, about 30 seconds, scraping down the bowl once. Give the dough a final stir to ensure that no flour pockets remain. The dough will be soft.

4. Divide the dough into 22 portions, each about 1 tablespoon, and roll them between your hands into balls about 1¼ to 1½ inches in diameter. Working in batches, drop five dough balls into the baking dish with the sugar and toss to coat. Set the dough balls on the prepared baking sheets, spacing them about 2 inches apart. Repeat with the remaining dough.

5. Bake one sheet at a time, rotating the baking sheets halfway through the baking time, until the cookies are browned, still puffy, and the edges have begun to set but the centers are still soft (the cookies will look raw between the cracks and seem underdone), about 11 minutes. Do not overbake.

6. Cool the cookies on the baking sheets for 5 minutes; using a wide metal spatula, transfer the cookies to a wire rack and cool to room temperature.

ERIN KNOWS BEST

Erin McMurrer is our test kitchen director. She oversees all the recipe testing and development in the test kitchen, but one of her most important jobs is to keep an eye on new test cooks to make sure they're keeping up with test kitchen standards. And like the proverbial mother with eyes in the back of her head, Erin doesn't miss much. You'll often hear her issuing gentle admonitions to new test cooks throughout the day. Where do the test cooks sometimes fall short? Cutting vegetables into perfect dice? Filleting fish properly? Efficiently frenching racks of lamb? Not even close. They sometimes neglect to thoroughly scrape out the contents of their measuring cups. Other than the waste factor, there is a second important reason Erin wants to make sure all the ingredients make it into the mixing bowl—it can often make or break a recipe.

To prove this point, we baked two batches of molasses spice cookies. In one batch we used a rubber spatula to scrape every last bit of molasses (an especially viscous ingredient) from the measuring cup and in the other, we simply poured the molasses from the cup, which left some residue behind (nearly 2 tablespoons!). The results were remarkable. The cookies made with less molasses were less flavorful and they were also dry and cakey as opposed to the cookies using the full amount of molasses, which were richly flavored, moist, and chewy.

So whether you're a test cook or home cook, heed Erin's advice and take a few extra minutes to scrape out your measuring cups—it makes a difference.

Molasses Spice Cookies with Dark Rum Glaze

If the glaze is too thick to drizzle, whisk in up to an additional ½ tablespoon rum.

Follow the recipe for Molasses Spice Cookies. Whisk 1 cup (4 ounces) confectioners' sugar and 2½ tablespoons dark rum together in a medium bowl until smooth. Drizzle or spread the glaze using the back of a spoon on the cooled cookies. Allow the glazed cookies to dry for at least 15 minutes.

CLASSIC CHOCOLATE CHIP COOKIES

WHY THIS RECIPE WORKS: Rich and buttery, with their soft cores and crispy edges, chocolate chip cookies are the American cookie-jar standard. Since Nestlé first began printing the recipe for Toll House cookies on the back of chocolate chip bags in 1939, generations of bakers have packed them into lunches and taken them to potlucks. But we wondered if this was really the best that a chocolate chip cookie could be. We wanted something more than the standard bake sale offering; we wanted a moist and chewy cookie with crisp edges and deep notes of toffee and butterscotch to balance its sweetness.

Melting the butter before combining it with the other ingredients gave us the chewy texture we wanted, and browning a portion of it added nutty flavor. Upping the brown sugar enhanced chewiness, while a combination of one whole egg and one egg yolk gave us supremely moist cookies. For the crisp edges and deep toffee flavor, we allowed the sugar to dissolve and rest in the melted butter. We baked the cookies until golden brown and just set, but still soft in the center. The resulting cookies were crisp, chewy, and gooey with chocolate and boasted a complex medley of sweet, buttery, caramel, and toffee flavors.

Classic Chocolate Chip Cookies

MAKES ABOUT 16 LARGE COOKIES

Avoid using a nonstick skillet to brown the butter; the dark color of the nonstick coating makes it difficult to gauge when the butter is browned. Use fresh, moist brown sugar instead of hardened brown sugar, which will make the cookies dry. This recipe works with light brown sugar, but the cookies will be less full-flavored. For our winning brand of chocolate chips, see page 740. If you're using smaller baking sheets, put fewer cookies on each sheet and bake them in batches.

1¾ cups (8¾ ounces) unbleached all-purpose flour
½ teaspoon baking soda
14 tablespoons (1¾ sticks) unsalted butter
¾ cup packed (5¼ ounces) dark brown sugar (see note)
½ cup (3½ ounces) granulated sugar
1 teaspoon table salt
2 teaspoons vanilla extract
1 large whole egg
1 large egg yolk
1¼ cups (7½ ounces) semisweet chocolate chips or chunks (see note)
¾ cup chopped pecans or walnuts, toasted (optional)

1. Adjust an oven rack to the middle position and heat the oven to 375 degrees. Line two large baking sheets with parchment paper.

2. Whisk the flour and baking soda together in a medium bowl; set aside.

3. Heat 10 tablespoons of the butter in a 10-inch skillet over medium-high heat until melted, about 2 minutes. Continue cooking, swirling the pan constantly until the butter is dark golden brown and has a nutty aroma, 1 to 3 minutes. Transfer the browned butter to a large heatproof bowl. Add the remaining 4 tablespoons butter and stir until completely melted.

4. Add the sugars, salt, and vanilla to the melted butter; whisk until fully incorporated. Add the whole egg and egg yolk; whisk until the mixture is smooth with no sugar lumps remaining, about 30 seconds. Let the mixture stand for 3 minutes, then whisk for 30 seconds. Repeat the process of resting and whisking two more times until the mixture is thick, smooth, and shiny. Using a rubber spatula, stir in the flour mixture until just combined, about 1 minute. Stir in the chocolate chips and nuts (if using), giving the dough a final stir to ensure that no flour pockets remain.

5. Divide the dough into 16 portions, each about 3 tablespoons. Place the cookies on the prepared baking sheets, spacing them about 2 inches apart.

6. Bake one sheet at a time, rotating the sheet halfway through the baking time, until the cookies are golden brown and still puffy, and the edges have begun to set but the centers are still soft, 10 to 14 minutes. Transfer the baking sheet to a wire rack; cool to room temperature.

THICK AND CHEWY CHOCOLATE CHIP COOKIES

WHY THIS RECIPE WORKS: Nowadays, chocolate chip cookies sold in gourmet shops and cafés always come jumbo-sized (think saucer plate). These cookies are incredibly appealing and satisfying—thick and chewy rounds loaded with as many chocolate chips as they can hold. We wanted our own version that retained the soft and tender texture of these café cookies, even after a day or two (not that they'd be hanging around that long).

One key element in achieving this cookie was melting the butter, which creates a product with a chewy texture. But to keep the cookie from becoming tough, we had to add a little extra fat, which we did in the form of an egg yolk; the added fat acts a tenderizer and prevents the cookies from hardening after several hours. The usual suspects of all-purpose flour, baking soda, an egg, brown sugar, and granulated sugar made an appearance in our cookie recipe, and vanilla provided a light flavor. A good amount of chocolate chips guaranteed that every bite was rich and chocolaty. Finally, we formed the dough into balls, then pulled each ball into two pieces and rejoined them with the uneven surface facing up; now our cookies had the rustic, craggy appearance we wanted.

Thick and Chewy Chocolate Chip Cookies
MAKES ABOUT 18 LARGE COOKIES
To ensure the proper texture, cool the cookies on the baking sheets. See page 711 for our top-rated baking sheet.

- 2 cups plus 2 tablespoons (about 10⅔ ounces) unbleached all-purpose flour
- ½ teaspoon baking soda
- ½ teaspoon table salt
- 12 tablespoons (1½ sticks) unsalted butter, melted and cooled
- 1 cup packed (7 ounces) light or dark brown sugar
- ½ cup (3½ ounces) granulated sugar
- 1 large whole egg
- 1 large egg yolk
- 2 teaspoons vanilla extract
- 1½ cups (9 ounces) semisweet chocolate chips

1. Adjust the oven racks to the upper-middle and lower-middle positions and heat the oven to 325 degrees. Line two large baking sheets with parchment paper.

2. Whisk the flour, baking soda, and salt together in a medium bowl; set aside.

3. In a stand mixer fitted with the paddle attachment, beat the butter and sugars at medium speed until smooth, about 1 minute. Add the whole egg, egg yolk, and vanilla and beat on medium-low speed until fully incorporated, about 30 seconds, scraping down the bowl and beater as needed with a rubber spatula. Add the dry ingredients and mix on low speed until combined, about 30 seconds. Mix in the chocolate chips until just incorporated.

4. Divide the dough into 18 portions, each about ¼ cup, and roll them between your hands into balls. Holding one dough ball with your fingers, pull the dough apart into two equal halves. Rotate the halves 90 degrees and, with the jagged surfaces facing up, join the halves together at their base, again forming a single ball, being careful not to smooth the dough's uneven surface. Place the cookies on the prepared baking sheets, spacing them about 2½ inches apart.

5. Bake until the cookies are light golden brown and the edges start to harden but the centers are still soft and puffy, 15 to 18 minutes, switching and rotating the baking sheets halfway through the baking time. Cool the cookies on the baking sheets.

THIN, CRISPY CHOCOLATE CHIP COOKIES

WHY THIS RECIPE WORKS: Too often, thin and crispy chocolate chip cookies are brittle and crumbly or tough and lacking flavor. We wanted cookies that were thin, almost like praline cookies, and packed a big crunch without breaking teeth or shattering into a million pieces when eaten. And they had to have the simple, gratifying flavors of deeply caramelized sugar and rich butter.

For cookies with a notable butterscotch flavor and sufficient crunch, we turned to a combination of light brown sugar and white sugar. Next we focused on the thickness of our cookies. When butter is creamed with sugar, air cells are created in the batter; these cells expand during baking, leading to cookies that rise—and cookies with height were not what we wanted. So we used melted butter and milk to create a batter that would spread (not rise) in the oven, resulting in cookies with

the perfect thin crispiness. A bit of baking soda and corn syrup promoted maximum browning and caramelization, and vanilla and salt gave our cookies the best flavor.

Thin and Crispy Chocolate Chip Cookies
MAKES ABOUT 40 COOKIES

The dough, en masse or shaped into balls and wrapped well, can be refrigerated for up to 2 days or frozen for up to 1 month; bring it to room temperature before baking.

1½ cups (7½ ounces) unbleached all-purpose flour
¾ teaspoon baking soda
¼ teaspoon table salt
8 tablespoons (1 stick) unsalted butter, melted and cooled
½ cup (3½ ounces) granulated sugar
⅓ cup packed (2⅓ ounces) light brown sugar
2 tablespoons light corn syrup
1 large egg yolk
2 tablespoons milk
1 tablespoon vanilla extract
¾ cup (4½ ounces) semisweet chocolate chips

1. Adjust an oven rack to the middle position and heat the oven to 375 degrees. Line two large baking sheets with parchment paper.

2. Whisk the flour, baking soda, and salt together in a medium bowl; set aside.

3. In a stand mixer fitted with the paddle attachment, beat the melted butter, granulated sugar, brown sugar, and corn syrup at low speed until thoroughly blended, about 1 minute. Add the egg yolk, milk, and vanilla; mix until fully incorporated and smooth, about 1 minute, scraping down the bowl and beater as needed. With the mixer still running on low, slowly add the dry ingredients and mix until just combined. Do not overbeat. Add the chocolate chips and mix until evenly distributed throughout the batter, about 5 seconds.

4. Divide the dough into 40 portions, each about 1 tablespoon, and roll them between your hands into balls. Place the cookies on the prepared baking sheets, spacing them about 2 inches apart. Bake, one sheet at a time, until the cookies are deep golden brown and flat, about 12 minutes, switching and rotating the baking sheets halfway through the baking time.

5. Cool the cookies on the baking sheet for 3 minutes. Using a wide metal spatula, transfer the cookies to a wire rack and cool to room temperature.

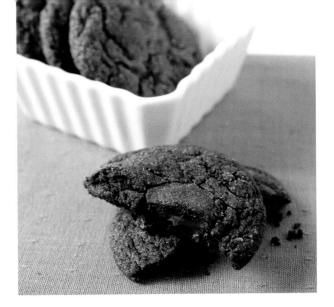

CHOCOLATE COOKIES

WHY THIS RECIPE WORKS: Cookie recipes that trumpet their extreme chocolate flavor always leave us a bit suspicious. While they provide plenty of intensity, these over-the-top confections also tend to be delicate and crumbly, more like cakey brownies than cookies. We set out to make an exceptionally rich chocolate cookie that we could sink our teeth into—without having it fall apart.

Our first batch, with modest amounts of cocoa powder and melted chocolate, baked up too cakey and tender—just what we didn't want. The chocolate was the culprit; its fat was softening the dough. Cutting out the chocolate made the cookies less cakey and tender, and more like cookies. To restore chocolate flavor without adding too much fat, we increased the cocoa powder and reduced the flour. Using an egg white rather than a whole egg gave us the structure we wanted, and adding dark corn syrup gave the cookies a nice chewiness and lent a hint of caramel flavor. For more richness, we folded in chopped bittersweet chocolate; the chunks stayed intact and added intense chocolate flavor. A dip in granulated sugar before baking gave the cookies a sweet crunch and an attractive crackled appearance once they were out of the oven.

Chocolate Cookies
MAKES ABOUT 16 COOKIES

We recommend using one of the test kitchen's favorite baking chocolates, Callebaut Intense Dark Chocolate or Ghirardelli Bittersweet Chocolate, but any high-quality dark, bittersweet, or semisweet chocolate will work. Light brown sugar can be substituted for the dark, as can light corn syrup for the dark, but with some sacrifice in flavor.

- ⅓ cup (2⅓ ounces) granulated sugar, plus ½ cup for coating
- 1½ cups (7½ ounces) unbleached all-purpose flour
- ¾ cup Dutch-processed cocoa powder
- ½ teaspoon baking soda
- ¼ teaspoon plus ⅛ teaspoon table salt
- ½ cup dark corn syrup (see note)
- 1 large egg white
- 1 teaspoon vanilla extract
- 12 tablespoons (1½ sticks) unsalted butter, softened
- ⅓ cup packed (2⅓ ounces) dark brown sugar (see note)
- 4 ounces bittersweet chocolate, chopped into ½-inch pieces (see note)

1. Adjust the oven racks to the upper-middle and lower-middle positions and heat the oven to 375 degrees. Line two large baking sheets with parchment paper. Place ½ cup of the granulated sugar in a shallow baking dish or pie plate. Whisk the flour, cocoa powder, baking soda, and salt together in a medium bowl. Whisk the corn syrup, egg white, and vanilla together in a small bowl.

2. In a stand mixer fitted with the paddle attachment, beat the butter, brown sugar, and remaining ⅓ cup granulated sugar at medium-high speed until light and fluffy, about 2 minutes. Decrease the speed to medium-low, add the corn syrup mixture, and beat until fully incorporated, about 20 seconds, scraping down the bowl and beater as needed with a rubber spatula. Decrease the speed to low, add the flour mixture and chopped chocolate, and mix until just incorporated, about 30 seconds, scraping down the bowl and beater as needed. Give the dough a final stir to ensure that no pockets of flour remain. Chill the dough for 30 minutes to firm slightly (do not chill longer than 30 minutes).

3. Divide the dough into 16 equal portions, each a generous 2 tablespoons, and roll them between your hands into balls about 1½ inches in diameter. Working in batches, drop eight dough balls into the baking dish with the sugar and toss to coat. Place the dough balls on the prepared baking sheet, spacing them about 2 inches apart; repeat with the second batch of eight. Bake, switching and rotating the sheets halfway through the baking time, until the cookies are puffed and cracked and the edges have begun to set but the centers are still soft (the cookies will look raw between the cracks and seem underdone), 10 to 11 minutes. Do not overbake.

4. Cool the cookies on the baking sheets for 5 minutes; using a wide metal spatula, transfer the cookies to a wire rack and cool to room temperature.

DOUBLE-CHOCOLATE COOKIES

WHY THIS RECIPE WORKS: Our goal in creating a traditional double-chocolate cookie recipe seemed more like a fantasy: The first bite of the cookie would reveal a center of hot fudge sauce, the texture would call to mind chocolate bread pudding, and the overall flavor would be of deep and complex chocolate. Was it possible?

In the end, the fulfillment of our fantasy relied on very basic ingredients: chocolate, sugar, eggs, butter, flour, baking powder, and salt. We used a modified creaming method with minimal beating to produce moist cookies that weren't cakey, and we let the batter rest for a half-hour to develop a certain fudginess. Ingredient proportions were all-important—for moist, rich cookies, we used more chocolate than flour. The more highly processed semisweet chocolate tasted smoother and richer than unsweetened, and Dutch-processed cocoa and instant coffee further enriched the chocolate flavor. At last, we had a cookie that was both rich and soft, with an intense chocolaty center.

Thick and Chewy Double-Chocolate Cookies

MAKES ABOUT 42 COOKIES

To melt the chocolate using a microwave, heat it at 50 percent power for 2 minutes; stir the chocolate and continue heating until melted, stirring once every additional minute. Resist the urge to bake the cookies longer than indicated; they may appear underbaked at first but will firm up as they cool.

- 2 cups (10 ounces) unbleached all-purpose flour
- ½ cup Dutch-processed cocoa powder
- 2 teaspoons baking powder
- ½ teaspoon table salt
- 16 ounces semisweet chocolate, chopped
- 4 large eggs
- 2 teaspoons vanilla extract
- 2 teaspoons instant coffee or espresso powder
- 10 tablespoons (1¼ sticks) unsalted butter, softened
- 1½ cups packed (10½ ounces) light brown sugar
- ½ cup (3½ ounces) granulated sugar

1. Whisk the flour, cocoa powder, baking powder, and salt together in a medium bowl; set aside.

2. Melt the chocolate in a medium heatproof bowl set over a saucepan of barely simmering water, stirring occasionally, until smooth; set aside to cool slightly. Whisk the eggs and vanilla together in a medium bowl, sprinkle the coffee powder over the top to dissolve, and set aside.

3. In a stand mixer fitted with the paddle attachment, beat the butter and sugars at medium speed until combined, about 45 seconds; the mixture will look granular. Decrease the speed to low, gradually add the egg mixture, and mix until incorporated, about 45 seconds. Add the melted chocolate in a steady stream and mix until combined, about 40 seconds, scraping down the bowl and beater as needed with a rubber spatula. With the mixer still running on low, add the dry ingredients and mix until just combined. Do not overbeat. Cover the bowl of dough with plastic wrap and let stand at room temperature until the consistency is scoopable and fudge-like, about 30 minutes.

4. Meanwhile, adjust the oven racks to the upper-middle and lower-middle positions and heat the oven to 350 degrees. Line two baking sheets with parchment paper. Divide the dough into 42 equal portions, each about 2 tablespoons, and roll them between your hands into balls about 1¾ inches in diameter. Set the dough balls on the prepared baking sheets, spacing them about 1½ inches apart.

5. Bake two sheets at a time, switching and rotating the baking sheets halfway through the baking time, until the edges have just begun to set but the centers are still very soft, about 10 minutes. Cool the cookies on the baking sheets for 10 minutes; using a wide metal spatula, transfer the cookies to a wire rack and cool to room temperature.

Thick and Chewy Triple-Chocolate Cookies

The addition of chocolate chips will slightly increase the yield of the cookies.

Follow the recipe for Thick and Chewy Double-Chocolate Cookies, adding 2 cups (12 ounces) semisweet chocolate chips to the batter after the dry ingredients are incorporated in step 3.

PEANUT BUTTER COOKIES

WHY THIS RECIPE WORKS: Recipes for peanut butter cookies tend to fall into one of two categories: sweet and chewy with a mild peanut flavor, and sandy and crumbly with a strong peanut flavor. What we wanted, of course, was the best of both worlds—that is, cookies that were crisp on the edges and chewy in the center, with lots of peanut flavor.

First off, we had to determine the amount and type of sugar. Granulated sugar was necessary for crisp edges and chewy centers, while dark brown sugar enriched the peanut flavor. As for flour, too little resulted in an oily cookie,

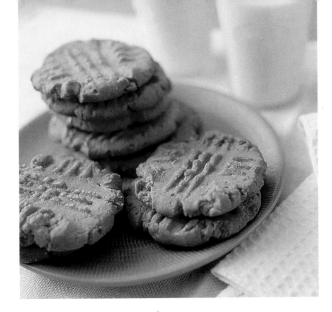

whereas too much made for dry cookies. Baking soda contributed to browning and amplified the peanut flavor and baking powder provided lift, making both leaveners necessary. Extra-crunchy peanut butter also helped the cookie rise and achieve a crisper edge and a softer center. But the best way to get the true peanut flavor we sought was to use peanuts and salt. Adding some roasted, salted peanuts, ground in a food processor, and then adding still more salt (directly to the batter as well in the form of salted rather than unsalted butter) produced a strong roasted nut flavor without sacrificing anything in terms of texture.

Peanut Butter Cookies

MAKES ABOUT 36 COOKIES

These cookies have a strong peanut flavor that comes from extra-crunchy peanut butter as well as from roasted salted peanuts that are ground in a food processor and worked into the dough. In our testing, we found that salted butter brings out the flavor of the nuts. If using unsalted butter, increase the salt to 1 teaspoon.

2½   cups (12½ ounces) unbleached all-purpose flour
½   teaspoon baking soda
½   teaspoon baking powder
½   teaspoon table salt
16   tablespoons (2 sticks) salted butter, softened (see note)
1   cup packed (7 ounces) dark brown sugar
1   cup (7 ounces) granulated sugar
1   cup extra-crunchy peanut butter, at room temperature
2   large eggs
2   teaspoons vanilla extract
1   cup (5 ounces) roasted salted peanuts, ground in a food processor to resemble bread crumbs, about 14 pulses

1. Adjust the oven racks to the upper-middle and lower-middle positions and heat oven to 350 degrees. Line two large baking sheets with parchment paper.

2. Whisk the flour, baking soda, baking powder, and salt together in a medium bowl; set aside.

3. In a stand mixer fitted with the paddle attachment, beat the butter and sugars at medium speed until light and fluffy, about 2 minutes, scraping down the bowl and beater as needed with a rubber spatula. Add the peanut butter and mix until fully incorporated, about 30 seconds; add the eggs, one at a time, and the vanilla and mix until combined, about 30 seconds. Decrease the speed to low and add the dry ingredients; mix until combined, about 30 seconds. Mix in the ground peanuts until just incorporated.

4. Divide the dough into 36 portions, each a generous 2 tablespoons, and roll them between your hands into balls about 2 inches in diameter. Place the dough balls on the prepared baking sheets, spacing them about 2½ inches apart. Press each dough ball twice, at perpendicular angles, with a dinner fork dipped in cold water to make a criss-cross design.

5. Bake, switching and rotating the sheets halfway through the baking time, until the cookies are puffy and slightly brown around the edges but not on top, 10 to 12 minutes; the cookies will not look fully baked. Cool the cookies on the baking sheets for 5 minutes; using a wide metal spatula, transfer the cookies to a wire rack and cool to room temperature.

ULTIMATE OATMEAL COOKIES

WHY THIS RECIPE WORKS: Oatmeal cookies can be great vehicles for additional flavors, but it's easy to get carried away and overload the dough with a crazy jumble of ingredients resulting in a poorly textured cookie monster. Our ultimate oatmeal cookie would have just the right amount of added ingredients and an ideal texture—crisp around the edges and chewy in the middle.

We wanted to add four flavor components—sweet, tangy, nutty, and chocolaty—to the underlying oat flavor. Bittersweet chocolate, dried sour cherries (or cranberries), and toasted pecans gave the right balance of flavors. We also analyzed the cookie dough ingredients and discovered that cookies made with brown sugar were moister and chewier than cookies made with granulated sugar. A combination of baking powder and baking soda (we doubled the usual amount) produced cookies that were light and crisp on the outside, but chewy, dense, and soft in the center. Finally, we focused on appearance to decide when to remove the cookies from the oven—they should be set but still look wet between the fissures; if they look matte rather than shiny, they've been overbaked.

Chocolate-Chunk Oatmeal Cookies with Pecans and Dried Cherries

MAKES ABOUT 16 LARGE COOKIES

We like these cookies made with pecans and dried sour cherries, but walnuts or skinned hazelnuts can be substituted for the pecans, and dried cranberries for the cherries. Quick oats used in place of the old-fashioned oats will yield a cookie with slightly less chewiness. These cookies keep for 4 to 5 days stored in an airtight container or zipper-lock bag, but they will lose their crisp exterior and become uniformly chewy after a day or so. To recrisp the cookies, place them on a baking sheet and in a 425-degree oven for 4 to 5 minutes. Make sure to let the cookies cool on the baking sheet for a few minutes before removing them, and eat them while they're warm.

- 1¼ cups (6¼ ounces) unbleached all-purpose flour
- ¾ teaspoon baking powder
- ½ teaspoon baking soda
- ½ teaspoon table salt
- 1¼ cups (3¾ ounces) old-fashioned oats (see note)
- 1 cup (4 ounces) pecans, toasted and chopped (see note)
- 1 cup dried sour cherries, chopped coarse (see note)
- 4 ounces bittersweet chocolate, chopped into chunks about the size of chocolate chips (about ¾ cup)
- 12 tablespoons (1½ sticks) unsalted butter, softened
- 1½ cups packed (10½ ounces) brown sugar, preferably dark
- 1 large egg
- 1 teaspoon vanilla extract

1. Adjust the oven racks to the upper-middle and lower-middle positions and heat the oven to 350 degrees. Line two large baking sheets with parchment paper.

2. Whisk the flour, baking powder, baking soda, and salt together in a medium bowl. In a second medium bowl, stir together the oats, pecans, cherries, and chocolate.

3. In a stand mixer fitted with the paddle attachment, beat the butter and sugar at medium speed until no sugar lumps remain, about 1 minute, scraping down the bowl and beater as needed with a rubber spatula. Add the egg and vanilla and beat on medium-low until fully incorporated, about 30 seconds, scraping down the bowl and beater as needed. Decrease the speed to low, add the flour mixture, and mix until just combined, about 30 seconds. With the mixer still running on low, gradually add the oat–nut mixture; mix until just incorporated. Give the dough a final stir to ensure that no flour pockets remain and the ingredients are evenly distributed.

4. Divide the dough into 16 portions, each about ¼ cup, and roll them between your hands into balls; stagger eight balls on each prepared baking sheet, spacing them about 2½ inches apart. Using your fingertips, gently press each dough ball to a 1-inch thickness. Bake the cookies for 20 to 22 minutes, switching and rotating the baking sheets halfway through the baking time, until the cookies are medium brown and the edges have begun to set but the centers are still soft (the cookies will seem underdone and will appear raw, wet, and shiny in the cracks).

5. Cool the cookies on the baking sheets for 5 minutes; using a wide metal spatula, transfer the cookies to a wire rack and cool to room temperature.

BIG AND CHEWY OATMEAL-RAISIN COOKIES

WHY THIS RECIPE WORKS: Big, moist, and craggy, oatmeal cookies are so good and so comforting, but also so hard to get just right. Too often, they have textural issues and are dry and brittle; other times, it's the flavor that's off, with cookies that lack any sign of oatiness. We wanted an oversize cookie with buttery oat flavor and the utmost chewiness.

After numerous rounds of testing, we discovered three key changes that made a significant difference in the research recipes we uncovered. First, we substituted baking powder for baking soda. The baking powder gave the dough more lift, which in turn made the cookies less dense and a bit chewier. Second, we eliminated the cinnamon recommended in lots of recipes; by taking away the cinnamon, we revealed more oat flavor. We wanted some spice, however, and chose nutmeg, which has a cleaner, subtler flavor that we like with oats. Finally, we increased the sugar in our cookies, and this made a huge difference in terms of texture and moistness.

Big and Chewy Oatmeal-Raisin Cookies

MAKES ABOUT 18 LARGE COOKIES

If you prefer a less sweet cookie, you can reduce the granulated sugar to ¾ cup, but you will lose some crispness. Do not overbake these cookies. The edges should be brown, but the rest of the cookie should be very light in color.

- 1½ cups (7½ ounces) unbleached all-purpose flour
- ½ teaspoon table salt
- ½ teaspoon baking powder
- ¼ teaspoon freshly grated nutmeg
- 16 tablespoons (2 sticks) unsalted butter, softened
- 1 cup packed (7 ounces) light brown sugar
- 1 cup (7 ounces) granulated sugar (see note)
- 2 large eggs
- 3 cups (9 ounces) old-fashioned oats
- 1½ cups raisins (optional)

1. Adjust the oven racks to the upper-middle and lower-middle positions and heat the oven to 350 degrees. Line two large baking sheets with parchment paper. Whisk the flour, salt, baking powder, and nutmeg together in a medium bowl; set aside.

2. In a stand mixer fitted with the paddle attachment, beat the butter and sugars at medium speed until light and fluffy, about 2 minutes. Add the eggs, one at a time, and mix until combined, about 30 seconds.

3. Decrease the speed to low and slowly add the dry ingredients until combined, about 30 seconds. Mix in the oats and raisins (if using) until just incorporated.

4. Divide the dough into 18 portions, each a generous 2 tablespoons, and roll them between your hands into balls about 2 inches in diameter. Place the dough balls on the prepared baking sheets, spacing them about 2 inches apart.

5. Bake, switching and rotating the sheets halfway through the baking time, until the cookies turn golden brown around the edges, 22 to 25 minutes. Cool the cookies on the baking sheets for 2 minutes; using a wide metal spatula, transfer the cookies to a wire rack and cool to room temperature.

Big and Chewy Oatmeal-Date Cookies

Follow the recipe for Big and Chewy Oatmeal-Raisin Cookies, substituting 1½ cups chopped dates for the raisins.

THIN AND CRISPY OATMEAL COOKIES

WHY THIS RECIPE WORKS: Thin and crispy oatmeal cookies can be irresistible—crunchy and delicate, these cookies really let the flavor of the oats take center stage. But the usual ingredients that give thick, chewy oatmeal cookies great texture—generous amounts of sugar and butter, a high ratio of oats to flour, raisins, and nuts—won't all fit in a thin, crispy cookie. We wanted to adjust the standard ingredients to create a crispy, delicate cookie in which the simple flavor of buttery oats really stands out.

Given this cookie's simplicity, creating a rich butter flavor was critical, so we kept almost the same amount of butter as in our standard big, chewy oatmeal cookie, but we scaled back the amount of sugar. Fine-tuning the amount and type of leavener led to a surprising result that solved our texture and shape problems. During baking, large carbon dioxide bubbles created by the baking soda and baking powder (upped from our traditional recipe) caused the cookies to puff up, collapse, and spread out, producing the thin, flat cookies we were looking for. Baking the cookies all the way through until they were fully set and evenly browned from center to edge made them crisp throughout but not tough.

Thin and Crispy Oatmeal Cookies

MAKES ABOUT 24 COOKIES

To ensure that the cookies bake evenly and are crisp throughout, bake them one sheet at a time. Place them on the baking sheet in three rows, with three cookies in the outer rows and two cookies in the center row. If you reuse a baking sheet, allow the cookies on it to cool for at least 15 minutes before transferring them to a wire rack, then reline the sheet with fresh parchment before baking more cookies. We developed this recipe using Quaker Old Fashioned Oats. Other brands of old-fashioned oats can be substituted but may cause the cookies to spread more. Do not use instant or quick oats.

- 1 **cup (5 ounces) unbleached all-purpose flour**
- ¾ **teaspoon baking powder**
- ½ **teaspoon baking soda**
- ½ **teaspoon table salt**
- 14 **tablespoons (1¾ sticks) unsalted butter, softened but still cool**
- 1 **cup (7 ounces) granulated sugar**
- ¼ **cup packed (1¾ ounces) light brown sugar**
- 1 **large egg**
- 1 **teaspoon vanilla extract**
- 2½ **cups (7½ ounces) old-fashioned oats (see note)**

1. Adjust an oven rack to the middle position and heat the oven to 350 degrees. Line three large baking sheets with parchment paper. Whisk the flour, baking powder, baking soda, and salt in a medium bowl; set aside.

2. In a stand mixer fitted with the paddle attachment, beat the butter and sugars at medium-low speed until just combined, about 20 seconds. Increase the speed to medium and continue to beat until light and fluffy, about 1 minute longer, scraping down the bowl and beater as needed with a rubber spatula. Add the egg and vanilla and beat on medium-low until fully incorporated, about

30 seconds, scraping down the bowl and beater as needed. Decrease the speed to low, add the flour mixture, and mix until just incorporated and smooth, about 10 seconds. With the mixer still running on low, gradually add the oats and mix until well incorporated, about 20 seconds. Give the dough a final stir to ensure that no flour pockets remain and the ingredients are evenly distributed.

3. Divide the dough into 24 portions, each about 2 tablespoons, and roll them between your hands into balls. Place the cookies on the prepared baking sheets, spacing them about 2½ inches apart, eight dough balls per sheet (see note). Using your fingertips, gently press each dough ball to a ¾-inch thickness.

4. Bake one sheet at a time until the cookies are deep golden brown, the edges are crisp, and the centers yield to slight pressure when pressed, 13 to 16 minutes, rotating the sheet halfway through the baking time. Cool the cookies completely on the sheet.

Salty Thin and Crispy Oatmeal Cookies

We prefer the texture and flavor of a coarse-grained sea salt, like Maldon or fleur de sel, but kosher salt can be used. If using kosher salt, reduce the amount sprinkled over the cookies to ¼ teaspoon.

Follow the recipe for Thin and Crispy Oatmeal Cookies, reducing the amount of salt in the dough to ¼ teaspoon. Lightly sprinkle ½ teaspoon coarse sea salt evenly over the flattened dough balls before baking.

COCONUT MACAROONS

WHY THIS RECIPE WORKS: Not that long ago, macaroons (cone-shaped cookies flavored with shredded coconut) were quite elegant and very popular. But today, they have deteriorated into lackluster mounds of beaten egg whites and coconut shreds or, at their worst, nothing more than a baked mixture of condensed milk and sweetened coconut. We set out to create a great coconut macaroon, with a pleasing texture and real, honest coconut flavor.

When we began looking at recipes for modern coconut macaroons, we found that they varied widely, some calling for vanilla or almond extract in addition to different kinds of coconut and sweeteners. We knew that narrowing the field when it came to the coconut and other flavorings would make a big difference in both taste and texture. After rounds of testing, we determined that unsweetened shredded coconut resulted in a less sticky, more appealing texture. But sweetened shredded coconut packed more flavor than the unsweetened coconut, so we decided to use both; together they worked very well in the cookie. To add one more layer of coconut flavor, we tried cream of coconut and hit the jackpot. As for the structure of our cookie, a few egg whites and some corn syrup ensured that the macaroons held together well and were moist and pleasantly chewy.

Triple-Coconut Macaroons

MAKES ABOUT 48 COOKIES

Cream of coconut, available canned, is a very sweet product commonly used in piña colada cocktails. Be sure to mix the can's contents thoroughly before using, as the mixture separates upon standing. Unsweetened desiccated coconut is commonly sold in natural foods stores and Asian markets. If you are unable to find any, use all sweetened flaked or shredded coconut, but reduce the amount of cream of coconut to ½ cup, omit the corn syrup, and toss 2 tablespoons cake flour with the coconut before adding the liquid ingredients. For larger macaroons, shape haystacks from a generous ¼ cup of batter and increase the baking time to 20 minutes.

    1   cup cream of coconut (see note)
    2   tablespoons light corn syrup
    4   large egg whites
    2   teaspoons vanilla extract
    ½   teaspoon table salt
    3   cups unsweetened, shredded, desiccated (dried)
        coconut (see note)
    3   cups sweetened flaked or shredded coconut

1. Adjust the oven racks to the upper-middle and lower-middle positions and heat the oven to 375 degrees. Line two baking sheets with parchment paper and lightly spray the parchment with vegetable oil spray.

2. Whisk the cream of coconut, corn syrup, egg whites, vanilla, and salt together in a small bowl; set aside. Combine the unsweetened and sweetened coconuts in a large bowl; toss together, breaking up clumps with your fingertips. Pour the liquid ingredients over the coconut and mix with a rubber spatula until evenly moistened. Chill for 15 minutes.

3. Drop heaping tablespoons of batter onto the prepared baking sheets, spacing them about 1 inch apart. Using moistened fingertips, form the cookies into loose haystacks.

Bake until light golden brown, about 15 minutes, switching and rotating the sheets halfway through the baking time.

4. Cool the cookies on the baking sheets until slightly set, about 2 minutes; using a wide metal spatula, transfer the cookies to a wire rack and cool to room temperature.

Chocolate-Dipped Triple-Coconut Macaroons

Using the two-stage melting process for the chocolate helps ensure that it will be at the proper consistency for dipping the cookies. To melt the 8 ounces of chocolate in a microwave, heat it at 50 percent power for 2 minutes; stir the chocolate and continue heating until melted, stirring once every additional minute.

Follow the recipe for Triple-Coconut Macaroons. Cool the baked macaroons to room temperature; line two large baking sheets with parchment paper. Chop 10 ounces semisweet chocolate; melt 8 ounces of the chocolate in a small heatproof bowl set over a saucepan of barely simmering water, stirring occasionally, until smooth. Off the heat, stir in the remaining 2 ounces of chocolate until smooth. Holding a macaroon by its pointed top, dip the bottom ½ inch up the sides in the chocolate, scrape off the excess, and place the macaroon on the prepared baking sheet. Repeat with the remaining macaroons. Refrigerate until the chocolate sets, about 15 minutes.

We had the best results baking these cookies one sheet at a time. When reusing a baking sheet, make sure that it has completely cooled before forming more cookies on it. Unbaked dough can be refrigerated in an airtight container for up to 4 days; to use, let it stand at room temperature until softened, about 45 minutes. Baked cookies will keep for more than a week if stored in an airtight container or zipper-lock bag.

- 1 **large egg yolk**
- 1 **tablespoon heavy cream**
- 1 **teaspoon vanilla extract**
- 16 **tablespoons (2 sticks) unsalted butter, softened but still cool**
- ⅔ **cup (4⅔ ounces) granulated sugar**
- ¼ **teaspoon table salt**
- 2 **cups (10 ounces) unbleached all-purpose flour**

1. Adjust an oven rack to the middle position and heat the oven to 375 degrees. Line two large baking sheets with parchment paper. Whisk the egg yolk, cream, and vanilla in a small bowl until combined; set aside.

2. In a stand mixer fitted with the paddle attachment, beat the butter, sugar, and salt at medium-high speed until light and fluffy, about 3 minutes, scraping down the bowl and beater as needed with a rubber spatula. With the mixer running at medium speed, add the yolk-cream mixture and beat until incorporated, about 30 seconds. With the mixer running at low speed, gradually beat in the flour until combined, scraping down the bowl and beater as needed. Give the dough a final stir to ensure that no flour pockets remain.

3. If using a cookie press to form the cookies, follow the manufacturer's instructions to fill the press. If using a pastry bag (see note), fit it with a star tip and fill the bag with half of the dough. Press or pipe cookies onto the prepared baking sheet, spacing them about 1½ inches apart, refilling

HOLIDAY SPRITZ COOKIES

WHY THIS RECIPE WORKS: Spritz cookies, those golden-swirled holiday cookies, often end up bland, gummy, and tasteless. How come they never taste as good as they look? Unfortunately, this Scandinavian treat has fallen victim to many recipe modifications, such as the use of vegetable shortening instead of butter, an overload of eggs, and an excess of starchy confectioners' sugar. We set out to spruce up spritz cookies and make them light, crisp, buttery treats—the life of any holiday party.

The success of these confections rests primarily in the management of a finicky ingredient list. Carefully balancing the butter, sugar, flour, egg (yolk only), heavy cream (just a drop), vanilla, and salt is the only recipe for success—a few simple ingredients gathered in the proper proportions. Creaming the butter and sugar in the traditional fashion worked well and produced a dough light enough to easily press or pipe the cookies. As for shaping, either a cookie press or a pastry bag can be used—it's up to you.

Spritz Cookies

MAKES ABOUT 72 SMALL COOKIES

If using a pastry bag, use a star tip to create the various shapes. For stars, a ½ to ⅝-inch tip (measure the diameter of the tip at the smallest point) works best, but for rosettes and S shapes, use a ⅜-inch tip. To create stars, see the photo; stars should be about 1 inch in diameter. To create rosettes, pipe the dough while moving the bag in a circular motion, ending at the center of the rosette; rosettes should be about 1¼ inches in diameter. To create S shapes, pipe the dough into compact S's; they should be about 2 inches long and 1 inch wide. If you make an error while piping, the dough can be scraped off the baking sheet and re-piped.

NOTES FROM THE TEST KITCHEN

PIPING SPRITZ COOKIES

Using a ½-inch star tip, hold the bag at a 90-degree angle to the baking sheet and pipe the dough straight down, about 1 inch in diameter. If you make an error while piping, the dough can be scraped off the baking sheet and re-piped.

the cookie press or pastry bag as needed. Bake one sheet at a time, until the cookies are light golden brown, 10 to 12 minutes, rotating the baking sheet halfway through the baking time. Cool the cookies on the baking sheet for 10 to 15 minutes; using a metal spatula, transfer them to a wire rack and cool to room temperature.

Spritz Cookies with Lemon Essence

Follow the recipe for Spritz Cookies, adding 1 teaspoon juice from 1 lemon to the yolk-cream mixture in step 1 and adding 1 teaspoon finely grated zest from 1 lemon to the butter along with the sugar and salt in step 2.

Almond Spritz Cookies

Grind ½ cup sliced almonds and 2 tablespoons of the flour in a food processor until powdery and evenly fine, about 12 pulses; combine the almond mixture with the remaining flour. Follow the recipe for Spritz Cookies, substituting ¾ teaspoon almond extract for the vanilla.

SABLÉ COOKIES

WHY THIS RECIPE WORKS: During the holidays, these French butter cookies offer sophistication and style. That is, if you can capture their elusive sandy texture (*sablé* is French for sandy), which separates them from sturdy American butter cookies. Most of the sablé recipes we came across had only slight differences in ingredient proportions—but they all baked up without the delicate crumbliness that defines this cookie. To create the hallmark sandy texture of sablés—light, with an inviting granular quality similar to shortbread—we would have to do some detective work.

We started with a basic recipe using the typical method of creaming butter and sugar, then adding egg and flour. We then chilled, sliced, and baked the dough—but these cookies were missing the delicate crumbliness that defines sablés. We needed to decrease the liquid in the dough so there would be less moisture to dissolve the sugar particles. Cutting back on butter helped, as did the inclusion of a hard-cooked egg yolk, an addition we came across in our research. Adding the mashed yolk during creaming eliminated moisture and perfected the texture of the cookies. Brushing the cookies with a beaten egg white and sprinkling them with coarse sugar before baking added a delicate crunch and an attractive sparkle.

Sablés (French Butter Cookies)
MAKES ABOUT 40 COOKIES

Turbinado sugar is commonly sold as Sugar in the Raw. Demerara sugar, sanding sugar, or another coarse sugar can be substituted. Make sure the cookie dough is well chilled and firm so that it can be uniformly sliced. After the dough has been wrapped in parchment, it can be double-wrapped in plastic wrap and frozen for up to 2 weeks.

- 1 large egg
- 10 tablespoons (1¼ sticks) unsalted butter, softened
- ⅓ cup plus 1 tablespoon (2¾ ounces) granulated sugar
- ¼ teaspoon table salt
- 1 teaspoon vanilla extract
- 1½ cups (7½ ounces) unbleached all-purpose flour
- 1 large egg white, lightly beaten with 1 teaspoon water
- 4 teaspoons turbinado sugar (see note)

1. Place the egg in a small saucepan, cover with water by 1 inch, and bring to a boil over high heat. Remove the pan from the heat, cover, and let sit for 10 minutes. Meanwhile, fill a small bowl with ice water. Using a slotted spoon, transfer the egg to the ice water and let stand for 5 minutes. Crack the egg and peel the shell. Separate the yolk from the white; discard the white. Press the yolk through a fine-mesh strainer into a small bowl.

2. In a stand mixer fitted with the paddle attachment, beat the butter, granulated sugar, salt, and cooked egg yolk on medium speed until light and fluffy, about 4 minutes, scraping down the bowl and beater as needed with a rubber spatula. Decrease the speed to low, add the vanilla, and mix until incorporated. Stop the mixer; add the flour and mix on low speed until just combined, about 30 seconds. Using a rubber spatula, press the dough into a cohesive mass.

FORMING SPIRAL COOKIES

1. Halve each batch of dough. Roll out each portion on parchment paper into an 8 by 6-inch rectangle, ¼ inch thick. Briefly chill the dough until firm enough to handle.

2. Using a bench scraper, place one plain cookie dough rectangle on top of one chocolate dough rectangle. Repeat to make two double rectangles.

3. Roll out each double rectangle on parchment into a 9 by 6-inch rectangle (if too firm, let rest until malleable). Then, starting at the long end, roll each into a tight log.

4. Twist the ends of the parchment to seal. Chill the logs for 1 hour. Slice the logs into ¼-inch-thick rounds.

FORMING PRETZEL COOKIES

1. Slice slightly chilled dough into ¼-inch-thick rounds and roll into balls.

2. Roll each ball into a 6-inch rope, tapering the ends.

3. Pick up one end of the rope and cross it over to form half of a pretzel shape.

4. Bring the second end over to complete the pretzel shape.

---

3. Divide the dough in half; roll each piece into a log about 6 inches long and 1¾ inches in diameter. Wrap each log in a 12-inch square of parchment paper and twist the ends to seal and firmly compact the dough into a tight cylinder. Chill until firm, about 1 hour.

4. Adjust the oven racks to the upper-middle and lower-middle positions and heat the oven to 350 degrees. Line two large baking sheets with parchment paper. Using a chef's knife, slice the dough into ¼-inch-thick rounds, rotating the dough so that it won't become misshapen from the weight of the knife. Place the cookies 1 inch apart on the baking sheets. Using a pastry brush, gently brush the cookies with the egg white mixture and sprinkle evenly with the turbinado sugar.

5. Bake until the centers of the cookies are pale golden brown with edges slightly darker than the centers, about 15 minutes, switching and rotating the baking sheets halfway through the baking time. Cool the cookies on the baking sheets for 5 minutes; using a thin metal spatula, transfer the cookies to a wire rack and cool to room temperature. (The cookies can be stored between sheets of parchment paper in an airtight container for up to 1 week.)

Chocolate Sablés

Follow the recipe for Sablés, reducing the flour to 1⅓ cups (6⅔ ounces) and adding ¼ cup Dutch-processed cocoa powder with the flour in step 2.

Black and White Spiral Cookies

MAKES ABOUT 80 COOKIES

Follow the recipes for Sablés and Chocolate Sablés through step 2. Following the "Forming Spiral Cookies" photos on page 577, form the dough into spiral logs. Proceed with the Sablés recipe from step 4, slicing the logs into ¼-inch-thick rounds, omitting the egg white mixture and turbinado sugar in both recipes, and baking as directed.

Chocolate Sandwich Cookies

MAKES ABOUT 40 COOKIES

Follow the recipe for Sablés through step 3. In step 4, slice one dough log into ⅛-inch-thick rounds, omitting the egg white mixture and turbinado sugar. Bake the cookies as directed in step 5, reducing the baking time to 10 to 13 minutes. Repeat with the second dough log. When all the cookies are completely cool, melt 3½ ounces dark or milk chocolate and cool slightly. Spread the melted chocolate on the bottom of one cookie. Place a second cookie on top, slightly off-center, so some chocolate shows. Repeat with the remaining melted chocolate and cookies.

Vanilla Pretzel Cookies

MAKES ABOUT 40 COOKIES

Follow the recipe for Sablés through step 3, increasing the vanilla extract to 1 tablespoon and reducing the chilling time to 30 minutes (the dough will not be fully hardened). Slice the dough into ¼-inch-thick rounds and roll into balls. Roll each ball into a 6-inch rope, tapering the ends. Following the "Forming Pretzel Cookies" photos on page 577, form the ropes into pretzel shapes. Proceed with the recipe, brushing with the egg white mixture, sprinkling with the turbinado sugar, and baking as directed.

HOLIDAY ROLLED COOKIES

WHY THIS RECIPE WORKS: Baking holiday cookies should be a fun endeavor but so often it's an exercise in frustration. The dough clings to the rolling pin, it rips and tears as it is rolled out, and the tactic of moving the dough in and out of the fridge to make it easier to work with turns a simple one-hour process into a half-day project. We wanted a simple recipe that would yield a forgiving, workable dough, producing cookies that would be sturdy enough to decorate yet tender enough to be worth eating.

Our first realization was that we had to use enough butter to stay true to the nature of a butter cookie but not so much that the dough became greasy. All-purpose flour had enough gluten to provide structure, while superfine sugar provided a fine, even crumb and a compact, crisp cookie. Cream cheese—a surprise ingredient—gave the cookies flavor and richness without altering their texture.

Glazed Butter Cookies

MAKES ABOUT 38 COOKIES

If you cannot find superfine sugar, process granulated sugar in a food processor for 30 seconds. If desired, the cookies can be finished with sprinkles or other decorations immediately after glazing. (see page 580)

BUTTER COOKIE DOUGH
- 2½ cups (12½ ounces) unbleached all-purpose flour
- ¾ cup (5⅔ ounces) superfine sugar (see note)
- ¼ teaspoon table salt
- 16 tablespoons (2 sticks) unsalted butter, cut into 16 pieces, softened
- 2 tablespoons cream cheese, at room temperature
- 2 teaspoons vanilla extract

GLAZE
- 1 tablespoon cream cheese, at room temperature
- 3 tablespoons milk
- 1½ cups (6 ounces) confectioners' sugar

1. FOR THE COOKIES: In a stand mixer fitted with the paddle attachment, mix the flour, sugar, and salt at low speed until combined, about 5 seconds. With the mixer running on low, add the butter 1 piece at a time; continue to mix until the mixture looks crumbly and slightly wet, 1 to 2 minutes longer. Beat in the cream cheese and vanilla until the dough just begins to form large clumps, about 30 seconds.

2. Knead the dough by hand in the bowl, about two to three turns, until it forms a large, cohesive mass. Transfer the dough to a clean work surface and divide it into two even pieces. Press each piece into a 4-inch disk, wrap the disks in plastic wrap, and refrigerate until the dough is firm but malleable, about 30 minutes. (The disks can be refrigerated for up to 3 days or frozen for up to 2 weeks; defrost in the refrigerator before using.)

3. Adjust an oven rack to the middle position and heat the oven to 375 degrees. Working with one piece of dough at a time, roll out the dough to an even ⅛-inch thickness between two large sheets of parchment paper; slide the rolled dough, still on the parchment, onto a baking sheet and refrigerate until firm, about 10 minutes.

4. Line two large baking sheets with parchment paper. Working with one sheet of dough at a time, cut into desired shapes using cookie cutters and place the cookies on the prepared sheet, spacing them about 1½ inches apart. Bake one sheet at a time, until the cookies are light golden brown, about 10 minutes, rotating the sheet halfway through the baking time. (The dough scraps can be patted together, chilled, and rerolled once.) Cool the cookies on the baking sheet for 3 minutes; using a wide metal spatula, transfer the cookies to a wire rack and cool to room temperature.

5. FOR THE GLAZE: Whisk the cream cheese and 2 tablespoons of the milk together in a medium bowl until combined and no lumps remain. Add the confectioners' sugar and whisk until smooth, adding the remaining 1 tablespoon milk as needed until the glaze is thin enough to spread easily. Using the back of a spoon, drizzle or spread a scant teaspoon of the glaze onto each cooled cookie. Allow the glazed cookies to dry for at least 30 minutes.

Jam Sandwiches

MAKES ABOUT 30 COOKIES

See the photos to prepare these cookies. Turbinado sugar is commonly sold as Sugar in the Raw. Demerara sugar, sanding sugar, or another coarse sugar can be substituted.

  1 **recipe Butter Cookie Dough, prepared through step 3**
  2 **tablespoons turbinado sugar (see note)**
1¼ **cups (12 ounces) raspberry jam, strained, simmered until reduced to 1 cup, and cooled to room temperature**

1. Line two large baking sheets with parchment paper. Using a 2-inch round fluted cookie cutter, cut rounds

---

NOTES FROM THE TEST KITCHEN

CUTTING AND FILLING JAM SANDWICHES

1. Using a 2-inch round fluted cookie cutter, cut out cookies from one piece of the dough.

2. Sprinkle the second piece of rolled dough evenly with turbinado sugar and cut out 2-inch rounds.

3. Using a ¾-inch round fluted cookie cutter, cut out the centers of the sugared rounds.

4. When the cookies have cooled, spread the reduced jam on the solid cookies, then place the cut-out cookies on top.

---

from one piece of rolled dough and bake on a prepared sheet in a 375-degree oven, rotating the baking sheet halfway through the baking time, until the cookies are light golden brown, 8 to 10 minutes.

2. Sprinkle the second piece of rolled dough evenly with the sugar.

3. Using a 2-inch round fluted cookie cutter, cut rounds of sugar-sprinkled dough. Using a ¾-inch round fluted cookie cutter, cut out the centers of the sugared rounds. Place the cookies on a prepared sheet and bake, rotating

DECORATING GLAZED BUTTER COOKIES

1. For a smooth, evenly glazed cookie, spoon a little glaze on the center of the cookie, then spread it out in an even layer using the back of a spoon.

2. After glazing the cookies, sprinkle with crushed candy canes, colored sugar, or chopped nuts.

3. To add detail to a cut-out cookie, make a piping bag by spooning some glaze into a zipper-lock bag, pushing the glaze to a bottom corner, and snipping off the corner of the bag with scissors.

4. After you've piped out-lines onto a cookie, go back and fill in with colored glazes.

5. Use the zipper-lock bag to pipe small dots on the cookie, then top with shiny bead-like decorations. When set, the glaze will hold the beads in place.

the baking sheet halfway through the baking time, until the cookies are light golden brown, about 8 minutes.

4. When the cookies have cooled, spread 1 teaspoon jam on the top of each solid cookie, then cover with a cut-out cookie. Let the filled cookies stand until set, about 30 minutes.

Lime-Glazed Coconut Snowballs

MAKES ABOUT 40 COOKIES

> 1 recipe Butter Cookie Dough, with 1 teaspoon grated lime zest added with the dry ingredients, prepared through step 2
>
> 1 recipe Glaze, with 3 tablespoons juice from 2 limes substituted for the milk
>
> 1½ cups sweetened shredded coconut, pulsed in a food processor until finely chopped, about 15 pulses

1. Line two baking sheets with parchment paper. Roll the dough between your hands into 1-inch balls. Place the balls on the prepared sheets, spacing them about 1½ inches apart. Bake one sheet at a time in a 375-degree oven until lightly browned, about 12 minutes. Cool to room temperature.

2. Dip the tops of the cookies into the glaze and scrape off the excess, then dip them into the coconut. Place the cookies on a wire rack and let stand until the glaze sets, about 20 minutes.

Chocolate-Cherry Bar Cookies with Hazelnuts

MAKES ABOUT 50 COOKIES

> 1 recipe Butter Cookie Dough, with 1 cup chopped dried cherries added with the dry ingredients, prepared through step 2
>
> 1½ cups (9 ounces) semisweet chocolate chips
>
> 1½ cups (6 ounces) hazelnuts, toasted, skinned, and chopped

1. Adjust an oven rack to the lower-middle position and heat the oven to 375 degrees. Line a 17 by 12-inch rimmed baking sheet with parchment paper. Press the dough evenly into the prepared sheet and bake until golden brown, about 20 minutes, rotating the sheet halfway through the baking time.

2. Immediately after removing the baking sheet from the oven, sprinkle evenly with the chocolate chips; let stand to melt, about 3 minutes.

3. Using an offset spatula, spread the chocolate into an even layer, then sprinkle the chopped hazelnuts evenly over the chocolate. Cool on a wire rack until just warm, 15 to 20 minutes.

4. Using a pizza wheel, cut on the diagonal into 1½-inch diamonds. Transfer the cookies to a wire rack to cool completely.

BEST SHORTBREAD

WHY THIS RECIPE WORKS: When made well, shortbread, with its moderately sweet, buttery flavor and distinctive sandy texture, is the perfect partner to a cup of tea or served alongside fruit for dessert, but often shortbread turns out bland and chalky. We wanted superlative shortbread with an alluring tawny brown crumb and pure, buttery richness.

In initial tests, we tinkered with various mixing methods and found that reverse creaming—mixing the flour and sugar before adding the butter, creating less aeration—yielded the most reliable results. To smooth out an objectionable granular texture, we swapped the white sugar for confectioners' sugar. Still, our shortbread was unpleasantly tough. The problems were gluten and moisture. Gluten, the protein matrix that lends baked goods structure and chew, forms naturally when liquid and all-purpose flour are combined, even without kneading. The liquid in our recipe was coming from butter, which contains 20 percent water. To curb gluten development, we replaced some of our flour with powdered old-fashioned oats. We ground some oats to a powder and supplemented it with a modest amount of cornstarch (using all oat powder muted the buttery flavor). The cookies were now perfectly crisp and flavorful, with an appealing hint of oat flavor.

As for the moisture problem, we took a hint from recipes from historic cookbooks: We cooked the dough briefly, then shut off the heat and let it sit in the still-warm oven. The batch was dry through and through, with an even golden brown exterior. Crisp and buttery, our shortbread was anything but bland.

FORMING AND BAKING THE SHORTBREAD

1. Press the dough into a closed springform pan collar; smooth with the back of a spoon.

2. Cut a hole in the center of the dough with a 2-inch biscuit cutter and remove the round of dough—place it on the baking sheet next to the collar; replace the cutter in the hole.

3. Open the collar, but leave it in place. Bake 5 minutes at 450 degrees, then 10 to 15 minutes at 250 degrees.

4. Score the partially baked shortbread into wedges, then poke 8 to 10 holes in each wedge.

5. Return the shortbread to the turned-off oven to dry; prop the door open with a wooden spoon or stick.

Best Shortbread

MAKES 16 WEDGES

Use the collar of a springform pan to form the shortbread into an even round. Mold the shortbread with the collar in the closed position, then open the collar, but leave it in place. This allows the shortbread to expand slightly but keeps it from spreading too far. The extracted round of dough in step 2 is baked alongside the rest of the shortbread. Wrapped well and stored at room temperature, the shortbread will keep for up to 7 days.

½ cup (1½ ounces) old-fashioned oats
1½ cups (7½ ounces) unbleached all-purpose flour
¼ cup cornstarch
⅔ cup (2⅔ ounces) confectioners' sugar
½ teaspoon table salt
14 tablespoons (1¾ sticks) unsalted butter, chilled, cut into ⅛-inch-thick slices

1. Adjust an oven rack to the middle position and heat the oven to 450 degrees. Pulse the oats in a spice grinder or blender until reduced to a fine powder, about ten 5-second pulses (you should have ¼ to ⅓ cup oat flour). In a stand mixer fitted with the paddle attachment, mix the oat flour, all-purpose flour, cornstarch, sugar, and salt on low speed until combined, about 5 seconds. Add the butter to the dry ingredients and continue to mix on low speed until the dough just forms and pulls away from the sides of the bowl, 5 to 10 minutes.

2. Place an upside-down (the grooved edge should be at the top) collar of a 9- or 9½-inch springform pan on a parchment-lined rimmed baking sheet (do not use the springform pan bottom). Following the photos on page 581, press the dough into the collar in an even ½-inch-thick layer, smoothing the top of the dough with the back of a spoon. Place a 2-inch biscuit cutter in the center of the dough and cut out the center. Place the extracted round alongside the springform collar on the baking sheet and replace the cutter in the center of the dough. Open the springform collar, but leave it in place.

3. Bake the shortbread for 5 minutes, then reduce the oven temperature to 250 degrees. Continue to bake until the edges turn pale golden, 10 to 15 minutes longer. Remove the baking sheet from the oven; turn off the oven. Remove the springform pan collar; use a chef's knife to score the surface of the shortbread into 16 even wedges, cutting halfway through the shortbread. Using a wooden skewer, poke 8 to 10 holes in each wedge. Return the shortbread to the oven and prop the door open with the handle of a wooden spoon, leaving a 1-inch gap at the top.

Allow the shortbread to dry in the turned-off oven until pale golden in the center (the shortbread should be firm but giving to the touch), about 1 hour.

4. Transfer the baking sheet to a wire rack; cool the shortbread to room temperature, at least 2 hours. Cut the shortbread at the scored marks to separate and serve.

NUT CRESCENT COOKIES

WHY THIS RECIPE WORKS: When nut crescent cookies are well made, they can be delicious: buttery, nutty, slightly crisp, slightly crumbly, with a melt-in-your mouth quality. Too often, however, they turn out bland and dry. We wanted to develop a recipe that would put them back in their proper place.

The ratio of 1 cup butter to 2 cups flour in almost all of the recipes we looked at is what worked for us. We tried three kinds of sugar in the batter: granulated, confectioners', and superfine. The last resulted in just what we wanted: cookies that melted in our mouths. In determining the amount, we had to remember that the cookies would be sweetened once more by their traditional coating of confectioners' sugar. Before rolling them, we let the cookies cool to room temperature; coating them with sugar while still warm results in the pasty outer layer we wanted to avoid.

Pecan or Walnut Crescent Cookies

MAKES ABOUT 48 SMALL COOKIES

If you cannot find superfine sugar, you can obtain a close approximation by processing regular granulated sugar in a food processor for about 30 seconds. If you don't have a food processor, you can finely grind the chopped nuts by rolling them between two large sheets of plastic wrap with a rolling pin, applying moderate pressure, until broken down to a coarse cornmeal-like texture.

- 2 cups (8 ounces) whole pecans or walnuts, chopped fine
- 2 cups (10 ounces) unbleached all-purpose flour
- ½ teaspoon table salt
- 16 tablespoons (2 sticks) unsalted butter, softened
- ⅓ cup (2½ ounces) superfine sugar (see note)
- 1½ teaspoons vanilla extract
- 1½ cups (6 ounces) confectioners' sugar

1. Adjust the oven racks to the upper-middle and lower-middle positions and heat the oven to 325 degrees. Line two large baking sheets with parchment paper.

2. Whisk 1 cup of the chopped nuts, the flour, and salt together in a medium bowl; set aside. Process the remaining 1 cup chopped nuts in a food processor (see note) until they are the texture of coarse cornmeal, 10 to 15 seconds (do not overprocess). Stir the nuts into the flour mixture and set aside.

3. In a stand mixer fitted with the paddle attachment, beat the butter and superfine sugar at medium-low speed until light and fluffy, about 2 minutes; add the vanilla, scraping down the bowl and beater with a rubber spatula. Add the flour mixture and beat on low speed until the dough just begins to come together but still looks scrappy, about 15 seconds. Scrape down the bowl and beater again with a rubber spatula; continue beating at low speed until the dough is cohesive, 6 to 9 seconds longer. Do not overbeat.

4. Divide the dough into 48 portions, each about 1 tablespoon, and roll them between your hands into 1¼-inch balls. Roll each ball between your palms into a rope that measures 3 inches long. Place the ropes on the prepared baking sheets and turn up the ends to form a crescent shape. Bake until the tops are pale golden and the bottoms are just beginning to brown, 17 to 19 minutes, switching and rotating the baking sheets halfway through the baking time.

5. Cool the cookies on the baking sheets for 2 minutes; using a wide metal spatula, transfer the cookies to a wire rack and cool to room temperature, about 30 minutes. Place the confectioners' sugar in a shallow baking dish or pie plate. Working with three or four cookies at a time, roll the cookies in the sugar to coat them thoroughly; gently shake off the excess. (The cookies can be stored in an airtight container for up to 5 days.) Before serving, roll the cookies in the confectioners' sugar again and tap off the excess.

Almond or Hazelnut Crescent Cookies

Almonds can be used raw for cookies that are light in both color and flavor or toasted to enhance the almond flavor and darken the crescents.

Follow the recipe for Pecan or Walnut Crescent Cookies, substituting 1¾ cups (7¾ ounces) whole blanched almonds (toasted, if desired) or 2 cups (8 ounces) toasted, skinned hazelnuts for the pecans or walnuts. If using almonds, add ½ teaspoon almond extract along with the vanilla extract.

MERINGUE COOKIES

WHY THIS RECIPE WORKS: A classic meringue cookie may have only two ingredients—egg whites and sugar—but it requires precise timing. Otherwise, you'll end up with a meringue that's as dense as Styrofoam or weepy, gritty, and cloyingly sweet. A great meringue cookie should emerge from the oven glossy and white, with a shatteringly crisp texture that dissolves instantly in your mouth.

We chose a basic French meringue over a fussier Italian meringue. The French version, in which egg whites are whipped with sugar, is the simpler of the two; the Italian meringue, in which hot sugar syrup is poured into the whites, produces cookies that are dense and candy-like. The key to glossy, evenly textured meringue was adding the sugar at just the right time—when the whites have been whipped enough to gain some volume, but still have enough free water left in them for the sugar to dissolve completely. Surprisingly, we found that cream of tartar wasn't necessary. Without it, the whites formed more slowly, giving a wider time frame in which to add the sugar. It was also important to form the cookies in a uniform shape, so we piped them from either a pastry bag or a zipper-lock bag with a corner cut off.

Meringue Cookies

MAKES ABOUT 48 SMALL COOKIES

Meringues may be a little soft immediately after being removed from the oven but will stiffen as they cool. To minimize stickiness on humid or rainy days, allow the meringues to cool in a turned-off oven for an additional hour (for a total of 2 hours) without opening the door, then transfer them immediately to airtight containers and seal. Cooled cookies can be kept in an airtight container for up to 2 weeks.

¾ cup (5¼ ounces) sugar
2 teaspoons cornstarch
4 large egg whites
¾ teaspoon vanilla extract
⅛ teaspoon table salt

1. Adjust the oven racks to the upper-middle and lower-middle positions and heat the oven to 225 degrees. Line two large baking sheets with parchment paper. Combine the sugar and cornstarch in a small bowl.

2. In a stand mixer fitted with the whisk attachment, beat the egg whites, vanilla, and salt together at high speed until very soft peaks start to form (the peaks should slowly lose their shape when the whip is removed), 30 to 45 seconds. Decrease the speed to medium and slowly add the sugar mixture in a steady stream down the side of the mixer bowl (the process should take about 30 seconds). Stop the mixer and scrape down the sides and bottom of the bowl with a rubber spatula. Increase the speed to high and beat until glossy and stiff peaks have formed, 30 to 45 seconds.

3. Working quickly, place the meringue in a pastry bag fitted with a ½-inch plain tip or a large zipper-lock bag with ½ inch of the corner cut off. Pipe meringues into

1¼-inch-wide mounds about 1 inch high on the baking sheets, six rows of four meringues on each sheet. Bake for 1 hour, switching and rotating the baking sheets halfway through the baking time. Turn off the oven and allow the meringues to cool in the oven for at least 1 hour. Remove the meringues from the oven and let cool to room temperature before serving, about 10 minutes.

Chocolate Meringue Cookies

Follow the recipe for Meringue Cookies, gently folding 2 ounces finely chopped bittersweet chocolate into the meringue mixture at the end of step 2.

Toasted Almond Meringue Cookies

Follow the recipe for Meringue Cookies, substituting ½ teaspoon almond extract for the vanilla extract. In step 3, sprinkle the meringues with ⅓ cup coarsely chopped toasted almonds and 1 teaspoon coarse sea salt, such as Maldon (optional), before baking.

BLONDIES

WHY THIS RECIPE WORKS: Blondies are first cousins to both brownies and chocolate chip cookies. Although blondies are baked in a pan like brownies, the flavorings are similar to those in chocolate chip cookies—vanilla, butter, and brown sugar. They're sometimes laced with nuts and chocolate chips or butterscotch chips. But even with these extras, blondies can be pretty bland, floury, and dry. We set out to fix the blondie so it would be chewy but not dense, sweet but not cloying, and loaded with nuts and chocolate.

We found that the key to chewy blondies was using melted, not creamed, butter because the creaming process incorporates too much air into the batter. For sweetening, light brown sugar lent the right amount of earthy, molasses flavor. And combined with a substantial amount of vanilla extract and salt (to sharpen the sweetness), the light brown sugar developed a rich butterscotch flavor. To add both texture and flavor to the cookies, we included chocolate chips and pecans. We also tried butterscotch chips, but we found that they did little for this recipe. On a whim, we included white chocolate chips with the semisweet chips, and we were surprised that they produced the best blondie yet.

Congo Bars

If you have trouble locating unsweetened shredded coconut, try a natural foods store or an Asian market. Keep a close eye on the coconut when toasting, as it can burn quickly.

Toast 1½ cups unsweetened shredded coconut on a rimmed baking sheet on the middle oven rack at 350 degrees, stirring two to three times, until light golden, 4 to 5 minutes. Transfer to a small bowl to cool. Follow the recipe for Blondies, adding the toasted coconut with the chocolate chips and nuts in step 3.

Blondies

MAKES 36 BARS

If you have trouble finding white chocolate chips, chop a bar of white chocolate into small chunks.

- 1½ cups (7½ ounces) unbleached all-purpose flour
- 1   teaspoon baking powder
- ½   teaspoon table salt
- 1½ cups packed (10½ ounces) light brown sugar
- 12 tablespoons (1½ sticks) unsalted butter, melted and cooled
- 2   large eggs
- 1½ teaspoons vanilla extract
- 1   cup (4 ounces) pecans, toasted and chopped coarse
- ½   cup (3 ounces) semisweet chocolate chips
- ½   cup (3 ounces) white chocolate chips (see note)

1. Adjust an oven rack to the middle position and heat the oven to 350 degrees. Line a 13 by 9-inch baking pan with two pieces of foil (see the photos on page 588) and spray with vegetable oil spray.

2. Whisk the flour, baking powder, and salt together in a medium bowl; set aside.

3. Whisk the brown sugar and melted butter together in a medium bowl until combined. Add the eggs and vanilla and mix well. Using a rubber spatula, fold the dry ingredients into the egg mixture until just combined. Do not overmix. Fold in the nuts and semisweet and white chocolate chips and turn the batter into the prepared pan, smoothing the top with a rubber spatula.

4. Bake until the top is shiny and cracked and feels firm to the touch, 22 to 25 minutes. Transfer the pan to a wire rack and cool completely. Loosen the edges with a paring knife and lift the bars from the pan using the foil sling. Cut into 2 by 1½-inch bars.

CLASSIC BROWNIES

WHY THIS RECIPE WORKS: Chewy and chocolaty, brownies should be a simple and utterly satisfying affair. But too often, brownies are heavy, dense, and remarkably low on chocolate flavor. We wanted old-fashioned brownies that had serious chocolate flavor. They had to be the simple treats we enjoyed in our youth—Mom's brownies—but altered to cater to adult tastes.

To get that tender texture and delicate chew, we shelved the all-purpose flour in favor of cake flour; a bit of baking powder further lightened the crumb. Getting the number of eggs just right prevented our brownies from being cakey or dry. As for chocolatiness, plenty of unsweetened chocolate provided maximum chocolate flavor—not too sweet, with profound chocolate notes. Nailing the baking time was essential—too little time in the oven and the brownies were gummy and underbaked, too much time and they were dry. Finally, for nut-lovers, we toasted pecans and topped the brownies with them just before baking; baked inside the brownies, they steam and get soft.

Classic Brownies

MAKES 24 BROWNIES

Be sure to test for doneness before removing the brownies from the oven. If underbaked (the toothpick has batter clinging to it), the texture of the brownies will be dense and gummy; if overbaked (the toothpick comes out completely clean), the brownies will be dry and cakey. To melt the chocolate using a microwave, heat it with the butter at 50 percent power for 2 minutes; stir the chocolate and continue heating until melted, stirring once every additional minute.

1¼ cups (5 ounces) cake flour

¾ teaspoon baking powder

½ teaspoon table salt

6 ounces unsweetened chocolate, chopped fine

12 tablespoons (1½ sticks) unsalted butter, cut into 6 pieces

2¼ cups (15¾ ounces) sugar

4 large eggs

1 tablespoon vanilla extract

1 cup (4 ounces) pecans or walnuts, toasted and coarsely chopped (optional)

1. Adjust an oven rack to the middle position and heat the oven to 325 degrees. Line a 13 by 9-inch baking pan with two pieces of foil (see the photos on page 588) and spray with vegetable oil spray.

2. Whisk the flour, baking powder, and salt in a medium bowl until combined; set aside.

3. Melt the chocolate and butter in a medium heatproof bowl set over a saucepan of barely simmering water, stirring occasionally, until smooth. Off the heat, gradually whisk in the sugar. Add the eggs, one at a time, whisking after each addition, until thoroughly combined. Whisk in the vanilla. Add the flour mixture in three additions,

folding with a rubber spatula until the batter is completely smooth and homogeneous.

4. Transfer the batter to the prepared pan; using a spatula, spread the batter into the corners of the pan and smooth the surface. Sprinkle the toasted nuts (if using) evenly over the batter. Bake until a toothpick or wooden skewer inserted into the center of the brownies comes out with a few moist crumbs attached, 30 to 35 minutes. Cool on a wire rack to room temperature, about 2 hours; loosen the edges with a paring knife and lift the brownies from the pan using the foil sling. Cut the brownies into 2-inch squares and serve. (The brownies can be stored in an airtight container at room temperature for up to 3 days.)

CHEWY BROWNIES

WHY THIS RECIPE WORKS: Brownies are a tricky business: Homemade recipes have better flavor, while boxed mixes claim best texture. Our goal was clear: a homemade brownie with chewiness (and a shiny, crisp, crackly top) to rival the boxed-mix standard—but flush with a rich, deep, all-natural chocolate flavor.

To start, we consulted our science editor to see if he knew of any tricks that boxed brownies use to achieve their chewy texture. He explained that boxed brownie mixes derive their chewy texture from the right combination of saturated (solid) and unsaturated (liquid) fats. Unsaturated vegetable oil and powdered solid fat combine in a ratio designed to deliver maximum chew. To get the same chew at home, we tested and tested until we finally homed in on the ratio that produced the chewiest brownie. To combat greasiness, we replaced some of the oil with egg yolks, whose emulsifiers prevent fat from separating and leaking out during baking.

We focused on flavor next. Because unsweetened chocolate contains a similar ratio of saturated and unsaturated fat to butter, we could replace some of the butter with unsweetened chocolate, thereby providing more chocolate flavor. Espresso powder improved the chocolate taste as well. And finally, folding in bittersweet chocolate chunks just before baking gave our chewy, fudgy brownies gooey pockets of melted chocolate and rounded out their complex chocolate flavor.

Chewy Brownies

MAKES 2 DOZEN 2-INCH BROWNIES

For an accurate measurement of boiling water, bring a full kettle of water to a boil, then measure out the desired amount. For the chewiest texture, it is important to let the brownies cool thoroughly before cutting. If your baking dish is glass, cool the brownies for 10 minutes, then remove them promptly from the pan (otherwise, the superior heat retention of glass can lead to overbaking). While any high-quality chocolate can be used, our preferred brands of bittersweet chocolate are Callebaut Intense Dark Chocolate and Ghirardelli Bittersweet Chocolate. Our preferred brand of unsweetened chocolate is Hershey's.

⅓ cup (1 ounce) Dutch-processed cocoa powder
1½ teaspoons instant espresso (optional)
½ cup plus 2 tablespoons boiling water (see note)
2 ounces unsweetened chocolate (see note), chopped fine
½ cup plus 2 tablespoons vegetable oil
4 tablespoons (½ stick) unsalted butter, melted
2 large whole eggs plus 2 large egg yolks
2 teaspoons vanilla extract
2½ cups (17½ ounces) sugar
1¾ cups (8¾ ounces) unbleached all-purpose flour
¾ teaspoon table salt
6 ounces bittersweet chocolate (see note), cut into ½-inch pieces

1. Adjust an oven rack to the lowest position and heat the oven to 350 degrees. Following the photos on page 588, line a 13 by 9-inch baking pan with a foil sling, lightly coat with vegetable oil spray, and set aside.

2. Whisk the cocoa, espresso powder (if using), and boiling water together in a large bowl until smooth. Add the unsweetened chocolate and whisk until the chocolate is melted. Whisk in the oil and melted butter. (The mixture may look curdled.) Add the whole eggs, egg yolks, and vanilla and continue to whisk until smooth and homogeneous. Whisk in the sugar until fully incorporated. Add the flour and salt and mix with a rubber spatula until combined. Fold in the bittersweet chocolate pieces.

3. Scrape the batter into the prepared pan and bake until a toothpick inserted halfway between the edge and the center comes out with just a few moist crumbs attached, 30 to 35 minutes. Transfer the pan to a wire rack and cool for 1½ hours.

4. Loosen the edges with a paring knife and lift the brownies from the pan using the foil sling. Return the brownies to the wire rack and let cool completely, about 1 hour. Cut into 2-inch squares and serve. (The brownies can be stored in an airtight container at room temperature for up to 4 days.)

FUDGY BROWNIES

WHY THIS RECIPE WORKS: Classic Brownies (page 585) boast a balance of cakey and chewy. We wanted a brownie that was distinctly chewy and very fudgy—a moist, dark, luscious brownie with a firm, smooth, velvety texture. It must pack an intense chocolate punch and have deep, resonant chocolate flavor, but it must fall just short of overwhelming the palate.

To develop a rich, deep chocolate flavor, we ultimately found it necessary to use three types of chocolate. Unsweetened chocolate laid a solid, intense foundation; semisweet chocolate provided a mellow, even somewhat sweet, flavor; and cocoa powder smoothed out any rough edges introduced by the unsweetened chocolate (which can contribute a sour, acrid flavor) and added complexity to what can be the bland flavor of semisweet chocolate. We focused on flour, butter, and eggs to arrive at the chewy texture we wanted. Too little flour and the batter was goopy; too much made the brownies dry and muted the chocolate flavor. We melted the butter instead of creaming softened butter with the sugar and eggs; as with our Classic Brownies, the melted butter produced a more dense and fudgy texture.

Fudgy Triple-Chocolate Brownies

MAKES 64 SMALL BROWNIES

To melt the chocolates in a microwave, heat them with the butter at 50 percent power for 2 minutes; stir the chocolate and continue heating until melted, stirring once every additional minute. Either Dutch-processed or natural cocoa powder works well in this recipe. These brownies are very rich, so we prefer to cut them into very small squares for serving.

5   ounces semisweet or bittersweet chocolate, chopped
2   ounces unsweetened chocolate, chopped
8   tablespoons (1 stick) unsalted butter, cut into quarters
3   tablespoons cocoa powder (see note)
3   large eggs
1¼ cups (8¾ ounces) sugar
2   teaspoons vanilla extract
½   teaspoon table salt
1   cup (5 ounces) unbleached all-purpose flour

1. Adjust an oven rack to the lower-middle position and heat the oven to 350 degrees. Following the photos, line an 8-inch square baking pan with two pieces of foil and spray with vegetable oil spray.

2. Melt the chocolates and butter in a medium heatproof bowl set over a saucepan of barely simmering water, stirring occasionally, until smooth. Whisk in the cocoa powder until smooth. Set aside to cool slightly.

3. Whisk the eggs, sugar, vanilla, and salt together in a medium bowl until combined, about 15 seconds. Whisk the warm chocolate mixture into the egg mixture. Using a wooden spoon, stir in the flour until just combined. Transfer the batter to the prepared pan; using a spatula, spread the batter into the corners and smooth the surface. Bake until slightly puffed and a toothpick or wooden skewer inserted into the center of the brownies comes out with a few moist crumbs attached, 35 to 40 minutes. Cool the brownies on a wire rack to room temperature, about 2 hours; loosen the edges with a paring knife and lift the brownies from the pan using the foil sling. Cut the brownies into 1-inch squares and serve. (Do not cut the brownies until ready to serve; the brownies can be wrapped in plastic wrap and refrigerated for up to 5 days.)

Triple-Chocolate Espresso Brownies

Follow the recipe for Fudgy Triple-Chocolate Brownies, whisking in 1½ tablespoons instant espresso or coffee powder along with the cocoa powder in step 2.

FUDGY LOW-FAT BROWNIES

WHY THIS RECIPE WORKS: We have tried many recipes for "healthy" brownies, but it usually takes just one bite to regret the effort. Either the texture is incredibly dry or the chocolate flavor is anemic. We wanted a moist, fudgy, chocolaty brownie that had a lower fat and calorie count than a traditional brownie, which can weigh in at over 200 calories and 12 grams of fat.

We knew the richness and flavor would have to come from somewhere if we were cutting back on butter and unsweetened chocolate. We started our tests with "alternative" ingredients, such as prune puree, applesauce, and yogurt, but they resulted in everything from oddly flavored brownies to flavorless hockey pucks. We had more success replacing some of the butter with low-fat sour cream, which yielded moist, fudgy brownies. A blend of cocoa powder and bittersweet chocolate (which has less fat per ounce than unsweetened chocolate) added

---

NOTES FROM THE TEST KITCHEN

MAKING A FOIL SLING

1. Place two sheets of aluminum foil perpendicular to each other in the baking pan, with the extra foil hanging over the edges of the pan.

2. Push the foil into the corners and up the sides of the pan, smoothing out any wrinkles in the foil.

3. After the bars or brownies have baked and cooled, use the foil sling to lift and transfer them to a cutting board before cutting into squares.

deep chocolate flavor. And to boost both the brownies' chocolate flavor and moisture without adding any fat, we used a shot of chocolate syrup. Our brownies were now rich and decadent, but with half the calories (just 110 per serving) and less than half the fat (only 4.5 grams) of traditional brownies.

Fudgy Low-Fat Brownies
MAKES 16 BROWNIES

For a truly fudgy consistency, don't overbake the brownies; as soon as a toothpick inserted into the center comes out with moist crumbs attached, the brownies are done. If the toothpick emerges with no crumbs, the brownies will be cakey. To melt the chocolate in a microwave, heat it with the butter at 50 percent power for 2 minutes; stir and continue heating until melted, stirring once every additional minute.

- ¾ **cup (3¾ ounces) unbleached all-purpose flour**
- ⅓ **cup Dutch-processed cocoa powder**
- ½ **teaspoon baking powder**
- ¼ **teaspoon table salt**
- 2 **ounces bittersweet chocolate, chopped**
- 2 **tablespoons unsalted butter**
- 1 **cup (7 ounces) sugar**
- 2 **tablespoons low-fat sour cream**
- 1 **tablespoon chocolate syrup**
- 2 **teaspoons vanilla extract**
- 1 **large whole egg**
- 1 **large egg white**

1. Adjust an oven rack to the middle position and heat the oven to 350 degrees. Line an 8-inch square baking pan with two pieces of foil (see photos on page 588) and spray with vegetable oil spray.

2. Whisk the flour, cocoa powder, baking powder, and salt together in a medium bowl. Melt the chocolate and butter in a large heatproof bowl set over a saucepan of barely simmering water, stirring occasionally, until smooth. Set aside to cool slightly, 2 to 3 minutes. Whisk in the sugar, sour cream, chocolate syrup, vanilla, whole egg, and egg white. Using a rubber spatula, fold the dry ingredients into the chocolate mixture until combined.

3. Transfer the batter to the prepared pan; using a spatula, spread the batter into the corners and smooth the surface. Bake until slightly puffed and a toothpick or wooden skewer inserted into the center of the brownies comes out with a few moist crumbs attached, 20 to 25 minutes.

Cool the brownies on a wire rack to room temperature, about 1 hour. Loosen the edges with a paring knife and lift the brownies from the pan using the foil sling. Cut the brownies into 2-inch squares and serve. (Do not cut the brownies until ready to serve; the brownies can be wrapped in plastic wrap and refrigerated for up to 3 days.)

RASPBERRY SQUARES

WHY THIS RECIPE WORKS: Raspberry squares are one of the best, and easiest, bar cookies to prepare, especially since the filling is ready-made (a jar of raspberry preserves). But sometimes the proportions are uneven, leaving one parched from too much sandy crust, or with a puckered face from an overload of tart filling. We were after a buttery, tender, golden brown crust and crumb topping with just the right amount of sweet and tart raspberry preserves in the middle.

For the tender, almost (but not quite) sandy crumb, we had to get the right combination of ingredients, especially the butter and sugar. Too much butter made the raspberry squares greasy, but too little left them on the dry side. We found that equal amounts of white and light brown sugar made for a deeper flavor than white alone; oats and nuts made a subtle contribution to flavor while also adding some textural interest. For a golden brown bottom crust, we prebaked it before layering it with raspberry preserves and sprinkling on the top crust, which was a small amount of the reserved bottom crust mixture.

Raspberry Squares

MAKES 25 SQUARES

For a nice presentation, trim ¼ inch off the outer rim of the uncut baked block. The outside edges of all cut squares will then be neat.

1½	cups (7½ ounces) unbleached all-purpose flour
1¼	cups (3¾ ounces) quick oats
½	cup pecans or almonds, chopped fine
⅓	cup (2⅓ ounces) granulated sugar
⅓	cup packed (2⅓ ounces) light brown sugar
¼	teaspoon baking soda
¼	teaspoon table salt
12	tablespoons (1½ sticks) unsalted butter, cut into 12 pieces and softened
1	cup raspberry preserves

1. Adjust an oven rack to the lower-middle position and heat the oven to 350 degrees. Line a 9-inch square baking pan with two pieces of foil (see the photos on page 588) and spray with vegetable oil spray.

2. Whisk the flour, oats, nuts, sugars, baking soda, and salt together in a large bowl. In a stand mixer fitted with the paddle attachment, beat the flour mixture and butter at low speed until well blended and the mixture resembles wet sand, about 2 minutes.

3. Transfer two-thirds of the mixture to the prepared pan. Press the crumbs evenly and firmly into the bottom of the pan. Bake until just starting to brown, about 20 minutes. Using a rubber spatula, spread the preserves evenly over the hot crust; sprinkle the remaining flour mixture evenly over the preserves. Bake until bubbling around the edges and the top is golden brown, about 30 minutes, rotating the pan halfway through the baking time. Cool on a wire rack to room temperature, 1 to 1½ hours. Lift the bars from the baking pan using the foil sling; cut the bars into 25 squares and serve.

KEY LIME BARS

WHY THIS RECIPE WORKS: Key lime pie is a luscious, bright, summery dessert, but like all pies, it's not very portable. Thus, we decided to bring all the essence of Key lime pie to a Key lime bar, creating a cookie that balanced tart and creamy flavors as well as soft and crispy textures.

To support our handheld bars, we needed a thicker, sturdier crust, which required more crumbs and butter than used in traditional pie crust. Tasters found the traditional graham cracker flavor too assertive in such a crust and preferred the more neutral flavor of animal crackers. As for the filling, it also had to be firmer. By adding cream cheese and an egg yolk to the usual sweetened condensed milk, lime juice, and lime zest, we created a firm, rich filling that didn't fall apart when the bars were picked up. Two issues remained: Were Key limes really key? Did we need a topping? While testers preferred Key lime juice to regular lime juice by a narrow margin, regular juice was judged acceptable, especially considering that we needed to squeeze far fewer regular limes (three) than Key limes (20) to get the same amount of juice. For a topping, a heavy streusel was rejected. The favorite was an optional toasted-coconut topping.

Key Lime Bars

MAKES 16 BARS

If you cannot find fresh Key limes, use regular (Persian) limes. Do not use bottled lime juice. Grate the zest from the limes before juicing them, avoiding the bitter white pith that lies just beneath the outermost skin. The optional coconut garnish adds textural interest and tames the lime flavor for those who find it too intense. The recipe can be doubled and baked in a 13 by 9-inch baking pan; you will need a double layer of extra-wide foil for the pan (each sheet about 20 inches in length) and should increase the baking times by a minute or two.

CRUST

- **5 ounces animal crackers**
- **3 tablespoons brown sugar**
- **Pinch table salt**
- **4 tablespoons (½ stick) unsalted butter, melted and cooled slightly**

FILLING

- **2 ounces cream cheese, at room temperature**
- **1 tablespoon grated zest from 1 lime**
- **Pinch table salt**
- **1 (14-ounce) can sweetened condensed milk**
- **1 large egg yolk**
- **½ cup juice from about 20 Key limes or from about 3 Persian limes (see note)**

GARNISH (OPTIONAL)

- **¾ cup sweetened shredded coconut, toasted until golden and crisp (see note)**

1. Adjust an oven rack to the middle position and heat the oven to 325 degrees. Line an 8-inch square baking pan with two pieces of foil (see the photos on page 588) and spray with vegetable oil spray.

2. FOR THE CRUST: Pulse the animal crackers in a food processor until broken down, about 10 pulses; process the crumbs until evenly fine, about 10 seconds (you should have about 1¼ cups crumbs). Add the brown sugar and salt; process to combine, 10 to 12 pulses (if large sugar lumps remain, break them apart with your fingers). Drizzle the butter over the crumbs and pulse until the crumbs are evenly moistened with the butter, about 10 pulses. Press the crumbs evenly and firmly into the bottom of the prepared pan. Bake until deep golden brown, 18 to

20 minutes. Cool on a wire rack while making the filling. Do not turn off the oven.

3. FOR THE FILLING: While the crust cools, in a medium bowl, stir the cream cheese, zest, and salt with a rubber spatula until softened, creamy, and thoroughly combined. Add the sweetened condensed milk and whisk vigorously until incorporated and no lumps of cream cheese remain; whisk in the egg yolk. Add the lime juice and whisk gently until incorporated (the mixture will thicken slightly).

4. Pour the filling into the crust; spread to the corners and smooth the surface with a rubber spatula. Bake until set and the edges begin to pull away slightly from the sides, 15 to 20 minutes. Cool on a wire rack to room temperature, 1 to 1½ hours. Cover with foil and refrigerate until thoroughly chilled, at least 2 hours.

5. Loosen the edges with a paring knife and lift the bars from the baking pan using the foil sling; cut the bars into 16 squares. Sprinkle with the toasted coconut (if using) and serve. (Leftovers can be refrigerated for up to 2 days; the crust will soften slightly. Let the bars stand at room temperature for about 15 minutes before serving.)

Triple Citrus Bars

Using three types of citrus (orange, lemon, and lime) gives these bars a slightly more complex, floral flavor.

Follow the recipe for Key Lime Bars, substituting 1½ teaspoons each grated lime zest, lemon zest, and orange zest for the lime zest, and using 6 tablespoons lime juice, 1 tablespoon lemon juice, and 1 tablespoon orange juice in place of all the lime juice.

NOTES FROM THE TEST KITCHEN

ZESTING CITRUS

Hold a rasp-style grater upside down with the fruit on the bottom and the inverted grater on the top. This method is neater and makes it easy to see exactly how much zest you have.

CHAPTER 22

A PIECE OF CAKE

Angel Food Cake   594

Rich Chocolate
Bundt Cake   595

Lemon Bundt Cake   596

Lemon Pound Cake   597

Applesauce Snack
Cake   598

Oatmeal Cake with
Broiled Icing   599

Apple Upside-Down
Cake   600

Apple Upside-Down
Cake with Almond   601

Apple Upside-Down
Cake with Lemon
and Thyme   601

Carrot Cake   602
    Cream Cheese Frosting

Light Carrot Cake   603
    Light Cream Cheese
    Frosting

Spice Cake   604

Strawberry Cream
Cake   605

Summer Peach Cake   607

Classic Gingerbread
Cake   608

Coconut Layer Cake   609

Easy Caramel Cake   610

Lemon Layer Cake with
Fluffy White Icing   611

Classic White Layer Cake
with Butter Frosting
and Raspberry-Almond
Filling   613

Classic Yellow Layer
Cake with Vanilla
Buttercream   614

Fluffy Yellow Layer Cake
with Milk Chocolate
Frosting   616

Old-Fashioned Chocolate
Layer Cake with Chocolate
Frosting   617

Chocolate Sheet Cake
with Easy Chocolate
Frosting   619

German Chocolate
Cake   620

Dark Chocolate
Cupcakes   621
    Easy Vanilla Bean
    Buttercream
    Easy Chocolate
    Buttercream
    Easy Coffee Buttercream

Ultimate Chocolate
Cupcakes with Ganache
Filling   623
    Creamy Chocolate
    Frosting

Chocolate-Raspberry
Torte   625

Flourless Chocolate
Cake   626

Hot Fudge Pudding
Cake   627

Individual Hot Fudge
Pudding Cakes   627

Bittersweet Chocolate
Roulade   628
    Espresso-Mascarpone
    Cream
    Dark Chocolate Ganache

Triple-Chocolate Mousse
Cake   630

Chocolate Volcano
Cakes with Espresso
Ice Cream   631

Tiramisù   632

Tiramisù with Cooked
Eggs   633

New York Cheesecake   633
    Strawberry Topping

Light New York
Cheesecake   635

Spiced Pumpkin
Cheesecake   636

Lemon Cheesecake   637

ANGEL FOOD CAKE

WHY THIS RECIPE WORKS: At its heavenly best, an angel food cake should be tall and perfectly shaped, have a snowy-white, tender crumb, and be encased in a thin, delicate golden crust. The difficulty with making a great angel food cake is that it requires a delicate balance of ingredients and proper cooking techniques. In particular, since this cake is leavened only with beaten egg whites, it is critical that you whip them correctly. Overbeaten egg whites produce a flatter cake.

First, we found it key to create a stable egg-white base, starting the whites at medium-low speed just to break them up into a froth and increasing the speed to medium-high speed to form soft, billowy mounds. Next, the sugar should be added, a tablespoon at a time. Once all the sugar is added, the whites become shiny and form soft peaks when the beater is lifted. A delicate touch is required when incorporating the remaining ingredients, such as the flour, which should be sifted over the batter and gently folded in. Angel food cakes are baked in a tube pan. We like to use a tube pan with a removable bottom but a pan without one can be lined with parchment paper. We avoid greasing the sides of the pan so that the cake can climb up and cling to the sides as it bakes—a greased pan will produce a disappointingly short cake. Follow our instructions and you'll be rewarded with the perfect tall, light yet firm angel food cake.

Angel Food Cake

SERVES 10 TO 12

If your tube pan has a removable bottom, you do not need to line it with parchment. Angel food cake can be served plain or dusted with confectioners' sugar.

- 1½ cups (10½ ounces) sugar
- ¾ cup (3 ounces) cake flour
- 12 large egg whites, at room temperature
- 1 teaspoon cream of tartar
- ¼ teaspoon table salt
- 1½ teaspoons juice from 1 lemon
- 1½ teaspoons vanilla extract
- ½ teaspoon almond extract

1. Adjust an oven rack to the lower-middle position and heat the oven to 325 degrees. Line the bottom of a 16-cup tube pan with parchment paper but do not grease. Whisk ¾ cup of the sugar and the flour together in a medium bowl.

2. In a stand mixer fitted with the whisk attachment, whip the egg whites and cream of tartar together on medium-low speed until foamy, about 1 minute. Increase the mixer speed to medium-high and whip the whites to soft, billowy mounds, about 1 minute. Gradually whip in the salt and remaining ¾ cup sugar, 1 tablespoon at a time, about 1 minute. Continue to whip the whites until they are shiny and form soft peaks, 1 to 3 minutes.

3. Whisk the lemon juice and extracts into the whipped whites by hand. Sift ¼ cup of the flour mixture over the top of the whites, then gently fold to combine with a large rubber spatula until just a few streaks of flour remain. Repeat with the remaining flour mixture, ¼ cup at a time.

4. Scrape the batter into the prepared pan and smooth the top. Wipe any drops of batter off the sides of the pan and lightly tap the pan against the countertop two or three times to settle the batter. Bake the cake until golden brown and the top springs back when pressed firmly, 50 to 60 minutes.

5. Invert the tube pan over a large metal kitchen funnel or the neck of a sturdy bottle (or, if your pan has "feet" that rise above the top edge of the pan, simply let the cake rest upside down). Cool the cake completely, upside down, 2 to 3 hours.

6. Run a small knife around the edge of the cake to loosen. Gently tap the pan upside down on the countertop to release the cake. Peel off the parchment paper, turn the cake right side up onto a serving platter, and serve.

CHOCOLATE BUNDT CAKE

WHY THIS RECIPE WORKS: A Bundt cake is the pinnacle of cake-baking simplicity. With its decorative shape, this cake doesn't require frosting or fussy finishing techniques. We wanted a cake that would deliver that moment of pure chocolate ecstasy with the first bite—a chocolate Bundt cake that tastes every bit as good as it looks, with a fine crumb, moist texture, and rich chocolate flavor.

We intensified the chocolate flavor by using both bittersweet chocolate and natural cocoa and dissolving them in boiling water, which "bloomed" their flavor. We used sour cream and brown sugar instead of white to add moisture and flavor. Finally, we further enhanced flavor with a little espresso powder and a generous amount of vanilla extract, both of which complemented the floral nuances of the chocolate.

Rich Chocolate Bundt Cake

SERVES 12

We prefer natural cocoa here because Dutch-processed cocoa will result in a compromised rise. For an accurate measurement of boiling water, bring a kettle of water to a boil, then measure out the desired amount. The cake can be served with just a dusting of confectioners' sugar but is easily made more impressive with lightly sweetened whipped cream and raspberries.

- **12** tablespoons (1½ sticks) unsalted butter, softened, plus 1 tablespoon, melted, for the pan
- **¾** cup natural cocoa powder, plus 1 tablespoon for the pan (see note)
- **6** ounces bittersweet chocolate, chopped coarse
- **1** teaspoon instant espresso powder (optional)
- **¾** cup boiling water (see note)
- **1** cup sour cream, at room temperature
- **1¾** cups (8¾ ounces) unbleached all-purpose flour
- **1** teaspoon table salt
- **1** teaspoon baking soda
- **2** cups packed (14 ounces) light brown sugar
- **1** tablespoon vanilla extract
- **5** large eggs, at room temperature
  Confectioners' sugar, for dusting (see note)

1. Stir together the 1 tablespoon melted butter and 1 tablespoon of the cocoa in a small bowl until a paste forms. Using a pastry brush, coat all the interior surfaces of a standard 12-cup Bundt pan. (If the mixture becomes too thick to brush on, microwave it for 10 to 20 seconds, or until warm and softened.) Adjust an oven rack to the lower-middle position and heat the oven to 350 degrees.

2. Combine the remaining ¾ cup cocoa, the chocolate, and espresso powder (if using) in a medium heatproof bowl. Pour the boiling water over and whisk until smooth. Cool to room temperature; then whisk in the sour cream. Whisk the flour, salt, and baking soda in a second bowl to combine.

3. In a stand mixer fitted with the paddle attachment, beat the remaining 12 tablespoons butter, the brown sugar, and vanilla on medium-high speed until pale and fluffy, about 3 minutes. Reduce the speed to medium and add the eggs one at a time, mixing for about 30 seconds after each addition and scraping down the bowl with a rubber spatula after the first two additions. Reduce to medium-low speed (the batter may appear separated); add about one-third of the flour mixture and half of the chocolate mixture and mix until just incorporated, about 20 seconds. Scrape the bowl and repeat using half of the remaining flour mixture and all of the remaining chocolate mixture; add the remaining flour mixture and beat until just incorporated, about 10 seconds. Scrape the bowl and mix on medium-low speed until the batter is thoroughly combined, about 30 seconds.

4. Transfer the batter to the prepared pan, smoothing the top with a rubber spatula. Lightly tap the pan against the countertop two or three times to settle the batter. Bake until a toothpick inserted into the center comes out with a few crumbs attached, 45 to 50 minutes, rotating the pan halfway through the baking time. Cool the cake in the pan on a wire rack for 10 minutes, then invert the cake directly onto the wire rack; cool to room temperature, about 2 hours. Dust with confectioners' sugar, transfer to a serving platter, cut into slices, and serve.

LEMON BUNDT CAKE

WHY THIS RECIPE WORKS: Lemons are tart, brash, and aromatic. Why, then, is it so hard to capture their assertive flavor in a straightforward Bundt cake? The flavor of lemon juice is drastically muted when exposed to the heat of an oven, and its acidity can wreak havoc on the delicate nature of baked goods. We wanted to develop a Bundt cake with potent lemon flavor without ruining its texture.

We developed a battery of tests challenging classic lemon Bundt cake ingredient proportions, finally deciding to increase the butter and to replace the milk with buttermilk. We also found that creaming was necessary to achieve a light and even crumb. But we still needed to maximize the lemon flavor; we couldn't get the flavor we needed from lemon juice alone without using so much that the cake fell apart when sliced. We turned to zest and found that three lemons' worth gave the cake a perfumed lemon flavor, though we needed to give the zest a brief soak in lemon juice to eliminate its fibrous texture. The final challenge was the glaze, and a simple mixture of lemon juice, buttermilk, and confectioners' sugar made the grade.

Lemon Bundt Cake

SERVES 12

The cake has a light, fluffy texture when eaten the day it is baked, but if well wrapped and held at room temperature overnight its texture becomes more dense—like that of pound cake—the following day.

CAKE

- 18 tablespoons (2¼ sticks) unsalted butter, at room temperature, plus 1 tablespoon, melted, for the pan
- 3 cups (15 ounces) unbleached all-purpose flour, plus 1 tablespoon for the pan
- 3 tablespoons grated zest plus 3 tablespoons juice from 3 lemons
- 1 teaspoon baking powder
- ½ teaspoon baking soda
- 1 teaspoon table salt
- ¾ cup buttermilk
- 1 teaspoon vanilla extract
- 3 large eggs plus 1 large egg yolk, at room temperature
- 2 cups (14 ounces) granulated sugar

GLAZE

- 2 cups (8 ounces) confectioners' sugar
- 2-3 tablespoons juice from 1 lemon
- 1 tablespoon buttermilk

1. FOR THE CAKE: Adjust an oven rack to the lower-middle position and heat the oven to 350 degrees. Stir together the 1 tablespoon melted butter and 1 tablespoon of the flour in a small bowl until a paste forms. Using a pastry brush, coat all the interior surfaces of a standard 12-cup Bundt pan. (If the mixture becomes too thick to brush on, microwave it for 10 to 20 seconds, or until warm and softened.) Mince the lemon zest to a fine paste (you should have about 2 tablespoons). Combine the zest and lemon juice in a small bowl; set aside to soften, 10 to 15 minutes.

2. Whisk the remaining 3 cups flour, the baking powder, baking soda, and salt in a large bowl. Combine the lemon juice mixture, buttermilk, and vanilla in a medium bowl. In a small bowl, gently whisk the whole eggs and yolk to combine. In a stand mixer fitted with the paddle attachment, beat the remaining 18 tablespoons butter and the granulated sugar at medium-high speed until pale and fluffy, about 3 minutes. Reduce to medium speed and add half of the eggs, mixing until incorporated, about 15 seconds; scrape down the bowl with a rubber spatula. Repeat with the remaining eggs; scrape down the bowl again. Reduce to low speed; add about one-third of the flour mixture, followed by half of the buttermilk mixture, mixing until just incorporated after each addition (about 5 seconds). Repeat using half of the remaining flour mixture and all of the remaining buttermilk mixture. Scrape down the bowl and add the remaining flour mixture; mix at medium-low speed until the batter is thoroughly combined, about 15 seconds. Transfer the batter to the prepared pan, smoothing the top with a rubber spatula. Lightly tap the pan against the countertop two or three times to settle the batter.

3. Bake until the top is golden brown and a toothpick inserted into the center comes out with no crumbs attached, 45 to 50 minutes, rotating the pan halfway through the baking time.

4. FOR THE GLAZE: While the cake is baking, whisk the confectioners' sugar, 2 tablespoons of the lemon juice, and the buttermilk until smooth, adding more lemon juice gradually as needed until the glaze is thick but still pourable. Cool the cake in the pan on a wire rack set over a baking sheet for 10 minutes, then invert the cake directly onto the rack. Pour half of the glaze over the warm cake and cool for 1 hour; pour the remaining glaze evenly over the top of the cake and continue to cool to room temperature, at least 2 hours. Cut into slices and serve.

LEMON POUND CAKE

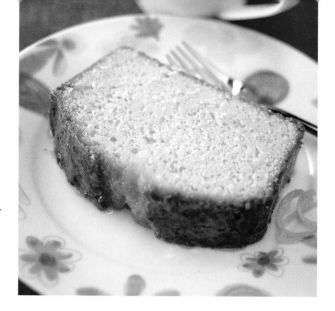

WHY THIS RECIPE WORKS: Pound cakes often turn out spongy, rubbery, heavy, and dry—and lemon pound cakes often lack true lemon flavor. We wanted to produce a superior pound cake (fine-crumbed, rich, moist, and buttery) while making the process as simple and foolproof as possible.

After less-than-successful results with a stand mixer and a hand mixer, we turned to the food processor to mix our cake. It ensured a perfect emulsification of the eggs, sugar, and melted butter (we found that a blender worked, too). Cake flour produced a tender crumb, but our cake was still a bit heavy. We fixed matters with the addition of baking powder, which increased lift and produced a consistent, fine crumb. Finally, in addition to mixing lemon zest into the cake batter, we glazed the finished cake with lemon sugar syrup—but first we poked holes all over the cake to ensure that the tangy, sweet glaze infused the cake with a blast of bright lemon flavor.

Lemon Pound Cake

MAKES ONE 8-INCH LOAF, SERVING 8

You can use a blender instead of a food processor to mix the batter. To add the butter, remove the center cap of the lid so it can be drizzled into the whirling blender with minimal splattering. This batter looks almost like a thick pancake batter and is very fluid.

CAKE

- **16** tablespoons (2 sticks) unsalted butter, plus 1 tablespoon, softened, for the pan
- **1½** cups (6 ounces) cake flour, plus 1 tablespoon for the pan
- **1** teaspoon baking powder
- **½** teaspoon table salt
- **1¼** cups (8¾ ounces) sugar
- **2** tablespoons grated zest plus 2 teaspoons juice from 1 lemon
- **4** large eggs, at room temperature
- **1½** teaspoons vanilla extract

GLAZE

- **½** cup (3½ ounces) sugar
- **¼** cup juice from 2 lemons

1. FOR THE CAKE: Adjust an oven rack to the middle position and heat the oven to 350 degrees. Grease an 8½ by 4½-inch loaf pan with 1 tablespoon of the softened butter; dust with 1 tablespoon of the flour, tapping out the excess. In a medium bowl, whisk together the remaining 1½ cups flour, the baking powder, and salt; set aside.

2. Melt the remaining 16 tablespoons butter in a small saucepan over medium heat. Whisk the melted butter thoroughly to reincorporate any separated milk solids.

3. In a food processor, pulse the sugar and zest until combined, about 5 pulses. Add the lemon juice, eggs, and vanilla; process until combined, about 5 seconds. With the machine running, add the melted butter through the feed tube in a steady stream (this should take about 20 seconds). Transfer the mixture to a large bowl. Sift the flour mixture over the egg mixture in three additions, whisking gently after each addition until just combined.

4. Pour the batter into the prepared pan and bake for 15 minutes. Reduce the oven temperature to 325 degrees and continue to bake until deep golden brown and a toothpick inserted in the center comes out clean, about 35 minutes, rotating the pan halfway through the baking time. Cool in the pan for 10 minutes, then turn onto a wire rack. Poke the top and sides of the cake throughout with a toothpick. Cool to room temperature, at least 1 hour. (The cooled cake can be wrapped tightly in plastic wrap and stored at room temperature for up to 5 days.)

5. FOR THE GLAZE: While the cake is cooling, bring the sugar and lemon juice to a boil in a small saucepan, stirring occasionally to dissolve the sugar. Reduce the heat to low and simmer until thickened slightly, about 2 minutes. Brush the top and sides of the cake with the glaze and cool to room temperature.

APPLESAUCE CAKE

WHY THIS RECIPE WORKS: Applesauce cakes run the gamut from dense, chunky fruitcakes to gummy "health" cakes without much flavor. We wanted a moist and tender cake that actually tasted like its namesake.

It was easy to achieve the looser, more casual crumb that is best suited to a rustic snack cake. Since this texture is similar to that of quick breads and muffins, we used the same technique, i.e., mixing the wet ingredients separately and then gently adding the dry ingredients by hand. The harder challenge was to develop more apple flavor—simply adding more applesauce made for a gummy cake and fresh apples added too much moisture. But two other sources worked well. Apple cider, reduced to a syrup, contributed a pleasing sweetness and a slight tang without excess moisture. And plumping dried apples in the cider while it was reducing added even more apple taste without making the cake chunky. With such great apple flavor, we didn't want the cake to be too sweet or rich, so we rejected the idea of topping the cake with a glaze or frosting. But we found we liked the modicum of textural contrast provided by a simple sprinkling of spiced granulated sugar.

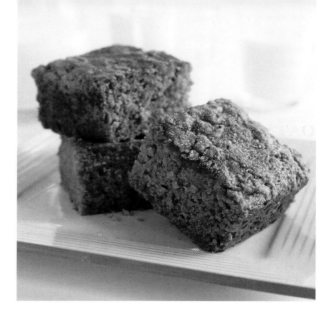

Applesauce Snack Cake

SERVES 9

This recipe can be easily doubled and baked in a 13 by 9-inch baking dish. If doubling the recipe, give the cider and dried apple mixture about 20 minutes to reduce, and bake the cake for about 45 minutes. The cake is very moist, so it is best to err on the side of overdone when testing its doneness. The test kitchen prefers the rich flavor of cider, but apple juice can be substituted.

- 1 cup apple cider (see note)
- ¾ cup (2 ounces) dried apples, cut into ½-inch pieces
- 1½ cups (7½ ounces) unbleached all-purpose flour
- 1 teaspoon baking soda
- ⅔ cup (4⅔ ounces) sugar
- ½ teaspoon ground cinnamon
- ¼ teaspoon ground nutmeg
- ⅛ teaspoon ground cloves
- 1 cup unsweetened applesauce, at room temperature
- 1 large egg, at room temperature, lightly beaten
- ½ teaspoon table salt
- 8 tablespoons (1 stick) unsalted butter, melted and cooled slightly
- 1 teaspoon vanilla extract

1. Adjust an oven rack to the middle position and heat the oven to 325 degrees. Cut a 16-inch length of parchment paper or foil and fold lengthwise to a 7-inch width. Grease an 8-inch square baking dish and fit the parchment into the dish, pushing it into the corners and up the sides; allow the excess to overhang the edges of the dish.

2. Bring the cider and dried apples to a simmer in a small saucepan over medium heat; cook until the liquid evaporates and the mixture appears dry, about 15 minutes. Cool to room temperature.

3. Whisk the flour and baking soda in a medium bowl to combine; set aside. In a second medium bowl, whisk the sugar, cinnamon, nutmeg, and cloves together. Measure 2 tablespoons of the sugar-spice mixture into a small bowl and set aside for the topping.

4. In a food processor, process the cooled dried-apple mixture and applesauce until smooth, 20 to 30 seconds, scraping down the sides of the bowl as needed; set aside. Whisk the egg and salt in a large bowl to combine. Add the sugar-spice mixture and whisk continuously until well combined and light colored, about 20 seconds. Add the butter in three additions, whisking after each addition. Add the applesauce mixture and vanilla and whisk to combine. Add the flour mixture to the wet ingredients; using a rubber spatula, fold gently until just combined and evenly moistened.

5. Transfer the batter to the prepared pan, smoothing the top with a rubber spatula. Lightly tap the pan against the countertop two or three times to settle the batter. Sprinkle the reserved 2 tablespoons sugar-spice mixture evenly over the batter. Bake until a toothpick inserted into the center comes out clean, 35 to 40 minutes, rotating the pan halfway through the baking time. Cool the cake to room temperature in the pan on a wire rack, about 2 hours. Remove the cake from the pan by lifting the parchment overhang and transfer to a cutting board. Cut the cake into squares and serve.

OATMEAL CAKE

WHY THIS RECIPE WORKS: While we love the broiled icing on this classic snack cake, we find that the cake itself is often dense, gummy, and bland. And the icing isn't always perfect, either; it can be saccharine sweet and tend toward greasiness. We wanted a moist, not dense, cake with buttery undertones topped by a broiled icing that features chewy coconut, crunchy nuts, and a butterscotch-like flavor.

We solved the problem of denseness by replacing some of the brown sugar with granulated sugar—less moist than brown sugar, granulated sugar lightened the cake's texture. We also reduced the proportion of flour to oats, using the minimum amount of flour needed to keep the cake from collapsing into crumbs. The cake was now sufficiently light, and its more moderate sweetness made it better suited to a sugary icing. We still had to tackle the gumminess, however, which was created partly by soaking the oats in water; the hydrated oats were a sticky mess when we stirred them into the batter. But simply folding in dried oats didn't work—they never fully hydrated during baking, and tasted raw and chewy in the finished cake. The answer proved to be soaking the oats in room-temperature rather than boiling water, minimizing the amount of released starch. As for the type of oats, quick-cooking worked best. Unlike the cake, the icing only required a few tweaks. Cutting back on the sugar

brought the sweetness in line, using melted butter (rather than creaming the butter into the sugar) simplified the recipe, and adding a splash of milk made the icing more pliable. Keeping the cake about 9 inches from the heating element produced the "crun-chewy" texture we wanted.

Oatmeal Cake with Broiled Icing
SERVES 9

Do not use old-fashioned or instant oats for this recipe. Be sure to use a metal baking dish; glass pans are not recommended when broiling. If you have a drawer-style broiler (underneath the oven), position the rack as far as possible from the broiler element and monitor the icing carefully as it cooks in step 5. A vertical sawing motion with a serrated knife works best for cutting through the crunchy icing and tender crumb.

CAKE
- 1 cup (3 ounces) quick-cooking oats (see note)
- ¾ cup water, at room temperature
- ¾ cup (3¾ ounces) unbleached all-purpose flour
- ½ teaspoon baking soda
- ½ teaspoon baking powder
- ½ teaspoon table salt
- ¼ teaspoon ground cinnamon
- ⅛ teaspoon ground nutmeg
- 4 tablespoons (½ stick) unsalted butter, softened
- ½ cup (3½ ounces) granulated sugar
- ½ cup packed (3½ ounces) light brown sugar
- 1 large egg, at room temperature
- ½ teaspoon vanilla extract

BROILED ICING
- ¼ cup packed (1¾ ounces) light brown sugar
- 3 tablespoons unsalted butter, melted and cooled
- 3 tablespoons milk
- ¾ cup sweetened shredded coconut
- ½ cup (2½ ounces) pecans, chopped

1. FOR THE CAKE: Adjust an oven rack to the middle position and heat the oven to 350 degrees. Cut two 16-inch lengths of aluminum foil and fold both lengthwise to 5-inch widths. Grease an 8-inch square metal baking dish. Fit the foil pieces into the baking dish, one overlapping the other, pushing them into the corners and up the sides of the pan; allow the excess to overhang the pan edges. Spray the foil lightly with vegetable oil spray.

2. Combine the oats and water in a medium bowl and let sit until the water is absorbed, about 5 minutes. In a second medium bowl, whisk the flour, baking soda, baking powder, salt, cinnamon, and nutmeg together.

3. In the bowl of a stand mixer fitted with the paddle attachment, beat the butter and sugars on medium speed until combined and the mixture has the consistency of damp sand, 2 to 4 minutes, scraping down the bowl with a rubber spatula halfway through mixing. Add the egg and vanilla; beat until combined, about 30 seconds. Add the flour mixture in two additions and mix until just incorporated, about 30 seconds. Add the soaked oats and mix until combined, about 15 seconds.

4. Give the batter a final stir with a rubber spatula to make sure it is thoroughly combined. Transfer the batter to the prepared pan and lightly tap it against the countertop two or three times to settle the batter; smooth the surface with the spatula. Bake the cake until a toothpick inserted into the center comes out with a few crumbs attached, 30 to 35 minutes, rotating the pan halfway through the baking time. Cool the cake slightly in the pan, at least 10 minutes.

5. FOR THE BROILED ICING: While the cake cools, adjust an oven rack about 9 inches from the broiler element and heat the broiler. In a medium bowl, whisk the brown sugar, melted butter, and milk together; stir in the coconut and pecans. Spread the mixture evenly over the warm cake. Broil until the topping is bubbling and golden, 3 to 5 minutes.

6. Cool the cake in the pan for 1 hour. To remove the cake from the pan, pick up the overhanging edges of the foil and transfer the cake to a platter. Gently push the side of the cake with a knife and remove the foil, one piece at a time. Cut the cake into squares and serve.

APPLE UPSIDE-DOWN CAKE

WHY THIS RECIPE WORKS: Ever since canned pineapple was introduced into this country in the early 1900s, pineapple has been synonymous with upside-down cake. But at one time, upside-down cakes were made with seasonal fruit, such as apples. We loved the idea of resurrecting apple upside-down cake. We wanted a rich buttery cake topped with tightly packed, burnished, sweet apples.

We started our testing with choosing the type of apple. Most apples turned mushy and watery and were simply too sweet, but crisp, tart Granny Smiths made the cut. Following the lead of recipes found in our research, we shingled the apples in the pan and poured the cake batter over the top. But once baked and inverted, our apple layer was shrunken and dry. The solution turned out to be increasing the number of apples, for a hefty layer of fruit.

This effort yielded better results, but we found the apples to be overcooked, so we turned to a method uncovered in our recipe for Deep-Dish Apple Pie (page 686)—we precooked half the apples by sautéing them on the stovetop, then we cut the remainder thin, so they baked through evenly. For the butter cake, we tested milk, buttermilk, yogurt, and sour cream. Sour cream won hands down—its subtle tang balanced the sweetness of the cake and complemented the caramelized apples. And another addition—cornmeal—gave the cake a hint of earthy flavor and a pleasantly coarse texture. Our final discovery came when we attempted to release the cake cleanly from the pan. Typical recipes instruct a 5 to 10-minute cooling period, but we found that a full 20 minutes was required to allow the apple filling to set. And turning the cake out onto a rack to finish cooling let the bottom of the cake breathe, preventing sogginess, which is typical of so many upside-down cakes.

Apple Upside-Down Cake
SERVES 8

We like the slight coarseness that cornmeal adds to the cake, but it's fine to omit it. Golden Delicious apples can be substituted for the Granny Smiths. You will need a 9-inch nonstick cake pan with sides that are at least 2 inches high; anything shallower and the cake will overflow. Alternatively, a 10-inch ovensafe stainless steel skillet (don't use cast iron) can be used to both cook the apples and bake the cake, with the following modifications: Cook the apples in the skillet and set them aside while mixing the batter (it's OK if the skillet is still warm when the batter is added) and increase the baking time by 7 to 9 minutes. If you don't have either a 2-inch-high cake pan or an ovensafe skillet, use an 8-inch square pan.

TOPPING

- 4 **tablespoons (½ stick) unsalted butter, cut into 4 pieces, plus extra for the pan**
- 4 **Granny Smith apples (about 2 pounds), peeled and cored (see note)**
- ⅔ **cup packed (4⅔ ounces) light brown sugar**
- 2 **teaspoons juice from 1 lemon**

CAKE

- 1 **cup (5 ounces) unbleached all-purpose flour**
- 1 **tablespoon cornmeal (optional; see note)**
- 1 **teaspoon baking powder**
- ½ **teaspoon table salt**
- ¾ **cup (5¼ ounces) granulated sugar**
- ¼ **cup packed (1¾ ounces) light brown sugar**
- 2 **large eggs, at room temperature**
- 6 **tablespoons (¾ stick) unsalted butter, melted and cooled slightly**
- ½ **cup sour cream**
- 1 **teaspoon vanilla extract**

1. FOR THE TOPPING: Butter the bottom and sides of a nonstick 9-inch-wide by 2-inch-high round cake pan; set aside. Adjust an oven rack to the lowest position and heat the oven to 350 degrees.

2. Halve the apples from pole to pole. Cut 2 apples into ¼-inch-thick slices; set aside. Cut the remaining 2 apples into ½-inch-thick slices. Melt the butter in a 12-inch skillet over medium-high heat. Add the ½-inch-thick apple slices and cook, stirring two or three times, until the apples begin to caramelize, 4 to 6 minutes. (Do not fully cook the apples.) Add the ¼-inch-thick apple slices, brown sugar, and lemon juice; continue cooking, stirring constantly, until the sugar dissolves and the apples are coated, about 1 minute longer. Transfer the apple mixture to the prepared pan and lightly press into an even layer. Set aside while preparing the cake.

3. FOR THE CAKE: Whisk the flour, cornmeal (if using), baking powder, and salt together in a medium bowl; set aside. Whisk the sugars and eggs together in a large bowl until thick and homogeneous, about 45 seconds. Slowly whisk in the butter until combined. Add the sour cream and vanilla; whisk until combined. Add the flour mixture and whisk until just combined. Pour the batter into the pan and spread evenly over the fruit. Lightly tap the pan against the countertop two or three times to settle the batter. Bake until the cake is golden brown and a toothpick inserted into the center comes out clean, 35 to 40 minutes, rotating the pan halfway through the baking time.

4. Cool the pan on a wire rack for 20 minutes. Run a small knife around the sides of the cake to loosen. Place a wire rack over the cake pan. Holding the rack tightly, invert the cake pan and wire rack together; lift off the cake pan. Place the wire rack over a baking sheet or large plate to catch any drips. If any fruit sticks to the pan bottom, remove and position it on top of the cake. Cool the cake for 20 minutes (or longer to cool it completely), then transfer it to a serving platter, cut into pieces, and serve.

Apple Upside-Down Cake with Almond

Follow the recipe for Apple Upside-Down Cake, combining ⅓ cup finely ground toasted almonds with the flour and adding 1 teaspoon almond extract with the sour cream and vanilla in step 3.

Apple Upside-Down Cake with Lemon and Thyme

Follow the recipe for Apple Upside-Down Cake, adding 1 teaspoon finely grated lemon zest and 1 teaspoon finely chopped fresh thyme leaves with the sour cream and vanilla in step 3.

CARROT CAKE

WHY THIS RECIPE WORKS: A relic of the health food craze, carrot cake was once heralded for its use of vegetable oil in place of butter and carrots as a natural sweetener. Sure, the carrots add some sweetness, but they also add a lot of moisture, which is why carrot cake is invariably soggy. And oil? It makes this cake dense and, well, oily. We didn't want a greasy cake. We wanted a moist, rich cake with a tight and tender crumb and balanced spice.

We started with all-purpose flour—cake flour proved too delicate to support the grated carrots that get mixed in. For lift, we liked a combination of baking soda and baking powder. Some carrot cakes use a heavy hand with the spices and taste too much like spice cake. We took a conservative approach and used modest amounts of cinnamon, nutmeg, and cloves. After trying varying amounts of grated carrots, we settled on 3 cups for a pleasantly moist texture. One and one-half cups of vegetable oil gave us a rich, but not greasy, cake. Cream cheese frosting is the perfect partner to carrot cake—we enriched our version with sour cream for extra tang and vanilla for depth of flavor.

Carrot Cake

SERVES 15 TO 18

You can serve the cake right out of the pan, in which case you'll only need 3 cups of frosting for the top of the cake.

- 2½ cups (12½ ounces) unbleached all-purpose flour
- 1¼ teaspoons ground cinnamon
- 1¼ teaspoons baking powder
- 1 teaspoon baking soda
- ½ teaspoon table salt
- ½ teaspoon ground nutmeg
- ⅛ teaspoon ground cloves
- 4 large eggs, at room temperature
- 1½ cups (10½ ounces) granulated sugar
- ½ cup packed (3½ ounces) light brown sugar
- 1½ cups vegetable oil
- 1 pound carrots (about 6 medium), peeled and grated (about 3 cups)
- 4 cups Cream Cheese Frosting (recipe follows; see note)

1. Adjust an oven rack to the middle position and heat the oven to 350 degrees. Grease a 13 by 9-inch baking pan, then line the bottom with parchment paper. Whisk the flour, cinnamon, baking powder, baking soda, salt, nutmeg, and cloves together in a medium bowl.

2. In a large bowl, whisk the eggs and sugars together until the sugars are mostly dissolved and the mixture is frothy. Continue to whisk, while slowly drizzling in the oil, until thoroughly combined and emulsified. Whisk in the flour mixture until just incorporated. Stir in the carrots.

3. Give the batter a final stir with a rubber spatula to make sure it is thoroughly combined. Scrape the batter into the prepared pan, smooth the top, and lightly tap the pan against the countertop two or three times to settle the batter. Bake the cake until a toothpick inserted in the center comes out with a few moist crumbs attached, 35 to 40 minutes, rotating the pan halfway through the baking time.

4. Cool the cake completely in the pan, set on a wire rack, about 2 hours. Run a small knife around the edge of the cake and flip the cake out onto a wire rack. Peel off the parchment paper, then flip the cake right side up onto a serving platter. Spread the frosting evenly over the top and sides of the cake and serve.

Cream Cheese Frosting

MAKES ABOUT 4 CUPS

If the frosting becomes too soft to work with, let it chill in the refrigerator until firm.

- 2 (8-ounce) packages cream cheese, softened
- 10 tablespoons (1¼ sticks) unsalted butter, cut into chunks and softened
- 2 tablespoons sour cream
- 1½ teaspoons vanilla extract
- ¼ teaspoon table salt
- 2 cups (8 ounces) confectioners' sugar

1. Beat the cream cheese, butter, sour cream, vanilla, and salt together in a large bowl with an electric mixer on medium-high speed until smooth, 2 to 4 minutes.

2. Reduce the mixer speed to medium-low, slowly add the confectioners' sugar, and beat until smooth, 4 to 6 minutes. Increase the mixer speed to medium-high and beat until the frosting is light and fluffy, 4 to 6 minutes.

LIGHT CARROT CAKE

WHY THIS RECIPE WORKS: Although carrot cake sounds healthy, most versions tip the scales at 500 calories and 31 grams of fat per slice. We wanted to create a moist and rich carrot cake and we wanted the cake to be lighter in both calories and fat.

We made four significant changes to satisfy our goal of a tasty dessert we could enjoy more than once in a while. We reduced the amount of oil from 1½ cups to ½ cup and also reduced the number of eggs from four to three. We whipped air into the eggs to keep the cake from being dense and leaden. And, finally, we replaced the cream cheese and butter in the frosting with Neufchâtel reduced-fat cream cheese and mixed it by hand to prevent it from being runny. In the end, we reduced the calories to 350 and the fat grams to 13 and still had a cake that was tender, moist, and flavorful.

Light Carrot Cake

SERVES 16

You can use either the large holes of a box grater or the large-holed shredding disk in a food processor for grating the carrots. Use a metal cake pan, not a glass or Pyrex pan, for best results. This cake is terrific with our Light Cream Cheese Frosting (recipe follows) or a simple dusting of confectioners' sugar.

2½	cups (12½ ounces) unbleached all-purpose flour
1¼	teaspoons baking powder
1	teaspoon baking soda
1¼	teaspoons ground cinnamon
½	teaspoon ground nutmeg
½	teaspoon table salt
⅛	teaspoon ground cloves
3	large eggs, at room temperature
1	cup packed (7 ounces) light brown sugar
1	cup (7 ounces) granulated sugar
½	cup vegetable oil
1	pound carrots (about 6 medium), peeled and grated (about 3 cups; see note)

1. Adjust an oven rack to the middle position and heat the oven to 350 degrees. Grease a 13 by 9-inch cake pan, then line the bottom with parchment paper. Whisk the flour, baking powder, baking soda, cinnamon, nutmeg, salt, and cloves together in a medium bowl.

2. Beat the eggs, brown sugar, and granulated sugar together in a large bowl with an electric mixer on medium speed until the mixture turns thick and creamy, 1 to 3 minutes. Reduce the mixer speed to low and slowly beat in the oil until thoroughly combined and emulsified, 30 to 60 seconds.

3. Sift half the flour mixture over the batter and gently whisk in by hand. Repeat with the remaining flour mixture and continue to whisk the batter gently until most of the lumps are gone (do not overmix). Using a rubber spatula, gently stir in the carrots.

4. Pour the batter into the prepared pan and smooth the top. Bake until a wooden skewer inserted into the center of the cake comes out with a few moist crumbs attached, 35 to 40 minutes, rotating the pan halfway through the baking time.

5. Cool the cake completely in the pan, about 2 hours. Run a paring knife around the edge of the cake and flip the cake out onto a wire rack. Peel off the parchment paper, then flip the cake right side up onto a serving platter. If desired, spread the frosting (see note) evenly over the top and sides of the cake and serve.

Light Cream Cheese Frosting

MAKES ABOUT 2 CUPS

12	ounces Neufchâtel (⅓ less fat) cream cheese, softened
1	teaspoon vanilla extract
1½	cups (6 ounces) confectioners' sugar

Mix the cream cheese and vanilla together in a large bowl with a rubber spatula. Add the confectioners' sugar and stir until thoroughly combined and smooth.

NOTES FROM THE TEST KITCHEN

TESTING FOR DONENESS

As a rule of thumb, we pull our cakes out of the oven when there are just a few crumbs still clinging to the skewer (wooden skewers work best). The residual heat will continue to bake the cake to perfection.

SPICE CAKE

WHY THIS RECIPE WORKS: The problem with spice cakes? Spice. Some variations suffer from spice overload, which makes them gritty and dusty. Others are so lacking in spice flavor that it seems as if a cinnamon stick has only been waved in their general direction. We wanted an old-fashioned, moist, and substantial spice cake with spices that were warm and bold without being overpowering, and a rich, but complementary, cream cheese frosting.

We needed a less-than-tender cake, one with a substantial and open crumb that could stand up to the spices. We found that all-purpose flour, rather than cake flour, added volume and heft. Butter and eggs added richness. Simply adding more spices didn't lead to increased spiciness; the spices simply smelled stronger than they tasted. Therefore, we needed to bloom the spices in butter, a process that intensified their aromas and gave the cake a heightened spice impact throughout. We used the classic mixture of cinnamon, cloves, cardamom, allspice, and nutmeg, but found that a tablespoon of grated fresh ginger and a couple of tablespoons of molasses gave the cake an extra zing. And reserving a little of the spice mixture to add to the cream cheese frosting united the frosting and the cake.

Spice Cake

SERVES 15 TO 18

Using fresh ginger instead of dried ground ginger gives this cake a brighter flavor. You can serve the cake right out of the pan, in which case you'll only need 3 cups of frosting for the top of the cake.

- 1 tablespoon ground cinnamon
- ¾ teaspoon ground cardamom
- ½ teaspoon ground allspice
- ½ teaspoon ground cloves
- ¼ teaspoon ground nutmeg
- 16 tablespoons (2 sticks) unsalted butter, cut into 16 pieces and softened
- 2¼ cups (11¼ ounces) all-purpose flour
- ½ teaspoon baking powder
- ½ teaspoon baking soda
- ½ teaspoon table salt
- 2 large whole eggs plus 3 large egg yolks, at room temperature
- 1 teaspoon vanilla extract
- 1¾ cups (12¼ ounces) sugar
- 2 tablespoons light or mild molasses
- 1 tablespoon minced or grated fresh ginger (see note)
- 1 cup buttermilk, room temperature
- 4 cups Cream Cheese Frosting (page 602; see note)

1. Adjust an oven rack to the middle position and heat the oven to 350 degrees. Grease a 13 by 9-inch baking pan, then line the bottom with parchment paper.

2. Combine the cinnamon, cardamom, allspice, cloves, and nutmeg in a small bowl; reserve ½ teaspoon of the spice mixture for the frosting. Melt 4 tablespoons of the butter in a small skillet over medium heat and continue to cook, swirling the pan constantly, until the butter is light brown, 3 to 6 minutes. Stir in the spice mixture and cook until fragrant, about 15 seconds. Set the mixture aside to cool slightly.

3. In a medium bowl, whisk the flour, baking powder, baking soda, and salt together. In a small bowl, whisk the whole eggs, egg yolks, and vanilla together.

4. In a stand mixer fitted with the paddle attachment, beat the remaining 12 tablespoons butter, the sugar, and molasses on medium-high speed until light and fluffy, 3 to 6 minutes; scrape down the bowl with a rubber spatula. Beat in the ginger, cooled butter-spice mixture, and half of the egg mixture until combined, about 30 seconds. Beat in the remaining egg mixture until combined, about 30 seconds, and scrape down the bowl again.

5. Reduce the mixer speed to low and beat in one-third of the flour mixture, followed by half of the buttermilk. Repeat with half of the remaining flour mixture and the remaining buttermilk. Beat in the remaining flour mixture until just combined; scrape down the bowl.

6. Give the batter a final stir with a rubber spatula to make sure it is thoroughly combined. Scrape the batter into the prepared pan, smooth the top, and lightly tap the pan against the countertop two or three times to settle the batter. Bake the cake until a toothpick inserted in the center comes out with a few moist crumbs attached, 30 to 35 minutes, rotating the pan halfway through the baking time.

7. Cool the cake completely in the pan, set on a wire rack, about 2 hours. Run a small knife around the edge of the cake and flip the cake out onto a wire rack. Peel off the parchment paper, then flip the cake right side up onto a serving platter. Stir the reserved spice mixture into the frosting, spread the frosting evenly over the top and sides of the cake, and serve.

STRAWBERRY CREAM CAKE

WHY THIS RECIPE WORKS: What could possibly ruin the heavenly trio of cake, cream, and ripe strawberries? How about soggy cake, bland berries, and squishy cream? We wanted a sturdy cake, a firm filling, and strawberry flavor fit for a starring role—a cake that would serve a formal occasion better than a simple strawberry shortcake.

To start, we had to solve three crucial problems. First, we realized that tender butter cakes couldn't support a substantial strawberry filling, so we developed a chiffon-style cake that combined the rich flavor of a butter cake with the light-yet-sturdy texture of a sponge cake. Second, we made a flavorful berry "mash" with half of the berries and then reduced the macerated juice in a sauce-pan (with a little kirsch) to help concentrate and round out the flavor. We sliced the rest of the berries and placed them around the edges of the cake for visual appeal. Another problem arose when the cake was sliced: The filling squirted out and the layers fell apart. To correct the problem, we reduced the number of layers from four to three and fortified the whipped-cream filling with cream cheese. This filling stayed put and didn't mar the glorious layers of this spectacular summertime cake.

Strawberry Cream Cake

SERVES 8 TO 10

You will need a cake pan with straight sides that are at least 2 inches high.

CAKE

- 1¼ cups (5 ounces) cake flour, plus extra for the pan
- 1½ teaspoons baking powder
- ¼ teaspoon table salt
- 1 cup (7 ounces) sugar
- 5 large eggs (2 whole and 3 separated), at room temperature
- 6 tablespoons (¾ stick) unsalted butter, melted and cooled slightly
- 2 tablespoons water
- 2 teaspoons vanilla extract

STRAWBERRY FILLING

- 2 pounds fresh strawberries (medium or large, about 2 quarts), washed, dried, and stemmed
- 4-6 tablespoons sugar
- 2 tablespoons kirsch
- Pinch table salt

WHIPPED CREAM

- 8 ounces cream cheese, at room temperature
- ½ cup (3½ ounces) sugar
- 1 teaspoon vanilla extract
- ⅛ teaspoon table salt
- 2 cups heavy cream

1. FOR THE CAKE: Adjust an oven rack to the lower-middle position and heat the oven to 325 degrees. Grease and flour a 9-inch-wide by 2-inch-high round cake pan or 9-inch springform pan and line it with parchment paper. Whisk the flour, baking powder, salt, and all but 3 table-spoons of the sugar in a mixing bowl. Whisk in 2 whole eggs and 3 yolks (reserving the whites), the butter, water, and vanilla; whisk until smooth.

2. In the clean bowl of a stand mixer fitted with the whisk attachment, beat the remaining 3 egg whites at medium-low speed until frothy, 1 to 2 minutes. With the machine running, gradually add the remaining 3 table-spoons sugar, increase the speed to medium-high, and beat until soft peaks form, 60 to 90 seconds. Stir one-third of the whites into the batter to lighten; add the remaining whites and gently fold into the batter until no white streaks remain. Transfer the batter to the prepared pan,

BUILDING A STRAWBERRY CREAM CAKE

1. With a serrated knife, use a sawing motion to cut the cake into three layers, rotating the cake as you go.

2. Place sliced berries evenly around the edges (they will be visible once the layers are assembled).

3. Cover the center of the cake completely with half of the pureed strawberries.

4. Spread one-third of the whipped cream over the berries, leaving a ½-inch border. Repeat the layering.

5. Press the last layer into place, spread with the remaining cream, and decorate with the remaining berries.

smoothing the top with a rubber spatula. Lightly tap the pan against the countertop two or three times to settle the batter. Bake until a toothpick inserted into the center comes out clean, 30 to 40 minutes, rotating the pan halfway through the baking time. Cool the cake in the pan on a wire rack for 10 minutes, then invert onto the wire rack and peel off the parchment. Invert the cake again and cool completely on the rack, about 2 hours.

3. FOR THE STRAWBERRY FILLING: Halve 24 of the best-looking berries and reserve. Quarter the remaining berries; toss with 4 to 6 tablespoons sugar (depending on the sweetness of the berries) in a medium bowl and let sit for 1 hour, stirring occasionally. Strain the juices from the berries and reserve (you should have about ½ cup). In a food processor, give the macerated berries 5 pulses (you should have about 1½ cups). In a small saucepan over medium-high heat, simmer the reserved juices and the kirsch until syrupy and reduced to about 3 tablespoons, 3 to 5 minutes. Pour the reduced syrup over the processed, macerated berries, add the salt, and toss to combine. Set aside until the cake has cooled.

4. FOR THE WHIPPED CREAM: When the cake has cooled, place the cream cheese, sugar, vanilla, and salt in the clean bowl of a stand mixer fitted with the whisk attachment. Whisk at medium-high speed until light and fluffy, 1 to 2 minutes, scraping down the bowl with a rubber spatula as needed. Reduce the speed to low and add the heavy cream in a slow, steady stream; when almost fully combined, increase the speed to medium-high and beat until the mixture holds stiff peaks, 2 to 2½ minutes more, scraping down the bowl as needed (you should have about 4½ cups).

5. TO ASSEMBLE THE CAKE: Line the edges of a cake platter with strips of parchment paper to keep the platter clean. Following the photos, use a serrated knife to cut the cake horizontally into three even layers. Place the bottom layer on the platter and arrange a ring of 20 strawberry halves, cut sides down and stem ends facing out, around the perimeter of the cake layer. Pour one-half of the pureed berry mixture (about ¾ cup) in the center, then spread to cover any exposed cake. Gently spread about one-third of the whipped cream (about 1½ cups) over the berry layer, leaving a ½-inch border from the edge. Place the middle cake layer on top and press down gently (the whipped cream layer should become flush with the cake edge). Repeat with 20 additional strawberry halves, the remaining berry mixture, and half of the remaining whipped cream; gently press the last cake layer on top. Spread the remaining whipped cream over the top; decorate with the remaining cut strawberries. Remove the parchment strips from the platter and serve.

SUMMER PEACH CAKE

WHY THIS RECIPE WORKS: Marrying cake with fresh summer peaches, this dessert is a bakery favorite, yet most versions are plagued by soggy cake and barely noticeable peach flavor. We wanted a buttery cake that was moist and not at all soggy, with a golden-brown exterior and plenty of peach flavor. Roasting chunks of peaches tossed in sugar and a little lemon juice helped concentrate their flavor and expel excess moisture before we combined them with our cake batter. However, during roasting, the peach chunks became swathed in a flavorful but unpleasantly gooey film. Coating our roasted peaches in panko bread crumbs before combining them with the batter ensured the film was absorbed by the crumbs, which then dissolved into the cake during baking. To amplify the peach flavor, we tossed the fruit with peach schnapps before roasting, and a little almond extract added to the batter lent a subtle complementary note. Fanning peach slices (macerated with a little more of the schnapps) over the top, sprinkled with almond extract–flavored sugar for a light glaze, ensured our cake looked as good as it tasted.

Summer Peach Cake

SERVES 8

To crush the panko bread crumbs, place them in a zipper-lock bag and smash them with a rolling pin. If you can't find panko, ¼ cup of plain, unseasoned bread crumbs can be substituted. Orange liqueur can be substituted for the peach schnapps. If using peak-of-season, farm-fresh peaches, omit the peach schnapps.

2½ **pounds peaches, halved, pitted, and cut into ½-inch wedges**

5 **tablespoons peach schnapps (see note)**

4 **teaspoons juice from 1 lemon**

6 **tablespoons plus ⅓ cup (5 ounces) granulated sugar**

1 **cup (5 ounces) unbleached all-purpose flour**

1¼ **teaspoons baking powder**

¾ **teaspoon table salt**

½ **cup packed (3½ ounces) light brown sugar**

2 **large eggs, at room temperature**

8 **tablespoons (1 stick) unsalted butter, melted and cooled**

¼ **cup sour cream**

1½ **teaspoons vanilla extract**

¼ **teaspoon plus ⅛ teaspoon almond extract**

⅓ **cup panko bread crumbs, crushed fine (see note)**

1. Adjust an oven rack to the middle position and heat the oven to 425 degrees. Line a rimmed baking sheet with aluminum foil and spray with vegetable oil spray. Grease and flour a 9-inch springform pan. Gently toss 24 peach wedges with 2 tablespoons of the schnapps, 2 teaspoons of the lemon juice, and 1 tablespoon of the granulated sugar in a bowl; set aside.

2. Cut the remaining peach wedges crosswise into 3 chunks. In a large bowl, gently toss the chunks with the remaining 3 tablespoons schnapps, remaining 2 teaspoons lemon juice, and 2 tablespoons more granulated sugar. Spread the peach chunks in a single layer on the prepared baking sheet and bake until the exuded juices begin to thicken and caramelize at the edges of the pan, 20 to 25 minutes. Transfer the pan to a wire rack and let the peaches cool to room temperature, about 30 minutes. Reduce the oven temperature to 350 degrees.

3. Whisk the flour, baking powder, and salt together in a bowl. Whisk ⅓ cup more granulated sugar, the brown sugar, and eggs together in a bowl until thick and thoroughly combined, about 45 seconds. Slowly whisk in the butter until combined. Add the sour cream, vanilla, and ¼ teaspoon of the almond extract; whisk until combined. Add the flour mixture and whisk until just combined.

4. Pour half of the batter into the prepared pan. Using an offset spatula, spread the batter evenly to the pan edges and smooth the top. Sprinkle the crushed panko evenly over the cooled peach chunks and gently toss to coat. Arrange the peach chunks on the batter in the pan in an even layer, gently pressing the peaches into the batter. Gently spread the remaining batter over the peach chunks and smooth the top. Arrange the reserved peach wedges, slightly overlapped, in a ring over the surface of the batter, placing the smaller wedges in the center. Stir the remaining 3 tablespoons granulated sugar and the remaining ⅛ teaspoon almond extract together in a small bowl until the sugar is moistened. Sprinkle the sugar mixture evenly over the top of the cake.

5. Bake until the center of the cake is set and a toothpick inserted in the center comes out clean, 50 to 60 minutes. Transfer the pan to a wire rack and let cool for 5 minutes. Run a thin knife between the cake and the sides of the pan; remove the sides of the pan. Let the cake cool completely, 2 to 3 hours, before serving.

CLASSIC GINGERBREAD

WHY THIS RECIPE WORKS: Most recipes for gingerbread suffer from a dense, sunken center, and flavors range from barely gingery to spicier than a curry dinner. Our ideal gingerbread should be moist through and through and utterly simple. Focusing on flavor first, we bumped up the ginger with both a hefty dose of ground ginger and grated fresh ginger. Cinnamon and freshly ground pepper helped produce a warm, complex, lingering heat. As for the liquid components, dark stout, gently heated to minimize its booziness, had a bittersweet flavor that brought out the caramel undertones of the molasses. Finally, swapping out the butter for vegetable oil and replacing some of the brown sugar with granulated let the spice flavors come through. To prevent a sunken center, we looked at our leaveners first. Baking powder isn't as effective at leavening if too many other acidic ingredients are present in the batter (in this case, molasses, brown sugar, and

stout). Incorporating the baking soda with the wet ingredients instead of the other dry ones helped to neutralize those acidic ingredients before they got incorporated into the batter and thus allowed the baking powder to do a better job. And while stirring is typically the enemy of tenderness since it develops the flour's gluten, our batter was so loose that vigorous stirring actually gave our bread the structure necessary to further ensure the center didn't collapse. With that, we had a flawless, even cake with plenty of spice and warmth.

Classic Gingerbread Cake

SERVES 8

This cake packs potent yet well-balanced spice. If you prefer less spice, you can decrease the amount of ground ginger to 1 tablespoon. Avoid opening the oven door until the minimum baking time has elapsed. Serve the gingerbread plain or with lightly sweetened whipped cream.

- ¾ **cup stout, such as Guinness**
- ½ **teaspoon baking soda**
- ⅔ **cup molasses**
- ¾ **cup (5¼ ounces) packed light brown sugar**
- ¼ **cup (1¾ ounces) granulated sugar**
- 1½ **cups (7½ ounces) unbleached all-purpose flour**
- 2 **tablespoons ground ginger**
- ½ **teaspoon baking powder**
- ½ **teaspoon table salt**
- ¼ **teaspoon ground cinnamon**
- ¼ **teaspoon ground black pepper**
- 2 **large eggs, at room temperature**
- ⅓ **cup vegetable oil**
- 1 **tablespoon grated fresh ginger**

1. Adjust an oven rack to the middle position and heat the oven to 350 degrees. Grease an 8-inch square baking pan, line with parchment paper, grease the parchment, and flour the pan.

2. Bring the stout to a boil in a medium saucepan over medium heat, stirring occasionally. Remove from the heat and stir in the baking soda (the mixture will foam vigorously). When the foaming subsides, stir in the molasses, brown sugar, and granulated sugar until dissolved; set aside. Whisk the flour, ground ginger, baking powder, salt, cinnamon, and pepper together in a large bowl.

3. Transfer the stout mixture to a second large bowl. Whisk in the eggs, oil, and grated ginger until combined. Whisk the wet mixture into the flour mixture in thirds, stirring vigorously until completely smooth after each addition.

4. Scrape the batter into the prepared pan, smooth the top with a rubber spatula, and gently tap the pan on the counter to release any air bubbles. Bake until the top of the cake is just firm to the touch and a toothpick inserted into the center comes out clean, 35 to 45 minutes. Let the cake cool in the pan on a wire rack, about 1½ hours, before serving.

COCONUT LAYER CAKE

WHY THIS RECIPE WORKS: Too often, a coconut cake is just plain white cake with plain white frosting sprinkled with shredded coconut, lacking any real coconut flavor. Coconut cake should be perfumed inside and out with the cool, subtle, mysterious essence of coconut. Its layers of snowy white cake should be moist and tender, with a delicate, yielding crumb, and the icing a silky, gently sweetened coat covered with a deep drift of downy coconut.

For this type of cake, we found a traditional butter cake to be best. To infuse this cake with maximum coconut flavor, we relied on coconut extract and cream of coconut in the cake and the buttercream icing. We also coated the cake with a generous amount of shredded coconut for more flavor and textural interest.

Coconut Layer Cake

SERVES 10 TO 12

Be sure to use cream of coconut (such as Coco López), and not coconut milk here. If you like, before decorating, toast the shredded coconut in a 350-degree oven, stirring often, until golden, about 10 minutes. Toasting the coconut, which is optional, adds a golden halo to the finished cake, as well as a nutty flavor.

CAKE

- 2¼ cups (9 ounces) cake flour, plus extra for the pans
- ¾ cup cream of coconut (see note)
- 5 large egg whites plus 1 large egg, at room temperature
- ¼ cup water
- 1 teaspoon coconut extract
- 1 teaspoon vanilla extract
- 1 cup (7 ounces) granulated sugar
- 1 tablespoon baking powder
- ¾ teaspoon table salt
- 12 tablespoons (1½ sticks) unsalted butter, cut into 12 pieces and softened

FROSTING

- 2 tablespoons heavy cream
- 1 teaspoon coconut extract
- 1 teaspoon vanilla extract
- Pinch table salt
- 16 tablespoons (2 sticks) unsalted butter, cut into chunks and softened
- ¼ cup cream of coconut (see note)
- 3 cups (12 ounces) confectioners' sugar
- 2 cups sweetened shredded coconut (see note)

1. FOR THE CAKE: Adjust an oven rack to the middle position and heat the oven to 325 degrees. Grease and flour two 9-inch round cake pans, then line the bottoms with parchment paper. Whisk the cream of coconut, egg whites, whole egg, water, and extracts together in a medium bowl.

2. In a stand mixer fitted with the paddle attachment, mix the flour, granulated sugar, baking powder, and salt on low speed until combined, about 30 seconds. Increase the speed to medium and beat the butter into the flour mixture, one piece at a time, about 30 seconds. Continue to beat the mixture until it resembles moist crumbs, about 1 minute.

3. Beat in all but ½ cup of the cream of coconut mixture, then increase the mixer speed to medium and beat the batter until smooth, light, and fluffy, about 1 minute. Reduce the mixer speed to low and slowly beat in the remaining cream of coconut mixture until the batter is combined, about 30 seconds.

4. Scrape the batter into the prepared pans, smooth the tops, and lightly tap the pans against the countertop two or three times to settle the batter. Bake the cakes until a toothpick inserted in the center comes out with a few crumbs attached, 30 to 35 minutes, rotating the pans halfway through the baking time.

5. Cool the cakes in the pans for 10 minutes. Run a small knife around the edge of the cakes, then flip them out onto a wire rack. Peel off the parchment paper, flip the cakes right side up, and cool completely before frosting, about 2 hours.

6. FOR THE FROSTING: In a small bowl, stir the cream, extracts, and salt together. In a stand mixer fitted with the paddle attachment, beat the butter and cream of coconut together on medium-high speed until smooth, about 20 seconds. Reduce the mixer speed to medium-low and gradually beat in the confectioners' sugar, then continue to beat until smooth, about 2 minutes. Beat in the cream mixture. Increase the mixer speed to medium-high and beat until the mixture is light and fluffy, about 4 minutes.

7. Line the edges of a cake platter with strips of parchment paper to keep the platter clean while you assemble the cake. Place one of the cake layers on the platter. Spread 1 cup of the frosting over the cake, right to the edges. Place the other cake layer on top and press lightly to adhere. Frost the cake with the remaining frosting. Press the coconut into the sides of the cake and sprinkle it over the top. Remove the parchment strips from the platter before serving.

EASY CARAMEL CAKE

WHY THIS RECIPE WORKS: A Southern favorite, caramel cake boasts a rich toffee-flavored caramel frosting spread over yellow cake layers. But the best part—the caramel frosting that develops a thin, crystalline crust on its exterior while remaining silky-smooth closer to the cake— is notoriously troublesome to make. We wanted an easier, even foolproof, caramel icing that would stay creamy long enough to frost a two-layer cake. First, we needed a cake sturdy enough to support the thick frosting. Using the reverse creaming method—beating the butter into the dry ingredients—and switching from cake flour to all-purpose flour gave us a tender, fine-crumbed cake with enough structure. For a truly easy frosting, we simmered brown sugar and butter before adding cream, and rather than use a candy thermometer we relied on simple visual cues to know when to add the cream and when to remove the mixture from the heat. To ensure that the frosting wouldn't stiffen before we frosted the cake, we beat in a little softened butter. The fat from the butter kept the frosting soft and spreadable for a few precious extra minutes. After about 30 minutes, it transformed into the classic coating of frosting that we were after.

NOTES FROM THE TEST KITCHEN

GETTING THE TIMING RIGHT

When a ring of bubbles appears around the perimeter of the pan, it's time to add the cream.

Easy Caramel Cake

SERVES 8

In step 5, the cooled frosting stays soft and spreadable longer than with other recipes, but it will harden over time. If the frosting does begin to stiffen, you can microwave it for about 10 seconds (or until it returns to a spreadable consistency).

CAKE

- ½ cup buttermilk, at room temperature
- 4 large eggs, at room temperature
- 2 teaspoons vanilla extract
- 2¼ cups (11¼ ounces) unbleached all-purpose flour
- 1½ cups (10⅛ ounces) granulated sugar
- 1½ teaspoons baking powder
- ½ teaspoon baking soda
- ¾ teaspoon table salt
- 16 tablespoons (2 sticks) unsalted butter, cut into 16 pieces and softened

FROSTING

- 12 tablespoons (1½ sticks) unsalted butter, cut into 12 pieces and softened
- 2 cups packed (14 ounces) dark brown sugar
- ½ teaspoon table salt
- ½ cup heavy cream
- 1 teaspoon vanilla extract
- 2½ cups (10 ounces) confectioners' sugar, sifted

1. FOR THE CAKE: Adjust an oven rack to the middle position and heat the oven to 350 degrees. Grease and flour two 9-inch cake pans, then line the bottoms with parchment paper. Whisk the buttermilk, eggs, and vanilla in a large measuring cup. With an electric mixer on low speed, mix the flour, granulated sugar, baking powder, baking soda, and salt until combined. Beat in the butter, 1 piece at a time, until only pea-size pieces remain. Pour in half of the buttermilk mixture and beat over medium-high speed until light and fluffy, about 1 minute. Slowly add the remaining buttermilk mixture to the bowl and beat until incorporated, about 15 seconds.

2. Scrape equal amounts of the batter into the prepared pans and bake until golden and a toothpick inserted in the center comes out clean, 20 to 25 minutes. Cool the cakes in the pans for 10 minutes, then turn out onto wire racks. Cool completely, at least 1 hour.

3. FOR THE FROSTING: Following the photo, heat 8 tablespoons of the butter, the brown sugar, and salt in a large saucepan over medium heat until small bubbles appear around the perimeter of the pan, 4 to 8 minutes.

than buttercream for our frosting, eventually landing on an old-fashioned classic: seven-minute icing. We needed to make some adjustments, as the traditional version was a little too sweet, slightly thick, and required holding a hand-held mixer for longer than was comfortable. We cut back on the sugar and added a squeeze of lemon juice to solve the first two problems. After some trial and error, we learned that if we heated the mixture to at least 160 degrees and then transferred it to the stand mixer for whipping (rather than holding a hand mixer for seven minutes), the end result was just as billowy and shiny as the old-fashioned version.

Whisk in the cream and cook until the ring of bubbles reappears, about 1 minute. Off the heat, whisk in the vanilla.

4. Transfer the hot frosting mixture to a bowl and, with the electric mixer on low speed, gradually mix in the confectioners' sugar until incorporated. Increase the speed to medium and beat until the frosting is pale brown and just warm, about 5 minutes. Add the remaining butter, 1 piece at a time, and beat until light and fluffy, about 2 minutes.

5. Line the edges of a cake platter with strips of parchment paper to keep the platter clean. Place 1 cake round on a serving platter. Spread ¾ cup of the frosting over the cake, then top with the second cake round. Spread the remaining frosting evenly over the top and sides of the cake. Serve.

LEMON LAYER CAKE

WHY THIS RECIPE WORKS: Most versions of lemon layer cake are poorly executed concoctions of heavy cake stacked with filling and frosting that taste more like butter than lemon. We wanted an old-fashioned cake in which tangy, creamy lemon filling divides layers of tender, delicate cake draped in sweet frosting—an ideal contrast of sweet and tart.

Most layer cakes are substantial butter cakes, but we suspected that the light, fresh flavor of lemon would be better served by something more ethereal. After trying a sponge cake and a classic yellow cake, we found that a white butter cake was the perfect compromise: a cake nicely flavored by butter yet light enough for our flavors, with a fine crumb and tender texture.

Lemon layer cake is often filled with lemon-scented buttercream, but this filling can mute the lemon flavor and make the cake far too rich. We preferred the brightness of lemon curd. We also wanted something lighter

Lemon Layer Cake with Fluffy White Icing
SERVES 10 TO 12

You will need a cake pan with straight sides that are at least 2 inches high. For neater slices, dip a knife into hot water before cutting the cake.

LEMON CURD FILLING
- **1** cup juice from about 6 lemons
- **1** teaspoon powdered gelatin
- **1½** cups (10½ ounces) sugar
- **⅛** teaspoon table salt
- **4** large whole eggs plus 6 large egg yolks (reserve the egg whites for the cake)
- **8** tablespoons (1 stick) unsalted butter, cut into ½-inch cubes and frozen

CAKE
- **2¼** cups (9 ounces) cake flour, plus extra for the pans
- **1** cup whole milk, at room temperature
- **6** large egg whites, at room temperature
- **2** teaspoons vanilla extract
- **1¾** cups (12¼ ounces) sugar
- **4** teaspoons baking powder
- **1** teaspoon table salt
- **12** tablespoons (1½ sticks) unsalted butter, cut into 12 pieces, softened but still cool

FLUFFY WHITE ICING
- **1** cup (7 ounces) sugar
- **2** large egg whites, at room temperature
- **¼** cup water
- **1** tablespoon juice from 1 lemon
- **1** tablespoon corn syrup

1. FOR THE FILLING: Measure 1 tablespoon of the lemon juice into a small bowl; sprinkle the gelatin over the top.

Heat the remaining lemon juice, the sugar, and salt in a medium saucepan over medium-high heat, stirring occasionally, until the sugar dissolves and the mixture is hot but not boiling. Whisk the eggs and yolks in a large bowl. Whisking constantly, slowly pour the hot lemon-sugar mixture into the eggs, then return the mixture to the saucepan. Cook over medium-low heat, stirring constantly with a heatproof spatula, until the mixture registers 170 degrees on an instant-read thermometer and is thick enough to leave a trail when the spatula is scraped along the pan bottom, 4 to 6 minutes. Immediately remove the pan from the heat and stir in the gelatin mixture until dissolved. Stir in the frozen butter until incorporated. Pour the filling through a fine-mesh strainer into a bowl (you should have 3 cups). Lay a sheet of plastic wrap directly on the surface and refrigerate until firm enough to spread, at least 4 hours.

2. FOR THE CAKE: Adjust an oven rack to the middle position and heat the oven to 350 degrees. Grease and flour two 9-inch-wide by 2-inch-high round cake pans and line with parchment paper. In a 2-cup liquid measure or medium bowl, whisk together the milk, egg whites, and vanilla.

3. In a stand mixer fitted with the paddle attachment, mix the flour, sugar, baking powder, and salt at low speed

until combined, about 30 seconds. With the mixer running at low speed, add the butter one piece at a time; continue beating until the mixture resembles moist crumbs with no visible butter chunks. Add all but ½ cup of the milk mixture to the crumbs and beat at medium speed until the mixture is pale and fluffy, about 1½ minutes. With the mixer running at low speed, add the remaining ½ cup milk mixture; increase the speed to medium and beat for 30 seconds more. Stop the mixer and scrape the sides of the bowl. Return the mixer to medium speed and beat for 20 seconds longer. Divide the batter evenly between the pans, smoothing the tops with a rubber spatula. Lightly tap the pan against the countertop two or three times to settle the batter.

4. Bake until a toothpick inserted in the center of the cakes comes out clean, 23 to 25 minutes, rotating the pans halfway through the baking time. Cool the cakes in the pans on a wire rack for 10 minutes. Run a small knife around the edges of the cakes, then flip them out onto a wire rack. Peel off the parchment paper, flip the cakes right side up, and cool completely before frosting, about 2 hours.

5. TO ASSEMBLE: Line the edges of a cake platter with strips of parchment paper to keep the platter clean while you assemble the cake. Use a serrated knife to cut each cake horizontally into two even layers. Place the bottom layer of one cake on the platter. Using a spatula, spread 1 cup of the lemon filling evenly on the cake, leaving a ½-inch border around the edge. Carefully place the upper cake layer on top of the filling. Spread 1 cup of the filling on top; repeat using the remaining filling and cake layers. Smooth out any filling that has leaked from the sides of the cake; cover with plastic wrap and refrigerate while making the icing.

6. FOR THE ICING: Combine all the ingredients in the bowl of a stand mixer or a large heatproof bowl and set over a medium saucepan filled with 1 inch of barely simmering water (do not let the bowl touch the water). Cook, stirring constantly, until the mixture registers 160 degrees on an instant-read thermometer, 5 to 10 minutes. Remove the bowl from the heat and transfer the mixture to a stand mixer fitted with the whisk attachment. Beat on medium speed until soft peaks form, about 5 minutes. Increase the speed to medium-high and continue to beat until the mixture has cooled to room temperature and stiff peaks form, 5 minutes longer. Using a spatula, spread the frosting evenly over the top and sides of the cake. Remove the parchment strips from the platter and serve.

OLD-FASHIONED BIRTHDAY CAKE

WHY THIS RECIPE WORKS: White layer cakes have been the classic birthday cake for more than 100 years. White cake is simply a basic butter cake made with egg whites instead of whole eggs. The whites produce the characteristic color, and they are also supposed to make the cake soft and fine-grained—that's what we wanted. Unfortunately, the white cakes that we have baked over the years, though good enough, always fell short of our high expectations. They came out a little dry and chewy—one might say cottony—and we noticed that they were riddled with tunnels and small holes. What were we doing wrong?

Every traditional recipe for white cake calls for stiffly beaten egg whites folded into the batter at the end. We began to suspect that it was the beaten egg whites that were forming the large air pockets and those unsightly holes in the baked cakes. We solved this problem by mixing the egg whites with the milk before beating them into the flour-and-butter mixture. The results were fantastic. The cake was not only fine-grained and free from holes but, to our surprise, it was also larger and lighter than the ones we'd prepared with beaten whites. And the method couldn't be simpler, quicker, or more foolproof. To make this cake birthday-special, we iced it with an easy butter frosting and added a layer of raspberry jam and chopped toasted almonds.

Classic White Layer Cake with Butter Frosting and Raspberry-Almond Filling

SERVES 10 TO 12

There will be enough frosting left to pipe a border around the base and top of the cake; to decorate the cake more elaborately, you should make 1½ times the frosting recipe. If desired, finish the sides of the cake with 1 cup of sliced almonds.

CAKE

2¼ cups (9 ounces) cake flour, plus extra for the pans
  1 cup whole milk, at room temperature
  6 large egg whites, at room temperature
  1 teaspoon vanilla extract
  1 teaspoon almond extract
1¾ cups (12¼ ounces) granulated sugar
  4 teaspoons baking powder
  1 teaspoon table salt
 12 tablespoons (1½ sticks) unsalted butter, cut into 12 pieces and softened

FROSTING AND FILLING

 16 tablespoons (2 sticks) unsalted butter, softened
  4 cups (1 pound) confectioners' sugar
  1 tablespoon vanilla extract
  1 tablespoon milk
     Pinch table salt
  ½ cup (2¼ ounces) blanched slivered almonds, toasted and chopped coarse
  ⅓ cup seedless raspberry jam

1. FOR THE CAKE: Adjust an oven rack to the middle position and heat the oven to 350 degrees. Grease and flour two 8- or 9-inch round cake pans, then line the bottoms with parchment paper. Whisk the milk, egg whites, and both extracts together in a small bowl.

2. In a stand mixer fitted with the paddle attachment, mix the flour, sugar, baking powder, and salt together on low speed until combined, about 30 seconds. Increase the speed to medium-low and beat the butter into the flour mixture, one piece at a time, about 30 seconds. Continue to beat the mixture until it resembles moist crumbs, about 1 minute.

3. Beat in all but ½ cup of the milk mixture, then increase the mixer speed to medium and beat until smooth, light, and fluffy, about 1 minute. Reduce the mixer speed to low and slowly beat in the remaining ½ cup milk mixture until the batter looks slightly curdled, about 15 seconds.

4. Give the batter a final stir with a rubber spatula to make sure it is thoroughly combined. Scrape the batter into the prepared pans, smooth the tops, and lightly tap the pans against the countertop two or three times to settle the batter. Bake the cakes until a toothpick inserted in the center comes out with a few crumbs attached, 20 to 25 minutes, rotating the pans halfway through the baking time.

5. Cool the cakes in the pans for 10 minutes. Run a small knife around the edge of the cakes, then flip them out onto a wire rack. Peel off the parchment paper, flip the cakes right side up, and cool completely before frosting, about 2 hours.

6. FOR THE FROSTING AND FILLING: In the bowl of a stand mixer fitted with the paddle attachment, beat the butter, confectioners' sugar, vanilla, milk, and salt on low speed until the sugar is moistened, about 30 seconds. Increase the speed to medium-high; beat, stopping twice to scrape down the bowl, until creamy and fluffy, about 1½ minutes.

7. Line the edges of a cake platter with strips of parchment to keep the platter clean while you assemble the cake. Place one cake layer on the platter. Combine ½ cup of the frosting with the almonds in a small bowl.

LINING CAKE PANS

1. Trace the outline of the bottom of the pan onto a sheet of parchment paper. Cut out the outline, cutting on the inside of the line so that the round fits snugly inside the pan.

2. Fit the trimmed piece of parchment into the pan.

Spread the almond frosting over the first layer. Carefully spread the jam on top, then cover with the second cake layer. Spread the remaining frosting evenly over the top and sides of the cake. Remove the parchment strips from the platter before serving.

CLASSIC YELLOW LAYER CAKE

WHY THIS RECIPE WORKS: Traditional yellow layer cake should melt in the mouth and taste of butter and eggs. But many recipes we tried came out crumbly, sugary, and hard. And the flavor? It tasted merely sweet. We wanted a yellow cake that was tender and buttery and could stand up to a slathering of frosting, if desired.

Most versions of yellow layer cake rely on the classic 1–2–3–4 formula (1 cup butter, 2 cups sugar, 3 cups flour, and four eggs—plus milk, baking powder, vanilla, and salt) and follow the classic way of mixing together the ingredients—creaming the butter and sugar, adding the eggs one at a time, and finally adding the milk and dry ingredients alternately. This worked okay, but we wanted something easier for this cake. The two-stage method fit the bill. In this technique, the dry ingredients are combined and then two-thirds of the milk and eggs are added and beaten until thick and fluffy. Then in the

second stage, the rest of the milk and eggs are poured in and the batter is beaten again. This technique is simpler and quicker, and produced a tender cake. The flavor still needed some improvement. We tackled the proportions of the ingredients, increasing the butter, eggs, and sugar. This cake turned out fine-grained, soft, and meltingly rich—just what we wanted. As for the frosting, we chose a traditional vanilla buttercream. Rich with egg yolks, butter, sugar, and corn syrup for sheen, this supple frosting is the perfect complement to our cake.

Classic Yellow Layer Cake with Vanilla Buttercream

SERVES 8 TO 10

Cake flour gives this buttery yellow cake its tender crumb; do not substitute all-purpose flour. When making the buttercream, make sure that the sugar mixture is poured into the egg yolks while still hot. For a decorative finish, press toasted sliced almonds on the sides of the cake.

CAKE

- 1¾ cups (7 ounces) cake flour (see note), plus extra for the pans
- ½ cup whole milk, at room temperature
- 4 large eggs, at room temperature
- 2 teaspoons vanilla extract
- 1½ cups (10½ ounces) sugar
- 2 teaspoons baking powder
- ¾ teaspoon table salt
- 16 tablespoons (2 sticks) unsalted butter, cut into 16 pieces and softened

VANILLA BUTTERCREAM

- 6 large egg yolks, at room temperature
- ¾ cup (5¼ ounces) sugar
- ½ cup light corn syrup
- 2½ teaspoons vanilla extract
- ¼ teaspoon table salt
- 4 sticks unsalted butter, cut into chunks and softened

1. FOR THE CAKE: Adjust an oven rack to the middle position and heat the oven to 350 degrees. Grease and flour two 8- or 9-inch round cake pans, then line the bottoms with parchment paper. Whisk the milk, eggs, and vanilla together in a small bowl.

2. In a stand mixer fitted with the paddle attachment, whisk the flour, sugar, baking powder, and salt together on low speed until combined, about 30 seconds. Increase the speed to medium-low and beat the butter into the flour mixture, one piece at a time, about 30 seconds. Continue to beat the mixture until it resembles moist crumbs, about 1 minute.

3. Beat in all but ½ cup of the milk mixture, then increase the mixer speed to medium and beat the batter until smooth, light, and fluffy, about 1 minute. Reduce the mixer speed to low and slowly beat in the remaining ½ cup milk mixture until the batter looks slightly curdled, about 15 seconds.

4. Give the batter a final stir with a rubber spatula to make sure it is thoroughly combined. Scrape the batter into the prepared pans and smooth the tops with a rubber spatula. Lightly tap the pans against the countertop two or three times to settle the batter. Bake the cakes until a toothpick inserted in the center comes out with a few crumbs attached, 20 to 25 minutes, rotating the pans halfway through the baking time.

5. Cool the cakes in the pans for 10 minutes. Run a small knife around the edge of the cakes, then flip them out onto a wire rack. Peel off the parchment paper, flip the cakes right side up, and cool completely before frosting, about 2 hours.

6. FOR THE FROSTING: Whip the egg yolks in a large bowl with an electric mixer on medium speed until slightly thickened and pale yellow, 4 to 6 minutes.

7. Meanwhile, bring the sugar and corn syrup to a boil in a small saucepan over medium heat, stirring occasionally to dissolve the sugar, about 3 minutes.

8. Without letting the hot sugar mixture cool off, turn the mixer to low and slowly pour the warm sugar syrup into the whipped egg yolks without hitting the side of the bowl or the beaters. Increase the mixer speed to medium-high and whip the mixture until it is light and fluffy and the bowl is no longer warm, 5 to 10 minutes.

9. Reduce the mixer speed to medium-low and add the vanilla and salt. Gradually add the butter, one piece at a time, until completely incorporated, about 2 minutes. Increase the mixer speed to medium-high and whip the buttercream until smooth and silky, about 2 minutes. (If the mixture looks curdled, wrap a hot wet towel around the bowl and continue to whip until smooth, 1 to 2 minutes.)

10. Line the edges of a cake platter with strips of parchment to keep the platter clean while you assemble the cake. Place one cake layer on the platter. Spread 1½ cups of the frosting evenly across the top of the cake with a spatula. Place the second cake layer on top, then spread the remaining frosting evenly over the top and sides of the cake. Remove the parchment strips from the platter before serving.

FLUFFY YELLOW CAKE

WHY THIS RECIPE WORKS: It's easy to create a supremely fluffy layer cake with additives, but most cakes made entirely from natural ingredients are either unpleasantly dense or too fragile to support layers of frosting. We wanted a frosted yellow layer cake with an ethereal texture and the great flavor of real butter and eggs.

Chiffon cakes are especially weightless, springy, and moist. But unlike butter cakes, they are too light to stand up to a serious slathering of frosting. We decided to blend the two types of cake. We adapted a chiffon technique (using a large quantity of whipped egg whites to get a high volume and light texture) to combine the ingredients from our butter cake recipe. This worked beautifully, creating a light, porous cake that was hefty enough to hold the frosting's weight. But the cake lacked moistness and some tenderness. A combination of fats (butter plus vegetable oil), kept the butter flavor intact while improving the moistness of the cake. For extra tenderness, we increased the sugar and substituted buttermilk for milk. The buttermilk not only introduced a new flavor dimension, but also allowed us to replace some of the baking powder with a little baking soda to ensure an even rise.

As for the frosting, a fluffy chocolate frosting is the perfect partner to this cake. A hefty amount of cocoa powder combined with melted chocolate gave the frosting a deep chocolate flavor. A combination of confectioners' sugar and corn syrup made it smooth and glossy. To keep the frosting from separating and turning greasy, we moved it out of the stand mixer and into the food processor. The faster machine minimized any risk of overbeating, as it blended the ingredients quickly without melting the butter or incorporating too much air. The result is a thick, fluffy chocolate frosting that spreads like a dream.

Fluffy Yellow Layer Cake with Milk Chocolate Frosting

SERVES 10 TO 12

Bring all the ingredients to room temperature before beginning. For the frosting, cool the chocolate to between 85 and 100 degrees before adding it to the butter mixture. The frosting can be made 3 hours in advance. For longer storage, refrigerate the frosting, covered, and let it stand at room temperature for 1 hour before using.

CAKE

- 2½ cups (10 ounces) cake flour, plus extra for the pans
- 1¾ cups (12¼ ounces) granulated sugar
- 1¼ teaspoons baking powder
- ¼ teaspoon baking soda
- ¾ teaspoon table salt
- 1 cup buttermilk, at room temperature
- 10 tablespoons (1¼ sticks) unsalted butter, melted and cooled slightly
- 3 tablespoons vegetable oil
- 2 teaspoons vanilla extract
- 6 large egg yolks plus 3 large egg whites, at room temperature

FROSTING

- 20 tablespoons (2½ sticks) unsalted butter, softened
- 1 cup (4 ounces) confectioners' sugar
- ¾ cup Dutch-processed cocoa powder
- Pinch table salt
- ¾ cup light corn syrup
- 1 teaspoon vanilla extract
- 8 ounces milk chocolate, melted and cooled slightly (see note)

1. FOR THE CAKE: Adjust an oven rack to the middle position and heat the oven to 350 degrees. Grease and flour two 9-inch-wide by 2-inch-high round cake pans and line with parchment paper. Whisk the flour, 1½ cups of the granulated sugar, the baking powder, baking soda, and salt together in a large bowl. In a 4-cup liquid measuring cup or medium bowl, whisk together the buttermilk, melted butter, oil, vanilla, and egg yolks.

2. In a stand mixer fitted with the whisk attachment, beat the egg whites at medium-high speed until foamy, about 30 seconds. With the machine running, gradually add the remaining ¼ cup granulated sugar; continue to beat until stiff peaks just form, 30 to 60 seconds (the whites should hold a peak but the mixture should appear moist). Transfer to a bowl and set aside.

3. Add the flour mixture to the now-empty mixing bowl. With the mixer still fitted with the whisk attachment, and

FROSTING A LAYER CAKE

1. Dollop a portion of frosting in the center of the cake and spread into an even layer right to the edge.

2. Lay the second layer on top. Brush away any large crumbs, dollop more frosting in the center, and spread slightly over the edge.

3. Gather a few tablespoons of frosting onto the top of the spatula, then gently smear it onto the side of the cake. Repeat to frost the sides completely.

4. For smooth sides, gently run the edge of the spatula around the cake. Or, to create billows in the frosting, press the back of a soup spoon into the frosting, then twirl the spoon as you lift it away.

running at low speed, gradually pour in the butter mixture and mix until almost incorporated (a few streaks of dry flour will remain), about 15 seconds. Stop the mixer and scrape the whisk and the sides of the bowl. Return the mixer to medium-low speed and beat until smooth and fully incorporated, 10 to 15 seconds.

4. Using a rubber spatula, stir one-third of the whites into the batter to lighten, then add the remaining whites and gently fold into the batter until no white streaks remain. Divide the batter evenly between the prepared pans, smoothing the tops with a rubber spatula. Lightly tap the pans against the countertop two or three times to settle the batter.

5. Bake until the cake layers begin to pull away from the sides of the pans and a toothpick inserted into the centers comes out clean, 20 to 22 minutes, rotating the pans halfway through the baking time. Cool the cakes in the pans on a wire rack for 10 minutes. Run a small knife around the edge of the cakes, then flip them out onto a wire rack. Peel off the parchment paper, flip the cakes right side up, and cool completely before frosting, about 2 hours.

6. FOR THE FROSTING: In a food processor, process the butter, confectioners' sugar, cocoa, and salt until smooth, about 30 seconds, scraping down the sides of the bowl as needed. Add the corn syrup and vanilla and process until just combined, 5 to 10 seconds. Scrape down the sides of the bowl, then add the chocolate and process until smooth and creamy, 10 to 15 seconds. The frosting can be used immediately or held (see note).

7. Line the edges of a cake platter with strips of parchment to keep the platter clean while you assemble the cake. Place one cake layer on the platter. Spread 1½ cups of the frosting evenly across the top of the cake with a spatula. Place the second cake layer on top, then spread the remaining frosting evenly over the top and sides of the cake. Remove the parchment strips from the platter before serving.

OLD-FASHIONED CHOCOLATE LAYER CAKE

WHY THIS RECIPE WORKS: Over the years, chocolate cakes have become denser, richer, and squatter. Many contemporary cakes are so intense that just a few forkfuls satisfy. These cakes taste great—it's hard to imagine a bad chocolate cake—but sometimes we'd rather have a real piece of cake, not a fudge-like confection. We wanted an old-style, mile-high chocolate layer cake with a tender, airy, open crumb and a soft, billowy frosting.

The mixing method was the key to getting the right texture. After trying a variety of techniques, we turned to ribboning, a popular old-fashioned method used for cakes like genoise (a moist, light sponge cake). Ribboning involves whipping eggs with sugar until they double in volume, then adding the butter, dry ingredients, and milk. The egg foam aerated the cake, giving it both structure and tenderness. To achieve a moist cake with rich chocolate flavor, we once again looked to historical sources, which suggested using buttermilk and making a "pudding" with a mixture of chocolate, water, and sugar. We simply melted unsweetened chocolate and cocoa powder in hot water over a double boiler, then stirred in sugar until it dissolved. Turning to the frosting, we

wanted to combine the best elements of classic chocolate frostings: the intense chocolate flavor of a ganache (a mixture of chocolate and cream) and the volume of a meringue or buttercream. The solution turned out to be a simple reversal of the conventional ganache procedure: We poured cold (rather than heated) cream into warm (rather than room-temperature) chocolate, waited for it to cool to room temperature, then whipped until fluffy.

Old-Fashioned Chocolate Layer Cake with Chocolate Frosting

SERVES 10 TO 12

For a smooth, spreadable frosting, use chopped semisweet chocolate, not chocolate chips—chocolate chips contain less cocoa butter than bar chocolate and will not melt as readily. As for other bar chocolate, bittersweet chocolate that is 60 percent cacao can be substituted but it will produce a stiffer, but still spreadable, frosting. Bittersweet chocolate with 70 percent cacao, however, should be avoided—it will produce a frosting that is crumbly and it will not spread. For best results, don't make the frosting until the cakes are cooled, and use the frosting as soon as it is ready. If the frosting gets too cold and stiff to spread easily, wrap the mixer bowl with a towel soaked in hot water and mix on low speed until the frosting appears creamy and smooth.

CAKE

- 1¾ cups (8¾ ounces) unbleached all-purpose flour, plus extra for the pans
- 4 ounces unsweetened chocolate, chopped coarse
- ¼ cup Dutch-processed cocoa powder
- ½ cup hot water
- 1¾ cups (12¼ ounces) sugar
- 1½ teaspoons baking soda
- 1 teaspoon table salt
- 1 cup buttermilk
- 2 teaspoons vanilla extract
- 4 large whole eggs plus 2 large egg yolks, at room temperature
- 12 tablespoons (1½ sticks) unsalted butter, very soft

FROSTING

- 1 pound semisweet chocolate, chopped fine (see note)
- 8 tablespoons (1 stick) unsalted butter
- ⅓ cup (2⅓ ounces) sugar
- 2 tablespoons corn syrup
- 2 teaspoons vanilla extract
- ¼ teaspoon table salt
- 1¼ cups heavy cream, chilled

1. FOR THE CAKE: Adjust an oven rack to the middle position and heat the oven to 350 degrees. Grease and flour two 9-inch-wide by 2-inch-high round cake pans and line with parchment paper. Combine the chocolate, cocoa powder, and hot water in a medium heatproof bowl set over a saucepan filled with 1 inch of barely simmering water, stirring occasionally until smooth. Add ½ cup of the sugar to the chocolate mixture and stir until thick and glossy, 1 to 2 minutes. Remove the bowl from the heat and set aside to cool.

2. Whisk the flour, baking soda, and salt in a medium bowl. Combine the buttermilk and vanilla in a small bowl. In the bowl of a stand mixer fitted with the whisk attachment, whisk the whole eggs and egg yolks on medium-low speed until combined, about 10 seconds. Add the remaining 1¼ cups sugar, increase the speed to high, and whisk until fluffy and lightened in color, 2 to 3 minutes. Replace the whisk with the paddle attachment. Add the cooled chocolate mixture to the egg-sugar mixture and mix on medium speed until thoroughly incorporated, 30 to 45 seconds, pausing to scrape down the sides of the bowl with a rubber spatula as needed. Add the softened butter 1 tablespoon at a time, mixing for about 10 seconds after each addition. Add about one-third of the flour mixture followed by half of the buttermilk mixture, mixing until incorporated after each addition (about 15 seconds). Repeat, using half of the remaining flour mixture and all of the remaining buttermilk mixture (the batter may appear separated). Scrape down the sides of the bowl and add the remaining flour mixture; mix at medium-low speed until the batter is thoroughly combined, about 15 seconds. Remove the bowl from the mixer and fold the batter once or twice with a rubber spatula to incorporate any remaining flour. Divide the batter evenly between the prepared pans, smoothing the tops with a rubber spatula. Lightly tap the pans against the countertop two or three times to settle the batter.

3. Bake the cakes until a toothpick inserted into the center comes out with a few crumbs attached, 25 to 30 minutes, rotating the pans halfway through the baking time. Cool the cakes in the pans on a wire rack for 15 minutes. Run a small knife around the edge of the cakes, then flip them out onto a wire rack. Peel off the parchment paper, flip the cakes right side up, and cool completely before frosting, about 2 hours.

4. FOR THE FROSTING: Melt the chocolate in a heatproof bowl set over a saucepan containing 1 inch of barely simmering water, stirring occasionally until smooth. Remove from the heat and set aside. Meanwhile, heat the butter in a small saucepan over medium-low heat until melted.

Increase the heat to medium; add the sugar, corn syrup, vanilla, and salt and stir with a heatproof spatula until the sugar is dissolved, 4 to 5 minutes. Add the melted chocolate, butter mixture, and cream to the clean bowl of a stand mixer and stir to thoroughly combine.

5. Place the mixer bowl over an ice bath and stir the mixture constantly with a rubber spatula until the frosting is thick and just beginning to harden against the sides of the bowl, 1 to 2 minutes (the frosting should be at 70 degrees). Place the bowl on a stand mixer fitted with the paddle attachment and beat on medium-high speed until the frosting is light and fluffy, 1 to 2 minutes. Stir with a rubber spatula until completely smooth.

6. Line the edges of a cake platter with strips of parchment to keep the platter clean while you assemble the cake. Place one cake layer on the platter. Spread 1½ cups of the frosting evenly across the top of the cake with a spatula. Place the second cake layer on top, then spread the remaining frosting evenly over the top and sides of the cake. Remove the parchment strips from the platter before serving.

CHOCOLATE SHEET CAKE

WHY THIS RECIPE WORKS: Sheet cakes, for all their simplicity, can still turn out dry, sticky, or flavorless and, on occasion, can even sink in the middle. We wanted to find a simple, dependable recipe, one that delivered a moist yet also tender and chocolaty cake.

We started with the mixing method—testing everything from creaming butter to beating yolks, whipping whites, and gently folding together everything in the end. The best of the lot was the most complicated to make, so we took a step back. The simplest technique we tried was simply whisking all the ingredients together without beating, creaming, or whipping. The recipe needed work, but the approach was clearly a good match for the simple all-purpose nature of a sheet cake. First we added buttermilk and baking soda to lighten the batter, since the original cake had been too dense. To increase the chocolate flavor, we reduced the sugar and flour, and decreased the butter. To further deepen the chocolate taste, we used semisweet chocolate in addition to the cocoa. We baked the cake at a low temperature for a long time—40 minutes—to produce a perfectly baked cake with a lovely flat top. Though this cake can be frosted with almost anything, we like a classic American milk chocolate frosting, which pairs well with the darker flavor of the cake.

Chocolate Sheet Cake with Easy Chocolate Frosting

SERVES 15 TO 18

We prefer Dutch-processed cocoa for the deeper chocolate flavor it gives the cake. The frosting needs about an hour to cool before it can be used, so begin making it when the cake comes out of the oven. You can also serve the cake lightly dusted with confectioners' sugar or with lightly sweetened whipped cream.

CAKE

- 12 tablespoons (1½ sticks) unsalted butter
- ¾ cup cocoa powder, preferably Dutch-processed (see note)
- 1¼ cups (6¼ ounces) unbleached all-purpose flour
- ½ teaspoon baking soda
- ¼ teaspoon table salt
- 8 ounces semisweet chocolate, chopped
- 4 large eggs, at room temperature
- 1½ cups (10½ ounces) granulated sugar
- 1 teaspoon vanilla extract
- 1 cup buttermilk

FROSTING

- ½ cup heavy cream
  Pinch table salt
- 1 tablespoon light or dark corn syrup
- 10 ounces milk chocolate, chopped
- ½ cup (2 ounces) confectioners' sugar
- 8 tablespoons (1 stick) cold unsalted butter, cut into 8 pieces

1. FOR THE CAKE: Adjust an oven rack to the middle position and heat the oven to 325 degrees. Grease a 13 by 9-inch baking pan, then line the bottom with parchment paper.

2. Sift together the cocoa, flour, baking soda, and salt in a medium bowl; set aside. Melt the chocolate and butter in a heatproof bowl set over a saucepan filled with 1 inch of barely simmering water, stirring occasionally until smooth. Whisk together the eggs, sugar, and vanilla in a medium bowl. Whisk in the buttermilk until smooth.

3. Whisk the chocolate into the egg mixture until combined. Whisk in the dry ingredients until the batter is smooth and glossy. Pour the batter into the prepared pan; bake until firm in the center when lightly pressed and a toothpick inserted in the center comes out clean, about 40 minutes, rotating the pan halfway through the baking time. Let the cake cool completely in the pan, set on a wire rack, about 2 hours. Run a small knife around the cake and flip the cake out onto a wire rack. Peel off the parchment paper, then flip the cake right side up onto a serving platter.

4. FOR THE FROSTING: Heat the cream, salt, and corn syrup in a microwave-safe measuring cup on high power until simmering, about 1 minute, or bring to a simmer in a small saucepan over medium heat.

5. Place the chocolate in a food processor. With the machine running, gradually add the hot cream mixture through the feed tube; process for 1 minute after the cream has been added. Stop the machine; add the confectioners' sugar and process to combine, about 30 seconds. With the machine running, add the butter through the feed tube one piece at a time; process until incorporated and smooth, about 20 seconds longer.

6. Transfer the frosting to a medium bowl and cool at room temperature, stirring frequently, until thick and spreadable, about 1 hour. Spread the frosting evenly over the top and sides of the cake and serve.

GERMAN CHOCOLATE CAKE

WHY THIS RECIPE WORKS: Most German chocolate cake recipes are similar, if not identical, to the one on the German's Sweet Chocolate box. Our tasters found several shortcomings in this recipe. It produced a cake that was too sweet, with chocolate flavor that was too mild, and with a texture so listless that the filling and cake together formed a soggy, sweet mush. We wanted a cake that was less sweet and more chocolaty than the original, but we didn't want to sacrifice the overall blend of flavors and textures that makes German chocolate cake so appealing in the first place.

The first order of business was to scale back the recipe by one quarter, which allowed us to fit the batter into two cake pans, thereby producing a cake with four thinner layers rather than three thicker layers. After testing, we discovered that the texture of the cake actually improved when we used whole eggs instead of laboriously separating the eggs, beating the whites, and folding them into the batter. We increased chocolate flavor with a combination of cocoa powder and good-quality semisweet or bittersweet chocolate. By adjusting the level and proportions of the sugar (both brown and white) and butter in the cake and filling, as well as toasting the pecans, we finished the necessary adjustments to create a definitely easier-to-make cake, with better texture and flavor than the original.

German Chocolate Cake

SERVES 12 TO 16

When you assemble the cake, the filling should be cool or cold. To be time-efficient, first make the filling, then use the refrigeration time to prepare, bake, and cool the cakes. For an accurate measurement of boiling water, bring a kettle of water to a boil, then measure out the desired amount. Note that the toasted pecans are stirred into the filling just before assembly to keep them from becoming soft and soggy.

FILLING

- 4   large egg yolks, at room temperature
- 1   (12-ounce) can evaporated milk
- 1   cup (7 ounces) granulated sugar
- ¼   cup packed (1¾ ounces) light brown sugar
- 6   tablespoons (¾ stick) unsalted butter, cut into 6 pieces
- ⅛   teaspoon table salt
- 2   teaspoons vanilla extract
- 2⅓   cups sweetened shredded coconut
- 1½   cups (6 ounces) finely chopped pecans, toasted (see note)

CAKE

- 4   ounces semisweet or bittersweet chocolate, chopped fine
- ¼   cup Dutch-processed cocoa powder
- ½   cup boiling water (see note)
- 2   cups (10 ounces) unbleached all-purpose flour, plus extra for the pans
- ¾   teaspoon baking soda
- 12   tablespoons (1½ sticks) unsalted butter, softened
- 1   cup (7 ounces) granulated sugar
- ⅔   cup packed (4⅔ ounces) light brown sugar
- ¾   teaspoon table salt
- 4   large whole eggs, at room temperature
- 1   teaspoon vanilla extract
- ¾   cup sour cream, at room temperature

1. FOR THE FILLING: Whisk the egg yolks in a medium saucepan; gradually whisk in the evaporated milk. Add the sugars, butter, and salt and cook over medium-high heat, whisking constantly, until the mixture is boiling, frothy, and slightly thickened, about 6 minutes. Transfer the mixture to a bowl, whisk in the vanilla, then stir in the coconut. Cool until just warm, cover with plastic wrap, and refrigerate until cool or cold, at least 2 hours or up to 3 days. (The pecans are stirred in just before cake assembly.)

2. FOR THE CAKE: Adjust an oven rack to the lower-middle position; heat the oven to 350 degrees. Combine the chocolate and cocoa in a small bowl; pour the boiling water over and let stand to melt the chocolate, about 2 minutes. Whisk until smooth; set aside until cooled to room temperature.

3. Meanwhile, grease and flour two 9-inch-wide by 2-inch-high round cake pans and line with parchment paper. Sift the flour and baking soda into a medium bowl or onto a sheet of parchment or waxed paper.

4. In a stand mixer fitted with the paddle attachment, beat the butter, sugars, and salt at medium-low speed until the sugar is moistened, about 30 seconds. Increase the speed to medium-high and beat until the mixture is light and fluffy, about 4 minutes, scraping down the bowl with a spatula halfway through. With the mixer running at medium speed, add the eggs one at a time, beating well after each addition and scraping down the bowl halfway through. Beat in the vanilla; increase the speed to medium-high and beat until light and fluffy, about 45 seconds. With the mixer running at low speed, add the chocolate mixture, then increase the speed to medium and beat until combined, about 30 seconds, scraping down the bowl once (the batter may appear curdled). Add about one-third of the flour mixture, followed by half of the sour cream, mixing until just incorporated after each addition (about 5 seconds). Repeat using half of the remaining flour mixture and all of the remaining sour cream. Scrape down the bowl and add the remaining flour mixture; mix at medium-low speed until the batter is thoroughly combined, about 15 seconds. Divide the batter evenly between the prepared cake pans, smoothing the tops with a rubber spatula. Lightly tap the pans against the countertop two or three times to settle the batter.

5. Bake the cakes until a toothpick inserted into the centers comes out clean, about 30 minutes, rotating the pans halfway through the baking time. Cool the cakes in the pans on a wire rack for 10 minutes. Run a small knife around the edges of the cakes, then flip them out onto a wire rack. Peel off the parchment, flip the cakes right side up, and cool completely before frosting, about 2 hours.

6. TO ASSEMBLE: Stir the toasted pecans into the chilled filling. Line the edges of a cake platter with strips of parchment paper to keep the platter clean while you assemble the cake. Use a serrated knife to cut each cake horizontally into two even layers. Place one bottom layer on the platter. Spread about 1 cup of the filling evenly across the top of the cake with a spatula. Carefully place the upper cake layer on top of the filling; repeat using the remaining filling and cake layers. Remove the parchment strips before serving.

CHOCOLATE CUPCAKES

WHY THIS RECIPE WORKS: Cupcakes shouldn't be complicated, but homemade versions can take a lot of time and store-bought mixes don't deliver good chocolate flavor. We wanted the consummate chocolate cupcake—one with a rich, buttery flavor, a light, moist, cakey texture, and just the right amount of sugar—but we wanted it to be almost as quick and easy to make as the cupcakes that come from a box.

For the mixing method, we found that the melted-butter method often used for mixing muffins, quick breads, and brownies—a method that requires no mixer and no time spent waiting for butter to soften—worked best. The same procedure won out over the more conventional creaming method for our cupcakes, delivering a light texture with a tender, fine crumb. Moving on to tackle our desire for deep chocolate flavor, we found that a combination of cocoa powder and bittersweet chocolate delivered deep chocolate flavor and that mixing the cocoa powder with the butter and chocolate as they melted (rather than adding the cocoa to the dry ingredients) made the chocolate flavor even stronger and richer. Sour cream gave our cupcakes moistness and a little tang, while just the right amounts of baking soda and baking powder helped them rise to a gently domed shape that was perfect for frosting.

Dark Chocolate Cupcakes
MAKES 12 CUPCAKES

Store leftover cupcakes (frosted or unfrosted) in the refrigerator, but let them come to room temperature before serving.

- 8 tablespoons (1 stick) unsalted butter, cut into 4 pieces
- 2 ounces bittersweet chocolate, chopped
- ½ cup cocoa powder, preferably Dutch-processed
- ¾ cup (3¾ ounces) unbleached all-purpose flour
- ¾ teaspoon baking powder
- ½ teaspoon baking soda
- 2 large eggs, at room temperature
- ¾ cup (5¼ ounces) sugar
- 1 teaspoon vanilla extract
- ½ teaspoon table salt
- ½ cup sour cream
- 1 recipe Easy Vanilla Bean Buttercream, Easy Chocolate Buttercream, or Easy Coffee Buttercream (recipes follow)

1. Adjust an oven rack to the lower-middle position and heat the oven to 350 degrees. Line a standard-size muffin pan with baking cup liners.

2. Melt the butter, chocolate, and cocoa in a medium heatproof bowl set over a saucepan filled with 1 inch of barely simmering water, stirring occasionally. Set aside to cool until just warm to the touch.

3. Whisk the flour, baking powder, and baking soda in a small bowl to combine.

4. Whisk the eggs in a medium bowl to combine; add the sugar, vanilla, and salt and whisk until fully incorporated. Add the cooled chocolate mixture and whisk until combined. Sift about one-third of the flour mixture over the chocolate mixture and whisk until combined; whisk in the sour cream until combined, then sift the remaining flour mixture over the batter and whisk until homogeneous and thick.

5. Divide the batter evenly among the muffin cups. Bake until a toothpick or wooden skewer inserted into the center of the cupcakes comes out clean, 18 to 20 minutes, rotating the pan halfway through the baking time.

6. Cool the cupcakes in the pan on a wire rack until cool enough to handle, about 15 minutes. Carefully lift each cupcake from the muffin pan and set on a wire rack. Cool to room temperature before icing, about 30 minutes. To frost: Mound about 2 tablespoons of icing on the center of each cupcake. Using a small spatula or butter knife, spread the icing to the edge of the cupcake, leaving a slight mound in the center.

Easy Vanilla Bean Buttercream

MAKES ABOUT 1½ CUPS, ENOUGH TO FROST 12 CUPCAKES

If you prefer to skip the vanilla bean, increase the extract to 1½ teaspoons. Any of the buttercream frostings can be made ahead and refrigerated; if refrigerated, however, the frosting must stand at room temperature to soften before use. If using a hand-held mixer, increase mixing times significantly (by at least 50 percent).

- 10 **tablespoons (1¼ sticks) unsalted butter, softened**
- ½ **vanilla bean, halved lengthwise (see note)**
- 1¼ **cups (5 ounces) confectioners' sugar**
  Pinch table salt
- 1 **tablespoon heavy cream**
- ½ **teaspoon vanilla extract**

In a stand mixer fitted with the whisk attachment, beat the butter at medium-high speed until smooth, about

20 seconds. Using a paring knife, scrape the seeds from the vanilla bean into the butter and beat the mixture at medium-high speed to combine, about 15 seconds. Add the confectioners' sugar and salt and beat at medium-low speed until most of the sugar is moistened, about 45 seconds. Scrape down the bowl and beat at medium speed until the mixture is fully combined, about 15 seconds. Scrape down the bowl, add the heavy cream and vanilla extract, and beat at medium speed until incorporated, about 10 seconds, then increase the speed to medium-high and beat until light and fluffy, about 4 minutes, scraping down the bowl once or twice.

Easy Chocolate Buttercream

Follow the recipe for Easy Vanilla Bean Buttercream, omitting the vanilla bean and heavy cream and reducing the sugar to 1 cup. After beating in the vanilla extract, reduce the speed to low and gradually beat in 4 ounces melted and cooled semisweet or bittersweet chocolate.

Easy Coffee Buttercream

Follow the recipe for Easy Vanilla Bean Buttercream, omitting the vanilla bean and dissolving 1½ teaspoons instant espresso powder in the heavy cream and vanilla extract.

ULTIMATE CHOCOLATE CUPCAKES

WHY THIS RECIPE WORKS: A cupcake catch-22 befalls bakery and homemade confections alike: If the cupcakes are packed with decent chocolate flavor, their structure is too crumbly for out-of-hand consumption. Conversely, if the cakes balance moisture and tenderness without crumbling, the core elements—cake and frosting—are barely palatable. We wanted a moist, tender (but not crumbly) crumb capped with just enough creamy, not-too-sweet frosting.

Figuring that a cupcake is just a pint-size cake, we made cupcakes using our favorite chocolate cake recipe. Tasters liked the real chocolate flavor, but their crumbly texture made them impossible to eat without a fork. Though we were loath to compromise the chocolate's intensity, we knew that to strengthen the batter we had to cut back on both kinds of chocolate. We tweaked the ingredients to achieve a perfectly portable batch of cupcakes before we turned our attention to working in more chocolate without disrupting the batter's structure. Mixing the cocoa with hot coffee eked out more chocolate flavor. To make the chocolate even more pronounced, we replaced the butter with more neutral-flavored vegetable oil.

Next, we tried enhancing the structure of the cupcake. That would give us a base for adding back extra chocolate without overtenderizing. To do this, we substituted bread flour for all-purpose flour. Specifically engineered for gluten development, bread flour turned out a cupcake that was markedly less crumble-prone, but not tough. For a final chocolate burst, we spooned ganache onto the cupcakes before baking, which gave them a truffle-like center. A velvety buttercream with just enough sweetness crowned the cake perfectly.

Ultimate Chocolate Cupcakes with Ganache Filling

MAKES 12 CUPCAKES

Use a high-quality bittersweet or semisweet chocolate for this recipe, such as one of the test kitchen's favorite baking chocolates, Callebaut Intense Dark Chocolate or Ghirardelli Bittersweet Chocolate. Though we highly recommend the ganache filling, you can omit it for a more traditional cupcake.

GANACHE FILLING

- 2   ounces bittersweet chocolate, chopped fine (see note)
- ¼   cup heavy cream
- 1   tablespoon confectioners' sugar

CHOCOLATE CUPCAKES

- 3   ounces bittersweet chocolate, chopped fine (see note)
- ⅓   cup (1 ounce) Dutch-processed cocoa powder
- ¾   cup hot coffee
- ¾   cup (4⅛ ounces) bread flour
- ¾   cup (5¼ ounces) granulated sugar
- ½   teaspoon table salt
- ½   teaspoon baking soda
- 6   tablespoons vegetable oil
- 2   large eggs
- 2   teaspoons white vinegar
- 1   teaspoon vanilla extract
- 1   recipe Creamy Chocolate Frosting (recipe follows)

1. FOR THE GANACHE FILLING: Place the chocolate, cream, and confectioners' sugar in a medium microwave-safe bowl. Microwave until the mixture is warm to the touch, 20 to 30 seconds. Whisk the mixture until smooth, then refrigerate until just chilled, no longer than 30 minutes.

2. FOR THE CUPCAKES: Adjust an oven rack to the middle position and heat the oven to 350 degrees. Line a standard-size muffin pan (cups have ½-cup capacity) with baking cup liners. Place the chocolate and cocoa in a medium bowl. Pour the hot coffee over the mixture and whisk until smooth. Refrigerate until completely cool, about 20 minutes. Whisk the flour, granulated sugar, salt, and baking soda together in a medium bowl and set aside.

3. Whisk the oil, eggs, vinegar, and vanilla into the cooled chocolate-cocoa mixture until smooth. Add the flour mixture and whisk until smooth.

4. Divide the batter evenly among the muffin pan cups. Place one slightly rounded teaspoon of the ganache filling on top of each cupcake. Bake until the cupcakes are set and just firm to the touch, 17 to 19 minutes. Cool the cupcakes in the muffin pan on a wire rack until cool enough to handle, about 10 minutes. Carefully lift each cupcake from the muffin pan and set on a wire rack. Cool to room temperature before frosting, about 1 hour.

5. TO FROST: Mound 2 to 3 tablespoons of the frosting on the center of each cupcake. Use a small icing spatula or butter knife to ice each cupcake. (The cupcakes can be made up to 24 hours in advance and stored unfrosted in an airtight container.)

Creamy Chocolate Frosting

MAKES ABOUT 2¼ CUPS

Cool the chocolate to between 85 and 100 degrees before adding it to the frosting. If the frosting seems too soft after adding the chocolate, chill it briefly in the refrigerator and then rewhip it until creamy.

⅓ cup (2⅓ ounces) sugar
2 large egg whites
    Pinch salt
12 tablespoons (1½ sticks) unsalted butter, cut into 12 pieces and softened
6 ounces bittersweet chocolate, melted and cooled (see note)
½ teaspoon vanilla extract

1. Combine the sugar, egg whites, and salt in the bowl of a stand mixer, then place the bowl over a pan of simmering water. Whisking gently but constantly, heat the mixture until slightly thickened and foamy and it registers 150 degrees on an instant-read thermometer, 2 to 3 minutes.

2. Using the whisk attachment, beat the mixture on medium speed in a stand mixer until it reaches the consistency of shaving cream and is slightly cooled, 1 to 2 minutes. Add the butter, one piece at a time, until smooth and creamy. (The frosting may look curdled after half of the butter has been added; it will smooth with additional butter.) Once all the butter is added, add the cooled melted chocolate and the vanilla and mix until combined. Increase the mixer speed to medium-high and beat until light, fluffy, and thoroughly combined, about 30 seconds, scraping the beater and sides of the bowl with a rubber spatula as necessary. (The frosting can be made up to 24 hours in advance and refrigerated in an airtight container. When ready to frost, place the frosting in a microwave-safe container and microwave briefly until just slightly softened, 5 to 10 seconds. Once warmed, stir until creamy.)

CHOCOLATE TORTE

WHY THIS RECIPE WORKS: Sachertorte, the classic Viennese dessert with layers of chocolate cake sandwiching apricot jam and enrobed in a creamy-rich chocolate glaze, always sounds more promising than it typically is in reality—dry, flavorless cake and sweet jam with little fruity complexity, all covered in a glaze that is nothing more than a thin, overly sugary coating. We set out to create a rich, deeply chocolaty dessert using Sachertorte as the inspiration, giving it our own spin by pairing the chocolate with raspberries.

For a rich, fudgy base, we started by baking our Flourless Chocolate Cake (page 626) in two 9-inch pans, so we could sandwich the two cakes together rather than deal with halving a single delicate cake. But when we tried to stack the layers, the dense cake tore and fell apart. Adding ground nuts gave it the structure it needed, plus a good boost of flavor. Since we were using the food processor to grind the nuts, we tweaked our cake recipe so that it could be prepared using the same appliance. The winning approach for our filling was to combine jam with lightly mashed fresh berries for a tangy-sweet mixture that clung to the cake. For the glaze, we kept things simple, melting bittersweet chocolate with heavy cream to create a rich-tasting, glossy ganache that poured smoothly over the cake. For simple but tasty decorating, we dotted fresh raspberries around the top of the torte and pressed sliced, toasted almonds along its sides.

NOTES FROM THE TEST KITCHEN

DECORATING CHOCOLATE-RASPBERRY TORTE

1. With the fully assembled cake placed on a cardboard round, hold the bottom of the cake in one hand and gently press the chopped nuts onto its side with the other hand.

2. Place one raspberry on the cake at 12 o'clock, then another at 6 o'clock. Place a third berry at 9 o'clock and a fourth at 3 o'clock. Continue to place raspberries directly opposite each other until all have been arranged in an evenly spaced circle.

Chocolate-Raspberry Torte

SERVES 12 TO 16

Be sure to use cake pans with at least 2-inch-tall sides.

CAKE

- **8 ounces bittersweet chocolate, chopped fine**
- **12 tablespoons (1½ sticks) unsalted butter, cut into ½-inch pieces**
- **2 teaspoons vanilla extract**
- **¼ teaspoon instant espresso powder**
- **1¾ cups (6⅛ ounces) sliced almonds, toasted**
- **¼ cup (1¼ ounces) unbleached all-purpose flour**
- **½ teaspoon table salt**
- **5 large eggs, at room temperature**
- **¾ cup (5¼ ounces) sugar**

FILLING

- **2½ ounces (½ cup) raspberries, plus 16 individual raspberries**
- **¼ cup seedless raspberry jam**

GLAZE

- **5 ounces bittersweet chocolate, chopped fine**
- **½ cup plus 1 tablespoon heavy cream**

1. FOR THE CAKE: Adjust an oven rack to the middle position and heat the oven to 325 degrees. Grease and flour two 9-inch round cake pans, line the bottoms with parchment paper, then grease and flour the parchment. Melt the chocolate and butter in a large heatproof bowl set over a saucepan filled with 1 inch of simmering water, stirring occasionally until smooth. Remove from the heat and let cool to room temperature, about 30 minutes. Stir in the vanilla and espresso powder.

2. Pulse ¾ cup of the almonds in a food processor until coarsely chopped, 6 to 8 pulses, and set aside. Process the remaining 1 cup almonds until very finely ground, about 45 seconds. Add the flour and salt and continue to process until combined, about 15 seconds. Transfer the almond-flour mixture to a medium bowl. Process the eggs until lightened in color and almost doubled in volume, about 3 minutes. With the processor running, slowly add the sugar and process until thoroughly combined, about 15 seconds. Using a whisk, gently fold the egg mixture into the chocolate mixture until some streaks of egg remain. Sprinkle half of the almond-flour mixture over the chocolate mixture and gently whisk until just combined. Sprinkle with the remaining almond-flour mixture and gently whisk until just combined.

3. Divide the batter evenly between the prepared pans and smooth the tops with a rubber spatula. Bake until the center is firm and a toothpick inserted in the center comes out with a few moist crumbs attached, 14 to 16 minutes. Transfer the cakes to a wire rack and let cool completely in the pans, about 30 minutes.

4. Run a paring knife around the sides of the cakes to loosen and invert the cakes onto cardboard rounds cut the same size as the diameter of the cake; discard the parchment. Using a wire rack, turn 1 cake right side up, then slide from the rack back onto the cardboard round.

5. FOR THE FILLING: Place ½ cup of the raspberries in a medium bowl and coarsely mash with a fork. Stir in the raspberry jam until just combined.

6. TO ASSEMBLE THE TORTE: Spread the raspberry mixture onto the cake layer that is right side up. Top with the second cake layer, leaving it upside down. Transfer the assembled cake, still on the cardboard round, to a wire rack set in a rimmed baking sheet.

7. FOR THE GLAZE: Melt the chocolate and cream in a medium heatproof bowl set over a saucepan filled with 1 inch of simmering water, stirring occasionally until smooth. Remove from the heat and gently whisk until very smooth. Pour the glaze onto the center of the assembled cake. Using an offset spatula, spread the glaze evenly over the top of the cake, letting it drip down the sides. Spread the glaze along the sides of the cake to coat evenly.

8. Using a fine-mesh strainer, sift the reserved chopped almonds to remove any fine bits. Holding the bottom of the cake on the cardboard round with 1 hand, gently press the sifted almonds onto the cake sides with the other hand. Arrange the remaining 16 raspberries around the circumference. Refrigerate the cake on the rack until the glaze is set, at least 1 hour or up to 24 hours (if refrigerating the cake for more than 1 hour, let sit at room temperature for about 30 minutes before serving). Transfer the cake to a platter and serve.

FLOURLESS CHOCOLATE CAKE

WHY THIS RECIPE WORKS: While all flourless chocolate cake recipes share common ingredients (chocolate, butter, and eggs), the techniques used to make them vary, as do the results. You can end up with anything from a fudge brownie to a bittersweet chocolate soufflé. We wanted something dense, moist, and ultra-chocolaty.

We started with the type of chocolate. A cake made with unsweetened chocolate was neither smooth nor silky enough for this kind of cake. Bittersweet or semisweet chocolate was ideal, with deep chocolate flavor and a smooth texture. Next we turned to the eggs—we compared cakes made with room temperature eggs and eggs taken straight from the fridge. The batter made with chilled eggs produced a denser foam and the resulting cake boasted a smooth, velvety texture. And the gentle, moist heat of a water bath further preserved the cake's lush texture.

Flourless Chocolate Cake

SERVES 12 TO 16

This cake is best when baked a day ahead to mellow its flavor. Even though the cake may not look done, pull it from the oven when an instant-read thermometer registers 140 degrees. (Do not let the tip of the thermometer hit the bottom of the pan.) It will continue to firm up as it cools. If you use a 9-inch springform pan instead of the preferred 8-inch pan, reduce the baking time to 18 to 20 minutes. See pages 740–741 for our top-rated brands of chocolate.

- 8 large eggs, chilled
- 1 pound bittersweet or semisweet chocolate, chopped (see note)
- ½ pound (2 sticks) unsalted butter, cut into ½-inch chunks
- ¼ cup strong coffee
- Confectioners' sugar or cocoa powder, for decoration

1. Adjust an oven rack to the lower-middle position and heat the oven to 325 degrees. Grease an 8-inch springform pan, then line the bottom with parchment paper. Wrap the outside of the pan with two 18-inch-square pieces of heavy-duty foil; set the springform pan in a roasting pan. Bring a kettle of water to a boil.

2. In a stand mixer fitted with the whisk attachment, beat the eggs at medium speed until doubled in volume, about 5 minutes.

3. Meanwhile, melt the chocolate and butter in a large heatproof bowl set over a saucepan filled with 1 inch of barely simmering water until smooth, stirring once or twice; stir in the coffee. Using a large rubber spatula, fold one-third of the egg mixture into the chocolate mixture until only a few streaks of egg are visible; fold the remaining egg mixture, in two additions, until the batter is totally homogeneous.

4. Scrape the batter into the prepared pan and smooth the surface with the spatula. Set the roasting pan on the oven rack and pour in enough boiling water to come about halfway up the sides of the pan. Bake until the cake has risen slightly, the edges are just beginning to set, a thin glazed crust (like a brownie) has formed on the surface, and an instant-read thermometer inserted halfway through the center of the cake registers 140 degrees, 22 to 25 minutes. Remove the pan from the water bath and set on a wire rack; cool to room temperature. Cover and refrigerate overnight to mellow the flavors. (The cake can be covered and refrigerated for up to 4 days.)

5. About 30 minutes before serving, remove the springform pan sides, then flip the cake out onto the wire rack. Peel off the parchment and flip the cake right side up onto a serving platter. Lightly dust the cake with confectioners' sugar or unsweetened cocoa powder, if desired, and serve.

HOT FUDGE PUDDING CAKE

WHY THIS RECIPE WORKS: Those who have eaten hot fudge pudding cake know its charms: unpretentious, moist, brownie-like chocolate cake sitting on a pool of thick, chocolate pudding–like sauce, baked together in one dish, as if by magic. Served warm with vanilla ice cream, this cake has a flavor that more than makes up for its homespun looks. But some recipes lack decent chocolate flavor; texture can be a problem, too. Instead of providing enough spoon-coating sauce to accompany the cake, some are dry, with a disproportionate amount of cake, while others are soupy, with a wet, sticky, underdone cake. We set out to master this humble dessert.

Pudding cake is made by sprinkling brownie batter with a mixture of sugar and cocoa, then pouring hot water on top, and baking. To bump up the chocolate flavor, we used a combination of Dutch-processed cocoa and bittersweet chocolate. We also added instant coffee to the water that is poured over the batter to cut the sweetness of the cake. We baked the cake slow and low to promote a good top crust and a silky sauce. And we found that letting the cake rest for 20 to 30 minutes before eating allows the sauce to become pudding-like and the cake brownie-like.

Hot Fudge Pudding Cake

SERVES 8

If you have cold brewed coffee on hand, it can be used in place of the instant coffee and water, but to make sure it isn't too strong, use 1 cup of cold coffee mixed with ½ cup of water. Serve the cake warm with vanilla or coffee ice cream.

2   **teaspoons instant coffee powder (see note)**
1½ **cups water**
1   **cup (7 ounces) granulated sugar**
⅔ **cup Dutch-processed cocoa powder**
⅓ **cup packed (2⅓ ounces) brown sugar**
6   **tablespoons (¾ stick) unsalted butter**
2   **ounces bittersweet or semisweet chocolate, chopped**
¾ **cup (3¾ ounces) unbleached all-purpose flour**
2   **teaspoons baking powder**
⅓ **cup whole milk**
1   **tablespoon vanilla extract**
¼ **teaspoon table salt**
1   **large egg yolk, at room temperature**

1. Adjust an oven rack to the lower-middle position and heat the oven to 325 degrees. Lightly grease an 8-inch square glass or ceramic baking dish. Stir the instant coffee into the water; set aside to dissolve. Stir together ⅓ cup of the granulated sugar, ⅓ cup of the cocoa, and the brown sugar in a small bowl, breaking up large clumps with your fingers; set aside. Melt the butter, the remaining ⅓ cup cocoa, and the chocolate in a small bowl set over a saucepan filled with 1 inch of barely simmering water; whisk until smooth and set aside to cool slightly. Whisk the flour and baking powder in a small bowl to combine; set aside. Whisk the remaining ⅔ cup granulated sugar, the milk, vanilla, and salt in a medium bowl until combined; whisk in the egg yolk. Add the chocolate mixture and whisk to combine. Add the flour mixture and whisk until the batter is evenly moistened.

2. Pour the batter into the prepared baking dish and spread evenly to the sides and corners. Sprinkle the cocoa-sugar mixture evenly over the batter (the cocoa mixture should cover the entire surface of the batter); pour the coffee mixture gently over the cocoa mixture. Bake until the cake is puffed and bubbling and just beginning to pull away from the sides of the baking dish, about 45 minutes, rotating the pan halfway through the baking time. (Do not overbake.) Cool the cake in the dish on a wire rack for about 25 minutes and serve.

Individual Hot Fudge Pudding Cakes

Follow the recipe for Hot Fudge Pudding Cake, heating the oven to 400 degrees and lightly greasing eight 6 to 8-ounce ramekins; set the ramekins on a baking sheet. Divide the batter evenly among the ramekins (about ¼ cup per ramekin) and level with the back of a spoon; sprinkle about 2 tablespoons cocoa-sugar mixture over the batter in each ramekin. Pour 3 tablespoons coffee mixture over the cocoa-sugar mixture in each ramekin. Bake until puffed and bubbling, about 20 minutes. (Do not overbake.) Cool the pudding cakes for about 15 minutes before serving (the cakes will fall as they cool).

BITTERSWEET CHOCOLATE ROULADE

WHY THIS RECIPE WORKS: A chocolate roulade can be a baker's nightmare—a hard-to-roll cake with a dry texture and a filling that won't stay put. We wanted a recipe for a true showcase roulade, a cake with a velvety texture and deep chocolate flavor, a thick, rich filling, and a decadent icing that covers it all.

We used bitter- or semisweet chocolate for maximum chocolate flavor. Six eggs gave our cake great support. A combination of cocoa and flour provided further structure and extra chocolate flavor. Once the cake was baked, we cooled it briefly in the pan, then unmolded it onto a kitchen towel rubbed with cocoa to prevent sticking. While the cake was still warm, we rolled it up with the towel inside, cooled it briefly, and then unrolled the cake—this method gave the cake a "memory" so it could be filled and re-rolled. For the filling, we made a simple espresso-flavored cream with just four ingredients, including the lush Italian cream cheese, mascarpone. Mascarpone provided both structural support and rich flavor. For the icing, we chose dark chocolate ganache, made with bittersweet chocolate and cognac for complex flavor.

Bittersweet Chocolate Roulade

SERVES 8 TO 10

We suggest that you make the filling and ganache first, then make the cake while the ganache is setting up. Or, if you prefer, the cake can be baked, filled, and rolled—but not iced—then wrapped in plastic wrap and refrigerated for up to 24 hours. If serving this cake in the style of a holiday yule log, make wood-grain striations in the ganache with a fork. The roulade is best served at room temperature.

- ¼ cup (1¼ ounces) unbleached all-purpose flour, plus extra for the pan
- 6 ounces bittersweet or semisweet chocolate, chopped fine
- 2 tablespoons cold unsalted butter, cut into 2 pieces
- 2 tablespoons cold water
- ¼ cup Dutch-processed cocoa powder, sifted, plus 1 tablespoon for unmolding
- ⅛ teaspoon table salt
- 6 large eggs, at room temperature and separated
- ⅓ cup (2⅓ ounces) sugar
- 1 teaspoon vanilla extract
- ⅛ teaspoon cream of tartar
- 1 recipe Espresso-Mascarpone Cream (recipe follows)
- 1 recipe Dark Chocolate Ganache (recipe follows)

1. Adjust an oven rack to the upper-middle position and heat the oven to 400 degrees. Spray a 17½ by 12-inch rimmed baking sheet with vegetable oil spray, cover the pan bottom with parchment paper, and spray the parchment with vegetable oil spray; dust with flour and tap out the excess.

2. Heat the chocolate, butter, and water in a small heatproof bowl set over a saucepan filled with 1 inch of barely simmering water, stirring occasionally until smooth. Set aside to cool slightly. Sift ¼ cup of the cocoa, the flour, and salt together into a small bowl and set aside.

3. In a stand mixer fitted with the whisk attachment, beat the egg yolks at medium-high speed until just combined, about 15 seconds. With the mixer running, add half of the sugar. Continue to beat, scraping down the sides of the bowl as necessary, until the yolks are pale yellow and the mixture falls in a thick ribbon when the whisk is lifted, about 8 minutes. Add the vanilla and beat to combine, scraping down the bowl once, about 30 seconds. Turn the mixture into a medium bowl; wash and dry the mixer bowl and whisk attachment.

4. In the clean bowl with the clean whisk attachment, beat the egg whites and cream of tartar at medium speed until foamy, about 30 seconds. With the mixer running, add about 1 teaspoon more sugar; continue beating until soft peaks form, about 40 seconds. Gradually add the remaining sugar and beat until the egg whites are glossy and hold stiff peaks when the whisk is lifted, about 1 minute longer. Do not overbeat.

5. Stir the chocolate mixture into the egg yolks. With a rubber spatula, stir one-quarter of the egg whites into the chocolate mixture to lighten it. Fold in the remaining egg whites until almost no streaks remain. Sprinkle the cocoa-flour mixture over the top and fold in quickly but gently.

6. Pour the batter into the prepared pan; using a spatula and working quickly, even the surface and smooth the batter into the pan corners. Lightly tap the pan against the countertop two or three times to settle the batter. Bake until the center of the cake springs back when touched with a finger, 8 to 10 minutes, rotating the pan halfway through the baking time. Cool the cake in the pan on a wire rack for 5 minutes.

7. While the cake is cooling, lay a clean kitchen towel over the work surface and sift the remaining 1 tablespoon cocoa over the towel; rub the cocoa into the towel. Run a small knife around the baking sheet to loosen the cake. Flip the cake onto the towel and peel off the parchment.

8. Roll the cake, towel and all, into a jellyroll shape. Cool for 15 minutes, then unroll the cake and towel. Using a spatula, immediately spread the filling evenly over the cake, almost to the edges. Roll up the cake gently but snugly around the filling. Set a large sheet of parchment paper on an overturned rimmed baking sheet and set the roulade, seam side down, on top. Trim both ends on the diagonal. Spread the ganache evenly over the roulade. Use a fork to make wood-grain striations, if desired, on the surface of the ganache before the icing has set. Refrigerate the cake, on the baking sheet, uncovered, to slightly set the icing, about 20 minutes.

9. Carefully slide two wide metal spatulas under the cake and transfer the cake to a serving platter. Cut into slices and serve.

Espresso-Mascarpone Cream

MAKES ABOUT 2½ CUPS

Mascarpone is a fresh Italian cheese. Its flavor is unique—mildly sweet and refreshing. It is sold in small containers in some supermarkets as well as most gourmet stores, cheese shops, and Italian markets.

½ cup heavy cream

2 teaspoons espresso powder or instant coffee

6 tablespoons confectioners' sugar

16½ ounces mascarpone cheese (generous 2 cups)

1. Bring the cream to a simmer in a small saucepan over high heat. Off the heat, stir in the espresso and confectioners' sugar; cool slightly.

2. With a spatula, beat the mascarpone in a medium bowl until softened. Gently whisk in the cooled cream mixture until combined. Cover with plastic wrap and refrigerate until ready to use.

Dark Chocolate Ganache

MAKES ABOUT 1½ CUPS

If your kitchen is cool and the ganache becomes too stiff to spread, set the bowl over a saucepan of simmering water, then stir briefly until it is smooth and icing-like.

¾ cup heavy cream

2 tablespoons unsalted butter

6 ounces high-quality bittersweet or
   semisweet chocolate, chopped

1 tablespoon cognac

Microwave the cream and butter in a microwave-safe measuring cup on high power until bubbling, about 1½ minutes. (Alternatively, bring to a simmer in a small saucepan over medium-high heat.) Place the chocolate in a food processor. With the machine running, gradually add the hot cream mixture and cognac through the feed tube and process until smooth and thickened, about 3 minutes. Transfer the ganache to a medium bowl and let stand at room temperature for 1 hour, until spreadable (the ganache should have the consistency of soft icing).

TRIPLE-CHOCOLATE MOUSSE CAKE

WHY THIS RECIPE WORKS: Triple chocolate mousse cake is a truly decadent dessert. Most times, though, the mousse texture is exactly the same from one layer to the next and the flavor is so overpoweringly rich it's hard to finish more than a few forkfuls. We set out to tweak this showy confection. By finessing one layer at a time, starting with the dark chocolate base and building to the top white chocolate tier, we aimed to create a triple-decker that was incrementally lighter in texture—and richness.

For simplicity's sake, we decided to build the whole dessert, layer by layer, in the same springform pan. For a base layer that had the heft to support the upper two tiers, we chose flourless chocolate cake instead of the typical mousse. Folding egg whites into the batter helped lighten the cake without affecting its structural integrity. For the middle layer, we started with a traditional chocolate mousse, but the texture seemed too heavy when combined with the cake, so we removed the eggs and cut back on the chocolate a bit—this resulted in the lighter, creamier layer we desired. And for the crowning layer to our cake, we made an easy white chocolate mousse by folding whipped cream into melted white chocolate—and to prevent the soft mousse from oozing during slicing, we added a little gelatin to the mix.

Triple-Chocolate Mousse Cake

SERVES 12 TO 16

This recipe requires a springform pan at least 3 inches high for all three layers to fit. It is imperative that each layer is made in sequential order. Cool the base completely before topping with the middle layer. We recommend Ghirardelli Bittersweet Chocolate for the base and middle layers; our other recommended brand of chocolate, Callebaut Intense Dark Chocolate, may be used but will produce drier, slightly less sweet results. Our preferred brand of white chocolate is Guittard Choc-Au-Lait White Chips. For best results, chill the mixer bowl before whipping the heavy cream. For neater slices, clean the knife thoroughly between slices.

BASE LAYER

- 6 tablespoons (¾ stick) unsalted butter, cut into 6 pieces
- 7 ounces bittersweet chocolate, chopped fine (see note)
- ¾ teaspoon instant espresso powder
- 4 large eggs, at room temperature and separated
- 1½ teaspoons vanilla extract
  Pinch table salt
- ⅓ cup packed (2⅓ ounces) light brown sugar, crumbled with fingers to remove lumps

MIDDLE LAYER

- 5 tablespoons hot water
- 2 tablespoons cocoa powder, preferably Dutch-processed
- 7 ounces bittersweet chocolate, chopped fine (see note)
- 1½ cups heavy cream, chilled
- 1 tablespoon granulated sugar
- ⅛ teaspoon table salt

TOP LAYER

- ¾ teaspoon powdered gelatin
- 1 tablespoon water
- 6 ounces white chocolate, chopped fine (see note)
- 1½ cups heavy cream, chilled
  Shaved chocolate or cocoa powder, for serving (optional)

1. FOR THE BASE LAYER: Adjust an oven rack to the middle position and heat the oven to 325 degrees.

Grease the bottom and sides of a 9-inch-wide by 3-inch-high round springform pan. Melt the butter, chocolate, and espresso powder in a large heatproof bowl set over a saucepan filled with 1 inch of barely simmering water, stirring occasionally until smooth. Remove from the heat and cool the mixture slightly, about 5 minutes. Whisk in the egg yolks and vanilla; set aside.

2. In a stand mixer fitted with the whisk attachment, beat the egg whites and salt at medium speed until frothy, about 30 seconds. Add half of the brown sugar and beat until combined, about 15 seconds. Add the remaining brown sugar and beat at high speed until soft peaks form when the whisk is lifted, about 1 minute longer, scraping down the sides of the bowl halfway through. Using a whisk, fold one-third of the beaten egg whites into the chocolate mixture to lighten. Using a rubber spatula, fold in the remaining egg whites until no white streaks remain. Carefully transfer the batter to the prepared pan, gently smoothing the top with a spatula.

3. Bake until the cake has risen, is firm around the edges, and the center has just set but is still soft (the center of the cake will spring back after pressing gently with a finger), 13 to 18 minutes. Transfer the cake to a wire rack to cool completely, about 1 hour. (The cake will collapse as it cools.) Do not remove the cake from the pan.

4. FOR THE MIDDLE LAYER: Combine the hot water and cocoa powder in a small bowl; set aside. Melt the chocolate in a large heatproof bowl set over a saucepan filled with 1 inch of barely simmering water, stirring occasionally until smooth. Remove from the heat and cool slightly, 2 to 5 minutes.

5. In the clean bowl of a stand mixer fitted with the whisk attachment, whip the heavy cream, sugar, and salt at medium speed until it begins to thicken, about 30 seconds. Increase the speed to high and whip until soft peaks form when the whisk is lifted, 15 to 60 seconds. Whisk the cocoa powder mixture into the melted chocolate until smooth. Using a whisk, fold one-third of the whipped cream mixture into the chocolate mixture to lighten. Using a rubber spatula, fold in the remaining whipped cream mixture until no white streaks remain. Spoon the mousse into the springform pan over the cooled cake and lightly tap the pan against the countertop two or three times to settle the mousse; gently smooth the top with a spatula. Wipe the inside edge of the pan with a damp cloth to remove any drips. Refrigerate the cake for at least 15 minutes while preparing the top layer.

6. FOR THE TOP LAYER: In a small bowl, sprinkle the gelatin over the water; let stand for at least 5 minutes. Place the white chocolate in a medium bowl. Bring ½ cup of the cream to a simmer in a small saucepan over medium-high heat. Remove from the heat; add the gelatin mixture and stir until fully dissolved. Pour the cream mixture over the white chocolate and whisk until the chocolate is melted and the mixture is smooth, about 30 seconds. Cool to room temperature, stirring occasionally, 5 to 8 minutes (the mixture will thicken slightly).

7. In the bowl of a stand mixer fitted with the whisk attachment, whip the remaining 1 cup cream at medium speed until it begins to thicken, about 30 seconds. Increase the speed to high and whip until soft peaks form when the whisk is lifted, 15 to 60 seconds. Using a whisk, fold one-third of the whipped cream into the white chocolate mixture to lighten. Using a rubber spatula, fold the remaining whipped cream into the white chocolate mixture until no white streaks remain. Spoon the white chocolate mousse into the pan over the bittersweet chocolate mousse layer. Smooth the top with a spatula. Return the cake to the refrigerator and chill until set, at least 2½ hours.

8. TO SERVE: Garnish the top of the cake with chocolate curls or dust with cocoa (if using). Run a thin knife between the cake and sides of the springform pan; remove the sides of the pan. Run the cleaned knife along the outside of the cake to smooth the sides. Serve.

CHOCOLATE VOLCANO CAKES WITH ESPRESSO ICE CREAM

WHY THIS RECIPE WORKS: A common restaurant dessert, volcano cake, or molten chocolate cake, is an intensely chocolate cake that boasts a warm, liquid center. In addition to its great flavor and alluring contrasting textures, the cake can often be made ahead and baked just before serving. The make-ahead appeal of such a cake inspired us to master this dessert for the home cook.

The initial recipes we tried revealed a host of problems with this cake—unbalanced chocolate flavor and a soggy or dry texture were just a few issues we faced. After testing various chocolates, we settled on a combination of bittersweet chocolate and unsweetened chocolate—this gave us maximum chocolate flavor. Chocolate alone seemed a little flat, so we added Grand Marnier for another layer of flavor. Whole eggs and egg yolks contributed richness and cornstarch helped make the batter remarkably stable. To help the cakes fall right out of the ramekins without a struggle, we buttered and sugared the ramekins before pouring in the batter. The cakes alone were great, but we felt they were even better when accompanied by a cold, creamy scoop of doctored "espresso" ice cream.

Chocolate Volcano Cakes with Espresso Ice Cream

SERVES 8

Use a bittersweet bar chocolate in this recipe, not chips—the chips include emulsifiers that will alter the cakes' texture. The cake batter can be mixed and portioned into the ramekins, wrapped tightly with plastic wrap, and refrigerated up to 24 hours in advance. The cold cake batter should be baked straight from the refrigerator.

ESPRESSO ICE CREAM

- 2 pints coffee ice cream, softened
- 1½ tablespoons finely ground espresso beans

CAKES

- 10 tablespoons (1¼ sticks) unsalted butter, cut into ½-inch pieces, plus extra for the ramekins
- 1½ cups (10½ ounces) granulated sugar, plus extra for the ramekins
- 8 ounces bittersweet chocolate, chopped fine (see note)
- 2 ounces unsweetened chocolate, chopped fine
- 2 tablespoons cornstarch
- 3 large eggs plus 4 large egg yolks, at room temperature
- 2 teaspoons Grand Marnier (or other orange-flavored liqueur)
- Confectioners' sugar, for dusting the cakes

1. FOR THE ICE CREAM: Transfer the ice cream to a medium bowl and, using a rubber spatula, fold in the ground espresso until incorporated. Press a sheet of plastic wrap directly on the ice cream to prevent freezer burn and return it to the freezer. (The ice cream can be prepared up to 24 hours ahead.)

2. FOR THE CAKES: Lightly coat eight 4-ounce ramekins with butter. Dust with sugar, tapping out any excess, and set aside.

3. Melt the bittersweet and unsweetened chocolates and the 10 tablespoons butter in a large heatproof bowl set over a pan filled with 1 inch of barely simmering water, stirring occasionally until smooth. In a large bowl, whisk the 1½ cups sugar and cornstarch together. Add the chocolate mixture and stir to combine. Add the whole eggs, egg yolks, and Grand Marnier and whisk until fully combined. Using a ½-cup measure, scoop the batter into each of the prepared ramekins. (The ramekins can be covered tightly with plastic wrap and refrigerated for up to 24 hours.)

4. Adjust an oven rack to the upper-middle position and heat the oven to 375 degrees. Place the filled ramekins on a rimmed baking sheet and bake until the tops of the cakes are set, have formed shiny crusts, and are beginning to crack, 16 to 20 minutes.

5. Transfer the ramekins to a wire rack and cool slightly, about 2 minutes. Run a small knife around the edge of each cake. Using a towel to protect your hand from the hot ramekins, invert each cake onto a small plate, then immediately invert again right side up onto eight individual plates. Sift confectioners' sugar over each cake. Remove the ice cream from the freezer and scoop a portion next to each cake. Serve immediately.

TIRAMISÙ

WHY THIS RECIPE WORKS: There's a reason restaurant menus (Italian or not) offer tiramisù. Delicate ladyfingers soaked in a spiked coffee mixture layered with a sweet, creamy filling make an irresistible combination. Preparing tiramisù, however, can be labor intensive and the dessert is not without its problems. Some versions are overly rich and the ladyfingers, which should be moist, sometimes turn soggy to the point of mush. We wanted to avoid these issues and find a streamlined approach—one that highlights the luxurious combination of flavors and textures that have made this dessert so popular.

Instead of hauling out a double boiler to make the fussy custard-based filling (called *zabaglione*), we instead simply whipped egg yolks, sugar, salt, rum (our preferred spirit), and mascarpone together. Salt is not traditional, but we found that it heightened the filling's subtle flavors. And to lighten the filling, we chose whipped cream instead of egg whites. For the coffee soaking mixture, we combined strong brewed coffee and espresso powder (along with more rum). To moisten the ladyfingers so that they were neither too dry nor too saturated, we dropped them one at a time into the spiked coffee mixture and, once they were moistened, rolled them over to moisten the other side for just a couple of seconds. For best flavor and texture, we discovered that it was important to allow the tiramisù to chill in the refrigerator for at least six hours.

Tiramisù

SERVES 10 TO 12

Brandy and even whiskey can stand in for the dark rum. The test kitchen prefers a tiramisù with a pronounced rum flavor; for a less potent rum flavor, halve the amount of rum added to the coffee mixture in step 1. Do not allow the mascarpone to warm to room temperature before using it; it has a tendency to break if allowed to do so.

2½ cups strong brewed coffee, at room temperature
9 tablespoons dark rum (see note)
1½ tablespoons instant espresso powder
6 large egg yolks, at room temperature
⅔ cup (4⅔ ounces) sugar
¼ teaspoon table salt
1½ pounds mascarpone (generous 3 cups; see note)
¾ cup heavy cream, chilled
14 ounces (42 to 60, depending on size) dried ladyfingers
3½ tablespoons cocoa powder, preferably Dutch-processed
¼ cup grated semisweet or bittersweet chocolate (optional)

1. Stir together the coffee, 5 tablespoons of the rum, and the espresso powder in a wide bowl or baking dish until the espresso dissolves; set aside.

2. In a stand mixer fitted with the whisk attachment, beat the egg yolks at low speed until just combined. Add the sugar and salt and beat at medium-high speed until pale yellow, 1½ to 2 minutes, scraping down the sides of the bowl with a rubber spatula once or twice. Add the remaining 4 tablespoons rum and beat at medium speed until just combined, 20 to 30 seconds; scrape the bowl. Add the mascarpone and beat at medium speed until no lumps remain, 30 to 45 seconds, scraping down the sides of the bowl once or twice. Transfer the mixture to a large bowl and set aside.

3. In the now-empty mixer bowl (no need to clean the bowl), beat the cream at medium speed until frothy, 1 to 1½ minutes. Increase the speed to high and continue to beat until the cream holds stiff peaks, 1 to 1½ minutes longer. Using a rubber spatula, fold one-third of the whipped cream into the mascarpone mixture to lighten, then gently fold in the remaining whipped cream until no white streaks remain. Set the mascarpone mixture aside.

4. Working one at a time, drop half of the ladyfingers into the coffee mixture, roll, remove, and transfer to a 13 by 9-inch glass or ceramic baking dish. (Do not submerge the ladyfingers in the coffee mixture; the entire process should take no longer than 2 to 3 seconds for each cookie.) Arrange the soaked cookies in a single layer in the baking dish, breaking or trimming the ladyfingers as needed to fit neatly into the dish.

5. Spread half of the mascarpone mixture over the ladyfingers; use a rubber spatula to spread the mixture to the sides and into the corners of the dish and smooth the surface. Place 2 tablespoons of the cocoa in a fine-mesh strainer and dust the cocoa over the mascarpone.

6. Repeat the dipping and arrangement of the ladyfingers; spread the remaining mascarpone mixture over the ladyfingers and dust with the remaining 1½ tablespoons cocoa. Wipe the edges of the dish with a dry paper towel. Cover with plastic wrap and refrigerate for 6 to 24 hours. Sprinkle with the grated chocolate (if using); cut into pieces and serve chilled.

Tiramisù with Cooked Eggs

This recipe involves cooking the yolks in a double boiler, which requires a little more effort and makes for a slightly thicker mascarpone filling, but the results are just as good as with our traditional method. You will need an additional ⅓ cup heavy cream.

Follow the recipe for Tiramisù through step 1. In step 2, add ⅓ cup cream to the egg yolks after the sugar and salt; do not whisk in the rum. Set the bowl with the yolks over a medium saucepan containing 1 inch gently simmering water; cook, constantly scraping along the bottom and sides of the bowl with a heatproof spatula, until the mixture coats the back of a spoon and registers 160 degrees on an instant-read thermometer, 4 to 7 minutes. Remove from the heat and stir vigorously to cool slightly, then set aside to cool to room temperature, about 15 minutes. Whisk in the remaining 4 tablespoons rum until combined. Transfer the bowl to a stand mixer fitted with the whisk attachment, add the mascarpone, and beat at medium speed until no lumps remain, 30 to 45 seconds. Transfer the mixture to a large bowl and set aside. Continue with the recipe from step 3, using the full amount of cream specified (¾ cup).

NEW YORK–STYLE CHEESECAKE

WHY THIS RECIPE WORKS: The ideal New York cheesecake should be a tall, bronze-skinned, and dense affair. At the core, it should be cool, thick, smooth, satiny, and creamy. The flavor should be pure and minimalist, sweet and tangy, and rich. But many recipes fall short—going wrong in a number of ways—with textures that range from fluffy to rubbery and leaden, and flavors that are starchy or overly citrusy. We wanted to find the secret to perfect New York cheesecake.

After trying a variety of crusts, we settled on the classic graham cracker crust—a simple combination of graham crackers, butter, and sugar. For the filling, cream cheese, boosted by the extra tang of a little sour cream, delivered the best flavor. A little lemon juice and vanilla added just the right sweet, bright accents without calling attention to themselves. A combination of eggs and egg yolks yielded a texture that was dense but not heavy. We found that the New York method worked better for this cheesecake than the typical water bath—baking the cake in a hot oven for 10 minutes then in a low oven for a full 90 minutes yielded the satiny texture we were after.

New York Cheesecake

SERVES 12

For neater slices, clean the knife thoroughly between slices. Serve as is or with Strawberry Topping (recipe follows).

CRUST

- **8 whole graham crackers, broken into 1-inch pieces**
- **7 tablespoons unsalted butter, melted and cooled**
- **3 tablespoons sugar**

FILLING

- **2½ pounds cream cheese, cut into chunks and softened**
- **1½ cups (10½ ounces) sugar**
- **⅛ teaspoon table salt**
- **⅓ cup sour cream**
- **2 teaspoons juice from 1 lemon**
- **2 teaspoons vanilla extract**
- **6 large eggs plus 2 large egg yolks, at room temperature**

1. FOR THE CRUST: Adjust an oven rack to the middle position and heat the oven to 325 degrees. Process the graham cracker pieces in a food processor to fine, even crumbs, about 30 seconds. Sprinkle 6 tablespoons of the melted butter and the sugar over the crumbs and pulse to incorporate. Sprinkle the mixture into a 9-inch springform pan. Press the crumbs firmly into an even layer using the bottom of a measuring cup. Bake the crust until fragrant and beginning to brown, 10 to 15 minutes. Cool the crust to room temperature, about 30 minutes.

2. FOR THE FILLING: Meanwhile, increase the oven temperature to 500 degrees. In the bowl of a stand mixer fitted with the paddle attachment, beat the cream cheese on medium-low speed until smooth, 1 to 3 minutes. Scrape down the bowl and beaters as needed.

3. Beat in ¾ cup of the sugar and the salt until incorporated, 1 to 3 minutes. Beat in the remaining ¾ cup sugar until incorporated, 1 to 3 minutes. Beat in the sour cream, lemon juice, and vanilla until incorporated, 1 to 3 minutes. Beat in the whole eggs and egg yolks, two at a time, until combined, 1 to 3 minutes.

4. Being careful not to disturb the baked crust, brush the inside of the prepared springform pan with the remaining 1 tablespoon melted butter. Set the pan on a rimmed baking sheet. Carefully pour the filling into the pan. Bake the cheesecake for 10 minutes.

5. Without opening the oven door, reduce the oven temperature to 200 degrees and continue to bake until the center of the cheesecake registers 150 degrees on an instant-read thermometer, about 1½ hours.

6. Transfer the cheesecake to a wire rack and run a knife around the edge of the cake. Cool the cheesecake until just barely warm, 2½ to 3 hours, running a knife around the edge of the cake every hour or so. Wrap the pan tightly in plastic wrap and refrigerate until cold, about 3 hours.

7. To unmold the cheesecake, wrap a wet, hot kitchen towel around the cake pan and let sit for 1 minute. Remove the sides of the pan and carefully slide the cake onto a cake platter. Let the cheesecake sit at room temperature for 30 minutes before serving.

Strawberry Topping

MAKES ABOUT 6 CUPS

This accompaniment to cheesecake is best served the same day it is made.

- **2 pounds fresh strawberries, cleaned, hulled, and cut lengthwise into ¼ to ⅛-inch slices**
- **½ cup (3½ ounces) sugar**
  Pinch table salt
- **1 cup strawberry jam**
- **2 tablespoons juice from 1 lemon**

1. Toss the berries, sugar, and salt in a medium bowl; let stand until the berries have released their juices and the

sugar has dissolved, about 30 minutes, tossing occasionally to combine.

2. Process the jam in a food processor until smooth, about 8 seconds; transfer to a small saucepan. Bring the jam to a simmer over medium-high heat; simmer, stirring frequently, until dark and no longer frothy, about 3 minutes. Stir in the lemon juice; pour the warm liquid over the strawberries and stir to combine. Let cool, then cover with plastic wrap and refrigerate until cold, at least 2 hours or up to 12 hours. To serve, spoon a portion of topping over each slice of cheesecake.

LIGHT CHEESECAKE

WHY THIS RECIPE WORKS: Of all the desserts that people long for in low-fat form, cheesecake is probably the most popular—but it's also the most difficult to lighten. Why? One modest slice of cheesecake boasts nearly 600 calories and about 40 grams of fat. Start removing the fat and sugar in the cake and flavor and texture can suffer terribly, as evidenced by the light recipes we tried. These cheesecakes were rubbery, gummy, and full of artificial flavors. We set out to develop a light cheesecake worth eating.

Three key steps produced our desired results. We replaced full-fat cream cheese and sour cream with a combination of light cream cheese, low-fat cottage cheese, and low-fat yogurt cheese. And to ensure a firm, not loose, filling, we drained the cottage cheese—this rid it of excess moisture. We cut the fat further by using a reduced number of whole eggs instead of whole eggs and yolks. And, finally, we pureed the filling in a food processor for an ultrasmooth texture. The result? A rich, creamy cheesecake with about half the calories and three-quarters less fat than the original.

Light New York Cheesecake

SERVES 12

You can buy low-fat yogurt cheese (also called labne) or make your own with low-fat yogurt—allow at least 10 hours for the yogurt to drain. To make 1 cup yogurt cheese, line a fine-mesh strainer with 3 paper coffee filters or a double layer of cheesecloth. Spoon 2 cups of plain low-fat yogurt into the lined strainer, cover, and refrigerate for 10 to 12 hours (about 1 cup of liquid will have drained out of the yogurt to yield 1 cup yogurt cheese). Serve cake as is, or with Strawberry Topping (page 634).

CRUST
- 9 whole graham crackers, broken into 1-inch pieces
- 4 tablespoons (½ stick) unsalted butter, melted
- 1 tablespoon sugar

FILLING
- 1 pound 1 percent cottage cheese
- 1 pound light cream cheese, cut into chunks and softened
- 8 ounces (1 cup) low-fat yogurt cheese (see note)
- 1½ cups (10½ ounces) sugar
- 1 tablespoon vanilla extract
- 1 teaspoon grated zest from 1 lemon
- ¼ teaspoon table salt
- 3 large eggs, at room temperature

1. FOR THE CRUST: Adjust an oven rack to the middle position and heat the oven to 325 degrees. Process the graham cracker pieces in a food processor to fine, even crumbs, about 30 seconds. Mix the cracker crumbs, melted butter, and sugar together, then pour into a 9-inch springform pan. Press the crumbs firmly into an even layer using the bottom of a measuring cup. Bake the crust until fragrant, 10 to 15 minutes. Cool on a wire rack, about 30 minutes.

2. FOR THE FILLING: Meanwhile, increase the oven temperature to 500 degrees. Line a medium bowl with a clean dish towel or several layers of paper towels. Spoon the cottage cheese into the bowl and let drain for 30 minutes.

3. Process the drained cottage cheese in a food processor until smooth and no visible lumps remain, about 1 minute, scraping down the bowl as needed. Dollop the cream cheese and yogurt cheese into the food processor and continue to process until smooth, 1 to 2 minutes, scraping down the bowl as needed. Add the sugar, vanilla, lemon zest, and salt and continue to process until smooth, about 1 minute. With the processor running, add the eggs one at a time and continue to process until smooth.

4. Being careful not to disturb the baked crust, spray the insides of the springform pan with vegetable oil spray. Set the pan on a rimmed baking sheet. Pour the processed cheese mixture into the cooled crust and bake for 10 minutes.

5. Without opening the oven door, reduce the oven temperature to 200 degrees and continue to bake until the center of the cheesecake registers 150 degrees on an instant-read thermometer, about 1½ hours.

6. Transfer the cake to a wire rack and run a paring knife around the edge of the cake. Cool until barely warm, 2½ to 3 hours, running a paring knife around the edge of the cake every hour or so. Wrap the pan tightly in plastic wrap and refrigerate until cold, about 3 hours.

7. To unmold the cheesecake, wrap a wet, hot kitchen towel around the springform pan and let stand for 1 minute. Remove the sides of the pan. Blot any excess moisture from the top of the cheesecake with paper towels and slide onto a cake platter. Let the cheesecake stand at room temperature for about 30 minutes before slicing.

PUMPKIN CHEESECAKE

WHY THIS RECIPE WORKS: Those who suffer from pumpkin pie ennui embrace pumpkin cheesecake as "a nice change," but the expectations are low. Undoubtedly, pumpkin cheesecake can be good in its own right, though it rarely is. Textures run the gamut from dry and dense to wet, soft, and mousse-like. Flavors veer from far too cheesy and tangy to pungently overspiced to totally bland. We wanted a creamy pumpkin cheesecake with a velvety smooth texture that tasted of sweet, earthy pumpkin as well as tangy cream cheese, that struck a harmonious spicy chord, and, of course, that had a crisp, buttery, cookie-crumb crust.

For a cookie crust that complemented the earthy, warm flavors of pumpkin, we spiced up a graham cracker crust with ginger, cinnamon, and cloves. For a smooth and creamy texture, we blotted canned pumpkin puree with paper towels to remove excess moisture—this solved the sogginess issue. For dairy, we liked heavy cream, not sour cream, for added richness. We also preferred white sugar to brown, which tended to overpower the pumpkin flavor. Whole eggs, vanilla, salt, lemon juice, and a moderate blend of spices rounded out our cake. And for a smooth, velvety texture, we baked the cheesecake in a water bath in a moderate oven.

Spiced Pumpkin Cheesecake

SERVES 12

Be sure to buy unsweetened canned pumpkin, not pumpkin pie filling, which is preseasoned and sweetened. For neater slices, clean the knife thoroughly between slices.

CRUST

- 8 whole graham crackers, broken into 1-inch pieces
- 7 tablespoons unsalted butter, melted and cooled
- 3 tablespoons sugar
- ½ teaspoon ground ginger
- ½ teaspoon ground cinnamon
- ¼ teaspoon ground cloves

FILLING

- 1 (15-ounce) can pumpkin puree (see note)
- 1⅓ cups (9⅓ ounces) sugar
- 1 teaspoon ground cinnamon
- ½ teaspoon ground ginger
- ¼ teaspoon ground nutmeg
- ¼ teaspoon ground cloves
- ¼ teaspoon ground allspice
- ½ teaspoon table salt
- 1½ pounds cream cheese, cut into chunks and softened
- 1 tablespoon juice from 1 lemon
- 1 tablespoon vanilla extract
- 5 large eggs, at room temperature
- 1 cup heavy cream

1. FOR THE CRUST: Adjust an oven rack to the middle position and heat the oven to 325 degrees. Process the graham cracker pieces in a food processor to fine, even crumbs, about 30 seconds. Sprinkle 6 tablespoons of the melted butter, the sugar, and spices over the crumbs and pulse to incorporate. Sprinkle the mixture into a 9-inch springform pan. Press the crumbs firmly into an even layer using the bottom of a measuring cup. Bake the crust until fragrant and beginning to brown, 10 to 15 minutes. Let the crust cool to room temperature, about 30 minutes. Once cool, wrap the outside of the pan with two sheets of heavy-duty foil and set in a large roasting pan lined with a dish towel. Bring a kettle of water to a boil.

2. FOR THE FILLING: Pat the pumpkin puree dry with several layers of paper towels. Whisk the sugar, spices, and salt together in a small bowl.

3. In a stand mixer fitted with the paddle attachment, beat the cream cheese on medium-low speed until smooth, about 1 minute. Scrape down the bowl and beaters as needed.

4. Beat in half of the sugar mixture until incorporated, about 1 minute. Beat in the remaining sugar mixture until incorporated, about 1 minute. Beat in the dried pumpkin, lemon juice, and vanilla until incorporated, about 1 minute. Beat in the eggs, one at a time, until combined, about 1 minute. Beat in the heavy cream until incorporated, about 1 minute.

5. Being careful not to disturb the baked crust, brush the inside of the springform pan with the remaining 1 tablespoon melted butter. Carefully pour the filling into the pan. Set the roasting pan, with the cheesecake, on the oven rack and pour the boiling water into the roasting pan until it reaches about halfway up the sides of the pan. Bake the cheesecake until the center registers 150 degrees on an instant-read thermometer, about 1½ hours.

6. Cool the cheesecake in the roasting pan for 45 minutes, then transfer to a wire rack and cool until barely warm, 2½ to 3 hours, running a knife around the edge of the cake every hour or so. Wrap the pan tightly in plastic wrap and refrigerate until cold, about 3 hours.

7. To unmold the cheesecake, wrap a wet, hot kitchen towel around the cake pan and let sit for 1 minute. Remove the sides of the pan and carefully slide the cake onto a cake platter. Let the cheesecake sit at room temperature for 30 minutes before serving.

LEMON CHEESECAKE

WHY THIS RECIPE WORKS: Cheesecake is decadently rich. We love it in its unadulterated form, but sometimes the fresh flavor of citrus can take cheesecake to a refreshing new level. We aimed to develop a creamy cheesecake with a bracing but not overpowering lemon flavor.

Graham crackers, our usual cookie for cheesecakes, were too overpowering for the filling's lemon flavor. Instead, we turned to biscuit-type cookies, such as animal crackers, for a mild-tasting crust that allowed the lemon flavor of the cheesecake to shine. For maximum lemon flavor, we ground lemon zest with a portion of the sugar. This released its flavorful oils dramatically. Grinding the zest also improved the filling's texture (minced lemon zest baked up into fibrous bits in the cake). Heavy cream, in addition to cream cheese, provided richness, and vanilla rounded out the flavors. For ultimate creaminess, we baked the cake in a water bath. And finally, for an additional layer of bright lemon flavor, we topped off the cake with lemon curd.

Lemon Cheesecake

SERVES 12

Be sure to zest the lemons before juicing them. For neater slices, clean the knife thoroughly between slices.

CRUST

5	ounces Nabisco Barnum's Animal Crackers or Social Tea Biscuits
7	tablespoons unsalted butter, melted and cooled
3	tablespoons sugar

FILLING

1¼	cups (8¾ ounces) sugar
1	tablespoon grated zest from 1 lemon
1½	pounds cream cheese, cut into chunks and softened
¼	teaspoon table salt
¼	cup juice from 2 lemons
2	teaspoons vanilla extract
4	large eggs, at room temperature
½	cup heavy cream

CURD

⅓	cup juice from 2 lemons
½	cup (3½ ounces) sugar
	Pinch table salt
2	large whole eggs plus 1 large egg yolk
2	tablespoons unsalted butter, cut into ½-inch pieces and frozen
1	tablespoon heavy cream
¼	teaspoon vanilla extract

1. FOR THE CRUST: Adjust an oven rack to the middle position and heat the oven to 325 degrees. Process the cookies in a food processor to fine, even crumbs, about 30 seconds. Sprinkle 6 tablespoons of the melted butter and the sugar over the crumbs and pulse to incorporate. Sprinkle the mixture into a 9-inch springform pan. Press the crumbs firmly into an even layer using the bottom of a measuring cup. Bake the crust until fragrant and beginning to brown, 10 to 15 minutes. Let the crust cool to room temperature, about 30 minutes. Once cool, wrap the outside of the pan with two sheets of heavy-duty foil and set in a large roasting pan lined with a dish towel. Bring a kettle of water to a boil.

2. FOR THE FILLING: Process ¼ cup of the sugar and the lemon zest in a food processor until the sugar is yellow and the zest is very fine, about 15 seconds. Pulse in the remaining 1 cup sugar to combine.

3. In a stand mixer fitted with the paddle attachment, beat the cream cheese on medium speed until smooth, about 1 minute. Scrape down the bowl and beaters as needed.

4. Beat in half of the lemon sugar and the salt until incorporated. Beat in the remaining lemon sugar until incorporated, about 1 minute. Beat in the lemon juice and vanilla until incorporated, about 1 minute. Beat in the eggs, one at a time, until combined, about 1 minute. Beat in the heavy cream until incorporated, about 1 minute.

5. Being careful not to disturb the baked crust, brush the inside of the prepared springform pan with the remaining 1 tablespoon melted butter. Carefully pour the filling into the pan. Set the roasting pan, with the cheesecake, on the oven rack and pour the boiling water into the roasting pan until it reaches about halfway up the sides of the springform pan. Bake the cheesecake until the center registers 150 degrees on an instant-read thermometer, about 1½ hours.

6. Cool the cheesecake in the roasting pan for 45 minutes, then transfer to a wire rack and cool until barely warm, 2½ to 3 hours, running a knife around the edge of the cake every hour or so. Wrap the pan tightly in plastic wrap and refrigerate until cold, about 3 hours.

7. FOR THE CURD: Meanwhile, cook the lemon juice, sugar, and salt together in a small saucepan over medium-high heat until the sugar dissolves and the mixture is hot (do not boil). In a medium bowl, whisk the whole eggs and egg yolk together until combined, then slowly whisk in the hot lemon mixture to temper. Return the mixture to the saucepan and cook over medium-low heat, stirring constantly, until the mixture is thickened and a spatula scraped along the bottom of the pan leaves a trail (170 degrees on an instant-read thermometer), 2 to 4 minutes.

8. Off the heat, stir in the frozen butter until melted and incorporated, then stir in the cream and vanilla. Strain the curd through a fine-mesh strainer into a small bowl. Press plastic wrap directly on the surface of the curd and refrigerate until needed.

9. TO FINISH THE CAKE: When the cheesecake is cold, spoon the lemon curd over the top of the cake and spread into an even layer. Wrap the pan tightly in plastic wrap and refrigerate until the curd and cake have set, at least 5 hours.

10. To unmold the cheesecake, wrap a wet, hot kitchen towel around the cake pan and let sit for 1 minute. Remove the sides of the pan and carefully slide the cake onto a cake platter. Let the cheesecake sit at room temperature for 30 minutes before serving.

CHAPTER 23

PUDDINGS AND SOUFFLÉS

Classic Bread Pudding   640

    Bourbon–Brown Sugar
Sauce

Chocolate–Hazelnut Slow
Cooker Bread Pudding   641

Stovetop Rice Pudding   642

Coconut Rice Pudding   642

Panna Cotta   643

    Raspberry Coulis

Classic Crème Brûlée   644

Espresso Crème
Brûlée   645

Classic Crème
Caramel   645

Chocolate
Pots de Crème   646

Milk Chocolate
Pots de Crème   647

Creamy Chocolate
Pudding   648

Dark Chocolate
Mousse   648

Chocolate-Orange
Mousse   649

Chocolate-Raspberry
Mousse   649

Premium Dark Chocolate
Mousse   649

Low-Fat Chocolate
Mousse   650

Grand Marnier Soufflé   650

Grand Marnier Soufflé
with Grated Chocolate   651

Chilled Lemon Soufflé   651

Chilled Lemon Soufflé
with White Chocolate   652

Individual Chilled
Lemon Soufflés   652

Make-Ahead Chocolate
Soufflés   653

Make-Ahead Mocha
Soufflés   653

Skillet Lemon Soufflé   654

Skillet Chocolate-Orange
Soufflé   654

Homemade Vanilla
Ice Cream   655

BREAD PUDDING

WHY THIS RECIPE WORKS: Contemporary versions of this humble dish vary in texture, from mushy, sweetened porridge to chewy, desiccated cousins of overcooked holiday stuffing. We wanted a dessert cart–worthy dish as refined as any French soufflé: a moist, creamy (but not eggy) interior and a crisp top crust.

After extensive testing of different types of bread, we chose challah for its rich flavor. We cut the bread into cubes, toasted them until lightly browned, and soaked the cubes with a batch of basic custard. Once the cubes were saturated, we transferred them to a baking dish and slid our pudding into a low-temperature oven to prevent curdling. The custard turned out creamy and smooth, but not as set as we'd have liked. Adding another egg or two would help, but tasters were already complaining that the pudding tasted somewhat eggy. It turns out that eggy flavor comes from the sulfur compounds in egg whites. We got rid of the whites and just used the yolks. We now had a luscious, silky custard with no trace of egginess.

For a crackly crust, we dotted the top of the pudding with additional toasted bread cubes. Then we brushed it with melted butter and sprinkled it with a flavorful mixture of white and brown sugar before transferring it to the oven. The crunchy, buttery, sugary crust was the perfect partner to the satiny-smooth custard that lay below.

Classic Bread Pudding

SERVES 8 TO 10

Challah is an egg-enriched bread that can be found in most bakeries and supermarkets. If you cannot find challah, a firm high-quality sandwich bread such as Arnold Country Classics White or Pepperidge Farm Farmhouse Hearty White may be substituted. If desired, serve this pudding with softly whipped cream or with Bourbon–Brown Sugar Sauce (recipe follows). Store leftovers tightly wrapped in the refrigerator. To retain a crisp top crust when reheating leftovers, cut the bread pudding into squares and heat, uncovered, in a 450-degree oven until warmed through, 6 to 8 minutes.

- 2 tablespoons light brown sugar
- ¾ cup (5¼ ounces) plus 1 tablespoon granulated sugar
- 1 (14-ounce) loaf challah bread, cut into ¾-inch cubes (about 10 cups; see note)
- 9 large egg yolks
- 4 teaspoons vanilla extract
- ¾ teaspoon table salt
- 2½ cups heavy cream
- 2½ cups milk
- 2 tablespoons unsalted butter, melted

1. Adjust the oven racks to the middle and lower-middle positions and heat the oven to 325 degrees. Combine the brown sugar and 1 tablespoon of the granulated sugar in a small bowl; set aside.

2. Spread the bread cubes in a single layer on two rimmed baking sheets. Bake, tossing occasionally, until just dry, about 15 minutes, switching the baking sheets halfway through the baking time. Cool the bread cubes for about 15 minutes; set aside 2 cups.

3. Whisk the egg yolks, remaining ¾ cup sugar, the vanilla, and salt together in a large bowl. Whisk in the cream and milk until combined. Add the remaining 8 cups cooled bread cubes and toss to coat. Transfer the mixture to a 13 by 9-inch baking dish and let stand, occasionally pressing the bread cubes into the custard, until the cubes are thoroughly saturated, about 30 minutes.

4. Spread the reserved bread cubes evenly over the top of the soaked bread mixture and gently press into the custard. Using a pastry brush, dab the melted butter over the top of the unsoaked bread pieces. Sprinkle the brown sugar mixture evenly over the top. Place the bread pudding on a rimmed baking sheet and bake on the middle rack until the custard has just set and pressing the center of the pudding with your finger reveals no runny liquid, 45 to 50 minutes. (An instant-read thermometer inserted into the center of the pudding should read 170 degrees.) Transfer to a wire rack and cool until the pudding is set and just warm, about 45 minutes. Serve.

Bourbon–Brown Sugar Sauce

MAKES ABOUT 1 CUP

- ½ cup packed (3½ ounces) light brown sugar
- 7 tablespoons heavy cream
- 2½ tablespoons unsalted butter
- 1½ tablespoons bourbon

Whisk the brown sugar and heavy cream in a small saucepan over medium heat until combined. Continue to cook, whisking frequently, until the mixture comes to a boil, about 5 minutes. Whisk in the butter and bring the mixture back to a boil, about 1 minute. Remove from the heat and whisk in the bourbon. Cool to just warm; serve with the bread pudding.

SLOW-COOKER BREAD PUDDING

WHY THIS RECIPE WORKS: Making bread pudding in a slow cooker may seem like a stretch, but we were determined to make a company-worthy version in the slow cooker that boasted both decadence and hands-off (and oven-freeing) convenience. Getting the texture of this dessert just right was the real challenge; early tests yielded mushy or dry puddings, not the creamy and moist texture we were after. After testing various types of bread, we agreed challah, with its rich flavor, had the upper hand. We cut the bread into cubes and toasted it in the oven before adding it to the slow cooker. This extra step dried out the bread so it would be able to soak up as much custard as possible. Once toasted, we transferred the bread to the slow cooker and added the custard (a combination of egg yolks, milk, heavy cream, sugar, and vanilla). Pressing the bread into the custard ensured every cube soaked up its share. A chocolate bread pudding seemed like the right indulgent route to take, and opting for nutella as our chief chocolaty component took our recipe to the next level. To give our recipe another chocolaty boost, we stirred in chocolate chips, which melted into the pudding and made this dessert that much more decadent.

Chocolate–Hazelnut Slow-Cooker Bread Pudding

SERVES 8 TO 10

- 1 (14-ounce) loaf challah bread, cut into 1-inch cubes (about 12 cups; see note on page 640)
- ½ cup chocolate chips
- 2 cups heavy cream
- 2 cups whole milk
- 9 large egg yolks
- 1 cup Nutella
- ¾ cup plus 1 tablespoon (5⅔ ounces) granulated sugar
- 4 teaspoons vanilla extract
- ¾ teaspoon table salt
- 2 tablespoons light brown sugar

1. Following the photos, line the slow cooker with an aluminum foil collar, then line with a foil sling, and spray with vegetable oil spray. Adjust the oven rack to the middle position and heat the oven to 225 degrees. Spread the bread over a rimmed baking sheet and bake, shaking the pan occasionally, until dry and crisp, about 40 minutes. Let the bread cool slightly, then transfer to a very large bowl.

2. Mix the chocolate chips into the dried bread; transfer to the prepared slow cooker. Whisk the cream, milk, egg yolks, Nutella, ¾ cup of the granulated sugar, the vanilla,

---

NOTES FROM THE TEST KITCHEN

PREPARING THE SLOW COOKER

1. TO MAKE A FOIL COLLAR:
Layer and fold sheets of heavy-duty foil until you have a six-layered foil rectangle that measures roughly 16 inches long by 4 inches wide. Press the collar into the back side of the slow cooker insert.

2. TO MAKE A FOIL SLING:
Fit two large sheets of heavy-duty foil into the slow cooker, perpendicular to one another and hanging over the edges of the slow cooker. Use the overhanging foil to lift the dish out of the slow cooker fully intact.

and salt together in a bowl, then pour the mixture evenly over the bread. Press gently on the bread to submerge.

3. Mix the remaining 1 tablespoon granulated sugar with the brown sugar then sprinkle over the top of the casserole. Cover and cook until the center is set, about 4 hours on low. Let cool for 30 minutes before serving.

STOVETOP RICE PUDDING

WHY THIS RECIPE WORKS: At its best, rice pudding is lightly sweet and tastes of its primary component, rice. At its worst, the rice flavor is lost to cloying sweetness, over-cooked milk, and a pasty, leaden consistency. We wanted a rice pudding with intact, tender grains bound loosely in a subtly sweet, creamy pudding.

For simple, straightforward rice flavor, we avoided aromatic rices like basmati and jasmine. Arborio rice, used for risotto, was stiff and gritty. Overall, medium-grain rice produced the best texture (with long-grain rice a close second). We found that cooking the rice in water rather than milk left its flavor intact. After the rice absorbed the water, we added sugar and equal amounts of milk and half-and-half, which delivered the proper degree of richness; the eggs and butter found in other recipes were just too overpowering. When we cooked the rice in water with the lid on the pan, then removed the lid while the rice simmered in the milk mixture, we got the results we wanted: distinct, tender grains of rice in a milky, subtly sweet sauce.

Stovetop Rice Pudding

SERVES 6 TO 8

We prefer pudding made with medium-grain rice, but long-grain rice works, too.

- 2 cups water
- 1 cup medium-grain rice (see note)
- ¼ teaspoon table salt
- 2½ cups whole milk
- 2½ cups half-and-half
- ⅔ cup (4⅔ ounces) sugar
- ½ cup raisins
- 1½ teaspoons vanilla extract
- 1 teaspoon ground cinnamon

1. Bring the water to a boil in a large saucepan. Stir in the rice and salt, cover, and simmer over low heat, stirring

once or twice, until the water is almost fully absorbed, 15 to 20 minutes.

2. Stir in the milk, half-and-half, and sugar. Increase the heat to medium-high and bring to a simmer, then reduce the heat to maintain a simmer. Cook, uncovered and stirring frequently, until the mixture starts to thicken, about 30 minutes. Reduce the heat to low and continue to cook, stirring every couple of minutes to prevent sticking and scorching, until a spoon is just able to stand up in the pudding, about 15 minutes longer.

3. Remove from the heat and stir in the raisins, vanilla, and cinnamon. Serve warm, at room temperature, or chilled. (To store, press plastic wrap directly onto the surface of the pudding and refrigerate for up to 2 days. If serving at room temperature or chilled, stir in up to 1 cup warm milk, 2 tablespoons at a time, as needed to loosen before serving.)

Coconut Rice Pudding

To toast the coconut, spread it out on a rimmed baking sheet and toast it in a 325-degree oven, stirring often, until light golden, 10 to 15 minutes.

Follow the recipe for Stovetop Rice Pudding, substituting coconut milk for the whole milk and garnishing with 1 cup shredded sweetened coconut, toasted, before serving.

PANNA COTTA

WHY THIS RECIPE WORKS: Though its name is lyrical, the literal translation of panna cotta, "cooked cream," does nothing to suggest its ethereal qualities. In fact, panna cotta is not cooked at all. Neither is it complicated with eggs, as is a custard. Instead, sugar and gelatin are melted in cream and milk, and the whole mixture is then turned into individual ramekins and chilled. Panna cotta is more often found on restaurant menus, but we wanted a version for the home cook—one that would guarantee a pudding with the rich flavor of cream and vanilla and a delicate texture.

After trying several different recipes, we concluded that we needed a higher proportion of cream to milk to achieve the creamiest flavor and texture. The amount of gelatin proved critical—too much turned the panna cotta rubbery; it needs to be just firm enough to unmold, so we used a light hand. And because gelatin sets more quickly at cold temperatures, we minimized the amount of heat by softening the gelatin in cold milk, then heating it very briefly until it was melted. To avoid premature hardening, we gradually added cold vanilla-infused cream to the gelatin mixture and stirred everything over an ice bath to incorporate the gelatin. Chilled until set and served with a raspberry sauce, our panna cotta was creamy, smooth, and light.

Panna Cotta

SERVES 8

A vanilla bean gives the panna cotta the deepest flavor, but 2 teaspoons of vanilla extract can be used instead. If you like, you can omit the Raspberry Coulis and simply serve the panna cotta with lightly sweetened berries. Though traditionally unmolded, panna cotta may be chilled and served in wine glasses and sauced on top. If you would like to make the panna cotta a day ahead, decrease the amount of gelatin to 2½ teaspoons, and chill the filled wine glasses or ramekins for 18 to 24 hours.

1	cup whole milk
2¾	teaspoons gelatin (see note)
3	cups heavy cream
1	vanilla bean, halved lengthwise (see note)
6	tablespoons sugar
	Pinch table salt
	Raspberry Coulis (recipe follows)

1. Pour the milk into a medium saucepan; sprinkle the surface evenly with the gelatin and let stand for 10 minutes.

Meanwhile, turn the contents of two ice cube trays (about 32 cubes) into a large bowl; add 4 cups cold water. Pour the cream into a large measuring cup or pitcher. With a paring knife, scrape the vanilla seeds into the cream; place the pod in the cream along with the seeds and set the mixture aside. Set eight 4-ounce ramekins on a rimmed baking sheet.

2. Heat the milk and gelatin mixture over high heat, stirring constantly, until the gelatin is dissolved and the mixture registers 135 degrees on an instant-read thermometer, about 1½ minutes. Off the heat, add the sugar and salt; stir until dissolved, about 1 minute.

3. Stirring constantly, slowly pour the cream with the vanilla into the saucepan containing the milk, then transfer the mixture to a medium bowl and set the bowl over the ice water bath. Stir frequently until thickened to the consistency of eggnog and the mixture registers 50 degrees on an instant-read thermometer, about 10 minutes. Strain the mixture into a large measuring cup or pitcher, then distribute evenly among the ramekins. Cover the baking sheet with plastic wrap, making sure that the plastic does not mar the surface of the cream; refrigerate until just set (the mixture should wobble when shaken gently), about 4 hours.

4. To serve, spoon a portion of the raspberry coulis onto eight individual serving plates. Pour 1 cup boiling water into a small wide-mouthed bowl, dip a ramekin filled with panna cotta into the water for 3 seconds and lift the ramekin out of the water. With a moistened finger, press lightly on the periphery of the panna cotta to loosen the edges. Dip the ramekin back into the hot water for another 3 seconds. Invert the ramekin over your palm and loosen the panna cotta by cupping your fingers between the panna cotta and the edges of the ramekin. Gently lower the panna cotta onto a serving plate with the coulis. Repeat the process with the remaining ramekins of panna cotta. Serve.

Raspberry Coulis

MAKES ABOUT 1½ CUPS

24	ounces (about 5 cups) frozen raspberries
⅓	cup (2⅓ ounces) sugar
¼	teaspoon juice from 1 lemon
	Pinch table salt

1. Place the frozen raspberries in a 4-quart saucepan. Cover and simmer over medium-high heat, stirring occasionally, for 10 to 12 minutes. Add the sugar and increase the heat to high. Boil for 2 minutes.

2. Strain the berries through a fine-mesh strainer into a bowl, using a rubber spatula to push the berries through the strainer; discard the seeds. Stir in the lemon juice and salt. Cover and refrigerate until chilled, at least 2 hours or up to 3 days.

CRÈME BRÛLÉE

WHY THIS RECIPE WORKS: Crème brûlée is all about the contrast between the crisp sugar crust and the silky custard underneath. But too often the crust is either stingy or rock-hard and the custard is heavy and tasteless. Because crème brûlée requires so few ingredients, we knew that finding just the right technique would be key in creating the quintessential version of this elegant dessert.

The texture of the custard should not be firm but rather soft and supple. The secret, we found, is using egg yolks—and lots of them—rather than whole eggs. Heavy cream gave the custard a luxurious richness. Sugar, a vanilla bean, and a pinch of salt were the only other additions. Despite instructions in many recipes to use scalded cream, we found that this technique was more likely to result in overcooked custard, so we thought we would leave the ingredients cold. The downside, however, was that we needed heat to extract flavor from the vanilla bean and dissolve the sugar. Our compromise was to heat only half of the cream with the sugar and vanilla bean and add the remaining cream cold, which worked perfectly. For the crust, we used crunchy turbinado sugar, which was easy to spread on the baked and chilled custards. A propane or butane torch worked better than the broiler for caramelizing the sugar, and because the blast of heat inevitably warms the custard beneath the crust, we chilled our crèmes brûlées once more before serving.

Classic Crème Brûlée

SERVES 8

Separate the eggs and whisk the yolks after the cream has finished steeping; if left to sit, the surface of the yolks will dry and form a film. A vanilla bean gives the custard the deepest flavor, but 2 teaspoons of vanilla extract, whisked into the yolks in step 4, can be used instead. The best way to judge doneness is with an instant-read thermometer. For the caramelized sugar crust, we recommend turbinado or Demerara sugar. Regular granulated sugar will work, too, but use only 1 scant teaspoon on each ramekin or 1 teaspoon on each shallow fluted dish. It's important to use 4 to 5-ounce ramekins.

4 cups heavy cream, chilled
⅔ cup (4⅔ ounces) granulated sugar
 Pinch table salt
1 vanilla bean, halved lengthwise (see note)
12 large egg yolks (see note)
8–12 teaspoons turbinado or Demerara sugar (see note)

1. Adjust an oven rack to the lower-middle position and heat the oven to 300 degrees.

2. Combine 2 cups of the cream, the sugar, and salt in a medium saucepan. With a paring knife, scrape the seeds from the vanilla bean into the pan, submerge the pod in the cream, and bring the mixture to a boil over medium heat, stirring occasionally to ensure that the sugar dissolves. Take the pan off the heat and let steep for 15 minutes.

3. Meanwhile, place a kitchen towel in the bottom of a large baking dish or roasting pan and arrange eight 4- or 5-ounce ramekins (or shallow fluted dishes) on the towel (making sure they do not touch). Bring a kettle or large saucepan of water to a boil.

4. After the vanilla bean has steeped, stir in the remaining 2 cups cream to cool down the mixture. Whisk the egg yolks in a large bowl until broken up and combined. Whisk about 1 cup of the cream mixture into the yolks until loosened and combined; repeat with 1 cup more cream. Add the remaining cream and whisk until evenly colored and thoroughly combined. Strain the mixture through a fine-mesh strainer into a large measuring cup or pitcher (or clean medium bowl); discard the solids in the strainer. Pour or ladle the mixture into the ramekins, dividing it evenly among them.

5. Carefully place the baking dish with the ramekins on the oven rack; pour the boiling water into the dish, taking care not to splash water into the ramekins, until the water reaches two-thirds of the way up the sides of the ramekins. Bake until the centers of the custards are just barely set and are no longer sloshy and register

170 to 175 degrees on an instant-read thermometer, 30 to 35 minutes (25 to 30 minutes for shallow fluted dishes). Begin checking the temperature about 5 minutes before the recommended time.

6. Transfer the ramekins to a wire rack and cool to room temperature, about 2 hours. Set the ramekins on a rimmed baking sheet, cover tightly with plastic wrap, and refrigerate until cold, at least 4 hours or up to 4 days.

7. Uncover the ramekins; if condensation has collected on the custards, blot the moisture with a paper towel. Sprinkle each with about 1 teaspoon turbinado sugar (1½ teaspoons for shallow fluted dishes); tilt and tap each ramekin for even coverage. Ignite a torch and caramelize the sugar. Refrigerate the ramekins, uncovered, to rechill, 30 to 45 minutes (but no longer); serve.

Espresso Crème Brûlée

Place ¼ cup espresso beans in a zipper-lock bag and crush lightly with a rolling pin or meat pounder until coarsely cracked. Follow the recipe for Classic Crème Brûlée, substituting the cracked espresso beans for the vanilla bean and whisking 1 teaspoon vanilla extract into the egg yolks in step 4 before adding the cream.

CRÈME CARAMEL

WHY THIS RECIPE WORKS: This simple, classic French dessert is essentially a baked custard, but what makes it really stand out is the caramel sauce. We found that making the caramel is relatively simple; what we needed to address was the custard, which should be silky smooth, modestly sweet, and firm but not rubbery.

We discovered that the proportion of egg whites to yolks in the custard was critical for the texture. Too many whites caused the custard to solidify too much, and too few left it almost runny. We settled on a formula of three whole eggs and two yolks. Light cream and milk for the dairy component provided the proper amount of richness. For contrast with the sweet caramel, we kept the amount of sugar in the custard to a minimum. The caramel comes together quickly; sugar is dissolved in water and cooked until caramel-colored. Baking the ramekins in a water bath was essential for even cooking and ensured a delicate custard; a dish towel on the bottom of the pan stabilized the ramekins and prevented the bottoms of the custards from overcooking. When we unmolded our crème caramel on serving plates, the sweet caramel sauce bathed the rounds of perfectly cooked custard.

Classic Crème Caramel

SERVES 8

You can vary the amount of sugar in the custard to suit your taste. Most tasters preferred the full ⅔ cup, but you can reduce that amount to as little as ½ cup to create a greater contrast between the custard and the caramel. Cook the caramel in a pan with a light-colored interior, since a dark surface makes it difficult to judge the color of the syrup. Caramel can leave a real mess in a pan, but it is easy to clean. Simply boil water in the pan for 5 to 10 minutes to loosen the hardened caramel.

CARAMEL

- ⅓ cup water
- 2 tablespoons light corn syrup
- ¼ teaspoon juice from 1 lemon
- 1 cup (7 ounces) sugar

CUSTARD

- 1½ cups whole milk
- 1½ cups light cream
- 3 large whole eggs, plus 2 large egg yolks
- ⅔ cup (4⅔ ounces) sugar (see note)
- 1½ teaspoons vanilla extract
- Pinch table salt

1. FOR THE CARAMEL: Combine the water, corn syrup, and lemon juice in a 2 to 3-quart saucepan. Pour the sugar into the center of the saucepan, taking care not to let the sugar granules touch the sides of the pan. Gently stir with a clean spatula to moisten the sugar thoroughly. Bring to a boil over medium-high heat and cook, without stirring, until the sugar is completely dissolved and the liquid is clear, 6 to 10 minutes. Reduce the heat to medium-low and continue to cook (swirling occasionally) until the caramel darkens to a honey color, 4 to 5 minutes longer. Remove the pan immediately from the heat and, working quickly but carefully (the caramel is above 300 degrees and will burn if it touches your skin), pour a portion of the caramel into each of eight ungreased 6-ounce ramekins. Allow the caramel to cool and harden, about 15 minutes. (The caramel-coated ramekins can be covered with plastic wrap and refrigerated for up to 2 days; return to room temperature before adding the custard.)

2. FOR THE CUSTARD: Adjust an oven rack to the middle position and heat the oven to 350 degrees. Heat the milk and cream in a medium saucepan over medium heat, stirring occasionally, until steam appears and/or the mixture registers 160 degrees on an instant-read thermometer, 6 to 8 minutes; remove from the heat. Meanwhile, gently whisk the whole eggs, egg yolks, and sugar in a large bowl until just combined. Off the heat, gently whisk the warm milk mixture, vanilla, and salt into the eggs until just combined but not at all foamy. Strain the mixture through a fine-mesh strainer into a large measuring cup or pitcher (or clean medium bowl); set aside.

3. Bring a kettle or large saucepan of water to a boil. Meanwhile, place a kitchen towel in the bottom of a large baking dish or roasting pan. Arrange the ramekins on the towel (making sure they do not touch). Divide the reserved custard mixture among the ramekins and carefully place the baking dish on the oven rack. Pour the boiling water into the dish, taking care not to splash water into the ramekins, until the water reaches halfway up the sides of the ramekins; cover the entire pan loosely with aluminum foil. Bake until a paring knife inserted halfway between the center and the edge of the custards comes out clean, 35 to 40 minutes. Transfer the custards to a wire rack and cool to room temperature. (The custards can be covered with plastic wrap and refrigerated for up to 2 days.)

4. To unmold, slide a paring knife around the perimeter of each ramekin, pressing the knife against the side of the dish. Hold a serving plate over the top of the ramekin and invert; set the plate on a work surface and shake the ramekin gently to release the custard. Repeat with the remaining ramekins and serve.

CHOCOLATE POTS DE CRÈME

WHY THIS RECIPE WORKS: Classic pots de crème can be finicky and laborious, requiring a hot water bath that threatens to splash the custards every time the pan is moved. In addition, the individual custards don't always cook at the same rate. We wanted a user-friendly recipe that delivered a decadent dessert with a satiny texture and intense chocolate flavor.

First we moved the dish out of the oven, concentrating on an unconventional approach in which the custard is cooked on the stovetop in a saucepan, then poured into ramekins. Our next challenge was developing the right amount of richness and body, which we did by choosing a combination of heavy cream and half-and-half, along with egg yolks only, for maximum richness. For intense chocolate flavor, we focused on bittersweet chocolate—and a lot of it. Our chocolate content was at least 50 percent more than in any other recipe we had encountered.

Chocolate Pots de Crème
SERVES 8

We prefer pots de crème made with 60 percent bittersweet chocolate (our favorite brands are Callebaut Intense Dark Chocolate and Ghirardelli Bittersweet Chocolate), but 70 percent bittersweet chocolate can also be used. If using a 70 percent bittersweet chocolate, reduce the amount of chocolate to 8 ounces. An instant-read thermometer is the most reliable way to judge when the custard has reached the proper temperature. However, you can also judge the progress of the custard by its thickness. Dip a wooden spoon into the custard and run your finger across the back. The custard is ready when it coats the spoon and a line drawn maintains neat edges. The pots de crème (minus the whipped cream garnish) can be covered tightly with plastic wrap and refrigerated for up to 3 days.

POTS DE CRÈME

- **10 ounces bittersweet chocolate, chopped fine (see note)**
- **5 large egg yolks**
- **5 tablespoons sugar**
- **¼ teaspoon table salt**
- **1½ cups heavy cream**
- **¾ cup half-and-half**
- **1 tablespoon vanilla extract**
- **½ teaspoon instant espresso powder mixed with 1 tablespoon water**

WHIPPED CREAM AND GARNISH

- **½ cup heavy cream, chilled**
- **2 teaspoons sugar**
- **½ teaspoon vanilla extract**
- **Cocoa, for dusting (optional)**
- **Chocolate shavings, for sprinkling (optional)**

1. FOR THE POTS DE CRÈME: Place the chocolate in a medium heatproof bowl; set a fine-mesh strainer over the bowl and set aside.

2. Whisk the egg yolks, sugar, and salt together in a medium bowl until combined, then whisk in the heavy cream and half-and-half. Transfer the mixture to a medium saucepan. Cook the mixture over medium-low heat, stirring constantly and scraping the bottom of the pot with a wooden spoon, until it is thickened and silky and registers 175 to 180 degrees on an instant-read thermometer, 8 to 12 minutes. (Do not let the custard overcook or simmer.)

3. Immediately pour the custard through the strainer over the chocolate. Let the mixture stand to melt the chocolate, about 5 minutes. Whisk gently until smooth, then whisk in the vanilla and dissolved espresso. Divide the mixture evenly among eight 5-ounce ramekins. Gently tap the ramekins against the counter to remove any air bubbles.

4. Cool the pots de crème to room temperature, then cover with plastic wrap and refrigerate until chilled, at least 4 hours or up to 3 days. Before serving, let the pots de crème stand at room temperature for 20 to 30 minutes.

5. FOR THE WHIPPED CREAM AND GARNISH: Using an electric mixer, whip the cream, sugar, and vanilla on medium-low speed until small bubbles form, about 30 seconds. Increase the speed to medium-high and continue to whip the mixture until it thickens and forms stiff peaks, about 1 minute. Dollop each pot de crème with about 2 tablespoons of the whipped cream and garnish with cocoa and/or chocolate shavings (if using). Serve.

Milk Chocolate Pots de Crème

Milk chocolate behaves differently in this recipe than bittersweet chocolate, and more of it must be used to ensure that the custard sets. And because of the increased amount of chocolate, it's necessary to cut back on the amount of sugar so that the custard is not overly sweet.

Follow the recipe for Chocolate Pots de Crème, substituting 12 ounces milk chocolate for the 10 ounces bittersweet chocolate. Reduce the amount of sugar to 2 tablespoons and proceed as directed.

CHOCOLATE PUDDING

WHY THIS RECIPE WORKS: Homemade chocolate pudding often suffers either from lackluster chocolate flavor, caused by a dearth of chocolate, or a grainy texture, caused by too much cocoa butter. We were after chocolate pudding that tasted deeply of chocolate and was thickened to a perfectly silky, creamy texture.

We found that using a moderate amount of bittersweet chocolate in combination with unsweetened cocoa and espresso powder helped us achieve maximum chocolate flavor. Cornstarch proved the right thickener for our pudding; using mostly milk, and just half a cup of heavy cream, along with three egg yolks ensured that our pudding had a silky smooth texture. Salt and vanilla enhanced the chocolate flavor for the perfect classic chocolate pudding.

Creamy Chocolate Pudding

SERVES 6

We recommend using one of the test kitchen's favorite baking chocolates, Callebaut Intense Dark Chocolate or Ghirardelli Bittersweet Chocolate, for this recipe, but any high-quality dark, bittersweet, or semisweet chocolate will work. This recipe was developed using a 60 percent cacao chocolate. Using a chocolate with a higher cacao percentage will result in a thicker pudding. Low-fat milk (1 percent or 2 percent) may be substituted for the whole milk with a small sacrifice in richness. Do not use skim milk as a substitute. Serve the pudding with lightly sweetened whipped cream and chocolate shavings.

- 2 teaspoons vanilla extract
- ½ teaspoon instant espresso powder
- ½ cup (3½ ounces) sugar
- 3 tablespoons Dutch-processed cocoa powder
- 2 tablespoons cornstarch
- ¼ teaspoon table salt
- 3 large egg yolks
- ½ cup heavy cream
- 2½ cups whole milk (see note)
- 5 tablespoons unsalted butter, cut into 8 pieces
- 4 ounces bittersweet chocolate, finely chopped (see note)

1. Stir together the vanilla extract and espresso powder in a bowl; set aside. Whisk the sugar, cocoa, cornstarch, and salt together in a large saucepan. Whisk in the egg yolks and cream until fully incorporated, making sure to scrape the corners of the saucepan. Whisk in the milk until incorporated.

2. Place the saucepan over medium heat and cook, whisking constantly, until the mixture is thickened and bubbling over the entire surface, 5 to 8 minutes. Cook for 30 seconds longer, remove from the heat, add the butter and chocolate, and whisk until melted and fully incorporated. Whisk in the vanilla mixture.

3. Strain the pudding through a fine-mesh strainer into a bowl. Place lightly greased parchment paper against the surface of the pudding, and place in a refrigerator to cool, at least 4 hours. Serve. (The pudding can be refrigerated for up to 2 days.)

CHOCOLATE MOUSSE

WHY THIS RECIPE WORKS: Rich, creamy, and dense, chocolate mousse can be delicious but too filling after a few mouthfuls. On the other hand, light and airy mousse usually lacks deep chocolate flavor. We wanted chocolate mousse with both a light, meltingly smooth texture and a substantial chocolate flavor.

To start, we addressed the mousse's dense, heavy texture. Most recipes for chocolate mousse contain butter. Could we do without it? We eliminated the butter and found that our mousse tasted less heavy. We further lightened the mousse's texture by reducing the number of egg whites and yolks. To make up for the lost volume of the eggs, we whipped the cream to soft peaks before adding it to the chocolate.

Next we tackled the mousse's flavor. We maximized the chocolate flavor with a combination of bittersweet chocolate and cocoa powder. And to further deepen the chocolate flavor, we found that a small amount of instant espresso powder, salt, and brandy did the trick.

Dark Chocolate Mousse

SERVES 6 TO 8

When developing this recipe, we used our winning brands of dark chocolate, Callebaut Intense Dark Chocolate and Ghirardelli Bittersweet Chocolate, which each contain about 60 percent cacao. If you want to use a chocolate with a higher percentage of cacao, see our variation, Premium Dark Chocolate Mousse (page 649). If you choose to make the mousse a day in advance, let it sit at room temperature for 10 minutes before serving. Serve with very lightly sweetened whipped cream and chocolate shavings, if desired.

- 8 ounces bittersweet chocolate, chopped fine (see note)
- 5 tablespoons water
- 2 tablespoons cocoa powder, preferably Dutch-processed
- 1 tablespoon brandy
- 1 teaspoon instant espresso powder
- 2 large eggs, separated
- 1 tablespoon sugar
- ⅛ teaspoon table salt
- 1 cup plus 2 tablespoons heavy cream, chilled

1. Melt the chocolate with the water, cocoa powder, brandy, and espresso powder in a medium heatproof bowl set over a saucepan filled with 1 inch of barely simmering water, stirring frequently until smooth. Remove from the heat.

2. Whisk the egg yolks, 1½ teaspoons of the sugar, and the salt in a medium bowl until the mixture lightens in color and thickens slightly, about 30 seconds. Pour the melted chocolate into the egg mixture and whisk until combined. Cool until just warmer than room temperature, 3 to 5 minutes.

3. Using an electric mixer, whip the egg whites at medium-low speed until frothy, 1 to 2 minutes. Add the remaining 1½ teaspoons sugar, increase the mixer speed to medium-high, and whip until soft peaks form when the whisk is lifted, about 1 minute. Whisk the last few strokes by hand, making sure to scrape any unbeaten whites from the bottom of the bowl. Using the whisk, stir about one-quarter of the whipped egg whites into the chocolate mixture to lighten it; gently fold in the remaining egg whites with a rubber spatula until a few white streaks remain.

4. In the now-empty bowl, whip the heavy cream at medium speed until it begins to thicken, about 30 seconds. Increase the speed to high and whip until soft peaks form when the whisk is lifted, about 15 seconds more. Using a rubber spatula, fold the whipped cream into the mousse until no white streaks remain. Spoon the mousse into six to eight individual serving dishes or goblets. Cover with plastic wrap and refrigerate until set and firm, at least 2 hours or up to 24 hours. Serve.

Chocolate-Orange Mousse

For best flavor, the orange zest needs to steep in the heavy cream overnight, so plan accordingly. Garnish each serving of mousse with a thin strip of orange zest, if desired.

Follow the recipe for Dark Chocolate Mousse with the following changes: Start by bringing the heavy cream to a simmer in a medium saucepan. Remove from the heat and transfer to a liquid measuring cup; add 3 strips orange zest (each about 2 inches long and ½ inch wide). Cool until just warm, cover, and refrigerate overnight. Remove and discard the zest; add more heavy cream, if necessary, to equal 1 cup plus 2 tablespoons. Continue with step 1, reducing the amount of water to 4 tablespoons and omitting the brandy. Once the chocolate is melted, stir in 2 tablespoons Grand Marnier and proceed as directed in step 2.

Chocolate-Raspberry Mousse

Chambord is our preferred brand of raspberry-flavored liqueur for this recipe. Serve the mousse with fresh raspberries, if desired.

Follow the recipe for Dark Chocolate Mousse, reducing the amount of water to 4 tablespoons, omitting the brandy, and, once the chocolate is melted at the end of step 1, stirring in 2 tablespoons raspberry-flavored liqueur.

Premium Dark Chocolate Mousse

This recipe is designed to work with a boutique chocolate that contains a higher percentage of cacao than the Callebaut or Ghirardelli chocolate recommended for our Dark Chocolate Mousse.

Follow the recipe for Dark Chocolate Mousse, replacing the bittersweet chocolate (containing about 60 percent cacao) with an equal amount of bittersweet chocolate containing 62 to 70 percent cacao. Increase the amount of water to 7 tablespoons, add 1 egg (for a total of 3 eggs), and increase the amount of sugar to 3 tablespoons (adding the extra 2 tablespoons sugar to the chocolate mixture in step 1).

LOW-FAT CHOCOLATE MOUSSE

WHY THIS RECIPE WORKS: When presented with the challenge of developing a low-fat chocolate mousse, we admit we were daunted. After all, traditional chocolate mousse gets its lush, creamy texture and decadent richness chiefly from heavy cream—and lots of it. We wanted to ditch the cream but preserve the rich chocolate flavor and silky, fluffy texture.

We found the solution in an Italian meringue (egg whites beaten until fluffy, and then cooked in hot sugar syrup). It made a fat-free base that mimicked the volume and texture of a traditional mousse made with heavy cream. Semisweet chocolate and Dutch-processed cocoa added rich chocolate flavor, and a surprise ingredient—melted white chocolate chips—mellowed and rounded out the flavors of each.

Low-Fat Chocolate Mousse
SERVES 6

The meringue and chocolate mixture are combined in two stages so the meringue doesn't collapse. For the best texture, chill the mousse overnight. The mousse can be refrigerated for up to 4 days.

- 4 ounces semisweet chocolate, broken into pieces
- ⅓ cup white chocolate chips
- 2 tablespoons Dutch-processed cocoa powder
- 6 tablespoons plus ½ cup water
- 1 teaspoon vanilla extract
- ½ cup (3½ ounces) sugar
- 3 large egg whites
- ¼ teaspoon cream of tartar

1. Melt the semisweet chocolate, white chocolate, cocoa powder, 6 tablespoons of the water, and the vanilla in a medium bowl set over a pot of barely simmering water, stirring until smooth. Set aside to cool slightly.

2. Bring the remaining ½ cup water and the sugar to a vigorous boil in a small saucepan over high heat. Boil until slightly thickened and large bubbles rise to the top, about 4 minutes. Remove from the heat.

3. With an electric mixer on medium-low speed, beat the egg whites in a large bowl until frothy, about 1 minute. Add the cream of tartar and beat, gradually increasing the speed to medium-high, until the whites hold soft peaks, about 2 minutes. With the mixer running, slowly pour the hot syrup into the whites (avoid pouring the syrup onto the beaters or it will splash). Increase the speed to high and beat until the meringue has cooled to just warm and becomes very thick and shiny, 2 to 3 minutes.

4. Whisk one-third of the meringue into the chocolate mixture until combined, then whisk in the remaining meringue. Spoon the mousse into six 6-ounce ramekins or pudding cups. Cover tightly with plastic wrap. Chill overnight.

GRAND MARNIER SOUFFLÉ

WHY THIS RECIPE WORKS: Home cooks are wary of attempting soufflés, which have the reputation of being difficult and temperamental and so are relegated to being eaten only in restaurants. The reality, however, is that they are relatively easy to make. To prove the point, we set out to develop a reliable recipe for a classic Grand Marnier soufflé.

The best soufflés have a crusty top layer above the rim of the dish and a contrasting rich, creamy, almost-fluid center, so we needed to produce height without making the entire dish foamy. For the base we began with a *bouillie*—a paste of flour and milk. Butter kept the egginess at bay, and increasing the usual amount of flour prevented the frothiness we wanted to avoid. An equal number of egg whites and yolks was the right proportion for rise versus richness. Adding a little sugar and some cream of tartar to the whites while we whipped them stabilized the whites so that they would hold their structure. We discovered that the sugar must be added gradually and partway through the beating process, not at the beginning, or the soufflé will not rise properly and will taste too sweet. We also found it important to remove the soufflé from the oven while the center was still loose and moist to prevent overcooking. With a luxuriously creamy interior and crusty top, our foolproof soufflé is an impressive dessert that can easily be made at home.

Grand Marnier Soufflé
SERVES 6 TO 8

Make the soufflé base and immediately begin beating the whites before the base cools too much. Once the whites have reached the proper consistency, they must be used at once. Do not open the oven door during the first 15 minutes of baking time; as the soufflé nears the end of its baking, you may check its progress by opening the oven door slightly. (Be careful here; if your oven runs hot, the top of the soufflé may burn.) A quick dusting of confectioners' sugar is a nice finishing touch, but a soufflé waits for no one, so be ready to serve it immediately.

SOUFFLÉ DISH PREPARATION
- 1 tablespoon unsalted butter, softened
- ¼ cup sugar
- 2 teaspoons sifted cocoa powder

- 5 tablespoons unbleached all-purpose flour
- ½ cup (3½ ounces) sugar
- ¼ teaspoon table salt
- 1 cup whole milk
- 2 tablespoons unsalted butter, at room temperature
- 5 large eggs, separated
- 1 tablespoon grated zest from 1 orange
- 3 tablespoons Grand Marnier
- ⅛ teaspoon cream of tartar

1. Adjust an oven rack to the upper-middle position and heat the oven to 400 degrees. Grease a 1½-quart porcelain soufflé dish with the butter, making sure to coat all of the interior surfaces. Stir the sugar and cocoa together in a small bowl; pour into the buttered soufflé dish and shake to coat the bottom and sides with a thick, even coating. Tap out the excess and set the dish aside.

2. FOR THE SOUFFLÉ: Whisk the flour, ¼ cup of the sugar, and the salt in a small saucepan. Gradually whisk in the milk, whisking until smooth and no lumps remain. Bring the mixture to a boil over high heat, whisking constantly, until thickened and the mixture pulls away from the sides of the pan, about 3 minutes. Scrape the mixture into a medium bowl; whisk in the butter until combined. Whisk in the yolks until incorporated; stir in the orange zest and Grand Marnier.

3. Using an electric mixer, whip the egg whites, cream of tartar, and 1 teaspoon more sugar at medium-low speed until combined, about 10 seconds. Increase the speed to medium-high and whip until frothy and no longer translucent, about 2 minutes. With the mixer running, sprinkle in half of the remaining sugar; continue whipping until the whites form soft, billowy peaks, about 30 seconds. With the mixer still running, sprinkle in the remaining sugar and whip until just combined, about 10 seconds. The whites should form soft peaks when the beater is lifted but should not appear Styrofoam-like or dry.

4. Using a rubber spatula, immediately stir one-quarter of the beaten whites into the soufflé base to lighten until almost no white streaks remain. Scrape the remaining whites into the base and fold in the whites with a balloon whisk until the mixture is just combined, gently flicking the whisk after scraping up the sides of the bowl to free any of the mixture caught in the whisk. Gently pour the mixture into the prepared dish and run your index finger through the mixture, tracing the circumference about ½ inch from the side of the dish, to help the soufflé

rise properly. Bake until the surface of the soufflé is deep brown, the center jiggles slightly when shaken, and the soufflé has risen 2 to 2½ inches above the rim of the dish, 20 to 25 minutes. Serve immediately.

Grand Marnier Soufflé with Grated Chocolate

A rotary cheese grater is the perfect tool for grating the chocolate, though a box grater works well, too.

Finely grate ½ ounce bittersweet chocolate (you should have about ⅓ cup). Follow the recipe for Grand Marnier Soufflé, folding the grated chocolate into the soufflé base along with the beaten egg whites.

CHILLED LEMON SOUFFLÉ

WHY THIS RECIPE WORKS: "Chilled lemon soufflé" can be interpreted in many ways, from cooled baked pudding cake to lemony, eggy foam. But no matter what the desired outcome, what typically results is a dense, rubbery mass or a mouthful of tart egg white foam. The delicate balance of ingredients is hard for home cooks to get right. We wanted to perfect the unusual marriage of cream and foam, sweet and sour, high lemony notes and rich custard.

A starting point of egg whites, gelatin, sugar, and lemon juice had none of the creaminess we desired, so we cooked a custard base of milk, egg yolks, and sugar, adding a little cornstarch to prevent the yolks from curdling. To our custard we then added lemon juice and gelatin (to stabilize the mixture so it would set up while chilling). Because this was to be a soufflé, not a pudding, we lightened the custard with whipped cream and beaten egg whites. The egg yolks and dairy tended to mute the lemon flavor, so for more citrus punch we included grated lemon zest. Now we had the balance of flavor and texture that we sought: a satisfying but light custard with bright lemon flavor.

Chilled Lemon Soufflé

SERVES 4 TO 6

To make this lemon soufflé "soufflé" over the rim of the dish, use a 1-quart soufflé dish and, following the photo on page 653, make a foil collar for it before beginning the recipe. For those less concerned about appearance, this dessert can be served from any 1½-quart serving bowl. For the best texture, serve the soufflé after 1½ hours of chilling. It may be chilled for up to 6 hours; though the texture will stiffen slightly because of the gelatin, it will taste just as good.

½ cup juice plus 2½ teaspoons grated zest from 3 lemons
1 (¼-ounce) package gelatin
1 cup whole milk
¾ cup (5¼ ounces) sugar
5 large egg whites plus 2 large egg yolks, at room temperature
¼ teaspoon cornstarch
Pinch cream of tartar
¾ cup heavy cream
Mint, raspberries, confectioners' sugar, or finely chopped pistachios, for garnish (optional)

1. Place the lemon juice in a small bowl; sprinkle the gelatin over and set aside.

2. Heat the milk and ½ cup of the sugar in a medium saucepan over medium-low heat, stirring occasionally, until steaming and the sugar is dissolved, about 5 minutes. Meanwhile, whisk the egg yolks, 2 tablespoons more sugar, and the cornstarch in a medium bowl until pale yellow and thickened. Whisking constantly, gradually add the hot milk to the yolks. Return the milk-egg mixture to the saucepan and cook, stirring constantly, over medium-low heat until the foam has dissipated to a thin layer and the mixture thickens to the consistency of heavy cream and registers 185 degrees on an instant-read thermometer, about 4 minutes. Pour the mixture through a fine-mesh strainer into a medium bowl; stir in the lemon juice mixture and zest. Set the bowl with the custard in a large bowl of ice water; stir occasionally to cool.

3. While the custard mixture is chilling, use an electric mixer to whip the egg whites and cream of tartar on medium speed until foamy, about 1 minute. Increase the speed to medium-high; gradually add the remaining 2 tablespoons sugar and continue to whip until glossy and the whites hold soft peaks when the beater is lifted, about 2 minutes longer. Do not overwhip. Remove the bowl containing the custard mixture from the ice water bath; gently whisk in about one-third of the egg whites, then fold in the remaining whites with a large rubber spatula until almost no white streaks remain.

4. In the same mixer bowl, whip the cream on medium-high speed until soft peaks form when the beater is lifted, 2 to 3 minutes. Fold the cream into the custard and egg-white mixture until no white streaks remain.

5. Pour into a 1½ quart soufflé dish or bowl (see note). Chill until set but not stiff, about 1½ hours; remove the foil collar, if using, and serve, garnishing if desired.

Chilled Lemon Soufflé with White Chocolate

The white chocolate in this variation subdues the lemony kick.

Follow the recipe for Chilled Lemon Soufflé, adding 2 ounces chopped white chocolate to the warm custard before adding the lemon juice mixture and the zest. Stir until melted and fully incorporated.

Individual Chilled Lemon Soufflés

Follow the recipe for Chilled Lemon Soufflé, dividing the batter equally among eight ¾-cup ramekins (filled to the rim) or six 6-ounce ramekins with foil collars (see page 653).

MAKE-AHEAD CHOCOLATE SOUFFLÉS

WHY THIS RECIPE WORKS: A chocolate soufflé is a grand dessert to serve dinner guests, but most cooks wouldn't risk the anxiety of all the last-minute preparation when entertaining. It seemed a shame to cross this dessert off the list of possibilities for a dinner party, so we challenged ourselves to find a way to make it in advance.

First we needed to perfect the soufflé recipe itself. We wanted the chocolate to be front and center, so we used a base of egg yolks beaten with sugar, with no flour or milk to mute the chocolate flavor. Instead of the equal number of egg yolks and whites that worked for our Grand Marnier Soufflé (page 650), two extra whites were necessary to lighten and lift our chocolaty base. Now that we had the flavor and texture we wanted, it was time to address the problem of making the soufflés ahead of time. To our amazement, the answer was simple: freezing. Adding a little confectioners' sugar to the egg whites helped stabilize them so they held up better in the freezer, and individual ramekins produced better results than a single large soufflé dish. Now we could make our dinner party dessert ahead of time, confident that we could pull perfectly risen, rich chocolate soufflés from the oven at the end of the meal.

Make-Ahead Chocolate Soufflés

SERVES 6 TO 8

The yolk whipping time in step 3 depends on the type of mixer you use; a stand mixer will take about 3 minutes, and a hand-held mixer will take about 8 minutes. If using 6-ounce ramekins, reduce the cooking time to 20 to 22 minutes. See the photo for making a collar for the ramekins.

RAMEKIN PREPARATION
- 2 tablespoons unsalted butter, softened
- 2 tablespoons granulated sugar

SOUFFLÉS
- 8 ounces bittersweet or semisweet chocolate, chopped coarse
- 4 tablespoons (½ stick) unsalted butter, cut into ½-inch pieces
- 1 tablespoon Grand Marnier
- ½ teaspoon vanilla extract
- ⅛ teaspoon table salt
- 6 large egg yolks plus 8 large egg whites
- ⅓ cup (2⅓ ounces) granulated sugar
- ¼ teaspoon cream of tartar
- 2 tablespoons confectioners' sugar

1. FOR THE RAMEKINS: Grease the inside of eight 8-ounce ramekins with the softened butter, then coat the inside of each dish evenly with the granulated sugar.

2. FOR THE SOUFFLÉS: Melt the chocolate and butter together in a medium heatproof bowl set over a saucepan filled with 1 inch of barely simmering water, stirring frequently until smooth. Remove from the heat and stir in the Grand Marnier, vanilla, and salt; set aside.

3. Using an electric mixer, whip the egg yolks and granulated sugar at medium speed until the mixture triples in volume and is thick and pale yellow, 3 to 8 minutes (see note). Fold the yolk mixture into the chocolate mixture. Thoroughly clean and dry the mixing bowl and the beaters.

4. Using the clean beaters, whip the egg whites at medium-low speed until frothy, 1 to 2 minutes. Add the cream of tartar, increase the mixer speed to medium-high, and whip until soft peaks form when the beaters are lifted, 1 to 2 minutes. Add the confectioners' sugar and continue to whip until stiff peaks form, 2 to 4 minutes (do not overwhip). Whisk the last few strokes by hand, making sure to scrape any unwhipped whites from the bottom of the bowl.

5. Vigorously stir one-quarter of the whipped egg whites into the chocolate mixture. Gently fold the remaining whites into the chocolate mixture until just incorporated. Carefully spoon the mixture into the prepared ramekins almost to the rim, wiping the excess filling from the rims with a wet paper towel. If making a foil collar for the ramekins, see the photo. (To serve right away, bake as directed in step 7, reducing the baking time to 12 to 15 minutes.)

6. TO STORE: Cover each ramekin tightly with plastic wrap and then foil and freeze for at least 3 hours or up to 1 month. (Do not thaw before baking.)

7. TO BAKE AND SERVE: Adjust an oven rack to the lower-middle position and heat the oven to 400 degrees. Unwrap the frozen ramekins and spread them out on a baking sheet. Bake the soufflés until fragrant, fully risen, and the exterior is set but the interior is still a bit loose and creamy, about 25 minutes. (To check the interior, use two spoons to pull open the top of one and peek inside.) Serve immediately.

Make-Ahead Mocha Soufflés

Follow the recipe for Make-Ahead Chocolate Soufflés, adding 1 tablespoon instant coffee or espresso powder dissolved in 1 tablespoon hot water to the melted chocolate with the vanilla in step 2.

SKILLET SOUFFLÉ

WHY THIS RECIPE WORKS: Having taken the mystique out of soufflé making and even developing a recipe for making soufflés ahead of time, we wondered if we could take our expertise one step further. If we could make a soufflé in a skillet, we would guarantee that this great dessert was in the realm of everyday cooking.

We theorized that the heat on the stovetop would activate the batter and ensure an even rise from the egg whites. To determine what to use for the soufflé base, we pitted the bases used in our other soufflés—béchamel and bouillie—against a simpler base of whipped egg yolks. All tasted fine, but the whipped egg yolks were so much less complicated that we decided to start there. A little flour added to the yolks kept the soufflé creamy rather than foamy. We decided that lemon would be the best flavoring, since it would shine through the eggy base well; lemon juice and zest provided bright, natural citrus flavor. We beat the egg whites separately, adding sugar partway through, folded them into the egg-lemon base, and poured the mixture into a buttered ovensafe skillet. After a few minutes on the stovetop the soufflé was just set around the edges and on the bottom (and the crust that eventually formed on the bottom was a bonus our tasters applauded), so we moved the skillet to the oven to finish. A few minutes later our soufflé was puffed, golden on top, and creamy in the middle—a successful transformation from fussy to easy.

Skillet Lemon Soufflé

SERVES 6

Don't open the oven door during the first 7 minutes of baking, but do check the soufflé regularly for doneness during the final few minutes in the oven. Be ready to serve the soufflé immediately after removing it from the oven. Using a 10-inch traditional (not nonstick) skillet is essential to getting the right texture and height in the soufflé.

- 5 large eggs, separated
- ¼ teaspoon cream of tartar
- ⅔ cup (4⅔ ounces) granulated sugar
- ⅛ teaspoon table salt
- ⅓ cup juice plus 1 teaspoon grated zest from 2 lemons
- 2 tablespoons unbleached all-purpose flour
- 1 tablespoon unsalted butter
  Confectioners' sugar, for dusting

1. Adjust an oven rack to the middle position and heat the oven to 375 degrees. Using an electric mixer, whip the egg whites and cream of tartar together on medium-low speed until foamy, about 1 minute. Slowly add ⅓ cup of the granulated sugar and the salt, then increase the mixer speed to medium-high, and continue to whip until stiff peaks form, 3 to 5 minutes. Gently transfer the whites to a clean bowl and set aside.

2. Using an electric mixer (no need to wash the mixing bowl), whip the egg yolks and the remaining ⅓ cup granulated sugar together on medium-high speed until pale and thick, about 1 minute. Whip in the lemon juice, zest, and flour until incorporated, about 30 seconds.

3. Fold one-quarter of the whipped egg whites into the yolk mixture until almost no white streaks remain. Gently fold in the remaining egg whites until just incorporated.

4. Melt the butter in a 10-inch ovensafe skillet over medium-low heat. Swirl the pan to coat it evenly with the melted butter, then gently scrape the soufflé batter into the skillet and cook until the edges begin to set and bubble slightly, about 2 minutes.

5. Transfer the skillet to the oven and bake the soufflé until puffed, the center jiggles slightly when shaken, and the surface is golden, 7 to 11 minutes. Using a potholder (the skillet handle will be hot), remove the skillet from the oven. Dust the soufflé with the confectioners' sugar and serve immediately.

Skillet Chocolate-Orange Soufflé

Grating the chocolate fine is key here; we find it easiest to use either a rasp grater or the fine holes of a box grater.

Follow the recipe for Skillet Lemon Soufflé, substituting 1 tablespoon grated zest from 1 orange for the lemon zest and ⅓ cup orange juice for the lemon juice. Gently fold 1 ounce finely grated bittersweet chocolate (about ½ cup) into the soufflé batter after incorporating all of the whites in step 3.

VANILLA ICE CREAM

WHY THIS RECIPE WORKS: Homemade vanilla ice cream is never as creamy or dense as the impossibly smooth "super-premium" ice cream found at gourmet markets or high-end ice cream shops. Instead of thick, dense, and velvety, ice cream made at home invariably turns out crumbly, fluffy, and icy. We wanted an incredibly creamy custard-based vanilla ice cream that would rival any pricey artisanal batch.

Creating smooth ice cream means reducing the size of the ice crystals; the smaller they are, the less perceptible they are. Our first move was to replace some of the sugar in our custard base with corn syrup, which interferes with crystal formation, making for a super-smooth texture. To speed up the freezing process, further ensuring small ice crystals, we froze a portion of the custard prior to churning, then mixed it with the remaining refrigerated custard. Finally, instead of freezing the churned ice cream in a tall container, we spread it into a thin layer in a cold metal baking pan and chilled it, which allowed the ice cream to firm up more quickly and delivered the flawlessly smooth texture we were after.

Homemade Vanilla Ice Cream

MAKES ABOUT 1 QUART

Two teaspoons of vanilla extract can be substituted for the vanilla bean; stir the extract into the cold custard in step 3. An instant-read thermometer is critical for the best results. Using a prechilled metal baking pan and working quickly in step 4 will help prevent melting and refreezing of the ice cream and will speed the hardening process. If using a canister-style ice-cream machine, be sure to freeze the empty canister at least 24 hours and preferably 48 hours before churning. For self-refrigerating ice-cream machines, prechill the canister by running the machine for 5 to 10 minutes before pouring in the custard. The ice cream can be stored for up to 5 days.

- 1 **vanilla bean**
- 1¾ **cups heavy cream**
- 1¼ **cups whole milk**
- ½ **cup plus 2 tablespoons (4⅖ ounces) sugar**
- ⅓ **cup light corn syrup**
- ¼ **teaspoon table salt**
- 6 **large egg yolks**

1. Place an 8- or 9-inch-square metal baking pan in the freezer. Cut the vanilla bean in half lengthwise. Using the tip of a paring knife, scrape out the vanilla seeds. Combine the vanilla bean, seeds, cream, milk, ¼ cup plus 2 tablespoons of the sugar, the corn syrup, and salt in a medium saucepan. Heat over medium-high heat, stirring occasionally, until the mixture is steaming steadily and registers 175 degrees on an instant-read thermometer, 5 to 10 minutes. Remove the saucepan from the heat.

2. While the cream mixture heats, whisk the egg yolks and the remaining ¼ cup sugar in a bowl until smooth, about 30 seconds. Slowly whisk 1 cup of the heated cream mixture into the egg yolk mixture. Return the mixture to the saucepan and cook over medium-low heat, stirring constantly, until the mixture thickens and registers 180 degrees, 7 to 14 minutes. Immediately pour the custard into a large bowl and let cool until no longer steaming, 10 to 20 minutes. Transfer 1 cup of the custard to a small bowl. Cover both bowls with plastic wrap. Place the large bowl in the refrigerator and the small bowl in the freezer and cool completely, at least 4 hours or up to 24 hours. (The small bowl of custard will freeze solid.)

3. Remove the custards from the refrigerator and freezer. Scrape the frozen custard from the small bowl into the large bowl of custard. Stir occasionally until the frozen custard has fully dissolved. Strain the custard through a fine-mesh strainer and transfer to an ice-cream machine. Churn until the mixture resembles thick soft-serve ice cream and registers about 21 degrees, 15 to 25 minutes. Transfer the ice cream to the frozen baking pan and press plastic wrap on the surface. Return to the freezer until firm around the edges, about 1 hour.

4. Transfer the ice cream to an airtight container, pressing firmly to remove any air pockets, and freeze until firm, at least 2 hours, before serving.

CHAPTER 24

CLASSIC FRUIT DESSERTS

Strawberry
Shortcakes   658

Sour Cherry Cobbler   659

Fresh Sour Cherry
Cobbler   660

Blueberry Cobbler   660

Peach Crisp   662

Peach Crisp for a
Crowd   662

Simple Raspberry
Gratin   662

Individual Fresh
Berry Gratins with
Zabaglione   663

Individual Fresh Berry
Gratins with Lemon
Zabaglione   664

Best Baked Apples   664

Skillet Apple Crisp   665

Skillet Apple Brown
Betty   666

Easy Apple Strudel   667
    Tangy Whipped Cream

Skillet Apple Pie   669

Bananas Foster   670

Crêpes Suzette   671

Crêpes with Sugar and
Lemon   672
    Crêpes with Chocolate
    and Orange
    Crêpes with Bananas
    and Nutella

Individual Summer
Berry Puddings   673

Large Summer Berry
Pudding   674

Caramelized Pears with
Blue Cheese and
Black Pepper–Caramel
Sauce   675

Strawberries with
Balsamic Vinegar   675

Berry Fool   676

Rhubarb Fool   677

Strawberry-Rhubarb
Fool   677

STRAWBERRY SHORTCAKES

WHY THIS RECIPE WORKS: While some cooks like to spoon strawberries over pound cake, sponge cake, and even angel food cake, our idea of strawberry shortcake definitely involves a biscuit. We wanted a juicy strawberry filling and mounds of freshly whipped cream sandwiched in between a lightly sweetened, tender biscuit.

While eggs are not traditional, we found that one whole egg gave our biscuits a light, tender texture. And we used just enough dairy (half-and-half or milk) to bind the dough together. A modest amount of sugar yielded a lightly sweetened biscuit. For the strawberries, we wanted to avoid both a mushy puree and dry chunks of fruit. We found our solution in a compromise—mashing a portion of the berries and slicing the rest for a chunky, juicy mixture that didn't slide off the biscuit. And lightly sweetened whipped cream, flavored with vanilla, provided a cool, creamy contrast to the berries and biscuits.

Strawberry Shortcakes

SERVES 6

Start the recipe by preparing the fruit, then set the fruit aside while preparing the biscuits to allow the juices to become syrupy.

FRUIT

- **8** cups (40 ounces) strawberries, hulled
- **6** tablespoons sugar

SHORTCAKE

- **2** cups (10 ounces) unbleached all-purpose flour, plus extra for the work surface and biscuit cutter
- **5** tablespoons sugar
- **1** tablespoon baking powder
- **½** teaspoon table salt
- **8** tablespoons (1 stick) unsalted butter, cut into ½-inch pieces and chilled
- **½** cup plus 1 tablespoon half-and-half or milk
- **1** large whole egg, lightly beaten
- **1** large egg white, lightly beaten

WHIPPED CREAM

- **1** cup heavy cream, chilled
- **1** tablespoon sugar
- **1** teaspoon vanilla extract

1. FOR THE FRUIT: Crush 3 cups of the strawberries in a large bowl with a potato masher. Slice the remaining 5 cups of berries and stir them into the crushed berries along with the sugar. Set aside until the sugar has dissolved and the berries are juicy, at least 30 minutes or up to 2 hours.

2. FOR THE SHORTCAKE: Adjust an oven rack to the lower-middle position and heat the oven to 425 degrees. Line a large baking sheet with parchment paper. Pulse the flour, 3 tablespoons of the sugar, the baking powder, and salt in a food processor until combined. Sprinkle the butter pieces over the top and pulse until the mixture resembles coarse meal, about 15 pulses. Transfer the mixture to a large bowl.

3. Whisk the half-and-half and lightly beaten whole egg together in a small bowl, then stir into the flour mixture with a rubber spatula until large clumps form. Turn the dough onto a lightly floured work surface and knead lightly until it comes together.

4. Pat the dough into a 9 by 6-inch rectangle, about ¾ inch thick. Do not overwork the dough. Using a floured 2¾-inch biscuit cutter, cut out six dough rounds. Arrange the shortcakes on the prepared baking sheet, spaced about 1½ inches apart. Brush the tops with the lightly beaten egg white and sprinkle evenly with the remaining 2 tablespoons sugar. (The unbaked shortcakes can be covered with plastic wrap and refrigerated for up to 2 hours.)

5. Bake until the shortcakes are golden brown, 12 to 14 minutes, rotating the sheet halfway through the baking time. Transfer the sheet to a wire rack and cool the shortcakes until warm, about 10 minutes.

6. FOR THE WHIPPED CREAM: In a medium bowl, whip the cream, sugar, and vanilla with an electric mixer on medium-low speed until frothy, about 1 minute. Increase the speed to high and continue to whip until the cream forms soft peaks, 1 to 3 minutes.

7. TO ASSEMBLE: When the shortcakes have cooled slightly, split them in half horizontally. Place each shortcake bottom on an individual plate, spoon a portion of the berries over each bottom, dollop with whipped cream, and cap with the shortcake tops. Serve immediately.

CHERRY COBBLER

WHY THIS RECIPE WORKS: Most cherry cobblers are no more than canned pie filling topped with dry, heavy biscuits. We wanted a filling that highlighted the unique, sweet-tart flavor of sour cherries and, on top, we wanted a tender, feather-light biscuit crust.

Because fresh sour cherries are so hard to find most of the year, we picked jarred Morello cherries—easy to find and available year-round. Embellishing the cherries with cherry juice, cinnamon, and vanilla was a step in the right direction but the filling still tasted a bit flat, so we switched out some of the juice for red wine and replaced the vanilla with almond extract. The resulting sauce was better, but a little thin. A small amount of cornstarch thickened the filling nicely. As for the biscuits, we favored

buttermilk biscuits, which have a light and fluffy texture. To ensure nicely browned biscuits that didn't become soggy over the filling, we parbaked them on their own ahead of time, then slid the biscuits over the warm cherry filling and put it in the oven to finish cooking.

Sour Cherry Cobbler
SERVES 12

Use the smaller amount of sugar in the filling if you prefer your fruit desserts on the tart side and the larger amount if you like them sweet. Serve with vanilla ice cream or lightly sweetened whipped cream.

BISCUIT TOPPING
- 2 cups (10 ounces) unbleached all-purpose flour
- ½ cup (3½ ounces) sugar
- ½ teaspoon baking powder
- ½ teaspoon baking soda
- ½ teaspoon table salt
- 6 tablespoons (¾ stick) unsalted butter, cut into ½-inch pieces and chilled
- 1 cup buttermilk

FILLING
- 8 cups jarred Morello cherries from 4 (24-ounce) jars, drained, 2 cups juice reserved
- ¾–1 cup (5¼ to 7 ounces) sugar (see note)
- 3 tablespoons plus 1 teaspoon cornstarch
  Pinch table salt
- 1 cup dry red wine
- 1 (3-inch) cinnamon stick
- ¼ teaspoon almond extract

1. Adjust an oven rack to the middle position and heat the oven to 425 degrees. Line a large baking sheet with parchment paper.

2. FOR THE BISCUIT TOPPING: Pulse the flour, 6 tablespoons of the sugar, the baking powder, baking soda, and salt in a food processor until combined. Sprinkle the butter pieces over the top and pulse until the mixture resembles coarse meal, about 15 pulses. Transfer the mixture to a large bowl; add the buttermilk and stir with rubber spatula until combined. Using a greased ¼-cup measure ice cream scoop, scoop 12 biscuits onto the prepared baking sheet, spacing them 1½ inches apart. Sprinkle the biscuits evenly with the remaining 2 tablespoons sugar and bake until lightly browned, about 15 minutes, rotating the sheet halfway through baking. (Do not turn the oven off.)

3. FOR THE FILLING: Meanwhile, arrange the drained cherries in an even layer in a 13 by 9-inch glass baking dish. Combine the sugar, cornstarch, and salt in a medium saucepan. Stir in the reserved cherry juice and wine and add the cinnamon stick; cook over medium-high heat, stirring frequently, until the mixture simmers and thickens, about 5 minutes. Discard the cinnamon stick, stir in the almond extract, and pour the hot liquid over the cherries in the baking dish.

4. TO BAKE: Arrange the hot biscuits in three rows of four biscuits over the warm filling. Bake the cobbler until the filling is bubbling and the biscuits are deep golden brown, about 10 minutes. Transfer the baking dish to a wire rack and cool for 10 minutes; serve.

Fresh Sour Cherry Cobbler

Morello or Montmorency cherries can be used in this cobbler made with fresh sour cherries. Do not use sweet Bing cherries. If the cherries do not release enough juice after 30 minutes in step 1, add cranberry juice to make up the difference.

1¼ cups (8¾ ounces) sugar
3 tablespoons plus 1 teaspoon cornstarch
    Pinch table salt
8 cups (4 pounds) fresh sour cherries, pitted, juice reserved (see note)
1 cup dry red wine
    Cranberry juice, as needed (see note)
1 recipe Biscuit Topping (see page 661)
1 (3-inch) cinnamon stick
¼ teaspoon almond extract

1. Whisk the sugar, cornstarch, and salt together in a large bowl; add the cherries and toss well to combine. Pour the wine over the cherries; let stand for 30 minutes. Drain the cherries in a colander set over a medium bowl. Combine the drained and reserved juices (from pitting the cherries); you should have 3 cups (if not, add cranberry juice to make this amount).

2. Meanwhile, prepare and bake the biscuit topping.

3. Arrange the drained cherries in an even layer in a 13 by 9-inch glass baking dish. Bring the juices, wine, and cinnamon stick to a simmer in a medium saucepan over medium-high heat, stirring frequently, until the mixture thickens, about 5 minutes. Discard the cinnamon stick, stir

in the almond extract, and pour the hot juices over the cherries in the baking dish.

4. Arrange the hot biscuits in three rows of four biscuits over the warm filling. Bake the cobbler until the filling is bubbling and the biscuits are deep golden brown, about 10 minutes. Transfer the baking dish to a wire rack and cool for 10 minutes; serve.

BLUEBERRY COBBLER

WHY THIS RECIPE WORKS: Too often, blueberry cobbler means a filling that is too sweet, overspiced, and unappealingly thick. We wanted a not-too-thin, not-too-thick filling where the blueberry flavor would be front and center. And over the fruit, we wanted a light, tender biscuit topping that could hold its own against the fruit filling, with an ingredient list simple enough to allow the blueberries to play a starring role.

We prepared a not-too-sweet filling using 6 cups of fresh berries and less than a cup of sugar. Cornstarch worked well as a thickener—it thickened the fruit's juice without leaving a starchy texture behind. A little lemon and cinnamon were all that were needed to enhance the filling without masking the blueberry flavor. For the topping, ease of preparation was our guiding principle, so we made light, rustic drop biscuits enriched with a little cornmeal. Adding the biscuit topping to the cobbler after the filling had baked on its own allowed the biscuits to brown evenly and cook through. A sprinkling of cinnamon sugar on the dropped biscuit dough added a pleasing sweet crunch.

Blueberry Cobbler
SERVES 6 TO 8

While the blueberries are baking, prepare the ingredients for the topping, but do not stir the wet ingredients into the dry ingredients until just before the berries come out of the oven. A standard or deep-dish 9-inch pie plate works well; an 8-inch square baking dish can also be used. Vanilla ice cream or lightly sweetened whipped cream is the perfect accompaniment. To reheat leftovers, put the cobbler in a 350-degree oven for 10 to 15 minutes, until heated through.

FILLING

½ cup (3½ ounces) sugar

1 tablespoon cornstarch

Pinch ground cinnamon

Pinch table salt

6 cups (30 ounces) fresh blueberries, rinsed and picked over

1½ teaspoons grated zest plus 1 tablespoon juice from 1 lemon

BISCUIT TOPPING

1 cup (5 ounces) unbleached all-purpose flour

¼ cup (1¾ ounces) plus 2 teaspoons sugar

2 tablespoons stone-ground cornmeal

2 teaspoons baking powder

¼ teaspoon baking soda

¼ teaspoon table salt

4 tablespoons (½ stick) unsalted butter, melted

⅓ cup buttermilk

½ teaspoon vanilla extract

⅛ teaspoon ground cinnamon

1. Adjust an oven rack to the lower-middle position and heat the oven to 375 degrees.

2. FOR THE FILLING: Whisk the sugar, cornstarch, cinnamon, and salt together in a large bowl. Add the berries and mix gently with a rubber spatula until evenly coated; add the lemon zest and juice and mix to combine.

Transfer the berry mixture to a 9-inch glass pie plate, place the pie plate on a rimmed baking sheet, and bake until the filling is hot and bubbling around the edges, about 25 minutes.

3. FOR THE BISCUIT TOPPING: Meanwhile, whisk the flour, ¼ cup of the sugar, the cornmeal, baking powder, baking soda, and salt together in a large bowl. Whisk the melted butter, buttermilk, and vanilla together in a small bowl. Mix the remaining 2 teaspoons sugar with the cinnamon in a second small bowl and set aside. One minute before the berries come out of the oven, add the wet ingredients to the dry ingredients; stir with a rubber spatula until just combined and no dry pockets remain.

4. TO ASSEMBLE AND BAKE: Remove the berries from the oven; increase the oven temperature to 425 degrees. Divide the biscuit dough into eight equal pieces and place them on the hot berry filling, spacing them at least ½ inch apart (they should not touch). Sprinkle each mound of dough evenly with the cinnamon sugar. Bake until the filling is bubbling and the biscuits are golden brown on top and cooked through, 15 to 18 minutes. Transfer the cobbler to a wire rack; cool for 20 minutes and serve.

PEACH CRISP

WHY THIS RECIPE WORKS: There is seldom anything crisp about most crisps. This simple fruit dessert usually comes out of the oven with a soggy, mushy topping—quite a letdown from the ideal of a warm, fruity filling covered in a crunchy, sweet topping. We set out to make peach crisp that wouldn't disappoint, one with the perfect balance of nicely thickened filling and a lightly sweetened, crisp topping.

We tried everything from Grape-Nuts to cookie crumbs and found the ideal topping mixture to be chopped nuts, butter, and flour. Cutting the butter into the flour is crucial for creating a crisp topping, and we found that a food processor was ideally suited to producing a mixture that resembles crumbly wet sand. Another issue to tackle was sugar: what kind and how much. White sugar alone was too bland, while brown sugar on its own was too strong tasting. A 50-50 mix of the two proved to be the perfect combination. We decided not to use too much sugar in the fruit filling so there would be some contrast with the topping. And we nixed the idea of a thickener—the filling without one had a nicely bright fresh fruit flavor and the topping remained crisp whether we used one or not.

Peach Crisp

SERVES 4 TO 6

Lightly sweetened whipped cream or vanilla ice cream is the perfect accompaniment, especially if serving the crisp warm. A standard or deep-dish 9-inch pie plate works well; an 8-inch square baking dish can also be used.

TOPPING

- 6 tablespoons unbleached all-purpose flour
- ¼ cup packed (1¾ ounces) light brown sugar
- ¼ cup (1¾ ounces) granulated sugar
- ¼ teaspoon ground cinnamon
- ¼ teaspoon ground nutmeg
- ¼ teaspoon table salt
- 5 tablespoons unsalted butter, cut into ½-inch pieces and chilled
- ¾ cup (about 4 ounces) coarsely chopped pecans, walnuts, or almonds

FILLING

- 3 pounds peaches (6 to 8 medium), peeled, pitted, and cut into ½-inch slices
- ¼ cup (1¾ ounces) granulated sugar
- ½ teaspoon grated zest plus 1½ tablespoons juice from 1 lemon

1. FOR THE TOPPING: Pulse the flour, sugars, cinnamon, nutmeg, and salt in a food processor until combined. Sprinkle the butter pieces over the top and pulse until the mixture resembles coarse meal, about 15 pulses. Add the nuts and pulse until the mixture clumps together and resembles wet sand, about 5 pulses; do not overmix. Transfer the mixture to a bowl and refrigerate while preparing the filling, at least 15 minutes.

2. FOR THE FILLING: Adjust an oven rack to the lower-middle position and heat the oven to 375 degrees. Combine the peaches, sugar, zest, and juice in a large bowl and toss gently to combine. Transfer the peach mixture to a 9-inch glass pie plate, place the pie plate on a rimmed baking sheet, and sprinkle the chilled topping evenly over the top.

3. Bake for 40 minutes. Increase the oven temperature to 400 degrees and continue to bake until the filling is bubbling and the topping is deep golden brown, about 5 minutes longer. Serve warm.

Peach Crisp for a Crowd

SERVES 10

Follow the recipe for Peach Crisp, doubling all the ingredients and using a 13 by 9-inch baking dish. Increase the baking time to 55 minutes and bake at 375 degrees without increasing the oven temperature.

RASPBERRY GRATIN

WHY THIS RECIPE WORKS: Quicker than a crisp and dressier than a shortcake, a gratin is a layer of fresh fruit piled into a shallow baking dish, dressed up with bread crumbs, and run under a broiler. The topping browns and the fruit is warmed just enough to release a bit of juice. We wanted to find the quickest, easiest route to this pleasing dessert.

We started with perfect raspberries: ripe, dry, unbruised, and clean. Tossing the sweet-tart berries with just a bit of sugar and kirsch (a clear cherry brandy; vanilla extract can be substituted) provided enough additional flavor and sweetness. For the topping, we combined soft white bread, brown sugar, cinnamon, and butter in the food processor and topped the berries with the fluffy crumbs. Instead of broiling the gratin, which can produce a crust that's burnt in spots, we simply baked it. We found that a moderately hot oven gave the berries more time to soften and browned the crust more evenly.

Simple Raspberry Gratin

SERVES 4 TO 6

If you prefer, you can substitute blueberries, blackberries, or strawberries for part or all of the raspberries. If using strawberries, hull them and slice them in half lengthwise if small or into quarters if large. Later in the summer season, ripe, peeled peaches or nectarines, sliced, can be used in combination with the blueberries or raspberries.

- 4 cups (20 ounces) fresh or frozen (not thawed) raspberries (see note)
- 1 tablespoon granulated sugar
- 1 tablespoon kirsch or vanilla extract (optional)
  Pinch table salt
- 3 slices high-quality white sandwich bread, torn into quarters
- ¼ cup packed (1¾ ounces) light or dark brown sugar
- 2 tablespoons unsalted butter, softened
  Pinch ground cinnamon

1. Adjust an oven rack to the lower-middle position and heat the oven to 400 degrees. Gently toss the raspberries, granulated sugar, kirsch (if using), and salt in a medium bowl. Transfer the mixture to a 9-inch glass pie plate.

2. Pulse the bread, brown sugar, butter, and cinnamon in a food processor until the mixture resembles coarse crumbs, about 10 pulses. Sprinkle the crumbs evenly over the fruit and bake until the crumbs are deep golden brown, 15 to 20 minutes. Transfer to a wire rack; cool for 5 minutes and serve.

FRESH BERRY GRATIN

WHY THIS RECIPE WORKS: Gratins can be very humble, as in our Simple Raspberry Gratin (page 662), where the topping is little more than sweetened bread crumbs. Or they can be a bit more sophisticated, as when they are topped with the foamy Italian custard called *zabaglione*. Zabaglione is made with just three simple ingredients— egg yolks, sugar, and alcohol—but it requires constant watching so that the mixture doesn't overcook. It also needs to be whisked just long enough to transform the egg yolks to the ideal thick, creamy texture. We were after a foolproof method for this topping for a gratin that could serve as an elegant finale to a special summer meal.

We chose to make individual gratins—perfect for entertaining—and settled on raspberries, strawberries, blueberries, and blackberries. We tossed the berries with sugar and a pinch of salt to draw out their juices and let the mixture sit while we worked on the custard. To prevent scrambled eggs, we kept the heat low; for the right texture, we didn't stop whisking when soft peaks formed—instead we waited until the custard became slightly thicker. As for flavor, tasters thought that zabaglione made with the traditional Marsala wine was a bit sweet and cloying on top of the berries. We switched to a crisp, dry Sauvignon Blanc and found that its clean flavor allowed the berries to shine. However, with that change, our zabaglione was almost runny. After trying to thicken it with cornstarch and gelatin (with disappointing results), we turned to whipped cream. After carefully folding a few tablespoons of whipped cream into the cooked and slightly cooled zabaglione base, we spooned it over the berries. Finally, we sprinkled the custard with a mixture of brown and white sugar before broiling for a crackly, caramelized crust.

Individual Fresh Berry Gratins with Zabaglione
SERVES 4

When making the zabaglione, make sure to cook the egg mixture in a glass bowl over water that is barely simmering; glass conducts heat more evenly and gently than metal. If the heat is too high, the yolks around the edges of the bowl will start to scramble. Constant whisking is required. Do not use frozen berries for this recipe. You will need four shallow 6-inch gratin dishes, but a broiler-safe pie plate or gratin dish can be used instead. To prevent scorching, pay close attention to the gratins when broiling.

BERRY MIXTURE
- **3 cups (about 15 ounces) mixed berries (raspberries, blueberries, blackberries, and strawberries; strawberries hulled and halved lengthwise if small, quartered if large), at room temperature (see note)**
- **2 teaspoons granulated sugar**
  Pinch table salt

ZABAGLIONE
- **3 large egg yolks**
- **3 tablespoons granulated sugar**
- **3 tablespoons dry white wine, such as Sauvignon Blanc**
- **2 teaspoons light brown sugar**
- **3 tablespoons heavy cream, chilled**

1. FOR THE BERRY MIXTURE: Toss the berries, sugar, and salt together in a medium bowl. Divide the berry mixture evenly among four shallow 6-ounce gratin dishes set on a rimmed baking sheet; set aside.

2. FOR THE ZABAGLIONE: Whisk the egg yolks, 2 tablespoons plus 1 teaspoon of the granulated sugar, and the wine together in a medium glass bowl until the sugar is dissolved, about 1 minute. Set the bowl over a saucepan of barely simmering water and cook, whisking constantly, until the mixture is frothy. Continue to cook, whisking constantly, until the mixture is slightly thickened, creamy, and glossy, 5 to 10 minutes (the mixture will form loose mounds when dripped from the whisk). Remove the bowl from the saucepan and whisk constantly for 30 seconds to cool slightly. Transfer the bowl to the refrigerator and chill until the egg mixture is completely cool, about 10 minutes.

3. Meanwhile, adjust an oven rack 6 inches from the broiler element and heat the broiler. Combine the brown sugar and the remaining 2 teaspoons granulated sugar in a small bowl.

4. Whisk the heavy cream in a large bowl until it holds soft peaks, 30 to 90 seconds. Using a rubber spatula, gently fold the whipped cream into the cooled egg mixture. Spoon the zabaglione over the berries and sprinkle the sugar mixture evenly on top; let stand at room temperature for 10 minutes, until the sugar dissolves.

5. Broil the gratins until the sugar is bubbly and caramelized, 1 to 4 minutes. Serve immediately.

Individual Fresh Berry Gratins with Lemon Zabaglione

Follow the recipe for Individual Fresh Berry Gratins with Zabaglione, replacing 1 tablespoon of the wine with 1 tablespoon juice from 1 lemon and adding 1 teaspoon grated zest from 1 lemon to the yolk mixture in step 2.

BAKED APPLES

WHY THIS RECIPE WORKS: This homey (and typically dowdy) dessert is often plagued with a mushy texture and one-dimensional, cloyingly sweet flavor. We wanted baked apples that were tender and firm with a filling that perfectly complemented their sweet, tart flavor.

We knew picking the right variety of apple was paramount to our success and, after extensive testing, we arrived at a surprising winner: Granny Smith was the best apple for the job, with its firm flesh and tart, fruity flavor. To ensure that our fruit avoided even the occasional collapse, we peeled the apples after cutting off the top. The skin traps steam from the extra moisture released by the breakdown of the apples' interior cells, and removing it allows the steam to escape and the apple to retain its tender-firm texture. Sautéing our apples cut side down intensified their flavor. Our filling base of tangy dried cranberries, brown sugar, and pecans benefited from some finessing by way of cinnamon, orange zest, and a pat of creamy butter. To punch up the flavor even more, we

intensified the nuttiness with chewy rolled oats, and diced apple was an obvious addition. A melon baller helped us to scoop out a spacious cavity that accommodated plenty of filling. We then capped off the filled apples with the tops we had previously lopped off. Once in the oven, the apples were basted with an apple cider and maple syrup sauce and emerged full of flavor—and far from frumpy.

Best Baked Apples

SERVES 6

If you don't have an ovensafe skillet, transfer the browned apples to a 13 by 9-inch baking dish and bake as directed. The recipe calls for seven apples; six are left whole and one is diced and added to the filling. Serve the apples with vanilla ice cream, if desired.

- 7 **large (about 6 ounces each) Granny Smith apples (see note)**
- 6 **tablespoons (¾ stick) unsalted butter, softened**
- ⅓ **cup dried cranberries, chopped coarse**
- ⅓ **cup coarsely chopped pecans, toasted**
- ¼ **cup packed (1¾ ounces) brown sugar**
- 3 **tablespoons old-fashioned oats**
- 1 **teaspoon finely grated zest from 1 orange**
- ½ **teaspoon ground cinnamon**
  Pinch table salt
- ⅓ **cup maple syrup**
- ⅓ **cup plus 2 tablespoons apple cider**

1. Adjust an oven rack to the middle position and heat the oven to 375 degrees. Peel, core, and cut 1 apple into ¼-inch dice. Combine 5 tablespoons of the butter, the cranberries, pecans, brown sugar, oats, orange zest, cinnamon, salt, and diced apple in a large bowl; set aside.

2. Shave a thin slice off the bottom (blossom end) of the remaining 6 apples to allow them to sit flat. Cut the top ½ inch off the stem end of the apples and reserve. Peel the apples and use a melon baller or small measuring spoon to remove a 1½-inch-diameter core, being careful not to cut through the bottom of the apple.

3. Melt the remaining 1 tablespoon butter in a 12-inch ovensafe nonstick skillet over medium heat. Once the foaming subsides, add the apples, stem side down, and cook until the cut surface is golden brown, about 3 minutes. Flip the apples, reduce the heat to low, and spoon the filling inside, mounding the excess filling over the cavities; top with the reserved apple caps. Add the maple syrup and ⅓ cup of the cider to the skillet. Transfer the skillet to the oven and bake until a skewer inserted into the apples meets little resistance, 35 to 40 minutes, basting every 10 minutes with the maple syrup mixture in the skillet.

4. Transfer the apples to a serving platter. Stir up to 2 tablespoons of the remaining cider into the sauce in the skillet to adjust the consistency. Pour the sauce over the apples and serve.

APPLE CRISP

WHY THIS RECIPE WORKS: Most apple crisp recipes are what you'd expect—unevenly cooked fruit and an unremarkable topping that rarely lives up to its crisp moniker. We wanted an exemplary apple crisp—a lush (but not mushy) sweet-tart apple filling covered with truly crisp morsels of buttery, sugary topping.

For apple crisp, we prefer crisp apples such as Golden Delicious, because they are hardier and turn tender, but not mushy. But they posed two problems. One, their mellower, more honeyed flesh lacked fruity punch. And while complete apple blowouts had been averted, the apples were still cooking unevenly. Stirring the fruit helped solve the problem but donning oven mitts to reach into a hot oven and stir bubbling fruit was a hassle. Instead, we turned to softening our fruit on the stovetop—in a skillet. The shallow, flared shape of the skillet also encouraged evaporation, browning, and better flavor overall. But to improve the flavor further, we turned to apple cider, first reducing it in the skillet to a syrupy consistency. This super-potent reduction contributed an intense, almost tarte Tatin–like fruity depth.

As for the topping, we added brown sugar to white to play up the apples' caramel notes. Rolled oats gave the topping character and chew. Chopped pecans not only improved the crunch factor, but added rich flavor as well. We then slid the skillet into the oven for a quick browning and to finish cooking the apples.

Skillet Apple Crisp

SERVES 6 TO 8

If your skillet is not ovensafe, prepare the recipe through step 3 and then transfer the filling to a 13 by 9-inch baking dish. Top the filling as directed and bake for an additional 5 minutes. We like Golden Delicious apples for this recipe, but any sweet, crisp apple such as Honeycrisp or Braeburn can be substituted. Do not use Granny Smith apples in this recipe. While old-fashioned oats are preferable in this recipe, quick-cooking oats can be substituted. Serve the apple crisp warm or at room temperature with vanilla ice cream or whipped cream.

TOPPING

- ¾ cup (3¾ ounces) unbleached all-purpose flour
- ¾ cup (3 ounces) pecans, chopped fine
- ¾ cup (2¼ ounces) old-fashioned oats (see note)
- ½ cup packed (3½ ounces) light brown sugar
- ¼ cup (1¾ ounces) granulated sugar
- ½ teaspoon ground cinnamon
- ½ teaspoon table salt
- 8 tablespoons (1 stick) unsalted butter, melted

FILLING

- 3 pounds Golden Delicious apples (about 7 medium), peeled, cored, halved, and cut into ½-inch-thick wedges (see note)
- ¼ cup (1¾ ounces) granulated sugar
- ¼ teaspoon ground cinnamon (optional)

1 cup apple cider
2 teaspoons juice from 1 lemon
2 tablespoons unsalted butter

1. FOR THE TOPPING: Adjust an oven rack to the middle position and heat the oven to 450 degrees. Combine the flour, pecans, oats, brown sugar, granulated sugar, cinnamon, and salt in a medium bowl. Stir in the butter until the mixture is thoroughly moistened and crumbly. Set aside while preparing the fruit filling.

2. FOR THE FILLING: Toss the apples, sugar, and cinnamon (if using) together in a large bowl; set aside. Bring the cider to a simmer in a 12-inch ovensafe skillet over medium heat; cook until reduced to ½ cup, about 5 minutes. Transfer the reduced cider to a bowl or liquid measuring cup; stir in the lemon juice and set aside.

3. Heat the butter in the now-empty skillet over medium heat. When the foaming subsides, add the apple mixture and cook, stirring frequently, until the apples are beginning to soften and become translucent, 12 to 14 minutes. (Do not fully cook the apples.) Remove the pan from the heat and gently stir in the cider mixture until the apples are coated.

4. Sprinkle the topping evenly over the fruit, breaking up any large chunks. Place the skillet on a baking sheet and bake until the fruit is tender and the topping is deep golden brown, 15 to 20 minutes. Cool on a wire rack until warm, at least 15 minutes, and serve.

APPLE BROWN BETTY

WHY THIS RECIPE WORKS: In its most basic form, apple brown betty contains only four ingredients: apples, bread crumbs, sugar, and butter. Sadly, this simple combination inevitably results in a soggy, mushy mess of a dessert—not the classic Colonial dish of tender, lightly spiced chunks of apple topped with buttery toasted bread crumbs. We decided it was time to give "Betty" a serious makeover.

For a lightly sweetened, crisp crumb topping, we toasted white sandwich bread crumbs with butter and a bit of sugar. The sweet/tart combination of Granny Smith and Golden Delicious apples made a not-too-sweet apple filling. Instead of baking the dessert, we prepared it in a skillet on the stovetop and cooked the apples in two batches to ensure even cooking. After preparing the bread crumbs, we removed them from the pan and

caramelized the apples. Adding brown sugar to the apples along with ginger and cinnamon gave the dessert a deepened, lightly spiced flavor. The addition of apple cider to the fruit brought moisture and a further dimension of apple flavor; a bit of lemon juice brightened the filling. For a thicker filling, we added a portion of the toasted bread crumbs to the apples and reserved the remainder for sprinkling over the top.

Skillet Apple Brown Betty

SERVES 6 TO 8

If your apples are especially tart, omit the lemon juice. If, on the other hand, your apples are exceptionally sweet, use the full amount. Leftovers can be refrigerated in an airtight container; topped with vanilla yogurt, they make an excellent breakfast.

BREAD CRUMBS
4 slices high-quality white sandwich bread, torn into quarters
3 tablespoons unsalted butter, cut into 4 pieces
2 tablespoons packed light brown sugar

FILLING
¼ cup packed (1¾ ounces) light brown sugar
¼ teaspoon ground ginger
¼ teaspoon ground cinnamon
Pinch table salt
3 tablespoons unsalted butter
1½ pounds Granny Smith apples (about 3 large), peeled, cored, and cut into ½-inch cubes (about 4 cups)
1½ pounds Golden Delicious apples (about 3 large), peeled, cored, and cut into ½-inch cubes (about 4 cups)
1¼ cups apple cider
1-3 teaspoons juice from 1 lemon (see note)

1. FOR THE BREAD CRUMBS: Pulse the bread, butter, and sugar in a food processor until coarsely ground, 5 to 7 pulses. Transfer the bread crumbs to a 12-inch skillet and toast over medium heat, stirring constantly, until they are deep golden brown, 8 to 10 minutes. Transfer to a paper towel–lined plate; wipe out the skillet.

2. FOR THE FILLING: Combine the sugar, spices, and salt in a small bowl. Melt 1½ tablespoons of the butter in the now-empty skillet over high heat. Stir in the Granny Smith apples and half of the sugar mixture. Distribute the apples in an even layer and cook, stirring two or three times, until medium brown, about 5 minutes; transfer to a medium bowl. Repeat with the remaining butter, the Golden Delicious apples, and the remaining sugar mixture, returning the first batch of apples to the skillet when the second batch is done.

3. Add the apple cider to the skillet and scrape the bottom and sides of the pan with a wooden spoon to loosen the browned bits; cook until the apples are tender but not mushy and the liquid has reduced and is just beginning to thicken, 2 to 4 minutes.

4. Remove the skillet from the heat; stir in the lemon juice (if using) and ⅓ cup of the toasted bread crumbs. Using a wooden spoon, lightly flatten the apples into an even layer in the skillet and evenly sprinkle with the remaining toasted bread crumbs. Spoon the warm betty into individual bowls and serve with vanilla ice cream, if desired.

EASY APPLE STRUDEL

WHY THIS RECIPE WORKS: Apple strudel, lightly spiced apples in a thin, flaky pastry, is meant to be savored by the forkful, preferably with a strong cup of coffee. We wanted all the flavor and charm of this apple dessert, but we didn't want to bother with the hours of preparation the paper-thin dough requires. So, chucking the notion of homemade strudel dough, we started with a simpler option—store-bought phyllo dough—and set out to simplify this classic dessert while keeping the rich apple filling and as much of the crisp, flaky texture as possible.

Replacing homemade strudel dough with purchased phyllo dough made for a crust with crisp, flaky layers in a fraction of the time. We brushed the phyllo sheets with melted butter to keep them crisp and flaky. A combination of Golden Delicious and McIntosh apples, sliced thin, gave us a filling with layered apple flavor and just the right texture. A small amount of bread crumbs, browned in butter, thickened the filling without weighing it down. Golden raisins, plumped on the stove with Calvados (apple brandy), added a sophisticated, fruity dimension to the apple filling; for brightness and to lighten the filling, we added in some fresh lemon juice. We found that the phyllo on most strudels, including this one, curled and shattered as it cooled; sprinkling sugar between the layers of phyllo "glued" them together in the oven and prevented this problem.

Easy Apple Strudel

SERVES 6

The best ways to thaw the phyllo are in the refrigerator overnight or at room temperature for 3 to 4 hours; it doesn't defrost well in the microwave. Make sure that the phyllo sheets you use for the strudel are not badly torn. If they have small cuts or tears in the same location (sometimes an entire package sustains cuts in the same spot), when forming the strudel, flip alternating layers so that the cuts will not line up, thereby creating a weak spot that can cause the strudel to burst during baking. To make the fresh bread crumbs, process one slice of high-quality white sandwich bread in a food processor until fine, 20 to 30 seconds. Serve the strudel warm with Tangy Whipped Cream (recipe follows) or regular whipped cream; if you choose to make the tangy whipped cream, make it before starting the strudel because it must stand at room temperature for about 1½ hours before serving.

½ cup golden raisins

2 tablespoons Calvados or apple cider

8 tablespoons (1 stick) unsalted butter, melted and cooled

¼ cup fresh bread crumbs (see note)

1 pound Golden Delicious apples (about 2 large), peeled, cored, and sliced ¼ inch thick

1 medium McIntosh apple, peeled, cored, and sliced ¼ inch thick

¼ cup (1¾ ounces) plus 2 tablespoons granulated sugar

⅓ cup finely chopped walnuts (optional), toasted

¼ teaspoon ground cinnamon

⅛ teaspoon table salt

1 teaspoon juice from 1 lemon

10 (14 by 9-inch) sheets phyllo, thawed (see note)

1½ teaspoons confectioners' sugar

1. Adjust an oven rack to the lower-middle position and heat the oven to 475 degrees. Line a large baking sheet with parchment paper. Bring the raisins and Calvados to a simmer in a small saucepan over medium heat. Cover, remove from the heat, and let stand until needed.

2. Combine 1 tablespoon of the butter and the bread crumbs in a small skillet and cook over medium heat, stirring frequently, until golden brown, about 2 minutes. Transfer the bread crumbs to a small bowl and set aside.

NOTES FROM THE TEST KITCHEN

ASSEMBLING STRUDEL

1. Brush 1 sheet of phyllo with melted butter and sprinkle with sugar. Place another sheet of phyllo next to it, overlapping the sheets. Brush with more butter and sprinkle with sugar. Repeat this process four times.

2. Mound the filling along the bottom edge of the phyllo, leaving a 2½-inch border on the bottom and a 2-inch border on the sides.

3. Fold the dough on the sides over the apples. Fold the dough on the bottom over the apples and continue to roll the dough around the filling to form the strudel.

4. After the strudel has been assembled and rolled, gently lay it seam side down on the prepared baking sheet.

3. Drain off and discard any remaining liquid from the raisins. Toss the apples, raisins, bread crumbs, ¼ cup of the granulated sugar, the walnuts (if using), cinnamon, salt, and lemon juice in a large bowl to combine.

4. Melt the remaining 7 tablespoons butter. Place a large sheet of parchment paper horizontally on a work surface. Following the photos, lay 1 sheet of phyllo on the left side of the sheet of parchment paper, then brush with melted butter and sprinkle with ½ teaspoon more of the granulated sugar. Place another sheet of phyllo on the right side of the parchment, overlapping the sheets by 1 inch, then brush with more butter and sprinkle with sugar. Repeat this process with the remaining 8 sheets of phyllo, more butter, and more sugar. Mound the filling along the bottom edge of the phyllo, leaving a 2½-inch border on the bottom and a 2-inch border on the sides. Fold the dough on the sides over the apples. Fold the dough on the bottom over the apples and continue to roll the dough around the filling to form the strudel.

5. Place the strudel, seam side down, on the prepared baking sheet; brush with the remaining butter and sprinkle with the remaining 1 teaspoon sugar. Cut four 1-inch crosswise vents into the top of the strudel and bake until golden brown, 15 minutes. Transfer the baking sheet to a wire rack and cool until warm, about 40 minutes.

6. Dust the strudel with the confectioners' sugar before serving; slice with a serrated knife and serve warm or at room temperature.

Tangy Whipped Cream
MAKES ABOUT 2 CUPS

Adding sour cream to whipped cream mimics the pleasantly tart flavor of the rich French-style whipped cream, crème fraîche.

- 1 cup heavy cream
- ½ cup sour cream
- 1 tablespoon sugar
- 1 teaspoon vanilla extract

Whip the heavy cream and sour cream in a large bowl with an electric mixer on medium-low speed until frothy, about 1 minute. Add the sugar and vanilla. Increase the mixer speed to high and continue to whip until the cream forms soft peaks, 1 to 3 minutes.

APPLE PANDOWDY

WHY THIS RECIPE WORKS: Apple pandowdy harks back to Colonial-era New England—the dessert takes a more rustic approach to apple pie in that it features just one pastry crust, placed on top of a lightly sweetened apple filling. During or after baking, the pastry is broken and pushed into the filling—a technique known as "dowdying." We found the idea of an easier approach to apple pie very appealing—no fussy crimping and only one piece of pastry dough to roll out, so we set out to make our own version—one with a flaky crust and tender, juicy apples.

For a juicy apple filling with bright fruit flavor, we added cider to the apples and sweetened the filling with maple syrup—the tart intensity of the cider deepened the apple flavor and maple syrup's rich character added the right degree of sweetness. Both additions also made for a pleasantly saucy filling. Parcooking the apples in a skillet until caramelized before adding the other ingredients helped to deepen their flavor. For the crust, we cut a standard pie crust into squares after rolling it over the fruit right in the skillet—this encouraged a multitude of crispy edges that contrast nicely with the tender fruit and recall (in a less dowdy way) the broken-up crusts of a traditional pandowdy.

Skillet Apple Pie

SERVES 6 TO 8

If your skillet is not ovensafe, precook the apples and stir in the cider mixture as instructed, then transfer the apples to a 13 by 9-inch baking dish. Roll out the dough to a 13 by 9-inch rectangle and cut the crust and bake the

pandowdy as instructed. If you do not have apple cider, reduced apple juice may be used as a substitute; simmer 1 cup apple juice in a small saucepan over medium heat until reduced to ½ cup (about 10 minutes). Serve the pandowdy warm or at room temperature with vanilla ice cream or whipped cream. Use a combination of sweet, crisp apples such as Golden Delicious and firm, tart apples such as Cortland or Empire.

CRUST

- 1 cup (5 ounces) unbleached all-purpose flour, plus extra for the work surface
- 1 tablespoon sugar
- ½ teaspoon table salt
- 2 tablespoons vegetable shortening, chilled
- 6 tablespoons (¾ stick) unsalted butter, cut into ¼-inch pieces and chilled
- 3–4 tablespoons ice water

FILLING

- ½ cup apple cider
- ⅓ cup maple syrup
- 2 tablespoons juice from 1 lemon
- 2 teaspoons cornstarch
- ⅛ teaspoon ground cinnamon (optional)
- 2 tablespoons unsalted butter
- 2½ pounds sweet and tart apples (about 4 large), peeled, cored, and cut into ½-inch-thick wedges (see note)
- 1 large egg white, lightly beaten
- 2 teaspoons sugar

1. FOR THE CRUST: Pulse the flour, sugar, and salt in a food processor until combined, about 4 pulses. Add the shortening and pulse until the mixture has the texture of coarse sand, about 10 pulses. Sprinkle the butter pieces over the flour mixture and pulse until the mixture is pale yellow and resembles coarse crumbs, with the butter bits no larger than small peas, about 10 pulses. Transfer the mixture to a medium bowl.

2. Sprinkle 3 tablespoons of the ice water over the mixture. With a rubber spatula, use a folding motion to mix, pressing down on the dough until the dough is slightly tacky and sticks together, adding up to 1 tablespoon more ice water if the dough does not come together. Flatten the dough into a 4-inch disk. Wrap the disk in plastic wrap and refrigerate for at least 1 hour or up to 2 days. Let the dough stand at room temperature for 15 minutes before rolling.

3. FOR THE FILLING: Adjust an oven rack to the upper-middle position (between 7 and 9 inches from the heating element) and heat the oven to 500 degrees. Whisk the cider, syrup, lemon juice, cornstarch, and cinnamon (if using) together in a medium bowl until smooth. Melt the butter in a 12-inch ovensafe skillet over medium-high heat. Add the apples and cook, stirring two or three times, until the apples begin to caramelize, about 5 minutes. (Do not fully cook the apples.) Remove the pan from the heat, add the cider mixture, and gently stir until the apples are well coated. Set aside to cool slightly.

4. TO ASSEMBLE AND BAKE: Roll the dough out on a lightly floured work surface to an 11-inch circle. Roll the dough loosely around the rolling pin and unroll over the apple filling. Brush the dough with the egg white and sprinkle with the sugar. With a sharp knife, gently cut the dough into six pieces by making one vertical cut followed by two evenly spaced horizontal cuts (perpendicular to the first cut). Bake until the apples are tender and the crust is a deep golden brown, about 20 minutes, rotating the skillet halfway through the baking time. Cool for 15 minutes and serve.

BANANAS FOSTER

WHY THIS RECIPE WORKS: Although the New Orleans dessert bananas Foster is quick and simple, with few ingredients (butter, brown sugar, rum, and bananas), things can go wrong. Sometimes the bananas are overcooked and mushy. Or the sauce can be too thin, overly sweet, or taste too strongly of alcohol. We wanted to fix these issues and come up with a quick, reliable dessert with tender bananas and a flavorful but not boozy sauce.

First we kept the amounts of butter and brown sugar in check—most recipes use a high ratio of butter to brown sugar, which makes for a thin, greasy sauce. For the rum, we found that a small amount was just enough to impart a definite rum flavor without turning the dessert into a cocktail. We decided to add some rum to the sauce and use the rest to flambé the bananas. We also enhanced the sauce with a little cinnamon and lemon zest, which added some complexity. As for the bananas, we cooked them in the sauce until soft, flipping them over halfway through cooking so they turned out tender, not mushy.

Bananas Foster

SERVES 4

While the bananas cook, scoop the ice cream into individual bowls so they are ready to go once the sauce has been flambéed. Before preparing this recipe, read "Tips for Fearless Flambé" on page 342.

- 4 tablespoons (½ stick) unsalted butter
- ½ cup packed (3½ ounces) dark brown sugar
- 1 (3-inch) cinnamon stick
- 1 (2-inch) strip zest from 1 lemon
- 4 tablespoons dark rum
- 2 large, firm, ripe bananas, peeled and quartered
- 1 pint vanilla ice cream, divided among four bowls

1. Combine the butter, sugar, cinnamon stick, zest, and 1 tablespoon of the rum in a 12-inch skillet. Cook over medium-high heat, stirring constantly, until the sugar dissolves and the mixture has thickened, about 2 minutes.

2. Reduce the heat to medium and add the bananas to the pan, spooning some sauce over each quarter. Cook until the bananas are glossy and golden on the bottom, about 1½ minutes. Flip the bananas; continue to cook until very soft but not mushy or falling apart, about 1½ minutes longer.

3. Off the heat, add the remaining 3 tablespoons rum and allow the rum to warm slightly, about 5 seconds. Wave a lit match over the pan until the rum ignites, shaking the pan to distribute the flame over the entire pan. When the flames subside (this will take 15 to 30 seconds), discard the cinnamon stick and zest and divide the bananas and sauce among the four bowls of ice cream. Serve.

CRÊPES SUZETTE

WHY THIS RECIPE WORKS: Classic French restaurants have mastered the fiery theatrics of this tableside treat—a sophisticated combination of crêpes, oranges, liqueur, and a showy flambé. We wanted to develop a recipe that would comfortably guide the home cook through the flambé process so this dessert could be prepared for an elegant dinner party.

For a foolproof flambé that didn't create a frightening fireball or, conversely, didn't burn at all, we ignited the alcohol (cognac) alone in the skillet before building the sauce. To build a delicate sauce with complex flavor, we enriched a reduction of butter, sugar, and fresh orange juice with additional orange juice, fresh orange zest, and triple sec (not the pricier Grand Marnier or Cointreau). For tender but sturdy crêpes that would stand up to the sauce without turning soggy, we skipped the usual resting of the batter, meant to relax the gluten, before cooking. Then, once the crêpes were cooked, we sprinkled them with sugar and ran them under the broiler for a sweet and crunchy coating.

Crêpes Suzette

SERVES 6

Note that it takes a few crêpes to get the heat of the pan right; your first two or three will almost inevitably be unusable. (To allow for practice, the recipe yields about 16 crêpes; only 12 are needed for the dish.) A dry measuring cup with a ¼-cup capacity is useful for portioning the batter. We prefer crêpes made with whole milk, but low-fat or skim milk can also be used. Before preparing this recipe, read "Tips for Fearless Flambé" on page 342.

CRÊPES

- 3 large eggs
- 1½ cups whole milk (see note)
- 1½ cups (7½ ounces) unbleached all-purpose flour
- ½ cup water
- 5 tablespoons unsalted butter, melted, plus extra for brushing the pan
- 3 tablespoons sugar
- 2 tablespoons cognac
- ½ teaspoon table salt

ORANGE SAUCE

- 4 tablespoons cognac
- 1¼ cups juice plus 1 tablespoon finely grated zest from 3 to 4 large oranges
- 6 tablespoons (¾ stick) unsalted butter, cut into 6 pieces
- ¼ cup (1¾ ounces) sugar
- 2 tablespoons orange-flavored liqueur, preferably triple sec

1. FOR THE CRÊPES: Combine the eggs, milk, flour, water, melted butter, sugar, cognac, and salt in a blender until a smooth batter forms, about 10 seconds. Transfer the batter to a medium bowl.

2. Using a pastry brush, brush the bottom and sides of a 10-inch nonstick skillet very lightly with melted butter and heat the skillet over medium heat. When the butter

stops sizzling, tilt the pan slightly to the right and begin pouring in a scant ¼ cup batter. Continue to pour the batter in a slow, steady stream, rotating your wrist and twirling the pan slowly counterclockwise until the pan bottom is covered with an even layer of batter. Cook until the crêpe starts to lose its opaqueness and turns spotty light golden brown on the bottom, loosening the crêpe from the side of the pan with a heatproof rubber spatula, 30 seconds to 1 minute. To flip the crêpe, loosen the edge with the spatula and, with your fingertips on the top side, slide the spatula under the crêpe and flip. Cook until dry on the second side, about 20 seconds.

3. Place the cooked crêpe on a plate and repeat the cooking process with the remaining batter, brushing the pan very lightly with butter before making each crêpe. As they are done, stack the crêpes on a plate (you will need 12 crêpes). (The crêpes can be double-wrapped in plastic wrap and refrigerated for up to 3 days; bring them to room temperature before making the sauce.)

4. FOR THE ORANGE SAUCE: Adjust an oven rack to the lower-middle position and heat the broiler. Add 3 tablespoons of the cognac to a broiler-safe 12-inch skillet; heat the pan over medium heat just until the vapors begin to rise from the cognac, about 5 seconds. Remove the pan from the heat and wave a lit match over the pan until the cognac ignites, shaking the pan until the flames subside, about 15 seconds; reignite if the flame dies too soon.

5. Add 1 cup of the orange juice, the butter, and 3 tablespoons of the sugar and simmer briskly over high heat, stirring occasionally, until many large bubbles appear and the mixture reduces to a thick syrup, 6 to 8 minutes (you should have just over ½ cup sauce). Transfer the sauce to a small bowl; do not wash the skillet. Stir the remaining ¼ cup orange juice, zest, liqueur, and the remaining 1 tablespoon cognac into the sauce; cover.

6. TO ASSEMBLE: Fold each crêpe in half, then in half again to form a wedge shape. Arrange nine folded crêpes around the edge of the now-empty skillet, with the rounded edges facing inward, overlapping as necessary to fit. Arrange the remaining three crêpes in the center of the pan. Sprinkle the crêpes evenly with the remaining 1 tablespoon sugar. Broil until the sugar caramelizes and the crêpes turn spotty brown, about 5 minutes. (Watch the crêpes constantly to prevent scorching; turn the pan as necessary.) Carefully remove the pan from the oven and pour half of the sauce over the crêpes, leaving some areas uncovered. Transfer the crêpes to individual serving dishes and serve immediately, passing the extra sauce separately.

CLASSIC CRÊPES

WHY THIS RECIPE WORKS: A crêpe is nothing but a thin pancake cooked quickly on each side and wrapped around a sweet or savory filling, but it has a reputation for being difficult. We wanted an easy method for crêpes that were thin and delicate yet rich and flavorfully browned in spots.

Finding the perfect ratio of milk to flour and sugar gave us rich-tasting, lightly sweet pancakes. We were surprised to find that neither the type of flour nor the mixing method seemed to matter, and a plain old 12-inch nonstick skillet worked as well as a specialty crêpe pan. What does matter is heating the pan properly (over low heat for at least 10 minutes), using the right amount of batter (we settled on ¼ cup), and flipping the crêpe at precisely the right moment, when the edges appear dry, matte, and lacy. To transform our perfectly cooked crêpes into decadent desserts, we whipped up a few sweet fillings: the simple classic of sugar and lemon; a decadent chocolate and orange; and a banana and Nutella sure to please kids and adults alike.

Crêpes with Sugar and Lemon
SERVES 4

The crêpes will give off steam as they cook, but if at any point the skillet begins to smoke, remove it from the heat immediately and turn down the heat. Stacking the crêpes on a wire rack allows excess steam to escape so they won't stick together. To allow for practice, the recipe yields 10 crêpes; only eight are needed for the filling.

- ½ teaspoon vegetable oil
- 1 cup (5 ounces) unbleached all-purpose flour
- 1 teaspoon sugar, plus 8 teaspoons for sprinkling
- ¼ teaspoon table salt
- 1½ cups whole milk
- 3 large eggs
- 2 tablespoons unsalted butter, melted and cooled
- Lemon wedges, for serving

1. Heat the oil in a 12-inch nonstick skillet over low heat for at least 10 minutes.

2. While the skillet is heating, whisk the flour, 1 teaspoon of the sugar, and the salt together in a medium bowl. In a separate bowl, whisk together the milk and eggs. Add half of the milk mixture to the dry ingredients and whisk until smooth. Add the butter and whisk until incorporated. Whisk in the remaining milk mixture until smooth.

3. Using a paper towel, wipe out the skillet, leaving a thin film of oil on the bottom and sides of the pan. Increase the heat to medium and let the skillet heat for 1 minute. After 1 minute, test the heat of the skillet by placing 1 teaspoon of the batter in the center; cook for 20 seconds. If the mini crêpe is golden brown on the bottom, the skillet is properly heated; if it is too light or too dark, adjust the heat accordingly and retest.

4. Pour ¼ cup batter into the far side of pan and tilt and shake gently until the batter evenly covers the bottom of the pan. Cook the crêpe without moving until the top surface is dry and the edges are starting to brown, loosening the crêpe from the side of the pan with a rubber spatula, about 25 seconds. Gently slide the spatula underneath the edge of the crêpe, grasp the edge with your fingertips, and flip the crêpe. Cook until the second side is lightly spotted, about 20 seconds. Transfer the cooked crêpe to a wire rack, inverting so the spotted side is facing up. Return the pan to the heat and heat for 10 seconds before repeating with the remaining batter. As the crêpes are done, stack on the wire rack.

5. Transfer the stack of crêpes to a large plate and invert a second plate over the crêpes. Microwave until the crêpes are warm, 30 to 45 seconds (45 to 60 seconds if the crêpes have cooled completely). Remove the top plate and wipe dry with a paper towel. Sprinkle half of the top crêpe with 1 teaspoon sugar. Fold the unsugared bottom half over the sugared half, then fold into quarters. Transfer the sugared crêpe to a second plate. Continue with the remaining crêpes. Serve immediately, passing the lemon wedges separately.

Crêpes with Chocolate and Orange

Follow the recipe for Crêpes with Sugar and Lemon, omitting the 8 teaspoons sugar for sprinkling and the lemon wedges. Using your fingertips, rub 1 teaspoon finely grated orange zest into ¼ cup sugar. Stir in 2 ounces finely grated bittersweet chocolate. In step 5, sprinkle 1½ tablespoons of the chocolate-orange mixture over half of each crêpe. Fold the crêpes into quarters. Serve immediately.

Crêpes with Bananas and Nutella

Follow the recipe for Crêpes with Sugar and Lemon, omitting the 8 teaspoons sugar for sprinkling and the lemon wedges. In step 5, spread 2 teaspoons Nutella over half of each crêpe, followed by eight to ten ¼-inch-thick banana slices. Fold the crêpes into quarters. Serve immediately.

SUMMER PUDDING

WHY THIS RECIPE WORKS: If any food speaks of summer, the English dessert called summer pudding does. Ripe, fragrant, lightly sweetened berries are gently cooked to coax out their juices and then packed into a bowl lined with slices of bread. The berry juices soak and soften the bread to make it meld with the fruit. We set out to master this summertime classic.

Instead of lining the mold with bread and then filling it with berries, we opted to layer bread (cut out with a biscuit cutter) and berries together in ramekins; this way, the layers of bread on the inside would almost melt into the fruit. Combining the berries—we used strawberries, raspberries, blueberries, and blackberries—with sugar

and lemon juice, and gently cooking the mixture for just five minutes, released just the right amount of juice and offset the tartness of the berries. Fresh bread became too gummy in the pudding, but day-old bread had just the right consistency. We used potato bread; its even, tight-crumbed, tender texture and light sweetness was a perfect match for the berries (challah makes a good substitute). To ensure that the puddings would come together and hold their shape, we weighted and refrigerated them for at least eight hours.

Individual Summer Berry Puddings
SERVES 6

The bread should be dry to the touch but not brittle. If working with fresh bread, dry the slices by heating them on an oven rack in a single layer in a 200-degree oven for about 1 hour, flipping them once halfway through the time. For this recipe, you will need six 6-ounce ramekins and a round cookie cutter of a slightly smaller diameter than the ramekins. If you don't have the right size cutter, use a paring knife and the bottom of a ramekin (most ramekins taper toward the bottom) as a guide for trimming the rounds. Challah will need to be cut into slices about ½ inch thick; if both potato bread and challah are unavailable, use high-quality white sandwich bread. Summer pudding can be made up to 24 hours before serving; held any longer, the berries begin to lose their freshness. Lightly sweetened whipped cream is the perfect accompaniment.

　4　cups (20 ounces) strawberries, hulled and sliced
　2　cups (about 10 ounces) raspberries
　1　cup (about 5 ounces) blueberries
　1　cup (about 5 ounces) blackberries
　¾　cup (5¼ ounces) sugar
　2　tablespoons juice from 1 lemon
　12　slices stale potato bread, challah, or high-quality white sandwich bread (see note)

1. Cook the strawberries, raspberries, blueberries, blackberries, and sugar in a large saucepan over medium heat, stirring occasionally, until the berries begin to release their juice and the sugar has dissolved, about 5 minutes. Off the heat, stir in the lemon juice; cool to room temperature.

2. While the berries are cooling, spray six 6-ounce ramekins with vegetable oil spray and place on a rimmed baking sheet. Use a cookie cutter to cut out 12 bread rounds that are slightly smaller in diameter than the ramekins.

3. Using a slotted spoon, place ¼ cup of the fruit mixture in each ramekin. Lightly soak one bread round in the fruit juice in the saucepan and place on top of the fruit in a ramekin; repeat with five more bread rounds and the remaining ramekins. Diving the remaining fruit among the ramekins. Lightly soak one bread round in the juice and place on top of the fruit in a ramekin (it should sit above the lip of the ramekin); repeat with the remaining five bread rounds and the remaining ramekins. Pour the remaining fruit juice over the bread and cover the ramekins loosely with plastic wrap. Place a second baking sheet on top of the ramekins and weight it with heavy cans. Refrigerate the puddings for at least 8 hours or up to 24 hours.

4. Remove the cans and baking sheet and uncover the puddings. Loosen the puddings by running a paring knife around the edge of each ramekin, unmold into individual bowls, and serve immediately.

Large Summer Berry Pudding

SERVES 6 TO 8

You will need a 9 by 5-inch loaf pan for this recipe. Because there is no need to cut out rounds for this version, you will need only about 8 slices bread, depending on their size.

Follow the recipe for Individual Summer Berry Puddings through step 1. While the berries are cooling, spray a 9 by 5-inch loaf pan with vegetable oil spray, line it with plastic wrap, and place it on a rimmed baking sheet. Trim the crusts from the bread and trim the slices to fit in a single layer in the loaf pan (you will need about 2½ slices per layer; there will be three layers). Using a slotted spoon, spread about 2 cups of the fruit mixture evenly over the bottom of the prepared pan. Lightly soak enough bread slices for one layer in the fruit juice in the saucepan and place on top of the fruit. Repeat with two more layers of fruit and bread. Pour the remaining fruit juice over the bread and cover loosely with plastic wrap. Place a second baking sheet on top of the loaf pan and weight it with heavy cans. Refrigerate the pudding for at least 8 hours or up to 24 hours. Remove the cans and baking sheet and uncover the pudding. Invert the pudding onto a serving platter, remove the loaf pan and plastic wrap, slice, and serve.

CARAMELIZED PEARS

WHY THIS RECIPE WORKS: Pears and blue cheese are a classic combination, but we wanted to up the flavor ante with another component—caramel. We had encountered this triple play in restaurants, where a caramel sauce is draped over seared pears, and a modest amount of pungent blue cheese provides a nice contrast to the dessert's sweetness. We decided to adapt this dish so it would be easy for the home cook to get it just right (meaning no mushy pears and no sticky, overcooked caramel).

To streamline the recipe, we cooked the pears right in the caramel sauce, instead of separately, saving time and eliminating some dirty dishes. We brought water and sugar (the basis for caramel sauce) to a boil in a skillet and slid the pears into the hot mixture to cook in the browning caramel. We added cream to the pan to transform the sticky sugar syrup into a smooth sauce that clung lightly to the pears. After removing the pears, we were able to season the sauce left in the skillet with just the right amount of black pepper and salt. For an attractive presentation, we stood the pears upright on a plate (we had already trimmed the bottom off each pear for a flat base) and drizzled the caramel sauce around them, then added wedges of strong blue cheese—the perfect foil to the sweet caramel.

Caramelized Pears with Blue Cheese and Black Pepper–Caramel Sauce

SERVES 6

Any type of pear can be used in this recipe, but the pears must be firm to withstand the heat. If desired, the pears can be served upright on a large platter instead of on individual plates, with the warm caramel sauce and the blue cheese passed separately. Many pepper mills do not have a sufficiently coarse setting; in that case, crush peppercorns with the back of a heavy pan or a rolling pin. See page 713 for information on our top-rated pepper mill.

⅓   **cup water**
⅔   **cup (4⅔ ounces) sugar**
3   **ripe, firm pears, halved, cored, and ¼ inch trimmed off the bottom (see note)**
⅔   **cup heavy cream**
    Table salt
¼   **teaspoon black peppercorns, crushed (see note)**
3   **ounces strong blue cheese (such as Stilton), cut into 6 wedges**

1. Pour the water into a 12-inch nonstick skillet, then pour the sugar into the center of the pan, being careful not to let it hit the sides of the pan. Bring to a boil over high heat, stirring occasionally, until the sugar is fully dissolved and the liquid is bubbling. Add the pears to the skillet, cut side down, cover, reduce the heat to medium-high, and cook until the pears are almost tender and a paring knife inserted into the center of the pears meets slight resistance, 13 to 15 minutes.

2. Uncover, reduce the heat to medium, and cook until the sauce is golden brown and the cut sides of the pears are beginning to brown, 3 to 5 minutes. Pour the heavy cream around the pears and cook, shaking the pan until the sauce is a smooth, deep caramel color and the cut sides of the pears are golden brown, 3 to 5 minutes.

3. Off the heat, transfer the pears, cut side up, to a wire rack set over a rimmed baking sheet and cool slightly. Season the sauce left in the pan with salt to taste and the crushed peppercorns, then transfer it to a small bowl.

4. Carefully (the pears will still be hot) stand each pear half upright on an individual plate and arrange a wedge of the blue cheese beside it. Drizzle the caramel sauce over the plate and the pear. Serve immediately.

STRAWBERRIES WITH BALSAMIC VINEGAR

WHY THIS RECIPE WORKS: Strawberries with balsamic vinegar may sound a bit trendy, but this combination actually goes back in time—hundreds of years at least—to northern Italy. We wanted to pay homage to this time-honored tradition and create our own dessert, with the vinegar enhancing but not overwhelming the flavor of bright, summer berries.

We didn't want to pay big bucks for a super-pricey balsamic vinegar, so we opted to use an inexpensive vinegar. To coax big flavor out of our bargain balsamic, we simmered it with some sugar to approximate the syrupy texture of an aged vinegar. Next we tried to enhance the flavor with honey or vanilla, but these flavors were too overpowering; a squirt of fresh lemon juice brought just the right amount of brightness. We tossed the berries with light brown sugar—rather than the traditional granulated sugar—for the most complex flavor. Once we mixed the sliced berries and sugar together, it took about 15 minutes for the sugar to dissolve and the berries to release their juice; if the strawberries sat any longer than this, they continued to soften and became quite mushy.

Strawberries with Balsamic Vinegar

SERVES 6

If you don't have light brown sugar on hand, sprinkle the berries with an equal amount of granulated sugar. Serve the berries and syrup as is or with a scoop of vanilla ice cream or a dollop of lightly sweetened whipped cream.

⅓   **cup balsamic vinegar**
2   **teaspoons granulated sugar**
½   **teaspoon juice from 1 lemon**
6   **cups (30 ounces) strawberries, hulled, sliced lengthwise ¼ inch thick if large, halved or quartered if small**
¼   **cup packed (1¾ ounces) light brown sugar (see note)**
    Ground black pepper

1. Bring the vinegar, granulated sugar, and lemon juice to a simmer in a small saucepan over medium heat. Simmer until the syrup is reduced by half (about 3 tablespoons), about 3 minutes. Transfer to a small bowl and cool completely.

2. Gently toss the berries and brown sugar in a large bowl. Let stand until the sugar dissolves and the berries exude some juice, 10 to 15 minutes. Pour the vinegar syrup over the berries, add pepper to taste, and toss to combine. Serve immediately.

BERRY FOOL

WHY THIS RECIPE WORKS: Traditionally, fruit fool is made by folding pureed stewed fruit (traditionally gooseberries) into sweet custard. Modern fool recipes skip the traditional custard and use whipped cream. But whipped cream blunts the fruit flavor and is too light and insubstantial—or, worse, it can turn the dessert soupy. We wanted a dessert with intense fruitiness and rich body—and we wanted to use raspberries or strawberries rather than the traditional gooseberries.

Gooseberries are naturally high in pectin—when exposed to heat, sugar, and acid, pectin breaks down and causes fruit to thicken, which made them ideal for fruit fool. We wanted to use raspberries and strawberries, which are low in pectin, so our first challenge was to thicken the fruit properly. We turned to gelatin to thicken our berries, but used a judicious hand (just 2 teaspoons), softening the gelatin in some uncooked berry puree, and then combined the softened mixture with some heated puree to help melt and distribute the gelatin. The result? A smooth, thickened puree with intense fruit flavor.

Now we just needed a richer, sturdier cream base to partner with the fruit puree. We liked the ease of using whipped cream rather than custard, so why not make whipped cream more custard-like? Combined with sour cream, the mixture was airy yet substantial, and the sour cream added just the right touch of richness, along with a tangy undertone. For even more fruit flavor, we layered the fruit puree and cream base with fresh berries that had been macerated in sugar to release excess juice. Finally, topping the dessert with crumbled sweet wheat crackers added a pleasant, nutty contrast.

Berry Fool

SERVES 6

Blueberries or blackberries can be substituted for raspberries in this recipe. You may also substitute frozen fruit for fresh, but there will be a slight compromise in texture. If using frozen fruit, reduce the amount of sugar in the puree by 1 tablespoon. The thickened fruit puree can be made up to 4 hours in advance; just make sure to whisk it well

in step 4 to break up any clumps before combining it with the whipped cream. For the best results, chill your beater and bowl before whipping the cream. We like the granular texture and nutty flavor of Carr's Whole Wheat Crackers, but graham crackers or gingersnaps will also work.

> 2 quarts strawberries (about 2 pounds), washed, dried, and stemmed
> 1 pint raspberries (about 12 ounces), washed and dried (see note)
> ½ cup (3½ ounces) plus 4 tablespoons sugar
> 2 teaspoons unflavored powdered gelatin
> 1 cup heavy cream
> ¼ cup sour cream
> ½ teaspoon vanilla extract
> 4 Carr's Whole Wheat Crackers, crushed fine (about ¼ cup; see note)
> 6 sprigs fresh mint (optional)

1. Process 1 quart of the strawberries, ½ pint of the raspberries, and ½ cup of the sugar in a food processor until the mixture is completely smooth, about 1 minute. Strain the berry puree through a fine-mesh strainer into a 4-cup liquid measuring cup (you should have about 2½ cups puree; reserve any excess for another use). Transfer ½ cup of the puree to a small bowl and sprinkle the gelatin over the top; stir until the gelatin is incorporated and let stand for at least 5 minutes. Heat the remaining 2 cups puree in a small saucepan over medium heat until it begins to bubble, 4 to 6 minutes. Remove the pan from the heat and stir in the gelatin mixture until dissolved. Transfer the gelatin-puree mixture to a medium bowl, cover with plastic wrap, and refrigerate until cold, about 2 hours.

2. Meanwhile, chop the remaining 1 quart strawberries into rough ¼-inch pieces. Toss the strawberries, remaining ½ pint raspberries, and 2 tablespoons more sugar together in a medium bowl. Set aside for 1 hour.

3. Place the cream, sour cream, vanilla, and remaining 2 tablespoons sugar in the chilled bowl of a stand mixer. Beat on low speed until bubbles form, about 30 seconds. Increase the mixer speed to medium and continue beating until the beaters leave a trail, about 30 seconds. Increase the mixer speed to high; continue beating until the mixture has nearly doubled in volume and holds stiff peaks, about 30 seconds. Transfer ⅓ cup of the whipped cream mixture to a small bowl and set aside.

4. Remove the thickened berry puree from the refrigerator and whisk until smooth. With the mixer running at medium speed, slowly add two-thirds of the puree to the whipped cream mixture; mix until incorporated, about 15 seconds. Using a spatula, gently fold in the remaining thickened puree, leaving streaks of puree.

5. Transfer the uncooked berries to a fine-mesh strainer; shake gently to remove any excess juice. Divide two-thirds of the berries evenly among six tall parfait or sundae glasses. Divide the creamy berry mixture evenly among the glasses, followed by the remaining uncooked berries. Top each glass with the reserved plain whipped cream mixture. Sprinkle with the crushed crackers and garnish with mint sprigs (if using). Serve immediately.

RHUBARB FOOL

WHY THIS RECIPE WORKS: A fool is a quick, everyday dessert that just so happens to have a quaint and quirky British name. When we decided to try our hand at this simple dessert—essentially cooked fruit with sweetened whipped cream folded in—we sided with tradition and used rhubarb as the foundation. Although fool is in itself no culinary feat, the challenges lie in the rhubarb, with its sometimes overpowering sourness and tendency to cook into a thick, drab gray mess. We knew that before we could finalize a fool, we would have to tame the rhubarb. We wanted the perfect balance in our fool—pinkish-red, sweet/tart, toothsome fruit mixed with light, sweet cream.

Baking, stewing, and sautéing the rhubarb all led to gray, mushy fruit. Eventually, we hit on soaking the rhubarb in cold water for 20 minutes—this removed some of the bitterness—and simmering it with orange juice. Its flavor was now round and full, and its color bright red. As for the whipped cream, we decided that a soft-to-medium peak gave the fool just enough body without

making it sliceable and stiff. For the best presentation and flavor, we arranged the rhubarb and whipped cream in layers rather than folding the two elements together. The alternating texture of fruit and cream made for a pleasing contrast of color and flavor.

Rhubarb Fool
SERVES 8

For a more elegant presentation, use a pastry bag to pipe the whipped cream into individual glasses. To make one large fool, double the recipe and layer the rhubarb and whipped cream in a 12-cup glass bowl.

2¼ **pounds rhubarb, trimmed and cut into 6-inch lengths**
⅓   **cup juice from 1 large orange**
1   **cup (7 ounces) plus 2 tablespoons sugar**
     Pinch table salt
2   **cups heavy cream, chilled**

1. Soak the rhubarb in cold water for 20 minutes. Drain, pat dry with paper towels, and cut crosswise into ½-inch-thick pieces.

2. Bring the orange juice, ¾ cup of the sugar, and the salt to a boil in a medium saucepan over medium-high heat. Add the rhubarb and return to a boil, then reduce the heat to medium-low and simmer, stirring two or three times, until the rhubarb begins to break down and is tender, 7 to 10 minutes. Transfer the rhubarb to a large bowl, cool to room temperature, cover with plastic wrap, and refrigerate until cold, at least 1 hour or up to 24 hours.

3. Whip the cream and remaining 6 tablespoons sugar in a large bowl with an electric mixer on medium-low speed until frothy, about 1 minute. Increase the speed to high and continue to whip until the cream forms soft peaks, 1 to 3 minutes.

4. To assemble, spoon about ¼ cup rhubarb into each of eight 8-ounce glasses, then layer about ¼ cup whipped cream on top. Repeat, ending with a dollop of cream; serve. (The fools can be refrigerated, covered with plastic wrap, for up to 6 hours.)

Strawberry-Rhubarb Fool

Follow the recipe for Rhubarb Fool, substituting 4 cups strawberries, hulled and quartered, for 1¼ pounds of the rhubarb and adding the strawberries to the saucepan with the rhubarb in step 2.

CHAPTER 25

KEEP YOUR FORK— THERE'S PIE!

Basic Double-Crust Pie Dough 680

Hand Mixed Basic Double-Crust Pie Dough 681

Basic Single-Crust Pie Dough 681

Hand Mixed Basic Single-Crust Pie Dough 681

Single-Crust Pie Dough for Custard Pies 681

All-Butter Double-Crust Pie Dough 682

Hand Mixed All-Butter Double-Crust Pie Dough 682

Foolproof Double-Crust Pie Dough 683

Foolproof Single-Crust Pie Dough 684

Graham Cracker Crust 685

Classic Apple Pie 685

Apple Pie with Crystallized Ginger 686

Apple Pie with Dried Fruit 686

Apple Pie with Fresh Cranberries 686

Deep-Dish Apple Pie 686

Lattice-Top Fresh Peach Pie 688

Fresh Strawberry Pie 689

Blueberry Pie 690

Summer Berry Pie 691

Sweet Cherry Pie 692

Pumpkin Pie 693

Pecan Pie 694

Triple-Chocolate-Chunk Pecan Pie 695

Key Lime Pie 696

Lemon Meringue Pie 697

Coconut Cream Pie 698

Chocolate Cream Pie 699

Classic Tart Dough 700

Lemon Tart 701

Free-Form Summer Fruit Tart 701

Fresh Fruit Tart with Pastry Cream 703

Mixed Berry Tart with Pastry Cream 703

Apple Galette 704

Free-Form Apple Tart 705

30-Minute Tarte Tatin 706

Pear Tatin 706

BASIC PIE DOUGH

WHY THIS RECIPE WORKS: Basic pie dough often contains vegetable shortening, which makes the dough easier to handle and yields a crust that is remarkably flaky. The primary issue with vegetable shortening crusts, however, is that they lack flavor. We set out to master basic pie dough by determining the right fat, the right proportion of fat to flour, and the right method for combining them.

Flakiness is important to a crust, but so is flavor—and nothing beats butter. We experimented with a variety of combinations and ultimately settled on a proportion of 3 parts butter to 2 parts shortening as optimal for both flavor and texture. We also settled on a ratio of 2 parts flour to 1 part fat. This crust is relatively high in fat, but we found that the 2–1 proportion produces dough that is easier to work with and a baked crust that is more tender and flavorful than any other. You can make this pie dough by hand, but the food processor is faster and easier and does the best job of cutting the fat into the flour.

Basic Double-Crust Pie Dough

MAKES ENOUGH FOR ONE 9-INCH PIE

The dough, wrapped tightly in plastic wrap, can be refrigerated for up to 2 days or frozen for up to 1 month. If frozen, let the dough thaw completely on the counter before rolling it out.

- 2½ **cups (12½ ounces) unbleached all-purpose flour, plus extra for the work surface**
- 2 **tablespoons sugar**
- 1 **teaspoon table salt**
- ½ **cup vegetable shortening, cut into ½-inch pieces and chilled**
- 12 **tablespoons (1½ sticks) unsalted butter, cut into ¼-inch pieces and chilled**
- 6–8 **tablespoons ice water**

1. Process the flour, sugar, and salt together in a food processor until combined. Scatter the shortening over the top and process until the mixture resembles coarse cornmeal, about 10 seconds. Scatter the butter pieces over the top and pulse the mixture until it resembles coarse crumbs, about 10 pulses. Transfer the mixture to a large bowl.

2. Sprinkle 6 tablespoons of the ice water over the mixture. Stir and press the dough together, using a stiff rubber spatula, until the dough sticks together. If the dough does not come together, stir in the remaining water, 1 tablespoon at a time, until it does.

3. Divide the dough into two even pieces. Turn each piece of dough onto a sheet of plastic wrap and flatten each into a 4-inch disk. Wrap each piece tightly in plastic wrap and refrigerate for 1 hour. Before rolling the dough out, let it sit on the counter to soften slightly, about 10 minutes.

Hand Mixed Basic Double-Crust Pie Dough

Freeze the butter in its stick form until very firm. Whisk the flour, sugar, and salt together in a large bowl. Add the chilled shortening and press it into the flour using a fork. Grate the frozen butter on the large holes of a box grater into the flour mixture, then cut the mixture together using two butter or dinner knives, until the mixture resembles coarse crumbs. Follow the recipe for Basic Double-Crust Pie Dough, adding the water as directed.

Basic Single-Crust Pie Dough

MAKES ENOUGH FOR ONE 9-INCH PIE

The dough, wrapped tightly in plastic wrap, can be refrigerated for up to 2 days or frozen for up to 1 month. If frozen, let the dough thaw completely on the counter before rolling it out.

1¼ cups (6¼ ounces) unbleached all-purpose flour, plus extra for the work surface
1 tablespoon sugar
½ teaspoon table salt
3 tablespoons vegetable shortening, cut into ½-inch pieces and chilled
5 tablespoons unsalted butter, cut into ¼-inch pieces and chilled
4–6 tablespoons ice water

1. Process the flour, sugar, and salt together in a food processor until combined. Scatter the shortening over the top and process until the mixture resembles coarse cornmeal, about 10 seconds. Scatter the butter pieces over the top and pulse the mixture until it resembles coarse crumbs, about 10 pulses. Transfer the mixture to a medium bowl.

2. Sprinkle 4 tablespoons of the ice water over the mixture. Stir and press the dough together, using a stiff rubber spatula, until the dough sticks together. If the dough does not come together, stir in the remaining water, 1 tablespoon at a time, until it does.

3. Turn the dough onto a sheet of plastic wrap and flatten into a 4-inch disk. Wrap the dough tightly in plastic wrap and refrigerate for 1 hour. Before rolling the dough out, let it sit on the counter to soften slightly, about 10 minutes.

4. Following the photos on page 680, roll the dough into a 12-inch circle and fit it into a pie plate. Following the photos at right, trim, fold, and crimp the edge of the dough. Wrap the dough-lined pie plate loosely in plastic wrap and place in the freezer until the dough is fully chilled and firm, about 30 minutes, before using.

Hand Mixed Basic Single-Crust Pie Dough

Freeze the butter in its stick form until very firm. Whisk the flour, sugar, and salt together in a medium bowl. Add the chilled shortening and press it into the flour using a fork. Grate the frozen butter on the large holes of a box grater into the flour mixture, then cut the mixture together using two butter or dinner knives, until the mixture resembles coarse crumbs. Follow the recipe for Basic Single-Crust Pie Dough, adding the water as directed.

Single-Crust Pie Dough for Custard Pies

We like rolling our single-crust dough in fresh graham cracker crumbs because it adds flavor and crisp textural appeal to many of our custard pies.

Crush 3 whole graham crackers to fine crumbs. (You should have about ½ cup crumbs.) Follow the recipe for Basic Single-Crust Pie Dough, dusting the work surface with the graham cracker crumbs instead of flour. Continue sprinkling the dough with the crumbs, both underneath and on top, as it is being rolled out.

NOTES FROM THE TEST KITCHEN

CRIMPING A SINGLE-CRUST PIE DOUGH

For a traditional single-crust pie, you need to make an evenly thick edge before crimping. Trim the pie dough so that it hangs over the pie plate by ½ inch, then tuck the dough underneath itself to form a tidy, even edge that sits on the lip of the pie plate.

FOR A FLUTED EDGE: Use the index finger of one hand and the thumb and index finger of the other to create fluted ridges perpendicular to the edge of the pie plate.

FOR A RIDGED EDGE: Press the tines of a fork into the dough to flatten it against the rim of the pie plate.

ALL-BUTTER PIE DOUGH

WHY THIS RECIPE WORKS: All-butter pie doughs possess great flavor, but they often fail to be flaky and are notoriously difficult to work with. We wanted an all-butter pie pastry that was easier to mix, handle, and roll, producing a pie crust with all the tenderness and flavor that the description "all-butter" promises.

We initially tried to make the dough easier to handle by reducing the amount of butter, but this resulted in bland flavor and dry texture. Rather than adding back the subtracted butter, we experimented with other forms of fat, including heavy cream, cream cheese, and sour cream. We found that sour cream not only added flavor but, because acid reduces gluten development, also helped keep the dough tender and flaky. And to mix the dough, we used a food processor, which brought the ingredients together quickly and evenly.

All-Butter Double-Crust Pie Dough

MAKES ENOUGH FOR ONE 9-INCH PIE

Freezing the butter for 10 to 15 minutes is crucial to the flaky texture of this crust. If preparing the dough in a very warm kitchen, refrigerate all of the ingredients before making the dough. The dough, wrapped tightly in plastic wrap, can be refrigerated for up to 2 days or frozen for up to 1 month. If frozen, let the dough thaw completely on the counter before rolling it out.

- ⅓ cup ice water, plus extra as needed
- 3 tablespoons sour cream
- 2½ cups (12½ ounces) unbleached all-purpose flour, plus extra for the work surface
- 1 tablespoon sugar
- 1 teaspoon table salt
- 16 tablespoons (2 sticks) unsalted butter, cut into ¼-inch pieces and frozen for 10 to 15 minutes (see note)

1. Mix ⅓ cup of the ice water and the sour cream in a small bowl until combined. Process the flour, sugar, and salt together in a food processor until combined. Following the photos, scatter the butter pieces over the top and pulse the mixture until the butter is the size of large peas, about 10 pulses.

2. Pour half of the sour cream mixture over the flour mixture and pulse until incorporated, about 3 pulses. Repeat with the remaining sour cream mixture. Pinch the dough with your fingers; if the dough feels dry and does

not hold together, sprinkle 1 to 2 tablespoons more ice water over the mixture and pulse until the dough forms large clumps and no dry flour remains, 3 to 5 pulses.

3. Divide the dough into two even pieces. Turn each piece of dough onto a sheet of plastic wrap and flatten each into a 4-inch disk. Wrap each piece tightly in plastic wrap and refrigerate for 1 hour. Before rolling the dough out, let it sit on the counter to soften slightly, about 10 minutes.

Hand Mixed All-Butter Double-Crust Pie Dough

Freeze the butter in its stick form until very firm. Whisk the flour, sugar, and salt together in a large bowl. Grate the frozen butter on the large holes of a box grater into the flour mixture, then cut the mixture together using two butter or dinner knives, until the mixture resembles coarse crumbs. Follow the recipe for All-Butter Double-Crust Pie Dough, adding the liquid as directed, stirring it with a rubber spatula.

NOTES FROM THE TEST KITCHEN

MAKING ALL-BUTTER DOUBLE-CRUST PIE DOUGH

1. Pulse the butter and flour mixture together in a food processor until the butter is the size of large peas, about 10 pulses.

2. After adding the sour cream and water mixture, pinch the dough with your fingers. If the dough is dry and does not hold together, sprinkle 1 to 2 tablespoons ice water over the mixture and pulse 3 to 5 times.

3. Divide the dough into two pieces and flatten each into a 4-inch disk. Wrap the disks tightly in plastic wrap and refrigerate for 1 hour. Before rolling the dough out, let it sit on the counter to soften slightly, about 10 minutes.

FOOLPROOF PIE DOUGH

WHY THIS RECIPE WORKS: Unless you're a practiced pie baker, it's hard to get the same results every time. While we think our All-Butter Pie Dough (page 682) and Basic Pie Dough (page 680) are great, we wanted a recipe for pie dough that rolls out easily every time and produces a tender, flaky crust.

The first step was to determine the right fat. As with our basic dough, a combination of butter and shortening provided the best balance of flavor and tenderness. Once again, the best tool to cut the fat into the flour was the food processor. To ensure the butter was incorporated evenly, we skipped cutting it into pieces and made a paste instead. Rather than starting with all the flour in the processor, we put aside 1 cup of flour and processed the remaining 1½ cups with all of the fat until it formed a unified paste. We added the reserved flour to the bowl and pulsed it until it was just evenly distributed. Finally, we tackled the tenderness issue, which is partially determined by the amount of water added. For the dough to roll easily, it needs a generous amount of water, but more water makes crusts tough. We found the answer in the liquor cabinet: vodka. While gluten (the protein that makes crust tough) forms readily in water, it doesn't form in ethanol, and vodka is 60 percent water and 40 percent ethanol. So adding ¼ cup of vodka produced a moist, easy-to-roll dough that stayed tender. (The alcohol vaporizes in the oven, so you won't taste it in the baked crust.)

Foolproof Double-Crust Pie Dough

MAKES ENOUGH FOR ONE 9-INCH PIE

Vodka is essential to the tender texture of this crust and imparts no flavor—do not substitute water. This dough is moister than most standard pie doughs and will require lots of flour to roll out (up to ¼ cup). The dough, wrapped tightly in plastic wrap, can be refrigerated for up to 2 days or frozen for up to 1 month. If frozen, let the dough thaw completely on the counter before rolling it out.

- 2½ cups (12½ ounces) unbleached all-purpose flour, plus extra for the work surface (see note)
- 2 tablespoons sugar
- 1 teaspoon table salt
- 12 tablespoons (1½ sticks) unsalted butter, cut into ¼-inch pieces and chilled
- ½ cup vegetable shortening, cut into 4 pieces and chilled
- ¼ cup vodka, chilled (see note)
- ¼ cup ice water

Viewers of our television show and readers of our recipes may wonder why we revisit the same recipes (roast chicken, mashed potatoes, and pie dough, to name a few) and develop alternate versions of them. Simply put, personal choice is a big factor. Take pie dough. There are few recipes that divide the test kitchen like the humble pie crust. Some in the test kitchen are purists when it comes to pie dough—they wouldn't dream of using anything but an all-butter dough. The flavor of our All-Butter Pie Dough (page 682) is undeniably buttery and delicious, but let's face it—this dough can be difficult to work with and isn't quite as flaky as a pie dough made with vegetable shortening. Next are the cooks who prefer the ease of working with a dough made with vegetable shortening as well as butter, like our Basic Pie Dough (page 680). Vegetable shortening, such as Crisco, is made from vegetable oil that has been hydrogenated, a process in which hydrogen gas is pumped into vegetable oil so it solidifies. Adding vegetable shortening makes the dough easier to work with and it does a good job of lightening and tenderizing the dough. That said, this pie dough still takes some patience to roll out.

The problem is that most pie dough recipes are stingy with the water (and thus really hard to roll out). Adding more water may seem to help matters, but once baked, the resulting crust is tougher. So to solve this problem, we developed a third pie dough, based on our Basic Pie Dough but with an unlikely ingredient—vodka.

While gluten (the protein that makes crust tough) forms readily in water, it doesn't form in ethanol, and vodka is 60 percent water and 40 percent ethanol. So adding ¼ cup of vodka and ¼ cup of water produces a moist, easy-to-roll dough that stays tender because the alcohol vaporizes in the oven, leaving the final crust with only about 6 tablespoons of water. This dough bakes into a crust that is tender and flavorful and that rolls out easily every time. For those in the test kitchen who demand an easy-to-roll pie dough, this is their dream recipe. (And for those who aren't practiced bakers and make a pie maybe once a year around the holidays, this dough makes a lot of sense.) Does that mean we're through developing pie doughs? Maybe, maybe not.

1. Process 1½ cups of the flour, the sugar, and salt together in a food processor until combined. Scatter the butter and shortening over the top and continue to process until incorporated and the mixture begins to form uneven clumps with no remaining floury bits, about 15 seconds.

2. Scrape down the workbowl and redistribute the dough evenly around the processor blade. Sprinkle the remaining 1 cup flour over the dough and pulse until the mixture has broken up into pieces and is evenly distributed around the bowl, 4 to 6 pulses.

3. Transfer the mixture to a medium bowl. Sprinkle the vodka and water over the mixture. Stir and press the dough together, using a stiff rubber spatula, until the dough sticks together.

4. Divide the dough into two even pieces. Turn each piece of dough onto a sheet of plastic wrap and flatten each into a 4-inch disk. Wrap each piece tightly in plastic wrap and refrigerate for 1 hour. Before rolling the dough out, let it sit on the counter to soften slightly, about 10 minutes.

Foolproof Single-Crust Pie Dough

MAKES ENOUGH FOR ONE 9-INCH PIE

Vodka is essential to the tender texture of this crust and imparts no flavor—do not substitute water. This dough is moister than most standard pie doughs and will require lots of flour to roll out (up to ¼ cup). The dough, wrapped tightly in plastic wrap, can be refrigerated for up to 2 days or frozen for up to 1 month. If frozen, let the dough thaw completely on the counter before rolling it out.

- 1¼ **cups (6¼ ounces) all-purpose flour**
- 1 **tablespoon sugar**
- ½ **teaspoon salt**
- 6 **tablespoons unsalted butter, cut into ¼-inch pieces and chilled**
- 4 **tablespoons vegetable shortening, cut into 2 pieces and chilled**
- 2 **tablespoons vodka, chilled**
- 2 **tablespoons ice water**

1. Process ¾ cups of the flour, the sugar, and salt together in a food processor until combined. Scatter the butter and shortening over the top and continue to process until incorporated and the mixture begins to form uneven clumps with no remaining floury bits, about 10 seconds.

2. Scrape down the workbowl and redistribute the dough evenly around the processor blade. Sprinkle the remaining ½ cup flour over the dough and pulse until the mixture has broken up into pieces and is evenly distributed around the bowl, 4 to 6 pulses.

3. Transfer the mixture to a medium bowl. Sprinkle the vodka and water over the mixture. Stir and press the dough together, using a stiff rubber spatula, until the dough sticks together.

4. Turn the dough onto a sheet of plastic wrap and flatten into a 4-inch disk. Wrap tightly in plastic wrap and refrigerate for 45 minutes or up to 2 days. Before rolling the dough out, let it sit on the counter to soften slightly, about 10 minutes.

GRAHAM CRACKER CRUST

WHY THIS RECIPE WORKS: Saving time is always a good idea—just as long as you're not sacrificing quality. But while store-bought graham cracker pie crusts are tempting (all you have to do is fill, chill, then serve), they taste stale and bland. We wanted a fresh-tasting homemade crust that wasn't too sweet, with a crisp texture.

Turns out, a classic graham cracker crust couldn't be easier to make: Combine crushed crumbs with a little butter and sugar to bind them, then use a measuring cup or flat-bottomed glass to pack the crumbs into the pie plate. And producing a perfect graham cracker crust has a lot to do with the type of graham crackers used. After experimenting with the three leading brands, we discovered subtle but distinct differences among them and found that these differences carried over into crumb crusts made with each kind of cracker. Here in the test kitchen, we prefer Nabisco Original Graham Crackers for their hearty molasses flavor.

NOTES FROM THE TEST KITCHEN

MAKING A GRAHAM CRACKER OR COOKIE CRUST

Press the crumb mixture firmly and evenly across the bottom of the pie plate, using the bottom of a measuring cup. Then tightly pack the crumbs against the sides of the pie plate, using your thumb and the measuring cup simultaneously.

Graham Cracker Crust

MAKES ENOUGH FOR ONE 9-INCH PIE

We don't recommend using store-bought graham cracker crumbs here as they can often be stale. Be sure to note whether the crust needs to be warm or cool before filling (the pie recipes will specify) and plan accordingly.

- 8 whole graham crackers, broken into 1-inch pieces
- 5 tablespoons unsalted butter, melted and cooled
- 3 tablespoons sugar

1. Adjust an oven rack to the middle position and heat the oven to 325 degrees. Process the graham cracker pieces in a food processor to fine, even crumbs, about 30 seconds. Sprinkle the butter and sugar over the crumbs and pulse to incorporate.

2. Sprinkle the mixture into a 9-inch pie plate. Following the photo on page 684, use the bottom of a measuring cup to press the crumbs into an even layer on the bottom and sides of the pie plate. Bake until the crust is fragrant and beginning to brown, 13 to 18 minutes. Following the particular pie recipe, use the crust while it is still warm or let it cool completely.

APPLE PIE

WHY THIS RECIPE WORKS: In the test kitchen, we have found that it's difficult to produce an apple pie with a filling that is tart as well as sweet and juicy. We wanted to develop a classic apple pie recipe—one with the clean, bright taste of apples that could be made year-round, based on apple types that are always available in the supermarket.

To arrive at the tartness and texture we were after, we had to use two kinds of apples in our pie, Granny Smith and McIntosh. The Grannies could be counted on for tartness and for keeping their shape during cooking; the Macs added flavor, and their otherwise frustrating tendency to become mushy was a virtue, providing a nice, juicy base for the harder Grannies. While many bakers add butter to their apple pie fillings, we found that it dulled the fresh taste of the apples and so did without it. Lemon juice, however, was essential, counterbalancing the sweetness of the apples. To give the apples the upper hand, we settled on quite modest amounts of cinnamon, nutmeg, and allspice.

Classic Apple Pie

SERVES 8

You can use All-Butter Double-Crust Pie Dough (page 682), Basic Double-Crust Pie Dough (page 680), or Foolproof Double-Crust Pie Dough (page 683) for this pie. The pie is best eaten when cooled to room temperature, or even the next day. Serve with vanilla ice cream or lightly sweetened whipped cream.

- 1 recipe double-crust pie dough (see note)
- 2 tablespoons unbleached all-purpose flour, plus extra for the work surface
- ¾ cup (5¼ ounces) plus 1 tablespoon sugar
- 1 teaspoon grated zest plus 1 tablespoon juice from 1 lemon
- ¼ teaspoon table salt
- ¼ teaspoon ground nutmeg
- ¼ teaspoon ground cinnamon
- ⅛ teaspoon ground allspice
- 2 pounds firm McIntosh apples (about 4 large), peeled, cored, and sliced ¼ inch thick
- 1½ pounds Granny Smith apples (about 3 large), peeled, cored, and sliced ¼ inch thick
- 1 large egg white, lightly beaten

1. Following the photos on page 680, roll one disk of dough into a 12-inch circle on a lightly floured work surface, then fit it into a 9-inch pie plate, letting the excess dough hang over the edge; cover with plastic wrap and refrigerate for 30 minutes. Roll the other disk of dough into a 12-inch circle on a lightly floured work surface, then transfer to a parchment-lined baking sheet; cover with plastic wrap and refrigerate for 30 minutes.

2. Adjust an oven rack to the lowest position, place a rimmed baking sheet on the rack, and heat the oven to 500 degrees.

3. Mix the flour, ¾ cup of the sugar, the zest, salt, nutmeg, cinnamon, and allspice together in a large bowl. Add the lemon juice and apples and toss until combined. Spread the apples with their juice into the dough-lined pie plate, mounding them slightly in the middle. Following the photos on page 687, loosely roll the second piece of dough around the rolling pin and gently unroll it over the pie. Trim, fold, and crimp the edges, and cut four vent holes in the top. Brush the dough with the egg white and sprinkle with the remaining 1 tablespoon sugar.

4. Place the pie on the heated baking sheet, reduce the oven temperature to 425 degrees, and bake until the crust is golden, about 25 minutes. Reduce the oven temperature to 375 degrees, rotate the baking sheet, and continue to bake until the juices are bubbling and the crust is deep golden brown, 30 to 35 minutes longer. Cool the pie on a wire rack to room temperature, about 4 hours. Serve.

Apple Pie with Crystallized Ginger

Follow the recipe for Classic Apple Pie, adding 3 tablespoons chopped crystallized ginger to the apple mixture.

Apple Pie with Dried Fruit

Toss 1 cup raisins, dried sweet cherries, or dried cranberries with the lemon juice plus 1 tablespoon applejack, brandy, or cognac. Follow the recipe for Classic Apple Pie, adding the dried fruit and liquid to the apple mixture.

Apple Pie with Fresh Cranberries

Follow the recipe for Classic Apple Pie, increasing the sugar to 1 cup (7 ounces) and adding 1 cup fresh or frozen cranberries to the apple mixture.

DEEP-DISH APPLE PIE

WHY THIS RECIPE WORKS: The problem with deep-dish apple pie is that the apples are often unevenly cooked (some mushy, some crunchy) and the exuded juice leaves the apples swimming in an ocean of liquid, producing a bottom crust that is a pale, soggy mess. Then there is the gaping hole left between the apples (which are shrunken from the loss of all that moisture) and the arching top crust, making it impossible to slice and serve a neat piece of pie. We wanted our piece of deep-dish pie to be a towering wedge of tender, juicy apples, fully framed by a buttery, flaky crust.

Precooking the apples solved the shrinking problem, helped the apples hold their shape, and prevented a flood of juices from collecting in the bottom of the pie plate, giving us a nicely browned bottom crust. Why didn't cooking the apples twice (once on the stovetop and once in the oven) cause them to become insipid and mushy? We learned that when the apples are gently heated, their pectin is converted to a heat-stable form that keeps them from becoming mushy when cooked further in the oven. All that was left to do was to choose the right combination of sweet and tart apples and stir in a little brown sugar, salt, lemon, and cinnamon, for flavor and sweetness.

Deep-Dish Apple Pie

SERVES 8

You can use All-Butter Double-Crust Pie Dough (page 682), Basic Double-Crust Pie Dough (page 680), or Foolproof Double-Crust Pie Dough (page 683) for this pie. Use a combination of tart and sweet apples for this pie. Good choices for tart are Granny Smiths, Empires, or Cortlands; for sweet we recommend Golden Delicious, Jonagolds, or Braeburns. Serve with vanilla ice cream or lightly sweetened whipped cream.

- 1 recipe double-crust pie dough (see note)
  Unbleached all-purpose flour, for the work surface
- 2½ pounds firm tart apples (about 5 large), peeled, cored, and sliced ¼ inch thick (see note)
- 2½ pounds firm sweet apples (about 5 large), peeled, cored, and sliced ¼ inch thick (see note)
- ½ cup (3½ ounces) plus 1 tablespoon granulated sugar
- ¼ cup packed (1¾ ounces) light brown sugar
- ½ teaspoon grated zest plus 1 tablespoon juice from 1 lemon
- ¼ teaspoon table salt
- ⅛ teaspoon ground cinnamon
- 1 large egg white, lightly beaten

1. Following the photos on page 680, roll one disk of dough into a 12-inch circle on a lightly floured work surface, then fit it into a 9-inch pie plate, letting the excess dough hang over the edge; cover with plastic wrap and

MAKING A DOUBLE-CRUST PIE

1. Loosely roll the chilled top crust around the rolling pin, then gently unroll it over the filled pie crust bottom.

2. Using scissors, trim all but ½ inch of the dough overhanging the edge of the pie plate.

3. Press the top and bottom crusts together, then tuck the edges underneath.

4. Crimp the dough evenly around the edge of the pie, using your fingers. Cut vent holes attractively in the center of the top crust with a paring knife (drier pies only require four vents, while very juicy pies require eight vents).

refrigerate for 30 minutes. Roll the other disk of dough into a 12-inch circle on a lightly floured work surface, then transfer to a parchment-lined baking sheet; cover with plastic wrap and refrigerate for 30 minutes.

2. Toss the apples, ½ cup of the granulated sugar, the brown sugar, zest, salt, and cinnamon together in a Dutch oven. Cover and cook over medium heat, stirring frequently, until the apples are tender when poked with a fork but still hold their shape, 15 to 20 minutes. Transfer the apples and their juice to a rimmed baking sheet and cool to room temperature, about 30 minutes.

3. Adjust an oven rack to the lowest position, place a rimmed baking sheet on the rack, and heat the oven to 425 degrees. Drain the cooled apples thoroughly through a colander, reserving ¼ cup of the juice. Stir the lemon juice into the reserved ¼ cup apple juice.

4. Spread the apples into the dough-lined pie plate, mounding them slightly in the middle, and drizzle with the lemon juice mixture. Following the photos, loosely roll the second piece of dough around the rolling pin and gently unroll it over the pie. Trim, fold, and crimp the edges and cut four vent holes in the top. Brush the dough with the egg white and sprinkle with the remaining 1 tablespoon sugar.

5. Place the pie on the heated baking sheet and bake until the crust is golden, about 25 minutes. Reduce the oven temperature to 375 degrees, rotate the baking sheet, and continue to bake until the juices are bubbling and the crust is deep golden brown, 25 to 30 minutes longer. Cool the pie on a wire rack until the filling has set, about 2 hours; serve slightly warm or at room temperature.

PEACH PIE

WHY THIS RECIPE WORKS: Fresh peach pies are often soupy or overly sweet, with a bottom crust that is soggy or undercooked. We wanted to create a filling that was juicy but not swimming in liquid, its flavors neither muscled out by spices nor overwhelmed by thickeners, and we wanted a crust that was well browned on the bottom.

We peeled and sliced the peaches and found that all they needed in the way of flavor was sugar, lemon juice, cinnamon, nutmeg, and a dash of salt. To thicken the juices, we used a little cornstarch, but still, we needed to do more. A lattice-top pie crust was our solution—while it requires a bit more work than making a regular double-crust pie, we found that it's worth the effort. Not only is it pretty and very traditional on peach pies, but it serves an important purpose: The structure of a lattice top allows for maximum evaporation while the pie cooks—the juices released by the fruit cook down slowly while baking so the filling isn't soupy. For easy assembly, we rolled and cut the dough, then froze it so the strips were firm and easy to handle.

Lattice-Top Fresh Peach Pie

SERVES 8

You can use All-Butter Double-Crust Pie Dough (page 682), Basic Double-Crust Pie Dough (page 680), or Foolproof Double-Crust Pie Dough (page 683) for this pie. A serrated peeler makes peeling peaches a whole lot easier and you can avoid the step of blanching the peaches. Serve with vanilla ice cream or lightly sweetened whipped cream.

- 1 recipe double-crust pie dough (see note)
  Unbleached all-purpose flour, for the work surface
- 2½ pounds ripe peaches (6 to 7 medium), peeled, pitted, and sliced ⅓ inch thick (see note)
- 1 cup (7 ounces) plus 1 tablespoon sugar
- 1 tablespoon cornstarch
- 1 tablespoon juice from 1 lemon
  Pinch ground cinnamon
  Pinch ground nutmeg
  Pinch table salt
- 1 large egg white, lightly beaten

1. Following the photos on page 680, roll one disk of dough into a 12-inch circle on a lightly floured work surface, then fit it into a 9-inch pie plate, letting the excess dough hang over the edge; cover with plastic wrap and refrigerate for 30 minutes to 1 hour.

2. Roll the other disk of dough into a 13½ by 10½-inch rectangle, then transfer to a parchment-lined baking sheet. Trim the dough to a 13 by 10-inch rectangle with straight edges and slice it lengthwise into eight 13-inch-long strips. Separate the strips slightly, cover with plastic wrap, and freeze until very firm, about 30 minutes.

3. Toss the peaches and 1 cup of the sugar together in a large bowl and let sit, tossing occasionally, until the peaches release their juice, about 1 hour. Adjust an oven rack to the lowest position, place a rimmed baking sheet on the rack, and heat the oven to 425 degrees.

4. Drain the peaches thoroughly through a colander, reserving ¼ cup of the juice. In a large bowl, toss the drained fruit, the reserved juice, cornstarch, lemon juice, cinnamon, nutmeg, and salt together until well combined.

5. Spread the peaches into the dough-lined pie plate and, following the photos, weave the chilled strips of dough over the top into a lattice. Let the strips soften for 5 to 10 minutes, then trim, fold, and crimp the edges. Lightly brush the lattice with the egg white and sprinkle with the remaining 1 tablespoon sugar.

6. Place the pie on the heated baking sheet and bake until the top crust is golden, about 25 minutes. Reduce the oven temperature to 375 degrees, rotate the baking sheet,

NOTES FROM THE TEST KITCHEN

MAKING A LATTICE TOP

Making a lattice-top pie crust is a bit more work than making a regular double-crust pie, but it is well worth the effort. Not only is it pretty and very traditional on fruit pies, but it also serves an important purpose: The structure of a lattice top allows for maximum evaporation while the pie cooks. This is especially important for stone fruit pies, such as cherry and peach, as it allows the juices released by the fruit to cook down slowly while baking so that the filling isn't too soupy.

1. Using the chilled strips of lattice, lay four parallel strips evenly over the filling. Weave a fifth strip in the opposite direction.

2. Continue to weave in the remaining three strips, one at a time, to create a lattice.

3. After letting the strips thaw and soften for a few minutes, trim the overhanging edges of the dough to ½ inch. Press the edges of the bottom crust and lattice strips together and fold underneath.

4. Crimp the dough evenly around the edges of the pie using your fingers. Crimping the dough gives the pie a decorative edge and an attractive, finished look.

and continue to bake until the juices are bubbling and the crust is deep golden brown, 25 to 35 minutes longer. Let the pie cool on a wire rack until the filling has set, about 2 hours; serve slightly warm or at room temperature.

STRAWBERRY PIE

WHY THIS RECIPE WORKS: Because uncooked berries shed so much liquid, the filling for strawberry pie is usually firmed up with a thickener, which produces results that range from stiff and bouncy to runny and gloppy. We wanted a strawberry pie featuring fresh berries lightly held together by a sheer, glossy glaze in a buttery shell. We knew that the success of our strawberry pie hinged on getting the thickener just right. When none of the thickeners we tried worked on their own, we decided to use a combination of two: pectin (in the form of a homemade strawberry jam) and cornstarch. By themselves, pectin produced a filling that was too firm and cornstarch one that was too loose, but together they created just the right supple, lightly clingy glaze. Fresh, flavorful strawberries make this dessert a perfect summery treat.

Fresh Strawberry Pie

SERVES 8

To account for any imperfect strawberries, the ingredient list calls for several more ounces of berries than will be used in the pie. If possible, seek out ripe, farmers' market–quality berries. Make sure to thoroughly dry the strawberries after washing. Make certain that you use fruit pectin engineered for low- or no-sugar recipes (we recommend Sure-Jell Premium Fruit Pectin) and not regular pectin; otherwise, the glaze will not set properly. The pie is at its best after two or three hours of chilling; as it continues to chill, the glaze becomes softer and wetter, though the pie will taste just as good.

- 1 recipe Foolproof Single-Crust Pie Dough (page 684), fitted into a 9-inch pie plate and chilled
- 3 pounds strawberries, hulled (9 cups)
- ¾ cup (5¼ ounces) sugar
- 2 tablespoons cornstarch
- 1½ teaspoons Sure-Jell for low-sugar recipes (see note)
  Pinch table salt
- 1 tablespoon juice from 1 lemon
- 1 cup heavy cream, cold
- 1 tablespoon sugar

1. Adjust an oven rack to the lowest position, place a rimmed baking sheet on the rack, and heat the oven to 425 degrees. Following the photos on page 694, line the chilled pie shell with a double layer of foil and fill with pie weights.

2. Bake the pie shell on the heated baking sheet for 15 minutes. Remove the weights and foil and continue to bake the crust until golden brown and crisp, 5 to 10 minutes longer. Transfer the pie crust to a wire rack and let cool to room temperature.

3. Select 6 ounces misshapen, underripe, or otherwise unattractive berries, halving those that are large; you should have about 1½ cups. Process the berries in a food processor to a smooth puree, 20 to 30 seconds, scraping down the bowl as needed (you should have about ¾ cup puree).

4. Whisk the sugar, cornstarch, Sure-Jell, and salt together in a medium saucepan. Stir in the berry puree, making sure to scrape the corners of the pan. Cook over medium-high heat, stirring constantly, and bring to a boil. Boil, scraping the bottom and sides of the pan to prevent scorching, for 2 minutes to ensure that the cornstarch is fully cooked (the mixture will appear frothy when it first reaches a boil, then will darken and thicken with further cooking). Transfer the glaze to a large bowl and stir in the lemon juice; let cool to room temperature.

5. Meanwhile, pick over the remaining berries and measure out 2 pounds of the most attractive ones; halve only any extra-large berries. Add the berries to the bowl with the glaze and fold gently with a rubber spatula until the berries are evenly coated. Scoop the berries into the cooled prebaked pie shell, piling into a mound. If any cut sides face up on top, turn them face down. If necessary, rearrange the berries so that holes are filled and the mound looks attractive. Refrigerate the pie until the filling is chilled and has set, about 2 hours. Serve within 5 hours of chilling.

6. FOR THE WHIPPED CREAM: Just before serving, beat the cream and sugar with an electric mixer on low speed until small bubbles form, about 30 seconds. Increase the speed to medium; continue beating until the beaters leave a trail, about 30 additional seconds. Increase the speed to high; continue beating until the cream is smooth, thick, and nearly doubled in volume and forms soft peaks, 30 to 60 seconds. 7. Cut the pie into wedges and serve with the whipped cream.

BLUEBERRY PIE

WHY THIS RECIPE WORKS: If the filling in blueberry pie doesn't jell, a sliced wedge can collapse into a soupy puddle topped by a sodden crust. Too much thickener and the filling can be so dense that cutting into it is like slicing through gummi bears. We wanted a pie that had a firm, glistening filling full of fresh, bright flavor and still-plump berries.

To thicken the pie, we favored tapioca because it didn't mute the fresh yet subtle blueberry flavor as cornstarch and flour did. The back of the tapioca box recommended 6 tablespoons, but this produced a stiff, congealed mass. Cooking and reducing half of the berries helped us cut down on the tapioca required, but not enough. A second inspiration came from a peeled and grated Granny Smith apple. Apples are high in pectin, a type of carbohydrate that acts as a thickener when cooked. Combined with a modest 2 tablespoons of tapioca, the

apple thickened the filling to a soft, even consistency that was neither gelatinous nor slippery. The crust posed a much simpler challenge. As with all of our fruit pies, baking on a preheated baking sheet on the bottom oven rack produced a crisp, golden bottom crust. And we found a fast, easy alternative to a lattice top in a small biscuit cutter, which we used to cut out circles in the top crust before transferring the dough onto the pie. The attractive, unusual-looking top crust vented the steam from the berries as successfully as a classic lattice top.

Blueberry Pie

SERVES 8

You can use All-Butter Double-Crust Pie Dough (page 682), Basic Double-Crust Pie Dough (page 680), or Foolproof Double-Crust Pie Dough (page 683) for this pie. This recipe was developed using fresh blueberries, but unthawed frozen blueberries (our favorite brands are Wyman's and Cascadian Farm) will work as well. In step 3, cook half the frozen berries over medium-high heat, without mashing, until reduced to 1¼ cups, 12 to 15 minutes. Grind the tapioca to a powder in a spice grinder or mini food processor. If using pearl tapioca, reduce the amount to 5 teaspoons. Serve with vanilla ice cream or lightly sweetened whipped cream.

  1 recipe double-crust pie dough (see note)
     Unbleached all-purpose flour, for the work surface
  6 cups (30 ounces) fresh blueberries (see note)
  1 Granny Smith apple, peeled, cored, and shredded on the large holes of a box grater
  ¾ cup (5¼ ounces) sugar
  2 tablespoons instant tapioca, ground (see note)
  2 teaspoons grated zest plus 2 teaspoons juice from 1 lemon
     Pinch table salt
  2 tablespoons unsalted butter, cut into ¼-inch pieces
  1 large egg white, lightly beaten

1. Following the photos on page 680, roll one disk of dough into a 12-inch circle on a lightly floured work surface, then fit it into a 9-inch pie plate, letting the excess dough hang over the edge; cover with plastic wrap and refrigerate for 30 minutes.

2. Roll the other disk of dough into a 12-inch circle on a lightly floured work surface. Following the photo on page 691, use a 1¼-inch round biscuit cutter to cut a round from the center of the dough. Cut 6 more rounds from the dough, 1½ inches from the edge of the center hole and equally spaced around the center hole. Transfer the dough to a parchment-lined baking sheet; cover with plastic wrap and refrigerate for 30 minutes.

3. Place 3 cups of the berries in a medium saucepan and set over medium heat. Using a potato masher, mash the berries several times to release the juices. Continue to cook, stirring frequently and mashing occasionally, until about half of the berries have broken down and the mixture is thickened and reduced to 1½ cups, about 8 minutes. Cool slightly.

4. Adjust an oven rack to the lowest position, place a rimmed baking sheet on the rack, and heat the oven to 400 degrees.

5. Place the shredded apple in a clean kitchen towel and wring dry. Transfer the apple to a large bowl and stir in the cooked berries, remaining 3 cups uncooked berries, sugar, tapioca, lemon zest and juice, and salt until combined. Spread the mixture into the dough-lined pie plate and scatter the butter pieces over the top.

6. Following the photos on page 687, loosely roll the second piece of dough around the rolling pin and gently unroll it over the pie. Trim, fold, and crimp the edges. Brush the dough with the egg white.

7. Place the pie on the heated baking sheet and bake until the crust is golden, about 25 minutes. Reduce the oven temperature to 350 degrees, rotate the baking sheet, and continue to bake until the juices are bubbling and the crust is deep golden brown, 30 to 40 minutes longer. Cool the pie on a wire rack to room temperature, about 4 hours. Serve.

NOTES FROM THE TEST KITCHEN

MAKING A CUT-OUT CRUST

1. Use a 1¼-inch biscuit cutter (or spice jar lid) to cut holes in the dough.

2. The cut-out crust vents the steam from the berry filling and is an easy alternative to a lattice-top pie.

SUMMER BERRY PIE

WHY THIS RECIPE WORKS: A fresh berry pie might seem like an easy-to-pull-off summer dessert, but most of the recipes we tried buried the berries in gluey thickeners or embedded them in bouncy gelatin. Our goal was to make a pie with great texture and flavor—and still keep it simple.

We started with the test kitchen's quick and easy homemade graham cracker crust. For the filling, we used a combination of raspberries, blackberries, and blueberries. After trying a few different methods, we found a solution that both bound the berries in the graham cracker crust and intensified their bright flavor. We processed a portion of berries in the food processor until they made a smooth puree, then we thickened the puree with cornstarch. Next, we tossed the remaining berries with warm jelly for a glossy coat and a shot of sweetness. Pressed gently into the puree, the berries stayed put and tasted great.

Summer Berry Pie

SERVES 8

Feel free to vary the amount of each berry as desired as long as you have 6 cups of berries total; do not substitute frozen berries here. Serve with lightly sweetened whipped cream.

- 2 cups (10 ounces) raspberries (see note)
- 2 cups (10 ounces) blackberries (see note)
- 2 cups (10 ounces) blueberries (see note)
- ½ cup (3½ ounces) sugar
- 3 tablespoons cornstarch
- ⅛ teaspoon table salt

1 tablespoon juice from 1 lemon
1 recipe Graham Cracker Crust (page 685), baked and
    cooled
2 tablespoons red currant or apple jelly

1. Gently toss the berries together in a large bowl. Process 2½ cups of the berries in a food processor until very smooth, about 1 minute (do not under-process). Strain the puree through a fine-mesh strainer into a small saucepan, pressing on the solids to extract as much puree as possible (you should have about 1½ cups); discard the solids.

2. In a small bowl, whisk the sugar, cornstarch, and salt together, then whisk into the strained puree. Bring the puree to a boil over medium heat, stirring constantly, and cook until it is as thick as pudding, about 7 minutes. Off the heat, stir in the lemon juice and set aside to cool slightly.

3. Pour the warm berry puree into the baked and cooled pie crust. Melt the jelly in a small saucepan over low heat, then pour over the remaining 3½ cups berries and toss to coat. Spread the berries evenly over the puree and lightly press them into the puree. Cover the pie loosely with plastic wrap and refrigerate until the filling is chilled and set, about 3 hours. Serve chilled or at room temperature.

CHERRY PIE

WHY THIS RECIPE WORKS: Great cherry pie is typically made with sour cherries because their soft, juicy flesh and bright, punchy flavor isn't dulled by oven heat or sugar. But cherry season is cruelly short and chances are the cherries that are available are the sweet variety. Sweet cherries have mellower flavors and meaty, firm flesh—traits that make them ideal for eating straight off the stem but don't translate well to baking. Our challenge was obvious: Develop a recipe for sweet cherry pie with all the intense, jammy flavor and softened but still intact fruit texture of the best sour cherry pie.

To mimic the bright, tart flavor of a sour cherry pie filling, we supplemented sweet cherries with chopped plums, which are tart and helped tame the cherries' sweet flavor. To fix the texture problem, we cut the cherries in half to expose their sturdy flesh. This step encouraged the cherries to soften and give up their juices. A splash of bourbon and lemon juice also offset the sweetness and added flavorful depth. To keep the filling juicy, rather than dry, we switched out the typical lattice pie crust in favor of a traditional top crust, which prevented any moisture from evaporating.

Sweet Cherry Pie

SERVES 8

You can use All-Butter Double-Crust Pie Dough (page 682), Basic Double-Crust Pie Dough (page 680), or Foolproof Double-Crust Pie Dough (page 683) for this recipe. The tapioca should be measured first, then ground in a coffee grinder or food processor for 30 seconds. If you are using frozen fruit, measure it frozen, but let it thaw before filling the pie. If not, you run the risk of partially cooked fruit and undissolved tapioca.

1 recipe double-crust pie dough (see note)
    Unbleached all-purpose flour, for the work surface
2 red plums, halved and pitted
6 cups (about 2 pounds) pitted sweet cherries or 6 cups
    pitted frozen cherries, halved (see note)
½ cup (3½ ounces) sugar
⅛ teaspoon table salt
1 tablespoon juice from 1 lemon
2 teaspoons bourbon (optional)
2 tablespoons instant tapioca, ground (see note)
⅛ teaspoon ground cinnamon (optional)
2 tablespoons unsalted butter, cut into ¼-inch pieces
1 large egg, lightly beaten with 1 teaspoon water

1. Following the photos on page 680, roll one disk of the dough into a 12-inch circle on a lightly floured work surface, then fit it into a 9-inch pie plate, letting the excess dough hang over the edge; cover with plastic wrap and refrigerate for 30 minutes. Roll the other disk of dough into a 12-inch circle on a lightly floured work surface, then transfer to a parchment-lined baking sheet; cover with plastic wrap and refrigerate for 30 minutes.

2. Adjust an oven rack to the lowest position, place a baking sheet on the rack and heat the oven to 400 degrees. Process the plums and 1 cup of the halved cherries in a food processor until smooth, about 1 minute, scraping down the sides of the bowl as necessary. Strain the puree through a fine-mesh strainer into a large bowl, pressing on the solids to extract the liquid; discard the solids. Stir in the remaining 5 cups halved cherries, sugar, salt, lemon juice, bourbon (if using), tapioca, and cinnamon (if using) into the puree; let stand for 15 minutes.

3. Transfer the cherry mixture, including all the juices, to the dough-lined plate. Scatter the butter pieces over the fruit. Following the photos on page 687, loosely roll the second piece of dough around the rolling pin and gently unroll it over the pie. Trim, fold, and crimp the edges, and cut eight evenly spaced vent holes in the top. Brush the dough with the egg mixture. Freeze the pie for 20 minutes.

4. Place the pie on the baking sheet and bake for 30 minutes. Reduce the oven temperature to 350 degrees and continue to bake until the juices bubble and the crust is deep golden brown, 30 to 40 minutes longer.

5. Cool the pie on a wire rack to room temperature, about 4 hours, before serving.

PUMPKIN PIE

WHY THIS RECIPE WORKS: Too often, pumpkin pie appears at the end of a Thanksgiving meal as a grainy, overspiced, canned-pumpkin custard encased in a soggy crust. We wanted to create a pumpkin pie recipe destined to be a new classic: velvety smooth, packed with pumpkin flavor, and redolent of just enough fragrant spices.

Canned pumpkin contains moisture, which dilutes a pie's flavor. To maximize flavor, we concentrated this liquid by cooking the pumpkin with sugar and spices, then whisked in heavy cream, milk, and eggs. This improved the flavor and the hot filling let the custard firm up quickly in the oven, preventing it from soaking into the crust. For spices, we chose nutmeg, cinnamon, and, surprisingly, freshly grated ginger. Sugar and maple syrup sweetened things, but tasters still craved a more complex pie. On a whim, we added mashed roasted yams to the filling and tasters appreciated the deeper flavor. To streamline the recipe we switched to canned candied yams and cooked them with the pumpkin. To keep the custard from curdling, we started the pie at a high temperature for 10 minutes, followed by a reduced temperature for the remainder of the baking time. This cut the baking time to less than one hour and the dual temperatures produced a creamy pie fully and evenly cooked from edge to center.

Pumpkin Pie

SERVES 8

If candied yams are unavailable, regular canned yams can be substituted. When the pie is properly baked, the center 2 inches of the pie should look firm but jiggle slightly. The pie finishes cooking with residual heat; to ensure that the filling sets, cool it at room temperature and not in the refrigerator. The crust and filling must both be warm when the filling is added. Serve with lightly sweetened whipped cream.

- 1 recipe Basic Single-Crust Pie Dough (see page 681), fitted into a 9-inch pie plate and chilled
- 1 cup heavy cream
- 1 cup whole milk
- 3 large whole eggs plus 2 large egg yolks
- 1 teaspoon vanilla extract
- 1 (15-ounce) can pumpkin puree
- 1 cup candied yams, drained (see note)
- ¾ cup (5¼ ounces) sugar
- ¼ cup maple syrup
- 2 teaspoons grated or minced fresh ginger
- 1 teaspoon table salt
- ½ teaspoon ground cinnamon
- ¼ teaspoon ground nutmeg

1. Adjust an oven rack to the lowest position, place a rimmed baking sheet on the rack, and heat the oven to 400 degrees. Following the photos, line the chilled pie shell with a double layer of foil and fill with pie weights.

2. Bake the pie shell on the heated baking sheet for 15 minutes. Remove the weights and foil and continue to bake the crust until golden brown and crisp, 5 to 10 minutes longer. Transfer the pie crust with the baking sheet to a wire rack. (The crust must still be warm when the filling is added.)

3. While the pie shell is baking, whisk the cream, milk, whole eggs, egg yolks, and vanilla together in a medium bowl. Bring the pumpkin puree, yams, sugar, maple syrup, ginger, salt, cinnamon, and nutmeg to a simmer in a large saucepan over medium heat and cook, stirring constantly and mashing the yams against the sides of the pot, until thick and shiny, 15 to 20 minutes.

4. Remove the pan from the heat and whisk in the cream mixture until fully incorporated. Strain the mixture through a fine-mesh strainer set over a medium bowl, using the back of a ladle or spatula to press the solids through the strainer. Whisk the mixture, then transfer to the warm prebaked pie crust.

5. Bake the pie on the baking sheet for 10 minutes. Reduce the oven temperature to 300 degrees and continue to bake until the edges of the pie are set and the center registers 175 degrees on an instant-read thermometer, 20 to 35 minutes longer. Cool the pie on a wire rack to room temperature, 2 to 3 hours, before serving.

PECAN PIE

WHY THIS RECIPE WORKS: Pecan pies can be overwhelmingly sweet, with no real pecan flavor. And they too often turn out curdled and separated. What's more, the weepy filling makes the bottom crust soggy and leathery. The fact that the crust usually seems underbaked to begin with doesn't help matters. We wanted to create a recipe for a not-too-sweet pie with a smooth-textured filling and a properly baked bottom crust.

We tackled this pie's problems by using brown sugar and reducing the amount, which helped bring out the pecan flavor. We also partially baked the crust, which kept it crisp. We found that it's important to add the hot filling to a warm pie crust as this helps keep the crust from getting soggy. In addition, we discovered that simulating a double boiler when you're melting the butter and making the filling is an easy way to maintain gentle heat, which helps ensure that the filling doesn't curdle.

Pecan Pie

SERVES 8

The crust must still be warm when the filling is added. To serve the pie warm, cool it thoroughly so that it sets completely, then warm it in a 250-degree oven for about 15 minutes and slice. Serve with vanilla ice cream or lightly sweetened whipped cream.

- 1 recipe Basic Single-Crust Pie Dough (page 681), fitted into a 9-inch pie plate and chilled
- 6 tablespoons (¾ stick) unsalted butter, cut into 1-inch pieces
- 1 cup packed (7 ounces) dark brown sugar
- ½ teaspoon table salt
- 3 large eggs
- ¾ cup light corn syrup
- 1 tablespoon vanilla extract
- 2 cups (8 ounces) pecans, toasted and chopped into small pieces

---

NOTES FROM THE TEST KITCHEN

BLIND BAKING A PIE CRUST

1. Line the chilled pie shell with a double layer of aluminum foil, covering the edges to prevent burning.

2. Fill the shell with pie weights and bake until dry and light in color. After baking, carefully remove the weights and let the crust cool (for a partially baked crust) or continue to bake until deep golden brown (for a fully baked crust).

1. Adjust an oven rack to the middle position and heat the oven to 375 degrees. Following the photos on page 694, line the chilled pie shell with a double layer of foil and fill with pie weights. Bake until the pie dough looks dry and is light in color, 25 to 30 minutes. Transfer the pie plate to a wire rack and remove the weights and foil. Adjust the oven rack to the lower-middle position and reduce the oven temperature to 275 degrees. (The crust must still be warm when the filling is added.)

2. Melt the butter in a heatproof bowl set in a skillet of water maintained at just below a simmer. Remove the bowl from the skillet and stir in the sugar and salt until the butter is absorbed. Whisk in the eggs, then the corn syrup and vanilla until smooth. Return the bowl to the hot water and stir until the mixture is shiny and hot to the touch and registers 130 degrees on an instant-read thermometer. Off the heat, stir in the pecans.

3. Pour the pecan mixture into the warm pie crust. Bake the pie until the filling looks set but yields like Jell-O when gently pressed with the back of a spoon, 50 to 60 minutes. Cool the pie on a wire rack until the filling has firmed up, about 2 hours; serve slightly warm (see note) or at room temperature.

Triple-Chocolate-Chunk Pecan Pie
SERVES 8

Use either just one type of chocolate listed or a combination of two or three types. See pages 740–741 for information on our top-rated brands of chocolate. The crust must still be warm when the filling is added.

- 1 recipe Basic Single-Crust Pie Dough (page 681), fitted into a 9-inch pie plate and chilled
- 3 tablespoons unsalted butter, cut into 3 pieces
- ¾ cup packed (5¼ ounces) dark brown sugar
- ½ teaspoon table salt
- 2 large eggs
- ½ cup light corn syrup
- 1 teaspoon vanilla extract
- 1 cup (4 ounces) pecans, toasted and chopped coarse
- 6 ounces semisweet, milk, and/or white chocolate, chopped coarse (see note)

1. Adjust an oven rack to the middle position and heat the oven to 375 degrees. Following the photos on page 694, line the chilled pie shell with a double layer of foil and fill with pie weights. Bake until the pie dough looks dry and is light in color, 25 to 30 minutes. Transfer the pie plate to a wire rack and remove the weights and foil. Adjust the oven rack to the lower-middle position and reduce the oven temperature to 275 degrees. (The crust must still be warm when the filling is added.)

2. Melt the butter in a heatproof bowl set in a skillet of water maintained at just below a simmer. Remove the bowl from the skillet and stir in the sugar and salt until the butter is absorbed. Whisk in the eggs, then the corn syrup and vanilla until smooth. Return the bowl to the hot water and stir until the mixture is shiny and hot to the touch and registers 130 degrees on an instant-read thermometer. Off the heat, stir in the pecans.

3. Pour the pecan mixture into the warm pie crust. Scatter the chocolate over the top and lightly press it into the filling with the back of a spoon. Bake the pie until the filling looks set but yields like Jell-O when gently pressed with the back of a spoon, 50 to 60 minutes. Cool the pie on a wire rack until the filling has firmed up, about 2 hours; serve slightly warm or at room temperature.

KEY LIME PIE

WHY THIS RECIPE WORKS: Some of us have been served Key lime pie in restaurants and found it disappointing, usually harsh and artificial tasting. We wanted a recipe for classic Key lime pie with a fresh flavor and silky filling. Traditional Key lime pie is usually not baked; instead, the combination of egg yolks, lime juice, and sweetened condensed milk firms up when chilled because the juice's acidity causes the proteins in the eggs and milk to bind.

Although we had suspected that the sweetened condensed milk was the party guilty of giving Key lime pies their "off" flavor, we found that the real culprit was the lime juice—bottled, reconstituted lime juice, that is. When we substituted the juice and zest from fresh limes, the pie became an entirely different experience: pungent and refreshing, cool and yet creamy, and very satisfying. We also discovered that while the pie filling will set without baking (most recipes call only for mixing and then chilling), it set much more nicely after being baked for only 15 minutes. We tried other, more dramatic, departures from the "classic" recipe—folding in egg whites, substituting heavy cream for condensed milk—but they didn't work. Just two seemingly minor adjustments to the recipe made all the difference in the world.

Key Lime Pie

SERVES 8

Despite this pie's name, we found that tasters could not tell the difference between pies made with regular supermarket limes (called Persian limes) and true Key limes. Since Persian limes are easier to find and juice, we recommend them. The timing here is different from other pies; you need to make the filling first, then prepare the crust.

PIE

- 4 large egg yolks
- 4 teaspoons grated zest plus ½ cup juice from 3 or 4 limes (see note)
- 1 (14-ounce) can sweetened condensed milk
- 1 recipe Graham Cracker Crust (page 685)

TOPPING (OPTIONAL)

- 1 cup heavy cream, chilled
- ¼ cup (1 ounce) confectioners' sugar

1. FOR THE PIE: Whisk the egg yolks and lime zest together in a medium bowl until the mixture has a light green tint, about 2 minutes. Whisk in the condensed milk until smooth, then whisk in the lime juice. Cover the mixture and set aside at room temperature until thickened, about 30 minutes.

2. Meanwhile, prepare and bake the crust. Transfer the pie plate to a wire rack and leave the oven at 325 degrees. (The crust must still be warm when the filling is added.)

3. Pour the thickened filling into the warm pie crust. Bake the pie until the center is firm but jiggles slightly when shaken, 15 to 20 minutes. Let the pie cool slightly on a wire rack, about 1 hour, then cover loosely with plastic wrap and refrigerate until the filling is chilled and set, about 3 hours.

4. FOR THE TOPPING (IF USING): Before serving, whip the cream and sugar together in a large bowl with an electric mixer on medium-low speed until frothy, about 1 minute. Increase the mixer speed to high and continue to whip until the cream forms soft peaks, 1 to 3 minutes. Spread the whipped cream attractively over the top of the pie and serve.

LEMON MERINGUE PIE

WHY THIS RECIPE WORKS: Most everybody loves lemon meringue pie—at least the bottom half of it. The most controversial part is the meringue. On any given day it can shrink, bead, puddle, deflate, burn, sweat, break down, or turn rubbery. We wanted a pie with a crisp, flaky crust and a rich filling that would balance the airy meringue, without blocking the clear lemon flavor. The filling should be soft but not runny; firm enough to cut but not stiff and gelatinous. Most important, we wanted a meringue that didn't break down and puddle on the bottom or "tear" on top.

We consulted a food scientist, who told us that the puddling underneath the meringue is from undercooking. The beading on top of the pie is from overcooking.

We discovered that if the filling is piping hot when the meringue is applied, the underside of the meringue will not undercook; if the oven temperature is relatively low, the top of the meringue won't overcook. Baking the pie in a relatively cool (325-degree) oven also produces the best-looking, most evenly baked meringue. To further stabilize the meringue and keep it from weeping (even on hot, humid days), we beat in a small amount of cornstarch.

Lemon Meringue Pie

SERVES 8

Make the pie crust, let it cool, and then begin work on the filling. As soon as the filling is made, cover it with plastic wrap to keep it hot and then start working on the meringue topping. You want to add hot filling to the pie crust, apply the meringue topping, and then quickly get the pie into the oven.

- 1 recipe Single-Crust Pie Dough for Custard Pies (page 681), fitted into a 9-inch pie plate and chilled

FILLING

- 1½ cups water
- 1 cup (7 ounces) sugar
- ¼ cup (1 ounce) cornstarch
- ⅛ teaspoon table salt
- 6 large egg yolks
- 1 tablespoon grated zest plus ½ cup juice from 3 lemons
- 2 tablespoons unsalted butter, cut into 2 pieces

MERINGUE

- ⅓ cup water
- 1 tablespoon cornstarch
- ½ cup (3½ ounces) sugar
- ¼ teaspoon cream of tartar
- 4 large egg whites
- ½ teaspoon vanilla extract

1. Adjust an oven rack to the middle position and heat the oven to 375 degrees. Following the photos on page 694, line the chilled pie shell with a double layer of foil and fill with pie weights. Bake until the pie dough looks dry and is light in color, 25 to 30 minutes. Remove the weights and foil and continue to bake the crust until deep golden brown, 10 to 12 minutes longer. Cool the crust to room temperature. Reduce the oven temperature to 325 degrees.

2. FOR THE FILLING: Bring the water, sugar, cornstarch, and salt to a simmer in a large saucepan over medium heat, whisking constantly. When the mixture starts to turn translucent, whisk in the egg yolks, 2 at a time. Whisk in the lemon zest and juice and the butter. Return the mixture to a brief simmer, then remove the pan from the heat. Lay a sheet of plastic wrap directly on the surface of the filling to keep warm and prevent a skin from forming.

3. FOR THE MERINGUE: Bring the water and cornstarch to a simmer in a small saucepan and cook, whisking occasionally, until thickened and translucent, 1 to 2 minutes. Set aside off the heat to cool slightly.

4. Combine the sugar and cream of tartar in a small bowl. In a large bowl, whip the egg whites and vanilla together with an electric mixer on medium-low speed until foamy, about 1 minute. Increase the mixer speed to medium-high, add the sugar mixture, 1 tablespoon at a time, and whip the whites until shiny and soft peaks form, 1 to 3 minutes. Add the cornstarch mixture, 1 tablespoon at a time, and continue to whip the meringue to stiff peaks, 1 to 3 minutes longer.

5. Meanwhile, remove the plastic wrap from the filling and return to very low heat during the last minute or so of beating the meringue (to ensure the filling is hot).

6. Pour the warm filling into the pie crust. Using a rubber spatula, immediately distribute the meringue evenly around the edge and then the center of the pie, attaching the meringue to the pie crust to prevent shrinking. Use the back of a spoon to create attractive swirls and peaks in the meringue. Bake until the meringue is golden brown, about 20 minutes. Cool the pie on a wire rack until the filling has set, about 2 hours. Serve.

COCONUT CREAM PIE

WHY THIS RECIPE WORKS: Most recipes for this diner dessert are nothing more than a redecorated vanilla cream pie. A handful of coconut shreds stirred into the filling or sprinkled on the whipped cream might be enough to give it a new name, but certainly not enough to give it flavor. We wanted a coconut cream pie with the exotic and elusive flavor of tropical coconut rather than a thinly disguised vanilla custard.

We found that using not-too-sweet graham crackers made a crust with a delicate, cookie-like texture that didn't overshadow the coconut filling. For the filling, we started with a basic custard, using a combination of unsweetened coconut milk and whole milk. For more coconut flavor, we stirred in unsweetened shredded coconut and cooked it so the shreds softened slightly in the hot milk. Lastly, we topped the pie with simple sweetened whipped cream and dusted it with crunchy shreds of toasted coconut.

Coconut Cream Pie

SERVES 8

Do not use low-fat coconut milk here because it does not have enough flavor. Also, don't confuse coconut milk with cream of coconut. The filling should be warm—neither piping hot nor room temperature—when poured into the cooled pie crust. To toast the coconut, place it in a small skillet over medium heat and cook, stirring frequently, for 3 to 5 minutes. It burns quite easily, so keep a close eye on it.

FILLING

- 1 (14-ounce) can coconut milk (see note)
- 1 cup whole milk
- ½ cup (1¼ ounces) unsweetened shredded coconut
- ⅔ cup (4⅔ ounces) sugar
- ¼ teaspoon table salt
- 5 large egg yolks
- ¼ cup (1 ounce) cornstarch
- 2 tablespoons unsalted butter, cut into 2 pieces
- 1½ teaspoons vanilla extract

- 1 recipe Graham Cracker Crust (page 685), baked and cooled

TOPPING

- 1½ cups heavy cream, chilled
- 1½ tablespoons sugar
- 1½ teaspoons dark rum (optional)
- ½ teaspoon vanilla extract
- 1 tablespoon unsweetened shredded coconut, toasted (see note)

1. FOR THE FILLING: Bring the coconut milk, whole milk, shredded coconut, ⅓ cup of the sugar, and the salt to a simmer in a medium saucepan over medium-high heat, stirring occasionally.

2. As the milk mixture begins to simmer, whisk the remaining ⅓ cup sugar, the egg yolks, and cornstarch together in a separate bowl. Slowly whisk 1 cup of the simmering coconut milk mixture into the yolk mixture to temper, then slowly whisk the tempered yolks back into the simmering saucepan. Reduce the heat to medium and cook, whisking vigorously, until the mixture is thickened and a few bubbles burst on the surface, about 30 seconds.

3. Off the heat, whisk in the butter and vanilla. Cool the mixture until just warm, stirring often, about 5 minutes.

4. Pour the warm filling into the baked and cooled pie crust. Lay a sheet of plastic wrap directly on the surface of the filling and refrigerate the pie until the filling is chilled and set, about 4 hours.

5. FOR THE TOPPING: Before serving, whip the cream, sugar, rum (if using), and vanilla together with an electric mixer on medium-low speed until frothy, about 1 minute. Increase the mixer speed to high and continue to whip until the cream forms soft peaks, 1 to 3 minutes. Spread the whipped cream attractively over the top of the pie and sprinkle with the toasted coconut.

CHOCOLATE CREAM PIE

WHY THIS RECIPE WORKS: Chocolate cream pies can look superb but are often gummy, gluey, overly sweet, and impossible to slice. We wanted a voluptuously creamy pie, with a well-balanced chocolate flavor somewhere between milkshake and melted candy bar, and a delicious, easy-to-slice crust.

After testing every type of cookie on the market, we hit on pulverized Oreos and a bit of melted butter for the tastiest, most tender, sliceable crumb crust. We found that the secret to perfect chocolate cream pie filling was to combine two different types of chocolate for a deeper, more complex flavor. Bittersweet or semisweet chocolate provides the main thrust of flavor, and intensely flavored unsweetened chocolate lends depth. One ounce of unsweetened chocolate may not seem like much, but it gives this pie great flavor. We also discovered that the custard's texture depended upon carefully pouring the egg yolk mixture into simmering half-and-half, then whisking in butter.

Chocolate Cream Pie

SERVES 8

For the best chocolate flavor and texture, we recommend either Callebaut semisweet and unsweetened chocolates or Hershey's Special Dark and Hershey's unsweetened chocolates. Other brands of chocolate sandwich cookies may be substituted for the Oreos, but avoid any "double-filled" cookies because the proportion of cookie to filling won't be correct. Do not combine the egg yolks and sugar in advance of making the filling—the sugar will begin to break down the yolks, and the finished cream will be pitted.

CRUST
- **16** Oreo cookies, broken into rough pieces (see note)
- **4** tablespoons (½ stick) unsalted butter, melted and cooled

FILLING
- **2½** cups half-and-half
- **⅓** cup (2⅓ ounces) sugar
- Pinch table salt
- **6** large egg yolks
- **2** tablespoons cornstarch
- **6** tablespoons (¾ stick) unsalted butter, cut into 6 pieces
- **6** ounces semisweet or bittersweet chocolate, chopped fine (see note)
- **1** ounce unsweetened chocolate, chopped fine (see note)
- **1** teaspoon vanilla extract

TOPPING
- **1½** cups heavy cream, chilled
- **2** tablespoons sugar
- **½** teaspoon vanilla extract

1. FOR THE CRUST: Adjust an oven rack to the middle position and heat the oven to 350 degrees. Pulse the cookies in a food processor until coarsely ground, about 15 pulses, then continue to process to fine, even crumbs, about 15 seconds. Sprinkle the butter over the crumbs and pulse to incorporate.

2. Sprinkle the mixture into a 9-inch pie plate. Following the photo on page 684, use the bottom of a measuring cup to press the crumbs into an even layer on the bottom and sides of the pie plate. Bake until the crust is fragrant and looks set, 10 to 15 minutes. Transfer the crust to a wire rack and cool completely.

3. FOR THE FILLING: Bring the half-and-half, 3 tablespoons of the sugar, and the salt to a simmer in a medium saucepan over medium-high heat, stirring occasionally.

4. As the half-and-half mixture begins to simmer, whisk the egg yolks, cornstarch, and remaining sugar together in a medium bowl until smooth. Slowly whisk about 1 cup of the simmering half-and-half mixture into the yolk mixture to temper, then slowly whisk the tempered yolks back into the simmering saucepan. Reduce the heat to medium and cook, whisking vigorously, until the mixture is thickened and a few bubbles burst on the surface, about 30 seconds.

5. Off the heat, whisk in the butter and chocolates until completely smooth and melted. Stir in the vanilla. Pour the warm filling into the baked and cooled pie crust. Lay a sheet of plastic wrap directly on the surface of the filling and refrigerate the pie until the filling is chilled and set, about 4 hours.

6. FOR THE TOPPING: Before serving, whip the cream, sugar, and vanilla together with an electric mixer on medium-low speed until frothy, about 1 minute. Increase the mixer speed to high and continue to whip until the cream forms soft peaks, 1 to 3 minutes. Spread the whipped cream attractively over the top of the pie.

CLASSIC TART DOUGH

WHY THIS RECIPE WORKS: The problem with most tarts is the crust—it's usually either too tough or too brittle. While regular pie crust is tender and flaky, classic tart crust should be fine-textured, buttery-rich, crisp, and crumbly—it is often described as being shortbread-like. We set out in the test kitchen to achieve the perfect tart dough, one that we could use in several of our tart recipes.

We found that using a full stick of butter made tart dough that tasted great and was easy to handle, yet still had a delicate crumb. Instead of using the hard-to-find superfine sugar and pastry flour that many other recipes call for, we used confectioners' sugar and all-purpose flour to achieve a crisp texture. Rolling the dough and fitting it into the tart pan was easy, and we had ample dough to patch any holes.

Classic Tart Dough

MAKES ENOUGH FOR ONE 9-INCH TART

Tart crust is sweeter, crisper, and less flaky than pie crust—it is more similar in texture to a cookie. The dough, wrapped tightly in plastic wrap, can be refrigerated for up to 2 days or frozen for up to 1 month. If frozen, let the dough thaw completely on the counter before rolling out.

- 1 **large egg yolk**
- 1 **tablespoon heavy cream**
- ½ **teaspoon vanilla extract**
- 1¼ **cups (6¼ ounces) unbleached all-purpose flour**
- ⅔ **cup (2⅔ ounces) confectioners' sugar**
- ¼ **teaspoon table salt**
- 8 **tablespoons (1 stick) unsalted butter, cut into ¼-inch pieces and chilled**

1. Whisk the egg yolk, cream, and vanilla together in a small bowl. Process the flour, sugar, and salt together in a food processor until combined. Scatter the butter pieces over the top and pulse until the mixture resembles coarse cornmeal, about 15 pulses.

2. With the machine running, add the egg mixture through the feed tube and continue to process until the dough just comes together around the processor blade, about 12 seconds.

3. Turn the dough onto a sheet of plastic wrap and flatten into a 6-inch disk. Wrap the dough tightly in plastic wrap and refrigerate for 1 hour. Before rolling the dough out, let it sit on the counter to soften slightly, about 10 minutes.

NOTES FROM THE TEST KITCHEN

MAKING A TART SHELL

1. After rolling the dough out into an 11-inch circle on a lightly floured work surface, wrap it loosely around the rolling pin and unroll the dough over a 9-inch tart pan with a removable bottom.

2. Lifting the edge of the dough, gently ease the dough into the pan. Press the dough into the corners and fluted sides of the pan.

3. Run the rolling pin over the top of the tart pan to remove any excess dough and make a clean edge.

4. If parts of the edge are too thin, reinforce them by pressing in some of the excess dough. If the edge is too thick, press some of the dough up over the edge of the pan and trim it away.

LEMON TART

WHY THIS RECIPE WORKS: Despite its apparent simplicity, there is much that can go wrong with a lemon tart. It can slip over the edge of sweet into cloying; its tartness can grab at your throat; it can be gluey or eggy or, even worse, metallic-tasting. Its crust can be too hard, too soft, too thick, or too sweet. We wanted a proper tart, one in which the filling is baked with the shell. For us, that meant only one thing: lemon curd.

For just enough sugar to offset the acid in the lemons, we used 3 parts sugar to 2 parts lemon juice, plus a whopping ¼ cup of lemon zest. To achieve a curd that was creamy and dense with a vibrant lemony yellow color, we used a combination of whole eggs and egg yolks. We cooked the curd over direct heat, then whisked in cold butter. And for a smooth, light texture, we strained the curd, then stirred in heavy cream just before baking.

Lemon Tart

SERVES 8 TO 10

Once the lemon curd ingredients have been combined, cook the curd immediately; otherwise it will have a grainy finished texture. Dust with confectioners' sugar before serving, or serve with lightly whipped cream.

- 1 recipe Classic Tart Dough (page 700)
  Unbleached all-purpose flour, for the work surface
- 7 large egg yolks plus 2 large whole eggs
- 1 cup (7 ounces) sugar
- ¼ cup grated zest plus ⅔ cup juice from 4 to 5 lemons
  Pinch table salt
- 4 tablespoons (½ stick) unsalted butter, cut into 4 pieces
- 3 tablespoons heavy cream

1. Roll the dough out to an 11-inch circle on a lightly floured work surface and, following the photos on page 700, fit it into a 9-inch tart pan with a removable bottom. Set the tart pan on a large plate and freeze the tart shell for 30 minutes.

2. Adjust an oven rack to the middle position and heat the oven to 375 degrees. Set the tart pan on a large baking sheet. Press a double layer of foil into the frozen tart shell and over the edges of the pan and fill with pie weights. Bake until the tart shell is golden brown and set, about 30 minutes, rotating the baking sheet halfway through.

3. Carefully remove the weights and foil and continue to bake the tart shell until it is fully baked and golden, 5 to 10 minutes longer. Transfer the tart crust with the baking sheet to a wire rack and cool the tart shell slightly while making the filling.

4. Whisk the egg yolks and whole eggs together in a medium saucepan. Whisk in the sugar until combined, then whisk in the lemon zest and juice and salt. Add the butter and cook over medium-low heat, stirring constantly, until the mixture thickens slightly and registers 170 degrees on an instant-read thermometer, about 5 minutes. Immediately pour the mixture through a fine-mesh strainer into a bowl and stir in the cream.

5. Pour the lemon filling into the warm tart shell. Bake the tart on the baking sheet until the filling is shiny and opaque and the center jiggles slightly when shaken, 10 to 15 minutes. Let the tart cool completely on the baking sheet, about 1½ hours. To serve, remove the outer metal ring of the tart pan, slide a thin metal spatula between the tart and the tart pan bottom, and carefully slide the tart onto a serving platter or cutting board.

FREE-FORM FRUIT TART

WHY THIS RECIPE WORKS: Few things are better than a summer fruit pie, but that takes time (and skill). What we wanted was simpler: a buttery, flaky crust paired with juicy summer fruit—with half the work of a regular pie. A free-form tart (a single layer of buttery pie dough folded up around fresh fruit) seemed the obvious solution.

Without the support of a pie plate, tender crusts are prone to leak juice, and this results in soggy bottoms. For our crust, we used a high proportion of butter to flour, which provided the most buttery flavor and tender texture without compromising the structure. We then turned to a French technique in pastry making called *fraisage*. To begin, butter is only partially cut into the dry ingredients. Then, with the heel of the hand, the cook presses the barely mixed dough firmly against the counter. As a result, the chunks of butter are pressed into long, thin sheets that create lots of flaky layers when the dough is baked. We rolled the dough into a 12-inch circle for a crust that was thick enough to contain a lot of fruit but thin enough to bake evenly and thoroughly. We placed the fruit in the middle, then lifted the dough up and back over the fruit and pleated it loosely to allow for shrinkage. The bright summer fruit needed only the simple addition of sugar.

Free-Form Summer Fruit Tart

SERVES 6

The dough, wrapped tightly in plastic wrap, can be refrigerated for up to 2 days or frozen for up to 1 month. If frozen, let the dough thaw completely on the counter before rolling it out. Though we prefer a tart made with a mix of stone fruits and berries, you can use only one type of fruit if you prefer. Taste the fruit before adding sugar to it; use the lesser amount if the fruit is very sweet, more if it is tart. However much sugar you use, do not add it to the fruit until you are ready to fill and form the tart. Serve with vanilla ice cream, lightly sweetened whipped cream, or crème fraîche.

MIXING A FLAKY DOUGH

1. Starting at one end of the rectangular pile of dough, smear a small amount of the dough against the work surface with the heel of your hand. Repeat this process (called *fraisage*) until the rest of the buttery crumbs have been worked.

2. Gather the smeared bits into another rectangular pile and repeat the smearing process until all of the crumbs have been worked again. This second time won't take as long and will result in large flakes of dough.

RUSTIC TART DOUGH

1½ cups (7½ ounces) unbleached all-purpose flour, plus extra for the work surface

½ teaspoon table salt

10 tablespoons (1¼ sticks) unsalted butter, cut into ½-inch pieces and chilled

4–6 tablespoons ice water

FILLING

1 pound peaches, nectarines, apricots, or plums, pitted and sliced into ½-inch-thick wedges (see note)

1 cup (5 ounces) blueberries, raspberries, or blackberries (see note)

3–5 tablespoons plus 1 tablespoon sugar (see note)

1. FOR THE RUSTIC TART DOUGH: Process the flour and salt in a food processor until combined. Scatter the butter pieces over the top and pulse until the mixture resembles coarse bread crumbs and the butter pieces are about the size of small peas, about 10 pulses. Continue to pulse, adding the water through the feed tube 1 tablespoon at a time, until the dough begins to form small curds that hold together when pinched with your fingers (the dough will be crumbly), about 10 pulses.

2. Following the photos, turn the dough crumbs out onto a lightly floured work surface and gather into a rectangular-shaped pile. Starting at the farthest end, use the heel of your hand to smear a small amount of dough against the work surface. Continue to smear the dough until all the crumbs have been worked. Gather the smeared crumbs together in another rectangular-shaped pile and repeat the process. Flatten the dough into a 6-inch disk, wrap it tightly in plastic wrap, and refrigerate for 1 hour. Before rolling the dough out, let it sit on the counter to soften slightly, about 10 minutes.

3. Roll the dough into a 12-inch circle between two large sheets of floured parchment paper. Slide the dough, still between the parchment sheets, onto a large baking sheet and refrigerate until firm, about 20 minutes.

4. FOR THE FILLING: Adjust an oven rack to the middle position and heat the oven to 375 degrees. Gently toss the fruit and sugar together in a large bowl. Remove the top sheet of parchment paper from the dough. Mound the fruit in the center of the dough, leaving a 2½-inch border around the edge. Following photo 2 on page 706, and being careful to leave a ½-inch border of dough around the fruit, fold the outermost 2 inches of dough over the fruit, pleating it every 2 to 3 inches as needed; gently pinch the pleated dough to secure, but do not press the dough into the fruit. Working quickly, brush the dough with water and sprinkle evenly with the additional 1 tablespoon sugar.

5. Bake the tart until the crust is deep golden brown and the fruit is bubbling, about 1 hour, rotating the baking sheet halfway through.

6. Cool the tart on the baking sheet on a wire rack for 10 minutes, then use the parchment paper to gently transfer the tart to a wire rack. Use a metal spatula to loosen the tart from the parchment and remove the parchment. Cool the tart on the rack until the juices have thickened, about 25 minutes. Serve warm or at room temperature.

FRESH FRUIT TART WITH PASTRY CREAM

WHY THIS RECIPE WORKS: Fresh fruit tarts usually offer little substance beyond their dazzling beauty, with rubbery or institutionalized pudding fillings, soggy crusts, and underripe, flavorless fruit. We set out to create a buttery, crisp crust filled with rich, lightly sweetened pastry cream, topped with fresh, glistening fruit.

We started with our classic tart dough as the crust and baked it until it was golden brown. We then filled the tart with pastry cream, made with half-and-half that was enriched with butter and thickened with just enough cornstarch to keep its shape without becoming gummy. For the fruit, we chose a combination of kiwi, which we peeled and sliced into half-moons, raspberries, and blueberries. We found that it was important not to wash the berries, as washing causes them to bruise and bleed and makes for a less than attractive tart (buy organic if you're worried about pesticide residues). The finishing touch: a drizzle with a jelly glaze for a glistening presentation.

Fresh Fruit Tart with Pastry Cream

SERVES 8 TO 10

The pastry cream can be made a day or two in advance, but do not fill the prebaked tart shell until just before serving. Once filled, the tart should be topped with fruit, glazed, and served within half an hour or so. Don't wash the berries or they will lose their flavor and shape.

PASTRY CREAM

- 2 **cups half-and-half**
- ½ **cup (3½ ounces) sugar**
- **Pinch table salt**
- 5 **large egg yolks**
- 3 **tablespoons cornstarch**
- 4 **tablespoons (½ stick) unsalted butter, cut into 4 pieces**
- 1½ **teaspoons vanilla extract**

TART SHELL AND FRUIT

- 1 **recipe Classic Tart Dough (page 700)**
  Unbleached all-purpose flour, for the work surface
- 2 **large kiwis, peeled, halved lengthwise, and sliced ⅜ inch thick**
- 2 **cups (10 ounces) raspberries (see note)**
- 1 **cup (5 ounces) blueberries (see note)**
- ½ **cup red currant or apple jelly**

1. FOR THE PASTRY CREAM: Bring the half-and-half, 6 tablespoons of the sugar, and the salt to a simmer in a medium saucepan over medium-high heat, stirring occasionally.

2. As the half-and-half mixture begins to simmer, whisk the egg yolks, cornstarch, and remaining 2 tablespoons sugar together in a medium bowl until smooth. Slowly whisk about 1 cup of the simmering half-and-half mixture into the yolks to temper, then slowly whisk the tempered yolks back into the simmering saucepan. Reduce the heat to medium and cook, whisking vigorously, until the mixture is thickened and a few bubbles burst on the surface, about 30 seconds.

3. Off the heat, stir in the butter and vanilla. Transfer the mixture to a medium bowl, lay a sheet of plastic wrap directly on the surface, and refrigerate the pastry cream until chilled and firm, about 3 hours.

4. FOR THE TART SHELL AND FRUIT: Roll the dough out to an 11-inch circle on a lightly floured work surface and, following the photos on page 700, fit it into a 9-inch tart pan with a removable bottom. Set the tart pan on a large plate and freeze the tart shell for 30 minutes.

5. Adjust an oven rack to the middle position and heat the oven to 375 degrees. Set the tart pan on a large baking sheet. Press a double layer of foil into the frozen tart shell and over the edges of the pan and fill with pie weights. Bake until the tart shell is golden brown and set, about 30 minutes, rotating the baking sheet halfway through.

6. Carefully remove the weights and foil and continue to bake the tart shell until it is fully baked and golden, 5 to 10 minutes longer. Transfer the tart shell with the baking sheet to a wire rack and cool the tart shell completely, about 1 hour.

7. Spread the chilled pastry cream evenly over the bottom of the cooled tart shell. Shingle the kiwi slices around the edge of the tart, then arrange three rows of raspberries inside the kiwi. Finally, arrange a mound of blueberries in the center.

8. Melt the jelly in a small saucepan over medium-high heat, stirring occasionally to smooth out any lumps. Using a pastry brush, dab the melted jelly over the fruit. To serve, remove the outer metal ring of the tart pan, slide a thin metal spatula between the tart and the tart pan bottom, and carefully slide the tart onto a serving platter or cutting board.

Mixed Berry Tart with Pastry Cream

Follow the recipe for Fresh Fruit Tart with Pastry Cream, omitting the kiwi and adding 2 cups (10 ounces) extra berries (including blackberries or quartered strawberries). Combine the berries in a large plastic bag and toss them gently to mix. Carefully spread the berries in an even layer over the tart. Glaze and serve as directed.

FRENCH APPLE TART

WHY THIS RECIPE WORKS: The French tart known as an apple galette should have a flaky crust and a substantial layer of nicely shingled sweet caramelized apples. But it's challenging to make a crust strong enough to hold the apples and still be eaten out of hand—most recipes create a crust that is tough, cracker-like, and bland. Our ideal galette has the buttery flakiness of a croissant but is strong enough to support a generous layer of caramelized apples.

Choosing the right flour put us on the right track. All-purpose flour contains too much gluten for this dough; it made the pastry tough. Lower-protein pastry flour created a flaky, tender, and sturdy pastry. As pastry flour is hard to find, we created a practical alternative by mixing regular all-purpose flour with instant flour. Technique also proved to be important. We used the French *fraisage* method of blending butter into dough (see page 701 for more information). The apple topping was simple. We found that any thinly sliced apple would work, although we slightly preferred Granny Smith.

Apple Galette

SERVES 10 TO 12

The most common brands of instant flour are Wondra and Shake & Blend; they are sold in canisters in the baking aisle. The galette can be made without instant flour, using 2 cups unbleached all-purpose flour and 2 tablespoons cornstarch; however, you might have to increase the amount of ice water. The dough, wrapped tightly in plastic wrap, can be refrigerated for up to 2 days or frozen for up to 1 month. If frozen, let the dough thaw completely on the counter before rolling out. Serve with ice cream, whipped cream, or crème fraîche.

DOUGH

- 1½ cups (7½ ounces) unbleached all-purpose flour, plus extra for the work surface
- ½ cup (2½ ounces) instant flour (see note)
- ½ teaspoon table salt
- ½ teaspoon sugar
- 12 tablespoons (1½ sticks) unsalted butter, cut into ¼-inch pieces and chilled
- 7–9 tablespoons ice water

TOPPING

- 1½ pounds Granny Smith apples (about 3 large), peeled, cored, and sliced ⅛ inch thick
- 2 tablespoons unsalted butter, cut into ¼-inch pieces
- ¼ cup (1¾ ounces) sugar
- 3 tablespoons apple jelly

1. FOR THE DOUGH: Process the flours, salt, and sugar together in a food processor until combined. Scatter the butter pieces over the top and pulse until the mixture resembles coarse cornmeal, about 15 pulses. Continue to pulse, adding the water through the feed tube 1 tablespoon at a time until the dough begins to form small curds that hold together when pinched with your fingers (the dough will be crumbly), about 10 pulses.

2. Following the photos on page 702, turn the dough crumbs onto a lightly floured work surface and gather into a rectangular-shaped pile. Starting at the farthest end, use the heel of your hand to smear a small amount of dough against the work surface. Continue to smear the dough until all the crumbs have been worked. Gather the smeared crumbs together in another rectangular-shaped pile and repeat the process. Press the dough into a 4-inch square, wrap it tightly in plastic wrap, and refrigerate for 1 hour. Before rolling the dough out, let it sit on the counter to soften slightly, about 10 minutes.

3. Adjust an oven rack to the middle position and heat the oven to 400 degrees. Cut a piece of parchment to measure exactly 16 by 12 inches. Following the photos on page 705, roll the dough out over the parchment, dusting with flour as needed, until it just overhangs the parchment. Trim the edges of the dough even with the parchment. Roll the outer 1 inch of the dough up to create a ½-inch-thick border. Slide the parchment paper with the dough onto a large rimmed baking sheet.

4. FOR THE TOPPING: Starting in one corner of the tart, shingle the apple slices onto the crust in tidy diagonal rows, overlapping them by a third. Dot with the butter and sprinkle evenly with the sugar. Bake the tart until the bottom is deep golden brown and the apples have

PREPARING APPLE GALETTE

1. Cut a piece of parchment to measure exactly 16 by 12 inches, then roll the dough out on top of the parchment until it just overhangs the edge and is about ⅛ inch thick.

2. Trim the dough so that the edges are even with the parchment paper. We use the parchment as a guide to cut a perfectly even rectangle of dough from which we can make a large thin crust.

3. Roll up 1 inch of each edge to create a ½-inch-thick border. This border is decorative and helps keep the apple slices in place.

4. Slide the parchment and dough onto a rimmed baking sheet. Starting in one corner, shingle the apple slices in tidy rows on the diagonal over the dough, overlapping each row by a third.

caramelized, 45 to 60 minutes, rotating the baking sheet halfway through.

5. Melt the jelly in a small saucepan over medium-high heat, stirring occasionally to smooth out any lumps. Brush the glaze over the apples and let the tart cool slightly on the baking sheet for 10 minutes. Slide the tart onto a large platter or cutting board and slice the tart in half lengthwise, then crosswise into square pieces. Serve warm or at room temperature.

FREE-FORM APPLE TART

WHY THIS RECIPE WORKS: Apple tarts are easier to make than apple pie, but they have their problems: The filling can dry out owing to the lack of a top crust, and the dough can be limp and tacky. We wanted a simple free-form tart with moist, flavorful apples neatly contained by a flaky, easy-to-handle dough.

Off the bat, we decided to borrow the crust from our Free-Form Summer Fruit Tart recipe (see page 701)—it's sturdy yet flaky, with a great buttery flavor. As with our Classic Apple Pie (see page 685), we favored a combination of Granny Smith and McIntosh apples. To ensure that the apples cooked through in a short amount of time, we sliced them ¼ inch thick. All the apples needed in the way of flavor enhancement was lemon juice, sugar, and cinnamon.

Free-Form Apple Tart

SERVES 6

Serve with vanilla ice cream or lightly sweetened whipped cream.

- 1 **pound Granny Smith apples (about 2 large), peeled, cored, and sliced ¼ inch thick**
- 1 **pound McIntosh apples (about 2 large), peeled, cored, and sliced ¼ inch thick**
- ½ **cup (3½ ounces) plus 1 tablespoon sugar**
- 1 **tablespoon juice from 1 lemon**
- ⅛ **teaspoon ground cinnamon**
- 1 **recipe Rustic Tart Dough (page 702), rolled into a 12-inch circle and chilled**

1. Adjust an oven rack to the middle position and heat the oven to 375 degrees. Toss the apples, ½ cup of the sugar, the lemon juice, and cinnamon together in a large bowl.

2. Remove the top sheet of parchment paper from the dough. Following the photos on page 706, stack some of the apples into a circular wall, leaving a 2½-inch border around the edge. Fill in the middle of the tart with the remaining apples. Being careful to leave a ½-inch border of dough around the fruit, fold the outermost 2 inches of dough over the fruit, pleating it every 2 to 3 inches as needed; gently pinch the pleated dough to secure, but do not press the dough into the fruit. Working quickly, brush the dough with water and sprinkle evenly with the remaining 1 tablespoon sugar.

MAKING A FREE-FORM TART

1. Discard the top piece of parchment. Stack the apple slices into a circular wall, leaving a 2½–inch border of dough. Fill the center with the remaining apples.

2. Fold 2 inches of the dough up over the fruit, leaving a ½-inch border between the fruit and the edge of the tart shell. This ½-inch space helps prevent the tart juices from leaking through the folds in the shell.

3. Bake the tart on a large rimmed baking sheet until the crust is deep golden brown and the apples are tender, about 1 hour, rotating the baking sheet halfway through.

4. Cool the tart on the baking sheet on a wire rack for 10 minutes, then use the parchment paper to gently transfer the tart to the wire rack. Use a metal spatula to loosen the tart from the parchment and remove the parchment. Cool the tart on the rack until the juices have thickened, about 25 minutes. Serve warm or at room temperature.

TARTE TATIN

WHY THIS RECIPE WORKS: Making a true tarte Tatin requires an investment of time and a certain amount of skill. Traditionally, the apples are cooked in a skillet until caramelized, then topped with homemade pastry and cooked in the oven. Before serving, the tart is masterfully flipped onto a serving platter. Yes, this version is great, but we wanted to simplify it enough for a weeknight dessert.

We first baked a sheet of store-bought puff pastry until it was beautifully golden brown. While the pastry baked, we caramelized the apples in a skillet until they were tender. We then spooned the apples over the pastry, arranging them in three even rows with a ½-inch border around the outside of the pastry. As a final touch, we created a simple sauce by adding heavy cream and Grand Marnier to the juices left behind after the apples were cooked.

30-Minute Tarte Tatin

SERVES 6 TO 8

To get this dessert on the table in 30 minutes, peel the apples while the oven preheats and the pastry thaws, and then bake the pastry while the apples are caramelizing. This dessert is especially good with Tangy Whipped Cream (page 668).

- 1 (9½ by 9-inch) sheet frozen puff pastry, thawed
- 8 tablespoons (1 stick) unsalted butter
- ¾ cup (5¼ ounces) sugar
- 2 pounds Granny Smith apples (about 4 large), peeled, quartered, and cored
- ¼ cup heavy cream
- 2 tablespoons Grand Marnier, spiced rum, or Calvados (optional)

1. Adjust an oven rack to the middle position and heat the oven to 400 degrees. Line a rimmed baking sheet with parchment paper. Unfold the puff pastry, lay it on the prepared baking sheet, and bake until golden brown and puffed, 15 to 20 minutes, rotating the baking sheet halfway through. Transfer the baked pastry sheet to a serving platter and press lightly to flatten if domed.

2. Meanwhile, melt the butter in a 12-inch nonstick skillet over high heat. Remove the pan from the heat and sprinkle evenly with the sugar. Lay the apples in the skillet, return the skillet to high heat, and cook until the juice in the pan turns a rich amber color and the apples are caramelized, about 15 minutes, turning the apples halfway through.

3. Remove the apples from the pan one at a time and arrange in three overlapping rows on the baked pastry sheet, leaving a ½-inch border. Spoon about half of the pan juice over the apples.

4. Whisk the cream and Grand Marnier (if using) into the remaining juice in the pan and bring to a simmer. Pour some sauce over the tart and serve, passing the remaining sauce separately.

Pear Tatin

We like to use Bosc or Bartlett pears here because they maintain their shape nicely when cooked. If you have it on hand, substitute Poire William (or other pear liqueur) for the Grand Marnier.

Follow the recipe for 30-Minute Tarte Tatin, substituting 2 pounds Bosc or Bartlett pears for the apples. Increase the cooking time by 5 to 10 minutes if necessary.

THE AMERICA'S TEST KITCHEN SHOPPING GUIDE

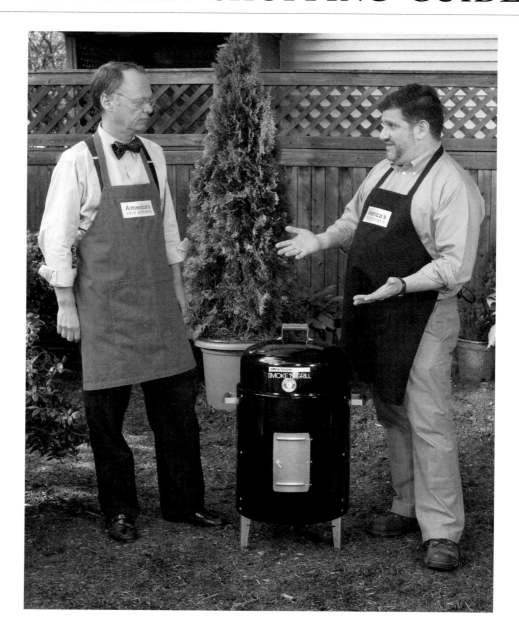

SHOPPING FOR EQUIPMENT

With a well-stocked kitchen, you'll be able to take on any recipe. But there's so much equipment out there on the market, how do you figure out what's what? Price often correlates with design, not performance. Over the years, our test kitchen has evaluated thousands of products. We've gone through copious rounds of testing and have identified the most important attributes in every piece of equipment, so when you go shopping you'll know what to look for. And because our test kitchen accepts no support from product manufacturers, you can trust our ratings. Prices in this chart are based on shopping at online retailers and will vary. See AmericasTestKitchen.com for updates to these testings.

KNIVES AND MORE	ITEM	WHAT TO LOOK FOR	TEST KITCHEN FAVORITES
MUST-HAVE ITEMS	CHEF'S KNIFE	• High-carbon stainless steel knife • Thin, curved 8-inch blade • Lightweight • Comfortable grip and nonslip handle	**Victorinox Fibrox 8-Inch Chef's Knife** (formerly Victorinox Forschner) $29.99
	PARING KNIFE	• 3- to 3½-inch blade • Thin, slightly curved blade with pointed tip • Comfortable grip	**Wüsthof Classic with PEtec 3½-Inch Paring Knife** (model #4066) $39.95 Best Buy: **Victorinox Fibrox 3¼-inch Paring Knife** $8.95
	SERRATED KNIFE	• 10- to 12-inch blade • Long, somewhat flexible, slightly curved blade • Pointed serrations that are uniformly spaced and moderately sized	**Wüsthof Classic 10-Inch Bread Knife** $109.95 Best Buy: **Victorinox Fibrox 10¼-Inch Bread Knife** $24.95
	SLICING KNIFE	• Tapered 12-inch blade for slicing large cuts of meat • Oval scallops (called a granton edge) carved into blade • Fairly rigid blade with rounded tip	**Victorinox Fibrox 12-Inch Granton Edge Slicing Knife** $39.95
	STEAK KNIVES	• Super-sharp, straight-edged blade • Sturdy, not wobbly, blade	**Victorinox Rosewood Straight Edge Steak Knife Set** (model #46059) $129.95 for a set of six Best Buy: **Chicago Cutlery 4-Piece Walnut Tradition Steak Knife Set** $22.95 for a set of four
	SANTOKU KNIFE	• 6½-inch blade • Narrow, curved, and short blade • Comfortable grip	**MAC Superior 6½-Inch Santoku Knife** $70

KNIVES AND MORE	ITEM	WHAT TO LOOK FOR	TEST KITCHEN FAVORITES
	BONING KNIFE	• 6-inch blade • Narrow, highly maneuverable and razor-sharp blade • Comfortable grip and nonslip handle	**Victorinox Fibrox 6-Inch Straight Boning Knife** (Flexible) $19.95
	MEAT CLEAVER	• Razor-sharp blade • Balanced weight between handle and blade • Comfortable grip	**Global 6-Inch Meat Cleaver** $166.95 Best Buy: **LamsonSharp 7¼-Inch Meat Cleaver** $51
	VEGETABLE CLEAVER	• Slim blade for slicing through thick, hard vegetables • Lightweight	**MAC Japanese Series 6½-Inch Japanese Vegetable Cleaver** $95
	HYBRID CHEF'S KNIFE	• High-carbon stainless steel knife • Lightweight • Thin blade that tapers from spine to cutting edge and from handle to tip	**Masamoto VG Gyutou, 8.2 Inches** $151
	MANDOLINE	• Razor-sharp blade(s) • Hand guard to shield fingers • Gripper tongs to grasp food • Measurement-marked dial for precision cuts • Storage for extra blades	**OXO Good Grips V-Blade Mandoline Slicer** $39.95 Best Buy: **Kyocera Adjustable Ceramic Mandoline Slicer** $24.95
	CARVING BOARD	• Heavy, sturdy board • Deep, wide trench to trap juices • Central well to hold meat snugly	**Williams-Sonoma Medium Maple Reversible Carving Board** $60
	CUTTING BOARD	• Roomy work surface at least 20 by 15 inches • Teak board for minimal maintenance • Durable edge-grain construction (wood grain runs parallel to surface of board)	**Proteak Edge Grain Teak Cutting Board** $84.99 Best Buy: **OXO Good Grips Carving and Cutting Board** $24.99
	KNIFE SHARPENER	• Diamond sharpening material for electric sharpeners • Easy to use and comfortable • Clear instructions	Electric: **Chef'sChoice Model 130 Professional Sharpening Station** $149.95 Manual: **AccuSharp Knife and Tool Sharpener** $10.95

MUST-HAVE ITEMS

KNIVES AND MORE	ITEM	WHAT TO LOOK FOR	TEST KITCHEN FAVORITES
	UNIVERSAL KNIFE BLOCK	• Holds up to nine knives • Narrow base for easy storage • Removable, dishwasher-safe lining	**Bodum Bistro Universal Knife Block** $45
	KNIFE BLOCK SET	• High-quality knives • Includes test kitchen's top-rated chef's knife, paring knife, serrated knife, slicing knife, boning knife, kitchen shears, and knife block	**Test Kitchen à la Carte Knife Set** $334.95
	MAGNETIC KNIFE STRIP	• 16½-inch strip that holds five knives, plus kitchen shears • Easy to install and clean • Bamboo surface that is gentle on blades	**Messermeister Bamboo Knife Magnet** $50 **Best Buy: Chicago Cutlery Magnetic Knife Storage Strip** $19.99
	CUT-RESISTANT GLOVE	• Tightly woven fabric for durability • Stretchy fabric for comfortable fit • Fits either right or left hand	**Microplane Specialty Series Cut Resistant Glove** $14.95

POTS AND PANS	ITEM	WHAT TO LOOK FOR	TEST KITCHEN FAVORITES
	TRADITIONAL SKILLETS	• Stainless steel interior and fully clad for even heat distribution • 12-inch diameter and flared sides • Comfortable, ovensafe handle • Cooking surface of at least 9 inches • Good to have smaller (8- or 10-inch) skillets too	**All-Clad Stainless 12-Inch Frypan** $154.99
	NONSTICK SKILLETS	• Dark, nonstick surface • 12- or 12½-inch diameter, thick bottom • Comfortable, ovensafe handle • Cooking surface of at least 9 inches • Good to have smaller (8- or 10-inch) skillets too	**T-Fal Professional Total Non-Stick 12½-Inch Fry Pan** $34.99
	CAST-IRON SKILLET	• Thick bottom and straight sides • Roomy interior (cooking surface of 9¼ inches or more) • Preseasoned	**Lodge Logic 12-Inch Skillet** $32.95

MUST-HAVE ITEMS

POTS AND PANS	ITEM	WHAT TO LOOK FOR	TEST KITCHEN FAVORITES
	ECO-FRIENDLY SKILLET	• PFOA-free (perfluorooctanoic acid) surfaces are nonstick and more durable than silicone coatings • Roomy interior (cooking surface of 9 inches or more) NOTE: We prefer our favorite nonstick skillet for its superior performance.	**Scanpan Professional 12½-Inch Fry Pan** $139.95
	DUTCH OVEN	• Enameled cast iron or stainless steel • Capacity of at least 6 quarts • Diameter of at least 9 inches • Tight-fitting lid • Wide, sturdy handles	**Le Creuset 7¼-Quart Round French Oven** $304.95 **All-Clad Stainless 8-Quart Stockpot** $294.95 Best Buy: **Tramontina 6.5-Quart Cast Iron Dutch Oven** $49
	SAUCEPANS	• Large saucepan with 3- to 4-quart capacity and small nonstick saucepan with 2- to 2½-quart capacity • Tight-fitting lids • Pans with rounded corners that a whisk can reach into • Long, comfortable handles that are angled for even weight distribution	Large: **All-Clad Stainless 4-Quart Saucepan** $224.95 Best Buy: **Cuisinart MultiClad Unlimited 4-Quart Saucepan** $69.99 Small: **Calphalon Contemporary Nonstick 2½-Quart Shallow Saucepan** $39.95
	RIMMED BAKING SHEETS	• Light-colored surface (heats and browns evenly) • Thick, sturdy pan • Dimensions of 18 by 13 inches • Good to have at least two	**Wear-Ever 13-Gauge Half Size Heavy Duty Sheet Pan by Vollrath** (formerly Lincoln Foodservice) $13
	SAUTÉ PAN	• Aluminum core surrounded by layers of stainless steel • Hefty but well-balanced pan • 9½- to 10-inch diameter • Helper handle and tight-fitting lid	**Viking Stainless 7-Ply 3-Quart Sauté Pan** $219.95 Best Buy: **Cuisinart Multiclad Pro Triple-Ply 3½-Quart Sauté Pan with Lid** $79.95
	OMELET PAN	• Gently sloped sides for easy turning and rolling of omelets • Nonstick finish • Heavy construction for durability and even heat distribution • 8-inch size for French omelets	**Original French Chef 8-Inch Black Nonstick Omelette Pan** $139.95

MUST-HAVE ITEMS

POTS AND PANS	ITEM	WHAT TO LOOK FOR	TEST KITCHEN FAVORITES
	STOCKPOT	• 12-quart capacity • Thick bottom to prevent scorching • Wide body for easy cleaning and storage • Flat or round handles that extend at least 1¾ inches	**All-Clad Stainless 12-Quart Stock Pot** $389.95 Best Buy: **Cuisinart Chef's Classic Stainless 12-Quart Stock Pot** $69.95
ROASTING PAN	• At least 15 by 11 inches • Stainless steel interior with aluminum core for even heat distribution • Upright handles for easy gripping • Light interior for better food monitoring	**Calphalon Contemporary Stainless Roasting Pan with V-Rack** $129.99
	V-RACK	• Fixed, not adjustable, to provide sturdiness • Tall, vertical handles positioned on long side of rack	**All-Clad Nonstick Roasting Rack** $24.95
	COOKWARE SET	• Fully clad stainless steel with aluminum core for even heat distribution • Moderately heavy, durable construction • Lids included • Ideal mix of pans includes 12-inch skillet, 10-inch skillet, 2-quart saucepan, 4-quart saucepan, 8-quart stockpot	**All-Clad Stainless Steel 10-Piece Cookware Set** $799.95 Best Buy: **Tramontina 18/10 Stainless Steel TriPly-Clad 8-Piece Cookware Set** $149.97

(left margin: MUST-HAVE ITEM)

HANDY TOOLS	ITEM	WHAT TO LOOK FOR	TEST KITCHEN FAVORITES
	KITCHEN SHEARS	• Take-apart scissors (for easy cleaning) • Super-sharp blades • Sturdy construction • Work for both right- and left-handed users	**Shun Classic Kitchen Shears** $39.99 Best Buy: **J. A. Henckels International Kitchen Shears—Take Apart** $14.95
	TONGS	• Scalloped edges • Slightly concave pincers • Length of 12 inches (to keep your hand far from the heat) • Open and close easily	**OXO Good Grips 12-Inch Locking Tongs** $12.95
	WOODEN SPOON	• Slim yet broad bowl • Stain-resistant bamboo • Comfortable handle	**SCI Bamboo Wood Cooking Spoon** $2.40
	SLOTTED SPOON	• Deep bowl • Long handle • Enough holes for quick draining	**OXO Good Grips Nylon Slotted Spoon** $6.99

(left margin: MUST-HAVE ITEMS)

HANDY TOOLS	ITEM	WHAT TO LOOK FOR	TEST KITCHEN FAVORITES
	BASTING SPOON	• Thin, shallow bowl • Handle at least 9 inches in length • Slight dip from handle to bowl	**Rösle Basting Spoon with Hook Handle** $28.95
	ALL-AROUND SPATULAS	• Head about 3 inches wide and 5½ inches long • 11 inches in length (tip to handle) • Long, vertical slots • Useful to have a metal spatula to use with traditional cookware and plastic for nonstick cookware	Metal: **Wüsthof Gourmet Fish Spatula** $34.95 Plastic: **Matfer Bourgeat Pelton Spatula** $11.95
	RUBBER SPATULA	• Wide, stiff blade with a thin edge that's flexible enough to conform to the curve of a mixing bowl • Heatproof	**Rubbermaid Professional 13½-Inch High Heat Scraper** $18.99
	OFFSET SPATULA	• Flexible blade offset from handle • Useful to have a small spatula for icing cookies and cupcakes and a large one for layer cakes and sheet cakes	Large: **Ateco Offset Spatula** $5.75 Small: **Wilton 9-Inch Angled Spatula** $4.79
	COOKIE SPATULA	• Small, silicone blade with thin, flexible edge • Angled handle	**OXO Good Grips Cookie Spatula** $6.99
	ALL-PURPOSE WHISK	• At least 10 wires • Wires of moderate thickness • Comfortable rubber handle • Balanced, lightweight feel	**OXO Good Grips 11-Inch Whisk** $9.99
	BALLOON WHISK	• Balloon-shaped whisk with long, thin wires for beating egg whites and whipping cream • Comfortable handle	**Rösle Balloon Whisk Beater** $30
	PEPPER MILL	• Six clearly marked fixed-grind settings that are easy to adjust • Easy to refill • Comfortable to hold	**Cole & Mason Derwent Precision Gourmet Pepper Mill** $40
	LADLE	• Stainless steel • Hook handle • Pouring rim to prevent dripping • Handle 9 to 10 inches in length	**Rösle Ladle with Pouring Rim** $29.95

MUST-HAVE ITEMS

MUST-HAVE ITEM

MUST-HAVE ITEMS

HANDY TOOLS	ITEM	WHAT TO LOOK FOR	TEST KITCHEN FAVORITES
MUST-HAVE ITEM	CAN OPENER	• Intuitive and easy to attach • Smooth turning motions • Magnet for no-touch lid disposal • Comfortable handle	**OXO Good Grips Magnetic Locking Can Opener** $21.99
	JAR OPENER	• Strong, sturdy clamp grip • Adjusts quickly to any size jar	**Amco Swing-A-Way Comfort Grip Jar Opener** $6.99
MUST-HAVE ITEM	GARLIC PRESS	• Large capacity that holds multiple garlic cloves • Curved plastic handles • Long handle and short distance between pivot point and plunger	**Kuhn Rikon Easy-Squeeze Garlic Press** $20 Best Buy: **Trudeau Garlic Press** $11.99
	SERRATED FRUIT PEELER	• Comfortable grip and nonslip handle • Sharp blade	**Messermeister Pro-Touch Serrated Swivel Peeler** $6.95
MUST-HAVE ITEM	VEGETABLE PEELER	• Sharp, carbon steel blade • 1-inch space between blade and peeler to prevent jamming • Lightweight and comfortable	**Kuhn Rikon Original 4-Inch Swiss Peeler** $3.50
	RASP GRATER	• Sharp teeth (require little effort or pressure when grating) • Maneuverable over round shapes • Comfortable handle	**Microplane Classic 40020 Zester/Grater** $14.95
MUST-HAVE ITEM	GRATER	• Paddle-style grater • Sharp, extra-large holes and generous grating plane • Rubber-lined feet for stability • Comfortable handle	**Rösle Coarse Grater** $35
	ROTARY GRATER	• Barrel at least 2 inches in diameter • Classic turn-crank design • Comfortable handle • Simple to disassemble for easy cleanup	**Zyliss All Cheese Grater** $19.95

HANDY TOOLS	ITEM	WHAT TO LOOK FOR	TEST KITCHEN FAVORITES
	MANUAL JUICER	• Hand-held squeezer with comfortable handle • Sturdy, enameled aluminum construction • Sized specifically for lemons, limes, and oranges	**Amco Enameled Citrus Squeezers** $11.95, lime $12.95, lemon $15.95, orange
	PORTION SCOOP	• Perfect half-sphere shape for easy portioning of batter and dough • Easy-to-squeeze handles to eject dough • Size number indicates how many portions per quart	**Fante's Stainless Portion Scoop #16 (2-ounce)** $13.99
	ICE CREAM SCOOP	• Stainless steel • Slim, comfortable handle • Thin bowl edge for easier scooping	**Rösle Ice Cream Scoop** $22.95
	MEAT POUNDER	• At least 1½ pounds in weight • Vertical handle for better leverage and control	**Norpro Grip-EZ Meat Pounder** $23.99
	BENCH SCRAPER	• Sturdy blade • Ruler marks (for easy measuring) • Comfortable handle with plastic, rubber, or nylon grip	**OXO Good Grips Stainless Steel Multi-Purpose Scraper and Chopper** $8.95
	BOWL SCRAPER	• Curved shape with comfortable grip • Rigid enough to move dough but flexible enough to scrape up batter • Thin, straight edge doubles as dough cutter or bench scraper	**iSi Basics Silicone Scraper Spatula** $5.99
	ROLLING PIN	• Moderate weight (1 to 1½ pounds) • 19-inch straight barrel • Slightly textured wooden surface to grip dough for easy rolling	**J.K. Adams Plain Maple Rolling Dowel** $13.95
	MIXING BOWLS	• Good to have both stainless steel and glass (for mixing, microwaving, and holding prepped ingredients) • Sets of 6 to 9 nesting bowls ranging in capacity from about 1¼ ounces to 4 quarts (for glass) and 2 cups to 8 quarts (for stainless steel)	**Little difference among various brands**

MUST-HAVE ITEMS

HANDY TOOLS	ITEM	WHAT TO LOOK FOR	TEST KITCHEN FAVORITES
	MINI PREP BOWLS	• Sturdy and somewhat heavy bowls to prevent tipping • Roomy 6-ounce capacity • Glass to resist stains and not absorb odors • Dishwasher- and microwave-safe	**Pyrex 6-Ounce Dessert Dishes, Set of 4** $6.99
	OVEN MITT	• Form-fitting and not overly bulky for easy maneuvering • Machine washable • Flexible, heat-resistant material	**Kool-Tek 15-Inch Oven Mitt by KatchAll** $44.95 Best Buy: **OrkaPlus Silicone Oven Mitt with Cotton Lining** $14.95
	COOKIE CUTTERS	• Metal cutters • Thin, sharp cutting edge and round or rubber-grip top • Depth of at least 1 inch	**Little difference among various brands**
	PASTRY BRUSH	• Silicone bristles (heat-resistant, durable, and easy to clean) • Perforated flaps (to trap liquid) • Angled head to reach tight spots • Comfortable handle	**OXO Good Grips Silicone Pastry Brush** $6.99
	SPLATTER SCREEN	• Diameter of at least 13 inches • Lollipop-shaped design • Tightly woven mesh face	**Amco 13-Inch Splatter Screen** $14.95
	BOUILLON STRAINER/ CHINOIS	• Conical shape • Depth of 7 to 8 inches • At least one hook on rim for stability	**Winco Reinforced Extra Fine Mesh Bouillon Strainer** $33.78
	COLANDER	• 4- to 7-quart capacity • Metal ring attached to the bottom for stability • Many holes for quick draining • Small holes so pasta doesn't slip through	**RSVP International Endurance Precision Pierced 5-Quart Colander** $32.95
	FINE-MESH STRAINER	• At least 6 inches in diameter (measured from inside edge to inside edge) • Sturdy construction	**CIA Masters Collection 6¾-Inch Fine Mesh Strainer** $27.50

MUST-HAVE ITEM

MUST-HAVE ITEMS

HANDY TOOLS	ITEM	WHAT TO LOOK FOR	TEST KITCHEN FAVORITES
	COLLAPSIBLE MINI COLANDER	• Compact yet sturdy • Folds down to height of 1 inch for easy storage • Removable plastic base to seal drainage holes and catch drips	**Progressive International Collapsible Mini Colander** $6.13
	FOOD MILL	• Interchangeable disks for fine, medium, and coarse purees • Stainless steel • Easy to turn	**Cuisipro Stainless Steel Food Mill** $105
	FAT SEPARATOR	• Pitcher-style • Wide-shaped spout for pouring • Strainer for catching solids • 4-cup capacity	**Trudeau Gravy Separator with Integrated Strainer** $13.29
	POTATO MASHER	• Solid mashing disk with small holes • Comfortable grip	**WMF Profi Plus Stainless Steel Potato Masher** $19
	SALAD SPINNER	• Solid bottom for washing greens in bowl • Ergonomic and easy-to-operate hand pump	**OXO Good Grips Salad Spinner** $29.99
	STEAMER BASKET	• Collapsible stainless steel basket with feet • Adjustable and removable center rod for easy removal from pot and easy storage	**Progressive Easy Reach Steamer Basket** $8.95
	MORTAR AND PESTLE	• Heavy, stable base with tall, narrow walls • Rough interior to help grip and grind ingredients • Comfortable, heavy pestle	**Frieling "Goliath" Mortar and Pestle Set** $49.95
	INNOVATIVE MORTAR AND PESTLE	• Heavy ceramic ball quickly crushes spices and garlic • Dishwasher-safe	**Jamie Oliver Flavour Shaker** $29.95

MUST-HAVE ITEMS

MEASURING EQUIPMENT	ITEM	WHAT TO LOOK FOR	TEST KITCHEN FAVORITES
MUST-HAVE ITEMS	DRY MEASURING CUPS	• Stainless steel cups (hefty and durable) • Measurement markings that are visible even once the cup is full • Evenly weighted and stable • Long handles that are level with the rim of the cup	**Amco Houseworks Professional Performance 4-Piece Measuring Cup Set** $14.95
	LIQUID MEASURING CUPS	• Crisp, unambiguous markings that include ¼ and ⅓ cup measurements • Heatproof, sturdy cup with handle • Good to have in a variety of sizes (1, 2, and 4 cups)	**Pyrex 2-Cup Measuring Cup** $5.99
	ADJUSTABLE MEASURING CUP	• Plunger-like bottom (with a tight seal between plunger and tube) that you can set to correct measurement, then push up to cleanly extract sticky ingredients (such as shortening or peanut butter) • 1- or 2-cup capacity • Dishwasher-safe	**KitchenArt Pro Adjust-A-Cup** $12.95
MUST-HAVE ITEMS	MEASURING SPOONS	• Long, comfortable handles • Rim of bowl flush with handle (makes it easy to "dip" into a dry ingredient and "sweep" across the top for accurate measuring) • Slim design	**Cuisipro Stainless Steel Measuring Spoon Set** $9.95
	KITCHEN RULER	• Stainless steel and easy to clean • 18 inches in length • Large, easy-to-read markings	**Empire 18-Inch Stainless Steel Ruler** $8.49
	DIGITAL SCALE	• Easy-to-read display not blocked by weighing platform • At least 7-pound capacity • Accessible buttons • Gram-to-ounce conversion feature • Roomy platform	**OXO Food Scale** $49.99 **Best Buy: Soehnle 65055 Digital Scale** $34.95

THERMOMETERS AND TIMERS	ITEM	WHAT TO LOOK FOR	TEST KITCHEN FAVORITES
MUST-HAVE ITEM	INSTANT-READ THERMOMETER	• Digital model with automatic shut-off • Quick-response readings in 10 seconds or less • Wide temperature range (-40 to 450 degrees) • Long stem that can reach interior of large cuts of meat • Water resistant	**ThermoWorks Splash-Proof Super-Fast Thermapen** $89 **Best Buys: ThermoWorks Super-Fast Pocket Thermometer** $19 **CDN ProAccurate Quick-Read Thermometer** $19.99

THERMOMETERS AND TIMERS	ITEM	WHAT TO LOOK FOR	TEST KITCHEN FAVORITES
MUST-HAVE ITEM	OVEN THERMOMETER	• Clearly marked numbers for easy readability • Hang model or stable base • Large temperature range (up to 600 degrees)	Cooper-Atkins Oven Thermometer (model #24HP) $6
	CANDY THERMOMETER	• Digital model • Easy-to-read console • Mounting clip (to attach probe to the pan)	CDN DTTC-S Combo Probe Thermometer, Timer, and Clock $24.95
	MEAT-PROBE THERMOMETER	• Long cord • Clear digital display	ThermoWorks Original Cooking Thermometer/Timer $19
	REFRIGERATOR/ FREEZER THERMOMETER	• Clear digital display • Wire probe for monitoring refrigerator and freezer simultaneously	Maverick Cold-Chek Digital Refrigerator/Freezer Thermometer $34.95
	REMOTE THERMOMETER	• Temperature probe attached to base that rests outside oven or grill and pager for notification • Easy to use	Taylor Wireless Thermometer with Remote Pager Plus Timer $21.95
MUST-HAVE ITEM	KITCHEN TIMER	• Lengthy time range (1 second to at least 10 hours) • Ability to count up after alarm goes off • Easy to use and read	Polder 3-in-1 Clock, Timer, and Stopwatch (model #898-95) $12
	INNOVATIVE TIMER	• Stovetop shape with individual timers in position of each burner and oven • Easy to read and use	5 in 1 DoneRight Kitchen Timer $24.95

BAKEWARE	ITEM	WHAT TO LOOK FOR	TEST KITCHEN FAVORITES
	GLASS BAKING DISH	• Dimensions of 13 by 9 inches • Large enough to hold casseroles and large crisps and cobblers • Handles	**Pyrex Bakeware 9 x 13-Inch Baking Dish** $12.99
	METAL BAKING PAN	• Dimensions of 13 by 9 inches • Straight sides • Nonstick coating for even browning and easy release of cakes and bar cookies • Handles	**Baker's Secret 9 x 13-Inch Nonstick Cake Pan** $7.49
	SQUARE BAKING PANS	• Straight sides • Light gold or dark nonstick surface for even browning and easy release of cakes • Good to have both 9-inch and 8-inch square pans	**Williams-Sonoma Nonstick Goldtouch Square Cake Pan** $26, 8-inch $27, 9-inch Best Buy: **Chicago Metallic Gourmetware 8-Inch Nonstick Square Cake Pan** $6.99
	ROUND CAKE PANS	• Straight sides • Nonstick coating for even browning and easy release of cakes • Good to have a set of both 9-inch and 8-inch round pans	**Chicago Metallic Professional Lifetime 9-Inch Nonstick Round Cake Pan** $12.99
	PIE PLATES	• Glass promotes even browning and allows progress to be monitored • ½-inch rim (makes it easy to shape decorative crusts) • Shallow angled sides prevent crusts from slumping • Good to have two	**Pyrex Bakeware 9-Inch Pie Plate** $2.99
	LOAF PANS	• Light gold or dark nonstick surface for even browning and easy release • Good to have both 8½ by 4½-inch and 9 by 5-inch pans	**Williams-Sonoma 8½ x 4½-Inch Nonstick Goldtouch Loaf Pan** $21 Best Buy: **Baker's Secret 9 x 5-Inch Nonstick Loaf Pan** $5
	SPRINGFORM PAN	• Rimless glass bottom allows you to monitor browning • Handles • Tight seal between band and bottom of pan (prevents leakage) • Flat, not rimmed, base that can double as serving plate	**Frieling's Handle-It Glass Bottom 9-Inch Springform Pan** $49.99 Best Buy: **Nordic Ware Pro Form 9-Inch LeakProof Springform Pan** $15

MUST-HAVE ITEMS

BAKEWARE	ITEM	WHAT TO LOOK FOR	TEST KITCHEN FAVORITES
	MUFFIN PAN	• Nonstick surface for even browning and easy release • Wide, extended rims and raised lip for easy handling • Cup capacity of ½ cup	**Wilton Avanti Everglide Metal-Safe Nonstick 12-Cup Muffin Pan** $13.99
	COOLING RACK	• Grid-style rack with tightly woven, heavy-gauge bars • Should fit inside a standard 18 by 13-inch rimmed baking sheet • Dishwasher-safe	**CIA Bakeware 12 x 17-Inch Cooling Rack** $15.95 Best Buy: **Libertyware Half-Size Sheet Pan Grate** $5.25
	BAKER'S COOLING RACK	• Sturdy rack • Four collapsible shelves • Unit folds down for easy storage	**Linden Sweden Baker's Cooling Rack** $19.99
	BISCUIT CUTTERS	• Sharp edges • A set with a variety of sizes	**Ateco 11-Piece Plain Round Cutter Set** $14.99
	BUNDT PAN	• Heavyweight cast aluminum • Silver platinum nonstick surface for even browning and easy release • Clearly defined ridges • 15-cup capacity	**Nordic Ware Anniversary Bundt Pan** (model #50037) $36
	MINI BUNDT PAN	• Tray-style model with six ¾-cup molds • Silver platinum nonstick surface for even browning and easy release • Clearly defined ridges	**Nordic Ware Platinum Anniversary Bundtlette Pan** $40
	TART PAN	• Tinned steel for even browning and easy release • Removable bottom • If you bake a lot, it's good to have multiple sizes, though 9 inches is standard	**Kaiser Tinplate 9-Inch Quiche Pan with Removable Bottom** $12
	TUBE PAN	• Heavy pan (at least 1 pound) • Heavy bottom for leak-free seal • Dark nonstick surface for even browning and easy release • 16-cup capacity • Feet on the rim	**Chicago Metallic Professional Nonstick Angel Food Cake Pan** $19.95

MUST-HAVE ITEMS

BAKEWARE	ITEM	WHAT TO LOOK FOR	TEST KITCHEN FAVORITES
	PULLMAN LOAF PAN	• Squared-off pan (4 by 4 inches) • Nonstick aluminized steel for easy cleanup • Light surface for even browning	**USA Pan 13 by 4-inch Pullman Loaf Pan and Cover** $33.95
	SLICING PAN	• Attached cutting grid • Dark nonstick surface for easy release	**Chicago Metallic Slice Solutions 9-Inch Brownie Pan** $19.99
	RAMEKINS	• Sturdy, high-fired porcelain (chip-resistant and safe for use in oven, broiler, microwave, and dishwasher) • For one all-purpose set, capacity of 6 ounces and diameter of 3 inches	**Apilco 6-Ounce Ramekins** $29 for a set of four
	BAKING STONE	• Substantial but not too heavy to handle • Dimensions of 16 by 14 inches • Clay, not cement, for evenly browned crusts	**The Baker's Catalogue Pizza Baking Stone by Old Stone Oven** $54.95

SMALL APPLIANCES	ITEM	WHAT TO LOOK FOR	TEST KITCHEN FAVORITES
MUST-HAVE ITEM	FOOD PROCESSOR	• 14-cup capacity • Sharp and sturdy blades • Wide feed tube • Should come with basic blades and discs: steel blade, dough blade, shredding/slicing disc	**Cuisinart Custom 14-Cup Food Processor** $199
	STAND MIXER	• Planetary action (stationary bowl and single mixing arm) • Powerful motor • Bowl size of at least 4½ quarts • Slightly squat bowl to keep ingredients in beater's range • Should come with basic attachments: paddle, dough hook, metal whisk	**Cuisinart 5.5 Quart Stand Mixer** $349.99 Best Buy: **KitchenAid Classic Plus Stand Mixer** $199.99
MUST-HAVE ITEM	HAND-HELD MIXER	• Lightweight model • Slim wire beaters without a central post • Digital display • Separate ejector buttons (not part of the speed dial) • Variety of speeds	**Cuisinart Power Advantage 7-Speed Hand Mixer** $49.95

SMALL APPLIANCES	ITEM	WHAT TO LOOK FOR	TEST KITCHEN FAVORITES
MUST-HAVE ITEM	BLENDER	• Mix of straight and serrated blades at different angles • Jar with curved base • At least 44-ounce capacity • Heavy base for stability	**Vitamix 5200** $449 **Breville BBL605XL The Hemisphere Control Blender** $200
	IMMERSION BLENDER	• Easy to operate and lightweight • Detachable shaft for easy cleaning • Wide blade cage so food can circulate	**KitchenAid 3-Speed Hand Blender** $59.99
	ELECTRIC EGG COOKER	• Boiling capacity of seven eggs • Well-fitting lid, not too tight, for safety • Audible timer • Easy to use	**West Bend Automatic Egg Cooker** $29.99
	ELECTRIC GRIDDLE	• Large cooking area (about 21 by 12 inches) • Attached pull-out grease trap (won't tip over) • Nonstick surface for easy cleanup	**BroilKing Professional Griddle** $99.99
	ELECTRIC JUICER	• Ideal for making a large amount of fruit or vegetable juice • Centrifugal, not masticating, model for fresher-tasting juice • 3-inch-wide feed tube • Easy to assemble and clean	**Breville Juice Fountain Plus** $149.99
	ADJUSTABLE ELECTRIC KETTLE	• Heats water to a range of different temperatures • Automatic shutoff • Separate base for cordless pouring • Visible water level	**Zojirushi Micom Water Boiler & Warmer** $114.95 Best Buy: **Chef'sChoice 688 Electric Smart Kettle** $99.99
	COFFEE MAKER	• Thermal carafe that keeps coffee hot and fresh with capacity of at least 10 cups • Short brewing time (6 minutes is ideal) • Copper, not aluminum, heating element • Easy-to-fill water tank • Clear, intuitive controls	**Technivorm Moccamaster KBT741 Coffeemaker** $299 Best Buy: **Bodum Chambord 8-Cup French Press** $39.95

SMALL APPLIANCES	ITEM	WHAT TO LOOK FOR	TEST KITCHEN FAVORITES
	MEAT GRINDER	• All-metal machine • Motorized grinder with reverse mode for unclogging stuck pieces • Easy to assemble	**Waring Pro Professional Meat Grinder** $199.99 Best Buy: **KitchenAid Food Grinder Attachment** $44.99
	DEEP FRYER	• Rotating basket that submerges food, reducing amount of oil needed • Window in lid to monitor cooking NOTE: We prefer to deep-fry in a Dutch oven for superior temperature control and larger capacity, but a deep fryer can be useful for french fries and other low-temperature fried foods.	**DeLonghi Cool Touch Roto Deep Fryer** $99.95
	PORTABLE INDUCTION BURNER	• Large cooking surface for even heating of pans • Basic push buttons and dial controls for ease of use	**Max Burton Induction Cook Top** $80
	ICE CREAM MAKER	• Minimum 1½-quart capacity • Removable canister and blade for easy cleaning	**Whynter SNÖ Professional Ice Cream Maker** $330.99 Best Buy: **Cuisinart Automatic Frozen Yogurt, Ice Cream, and Sorbet Maker** (model #ICE-21) $49.95
	ICE CREAM CONE MAKER	• Easy to use • Solidly constructed • Channel around edge to catch excess batter for easy cleanup	**Chef'sChoice Waffle Cone Express** $49.95
	PRESSURE COOKER	• Solidly built • Stovetop model with low sides and wide base for easy access and better browning and heat retention • Easy-to-read pressure indicator	**Fissler Vitaquick 8-Liter Pressure Cooker** (8½ quart) $280 Best Buy: **Fagor Duo 8-Quart Pressure Cooker** $89.99

SMALL APPLIANCES	ITEM	WHAT TO LOOK FOR	TEST KITCHEN FAVORITES
	SLOW COOKER	• At least 6-quart capacity • Insert handles • Clear lid to see progress of food • Dishwasher-safe insert • Intuitive control panel with programmable timer and warming mode	**Crock-Pot Touchscreen Slow Cooker** $129.99
	TOASTER OVEN	• Quartz heating elements for steady, controlled heat • Roomy but compact interior • Simple to use	**Breville The Smart Oven** $249.95 Best Buy: **Hamilton Beach Set & Forget Toaster Oven with Convection Cooking** $99.99
	WAFFLE IRON	• Audible alert • Heat-resistant handles • Multiple doneness settings	**Chef'sChoice WafflePro Express** $69.95

GRILLING EQUIPMENT	ITEM	WHAT TO LOOK FOR	TEST KITCHEN FAVORITES
	GAS GRILL	• Large grilling area (at least 350 square inches) • Built-in thermometer • Two burners for varying heat levels (three is even better) • Attached table • Fat drainage system	**Weber Spirit E-210** $399
	CHARCOAL GRILL	• Large grilling area • Deep grill cover to fit large food items (such as a turkey) • Hinged cooking grate to tend the fire • Ash catcher for easier cleanup	**Weber One-Touch Gold 22½-Inch Charcoal Grill** $149
	SMOKER	• Large cooking area • Water pan • Multiple vents for precise temperature control	**Weber Smokey Mountain Cooker Smoker, 18½ Inch** $299

GRILLING EQUIPMENT	ITEM	WHAT TO LOOK FOR	TEST KITCHEN FAVORITES
	CHIMNEY STARTER	• 6-quart capacity • Holes in the canister so air can circulate around the coals • Sturdy construction • Heat-resistant handle • Dual handle for easy control	**Weber Rapidfire Chimney Starter** $14.99
	GRILL TONGS	• 16 inches in length • Scalloped, not sharp and serrated, edges • Open and close easily • Lightweight • Moderate amount of springy tension	**OXO Good Grips 16-Inch Locking Tongs** $14.99
	GRILL BRUSH	• Long handle (about 14 inches) • Large woven-mesh detachable stainless steel scrubbing pad	**Tool Wizard BBQ Brush** $9.99
	BASTING BRUSH	• Silicone bristles • Angled brush head • Handle between 8 and 13 inches • Heat-resistant	**Elizabeth Karmel's Grill Friends Super Silicone Angled Barbecue Basting Brush** $8.99
	SKEWERS	• Flat and metal • $\frac{3}{16}$ inch thick	**Norpro 12-Inch Stainless Steel Skewers** $8 for a set of six
	GRILL GLOVES	• Excellent heat protection • Gloves, rather than mitts, for dexterity • Long sleeves to protect forearms	**Steven Raichlen Best of Barbecue Extra Long Suede Gloves** $29.99
	RIB RACK	• Sturdily supports six racks of ribs • Doubles as roasting rack (when flipped upside down) • Nonstick coating for easy cleanup	**Charcoal Companion Non-Stick Reversible Roasting/Rib Rack** $14.95
	GRILL LIGHTER	• Flexible neck • Refillable chamber with large, easy-to-read fuel window • Comfortable grip	**Zippo Flexible Neck Utility Lighter** $19.95
	DISPOSABLE GRILL	• Kit includes aluminum pan, metal grate, and charcoal • Large grilling area (about 12 by 10 inches) • After use, can be thrown away or recycled	**EZ Grill Disposable Instant Grill, Large** $9.99

GRILLING EQUIPMENT	ITEM	WHAT TO LOOK FOR	TEST KITCHEN FAVORITES
	OUTDOOR GRILL PAN	• Narrow slits and raised sides so food can't fall through or off • Sturdy construction with handles	**Weber Style 6435 Professional Grade Grill Pan** $19.99
	GRILL GRATE SET	• Stainless steel grate for 22½-inch charcoal grill • Removable inner circle of grate can be replaced with crosshatched sear grate (shown), griddle, or wok (sold separately)	**Weber Original Gourmet BBQ System, Griddle or Sear Grate Set** $64.99
	GRILLING FAN	• Battery-operated fan that circulates smoke and heat in grill to speed up cooking • Attaches to rotisserie notch in gas grill	**Charcoal Companion TurboQue** $23.69
	HEARTH GRILL	• Cast-iron grill rests in frame that fits into fireplace • Adjustable height • Generous cooking area (23½ by 30 inches) • Wood handles (easy to move grate when hot)	**Napastyle Tuscan Hearth Grill, Large** $199
	SMOKER BOX	• Cast iron for slow heating and steady smoke • Easy to fill, empty, and clean	**GrillPro Cast Iron Smoker Box made by Onward Manufacturing Company** $8.50
	GRILLING BASKET FOR WHOLE FISH	• Two-piece metal cage with nonstick coating to keep fish from sticking • Wires less than 2 inches apart to secure both large and small fish • Removable handle for easy cleanup	**Charcoal Companion Ultimate Nonstick Fish-Grilling Basket** $24.99
	VERTICAL ROASTER	• Helps poultry cook evenly • 8-inch shaft keeps chicken above fat and drippings in pan • Attached basin catches drippings for pan sauce • Sturdy construction	**Norpro Vertical Roaster with Infuser** $29.95 Best Buy: **Elizabeth Karmel's Grill Friends Porcelain Chicken Sitter Stand, 12 Inches** $12.99

SPECIALTY PIECES	ITEM	WHAT TO LOOK FOR	TEST KITCHEN FAVORITES
	APPLE CORER	• Comfortable grip • Sharp teeth • Blade diameter greater than ¾ inch and length greater than 3½ inches	**OXO Good Grips Corer** $9.99
	APPLE SLICER	• Sharp, serrated corer with 1-inch diameter • Ability to cut 8 or 16 slices • Comfortable handle	**Williams-Sonoma Dial-a-Slice Apple Divider** $19.95
	STRAWBERRY HULLER	• Huller with four spring-loaded metal prongs that slice out leaves, stem, and core • Easy and safe to use • Compact for easy storage	**Chef'n StemGem Strawberry-Stem Remover** $7.95
	PINEAPPLE SLICER	• Corkscrew design • Easy to use • Narrow slicing base for easy storage	**OXO Good Grips Ratcheting Pineapple Slicer** $19.99
	CORN STRIPPER	• Safer than using chef's knife • Attached cup to catch kernels • Comfortable grip and sharp blade	**OXO Good Grips Corn Stripper** $12.99
	NUT CHOPPER	• Sharp, sturdy stainless steel chopping tines • Dishwasher-safe	**Progressive International Heavy Duty Nut Chopper** $8.89
	NUTCRACKER	• Lever-style model • Solidly built • Extra-long handle for good leverage and easy cracking	**Get Crackin' Heavy Duty Steel Lever Nutcracker** $36
	GRILL PAN	• Cast-iron pan with enamel coating for heat retention and easy cleanup • Tall ridges (4 to 5.5 mm high) to keep food above rendered fat • Generous cooking area	**Staub 12-Inch American Square Grill Pan and Press** $159.90 Best Buy: **Lodge Logic Pre-Seasoned Square Grill Pan and Ribbed Panini Press** $18.97

SPECIALTY PIECES	ITEM	WHAT TO LOOK FOR	TEST KITCHEN FAVORITES
	STOVETOP GRIDDLE	• Anodized aluminum for even heating • Nonstick coating • Lightweight (about 4 pounds) • Heat-resistant loop handles • At least 17 by 9 inches (large enough to span two burners) • Pour spout for draining grease	**Anolon Advanced Double Burner Griddle** $59.95
	KITCHEN TORCH	• Easy one-hand operation • Triggered by thumb instead of forefinger (more comfortable) • Safety switch can easily be flicked off with thumb	**Bernzomatic Trigger-Start Micro Torch** $28.99
	MILK FROTHER	• Easy to use and clean • Immersion blender–style wand • Battery operated	**Aerolatte Milk Frother** $15
	OYSTER KNIFE	• Sturdy, flat blade with slightly curved tip for easy penetration • Slim, nonstick handle for secure, comfortable grip	**R. Murphy New Haven Oyster Knife** $16.95
	SEAFOOD SCISSORS	• Thin, curved blades to fit into shells • Strong and sturdy	**Progressive International Seafood Scissors** $9.95
	SILICONE SALT PIG	• Ceramic base keeps salt at hand for seasoning • One-touch closeable silicone lid • 1-cup capacity	**Prepara Pop Savor** $19.99
	SILICONE MICROWAVE LID	• Thin, silicone round to cover splatter-prone food during microwave heating • Easy to clean • Doubles as jar opener	**Piggy Steamer** $18
	RECIPE HOLDER	• Holds pages at perfect angle for viewing • Compact yet sturdy • Strong magnet	**Architec Recipe Rock** $9.99

SPECIALTY PIECES	ITEM	WHAT TO LOOK FOR	TEST KITCHEN FAVORITES
	OIL MISTER	• Clear plastic makes it easy to monitor oil level • Consistent, fine spray • Easy to refill • Dishwasher safe	**Orka Flavor and Oil Mister with Filter** $11.99
	MICROWAVE RICE COOKER	• Sturdy and compact • 6-cup capacity • Easy to clean	**Progressive International Microwave Rice Cooker Set** $8.99
	MICROWAVE CHIP MAKER	• Perforated 11-inch silicone disk that holds 15 to 20 chips • Slicer that produces wafer-thin chips	**Topchips Chips Maker** $19.99
	PASTRY BAG	• Plastic-coated canvas pastry bag (for durability and easy cleanup) or disposable bags • Large bag (about 18 inches in length) for easier gripping and twisting • Accommodates standard-size tips	**Ateco 18-Inch Plastic-Coated Pastry Bag** $5.95
	CHEESE WIRE	• Comfortable plastic handles • Narrow wire	**Fante's Handled Cheese Wire** $2.99
	PIZZA WHEEL	• Clear plastic wheel to prevent damage to pans • Comfortable, soft-grip handle • Thumb guard to protect fingers	**OXO Good Grips 4-Inch Pizza Wheel for Nonstick Pans** $19.49
	POTATO RICER	• Hopper with many holes so more food can travel through • Comfortable handles • Easy to assemble and clean	**RSVP International Classic Kitchen Basics Potato Ricer** $13.95
	PANCAKE BATTER DISPENSER	• Tall plastic cylinder • Easy to use • Heat-resistant silicone tip	**Tovolo Pancake Pen** $9.99

SPECIALTY PIECES	ITEM	WHAT TO LOOK FOR	TEST KITCHEN FAVORITES
	INSULATED ICE CREAM KEEPER	• Foam-core insulated base and gel pack–lined lid • Can hold 1 pint of ice cream • Keeps ice cream frozen for 90 minutes	Zak! Designs Ice Cream Tubbie $11.99
	QUICK POPSICLE MAKER	• Nonstick cast-aluminum mold with proprietary solution inside base to ensure quick freezing • Slots for three popsicles • Reusable plastic popsicle sticks	Zoku Quick Pop Maker $49.95
	CUPCAKE AND CAKE CARRIER	• Fits both round and square cakes and cupcakes • Snap locks • Nonskid base • Collapses for easy storage	Progressive Collapsible Cupcake and Cake Carrier $29.99
	REVOLVING CAKE STAND	• Elevated rotating stand so you can hold the spatula steady for easy frosting	Ateco Professional Icing Turntable $59.99 Best Buy: Ateco Plastic Revolving Cake Stand $24.75
	CREAM WHIPPER	• Slim canister for one-handed squeezing • Slender metal tip to make rosettes and mounds	Liss Professional Polished Stainless Steel Cream Whipper (1-pint) $99
	SPICE/COFFEE GRINDER	• Electric, not manual, grinders • Deep bowl to hold ample amount of coffee beans • Easy-to-control texture of grind • Good to have two, one each for coffee grinding and spice grinding	Krups Fast-Touch Coffee Mill $19.99
	MOKA POT	• Classic design that uses steam pressure to force hot water from bottom chamber up through coffee grounds • Stovetop, not electric, model • Easy to use	Bialetti 3-Cup Moka Express $24.95

SPECIALTY PIECES	ITEM	WHAT TO LOOK FOR	TEST KITCHEN FAVORITES
	MANUAL ESPRESSO MAKER	• Includes milk foamer, measuring scoop, and adapter for making two shots simultaneously • Easy and intuitive to use	**Presso Espresso Machine** $150
	TEAPOT	• Contained ultrafine-mesh strainer keeps tea leaf dregs separate • One-piece design for easy cleaning	**Adagio Teas IngenuiTEA** $19
	WINE OPENER	• Lever-style design with long handle for leverage • Comes with foil cutter and extra corkscrew worm • Compact and easy to use	**Oggi Nautilus Corkscrew** $24.99
	ELECTRIC WINE OPENER	• Sturdy, quiet corkscrew • Broad base that rests firmly on bottle	**Waring Pro Professional Cordless Wine Opener** $39.95
	WINE AERATOR	• Long, tubelike design that exposes wine to air as it is being poured • Neat, hands-free aerating	**Nuance Wine Finer** $29.95
	COCKTAIL SHAKER	• Double-walled canister to prevent condensation for slip-free gripping • Convenient pop-up spout • Tight-sealing lid	**Metrokane Fliptop Cocktail Shaker** $29.95
	ICE TRAY/ BUCKET	• Makes and stores ice and doubles as ice bucket • Tight-sealing lid • Soft silicone	**IceOrb by Fusionbrands** $16

SPECIALTY PIECES	ITEM	WHAT TO LOOK FOR	TEST KITCHEN FAVORITES
	COOLER	• Insulating layer of plastic lining • Lightweight, durable, sturdy, and easy to move, even when full • Easy to clean	**California Cooler Bags T-Rex Large Collapsible Rolling Cooler** $75
	SELTZER MAKER	• Easy to use and easy to control level of fizz • Large charger (producing about 60 liters of seltzer)	**Penguin Starter Kit by SodaStream** $199.95
	SOUS VIDE MACHINE	• Slowly cooks vacuum-sealed food in water bath at precise temperatures • Easy to set up and use	**SousVide Supreme** $399
	VACUUM ROBOT	• Easy to use and program for future use • Recharging dock • Sensor towers to restrict to specified area • Large vacuum intake	**iRobot Roomba** (model #560) $349.99
	COMPOST BUCKET	• Plastic pail to collect food scraps for composter • Carbon filter prevents odors from escaping and allows oxygen to enter so decomposition can occur • Easy to open lid that latches securely in place • 2.4-gallon capacity	**Exaco Trading Kitchen Compost Waste Collector** $19.98
	FIRE EXTINGUISHER	• Easy to operate • Powerful, controlled spray	**Kidde Kitchen Fire Extinguisher** (model #21005753/FX10K) $32

KITCHEN SUPPLIES	ITEM	WHAT TO LOOK FOR	TEST KITCHEN FAVORITES
MUST-HAVE ITEMS	PARCHMENT PAPER	• Sturdy paper for heavy doughs • Easy release of baked goods • At least 14 inches wide	**Reynolds Parchment Paper** $3.69
	PLASTIC WRAP	• Clings tightly and resticks well • Packaging with sharp teeth that aren't exposed (to avoid snags on clothing and skin) • Adhesive pad to hold cut end of wrap	**Glad Cling Wrap Clear Plastic** $2.59
	FOOD STORAGE CONTAINER	• Snap-style seal with ridge on underside to ensure tight seal • Low, flat rectangle for easy storage and more efficient heating and chilling • Made of plastic free of BPA (bisphenol-A)	**Snapware Airtight 8-Cup Rectangle Food Storage Container** $8.99
	SOAP-FILLED DISH BRUSH	• Handle for easy gripping and to keep hands dry • Tight seal to prevent soap from leaking	**OXO Steel Soap Squirting Dish Brush** $11.99
	ALL-PURPOSE CLEANERS	• Natural, green product • Cut through grease and food splatters quickly and efficiently • Pleasant, not overpowering, scent	**Method All-Purpose Natural Surface Cleaner, French Lavender** $3.79
	CAST-IRON POT SCRUBBER	• 4-inch square of chain mail made of 16-gauge stainless steel • Ideal for cleaning cast-iron cookware and all other cookware surfaces except nonstick	**KnappMade CM Scrubber** $19.98

SHOPPING FOR INGREDIENTS

Using the best ingredients is one way to guarantee success in the kitchen. But how do you know what to buy? Shelves are filled with a dizzying array of choices—and price does not equal quality. Over the years, the test kitchen's blind tasting panels have evaluated thousands of ingredients, brand by brand, side by side, plain and in prepared applications, to determine which brands you can trust and which brands to avoid. In the chart that follows, we share the results, revealing our top-rated choices and the attributes that made them stand out among the competition. And because our test kitchen accepts no support from product manufacturers, you can trust our ratings. See AmericasTestKitchen.com for updates to these tastings.

	TEST KITCHEN FAVORITE	WHY WE LIKE IT	RUNNERS-UP
	ANCHOVIES **Ortiz Oil-Packed Spanish**	• Pleasantly fishy, salty flavor, not overwhelming or bland • Firm, meaty texture, not mushy • Already filleted and ready to use, unlike salt-packed variety	Flott Salt-Packed
	APPLESAUCE **Musselman's Lite**	• An unusual ingredient, sucralose, sweetens this applesauce without overpowering its fresh, bright apple flavor • Pinch of salt boosts flavor above weak, bland, and too-sweet competitors • Coarse, almost chunky texture, not slimy like applesauces sweetened with corn syrup	Musselman's Home Style
	BACON, SUPERMARKET **Farmland Hickory Smoked**	• Good balance of saltiness and sweetness • Smoky and full flavored, not one-dimensional • Very meaty, not too fatty or insubstantial • Crisp yet hearty texture, not tough or dry	Boar's Head Brand Naturally Smoked Sliced and Hormel Black Label Original
	BARBECUE SAUCE **Bull's-Eye Original**	• Spicy, fresh tomato taste • Good balance of tanginess, smokiness, and sweetness • Robust flavor from molasses • Sweetened with sugar and molasses, not high-fructose corn syrup, which caramelizes and burns quickly	
	BEANS, CANNED BAKED **B&M Vegetarian**	• Firm and pleasant texture with some bite • Sweetened with molasses for complexity and depth	Bush's Best Original and Van Camp's Original
	BEANS, CANNED BLACK **Bush's Best**	• Clean, mild, and slightly earthy flavor • Firm, almost al dente texture, not mushy or pasty • Good amount of salt	Goya and Progresso
	BEANS, CANNED CHICKPEAS **Pastene**	• Firm yet tender texture bests pasty and dry competitors • Clean chickpea flavor • Enough salt to enhance but not overwhelm the flavor	Goya

	TEST KITCHEN FAVORITE	WHY WE LIKE IT	RUNNERS-UP
	BEANS, CANNED RED KIDNEY **Goya**	• Sweet with strong bean flavor • Beautiful red, plump beans • Smooth, creamy texture, not mushy, chalky, or too firm • Flavor boost from added sugar and salt	S&W
	BEANS, REFRIED **Taco Bell Home Originals**	• Well-seasoned mixture • Super-smooth texture, not overly thick, pasty, or gluey	Goya Traditional Refried Pinto Beans and Old El Paso
	BREAD, WHITE SANDWICH **Arnold Country Classics**	• Subtle sweetness, not tasteless or sour • Perfect structure, not too dry or too soft	Pepperidge Farm Farmhouse Hearty White
	BREAD, WHOLE-WHEAT SANDWICH **Pepperidge Farm 100% Whole Wheat**	• Whole-grain, nutty, earthy flavor • Dense, chewy texture, not gummy or too soft • Not too sweet, contains no corn syrup and has low sugar level (unlike competitors) NOTE: Available only east of the Mississippi River.	Rudi's Organic Bakery Honey Sweet Whole Wheat
	BREAD CRUMBS, PANKO **Ian's Panko**	• Crisp, with a substantial crunch • Not too delicate, stale, sandy, or gritty • Oil-free and without seasonings or undesirable artificial flavors	
	BROTH, BEEF **Rachael Ray Stock-in-a-Box All-Natural Beef Flavored Stock**	• Deep beefy profile with rich notes and gelatin-like body • Flavor-enhancing ingredients such as tomato paste and yeast extract	College Inn Bold Stock Tender Beef Flavor
	BROTH, CHICKEN **Swanson Certified Organic Free Range**	• Strong chicken flavor, not watery, beefy, or vegetal • Hearty and pleasant aroma • Roasted notes, not sour, rancid, or salty like some competitors • Flavor-boosting ingredients include carrots, celery, and onions	Better Than Bouillon Chicken Base and Swanson Natural Goodness

	TEST KITCHEN FAVORITE	WHY WE LIKE IT	RUNNERS-UP
	BROTH, VEGETABLE **Swanson Vegetarian**	• Balanced vegetable flavor with carrot and celery nuances • High concentration of vegetable product not found in competitors • High sodium content enhances vegetable flavors NOTE: Despite this broth's high concentration of artificial additives and salt, it is the only broth we found with acceptable flavor.	
	BROWNIE MIX **Ghirardelli Chocolate Supreme**	• Rich, balanced chocolate flavor from both natural and Dutch-processed cocoa • Moist, chewy, and fudgy with perfect texture	Barefoot Contessa Outrageous
	BUTTER, UNSALTED **Plugrá European-Style**	• Sweet and creamy • Complex tang and grassy flavor • Moderate amount of butterfat so that it's decadent and glossy but not so rich that baked goods are greasy	Land O'Lakes and Vermont Creamery European-Style
	CHEESE, AMERICAN, PRESLICED **Land O'Lakes**	• Strong cheesy flavor, unlike some competitors • Slightly rubbery but pleasantly gooey when melted • Higher content of cheese culture contributes to better flavor	Kraft Deli Deluxe White
	CHEESE, ASIAGO **BelGioioso**	• Sharp, tangy, and complex flavor, not mild • Firm and not too dry • Melts, shreds, and grates well	
	CHEESE, BLUE For dressings and dips: **Stella**	• Sweet, balanced, and mild flavor, not too pungent • Wet and extremely crumbly texture similar to feta	Danish Blue
	For eating out of hand: **Stilton**	• Balance of buttery, nutty, sweet, and salty flavors • Fairly firm with sliceable yet crumbly texture	Roquefort

	TEST KITCHEN FAVORITE	WHY WE LIKE IT	RUNNERS-UP
	CHEESE, CHEDDAR, EXTRA-SHARP **Cabot Private Stock**	• Balance of salty, creamy, and sweet flavors • Considerable but well-rounded sharpness, not overwhelming • Firm, crumbly texture, not moist, rubbery, or springy • Aged at least 12 months for complex flavor	Cabot Extra-Sharp, Grafton Village Cheese Company Premium, Cabot Sharp, and Tillamook Special Reserve
	CHEESE, CHEDDAR, PRESLICED **Tillamook Sharp**	• Slightly crumbly, not rubbery or processed, texture characteristic of block cheddar • Strong, tangy, and salty flavor, not bland or too mild	Cabot All Natural Sharp and Cracker Barrel Natural Sharp
	CHEESE, CHEDDAR, PREMIUM **Milton Creamery Prairie Breeze**	• Earthy complexity with nutty, buttery, and fruity flavors • Dry and crumbly with crystalline crunch, not rubbery or overly moist • Aged no more than 12 months to prevent overly sharp flavor	Cabot Clothbound, Tillamook Vintage White Extra Sharp, and Beecher's Flagship Reserve
	CHEESE, CHEDDAR, REDUCED-FAT **Cracker Barrel Reduced Fat Sharp**	• Ample creaminess • Strong cheesy flavor • Good for cooking	Cabot 50% Light Sharp
	CHEESE, CHEDDAR, SHARP **Cabot Sharp Vermont**	• Sharp, clean, and tangy flavor • Firm, crumbly texture, not moist, rubbery, or springy • Aged a minimum of 12 months for complex flavor	Tillamook Sharp, Cracker Barrel Sharp White, and Grafton Village Cheese Company
	CHEESE, COTTAGE **Hood Country Style**	• Rich, well-seasoned, and buttery flavor • Velvety, creamy texture • Pillowy curds	Friendship 4% California Style and Breakstone's 4% Small Curd
	CHEESE, CREAM **Philadelphia**	• Rich, tangy, and milky flavor • Thick, creamy texture, not pasty, waxy, or chalky	Organic Valley
	CHEESE, FETA **Mt. Vikos Traditional Feta**	• Strong tangy, salty flavor • Creamy, dense texture • Pleasing crumbly texture	Valbreso Feta
	CHEESE, FONTINA For eating out of hand: **Fontina Val d'Aosta**	• Strong, earthy aroma • Somewhat elastic texture with small irregular holes • Grassy, nutty flavor—but can be overpowering in cooked dishes	
	For cooking: **BelGioioso**	• Semisoft, super-creamy texture • Mildly tangy, nutty flavor • Melts well	

	TEST KITCHEN FAVORITE	WHY WE LIKE IT	RUNNERS-UP
	CHEESE, GOAT **Vermont Butter & Cheese** **Company Chèvre**	• Buttery, tangy flavor with a clean taste, not overpowering • Creamy yet firm texture, not chalky, pasty, or too soft • No offensive flavors as in some competitors	Westfield Farm Capri
	CHEESE, GRUYÈRE **Emmi Le Gruyère Reserve**	• Grassy, salty flavor, not bland or pedestrian • Creamy yet dry texture, not plasticky like some competitors • Aged a minimum of 10 months for strong and complex flavor • Melts especially well	Gruyère Salé
	CHEESE, MONTEREY JACK **Cabot**	• Mild flavor with an acidic tang, mellows when melted • Smooth, creamy consistency, not grainy	
	CHEESE, MOZZARELLA **Sorrento Whole Milk**	• Creamy and buttery with clean dairy flavor • Soft, not rubbery, chew	Kraft Low-Moisture Part Skim, Boar's Head Whole-Milk Low Moisture, and Kraft Shredded Low-Moisture Part-Skim
	CHEESE, PARMESAN **Boar's Head Parmigiano-** **Reggiano**	• Rich and complex flavor balances tanginess and nuttiness • Dry, crumbly texture yet creamy with a crystalline crunch, not rubbery or dense • Aged a minimum of 12 months for better flavor and texture	Il Villagio Parmigiano-Reggiano and BelGioioso
	CHEESE, PROVOLONE **Provolone Vernengo**	• Bold, nutty, and tangy flavor, not plasticky or bland • Firm, dry texture	BelGioioso Sliced Mild
	CHEESE, RICOTTA, **PART-SKIM** **Calabro**	• Clean, fresh flavor, not rancid or sour from addition of gums or stabilizers • Creamy texture with perfect curds, unlike chalky, grainy, and soggy competitors	Freshly made ricotta cheese without gums or stabilizers
	CHEESE, SWISS For eating out of hand: **Emmenthaler**	• Subtle flavor with sweet, buttery, nutty, and fruity notes • Firm yet gently giving texture, not rubbery • Aged longer for better flavor, resulting in larger eyes • Mildly pungent yet balanced	For eating out of hand or cooking: Sargento Baby, Sargento Deli Style Aged, and Boar's Head Gold Label Imported
	For cooking: **Jarlsberg**	• Creamy texture • Salty mildness preferable for grilled cheese sandwiches	

	TEST KITCHEN FAVORITE	WHY WE LIKE IT	RUNNERS-UP
	CHICKEN, WHOLE **Mary's Free Range** **Air-Chilled**	• Great, savory chicken flavor • Very tender • Air-chilled for minimum water retention and cleaner flavor	
	Bell & Evans **Air-Chilled** **Premium Fresh**	• Firm and tender texture • Full chicken flavor • Moist and juicy	
	CHICKEN, BREASTS, **BONELESS SKINLESS** **Bell & Evans Air-Chilled**	• Juicy and tender with clean chicken flavor • Not salted or brined • Air-chilled • Aged on bone for at least six hours after slaughter for significantly more tender meat	
	CHILI POWDER **Spice Islands**	• Blend of chile peppers with added seasonings, not assertively hot, overly smoky, or one-dimensional • Balance of sweet and smoky flavors • Potent but not overwhelming	The El Paso Chile Company Chili Spices and Fixin's and Pendery's Top Hat Chile Blend
	CHOCOLATE, DARK **Callebaut Intense Dark** **L-60-40NV** **(60% Cacao)**	• Creamy texture, not grainy or chalky • Rich and earthy, complex flavor with notes of caramel, smoke, and espresso • Balance of sweetness and bitterness	Ghirardelli Bittersweet Chocolate Baking Bar (60% Cacao)
	CHOCOLATE, MILK **Dove Silky Smooth**	• Intense, full, rich chocolate flavor • Super-creamy texture from abundant milk fat and cocoa butter • Not overwhelmingly sweet	Endangered Species All-Natural Smooth and Green & Black's Organic
	CHOCOLATE, MILK CHIPS **Hershey's**	• Bold chocolate flavor outshines too-sweet, weak chocolate flavor of other chips • Complex with caramel and nutty notes • Higher fat content makes texture creamier than grainy, artificial competitors	
	CHOCOLATE, **SEMISWEET CHIPS** **Ghirardelli 60% Cacao** **Bittersweet**	• Intense, complex flavor beats one-dimensional flavor of competitors • Low sugar content highlights chocolate flavor • High amount of cocoa butter ensures creamy, smooth texture, not gritty and grainy • Wider, flatter shape and high percentage of fat help chips melt better in cookies	Hershey's Special Dark Mildly Sweet

	TEST KITCHEN FAVORITE	WHY WE LIKE IT	RUNNERS-UP
	CHOCOLATE, UNSWEETENED **Hershey's Unsweetened Baking Bar**	• Well-rounded, complex flavor • Assertive chocolate flavor and deep notes of cocoa	Valrhona Cacao Pate Extra 100% and Scharffen Berger Unsweetened Dark
	CHOCOLATE, WHITE CHIPS **Guittard Choc-Au-Lait**	• Creamy texture, not waxy or crunchy • Silky smooth meltability from high fat content • Complex flavor like high-quality real chocolate, no artificial or off-flavors	Ghirardelli Classic White
	CINNAMON **Penzeys Extra Fancy Vietnamese Cassia**	• Warm, fragrant aroma with clove, fruity, and slightly smoky flavors • Mellow start with spicy finish • Strong yet not overpowering • Not harsh, bitter, dusty, or gritty NOTE: Available through mail order, Penzeys (800-741-7787, Penzeys.com).	Smith and Truslow Freshly Ground Organic and Adams Ground
	COCOA POWDER **Hershey's Natural Unsweetened**	• Full, strong chocolate flavor • Complex flavor with notes of coffee, cinnamon, orange, and spice	Droste
	COCONUT MILK For savory recipes: **Chaokoh**	• Strong coconut flavor • Smooth and creamy texture superior to competitors • Not very sweet, ideal for savory recipes like soups and stir-fries	
	For sweet recipes: **Ka-Me**	• Rich, velvety texture, not too thin or watery • Fruity and complex flavor, not mild or bland • Ideal sweetness for desserts	
	COFFEE, WHOLE BEAN, SUPERMARKET Dark roast: **Millstone Colombian Supremo**	• Deep, complex, and balanced flavor without metallic, overly acidic, or otherwise unpleasant notes • Smoky and chocolaty with a bitter, not burnt, finish	Starbucks Coffee House Blend
	Lighter roast: **Green Mountain Coffee Our Blend**	• Soft, complex, and balanced flavor • Pleasantly acidic with notes of caramel and fruit	Eight O'Clock Coffee Original

	TEST KITCHEN FAVORITE	WHY WE LIKE IT	RUNNERS-UP
	COFFEE, DECAF **Maxwell House Decaf Original Roast**	• Smooth, mellow flavor without being acidic or harsh • Complex, with a slightly nutty aftertaste • Made with only flavorful Arabica beans	Peet's Decaf House Blend Ground and Starbucks Coffee Decaf House Blend
	CORNMEAL **Arrowhead Mills Whole Grain**	• Clean, pure corn flavor comes from using whole-grain kernels • Ideal texture resembling slightly damp, fine sand, not too fine or too coarse	
	CRABMEAT **Phillips Premium Crab Jumbo**	• Moist, plump, meaty chunks • Taste comparable to freshly picked crabmeat	Miller's Select Lump
	CURRY POWDER **Penzeys Sweet**	• Balanced, neither too sweet nor too hot • Complex and vivid earthy flavor, not thin, bland, or one-dimensional NOTE: Available through mail order, Penzeys (800-741-7787, Penzeys.com).	
	DINNER ROLLS, FROZEN **Rhodes Frozen White Dinner Rolls**	• Sweet, yeasty, and fresh flavor • Neither overly sweet nor overly salty	
	FIVE-SPICE POWDER **Dean & Deluca**	• Nice depth, not one-dimensional • Balanced heat and sweetness NOTE: Available through mail order, Dean & Deluca (800-221-7714, DeanDeLuca.com).	Kalustyan's and Penzeys
	FLOUR, ALL-PURPOSE **King Arthur Unbleached**	• Fresh, toasty flavor • No metallic taste or other off-flavors • Consistent results across recipes • Made tender, flaky pie crust, hearty biscuits, crisp cookies, and chewy, sturdy bread	Gold Medal Enriched Bleached Presifted, Gold Medal Unbleached, and Heckers/Ceresota Unbleached Enriched Presifted
	Pillsbury Unbleached Enriched	• Clean, toasty, and hearty flavor • No metallic or other off-flavors • Consistent results across recipes • Made flaky pie crust, chewy cookies, and tender biscuits, muffins, and cakes	

	TEST KITCHEN FAVORITE	WHY WE LIKE IT	RUNNERS-UP
	FLOUR, WHOLE-WHEAT **King Arthur Premium**	• Finely ground for hearty but not overly coarse texture in bread and pancakes • Sweet, nutty flavor	Bob's Red Mill Organic
	GIARDINIERA **Pastene**	• Sharp, vinegary tang • Crunchy mix of vegetables • Mellow heat that's potent but not overpowering	Scala Hot
	GNOCCHI **Gia Russa**	• Tender, pillowlike texture • Nice potato flavor • Slightly sour taste that disappears when paired with tomato sauce	De Cecco
	HAM, BLACK FOREST DELI For cooking: **Dietz & Watson** For eating on its own: **Abraham's Black Forest Prosciutto Ham**	• Good texture • Nice ham flavor • Concentrated, silky texture • Intense ham flavor with bold smokiness	
	HAM, SPIRAL-SLICED, HONEY-CURED **Cook's Spiral Sliced Hickory Smoked Honey**	• Good balance of smokiness, saltiness, and sweetness • Moist, tender yet firm texture, not dry or too wet • Clean, meaty ham flavor	
	HOISIN SAUCE **Kikkoman**	• Balances sweet, salty, pungent, and spicy flavors • Initial burn mellows into harmonious and aromatic blend without bitterness	
	HORSERADISH **Boar's Head Pure Horseradish**	• No preservatives, just horseradish, vinegar, and salt (found in refrigerated section) • Natural flavor and hot without being overpowering	

	TEST KITCHEN FAVORITE	WHY WE LIKE IT	RUNNERS-UP
	HOT DOGS **Nathan's Famous** **Beef Franks**	• Meaty, robust, and hearty flavor, not sweet, sour, or too salty • Juicy but not greasy • Firm, craggy texture, not rubbery, mushy, or chewy	Johnsonville Stadium Style Beef Franks and Hebrew National Beef Franks
	HOT FUDGE SAUCE **Hershey's Hot Fudge** **Topping**	• True fudge flavor, not weak or overly sweet • Thick, smooth, and buttery texture	
	HOT SAUCE **Huy Fong Sriracha Hot** **Chili Sauce and Frank's** **RedHot Original**	• Right combination of punchy heat, saltiness, sweetness, and garlic • Full, rich flavor • Mild heat that's not too hot	Original Louisiana, Tapatio Salsa Picante
	ICE CREAM BARS **Dove Bar Vanilla Ice Cream** **with Milk Chocolate**	• Rich, prominent chocolate flavor • Thick, crunchy chocolate coating • Dense, creamy, ice cream with pure vanilla flavor • Milk chocolate, not coconut oil, listed first in coating ingredients	Häagen-Dazs Vanilla Milk Chocolate All Natural, Blue Bunny Big Alaska, and Good Humor Milk Chocolate
	ICE CREAM, CHOCOLATE **Ben & Jerry's**	• Deep, concentrated chocolate flavor, not too light or sweet • Dense and creamy texture	Friendly's Rich & Creamy Classic Chocolate Ice Cream
	ICE CREAM, VANILLA **Ben & Jerry's**	• Complex yet balanced vanilla flavor from real vanilla extract • Sweetness solely from sugar, rather than corn syrup • Creamy richness from both egg yolks and small amount of stabilizers	Häagen-Dazs Vanilla
	ICED TEA Loose leaf: **Tazo Iced** **Black Tea**	• Distinctive flavor with herbal notes • Balanced level of strength and astringency	Luzianne and Tetley Premium Blend
	Bottled, with lemon: **Lipton PureLeaf**	• Bright, balanced, and natural tea and lemon flavors • Uses concentrated tea leaves to extract flavor	Gold Peak

	TEST KITCHEN FAVORITE	WHY WE LIKE IT	RUNNERS-UP
	KETCHUP **Heinz Organic**	• Clean, pure sweetness from sugar, not high-fructose corn syrup • Bold, harmonious punch of saltiness, sweetness, tang, and tomato flavor	Hunt's and Simply Heinz
	LEMONADE **Newman's Own Old Fashioned Roadside Virgin**	• Natural-tasting lemon flavor, without artificial flavors or off-notes • Perfect balance of tartness and sweetness, unlike many overly sweet competitors	Florida's Natural and Minute Maid Premium Frozen Concentrated
	MACARONI & CHEESE **Kraft Homestyle Classic Cheddar**	• Reinforces flavor with blue and cheddar cheeses • Uses creamy, clingy liquid cheese sauce • Dry noodles, rather than frozen, for substantial texture and bite • Crunchy, buttery breadcrumb topping	Kraft Velveeta Original
	MAPLE SYRUP **Maple Grove Farms Grade A Dark Amber**	• Clean yet rich maple flavor, not too mild, harsh, or artificial in flavor • Moderate sweetness bests overwhelmingly sugary competitors • Ideal consistency, neither too thin nor too thick like pancake syrups made from corn syrup	Highland Sugarworks Grade B (especially in baking) and Camp Grade A Dark Amber
	MAYONNAISE **Blue Plate Real**	• Great balance of taste and texture • Richer, deeper flavor from using egg yolks alone (no egg whites) • Short ingredient list that's close to homemade NOTE: Hellmann's is known as Best Foods west of the Rockies.	Hellmann's Real, Hellmann's Light, and Spectrum Organic
	MAYONNAISE, LIGHT **Hellmann's Light**	• Bright, balanced flavor close to full-fat counterpart, not overly sweet like other light mayos • Not as creamy as full-fat but passable texture NOTE: Hellmann's is known as Best Foods west of the Rockies.	Hellmann's Canola Cholesterol Free
	MIRIN (JAPANESE RICE WINE) **Eden Mirin Rice Cooking Wine**	• Roasted flavor that is caramel-like and rich • Subtle salty-sweet and balanced flavor	Sushi Chef Mirin Sweetened Sake and Kikkoman Aji-Mirin Sweet Cooking Rice Seasoning

	TEST KITCHEN FAVORITE	WHY WE LIKE IT	RUNNERS-UP
	MOLASSES **Brer Rabbit All Natural Unsulphured Mild Flavor**	• Acidic yet balanced • Strong and straightforward raisin-y taste • Pleasantly bitter bite	Plantation Barbados Unsulphured and Grandma's Molasses Unsulphured Original
	MUSTARD, YELLOW **Annie's Naturals Organic**	• Lists mustard seeds second in the ingredients for rich mustard flavor • Good balance of heat and tang • Relatively low salt content	Gulden's, French's Classic, and Westbrae Natural
	MUSTARD, DIJON **Grey Poupon**	• Potent, bold, and very hot, not weak or mild • Good balance of sweetness, tanginess, and sharpness • Not overly acidic, sweet, or one-dimensional like competitors	Maille Dijon Originale Traditional and Roland Extra Strong
	MUSTARD, WHOLE-GRAIN **Grey Poupon Harvest Coarse Ground**	• Spicy, tangy burst of mustard flavor • High salt content amplifies flavor • Contains no superfluous ingredients that mask mustard flavor • Big, round seeds add pleasant crunch • Just enough vinegar, not too sour or thin	Grey Poupon Country Dijon
	OATS, ROLLED For hot cereal: **Bob's Red Mill Organic Extra Thick**	• Rich oat flavor with nutty, barley, and toasty notes • Creamy, cohesive texture • Plump grains with decent chew	
	For baking: **Quaker Old-Fashioned**	• Plump, almost crunchy texture with a slight chew, not gluey or mushy • Hearty, oaty, and toasty flavor • Subtly sweet with a natural taste	
	OATS, STEEL-CUT **Bob's Red Mill Organic**	• Rich and complex oat flavor with buttery, earthy, nutty, and whole-grain notes • Creamy yet toothsome texture • Moist but not sticky NOTE: Not recommended for baking	Arrowhead Mills Organic Hot Cereal, Country Choice Organic, and Hodgson's Mill Premium
	OLIVE OIL, CALIFORNIA **California Olive Ranch Arbequina**	• Round and full, sweet olive flavor with little bitterness or pungency • Complex with fruity, nutty, and buttery notes and fresh, pure olive aftertaste	Sciabica's Sevillano Variety Fall Harvest

	TEST KITCHEN FAVORITE	WHY WE LIKE IT	RUNNERS-UP
	OLIVE OIL, EXTRA-VIRGIN **Columela**	• Buttery flavor that is sweet and full with a peppery finish • Aromatic and fruity, not bland or bitter • Clean taste, comparable to a fresh-squeezed olive, outshines bland, greasy competitors	Lucini Italia Premium Select and Colavita
	OLIVE OIL, PURE **DaVinci 100% Pure**	• Peppery, fruity flavor, not too bland or mild like some competitors • Grassy and herbaceous notes, not boring or flavorless • Closest to extra-virgin olive oil among samples tasted although significantly more mild	Colavita and Filippo Berio
	ORANGE JUICE **Natalie's Orchid Island** **Juice Company**	• Blend of Hamlin, Pineapple, and Valencia oranges • Fresh, sweet, and fruity flavor without overly acidic, sour, or from-concentrate taste • Gentler pasteurization helps retain fresh-squeezed flavor • Pleasant amount of light pulp	Tropicana Pure Premium 100% Pure and Natural with Some Pulp
	OYSTER CRACKERS **Sunshine Krispy**	• Wheaty, toasty flavor • Flaky, delicate crackers that retain their crispness in soup	Olde Cape Cod All-Natural (also sold as Westminster Crackers)
	PANCAKE MIX **Hungry Jack Buttermilk**	• Flavorful balance of sweetness and tang well-seasoned with sugar and salt • Light, extra fluffy texture • Requires vegetable oil (along with milk and egg) to reconstitute the batter	Aunt Jemima Original
	PAPRIKA **The Spice House Hungarian** **Sweet**	• Complex flavor with earthy, fruity notes • Bright and bold, not bland and boring • Rich, toasty aroma NOTE: Available only through mail order, The Spice House (312-274-0378, TheSpiceHouse.com).	Penzeys Hungary Sweet (available through mail order, Penzeys, 800-741-7787, Penzeys.com)
	PASTA, CHEESE RAVIOLI **Rosetto**	• Creamy, plush, and rich blend of ricotta, Romano, and Parmesan cheeses • Pasta with nice, springy bite • Perfect dough-to-filling ratio	Buitoni Four Cheese and Celentano

	TEST KITCHEN FAVORITE	WHY WE LIKE IT	RUNNERS-UP
	PASTA, CHEESE TORTELLINI **Barilla Three Cheese**	• Robustly flavored filling from combination of ricotta, Emmentaler, and Grana Padano cheeses • Tender pasta that's sturdy enough to withstand boiling but not so thick that it becomes doughy	Seviroli and Buitoni Three Cheese
	PASTA, EGG NOODLES **Light 'n Fluffy Extra Wide**	• Balanced, buttery flavor with no off-flavors • Light and fluffy texture, not gummy or starchy	Black Forest Girl Extra Broad
	PASTA, ELBOW MACARONI **Barilla Elbows**	• Rich, wheaty taste with no off-flavors • Pleasantly hearty texture, not mushy or chewy • Ridged surface and slight twist in shape hold sauce especially well	Mueller's, Ronzoni Smart Taste, and Ronzoni
	PASTA, FRESH **Buitoni Fettuccine**	• Firm but yielding, slightly chewy texture, not too delicate, gummy, or heavy • Faint but discernible egg flavor with no chemical, plasticky, or otherwise unpleasant flavors • Rough, porous surface absorbs sauce better than dried pasta	
	PASTA, LASAGNA NOODLES No-boil: **Barilla**	• Taste and texture of fresh pasta • Delicate, flat noodles	Ronzoni and Pasta DeFino
	Whole-wheat: **Bionaturae Organic 100% Whole Wheat**	• Complex nutty, rich wheat flavor • Substantial chewy texture without any grittiness	DeLallo 100% Organic
	PASTA, PENNE **Mueller's Penne Rigate**	• Hearty texture, not insubstantial or gummy • Wheaty, slightly sweet flavor, not bland	Benedetto Cavalieri Penne Rigate and DeCecco
	PASTA, SPAGHETTI **De Cecco Spaghetti No. 12**	• Rich, nutty, wheaty flavor • Firm, ropy strands with good chew, not mushy, gummy, or mealy	Rustichella D'Abruzzo Pasta Abruzzese di Semola di Grano Duro, Garofalo, and DeLallo Spaghetti No. 4

	TEST KITCHEN FAVORITE	WHY WE LIKE IT	RUNNERS-UP
	PASTA, SPAGHETTI, WHOLE-WHEAT Bionaturae Organic 100% Whole Wheat	• Chewy, firm, and toothsome, not mushy or rubbery • Full and nutty wheat flavor	Barilla PLUS Multigrain
	PASTA SAUCE Bertolli Tomato & Basil	• Fresh-cooked, balanced tomato flavor, not overly sweet • Pleasantly chunky, not too smooth or pasty • Not overseasoned with dry herbs like competitors	Francesco Rinaldi Traditional Marinara, Prego Marinara Italian, and Barilla Marinara
	PASTA SAUCE, PREMIUM Victoria Marinara Sauce	• Nice, bright acidity that speaks of real tomatoes • Robust flavor comparable to homemade	Classico Marinara with Plum Tomatoes and Olive Oil
	PEANUT BUTTER, CREAMY Skippy	• Smooth, creamy, and spreadable • Good balance of sweet and salty flavors	Jif Natural and Reese's
	PEPPERCORNS, BLACK Kalustyan's Indian Tellicherry	• Enticing and fragrant, not musty, aroma with flavor to back it up and moderate heat • Fresh, complex flavor at once sweet and spicy, earthy and smoky, fruity and floral NOTE: Available only by mail order, Kalustyan's (800-352-3451, Kalustyans.com).	Morton & Bassett Organic Whole (widely available)
	PEPPERS, ROASTED RED Dunbars Sweet	• Balance of smokiness and sweetness • Mild, sweet, and earthy red pepper flavor • Firm texture, not slimy or mushy • Packed in simple yet strong brine of salt and water without distraction of other strongly flavored ingredients	Cento
	PEPPERONI Margherita Italian Style	• Nice balance of meatiness and spice • Tangy, fresh flavor with hints of fruity licorice and peppery fennel • Thin slices with the right amount of chew	Boar's Head
	PICKLES, BREAD-AND-BUTTER Bubbies	• Subtle, briny tang • All-natural solution that uses real sugar, not high-fructose corn syrup	

	TEST KITCHEN FAVORITE	WHY WE LIKE IT	RUNNERS-UP
	PICKLES, WHOLE KOSHER DILL **Boar's Head**	• Authentic, garlicky flavor and firm, snappy crunch • Balanced salty, sour, and garlic flavors • Fresh and refrigerated, not processed and shelf-stable	Claussen
	PIZZA, CHEESE, FROZEN **California Pizza Kitchen Crispy Thin Crust Margherita**	• Pleasing combination of flavors and fresh taste with no offensive off-flavors • Low in preservatives as compared to the competition • Chunks of tomato in place of sauce	Tombstone Extra Cheese Original and Amy's
	POPCORN, MICROWAVE **Freshly popped kernels with butter and salt**	• Homemade with a modest amount of butter and salt • Far better clean butter flavor than artificial-tasting prepackaged popcorns	
	PORK, PREMIUM **Snake River Farms American Kurobuta (Berkshire) Pork**	• Deep pink tint, which indicates higher pH level and more flavorful meat • Tender texture and juicy, intensely porky flavor	D'Artagnan Berkshire Pork Chops (Milanese-Style Cut) and Eden Farms French-Cut Kurobuta Pork
	POTATO CHIPS **Lay's Kettle Cooked Original**	• Big potato flavor, no offensive off-flavors • Perfectly salted • Slightly thick chips that aren't too delicate or brittle • Not too greasy	Herr's Crisp 'N Tasty and Utz
	POTATO CHIPS, REDUCED FAT **Cape Cod 40% Reduced Fat**	• Real potato flavor with excellent crunch and texture • Contain only potatoes, canola oil, and salt • With less sodium than many competitors, they have just the right balance of salt	Lay's Kettle Cooked Reduced Fat Extra Crunchy
	PRESERVES, RASPBERRY **Smucker's**	• Clean, strong raspberry flavor, not too tart or sweet • Not overly seedy • Ideal, spreadable texture, not too thick, artificial, or overprocessed	Trappist Red Raspberry Jam
	PRESERVES, STRAWBERRY **Welch's**	• Big, distinct strawberry flavor • Natural-tasting and not overwhelmingly sweet • Thick and spreadable texture, not runny, slimy, or too smooth	Smucker's and Smucker's Simply Fruit Spreadable Fruit
	RELISH, SWEET PICKLE **Cascadian Farm**	• Piquant, sweet flavor, lacks out-of-place flavors such as cinnamon and clove present in competitors • Fresh and natural taste, free of yellow dye #5 and high-fructose corn syrup • Good texture, not mushy like competitors	Heinz Premium

	TEST KITCHEN FAVORITE	WHY WE LIKE IT	RUNNERS-UP
	RICE, ARBORIO **RiceSelect**	• Creamier than competitors • Smooth grains • Characteristic good bite of Arborio rice in risotto where al dente is ideal	Riso Baricella and Rienzi
	RICE, BASMATI **Tilda Pure**	• Very long grains expand greatly with cooking, a result of being aged for a minimum of one year, as required in India • Ideal, fluffy texture, not dry, gummy, or mushy • Nutty taste with no off-flavors • Sweet aroma	Kohinoor Super
	RICE, BROWN **Goya Brown Rice Natural** **Long Grain**	• Firm yet tender grains • Bold, toasty, nutty flavor	Lundberg Organic Long Grain Brown
	RICE, LONG-GRAIN WHITE **Lundberg Organic** **Long Grain White Rice**	• Nutty, buttery, and toasty flavor • Distinct, smooth grains that offer some chew without being overly chewy	Carolina Enriched Extra Long-Grain and Canilla Extra Long-Grain Enriched
	RICE, READY **Minute Ready to Serve** **White Rice**	• Parboiled long-grain white rice that is ready in less than 2 minutes • Toasted, buttery flavor • Firm grains with al dente bite	
	SALSA, HOT **Pace Hot Chunky**	• Good balance of bright tomato, chile, and vegetal flavors • Chunky, almost crunchy texture, not mushy or thin • Spicy and fiery but not overpowering	Newman's Own All Natural Chunky Hot and Herdez Hot Salsa Casera
	SALT **Maldon Sea Salt**	• Light and airy texture • Delicately crunchy flakes • Not so coarse as to be overly crunchy or gritty nor so fine as to disappear	Fleur de Sel de Camargue, Morton Coarse Kosher, and Diamond Crystal Kosher
	SAUSAGE, BREAKFAST **Farmland Fully Cooked** **Pork Links**	• Big pork flavor, not bland or overly spiced • Good balance of saltiness and sweetness with pleasantly lingering spiciness • Tender, super-juicy meat, not rubbery, spongy, or greasy	Farmland Original Pork Links
	SOUP, CANNED CHICKEN **NOODLE** **Muir Glen Organic**	• Organic chicken and vegetables and plenty of seasonings give it a fresh taste and spicy kick • Firm, not mushy, vegetables and noodles • No off-flavors	Progresso Traditional

	TEST KITCHEN FAVORITE	WHY WE LIKE IT	RUNNERS-UP
	SOUP, CANNED TOMATO **Progresso Vegetable** **Classics Hearty Tomato**	• Includes fresh, unprocessed tomatoes, not just tomato puree like some competitors • Tangy, slightly herbaceous flavor • Balanced seasoning and natural sweetness • Medium body and slightly chunky texture	Imagine Organic Vine Ripened
	SOY SAUCE For cooking: **Lee Kum Kee** **Tabletop**	• Pleasantly salty yet sweet with high sodium and sugar content • Depth of flavor balances salty, sweet, roasted, and fruity notes • Aromatic in rice and teriyaki	
	For dipping: **Ohsawa** **Nama Shoyu Organic** **Unpasteurized**	• Lower sodium content allows clean, mellow taste to shine in uncooked applications • Rich and nuanced flavor with sweet, floral, and caramel notes resulting from traditional, slow-brewed production	
	SWEETENED **CONDENSED MILK** **Borden Eagle Brand** **Whole Milk**	• Made with whole milk; creamier in desserts and balances more assertive notes from other ingredients	Nestlé Carnation and Parrot
	TARTAR SAUCE **Legal Sea Foods**	• Creamy, nicely balanced sweet/tart base • Lots of vegetable chunks	McCormick Original
	TEA, BLACK For plain tea: **Twinings** **English Breakfast**	• Bright, bold, and flavorful yet not too strong • Fruity, floral, and fragrant • Smooth, slightly astringent profile preferred for tea without milk	PG Tips
	For tea with milk: **Tazo Awake**	• Clean, strong taste • Smoky and fruity with notes of clove, cinnamon, and vanilla • Aromatic but not overwhelming • Good balance of flavor and intensity • More astringent profile stands up to milk	Tetley Specialty English Breakfast
	TERIYAKI SAUCE **Annie Chun's All Natural**	• Distinct teriyaki flavor without offensive or dominant flavors, unlike competitors • Smooth, rich texture, not too watery or gluey	

	TEST KITCHEN FAVORITE	WHY WE LIKE IT	RUNNERS-UP
	TOMATOES, CANNED CRUSHED **Tuttorosso in Thick Puree with Basil**	• Chunky texture, not pasty, mushy, or watery • Bright, fresh tomato taste • Balance of saltiness, sweetness, and acidity NOTE: Available only in New England, Mid-Atlantic region, and Florida.	Muir Glen Organic with Basil and Hunt's Organic
	TOMATOES, CANNED DICED **Hunt's**	• Bright, fresh tomato flavor that balances sweet and tart • Firm yet tender texture	Muir Glen Organic
	TOMATOES, CANNED PUREED **Hunt's Tomato Puree**	• Full tomato flavor without any bitter, sour, or tinny notes • Pleasantly thick, even consistency, not watery or thin	Progresso, Cento, and Muir Glen Organic
	TOMATOES, CANNED WHOLE **Muir Glen Organic**	• Pleasing balance of bold acidity and fruity sweetness • Firm yet tender texture, even after hours of simmering	Hunt's
	TOMATO PASTE **Goya**	• Bright, robust tomato flavors • Balance of sweet and tart flavors	Pastene and Contadina
	TORTILLA CHIPS **Santitas Authentic Mexican Style White Corn**	• Mild and pleasantly salty flavor, not bland, artificial, or rancid • Sturdy yet crunchy and crisp texture, not brittle, stale, or cardboardlike	Tostitos 100% White Corn Restaurant Style, Green Mountain Gringo All Natural, and Tostitos Natural Yellow Corn Restaurant Style
	TORTILLAS, FLOUR **Tyson Mexican Original**	• Thin and flaky texture, not doughy or stale • Mild, pleasantly wheaty flavor without sour taste or off-flavors NOTE: Available only in the Northeast.	Mission
	TOSTADAS, CORN **Mission Tostadas Estilo Casero**	• Crisp, crunchy texture • Good corn flavor • Flavor and texture that are substantial enough to stand up to hearty toppings	Charras

	TEST KITCHEN FAVORITE	WHY WE LIKE IT	RUNNERS-UP
	TUNA, CANNED **Wild Planet Wild Albacore**	• Rich, fresh-tasting, and flavorful, but not fishy • Hearty, substantial chunks of tuna	American Tuna Pole Caught Wild Albacore and Starkist Selects Solid White Albacore
	TUNA, CANNED PREMIUM **Nardin Bonito Del Norte Ventresca Fillets**	• Creamy, delicate meat and tender yet firm fillets • Full, rich tuna flavor	Tonnino Tuna Ventresca Yellowfin in Olive Oil
	TURKEY, WHOLE **Empire Kosher**	• Moist and dense texture without being watery, chewy, or squishy • Meaty, full turkey flavor • Buttery white meat • Koshering process renders brining unnecessary	Good Shepherd Ranch Heritage (available through mail order, Good Shepherd Turkey Ranch Inc., 785-227-5149, ReeseTurkeys.net)
	VANILLA BEANS **McCormick Madagascar**	• Moist, seed-filled pods • Complex, robust flavor with caramel notes	Spice Islands Bourbon
	VANILLA EXTRACT **McCormick Pure**	• Strong, rich vanilla flavor where others are weak and sharp • Complex flavor with spicy, caramel notes and a sweet undertone	Rodelle Pure and Gold Medal Imitation by C.F. Sauer Co.
	VEGETABLE OIL **Crisco Natural Blend Oil**	• Unobtrusive, mild flavor for stir-frying and sautéing and for use in baked goods and in uncooked applications such as mayonnaise and vinaigrette • Neutral taste and absence of fishy or metallic flavors when used for frying	Mazola Canola Oil
	VINEGAR, APPLE CIDER **Spectrum Naturals Organic Unfiltered**	• Good balance of sweet and tart • Distinct apple flavor with a floral aroma and assertive, tangy qualities	Maille
	VINEGAR, BALSAMIC **Lucini Gran Riserva Balsamico**	• Sweet, nuanced flavor lacking any harshness or astringency • Smooth and thick like traditional balsamic, not too thin or light • Balance of tanginess and sweetness with complexity and a slight acidic zing	Monari Federzoni of Modena and Ortalli of Modena

	TEST KITCHEN FAVORITE	WHY WE LIKE IT	RUNNERS-UP
	VINEGAR, RED WINE **Laurent Du Clos**	• Crisp red wine flavor balanced by stronger than average acidity and subtle sweetness • Complex yet pleasing taste from multiple varieties of grapes	Pompeian Gourmet and Spectrum Naturals Organic
	VINEGAR, WHITE WINE For cooking: **Colavita Aged**	• Balance of tanginess and subtle sweetness, not overly acidic or weak • Fruity, bright, and perfumed	
	For vinaigrettes: **Spectrum Naturals Organic**	• Rich, dark flavor tastes fermented and malty, not artificial or harsh • Fruity flavor with caramel, earthy, and nutty notes	
	YEAST **SAF-Instant**	• Steady, predictable rise • Clean, clear aroma and flavor, not heady, strong, or otherwise off-tasting • Perfect crumb in yeasted coffee cake, airy crumb and crisp crust in baguettes	Red Star, Fermipan Instant, and Fleischmann's
	YOGURT, GREEK NONFAT **Olympus Traditional Greek Nonfat Yogurt Strained, Plain**	• Smooth, creamy consistency, not watery or puddinglike from added thickeners, such as pectin or gelatin • Pleasantly tangy, well-balanced flavor, not sour or metallic	Voskos Greek Plain Nonfat, Brown Cow Plain Greek 0% Fat, and Dannon Greek Plain 0% Fat
	YOGURT, GREEK FULL-FAT **Olympus Traditional Greek Yogurt Strained, Plain 10% Fat**	• Rich taste and satiny texture, not thin, watery, or soupy • Buttery, tangy flavor	Greek Gods Traditional Plain and Fage Total
	YOGURT, LOW-FAT STRAWBERRY **Dannon Fruit on the Bottom**	• Good strawberry flavor, not too sweet, sour, or bland • Pleasantly thick, not watery or runny • No artificial, plasticky, or otherwise unwelcome flavors as in many competitors	Wallaby Organic Creamy Australian-Style and Fage 2% All Natural Greek Strained
	YOGURT, WHOLE-MILK **Brown Cow Cream Top Plain**	• Rich, well-rounded flavor, not sour or bland • Especially creamy, smooth texture, not thin or watery • Higher fat content contributes to flavor and texture	Stonyfield Farm Organic Plain

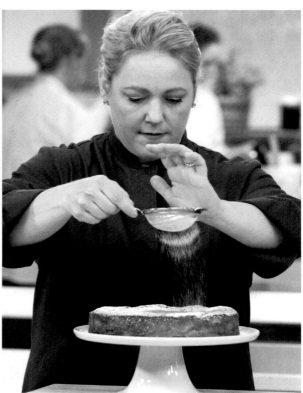

2013 EPISODE DIRECTORY

EPISODE ONE
Big, Bold Chicken Braises
Chicken Marbella   773
Filipino Chicken Adobo   771

EPISODE TWO
Rethinking Seafood Classics
Best Crab Cakes   788
Grill-Smoked Salmon   790

EPISODE THREE
Great Italian Pasta Sauces
Pasta all'Amatriciana   766
Quick Mushroom Ragu   766

EPISODE FOUR
Chicken Classics, Improved
Skillet Chicken Fajitas   770
Classic Chicken Salad   758

EPISODE FIVE
Irish Comfort Classics
Shepherd's Pie   781
Corned Beef and Cabbage   781

EPISODE SIX
Simple and Satisfying Vegetable Mains
Mushroom and Leek Galette   792
Farmhouse Vegetable and Barley Soup   759

EPISODE SEVEN
Meat and Potatoes à la Française
Pot-Roasted Pork Loin   784
Potato Casserole with Bacon and Caramelized Onion   785

EPISODE EIGHT
Company's Coming
Best Prime Rib   778
Roasted Brussels Sprouts   794

EPISODE NINE
Chili and Stew Go Vegetarian
Best Vegetarian Chili   762
Italian Vegetable Stew   760

EPISODE TEN
Pork Chops and Lentil Salad
Red Wine–Braised Pork Chops   784
Lentil Salads   758

EPISODE ELEVEN
Two Ways with Fish
Poached Fish Fillets   789
Easy Salmon Cakes   789

EPISODE TWELVE
Indian Classics Made Easy
Indian Flatbread (Naan)   801
Indian-Style Spinach with Fresh Cheese (Saag Paneer)   793

EPISODE THIRTEEN
Asian Takeout Favorites
Sichuan Stir-Fried Pork in Garlic Sauce   787
Thai-Style Stir-Fried Noodles with Chicken and Broccolini   768

EPISODE FOURTEEN
A Taste of Spain
Catalan-Style Beef Stew with Mushrooms   761
Spanish-Style Toasted Pasta with Shrimp   767

EPISODE FIFTEEN
Ultimate Italian
Fresh Pasta Without a Machine   763
Ragu alla Bolognese   765

EPISODE SIXTEEN
Skewered and Wrapped
Grilled Beef Satay   776
Chinese Chicken Lettuce Wraps   769

EPISODE SEVENTEEN
Turkey on the Grill
Simple Grill-Roasted Turkey   775
Cranberry Chutney with Apples and Crystallized Ginger   795

EPISODE EIGHTEEN
Perfecting Summer Classics
Spice-Rubbed Grilled Steak   777
Raspberry Sorbet   807

EPISODE NINETEEN
Short Ribs and Chops Hit the Grill
Grilled Beef Short Ribs   779
Grilled Boneless Pork Chops   782

EPISODE TWENTY
Grilled Turkey Burgers and Buns
Juicy Grilled Turkey Burgers   773
Potato Burger Buns   800

EPISODE TWENTY-ONE
Spicing Up the Grill
Spicy Pork Tacos (al Pastor)   786
Jerk Chicken   772

EPISODE TWENTY-TWO
Breakfast Standbys
Ten-Minute Steel-Cut Oatmeal   797
Home Fries   795

EPISODE TWENTY-THREE
Sunday Brunch
Cinnamon Swirl Bread   799
Baked Eggs Florentine   796

EPISODE TWENTY-FOUR
Spicy Fall Sweets
Pumpkin Bread   798
Gingersnaps   803

EPISODE TWENTY-FIVE
Great American Classics
Carrot Layer Cake   805
Peanut Butter Sandwich Cookies   802

EPISODE TWENTY-SIX
French Sweets, Refined and Rustic
Chocolate Truffles   806
French Apple Cake   804

CLASSIC CHICKEN SALAD

WHY THIS RECIPE WORKS: Recipes for chicken salad are only as good as the chicken itself. If the chicken is dry or flavorless, no amount of dressing or add-ins will camouflage it. To ensure silky, juicy, and flavorful chicken, we used a method based on *sous vide* cooking (submerging vacuum-sealed foods in a temperature-controlled water bath.) Our ideal formula was four chicken breasts and 6 cups of cold water heated to 170 degrees and then removed from the heat, covered, and left to stand for about 15 minutes. This yielded incomparably moist chicken that was perfect for chicken salad.

Classic Chicken Salad

SERVES 4 TO 6

To ensure that the chicken cooks through, don't use breasts that weigh more than 8 ounces or are thicker than 1 inch. Make sure to start with cold water in step 1. We like the combination of parsley and tarragon, but 2 table-spoons of one or the other is fine. This salad can be served in a sandwich or spooned over leafy greens.

    Salt and pepper
4 **(6- to 8-ounce) boneless, skinless chicken breasts, no more than 1 inch thick, trimmed**
½ **cup mayonnaise**
2 **tablespoons lemon juice**
1 **teaspoon Dijon mustard**
2 **celery ribs, minced**
1 **shallot, minced**
1 **tablespoon minced fresh parsley**
1 **tablespoon minced fresh tarragon**

1. Dissolve 2 tablespoons salt in 6 cups cold water in Dutch oven. Submerge chicken in water. Heat pot over medium heat until water registers 170 degrees. Turn off heat, cover pot, and let stand until chicken registers 165 degrees, 15 to 17 minutes.

2. Transfer chicken to paper towel–lined baking sheet. Refrigerate until chicken is cool, about 30 minutes. While chicken cools, whisk mayonnaise, lemon juice, mustard, and ¼ teaspoon pepper together in large bowl.

3. Pat chicken dry with paper towels and cut into ½-inch pieces. Transfer chicken to bowl with mayonnaise mixture. Add celery, shallot, parsley, and tarragon; toss to combine. Season with salt and pepper to taste. Serve. (Salad can be refrigerated for up to 2 days.)

Curried Chicken Salad with Cashews

Microwave 1 teaspoon vegetable oil, 1 teaspoon curry powder, and ⅛ teaspoon cayenne pepper together, uncovered, until oil is hot, about 30 seconds. Add curry oil to mayonnaise and substitute lime juice for lemon juice and 1 teaspoon grated fresh ginger for mustard in step 2. Substitute 2 tablespoons minced fresh cilantro for parsley and tarragon, and add ½ cup coarsely chopped toasted cashews and ⅓ cup golden raisins to salad with celery.

Waldorf Chicken Salad

Add ½ teaspoon ground fennel seeds to mayonnaise mixture in step 2. Substitute 1 teaspoon minced fresh thyme for parsley and add 1 peeled Granny Smith apple, cut into ¼-inch pieces, and ½ cup coarsely chopped toasted walnuts to salad with celery.

Chicken Salad with Red Grapes and Smoked Almonds

Add ¼ teaspoon grated lemon zest to mayonnaise mixture in step 2. Substitute 1 teaspoon minced fresh rosemary for tarragon, and add 1 cup quartered red grapes and ½ cup coarsely chopped smoked almonds to salad with celery.

LENTIL SALADS

WHY THIS RECIPE WORKS: The most important step in making a lentil salad is perfecting the cooking of the lentils so they maintain their shape and firm-tender bite. It turns out there are two key steps. The first is to brine the lentils in warm salt water. With brining, the lentils' skins soften, which leads to fewer blowouts. The second step is to cook the lentils in the oven, which heats them gently and uniformly. Once we had perfectly cooked lentils, all we had left to do was to pair the earthy beans with a tart vinaigrette and boldly flavored mix-ins.

Lentil Salad with Olives, Mint, and Feta

SERVES 4 TO 6

French green lentils, or *lentilles du Puy,* are our preferred choice for this recipe, but it works with any type of lentil except red or yellow. Brining helps keep the lentils intact, but if you don't have time, they'll still taste good without it. The salad can be served warm or at room temperature.

1 cup lentils, picked over and rinsed
  Salt and pepper
6 cups water
2 cups low-sodium chicken broth
5 garlic cloves, lightly crushed and peeled
1 bay leaf
5 tablespoons extra-virgin olive oil
3 tablespoons white wine vinegar
½ cup pitted kalamata olives, chopped coarse
½ cup minced fresh mint
1 large shallot, minced
1 ounce feta cheese, crumbled (¼ cup)

1. Place lentils and 1 teaspoon salt in bowl. Cover with 4 cups warm water (about 110 degrees) and soak for 1 hour. Drain well. (Drained lentils can be refrigerated for up to 2 days before cooking.)

2. Adjust oven rack to middle position and heat oven to 325 degrees. Combine drained lentils, 2 cups water, broth, garlic, bay leaf, and ½ teaspoon salt in ovenproof medium saucepan. Cover and bake until lentils are tender but remain intact, 40 minutes to 1 hour. Meanwhile, whisk oil and vinegar together in large bowl.

3. Drain lentils well; remove and discard garlic and bay leaf. Add drained lentils, olives, mint, and shallot to dressing and toss to combine. Season with salt and pepper to taste. Transfer to serving dish, sprinkle with feta, and serve.

Lentil Salad with Spinach, Walnuts, and Parmesan Cheese

Substitute sherry vinegar for white wine vinegar. Place 4 ounces baby spinach and 2 tablespoons water in bowl. Cover and microwave until spinach is wilted and volume is halved, 3 to 4 minutes. Remove bowl from microwave and keep covered for 1 minute. Transfer spinach to colander; gently press to release liquid. Transfer spinach to cutting board and chop coarse. Return to colander and press again. Substitute chopped spinach for olives and mint and ¾ cup coarsely grated Parmesan cheese for feta. Sprinkle with ⅓ cup coarsely chopped toasted walnuts before serving.

Lentil Salad with Hazelnuts and Goat Cheese

Substitute red wine vinegar for white wine vinegar and add 2 teaspoons Dijon mustard to dressing in step 2. Omit olives and substitute ¼ cup chopped parsley for mint. Substitute ½ cup crumbled goat cheese for feta and sprinkle with ⅓ cup coarsely chopped toasted hazelnuts before serving.

Lentil Salad with Carrots and Cilantro

Substitute lemon juice for white wine vinegar. Toss 2 carrots, peeled and cut into 2-inch-long matchsticks, with 1 teaspoon ground cumin, ½ teaspoon ground cinnamon, and ⅛ teaspoon cayenne pepper in bowl. Cover and microwave until carrots are tender but still crisp, 2 to 4 minutes. Substitute carrots for olives and ¼ cup minced fresh cilantro for mint. Omit shallot and feta.

FARMHOUSE VEGETABLE AND BARLEY SOUP

WHY THIS RECIPE WORKS: Most recipes for hearty winter vegetable soups, it turns out, are neither quick nor easy. For a satisfying soup that doesn't take the better part of a day to make, we started with canned vegetable broth. To this we added soy sauce and ground dried porcini mushrooms. These ingredients added a savory, almost meaty flavor to the soup base. To make the soup more filling, we added barley to the hearty combination of carrots, potatoes, leeks, cabbage, and turnips.

Farmhouse Vegetable and Barley Soup
SERVES 6 TO 8

We prefer an acidic, unoaked white wine such as Sauvignon Blanc for this recipe. We love the richness added by the Lemon-Thyme Butter and the crunch of Herbed Croutons (recipes follow) but the soup can also be garnished with crisp bacon or crumbled cheddar cheese. You will need at least a 6-quart Dutch oven for this recipe.

⅛ ounce dried porcini mushrooms, rinsed
8 sprigs fresh parsley plus 3 tablespoons minced
4 sprigs fresh thyme
1 bay leaf
2 tablespoons unsalted butter
1½ pounds leeks, white and light green parts sliced ½ inch thick and washed thoroughly
2 carrots, peeled and cut into ½-inch pieces
2 celery ribs, cut into ¼-inch pieces
⅓ cup dry white wine
2 teaspoons soy sauce
  Salt and pepper
6 cups water
4 cups low-sodium chicken broth or vegetable broth
½ cup pearl barley
1 garlic clove, peeled and smashed

1½ **pounds Yukon Gold potatoes, peeled and cut into**
½-inch pieces
1 **turnip, peeled and cut into ¾-inch pieces**
1½ **cups chopped green cabbage**
1 **cup frozen peas**
1 **teaspoon lemon juice**

1. Grind porcini with spice grinder until they resemble fine meal, 10 to 30 seconds. Measure out 2 teaspoons porcini powder; reserve remainder for another use. Using kitchen twine, tie together parsley sprigs, thyme sprigs, and bay leaf.

2. Melt butter in large Dutch oven over medium heat. Add leeks, carrots, celery, wine, soy sauce, and 2 teaspoons salt. Cook, stirring occasionally, until liquid has evaporated and celery is softened, about 10 minutes.

3. Add water, chicken broth, barley, porcini powder, herb bundle, and garlic; increase heat to high and bring to boil. Reduce heat to medium-low and simmer, partially covered, for 25 minutes.

4. Add potatoes, turnip, and cabbage; return to simmer and cook until barley, potatoes, turnip, and cabbage are tender, 18 to 20 minutes.

5. Remove pot from heat and remove herb bundle. Stir in peas, lemon juice, and minced parsley; season with salt and pepper to taste. Serve, passing Lemon-Thyme Butter separately.

Lemon-Thyme Butter

MAKES 6 TABLESPOONS

6 **tablespoons unsalted butter, softened**
1 **tablespoon minced fresh thyme**
¾ **teaspoon finely grated lemon zest plus ¼ teaspoon juice**
 Pinch salt

Combine all ingredients in bowl.

Herbed Croutons

MAKES ABOUT 2½ CUPS

Our favorite brand of sandwich bread is Arnold Country Classic White Bread.

1 **tablespoon unsalted butter**
1 **teaspoon minced fresh parsley**
½ **teaspoon minced fresh thyme**
4 **slices hearty white sandwich bread, cut into ½-inch pieces**
 Salt and pepper

Melt butter in 10-inch skillet over medium heat. Add parsley and thyme; cook, stirring constantly, for 20 seconds. Add bread and cook, stirring frequently, until light golden brown, 5 to 10 minutes. Season with salt and pepper to taste.

ITALIAN VEGETABLE STEW

WHY THIS RECIPE WORKS: Italy's *ciambotta* is a ratatouille-like stew chock-full of veggies that makes for a hearty one-bowl meal with nary a trace of meat. We wanted to avoid the sad fate of most recipes, which end in mushy vegetables drowning in a weak broth. In order to optimize the texture of the zucchini and peppers, we employed the dry heat of a skillet. To address the broth, we embraced eggplant's natural tendency to fall apart and cooked it until it completely assimilated into a thickened tomato-enriched sauce. Finally, we found that a traditional *pestata* of garlic and herbs provided the biggest flavor punch when added near the end of cooking.

Italian Vegetable Stew (Ciambotta)

SERVES 6 TO 8

Serve this hearty vegetable stew with crusty bread.

PESTATA
⅓ **cup chopped fresh basil**
⅓ **cup fresh oregano leaves**
6 **garlic cloves, minced**
2 **tablespoons extra-virgin olive oil**
¼ **teaspoon red pepper flakes**

STEW
12 **ounces eggplant, peeled and cut into ½-inch pieces**
 Salt
¼ **cup extra-virgin olive oil**
1 **large onion, chopped**
1 **pound russet potatoes, peeled and cut into ½-inch pieces**
2 **tablespoons tomato paste**
2¼ **cups water**
1 **(28-ounce) can whole peeled tomatoes, drained with juice reserved, chopped coarse**
2 **zucchini (8 ounces each), halved lengthwise, seeded, and cut into ½-inch pieces**
2 **red or yellow bell peppers, stemmed, seeded, and cut into ½-inch pieces**
1 **cup shredded fresh basil**

1. FOR THE PESTATA: Process all ingredients in food processor until finely ground, about 1 minute, scraping down sides as needed. Set aside.

2. FOR THE STEW: Toss eggplant with 1½ teaspoons salt in bowl. Line surface of large plate with double layer of coffee filters and lightly spray with vegetable oil spray. Spread eggplant in even layer over coffee filters. Microwave eggplant, uncovered, until dry to touch and slightly shriveled, 8 to 12 minutes, tossing once halfway through to ensure that eggplant cooks evenly.

3. Heat 2 tablespoons oil in Dutch oven over high heat until shimmering. Add eggplant, onion, and potatoes; cook, stirring frequently, until eggplant browns and surface of potatoes becomes translucent, about 2 minutes. Push vegetables to sides of pot; add 1 tablespoon oil and tomato paste to clearing. Cook paste, stirring frequently, until brown fond develops on bottom of pot, about 2 minutes. Add 2 cups water and chopped tomatoes and juice, scraping up any browned bits, and bring to boil. Reduce heat to medium, cover, and gently simmer until eggplant is completely broken down and potatoes are tender, 20 to 25 minutes.

4. Meanwhile, heat remaining 1 tablespoon oil in 12-inch skillet over high heat until smoking. Add zucchini, bell peppers, and ½ teaspoon salt; cook, stirring occasionally, until vegetables are browned and tender, 10 to 12 minutes. Push vegetables to sides of skillet; add pestata and cook until fragrant, about 1 minute. Stir pestata into vegetables and transfer vegetables to bowl. Add remaining ¼ cup water to skillet off heat, scraping up browned bits.

5. Remove Dutch oven from heat and stir reserved vegetables and water from skillet into vegetables in Dutch oven. Cover pot and let stand for 20 minutes to allow flavors to meld. Stir in basil and season with salt to taste; serve.

CATALAN-STYLE BEEF STEW

WHY THIS RECIPE WORKS: Supremely meaty and complexly flavored, Spanish beef stew is a little different than its American counterpart. It starts with a *sofrito,* a slow-cooked jamlike mixture of onions, spices, and herbs that builds a flavor-packed base. We normally use chuck eye for stew, but swapped it out for boneless beef short ribs, feeling that they gave us a beefier-tasting stew. We finished the stew with a mixture of toasted bread, toasted almonds, garlic, and parsley. This mixture, called a *picada,* brightened the stew's flavor and thickened the broth.

Catalan-Style Beef Stew with Mushrooms
SERVES 4 TO 6

While we developed this recipe with Albariño, a dry Spanish white wine, you can also use a Sauvignon Blanc. Remove the woody base of the oyster mushroom stems before cooking. An equal amount of quartered button mushrooms may be substituted for the oyster mushrooms. Serve the stew with boiled or mashed potatoes or rice.

STEW
- 2   tablespoons olive oil
- 2   large onions, chopped fine
- ½   teaspoon sugar
-     Kosher salt and pepper
- 2   plum tomatoes, halved lengthwise, pulp grated on large holes of box grater, and skins discarded
- 1   teaspoon smoked paprika
- 1   bay leaf
- 1½ cups dry white wine
- 1½ cups water
- 1   large sprig fresh thyme
- ¼   teaspoon ground cinnamon
- 2½ pounds boneless beef short ribs, trimmed and cut into 2-inch cubes

PICADA
- ¼   cup whole blanched almonds
- 2   tablespoons olive oil
- 1   slice hearty white sandwich bread, crusts removed, torn into 1-inch pieces
- 2   garlic cloves, peeled
- 3   tablespoons minced fresh parsley

- 8   ounces oyster mushrooms, trimmed
- 1   teaspoon sherry vinegar

1. FOR THE STEW: Adjust oven rack to middle position and heat oven to 300 degrees. Heat oil in Dutch oven over medium-low heat until shimmering. Add onions, sugar, and ½ teaspoon salt; cook, stirring often, until onions are deeply caramelized, 30 to 40 minutes. Add tomatoes, smoked paprika, and bay leaf; cook, stirring often, until darkened and thick, 5 to 10 minutes.

2. Add wine, water, thyme, and cinnamon to pot, scraping up any browned bits. Season beef with 1½ teaspoons salt and ½ teaspoon pepper and add to pot. Increase heat to high and bring to simmer. Transfer to oven and cook, uncovered. After 1 hour stir stew to redistribute meat, return to oven, and continue to cook, uncovered, until meat is tender, 1½ to 2 hours longer.

3. FOR THE PICADA: While stew is in oven, heat almonds and 1 tablespoon oil in 10-inch skillet over medium heat; cook, stirring often, until almonds are golden brown, 3 to 6 minutes. Using slotted spoon, transfer almonds to food processor. Return now-empty skillet to medium heat, add bread, and cook, stirring often, until toasted, 2 to 4 minutes; transfer to food processor with almonds. Add garlic and process until mixture is finely ground, about 20 seconds, scraping down bowl as needed. Transfer mixture to bowl, stir in parsley, and set aside.

4. Return again-empty skillet to medium heat. Heat remaining 1 tablespoon oil until shimmering. Add mushrooms and ½ teaspoon salt; cook, stirring often, until tender, 5 to 7 minutes. Transfer to bowl and set aside.

5. Remove bay leaf and thyme sprig. Stir picada, mushrooms, and vinegar into stew. Season with salt and pepper to taste and serve.

BEST VEGETARIAN CHILI

WHY THIS RECIPE WORKS: Vegetarian chilis are often little more than a mishmash of beans and vegetables. In order to create a robust, complex-flavored chili—not just a bean and vegetable stew—we found replacements for the different ways in which meat adds depth and savory flavor to chili. Walnuts, soy sauce, dried shiitake mushrooms, and tomatoes add hearty savoriness. Bulgur fills out the chili, giving it a substantial texture. The added oil and nuts lend a richness to the chili, for full, lingering flavor.

Best Vegetarian Chili
SERVES 6 TO 8

We prefer to make this chili with whole dried chiles, but it can be prepared with jarred chili powder. If using chili powder, grind the shiitakes and oregano and add them to the pot with ¼ cup of chili powder in step 4. Pinto, black, red kidney, small red, cannellini, or navy beans can be used in this recipe, either a single variety or a combination of beans. For a spicier chili use both jalapeños. Serve the chili with diced avocado, chopped red onion, lime wedges, sour cream, and shredded Monterey Jack or cheddar cheese. You will need at least a 6-quart Dutch oven for this recipe.

Salt
1 pound (2½ cups) dried beans, rinsed and picked over
2 dried ancho chiles
2 dried New Mexican chiles
½ ounce shiitake mushrooms, chopped coarse
4 teaspoons dried oregano
½ cup walnuts, toasted
1 (28-ounce) can diced tomatoes, drained with juice reserved
3 tablespoons tomato paste
1-2 jalapeño chiles, stemmed and chopped coarse
6 garlic cloves, minced
3 tablespoons soy sauce
¼ cup vegetable oil
2 pounds onions, chopped fine
1 tablespoon ground cumin
7 cups water
⅔ cup medium-grain bulgur
¼ cup chopped fresh cilantro

1. Bring 4 quarts water, 3 tablespoons salt, and beans to boil in Dutch oven over high heat. Remove pot from heat, cover, and let stand 1 hour. Drain beans and rinse well.

2. Adjust oven rack to middle position and heat oven to 300 degrees. Arrange ancho and New Mexican chiles on rimmed baking sheet and toast until fragrant and puffed, about 8 minutes. Transfer to plate and let cool, about 5 minutes. Stem and seed toasted chiles. Working in batches, grind toasted chiles, shiitakes, and oregano in spice grinder or with mortar with pestle until finely ground.

3. Process walnuts in food processor until finely ground, about 30 seconds. Transfer to bowl. Process drained tomatoes, tomato paste, jalapeño(s), garlic, and soy sauce in food processor until tomatoes are finely chopped, about 45 seconds, scraping down bowl as needed.

4. Heat oil in Dutch oven over medium-high heat until shimmering. Add onions and 1¼ teaspoons salt; cook, stirring occasionally until onions begin to brown, 8 to 10 minutes. Lower heat to medium, add ground chile mixture and cumin, and cook, stirring constantly, until fragrant, about 1 minute. Add rinsed beans and water and bring to boil. Cover pot, transfer to oven, and cook 45 minutes.

5. Remove pot from oven. Stir in bulgur, ground walnuts, tomato mixture and reserved tomato juice. Return to oven and cook until beans are fully tender, about 2 hours.

6. Remove pot from oven, stir chili well, and let stand, uncovered, for 20 minutes. Stir in cilantro and serve. (Chili can be made up to 3 days in advance.)

FRESH PASTA

WHY THIS RECIPE WORKS: Not everyone has a pasta machine and rolling out pasta dough by hand is no easy task. For an easy-to-roll pasta dough (that would still cook up into delicate, springy noodles), we added six extra egg yolks and a couple tablespoons of olive oil to our dough. In addition, we incorporated an extended resting period to allow the gluten network to relax. To roll and cut the pasta, we first divided the pasta into smaller manageable pieces, then used a rolling pin to roll the dough and a sharp knife to cut the dough into noodles.

Fresh Pasta without a Machine

MAKES 1 POUND; SERVES 4 TO 6

If using a high-protein all-purpose flour like King Arthur brand, increase the number of egg yolks to 7. The longer the dough rests in step 2, the easier it will be to roll out. When rolling out the dough, avoid adding too much flour, which may result in excessive snapback.

- 2 **cups (10 ounces) all-purpose flour**
- 2 **large eggs plus 6 large yolks**
- 2 **tablespoons olive oil**
- 1 **tablespoon salt**
- 1 **recipe sauce (recipes follow)**

1. Process flour, eggs and yolks, and oil together in food processor until mixture forms cohesive dough that feels soft and is barely tacky to touch, about 45 seconds. (If dough sticks to fingers, add up to ¼ cup flour, 1 tablespoon at a time, until barely tacky. If dough doesn't become cohesive, add up to 1 tablespoon water, 1 teaspoon at a time, until it just comes together; process 30 seconds longer.)

2. Turn dough ball out onto dry counter and knead until smooth, 1 to 2 minutes. Shape dough into 6-inch-long cylinder. Wrap with plastic wrap and set aside at room temperature to rest for at least 1 hour or up to 4 hours.

3. Cut cylinder crosswise into 6 equal pieces. Working with 1 piece of dough (rewrap remaining dough), dust both sides with flour, place cut side down on clean counter, and press into 3-inch square. Using heavy rolling pin, roll into 6-inch square. Dust both sides of dough lightly with flour. Starting at center of square, roll dough away from you in 1 motion. Return rolling pin to center of dough and roll toward you in 1 motion. Repeat steps of rolling until dough sticks to counter and measures roughly 12 inches long. Lightly dust both sides of dough with flour and continue rolling dough until it measures roughly 20 inches long and 6 inches wide, frequently lifting dough to release it from counter. (You should be able to easily see outline of your fingers through dough.) If dough firmly sticks to counter and wrinkles when rolled out, dust dough lightly with flour.

4. Transfer pasta sheet to clean dish towel and let stand, uncovered, until firm around edges, about 15 minutes; meanwhile, roll out remaining dough. Starting with 1 short end, gently fold pasta sheet at 2-inch intervals until sheet has been folded into flat, rectangular roll. With sharp chef's knife, slice crosswise into ³⁄₁₆-inch-wide noodles. Use fingers to unfurl pasta and transfer to baking sheet. Repeat folding and cutting remaining sheets of dough. Cook noodles within 1 hour.

5. Bring 4 quarts water to boil in large pot. Add pasta and salt and cook, stirring often, until al dente, about 3 minutes. Reserve 1 cup cooking water, then drain pasta. Toss with sauce; serve immediately.

TO MAKE AHEAD: Follow recipe through step 4, transfer baking sheet of pasta to freezer, and freeze until pasta is firm. Transfer to zipper-lock bag and store for up to 2 weeks. Cook frozen pasta straight from freezer as directed in step 5.

Tomato and Browned Butter Sauce

MAKES 3 CUPS; ENOUGH FOR 1 POUND PASTA

- 1 **(28-ounce) can whole peeled tomatoes**
- 4 **tablespoons unsalted butter, cut into 4 pieces**
- 2 **garlic cloves, minced**
- ½ **teaspoon sugar**
  Salt and pepper
- 2 **teaspoons sherry vinegar**
- 3 **tablespoons chopped fresh basil**
  Grated Parmesan cheese

1. Process tomatoes and their juice in food processor until smooth, about 30 seconds. Melt 3 tablespoons butter in 12-inch skillet over medium-high heat, swirling occasionally, until butter is dark brown and releases nutty aroma, about 1½ minutes. Stir in garlic and cook for 10 seconds. Stir in processed tomatoes, sugar, and ½ teaspoon salt and simmer until sauce is slightly reduced, about 8 minutes. Remove pan from heat; whisk in remaining 1 tablespoon butter and vinegar. Season with salt and pepper to taste; cover to keep warm.

2. To serve, return pan to medium heat. Add pasta, ¼ cup reserved cooking water, and basil; toss to combine.

Season with salt and pepper to taste and add remaining cooking water as needed to adjust consistency. Serve immediately, passing Parmesan separately.

Walnut Cream Sauce

MAKES 2 CUPS; ENOUGH FOR 1 POUND PASTA

- 1½ **cups (6 ounces) walnuts, toasted**
- ¾ **cup dry white wine**
- ½ **cup heavy cream**
- 1 **ounce Parmesan cheese, grated (½ cup)**
     Salt and pepper
- ¼ **cup minced fresh chives**

1. Process 1 cup walnuts in food processor until finely ground, about 10 seconds. Transfer to small bowl. Pulse remaining ½ cup walnuts in food processor until coarsely chopped, 3 to 5 pulses. Bring wine to simmer in 12-inch skillet over medium-high heat; cook until reduced to ¼ cup, about 3 minutes. Whisk in cream, ground and chopped walnuts, Parmesan, ¼ teaspoon salt, and ½ teaspoon pepper. Remove pan from heat and cover to keep warm.

2. To serve, return pan to medium heat. Add pasta, ½ cup reserved cooking water, and chives; toss to combine. Season with salt and pepper to taste and add remaining cooking water as needed to adjust consistency. Serve immediately.

NOTES FROM THE TEST KITCHEN

ROLLING AND CUTTING PASTA DOUGH BY HAND

What's the trick to turning a lump of pasta into long, silky, strands—without a pasta roller? Starting with a soft, malleable dough is half the battle. The other half: dividing the dough into small, manageable pieces and working with them one at a time.

1. Shape dough into 6-inch cylinder; wrap in plastic wrap and let rest for at least 1 hour. Divide into 6 equal pieces. Reserve 1 piece; rewrap remaining 5.

2. Working with reserved piece, dust both sides with flour, then press cut side down into 3-inch square. With rolling pin, roll into 6-inch square, then dust both sides again with flour.

3. Roll dough to 12 by 6 inches, rolling from center of dough 1 way at a time, then dust with flour. Continue rolling to 20 by 6 inches, lifting frequently to release from counter. Transfer dough to clean dish towel and air-dry for about 15 minutes.

4. Starting with short end, gently fold dried sheet at 2-inch intervals to create flat, rectangular roll.

5. With sharp knife, cut into ³⁄₁₆-inch-wide noodles.

6. Use fingers to unfurl pasta; transfer to baking sheet.

RAGU ALLA BOLOGNESE

WHY THIS RECIPE WORKS: There are many different ways to interpret what "real" bolognese sauce is. But no matter what the ingredients are, the sauce should be hearty and rich, but not cloying, with a velvety texture that lightly clings to the noodles. For our version we used six different types of meats: ground beef, pork, and veal; pancetta; mortadella (bologna-like Italian deli meat); and chicken livers. These meats and the combination of red wine and tomato paste gave us a rich, complex sauce with balanced acidity. The final addition of gelatin lent the sauce an ultra-silky texture.

Ragu alla Bolognese

MAKES ABOUT 6 CUPS

This recipe makes enough sauce for 2 pounds of pasta. Eight teaspoons of gelatin is equivalent to one (1-ounce) box of gelatin. If you can't find ground veal, use an additional ¾ pound of ground beef.

- 1 cup low-sodium chicken broth
- 1 cup beef broth
- 8 teaspoons unflavored gelatin
- 1 onion, chopped coarse
- 1 large carrot, peeled and chopped coarse
- 1 celery rib, chopped coarse
- 4 ounces pancetta, chopped
- 4 ounces mortadella, chopped
- 6 ounces chicken livers, trimmed
- 3 tablespoons extra-virgin olive oil
- ¾ pound 85 percent lean ground beef
- ¾ pound ground veal
- ¾ pound ground pork
- 3 tablespoons minced fresh sage
- 1 (6-ounce) can tomato paste
- 2 cups dry red wine
  Salt and pepper
- 1 pound pappardelle or tagliatelle
  Grated Parmesan cheese

1. Combine chicken broth and beef broth in bowl; sprinkle gelatin over top and set aside. Pulse onion, carrot, and celery together in food processor until finely chopped, about 10 pulses, scraping down bowl as needed; transfer to separate bowl. Pulse pancetta and mortadella together in now-empty food processor until finely chopped, about 25 pulses, scraping down bowl as needed; transfer to second bowl. Process chicken livers in now-empty food processor until pureed, about 5 seconds; transfer to third bowl.

2. Heat oil in Dutch oven over medium-high heat until shimmering. Add beef, veal, and pork; cook, breaking up pieces with wooden spoon, until all liquid has evaporated and meat begins to sizzle, 10 to 15 minutes. Add pancetta mixture and sage; cook, stirring frequently, until pancetta is translucent, 5 to 7 minutes, adjusting heat as needed to keep fond from burning. Add chopped vegetables and cook, stirring frequently, until softened, 5 to 7 minutes. Add tomato paste and cook, stirring constantly, until rust-colored and fragrant, about 3 minutes.

3. Stir in wine, scraping up any browned bits. Simmer until sauce has thickened, about 5 minutes. Stir in broth mixture and return to simmer. Reduce heat to low and cook at bare simmer until thickened (wooden spoon should leave trail when dragged through sauce), about 1½ hours.

4. Stir in pureed chicken livers, bring to boil, and remove from heat. Season with salt and pepper to taste; cover and keep warm.

5. Bring 4 quarts water to boil in large pot. Add pasta and 1 tablespoon salt and cook, stirring often, until al dente. Reserve ¾ cup cooking water, then drain pasta and return it to pot. Add half of sauce and cooking water to pasta and toss to combine. Transfer to serving bowl and serve, passing Parmesan separately. (Leftover sauce may be refrigerated for up to 3 days or frozen for up to 1 month.)

PASTA ALL'AMATRICIANA

WHY THIS RECIPE WORKS: To create an authentic-tasting version of *pasta all'amatriciana* we needed an alternative to hard-to-find *guanciale,* or cured pork jowl. Humble salt pork, though an unlikely solution, provided the rich, clean meatiness we were after. To ensure tender bites of pork throughout, we first simmered it in water to gently cook it and render fat, a step that allowed the meat to quickly turn golden once the water evaporated. Finally, to ensure the grated Pecorino Romano didn't clump in the hot sauce, we first mixed it with a little cooled rendered pork fat. Now the flavor of pork, tomato, chili flakes, and Pecorino shone through in each bite.

Pasta all'Amatriciana

SERVES 4 TO 6

Look for salt pork that is roughly 70 percent fat and 30 percent lean meat; leaner salt pork may not render enough fat. If difficult to slice, the salt pork can be put in the freezer for 15 minutes to firm up. In this dish, it is essential to use high-quality imported Pecorino Romano—not the bland domestic cheese labeled "Romano."

    8   ounces salt pork, rind removed, rinsed thoroughly, and
        patted dry
    ½   cup water
    ½   teaspoon red pepper flakes
    2   tablespoons tomato paste
    ¼   cup red wine
    1   (28-ounce) can diced tomatoes
    2   ounces Pecorino Romano, grated fine (1 cup)
    1   pound spaghetti
    1   tablespoon salt

1. Slice salt pork into ¼-inch-thick strips, then cut each strip crosswise into ¼-inch pieces. Bring pork and water to simmer in 10-inch nonstick skillet over medium heat; cook until water evaporates and pork begins to sizzle, 5 to 8 minutes. Reduce heat to medium-low and continue to cook, stirring frequently, until fat renders and pork turns golden, 5 to 8 minutes longer. Using slotted spoon, transfer salt pork to bowl. Pour off all but 1 tablespoon fat from skillet. Reserve remaining fat.

2. Return skillet to medium heat and add tomato paste and pepper flakes; cook, stirring constantly, for 20 seconds. Stir in wine and cook for 30 seconds. Stir in tomatoes and their juice and rendered pork and bring to simmer. Cook, stirring frequently, until thickened, 12 to 16 minutes. While sauce simmers, stir 2 tablespoons reserved fat and ½ cup Pecorino together in bowl to form paste.

3. Meanwhile, bring 4 quarts water to boil in large Dutch oven. Add pasta and salt and cook, stirring often, until al dente. Reserve 1 cup cooking water, then drain pasta and return it to pot.

4. Add sauce, ⅓ cup cooking water, and Pecorino mixture to pasta and toss well to coat, adding cooking water as needed to adjust consistency. Serve, passing remaining ½ cup Pecorino separately.

MUSHROOM RAGU

WHY THIS RECIPE WORKS: We wanted a mushroom ragu that combined the naturally hearty texture of fresh mushrooms with the concentrated flavor of dried ones—and that could be on the table in about 30 minutes. Using pancetta and its fat in our Quick Mushroom Ragu compensated for the lean nature of the mushrooms and made our mushroom ragu meatier. Portobello mushrooms gave our dish bulk, while smoky porcini gave it concentrated flavor. Adding tomato paste and fresh crushed tomatoes to our mushrooms after they'd browned sweetened our sauce but also let the mushrooms shine through. Finally, fresh rosemary finished our dish with brightness.

Spaghetti with Quick Mushroom Ragu

SERVES 4

Use a spoon to scrape the dark brown gills from the portobellos.

    1   cup low-sodium chicken broth
    1   ounce dried porcini mushrooms, rinsed
    4   ounces pancetta, cut into ½-inch pieces
    8   ounces portobello mushroom caps, gills removed,
        caps cut into ½-inch pieces (about 1½ cups)
    3   tablespoons extra-virgin olive oil
    4   medium garlic cloves, peeled and sliced thin
    1   tablespoon tomato paste
    2   teaspoons minced fresh rosemary leaves
    1   (14.5-ounce) can whole peeled tomatoes, roughly
        crushed by hand
        Salt and pepper
    1   pound spaghetti
        Grated Pecorino Romano cheese

1. Microwave broth and porcini in covered bowl until steaming, about 1 minute. Let sit until softened, about 10 minutes. Drain mushrooms through fine-mesh strainer lined with coffee filter into medium bowl, reserve broth, and chop mushrooms fine.

2. Heat pancetta in 12-inch skillet over medium heat; cook, stirring occasionally, until rendered and crisp, 7 to 10 minutes. Add portobellos, chopped porcini, oil, garlic, tomato paste, and rosemary; cook, stirring occasionally, until all liquid has evaporated and tomato paste starts to brown, 5 to 7 minutes. Add reserved broth and crushed tomatoes and their juice; increase heat to high and bring to simmer. Reduce heat to medium-low and simmer until thickened, 15 to 20 minutes. Season with salt and pepper to taste.

3. While sauce simmers, bring 4 quarts water to boil in large Dutch oven. Add pasta and 1 tablespoon salt; cook, stirring often, until al dente. Reserve ½ cup cooking water, then drain pasta and return it to pot. Add sauce to pasta and toss to combine. Add reserved cooking water as needed to adjust consistency and season with salt and pepper to taste. Serve, passing Pecorino separately.

SPANISH-STYLE PASTA WITH SHRIMP

WHY THIS RECIPE WORKS: Traditional recipes for *fideuà* can take several hours to prepare. We wanted to speed up the process but keep the deep flavors of the classic recipes. To replace the slow-cooked fish stock of the classics, we made a quick shrimp stock using the shrimp's shells, a combination of chicken broth and water, and a bay leaf. We also streamlined the *sofrito*, the aromatic base common in Spanish cooking, by finely mincing the onion and using canned tomatoes (instead of fresh), which helped the recipe components soften and brown more quickly. The final tweak to our recipe was boosting the flavor of the shrimp by quickly marinating them in olive oil, garlic, salt, and pepper.

Spanish-Style Toasted Pasta with Shrimp
SERVES 4

In step 5, if your skillet is not broiler-safe, once the pasta is tender transfer the mixture to a broiler-safe 13 by 9-inch baking dish lightly coated with olive oil; scatter the shrimp over the pasta and stir them in to partially submerge. Broil and serve as directed. Serve this dish with lemon wedges and Aïoli (recipe follows), stirring it into individual portions at the table.

- 3 tablespoons plus 2 teaspoons extra-virgin olive oil
- 3 garlic cloves, minced
  Salt and pepper
- 1½ pounds extra-large shrimp (21 to 25 per pound), peeled and deveined, shells reserved
- 2¾ cups water

- 1 cup low-sodium chicken broth
- 1 bay leaf
- 8 ounces spaghettini or thin spaghetti, broken into 1- to 2-inch lengths
- 1 onion, chopped fine
- 1 (14.5-ounce) can diced tomatoes, drained and chopped fine
- 1 teaspoon paprika
- 1 teaspoon smoked paprika
- ½ teaspoon anchovy paste
- ¼ cup dry white wine
- 1 tablespoon chopped fresh parsley
  Lemon wedges
- 1 recipe Aïoli (optional) (recipe follows)

1. Combine 1 tablespoon oil, 1 teaspoon garlic, ¼ teaspoon salt, and ⅛ teaspoon pepper in medium bowl. Add shrimp, toss to coat, and refrigerate until ready to use.

2. Place reserved shrimp shells, water, chicken broth, and bay leaf in medium bowl. Cover and microwave until liquid is hot and shells have turned pink, about 6 minutes. Set aside until ready to use.

3. Toss spaghettini and 2 teaspoons oil in broiler-safe 12-inch skillet until spaghettini is evenly coated. Toast spaghettini over medium-high heat, stirring frequently, until browned and nutty in aroma (spaghettini should be color of peanut butter), 6 to 10 minutes. Transfer spaghettini to bowl. Wipe out skillet with paper towel.

4. Heat remaining 2 tablespoons oil in now-empty skillet over medium-high heat until shimmering. Add onion and ¼ teaspoon salt; cook, stirring frequently, until onion is softened and beginning to brown around edges, 4 to 6 minutes. Add tomatoes and cook, stirring occasionally, until mixture is thick, dry, and slightly darkened in color, 4 to 6 minutes. Reduce heat to medium and add remaining garlic, paprika, smoked paprika, and anchovy paste. Cook until fragrant, about 1½ minutes. Add spaghettini and stir to combine. Adjust oven rack 5 to 6 inches from broiler element and heat broiler.

5. Pour shrimp broth through fine-mesh strainer into skillet. Add wine, ¼ teaspoon salt, and ½ teaspoon pepper and stir well. Increase heat to medium-high and bring to simmer. Cook uncovered, stirring occasionally, until liquid is slightly thickened and spaghettini is just tender, 8 to 10 minutes. Scatter shrimp over spaghettini and stir shrimp into spaghettini to partially submerge. Transfer skillet to oven and broil until shrimp are opaque and surface of spaghettini is dry with crisped, browned spots, 5 to 7 minutes. Remove from oven and let stand, uncovered, for 5 minutes. Sprinkle with parsley and serve immediately, passing lemon wedges and aïoli, if using, separately.

Spanish-Style Toasted Pasta with Shrimp and Clams

Reduce amount of shrimp to 1 pound and water to 2½ cups. In step 5, cook pasta until almost tender, about 6 minutes. Scatter 1½ pounds scrubbed littleneck or cherrystone clams over pasta, cover skillet, and cook until clams begin to open, about 3 minutes. Scatter shrimp over pasta, stir to partially submerge shrimp and clams, and proceed with recipe as directed.

Aïoli

MAKES ¾ CUP

- 1 garlic clove, grated fine
- 2 large egg yolks
- 4 teaspoons lemon juice
- ¼ teaspoon salt
- ⅛ teaspoon sugar
  Ground white pepper
- ¾ cup olive oil

In large bowl, combine garlic, egg yolks, lemon juice, salt, sugar, and pepper to taste until combined. Whisking constantly, very slowly drizzle oil into egg mixture until thick and creamy. Season with salt and pepper to taste.

NOTES FROM THE TEST KITCHEN

IT'S A SNAP

Since traditional short *fideos* noodles are hard to find, we came up with an easy way to break long strands into even lengths.

1. Loosely fold 4 ounces of spaghettini in clean dish towel, keeping pasta flat, not bunched. Position so that 1 to 2 inches of pasta rests on counter and remainder of pasta hangs off edge.

2. Pressing bundle against counter, press down on long end of towel to break strands into pieces, sliding bundle back over edge after each break.

STIR-FRIED THAI NOODLES WITH CHICKEN AND BROCCOLINI

WHY THIS RECIPE WORKS: We wanted to create a version of *pad see ew*—the traditional Thai dish of chewy, lightly charred rice noodles, with chicken, crisp broccoli, and moist egg, bound with a sweet and salty soy-based sauce—that would work in the American home kitchen. We substituted supermarket ingredients for hard-to-find fresh rice noodles, Chinese broccoli, and sweet Thai soy sauce, but it was simulating the high heat of a restaurant wok burner on a lower-output home stovetop that was the real challenge. Since we were already using maximum heat, we increased the surface area by using a 12-inch nonstick skillet, and we cooked the dish in batches, combining all of the components right before serving. Most important, we found that eliminating much of the stirring in our stir-fry helped us achieve the all-important char that characterizes pad see ew.

Thai-Style Stir-Fried Noodles with Chicken and Broccolini

SERVES 4

The flat pad thai–style rice noodles that are used in this recipe can be found in the Asian section of most supermarkets. If you can't find broccolini, you can substitute an equal amount of conventional broccoli, but be sure to trim and peel the stalks before cutting.

CHILE VINEGAR
- ⅓ cup white vinegar
- 1 serrano chile, stemmed and sliced into thin rings

STIR-FRY
- 2 (6-ounce) boneless, skinless chicken breasts, trimmed and cut against grain into ¼-inch-thick slices
- 1 teaspoon baking soda
- 8 ounces (¼-inch-wide) rice noodles
- ¼ cup vegetable oil
- ¼ cup oyster sauce
- 1 tablespoon plus 2 teaspoons soy sauce
- 2 tablespoons packed dark brown sugar
- 1 tablespoon white vinegar
- 1 teaspoon molasses
- 1 teaspoon fish sauce
- 3 garlic cloves, sliced thin
- 3 large eggs
- 10 ounces broccolini, florets cut into 1-inch pieces, stalks cut on bias into ½-inch pieces (5 cups)

1. FOR THE CHILE VINEGAR: Combine vinegar and serrano in bowl. Let stand at room temperature for at least 15 minutes.

2. FOR THE STIR-FRY: Combine chicken with 2 tablespoons water and baking soda in bowl. Let sit at room temperature for 15 minutes. Rinse chicken in cold water and drain well.

3. Bring 6 cups water to boil. Place noodles in large bowl. Pour boiling water over noodles. Stir, then soak until noodles are almost tender, about 8 minutes, stirring once halfway through. Drain and rinse with cold water. Drain well and toss with 2 teaspoons oil.

4. Whisk oyster sauce, soy sauce, sugar, vinegar, molasses, and fish sauce together in bowl.

5. Heat 2 teaspoons oil and garlic in 12-inch nonstick skillet over high heat, stirring occasionally, until garlic is deep golden brown, 1 to 2 minutes. Add chicken and 2 tablespoons sauce mixture, toss to coat, and spread chicken into even layer. Cook, without stirring, until chicken begins to brown, 1 to 1½ minutes. Flip chicken and cook, without stirring, until second side begins to brown, 1 to 1½ minutes. Push chicken to 1 side of skillet. Add 2 teaspoons oil to cleared side of skillet. Add eggs to clearing. Using rubber spatula, stir eggs gently and cook until set but still wet. Stir eggs into chicken and continue to cook, breaking up large pieces of egg, until eggs are fully cooked, 30 to 60 seconds. Transfer chicken mixture to bowl.

6. Heat 2 teaspoons oil in now-empty skillet until smoking. Add broccolini and 2 tablespoons sauce and toss to coat. Cover skillet and cook for 2 minutes, stirring once halfway through cooking. Remove lid and continue to cook until broccolini is crisp and very brown in spots, 2 to 3 minutes, stirring once halfway through cooking. Transfer broccolini to bowl with chicken mixture.

7. Heat 2 teaspoons oil in now-empty skillet until smoking. Add half of noodles and 2 tablespoons sauce and toss to coat. Cook until noodles are starting to brown in spots, about 2 minutes, stirring halfway through cooking. Transfer noodles to bowl with chicken mixture. Repeat with remaining 2 teaspoons oil, noodles, and sauce. When second batch of noodles is cooked, add contents of bowl back to skillet and toss to combine. Cook, without stirring, until everything is warmed through, 1 to 1½ minutes. Transfer to platter and serve immediately, passing chile vinegar separately.

CHINESE CHICKEN LETTUCE WRAPS

WHY THIS RECIPE WORKS: This dish, popularized by chain restaurants, is based on a Cantonese dish called *sung choy bao*. Most recipes for this dish suffer from a similar fate—stringy, tasteless meat drowned in a bland sauce. To remedy this, we started with flavorful chicken thighs and marinated them in soy sauce and rice wine. To keep the meat from drying out when stir-fried, we coated it in a velvetizing cornstarch slurry, which helped it retain moisture as it cooked.

Chinese Chicken Lettuce Wraps

SERVES 4 AS A MAIN DISH OR 6 AS AN APPETIZER

To make it an entrée, serve this dish with steamed white rice.

CHICKEN
- 1 pound boneless, skinless chicken thighs, trimmed and cut into 1-inch pieces
- 2 teaspoons Chinese rice wine or dry sherry
- 2 teaspoons soy sauce
- 2 teaspoons toasted sesame oil
- 2 teaspoons cornstarch

SAUCE
- 3 tablespoons oyster sauce
- 1 tablespoon Chinese rice wine or dry sherry
- 2 teaspoons soy sauce
- 2 teaspoons toasted sesame oil
- ½ teaspoon sugar
- ¼ teaspoon red pepper flakes

STIR-FRY
- 2 tablespoons vegetable oil
- 2 celery ribs, cut into ¼-inch pieces
- 6 ounces shiitake mushrooms, stemmed and sliced thin
- ½ cup water chestnuts, cut into ¼-inch pieces
- 2 scallions, white parts minced, green parts sliced thin
- 2 garlic cloves, minced
- 1 head Bibb lettuce (8 ounces), washed and dried, leaves separated and left whole
    Hoisin sauce

1. FOR THE CHICKEN: Place chicken pieces on large plate in single layer. Freeze meat until firm and starting to harden around edges, about 20 minutes.

2. Whisk rice wine, soy sauce, oil, and cornstarch together in bowl. Pulse half of meat in food processor until coarsely chopped into ¼- to ⅛-inch pieces, about 10 pulses. Transfer meat to bowl with rice wine mixture and repeat with remaining chunks. Toss chicken to coat and refrigerate for 15 minutes.

3. FOR THE SAUCE: Whisk all ingredients together in bowl; set aside.

4. FOR THE STIR-FRY: Heat 1 tablespoon oil in 12-inch nonstick skillet over high heat until smoking. Add chicken and cook, stirring constantly, until opaque, 3 to 4 minutes. Transfer to bowl and wipe out skillet.

5. Heat remaining 1 tablespoon oil in now-empty skillet over high heat until smoking. Add celery and mushrooms; cook, stirring constantly, until mushrooms have reduced in size by half and celery is crisp-tender, 3 to 4 minutes. Add water chestnuts, scallion whites, and garlic; cook, stirring constantly, until fragrant, about 1 minute. Whisk sauce to recombine. Return chicken to skillet; add sauce and toss to combine. Spoon into lettuce leaves and sprinkle with scallion greens. Serve, passing hoisin sauce separately.

SKILLET CHICKEN FAJITAS

WHY THIS RECIPE WORKS: To create indoor chicken fajitas that didn't require a slew of compensatory garnishes to be tasty, we took a fresh look at the key ingredients. For well-charred, juicy chicken we marinated boneless, skinless breasts in a potent mix of smoked paprika, garlic, cumin, cayenne, and sugar before searing them on one side and finishing them gently in a low oven. We revamped the usual bland mix of bell pepper and onion by charring poblano chiles and thinly sliced onion, and then cooking them down with cream and lime. Finally, we finish the dish with moderate amounts of complementary garnishes: pickled radish, queso fresco, and minced cilantro.

Skillet Chicken Fajitas

SERVES 4

We like to serve these fajitas with crumbled queso fresco or feta in addition to the other garnishes listed.

CHICKEN

- ¼ cup vegetable oil
- 2 tablespoons lime juice
- 4 garlic cloves, peeled and smashed
- 1½ teaspoons smoked paprika
- 1 teaspoon sugar
- 1 teaspoon salt
- ½ teaspoon ground cumin

- ½ teaspoon pepper
- ¼ teaspoon cayenne pepper
- 1½ pounds boneless, skinless chicken breasts, trimmed and pounded to ½-inch thickness

RAJAS CON CREMA

- 1 pound (3 to 4) poblano chiles, stemmed, halved, and seeded
- 1 tablespoon vegetable oil
- 1 onion, halved and sliced ¼ inch thick
- 2 garlic cloves, minced
- ¼ teaspoon dried thyme
- ¼ teaspoon dried oregano
- ½ cup heavy cream
- 1 tablespoon lime juice
- ½ teaspoon salt
- ¼ teaspoon pepper

- 8–12 (6-inch) flour tortillas, warmed
- ¼ cup minced fresh cilantro
  Spicy Pickled Radishes (recipe follows)
  Lime wedges

1. FOR THE CHICKEN: Whisk 3 tablespoons oil, lime juice, garlic, paprika, sugar, salt, cumin, pepper, and cayenne together in bowl. Add chicken and toss to coat. Cover and let stand at room temperature for at least 30 minutes or up to 1 hour.

2. FOR THE RAJAS CON CREMA: Meanwhile, adjust oven rack to highest position and heat broiler. Line rimmed baking sheet with aluminum foil, then arrange poblanos skin side up on baking sheet and press to flatten. Broil until skin is charred and puffed, 4 to 10 minutes, rotating baking sheet halfway through cooking. Transfer poblanos to bowl, cover, and let steam for 10 minutes. Rub most of skin from poblanos (leaving a little attached for flavor); slice into ¼-inch-thick strips. Adjust oven racks to middle and lowest positions and heat oven to 200 degrees.

3. Heat oil in 12-inch nonstick skillet over high heat until just smoking. Add onion and cook until charred and just softened, about 3 minutes. Add garlic, thyme, and oregano and cook until fragrant, about 15 seconds. Add cream and cook, stirring frequently, until reduced and cream lightly coats onion, 1 to 2 minutes. Add poblano strips, lime juice, salt, and pepper and toss to coat. Transfer vegetables to bowl, cover with foil, and place on middle oven rack. Wipe out skillet with paper towels.

4. Remove chicken from marinade and wipe off excess. Heat remaining 1 tablespoon oil in now-empty skillet over high heat until just smoking. Add chicken and cook without moving it until bottom side is well charred, about

4 minutes. Flip chicken; transfer skillet to lower oven rack. Bake until chicken registers 160 degrees, 7 to 10 minutes. Transfer to cutting board and let rest for 5 minutes; do not wash out skillet.

5. Slice chicken crosswise into ¼-inch-thick strips. Return chicken strips to skillet and toss to coat with pan juices. To serve, spoon few pieces of chicken into center of warmed tortilla and top with spoonful of vegetable mixture, cilantro, and pickled radishes. Serve with lime wedges.

Spicy Pickled Radishes

MAKES ABOUT 1¾ CUPS

If you'd like a less spicy version of these pickled radishes, omit the seeds from the jalapeño.

- 10 radishes, trimmed and sliced thin
- ½ cup lime juice (4 limes)
- ½ jalapeño chile, stemmed and sliced thin
- 1 teaspoon sugar
- ¼ teaspoon salt

Combine all ingredients in bowl. Cover and let stand at room temperature for 30 minutes (or refrigerate for up to 24 hours).

FILIPINO CHICKEN ADOBO

WHY THIS RECIPE WORKS: Adobo is the national dish of the Philippines, and chicken adobo is among the most popular versions. The dish consists of chicken simmered in a mixture of vinegar, soy sauce, garlic, bay leaves, and black pepper. The problem with most recipes we found was that they were aggressively tart and salty. Our secret to taming both of these elements was coconut milk. The coconut milk's richness tempered the bracing acidity of the vinegar and masked the briny soy sauce, bringing the sauce into balance. But the fat from the coconut milk and the chicken skin made the sauce somewhat greasy. To combat this, we borrowed a technique used in French bistros. We placed the meat skin side down in a cold pan and then turned up the heat. As the pan gradually got hotter, the fat under the chicken's skin melted away as the exterior browned.

Filipino Chicken Adobo

SERVES 4

Light coconut milk can be substituted for regular coconut milk. Serve this dish over rice.

- 8 (5- to 7-ounce) bone-in chicken thighs, trimmed
- ⅓ cup soy sauce
- 1 (13½-ounce) can coconut milk
- ¾ cup cider vinegar
- 8 garlic cloves, peeled
- 4 bay leaves
- 2 teaspoons pepper
- 1 scallion, sliced thin

1. Toss chicken with soy sauce in large bowl. Refrigerate for at least 30 minutes or up to 1 hour.

2. Remove chicken from soy sauce, allowing excess to drip back into bowl. Transfer chicken, skin side down, to 12-inch nonstick skillet; set aside soy sauce.

3. Place skillet over medium-high heat and cook until chicken skin is browned, 7 to 10 minutes. While chicken is browning, whisk coconut milk, vinegar, garlic, bay leaves, and pepper into soy sauce.

4. Transfer chicken to plate and discard fat in skillet. Return chicken to skillet skin side down, add coconut milk mixture, and bring to boil. Reduce heat to medium-low and simmer, uncovered, for 20 minutes. Flip chicken skin side up and continue to cook, uncovered, until chicken registers 175 degrees, about 15 minutes. Transfer chicken to platter and tent loosely with aluminum foil.

5. Remove bay leaves and skim any fat off surface of sauce. Return skillet to medium-high heat and cook until sauce is thickened, 5 to 7 minutes. Pour sauce over chicken, sprinkle with scallion, and serve.

JERK CHICKEN

WHY THIS RECIPE WORKS: Traditional Jamaican jerk recipes rely on island ingredients for both marinade and cooking technique. Fortunately, we were able to achieve the characteristic spicy-sweet-fresh-smoky balance with the right combination of stateside staples. Keeping the marinade pastelike and cooking the meat first over indirect heat prevented the jerk flavors from dripping or peeling off during grilling. Enhancing our hickory chip packet with a few spice-cabinet ingredients allowed our jerk chicken recipe to mimic the unique smoke of authentic pimento wood.

Jerk Chicken

SERVES 4

For a milder dish, use one seeded chile. If you prefer your food very hot, use up to all three chiles including their seeds and ribs. Scotch bonnet chiles can be used in place of the habaneros. Wear gloves when working with the chiles.

JERK MARINADE

1½ tablespoons whole coriander seeds
1 tablespoon whole allspice berries
1 tablespoon whole peppercorns
1–3 habanero chiles, stemmed, quartered, and seeds and ribs reserved, if using
8 scallions, chopped
6 garlic cloves, peeled
3 tablespoons vegetable oil
2 tablespoons soy sauce
2 tablespoons finely grated lime zest (3 limes), plus lime wedges for serving
2 tablespoons yellow mustard
1 tablespoon dried thyme
1 tablespoon ground ginger
1 tablespoon packed brown sugar
2¼ teaspoons salt
2 teaspoons dried basil
½ teaspoon dried rosemary
½ teaspoon ground nutmeg

CHICKEN

3 pounds bone-in chicken pieces (split breasts cut in half, drumsticks, and/or thighs)
2 tablespoons whole allspice berries
2 tablespoons dried thyme
2 tablespoons dried rosemary
2 tablespoons water
1 cup wood chips, soaked in water for 15 minutes and drained

1. FOR THE JERK MARINADE: Grind coriander seeds, allspice berries, and peppercorns in spice grinder or mortar and pestle until coarsely ground. Transfer spices to blender jar. Add habanero(s), scallions, garlic, oil, soy sauce, lime zest, mustard, thyme, ginger, brown sugar, salt, basil, rosemary, and nutmeg and process until smooth paste forms, 1 to 3 minutes, scraping down sides of blender jar as necessary. Transfer marinade to gallon-size zipper-lock bag.

2. FOR THE CHICKEN: Place chicken pieces in bag with marinade and toss to coat; press out as much air as possible and seal bag. Let stand at room temperature for 30 minutes while preparing grill, flipping bag after

15 minutes. (Marinated chicken can be refrigerated for up to 24 hours.)

3. Combine allspice berries, thyme, rosemary, and water in bowl and set aside to moisten for 15 minutes. Using large piece of heavy-duty aluminum foil, wrap soaked chips and moistened allspice mixture in foil packet and cut several vent holes in top.

4A. FOR A CHARCOAL GRILL: Open bottom vent halfway. Arrange 1 quart unlit charcoal briquettes in single layer over half of grill. Light large chimney starter one-third filled with charcoal briquettes (2 quarts). When top coals are partially covered with ash, pour evenly over unlit briquettes, keeping coals arranged over half of grill. Place wood chip packet on coals. Set cooking grate in place, cover, and open lid vent halfway. Heat grill until hot and wood chips are smoking, about 5 minutes.

4B. FOR A GAS GRILL: Place wood chip packet over primary burner. Turn all burners to high, cover, and heat grill until hot and wood chips begin to smoke, 15 to 25 minutes. Turn primary burner to medium and turn off other burner(s).

5. Clean and oil cooking grate. Place chicken, with marinade clinging and skin side up, as far away from fire as possible, with thighs closest to fire and breasts furthest away. Cover (positioning lid vent over chicken if using charcoal) and cook for 30 minutes.

6. Move chicken, skin side down, to hotter side of grill; cook until browned and skin renders, 3 to 6 minutes. Using tongs, flip chicken pieces and cook until browned on second side and breasts register 160 degrees and thighs/drumsticks register 175 degrees, 5 to 12 minutes longer.

7. Transfer chicken to serving platter, tent loosely with foil, and let rest for 5 to 10 minutes. Serve warm or at room temperature with lime wedges.

CHICKEN MARBELLA

WHY THIS RECIPE WORKS: More than 25 years ago, this dinner-party mainstay put *The Silver Palate Cookbook* on the map. We wanted to retool the recipe for today's tastes. To save time and boost flavor, we ditched the original marinade and made a paste of the prunes, olives, capers, garlic, and oregano, which we spread on the chicken and caramelized into the sauce. Instead of using whole birds, which require butchering, we chose easy-prep chicken parts. To intensify the dish's meaty flavor and to create complexity, we added anchovies and pepper flakes and browned the chicken skin in a skillet before baking it through.

Chicken Marbella

SERVES 4 TO 6

Any combination of split breasts and leg quarters can be used in this recipe.

PASTE

⅓ cup pitted green olives, rinsed
⅓ cup pitted prunes
3 tablespoons extra-virgin olive oil
2 tablespoons capers, rinsed
4 garlic cloves, peeled
3 anchovy fillets, rinsed
½ teaspoon dried oregano
½ teaspoon pepper
¼ teaspoon kosher salt
  Pinch red pepper flakes

CHICKEN

2½–3 pounds bone-in split chicken breasts and/or leg quarters, trimmed
  Kosher salt and pepper
2 teaspoons olive oil
¾ cup low-sodium chicken broth
⅓ cup white wine
⅓ cup pitted green olives, rinsed and halved
1 tablespoon capers, rinsed
2 bay leaves
⅓ cup pitted prunes, chopped coarse
1 tablespoon unsalted butter
1 teaspoon red wine vinegar
2 tablespoons minced fresh parsley

1. FOR THE PASTE: Adjust oven rack to middle position and heat oven to 400 degrees. Pulse all ingredients together in food processor until finely chopped, about 10 pulses. Scrape down bowl and continue to process until mostly smooth, 1 to 2 minutes. Transfer to bowl. (Paste can be refrigerated for up to 24 hours.)

2. FOR THE CHICKEN: Pat chicken dry with paper towels. Sprinkle chicken pieces with 1½ teaspoons salt and season with pepper.

3. Heat oil in 12-inch skillet over medium-high heat until just smoking. Add chicken, skin side down, and cook without moving until well browned, 5 to 8 minutes. Transfer chicken to large plate. Drain off all but 1 teaspoon fat from skillet and return to medium-low heat.

4. Add ⅓ cup paste to skillet and cook, stirring constantly, until fragrant and fond forms on bottom of pan, 1 to 2 minutes. Stir in broth, wine, olives, capers, and bay leaves, scraping up any browned bits. Return chicken, skin side up, to pan (skin should be above surface of liquid) and transfer to oven. Cook, uncovered, for 15 minutes.

5. Remove skillet from oven and use back of spoon to spread remaining paste over chicken pieces; sprinkle prunes around chicken. Continue to roast until paste begins to brown, breasts register 160 degrees, and leg quarters register 175 degrees, 7 to 12 minutes longer.

6. Transfer chicken to serving platter and tent loosely with aluminum foil. Remove bay leaves from sauce and whisk in butter, vinegar, and 1 tablespoon parsley; season with salt and pepper to taste. Pour sauce around chicken, sprinkle with remaining 1 tablespoon parsley, and serve.

TURKEY BURGERS

WHY THIS RECIPE WORKS: To create juicy, well-textured turkey burgers, we ditched store-bought ground turkey in favor of home-ground turkey thighs, which boast more fat and flavor. To ensure that our turkey burger recipe delivered maximum juiciness, we incorporated a paste with a portion of the ground turkey, gelatin, soy sauce, and baking soda, which trapped juice within the burgers. Finally, we added coarsely chopped raw white mushrooms to keep the meat from binding together too firmly.

Juicy Grilled Turkey Burgers

SERVES 6

If you are able to purchase boneless, skinless turkey thighs, substitute 1½ pounds for the bone-in thigh. To ensure the best texture, don't let the burgers stand for more than an hour before cooking. Serve the burgers with Malt Vinegar–Molasses Burger Sauce, Chile-Lime Burger Sauce, or Apricot-Mustard Burger Sauce.

1 (2-pound) bone-in turkey thigh, skinned, boned, trimmed, and cut into ½-inch pieces
1 tablespoon unflavored gelatin
3 tablespoons low-sodium chicken broth
6 ounces white mushrooms, trimmed
1 tablespoon soy sauce
  Pinch baking soda
2 tablespoons vegetable oil, plus extra for brushing
  Kosher salt and pepper
6 large hamburger buns

1. Place turkey pieces on large plate in single layer. Freeze meat until very firm and hardened around edges, 35 to 45 minutes. Meanwhile, sprinkle gelatin over chicken broth in small bowl and let sit until gelatin softens, about 5 minutes. Pulse mushrooms in food processor until coarsely chopped, about 7 pulses, stopping and redistributing mushrooms around bowl as needed to ensure even grinding. Set mushrooms aside; do not wash food processor.

2. Pulse one-third of turkey in food processor until coarsely chopped into ⅛-inch pieces, 18 to 22 pulses, stopping and redistributing turkey around bowl as needed to ensure even grinding. Transfer meat to large bowl and repeat two more times with remaining turkey.

3. Return ½ cup (about 3 ounces) ground turkey to bowl of food processor along with softened gelatin, soy sauce, and baking soda. Process until smooth, about 2 minutes, scraping down bowl as needed. With processor running, slowly drizzle in oil, about 10 seconds; leave paste in food processor. Return mushrooms to food processor with paste and pulse to combine, 3 to 5 pulses, stopping and redistributing mixture as needed to ensure even mixing. Transfer mushroom mixture to bowl with ground turkey and use hands to evenly combine.

4. With lightly greased hands, divide meat mixture into 6 balls. Flatten into ¾-inch-thick patties about 4 inches in diameter; press shallow indentation into center of each burger to ensure even cooking. (Shaped patties can be frozen for up to 1 month. Frozen patties can be cooked straight from freezer.)

5A. FOR A CHARCOAL GRILL: Open bottom vent completely. Light large chimney starter filled with charcoal briquettes (6 quarts). When top coals are partially covered with ash, pour evenly over half of grill. Set cooking grate in place, cover, and open lid vent completely. Heat grill until hot, about 5 minutes.

5B. FOR A GAS GRILL: Turn all burners to high, cover, and heat grill until hot, about 15 minutes. Leave primary burner on high and turn off other burner(s).

6. Clean and oil cooking grate. Brush 1 side of patties with oil and season with salt and pepper. Using spatula, flip patties, brush with oil, and season second side. Place burgers over hot part of grill and cook until burgers are well browned on both sides and register 160 degrees, 4 to 7 minutes per side. (If cooking frozen burgers: After burgers are browned on both sides, transfer to cool side of grill, cover, and continue to cook until burgers register 160 degrees.)

7. Transfer burgers to plate and let rest for 5 minutes. While burgers rest, grill buns over hot side of grill. Transfer burgers to buns, add desired toppings, and serve.

Malt Vinegar–Molasses Burger Sauce
MAKES ABOUT 1 CUP

- ¾ cup mayonnaise
- 4 teaspoons malt vinegar
- ½ teaspoon molasses
- ¼ teaspoon Worcestershire sauce
- ¼ teaspoon salt
- ¼ teaspoon pepper

Whisk all ingredients together in bowl.

Chile-Lime Burger Sauce
MAKES ABOUT 1 CUP

- ¾ cup mayonnaise
- 2 teaspoons chile-garlic paste
- 2 teaspoons lime juice
- 1 scallion, sliced thin
- ¼ teaspoon fish sauce
- ⅛ teaspoon sugar

Whisk all ingredients together in bowl.

Apricot-Mustard Burger Sauce
MAKES ABOUT 1 CUP

- ¾ cup mayonnaise
- 5 teaspoons apricot preserves
- 1 tablespoon lemon juice
- 1 tablespoon Dijon mustard
- 1 tablespoon whole-grain mustard
- ¼ teaspoon salt

Whisk all ingredients together in bowl.

GRILL-ROASTED TURKEY

WHY THIS RECIPE WORKS: Besides freeing up your oven for other dishes, roasting your turkey out on the grill also means that you needn't worry about constantly monitoring the bird to ensure a perfectly juicy, tender turkey. To make grilling turkey foolproof, we divided our coals into two piles on either side of the grill so that the turkey thighs would receive the highest heat. A combination of lit coals and unlit briquettes yielded a longer-burning fire, making replenishing coals unnecessary. The addition of a pan of water stabilized the temperature inside the grill for even cooking and a quick salt rub before grilling yielded seasoned meat and crispy skin.

Simple Grill-Roasted Turkey

SERVES 10 TO 12

Table salt is not recommended for this recipe because it is too fine. If using a kosher or self-basting turkey (such as a frozen Butterball), do not salt it in step 1. Check the wings halfway through roasting; if they are getting too dark, fold a 12 by 8-inch piece of foil in half lengthwise and then again crosswise and slide the foil between the wing and the cooking grate to shield the wings from the flame. As an accompaniment, try our Gravy for Simple Grill-Roasted Turkey (recipe follows).

1 (12- to 14-pound) turkey, neck and giblets removed and reserved for gravy
Kosher salt and pepper
1 teaspoon baking powder
1 tablespoon vegetable oil
Large disposable aluminum roasting pan (if using charcoal) or 2 disposable aluminum pie plates (if using gas)

1. Place turkey breast side down on work surface. Make two 2-inch incisions below each thigh and breast along back of turkey (4 incisions total). Using fingers or handle of wooden spoon, carefully separate skin from thighs and breast. Rub 4 teaspoons salt evenly inside cavity of turkey, 1 tablespoon salt under skin of each side of breast, and 1 teaspoon salt under skin of each leg.

2. Combine 1 teaspoon salt, 1 teaspoon pepper, and baking powder in small bowl. Pat turkey dry with paper towels and evenly sprinkle baking powder mixture all over. Rub in mixture with hands, coating entire surface evenly. Wrap turkey tightly with plastic wrap; refrigerate for 24 to 48 hours.

3. Remove turkey from refrigerator and discard plastic. Tuck wings underneath turkey. Using hands, rub oil evenly over entire surface.

4A. FOR A CHARCOAL GRILL: Open bottom vent halfway and place disposable pan filled with 3 cups water in center of grill. Arrange 1½ quarts unlit charcoal briquettes on either side of pan in even layer. Light large chimney starter two-thirds filled with charcoal briquettes

(4 quarts). When top coals are partially covered with ash, pour 2 quarts of lit coals on top of each pile of unlit coals. Set cooking grate in place, cover, and open lid vent halfway. Heat grill until hot, about 5 minutes.

4B. FOR A GAS GRILL: Place 2 disposable pie plates with 2 cups water in each directly on 1 burner over which turkey will be cooked. Turn all burners to high, cover, and heat grill until hot, about 15 minutes. Turn primary burner (burner opposite pie plates) to medium and turn other burner(s) off. Adjust primary burner as needed to maintain grill temperature of 325 degrees.

5. Clean and oil cooking grate. Place turkey, breast side up, in center of charcoal grill or on cooler side of gas grill, making sure bird is over disposable pans and not over flame. Cover (placing vents over turkey on charcoal grill) and cook until breasts register 160 degrees and thighs/drumsticks register 175 degrees, 2½ to 3 hours, rotating turkey after 1¼ hours if using gas grill.

6. Transfer turkey to carving board and let rest, uncovered, for 45 minutes. Carve turkey and serve.

Gravy for Simple Grill-Roasted Turkey

MAKES 6 CUPS

1 tablespoon vegetable oil
Reserved turkey neck and giblets
1 pound onions, chopped coarse
4 cups low-sodium chicken broth
4 cups beef broth
2 small carrots, peeled and chopped coarse
2 small celery ribs, chopped coarse
3 tablespoons unsalted butter
½ cup all-purpose flour
2 bay leaves
½ teaspoon dried thyme
10 whole black peppercorns
Salt and pepper

1. Heat oil in Dutch oven over medium-high heat until shimmering. Add turkey neck and giblets; cook, stirring occasionally, until browned, about 5 minutes. Add half of onions and cook, stirring occasionally, until softened, about 3 minutes. Reduce heat to low; cover and cook, stirring occasionally, until turkey parts and onions release their juices, about 20 minutes.

2. Add chicken broth and beef broth; increase heat to high and bring to boil. Reduce heat to low and simmer, uncovered, skimming any scum that rises to surface, until broth is rich and flavorful, about 30 minutes. Strain broth into large bowl (you should have about 8 cups), reserving giblets, if desired; discard neck. Reserve broth. If using, when cool enough to handle, remove gristle from gizzard; dice giblets and set aside. (Broth can be refrigerated for up to 2 days.)

3. Pulse carrots in food processor until broken into rough ¼-inch pieces, about 5 pulses. Add celery and remaining onions; pulse until all vegetables are broken into ⅛-inch pieces, about 5 pulses.

4. Melt butter in now-empty Dutch oven over medium-high heat. Add vegetables and cook, stirring frequently, until softened and well browned, about 10 minutes. Reduce heat to medium; stir in flour and cook, stirring constantly, until thoroughly browned and fragrant, 5 to 7 minutes. Whisking constantly, gradually add reserved broth; bring to boil, skimming off any foam that forms on surface. Reduce heat to medium-low and add bay leaves, thyme, and peppercorns; simmer, stirring occasionally, until thickened and reduced to 6 cups, 30 to 35 minutes.

5. Strain gravy through fine-mesh strainer into clean saucepan, pressing on solids to extract as much liquid as possible; discard solids. Stir in diced heart and gizzard, if using. Season with salt and pepper to taste. Serve hot.

GRILLED BEEF SATAY

WHY THIS RECIPE WORKS: In the hands of American cooks, satay often comes out thick and chewy or overly marinated and mealy. To return this dish to its streetwise roots, we sliced beefy-flavored flank steak thin across the grain and threaded it onto bamboo skewers. To add flavor, we used an aromatic basting sauce consisting of authentic Thai ingredients, rather than the overtenderizing marinade used in many recipes. And to ensure that the quick-cooking beef achieved a burnished exterior, we corralled the coals in an aluminum pan in the center of the grill to bring them closer to the meat.

Grilled Beef Satay

SERVES 6

Bamboo skewers soaked in water for 30 minutes can be substituted for metal skewers. The aluminum pan used for charcoal grilling should be at least 2¾ inches deep; you will not need the pan for a gas grill. Kitchen shears work well for punching the holes in the pan. Unless you have a very high-powered gas grill, these skewers will not be as well seared as they would be with charcoal. Serve with Peanut Sauce (recipe follows). To make it a meal, serve this dish with steamed white rice.

BASTING SAUCE
- ¾ cup regular or light coconut milk
- 3 tablespoons packed dark brown sugar
- 3 tablespoons fish sauce
- 2 tablespoons vegetable oil
- 3 shallots, minced
- 2 lemon grass stalks, trimmed to bottom 6 inches and minced
- 2 tablespoons grated fresh ginger
- 1½ teaspoons ground coriander
- ¾ teaspoon red pepper flakes
- ½ teaspoon ground cumin
- ½ teaspoon salt

BEEF
- 2 tablespoons vegetable oil
- 2 tablespoons packed dark brown sugar
- 1 tablespoon fish sauce
- 1 (1½- to 1¾-pound) flank steak, halved lengthwise and sliced on slight angle against grain into ¼-inch-thick slices
- Disposable aluminum deep roasting pan

1. FOR THE BASTING SAUCE: Whisk all ingredients together in bowl. Reserve one-third of sauce in separate bowl.

2. FOR THE BEEF: Whisk oil, sugar, and fish sauce together in medium bowl. Toss beef with marinade and let stand at room temperature for 30 minutes. Weave beef onto 12-inch metal skewers, 2 to 4 pieces per skewer, leaving 1½ inches at top and bottom of skewer exposed. You should have 10 to 12 skewers.

3A. FOR A CHARCOAL GRILL: Punch twelve ½-inch holes in bottom of disposable roasting pan. Open bottom vent completely and place roasting pan in center of grill. Light large chimney starter mounded with charcoal briquettes (7 quarts). When top coals are partially covered with ash, pour into roasting pan. Set cooking grate over coals with grates parallel to long side of roasting pan, cover, and open lid vent completely. Heat grill until hot, about 5 minutes.

3B. FOR A GAS GRILL: Turn all burners to high, cover, and heat grill until hot, about 15 minutes. Leave all burners on high.

4. Clean and oil cooking grate. Place beef skewers on grill (directly over coals if using charcoal) perpendicular to grate. Brush meat with reserved one-third of basting sauce and cook (covered if using gas) until browned, about 3 minutes. Flip skewers, brush with half of remaining basting sauce, and cook until browned on second side, about 3 minutes. Brush meat with remaining basting sauce and cook 1 minute longer. Transfer to large platter and serve with Peanut Sauce.

NOTES FROM THE TEST KITCHEN

HOW TO PREP LEMON GRASS

When buying lemon grass, look for green (not brown) stalks that are firm and fragrant.

1. Trim dry leafy top (this part is usually green) and tough bottom of each stalk.

2. Peel and discard dry outer layer until moist, tender inner stalk is exposed.

3. Smash peeled stalk with bottom of heavy saucepan to release maximum flavor from fibrous stalk.

4. Cut smashed stalk into long, thin strips; cut crosswise to mince.

Peanut Sauce
MAKES ABOUT 1½ CUPS

- 1 **tablespoon vegetable oil**
- 1 **tablespoon Thai red curry paste**
- 1 **tablespoon packed dark brown sugar**
- 2 **garlic cloves, minced**
- 1 **cup regular or light coconut milk**
- ⅓ **cup chunky peanut butter**
- ¼ **cup dry-roasted unsalted peanuts, chopped**
- 1 **tablespoon lime juice**
- 1 **tablespoon fish sauce**
- 1 **teaspoon soy sauce**

Heat oil in small saucepan over medium heat until shimmering. Add curry paste, sugar, and garlic; cook, stirring constantly, until fragrant, about 1 minute. Add coconut milk and bring to simmer. Whisk in peanut butter until smooth. Remove from heat and stir in peanuts, lime juice, fish sauce, and soy sauce. Cool to room temperature.

SPICE-RUBBED STEAK ON THE GRILL

WHY THIS RECIPE WORKS: In this recipe, we use a two-stage rub to make the most of a comparatively inexpensive steak, the shell sirloin. We started with a savory rub of salt, onion powder, garlic powder, fish sauce, and tomato paste. This *umami*-rich rub made the steaks more savory and enhanced juiciness. For the second stage, we made our own coarsely ground rub based on toasted whole spices and dried chiles. By grinding our own spices, instead of using store-bought ground spices, we created a rub with much deeper flavor.

Grilled Steak with New Mexican Chile Rub
SERVES 6 TO 8

Shell sirloin steak is also known as top butt, butt steak, top sirloin butt, top sirloin steak, and center-cut roast. Spraying the rubbed steaks with oil helps the spices bloom, preventing a raw flavor.

STEAK
- 2 **teaspoons tomato paste**
- 2 **teaspoons fish sauce**
- 1½ **teaspoons kosher salt**

½ teaspoon onion powder

½ teaspoon garlic powder

2 (1½- to 1¾-pound) boneless shell sirloin steaks, 1 to 1¼ inches thick, trimmed

SPICE RUB

2 dried New Mexican chiles, stemmed and seeded, flesh torn into ½-inch pieces

4 teaspoons cumin seeds

4 teaspoons coriander seeds

½ teaspoon red pepper flakes

½ teaspoon black peppercorns

1 tablespoon sugar

1 tablespoon paprika

¼ teaspoon ground cloves

Vegetable oil spray

1. FOR THE STEAK: Combine tomato paste, fish sauce, salt, onion powder, and garlic powder in bowl. Pat steaks dry with paper towels. With sharp knife, cut ¹⁄₁₆-inch-deep slits on both sides of steaks, spaced ½ inch apart, in crosshatch pattern. Rub salt mixture evenly on both sides of steaks. Place steaks on wire rack set in rimmed baking sheet; let stand at room temperature for at least 1 hour. After 30 minutes, prepare grill.

2. FOR THE SPICE RUB: Toast chiles, cumin seeds, coriander seeds, pepper flakes, and peppercorns in 10-inch skillet over medium-low heat, stirring frequently, until just beginning to smoke, 3 to 4 minutes. Transfer to plate to cool, about 5 minutes. Grind spices in spice grinder or in mortar with pestle until coarsely ground. Transfer spices to bowl and stir in sugar, paprika, and cloves.

3A. FOR A CHARCOAL GRILL: Open bottom vent completely. Light large chimney starter mounded with charcoal briquettes (7 quarts). When top coals are partially covered with ash, pour two-thirds evenly over grill, then pour remaining coals over half of grill. Set cooking grate in place, cover, and open lid vent completely. Heat grill until hot, about 5 minutes.

3B. FOR A GAS GRILL: Turn all burners to high, cover, and heat grill until hot, about 15 minutes. Leave primary burner on high and turn other burner(s) to medium.

4. Clean and oil cooking grate. Sprinkle half of spice rub evenly over 1 side of steaks and press to adhere until spice rub is fully moistened. Lightly spray rubbed side of steak with vegetable oil spray, about 3 seconds. Flip steaks and repeat process of sprinkling with spice rub and spraying with oil spray on second side.

5. Place steaks over hotter side of grill and cook until browned and charred on both sides and center registers

120 to 125 degrees (for medium-rare) or 130 to 135 degrees (for medium), 6 to 8 minutes. If steaks have not reached desired temperature, move to cooler side of grill and continue to cook. Transfer steaks to clean wire rack set in rimmed baking sheet, tent loosely with aluminum foil, and let rest for 10 minutes. Slice meat thin against grain and serve.

Grilled Steak with Ancho Chile–Coffee Rub

Substitute 1 dried ancho chile for New Mexican chiles, 2 teaspoons ground coffee for paprika, and 1 teaspoon cocoa powder for ground cloves.

Grilled Steak with Spicy Chipotle Chile Rub

Substitute 2 dried chipotle chiles for New Mexican chiles, 1 teaspoon dried oregano for paprika, and ½ teaspoon ground cinnamon for ground cloves.

THE BEST PRIME RIB

WHY THIS RECIPE WORKS: The perfect prime rib should have a deep-colored, substantial crust encasing a tender, juicy rosy-pink center. To achieve this perfect roast, we started by salting the roast overnight. The salt enhanced the beefy flavor while dissolving some of the proteins, yielding a buttery-tender roast. To further enhance tenderness, we cooked the roast at a very low temperature, which allowed the meat's enzymes to act as natural tenderizers, breaking down its tough connective tissue. A brief stint under the broiler before serving ensured a crisp, flavorful crust.

Best Prime Rib
SERVES 6 TO 8

Look for a roast with an untrimmed fat cap (ideally ½ inch thick). We prefer the flavor and texture of Prime beef, but Choice grade will work as well. Monitoring the roast with a meat-probe thermometer is best. If you use an instant-read thermometer, open the oven door as little as possible and remove the roast from the oven while taking its temperature. If the roast has not reached the correct temperature in the time range specified in step 3, heat the oven to 200 degrees, wait for five minutes, then shut it off, and continue to cook the roast until it reaches the desired temperature.

1 (7-pound) first-cut beef standing rib roast (3 bones), meat removed from bones, bones reserved
Kosher salt and pepper
2 teaspoons vegetable oil

1. Using sharp knife, cut slits in surface layer of fat, spaced 1 inch apart, in crosshatch pattern, being careful to cut down to, but not into, meat. Rub 2 tablespoons salt over entire roast and into slits. Place meat back on bones (to save space in refrigerator), transfer to large plate, and refrigerate, uncovered, for at least 24 hours or up to 4 days.

2. Adjust oven rack to middle position and heat oven to 200 degrees. Set wire rack in rimmed baking sheet. Heat oil in 12-inch skillet over high heat until just smoking. Sear sides and top of roast (reserving bones) until browned, 6 to 8 minutes total (do not sear side where roast was cut from bones). Place meat back on ribs so bones fit where they were cut and let cool for 10 minutes; tie meat to bones with 2 lengths of kitchen twine between ribs. Transfer roast, fat side up, to prepared wire rack and season with pepper. Roast until meat registers 110 degrees, 3 to 4 hours.

3. Turn off oven; leave roast in oven, opening door as little as possible, until meat registers about 120 degrees (for rare) or about 125 degrees (for medium-rare,) 30 minutes to 1¼ hours longer.

4. Remove roast from oven (leave roast on baking sheet), tent loosely with aluminum foil, and let rest for at least 30 minutes or up to 1¼ hours.

5. Adjust oven rack to about 8 inches from broiler element and heat broiler. Remove foil from roast, form into 3-inch ball, and place under ribs to elevate fat cap. Broil until top of roast is well browned and crisp, 2 to 8 minutes.

6. Transfer roast to carving board; cut twine and remove ribs from roast. Slice meat into ¾-inch-thick slices. Season with salt to taste, and serve.

GRILLED SHORT RIBS

WHY THIS RECIPE WORKS: Beef short ribs can require a lot of time and tending on the grill. We began our testing by coating our ribs with a simple spice rub. We jump-started the cooking process by giving the ribs a pit stop in the oven. In a foil-covered baking dish, the fat was rendered from the ribs, and the tough, chewy collagen began to transform into moisture-retaining gelatin. Then we headed out to the grill to complete the cooking while lacquering on one of our flavorful glazes.

Grill-Roasted Beef Short Ribs

SERVES 4 TO 6

Make sure to choose ribs that are 4 to 6 inches in length and have at least 1 inch of meat on top of the bone.

SPICE RUB
2 tablespoons kosher salt
1 tablespoon packed brown sugar
2 teaspoons pepper
2 teaspoons ground cumin
2 teaspoons garlic powder
1¼ teaspoons paprika
¾ teaspoon ground fennel
⅛ teaspoon cayenne pepper

SHORT RIBS
5 pounds bone-in English-style beef short ribs, trimmed
2 tablespoons red wine vinegar

1 recipe glaze (recipes follow)

NOTES FROM THE TEST KITCHEN

PREPARING PRIME RIB

1. Removing ribs makes it easier to sear prime rib in skillet. Run sharp knife down length of bones, following contours as closely as possible to remove ribs.

2. Score fat cap in 1-inch crosshatch pattern to allow salt to contact meat directly and to improve fat rendering and crisping.

3. After searing meat, place meat back on ribs so bones fit where they were cut and let cool for 10 minutes; tie meat to bones with 2 lengths of kitchen twine between ribs. The bones provide insulation to the meat so it cooks evenly.

1. FOR THE SPICE RUB: Combine all ingredients in bowl. Measure out 1 teaspoon rub and set aside for glaze.

2. FOR THE SHORT RIBS: Adjust oven rack to middle position and heat oven to 300 degrees. Sprinkle ribs with spice rub, pressing into all sides of ribs. Arrange ribs, bone side down, in 13 by 9-inch baking dish, placing thicker ribs around perimeter of baking dish and thinner ribs in center. Sprinkle vinegar evenly over ribs. Cover baking dish tightly with aluminum foil. Bake until thickest ribs register 165 to 170 degrees, 1½ to 2 hours.

3A. FOR A CHARCOAL GRILL: Open bottom vent halfway. Arrange 2 quarts unlit charcoal into steeply banked pile against 1 side of grill. Light large chimney starter half filled with charcoal (3 quarts). When top coals are partially covered with ash, pour on top of unlit charcoal to cover one-third of grill with coals steeply banked against side of grill. Set cooking grate in place, cover, and open lid vent halfway. Heat grill until hot, about 5 minutes.

3B. FOR A GAS GRILL: Turn all burners to high, cover, and heat grill until hot, about 15 minutes. Leave primary burner on medium and turn off other burner(s). Adjust primary burner as needed to maintain grill temperature of 275 to 300 degrees.

4. Clean and oil cooking grate. Place short ribs, bone side down, on cooler side of grill about 2 inches from flames. Brush with ¼ cup glaze. Cover and cook until ribs register 195 degrees, 1¾ to 2¼ hours, rotating and brushing ribs with ¼ cup glaze every 30 minutes. Transfer ribs to large platter, tent loosely with foil, and let rest for 5 to 10 minutes before serving.

Mustard Glaze

MAKES ABOUT 1 CUP

- ½ cup Dijon mustard
- ½ cup red wine vinegar
- ¼ cup packed brown sugar
- 1 teaspoon reserved spice rub
- ⅛ teaspoon cayenne pepper

Whisk all ingredients together in bowl.

Blackberry Glaze

MAKES ABOUT 1 CUP

- 10 ounces (2 cups) fresh or frozen blackberries
- ½ cup ketchup
- ¼ cup bourbon
- 2 tablespoons packed brown sugar
- 1½ tablespoons soy sauce
- 1 teaspoon reserved spice rub
- ⅛ teaspoon cayenne pepper

Bring all ingredients to simmer in small saucepan over medium-high heat. Simmer, stirring frequently to break up blackberries, until reduced to 1¼ cups, about 10 minutes. Strain through fine-mesh strainer, pressing on solids to extract as much liquid as possible. Discard solids.

Hoisin-Tamarind Glaze

MAKES ABOUT 1 CUP

- 1 cup water
- ⅓ cup hoisin sauce
- ¼ cup tamarind paste
- 1 (2-inch) piece ginger, peeled and sliced into ½-inch-thick rounds
- 1 teaspoon reserved spice rub
- ⅛ teaspoon cayenne pepper

Bring all ingredients to simmer in small saucepan over medium-high heat. Simmer, stirring frequently, until reduced to 1¼ cups, about 10 minutes. Strain through fine-mesh strainer, pressing on solids to extract as much liquid as possible. Discard solids.

SHEPHERD'S PIE

WHY THIS RECIPE WORKS: Shepherd's pie, a hearty mix of meat, gravy, and mashed potatoes can take the better part of a day to prepare. And while the dish is indeed satisfying, traditional versions are simply too rich. We wanted to scale back its preparation and lighten the dish to fit in better with modern sensibilities. Per other modern recipes, we chose ground beef as our filling over ground lamb. To prevent the beef from turning dry and crumbly, we tossed it with a little baking soda (diluted in water) before browning it. This unusual step raises the pH level of the beef, resulting in more tender meat. An onion and mushroom gravy, spiked with Worcestershire sauce, complemented the beef filling. For the mashed potatoes, we took our cue from an Irish dish called champ and cut way back on the dairy in favor of fresh scallions, which made for a lighter, more flavorful topping that was a good match for meat filling underneath.

Shepherd's Pie

SERVES 4 TO 6

This recipe was developed with 93 percent lean ground beef. Using ground beef with a higher percentage of fat will make the dish too greasy.

- 1½ pounds 93 percent lean ground beef
- 2 tablespoons plus 2 teaspoons water
- Salt and pepper
- ½ teaspoon baking soda
- 2½ pounds russet potatoes, peeled and cut into 1-inch chunks
- 4 tablespoons unsalted butter, melted
- ½ cup milk
- 1 large egg yolk
- 8 scallions, green parts only, sliced thin
- 2 teaspoons vegetable oil
- 1 onion, chopped
- 4 ounces white mushrooms, trimmed and chopped
- 1 tablespoon tomato paste
- 2 garlic cloves, minced
- 2 tablespoons Madeira or ruby port
- 2 tablespoons all-purpose flour
- 1¼ cups beef broth
- 2 teaspoons Worcestershire sauce
- 2 sprigs fresh thyme
- 1 bay leaf
- 2 carrots, peeled and chopped
- 2 teaspoons cornstarch

1. Toss beef with 2 tablespoons water, 1 teaspoon salt, ¼ teaspoon pepper, and baking soda in bowl until thoroughly combined. Let sit for 20 minutes.

2. Meanwhile, place potatoes in medium saucepan; add water to just cover and 1 tablespoon salt. Bring to boil over high heat. Reduce heat to medium-low and simmer until potatoes are soft and tip of paring knife inserted into potato meets no resistance, 8 to 10 minutes. Drain potatoes and return to saucepan. Return saucepan to low heat and cook, shaking pot occasionally, until any surface moisture on potatoes has evaporated, about 1 minute. Remove pan from heat and mash potatoes well with potato masher. Stir in butter. Whisk together milk and egg yolk in small bowl, then stir into potatoes. Stir in scallions and season with salt and pepper to taste. Cover and set aside.

3. Heat oil in broiler-safe 10-inch skillet over medium heat until shimmering. Add onion, mushrooms, ½ teaspoon salt, and ¼ teaspoon pepper; cook, stirring occasionally, until vegetables are just starting to soften and dark bits form on bottom of skillet, 4 to 6 minutes. Stir in

tomato paste and garlic; cook until bottom of skillet is dark brown, about 2 minutes. Add Madeira and cook, scraping up any browned bits, until evaporated, about 1 minute. Stir in flour and cook 1 minute. Add broth, Worcestershire, thyme sprigs, bay leaf, and carrots; bring to boil, scraping up any browned bits. Reduce heat to medium-low, add beef in 2-inch pieces to broth and bring to gentle simmer. Cover and cook until beef is cooked through, 10 to 12 minutes, stirring and breaking up meat chunks with 2 forks halfway through. Stir cornstarch and remaining 2 teaspoons water together in bowl. Stir cornstarch mixture into filling and continue to simmer for 30 seconds. Remove thyme sprigs and bay leaf. Season with salt and pepper to taste.

4. Adjust oven rack 5 inches from broiler element and heat broiler. Place mashed potatoes in large zipper-lock bag and snip off 1 corner to create 1-inch opening. Pipe potatoes in even layer over filling, making sure to cover entire surface. Smooth potatoes with back of spoon, then use tines of fork to make ridges over surface. Place skillet on rimmed baking sheet and broil until potatoes are golden brown and crusty and filling is bubbly, 10 to 15 minutes. Let cool for 10 minutes before serving.

CORNED BEEF AND CABBAGE

WHY THIS RECIPE WORKS: Corned beef and cabbage is a hearty winter favorite, but too many recipes result in overly salty beef and washed-out, mushy vegetables. To control the salt level in our beef, we eschewed commercially corned beef and set out to make our own with an easy dry rub. We cooked our corned beef in the oven so it would benefit from the oven's slow, steady, and gentle heat. Cooking the vegetables separately in the meat's broth (while the meat rested) allowed the vegetables to be enriched by the meat's juices, but still retain their own flavor.

New England–Style Home-Corned Beef and Cabbage

SERVES 8

Leave a bit of fat attached to the brisket for better texture and flavor. A similar size point-cut brisket can be used in this recipe. The meat is cooked fully when it is tender, the muscle fibers have loosened visibly, and a skewer slides in with minimal resistance. Serve this dish with horseradish, either plain or mixed with whipped cream or sour cream, or with grainy mustard.

CORNED BEEF

½ cup kosher salt

1 tablespoon cracked black peppercorns

1 tablespoon dried thyme

2¼ teaspoons ground allspice

1½ teaspoons paprika

2 bay leaves, crumbled

1 (4- to 5-pound) beef brisket, flat cut, trimmed

VEGETABLES

1½ pounds carrots, peeled and halved crosswise, thick end halved lengthwise

1½ pounds small red potatoes

1 small rutabaga (1 pound), peeled and halved crosswise; each half cut into 6 chunks

1 small head green cabbage (2 pounds), uncored, cut into 8 wedges

1. FOR THE CORNED BEEF: Combine salt, peppercorns, thyme, allspice, paprika, and bay leaves in bowl.

2. Using metal skewer, poke about 30 holes on each side of brisket. Rub each side evenly with salt mixture. Place brisket in 2-gallon zipper-lock bag, forcing out as much air as possible. Place in 13 by 9-inch baking dish, cover with second, similar-size pan, and weight with 2 bricks or heavy cans of similar weight. Refrigerate 5 to 7 days, turning once a day.

3. Rinse brisket and pat it dry. Place brisket in Dutch oven and cover brisket with water by 1 inch. Bring to boil over high heat, skimming any scum that rises to surface. Reduce heat to medium-low, cover, and simmer until skewer inserted in thickest part of brisket slides in and out with ease, 2 to 3 hours.

4. Adjust oven rack to middle position and heat oven to 200 degrees. Transfer meat to large platter, ladle 1 cup cooking liquid over meat, cover with aluminum foil and place in oven to keep warm.

5. FOR THE VEGETABLES: Add carrots, potatoes, and rutabaga to Dutch oven and bring to a boil over high heat. Reduce heat to medium-low, cover, and simmer until vegetables begin to soften, about 7 minutes.

6. Add cabbage, increase heat to high and return to boil. Reduce heat to medium-low, cover, and simmer until all vegetables are tender, 13 to 18 minutes.

7. Meanwhile, remove meat from oven, transfer to carving board, and slice against grain into ¼-inch slices. Return meat to platter. Transfer vegetables to meat platter, moisten with additional broth, and serve.

GRILLED PORK CHOPS

WHY THIS RECIPE WORKS: To produce juicy, well-charred boneless center-cut loin chops on the grill, we used a two-pronged approach. We brined the chops to improve their ability to hold on to juices during cooking, provide seasoning throughout, and increase their tenderness. To ensure we'd get a substantial browned crust before the interior overcooked, we looked to a unique coating of anchovy paste and honey. The anchovies' amino acids couple with the fructose from honey to rapidly begin the flavorful Maillard browning reaction.

Easy Grilled Boneless Pork Chops

SERVES 4 TO 6

If your pork is enhanced, do not brine it in step 1. Very finely mashed anchovy fillets (rinsed and dried before mashing) can be used instead of anchovy paste.

6 (6- to 8-ounce) boneless pork chops, ¾ to 1 inch thick

3 tablespoons salt

1 tablespoon vegetable oil

1½ teaspoons honey

1 teaspoon anchovy paste

½ teaspoon pepper

1 recipe relish (optional) (recipes follow)

1. Cut 2 slits about 1 inch apart through outer layer of fat and connective tissue on each chop to prevent buckling. Dissolve salt in 1½ quarts cold water in large container. Submerge chops in brine and let stand at room temperature for 30 minutes.

2. Whisk together oil, honey, anchovy paste, and pepper to form smooth paste. Remove pork from brine and pat dry with paper towels. Using spoon, spread half of oil mixture evenly over 1 side of each chop (about ¼ teaspoon per side).

3A. FOR A CHARCOAL GRILL: Open bottom vent completely. Light chimney starter filled with charcoal briquettes (6 quarts). When top coals are partially covered with ash, pour evenly over half of grill. Set cooking grate in place, cover, and open lid vent completely. Heat grill until hot, about 5 minutes.

3B. FOR A GAS GRILL: Turn all burners to high, cover, and heat grill until hot, about 15 minutes. Leave primary burner on high and turn off other burner(s).

4. Clean and oil cooking grate. Place chops, oiled side down, over hot part of grill and cook, uncovered, until well browned on first side, 4 to 6 minutes. While chops are grilling, spread remaining oil mixture evenly over second side of chops. Flip chops and continue to cook until chops register 140 degrees, 4 to 6 minutes longer (if chops are well browned but register less than 140 degrees, move to cooler part of grill to finish cooking). Transfer chops to plate and let rest for 5 minutes. Serve with relish, if using.

Onion, Olive, And Caper Relish
MAKES ABOUT 2 CUPS

- ¼ cup olive oil
- 2 onions, cut into ¼-inch pieces
- 6 garlic cloves, sliced thin
- ½ cup pitted kalamata olives, chopped coarse
- ¼ cup capers, rinsed
- 3 tablespoons balsamic vinegar
- 2 tablespoons minced fresh parsley
- 1 teaspoon minced fresh marjoram
- 1 teaspoon sugar
- ½ teaspoon anchovy paste
- ½ teaspoon pepper
- ¼ teaspoon salt

Heat 2 tablespoons oil in 10-inch nonstick skillet over medium heat until shimmering. Add onions and cook until softened, about 5 minutes. Stir in garlic and cook until fragrant, about 30 seconds. Transfer onion mixture to medium bowl; stir in remaining 2 tablespoons oil, olives, capers, vinegar, parsley, marjoram, sugar, anchovy paste, pepper, and salt. Serve warm or at room temperature.

Tomato, Fennel, and Almond Relish
MAKES ABOUT 2 CUPS

- ¼ cup olive oil
- 1 fennel bulb, stalks discarded, bulb halved, cored, and cut into ¼-inch pieces
- 6 garlic cloves, sliced thin
- 2 tomatoes, cored and cut into ½-inch pieces
- ¼ cup green olives, pitted and chopped coarse
- 3 tablespoons sherry vinegar
- ¼ cup slivered almonds, toasted
- 3 tablespoons minced fresh parsley
- 1 teaspoon sugar
- Salt and pepper

Heat 2 tablespoons oil in 10-inch skillet over medium heat until shimmering. Add fennel and cook until slightly

softened, about 5 minutes. Stir in garlic and cook until fragrant, about 30 seconds. Stir in tomatoes and continue to cook until tomatoes break down slightly, about 5 minutes. Transfer fennel mixture to medium bowl; stir in remaining 2 tablespoons oil, olives, vinegar, almonds, parsley, sugar, ¾ teaspoon salt, and ½ teaspoon pepper. Serve warm or at room temperature.

Orange, Jícama, and Pepita Relish
MAKES ABOUT 3 CUPS

- 1 orange
- ¼ cup olive oil
- 2 jalapeños, stemmed, seeded, and sliced into thin rings
- 3 shallots, sliced thin
- 6 garlic cloves, sliced thin
- 2 cups jícama, peeled and cut into ¼-inch pieces
- ¼ cup pepitas, toasted
- 3 tablespoons chopped fresh cilantro
- 3 tablespoons lime juice (2 limes)
- 1 teaspoon sugar
- Salt and pepper

Cut away peel and pith from orange. Quarter orange, then slice crosswise into ¼ inch-thick pieces. Heat 2 tablespoons oil in 10-inch skillet over medium heat until shimmering. Add jalapeños and shallots and cook until slightly softened, about 5 minutes. Stir in garlic and cook until fragrant, about 30 seconds. Transfer jalapeño-shallot mixture to medium bowl; stir in orange, jícama, pepitas, cilantro, lime juice, sugar, ¾ teaspoon salt, and ½ teaspoon pepper. Serve warm or at room temperature.

BRAISED PORK CHOPS

WHY THIS RECIPE WORKS: When braising pork chops, we found it's important to avoid lean loin chops that have a tendency to dry out when even slightly overcooked. For moist, tender chops, we began with blade chops, which, like other braising cuts, have a larger amount of fat and connective tissue. We trimmed the chops of excess fat and connective tissue to prevent buckling when cooked, and used those trimmings to build a rich and flavorful braising liquid. When the chops were done braising, we used the same liquid as the foundation for a quick and tasty sauce.

Red Wine–Braised Pork Chops

SERVES 4

Look for chops with a small eye and a large amount of marbling, as these are the best suited to braising. The pork scraps can be removed when straining the sauce in step 4 and served alongside the chops. (They taste great.)

    Salt and pepper
    4 (10- to 12-ounce) bone-in pork blade chops, 1 inch thick
    2 teaspoons vegetable oil
    2 onions, halved and sliced thin
    5 sprigs fresh thyme plus ¼ teaspoon minced
    2 garlic cloves, peeled
    2 bay leaves
    1 (½-inch) piece ginger, peeled and crushed
    ⅛ teaspoon ground allspice
    ½ cup red wine
    ¼ cup ruby port
    2 tablespoons plus ½ teaspoon red wine vinegar
    1 cup low-sodium chicken broth
    2 tablespoons unsalted butter
    1 tablespoon minced fresh parsley

1. Dissolve 3 tablespoons salt in 1½ quarts cold water in large container. Submerge chops in brine, cover, and refrigerate for 30 minutes or up to 1 hour.

2. Adjust oven rack to lower-middle position and heat oven to 275 degrees. Remove chops from brine and pat dry with paper towels. Trim off meat cap and any fat and cartilage opposite rib bones. Cut trimmings into 1-inch pieces. Heat oil in Dutch oven over medium-high heat until shimmering. Add trimmings and brown on all sides, 6 to 9 minutes.

3. Reduce heat to medium and add onions, thyme sprigs, garlic, bay leaves, ginger, and allspice. Cook, stirring occasionally, until onions are golden brown, 5 to 10 minutes. Stir in wine, port, and 2 tablespoons vinegar and cook until reduced to thin syrup, 5 to 7 minutes. Add chicken broth, spread onions and pork scraps into even layer, and bring to simmer. Arrange pork chops on top of pork scraps and onions.

4. Cover, transfer to oven, and cook until meat is tender, 1¼ to 1½ hours. Remove from oven and let chops rest in pot, covered, for 30 minutes. Transfer chops to serving platter and tent with aluminum foil. Strain braising liquid through fine-mesh strainer; discard solids. Transfer braising liquid to fat separator and let stand for 5 minutes.

5. Wipe out now-empty pot with wad of paper towels. Return defatted braising liquid to pot and cook over medium-high heat until reduced to 1 cup, 3 to 7 minutes.

Off heat, whisk in butter, minced thyme, and remaining ½ teaspoon vinegar. Season with salt and pepper to taste. Pour sauce over chops, sprinkle with parsley, and serve.

FRENCH-STYLE POT-ROASTED PORK LOIN

WHY THIS RECIPE WORKS: *Enchaud périgourdin* is a fancy name for what's actually a relatively simple French dish: slow-cooked pork loin. But given that American pork is so lean, this cooking method leads to bland, stringy pork. Butterflying the pork allowed us to salt a maximum amount of surface area for a roast that was thoroughly seasoned throughout. Searing just three sides of the roast, rather than all four, prevented the bottom of the roast from overcooking from direct contact with the pot. To improve the flavor and texture of our center-cut loin, we lowered the oven temperature (to 225 degrees) and removed the roast from the oven when it was medium-rare. And while we eliminated the hard-to-find trotter (or pig's foot), we added butter for richness and sprinkled in gelatin to lend body to the sauce.

French-Style Pot-Roasted Pork Loin

SERVES 4 TO 6

We strongly prefer the flavor of natural pork in this recipe, but if enhanced pork (injected with a salt solution) is used, reduce the salt to 2 teaspoons (1 teaspoon per side) in step 2.

    2 tablespoons unsalted butter, cut into 2 pieces
    6 garlic cloves, sliced thin
    1 (2½-pound) boneless center-cut pork loin roast, trimmed
       Kosher salt and pepper
    1 teaspoon sugar
    2 teaspoons herbes de Provence
    2 tablespoons vegetable oil
    1 Granny Smith apple, peeled, cored, and cut into ¼-inch pieces
    1 onion, chopped fine
    ⅓ cup dry white wine
    2 sprigs fresh thyme
    1 bay leaf
    1 tablespoon unflavored gelatin
  ¼–¾ cup low-sodium chicken broth
    1 tablespoon minced fresh parsley

1. Adjust oven rack to lower-middle position and heat oven to 225 degrees. Melt 1 tablespoon butter in 8-inch skillet over medium-low heat. Add half of garlic and cook, stirring frequently, until golden, 5 to 7 minutes. Transfer mixture to bowl and refrigerate.

2. Position roast fat side up. Insert knife one-third of way up from bottom of roast along 1 long side and cut horizontally, stopping ½ inch before edge. Open up flap. Keeping knife parallel to cutting board, cut through thicker portion of roast about ½ inch from bottom of roast, keeping knife level with first cut and stopping about ½ inch before edge. Open up this flap. If uneven, cover with plastic wrap and use meat pounder to even out. Sprinkle 1 tablespoon salt over both sides of loin (½ tablespoon per side) and rub into pork until slightly tacky. Sprinkle sugar over inside of loin, then spread with cooled toasted garlic mixture. Starting from short side, fold roast back together like business letter (keeping fat on outside) and tie with twine at 1-inch intervals. Sprinkle tied roast evenly with herbes de Provence and season with pepper.

3. Heat 1 tablespoon oil in Dutch oven over medium heat until just smoking. Add roast, fat side down, and brown on fat side and sides (do not brown bottom of roast), 5 to 8 minutes. Transfer to large plate. Add remaining 1 tablespoon oil, apple, and onion to pot; cook, stirring frequently, until onion is softened and browned, 5 to 7 minutes. Stir in remaining garlic and cook until fragrant,

about 30 seconds. Stir in wine, thyme, and bay leaf; cook for 30 seconds. Return roast, fat side up, to pot; place large sheet of aluminum foil over pot and cover tightly with lid. Transfer pot to oven and cook until pork registers 140 degrees, 50 minutes to 1½ hours (short, thick roasts will take longer than long, thin ones).

4. Transfer roast to carving board, tent loosely with foil, and let rest for 20 minutes. While pork rests, sprinkle gelatin over ¼ cup chicken broth and let sit until gelatin softens, about 5 minutes. Remove and discard thyme sprigs and bay leaf from jus. Pour jus into 2-cup measuring cup and, if necessary, add chicken broth to measure 1¼ cups. Return jus to pot and bring to simmer over medium heat. Whisk softened gelatin mixture, remaining 1 tablespoon butter, and parsley into jus and season with salt and pepper to taste; remove from heat and cover to keep warm. Slice pork into ½-inch-thick slices, adding any accumulated juices to sauce. Serve pork, passing sauce separately.

French-Style Pot-Roasted Pork Loin with Port and Figs

Substitute ¾ cup chopped dried figs for apple and port for white wine. Add 1 tablespoon balsamic vinegar to sauce with butter in step 4.

FRENCH POTATO CASSEROLE

WHY THIS RECIPE WORKS: In the old days, this casserole of potatoes and onions was baked beneath a roast, which allowed the casserole to be seasoned by the savory fat and juices of the roast. To get the same luxurious results without the roast, we started by rendering a small amount of bacon, which lent the dish a meaty flavor with a hint of smokiness. We then browned the onions in the rendered bacon fat, which gave the dish remarkable complexity.

Potato Casserole with Bacon and Caramelized Onion
SERVES 6 TO 8

Do not rinse or soak the potatoes, as this will wash away their starch, which is essential to the dish. A mandoline makes slicing the potatoes much easier. For the proper texture, make sure to let the casserole stand for 20 minutes before serving.

3 slices thick-cut bacon, cut into ½-inch pieces
1 large onion, halved and sliced thin
1¼ teaspoons salt
2 teaspoons chopped fresh thyme
½ teaspoon pepper
1¼ cups low-sodium chicken broth
1¼ cups beef broth
3 pounds Yukon Gold potatoes, peeled
2 tablespoons unsalted butter, cut into 4 pieces

1. Adjust oven rack to lower-middle position and heat oven to 425 degrees. Grease 13 by 9-inch baking dish.

2. Cook bacon in medium saucepan over medium-low heat until crisp, 10 to 13 minutes. Using slotted spoon, transfer bacon to paper towel–lined plate. Remove and discard all but 1 tablespoon fat from pot. Return pot to medium heat and add onion and ¼ teaspoon salt; cook, stirring frequently, until onion is soft and golden brown, about 25 minutes, adjusting heat and adding water 1 tablespoon at a time if onion or bottom of pot becomes too dark. Transfer onion to large bowl; add bacon, thyme, remaining 1 teaspoon salt, and pepper. Add broths to now-empty saucepan and bring to simmer over medium-high heat, scraping bottom of pan to loosen any browned bits.

3. Slice potatoes ⅛ inch thick. Transfer to bowl with onion mixture and toss to combine. Transfer to prepared baking dish. Firmly press down on mixture to compress into even layer. Carefully pour hot broth over top of potatoes. Dot surface evenly with butter.

4. Bake, uncovered, until potatoes are tender and golden brown on edges and most of liquid has been absorbed, 45 to 55 minutes. Transfer to wire rack and let stand for 20 minutes to fully absorb broth before cutting and serving.

TACOS AL PASTOR

WHY THIS RECIPE WORKS: In Mexico, super-thin slices of pork butt and pork fat are marinated in chiles and tomato, stacked and roasted on a spit, and shaved, hot and crispy, into a corn tortilla. To mimic this popular taco filling, which is often garnished with sweet pineapple, without any special equipment, we had to get creative. We braised ½-inch-thick slabs of pork butt in a mix of guajillo chiles, tomatoes, and spices until tender, before basting them with sauce on the grill until crisped and charred. Chopped into bite-size strips and topped with grilled pineapple, our simple homemade spicy pork filling lives up to the original.

Spicy Pork Tacos (al Pastor)
SERVES 6 TO 8

Boneless pork butt is often labeled Boston butt in the supermarket. If you can't find guajillo chiles, New Mexican chiles may be substituted, although the dish may be spicier. To warm tortillas, place them on a plate, cover with a damp dish towel, and microwave for 60 to 90 seconds. Keep tortillas covered and serve immediately.

10 large dried guajillo chiles, wiped clean
1½ cups water
1¼ pounds plum tomatoes, cored and quartered
8 garlic cloves, peeled
4 bay leaves
Salt and pepper
¾ teaspoon sugar
½ teaspoon ground cumin
⅛ teaspoon ground cloves
1 (3-pound) boneless pork butt roast
1 lime, cut into 8 wedges
½ pineapple, peeled, cored, and cut into ½-inch-thick rings
Vegetable oil
18 (6-inch) corn tortillas, warmed
1 small onion, chopped fine
½ cup coarsely chopped fresh cilantro

1. Toast guajillos in large Dutch oven over medium-high heat until softened and fragrant, 2 to 4 minutes. Transfer to large plate and, when cool enough to handle, remove stems.

2. Return toasted guajillos to now-empty Dutch oven, add water, tomatoes, garlic, bay leaves, 2 teaspoons salt, ½ teaspoon pepper, sugar, cumin, and cloves, and bring to simmer over medium-high heat. Cover, reduce heat, and simmer, stirring occasionally, until guajillos are softened and tomatoes mash easily, about 20 minutes.

3. While sauce simmers, trim excess fat from exterior of pork, leaving ¼-inch-thick fat cap. Slice pork against grain into ½-inch-thick slabs.

4. Transfer guajillo-tomato mixture to blender and process until smooth, about 1 minute. Strain puree through fine-mesh strainer, pressing on solids to extract as much liquid as possible. Return puree to pot, submerge pork slices in liquid, and bring to simmer over medium heat. Partially cover, reduce heat, and gently simmer until pork is tender but still holds together, 1½ to 1¾ hours, flipping and rearranging pork halfway through cooking. (Pork can be left in sauce, cooled to room temperature, and refrigerated for up to 2 days.)

5. Transfer pork to large plate, season both sides with

salt, and cover tightly with aluminum foil. Whisk sauce to combine. Transfer ½ cup sauce to bowl for grilling; pour off all but ½ cup remaining sauce from pot and reserve for another use. Squeeze 2 lime wedges into sauce in pot and add spent wedges; season with salt to taste.

6A. FOR A CHARCOAL GRILL: Open bottom vent halfway. Light large chimney starter filled with charcoal briquettes (6 quarts). When top coals are partially covered with ash, pour evenly over grill. Set cooking grate in place, cover, and open lid vent halfway. Heat grill until hot, about 5 minutes.

6B. FOR A GAS GRILL: Turn all burners to high, cover, and heat grill until hot, about 15 minutes. Turn all burners to medium.

7. Clean and oil cooking grate. Brush 1 side of pork with ¼ cup reserved sauce. Place pork on 1 side of grill, sauce side down, and cook until well browned and crisp, 5 to 7 minutes. Brush pork with remaining ¼ cup reserved sauce, flip, and continue to cook until second side is well browned and crisp, 5 to 7 minutes longer. Transfer to carving board. Meanwhile, brush both sides of pineapple rings with vegetable oil and season with salt to taste. Place on other half of grill and cook until pineapple is softened and caramelized, 10 to 14 minutes; transfer pineapple to carving board.

8. Coarsely chop grilled pineapple and transfer to serving bowl. Using tongs or carving fork to steady hot pork, slice each piece crosswise into ⅛-inch pieces. Bring remaining ½ cup sauce in pot to simmer, add sliced pork, remove pot from heat, and toss to coat pork well. Season with salt to taste.

9. Spoon small amount of pork into each warm tortilla and serve, passing chopped pineapple, remaining 6 lime wedges, onion, and cilantro separately.

SICHUAN STIR-FRIED PORK IN GARLIC SAUCE

WHY THIS RECIPE WORKS: Recipes for this Sichuan staple are imbalanced. Some taste cloyingly sweet, while others overdo it on the vinegar. And the pork is usually dry, chewy, and stringy. We wanted a version as good as anything we'd order in a Sichuan restaurant. To re-create the succulent pork found in the best restaurant stir-fries (usually achieved by low-temperature deep frying), we soaked the pork in a baking soda solution, which tenderizes and moisturizes the meat, and then coated it in a velvetizing cornstarch slurry, which helps it retain moisture as it cooks. And the secret to the sauce's silken texture and rich flavor? Ketchup and fish sauce, both high in flavor-enhancing glutamates.

Sichuan Stir-Fried Pork in Garlic Sauce
SERVES 4 TO 6

If Chinese black vinegar is unavailable, substitute 2 teaspoons balsamic vinegar and 2 teaspoons rice vinegar. If Asian broad-bean chili paste is unavailable, substitute 2 teaspoons Asian chili-garlic paste or Sriracha sauce. Serve with steamed white rice.

SAUCE
- ½ cup low-sodium chicken broth
- 2 tablespoons sugar
- 2 tablespoons soy sauce
- 4 teaspoons Chinese black vinegar
- 1 tablespoon toasted sesame oil
- 1 tablespoon Chinese rice wine or dry sherry
- 2 teaspoons ketchup
- 2 teaspoons fish sauce
- 2 teaspoons cornstarch

PORK
- 12 ounces boneless country-style pork ribs, trimmed
- 1 teaspoon baking soda
- 2 teaspoons Chinese rice wine or dry sherry
- 2 teaspoons cornstarch

STIR-FRY
- 2 scallions, white parts minced, green parts sliced thin
- 4 garlic cloves, minced
- 2 tablespoons Asian broad-bean chili paste
- ¼ cup vegetable oil
- 6 ounces shiitake mushrooms, stemmed and sliced thin
- 2 celery ribs, cut on bias into ¼-inch slices

1. FOR THE SAUCE: Whisk all ingredients together in bowl; set aside.

2. FOR THE PORK: Cut pork into 2-inch lengths, then cut each length into ¼-inch matchsticks. Combine pork with ½ cup cold water and baking soda in bowl. Let sit at room temperature for 15 minutes.

3. Rinse pork in cold water. Drain well and pat dry with paper towels. Whisk rice wine and cornstarch together in bowl. Add pork and toss to coat.

4. FOR THE STIR-FRY: Combine scallion whites, garlic, and chili paste in bowl.

5. Heat 1 tablespoon oil in 12-inch nonstick skillet over high heat until just smoking. Add mushrooms and cook, stirring frequently, until tender, 2 to 4 minutes. Add celery and continue to cook until celery is crisp-tender, 2 to 4 minutes. Transfer vegetables to separate bowl.

6. Add remaining 3 tablespoons oil to now-empty skillet and place over medium-low heat. Add scallion-garlic mixture and cook, stirring frequently, until fragrant, about 30 seconds. Transfer 1 tablespoon scallion-garlic oil to small bowl and set aside. Add pork to skillet and cook, stirring frequently, until no longer pink, 3 to 5 minutes. Whisk sauce mixture to recombine and add to skillet. Increase heat to high and cook, stirring constantly, until sauce is thickened and pork is cooked through, 1 to 2 minutes. Return vegetables to skillet and toss to combine. Transfer to serving platter, sprinkle with scallion greens and reserved scallion-garlic oil, and serve.

BEST CRAB CAKES

WHY THIS RECIPE WORKS: We wanted to come up with the best possible crab cakes—sweet, plump meat delicately seasoned and seamlessly held together with a binder that didn't mask seafood flavor. And we didn't want shopping to be an issue—our crab cakes should work with either fresh crabmeat or the pasteurized variety found at the supermarket. Instead of flavor-muting bread crumbs, gloppy mayo, and eggs, we bound our cakes with a delicate shrimp mousse, which also enhanced the crabmeat's natural sweetness. Classic components like Old Bay seasoning and lemon juice bolstered the crab's flavor and panko bread crumbs helped ensure a crisp crust.

Best Crab Cakes

SERVES 4

Either fresh or pasteurized crabmeat can be used in this recipe. With packaged crab, if the meat smells clean and fresh when you first open the package, skip steps 1 and 4 and simply blot away any excess liquid. Serve the crab cakes with lemon wedges.

- 1 **pound lump crabmeat, picked over for shells**
- 1 **cup milk**
- 1½ **cups panko bread crumbs**
   Salt and pepper
- 2 **celery ribs, chopped**
- ½ **cup chopped onion**
- 1 **garlic clove, peeled and smashed**
- 1 **tablespoon unsalted butter**
- 4 **ounces shrimp, peeled, deveined, and tails removed**
- ¼ **cup heavy cream**

- 2 **teaspoons Dijon mustard**
- 1 **teaspoon lemon juice**
- ½ **teaspoon hot sauce**
- ½ **teaspoon Old Bay seasoning**
- ¼ **cup vegetable oil**

1. Place crabmeat and milk in bowl, making sure crab is totally submerged. Cover and refrigerate for 20 minutes.

2. Meanwhile, place ¾ cup panko in small zipper-lock bag and finely crush with rolling pin. Transfer crushed panko to 10-inch nonstick skillet and add remaining ¾ cup panko. Toast over medium-high heat, stirring constantly, until golden brown, about 5 minutes. Transfer panko to shallow dish and stir in ¼ teaspoon salt and pepper to taste. Wipe out skillet.

3. Pulse celery, onion, and garlic together in food processor until finely chopped, 5 to 8 pulses, scraping down bowl as needed. Transfer vegetables to large bowl. Rinse processor bowl and blade. Melt butter in now-empty skillet over medium heat. Add chopped vegetables, ½ teaspoon salt, and ⅛ teaspoon pepper; cook, stirring frequently, until vegetables are softened and all moisture has evaporated, 4 to 6 minutes. Return vegetables to large bowl and let cool to room temperature. Rinse out pan and wipe clean.

4. Strain crabmeat through fine-mesh strainer, pressing firmly to remove milk but being careful not to break up lumps of crabmeat.

5. Pulse shrimp in now-empty food processor until finely ground, 12 to 15 pulses, scraping down bowl as needed. Add cream and pulse to combine, 2 to 4 pulses, scraping down bowl as needed. Transfer shrimp puree to bowl with cooled vegetables. Add mustard, lemon juice, hot sauce, and Old Bay; stir until well combined. Add crabmeat and fold gently with rubber spatula, being careful not to overmix and break up lumps of crabmeat. Divide mixture into 8 balls and firmly press into ½-inch-thick patties. Place cakes in rimmed baking sheet lined with parchment paper, cover tightly with plastic wrap, and refrigerate for 30 minutes.

6. Coat each cake with panko, firmly pressing to adhere crumbs to exterior. Heat 1 tablespoon oil in now-empty skillet over medium heat until shimmering. Place 4 cakes in skillet and cook without moving them until golden brown, 3 to 4 minutes. Using 2 spatulas, carefully flip cakes. Add 1 tablespoon oil, reduce heat to medium-low, and continue to cook until second side is golden brown, 4 to 6 minutes. Transfer cakes to platter. Wipe out skillet and repeat with remaining 4 cakes and remaining 2 tablespoons oil. Serve immediately.

EASY SALMON CAKES

WHY THIS RECIPE WORKS: Most salmon cakes are mushy and overly fishy, camouflaged by gluey binders and heavy-handed seasoning. Our goal was a quick and simple recipe for salmon cakes that first and foremost tasted like salmon, with a moist, delicate texture. To simplify preparation, we broke out our food processor. Pulsing small pieces of salmon (raw was preferred over cooked, which turned fishy), allowed for more even chopping and resulted in small, discrete pieces of fish. We also found a way to ditch the egg and flour steps of the breading process. Instead, we coated the salmon cakes with panko, which we had also used as a binder.

Easy Salmon Cakes
SERVES 4

If buying a skin-on salmon fillet, purchase 1⅓ pounds fish. This will yield 1¼ pounds fish after skinning. When processing the salmon, it is OK to have some pieces that are larger than ¼ inch. It is important to avoid over-processing the fish. Serve the salmon cakes with lemon wedges and/or tartar sauce.

- 3 tablespoons plus ¾ cup panko bread crumbs
- 2 tablespoons minced fresh parsley
- 2 tablespoons mayonnaise
- 4 teaspoons lemon juice
- 1 scallion, sliced thin
- 1 small shallot, minced
- 1 teaspoon Dijon mustard
- ¾ teaspoon salt
- ¼ teaspoon pepper
  Pinch cayenne pepper
- 1 (1¼-pound) skinless salmon fillet, cut into 1-inch pieces
- ½ cup vegetable oil

1. Combine 3 tablespoons panko, parsley, mayonnaise, lemon juice, scallion, shallot, mustard, salt, pepper, and cayenne in bowl. Working in 3 batches, pulse salmon in food processor until coarsely chopped into ¼-inch pieces, about 2 pulses, transferring each batch to bowl with panko mixture. Gently mix until uniformly combined.

2. Place remaining ¾ cup panko in shallow dish. Using ⅓-cup measure, scoop level amount of salmon mixture and transfer to baking sheet; repeat to make 8 cakes. Carefully coat each cake with bread crumbs, gently patting into disk measuring 2¾ inches in diameter and 1 inch high. Return coated cakes to baking sheet.

3. Heat oil in 12-inch skillet over medium-high heat until shimmering. Place salmon cakes in skillet and cook without moving until bottoms are golden brown, about 2 minutes. Carefully flip cakes and cook until second side is golden brown, 2 to 3 minutes. Transfer cakes to paper towel–lined plate to drain for 1 minute. Serve.

Easy Salmon Cakes with Smoked Salmon, Capers, and Dill

Reduce fresh salmon to 1 pound and salt to ½ teaspoon. Substitute 1 tablespoon minced fresh dill for parsley. Add 4 ounces finely chopped smoked salmon and 1 table-spoon chopped capers to bowl with salmon mixture.

POACHED FISH FILLETS WITH SHERRY-TOMATO VINAIGRETTE

WHY THIS RECIPE WORKS: This restaurant-style dish requires a potful of pricey olive oil and promises super-moist, delicately cooked fish. Using a small skillet and flipping the fish halfway through cooking allowed us to cut back to ¾ cup of oil, which we employed to crisp flavorful garnishes and finally blended into a creamy vinaigrette.

Poached Fish Fillets with Crispy Artichokes and Sherry-Tomato Vinaigrette
SERVES 4

Fillets of meaty white fish like cod, halibut, sea bass, or snapper work best in this recipe. Just make sure the fillets are at least 1 inch thick. A neutral oil such as canola can be substituted for the pure olive oil. The onion half in step 3 is used to displace the oil; a 4-ounce porcelain ramekin may be used instead. Serve with couscous or steamed white rice.

FISH

- 4 (6-ounce) skinless white fish fillets, 1 inch thick
  Kosher salt
- 4 ounces frozen artichoke hearts, thawed, patted dry, and sliced in half lengthwise
- 1 tablespoon cornstarch
- ¾ cup olive oil
- 3 garlic cloves, minced
- ½ onion, peeled

VINAIGRETTE

- 4 ounces cherry tomatoes
- ½ small shallot, peeled
- 4 teaspoons sherry vinegar
- Kosher salt and pepper

- 2 ounces cherry tomatoes, cut into ⅛-inch-thick rounds
- 1 tablespoon minced fresh parsley

1. FOR THE FISH: Adjust oven racks to middle and lower-middle positions and heat oven to 250 degrees. Pat fish dry with paper towels and season each fillet with ¼ teaspoon salt. Let sit at room temperature for 20 minutes.

2. Meanwhile, toss artichokes with cornstarch in bowl to coat. Heat ½ cup oil in 10-inch nonstick ovenproof skillet over medium heat until shimmering. Shake excess cornstarch from artichokes and add to skillet; cook, stirring occasionally, until crisp and golden, 2 to 4 minutes. Add garlic and continue to cook until garlic is golden, 30 to 60 seconds. Strain oil through fine-mesh strainer into bowl. Transfer artichokes and garlic to ovenproof paper towel–lined plate and season with salt. Do not wash strainer.

3. Return strained oil to skillet and add remaining ¼ cup oil. Place onion half in center of pan. Let oil cool until it registers about 180 degrees, 5 to 8 minutes. Arrange fish fillets, skinned side up, around onion (oil should come roughly halfway up fillets). Spoon a little oil over each fillet, cover skillet, transfer to middle oven rack, and cook for 15 minutes.

4. Remove skillet from oven. Using 2 spatulas, carefully flip fillets. Cover skillet, return to middle rack, and place plate with artichokes and garlic on lower-middle rack. Continue to cook fish until it registers 130 to 135 degrees, 9 to 14 minutes longer. Gently transfer fish to serving platter, reserving ½ cup oil, and tent fish loosely with aluminum foil. Turn off oven, leaving plate of artichokes in oven.

5. FOR THE VINAIGRETTE: Process cherry tomatoes, shallot, vinegar, ¾ teaspoon salt, and ½ teaspoon pepper with reserved ½ cup fish cooking oil in blender until smooth, 1 to 2 minutes. Add any accumulated fish juices from platter, season with salt to taste, and blend for 10 seconds. Strain sauce through fine-mesh strainer; discard solids.

6. To serve, pour vinaigrette around fish. Garnish each fillet with warmed crisped artichokes and garlic, tomato rounds, and parsley. Serve immediately.

Poached Fish Fillets with Jalapeño Vinaigrette

To make this dish spicier, add some of the reserved chile seeds to the vinaigrette in step 5. Serve with steamed white rice.

For fish, substitute 2 jalapeño chiles, stemmed, seeded, and cut into ⅛-inch-thick rings, for artichoke hearts and reduce cornstarch to 2 teaspoons. For vinaigrette, process 4 jalapeños, stemmed, halved, and seeded (seeds reserved); ½ small shallot, peeled; 6 sprigs fresh cilantro; 8 teaspoons lime juice; and ½ teaspoon kosher salt with ½ cup reserved fish cooking oil as directed in step 5. Garnish fish with 2 tablespoons fresh cilantro leaves and ½ avocado, cut into ¼-inch pieces.

Poached Fish Fillets with Crispy Scallions and Miso-Ginger Vinaigrette

For fish, substitute 8 scallion whites, sliced ¼ inch thick, for artichoke hearts; omit garlic; and reduce cornstarch to 2 teaspoons. For vinaigrette, process 6 scallion greens, 8 teaspoons lime juice, 2 tablespoons mirin, 4 teaspoons white miso paste, 2 teaspoons minced ginger, and ½ teaspoon sugar with ½ cup reserved fish cooking oil as directed in step 5. Garnish fish with 2 thinly sliced scallion greens and 2 halved and thinly sliced radishes.

GRILL-SMOKED SALMON

WHY THIS RECIPE WORKS: We wanted to capture the intense, smoky flavor of hot-smoked fish and the firm but silky texture of the cold-smoked type, but we also wanted to skip specialized equipment and make this dish less of a project recipe. To prepare the salmon for smoking, we quick-cured the fish with a mixture of salt and sugar to draw moisture from the flesh, which firmed it up, and we seasoned it inside and out. We then cooked the fish indirectly over a gentle fire with ample smoke to produce salmon that was sweet, smoky, and tender. We also cut our large fillet into individual serving-size portions. This small step delivered big: First, it ensured more thorough smoke exposure (without increasing the time) by creating more surface area. Second, the smaller pieces of delicate salmon were far easier to get off the grill intact than one large fillet.

Grill-Smoked Salmon

SERVES 6

Use center-cut salmon fillets of similar thickness so that they cook at the same rate. The best way to ensure uniformity is to buy a 2½- to 3-pound whole center-cut fillet and cut it into six pieces. Avoid mesquite wood chunks for this recipe. Serve the salmon with lemon wedges or with our "Smoked Salmon Platter" Sauce or Apple-Mustard Sauce.

- 2 **tablespoons sugar**
- 1 **tablespoon kosher salt**
- 6 **(6- to 8-ounce) center-cut skin-on salmon fillets**
- 2 **wood chunks soaked in water for 30 minutes and drained (if using charcoal) or 2 cups wood chips, half of chips soaked in water for 15 minutes and drained (if using gas)**

1. Combine sugar and salt in bowl. Set wire rack in rimmed baking sheet, set salmon on rack, and sprinkle flesh side evenly with sugar mixture. Refrigerate, uncovered, for 1 hour. With paper towels, brush any excess salt and sugar from salmon and blot dry. Return fish on wire rack to refrigerator, uncovered, while preparing grill.

2A. FOR A CHARCOAL GRILL: Open bottom vent halfway. Light large chimney starter one-third filled with charcoal briquettes (2 quarts). When top coals are partially covered with ash, pour into steeply banked pile against side of grill. Place wood chunks on top of coals. Set cooking grate in place, cover, and open lid vent halfway. Heat grill until hot and wood chunks begin to smoke, about 5 minutes.

2B. FOR A GAS GRILL: Combine soaked and unsoaked chips. Use large piece of heavy-duty aluminum foil to wrap chips into foil packet and cut several vent holes in top. Place wood chip packet directly on primary burner. Turn primary burner to high (leave other burners off), cover, and heat grill until hot and wood chips begin to smoke, 15 to 25 minutes. Turn primary burner to medium. (Adjust primary burner as needed to maintain grill temperature of 275 to 300 degrees.)

3. Clean and oil cooking grate. Fold piece of heavy-duty foil into 18 by 6-inch rectangle. Place foil rectangle over cool side of grill and place salmon pieces on foil, spaced at least ½ inch apart. Cover grill (positioning lid vent over fish if using charcoal) and cook until center of thickest part of fillet registers 125 degrees and is still translucent when checked with tip of paring knife, 30 to 40 minutes. Transfer to platter and serve, or allow to cool to room temperature.

"Smoked Salmon Platter" Sauce

MAKES 1½ CUPS

This sauce incorporates the three garnishes that are commonly served on a smoked salmon platter—hard-cooked egg, capers, and dill.

- 1 **large egg yolk, plus 1 large hard-cooked egg, chopped fine**
- 2 **teaspoons Dijon mustard**
- 2 **teaspoons sherry vinegar**
- ½ **cup vegetable oil**
- 2 **tablespoons capers, rinsed, plus 1 teaspoon caper brine**
- 2 **tablespoons minced shallot**
- 2 **tablespoons minced fresh dill**

Whisk egg yolk, mustard, and vinegar together in medium bowl. Whisking constantly, slowly drizzle in oil until emulsified, about 1 minute. Gently fold in capers and brine, hard-cooked egg, shallot, and dill.

Apple-Mustard Sauce

MAKES 1½ CUPS

This sweet and tangy sauce is a perfect complement to our Grill-Smoked Salmon.

- 2 **Honeycrisp or Granny Smith apples, peeled, cored, and cut into ¼-inch dice**
- ¼ **cup whole-grain mustard**
- 2 **tablespoons Dijon mustard**
- 2 **tablespoons minced fresh chervil or parsley**
- 1 **tablespoon cider vinegar**
- 1 **tablespoon honey**
- ¼ **teaspoon salt**

Combine all ingredients in bowl.

MUSHROOM AND LEEK GALETTE WITH GORGONZOLA

WHY THIS RECIPE WORKS: Most vegetable tarts rely on the same pastry dough used for fruit tarts. But vegetable tarts are more prone to leaking liquid into the crust or falling apart when the tart is sliced. We needed a crust that was extra sturdy and boasted a complex flavor of its own. To increase the flavor of the crust and keep it tender, we swapped out part of the white flour for nutty whole wheat, and we used butter rather than shortening. To punch up its flaky texture and introduce more structure, we gave the crust a series of folds to create numerous interlocking layers. For a filling that was both flavorful and cohesive, we paired mushrooms and leeks with rich, potent binders like Gorgonzola cheese and crème fraîche.

Mushroom and Leek Galette with Gorgonzola

SERVES 6

Cutting a few small holes in the dough prevents it from lifting off the pan as it bakes. A pizza stone helps to crisp the crust but is not essential. An overturned baking sheet can be used in place of the pizza stone.

DOUGH

1¼ cups (6¼ ounces) all-purpose flour
½   cup (2¾ ounces) whole-wheat flour
1   tablespoon sugar
¾   teaspoon salt
10 tablespoons unsalted butter, cut into
    ½-inch pieces and chilled
7   tablespoons ice water
1   teaspoon distilled white vinegar

FILLING

1¼ pounds shiitake mushrooms, stemmed and sliced thin
5   teaspoons olive oil
1   pound leeks, white and light green parts only, sliced
    ½ inch thick and washed thoroughly (3 cups)
1   teaspoon minced fresh thyme
2   tablespoons crème fraîche
1   tablespoon Dijon mustard
    Salt and pepper
3   ounces Gorgonzola cheese, crumbled (¾ cup)
1   large egg, lightly beaten
    Kosher salt
2   tablespoons minced fresh parsley

1. FOR THE DOUGH: Pulse all-purpose flour, whole-wheat flour, sugar, and salt together in food processor until combined, 2 to 3 pulses. Add butter and pulse until it forms pea-size pieces, about 10 pulses. Transfer mixture to medium bowl.

2. Sprinkle water and vinegar over mixture. With rubber spatula, use folding motion to mix until loose, shaggy mass forms with some dry flour remaining (do not overwork). Transfer mixture to center of large sheet of plastic wrap, press gently into rough 4-inch square, and wrap tightly. Refrigerate for at least 45 minutes.

3. Transfer dough to lightly floured counter. Roll into 11 by 8-inch rectangle with short side of rectangle parallel to edge of counter. Using bench scraper, bring bottom third of dough up, then fold upper third over it, folding like business letter into 8 by 4-inch rectangle. Turn dough 90 degrees counterclockwise. Roll out dough again into 11 by 8-inch rectangle and fold into thirds again. Turn dough 90 degrees counterclockwise and repeat rolling and folding into thirds.

After last fold, fold dough in half to create 4-inch square. Press top of dough gently to seal. Wrap in plastic and refrigerate for at least 45 minutes or up to 2 days.

4. FOR THE FILLING: Microwave mushrooms in covered bowl until just tender, 3 to 5 minutes. Transfer to colander to drain; return to bowl. Meanwhile, heat 1 tablespoon oil in 12-inch skillet over medium heat until shimmering. Add leeks and thyme, cover, and cook, stirring occasionally, until leeks are tender and beginning to brown, 5 to 7 minutes. Transfer to bowl with mushrooms. Stir in crème fraîche and mustard. Season with salt and pepper to taste. Set aside.

5. Adjust oven rack to lower-middle position, place pizza stone on rack, and heat oven to 400 degrees. Line rimmed baking sheet with parchment paper. Remove dough from refrigerator and let stand at room temperature for 15 to 20 minutes. Roll out on generously floured counter (use up to ¼ cup flour) to 14-inch circle about ⅛ inch thick. (Trim edges as needed to form rough circle.) Transfer dough to prepared baking sheet. With tip of paring knife, cut five ¼-inch circles in dough (one at center and four evenly spaced halfway from center to edge of dough). Brush top of dough with 1 teaspoon oil.

6. Spread half of filling evenly over dough, leaving 2-inch border around edge. Sprinkle with half of Gorgonzola, cover with remaining filling, and top with remaining Gorgonzola. Drizzle remaining 1 teaspoon oil over filling. Gently grasp 1 edge of dough and fold up outer 2 inches over filling. Repeat around circumference of tart, overlapping dough every 2 to 3 inches; gently pinch pleated dough to secure but do not press dough into filling. Brush dough with egg and sprinkle evenly with kosher salt.

7. Lower oven temperature to 375 degrees. Bake until crust is deep golden brown and filling is beginning to brown, 35 to 45 minutes. Let tart cool on baking sheet

NOTES FROM THE TEST KITCHEN

PLEATING A FREE-FORM TART

It's surprisingly simple to create pleated edges around free-form tarts.

Gently grasp 1 edge of dough and make 2-inch-wide fold over filling. Lift and fold another segment of dough over first fold to form pleat. Repeat every 2 to 3 inches.

on wire rack for 10 minutes. Using offset or wide metal spatula, loosen tart from parchment and carefully slide tart off parchment onto cutting board. Sprinkle with parsley, cut into wedges, and serve.

Potato and Shallot Galette with Goat Cheese

Substitute 1 pound Yukon Gold potatoes, sliced ¼ inch thick, for mushrooms and increase microwave cooking time to 4 to 8 minutes. Substitute 4 ounces thinly sliced shallots for leeks and rosemary for thyme. Increase amount of crème fraîche to ¼ cup and substitute ¼ cup chopped pitted kalamata olives and 1 teaspoon finely grated lemon zest for Dijon mustard. Substitute goat cheese for Gorgonzola.

Butternut Squash Galette with Gruyère

1. Microwave 6 ounces baby spinach and ¼ cup water in bowl until spinach is wilted and decreased in volume by half, 3 to 4 minutes. Using potholders, remove bowl from microwave and keep covered for 1 minute. Carefully remove plate and transfer spinach to colander. Gently press spinach with rubber spatula to release excess liquid. Transfer spinach to cutting board and chop coarse. Return spinach to colander and press again with rubber spatula; set aside.

2. Substitute 1¼ pounds butternut squash, peeled and cut into ½-inch cubes, for mushrooms and increase microwave cooking time to about 8 minutes. Substitute 1 thinly sliced red onion for leeks and ½ teaspoon minced fresh oregano for thyme. Substitute 1 teaspoon sherry vinegar for Dijon mustard and stir reserved spinach and 3 ounces shredded Gruyère cheese into filling along with crème fraîche and vinegar in step 4. Omit Gorgonzola.

SAAG PANEER

WHY THIS RECIPE WORKS: *Saag paneer,* soft cubes of creamy cheese in a spicy pureed spinach sauce is an Indian restaurant classic. We found that re-creating this dish at home wasn't so difficult. We made our own cheese by heating a combination of whole milk and buttermilk, squeezing the curds of moisture, then weighting the cheese down until it was firm enough to slice. As for the spinach sauce, instead of cooking the spinach in batches on the stovetop, we simply wilted it all in the microwave. The addition of mustard greens gave our sauce additional complexity that worked well with the dish's warm spices. Canned diced tomatoes brightened the dish. And buttery cashews—both pureed and chopped gave our Indian classic a subtle nutty richness.

Indian-Style Spinach with Fresh Cheese (Saag Paneer)

SERVES 4 TO 6

To ensure that the cheese is firm, wring it tightly in step 2 and be sure to use two plates that nestle together snugly. Use commercially produced cultured buttermilk in this recipe. We found that some locally produced buttermilks didn't sufficiently coagulate the milk. Serve with basmati rice.

CHEESE
- **3** quarts whole milk
- **3** cups buttermilk
- **1** tablespoon salt

SPINACH SAUCE
- **1** (10-ounce) bag curly-leaf spinach, rinsed
- **12** ounces mustard greens, stemmed and rinsed
- **3** tablespoons unsalted butter
- **1** teaspoon cumin seeds
- **1** teaspoon ground coriander
- **1** teaspoon paprika
- **½** teaspoon ground cardamom
- **¼** teaspoon ground cinnamon
- **1** onion, chopped fine
   Salt and pepper
- **3** garlic cloves, minced
- **1** tablespoon grated fresh ginger
- **1** jalapeño chile, stemmed, seeded, and minced
- **1** (14.5-ounce) can diced tomatoes, drained and chopped coarse
- **½** cup roasted cashews, chopped coarse
- **1** cup water
- **1** cup buttermilk
- **3** tablespoons chopped fresh cilantro

1. FOR THE CHEESE: Line colander with triple layer of cheesecloth and set in sink. Bring milk to boil in Dutch oven over medium-high heat. Whisk in buttermilk and salt, turn off heat, and let stand for 1 minute. Pour milk mixture through cheesecloth and let curds drain for 15 minutes.

2. Pull edges of cheesecloth together to form pouch. Twist edges of cheesecloth together, firmly squeezing out as much liquid as possible from cheese curds. Place taut, twisted cheese pouch between 2 large plates and weigh down top plate with heavy Dutch oven. Set aside at room temperature until cheese is firm and set, at least 45 minutes. Remove cheesecloth and cut cheese into ½-inch pieces. (Left uncut, cheese can be wrapped in plastic wrap and refrigerated for up to 3 days.)

3. FOR THE SPINACH SAUCE: Place spinach in large bowl, cover, and microwave until wilted, about 3 minutes. When cool enough to handle, chop enough spinach to measure ⅓ cup and set aside. Transfer remaining spinach to blender and wipe out bowl. Place mustard greens in now-empty bowl, cover, and microwave until wilted, about 4 minutes. When cool enough to handle, chop enough mustard greens to measure ⅓ cup and transfer to bowl with chopped spinach. Transfer remaining mustard greens to blender.

4. Meanwhile, melt butter in 12-inch skillet over medium-high heat. Add cumin seeds, coriander, paprika, cardamom, and cinnamon and cook until fragrant, about 30 seconds. Add onion and ¾ teaspoon salt; cook, stirring frequently, until softened, about 3 minutes. Add garlic, ginger, and jalapeño; cook, stirring frequently, until lightly browned and just beginning to stick to pan, 2 to 3 minutes. Stir in tomatoes and cook mixture until pan is dry and tomatoes are beginning to brown, 3 to 4 minutes. Remove skillet from heat.

5. Transfer half of onion mixture to blender with greens. Add ¼ cup cashews and water; process until smooth, about 1 minute. Return puree to skillet.

6. Return skillet to medium-high heat, stir in chopped greens and buttermilk, and bring to simmer. Reduce heat to low, cover, and cook until flavors have blended, 5 minutes. Season with salt and pepper to taste. Gently fold in cheese cubes and cook until just heated through, 1 to 2 minutes. Transfer to serving dish, sprinkle with remaining ¼ cup cashews and cilantro, and serve.

ROASTED BRUSSELS SPROUTS

WHY THIS RECIPE WORKS: Roasting is a simple and quick way to produce Brussels sprouts that are well caramelized on the outside and tender on the inside. To ensure we achieved this balance, we started out roasting the "tiny cabbages," covered, with a little bit of water. This created a steamy environment, which cooked the vegetable through. We then removed the foil and allowed the exterior to dry out and caramelize.

Roasted Brussels Sprouts
SERVES 6 TO 8

If you are buying loose Brussels sprouts, select those that are about 1½ inches long. Quarter Brussels sprouts longer than 2½ inches; don't cut sprouts shorter than 1 inch.

2¼ **pounds Brussels sprouts, trimmed and halved**
3 **tablespoons olive oil**
1 **tablespoon water**
   Salt and pepper

1. Adjust oven rack to upper-middle position and heat oven to 500 degrees. Toss Brussels sprouts, oil, water, ¾ teaspoon salt, and ¼ teaspoon pepper together in large bowl until sprouts are coated. Transfer sprouts to rimmed baking sheet and arrange cut sides down.

2. Cover baking sheet tightly with aluminum foil and roast for 10 minutes. Remove foil and continue to cook until Brussels sprouts are well browned and tender, 10 to 12 minutes longer. Transfer to serving platter, season with salt and pepper to taste, and serve.

Roasted Brussels Sprouts with Garlic, Red Pepper Flakes, and Parmesan

While Brussels sprouts roast, heat 3 tablespoons olive oil in 8-inch skillet over medium heat until shimmering. Add 2 minced garlic cloves and ½ teaspoon red pepper flakes; cook until garlic is golden and fragrant, about 1 minute. Remove from heat. Toss roasted Brussels sprouts with garlic oil and season with salt and pepper to taste. Transfer to platter and sprinkle with ¼ cup grated Parmesan cheese before serving.

Roasted Brussels Sprouts with Bacon and Pecans

While Brussels sprouts roast, cook 4 slices bacon in 10-inch skillet over medium heat until crisp, 7 to 10 minutes. Using slotted spoon, transfer bacon to paper towel–lined plate and reserve 1 tablespoon bacon fat. Finely chop bacon. Toss roasted Brussels sprouts with 2 tablespoons olive oil, reserved bacon fat, chopped bacon, and ½ cup finely chopped toasted pecans. Season with salt and pepper to taste; transfer to platter and serve.

HOME FRIES

WHY THIS RECIPE WORKS: Making home fries the traditional way takes about an hour of standing over a hot skillet, after which you get only three servings at most. We wanted a quicker, more hands-off method for making a larger amount. To speed things up, we developed a hybrid cooking technique: First, we parboiled diced russet potatoes, and then we coated them in oil and cooked them in a very hot oven. We discovered that boiling the potatoes with baking soda quickly breaks down their exterior while leaving their insides nearly raw, ensuring home fries with a crisp, brown crust and a moist, fluffy interior. We added diced onions in the last 20 minutes of oven time and finished the home fries with chives to reinforce the onion flavor.

Home Fries

SERVES 6 TO 8

Don't skip the baking soda in this recipe. It's critical for home fries with just the right crisp texture.

- 3½ pounds russet potatoes, peeled and cut into ¾-inch dice
- ½ teaspoon baking soda
- 3 tablespoons unsalted butter, cut into 12 pieces
  Kosher salt and pepper
  Pinch cayenne pepper
- 3 tablespoons vegetable oil
- 2 onions, cut into ½-inch dice
- 3 tablespoons minced chives

1. Adjust oven rack to lowest position, place rimmed baking sheet on rack, and heat oven to 500 degrees.

2. Bring 10 cups water to boil in Dutch oven over high heat. Add potatoes and baking soda. Return to boil and cook for 1 minute. Drain potatoes. Return potatoes to Dutch oven and place over low heat. Cook, shaking pot occasionally, until any surface moisture has evaporated, about 2 minutes. Remove from heat. Add butter, 1½ teaspoons salt, and cayenne; mix with rubber spatula until potatoes are coated with thick, starchy paste, about 30 seconds.

3. Remove baking sheet from oven and drizzle with 2 tablespoons oil. Transfer potatoes to baking sheet and spread into even layer. Roast for 15 minutes. While potatoes roast, combine onions, remaining 1 tablespoon oil, and ½ teaspoon salt in bowl.

4. Remove baking sheet from oven. Using thin, sharp metal spatula, scrape and turn potatoes. Clear about 8 by 5-inch space in center of baking sheet and add onion mixture. Roast for 15 minutes.

5. Scrape and turn again, mixing onions into potatoes. Continue to roast until potatoes are well browned and onions are softened and beginning to brown, 5 to 10 minutes. Stir in chives and season with salt and pepper to taste. Serve immediately.

HOLIDAY CRANBERRY CHUTNEY

WHY THIS RECIPE WORKS: There's nothing wrong with the simplicity of a plain old sweet-tart cranberry sauce made with back-of-the-bag instructions, but sometimes we want more. To create a more complexly flavored sauce, we looked to Indian chutneys. Adding vinegar, aromatics, and spices to slow-cooked cranberries and fruit yielded a jammy relish with kick and savor.

Cranberry Chutney with Apples and Crystallized Ginger

MAKES ABOUT 3 CUPS

If using frozen cranberries, thaw them before cooking.

- 1 teaspoon vegetable oil
- 1 shallot, minced
- 2 teaspoons finely grated fresh ginger
- ½ teaspoon salt
- ⅔ cup water
- ¼ cup cider vinegar
- 1 cup packed brown sugar
- 12 ounces (3 cups) fresh or frozen cranberries
- 2 Granny Smith apples, peeled, cored, and cut into ¼-inch pieces
- ⅓ cup minced crystallized ginger

1. Heat oil in medium saucepan over medium heat until shimmering. Add shallot, fresh ginger, and salt; cook, stirring occasionally, until shallot has softened, 1 to 2 minutes.

2. Add water, vinegar, and sugar. Increase heat to high and bring to simmer, stirring to dissolve sugar. Add 1½ cups cranberries and apples; return to simmer. Reduce heat to medium-low and simmer, stirring occasionally, until cranberries have almost completely broken down and mixture has thickened, about 15 minutes.

3. Add remaining 1½ cups cranberries and crystallized ginger; continue to simmer, stirring occasionally, until cranberries just begin to burst, 5 to 7 minutes. Transfer to serving bowl and cool for at least 1 hour before serving. (Sauce can be refrigerated for up to 3 days.)

Spicy Cranberry Chutney

Increase oil to 2 teaspoons and substitute 1 stemmed and seeded red bell pepper cut into ¼-inch pieces and 2 seeded and minced jalapeño chiles for fresh ginger in step 1. Increase cooking time in step 1 to 5 minutes. Increase water to ¾ cup and omit apples and crystallized ginger.

Cranberry Chutney with Fennel and Golden Raisins

Increase oil to 2 teaspoons and substitute 1 cored fennel bulb cut into ¼-inch pieces and ½ teaspoon fennel seeds for fresh ginger in step 1. Increase cooking time in step 1 to 5 minutes. Increase water to 1 cup, omit apples, and substitute ⅓ cup golden raisins for crystallized ginger.

Cranberry-Orange Chutney

Starting with 2 oranges, remove four 2-inch-wide strips zest from 1 orange, then peel both oranges and remove segments. Set aside zest and segments. Increase fresh ginger to 4 teaspoons and add 1 teaspoon yellow mustard seeds to oil together with fresh ginger in step 1. Increase water to ¾ cup and add orange zest and segments to pot with cranberries in step 2. Omit apples and crystallized ginger.

Cranberry Chutney with Pear, Lemon, and Rosemary

Remove two 2-inch-wide strips zest from 1 lemon, then peel and remove segments. Set aside zest and segments. Substitute 2 teaspoons chopped fresh rosemary for fresh ginger. Substitute 2 peeled Bosc pears cut into ¼-inch pieces for apples; omit crystallized ginger. Add lemon zest and segments to pot with cranberries in step 2.

BAKED EGGS

WHY THIS RECIPE WORKS: Baked eggs can be hard to get right. We wanted a creamy, slightly runny yolk and a tender white—in the same ramekin. The answer turned out to be insulation—that is, adding a spinach cream sauce to provide a barrier between the egg and the very hot sides of the ramekin. We also found that pulling the eggs from the oven before they were done and allowing carryover cooking to finish the job, delivered first-rate baked eggs.

Baked Eggs Florentine
SERVES 6

In order for the eggs to cook properly, it is imperative to add them to the hot, filling–lined ramekins quickly. Prepare by cracking eggs into separate bowls or teacups while the filled ramekins are heating. Use 6-ounce ramekins with 3¼-inch diameters, measured from the inner lip. We developed this recipe using a glass baking dish; if using a metal baking pan, reduce the oven temperature to 425 degrees. This recipe can be doubled and baked in two 13 by 9-inch dishes. If doubling, increase the baking times in steps 3 and 4 by 1 minute.

  2 tablespoons unsalted butter
  1 large shallot, minced
  1 tablespoon all-purpose flour
  ¾ cup half-and-half
 10 ounces frozen spinach, thawed and squeezed dry
  2 ounces Parmesan cheese, grated (1 cup)
     Salt and pepper
  ⅛ teaspoon dry mustard
  ⅛ teaspoon ground nutmeg
     Pinch cayenne pepper
     Vegetable oil spray
  6 large eggs

1. Adjust oven rack to middle position and heat oven to 500 degrees.

2. Melt butter in medium saucepan over medium heat. Add shallot and cook, stirring occasionally, until softened, about 3 minutes. Stir in flour and cook, stirring constantly, for 1 minute. Gradually whisk in half-and-half; bring mixture to boil, whisking constantly. Simmer, whisking frequently, until thickened, 2 to 3 minutes. Remove pan from heat and stir in spinach, Parmesan, ¾ teaspoon salt, ½ teaspoon pepper, mustard, nutmeg, and cayenne.

3. Lightly spray six 6-ounce ramekins with oil spray. Evenly divide spinach filling among ramekins. Using back of spoon, push filling 1 inch up sides of ramekins, making shallow indentation in center of filling large enough to hold egg. Place filled ramekins in 13 by 9-inch glass baking dish. Bake ramekins until filling just starts to brown, about 7 minutes, rotating dish halfway through baking.

4. While filling is heating, crack eggs (taking care not to break yolks) into individual cups or bowls. Remove baking dish with ramekins from oven and place on wire rack. Gently pour eggs from cups into hot ramekins, centering yolk in filling. Lightly spray surface of each egg with oil spray and sprinkle each with pinch of salt. Return baking dish to oven and bake until whites are just opaque but still tremble, 6 to 8 minutes, rotating dish halfway through baking.

5. Remove dish from oven and, using tongs, transfer ramekins to wire rack. Let stand until whites are firm and set (yolks should still be runny), about 10 minutes. Serve immediately.

TO MAKE AHEAD: Follow recipe through step 3, skipping step of baking lined ramekins. Wrap ramekins with plastic wrap and refrigerate for up to 3 days. To serve, heat lined ramekins, directly from refrigerator, for additional 3 to 4 minutes (10 to 11 minutes total) before proceeding with recipe.

Baked Eggs Lorraine

Wash 1 pound leeks and slice white and light green parts thin. Cook 2 slices bacon cut into ½-inch pieces in medium saucepan over medium heat until crisp, about 10 minutes. Transfer bacon to paper towel–lined plate. Add leeks and cook until softened, about 10 minutes. Transfer leeks to plate with bacon. Proceed with recipe, omitting shallot and reducing butter to 1 tablespoon. Substitute bacon and leek mixture for spinach and ½ cup shredded Gruyère cheese for Parmesan.

FASTER STEEL-CUT OATMEAL

WHY THIS RECIPE WORKS: Most oatmeal fans agree that the steel-cut version of the grain offers the best flavor and texture, but many balk at the 40-minute cooking time. We decrease the cooking time to only 10 minutes by stirring steel-cut oats into boiling water the night before. This enables the grains to hydrate and soften overnight. In the morning, more water (or fruit juice or milk) is added and the mixture is simmered for 4 to 6 minutes, until thick and creamy. A brief resting period off the heat ensures the perfect consistency.

Ten-Minute Steel-Cut Oatmeal

SERVES 4

The oatmeal will continue to thicken as it cools. If you prefer a looser consistency, thin the oatmeal with boiling water. Customize your oatmeal with toppings such as brown sugar, toasted nuts, maple syrup, or dried fruit.

- **4 cups water**
- **1 cup steel-cut oats**
- **¼ teaspoon salt**

1. Bring 3 cups water to boil in large saucepan over high heat. Remove pan from heat; stir in oats and salt. Cover pan and let stand overnight.

2. Stir remaining 1 cup water into oats and bring to boil over medium-high heat. Reduce heat to medium and cook, stirring occasionally, until oats are softened but still retain some chew and mixture thickens and resembles warm pudding, 4 to 6 minutes. Remove pan from heat and let stand for 5 minutes. Stir and serve, passing desired toppings separately.

Apple-Cinnamon Steel-Cut Oatmeal

Increase salt to ½ teaspoon. Substitute ½ cup apple cider and ½ cup whole milk for water in step 2. Stir ½ cup peeled, grated sweet apple, 2 tablespoons packed dark brown sugar, and ½ teaspoon ground cinnamon into oatmeal with cider and milk. Sprinkle each serving with 2 tablespoons coarsely chopped toasted walnuts.

Carrot-Spice Steel-Cut Oatmeal

Increase salt to ¾ teaspoon. Substitute ½ cup carrot juice and ½ cup whole milk for water in step 2. Stir ½ cup finely grated carrot, ¼ cup packed dark brown sugar, ⅓ cup dried currants, and ½ teaspoon ground cinnamon into oatmeal with carrot juice and milk. Sprinkle each serving with 2 tablespoons coarsely chopped toasted pecans.

Cranberry-Orange Steel-Cut Oatmeal

Increase salt to ½ teaspoon. Substitute ½ cup orange juice and ½ cup whole milk for water in step 2. Stir ½ cup dried cranberries, 3 tablespoons packed dark brown sugar, and ⅛ teaspoon ground cardamom into oatmeal with orange juice and milk. Sprinkle each serving with 2 tablespoons toasted sliced almonds.

Banana-Coconut Steel-Cut Oatmeal

Increase salt to ½ teaspoon. Substitute 1 cup canned coconut milk for water in step 2. Stir ½ cup toasted shredded coconut, 2 diced bananas, and ½ teaspoon vanilla extract into oatmeal before serving.

Peanut, Honey, and Banana Steel-Cut Oatmeal

Increase salt to ½ teaspoon. Substitute ½ cup whole milk for ½ cup water in step 2. Stir 3 tablespoons honey into oatmeal with milk and water. Add ¼ cup of peanut butter and 1 tablespoon unsalted butter to oatmeal after removing from heat in step 2. Stir 2 diced bananas into oatmeal before serving. Sprinkle each serving with 2 tablespoons coarsely chopped toasted peanuts.

PUMPKIN BREAD

WHY THIS RECIPE WORKS: Although most recipes for pumpkin bread are pleasantly sweet and spicy, they're nothing to write home about. For a bread with rich pumpkin flavor and enough spices to enhance rather than overwhelm the flavor of our pumpkin, we used a few strategies. To rid canned pumpkin puree of its raw flavor and bring out its richness, we cooked it on top of the stove just until it began to caramelize. To replace some of the lost moisture from cooking the puree and offset some of the sweetness, we added softened cream cheese to the mix. A modest hand with spices and a sweet streusel sprinkled over the top of the bread gave us perfect pumpkin bread.

Pumpkin Bread

MAKES 2 LOAVES

The test kitchen's preferred loaf pan measures 8½ by 4½ inches; if using a 9 by 5-inch loaf pan, start checking for doneness 5 minutes early.

TOPPING

    5 tablespoons packed (2¼ ounces) light brown sugar
    1 tablespoon all-purpose flour
    1 tablespoon unsalted butter, softened
    1 teaspoon ground cinnamon
    ⅛ teaspoon salt

BREAD

    2 cups (10 ounces) all-purpose flour
    1½ teaspoons baking powder
    ½ teaspoon baking soda
    1 (15-ounce) can unsweetened pumpkin puree
    1 teaspoon salt
    1½ teaspoons ground cinnamon
    ¼ teaspoon ground nutmeg
    ⅛ teaspoon ground cloves
    1 cup (7 ounces) granulated sugar
    1 cup packed (7 ounces) light brown sugar
    ½ cup vegetable oil
    4 ounces cream cheese, cut into 12 pieces
    4 large eggs
    ¼ cup buttermilk
    1 cup walnuts, toasted and chopped fine

1. FOR THE TOPPING: Using fingers, mix all ingredients together in bowl until well combined and topping resembles wet sand; set aside.

2. FOR THE BREAD: Adjust oven rack to middle position and heat oven to 350 degrees. Grease two 8½ by 4½-inch loaf pans. Whisk flour, baking powder, and baking soda together in bowl.

3. Combine pumpkin puree, salt, cinnamon, nutmeg, and cloves in large saucepan over medium heat. Cook mixture, stirring constantly, until reduced to 1½ cups, 6 to 8 minutes. Remove pot from heat; stir in granulated sugar, brown sugar, oil, and cream cheese until combined. Let mixture stand for 5 minutes. Whisk until no visible pieces of cream cheese remain and mixture is homogeneous.

4. Whisk together eggs and buttermilk. Add egg mixture to pumpkin mixture and whisk to combine. Fold flour mixture into pumpkin mixture until combined (some small lumps of flour are OK). Fold walnuts into batter. Scrape batter into prepared pans. Sprinkle topping evenly over top of each loaf. Bake until skewer inserted in center of loaf comes out clean, 45 to 50 minutes. Let loaves cool in pans on wire rack for 20 minutes. Remove loaves from pans and let cool for at least 1½ hours. Serve warm or at room temperature.

Pumpkin Bread with Candied Ginger

Substitute ½ teaspoon ground ginger for cinnamon in topping. Fold ⅓ cup minced crystallized ginger into batter after flour mixture has been added in step 4.

CINNAMON SWIRL BREAD

WHY THIS RECIPE WORKS: This American classic frequently disappoints due to either precious little cinnamon flavor or, just as bad, a gloppy, oozing filling reminiscent of sticky buns. The bread itself is often an afterthought of pedestrian white bread, or else it's a cakey, dense affair. We swapped in an airy, cottony Japanese white bread called *shokupan* and created a filling with a balanced mixture of cinnamon, confectioners' sugar, and vanilla. To ensure that our filling stayed put and could be tasted with every bite, we traded the traditional swirl shape for a simple yet elegant Russian braid.

Cinnamon Swirl Bread

MAKES 2 LOAVES

To achieve the proper dough consistency, make sure to weigh your ingredients. The dough will appear very wet and sticky until the final few minutes of kneading; do not be tempted to add supplemental flour.

DOUGH

8	tablespoons unsalted butter
3¾	cups (20⅔ ounces) bread flour
¾	cup (2¾ ounces) nonfat dry milk powder
⅓	cup (2⅓ ounces) granulated sugar
1	tablespoon instant or rapid-rise yeast
1½	cups (12 ounces) water, heated to 110 degrees
1	large egg, lightly beaten
1½	teaspoons salt
1½	cups (7½ ounces) golden raisins

FILLING

1	cup (4 ounces) confectioners' sugar
3	tablespoons ground cinnamon
1	teaspoon vanilla extract
½	teaspoon salt
1	large egg, lightly beaten with pinch salt

1. FOR THE DOUGH: Cut butter into 32 pieces and toss with 1 tablespoon flour; set aside to soften while mixing dough. Whisk remaining flour, milk powder, sugar, and yeast together in bowl of stand mixer fitted with dough hook.

Add water and egg and mix on medium-low speed until cohesive mass forms, about 2 minutes, scraping down bowl as needed. Cover mixing bowl with plastic wrap and let stand for 20 minutes.

2. Adjust oven rack to middle position and place loaf or cake pan on bottom of oven. Grease large bowl. Remove plastic from mixer bowl, add salt, and mix on medium-low speed until dough is smooth and elastic and clears sides of bowl, 7 to 15 minutes. With mixer running, add butter a few pieces at a time, and continue to knead until butter is fully incorporated and dough is smooth and elastic and clears sides of bowl, 3 to 5 minutes longer. Add raisins and mix until incorporated, 30 to 60 seconds. Transfer dough to prepared bowl and, using bowl scraper or rubber spatula, fold dough over itself by gently lifting and folding edge of dough toward middle. Turn bowl 90 degrees; fold again. Turn bowl and fold dough 6 more times (total of 8 folds). Cover tightly with plastic and transfer to middle rack of oven. Pour 3 cups boiling water into loaf pan in oven, close oven door, and allow dough to rise for 45 minutes.

3. Remove bowl from oven and gently press down on center of dough to deflate. Repeat folding (making total of 8 folds), re-cover, and return to oven until doubled in volume, about 45 minutes.

4. FOR THE FILLING: Whisk all ingredients together in bowl until well combined; set aside.

5. Grease two 8½ by 4½-inch loaf pans. Transfer dough to lightly floured counter and divide into 2 pieces. Working with 1 piece of dough, pat into rough 6 by 11-inch rectangle. With short side facing you, fold long sides in like a business letter to form 3 by 11-inch rectangle. Roll dough away from you into ball. Dust ball with flour and flatten with rolling pin into 7 by 18-inch rectangle with even ¼-inch thickness. Using spray bottle, spray dough lightly with water. Sprinkle half of filling mixture evenly over dough, leaving ¼-inch border on sides and ¾-inch border on top and bottom; spray filling lightly with water. (Filling should be speckled with water over entire surface.) With short side facing you, roll dough away from you into firm cylinder. Turn loaf seam side up and pinch closed; pinch ends closed. Dust loaf lightly on all sides with flour and let rest for 10 minutes. Repeat with second ball of dough and remaining filling.

6. Working with 1 loaf at a time, use bench scraper to cut loaf in half lengthwise; turn halves so cut sides are facing up. Gently stretch each half into 14-inch length. Line up pieces of dough and pinch 2 ends of strips together. Take piece on left and lay over piece on right. Repeat, keeping cut side up, until pieces of dough are tightly twisted. Pinch ends together. Transfer loaf, cut side up, to prepared loaf pan; push any exposed raisins into seams of braid. Repeat with second loaf. Cover loaves loosely with plastic, return to oven, and allow to rise for 45 minutes. Remove loaves and water pan from oven; heat oven to 350 degrees. Allow loaves to rise at room temperature until almost doubled in size, about 45 minutes (tops of loaves should rise about 1 inch over lip of pans).

7. Brush loaves with egg mixture. Bake until crust is well browned, about 25 minutes. Reduce oven temperature to 325 degrees, tent loaves with aluminum foil, and continue to bake until internal temperature registers 200 degrees, 15 to 25 minutes longer.

8. Transfer pans to wire rack and let cool for 5 minutes. Remove loaves from pans, return to rack, and cool to room temperature before slicing, about 2 hours.

POTATO BURGER BUNS

WHY THIS RECIPE WORKS: Mashed potatoes are hefty and substantial, but in a potato rolls recipe, they give the crumb a light, tender, moist texture. That's because the starches in potatoes dilute the gluten-forming proteins in flour, which weakens the structural network of the dough and makes it softer, moister, and more tender. For the lightest potato rolls, we combined ½ pound of mashed russet potatoes with high-protein bread flour. This created a potato roll dough with a stable structure, producing rolls that were not only perfectly risen but also light and airy.

Potato Burger Buns

MAKES 9 ROLLS

Don't salt the cooking water for the potatoes. A pound of russet potatoes should yield just over 1 very firmly packed cup (½ pound) of mash. To ensure optimum rise, your dough should be warm; if your potatoes or potato water is too hot to touch, let cool before proceeding with the recipe. This dough looks very dry when mixing begins but will soften as mixing progresses. If you prefer, you may portion the rolls by weight in step 5 (2.75 ounces of dough per roll).

- 1 **pound russet potatoes, peeled and cut into 1-inch pieces**
- 2 **tablespoons unsalted butter, cut into 4 pieces**
- 2¼ **cups (12⅓ ounces) bread flour**
- 1 **tablespoon sugar**
- 2 **teaspoons instant or rapid-rise yeast**
- 1 **teaspoon salt**
- 2 **large eggs, 1 lightly beaten with 1 teaspoon water and pinch salt**
- 1 **tablespoon sesame seeds (optional)**

1. Place potatoes in medium saucepan and add water to just cover. Bring to boil over high heat; reduce heat to medium-low and simmer until potatoes are cooked through, 8 to 10 minutes.

2. Transfer 5 tablespoons cooking water to bowl to cool; drain potatoes. Return potatoes to saucepan and place over low heat. Cook, shaking pot occasionally, until any surface moisture has evaporated, about 1 minute. Remove from heat. Process potatoes through ricer or food mill or mash well with potato masher. Measure 1 very firmly packed cup potatoes and transfer to bowl. Reserve any remaining potatoes for another use. Stir in butter until melted.

3. Combine flour, sugar, yeast, and salt in bowl of stand mixer. Add warm potato mixture to flour mixture and mix with hands until combined (some large lumps are OK). Add 1 egg and reserved potato water; mix with dough hook on low speed until dough is soft and slightly sticky, 8 to 10 minutes.

4. Shape dough into ball and place in lightly greased container. Cover tightly with plastic wrap and allow to rise at room temperature until almost doubled in volume, 30 to 40 minutes.

5. Turn out dough onto counter, dusting with flour only if dough is too sticky to handle comfortably. Pat gently into 8-inch square of even thickness. Using bench scraper or chef's knife, cut dough into 9 pieces (3 rows by 3 rows). Separate pieces and cover loosely with plastic.

6. Working with 1 piece of dough at a time and keeping remaining pieces covered, form dough pieces into smooth, taut rounds. (To round, set piece of dough on unfloured work surface. Loosely cup hand around dough and, without applying pressure to dough, move hand in small circular motions. Tackiness of dough against work surface and circular motion should work dough into smooth, even ball, but if dough sticks to hands, lightly dust fingers with flour.) Cover rounds with plastic and allow to rest for 15 minutes.

7. Line 2 rimmed baking sheets with parchment paper. On lightly floured surface, firmly press each dough round into 3½-inch disk of even thickness, expelling large pockets of air. Arrange on prepared baking sheets. Cover loosely with plastic and let rise at room temperature until almost doubled in size, 30 to 40 minutes. While rolls rise, adjust oven racks to middle and upper-middle positions and heat oven to 425 degrees.

8. Brush rolls gently with egg wash and sprinkle with sesame seeds, if using. Bake rolls until deep golden brown, 15 to 18 minutes, rotating and switching baking sheets halfway through baking. Transfer baking sheets to wire racks and let cool for 5 minutes. Transfer rolls from baking sheets to wire racks. Serve warm or at room temperature.

Potato Dinner Rolls
MAKES 12 ROLLS

Line rimmed baking sheet with parchment paper. In step 5, divide dough square into 12 pieces (3 rows by 4 rows). Shape pieces into smooth, taut rounds as directed in step 6. Transfer rounds to prepared baking sheet and let rise at room temperature until almost doubled in size, 30 to 40 minutes. Bake on upper-middle rack until rolls are deep golden brown, 12 to 14 minutes, rotating baking sheet halfway through baking.

NAAN

WHY THIS RECIPE WORKS: Even in India, naan is considered "restaurant" bread. This may be because it calls for a traditional tandoor oven, which few home cooks own. We wanted an ideal version of this bread—light and airy, with a pliant, chewy crust—that we could easily make at home. We started with a moist dough with a fair amount of fat, which created a soft bread that was pleasantly chewy, but the real secret was the cooking method. While we thought a grill or preheated pizza stone would be the best cooking method, we discovered that they cooked the bread unevenly. A much better option was a covered skillet. The skillet delivers heat to the bottom and the top of the bread, producing loaves that are nicely charred but still moist.

Indian Flatbread (Naan)
MAKES 4 BREADS

This recipe works best with a high-protein all-purpose flour such as King Arthur brand. Do not use nonfat yogurt in this recipe. A 12-inch nonstick skillet may be used in place of the cast-iron skillet. For efficiency, stretch the next ball of dough while each naan is cooking.

½   cup ice water
⅓   cup plain whole-milk yogurt
3   tablespoons plus 1 teaspoon vegetable oil
1   large egg yolk
2   cups (10 ounces) all-purpose flour
1¼ teaspoons sugar
½   teaspoon instant or rapid-rise yeast
1¼ teaspoons salt
1½ tablespoons unsalted butter, melted

1. In measuring cup or small bowl, combine water, yogurt, 3 tablespoons oil, and egg yolk. Process flour, sugar, and yeast together in food processor until combined, about 2 seconds. With processor running, slowly add water mixture; process until dough is just combined and no dry flour remains, about 10 seconds. Let dough stand for 10 minutes.

2. Add salt to dough and process until dough forms satiny, sticky ball that clears sides of workbowl, 30 to 60 seconds. Transfer dough to lightly floured counter and knead until smooth, about 1 minute. Shape dough into tight ball and place in large, lightly oiled bowl. Cover tightly with plastic wrap and refrigerate for 16 to 24 hours.

3. Adjust oven rack to middle position and heat oven to 200 degrees. Place heatproof plate on rack. Transfer dough to lightly floured counter and divide into 4 equal pieces. Shape each piece into smooth, tight ball. Place dough balls on lightly oiled baking sheet, at least 2 inches apart; cover loosely with plastic coated with vegetable oil spray. Let stand for 15 to 20 minutes.

4. Transfer 1 ball to lightly floured counter and sprinkle with flour. Using hands and rolling pin, press and roll piece of dough into 9-inch round of even thickness, sprinkling dough and counter with flour as needed to prevent sticking. Using fork, poke entire surface of round 20 to 25 times. Heat remaining 1 teaspoon oil in 12-inch cast-iron skillet over medium heat until shimmering. Wipe oil out of skillet completely with paper towels. Mist top of dough lightly with water. Place dough in pan, moistened side down; mist top surface of dough with water; and cover. Cook until bottom is browned in spots across surface, 2 to 4 minutes. Flip naan, cover, and continue to cook on second side until lightly browned, 2 to 3 minutes longer. (If naan puffs up, gently poke with fork to deflate.) Flip naan, brush top with about 1 teaspoon melted butter, transfer to plate in oven, and cover plate tightly with aluminum foil. Repeat rolling and cooking remaining 3 dough balls. Once last naan is baked, serve immediately.

Quicker Indian Flatbread

This variation, which can be prepared in about 2 hours, forgoes the overnight rest, but the dough may be a little harder to roll out.

After shaping dough in step 2, let dough rise at room temperature for 30 minutes. After 30 minutes, fold partially risen dough over itself 8 times by gently lifting and folding edge of dough toward middle, turning bowl 90 degrees after each fold. Cover with plastic wrap and let rise for 30 minutes. Repeat folding, turning, and rising 1 more time, for total of three 30-minute rises. After last rise, proceed with recipe from step 3.

PEANUT BUTTER SANDWICH COOKIES

WHY THIS RECIPE WORKS: We wanted a cookie so packed with peanut flavor that it needed no crosshatch to identify it. In the research for our testing, we found that peanut butter flavor molecules can be trapped by flour in baked applications, so we ratcheted up the flavor's intensity by sandwiching an uncooked peanut butter filling between our cookies. Adding a full cup of confectioners' sugar to the filling made it firm enough to stay in place, and we balanced the sweetness with a relatively low-sugar cookie component. Extra liquid and extra baking soda gave our cookies the thin, flat dimensions and sturdy crunch that are vital to a sandwich cookie.

Peanut Butter Sandwich Cookies
MAKES 24 COOKIES

Do not use unsalted peanut butter for this recipe.

COOKIES

- 1¼ cups (6¼ ounces) raw peanuts, toasted and cooled
- ¾ cup (3¾ ounces) all-purpose flour
- 1 teaspoon baking soda
- ½ teaspoon salt
- 3 tablespoons unsalted butter, melted
- ½ cup creamy peanut butter
- ½ cup (3½ ounces) granulated sugar
- ½ cup packed (3½ ounces) light brown sugar
- 3 tablespoons whole milk
- 1 large egg

FILLING

- ¾ cup creamy peanut butter
- 3 tablespoons unsalted butter
- 1 cup (4 ounces) confectioners' sugar

1. FOR THE COOKIES: Adjust oven racks to upper-middle and lower-middle positions and heat oven to 350 degrees. Line 2 baking sheets with parchment paper. Pulse peanuts

NOTES FROM THE TEST KITCHEN

FILLING COOKIES EVENLY

1. Using #60 scoop or tablespoon measure, portion warm filling onto bottom cookies (turned upside down).

2. Rather than spreading filling with knife or offset spatula, top bottom cookie with second cookie and press gently until filling spreads to edges.

in food processor until finely chopped, about 8 pulses. Whisk flour, baking soda, and salt together in bowl. Whisk melted butter, peanut butter, granulated sugar, brown sugar, milk, and egg together in second bowl. Stir flour mixture into peanut butter mixture with rubber spatula until combined. Stir in peanuts until evenly distributed.

2. Using #60 scoop or tablespoon measure, place 12 mounds, evenly spaced, on each prepared baking sheet. Using damp hand, flatten mounds until 2 inches in diameter.

3. Bake until deep golden brown and firm to touch, 15 to 18 minutes, switching and rotating baking sheets halfway through baking. Let cookies cool on baking sheets for 5 minutes. Transfer cookies to wire rack and let cool completely, about 30 minutes. Repeat portioning and baking remaining dough.

4. FOR THE FILLING: Microwave peanut butter and butter together until butter is melted and warm, about 40 seconds. Using rubber spatula, stir in confectioners' sugar until combined.

5. TO ASSEMBLE: Place 24 cookies upside down on counter. Place 1 level tablespoon (or #60 scoop) warm filling in center of each cookie. Place second cookie on top of filling, right side up, pressing gently until filling spreads to edges. Allow filling to set for 1 hour before serving. Assembled cookies can be stored at room temperature for up to 3 days.

Peanut Butter Sandwich Cookies with Honey-Cinnamon Filling

Omit butter from filling. Stir 5 tablespoons honey and ½ teaspoon ground cinnamon into warm peanut butter before adding confectioners' sugar.

Peanut Butter Sandwich Cookies with Milk Chocolate Filling

Reduce peanut butter to ½ cup and omit butter from filling. Stir 6 ounces finely chopped milk chocolate into warm peanut butter until melted, microwaving for 10 seconds at a time if necessary, before adding confectioners' sugar.

GINGERSNAPS

WHY THIS RECIPE WORKS: We wanted to put the "snap" back in gingersnap cookies. This meant creating a cookie that not only breaks cleanly in half and crunches satisfyingly with every bite but also has an assertive ginger flavor and heat. The key to texture was reducing the moisture in the final baked cookie. We achieved this by reducing the amount of sugar (which holds on to moisture), increasing the baking soda (which created cracks in the dough where more moisture could escape), and lowering the oven temperature (which increased the baking time.) For flavor we doubled the normal amount of dried ginger but also added fresh ginger, black pepper, and cayenne to ensure our cookie had real "snap."

Gingersnaps

MAKES 80 1½-INCH COOKIES

For the best results, use fresh spices. For efficiency, form the second batch of cookies while the first batch bakes. The 2 teaspoons of baking soda are essential to getting the right texture.

- 2½ cups (12½ ounces) all-purpose flour
- 2 teaspoons baking soda
- ½ teaspoon salt
- 12 tablespoons unsalted butter
- 2 tablespoons ground ginger
- 1 teaspoon ground cinnamon
- ¼ teaspoon ground cloves
- ¼ teaspoon pepper

Pinch cayenne
1¼ cups packed (8¾ ounces) dark brown sugar
¼ cup molasses
2 tablespoons finely grated fresh ginger
1 large egg plus 1 large yolk
½ cup (3½ ounces) granulated sugar

1. Whisk flour, baking soda, and salt together in bowl. Heat butter in 10-inch skillet over medium heat until melted. Lower heat to medium-low and continue to cook, swirling pan frequently, until foaming subsides and butter is just beginning to brown, 2 to 4 minutes. Transfer butter to large bowl and whisk in ground ginger, cinnamon, cloves, pepper, and cayenne. Let cool slightly, about 2 minutes. Add brown sugar, molasses, and fresh ginger to butter mixture and whisk to combine. Add egg and yolk and whisk to combine. Add flour mixture and stir until just combined. Cover dough tightly with plastic wrap and refrigerate until firm, about 1 hour.

2. Adjust oven racks to upper-middle and lower-middle positions and heat oven to 300 degrees. Line 2 baking sheets with parchment paper. Place granulated sugar in shallow dish. Divide dough into heaping teaspoon portions; roll dough into 1-inch balls. Working in batches of 10, roll balls in sugar to coat. Evenly space dough balls on prepared baking sheets, 20 dough balls per sheet.

3. Place 1 sheet on upper rack and bake for 15 minutes. Transfer partially baked top sheet to lower rack, rotating 180 degrees, and place second sheet of dough balls on upper rack. Continue to bake until cookies on lower tray just begin to darken around edges, 10 to 12 minutes longer. Remove lower sheet of cookies and transfer upper sheet to lower rack, rotating 180 degrees, and continue to bake until cookies begin to darken around edges, 15 to 17 minutes longer. Slide baked cookies, still on parchment, to wire rack and let cool completely before serving. Let baking sheets cool slightly and line with parchment again. Repeat step 2 with remaining dough balls. (Cooled cookies can be stored at room temperature for up to 2 weeks.)

TO MAKE AHEAD: Dough can be refrigerated for up to 2 days or frozen for up to 1 month. Let frozen dough thaw overnight in refrigerator before proceeding with recipe. Let dough stand at room temperature for 30 minutes before shaping.

FRENCH APPLE CAKE

WHY THIS RECIPE WORKS: For our own version of this classic French dessert, we wanted the best of both worlds: a dessert with a custardy, apple-rich base beneath a light, cakelike topping. To ensure that the apple slices softened fully, we microwaved them briefly to break the enzyme responsible for firming up pectin. And to create two differently textured layers from one batter, we divided the batter and added egg yolks to one part to make the custardy base and added flour to the rest to form the cake layer above it.

French Apple Cake
SERVES 8 TO 10

The microwaved apples should be pliable but not completely soft when cooked. To test for doneness, take one apple slice and try to bend it. If it snaps in half, it's too firm; microwave it for an additional 30 seconds and test again. If Calvados is unavailable, 1 tablespoon of apple brandy or white rum can be substituted.

1½ pounds Granny Smith apples, peeled, cored, cut into 8 wedges, and sliced ⅛ inch thick crosswise
1 tablespoon Calvados
1 teaspoon lemon juice
1 cup (5 ounces) plus 2 tablespoons all-purpose flour
1 cup (7 ounces) plus 1 tablespoon granulated sugar
2 teaspoons baking powder
½ teaspoon salt
1 large egg plus 2 large yolks
1 cup vegetable oil
1 cup whole milk
1 teaspoon vanilla extract
Confectioners' sugar

1. Adjust oven rack to lower-middle position and heat oven to 325 degrees. Spray 9-inch springform pan with vegetable oil spray. Place prepared pan on rimmed baking sheet lined with aluminum foil. Place apple slices in microwave-safe pie plate, cover, and microwave until apples are pliable and slightly translucent, about 3 minutes. Toss apple slices with Calvados and lemon juice and let cool for 15 minutes.

2. Whisk 1 cup flour, 1 cup granulated sugar, baking powder, and salt together in bowl. Whisk egg, oil, milk, and vanilla together in second bowl until smooth. Add dry ingredients to wet ingredients and whisk until just combined. Transfer 1 cup batter to separate bowl and set aside.

3. Add egg yolks to remaining batter and whisk to combine. Using spatula, gently fold in cooled apples. Transfer batter to prepared pan; using offset spatula, spread batter evenly to pan edges, gently pressing on apples to create even, compact layer, and smooth surface.

4. Whisk remaining 2 tablespoons flour into reserved batter. Pour over batter in pan and spread batter evenly to pan edges and smooth surface. Sprinkle remaining 1 tablespoon granulated sugar evenly over cake.

5. Bake until center of cake is set, toothpick inserted in center comes out clean, and top is golden brown, about 1¼ hours. Transfer pan to wire rack; let cool for 5 minutes. Run paring knife around sides of pan and let cool completely, 2 to 3 hours. Dust lightly with confectioners' sugar, cut into wedges, and serve.

BEST CARROT LAYER CAKE

WHY THIS RECIPE WORKS: This American classic has a lot going for it: moist cake, delicate spices, tangy cream cheese frosting. But its presentation could use some refinement. We wanted to reengineer humble carrot cake as a four-tier, nut-crusted confection that could claim its place among the most glamorous desserts. To start, we found that baking this cake in a half sheet pan meant that it baked and cooled in far less time than a conventional layer cake, and—cut into quarters—it produced four thin, level layers that did not require splitting or trimming before frosting. Adding extra baking soda raised the pH of the batter, ensuring that the coarsely shredded carrots softened during the shortened baking time. Buttermilk powder in the frosting reinforced the tangy flavor of the cream cheese without making the frosting too soft.

Carrot Layer Cake
SERVES 10 TO 12

Shred the carrots on the large holes of a box grater or in a food processor fitted with the shredding disk. Do not substitute liquid buttermilk for the buttermilk powder. To ensure the proper spreading consistency for the frosting, use cold cream cheese. If your baked cake is of an uneven thickness, adjust the orientation of the layers as they are stacked to produce a level cake. Assembling this cake on a cardboard cake round trimmed to about a 6 by 8-inch rectangle makes it easy to press the pecans onto the sides of the frosted cake.

CAKE
1¾ cups (8¾ ounces) all-purpose flour
2 teaspoons baking powder
1 teaspoon baking soda
1½ teaspoons ground cinnamon
¾ teaspoon ground nutmeg
½ teaspoon salt
¼ teaspoon ground cloves
1¼ cups packed (8¾ ounces) light brown sugar
¾ cup vegetable oil
3 large eggs
1 teaspoon vanilla extract
2⅔ cups shredded carrots (4 carrots)
⅔ cup dried currants

FROSTING
3 cups (12 ounces) confectioners' sugar
16 tablespoons unsalted butter, softened
⅓ cup buttermilk powder
2 teaspoons vanilla extract
¼ teaspoon salt
12 ounces cream cheese, chilled and cut into 12 equal pieces
2 cups (8 ounces) pecans, toasted and chopped coarse

1. FOR THE CAKE: Adjust oven rack to middle position and heat oven to 350 degrees. Grease 18 by 13-inch rimmed baking sheet, line with parchment paper, and grease parchment. Whisk flour, baking powder, baking soda, cinnamon, nutmeg, salt, and cloves together in large bowl.

2. Whisk sugar, oil, eggs, and vanilla together in second bowl until mixture is smooth. Stir in carrots and currants. Add flour mixture and fold with rubber spatula until mixture is just combined.

3. Transfer batter to prepared sheet and smooth surface with offset spatula. Bake until center of cake is firm to touch, 15 to 18 minutes. Cool in pan on wire rack for 5 minutes. Invert cake onto wire rack (do not remove parchment), then reinvert onto second wire rack. Cool cake completely, about 30 minutes.

4. FOR THE FROSTING: Using stand mixer fitted with paddle, beat sugar, butter, buttermilk powder, vanilla, and salt together on low speed until smooth, about 2 minutes, scraping down bowl as needed. Increase speed to medium-low; add cream cheese, 1 piece at a time; and mix until smooth, about 2 minutes.

5. Transfer cooled cake to cutting board, parchment side down. Using sharp chef's knife, cut cake and parchment in half crosswise, then lengthwise into 4 even quarters.

6. Place 6 by 8-inch cardboard rectangle on cake platter. Place 1 cake layer, parchment side up, on cardboard and carefully remove parchment. Using offset spatula, spread ⅔ cup frosting evenly over top, right to edge of cake. Repeat with 2 more layers of cake, pressing lightly to adhere and frosting each layer with ⅔ cup frosting. Top with last cake layer and spread 1 cup frosting evenly over top. Spread remaining frosting evenly over sides of cake. (It's fine if some crumbs show through frosting on sides, but if you go back to smooth top of cake, be sure that spatula is free of crumbs.)

7. Hold cake with 1 hand and gently press chopped pecans onto sides with other hand. Chill for at least 1 hour before serving. (The frosted cake can be refrigerated for up to 24 hours before serving.)

CHOCOLATE TRUFFLES

WHY THIS RECIPE WORKS: The problem with many homemade truffles is that they have a dry, grainy texture. There are three keys to creating creamy, silky-smooth truffles. First, start with melted chocolate. Melting the chocolate before adding the cream allowed us to stir—rather than whisk—the two together, reducing the incorporation of air that can cause grittiness. Second, add corn syrup and butter. Corn syrup smoothed over the gritty texture of the sugar, and butter introduced silkiness. Finally, cooling down the ganache gradually before chilling prevented the formation of grainy crystals.

Chocolate Truffles

MAKES 64 TRUFFLES

In step 5, running your knife under hot water and wiping it dry makes cutting the chocolate easier. We recommend using Callebaut Intense Dark L-60–40NV or Ghirardelli Bittersweet Chocolate Baking Bar. If giving the truffles as a gift, set them in 1½-inch candy cup liners in a gift box and keep them chilled.

GANACHE
- 2 cups (12 ounces) bittersweet chocolate, roughly chopped
- ½ cup heavy cream
- 2 tablespoons light corn syrup
- ½ teaspoon vanilla extract
  Pinch salt
- 1½ tablespoons unsalted butter, cut into 8 pieces and softened

COATING
- 1 cup (3 ounces) Dutch-processed cocoa
- ¼ cup (1 ounce) confectioners' sugar

1. FOR THE GANACHE: Lightly coat 8-inch baking dish with vegetable oil spray. Make parchment sling by folding 2 long sheets of parchment so that they are as wide as baking pan. Lay sheets of parchment in pan perpendicular to each other, with extra hanging over edges of pan. Push parchment into corners and up sides of pan, smoothing flush to pan.

2. Microwave chocolate in medium bowl at 50 percent power, stirring occasionally, until mostly melted and few small chocolate pieces remain, 2 to 3 minutes; set aside. Microwave cream in measuring cup until warm to touch, about 30 seconds. Stir corn syrup, vanilla, and salt into cream and pour mixture over chocolate. Cover bowl with plastic wrap, set aside for 3 minutes, and then stir with wooden spoon to combine. Stir in butter, one piece at a time, until fully incorporated.

3. Using rubber spatula, transfer ganache to prepared pan and set aside at room temperature for 2 hours. Cover pan and transfer to refrigerator; chill for at least 2 hours. (Ganache can be stored, refrigerated, for up to 2 days.)

4. FOR THE COATING: Sift cocoa and sugar through fine-mesh strainer into large bowl. Sift again into large cake pan and set aside.

5. Gripping overhanging parchment, lift ganache from pan. Cut ganache into sixty-four 1-inch squares (8 rows by 8 rows). (If ganache cracks during slicing, let sit at room temperature for 5 to 10 minutes and then proceed.) Dust hands lightly with cocoa mixture to prevent ganache from sticking and roll each square into ball. Transfer balls to cake pan with cocoa mixture and roll to evenly coat. Lightly shake truffles in hand over pan to remove excess coating. Transfer coated truffles to airtight container and repeat until all ganache squares are rolled and coated. Cover container and refrigerate for at least 2 hours or up to 1 week. Let truffles sit at room temperature for 5 to 10 minutes before serving.

Hazelnut-Mocha Truffles

Substitute 2 tablespoons Frangelico (hazelnut-flavored liqueur) and 1 tablespoon espresso powder for vanilla. For coating, omit confectioners' sugar and use enough cocoa to coat hands while shaping truffles. Roll shaped truffles in 1½ cups finely chopped toasted hazelnuts.

RASPBERRY SORBET

WHY THIS RECIPE WORKS: For our raspberry sorbet recipe, we super-chilled the base and used just the right ratio of sweeteners to water to ensure the finest-textured ice crystals possible. We also bumped up the berries' natural amount of pectin to give the sorbet stability both in the freezer and out.

Raspberry Sorbet

MAKES 1 QUART

Super-chilling part of the sorbet base before transferring it to the ice cream machine will keep ice crystals to a minimum. If using a canister-style ice cream machine, be sure to freeze the empty canister for at least 24 hours and preferably 48 hours before churning. For self-refrigerating machines, prechill the canister by running the machine for five to 10 minutes before pouring in the sorbet mixture. Allow the sorbet to sit at room temperature for five minutes to soften before serving. Fresh or frozen berries may be used. If using frozen berries, thaw them before proceeding. Make certain that you use Sure-Jell engineered for low- or no-sugar recipes (packaged in a pink box) and not regular Sure-Jell (in a yellow box).

- 1 cup water
- 1 teaspoon Sure-Jell for Less or No Sugar Needed Recipes
- ⅛ teaspoon salt
- 1¼ pounds (4 cups) raspberries
- ½ cup (3½ ounces) plus 2 tablespoons sugar
- ¼ cup light corn syrup

1. Combine water, Sure-Jell, and salt in medium saucepan. Heat over medium-high heat, stirring occasionally, until Sure-Jell is fully dissolved, about 5 minutes.

Remove saucepan from heat and allow mixture to cool slightly, about 10 minutes.

2. Process raspberries, sugar, corn syrup, and water mixture in blender or food processor until smooth, about 30 seconds. Strain mixture through fine-mesh strainer, pressing on solids to extract as much liquid as possible. Transfer 1 cup mixture to small bowl and place remaining mixture in large bowl. Cover both bowls with plastic wrap. Place large bowl in refrigerator and small bowl in freezer and cool completely, at least 4 hours or up to 24 hours. (Small bowl of base will freeze solid.)

3. Remove mixtures from refrigerator and freezer. Scrape frozen base from small bowl into large bowl of base. Stir occasionally until frozen base has fully dissolved. Transfer mixture to ice cream machine and churn until mixture has consistency of thick milkshake and color lightens, 15 to 25 minutes.

4. Transfer sorbet to airtight container, pressing firmly to remove any air pockets, and freeze until firm, at least 2 hours. Serve. (Sorbet can be frozen for up to 5 days.)

Raspberry–Lime Rickey Sorbet

Reduce water to ¾ cup. Add 2 teaspoons grated lime zest and ¼ cup lime juice to blender with raspberries.

Raspberry-Port Sorbet

Substitute ruby port for water in step 1.

Raspberry Sorbet with Ginger and Mint

Substitute ginger beer for water in step 1. Add 2-inch piece of peeled and thinly sliced ginger and ¼ cup mint leaves to blender with raspberries. Decrease amount of sugar to ½ cup.

CONVERSIONS AND EQUIVALENCIES

Some say cooking is a science and an art. We would say that geography has a hand in it, too. Flour milled in the United Kingdom and elsewhere will feel and taste different from flour milled in the United States. So, while we cannot promise that the loaf of bread you bake in Canada or England will taste the same as a loaf baked in the States, we can offer guidelines for converting weights and measures. We also recommend that you rely on your instincts when making our recipes. Refer to the visual cues provided. If the bread dough hasn't "come together in a ball," as described, you may need to add more flour—even if the recipe doesn't tell you so. You be the judge.

The recipes in this book were developed using standard U.S. measures following U.S. government guidelines. The charts below offer equivalents for U.S., metric, and imperial (U.K.) measures. All conversions are approximate and have been rounded up or down to the nearest whole number. For example:

EXAMPLE:

1 teaspoon = 4.929 milliliters, rounded up to 5 milliliters
1 ounce = 28.349 grams, rounded down to 28 grams

VOLUME CONVERSIONS

U.S.	METRIC
1 teaspoon	5 milliliters
2 teaspoons	10 milliliters
1 tablespoon	15 milliliters
2 tablespoons	30 milliliters
¼ cup	59 milliliters
⅓ cup	79 milliliters
½ cup	118 milliliters
¾ cup	177 milliliters
1 cup	237 milliliters
1¼ cups	296 milliliters
1½ cups	355 milliliters
2 cups	473 milliliters
2½ cups	591 milliliters
3 cups	710 milliliters
4 cups (1 quart)	0.946 liter
1.06 quarts	1 liter
4 quarts (1 gallon)	3.8 liters

WEIGHT CONVERSIONS

OUNCES	GRAMS
½	14
¾	21
1	28
1½	43
2	57
2½	71
3	85
3½	99
4	113
4½	128
5	142
6	170
7	198
8	227
9	255
10	283
12	340
16 (1 pound)	454

CONVERSIONS FOR INGREDIENTS COMMONLY USED IN BAKING

Baking is an exacting science. Because measuring by weight is far more accurate than measuring by volume, and thus more likely to achieve reliable results, in our recipes we provide ounce measures in addition to cup measures for many ingredients. Refer to the chart below to convert these measures into grams.

INGREDIENT	OUNCES	GRAMS
Flour		
1 cup all-purpose flour*	5	142
1 cup cake flour	4	113
1 cup whole-wheat flour	5½	156
Sugar		
1 cup granulated (white) sugar	7	198
1 cup packed brown sugar (light or dark)	7	198
1 cup confectioners' sugar	4	113
Cocoa Powder		
1 cup cocoa powder	3	85
Butter†		
4 tablespoons (½ stick, or ¼ cup)	2	57
8 tablespoons (1 stick, or ½ cup)	4	113
16 tablespoons (2 sticks, or 1 cup)	8	227

* U.S. all-purpose flour, the most frequently used flour in this book, does not contain leaveners, as some European flours do. These leavened flours are called self-rising or self-raising. If you are using self-rising flour, take this into consideration before adding leavening to a recipe.

† In the United States, butter is sold both salted and unsalted. We generally recommend unsalted butter. If you are using salted butter, take this into consideration before adding salt to a recipe.

OVEN TEMPERATURES

FAHRENHEIT	CELSIUS	GAS MARK (imperial)
225	105	¼
250	120	½
275	135	1
300	150	2
325	165	3
350	180	4
375	190	5
400	200	6
425	220	7
450	230	8
475	245	9

CONVERTING TEMPERATURES FROM AN INSTANT-READ THERMOMETER

We include doneness temperatures in many of our recipes, such as those for poultry, meat, and bread. We recommend an instant-read thermometer for the job. Refer to the table above to convert Fahrenheit degrees to Celsius. Or, for temperatures not represented in the chart, use this simple formula:

Subtract 32 degrees from the Fahrenheit reading, then divide the result by 1.8 to find the Celsius reading.

EXAMPLE:
"Roast chicken until thighs register 175 degrees."
To convert:

175° F − 32 = 143°
143° ÷ 1.8 = 79.44°C, rounded down to 79°C

INDEX

Note: Page references in *italics* indicate photographs.

A

Aïoli, 768
All-Butter Double-Crust Pie Dough, 682
All-Purpose Corn Bread, 550–51
All-Purpose Turkey Gravy, 127, *127*
Almond(s)
  Apple Upside-Down Cake with, 601
  Chocolate-Raspberry Torte, 624–25, *625*
  -Crusted Chicken with Wilted Spinach Salad, 33–34
  and Golden Raisins, Sautéed Baby Spinach with, 484
  Green Beans Amandine, 482–83
  Nut-Crusted Chicken Breasts with Lemon and Thyme, *85,* 85–86
  Oranges, and Olives, Rice Salad with, 45–46, *46*
  or Hazelnut Crescent Cookies, 583
  Pan-Seared Scallops with Wilted Spinach, Watercress, and Orange Salad, 34–35, *35*
  Peach Crisp, 661–62
  Peach Crisp for a Crowd, 662
  Picada, 761–62
  -Raspberry Filling and Butter Frosting, Classic White Layer Cake with, 613–14
  Raspberry Squares, *589,* 589–90
  Shallots, and Garlic, Couscous with, 500
  Smoked, and Red Grapes, Chicken Salad with, 758
  Spritz Cookies, 576
  Toasted, and Lemon, Roasted Carrots and Fennel with, 479
  Toasted, Meringue Cookies, 584
  Tomato, and Fennel Relish, 783
  and Tomato Pesto, Pasta with (Pesto alla Trapanese), 247–48, *248*
  Vinaigrette, 461
Almost Hands-Free Risotto with Parmesan and Herbs, 499
Almost No-Knead Bread, 553–54
American Potato Salad with Hard-Cooked Eggs and Sweet Pickles, 46
Anchovies
  Chicken Marbella, 773
  and Mustard, Madeira Pan Sauce with, 144–45
  Olive and Sun-Dried Tomato Stuffing, 441
  Pissaladière, 318–19, *319*
  Salsa Verde, 435–36
  Spaghetti Puttanesca, 245–46
  taste tests on, 735

Angel Food Cake, 594, *594*
Antipasto Pasta Salad, 44–45, *45*
Appetizers
  Beef Satay, 377
  Charcoal-Grilled Baba Ghanoush, 473
  Cheesy Nachos with Guacamole and Salsa, 347, *347*
  Chinese Chicken Lettuce Wraps, 769–70
  Creamy Herbed Spinach Dip, 484–85
  Frico, 293
  Gas-Grilled Baba Ghanoush, 473
  Potstickers with Scallion Dipping Sauce, *372,* 372–73
  Shrimp Cocktail, 208–9
  Shrimp Tempura, 375–76
  Spiced Pecans with Rum Glaze, 501
Apple
  Cake, French, 804–5
Apple Cider
  Cider and Brown Sugar Glaze, 185
  Cider-Glazed Pork Chops, *156,* 156–57
  Sauce, 173–74
  Sautéed Chicken Cutlets with Mustard-Cider Sauce, 84
Apple(s)
  Apple Cider Sauce, 173–74
  Applesauce Snack Cake, 598, *598*
  Bacon, Sage, and Caramelized Onions, Bread Stuffing with, 118–19
  Baked, Best, *664,* 664–65
  Brown Betty, Skillet, 666–67
  -Cinnamon Steel-Cut Oatmeal, 797
  -Cranberry Filling, Charcoal-Grilled Pork Loin with, *442,* 442–43
  -Cranberry Filling, Gas-Grilled Pork Loin with, 443
  Crisp, Skillet, *665,* 665–66
  and Crystallized Ginger, Cranberry Chutney with, 795–96
  and Currants, Curried Tuna Salad with, 218
  and Fennel Chopped Salad, 36–37
  -Ginger Chutney, 161
  Glaze, Spicy, Grilled Salmon with, 463
  Leeks, and Bacon, Baked Bread Stuffing with, 133
  -Mustard Sauce, 791
  Pancake, German, 518–19

Apple(s) *(cont.)*
  Pie
    Classic, 685–86
    with Crystallized Ginger, 686
    Deep-Dish, *686,* 686–87
    with Dried Fruit, 686
    with Fresh Cranberries, 686
    Skillet, *669,* 669–70
  Simple Applesauce, 476
  Strudel, Easy, *667,* 667–68
  Tart
    Free-Form, 705–6
    French (Apple Galette), *704,* 704–5
    30-Minute Tarte Tatin, 706
  Upside-Down Cake, *600,* 600–601
    with Almond, 601
    with Lemon and Thyme, 601
  Waldorf Chicken Salad, 758
Applesauce
  Simple, 476
  Snack Cake, 598, *598*
  taste tests on, 735
Appliances, small, buying guide, 722–25
Apricot(s)
  and Chickpeas, Moroccan Chicken with, 75
  and Corn Muffins with Orange Essence, 534
  Free-Form Summer Fruit Tart, 701–2
  -Mustard Burger Sauce, 774
Argentine Steaks with Chimichurri Sauce, Charcoal-Grilled, *432,* 432–33
Argentine Steaks with Chimichurri Sauce, Gas-Grilled, 433
Argentinian-Style Fresh Parsley and Garlic Sauce (Chimichurri), 145
Artichokes, Crispy, and Sherry-Tomato Vinaigrette, Poached Fish Fillets with, 789–90
Arugula
  Asparagus, Walnuts, and Blue Cheese, Cavatappi with, 251–52
  and Flank Steak Sandwiches with Red Onion, 146–47
  Goat Cheese, and Sun-Dried Tomato Pesto, Campanelle with, 248–49
  Pan-Seared Scallops with Wilted Spinach, Watercress, and Orange Salad, 34–35, *35*
  Salad with Figs, Prosciutto, Walnuts, and Parmesan, 31
  Salad with Herbed Baked Goat Cheese and Vinaigrette, 32–33
  Spicy Salad with Mustard and Balsamic Vinaigrette, 30
Asian Barbecue Glaze, 196
Asparagus
  Arugula, Walnuts, and Blue Cheese, Cavatappi with, 251–52
  Basil, and Balsamic Glaze, Campanelle with, 250–51
  Broiled, 476

Asparagus *(cont.)*
  Ham, and Gruyère Frittata, 514
  Pan-Roasted, 477
  Shrimp, and Yellow Pepper, Stir-Fried, with Lemon Sauce, 388
  Spring Vegetable Pasta, 249–50, *250*
  trimming tough ends, 251
Austrian-Style Potato Salad, 47, *47*
Avocado(s)
  Chunky Guacamole, 348
  dicing, 348
  and Orange, Shrimp Salad with, 210
  -Orange Salsa, 199
  Salsa, 213–14

B

Baba Ghanoush, Charcoal-Grilled, 473
Baba Ghanoush, Gas-Grilled, 473
Bacon
  Apples, Sage, and Caramelized Onions, Bread Stuffing with, 118–19
  and Caramelized Onion, Potato Casserole with, 785–86
  Cheeseburgers, Well-Done Grilled, 425
  Leeks, and Apple, Baked Bread Stuffing with, 133
  Onion, and Gruyère, Quick Cheese Bread with, 550
  Onion, and Pepper Jack Cheese, Scrambled Eggs with, 505–6
  and Onion Tart, French, 317–18
  Oven-Fried, 509
  and Pecans, Roasted Brussels Sprouts with, 794
  Peppered, and Aged Cheddar, Juicy Pub-Style Burgers with, 232
  Quiche Lorraine, *515,* 515–16
  and Roasted Red Peppers, Latino-Style Chicken and Rice with, 77
  Spaghetti alla Carbonara, 265
  taste tests on, 735
  Tomato, and Onion, Pasta with (Pasta all'Amatriciana), 246, *246*
  Warm, Dressing, Wilted Spinach Salad with, *31,* 31–32
Baked Bread Stuffing
  with Fresh Herbs, 133
  with Leeks, Bacon, and Apple, 133
  with Sausage, Dried Cherries, and Pecans, 132
Baked Eggs Florentine, 796–97
Baked Eggs Lorraine, 797
Baked Manicotti, 270–71, *271*
Baked Sole Fillets with Herbs and Bread Crumbs, *202,* 202–3
Bakeware, buying guide, 720–22
Balsamic-Mustard Vinaigrette, Foolproof, 28

Balsamic Vinegar, Strawberries with, 675–76

Balsamic vinegar, taste tests on, 754

Banana(s)

Bread, Classic, 523–24

Bread, Ultimate, *522,* 522–23

-Coconut Steel-Cut Oatmeal, 798

Foster, 670

frozen, uses for, 75

and Nutella, Crêpes with, 673

Peanut, and Honey Steel-Cut Oatmeal, 798

Barbecued Baby Back Ribs for a Charcoal Grill, *453,* 453–54

Barbecued Baby Back Ribs for a Gas Grill, 454

Barbecued Beef Brisket, Charcoal-Grilled, 436–37, *437*

Barbecued Beef Brisket, Gas-Grilled, 437

Barbecued Beef Ribs, Texas-Style, for a Charcoal Grill, 454–55, *455*

Barbecued Beef Ribs, Texas-Style, for a Gas Grill, 456

Barbecued Pulled Chicken for a Charcoal Grill, 418–19

Barbecued Pulled Chicken for a Crowd, 419

Barbecued Pulled Chicken for a Gas Grill, 419

Barbecued Pulled Pork for a Charcoal Grill, 446–47

Barbecued Pulled Pork for a Gas Grill, 447

Barbecued Salmon for a Charcoal Grill, 463–64

Barbecued Salmon for a Gas Grill, 464

Barbecued Spareribs, Memphis-Style, on a Charcoal Grill, 450–51

Barbecued Spareribs, Memphis-Style, on a Gas Grill, 451–52

Barbecue Glaze, 422–23

Barbecue Sauce

Eastern North Carolina, 448

Kansas City, 449–50

Lexington Vinegar, 184

Quick, 453

South Carolina Mustard, 184

Sweet and Tangy, 183–84

taste tests on, 735

for Texas-Style Beef Ribs, 456

Barley and Vegetable Soup, Farmhouse, 759–60

Bars

Blondies, 584–85, *585*

Brownies

Chewy, 586–87, *587*

Classic, 585–86, *586*

Fudgy Low-Fat, 588–89

Fudgy Triple-Chocolate, 587–88

Triple-Chocolate Espresso, 588

Chocolate-Cherry, with Hazelnuts, 580–81

Congo, 585

Key Lime, *590,* 590–91

Raspberry Squares, *589,* 589–90

Triple Citrus, 591

Basic Double-Crust Pie Dough, 680

Basic Polenta, 297, *297*

Basic Single-Crust Pie Dough, 681

Basic Spice Rub for Pork Chops, 439

Basic White Rice, 382

Basil

Asparagus, and Balsamic Glaze, Campanelle with, 250–51

–Cherry Tomato Vinaigrette, Chunky, 201

Farfalle with Pesto, 247

and Garlic, Fresh Tomato Sauce with, 240–41

Pasta Caprese, *242,* 242–43

Pasta Salad with Pesto, 43–44

Pestata, 760

Thai-Style Chicken with, 398–99

Tomatoes, and Mozzarella, Deep-Dish Pizza with, 282–83, *283*

Vinaigrette, 468

washing and storing, 30

Bean(s)

baked canned, taste tests on, 735

Barbecue, Smoky Kansas City, 450

Black, and Rice, Cuban-Style, 78

Black, Soup, 350–51, *351*

black, taste tests on, 735

Boston Baked, 481

chickpeas, taste tests on, 735

Chili, Best Vegetarian, 762

Cincinnati Chili, *223,* 223–24

Hearty Ham and Split Pea Soup with Potatoes, 19

Hearty Minestrone, *21,* 21–22

Indian-Style Curry with Potatoes, Cauliflower, Peas, and Chickpeas, *409,* 409–10

Indian-Style Curry with Sweet Potatoes, Eggplant, Green Beans, and Chickpeas, 410

Kidney, Beef Chili with, 365–66

Mediterranean Chopped Salad, 36, *36*

Modern Ham and Split Pea Soup, 18, *18*

Moroccan Chicken with Chickpeas and Apricots, 75

Our Favorite Chili, 8–9, *9*

and Pasta Soup, Italian (Pasta e Fagioli), *293,* 293–94

red kidney, taste tests on, 736

Refried, 369

refried, taste tests on, 736

Simplified Cassoulet with Pork and Kielbasa, 337–38

Skillet Tamale Pie, 54

Stew, Hearty Tuscan, 294–95, *295*

White Chicken Chili, 367–68

see also Green Bean(s); Lentil

Bean Sprouts

Pad Thai, 403–4

and Peas, Fried Rice with, 381–82

Beef

Braised in Barolo, 310–11

Brisket

Barbecued, Charcoal-Grilled, 436–37, *437*

Barbecued, Gas-Grilled, 437

Onion-Braised, 170–72, *171*

broth, taste tests on, 736

Burgers

Best Old-Fashioned, 229–30, *230*

Charcoal-Grilled Hamburgers, 423–24

Gas-Grilled Hamburgers, 424

Grilled Cheeseburgers, 424

Juicy Pub-Style, 230–31

Juicy Pub-Style, with Crispy Shallots and Blue Cheese, 231, *231*

Juicy Pub-Style, with Pan-Roasted Mushrooms and Gruyère, 232

Juicy Pub-Style, with Peppered Bacon and Aged Cheddar, 232

Juicy Pub-Style, with Sautéed Onions and Smoked Cheddar, 232

Well-Done Charcoal-Grilled Hamburgers, 424–25, *425*

Well-Done Gas-Grilled Hamburgers, 425

Well-Done Grilled Bacon Cheeseburgers, 425

Chili Con Carne, *366,* 366–67

Chili with Kidney Beans, 365–66

Cincinnati Chili, *223,* 223–24

Classic Stuffed Bell Peppers, 228–29, *229*

Empanadas, *352,* 352–53

Fettuccine with Slow-Simmered Bolognese Sauce, 258–59

Glazed All-Beef Meat Loaf, 226–27, *227*

Home-Corned, and Cabbage, New England–Style, 781–82

hot dogs, taste tests on, 744

Kebabs with Lemon and Rosemary Marinade, Charcoal-Grilled, 456–57

Kebabs with Lemon and Rosemary Marinade, Gas-Grilled, 457

Lasagna with Hearty Tomato-Meat Sauce, 274–75

Meat Loaf with Brown Sugar–Ketchup Glaze, 227–28

Our Favorite Chili, 8–9, *9*

Pasta and Slow-Simmered Tomato Sauce with Meat (Sunday Gravy), 260–61

Pasta with Hearty Italian Meat Sauce (Sunday Gravy), 256–57

Pasta with Weeknight Bolognese Sauce, *259,* 259–60

Pot Roast

Old-Fashioned, 63

Old-Fashioned, with Root Vegetables, 64

Simple, 62, *62*

Prime Rib, 170

Best, 778–79

carving, 170

preparing, 779

Beef *(cont.)*

Ragu alla Bolognese, 765

Ribs, Short

boning, 67

Braised, *66,* 66–67

Grill-Roasted, 779–80

Slow-Cooker Beer-Braised, 68, *68*

Ribs, Texas-Style

Barbecued, for a Charcoal Grill, 454–55, *455*

Barbecued, for a Gas Grill, 456

Barbecue Sauce for, 456

Roast

Inexpensive Charcoal-Grill-Roasted, with Garlic and Rosemary for a Charcoal Grill, 433–34

Inexpensive Gas-Grill-Roasted, with Garlic and Rosemary for a Gas Grill, 434

resting, before carving, 169

Slow-Roasted, 164–65

Tenderloin, *165,* 165–66

Tenderloin, Horseradish-Crusted, *166,* 166–67

Tenderloin with Caramelized Onion and Mushroom Stuffing, *167,* 167–69

salting, effect of, 164

Satay, 377

Satay, Grilled, 776–77

Sauce Base, 140

Shepherd's Pie, 780–81

Simple Italian-Style Meat Sauce, *257,* 257–58

Skillet Lasagna, 51–52, *52*

Skillet Tamale Pie, 54

Spaghetti and Meatballs, *261,* 261–62

Spaghetti and Meatballs, Classic, for a Crowd, 263–64

Steak

Argentine, with Chimichurri Sauce, Charcoal-Grilled, *432,* 432–33

Argentine, with Chimichurri Sauce, Gas-Grilled, 433

au Poivre with Brandied Cream Sauce, 338–39

blade, trimming, 64

Chicken-Fried, 225, *225*

Diane, 340–41, *341*

Fajitas for a Charcoal Grill, 358–59

Fajitas for a Gas Grill, 359

Filet Mignon, Pan-Seared, 144, *144*

Filet Mignon, Pepper-Crusted, *145,* 145–46

Filets Mignons, Charcoal-Grilled, 431

Filets Mignons, Gas-Grilled, 431

Flank, and Arugula Sandwiches with Red Onion, 146–47

flank, butterflying, 428

Flank, Charcoal-Grilled Marinated, 425–26

Flank, Gas-Grilled Marinated, 426

Flank, Grilled Stuffed, for a Charcoal Grill, *427,* 427–28

Flank, Grilled Stuffed, for a Gas Grill, 428

Flank, Grilled Stuffed, with Spinach and Pine Nuts, 428

Beef, Steak *(cont.)*

flank, slicing across the grain, 147

flank, stuffing, 428

Frites, *339,* 339–40

Grilled, with Ancho Chile–Coffee Rub, 778

Grilled, with New Mexican Chile Rub, 777–78

Grilled, with Spicy Chipotle Chile Rub, 778

Grilled Thai, Salad for a Charcoal Grill, 405–6

Grilled Thai, Salad for a Gas Grill, 406

Pan-Seared, 138

Pan-Seared Inexpensive, 142–43, *143*

Pan-Seared Thick-Cut, 140–41, *141*

Restaurant-Style Steak Sauces for, 139–40

searing two at same time, 142

Strip or Rib, Charcoal-Grilled, 430

Strip or Rib, Gas-Grilled, 430–31

Tacos, 355–56

Tips, Charcoal-Grilled, 429

Tips, Gas-Grilled, 429

Stew

Beer, and Onion, Belgian (Carbonnade à la Flamande), 64–65, *65*

Best, *7,* 7–8

Burgundy, 334–35

Burgundy, Slow-Cooker, 335–36

Catalan-Style, with Mushrooms, 761–62

Daube Provençal, 332–33, *333*

Hungarian, 65–66

Stir-Fried

and Broccoli with Oyster Sauce, *389,* 389–90

Tangerine, with Onion and Snow Peas, 391

Teriyaki, with Green Beans and Shiitakes, 390–91

Thai-Style, with Chiles and Shallots, *402,* 402–3

Stroganoff, Skillet, 55, *55*

Tacos, 354, *355*

Tenderloin

Grill-Roasted, for a Charcoal Grill, 434–35, *435*

Grill-Roasted, for a Gas Grill, 435

Horseradish-Crusted, *166,* 166–67

and Vegetable Soup, Quick, 9–10, *10*

see also Veal

Beer

Beef, and Onion Stew, Belgian (Carbonnade à la Flamande), 64–65, *65*

-Braised Short Ribs, Slow-Cooker, 68, *68*

Classic Gingerbread Cake, *608,* 608–9

Beer Can Chicken, Grill-Roasted, for a Charcoal Grill, 420–21

Beer Can Chicken, Grill-Roasted, for a Gas Grill, 421

Behind the scenes

brining tips, 129

brining turkey, 113, 129

buying chicken, 98

Behind the scenes *(cont.)*

chimney starters, 415

chopping onions, 315

cooking and serving pasta, 245

cooking in skillets, 53

cooking pork, 159

creating TV scripts and filming shows, 22

developing pie dough recipes, 683

equipment hall of shame, 487

essential kitchen tools, 286

flambéing food, 342

heating oil in skillets, 199

hiring test cooks, 219

kosher chicken, 155

making pan sauces with fond, 338

mincing garlic, 224, 275

mise en place, 336

natural pork, flavor of, 155

pasta cooking gadgets, 253

preventing food from sticking to grill, 461

rating equipment, 13, 431

reducing sauces and liquids, 146

resting meat before carving, 169

salting, or "dry-brining" meat, 164

sharpening knives, 494

stir-frying, 386

storing tomatoes, 240

taste testing ingredients, 34, 221

testing recipes, 420, 506, 565

test kitchen freezer items, 75

using rulers in cooking, 571

washing and storing greens, 30

weighing and measuring ingredients, 551

Belgian Beef, Beer, and Onion Stew (Carbonnade à la Flamande), 64–65, *65*

Belgian-Style Dipping Sauce, 235

Berry(ies)

Blackberry Glaze, 780

Fool, *676,* 676–77

Free-Form Summer Fruit Tart, 701–2

Fresh, Gratins, Individual, with Lemon Zabaglione, 664

Fresh, Gratins, Individual, with Zabaglione, *663,* 663–64

Mixed, Tart with Pastry Cream, 703

Summer, Pie, *691,* 691–92

Summer, Pudding, Large, 674

Summer, Puddings, Individual, 673–74

see also Blueberry(ies); Cranberry(ies); Raspberry(ies); Strawberry(ies)

Best Baked Apples, *664,* 664–65

Best Beef Stew, *7,* 7–8

Best Crab Cakes, 788

Best Drop Biscuits, 546–47, *547*

Best Old-Fashioned Burgers, 229–30, *230*

Best Prime Rib, 778–79
Best Shortbread, 581–82
Best Vegetarian Chili, 762
Best Whole Wheat Sandwich Bread, 556–58
Big and Chewy Oatmeal-Date Cookies, 572
Big and Chewy Oatmeal-Raisin Cookies, 572
Biscuits
    Best Drop, 546–47, *547*
    Cheddar, 546
    Cream, 546
    Cream, with Fresh Herbs, 546
Bittersweet Chocolate Roulade, 628–29
Black and White Spiral Cookies, *576,* 578
Black Bean(s)
    and Rice, Cuban-Style, 78
    Skillet Tamale Pie, 54
    Soup, 350–51, *351*
Blackberry(ies)
    Free-Form Summer Fruit Tart, 701–2
    Glaze, 780
    Individual Fresh Berry Gratins with Lemon Zabaglione, 664
    Individual Fresh Berry Gratins with Zabaglione,
        663, 663–64
    Individual Summer Berry Puddings, 673–74
    Large Summer Berry Pudding, 674
    Mixed Berry Tart with Pastry Cream, 703
    Summer Berry Pie, *691,* 691–92
Blanched Green Beans, 481–82
Blondies, 584–85, *585*
Blueberry(ies)
    Boy Bait, *536,* 536–37
    Cobbler, 660–61, *661*
    Free-Form Summer Fruit Tart, 701–2
    Fresh Fruit Tart with Pastry Cream, 702–3, *703*
    Honeydew, and Mango with Lime-Ginger Reduction, 543
    Individual Fresh Berry Gratins with Lemon Zabaglione, 664
    Individual Fresh Berry Gratins with Zabaglione,
        663, 663–64
    Individual Summer Berry Puddings, 673–74
    Large Summer Berry Pudding, 674
    Mixed Berry Tart with Pastry Cream, 703
    Muffins, *531,* 531–32
    Nectarines, and Raspberries with Champagne-Cardamom
        Reduction, 543
    Pancakes, *517,* 517–18
    Pie, *690,* 690–91
    Scones, 524–26, *525*
    Summer Berry Pie, *691,* 691–92
Blue Cheese
    Asparagus, Arugula, and Walnuts, Cavatappi with, 251–52
    and Black Pepper–Caramel Sauce, Caramelized Pears with,
        674, 674–75
    –Chive Butter, 146

Blue Cheese *(cont.)*
    Creamy Baked Four-Cheese Pasta, *268,* 268–69
    and Crispy Shallots, Juicy Pub-Style Burgers with, 231, *231*
    Dressing, Rich and Creamy, Leafy Green Salad with, 29–30
    Four-Cheese Lasagna, 271–73
    Gorgonzola-Cream Sauce, 268
    Mushroom and Leek Galette with Gorgonzola, 791–93
    Pear and Cranberry Chopped Salad, 35–36
    taste tests on, 737
Bok Choy and Crispy Noodle Cake, Stir-Fried Chicken
    with, *385,* 385–86
Boston Baked Beans, 481
Bourbon–Brown Sugar Sauce, 641
Braised Beef Short Ribs, *66,* 66–67
Braised Turkey, 127–28
Brandied Cream Sauce, Steak au Poivre with, 338–39
Brandy and Green Peppercorn Sauce, Restaurant-Style,
    for Pan-Seared Steaks, 139–40
Bran Muffins, 532–33, *533*
Breaded Chicken Cutlets, 84–85
Breaded Pork Cutlets (Pork Schnitzel), *174,* 174–75
Bread Pudding
    Breakfast Strata with Sausage, Mushrooms, and Monterey
        Jack, 517
    Breakfast Strata with Spinach and Gruyère, *516,* 516–17
    Chocolate-Hazelnut Slow Cooker, 641–42
    Classic, 640, *640*
Bread(s)
    Almost No-Knead, 553–54
    Banana, Classic, 523–24
    Banana, Ultimate, *522,* 522–23
    Biscuits
        Best Drop, 546–47, *547*
        Cheddar, 546
        Cream, 546
        Cream, with Fresh Herbs, 546
    Cheese, Quick, 549–50, *550*
    Cheese, Quick, with Bacon, Onion, and Gruyère, 550
    Ciabatta, 554–56, *555*
    Cinnamon-Swirl, 799
    Corn Bread
        All-Purpose, 550–51
        Golden, 122
        Southern, 551–52
        Spicy Jalapeño-Cheddar, 551
    Country, Rustic, 552–53
    Croissants, 527–31
    Croutons
        Buttery, 18
        Classic, 12
        Garlic, 23
        Herbed, 760
    crumbs, panko, taste tests on, 736

Bread(s) *(cont.)*

French Toast, *521,* 521–22

frozen dinner rolls, taste tests on, 742

Garlic, Cheesy, 292–93

Garlic, Classic, 292

Indian Flatbread, Quicker, 802

Indian Flatbread (Naan), 801–2

Muffins

Blueberry, *531,* 531–32

Bran, 532–33, *533*

Corn, 533–34

Corn and Apricot, with Orange Essence, 534

Cranberry-Pecan, 534–35

Multigrain, *558,* 558–59

Potato Burger Buns, 800–801

Potato Dinner Rolls, 801

Pumpkin, 798

Pumpkin, with Candied Ginger, 798

Quick Cinnamon Buns with Buttermilk Icing, *537,* 537–38

Rosemary Focaccia, *278,* 278–79

Rustic Dinner Rolls, 547–48, *548*

Salad, Italian (Panzanella), 38–39, *39*

Scones

Blueberry, 524–26, *525*

Cream, 524

Oatmeal, 526–27, *527*

Oatmeal, Glazed Maple-Pecan, 527

Soda, Irish, 548–49

Soda, Whole Wheat, 549

Sticky Buns with Pecans, 538–39

white sandwich, taste tests on, 736

Whole Wheat Sandwich, Best, 556–58

whole wheat sandwich, taste tests on, 736

Bread stuffings and dressings

Bread Stuffing

with Bacon, Apples, Sage, and Caramelized Onions, 118–19

Baked, with Fresh Herbs, 133

Baked, with Leeks, Bacon, and Apple, 133

Baked, with Sausage, Dried Cherries, and Pecans, 132

Mushroom-Leek, with Herbs, 103

Sausage Dressing, 120–21, *122*

stuffing into turkey, 117

Breakfast Strata with Sausage, Mushrooms, and Monterey Jack, 517

Breakfast Strata with Spinach and Gruyère, *516,* 516–17

Brining techniques, 113, 129

Broccoli

and Beef, Stir-Fried, with Oyster Sauce, *389,* 389–90

and Cheddar, Skillet Chicken and Rice with, 58

-Cheese Soup, 16–17, *17*

Broccoli *(cont.)*

Chicken, and Mushrooms, Thai Green Curry with, *399,* 399–400

Chicken, and Ziti, Skillet, 50–51

Roasted, *477,* 477–78

Roasted, with Garlic, 478

Broccolini and Chicken, Thai-Style Stir-Fried Noodles with, 768–69

Broccoli Rabe and Sausage, Orecchiette with, 253

Broiled Asparagus, 476

Broiled Salmon with Mustard and Crisp Dilled Crust, 193–94

Broth

beef, taste tests on, 736

chicken, taste tests on, 736

vegetable, taste tests on, 737

Brown Betty, Skillet Apple, 666–67

Browned Butter and Sage Sauce, 267

Brownies

brownie mixes, taste tests on, 737

Chewy, 586–87, *587*

Classic, 585–86, *586*

Fudgy Low-Fat, 588–89

Fudgy Triple-Chocolate, 587–88

Triple-Chocolate Espresso, 588

Brown Sugar Cookies, 562–63, *563*

Brussels Sprouts, Roasted, 794

with Bacon and Pecans, 794

with Garlic, Red Pepper Flakes, and Parmesan, 794

Buffalo Wings, 108–9

Bulgur

Bean Chili, 762

Buns

Potato Burger, 800–801

Quick Cinnamon, with Buttermilk Icing, *537,* 537–38

Sticky, with Pecans, 538–39

Burgers

Best Old-Fashioned, 229–30, *230*

Charcoal-Grilled Hamburgers, 423–24

Gas-Grilled Hamburgers, 424

Grilled Cheeseburgers, 424

Juicy Pub-Style, 230–31

with Crispy Shallots and Blue Cheese, 231, *231*

with Pan-Roasted Mushrooms and Gruyère, 232

with Peppered Bacon and Aged Cheddar, 232

with Sautéed Onions and Smoked Cheddar, 232

Turkey, Juicy Grilled, 773–74

Well-Done Charcoal-Grilled Hamburgers, 424–25

Well-Done Gas-Grilled Hamburgers, 425

Well-Done Grilled Bacon Cheeseburgers, 425

Burger Sauce, Classic, 230

Burger Sauce, Pub-Style, 231
Butter
    Blue Cheese–Chive, 146
    Browned, and Sage Sauce, 267
    Browned, and Tomato Sauce, 764
    Chipotle and Garlic, with Lime and Cilantro, 166
    Chipotle-Garlic, with Lime and Cilantro, 201
    Cookies, French (Sablés), *576,* 576–77
    freezing, 75
    Lemon, Garlic, and Parsley, 432
    Lemon-Thyme, 760
    Mustard-Garlic, with Thyme, 102
    Roasted Red Pepper and Smoked Paprika, 432
    Shallot and Parsley, 166
    Thai Chili, 142
    unsalted, taste tests on, 737
Buttermilk
    Coleslaw, Creamy, 41–42
    Indian-Style Spinach with Fresh Cheese (Saag Paneer), 793–94
    Mashed Potatoes, 491
    Waffles, 519–20
    Waffles, Easy, *520,* 520–21
Butternut Squash Galette with Gruyère, 793
Butternut Squash Risotto, 298–99, *299*
Butternut Squash Soup, 15, *15*
Buttery Croutons, 18

C

Cabbage
    Creamy Buttermilk Coleslaw, 41–42
    Creamy Coleslaw, 41
    Hearty Minestrone, *21,* 21–22
    New England–Style Home-Corned Beef and, 781–82
    Pork Lo Mein, 393–94, *394*
    Potstickers with Scallion Dipping Sauce, *372,* 372–73
    Salad, Confetti, with Spicy Peanut Dressing, 42
    shredding, 42
    Stir-Fried Portobellos with Ginger-Oyster Sauce, 397–98, *398*
    Stir-Fried Portobellos with Sweet Chili-Garlic Sauce, 398
Cakes
    Angel Food, 594, *594*
    Apple, French, 804–5
    Applesauce Snack, 598, *598*
    Apple Upside-Down, *600,* 600–601
        with Almond, 601
        with Lemon and Thyme, 601
    Caramel, Easy, 610–11, *611*
    Carrot, 601–2, *602*
    Carrot, Light, 603

Cakes *(cont.)*
    Carrot Layer, 805–6
    Coconut Layer, 609–10
    Gingerbread, Classic, *608,* 608–9
    Lemon
        Bundt, 596
        Layer, with Fluffy White Icing, 611–12, *612*
        Pound, 597, *597*
    lining cake pans for, 614
    Oatmeal, with Broiled Icing, *599,* 599–600
    Peach, Summer, 607, *607*
    Spice, 604
    Strawberry Cream, *605,* 605–6
    testing for doneness, 603
    Tiramisù, 632–33, *633*
    Tiramisù with Cooked Eggs, 633
    White Layer, Classic, with Butter Frosting and
        Raspberry-Almond Filling, 613–14
    Yellow Layer, Classic, with Vanilla Buttercream, 614–15
    Yellow Layer, Fluffy, with Milk Chocolate Frosting,
        615, 615–17
    see also Cheesecakes; Chocolate Cakes; Coffee Cakes
Campanelle with Arugula, Goat Cheese, and Sun-Dried
    Tomato Pesto, 248–49
Campanelle with Asparagus, Basil, and Balsamic Glaze,
    250–51
Candied Sweet Potato Casserole, 135, *135*
Candy. *See* Truffles
Caper(s)
    Chicken Marbella, 773
    Chicken Piccata, 302
    -Lemon Sauce, 154
    Onion, and Olive Relish, 783
    Salsa Verde, 435–36
    Smoked Salmon, and Dill, Easy Salmon Cakes with, 789
    "Smoked Salmon Platter" Sauce, 791
    -Tomato Pan Sauce, 143
Caramel Cake, Easy, 610–11, *611*
Caramelized Pears with Blue Cheese and Black
    Pepper–Caramel Sauce, *674,* 674–75
Caramel Sauce, 519
Carbonnade à la Flamande (Belgian Beef, Beer, and
    Onion Stew), 64–65, *65*
Carrot(s)
    Baby, Quick Roasted, 479
    Cake, 601–2, *602*
    Cake, Light, 603
    Chicken and Dumplings, *69,* 69–70
    and Cilantro, Lentil Salad with, 759
    Glazed, 479–80
    Hearty Minestrone, *21,* 21–22
    Layer Cake, 805–6

Carrot(s) *(cont.)*

Mashed Potatoes and Root Vegetables, 489–90, *490*

New England–Style Home-Corned Beef and Cabbage, 781–82

Old-Fashioned Pot Roast with Root Vegetables, 64

Quick Beef and Vegetable Soup, 9–10, *10*

Raisins, and Pine Nuts, Couscous with, 500

Roasted, 478, *478*

    and Fennel with Toasted Almonds and Lemon, 479

    and Parsnips with Rosemary, 479

Skillet Chicken Pot Pie with Biscuit Topping, 52–54

-Spice Steel-Cut Oatmeal, 797

Cashews

Curried Chicken Salad with, 758

Garlicky Eggplant, and Scallions, Stir-Fried Shrimp with, 396

Cassoulet, Simplified, with Pork and Kielbasa, 337–38

Catalan-Style Beef Stew with Mushrooms, 761–62

Cauliflower, Potatoes, Peas, and Chickpeas, Indian-Style Curry with, *409,* 409–10

Cavatappi with Asparagus, Arugula, Walnuts, and Blue Cheese, 251–52

Charcoal-grilled dishes. *See under* **Grilled dishes**

Cheddar

Aged, and Peppered Bacon, Juicy Pub-Style Burgers with, 232

Biscuits, 546

and Broccoli, Skillet Chicken and Rice with, 58

Broccoli-Cheese Soup, 16–17, *17*

Cheese, Sausage, and Sweet Pepper, Scrambled Eggs with, 506–7

Cheesy Nachos with Guacamole and Salsa, 347, *347*

Chicken Enchiladas with a Red Chili Sauce, 359–60, *360*

Cincinnati Chili, *223,* 223–24

Classic Grilled Cheese Sandwiches, 219–20

Classic Macaroni and Cheese, 220, *220*

extra-sharp, taste tests on, 738

Family-Sized Cheese Omelet, 509–10

and Ham, Stuffed Chicken Cutlets with, 86–87

-Jalapeño Corn Bread, Spicy, 551

Light Macaroni and Cheese, 222

premium, taste tests on, 738

presliced, taste tests on, 738

Quesadillas, 348–49

Quick Cheese Bread, 549–50, *550*

reduced-fat, taste tests on, 738

Scalloped Potatoes, 493–94

sharp, taste tests on, 738

Skillet Tamale Pie, 54

Smoked, and Sautéed Onions, Juicy Pub-Style Burgers with, 232

Stovetop Macaroni and Cheese, 221

Twice-Baked Potatoes, 494–95

Cheese

American, presliced, taste tests on, 737

Asiago, taste tests on, 737

Asparagus, Ham, and Gruyère Frittata, 514

Baked Eggs Lorraine, 797

Baked Manicotti, 270–71, *271*

Baked Ziti, *269,* 269–70

Baked Ziti, Skillet, 50, *50*

Bread, Quick, 549–50, *550*

Bread, Quick, with Bacon, Onion, and Gruyère, 550

Breakfast Strata with Sausage, Mushrooms, and Monterey Jack, 517

Breakfast Strata with Spinach and Gruyère, *516,* 516–17

Butternut Squash Galette with Gruyère, 793

Cheesy Garlic Bread, 292–93

Cheesy Nachos with Guacamole and Salsa, 347, *347*

Chicken Milanese, 85

Classic French Onion Soup, *314,* 314–15

cottage cheese, taste tests on, 738

Denver Omelet, *510,* 510–11

Enchiladas Verdes, 360–62, *361*

Espresso-Mascarpone Cream, 629

Fennel and Apple Chopped Salad, 36–37

Fontina, taste tests on, 738

Four- , Baked Pasta, Creamy, *268,* 268–69

Four- , Lasagna, 271–73

Fresh, and Spinach, Indian-Style, (Saag Paneer), 793–94

Frico, 293

and Garlic, French Mashed Potatoes with (Aligot), *323,* 323–24

Goat, and Hazelnuts, Lentil Salad with, 759

Goat, Herbed Baked, and Vinaigrette, Salad with, 32–33

Goat, Leek, and Prosciutto Frittata, 514–15

Goat, Potato and Shallot Galette with, 793

goat, taste tests on, 739

Grilled, Sandwiches, Classic, 219–20

Grilled Cheeseburgers, 424

Grilled Stuffed Flank Steak for a Charcoal Grill, *427,* 427–28

Grilled Stuffed Flank Steak for a Gas Grill, 428

Gruyère, taste tests on, 739

Juicy Pub-Style Burgers with Pan-Roasted Mushrooms and Gruyère, 232

Lasagna with Hearty Tomato-Meat Sauce, 274–75

Light New York Cheesecake, 634–35

Macaroni and, Classic, 220, *220*

Macaroni and, Stovetop, 221

Monterey Jack, taste tests on, 739

Omelet, Family-Sized, 509–10

Pasta all'Amatriciana, 765–66

Pepper Jack, Bacon, and Onion, Scrambled Eggs with, 505–6

provolone, taste tests on, 739

Cheese *(cont.)*

Quesadillas, 348–49

Quiche Lorraine, *515,* 515–16

ravioli, taste tests on, 747

ricotta, taste tests on, 739

Skillet Lasagna, 51–52, *52*

Spaghetti with Pecorino Romano and Black Pepper, 239

Streamlined French Onion Soup, 315–16

Stuffed Chicken Breasts, Gas-Grilled, 417

Stuffed Chicken Breasts with Prosciutto and Fontina, Charcoal-Grilled, 415–17

Swiss, taste tests on, 739

Tiramisù, 632–33, *633*

Tiramisù with Cooked Eggs, 633

and Tomato Pizzas, Grilled, for a Charcoal Grill, 288–90, *289*

and Tomato Pizzas, Grilled, for a Gas Grill, 290

tortellini, taste tests on, 748

Vegetable Lasagna, *272,* 273–74

Well-Done Grilled Bacon Cheeseburgers, 425

see also Blue Cheese; Cheddar; Cream Cheese; Feta; Mozzarella; Parmesan

Cheesecakes

Lemon, 636–37

New York, 633–34, *634*

New York, Light, 634–35

Spiced Pumpkin, 635–36

Cherry(ies)

Apple Pie with Dried Fruit, 686

-Chocolate Bars with Hazelnuts, 580–81

Dried, and Pecans, Chocolate-Chunk Oatmeal Cookies with, 570–71

Dried, and Pecans, Couscous with, 500

Dried, –Port Sauce with Onions and Marmalade, 176

Dried, Sausage, and Pecans, Baked Bread Stuffing with, 132

-Port Glaze, 187

-Port Reduction, 146

Sour, Cobbler, *659,* 659–60

Sour, Fresh, Cobbler, 660

Sweet, Pie, *692,* 692–93

Cherry Tomato Salad with Feta and Olives, 37–38, *38*

Chewy Brownies, 586–87, *587*

Chewy Sugar Cookies, 562

Chicago-Style Deep-Dish Pizza, *284,* 284–85

Chicken

Adobo, Filipino, 771

Almond-Crusted, with Wilted Spinach Salad, 33–34

Barbecued Pulled

for a Charcoal Grill, 418–19

for a Crowd, 419

for a Gas Grill, 419

Beer Can, Grill-Roasted, for a Charcoal Grill, 420–21

Chicken *(cont.)*

Beer Can, Grill-Roasted, for a Gas Grill, 421

Biryani, 407–8

Breasts

Bone-In, Charcoal-Grilled, 414, *414*

Bone-In, Gas-Grilled, 414–15

boneless skinless, taste tests on, 740

butterflying, 87

Nut-Crusted, with Lemon and Thyme, *85,* 85–86

Nut-Crusted, with Orange and Oregano, 86

Pan-Roasted, with Sage-Vermouth Sauce, 92–93, *93*

Pan-Seared, 87–88, *88*

Skillet-Roasted, with Potatoes, *56,* 56–57

split, trimming, 92

Stuffed, French-Style, *326,* 326–27

Stuffed, Gas-Grilled, 417

Stuffed with Prosciutto and Fontina, Charcoal-Grilled, 415–17

Broccoli, and Mushrooms, Thai Green Curry with, *399,* 399–400

Broccoli, and Ziti, Skillet, 50–51

and Broccolini, Thai-Style Stir-Fried Noodles with, 768–69

broth, taste tests on, 736

buying, tips for, 98

Canzanese, *306,* 306–7

Chili, White, 367–68

Chinese, Lettuce Wraps, 769–70

with 40 Cloves of Garlic, 329–30

Coq au Vin, *328,* 328–29

Cutlets

Breaded, 84–85

Parmesan-Crusted, 302–3

Sautéed, with Mustard-Cider Sauce, 84

Stuffed, with Ham and Cheddar, 86–87

and Dumplings, *69,* 69–70

and Dumplings, Lighter, 70–71

Enchiladas Verdes, 360–62, *361*

Enchiladas with a Red Chili Sauce, 359–60, *360*

Fajitas, Skillet, 770

Fajitas for a Charcoal Grill, 356–57, *357*

Fajitas for a Gas Grill, 357

Francese, 303–4, *304*

Fricassee, Quick, *325,* 325–26

Fried

Crispy, 105–6, *106*

Easier, 106–7, *107*

Oven-, 107–8, *108*

Italian-Style Charcoal-Grilled, 307–8, *308*

Italian-Style Gas-Grilled, 308

Jerk, 771–72

Kiev, *89,* 89–90

kosher, flavor of, 155

Chicken (*cont.*)

Marbella, 773

Marsala, 300

Milanese, 85

Moroccan, with Chickpeas and Apricots, 75

Moroccan, with Olives and Lemon, *74,* 74–75

Noodle Soup

Classic, 4

Hearty, *5,* 5–6

Old-Fashioned Slow-Cooker, 6–7

Orange-Flavored, 384–85

Oven-Barbecued, Sweet and Tangy, 90–91

Paella, *79,* 79–80

Parmesan, Lighter, 300–301, *301*

Piccata, 302

Picnic, Spice-Rubbed, *91,* 91–92

in a Pot, French, 330–31, *331*

Pot Pie, Skillet, with Biscuit Topping, 52–54

Pot Pie with Savory Crumble Topping, 71–73, *72*

Provençal, 331–32

Ragu alla Bolognese, 765

and Rice

Latino-Style, *76,* 76–77

Latino-Style, with Bacon and Roasted Red Peppers, 77

Latino-Style, with Ham, Peas, and Orange, 77

Skillet, Curried, 58

Skillet, with Broccoli and Cheddar, 58

Skillet, with Peas and Scallions, 57

Roast

applying butter under the skin, 94

carving, 95

Crisp-Skinned, 96–97

Glazed, 98–100, *99*

High-Roast Butterflied, with Potatoes, 101–2

Lemon, Classic, *97,* 97–98

Perfect, 93–94

Peruvian, with Garlic and Lime, 104–5, *105*

Stovetop, with Lemon-Herb Sauce, *100,* 100–101

"Stuffed" Butterflied, 102–3, *103*

Weeknight, 94–95

Salad

Classic, 758

Curried, with Cashews, 758

with Red Grapes and Smoked Almonds, 758

Waldorf, 758

Saltimbocca, 305, *305*

Shredded, Sesame Noodles with, 380, *380*

Simplified Cassoulet with Pork and Kielbasa, 337–38

Skillet Jambalaya, 59

Smoked, for a Charcoal Grill, *417,* 417–18

Smoked, for a Gas Grill, 418

Soup, Thai-Style, 377–78, *378*

Stir-Fried, and Zucchini with Ginger Sauce, 387

Chicken (*cont.*)

Stir-Fried, with Bok Choy and Crispy Noodle Cake, *385,* 385–86

Tandoori, 411, *411*

Teriyaki, 383–84

Thai Grilled, on a Gas Grill, 405

Thai Grilled, with Spicy, Sweet, and Sour Dipping Sauce, 404–5

Thai-Style, with Basil, 398–99

Tikka Masala, 406–7, *407*

Tortilla Soup, *349,* 349–50

whole

butterflying, 102

cutting up, 330

taste tests on, 740

Wings, Buffalo, 108–9

wings, cutting up, 109

Chicken-Fried Steaks, 225, *225*

Chickpeas

and Apricots, Moroccan Chicken with, 75

Cauliflower, Potatoes, and Peas, Indian-Style Curry with, *409,* 409–10

Mediterranean Chopped Salad, 36, *36*

Sweet Potatoes, Green Beans, and Eggplant, Indian-Style Curry with, 410

taste tests on, 735

Chile(s)

Ancho, –Coffee Rub, Grilled Steak with, 778

Bean Chili, 762

Chipotle, Rub, Spicy, Grilled Steak with, 778

Chipotle, Sauce, Creamy, 212–13

Chipotle and Garlic Butter with Lime and Cilantro, 166

Chipotle-Garlic Butter with Lime and Cilantro, 201

Coca-Cola Glaze with Lime and Jalapeño, 186

–Garlic Wet Paste Marinade, 427

Green Curry Paste, 400

Jerk Chicken, 771–72

–Lime Burger Sauce, 774

–Lime Vinaigrette, 468

New Mexican, Rub, Grilled Steak with, 777–78

Orange-Chipotle Glaze, 415

Our Favorite Chili, 8–9, *9*

Pan-Seared Shrimp with Chipotle-Lime Glaze, 205

Poached Fish Fillets with Jalapeño Vinaigrette, 790

Red Curry Paste, 401

and Shallots, Stir-Fried Thai-Style Beef with, *402,* 402–3

Skillet Chicken Fajitas, 770

Spicy Jalapeño-Cheddar Corn Bread, 551

Spicy Pickled Radishes, 771

Spicy Pork Tacos (al Pastor), 786–87

Chili

    Beef, with Kidney Beans, 365–66

    Best Vegetarian Chili, 762

    Chicken, White, 367–68

    Cincinnati, *223,* 223–24

    Con Carne, *366,* 366–67

    Our Favorite, 8–9, *9*

Chili-Mustard Spice Rub, 445

Chili Oil, 375

Chili powder, taste tests on, 740

Chilled Lemon Soufflé, 651–52

    Individual, 652

    with White Chocolate, 652

Chimichurri (Argentinian-Style Fresh Parsley and Garlic Sauce), 145

Chimichurri Sauce, 432–33

Chinese Chicken Lettuce Wraps, 769–70

Chipotle

    Chile Sauce, Creamy, 212–13

    -Garlic Butter with Lime and Cilantro, 201

    and Garlic Butter with Lime and Cilantro, 166

    Garlic-Chile Wet Paste Marinade, 427

    -Lime Glaze, Pan-Seared Shrimp with, 205

    -Orange Glaze, 415

Chive and Black Pepper Dipping Sauce, 235

Chive–Blue Cheese Butter, 146

Chocolate

    Blondies, 584–85, *585*

    Brownies

        Chewy, 586–87, *587*

        Classic, 585–86, *586*

        Fudgy Low-Fat, 588–89

        Fudgy Triple-Chocolate, 587–88

        Triple-Chocolate Espresso, 588

    -Cherry Bars with Hazelnuts, 580–81

    chips, taste tests on, 740, 741

    Chunk, Triple- , Pecan Pie, 695

    cocoa powder, taste tests on, 741

    Congo Bars, 585

    Cookies, 568, *568*

        Black and White Spiral, *576,* 578

        Chocolate Chip, Classic, 565–66, *566*

        Chocolate Chip, Thick and Chewy, 566–67

        Chocolate Chip, Thin and Crispy, 567

        Chocolate-Chunk Oatmeal, with Pecans and Dried Cherries, 570–71

        Double-Chocolate, Thick and Chewy, 569

        Meringue, 584

        Sablés, *576,* 578

        Sandwich, *576,* 578

        Triple-Chocolate, Thick and Chewy, 569

    Cream Pie, 698–99, *699*

    Cupcakes, Dark, 621–22

Chocolate *(cont.)*

    Cupcakes, Ultimate, with Ganache Filling, 622–23, *623*

    dark, taste tests on, 740

    -Dipped Triple-Coconut Macaroons, 574, *574*

    Frosting, Creamy, 624

    Ganache, Dark, 629

    Hazelnut-Mocha Truffles, 806

    -Hazelnut Slow Cooker Bread Pudding, 641–42

    hot fudge sauce, taste tests on, 744

    Milk (chocolate)

        chips, taste tests on, 740

        Filling, Peanut Butter Sandwich Cookies with, 803

        Frosting, Fluffy Yellow Layer Cake with, *615,* 615–17

        Pots de Crème, 647

        taste tests on, 740

    Mousse

        Dark, 648–49, *649*

        Low-Fat, 649–50

        Orange, 649

        Premium Dark, 649

        Raspberry, 649

    and Orange, Crêpes with, 673

    Pots de Crème, *646,* 646–47

    Pots de Crème, Milk Chocolate, 647

    Pudding, Creamy, *647,* 647–48

    Soufflés

        Grand Marnier, with Grated Chocolate, 651

        Make-Ahead, 652–53

        Make-Ahead Mocha, 653

        Skillet Chocolate-Orange, 654

    Truffles, 806

    unsweetened, taste tests on, 741

    White, Chilled Lemon Soufflé with, 652

    white, chips, taste tests on, 741

    see also Chocolate Cakes

Chocolate Cakes

    Bittersweet, Roulade, 628–29

    Bundt, Rich, 595, *595*

    Chocolate-Raspberry Torte, 624–25, *625*

    Cupcakes, Dark, 621–22

    Cupcakes, Ultimate, with Ganache Filling, 622–23, *623*

    Flourless, 626, *626*

    German, *620,* 620–21

    Hot Fudge Pudding Cake, 627

    Hot Fudge Pudding Cakes, Individual, 627

    Layer, Old-Fashioned, with Chocolate Frosting, 617–18

    Sheet, with Easy Chocolate Frosting, 618–19, *619*

    Triple- , Mousse, *629,* 629–31

    Volcano, with Espresso Ice Cream, 631–32

Chowder, Lighter Corn, 24

Chowder, New England Clam, 25, *25*

Chunky Cherry Tomato–Basil Vinaigrette, 201

Chunky Guacamole, 348

Chutney
  Cilantro-Mint, 410
  Cranberry
    with Apples and Crystallized Ginger, 795–96
    with Fennel and Golden Raisins, 796
    -Orange, 796
    with Pear, Lemon, and Rosemary, 796
    Spicy, 796
  Ginger-Apple, 161
  Sweet-and-Sour, 193
Ciabatta, 554–56, *555*
Ciambotta (Italian Vegetable Stew), 760–61
Cider. *See* Apple Cider
Cilantro
  and Carrots, Lentil Salad with, 759
  Chimichurri Sauce, 432–33
  Garlicky Lime Sauce with, 176
  and Garlic Marinade with Garam Masala, 458
  Grilled Thai Beef Salad for a Charcoal Grill,
    405–6
  Grilled Thai Beef Salad for a Gas Grill, 406
  -Mint Chutney, 410
Cincinnati Chili, *223,* 223–24
Cinnamon
  Buns, Quick, with Buttermilk Icing, *537,* 537–38
  Orange, and Star Anise Glaze, 186
  -Swirl Bread, 799
  taste tests on, 741
Clam(s)
  Chowder, New England, 25, *25*
  Indoor Clambake, 214–15, *215*
  and Shrimp, Spanish-Style Toasted Pasta with, 768
Classic Apple Pie, 685–86
Classic Banana Bread, 523–24
Classic Bread Pudding, 640, *640*
Classic Burger Sauce, 230
Classic Chicken Noodle Soup, 4
Classic Chicken Salad, 758
Classic Chocolate Chip Cookies, 565–66, *566*
Classic Cranberry Sauce, 131
Classic Cream of Tomato Soup, 11
Classic Crème Brûlée, *644,* 644–45
Classic Crème Caramel, *645,* 645–46
Classic Croutons, 12
Classic French Fries, 234
Classic French Onion Soup, *314,* 314–15
Classic Garlic Bread, 292
Classic Gazpacho, 22–23
Classic Gingerbread Cake, *608,* 608–9
Classic Greek Salad, 39
Classic Green Bean Casserole, *133,* 133–34
Classic Grilled Cheese Sandwiches, 219–20
Classic Macaroni and Cheese, 220, *220*

Classic Mashed Potatoes, 487–88
Classic Roast Lemon Chicken, *97,* 97–98
Classic Roast Stuffed Turkey, *117,* 117–18
Classic Roast Turkey, 112, *112*
Classic Spaghetti and Meatballs for a Crowd,
    263–64
Classic Stuffed Bell Peppers, 228–29, *229*
Classic Tart Dough, 700
Classic Tuna Salad, 218, *218*
Classic White Layer Cake with Butter Frosting and
    Raspberry-Almond Filling, 613–14
Classic Yellow Layer Cake with Vanilla Buttercream,
    614–15
Cobblers
  Blueberry, 660–61, *661*
  Fresh Sour Cherry, 660
  Sour Cherry, *659,* 659–60
Coca-Cola Glaze with Lime and Jalapeño, 186
Cocktail Sauce, 209
Cocoa powder, taste tests on, 741
Coconut
  -Banana Steel-Cut Oatmeal, 798
  Congo Bars, 585
  Cream Pie, 698
  German Chocolate Cake, 620, *620,* 620–21
  Layer Cake, 609–10
  milk, taste tests on, 741
  Mulligatawny Soup, 19–20, *20*
  Oatmeal Cake with Broiled Icing, *599,* 599–600
  Rice Pudding, 642
  Snowballs, Lime-Glazed, 580
  Triple-, Macaroons, 573–74
  Triple-, Macaroons, Chocolate-Dipped, 574, *574*
Coffee
  Chocolate Volcano Cakes with Espresso Ice Cream,
    631–32
  decaf, taste tests on, 742
  Espresso Crème Brûlée, 645
  Espresso-Mascarpone Cream, 629
  Hazelnut-Mocha Truffles, 806
  Make-Ahead Mocha Soufflés, 653
  Tiramisù, 632–33, *633*
  Tiramisù with Cooked Eggs, 633
  whole bean, taste tests on, 741
Coffee Cakes
  Blueberry Boy Bait, *536,* 536–37
  Cream Cheese, *541,* 541–42
  New York–Style Crumb Cake, *535,* 535–36
  Sour Cream, with Brown Sugar–Pecan Streusel, 540
Coleslaw, Creamy, 41
Coleslaw, Creamy Buttermilk, 41–42
Confetti Cabbage Salad with Spicy Peanut Dressing, 42
Congo Bars, 585

Cookies
Best Shortbread, 581–82
Black and White Spiral, *576, 578*
Brown Sugar, 562–63, *563*
Butter, French (Sablés), *576,* 576–77
Butter, Glazed, 578–79
Chocolate, 568, *568*
    Double-, Thick and Chewy, 569
    Sablés, *576,* 578
    Sandwich, *576,* 578
    Triple-, Thick and Chewy, 569
Chocolate Chip
    Classic, 565–66, *566*
    Thick and Chewy, 566–67
    Thin and Crispy, 567
Crescent, Almond or Hazelnut, 583
Crescent, Pecan or Walnut, *582,* 582–83
Gingersnaps, 803–4
holiday rolled, 578–81
holiday spritz, 575–76
Jam Sandwiches, 579–80
Lime-Glazed Coconut Snowballs, 580
Meringue, 583–84, *584*
    Chocolate, 584
    Toasted Almond, 584
Molasses Spice, 564, *564*
Molasses Spice, with Dark Rum Glaze, 565
Oatmeal
    Chocolate-Chunk, with Pecans and Dried Cherries, 570–71
    -Date, Big and Chewy, 572
    -Raisin, Big and Chewy, 572
    Salty Thin and Crispy, 573
    Thin and Crispy, 572–73, *573*
Peanut Butter, 569–70, *570*
    Sandwich, 802–3
    Sandwich, with Honey-Cinnamon Filling, 803
    Sandwich, with Milk Chocolate Filling, 803
Sablés (French Butter Cookies), *576,* 576–77
Spritz, 575, *575*
    Almond, 576
    with Lemon Essence, 576
Sugar, Chewy, 562
Triple-Coconut Macaroons, 573–74
Triple-Coconut Macaroons, Chocolate-Dipped, 574, *574*
Vanilla Pretzel, *576,* 578
see also Bars
Cool and Creamy Macaroni Salad, 43, *43*
Coq au Vin, *328,* 328–29
Corn
Chowder, Lighter, 24
Fritters, 480, *480*
Indoor Clambake, 214–15, *215*
Mexican-Style Charcoal-Grilled, 470–71, *471*
Mexican-Style Gas-Grilled, 471

Corn Bread
All-Purpose, 550–51
Golden, 122
Sausage Dressing, 120–21, *122*
Southern, 551–52
Spicy Jalapeño-Cheddar, 551
Cornish Game Hens
Grill-Roasted, for a Charcoal Grill, *421,* 421–23
Grill-Roasted, for a Gas Grill, 423
Cornmeal
All-Purpose Corn Bread, 550–51
Basic Polenta, 297, *297*
Corn and Apricot Muffins with Orange Essence, 534
Corn Muffins, 533–34
Golden Corn Bread, 122
No-Fuss Creamy Parmesan Polenta, 500–501
Skillet Tamale Pie, 54
Southern Corn Bread, 551–52
Spicy Jalapeño-Cheddar Corn Bread, 551
taste tests on, 742
Corn Muffins, 533–34
and Apricot, with Orange Essence, 534
Couscous
with Carrots, Raisins, and Pine Nuts, 500
with Dates and Pistachios, 500
with Dried Cherries and Pecans, 500
with Shallots, Garlic, and Almonds, 500
Simple, 499–500
Crab
Cakes, Best, 788
Cakes, Maryland, 212, *212*
taste tests on, 742
Towers with Avocado and Gazpacho Salsas, *213,* 213–14
Crackers, oyster, taste tests on, 747
Cranberry(ies)
-Apple Filling, Charcoal-Grilled Pork Loin with, *442,* 442–43
-Apple Filling, Gas-Grilled Pork Loin with, 443
Apple Pie with Dried Fruit, 686
Best Baked Apples, *664,* 664–65
Chutney
    with Apples and Crystallized Ginger, 795–96
    with Fennel and Golden Raisins, 796
    -Orange, 796
    with Pear, Lemon, and Rosemary, 796
    Spicy, 796
Dried, and Pecans, Wild Rice Pilaf with, 498–99
Fresh, Apple Pie with, 686
and Orange, Slow-Cooker Pork Loin with, *181,* 181–82
-Orange Steel-Cut Oatmeal, 797
and Pear Chopped Salad, 35–36
-Pecan Muffins, 534–35
Sauce, Classic, 131

Cream Biscuits, 546
  Cheddar, 546
  with Fresh Herbs, 546
Cream Cheese
  Carrot Layer Cake, 805–6
  Coffee Cake, *541,* 541–42
  Frosting, 602
  Frosting, Light, 603
  Lemon Cheesecake, 636–37
  New York Cheesecake, 633–34, *634*
  New York Cheesecake, Light, 634–35
  Spiced Pumpkin Cheesecake, 635–36
  taste tests on, 738
Creamless Creamy Tomato Soup, 11–12, *12*
Cream Scones, 524
Creamy Baked Four-Cheese Pasta, *268,* 268–69
Creamy Buttermilk Coleslaw, 41–42
Creamy Chipotle Chile Sauce, 212–13
Creamy Chocolate Frosting, 624
Creamy Chocolate Pudding, *647,* 647–48
Creamy Coleslaw, 41
Creamy Gazpacho Andaluz, 23–24
Creamy Herbed Spinach Dip, 484–85
Creamy Mashed Potatoes, 488–89, *489*
Creamy Mushroom Soup, 14
Creamy Pea Soup, 13
Crème Brûlée, Classic, *644,* 644–45
Crème Brûlée, Espresso, 645
Crème Caramel, Classic, *645,* 645–46
Creole-Style Shrimp and Sausage Gumbo, *80,* 80–81
Crêpes
  with Bananas and Nutella, 673
  with Chocolate and Orange, 673
  with Sugar and Lemon, *672,* 672–73
  Suzette, 670–71
Crisp, Peach, 661–62
Crisp, Peach, for a Crowd, 662
Crisp-Skin High-Roast Butterflied Turkey with
    Sausage Dressing, 120–22
Crisp-Skinned Roast Chicken, 96–97
Crisp Thin-Crust Pizza, 280
Crispy Fried Chicken, 105–6, *106*
Crispy Pan-Fried Pork Chops, 151, *151*
Crispy Roasted Potatoes, 491–92
Crispy Smashed Potatoes, *495,* 495–96
Croissants, 527–31
Croutons
  Buttery, 18
  Classic, 12
  Garlic, 23
  Herbed, 760
Crunchy Baked Pork Chops, *158,* 158–59
Crunchy Oven-Fried Fish, 190, *190*

Crust, Graham Cracker, 684–85
Cuban-Style Black Beans and Rice, 78
Cucumber(s)
  Cherry Tomato Salad with Feta and Olives, 37–38, *38*
  Classic Gazpacho, 22–23
  Classic Greek Salad, 39
  Creamy Gazpacho Andaluz, 23–24
  Fennel and Apple Chopped Salad, 36–37
  Gazpacho Salsa, 213–14
  Italian Bread Salad (Panzanella), 38–39, *39*
  Mediterranean Chopped Salad, 36, *36*
  Pear and Cranberry Chopped Salad, 35–36
  and Pineapple Salsa with Mint, 467
  Relish, Spicy, 198
  Salad, Sesame Lemon, 40
  seeding and chopping, 40
  see also Pickles
Cupcakes, Dark Chocolate, 621–22
Cupcakes, Ultimate Chocolate, with Ganache Filling,
    622–23, *623*
Curried dishes
  Curried Chicken Salad with Cashews, 758
  Curried Tuna Salad with Apples and Currants, 218
  Indian Curry, 408–9
  Indian-Style Curry with Potatoes, Cauliflower, Peas, and
    Chickpeas, *409,* 409–10
  Indian-Style Curry with Sweet Potatoes, Eggplant, Green
    Beans, and Chickpeas, 410
  Mulligatawny Soup, 19–20, *20*
  Skillet Curried Chicken and Rice, 58
  Thai Green Curry with Chicken, Broccoli, and Mushrooms,
    399, 399–400
  Thai Red Curry with Shrimp, Pineapple, and Peanuts,
    400–401
  Thai-Style Chicken Soup, 377–78, *378*
Curry Paste, Green, 400
Curry Paste, Red, 401
Curry powder, taste tests on, 742

D

Dark Chocolate Cupcakes, 621–22
Dark Chocolate Ganache, 629
Dark Chocolate Mousse, 648–49, *649*
Date(s)
  -Oatmeal Cookies, Big and Chewy, 572
  and Pistachios, Couscous with, 500
Daube Provençal, 332–33, *333*
Deep-Dish Apple Pie, *686,* 686–87
Deep-Dish Pizza with Tomatoes, Mozzarella, and Basil,
    282–83, *283*
Denver Omelet, *510,* 510–11

Desserts
cakes, 594–637, 804–5
cookies and bars, 562–91, 802–4
frozen, 655, 807
fruit desserts, 658–77
pies and tarts, 680–706
puddings and soufflés, 640–55
truffles, 806
see also specific dessert categories above
Dill
-Mustard Sauce, 464
"Smoked Salmon Platter" Sauce, 791
Diner-Style Home Fries, 508
Dips and spreads
Aïoli, 768
Belgian-Style Dipping Sauce, 235
Charcoal-Grilled Baba Ghanoush, 473
Chive and Black Pepper Dipping Sauce, 235
Chunky Guacamole, 348
Cocktail Sauce, 209
Creamy Herbed Spinach Dip, 484–85
Garlic Mayonnaise, 513–14
Garlic-Soy Mayonnaise, 147
Gas-Grilled Baba Ghanoush, 473
One-Minute Salsa, 347
Scallion Dipping Sauce, *372,* 372–73
Spicy Mayonnaise, 105
Spicy Peanut Dipping Sauce, 377
Dressing, Sausage, 120–21, *122*
Dried Cherry–Port Sauce with Onions and Marmalade, 176
Drinks
Fresh Margaritas, 346
Sangria, 346–47
Dry Rub for Barbecue, 447
Dumplings, Chinese Steamed (Shu Mai), 373–75, *375*

E

Easier French Fries, 235, *235*
Easier Fried Chicken, 106–7, *107*
Easiest Kansas City Sticky Ribs, 449
Eastern North Carolina Barbecue Sauce, 448
Easy Apple Strudel, *667,* 667–68
Easy Buttermilk Waffles, *520,* 520–21
Easy Caramel Cake, 610–11, *611*
Easy Chocolate Buttercream, 622
Easy Coffee Buttercream, 622
Easy Grilled Boneless Pork Chops, 782–83
Easy Salmon Cakes, 789
Easy Salmon Cakes with Smoked Salmon, Capers, and Dill, 789

Easy Vanilla Bean Buttercream, 622
Eggplant
Charcoal-Grilled Baba Ghanoush, 473
Garlicky, Scallions, and Cashews, Stir-Fried Shrimp with, 396
Gas-Grilled Baba Ghanoush, 473
Italian Vegetable Stew (Ciambotta), 760–61
Parmesan, 295–96
Pork, and Onion, Stir-Fried, with Garlic and Black Pepper, 392
Sweet Potatoes, Green Beans, and Chickpeas, Indian-Style Curry with, 410
Vegetable Lasagna, *272, 273*–74
Eggs
Asparagus, Ham, and Gruyère Frittata, 514
Baked, Florentine, 796–97
Baked, Lorraine, 797
Fried, 507
Hard-Cooked, and Sweet Pickles, American Potato Salad with, 46
Hard-Cooked, Foolproof, 32
Huevos Rancheros, 368–69
Indonesian-Style Fried Rice (Nasi Goreng), 382–83
Leek, Prosciutto, and Goat Cheese Frittata, 514–15
Omelets
Cheese, Family-Sized, 509–10
Denver, *510,* 510–11
French, *511,* 511–12
Pad Thai, 403–4
Poached, 507–8
Scrambled
with Bacon, Onion, and Pepper Jack Cheese, 505–6
Fluffy, 504
Rich and Creamy, *504,* 504–5
Rich and Creamy, for Two, 505
with Sausage, Sweet Pepper, and Cheddar Cheese, 506–7
"Smoked Salmon Platter" Sauce, 791
Spaghetti alla Carbonara, 265
Spanish Tortilla with Chorizo and Scallions, 513
Spanish Tortilla with Roasted Red Peppers and Peas, 512–13, *513*
Wilted Spinach Salad with Warm Bacon Dressing, *31,* 31–32
see also Soufflés
Empanadas, Beef, *352,* 352–53
Enchiladas, Chicken, with a Red Chili Sauce, 359–60, *360*
Enchiladas Verdes, 360–62, *361*
Equipment, ratings of
bakeware, 720–22
behind the scenes look at, 13, 431, 487
grilling equipment, 725–27
handy tools, 712–17
kitchen supplies, 734

Equipment, ratings of *(cont.)*

knives and more, 708–10

measuring equipment, 718

pots and pans, 710–12

small appliances, 722–25

specialty pieces, 728–33

thermometers and timers, 718–19

useless equipment and gadgets, 487

Espresso

Crème Brûlée, 645

Hazelnut-Mocha Truffles, 806

Ice Cream, Chocolate Volcano Cakes with, 631–32

-Mascarpone Cream, 629

F

Fajitas

Chicken, for a Charcoal Grill, 356–57, *357*

Chicken, for a Gas Grill, 357

Chicken, Skillet, 770

Steak, for a Charcoal Grill, 358–59

Steak, for a Gas Grill, 359

Family-Sized Cheese Omelet, 509–10

Farfalle

with Pesto, 247

with Tomatoes, Olives, and Feta, 243

Farmhouse Vegetable and Barley Soup, 759–60

Faux Leftover Rice, 383

Fennel

and Apple Chopped Salad, 36–37

and Carrots, Roasted, with Toasted Almonds and Lemon, 479

and Golden Raisins, Cranberry Chutney with, 796

Tomato, and Almond Relish, 783

trimming and coring, 37

Feta

Classic Greek Salad, 39

Mediterranean Chopped Salad, 36, *36*

Olives, and Mint, Lentil Salad with, 758–59

and Olives, Cherry Tomato Salad with, 37–38, *38*

and Olives, Fresh Tomato Sauce with, 470

and Spinach Pie, Greek (Spanakopita), *73*, 73–74

taste tests on, 738

Tomatoes, and Olives, Farfalle with, 243

and Tomatoes, Greek-Style Shrimp with, 207–8, *208*

Fettuccine Alfredo, 265–66, *266*

Fettuccine with Slow-Simmered Bolognese Sauce, 258–59

Figs

and Port, French-Style Pot-Roasted Pork Loin with, 785

Prosciutto, Walnuts, and Parmesan, Arugula Salad with, 31

Filipino Chicken Adobo, 771

Fish

and Chips, 191–92, *192*

Fillets, Poached

with Crispy Artichokes and Sherry-Tomato Vinaigrette, 789–90

with Crispy Scallions and Miso-Ginger Vinaigrette, 790

with Jalapeño Vinaigrette, 790

Fillets, Thick-Cut, Pan-Roasted, 201–2

Halibut Steaks, Pan-Roasted, *200*, 200–201

halibut steaks, trimming and serving, 200

Meunière with Browned Butter and Lemon, 342–43, *343*

Oven-Fried, Crunchy, 190, *190*

Red Snapper, Charcoal-Grilled Blackened, 465–66, *466*

Red Snapper, Gas-Grilled Blackened, 466

Sole Fillets, Baked, with Herbs and Bread Crumbs, *202*, 202–3

see also Anchovies; Salmon; Shellfish; Tuna

Five-spice powder, taste tests on, 742

Flambéed Pan-Roasted Lobster, 210–11

Flame tamer, improvising, 260

Flank Steak and Arugula Sandwiches with Red Onion, 146–47

Flour

all-purpose, taste tests on, 742

weighing, 551

whole-wheat, taste tests on, 743

Flourless Chocolate Cake, 626, *626*

Fluffy Mashed Potatoes, 490

Fluffy Scrambled Eggs, 504

Fluffy Yellow Layer Cake with Milk Chocolate Frosting, *615*, 615–17

Focaccia, Rosemary, *278*, 278–79

Foil tray for a grill, creating, 463

Fool

Berry, *676*, 676–77

Rhubarb, 677

Strawberry-Rhubarb, 677

Foolproof Double-Crust Pie Dough, 683–84

Foolproof Hard-Cooked Eggs, 32

Foolproof Single-Crust Pie Dough, 684

Foolproof Vinaigrette, 28, *28*

Balsamic-Mustard, 28

Herb, 28

Lemon, 28

Walnut, 28

Four-Cheese Lasagna, 271–73

Free-Form Apple Tart, 705–6

Free-Form Summer Fruit Tart, 701–2

French Apple Cake, 804–5

French Apple Tart, *704*, 704–5

French Butter Cookies (Sablés), *576,* 576–77
French Chicken in a Pot, 330–31, *331*
French Mashed Potatoes with Cheese and Garlic (Aligot), *323,* 323–24
French Omelets, *511,* 511–12
French Onion and Bacon Tart, 317–18
French Onion Soup, Classic, *314,* 314–15
French Onion Soup, Streamlined, 315–16
French Potato Salad, 316–17, *317*
French-Style Pot-Roasted Pork Loin, 177–78, 784–85
French-Style Pot-Roasted Pork Loin with Port and Figs, 785
French-Style Stuffed Chicken Breasts, *326,* 326–27
French Toast, *521,* 521–22
Fresh Fruit Tart with Pastry Cream, 702–3, *703*
Fresh Margaritas, 346
Fresh Pasta without a Machine, 763–64
Fresh Sour Cherry Cobbler, 660
Fresh Strawberry Pie, *689,* 689–90
Fresh Tomato Relish, 198
Fresh Tomato Sauce with Feta and Olives, 470
Frico, 293
Fried Eggs, 507
Fried Rice
    Indonesian-Style (Nasi Goreng), 382–83
    with Peas and Bean Sprouts, 381–82
    with Shrimp, Pork, and Shiitakes, 381
Frittata, Asparagus, Ham, and Gruyère, 514
Frittata, Leek, Prosciutto, and Goat Cheese, 514–15
Fritters, Corn, 480, *480*
Frostings
    Chocolate, Creamy, 624
    Cream Cheese, 602
    Cream Cheese, Light, 603
    Dark Chocolate Ganache, 629
    Easy Chocolate Buttercream, 622
    Easy Coffee Buttercream, 622
    Easy Vanilla Bean Buttercream, 622
    see also specific cake recipes
Frozen desserts
    Homemade Vanilla Ice Cream, 655, *655*
    Raspberry Sorbet, 807
      with Ginger and Mint, 807
      –Lime Rickey, 807
      -Port, 807
Fruit
    Dried, Apple Pie with, 686
    Fresh, Tart with Pastry Cream, 702–3, *703*
    Salads, 542–43
    Summer, Tart, Free-Form, 701–2
    see also Fruit desserts; *specific fruits*

Fruit desserts
    Bananas Foster, 670
    Best Baked Apples, *664,* 664–65
    Caramelized Pears with Blue Cheese and Black Pepper–Caramel Sauce, *674,* 674–75
    Cobblers
      Blueberry, 660–61, *661*
      Fresh Sour Cherry, 660
      Sour Cherry, *659,* 659–60
    Crêpes
      with Bananas and Nutella, 673
      with Chocolate and Orange, 673
      with Sugar and Lemon, *672,* 672–73
      Suzette, 670–71
    Easy Apple Strudel, *667,* 667–68
    Fools
      Berry, *676,* 676–77
      Rhubarb, 677
      Strawberry-Rhubarb, 677
    Gratins
      Individual Fresh Berry, with Lemon Zabaglione, 664
      Individual Fresh Berry, with Zabaglione, *663,* 663–64
      Simple Raspberry, 662–63
    Peach Crisp, 661–62
    Peach Crisp for a Crowd, 662
    Skillet Apple Brown Betty, 666–67
    Skillet Apple Crisp, *665,* 665–66
    Skillet Apple Pie, *669,* 669–70
    Strawberries with Balsamic Vinegar, 675–76
    Strawberry Shortcakes, *658,* 658–59
    Summer Berry Pudding, Large, 674
    Summer Berry Puddings, Individual, 673–74
Fudgy Low-Fat Brownies, 588–89
Fudgy Triple-Chocolate Brownies, 587–88

G

Galettes
    Apple, *704,* 704–5
    Butternut Squash, with Gruyère, 793
    Mushroom and Leek, with Gorgonzola, 791–93
    Potato, Simplified, *321,* 321–22
    Potato and Shallot, with Goat Cheese, 793
Game Hens, Cornish
    Grill-Roasted, for a Charcoal Grill, *421,* 421–23
    Grill-Roasted, for a Gas Grill, 423
Garlic
    Bread, Cheesy, 292–93
    Bread, Classic, 292
    -Chile Wet Paste Marinade, 427
    and Cilantro Marinade with Garam Masala, 458

Garlic *(cont.)*

Croutons, 23

40 Cloves of , Chicken with, 329–30

and Fresh Parsley Sauce, Argentinian-Style (Chimichurri), 145

Garlicky Lime Sauce with Cilantro, 176

Garlicky Shrimp Pasta, *254,* 254–55

Garlicky Shrimp with Buttered Bread Crumbs, 205–6, *206*

Ginger, and Soy Marinade, 430

-Ginger-Sesame Wet Paste Marinade, 426

Gremolata, 310

Lemon, and Parsley Butter, 432

-Lemon Butter, Pan-Seared Shrimp with, 205

-Lemon Sauce, Spicy, 470

-Lemon Spinach, Sautéed, 483–84

Mayonnaise, 513–14

mincing, ahead of time, 275

mincing, with garlic press, 224

Oil, Spicy, 290

and Oil, Pasta with, 238

and Olive Oil Mashed Potatoes, 488

Pestata, 760

Picada, 761–62

Roasted, and Rosemary Butter, Salt-Baked Potatoes with, 492–93

and Rosemary, Charcoal-Grilled Potatoes with, 471–72, *472*

and Rosemary, Gas-Grilled Potatoes with, 473

Sauce, Sichuan Stir-Fried Pork in, 787–88

-Shallot-Rosemary Wet Paste Marinade, 426

Shrimp, Spanish-Style, 206–7, *207*

Shrimp fra Diavolo, 255, *255*

Shrimp Scampi, 311

-Soy Mayonnaise, 147

-Studded Roast Pork Loin, 180–81

and Thyme Sauce, 153

Gas-grilled dishes. *See under* Grilled dishes

Gazpacho, Classic, 22–23

Gazpacho Andaluz, Creamy, 23–24

Gazpacho Salsa, 213–14

German Apple Pancake, 518–19

German Chocolate Cake, *620,* 620–21

Giardiniera, taste tests on, 743

Giblet Pan Gravy, 113

Giblet Pan Gravy for a Crowd, 114–15

Ginger

-Apple Chutney, 161

Candied, Pumpkin Bread with, 798

Classic Gingerbread Cake, *608,* 608–9

Crystallized, and Apples, Cranberry Chutney with, 795–96

Crystallized, Apple Pie with, 686

Garlic, and Soy Marinade, 430

-Garlic-Sesame Wet Paste Marinade, 426

Gingersnaps, 803–4

Ginger *(cont.)*

-Hoisin Glaze, Pan-Seared Shrimp with, 205

and Mint, Raspberry Sorbet with, 807

-Miso Vinaigrette and Crispy Scallions, Poached Fish Fillets with, 790

-Soy Glaze, 415

-Soy Sauce with Scallions, 199

and Tangerine Relish, 197–98

Warm-Spiced Parsley Marinade with, 458

Gingerbread Cake, Classic, *608,* 608–9

Gingersnaps, 803–4

Glazed All-Beef Meat Loaf, 226–27, *227*

Glazed Butter Cookies, 578–79

Glazed Carrots, 479–80

Glazed Maple-Pecan Oatmeal Scones, 527

Glazed Roast Chicken, 98–100, *99*

Glazed Salmon, 195–96, *196*

Glazed Spiral-Sliced Ham, *186,* 186–87

Glazes

Asian Barbecue, 196

Barbecue, 422–23

Blackberry, 780

Cherry-Port, 187

Cider and Brown Sugar, 185

Coca-Cola, with Lime and Jalapeño, 186

Hoisin-Tamarind, 780

Maple-Orange, 187

Mustard, 780

Orange, Cinnamon, and Star Anise, 186

Orange-Chipotle, 415

Orange-Miso, 196

Pineapple-Ginger, Spicy, 186

Pomegranate-Balsamic, 196

Soy-Ginger, 415

Soy-Mustard, 196

Gnocchi

Potato, with Browned Butter and Sage Sauce, 266–67, *267*

taste tests on, 743

Golden Corn Bread, 122

Gorgonzola-Cream Sauce, 268

Graham Cracker Crust, 684–85

Grains

Bean Chili, 762

Best Whole Wheat Sandwich Bread, 556–58

Bran Muffins, 532–33, *533*

Farmhouse Vegetable and Barley Soup, 759–60

freezing, 75

Multigrain Bread, *558,* 558–59

Whole Wheat Soda Bread, 549

see also Cornmeal; Oats; Rice

Grand Marnier Soufflé, 650–51

Grand Marnier Soufflé with Grated Chocolate, 651

Grapes
    and Balsamic Vinegar, Tuna Salad with, 218
    Red, and Smoked Almonds, Chicken Salad with, 758
    and Strawberries with Balsamic and Red Wine Reduction,
        542–43
Gratins
    Individual Fresh Berry, with Lemon Zabaglione, 664
    Individual Fresh Berry, with Zabaglione, *663*, 663–64
    Simple Raspberry, 662–63
Gravy
    All-Purpose, Quick, 161
    for Grill-Roasted Turkey, 775–76
    Pan, Giblet, 113
    Pan, Giblet, for a Crowd, 114–15
    Slow-Roasted Turkey with, *119*, 119–20
    Turkey, 122–23
    Turkey, All-Purpose, 127, *127*
    Turkey, Make-Ahead, 117
Greek Salad, Classic, 39
Greek Spinach and Feta Pie (Spanakopita), *73*, 73–74
Greek-Style Shrimp with Tomatoes and Feta, 207–8, *208*
Green Bean(s)
    Amandine, 482–83
    Blanched, 481–82
    Casserole, Classic, *133*, 133–34
    "Casserole," Quick, 134
    Pork, and Red Bell Pepper, Stir-Fried, with Gingery Oyster
        Sauce, *392*, 393
    Roasted, 483
    with Sautéed Shallots and Vermouth, 482
    and Shiitakes, Teriyaki Stir-Fried Beef with, 390–91
    Sweet Potatoes, Eggplant, and Chickpeas, Indian-Style
        Curry with, 410
    with Toasted Hazelnuts and Brown Butter, 482, *482*
    trimming quickly, 390
Green Curry Paste, 400
Greens
    Chinese Chicken Lettuce Wraps, 769–70
    Classic Greek Salad, 39
    Fennel and Apple Chopped Salad, 36–37
    Hearty Tuscan Bean Stew, 294–95, *295*
    Indian-Style Spinach with Fresh Cheese (Saag Paneer), 793–94
    Leafy Green Salad with Red Wine Vinaigrette, 29, *29*
    Leafy Green Salad with Rich and Creamy Blue Cheese
        Dressing, 29–30
    Mediterranean Chopped Salad, 36, *36*
    Pan-Seared Scallops with Wilted Spinach, Watercress, and
        Orange Salad, 34–35, *35*
    Pear and Cranberry Chopped Salad, 35–36
    Simple Sautéed Swiss Chard, 486
    Thai Pork Lettuce Wraps, *376*, 376–77
    Tough, Quick-Cooked, 485
    washing and storing, 30
    see also Arugula; Cabbage; Spinach

Gremolata, 310
Grilled dishes (beef)
    Argentine Steaks with Chimichurri Sauce,
        Charcoal-Grilled, *432*, 432–33
    Argentine Steaks with Chimichurri Sauce, Gas-Grilled, 433
    Beef Brisket, Barbecued, Charcoal-Grilled, 436–37, *437*
    Beef Brisket, Barbecued, Gas-Grilled, 437
    Beef Kebabs with Lemon and Rosemary Marinade,
        Charcoal-Grilled, 456–57
    Beef Kebabs with Lemon and Rosemary Marinade,
        Gas-Grilled, 457
    Beef Ribs, Texas-Style Barbecued, for a Charcoal Grill,
        454–55, *455*
    Beef Ribs, Texas-Style Barbecued, for a Gas Grill, 456
    Beef Salad, Grilled Thai, for a Charcoal Grill, 405–6
    Beef Salad, Grilled Thai, for a Gas Grill, 406
    Beef Satay, Grilled, 776–77
    Beef Short Ribs, Grill-Roasted, 779–80
    Beef Tenderloin, Grill-Roasted, for a Charcoal Grill,
        434–35, *435*
    Beef Tenderloin, Grill-Roasted, for a Gas Grill, 435
    Cheeseburgers, Bacon, Well-Done Grilled, 425
    Cheeseburgers, Grilled, 424
    Filets Mignons, Charcoal-Grilled, 431
    Filets Mignons, Gas-Grilled, 431
    Hamburgers, Charcoal-Grilled, 423–24
    Hamburgers, Gas-Grilled, 424
    Hamburgers, Well-Done Charcoal-Grilled, 424–25
    Hamburgers, Well-Done Gas-Grilled, 425
    Inexpensive Charcoal-Grill-Roasted Beef with Garlic
        and Rosemary for a Charcoal Grill, 433–34
    Inexpensive Gas-Grill-Roasted Beef with Garlic and
        Rosemary for a Gas Grill, 434
    Marinated Flank Steak, Charcoal-Grilled, 425–26
    Marinated Flank Steak, Gas-Grilled, 426
    Steak, Grilled, with Ancho Chile–Coffee Rub, 778
    Steak, Grilled, with New Mexican Chile Rub, 777–78
    Steak, Grilled, with Spicy Chipotle Chile Rub, 778
    Steak Fajitas for a Charcoal Grill, 358–59
    Steak Fajitas for a Gas Grill, 359
    Steak Tips, Charcoal-Grilled, 429
    Steak Tips, Gas-Grilled, 429
    Strip or Rib Steaks, Charcoal-Grilled, 430
    Strip or Rib Steaks, Gas-Grilled, 430–31
    Stuffed Flank Steak, Grilled, for a Charcoal Grill,
        427, 427–28
    Stuffed Flank Steak, Grilled, for a Gas Grill, 428
    Stuffed Flank Steak, Grilled, with Spinach and Pine Nuts, 428
Grilled dishes (lamb)
    Rack of Lamb, Charcoal-Grilled, *459*, 459–60
    Rack of Lamb, Gas-Grilled, 460
    Shish Kebabs, Charcoal-Grilled, 457–58
    Shish Kebabs, Gas-Grilled, 458

Grilled dishes (pizza)
Grilled Tomato and Cheese Pizzas for a Charcoal Grill, 288–90, *289*
Grilled Tomato and Cheese Pizzas for a Gas Grill, 290

Grilled dishes (pork)
Baby Back Ribs, Barbecued, for a Charcoal Grill, *453*, 453–54
Baby Back Ribs, Barbecued, for a Gas Grill, 456
Kansas City Sticky Ribs, Easiest, 449
Kansas City Sticky Ribs for a Charcoal Grill, 448–49, *449*
Kansas City Sticky Ribs for a Gas Grill, 449
Pork Chops, Boneless, Easy Grilled, 782–83
Pork Chops, Charcoal-Grilled, 438
Pork Chops, Gas-Grilled, 438
Pork Chops, Grill-Smoked, for a Charcoal Grill, *439*, 439–40
Pork Chops, Grill-Smoked, for a Gas Grill, 440
Pork Loin, Charcoal-Grilled, with Apple-Cranberry Filling, *442*, 442–43
Pork Loin, Gas-Grilled, with Apple-Cranberry Filling, 443
Pork Loin, Grill-Roasted, for a Charcoal Grill, 444
Pork Loin, Grill-Roasted, for a Gas Grill, 445
Pork Rib Roast, Bone-In, Charcoal-Grilled, *445*, 445–46
Pork Rib Roast, Bone-In, Gas-Grilled, 446
Pork Tenderloin, Stuffed, Charcoal-Grilled, 441
Pork Tenderloin, Stuffed, Gas-Grilled, 441
Pulled Pork, Barbecued, for a Charcoal Grill, 446–47
Pulled Pork, Barbecued, for a Gas Grill, 447
Spareribs, Memphis-Style Barbecued, on a Charcoal Grill, 450–51
Spareribs, Memphis-Style Barbecued, on a Gas Grill, 451–52
Spicy Pork Tacos (al Pastor), 786–87

Grilled dishes (poultry)
Chicken, Barbecued Pulled, for a Charcoal Grill, 418–19
Chicken, Barbecued Pulled, for a Crowd, 419
Chicken, Barbecued Pulled, for a Gas Grill, 419
Chicken, Beer Can, Grill-Roasted, for a Charcoal Grill, 420–21
Chicken, Beer Can, Grill-Roasted, for a Gas Grill, 421
Chicken, Italian-Style Charcoal-Grilled, 307–8, *308*
Chicken, Italian-Style Gas-Grilled, 308
Chicken, Jerk, 771–72
Chicken, Smoked, for a Charcoal Grill, *417*, 417–18
Chicken, Smoked, for a Gas Grill, 418
Chicken, Thai Grilled, on a Gas Grill, 405
Chicken, Thai Grilled, with Spicy, Sweet, and Sour Dipping Sauce, 404–5
Chicken Breasts, Bone-In, Charcoal-Grilled, 414, *414*
Chicken Breasts, Bone-In, Gas-Grilled, 414–15
Chicken Breasts, Stuffed, Gas-Grilled, 417

Grilled dishes (poultry) *(cont.)*
Chicken Breasts, Stuffed, with Prosciutto and Fontina, Charcoal-Grilled, 415–17
Chicken Fajitas for a Charcoal Grill, 356–57, *357*
Chicken Fajitas for a Gas Grill, 357
Cornish Game Hens, Grill-Roasted, for a Charcoal Grill, *421*, 421–23
Cornish Game Hens, Grill-Roasted, for a Gas Grill, 423
Turkey, Grill-Roasted, for a Charcoal Grill, 128–29
Turkey, Grill-Roasted, for a Gas Grill, 129
Turkey, Simple Grill-Roasted, 774–75
Turkey Breast, Boneless, Charcoal Grill–Roasted, *130*, 130–31
Turkey Breast, Boneless, Gas Grill–Roasted, 131
Turkey Burgers, Juicy Grilled, 773–74

Grilled dishes (seafood)
Grill-Smoked Salmon, 790–91
Red Snapper, Blackened, Charcoal-Grilled, 465–66, *466*
Red Snapper, Blackened, Gas-Grilled, 466
Salmon, Barbecued, for a Charcoal Grill, 463–64
Salmon, Barbecued, for a Gas Grill, 464
Salmon, Glazed, Charcoal-Grilled, 462, *462*
Salmon, Glazed, Gas-Grilled, 462
Salmon, Grilled, with Orange-Sesame Glaze, 463
Salmon, Grilled, with Spicy Apple Glaze, 463
Salmon Fillets, Charcoal-Grilled, 460–61
Salmon Fillets, Gas-Grilled, 461
Sea Scallops, Charcoal-Grilled, *467*, 467–68
Sea Scallops, Gas-Grilled, 468
Shrimp Skewers, Charcoal-Grilled, *469*, 469–70
Shrimp Skewers, Gas-Grilled, 470
Tuna Steaks with Red Wine Vinegar and Mustard Vinaigrette, Charcoal-Grilled, *464*, 464–65
Tuna Steaks with Red Wine Vinegar and Mustard Vinaigrette, Gas-Grilled, 465

Grilled dishes (vegetables)
Baba Ghanoush, Charcoal-Grilled, 473
Baba Ghanoush, Gas-Grilled, 473
Beans, Barbecue, Smoky Kansas City, 450
Corn, Mexican-Style Charcoal-Grilled, 470–71, *471*
Corn, Mexican-Style Gas-Grilled, 471
Potatoes with Garlic and Rosemary, Charcoal-Grilled, 471–72, *472*
Potatoes with Garlic and Rosemary, Gas-Grilled, 473

Grills
chimney starters for, 415
creating foil tray for, 463
grilling equipment, buying guide, 725–27
preventing food from sticking to, 461

Guacamole, Chunky, 348

Gumbo, Creole-Style Shrimp and Sausage, *80*, 80–81

H

Halibut Steaks
   Pan-Roasted, *200,* 200–201
   trimming and serving, 200
Ham
   Asparagus, and Gruyère Frittata, 514
   Black Forest deli, taste tests on, 743
   and Cheddar, Stuffed Chicken Cutlets with, 86–87
   Denver Omelet, *510,* 510–11
   Fresh, Roast, 184–85, *185*
   Fried Rice with Shrimp, Pork, and Shiitakes, 381
   Peas, and Orange, Latino-Style Chicken and Rice with, 77
   Spiral-Sliced, Glazed, *186,* 186–87
   spiral-sliced, taste tests on, 743
   and Split Pea Soup, Modern, 18, *18*
   and Split Pea Soup with Potatoes, Hearty, 19
   see also Prosciutto
Hamburgers. *See* Burgers
Hand Mixed All-Butter Double-Crust Pie Dough, 682
Hand Mixed Basic Double-Crust Pie Dough, 681
Hand Mixed Basic Single-Crust Pie Dough, 681
Hazelnut(s)
   Chocolate-Cherry Bars with, 580–81
   and Goat Cheese, Lentil Salad with, 759
   -Mocha Truffles, 806
   Nut-Crusted Chicken Breasts with Orange and Oregano, 86
   or Almond Crescent Cookies, 583
   Toasted, and Brown Butter, Green Beans with, 482, *482*
Hearty Chicken Noodle Soup, *5,* 5–6
Hearty Ham and Split Pea Soup with Potatoes, 19
Hearty Lentil Soup, 17
Hearty Minestrone, *21,* 21–22
Hearty Tuscan Bean Stew, 294–95, *295*
Herb(s)
   and Bread Crumbs, Baked Sole Fillets with, *202,* 202–3
   and Caper Vinaigrette, Poached Salmon with, *194,* 194–95
   freezing, 75
   Fresh, Baked Bread Stuffing with, 133
   Fresh, Cream Biscuits with, 546
   and Fresh Tomatoes, Pasta with, 240
   Herbed Croutons, 760
   Herbed Roast Turkey, 124–26
   Pestata, 760
   Sauce, Restaurant-Style, for Pan-Seared Steaks, 139
   Vinaigrette, Foolproof, 28
   see also specific herbs
High-Roast Butterflied Chicken with Potatoes, 101–2
Hoisin sauce, taste tests on, 743
Hoisin-Tamarind Glaze, 780
Home-Fried Taco Shells, 355
Home-Fries, 795
Homemade Vanilla Ice Cream, 655, *655*

Honeydew, Mango, and Blueberries with Lime-Ginger Reduction, 543
Horseradish
   Cocktail Sauce, 209
   Cream Sauce, 165
   Cream Sauce with Chives, 464
   -Crusted Beef Tenderloin, *166,* 166–67
   and Lime, Tuna Salad with, 218
   taste tests on, 743
Hot and Sour Soup, 378–79, *379*
Hot dogs, taste tests on, 744
Hot Fudge Pudding Cake, 627
Hot Fudge Pudding Cakes, Individual, 627
Hot sauce, taste tests on, 744
Huevos Rancheros, 368–69
Hungarian Beef Stew, 65–66

I

Ice Cream
   bars, taste tests on, 744
   chocolate, taste tests on, 744
   Espresso, Chocolate Volcano Cakes with, 631–32
   Vanilla, Homemade, 655, *655*
   vanilla, taste tests on, 744
Indian Curry, 408–9
Indian Flatbread, Quicker, 802
Indian Flatbread (Naan), 801–2
Indian-Style Curry with Potatoes, Cauliflower, Peas, and Chickpeas, *409,* 409–10
Indian-Style Curry with Sweet Potatoes, Eggplant, Green Beans, and Chickpeas, 410
Indian-Style Spinach with Fresh Cheese (Saag Paneer), 793–94
Individual Chilled Lemon Soufflés, 652
Individual Fresh Berry Gratins with Lemon Zabaglione, 664
Individual Fresh Berry Gratins with Zabaglione, *663,* 663–64
Individual Hot Fudge Pudding Cakes, 627
Individual Summer Berry Puddings, 673–74
Indonesian-Style Fried Rice (Nasi Goreng), 382–83
Indoor Clambake, 214–15, *215*
Indoor Pulled Pork with Sweet and Tangy Barbecue Sauce, *183,* 183–84
Inexpensive Charcoal-Grill-Roasted Beef with Garlic and Rosemary for a Charcoal Grill, 433–34
Inexpensive Gas-Grill-Roasted Beef with Garlic and Rosemary for a Gas Grill, 434
Ingredients, tastings of
   behind the scenes look at, 34, 221
   buying guide, 735–55

Irish Soda Bread, 548–49
Italian Bread Salad (Panzanella), 38–39, *39*
Italian-Style Charcoal-Grilled Chicken,
    307–8, *308*
Italian-Style Gas-Grilled Chicken, 308
Italian Vegetable Stew (Ciambotta), 760–61

J

Jambalaya, Skillet, 59
Jam Sandwiches, 579–80
Jerk Chicken, 771–72
Jícama, Orange, and Pepita Relish, 783
Juicy Grilled Turkey Burgers, 773–74
Juicy Pub-Style Burgers, 230–31
    with Crispy Shallots and Blue Cheese, 231, *231*
    with Pan-Roasted Mushrooms and Gruyère, 232
    with Peppered Bacon and Aged Cheddar, 232
    with Sautéed Onions and Smoked Cheddar, 232

K

Kale
    Hearty Tuscan Bean Stew, 294–95, *295*
    Quick-Cooked Tough Greens, 485
Kansas City Barbecue Beans, Smoky, 450
Kansas City Barbecue Sauce, 449–50
Kansas City Sticky Ribs
    for a Charcoal Grill, 448–49, *449*
    Easiest, 449
    for a Gas Grill, 449
Ketchup, taste tests on, 745
Key Lime Bars, *590,* 590–91
Key Lime Pie, 696, *696*
Kitchen supplies, buying guide, 734
Knives, buying guide, 708–10
Knives, sharpening, 494
Kung Pao Shrimp, *396,* 396–97

L

Lamb
    Indian Curry, 408–9
    Rack of
        Charcoal-Grilled, *459,* 459–60
        Gas-Grilled, 460
        trimming fat from, 460
    Shish Kebabs, Charcoal-Grilled, 457–58
    Shish Kebabs, Gas-Grilled, 458

Large Summer Berry Pudding, 674
Lasagna
    Four-Cheese, 271–73
    with Hearty Tomato-Meat Sauce, 274–75
    noodles, taste tests on, 748
    Skillet, 51–52, *52*
    Vegetable, *272,* 273–74
Latino-Style Chicken and Rice, *76,* 76–77
    with Bacon and Roasted Red Peppers, 77
    with Ham, Peas, and Orange, 77
Lattice-Top Fresh Peach Pie, 687–88
Leafy Green Salad with Red Wine Vinaigrette, 29, *29*
Leafy Green Salad with Rich and Creamy Blue Cheese
        Dressing, 29–30
Leek(s)
    Bacon, and Apple, Baked Bread Stuffing with, 133
    Baked Eggs Lorraine, 797
    and Mushroom Galette with Gorgonzola, 791–93
    -Potato Soup, Rustic, 15–16
    Prosciutto, and Goat Cheese Frittata, 514–15
Lemonade, taste tests on, 745
Lemon grass
    cutting, 401
    preparing, 777
Lemon(s)
    Brown Butter Sauce, 204
    Bundt Cake, 596
    -Caper Sauce, 154
    Cheesecake, 636–37
    Chicken Francese, 303–4, *304*
    Chicken Piccata, 302
    and Chive Pan Sauce, 88
    Essence, Spritz Cookies with, 576
    Fresh Margaritas, 346
    Garlic, and Parsley Butter, 432
    -Garlic Sauce, Spicy, 470
    Gremolata, 310
    -Herb Sauce, Stovetop Roast Chicken with,
        100, 100–101
    Layer Cake with Fluffy White Icing, 611–12, *612*
    Meringue Pie, 696–97, *697*
    and Olive Oil, Spaghetti with (al Limone), 238–39, *239*
    Pound Cake, 597, *597*
    Roast Chicken, Classic, *97,* 97–98
    Salsa Verde, 435–36
    Soufflé
        Chilled, 651–52
        Chilled, Individual, 652
        Chilled, with White Chocolate, 652
        Skillet, 654, *654*
    -Tarragon Pan Sauce, 95
    Tart, 700–701

Lemon(s) *(cont.)*
  -Thyme Butter, 760
  Triple Citrus Bars, 591
  Vinaigrette, Foolproof, 28
  zesting, 591
Lentil
  Salad
    with Carrots and Cilantro, 759
    with Hazelnuts and Goat Cheese, 759
    with Olives, Mint, and Feta, 758–59
    with Spinach, Walnuts, and Parmesan Cheese, 759
  Soup, Hearty, 17
Lexington Vinegar Barbecue Sauce, 184
Light Carrot Cake, 603
Light Cream Cheese Frosting, 603
Lighter Chicken and Dumplings, 70–71
Lighter Chicken Parmesan, 300–301, *301*
Lighter Corn Chowder, 24
Light Macaroni and Cheese, 222
Light New York Cheesecake, 634–35
Lime(s)
  -Chile Burger Sauce, 774
  -Chile Vinaigrette, 468
  Fresh Margaritas, 346
  and Garlic, Peruvian Roast Chicken with, 104–5, *105*
  -Glazed Coconut Snowballs, 580
  and Jalapeño, Coca-Cola Glaze with, 186
  Key, Bars, *590,* 590–91
  Key, Pie, 696, *696*
  Rickey–Raspberry Sorbet, 807
  Sauce, Garlicky, with Cilantro, 176
  Spicy Pickled Radishes, 771
  Triple Citrus Bars, 591
  zesting, 591
Livers
  Ragu alla Bolognese, 765
Lobster
  Flambéed Pan-Roasted, 210–11
  Indoor Clambake, 214–15, *215*
Lo Mein, Pork, 393–94, *394*
Low-Fat Chocolate Mousse, 649–50

M

Macaroni
  and Cheese, Classic, 220, *220*
  and Cheese, Light, 222
  and Cheese, Stovetop, 221
  and cheese, taste tests on, 745
  Salad, Cool and Creamy, 43, *43*
  taste tests on, 748

Macaroons, Triple-Coconut, 573–74
Macaroons, Triple-Coconut, Chocolate-Dipped, 574, *574*
Madeira Pan Sauce with Mustard and Anchovies, 144–45
Make-Ahead Chocolate Soufflés, 652–53
Make-Ahead Mocha Soufflés, 653
Make-Ahead Turkey Gravy, 117
Malt Vinegar–Molasses Burger Sauce, 774
Mango, Honeydew, and Blueberries with Lime-Ginger
    Reduction, 543
Maple (syrup)
  Best Baked Apples, *664,* 664–65
  -Glazed Pork Roast, *179,* 179–80
    with Orange Essence, 180
    with Rosemary, 180
    with Smoked Paprika, 180
    with Star Anise, 180
  -Glazed Pork Tenderloin, 176–77, *177*
  -Mustard Sauce, 173
  -Orange Glaze, 187
  -Pecan Oatmeal Scones, Glazed, 527
  Skillet Apple Pie, *669,* 669–70
  taste tests on, 745
Margaritas, Fresh, 346
Marinades
  Garlic, Ginger, and Soy, 430
  Garlic and Cilantro, with Garam Masala, 458
  Garlic-Chile Wet Paste, 427
  Garlic-Ginger-Sesame Wet Paste, 426
  Garlic-Shallot-Rosemary Wet Paste, 426
  Parsley, Warm-Spiced, with Ginger, 458
  Southwestern, 429
Marinara Sauce, *244,* 244–45
Marmalade
  Maple-Orange Glaze, 187
  and Onions, Dried Cherry–Port Sauce with, 176
Maryland Crab Cakes, 212, *212*
Mashed Potatoes
  Buttermilk, 491
  Classic, 487–88
  Creamy, 488–89, *489*
  Fluffy, 490
  French, with Cheese and Garlic (Aligot), *323,* 323–24
  Garlic and Olive Oil, 488
  and Root Vegetables, 489–90, *490*
Mashed Sweet Potatoes, 496
Mayonnaise
  Aïoli, 768
  Garlic, 513–14
  Garlic-Soy, 147
  Spicy, 105
  taste tests on, 745
Measuring equipment, buying guide, 718

Meat
resting, before carving, 169
roasts, "double-butterflying," 785
salting, effect of, 164
see also Beef; Lamb; Pork; Veal

Meatballs
Pasta with Hearty Italian Meat Sauce (Sunday Gravy), 256–57
Spaghetti and, *261,* 261–62
Spaghetti and, Classic, for a Crowd, 263–64

Meat Loaf
All-Beef, Glazed, 226–27, *227*
with Brown Sugar–Ketchup Glaze, 227–28

Meat loaf mix
Fettuccine with Slow-Simmered Bolognese Sauce, 258–59
Lasagna with Hearty Tomato-Meat Sauce, 274–75
Meat Loaf with Brown Sugar–Ketchup Glaze, 227–28
Pasta with Hearty Italian Meat Sauce (Sunday Gravy), 256–57
Pasta with Weeknight Bolognese Sauce, *259,* 259–60
Skillet Lasagna, 51–52, *52*

Mediterranean Chopped Salad, 36, *36*
Memphis-Style Barbecued Spareribs on a Charcoal Grill, 450–51
Memphis-Style Barbecued Spareribs on a Gas Grill, 451–52
Meringue Cookies, 583–84, *584*
Chocolate, 584
Toasted Almond, 584

Mexican Pulled Pork (Carnitas), *363,* 363–64
Mexican Rice, 364–65, *365*
Mexican-Style Charcoal-Grilled Corn, 470–71, *471*
Mexican-Style Gas-Grilled Corn, 471
Mid–South Carolina Mustard Sauce, 448
Milk Chocolate Pots de Crème, 647
Minestrone, Hearty, *21,* 21–22
Mint
-Cilantro Chutney, 410
and Ginger, Raspberry Sorbet with, 807
Grilled Thai Beef Salad for a Charcoal Grill, 405–6
Grilled Thai Beef Salad for a Gas Grill, 406
Olives, and Feta, Lentil Salad with, 758–59
Pineapple and Cucumber Salsa with, 467

Mirin, taste tests on, 745
Mise en place, meaning of, 336
Miso
-Ginger Vinaigrette and Crispy Scallions, Poached Fish Fillets with, 790
-Orange Glaze, 196

Mixed Berry Tart with Pastry Cream, 703
Mocha Soufflés, Make-Ahead, 653
Modern Ham and Split Pea Soup, 18, *18*
Molasses
Boston Baked Beans, 481
Classic Gingerbread Cake, *608,* 608–9
-Malt Vinegar Burger Sauce, 774
Spice Cookies, 564, *564*
Spice Cookies with Dark Rum Glaze, 565
taste tests on, 746

Moroccan Chicken with Chickpeas and Apricots, 75
Moroccan Chicken with Olives and Lemon, 74, 74–75
Mousse
Chocolate, Low-Fat, 649–50
Chocolate-Orange, 649
Chocolate-Raspberry, 649
Dark Chocolate, 648–49, *649*
Premium Dark Chocolate, 649

Mozzarella
Baked Manicotti, 270–71, *271*
Baked Ziti, *269,* 269–70
Chicago-Style Deep-Dish Pizza, *284,* 284–85
Crisp Thin-Crust Pizza, 280
Eggplant Parmesan, 295–96
French Mashed Potatoes with Cheese and Garlic (Aligot), *323,* 323–24
Lasagna with Hearty Tomato-Meat Sauce, 274–75
Lighter Chicken Parmesan, 300–301, *301*
New York–Style Thin-Crust Pizza, *281,* 281–82
Pasta Caprese, *242,* 242–43
Pepperoni Pan Pizza, 286–87
Skillet Baked Ziti, 50, *50*
taste tests on, 739
Tomatoes, and Basil, Deep-Dish Pizza with, 282–83, *283*
and Tomato Tart, *290,* 290–91
Vegetable Lasagna, *272,* 273–74

Muffins
Blueberry, *531,* 531–32
Bran, 532–33, *533*
Corn, 533–34
Corn and Apricot, with Orange Essence, 534
Cranberry-Pecan, 534–35

Mulligatawny Soup, 19–20, *20*
Multigrain Bread, 558, 558–59
Mushroom(s)
Antipasto Pasta Salad, 44–45, *45*
Beef Burgundy, 334–35
and Caramelized Onion Stuffing, Roast Beef Tenderloin with, *167,* 167–69
Catalan-Style Beef Stew with, 761–62

Mushroom(s) *(cont.)*
  Chicken, and Broccoli, Thai Green Curry with, *399*, 399–400
  Chicken Marsala, 300
  Classic Green Bean Casserole, *133*, 133–34
  French-Style Stuffed Chicken Breasts, *326*, 326–27
  -Leek Bread Stuffing with Herbs, 103
  and Leek Galette with Gorgonzola, 791–93
  Pan-Roasted, and Gruyère, Juicy Pub-Style Burgers with, 232
  Quick Beef and Vegetable Soup, 9–10, *10*
  Quick Chicken Fricassee, *325*, 325–26
  Quick Green Bean "Casserole," 134
  Quick Ragu, Spaghetti with, 766–67
  –Red Wine Pan Sauce, 141–42
  Risotto, 297–98
  Sausage, and Monterey Jack, Breakfast Strata with, 517
  Sautéed, and Thyme, Pasta with, *252*, 252–53
  Skillet Beef Stroganoff, 55, *55*
  Slow-Cooker Beef Burgundy, 335–36
  Soup, Creamy, 14
  Stir-Fried Portobellos with Ginger-Oyster Sauce, 397–98, *398*
  Stir-Fried Portobellos with Sweet Chili-Garlic Sauce, 398
  Teriyaki Stir-Fried Beef with Green Beans and Shiitakes, 390–91
  Turkey Tetrazzini, 222–23
  Wild, Sautéed, 14
Mussels
  Indoor Clambake, 214–15, *215*
  Paella, *79*, 79–80
Mustard
  and Anchovies, Madeira Pan Sauce with, 144–45
  -Apple Sauce, 791
  -Apricot Burger Sauce, 774
  -Balsamic Vinaigrette, Foolproof, 28
  Barbecue Sauce, South Carolina, 184
  -Chili Spice Rub, 445
  -Cider Sauce, Sautéed Chicken Cutlets with, 84
  -Cider Sauce, Sautéed Pork Cutlets with, 150, *150*
  -Cream Pan Sauce, 143
  Dijon, taste tests on, 746
  -Dill Sauce, 464
  -Garlic Butter with Thyme, 102
  Glaze, 780
  -Maple Sauce, 173
  Sauce, Mid–South Carolina, 448
  -Shallot Sauce with Thyme, 181
  -Soy Glaze, 196
  whole-grain, taste tests on, 746
  yellow, taste tests on, 746

N

Naan (Indian Flatbread), 801–2
Nachos, Cheesy, with Guacamole and Salsa, 347, *347*
Nectarines
  Blueberries, and Raspberries with Champagne-Cardamom Reduction, 543
  Free-Form Summer Fruit Tart, 701–2
New England Clam Chowder, 25, *25*
New England–Style Home-Corned Beef and Cabbage, 781–82
New York Cheesecake, 633–34, *634*
New York Cheesecake, Light, 634–35
New York–Style Crumb Cake, *535*, 535–36
New York–Style Thin-Crust Pizza, *281*, 281–82
No-Fuss Creamy Parmesan Polenta, 500–501
Noodle(s)
  Cake, Crispy, and Bok Choy, Stir-Fried Chicken with, *385*, 385–86
  Classic Chicken Noodle Soup, 4
  egg, taste tests on, 748
  Hearty Chicken Noodle Soup, *5*, 5–6
  Old-Fashioned Slow-Cooker Chicken Noodle Soup, 6–7
  Pad Thai, 403–4
  Pork Lo Mein, 393–94, *394*
  Sesame, with Shredded Chicken, 380, *380*
  Skillet Beef Stroganoff, 55, *55*
  Thai-Style Stir-Fried, with Chicken and Broccolini, 768–69
Nutella
  and Bananas, Crêpes with, 673
  Chocolate-Hazelnut Slow Cooker Bread Pudding, 641–42
Nut(s)
  Almond or Hazelnut Crescent Cookies, 583
  Chocolate-Cherry Bars with Hazelnuts, 580–81
  Couscous with Dates and Pistachios, 500
  -Crusted Chicken Breasts with Lemon and Thyme, *85*, 85–86
  -Crusted Chicken Breasts with Orange and Oregano, 86
  Curried Chicken Salad with Cashews, 758
  freezing, 75
  Green Beans with Toasted Hazelnuts and Brown Butter, 482, *482*
  Hazelnut-Mocha Truffles, 806
  Lentil Salad with Hazelnuts and Goat Cheese, 759
  Pasta Salad with Pesto, 43–44
  Pear and Cranberry Chopped Salad, 35–36
  Pine, and Spinach, Grilled Stuffed Flank Steak with, 428
  Pine, Carrots, and Raisins, Couscous with, 500
  Stir-Fried Shrimp with Garlicky Eggplant, Scallions, and Cashews, 396
  Toasted, and Parsley Pesto, Penne with, 249
  see also Almond(s); Peanut(s); Pecan(s); Walnut(s)

O

Oatmeal Cake with Broiled Icing, *599, 599–600*
Oatmeal Scones, 526–27, *527*
Oats
Apple-Cinnamon Steel-Cut Oatmeal, 797
Banana-Coconut Steel-Cut Oatmeal, 798
Big and Chewy Oatmeal-Date Cookies, 572
Big and Chewy Oatmeal-Raisin Cookies, 572
Carrot-Spice Steel-Cut Oatmeal, 797
Chocolate-Chunk Oatmeal Cookies with Pecans and Dried
Cherries, 570–71
Cranberry-Orange Steel-Cut Oatmeal, 797
Glazed Maple-Pecan Oatmeal Scones, 527
Multigrain Bread, *558,* 558–59
Oatmeal Cake with Broiled Icing, *599,* 599–600
Oatmeal Scones, 526–27, *527*
Peanut, Honey, and Banana Steel-Cut Oatmeal, 798
Raspberry Squares, *589,* 589–90
rolled, taste tests on, 746
Salty Thin and Crispy Oatmeal Cookies, 573
Skillet Apple Crisp, *665,* 665–66
steel-cut, taste tests on, 746
Ten-Minute Steel-Cut Oatmeal, 797
Thin and Crispy Oatmeal Cookies, 572–73, *573*
Oil
Chili, 375
Olive, and Garlic Mashed Potatoes, 488
olive, taste tests on, 746, 747
Spicy Garlic, 290
vegetable, taste tests on, 754
Old-Fashioned Beef Pot Roast, 63
Old-Fashioned Chocolate Layer Cake with Chocolate
Frosting, 617–18
Old-Fashioned Pot Roast with Root Vegetables, 64
Old-Fashioned Slow-Cooker Chicken Noodle Soup, 6–7
Old-Fashioned Stuffed Turkey, *115,* 115–16
Olive Oil
and Garlic Mashed Potatoes, 488
and Lemon, Spaghetti with (al Limone), 238–39, *239*
Spicy Garlic Oil, 290
taste tests on, 746, 747
Olive(s)
Beef Empanadas, *352,* 352–53
Chicken Marbella, 773
Chicken Provençal, 331–32
Classic Greek Salad, 39
Daube Provençal, 332–33, *333*
and Feta, Cherry Tomato Salad with, 37–38, *38*
and Feta, Fresh Tomato Sauce with, 470
Latino-Style Chicken and Rice, *76,* 76–77
and Lemon, Moroccan Chicken with, *74,* 74–75
Mediterranean Chopped Salad, 36, *36*

Olive(s) *(cont.)*
Mint, and Feta, Lentil Salad with, 758–59
Onion, and Caper Relish, 783
Oranges, and Almonds, Rice Salad with, 45–46, *46*
Pesto, Spaghetti with, 249
Pissaladière, 318–19, *319*
Spaghetti Puttanesca, 245–46
and Sun-Dried Tomato Stuffing, 441
Tomatoes, and Feta, Farfalle with, 243
Vegetable Lasagna, *272,* 273–74
Vinaigrette, 461
Omelets
Cheese, Family-Sized, 509–10
Denver, *510,* 510–11
French, *511,* 511–12
One-Minute Salsa, 347
Onion(s)
and Bacon Tart, French, 317–18
Beef, and Beer Stew, Belgian (Carbonnade à la Flamande),
64–65, *65*
Beef Burgundy, 334–35
Best Beef Stew, *7,* 7–8
-Braised Beef Brisket, 170–72, *171*
Caramelized, and Bacon, Potato Casserole with, 785–86
Caramelized, and Mushroom Stuffing, Roast Beef
Tenderloin with, *167,* 167–69
Caramelized, Bacon, Apples, and Sage, Bread Stuffing with,
118–19
chopping, without tears, 315
Classic Green Bean Casserole, *133,* 133–34
Hungarian Beef Stew, 65–66
and Marmalade, Dried Cherry–Port Sauce with, 176
Olive, and Caper Relish, 783
Pickled, Sweet and Spicy, 356
Pissaladière, 318–19, *319*
Potatoes Lyonnaise, *324,* 324–25
Relish, 410
Rings, Oven-Fried, *232,* 232–33
Sautéed, and Smoked Cheddar, Juicy Pub-Style Burgers
with, 232
Slow-Cooker Beef Burgundy, 335–36
Slow-Cooker Beer-Braised Short Ribs, 68, *68*
Smothered Pork Chops, *157,* 157–58
Soup, Classic French, *314,* 314–15
Soup, Streamlined French, 315–16
Sweet-and-Sour Chutney, 193
Orange(s)
Almond-Crusted Chicken with Wilted Spinach Salad, 33–34
and Avocado, Shrimp Salad with, 210
-Avocado Salsa, 199
-Chipotle Glaze, 415
and Chocolate, Crêpes with, 673

Orange(s) *(cont.)*

-Chocolate Mousse, 649

-Chocolate Soufflé, Skillet, 654

Cinnamon, and Star Anise Glaze, 186

-Cranberry Chutney, 796

-Cranberry Steel-Cut Oatmeal, 797

Crêpes Suzette, 670–71

-Flavored Chicken, 384–85

Ham, and Peas, Latino-Style Chicken and Rice with, 77

Jícama, and Pepita Relish, 783

juice, taste tests on, 747

-Miso Glaze, 196

Olives, and Almonds, Rice Salad with, 45–46, *46*

Salsa with Cuban Flavors, 446

Sangria, 346–47

segmenting, 214

-Sesame Glaze, Grilled Salmon with, 463

Triple Citrus Bars, 591

Wilted Spinach, and Watercress Salad, Pan-Seared Scallops with, 34–35, *35*

zesting, 591

Orecchiette with Broccoli Rabe and Sausage, 253

Osso Buco, 309–10

Our Favorite Chili, 8–9, *9*

Oven-Barbecued Spareribs, 452–53

Oven-Fried Bacon, 509

Oven-Fried Chicken, 107–8, *108*

Oven-Fried Onion Rings, *232*, 232–33

Oven-Roasted Pork Chops, 153

Oven-Roasted Salmon, 197, *197*

Oyster crackers, taste tests on, 747

P

Pad Thai, 403–4

Paella, *79*, 79–80

Pancake, German Apple, 518–19

Pancake mix, taste tests on, 747

Pancakes, Blueberry, *517*, 517–18

Pandowdy, Apple, *669*, 669–70

Panna Cotta, 643

Pan-Roasted Asparagus, 477

Pan-Roasted Chicken Breasts with Sage-Vermouth Sauce, 92–93, *93*

Pan-Roasted Halibut Steaks, *200*, 200–201

Pan-Roasted Thick-Cut Fish Fillets, 201–2

Pan-Seared Chicken Breasts, 87–88, *88*

Pan-Seared Filet Mignon, 144, *144*

Pan-Seared Inexpensive Steaks, 142–43, *143*

Pan-Seared Oven-Roasted Pork Tenderloins, 175

Pan-Seared Salmon, 192–93

Pan-Seared Scallops, 203–4

Pan-Seared Scallops with Wilted Spinach, Watercress, and Orange Salad, 34–35, *35*

Pan-Seared Sesame-Crusted Tuna Steaks, *198*, 198–99

Pan-Seared Shrimp, 204

with Chipotle-Lime Glaze, 205

with Garlic-Lemon Butter, 205

with Ginger-Hoisin Glaze, 205

Pan-Seared Steaks, 138

Pan-Seared Thick-Cut Pork Chops, *12*, 152

Pan-Seared Thick-Cut Steaks, 140–41, *141*

Paprika, Smoked, and Roasted Red Pepper Butter, 432

Paprika, taste tests on, 747

Parmesan

Baked Eggs Florentine, 796–97

Baked Manicotti, 270–71, *271*

Broccoli-Cheese Soup, 16–17, *17*

Chicken, Lighter, 300–301, *301*

Chicken Milanese, 85

Creamy Baked Four-Cheese Pasta, *268*, 268–69

-Crusted Chicken Cutlets, 302–3

Deep-Dish Pizza with Tomatoes, Mozzarella, and Basil, 282–83, *283*

Eggplant, 295–96

Fettuccine Alfredo, 265–66, *266*

Figs, Prosciutto, and Walnuts, Arugula Salad with, 31

Four-Cheese Lasagna, 271–73

Garlic, and Red Pepper Flakes, Roasted Brussels Sprouts with, 794

Grilled Tomato and Cheese Pizzas for a Charcoal Grill, 288–90, *289*

Grilled Tomato and Cheese Pizzas for a Gas Grill, 290

and Herbs, Almost Hands-Free Risotto with, 499

Lasagna with Hearty Tomato-Meat Sauce, 274–75

New York–Style Thin-Crust Pizza, *281*, 281–82

Pasta Salad with Pesto, 43–44

Polenta, No-Fuss Creamy, 500–501

Quick Cheese Bread, 549–50, *550*

Quick Cheese Bread with Bacon, Onion, and Gruyère, 550

Sauce with Pancetta and Walnuts, 268

Skillet Lasagna, 51–52, *52*

Spinach, and Walnuts, Lentil Salad with, 759

taste tests on, 739

Vegetable Lasagna, *272*, 273–74

Parsley

Chimichurri Sauce, 432–33

Fresh, and Garlic Sauce, Argentinian-Style (Chimichurri), 145

Gremolata, 310

Lemon, and Garlic Butter, 432

Parsley (*cont.*)

Marinade, Warm-Spiced, with Ginger, 458

Picada, 761–62

Salsa Verde, 435–36

and Shallot Butter, 166

and Toasted Nut Pesto, Penne with, 249

Parsnips

and Carrots, Roasted, with Rosemary, 479

Mashed Potatoes and Root Vegetables,
489–90, *490*

Old-Fashioned Pot Roast with Root Vegetables, 64

Pasta

all'Amatriciana, 765–66

and Bean Soup, Italian (Pasta e Fagioli), *293,* 293–94

Campanelle with Arugula, Goat Cheese, and Sun-Dried
Tomato Pesto, 248–49

Campanelle with Asparagus, Basil, and Balsamic Glaze,
250–51

Caprese, *242,* 242–43

Cavatappi with Asparagus, Arugula, Walnuts, and Blue
Cheese, 251–52

cheese ravioli, taste tests on, 747

cooking, 245

cooking gadgets, note about, 253

with Creamy Tomato Sauce, *241,* 241–42

draining and serving, 245

Farfalle

with Pesto, 247

with Tomatoes, Olives, and Feta, 243

Fettuccine Alfredo, 265–66, *266*

Fettuccine with Slow-Simmered Bolognese Sauce,
258–59

Four-Cheese, Creamy Baked, *268,* 268–69

fresh, taste tests on, 748

Fresh, without a Machine, 763–64

with Fresh Tomatoes and Herbs, 240

and Fresh Tomato Sauce with Garlic and Basil,
240–41

with Garlic and Oil, 238

gnocchi, taste tests on, 743

with Hearty Italian Meat Sauce (Sunday Gravy), 256–57

long-strand, breaking into pieces, 768

Manicotti, Baked, 270–71, *271*

Orecchiette with Broccoli Rabe and Sausage, 253

Penne

taste tests on, 748

with Toasted Nut and Parsley Pesto, 249

with Vodka Sauce (Penne alla Vodka), *264,* 264–65

Pork Lo Mein, 393–94, *394*

Potato Gnocchi with Browned Butter and Sage Sauce,
266–67, *267*

Pasta (*cont.*)

Ragu alla Bolognese, 765

Salad

Antipasto, 44–45, *45*

Macaroni, Cool and Creamy, 43, *43*

with Pesto, 43–44

Sauces

Marinara, *244,* 244–45

Meat, Simple Italian-Style, *257,* 257–58

taste tests on, 749

Tomato, Quick, *243,* 243–44

with Sautéed Mushrooms and Thyme, *252,* 252–53

Shrimp, Garlicky, *254,* 254–55

Shrimp fra Diavolo, 255, *255*

and Slow-Simmered Tomato Sauce with Meat (Sunday
Gravy), 260–61

Spring Vegetable, 249–50, *250*

Toasted, Spanish-Style, with Shrimp, 767

Toasted, Spanish-Style, with Shrimp and Clams, 768

with Tomato, Bacon, and Onion (Pasta all'Amatriciana),
246, *246*

with Tomato and Almond Pesto (Pesto alla Trapanese),
247–48, *248*

tortellini, taste tests on, 748

with Weeknight Bolognese Sauce, *259,* 259–60

Ziti

Baked, *269,* 269–70

Chicken and Broccoli, Skillet, 50–51

Skillet Baked, 50, *50*

see also Couscous; Lasagna; Macaroni; Noodle(s); Spaghetti

Pastry Cream, Fresh Fruit Tart with,
702–3, *703*

Peach(es)

Cake, Summer, 607, *607*

Crisp, 661–62

Crisp for a Crowd, 662

Free-Form Summer Fruit Tart, 701–2

Fresh, Pie, Lattice-Top, 687–88

Sauce, Slow-Roasted Pork Shoulder with,
182, 182–83

Peanut Butter

Confetti Cabbage Salad with Spicy Peanut Dressing, 42

Cookies, 569–70, *570*

Peanut, Honey, and Banana Steel-Cut Oatmeal, 798

Peanut Sauce, 777

Sandwich Cookies, 802–3

Sandwich Cookies with Honey-Cinnamon Filling, 803

Sandwich Cookies with Milk Chocolate Filling, 803

Sesame Noodles with Shredded Chicken, 380, *380*

Spicy Peanut Dipping Sauce, 377

taste tests on, 749

Peanut(s)
Pad Thai, 403–4
Peanut Butter Cookies, 569–70, *570*
Peanut Butter Sandwich Cookies, 802–3
with Honey-Cinnamon Filling, 803
with Milk Chocolate Filling, 803
Sauce, 777
Shrimp, and Pineapple, Thai Red Curry with,
400–401

Pear(s)
Caramelized, with Blue Cheese and Black Pepper–Caramel
Sauce, *674,* 674–75
and Cranberry Chopped Salad, 35–36
Lemon, and Rosemary, Cranberry Chutney with, 796
Tatin, 706

Pea(s)
and Bean Sprouts, Fried Rice with, 381–82
Best Beef Stew, *7,* 7–8
Cauliflower, Potatoes, and Chickpeas, Indian-Style Curry
with, *409,* 409–10
Chicken and Dumplings, *69,* 69–70
Ham, and Orange, Latino-Style Chicken and Rice with, 77
and Roasted Red Peppers, Spanish Tortilla with,
512–13, *513*
and Scallions, Skillet Chicken and Rice with, 57
Skillet Chicken Pot Pie with Biscuit Topping, 52–54
Skillet Curried Chicken and Rice, 58
Snow, and Onion, Tangerine Stir-Fried Beef with, 391
Snow, and Red Bell Pepper, Stir-Fried Shrimp with, in Hot
and Sour Sauce, 395, *395*
Snow, Tofu, and Red Onion, Stir-Fried, with Hot and Sour
Sauce, 388–89
Soup, Creamy, 13
Spring Vegetable Pasta, 249–50, *250*
Turkey Tetrazzini, 222–23

Pecan(s)
and Bacon, Roasted Brussels Sprouts with, 794
Best Baked Apples, *664,* 664–65
Blondies, 584–85, *585*
–Brown Sugar Streusel, Sour Cream Coffee Cake with, 540
Candied Sweet Potato Casserole, 135, *135*
Carrot Layer Cake, 805–6
Congo Bars, 585
-Cranberry Muffins, 534–35
and Dried Cherries, Chocolate-Chunk Oatmeal Cookies
with, 570–71
and Dried Cherries, Couscous with, 500
and Dried Cranberries, Wild Rice Pilaf with, 498–99
German Chocolate Cake, *620,* 620–21
Glazed Maple-Pecan Oatmeal Scones, 527
Oatmeal Cake with Broiled Icing, *599,* 599–600

Pecan(s) *(cont.)*
or Walnut Crescent Cookies, *582,* 582–83
Peach Crisp, 661–62
Peach Crisp for a Crowd, 662
Pie, 694–95, *695*
Pie, Triple-Chocolate Chunk, 695
Raspberry Squares, *589,* 589–90
Sausage, and Dried Cherries, Baked Bread Stuffing with,
132
Skillet Apple Crisp, *665,* 665–66
Spiced, with Rum Glaze, 501
Sticky Buns with, 538–39

Penne
taste tests on, 748
with Toasted Nut and Parsley Pesto, 249
with Vodka Sauce (Penne alla Vodka), *264,* 264–65

Pepita, Orange, and Jícama Relish, 783
Peppercorns, black, taste tests on, 749
Pepper-Crusted Filet Mignon, *145,* 145–46
Pepperoni
Antipasto Pasta Salad, 44–45, *45*
Pan Pizza, 286–87
taste tests on, 749

Pepper(s)
Antipasto Pasta Salad, 44–45, *45*
Bell, Classic Stuffed, 228–29, *229*
Chicken Fajitas for a Charcoal Grill, 356–57, *357*
Chicken Fajitas for a Gas Grill, 357
Classic Gazpacho, 22–23
Classic Greek Salad, 39
Creamy Gazpacho Andaluz, 23–24
Denver Omelet, *510,* 510–11
Gazpacho Salsa, 213–14
Italian Vegetable Stew (Ciambotta), 760–61
Mediterranean Chopped Salad, 36, *36*
Pear and Cranberry Chopped Salad, 35–36
Roasted Red
and Bacon, Latino-Style Chicken and Rice with, 77
and Basil, Shrimp Salad with, 210
and Peas, Spanish Tortilla with, 512–13, *513*
and Smoked Paprika Butter, 432
taste tests on, 749
Steak Fajitas for a Charcoal Grill, 358–59
Steak Fajitas for a Gas Grill, 359
stemming and seeding, 359
Sweet, and Vinegar, Pork Chops with, 308–9
Sweet, Sausage, and Cheddar Cheese, Scrambled Eggs
with, 506–7
see also Chile(s)

Perfect Roast Chicken, 93–94
Peruvian Roast Chicken with Garlic and Lime, 104–5, *105*

Pestata, 760
Pesto
   Farfalle with, 247
   Olive, Spaghetti with, 249
   Pasta Salad with, 43–44
   Sun-Dried Tomato, Arugula, and Goat Cheese, Campanelle
      with, 248–49
   Toasted Nut and Parsley, Penne with, 249
   Tomato and Almond, Pasta with (Pesto alla Trapanese),
      247–48, *248*
Picada, 761–62
Pickled Onions, Sweet and Spicy, 356
Pickled Radishes, Spicy, 771
Pickles
   Austrian-Style Potato Salad, 47, *47*
   bread-and-butter, taste tests on, 749
   kosher dill, taste tests on, 750
   Sweet, and Hard-Cooked Eggs, American Potato Salad
      with, 46
Pie Dough
   All-Butter Double-Crust, 682
   All-Butter Double-Crust, Hand Mixed, 682
   Basic Double-Crust, 680
   Basic Double-Crust, Hand Mixed, 681
   Basic Single-Crust, 681
   Basic Single-Crust, Hand Mixed, 681
   blind-baking, 694
   cut-out crusts for, 691
   Foolproof Double-Crust, 683–84
   Foolproof Single-Crust, 684
   recipes for, behind the scenes, 683
   rolling and fitting, 680
   single-crust, crimping, 681
   Single-Crust, For Custard Pies, 681
Pies (dessert)
   Apple
      Classic, 685–86
      with Crystallized Ginger, 686
      Deep-Dish, *686,* 686–87
      with Dried Fruit, 686
      with Fresh Cranberries, 686
      Skillet, *669,* 669–70
   blind-baking crust for, 694
   Blueberry, *690,* 690–91
   Chocolate Cream, 698–99, *699*
   Coconut Cream, 698
   cut-out top crusts, forming, 691
   double-crust, forming, 687
   Key Lime, 696, *696*
   lattice-top, forming, 688
   Lemon Meringue, 696–97, *697*
   Peach, Fresh, Lattice-Top, 687–88

Pies (dessert) *(cont.)*
   Pecan, 694–95, *695*
   Pecan, Triple-Chocolate Chunk, 695
   Pumpkin, *693,* 693–94
   Strawberry, Fresh, *689,* 689–90
   Summer Berry, *691,* 691–92
   Sweet Cherry, *692,* 692–93
   see also Tarts (dessert)
Pies (savory)
   Greek Spinach and Feta (Spanakopita), *73,* 73–74
   Shepherd's, 780–81
   Skillet Tamale, 54
Pineapple
   and Cucumber Salsa with Mint, 467
   -Ginger Glaze, Spicy, 186
   Shrimp, and Peanuts, Thai Red Curry with, 400–401
   Spicy Pork Tacos (al Pastor), 786–87
Pine Nuts
   Carrots, and Raisins, Couscous with, 500
   Pasta Salad with Pesto, 43–44
   and Spinach, Grilled Stuffed Flank Steak with, 428
Pissaladière, 318–19, *319*
Pistachios
   and Dates, Couscous with, 500
   Nut-Crusted Chicken Breasts with Orange and Oregano,
      86
   Pear and Cranberry Chopped Salad, 35–36
Pizza
   Bianca, *287,* 287–88
   cheese, frozen, taste tests on, 750
   Deep-Dish, Chicago-Style, *284,* 284–85
   Deep-Dish, with Tomatoes, Mozzarella, and Basil,
      282–83, *283*
   dough, preparing without a mixer, 287
   Pepperoni Pan, 286–87
   Quick Tomato Sauce for, 280–81
   Thin-Crust, Crisp, 280
   Thin-Crust, New York–Style, *281,* 281–82
   Tomato and Cheese, Grilled, for a Charcoal Grill,
      288–90, *289*
   Tomato and Cheese, Grilled, for a Gas Grill, 290
Poached Eggs, 507–8
Poached Fish Fillets
   with Crispy Artichokes and Sherry-Tomato Vinaigrette,
      789–90
   with Crispy Scallions and Miso-Ginger Vinaigrette, 790
   with Jalapeño Vinaigrette, 790
Poached Salmon with Herb and Caper Vinaigrette,
   194, 194–95
Polenta, Basic, 297, *297*
Polenta, No-Fuss Creamy Parmesan, 500–501
Pomegranate-Balsamic Glaze, 196

Pommes Anna, 322–23

Popcorn, taste tests on, 750

Pork

  butt, cutting in half, 184

  Chops

    Basic Spice Rub for, 439

    Boneless, Easy Grilled, 782–83

    Charcoal-Grilled, 438

    Cider-Glazed, *156,* 156–57

    cooking tip, 156

    Crispy Pan-Fried, 151, *151*

    Crunchy Baked, *158,* 158–59

    Gas-Grilled, 438

    Grill-Smoked, for a Charcoal Grill, *439,* 439–40

    Grill-Smoked, for a Gas Grill, 440

    Oven-Roasted, 153

    Pan-Seared Thick-Cut, 152, *152*

    Red Wine–Braised, 783–84

    Skillet-Barbecued, *154,* 154–55

    Smothered, *157,* 157–58

    Stuffed, 159–61

    with Vinegar and Sweet Peppers, 308–9

  Cutlets, Breaded (Pork Schnitzel), *174,* 174–75

  Cutlets, Sautéed, with Mustard-Cider Sauce, 150, *150*

  Fettuccine with Slow-Simmered Bolognese Sauce, 258–59

  Hot and Sour Soup, 378–79, *379*

  internal cooking temperatures, 159

  and Kielbasa, Simplified Cassoulet with, 337–38

  Lasagna with Hearty Tomato-Meat Sauce, 274–75

  Lettuce Wraps, Thai, *376,* 376–77 Loin

    with Apple-Cranberry Filling, Charcoal-Grilled, *442,* 442–43

    with Apple-Cranberry Filling, Gas-Grilled, 443

    cutting open and stuffing, 443

    double-butterflying, 178

    French-Style Pot-Roasted, 177–78, 784–85

    French-Style Pot-Roasted, with Port and Figs, 785

    Grill-Roasted, for a Charcoal Grill, 444

    Grill-Roasted, for a Gas Grill, 445

    Roast, Garlic-Studded, 180–81

    Slow-Cooker, with Cranberries and Orange, *181,* 181–82

  Lo Mein, 393–94, *394*

  Meat Loaf with Brown Sugar–Ketchup Glaze, 227–28

  natural versus enhanced, 155

  Pasta all'Amatriciana, 765–66

  Pasta with Hearty Italian Meat Sauce (Sunday Gravy), 256–57

  Pasta with Weeknight Bolognese Sauce, *259,* 259–60

  Potstickers with Scallion Dipping Sauce, *372,* 372–73

  premium, taste tests on, 750

Pork *(cont.)*

  Pulled

    Barbecued, for a Charcoal Grill, 446–47

    Barbecued, for a Gas Grill, 447

    Indoor, with Sweet and Tangy Barbecue Sauce, *183,* 183–84

    Mexican (Carnitas), *363,* 363–64

  Ragu alla Bolognese, 765

  Rib Roast, Bone-In, Charcoal-Grilled, *445,* 445–46

  Rib Roast, Bone-In, Gas-Grilled, 446

  Ribs

    Barbecued Baby Back, for a Charcoal Grill, *453,* 453–54

    Barbecued Baby Back, for a Gas Grill, 456

    Kansas City Sticky, Easiest, 449

    Kansas City Sticky, for a Charcoal Grill, 448–49, *449*

    Kansas City Sticky, for a Gas Grill, 449

    Memphis-Style Barbecued Spareribs on a Charcoal Grill, 450–51

    Memphis-Style Barbecued Spareribs on a Gas Grill, 451–52

    Oven-Barbecued Spareribs, 452–53

  Roast

    "double-butterflying," 785

    Maple-Glazed, *179,* 179–80

    Maple-Glazed, with Orange Essence, 180

    Maple-Glazed, with Rosemary, 180

    Maple-Glazed, with Smoked Paprika, 180

    Maple-Glazed, with Star Anise, 180

  salting, effect of, 164

  Shoulder, Slow-Roasted, with Peach Sauce, *182,* 182–83

  Shu Mai (Steamed Chinese Dumplings), 373–75, *375*

  Sichuan Stir-Fried, in Garlic Sauce, 787–88

  Skillet Lasagna, 51–52, *52*

  Stir-Fried, Eggplant, and Onion with Garlic and Black Pepper, 392

  Stir-Fried, Green Beans, and Red Bell Pepper with Gingery Oyster Sauce, *392,* 393

  Tacos, Spicy (al Pastor), 786–87

  Tenderloin

    Maple-Glazed, 176–77, *177*

    Medallions, Thick-Cut, *172,* 172–73

    medallions, tying, 173

    Pan-Seared Oven-Roasted, 175

    Stuffed, Charcoal-Grilled, 441

    Stuffed, Gas-Grilled, 441

    tail end, tying into medallion, 173

  Tostadas, Spicy Mexican Shredded, *362,* 362–63

  see also Bacon; Ham; Sausage(s)

Port

  -Cherry Glaze, 187

  -Cherry Reduction, 146

  –Dried Cherry Sauce with Onions and Marmalade, 176

  -Raspberry Sorbet, 807

  Wine Sauce, Restaurant-Style, for Pan-Seared Steaks, 140

Potato(es)

Best Beef Stew, 7, 7–8
Burger Buns, 800–801
Casserole with Bacon and Caramelized Onion, 785–86
Cauliflower, Peas, and Chickpeas, Indian-Style Curry with, *409,* 409–10
chips, taste tests on, 750
Diner-Style Home Fries, 508
Dinner Rolls, 801
Fish and Chips, 191–92 *192*
Fries
    French, Classic, 234
    French, Easier, 235, *235*
    Steak, *233,* 233–34
Galette, Simplified, *321,* 321–22
with Garlic and Rosemary, Charcoal-Grilled, 471–72, *472*
with Garlic and Rosemary, Gas-Grilled, 473
Gnocchi with Browned Butter and Sage Sauce, 266–67, *267*
Hearty Ham and Split Pea Soup with, 19
High-Roast Butterflied Chicken with, 101–2
Home Fries, 795
Indoor Clambake, 214–15, *215*
-Leek Soup, Rustic, 15–16
Lighter Corn Chowder, 24
Lyonnaise, *324,* 324–25
Mashed
    Buttermilk, 491
    Classic, 487–88
    Creamy, 488–89, *489*
    Fluffy, 490
    French, with Cheese and Garlic (Aligot), *323,* 323–24
    Garlic and Olive Oil, 488
    and Root Vegetables, 489–90, *490*
New England Clam Chowder, 25, *25*
New England–Style Home-Corned Beef and Cabbage, 781–82
Old-Fashioned Pot Roast with Root Vegetables, 64
Pommes Anna, 322–23
Roasted, Crispy, 491–92
Salad
    American, with Hard-Cooked Eggs and Sweet Pickles, 46
    Austrian-Style, 47, *47*
    French, 316–17, *317*
Salt-Baked, with Roasted Garlic and Rosemary Butter, 492–93
Salt-Baked, with Roasted Shallot and Thyme Butter, 493
Scalloped, 493–94
and Shallot Galette with Goat Cheese, 793

Potato(es) *(cont.)*

Shepherd's Pie, 780–81
skewering, for the grill, 472
Skillet-Roasted, 492
Skillet-Roasted Chicken Breasts with, *56,* 56–57
Smashed, 486–87
Smashed, Crispy, *495,* 495–96
Spanish Tortilla with Chorizo and Scallions, 513
Spanish Tortilla with Roasted Red Peppers and Peas, 512–13, *513*
Steak Frites, *339,* 339–40
Sweet
    Casserole, Candied, 135, *135*
    Eggplant, Green Beans, and Chickpeas, Indian-Style Curry with, 410
    Mashed, 496
    Twice-Baked, 494–95
Pot Pie, Chicken, with Savory Crumble Topping, 71–73, *72*
Pot Pie, Skillet Chicken, with Biscuit Topping, 52–54
Pots and pans
best, for stir-fries, 386
buying guide, 710–12
heating oil in skillets, 199
skillets, versatility of, 53
Pots de Crème, Chocolate, *646,* 646–47
Pots de Crème, Milk Chocolate, 647
Potstickers with Scallion Dipping Sauce, *372,* 372–73
Poultry. *See* Chicken; Cornish Game Hens; Turkey
Premium Dark Chocolate Mousse, 649
Prime Rib, 170
Prosciutto
Chicken Saltimbocca, 305, *305*
Figs, Walnuts, and Parmesan, Arugula Salad with, 31
and Fontina, Stuffed Chicken Breasts with, Charcoal-Grilled, 415–17
Grilled Stuffed Flank Steak for a Charcoal Grill, *427,* 427–28
Grilled Stuffed Flank Steak for a Gas Grill, 428
Leek, and Goat Cheese Frittata, 514–15
Stuffed Chicken Breasts, Gas-Grilled, 417
Prunes
Chicken Marbella, 773
Pub-Style Burger Sauce, 231
Puddings and soufflés (dessert)
Bread Pudding
    Chocolate-Hazelnut Slow Cooker, 641–42
    Classic, 640, *640*
Chilled Lemon Soufflé, 651–52
    Individual, 652
    with White Chocolate, 652

Puddings and soufflés (dessert) *(cont.)*

Classic Crème Caramel, *645,* 645–46

Creamy Chocolate Pudding, *647,* 647–48

Crème Brûlée, Classic, *644,* 644–45

Crème Brûlée, Espresso, 645

Grand Marnier Soufflé, 650–51

Grand Marnier Soufflé with Grated Chocolate, 651

Homemade Vanilla Ice Cream, 655, *655*

Make-Ahead Chocolate Soufflés, 652–53

Make-Ahead Mocha Soufflés, 653

Mousse

Chocolate, Low-Fat, 649–50

Chocolate-Orange, 649

Chocolate-Raspberry, 649

Dark Chocolate, 648–49, *649*

Premium Dark Chocolate, 649

Panna Cotta, 643

Pots de Crème, Chocolate, *646,* 646–47

Pots de Crème, Milk Chocolate, 647

Rice Pudding, Coconut, 642

Rice Pudding, Stovetop, 642, *642*

Skillet Soufflé, Chocolate-Orange, 654

Skillet Soufflé, Lemon, 654, *654*

Pumpkin

Bread, 798

Bread with Candied Ginger, 798

Cheesecake, Spiced, 635–36

Pie, *693,* 693–94

Q

Quesadillas, 348–49

Quiche Lorraine, *515,* 515–16

Quick All-Purpose Gravy, 161

Quick Barbecue Sauce, 453

Quick Beef and Vegetable Soup, 9–10, *10*

Quick Cheese Bread, 549–50, *550*

Quick Cheese Bread with Bacon, Onion, and Gruyère, 550

Quick Chicken Fricassee, *325,* 325–26

Quick Cinnamon Buns with Buttermilk Icing, *537,* 537–38

Quick-Cooked Tough Greens, 485

Quicker Indian Flatbread, 802

Quick Green Bean "Casserole," 134

Quick Roasted Acorn Squash with Brown Sugar, 496–97, *497*

Quick Roasted Baby Carrots, 479

Quick Tomato Sauce, *243,* 243–44

Quick Tomato Sauce for Pizza, 280–81

R

Radishes, Spicy Pickled, 771

Ragu alla Bolognese, 765

Raisins

Apple Pie with Dried Fruit, 686

Beef Empanadas, *352,* 352–53

Big and Chewy Oatmeal-Raisin Cookies, 572

Bran Muffins, 532–33, *533*

Carrots, and Pine Nuts, Couscous with, 500

Cinnamon-Swirl Bread, 799

Coconut Rice Pudding, 642

Easy Apple Strudel, *667,* 667–68

Golden, and Almonds, Sautéed Baby Spinach with, 484

Golden, and Fennel, Cranberry Chutney with, 796

Skillet Curried Chicken and Rice, 58

Stovetop Rice Pudding, 642, *642*

Raspberry(ies)

Berry Fool, *676,* 676–77

-Chocolate Mousse, 649

-Chocolate Torte, 624–25, *625*

Coulis, 643–44

Free-Form Summer Fruit Tart, 701–2

Fresh Fruit Tart with Pastry Cream, 702–3, *703*

Gratin, Simple, 662–63

Individual Fresh Berry Gratins with Lemon Zabaglione, 664

Individual Fresh Berry Gratins with Zabaglione, *663,* 663–64

Individual Summer Berry Puddings, 673–74

Large Summer Berry Pudding, 674

Mixed Berry Tart with Pastry Cream, 703

Nectarines, and Blueberries with Champagne-Cardamom Reduction, 543

Sorbet, 807

with Ginger and Mint, 807

–Lime Rickey, 807

-Port, 807

Summer Berry Pie, *691,* 691–92

Raspberry jam

Chocolate-Raspberry Torte, 624–25, *625*

Classic White Layer Cake with Butter Frosting and Raspberry-Almond Filling, 613–14

Jam Sandwiches, 579–80

Raspberry Squares, *589,* 589–90

taste tests on, 750

Ravioli, cheese, taste tests on, 747

Red Curry Paste, 401

Red Snapper, Charcoal-Grilled Blackened, 465–66, *466*

Red Snapper, Gas-Grilled Blackened, 466

Red Wine

Beef Braised in Barolo, 310–11

Beef Burgundy, 334–35

Beef Burgundy, Slow-Cooker, 335–36

Red Wine (cont.)
    Braised Beef Short Ribs, 66, 66–67
    –Braised Pork Chops, 783–84
    Coq au Vin, 328, 328–29
    Daube Provençal, 332–33, 333
    –Mushroom Pan Sauce, 141–42
    Pan Sauce, 138
    Sangria, 346–47
    Sauce Base, 140
    Sauce Base for Steak Diane, 341–42
Refried Beans, 369
Relish
    Cucumber, Spicy, 198
    Onion, 410
    Onion, Olive, and Caper, 783
    Orange, Jícama, and Pepita, 783
    sweet pickle, taste tests on, 750
    Tangerine and Ginger, 197–98
    Tomato, Fennel, and Almond, 783
    Tomato, Fresh, 198
Rémoulade, 467
Restaurant-Style Brandy and Green Peppercorn Sauce
        for Pan-Seared Steaks, 139–40
Restaurant-Style Herb Sauce for Pan-Seared Steaks,
        139
Restaurant-Style Port Wine Sauce for Pan-Seared Steaks,
        140
Rhubarb Fool, 677
Rhubarb-Strawberry Fool, 677
Rice
    Almost Hands-Free Risotto with Parmesan and Herbs, 499
    Arborio, taste tests on, 751
    Basmati, taste tests on, 751
    and Black Beans, Cuban-Style, 78
    brown, taste tests on, 751
    Butternut Squash Risotto, 298–99, 299
    Chicken and
        Latino-Style, 76, 76–77
        Latino-Style, with Bacon and Roasted Red Peppers, 77
        Latino-Style, with Ham, Peas, and Orange, 77
        Skillet, Curried, 58
        Skillet, with Broccoli and Cheddar, 58
        Skillet, with Peas and Scallions, 57
    Chicken Biryani, 407–8
    Classic Stuffed Bell Peppers, 228–29, 229
    Faux Leftover, 383
    Fried
        Indonesian-Style (Nasi Goreng), 382–83
        with Peas and Bean Sprouts, 381–82
        with Shrimp, Pork, and Shiitakes, 381
    Mexican, 364–65, 365
    Mushroom Risotto, 297–98

Rice (cont.)
    Paella, 79, 79–80
    Pilaf, 497–98
    Pudding, Coconut, 642
    Pudding, Stovetop, 642, 642
    ready, taste tests on, 751
    Salad with Oranges, Olives, and Almonds, 45–46, 46
    Skillet Jambalaya, 59
    White, Basic, 382
    white, long-grain, taste tests on, 751
    Wild, Pilaf with Pecans and Dried Cranberries, 498–99
Rich and Creamy Scrambled Eggs, 504, 504–5
Rich and Creamy Scrambled Eggs for Two, 505
Rich Chocolate Bundt Cake, 595, 595
Risotto
    Almost Hands-Free, with Parmesan and Herbs, 499
    Butternut Squash, 298–99, 299
    Mushroom, 297–98
Roast Beef Tenderloin, 165, 165–66
Roast Beef Tenderloin with Caramelized Onion and
        Mushroom Stuffing, 167, 167–69
Roasted Broccoli, 477, 477–78
Roasted Broccoli with Garlic, 478
Roasted Brussels Sprouts, 794
    with Bacon and Pecans, 794
    with Garlic, Red Pepper Flakes, and Parmesan, 794
Roasted Carrots, 478, 478
    and Fennel with Toasted Almonds and Lemon, 479
    and Parsnips with Rosemary, 479
Roasted Green Beans, 483
Roasted Red Pepper and Smoked Paprika Butter,
        432
Roast Fresh Ham, 184–85, 185
Roast Salted Turkey, 123, 123–24
Roast Turkey for a Crowd, 114
Rolls, Dinner
    frozen, taste tests on, 742
    Potato, 801
    Rustic, 547–48, 548
Rosemary
    Focaccia, 278, 278–79
    –Garlic-Shallot Wet Paste Marinade, 426
    Pear, and Lemon, Cranberry Chutney with, 796
    Pizza Bianca, 287, 287–88
    and Roasted Garlic Butter, Salt-Baked Potatoes with,
        492–93
Rubs
    Dry, for Barbecue, 447
    Spice, 421
    Spice, Basic, for Pork Chops, 439
    Spice, Chili-Mustard, 445
    Spicy Chili, 437

Rum
    Bananas Foster, 670
    Dark, Glaze, Molasses Spice Cookies with, 565
    Glaze, Spiced Pecans with, 501
    Tiramisù, 632–33, *633*
    Tiramisù with Cooked Eggs, 633
Rustic Country Bread, 552–53
Rustic Dinner Rolls, 547–48, *548*
Rustic Potato-Leek Soup, 15–16

S

Saag Paneer (Indian-Style Spinach with Fresh Cheese), 793–94
Sablés (French Butter Cookies), *576,* 576–77
Sage
    and Browned Butter Sauce, 267
    Chicken Saltimbocca, 305, *305*
    -Vermouth Sauce, Pan-Roasted Chicken Breasts with, 92–93, *93*
Salad dressings. *See* **Vinaigrettes**; *specific salad recipes*
Salads
    Arugula, with Figs, Prosciutto, Walnuts, and Parmesan, 31
    Beef, Grilled Thai, for a Charcoal Grill, 405–6
    Beef, Grilled Thai, for a Gas Grill, 406
    Cabbage, Confetti, with Spicy Peanut Dressing, 42
    Cherry Tomato, with Feta and Olives, 37–38, *38*
    Chicken
        Classic, 758
        Curried, with Cashews, 758
        with Red Grapes and Smoked Almonds, 758
        Waldorf, 758
    Chopped
        Fennel and Apple, 36–37
        Mediterranean, 36, *36*
        Pear and Cranberry, 35–36
    Creamy Buttermilk Coleslaw, 41–42
    Creamy Coleslaw, 41
    Cucumber, Sesame Lemon, 40
    Fruit, 542–43
    Greek, Classic, 39
    with Herbed Baked Goat Cheese and Vinaigrette, 32–33
    Italian Bread (Panzanella), 38–39, *39*
    Leafy Green, with Red Wine Vinaigrette, 29, *29*
    Leafy Green, with Rich and Creamy Blue Cheese Dressing, 29–30
    Lentil
        with Carrots and Cilantro, 759
        with Hazelnuts and Goat Cheese, 759
        with Olives, Mint, and Feta, 758–59
        with Spinach, Walnuts, and Parmesan Cheese, 759

Salads *(cont.)*
    Macaroni, Cool and Creamy, 43, *43*
    Pasta, Antipasto, 44–45, *45*
    Pasta, with Pesto, 43–44
    Potato
        American, with Hard-Cooked Eggs and Sweet Pickles, 46
        Austrian-Style, 47, *47*
        French, 316–17, *317*
    Rice, with Oranges, Olives, and Almonds, 45–46, *46*
    Shrimp, *209,* 209–10
        with Avocado and Orange, 210
        with Roasted Red Pepper and Basil, 210
    Spicy, with Mustard and Balsamic Vinaigrette, 30
    Thai Pork Lettuce Wraps, *376,* 376–77
    Tuna
        with Balsamic Vinegar and Grapes, 218
        Classic, 218, *218*
        Curried, with Apples and Currants, 218
        with Lime and Horseradish, 218
    Wilted Spinach
        Almond-Crusted Chicken with, 33–34
        with Warm Bacon Dressing, *31,* 31–32
        Watercress, and Orange, Pan-Seared Scallops with, 34–35, *35*
Salmon
    Barbecued, for a Charcoal Grill, 463–64
    Barbecued, for a Gas Grill, 464
    Broiled, with Mustard and Crisp Dilled Crust, 193–94
    Cakes, Easy, 789
    Cakes, Easy, with Smoked Salmon, Capers, and Dill, 789
    fillet, skinning, 195
    Fillets, Charcoal-Grilled, 460–61
    Fillets, Gas-Grilled, 461
    Glazed, 195–96, *196*
        Charcoal-Grilled, 462, *462*
        Gas-Grilled, 462
    Grilled, with Orange-Sesame Glaze, 463
    Grilled, with Spicy Apple Glaze, 463
    Grill-Smoked, 790–91
    Oven-Roasted, 197, *197*
    Pan-Seared, 192–93
    Poached, with Herb and Caper Vinaigrette, *194,* 194–95
Salsas
    Avocado, 213–14
    Avocado-Orange, 199
    Gazpacho, 213–14
    hot, taste tests on, 751
    One-Minute, 347
    Orange, with Cuban Flavors, 446
    Pineapple and Cucumber, with Mint, 467
    Salsa Verde, 435–36

Salt, sea, taste tests on, 751
Salt-Baked Potatoes with Roasted Garlic and Rosemary
    Butter, 492–93
Salt-Baked Potatoes with Roasted Shallot and Thyme
    Butter, 493
Salted Roast Turkey, *123,* 123–24
Salty Thin and Crispy Oatmeal Cookies, 573
Sandwiches
    Flank Steak and Arugula, with Red Onion, 146–47
    Grilled Cheese, Classic, 219–20
    Tuna Salad
        with Balsamic Vinegar and Grapes, 218
        Classic, 218, *218*
        Curried, with Apples and Currants, 218
        with Lime and Horseradish, 218
    see also Burgers
Sangria, 346–47
Satay, Beef, 377
Sauces
    Apple Cider, 173–74
    Apple-Mustard, 791
    Bolognese, Slow-Simmered, Pasta with, 258–59
    Bolognese, Weeknight, Pasta with, *259,* 259–60
    Bourbon–Brown Sugar, 641
    Brandy and Green Peppercorn, Restaurant-Style, for Pan-
        Seared Steaks, 139–40
    Browned Butter and Sage, 267
    Burger
        Apricot-Mustard, 774
        Chile-Lime, 774
        Malt Vinegar–Molasses, 774
    Burger, Classic, 230
    Burger, Pub-Style, 231
    Caramel, 519
    Chimichurri, 432–33
    Chipotle Chile, Creamy, 212–13
    Cranberry, Classic, 131
    Dipping
        Belgian-Style, 235
        Chive and Black Pepper, 235
        Cocktail, 209
        Scallion, *372,* 372–73
        Spicy Peanut, 377
    Dried Cherry–Port, with Onions and Marmalade, 176
    Fresh Parsley and Garlic, Argentinian-Style (Chimichurri),
        145
    Garlic and Thyme, 153
    Garlicky Lime, with Cilantro, 176
    Ginger-Soy, with Scallions, 199
    Gorgonzola-Cream, 268
    Herb, Restaurant-Style, for Pan-Seared Steaks, 139
    Horseradish Cream, 165

Sauces *(cont.)*
    Horseradish Cream, with Chives, 464
    hot, taste tests on, 744
    hot fudge, taste tests on, 744
    Lemon
        Brown Butter, 204
        -Caper, 154
        and Chive Pan, 88
        -Garlic, Spicy, 470
    Madeira Pan, with Mustard and Anchovies, 144–45
    Maple-Mustard, 173
    Marinara, *244,* 244–45
    Meat, Hearty Italian (Sunday Gravy), Pasta with, 256–57
    Meat, Simple Italian-Style, *257,* 257–58
    Mushroom Ragu, Spaghetti with Quick, 766–67
    Mustard
        -Cream Pan, 143
        -Dill, 464
        Mid–South Carolina, 448
        -Shallot, with Thyme, 181
    pan, using fond for, 338
    Parmesan, with Pancetta and Walnuts, 268
    pasta, taste tests on, 749
    Peanut, 777
    Port-Cherry Reduction, 146
    Port Wine, Restaurant-Style, for Pan-Seared Steaks, 140
    Ragu alla Bolognese, 765
    Raspberry Coulis, 643–44
    reducing, tip for, 146
    Red Wine–Mushroom Pan, 141–42
    Red Wine Pan, 138
    Rémoulade, 467
    Sauce Base, 140
    Sauce Base for Steak Diane, 341–42
    Shallot Butter, 139
    "Smoked Salmon Platter," 791
    Tarragon-Lemon Pan, 95
    Tartar, Sweet and Tangy, 191
    teriyaki, taste tests on, 752
    Thyme–Sherry Vinegar Pan, 95
    Tomato
        and Browned Butter, 764
        -Caper Pan, 143
        Marinara, *244,* 244–45
        Quick, *243,* 243–44
        Quick, for Pizza, 280–81
        Simple, 301
        Slow-Simmered, with Meat, Pasta and (Sunday Gravy),
            260–61
    Vodka, Penne with (Penne alla Vodka), *264,* 264–65
    Walnut Cream, 764
    see also Barbecue Sauce; Gravy; Salsas

Sausage(s)

Antipasto Pasta Salad, 44–45, *45*

breakfast, taste tests on, 751

and Broccoli Rabe, Orecchiette with, 253

Dressing, 120–21, *122*

Dried Cherries, and Pecans, Baked Bread Stuffing with, 132

Indoor Clambake, 214–15, *215*

Mushrooms, and Monterey Jack, Breakfast Strata with, 517

Paella, *79,* 79–80

Pasta with Hearty Italian Meat Sauce (Sunday Gravy), 256–57

pepperoni, taste tests on, 749

Pepperoni Pan Pizza, 286–87

and Shrimp Gumbo, Creole-Style, *80,* 80–81

Simplified Cassoulet with Pork and Kielbasa, 337–38

Skillet Jambalaya, 59

Spanish Tortilla with Chorizo and Scallions, 513

Sweet Pepper, and Cheddar Cheese, Scrambled Eggs with, 506–7

Sautéed Baby Spinach with Almonds and Golden Raisins, 484

Sautéed Chicken Cutlets with Mustard-Cider Sauce, 84

Sautéed Garlic-Lemon Spinach, 483–84

Sautéed Pork Cutlets with Mustard-Cider Sauce, 150, *150*

Sautéed Wild Mushrooms, 14

Scallion(s)

Crispy, and Miso-Ginger Vinaigrette, Poached Fish Fillets with, 790

Dipping Sauce, *372,* 372–73

Scalloped Potatoes, 493–94

Scallops

Pan-Seared, 203–4

Pan-Seared, with Wilted Spinach, Watercress, and Orange Salad, 34–35, *35*

preparing for cooking, 203

Sea, Charcoal-Grilled, *467,* 467–68

Sea, Gas-Grilled, 468

wet, compared with dry, 203

Scones

Blueberry, 524–26, *525*

Cream, 524

Oatmeal, 526–27, *527*

Oatmeal, Glazed Maple-Pecan, 527

Scrambled Eggs

with Bacon, Onion, and Pepper Jack Cheese, 505–6

Fluffy, 504

Rich and Creamy, *504,* 504–5

Rich and Creamy, for Two, 505

with Sausage, Sweet Pepper, and Cheddar Cheese, 506–7

Sesame oil

Garlic-Ginger-Sesame Wet Paste Marinade, 426

Grilled Salmon with Orange-Sesame Glaze, 463

Sesame seeds

Sesame-Crusted Pan-Seared Tuna Steaks, *198,* 198–99

Sesame Lemon Cucumber Salad, 40

Sesame Noodles with Shredded Chicken, 380, *380*

Shallot(s)

Butter Sauce, 139

Crispy, and Blue Cheese, Juicy Pub-Style Burgers with, 231, *231*

Garlic, and Almonds, Couscous with, 500

-Garlic-Rosemary Wet Paste Marinade, 426

-Mustard Sauce with Thyme, 181

and Parsley Butter, 166

and Potato Galette with Goat Cheese, 793

Quick Green Bean "Casserole," 134

Roasted, and Thyme Butter, Salt-Baked Potatoes with, 493

Sautéed, and Vermouth, Green Beans with, 482

Shellfish

Best Crab Cakes, 788

Clambake, Indoor, 214–15, *215*

Clam Chowder, New England, 25, *25*

Crab Cakes, Maryland, 212, *212*

crabmeat, taste tests on, 742

Crab Towers with Avocado and Gazpacho Salsas, *213,* 213–14

Lobster, Flambéed Pan-Roasted, 210–11

Paella, *79,* 79–80

Spanish-Style Toasted Pasta with Shrimp and Clams, 768

see also Scallops; Shrimp

Shepherd's Pie, 780–81

Shish Kebabs, Charcoal-Grilled, 457–58

Shish Kebabs, Gas-Grilled, 458

Shortbread, Best, 581–82

Shortcakes, Strawberry, *658,* 658–59

Shrimp

Best Crab Cakes, 788

and Clams, Spanish-Style Toasted Pasta with, 768

Cocktail, 208–9

deveining, 205

fra Diavolo, 255, *255*

Garlic, Spanish-Style, 206–7, *207*

Garlicky, with Buttered Bread Crumbs, 205–6, *206*

Greek-Style, with Tomatoes and Feta, 207–8, *208*

Indonesian-Style Fried Rice (Nasi Goreng), 382–83

Kung Pao, *396,* 396–97

Pad Thai, 403–4

Paella, *79,* 79–80

Pan-Seared, 204

    with Chipotle-Lime Glaze, 205

    with Garlic-Lemon Butter, 205

    with Ginger-Hoisin Glaze, 205

Shrimp (cont.)

Pasta, Garlicky, *254,* 254–55

Pineapple, and Peanuts, Thai Red Curry with, 400–401

Pork, and Shiitakes, Fried Rice with, 381

Salad, *209,* 209–10

with Avocado and Orange, 210

with Roasted Red Pepper and Basil, 210

and Sausage Gumbo, Creole-Style, *80,* 80–81

Scampi, 311

Shu Mai (Steamed Chinese Dumplings), 373–75, *375*

skewering, for the grill, 469

Skewers, Charcoal-Grilled, *469,* 469–70

Skewers, Gas-Grilled, 470

Skillet Jambalaya, 59

Spanish-Style Toasted Pasta with, 767

Stir-Fried

Asparagus, and Yellow Pepper with Lemon Sauce, 388

with Garlicky Eggplant, Scallions, and Cashews, 396

with Snow Peas and Red Bell Pepper in Hot and Sour Sauce, 395, *395*

Tempura, 375–76

Shu Mai (Steamed Chinese Dumplings), 373–75, *375*

Sichuan Stir-Fried Pork in Garlic Sauce, 787–88

Simple Applesauce, 476

Simple Couscous, 499–500

Simple Grill-Roasted Turkey, 774–75

Simple Italian-Style Meat Sauce, *257,* 257–58

Simple Pot Roast, 62, *62*

Simple Raspberry Gratin, 662–63

Simple Sautéed Swiss Chard, 486

Simple Tomato Sauce, 301

Simplified Cassoulet with Pork and Kielbasa, 337–38

Simplified Potato Galette, *321,* 321–22

Single-Crust Pie Dough For Custard Pies, 681

Skillet Apple Brown Betty, 666–67

Skillet Apple Crisp, *665,* 665–66

Skillet Apple Pie, *669,* 669–70

Skillet Baked Ziti, 50, *50*

Skillet-Barbecued Pork Chops, *154,* 154–55

Skillet Beef Stroganoff, 55, *55*

Skillet Chicken, Broccoli, and Ziti, 50–51

Skillet Chicken and Rice with Broccoli and Cheddar, 58

Skillet Chicken and Rice with Peas and Scallions, 57

Skillet Chicken Fajitas, 770

Skillet Chicken Pot Pie with Biscuit Topping, 52–54

Skillet Curried Chicken and Rice, 58

Skillet Jambalaya, 59

Skillet Lasagna, 51–52, *52*

Skillet-Roasted Chicken Breasts with Potatoes, *56,* 56–57

Skillet-Roasted Potatoes, 492

Skillet Soufflé, Chocolate-Orange, 654

Skillet Soufflé, Lemon, 654, *654*

Skillet Tamale Pie, 54

Slow-Cooker Beef Burgundy, 335–36

Slow-Cooker Beer-Braised Short Ribs, 68, *68*

Slow-Cooker Chicken Noodle Soup, Old-Fashioned, 6–7

Slow-Cooker Pork Loin with Cranberries and Orange, *181,* 181–82

Slow-Roasted Beef, 164–65

Slow-Roasted Pork Shoulder with Peach Sauce, *182,* 182–83

Slow-Roasted Turkey with Gravy, *119,* 119–20

Smashed Potatoes, 486–87

Smoked Paprika and Roasted Red Pepper Butter, 432

"Smoked Salmon Platter" Sauce, 791

Smoky Kansas City Barbecue Beans, 450

Smothered Pork Chops, *157,* 157–58

Soda Bread, Irish, 548–49

Soda Bread, Whole Wheat, 549

Sole Fillets, Baked, with Herbs and Bread Crumbs, *202,* 202–3

Sorbet, Raspberry, 807

with Ginger and Mint, 807

–Lime Rickey, 807

–Port, 807

Soufflés

Chilled Lemon, 651–52

Individual, 652

with White Chocolate, 652

Grand Marnier, 650–51

Grand Marnier, with Grated Chocolate, 651

Make-Ahead Chocolate, 652–53

Make-Ahead Mocha, 653

making foil collars for, 653

Skillet Chocolate-Orange, 654

Skillet Lemon, 654, *654*

Soups

Beef and Vegetable, Quick, 9–10, *10*

Black Bean, 350–51, *351*

Broccoli-Cheese, 16–17, *17*

Butternut Squash, 15, *15*

Chicken, Thai-Style, 377–78, *378*

Chicken Noodle

canned, taste tests on, 751

Classic, 4

Hearty, *5,* 5–6

Old-Fashioned Slow-Cooker, 6–7

Classic Gazpacho, 22–23

Creamy Gazpacho Andaluz, 23–24

French Onion, Classic, *314,* 314–15

French Onion, Streamlined, 315–16

Ham and Split Pea, Modern, 18, *18*

Ham and Split Pea, with Potatoes, Hearty, 19

Hearty Minestrone, *21,* 21–22

Soups *(cont.)*

Hearty Tuscan Bean Stew, 294–95, *295*

Hot and Sour, 378–79, *379*

Italian Pasta and Bean (Pasta e Fagioli), *293,* 293–94

Lentil, Hearty, 17

Lighter Corn Chowder, 24

Mulligatawny, 19–20, *20*

Mushroom, Creamy, 14

New England Clam Chowder, 25, *25*

Pea, Creamy, 13

Potato-Leek, Rustic, 15–16

Tomato

canned, taste tests on, 751

Classic Cream of, 11

Creamless Creamy, 11–12, *12*

Tortilla, *349,* 349–50

Vegetable and Barley, Farmhouse, 759–60

see also Stews

Sour Cherry, Fresh, Cobbler, 660

Sour Cherry Cobbler, *659,* 659–60

Sour Cream Coffee Cake with Brown Sugar–Pecan Streusel, 540

South Carolina Mustard Barbecue Sauce, 184

Southern Corn Bread, 551–52

Southwestern Marinade, 429

Soy (sauce)

Garlic, and Ginger Marinade, 430

-Ginger Glaze, 415

-Ginger Sauce with Scallions, 199

-Mustard Glaze, 196

taste tests on, 752

Spaghetti

alla Carbonara, 265

Cincinnati Chili, *223,* 223–24

with Lemon and Olive Oil (al Limone), 238–39, *239*

and Meatballs, *261,* 261–62

and Meatballs, Classic, for a Crowd, 263–64

with Olive Pesto, 249

Pasta all'Amatriciana, 765–66

Pasta with Garlic and Oil, 238

with Pecorino Romano and Black Pepper, 239

Puttanesca, 245–46

with Quick Mushroom Ragu, 766–67

taste tests on, 748

Turkey Tetrazzini, 222–23

whole-wheat, taste tests on, 749

Spanish-Style Garlic Shrimp, 206–7, *207*

Spanish-Style Toasted Pasta with Shrimp, 767

Spanish-Style Toasted Pasta with Shrimp and Clams, 768

Spanish Tortilla with Chorizo and Scallions, 513

Spanish Tortilla with Roasted Red Peppers and Peas, 512–13, *513*

Spice Cake, 604

Spiced Pecans with Rum Glaze, 501

Spiced Pumpkin Cheesecake, 635–36

Spice Rub, 421

Basic, for Pork Chops, 439

Chili-Mustard, 445

Spice-Rubbed Picnic Chicken, *91,* 91–92

Spicy Chili Rub, 437

Spicy Cranberry Chutney, 796

Spicy Cucumber Relish, 198

Spicy Garlic Oil, 290

Spicy Jalapeño-Cheddar Corn Bread, 551

Spicy Lemon-Garlic Sauce, 470

Spicy Mayonnaise, 105

Spicy Mexican Shredded Pork Tostadas, *362,* 362–63

Spicy Peanut Dipping Sauce, 377

Spicy Pickled Radishes, 771

Spicy Pineapple-Ginger Glaze, 186

Spicy Pork Tacos (al Pastor), 786–87

Spicy Salad with Mustard and Balsamic Vinaigrette, 30

Spinach

Baby, Sautéed, with Almonds and Golden Raisins, 484

Baked Eggs Florentine, 796–97

Broccoli-Cheese Soup, 16–17, *17*

Butternut Squash Galette with Gruyère, 793

Dip, Creamy Herbed, 484–85

and Feta Pie, Greek (Spanakopita), *73,* 73–74

with Fresh Cheese, Indian-Style, (Saag Paneer), 793–94

and Gruyère, Breakfast Strata with, *516,* 516–17

and Pine Nuts, Grilled Stuffed Flank Steak with, 428

Sautéed Garlic-Lemon, 483–84

Vegetable Lasagna, *272,* 273–74

Walnuts, and Parmesan Cheese, Lentil Salad with, 759

Wilted

Salad, Almond-Crusted Chicken with, 33–34

Salad with Warm Bacon Dressing, *31,* 31–32

Watercress, and Orange Salad, Pan-Seared Scallops with, 34–35, *35*

Split Pea and Ham Soup, Modern, 18, *18*

Split Pea and Ham Soup with Potatoes, Hearty, 19

Spreads. *See* Dips and spreads

Spring Vegetable Pasta, 249–50, *250*

Spritz Cookies, 575, *575*

Almond, 576

with Lemon Essence, 576

Squash

Acorn, Quick Roasted, with Brown Sugar, 496–97, *497*

Butternut, Galette with Gruyère, 793

Butternut, Risotto, 298–99, *299*

Butternut, Soup, 15, *15*

Hearty Minestrone, *21,* 21–22

Squash *(cont.)*
Stir-Fried Chicken and Zucchini with Ginger Sauce, 387
Summer Vegetable Gratin, *320,* 320–21
Vegetable Lasagna, *272,* 273–74
see also Pumpkin
Star Anise
Maple-Glazed Pork Roast with, 180
Orange, and Cinnamon Glaze, 186
Steak, beef. *See under* **Beef**
Steak Fries, *233,* 233–34
Stews
Bean, Hearty Tuscan, 294–95, *295*
Beef, Beer, and Onion, Belgian (Carbonnade à la Flamande), 64–65, *65*
Beef, Best, *7,* 7–8
Beef, Catalan-Style, with Mushrooms, 761–62
Beef, Hungarian, 65–66
Beef Burgundy, 334–35
Beef Burgundy, Slow-Cooker, 335–36
Chicken and Dumplings, *69,* 69–70
Chicken and Dumplings, Lighter, 70–71
Daube Provençal, 332–33, *333*
Vegetable, Italian (Ciambotta), 760–61
see also Chili
Sticky Buns with Pecans, 538–39
Stir-fries
best pans for, 386
Chinese Chicken Lettuce Wraps, 769–70
Fried Rice with Peas and Bean Sprouts, 381–82
Fried Rice with Shrimp, Pork, and Shiitakes, 381
Indonesian-Style Fried Rice (Nasi Goreng), 382–83
Kung Pao Shrimp, *396,* 396–97
Pad Thai, 403–4
Pork Lo Mein, 393–94, *394*
Sichuan Stir-Fried Pork in Garlic Sauce, 787–88
Stir-Fried Beef and Broccoli with Oyster Sauce, *389,* 389–90
Stir-Fried Chicken and Zucchini with Ginger Sauce, 387
Stir-Fried Chicken with Bok Choy and Crispy Noodle Cake, *385,* 385–86
Stir-Fried Pork, Eggplant, and Onion with Garlic and Black Pepper, 392
Stir-Fried Pork, Green Beans, and Red Bell Pepper with Gingery Oyster Sauce, *392,* 393
Stir-Fried Portobellos with Ginger-Oyster Sauce, 397–98, *398*
Stir-Fried Portobellos with Sweet Chili-Garlic Sauce, 398
Stir-Fried Shrimp, Asparagus, and Yellow Pepper with Lemon Sauce, 388
Stir-Fried Shrimp with Garlicky Eggplant, Scallions, and Cashews, 396

Stir-fries *(cont.)*
Stir-Fried Shrimp with Snow Peas and Red Bell Pepper in Hot and Sour Sauce, 395, *395*
Stir-Fried Thai-Style Beef with Chiles and Shallots, *402,* 402–3
Stir-Fried Tofu, Snow Peas, and Red Onion with Hot and Sour Sauce, 388–89
Tangerine Stir-Fried Beef with Onion and Snow Peas, 391
Teriyaki Stir-Fried Beef with Green Beans and Shiitakes, 390–91
Thai-Style Chicken with Basil, 398–99
Thai-Style Stir-Fried Noodles with Chicken and Broccolini, 768–69
Stovetop Macaroni and Cheese, 221
Stovetop Rice Pudding, 642, *642*
Stovetop Roast Chicken with Lemon-Herb Sauce, *100,* 100–101
Strata, Breakfast, with Sausage, Mushrooms, and Monterey Jack, 517
Strata, Breakfast, with Spinach and Gruyère, *516,* 516–17
Strawberry(ies)
with Balsamic Vinegar, 675–76
Berry Fool, *676,* 676–77
Cream Cake, *605,* 605–6
and Grapes with Balsamic and Red Wine Reduction, 542–43
Individual Fresh Berry Gratins with Lemon Zabaglione, 664
Individual Fresh Berry Gratins with Zabaglione, *663,* 663–64
Individual Summer Berry Puddings, 673–74
Large Summer Berry Pudding, 674
Mixed Berry Tart with Pastry Cream, 703
Pie, Fresh, *689,* 689–90
preserves, taste tests on, 750
-Rhubarb Fool, 677
Shortcakes, *658,* 658–59
Topping, 634
Streamlined French Onion Soup, 315–16
Strudel, Easy Apple, *667,* 667–68
Stuffed Chicken Cutlets with Ham and Cheddar, 86–87
Stuffed Pork Chops, 159–61
"Stuffed" Roast Butterflied Chicken, 102–3, *103*
Stuffings and dressings
Bread Stuffing
with Bacon, Apples, Sage, and Caramelized Onions, 118–19
Baked, with Fresh Herbs, 133
Baked, with Leeks, Bacon, and Apple, 133
Baked, with Sausage, Dried Cherries, and Pecans, 132
Mushroom-Leek, with Herbs, 103
inserting into turkey, 117
Sausage Dressing, 120–21, *122*
Sugar, Brown, Cookies, 562–63, *563*
Sugar Cookies, Chewy, 562

Summer Berry Pie, *691,* 691–92
Summer Peach Cake, 607, *607*
Summer Vegetable Gratin, *320,* 320–21
Sweet-and-Sour Chutney, 193
Sweet and Spicy Pickled Onions, 356
Sweet and Tangy Barbecue Sauce, 183–84
Sweet and Tangy Oven-Barbecued Chicken, 90–91
Sweet and Tangy Tartar Sauce, 191
Sweet Cherry Pie, *692,* 692–93
Sweetened condensed milk, taste tests on, 752
Sweet Potato(es)
    Casserole, Candied, 135, *135*
    Eggplant, Green Beans, and Chickpeas, Indian-Style Curry
        with, 410
    Mashed, 496
Swiss Chard, Simple Sautéed, 486

Tacos
    Beef, 354, *355*
    Pork, Spicy (al Pastor), 786–87
    Steak, 355–56
Taco Shells, Home-Fried, 355
Tamale Pie, Skillet, 54
Tamarind-Hoisin Glaze, 780
Tandoori Chicken, 411, *411*
Tangerine and Ginger Relish, 197–98
Tangerine Stir-Fried Beef with Onion and Snow Peas, 391
Tangy Whipped Cream, 668
Tarragon-Lemon Pan Sauce, 95
Tartar Sauce
    Sweet and Tangy, 191
    taste tests on, 752
Tart Dough, Classic, 700
Tarts (dessert)
    Apple, Free-Form, 705–6
    Apple Galette, *704,* 704–5
    Fresh Fruit, with Pastry Cream, 702–3, *703*
    Lemon, 700–701
    Mixed Berry, with Pastry Cream, 703
    Pear Tatin, 706
    preparing shell for, 700
    Summer Fruit, Free-Form, 701–2
    30-Minute Tarte Tatin, 706
Tarts (savory)
    Onion and Bacon, French, 317–18
    Pissaladière, 318–19, *319*
    Tomato and Mozzarella, *290,* 290–91
    see also Galettes

Tea
    black, taste tests on, 752
    iced, taste tests on, 744
Ten-Minute Steel-Cut Oatmeal, 797
Tequila
    Fresh Margaritas, 346
Teriyaki sauce, taste tests on, 752
Teriyaki Stir-Fried Beef with Green Beans and Shiitakes,
    390–91
Texas-Style Barbecued Beef Ribs for a Charcoal Grill,
    454–55, *455*
Texas-Style Barbecued Beef Ribs for a Gas Grill, 456
Thai Chili Butter, 142
Thai Green Curry with Chicken, Broccoli, and
    Mushrooms, *399,* 399–400
Thai Grilled Chicken on a Gas Grill, 405
Thai Grilled Chicken with Spicy, Sweet, and Sour
    Dipping Sauce, 404–5
Thai Pork Lettuce Wraps, *376,* 376–77
Thai Red Curry with Shrimp, Pineapple, and Peanuts,
    400–401
Thai-Style Chicken Soup, 377–78, *378*
Thai-Style Chicken with Basil, 398–99
Thai-Style Stir-Fried Noodles with Chicken and
    Broccolini, 768–69
Thermometers, buying guide, 718–19
Thick and Chewy Chocolate Chip Cookies, 566–67
Thick and Chewy Double-Chocolate Cookies, 569
Thick and Chewy Triple-Chocolate Cookies, 569
Thick-Cut Pork Tenderloin Medallions,
    172, 172–73
Thin and Crispy Chocolate Chip Cookies, 567
Thin and Crispy Oatmeal Cookies,
    572–73, *573*
30-Minute Tarte Tatin, 706
Thyme
    and Garlic Sauce, 153
    -Lemon Butter, 760
    Mustard-Garlic Butter with, 102
    Mustard-Shallot Sauce with, 181
    and Roasted Shallot Butter, Salt-Baked Potatoes with,
        493
    –Sherry Vinegar Pan Sauce, 95
Timers, kitchen, buying guide, 718–19
Tiramisù, 632–33, *633*
Tiramisù with Cooked Eggs, 633
Tofu
    Hot and Sour Soup, 378–79, *379*
    Stir-Fried, Snow Peas, and Red Onion with Hot and Sour
        Sauce, 388–89

Tomatillos

Enchiladas Verdes, 360–62, *361*

Tomato(es)

and Almond Pesto, Pasta with (Pesto alla Trapanese),
247–48, *248*

Bacon, and Onion, Pasta with (Pasta all'Amatriciana),
246, *246*

Baked Manicotti, 270–71, *271*

Beef Chili with Kidney Beans, 365–66

canned crushed, taste tests on, 753

canned diced, taste tests on, 753

canned pureed, taste tests on, 753

canned whole, taste tests on, 753

and Cheese Pizza, Grilled, for a Charcoal Grill,
288–90, *289*

and Cheese Pizzas, Grilled, for a Gas Grill, 290

Cherry, –Basil Vinaigrette, Chunky, 201

Cherry, Salad with Feta and Olives, 37–38, *38*

Chicken Tikka Masala, 406–7, *407*

Classic Gazpacho, 22–23

Classic Greek Salad, 39

Classic Spaghetti and Meatballs for a Crowd, 263–64

Creamy Gazpacho Andaluz, 23–24

Crisp Thin-Crust Pizza, 280

Eggplant Parmesan, 295–96

Fennel, and Almond Relish, 783

and Feta, Greek-Style Shrimp with, 207–8, *208*

Fettuccine with Slow-Simmered Bolognese Sauce,
258–59

Fresh, and Herbs, Pasta with, 240

Fresh, Relish, 198

Gazpacho Salsa, 213–14

Huevos Rancheros, 368–69

Italian Bread Salad (Panzanella), 38–39, *39*

–Meat Sauce, Hearty, Lasagna with, 274–75

Mediterranean Chopped Salad, 36, *36*

Mozzarella, and Basil, Deep-Dish Pizza with, 282–83, *283*

and Mozzarella Tart, *290,* 290–91

and Mushroom Sauce, Spaghetti with, 766–67

New York–Style Thin-Crust Pizza, *281,* 281–82

Olives, and Feta, Farfalle with, 243

One-Minute Salsa, 347

Pasta all'Amatriciana, 765–66

Pasta Caprese, *242,* 242–43

Pasta with Hearty Italian Meat Sauce (Sunday Gravy),
256–57

Pasta with Weeknight Bolognese Sauce, *259,* 259–60

Penne with Vodka Sauce (Penne alla Vodka),
264, 264–65

Tomato(es) *(cont.)*

Sauce

Creamy, Pasta with, *241,* 241–42

Fresh, with Feta and Olives, 470

Fresh, with Garlic and Basil, Pasta with, 240–41

Marinara, *244,* 244–45

with Meat, Slow-Simmered, Pasta and (Sunday Gravy),
260–61

Quick, *243,* 243–44

Quick, for Pizza, 280–81

Simple, 301

Tomato-Caper Pan, 143

–Sherry Vinaigrette and Crispy Artichokes, Poached Fish
Fillets with, 789–90

Shrimp fra Diavolo, 255, *255*

Simple Italian-Style Meat Sauce, *257,* 257–58

Skillet Baked Ziti, 50, *50*

Skillet Lasagna, 51–52, *52*

Soup, Classic Cream of, 11

Soup, Creamless Creamy, 11–12, *12*

Spaghetti and Meatballs, *261,* 261–62

Spaghetti Puttanesca, 245–46

storing, 240

Sun-Dried, and Olive Stuffing, 441

Sun-Dried, Arugula, and Goat Cheese Pesto, Campanelle
with, 248–49

Vegetable Lasagna, *272,* 273–74

Tomato paste, taste tests on, 753

Tools, handy, buying guide, 712–17

Tools, specialty, buying guide, 728–33

Tortellini, taste tests on, 748

Tortilla, Spanish, with Chorizo and Scallions, 513

**Tortilla, Spanish, with Roasted Red Peppers and Peas,
512–13, *513***

Tortilla(s)

Beef Tacos, 354, *355*

Cheesy Nachos with Guacamole and Salsa, 347, *347*

Chicken Enchiladas with a Red Chili Sauce, 359–60, *360*

Chicken Fajitas for a Charcoal Grill, 356–57, *357*

Chicken Fajitas for a Gas Grill, 357

chips, taste tests on, 753

flour, taste tests on, 753

Home-Fried Taco Shells, 355

Huevos Rancheros, 368–69

Quesadillas, 348–49

Skillet Chicken Fajitas, 770

Soup, *349,* 349–50

Spicy Mexican Shredded Pork Tostadas, *362,* 362–63

Spicy Pork Tacos (al Pastor), 786–87

Steak Fajitas for a Charcoal Grill, 358–59

Steak Fajitas for a Gas Grill, 359

Steak Tacos, 355–56

Tostadas
  corn, taste tests on, 753
  Spicy Mexican Shredded Pork, *362,* 362–63
Triple-Chocolate Chunk Pecan Pie, 695
Triple-Chocolate Espresso Brownies, 588
Triple-Chocolate Mousse Cake, *629,* 629–31
Triple Citrus Bars, 591
Triple-Coconut Macaroons, 573–74
Triple sec
  Fresh Margaritas, 346
  Sangria, 346–47
Truffles
  Chocolate, 806
  Hazelnut-Mocha, 806
Tuna
  canned, taste tests on, 754
  Salad, Classic, 218, *218*
  Salad, Curried, with Apples and Currants, 218
  Salad with Balsamic Vinegar and Grapes, 218
  Salad with Lime and Horseradish, 218
  Steaks, Pan-Seared Sesame-Crusted, *198,* 198–99
  Steaks with Red Wine Vinegar and Mustard Vinaigrette,
    Charcoal-Grilled, *464,* 464–65
  Steaks with Red Wine Vinegar and Mustard Vinaigrette,
    Gas-Grilled, 465
Turkey
  Braised, 127–28
  Breast
    Boneless, Charcoal Grill–Roasted, *130,* 130–31
    Boneless, Gas Grill–Roasted, 131
    carving, 126
    deboning, 131
  brining, 113, 129
  Burgers, Juicy Grilled, 773–74
  Grill-Roasted
    for a Charcoal Grill, 128–29
    for a Gas Grill, 129
    Gravy for, 775–76
    Simple, 774–75
  how to butterfly, 121
  inserting stuffing into, 117
  Roast
    Classic, 112, *112*
    Classic Stuffed, *117,* 117–18
    Crisp-Skin High-Roast Butterflied, with Sausage
      Dressing, 120–22
    for a Crowd, 114
    Herbed, 124–26
    Old-Fashioned Stuffed, *115,* 115–16
    Salted, *123,* 123–24
    Slow-Roasted, with Gravy, *119,* 119–20
    Tetrazzini, 222–23
  whole, taste tests on, 754

Turkey Gravy, 122–23
  All-Purpose, 127, *127*
  Giblet Pan, 113
  Giblet Pan, for a Crowd, 114–15
  Make-Ahead, 117
  Slow-Roasted Turkey with, *119,* 119–20
Twice-Baked Potatoes, 494–95

U

Ultimate Banana Bread, *522,* 522–23
Ultimate Chocolate Cupcakes with Ganache Filling,
  622–23, *623*

V

Vanilla
  beans, taste tests on, 754
  extract, taste tests on, 754
  Ice Cream, Homemade, 655, *655*
  Pretzel Cookies, *576,* 578
Veal
  Fettuccine with Slow-Simmered Bolognese Sauce,
    258–59
  Lasagna with Hearty Tomato-Meat Sauce, 274–75
  Meat Loaf with Brown Sugar–Ketchup Glaze,
    227–28
  Osso Buco, 309–10
  Pasta with Hearty Italian Meat Sauce (Sunday Gravy),
    256–57
  Pasta with Weeknight Bolognese Sauce,
    259, 259–60
  Ragu alla Bolognese, 765
  Skillet Lasagna, 51–52, *52*
Vegetable(s)
  and Barley Soup, Farmhouse, 759–60
  and Beef Soup, Quick, 9–10, *10*
  broth, taste tests on, 737
  giardiniera, taste tests on, 743
  Hearty Minestrone, *21,* 21–22
  Lasagna, *272,* 273–74
  Root, and Potatoes, Mashed, 489–90, *490*
  Root, Old-Fashioned Pot Roast with, 64
  Stew, Italian (Ciambotta), 760–61
  Summer, Gratin, *320,* 320–21
  see also specific vegetables
Vermouth-Sage Sauce, Pan-Roasted Chicken Breasts with,
  92–93, *93*

Vinaigrettes
  Almond, 461
  Basil, 468
  Cherry Tomato–Basil, Chunky, 201
  Chile-Lime, 468
  Foolproof, 28, *28*
  Foolproof Balsamic-Mustard, 28
  Foolproof Herb, 28
  Foolproof Lemon, 28
  Foolproof Walnut, 28
  Olive, 461
Vinegar
  apple cider, taste tests on, 754
  Balsamic, Strawberries with, 675–76
  balsamic, taste tests on, 754
  Barbecue Sauce, Lexington, 184
  Eastern North Carolina Barbecue Sauce, 448
  Malt, –Molasses Burger Sauce, 774
  red wine, taste tests on, 755
  and Sweet Peppers, Pork Chops with, 308–9
  white wine, taste tests on, 755
  see also Vinaigrettes
Vodka Sauce, Penne with (Penne alla Vodka),
  264, 264–65

Watercress, Wilted Spinach, and Orange Salad,
  Pan-Seared Scallops with, 34–35, *35*
Weeknight Roast Chicken, 94–95
Well-Done Charcoal-Grilled Hamburgers, 424–25
Well-Done Gas-Grilled Hamburgers, 425
Well-Done Grilled Bacon Cheeseburgers, 425
Whipped Cream, Tangy, 668
White Chicken Chili, 367–68
Whole Wheat Sandwich Bread, Best, 556–58
Whole Wheat Soda Bread, 549
Wild Rice Pilaf with Pecans and Dried Cranberries,
  498–99
Wilted Spinach, Watercress, and Orange Salad,
  Pan-Seared Scallops with, 34–35, *35*
Wilted Spinach Salad, Almond-Crusted Chicken with,
  33–34
Wilted Spinach Salad with Warm Bacon Dressing,
  31, 31–32
Wine
  Chicken Marsala, 300
  Madeira Pan Sauce with Mustard and Anchovies, 144–45
  Pan-Roasted Chicken Breasts with Sage-Vermouth Sauce,
    92–93, *93*
  see also Port; Red Wine

W

Waffles, Buttermilk, 519–20
Waffles, Buttermilk, Easy, *520,* 520–21
Waldorf Chicken Salad, 758
Walnut(s)
  Asparagus, Arugula, and Blue Cheese, Cavatappi with, 251–52
  Bean Chili, 762
  Classic Banana Bread, 523–24
  Cream Sauce, 764
  Fennel and Apple Chopped Salad, 36–37
  Figs, Prosciutto, and Parmesan, Arugula Salad with, 31
  or Pecan Crescent Cookies, *582,* 582–83
  and Pancetta, Parmesan Sauce with, 268
  Peach Crisp, 661–62
  Peach Crisp for a Crowd, 662
  Pumpkin Bread, 798
  Pumpkin Bread with Candied Ginger, 798
  Spinach, and Parmesan Cheese, Lentil Salad with, 759
  Waldorf Chicken Salad, 758
Warm-Spiced Parsley Marinade with Ginger, 458

Y

Yeast, taste tests on, 755
Yogurt
  Greek, taste tests on, 755
  low-fat strawberry, taste tests on, 755
  whole milk, taste tests on, 755

Z

Zabaglione, Individual Fresh Berry Gratins with,
  663, 663–64
Zabaglione, Lemon, Individual Fresh Berry Gratins
  with, 664
Zucchini
  and Chicken, Stir-Fried, with Ginger Sauce, 387
  Hearty Minestrone, *21,* 21–22
  Italian Vegetable Stew (Ciambotta), 760–61
  Summer Vegetable Gratin, *320,* 320–21
  Vegetable Lasagna, *272,* 273–74